West's
PARALEGAL TODAY
THE LEGAL TEAM AT WORK

Third Edition

The West Legal Studies Series

Your options keep growing with West Legal Studies

Each year our list continues to offer you more options for every area of the law to meet your course or on-the-job reference requirements. We now have over 140 titles from which to choose in the following areas:

Administrative Law	Family Law
Alternative Dispute Resolution	Federal Taxation
Bankruptcy	Intellectual Property
Business Organizations/Corporations	Introduction to Law
Civil Litigation and Procedure	Introduction to Paralegalism
CLA Exam Preparation	Law Office Management
Client Accounting	Law Office Procedures
Computer in the Law Office	Legal Research, Writing, and Analysis
Constitutional Law	Legal Terminology
Contract Law	Paralegal Employment
Criminal Law and Procedure	Real Estate Law
Document Preparation	Reference Materials
Environmental Law	Torts and Personal Injury Law
Ethics	Will, Trusts, and Estate Administration

You will find unparalleled, practical support

Each book is augmented by instructor and student supplements to ensure the best learning experience possible. We also offer custom publishing and other benefits such as West's Student Achievement Award. In addition, our sales representatives are ready to provide you with dependable service.

We want to hear from you

Our best contribution for improving the quality of our books and instructional materials is feedback from the people who use them. If you have a question, concern, or observation about any of our materials, or if you have a product proposal or manuscript, we want to hear from you. Please contact your local representative or write us at the following address:

West Legal Studies, 5 Maxwell Drive, P. O. Box 8007, Clifton Park, New York 12065

For additional information point your browser at
http://www.westlegalstudies.com

THOMSON
™
DELMAR LEARNING

West's
PARALEGAL TODAY
THE LEGAL TEAM AT WORK

Third Edition

ROGER LEROY MILLER &
MARY MEINZINGER URISKO

THOMSON
DELMAR LEARNING™

Australia Canada Mexico Singapore Spain United Kingdom United States

THOMSON
™
DELMAR LEARNING

WEST LEGAL STUDIES

WEST'S PARALEGAL TODAY
The Legal Team at Work, Third Edition
Roger LeRoy Miller and Mary Meinzinger Urisko

Career Education Strategic Business Unit:
Vice President:
Dawn Gerrain

Director of Editorial:
Sherry Gomoll

Acquisitions Editor:
Pamela Fuller

Developmental Editor:
Melissa Riveglia

Editorial Assistant:
Sarah Duncan

Director of Production:
Wendy A. Troeger

Production Manager:
Carolyn Miller

Production Editor:
Betty L. Dickson

Technology Project Manager:
Joseph Saba

Director of Marketing:
Donna J. Lewis

Channel Manager:
Wendy Mapstone

Cover Design:
Dutton and Sherman Design

Library of Congress Cataloging-in-Publication Data

Miller, Roger LeRoy.
    West's paralegal today: the legal team at work/Roger LeRoy Miller and Mary Meinzinger Urisko.—3rd ed.
        p. cm.—(West Legal Studies series)
    Includes index.
    ISBN 1-4018-1082-9
    1. Legal assistants—United States. I. Urisko, Mary M. II. Title. III. Series.

KF320.L4M55 2004
340'.023'73—dc21

2003043786

NOTICE TO THE READER

DEDICATION

To Penny and Dick:

Friends from the past.

Friends for today.

Friends for tomorrow.

Thanks.

R.L.M.

To Meghan and Katie,

the lights of my life.

I love you.

M.M.U.

Contents in Brief

CONTENTS

CHAPTER 2
Career Opportunties   24

Chapter 3
Ethics and Professional Responsibility 66

Chapter 4
The Inner Workings of the Law Office 109

PART 2:
INTRODUCTION TO LAW   141

CHAPTER 5
Sources of American Law   142

CHAPTER 6

The Court System and
Alternative Dispute Resolution   177

CHAPTER 8
Contracts and Intellectual Property Law   245

CHAPTER 9
Real Property, Estates, and Family Law   282

CHAPTER 10

Agency, Business Organizations, and Employment   321

Chapter 11
Administrative Law and Government Regulation 357

PART 3:
LEGAL PROCEDURES AND PARALEGAL SKILLS   393

CHAPTER 12
CIVIL LITIGATION—BEFORE THE TRIAL   394

CHAPTER 13

Conducting Interviews and Investigations 446

CHAPTER 14

Trial Procedures 488

CHAPTER 15
Criminal Law and Procedures   522

PREFACE

One of the fastest-growing occupations in America today is that of the paralegal, or legal assistant. It seems fitting, then, that you and your students should have a new textbook that reflects the excitement surrounding paralegal studies today. *West's Paralegal Today: The Legal Team at Work,* Third Edition, we believe, imparts this excitement to your students. They will find paralegal studies accessible and interesting. This book is up to date, colorful, and visually attractive, which encourages learning. We are certain that you and your students will find this text extremely effective.

West's Paralegal Today, Third Edition, makes the paralegal field come alive for the student. We use real-world examples, present numerous boxed-in features, and support the text with the most extensive supplements package ever offered for an introductory paralegal textbook. *West's Paralegal Today,* Third Edition, draws on the expertise of publishers that have had a long history of encouraging excellence in legal education.

All of the basic areas of paralegal studies are covered in *West's Paralegal Today,* Third Edition. These include careers, ethics and professional responsibility, pretrial preparation, trial procedures, criminal law, legal interviewing and investigation, legal research and analysis, computer-assisted legal research, and legal writing. We have added more in-depth coverage of substantive law, including contracts, intellectual property, torts, product liability, real property, estates, business organizations, and family law. In addition, there are a number of key features, which we describe in this preface.

A PRACTICAL, REALISTIC APPROACH

There sometimes exists an enormous gulf between classroom learning and on-the-job realities. We have tried to bridge this gulf in *West's Paralegal Today,* Third Edition, by offering a text full of practical advice and "hands-on" activities.

Exercises at the end of each chapter provide opportunities for your students to apply the concepts and skills discussed in the chapter. Many of the book's other key features, which you will read about shortly, were designed specifically to give students a glimpse of the types of situations and demands that they may encounter on the job as professional paralegals. A special introduction to the student, which appears just before Chapter 1, contains practical advice and tips on how to master the legal concepts and procedures presented in this text—advice and tips that your students can also apply later, on the job.

West's Paralegal Today, Third Edition, also realistically portrays paralegal working environments and on-the-job challenges. In Chapter 1, we present a hypothetical case scenario to pique the student's interest and illustrate the different duties that paralegals might perform in an actual case. Each chapter also contains realistic factual situations in which a paralegal's ethical obligations are challenged. These situations give students a better understanding of how seemingly abstract ethical rules affect the day-to-day tasks performed by attorneys and paralegals in the legal workplace.

TECHNOLOGY

We have attempted to make sure that *West's Paralegal Today*, Third Edition, is the most modern and up-to-date text available in today's marketplace. To that end, we have included in the Third Edition a number of new features and materials indicating how the latest developments in technology are affecting the law, the legal workplace, and paralegal tasks. Among other things, these features and materials will help your students learn how to take advantage of technology, including the Internet, to enhance their efficiency and productivity as paralegals.

A Chapter on CALR

An entire chapter on computer-assisted legal research (Chapter 17) shows students how they can do legal research and investigation using CD-ROMs, the legal databases provided by Westlaw® and Lexis®, and online information available at various Web sites.

A Feature Focusing on Technology

The *Technology and Today's Paralegal* feature, which was added to the Second Edition, has been retained and updated for the Third Edition. Each of these boxed-in features, which appear throughout the text, focuses on how technology is affecting a specific aspect of paralegal work or on how paralegals can use technology to their benefit. For the Third Edition, we have added a "Technology Tip"

From Chapter 3 . . .

TECHNOLOGY AND TODAY'S PARALEGAL

Is E-Mail "Confidential"?

The widespread use of the Internet by lawyers and paralegals has raised a host of ethical issues, many of which you will read about in later chapters of this book. Here, we look at a question of particular importance to all legal professionals, including paralegals: Does communicating with a client via e-mail constitute a violation of the confidentiality rule?

STATE BAR ASSOCIATIONS CONSIDER THE ISSUE

The problem with using e-mail to communicate with clients is that there is an increased risk that an unauthorized person will intercept (and read) the e-mail. When state bar associations first considered whether e-mail communications violate the duty of confidentiality, most concluded that lawyers should not use e-mail for sensitive client communications unless the e-mail is encrypted (encoded using some type of encryption software). In 1997, however, a number of states reached the opposite conclusion—finding that unencrypted e-mail communications with clients do not violate an attorney's ethical obligations, at least under normal circumstances. Some states, such as Vermont, went on to say that while encryption is not required, it may be prudent to use encryption in situations where the message being conveyed is "of a very sensitive nature."

THE ABA TAKES A STAND

In 1999, the ABA attempted to settle the controversy by issuing a formal opinion (Opinion No. 99-413), which

concludes that "lawyers have a reasonable expectation of privacy in communications made by all forms of e-mail, including unencrypted e-mail sent on the Internet, despite some risk of interception and disclosure." Although the opinion authorizes lawyers to use e-mail to communicate with clients, it also cautions that, "particularly strong measures are warranted to guard against the disclosure of highly sensitive information." While the ABA's opinion provides some guidance, experts point out that when the opinion was formulated, encryption software was much more costly and burdensome than it is today.

TECHNOLOGY TIP

Despite the trend toward acknowledging e-mail as a confidential medium, as a paralegal you should be very cautious when communicating with clients over the Internet. The National Federation of Paralegal Associations (NFPA) advises that the best way to avoid possible confidentiality problems is simply not to put any confidential information on the Internet. NFPA also suggests that legal professionals consider using encryption for e-mail with clients and establish office procedures regarding e-mail (which could include a disclaimer that e-mail messages may not be secure).

at the conclusion of each feature that boils down the information contained in the feature into concrete suggestions for the paralegal student. For example, in Chapter 2 (Career Opportunities) we have included a feature called "Online Job Searching." The feature offers guidelines to students on how they can find employment opportunities using the Internet. Titles of other features include the following:

- Cyberspace Communications (Chapter 4).
- Filing Court Documents Electronically (Chapter 6).
- Online Access to Information in Product Liability Suits (Chapter 7).
- Contract Forms (Chapter 8).
- Electronic Discovery (Chapter 12).
- Courtroom Technology (Chapter 14).

Margin Web Sites

Every chapter includes several features titled *On the Web* in the margins. These features offer Web sites that students can access for further information on the topic being discussed in the text.

From Chapter 1 . . .

On the Web
For more information on the definitions of *paralegal* and *legal assistant* given by the ABA, NALA, NFPA, and AAfPE, go to the following Web sites:
ABA: http://www.abanet.org
NALA: http://www.nala.org
NFPA: http://www.paralegals.org
AAfPE: http://www.aafpe.org

On the Web
NALA is implementing an online campus for continuing legal education (CLE) at http://www.nalacampus.com. For information on NFPA's online CLE offerings, go to http://www.paralegals.org/CLE/home.html.

Chapter-Ending Internet Exercises

To help your students learn how to navigate the Web and find various types of information online, we have included at the end of each chapter one or more Internet exercises in a section titled *Using Internet Resources*. Each exercise directs the student to a specific Web site and asks a series of questions about the materials available at that site.

From Chapter 8 . . .

✻ USING INTERNET RESOURCES

1. Go to FindLaw's site on contracts, which is located at http://www.findlaw.com/01topics/07contracts/index.html.

   a. Under "FindLaw Resources," click on "FindLaw Summaries of Law—Contract Law." There, you will find a collection of articles on particular topics of interest. Scroll down to the listing titled "Contracts Law." Click on it, and browse around to see what information is available. Click on "Consideration," and read the summary provided. How many examples are given? Click on "Typical Contract Provisions," and read this section. How many different types of clauses are discussed? Note on a piece of paper the types of clauses identified.

   b. Return to the FindLaw page indicated above. Now click on "FindLaw Corporate Deals—Sample Contracts," under "FindLaw Resources." There, you can access contracts listed by industry, by type, or by company name, or you can browse through the most recent contracts added to the site. Using any of the methods available, select a contract to view. Note the name of the contract and its general purpose. Does the contract use all of the clauses you noted in part a of this question (typical contract provisions)? Does it use any? Which of the typical clauses are used?

   c. Return to the main FindLaw page again. Spend a few minutes browsing to see all that is available at (or through) this site. How do you think this site

WEST'S PARALEGAL ONLINE RESOURCE CENTER

The West Legal Studies Web site, at http://www.westlegalstudies.com, continues to offer numerous resources for paralegal professionals, instructors, and students. At this site, you and your students will find many links to legal and paralegal information sites. This site also hosts a page dedicated to *West's Paralegal Today*, Third Edition, where you and your students can find text updates, hot links, and other resources.

THE ORGANIZATION OF THIS TEXTBOOK

As every paralegal instructor knows, ideally materials should be presented in such a way that students can build their skills and knowledge bases block by block. This is difficult because, no matter where you begin, you will need to refer to some information that has not yet been presented to the student. For example, if you try to explain what paralegals do on the first or second day of class, you will necessarily have to mention terms that may be unfamiliar to the students, such as *litigation* or *substantive law* or *procedural law*. In writing this text, the authors have attempted, whenever possible, to organize the topics covered in such a way that the student is never mystified by terms and concepts not yet discussed.

We realize that no one way of organizing the coverage of topics in a paralegal text will be suitable for all instructors, but we have attempted to accommodate your needs as much as possible by organizing the text into three basic parts. Part 1 (Chapters 1–4) focuses primarily on the paralegal profession—its origins and development, the wide array of paralegal careers, the threshold ethical responsibilities of the profession, and the requirements and procedures that students can expect to find in the legal workplace. Part 2 (Chapters 5–11) focuses on substantive law and has been expanded to provide better coverage in basic areas of law. These areas include torts, contracts, intellectual property, estates, real property, business organizations, and employment, among others. Part 2 also covers administrative law and government regulation. In addition, coverage of several areas of law—such as product liability and family law—has been added. Part 3 (Chapters 12–18) looks in detail at legal procedures and paralegal skills. The student learns about the basic procedural requirements in civil and criminal litigation, as well as the skills involved in conducting interviews and investigations, legal research and analysis, and legal writing.

It is our hope that this organization of the materials will allow the greatest flexibility for instructors. Although to a certain extent each chapter in this text builds on information contained in previous chapters, the chapters and parts can also be used independently. In other words, those instructors who wish to alter the presentation of topics to fit their course outlines, or who wish to use selected chapters or parts only, will find it relatively easy to do so.

KEY FEATURES

In addition to the *Technology and Today's Paralegal* features, which we have already discussed, every chapter in this text has the following features. Each feature is set apart and used both to instruct and to pique the interest of your paralegal students.

Developing Paralegal Skills

These boxed-in features present hypothetical examples of paralegals at work to help your students develop crucial paralegal skills. The features include checklists and practical tips. Some examples are the following:

- Avoiding UPL Problems (Chapter 3).
- Medical Records (Chapter 7).
- Monitoring the *Federal Register* (Chapter 11).
- Locating Assets (Chapter 14).
- Effective Editing (Chapter 18).

From Chapter 2 . . .

> **DEVELOPING PARALEGAL SKILLS**
> **Building an Ethical Wall**
>
> Lana Smith, a paralegal, has been asked by her supervising attorney to set up an ethical wall because a new attorney, Sandra Piper, has been hired from the law firm of Nunn & Bush. While employed by Nunn & Bush, Piper represented the defendant, Seski Manufacturing, in the ongoing case of *Tymes v. Seski Manufacturing Co.* Lana's firm represents the plaintiff, Joseph Tymes, in that same case, so Piper's work for Nunn & Bush creates a conflict of interest. Lana makes a list of the walling-off procedures to use to ensure that the firm cannot be accused of violating the rules on conflict of interest.
>
> CHECKLIST FOR BUILDING AN ETHICAL WALL
> - Prepare a memo to the office manager regarding the conflict and the need for special arrangements.
> - Prepare a memo to the team representing Tymes to inform them of the conflict of interest and the special procedures to be used.
> - Prepare a memo to the firm giving the case name, the nature of the conflict, the parties involved, and instructions to maintain a blanket of silence with respect to Sandra Piper.
> - Arrange for Piper's office to be on a different floor from the team to demonstrate, if necessary, that the firm took steps to prevent Piper and the team from having access to one another or each other's files.
> - Arrange with the office manager for special computer passwords to be issued to the team members so that access to computer files on the *Tymes* case is restricted to team members only.
> - Place "ACCESS RESTRICTED" stickers on the files for the *Tymes* case.
> - Develop a security procedure for signing out and tracking the case files in the *Tymes* case—to prevent inadvertent disclosure of the files to Piper or her staff members.

Ethical Concerns

Every chapter presents one or more *Ethical Concerns*. These features typically take a student into a hypothetical situation that clearly presents an ethical problem. When possible, students are told what they should and should not do in the particular situations being discussed. Some examples are the following:

- Electronic Filing and Privacy Issues (Chapter 6).
- Confidentiality and Product Liability (Chapter 7).
- Potential Conflicts of Interest (Chapter 8).
- Keeping Client Information Confidential (Chapter 12).

From Chapter 8 . . .

ETHICAL CONCERN
Intellectual Property and Confidentiality

Working as a paralegal for an intellectual property firm can be an exciting profession. It can also present challenges for paralegals in the area of confidentiality. For example, suppose you are working for a firm that represents a motion picture company in an action against the creator of software that breaks the code of encrypted DVDs (digital versatile disks). The software is available free of charge on the Internet at a specific Web site and allows users to make "pirated" copies of DVD movies without the copyright owner's permission. Your brother, a computer wiz, has been making copies of DVDs from his home computer for the last six months. You don't know which software he uses, and you did not realize that he was violating copyright law until you began working on this case. The firm you work for is proposing to settle the case in exchange for the software creator's agreement to stop making the software available on the Internet and to hand over a list of all the users who have downloaded the software. Can you warn your brother about the proposed settlement? No, clearly you cannot divulge the client's information to anyone, including members of your own family. This is just one example of how paralegals working in intellectual property law might be tempted to disclose confidential information.

From Chapter 2 . . .

PARALEGAL PROFILE
Real Estate Paralegal

TERRYE PRYBYLSKI *is a real estate paralegal at a full-service law firm that has represented businesses and individuals since 1890, when the industrial age created a boomtown for the city of Detroit. The firm handled Detroit's incredible growth and survived and prospered during the trials of the twentieth century, including the stock market crash, two World Wars, the introduction of unions, race riots, and the onset of the information age and the explosion of technology. Today, the firm has approximately a hundred attorneys and twenty paralegals in offices located throughout Michigan. Prybylski works in the real estate group's transactional practice in downtown Detroit.*

Prybylski has been a paralegal since 1992. She earned a postgraduate paralegal–legal assistant certificate from the American Institute for Paralegal Studies, Inc., and a master of business administration degree from the University of Detroit–Mercy.

Before specializing in real estate, Prybylski worked as a paralegal at a natural gas utility company and a national bank, where she was considered a "jack of all trades." At the bank, she worked in the areas of litigation and corporate, employment, banking, and regulatory law in addition to real estate law. She is a member of the State Bar of Michigan–Legal Assistants Section, Detroit Metropolitan Bar Association, and National Association of Legal Assistants (NALA) and is a notary public.

What do you like best about your work?
"What I like best about my work is the diversity of the client base and the variety of duties that I perform. I interact with developers, national banks, national and local tenants (particularly retail clients), corporate owners, individual buyers and sellers, surveyors, environmental consulting firms, title companies, and local governments. Each deal is unique, with its own specific set of circumstances, and each poses a challenge."

What is the greatest challenge that you face in your area of work?
"I am responsible for obtaining the title work, surveys, zoning letters, certificates of occupancy, corporate documents, and related due diligence. It is not uncommon for a transaction to involve multiple properties located in a variety of states. It is often a challenge to coordinate the acquisition of all of the required information from the various sources in a timely manner. Time frames and closing dates do not always allow for the time desired, and it takes persistence and a great deal of organizational skill to guarantee that all of the required elements have been obtained, reviewed, and approved prior to the closing date."

What advice do you have for would-be paralegals in your area of work?
"You must recognize the important role you play in the grand scheme of things. Not all of your assignments will be glamorous, but your efforts are vital to the success of the matter. A simple mistake—such as an incorrect legal description of property, an incorrect tax parcel identification number, or failure to conform to geographical recording requirements—will result in a document's not being recorded in a timely manner. This may have serious consequences for the client. It is important to perform all job duties with professionalism. Even a mundane task, such as compiling the closing binder, must be done to the best of your ability because your work product reflects on you and your firm's reputation."

What are some tips for success as a paralegal in your area of work?
"Knowing how to navigate on the Internet is crucial. I have discovered valuable resources and obtained all sorts of useful information in a fraction of the time that more traditional methods would take to obtain the same results. Information on business entities, whom to contact for zoning approval at the county level, statutes, local surveyors, and other data are now available online. Being detail oriented and accurate is a necessity for a real estate paralegal. This comes into play in many aspects of the job, such as when reviewing surveys, title work, and legal descriptions. In any area of specialization, a good paralegal is a team player who is willing to go the distance to do whatever it takes to get the job done. Excellent verbal and written communication skills, as well as a willingness to learn and experience new challenges, will guarantee success in your profession."

Paralegal Profiles

Every chapter includes a profile of a paralegal who is currently working in a specific area of law. These profiles open with a short biography of the paralegal and then present the paralegal's own answers to questions asked by the interviewer. The paralegal tells of his or her greatest challenges on the job, gives suggestions about what he or she thinks students should concentrate on when studying to become paralegals, and offers tips for being a successful paralegal in his or her line of work. This feature gives your students insights into various legal specialties and the diversity of paralegal working environments.

Featured Guest Articles

Each chapter features a contributed article written by an educator or an expert in the field. These articles offer your students practical tips on some aspect of paralegal work relating to the topic covered in the chapter. Some examples are the following:

- "Mediation: Career Opportunities for Paralegals," by Fernaundra Ferguson, an assistant professor in the Criminal Justice and Legal Studies Department of the University of West Florida (Chapter 6).

- "Strategies for Protecting Intellectual Property: The Intellectual Property Audit," by Deborah E. Bouchoux, instructor and member of the advisory board for the legal assistant program at Georgetown University in Washington, D.C. (Chapter 8).

- "Ten Tips for Effective Client-Centered Interviewing," by Daniel G. Cantone, sole practitioner and adjunct professor at Syracuse University (Chapter 13).

- "Keeping Current on Computer Technology," by Brent Roper, an attorney with a master's degree in business administration who has published a number of textbooks and articles on law office computing and law office management (Chapter 17).

From Chapter 12 . . .

FEATURED GUEST: P. DAVID PALMIERE
Ten Tips for the Effective Use of Interrogatories

BIOGRAPHICAL NOTE

P. David Palmiere received his bachelor's degree magna cum laude in economics from the University of Michigan in 1972 and his law degree from the University of Michigan Law School in 1975. Palmiere, currently a member of the firm of Secrest, Wardle, Lynch, Hampton, Truex & Morley in Farmington Hills, Michigan, has practiced litigation for more than twenty-five years in courts from California to New York.

For the past twenty-four years, Palmiere has also been an adjunct professor in an ABA-accredited legal-assistant program at Oakland University in Rochester, Michigan, where he teaches litigation and also assisted in designing the litigation specialty curriculum. Palmiere has been a guest lecturer at Wayne State University School of Law and a featured speaker at the state convention of the Legal Assistants Association of Michigan.

Interrogatories are written questions to an opposing party requiring written answers. Interrogatories are a mainstay of discovery, but often interrogatory effort is wasted because of poor topic selection or ineffective drafting. Here are some guidelines for the effective use of interrogatories.

1. Interrogatories and Answers Are a Struggle between Adversaries. Good answers start with good questions. An interrogatory (question) is wasted if the answer is not meaningful. There are sanctions for bad faith answers to good questions. Ambiguous questions, however, allow the opponent to dodge the question without incurring sanctions. The more direct, crisp, and clear your phrasing, the more a fear of sanctions will compel informative answers. Always assume that your opponent will seize any excuse to decline to answer, and minimize such opportunities. If your questions pass the clarity test, they will probably be effective.

2. Limit Interrogatories to Appropriate Subjects. There are five basic discovery tools: interrogatories, requests for production of documents and things, requests for admission, depositions, and physical or mental examinations of persons. Each tool has its own role in discovery. Interrogatories are best used to elicit concrete items of factual information, such as names, addresses, dates, times, and places. Interrogatories are usually ineffective in asking for narrative accounts of complex facts or for the basis for opinions—tasks that are more appropriate to a deposition. Similarly, instead of wasting interrogatories asking for specifics about documents (other than who has them), it is better practice to join the interrogatories to a request for production of the documents themselves. Limit interrogatories to their most appropriate purpose—learning hard, factual data.

3. Use Contention Interrogatories. One exception to the foregoing is a "contention interrogatory," which asks the opponent for all facts supporting some assertion from the opponent's pleading. If the defendant asserts that the plaintiff's claim is barred by the statute of limitations, the plaintiff's contention interrogatory says, "Please state each fact that supports your contention that the plaintiff's claim is barred by the statute of limitations." Contention interrogatories can effectively smoke out and dispose of sham issues. Note, however, that contention interrogatories have a major blind spot: they do not elicit, except indirectly, information to *refute* the opponent's contentions. Other questions are needed for that.

4. Use Several Sets of Interrogatories at Strategic Points during the Discovery Process. Interrogatories are primarily used early in the case to gather leads for further investigation. But interrogatories are not "just for breakfast." They are also useful to follow up on leads developed in other discovery, such as document productions or depositions. As you

---

FEATURED GUEST, *Continued*

read every new document and deposition, list new or unanswered questions, and consider interrogatories as the tool of choice for following up on the matter.

5. Be Aware of Court Rules Concerning Interrogatories. The court hearing the case will have rules about interrogatories. Know those rules. For example, the Federal Rules of Civil Procedure allow interrogatories only *after* the lawyers have conferred about a discovery schedule. The federal rules also require court permission to ask more than twenty-five questions, including subparts. State courts have their own rules limiting or affecting the use of interrogatories. These limitations must be observed.

6. Each Interrogatory Must Stand on Its Own—The "Stranger in the Street" Test. Interrogatory questions are often flawed because they lack context. Give every question this test: If a stranger approached you in the street, and asked the question just as you have written it, without more, could you answer it? For example, a stranger approaches you and says, "What time was it?" Your natural response would be, "What time was *what*?" or "What are you talking about?" This question does not pass the "stranger in the street" test. Any question that fails the test will probably not bring a meaningful answer from the opponent.

7. Use Definitions to Supply Context for Questions. Open your interrogatories with definitions of terms to be used, such as "the incident." Be sure that your definitions are nonargumentative— for example, if a plaintiff defines "the incident" as "the collision caused by defendant's negligence," the defendant will object to every question using the term. Then, in the interrogatories, you may ask what time "the incident" took place or who saw any part of "the incident" without having to repeat the entire description to supply the necessary context. Once you define a term, however, use it consistently. Remember that this word now has a special meaning and cannot be used as if it were ordinary English.

8. Some Questions You Always Ask. Questions that you should always ask include questions about eyewitnesses, about the opponent's trial witnesses, and about the opponent's expert witnesses. Ask these even if you ask nothing else.

9. Master Standard Phrasing. Like other legal drafting, interrogatories tend to fall into standard patterns and phrases. Master these. Many lawyers begin each interrogatory, "Please state . . . ." If you do so, each item that follows must be an item of information. (Students often submit questions reading, "Please state each car that you own." One cannot "state" a car, but only

information about the car, which is not what the question asks.) When an interrogatory contains a condition, description, or qualification, place it at the beginning of the question: "For each lawsuit to which you have ever been a party, please state . . . ." This phrasing is an effective substitute for questions that would otherwise have an "if-then" structure ("If you have ever been a party to a lawsuit, then please state . . ."). Drafting will be simpler if you use singular word forms rather than plural. When using subparts, make sure each one follows grammatically from the body of the main question.

10. Make Effective Use of the Duty to Supplement Responses. Federal Rule 26(e) and many state rules establish a duty to supplement interrogatory responses. This duty is often overlooked. Send periodic letters to the opposition, requesting supplements of prior interrogatory answers under the applicable rule. This places your side in a strong position to object if surprises are sprung at the trial.

Today's Professional Paralegal

Near the end of every chapter we have included a special feature entitled *Today's Professional Paralegal*. This important feature exposes your students to situations that they are likely to encounter on the job and offers guidance on how certain types of problems can be resolved. Some examples are the following:

- Developing a Life-Care Plan (Chapter 7).
- Trademark Searches (Chapter 8).
- Family Law Specialists: Investigations (Chapter 9).
- Mapping Out a Research Strategy (Chapter 16).

From Chapter 4 . . .

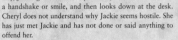
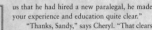

TODAY'S PROFESSIONAL PARALEGAL

Managing Conflict in the Legal Workplace

On Cheryl Hardy's first day at her new job as a legal assistant at Comp-Lease, Inc., a computer leasing corporation, Cheryl is introduced to the department staff by her boss, Dennis Hoyt. Dennis then takes her to meet the legal team. When she meets Jackie, the team secretary, Jackie gives her a frosty "Hello," without a handshake or smile, and then looks down at the desk. Cheryl does not understand why Jackie seems hostile. She has just met Jackie and has not done or said anything to offend her.

After her lunch break, Cheryl is given her first lease package to prepare. The work consists of drafting a lease (rental) agreement and giving it to the secretary to input into the computer and print out the agreement form. Cheryl prepares the draft and gives it to Jackie. Cheryl is very polite and tells Jackie not to rush because the agreement does not have to be sent out for two days. When Cheryl asks Jackie for the lease two days later, it is not done. Jackie tells Cheryl to check with her after lunch to see how it is coming. "Great," thinks Cheryl to herself, as she walks back to her desk. "My first week on the job and I'll be in trouble because of Jackie."

ANALYZING THE PROBLEM

Cheryl decides to talk to a co-worker, Sandy, about the problem. At lunch, Cheryl explains the situation to Sandy. "She probably resents you," says Sandy. "You see, Jackie has always wanted to be a paralegal. The company has a policy that you have to have a degree or a certificate, even if you have experience, and so she cannot move into a paralegal position without some education. She has not been able to attend a paralegal training program because of family obligations and the expense involved. I'm sure that she knows that you were a legal secretary and that you worked your way through school. When Dennis told

us that he had hired a new paralegal, he made your experience and education quite clear."

"Thanks, Sandy," says Cheryl. "That clears up the situation a lot. Now I can understand why she reacted the way she did to me."

SOLVING THE PROBLEM

Cheryl has an idea. She invites Jackie to lunch. Jackie talks about her interest in becoming a paralegal, her frustration with the company's policy, and her inability to get a certificate or degree because of her family obligations and the cost of going back to school. Cheryl tells Jackie that she was in a similar situation and that she got a scholarship from her school to pay for most of her education. She tells Jackie that she might be able to get one, too. She encourages Jackie by telling her, truthfully, that she is obviously bright enough to be a paralegal. Cheryl gives Jackie the name and phone number of Lois Allison, the director of the program that Cheryl attended. "Why don't you call her and tell her that I referred you? Explain that you are in the same situation that I was in when I started. She can tell you what might be available," suggested Cheryl.

When Cheryl returns to her office from lunch, she calls Lois Allison. She explains Jackie's situation and tells Lois that Jackie might be calling to get information on the program and scholarships. Lois replies that she will be happy to talk to Jackie and to help her if she can.

Later that afternoon, when Cheryl gives Jackie a lease package to prepare, Jackie prepares it right away. She even brings it into Cheryl's office, which she does not have to do. "I just want to thank you for going out of your way for me," says Jackie. "I called Lois Allison, and she wants me to come in and fill out some application forms. She thinks that I might qualify for a scholarship. So I might get to go to school after all." Cheryl smiles and replies, "I am glad that Lois could help you."

OTHER SPECIAL PEDAGOGICAL FEATURES

We have included in *West's Paralegal Today*, Third Edition, a number of additional pedagogical features, including those discussed below.

Chapter Outlines

On every chapter-opening page, a *Chapter Outline* lists the first-level headings within the chapter. These outlines allow you and your students to tell at a glance what topics are covered in the chapters.

Chapter Objectives

In every chapter, just following the *Chapter Outline*, we list five or six chapter objectives. Your students will know immediately what is expected of them as they read each chapter.

Margin Web Sites

As already mentioned, *On the Web* features appear in the page margins throughout the text. These features direct students to specific Web sites for further information on the topics being discussed. Note that Web sites are sometimes deleted and URLs are frequently changed as sites are redesigned. If you or your students encounter difficulties accessing one of the margin Web sites, refer to the instructions that appear in the Introduction to the Student, following this preface.

Vocabulary and Margin Definitions

Legal terminology is often a major challenge for beginning paralegal students. We have used an important pedagogical device—margin definitions—to help your students understand legal terms. Whenever an important term is introduced, it appears in boldface type and is defined. In addition, the term is listed and defined in the margin of the page, alongside the paragraph in which the boldfaced term appears.

At the end of each chapter, all terms that have been boldfaced within the chapter are listed in alphabetical order in a section called *Key Terms and Concepts*. Your students can briefly examine this list to make sure that they understand all of the important terms introduced in the chapter. If they do not understand a term completely, they can return to the chapter materials and review the term.

All boldfaced terms are again listed and defined in the *Glossary* at the end of the text. Spanish equivalents to many important legal terms in English are provided in a separate glossary.

Chapter Summaries

We have added a graphic chapter summary at the conclusion of each chapter for the Third Edition. These summaries illustrate the important concepts from the

estate administration
The process in which a decedent's personal representative settles the affairs of the decedent's estate (collects assets, pays debts and taxes, and distributes the remaining assets to heirs); the process is usually overseen by a probate court.

joint tenancy
The joint ownership of property by two or more co-owners in which each co-owner owns an undivided portion of the property. On the death of one of the joint tenants, his or her interest automatically passes to the surviving joint tenant or tenants.

✄ CHAPTER SUMMARY

From Chapter 6 . . .

Basic Judicial Requirements	1. *Jurisdiction*—Before a court can hear a case, it must have jurisdiction over the person against whom the suit is brought (*in personam* jurisdiction) or the property involved in the suit (*in rem* jurisdiction), as well as jurisdiction over the subject matter.
	a. Limited versus general jurisdiction—Limited jurisdiction exists when a court is limited to a specific subject matter, such as probate or divorce. General jurisdiction exists when a court can hear any kind of case.
	b. Original versus appellate jurisdiction—Courts that have authority to hear a case for the first time (trial courts) have original jurisdiction. Courts of appeals, or reviewing courts, have appellate jurisdiction; generally, these courts do not have original jurisdiction.
	c. Federal jurisdiction—Arises (1) when a federal question is involved (when the plaintiff's cause of action is based, at least in part, on the U.S. Constitution, a treaty, or a federal law) or (2) when a case involves diversity of citizenship (as in disputes between citizens of different states, between a foreign country and citizens of a state or states, or between citizens of a state and citizens or subjects of a foreign country) and the amount in controversy exceeds $75,000.
	d. Concurrent versus exclusive jurisdiction—Concurrent jurisdiction exists when two different courts have authority to hear the same case. Exclusive jurisdiction exists when only state courts or only federal courts have authority to hear a case.
	2. *Jurisdiction in cyberspace*—Because the Internet does not have physical boundaries, traditional jurisdictional concepts have been difficult to apply in cases involving activities conducted via the Web. Gradually, the courts are developing standards to use in determining when jurisdiction over a Web owner or operator in another state is proper.
	3. *Venue*—Venue has to do with the most appropriate location for a trial, which is usually the geographic area where the event leading to the dispute took place or where the parties reside.
	4. *Standing to sue*—A legally protected and tangible interest in a matter sufficient to justify seeking relief through the court system. The controversy at issue must also be a justiciable controversy—one that is real and substantial, as opposed to hypothetical or academic.
	5. *Judicial procedures*—Rules of procedure prescribe the way in which disputes are handled in the courts. The Federal Rules of Civil Procedure govern all civil litigation in federal courts. Each state has its own procedural rules (often similar to the federal rules), and each court within a state has specific court rules that must be followed.
State Court Systems	1. *Trial courts*—Courts of original jurisdiction, in which legal actions are initiated. State trial courts have either general jurisdiction or limited jurisdiction.
	2. *Intermediate appellate courts*—Many states have intermediate appellate courts that review the proceedings of the trial courts; generally these courts do not have original jurisdiction. Appellate courts ordinarily examine questions of law and procedure while deferring to the trial court's findings of fact.

chapter and show how the concepts are related to one another. The major topics discussed in the chapter appear in the left-hand column of the summary, with a synopsis of the concepts discussed under each topic listed in the right-hand column. This new, visually appealing format facilitates the student's review of the chapter contents.

Exhibits and Forms

When appropriate, we present exhibits illustrating important forms or concepts relating to paralegal work. Many exhibits are filled in with hypothetical data. Exhibits and forms in *West's Paralegal Today*, Third Edition, include those listed below:

- A Sample Retainer Agreement (Chapter 4).
- A Sample Complaint (Chapter 12).
- Major Procedural Steps in a Criminal Case (Chapter 15).
- An Investigation Plan (Chapter 13).

CHAPTER-ENDING MATERIALS FOR REVIEW AND STUDY

Every chapter contains numerous chapter-ending pedagogical materials. These materials are designed to provide a wide variety of assignments for your students. The chapter-ending pedagogy begins with the *Key Terms and Concepts*, followed by the chapter summaries, which we have already mentioned. Next are the materials described below.

Questions for Review

In every chapter are ten relatively straightforward questions for review. These questions are designed to test the student's knowledge of the basic concepts discussed in the chapter.

Ethical Questions

Because of the importance of ethical issues in paralegal training, we have also included at the end of each chapter two or more ethical questions. Each question presents a hypothetical situation, which is followed by one or two questions about what the paralegal should do to solve the dilemma.

Practice Questions and Assignments

The "hands-on" approach to learning paralegal skills is emphasized in the practice questions and assignments. There are several of these questions and assignments at the end of each chapter. A particular situation is presented, and the student is asked to actually carry out an assignment.

Questions for Critical Analysis

Every chapter has several questions for critical analysis. These questions are designed to elicit critical analysis and discussion of issues relating to the topics covered in the chapter.

Projects

There are two or more projects at the end of every chapter. These are specific work tasks that your students can carry out. Often, these projects involve obtaining information from sources that paralegals may deal with on the job, such as a library, a court, a prosecutor's office, or a police department.

Using Internet Resources

As already mentioned, concluding the chapter-ending materials in each chapter is a section titled *Using Internet Resources*. The Internet exercises presented in these sections are designed to familiarize students with useful Web sites and with the extensive array of resources available online.

APPENDICES

To make this text a reference source for your students, we have included the appendices listed below:

A   NALA's Code of Ethics and Professional Responsibility
B   NALA's Model Standards and Guidelines for the Utilization of Legal Assistants
C   NFPA's Model Code of Ethics and Professional Responsibility and Guidelines for Enforcement
D   The ABA's Model Guidelines for the Utilization of Legal Assistant Services
E   Paralegal Ethics and Regulation: How to Find State-Specific Information
F   Paralegal Associations
G   State and Major Local Bar Associations
H   Information on NALA's CLA and CLAS Examinations
I   Information on NFPA's PACE Examination
J   The Constitution of the United States
K   Spanish Equivalents for Important Legal Terms in English

NEW CHAPTERS AND SIGNIFICANT CHANGES TO THE THIRD EDITION

The authors have made a number of significant changes and additions to *West's Paralegal Today* for the Third Edition. We think that we have improved the text greatly, thanks in part to the many suggestions we have received from users of previous editions as well as from other paralegal educators and legal professionals.

New Chapters, Features, and Other Changes

Generally, all elements in the book—including the text, exhibits, features, and end-of-chapter pedagogy—have been updated as necessary. Significant additions and changes to the Third Edition include the following:

• **Two new chapters on substantive law**—Two chapters have been added to cover substantive law in greater depth. These additional chapters provide an expanded discussion of important concepts in torts, contracts, intellectual property, business organizations, real property, estates, administrative law, and employment.

• **Family law and product liability**—We have also added family law and product liability to the list of topics discussed.

• *Technology and Today's Paralegal*—As mentioned, this feature appears in every chapter and has been updated and modified to include practical technology tips for the paralegal student.

- **New *Featured Guests***—Most of the *Featured Guest* articles are new to this edition.
- **Graphic chapter summaries**—Each chapter now concludes with an in-depth summary presented in a visually appealing format.
- **Coverage of regulatory developments**—Current developments pertaining to paralegal licensing are discussed in Chapter 3.
- **Updated ethical rules**—The rules of ethical conduct for attorneys and other legal professionals have been updated as necessary.
- **Updated appendices**—All appendices have been updated as necessary.

For Users of the Second Edition

Those of you who have used the Second Edition of this text will probably want to know some of the other changes that have been made for the Third Edition. Besides those just mentioned, we have made the following changes to *West's Paralegal Today* for this edition:

- **Chapter 1** (Today's Professional Paralegal)—This chapter has been revised substantially and now includes a hypothetical case situation to illustrate the kinds of tasks that paralegals might perform and to stimulate students' interest.
- **Chapter 2** (Career Opportunities)—Updated information on where paralegals work, paralegal specialties, and paralegal compensation is provided in this chapter. Additional information on locating employers online is also included. A sample résumé of a paralegal without experience has been added to assist beginning paralegals in the application process.
- **Chapter 3** (Ethics and Professional Responsibility)—The 2002 Revisions to the American Bar Association's Model Rules of Professional Conduct have been incorporated into the discussion to keep paralegals up to date on ethical rules. In addition, recent developments regarding state regulation of paralegals and the unauthorized practice of law are discussed.
- **Chapter 5** (Sources of American Law)—More information has been added on the schools of legal thought and how different theories can affect how a judge interprets and applies the law to a specific set of facts. The sections on constitutional law and statutory law have been expanded.
- **Chapter 6** (The Court System and Alternative Dispute Resolution)—New sections have been added to address topics of growing concern—jurisdiction in cyberspace and online dispute resolution.
- **Chapter 7, 8, 9, 10** (Tort Law and Product Liability; Contracts and Intellectual Property Law; Real Property, Estates, and Family Law; Agency, Business Organizations, and Employment)—Chapters 7 and 8 of the Second Edition have been expanded and reorganized into four separate chapters to provide greater depth of coverage; additionally, the topics of product liability and family law are now included. Chapters 8 and 9 are largely new material and incorporate an up-to-date discussion of electronic contracting.
- **Chapter 11** (Administrative Law and Government Regulation)—This chapter has been streamlined and revised to focus more on major concepts in administrative law and procedure and less on naming the various administrative agencies and acts.
- **Chapter 12** (Civil Litigation—Before the Trial)—Chapter 10 from the Second Edition has been revised substantially and includes many new exhibits and more practical examples, in addition to an entirely new section and feature on electronic evidence.

- **Chapter 13** (Conducting Interviews and Investigations)—This chapter now precedes the chapter on trial procedures to stress the importance of factual investigation prior to trial. More examples and visually appealing exhibits have been added to illustrate key concepts, such as the types of interview questions. We have also added techniques for active listening, more online resources, and an expanded discussion of hearsay evidence.
- **Chapter 15** (Criminal Law and Procedures)—Chapter 12 from the Second Edition has been revised and streamlined for this chapter. New sections have been added on the different types of crimes, including cyber crimes. We have also expanded the discussion of the constitutional challenges and typical motions filed in criminal prosecutions.
- **Chapter 16** (Legal Research and Analysis)—This chapter integrates elements of Chapters 14 and 16 in the Second Edition into one comprehensive chapter that demonstrates how to find and analyze the law.

SUPPLEMENTAL TEACHING/LEARNING MATERIALS

West's Paralegal Today, Third Edition, is accompanied by what is arguably the largest number of teaching and learning supplements available for any text of its kind. We understand that instructors face a difficult task in finding the time necessary to teach the materials that they wish to cover during each term. In conjunction with a number of our colleagues, we have developed supplementary teaching materials that we believe are the best obtainable today. Each component of the supplements package is described below.

Instructor's Manual

Written by the authors of the text, the *Instructor's Manual* contains the following:

- A sample course syllabus.
- Chapter/lecture outlines.
- Teaching suggestions.
- Answers to text exercises and questions.
- Transparency masters and handouts are available online.
- PowerPoint presentations.

Online Resource

- At http://www.westlegalstudies.com, students can review chapter objectives to reinforce chapter-learning goals and read study tips dealing with issues found in the chapters of the text. This resource also contains extensive outlines for each chapter that will help students organize information and show how the concepts in the text relate to each other. In addition, students will discover practical advice that will help ease the way through studying, test-taking, writing essays, and more.
- Also at http://www.westlegalstudies.com, student interactive online quizzing is available. With the click of a mouse, students can access this robust technology study alternative that can help better prepare them for classroom exams. Interactive online quizzing provides students a chance to answer review questions directly relating to the text for each chapter. Each selected answer presents students with instant feedback and clarifies the rationale for correct and incorrect choices. This self-assessment tool can be accessed at school or at home, giving students more flexibility and opportunity to study.

Computerized Test Bank

Prepared by Susan Howery of Yavapai College, the Test Bank is available in a computerized format on CD-ROM. The platforms supported include Windows™ 98, ME, 2000, XP or a more recent version and Macintosh® system 8.5 or a more recent version including OS X in Classic mode.

- Multiple methods of question selection.
- Multiple outputs—that is, print, ASCII, RTF.
- Graphic support (black and white).
- Random questioning output.
- Special character support.

Citation-At-A-Glance

This handy reference card provides a quick, portable reference to the basic rules of citation for the most commonly cited legal sources, including judicial opinions, statutes, and secondary sources, such as legal encyclopedias and legal periodicals. *Citation-At-A-Glance* uses the rules set forth in *The Bluebook: A Uniform System of Citation*. A free copy of this valuable supplement is included with every student text.

Web Page

Come visit our Web site at **http://www.westlegalstudies.com**, where you will find valuable information specific to this book and other West Legal Studies texts.

Strategies for Paralegal Educators

Strategies and Tips for Paralegal Educators, a pamphlet by Anita Tebbe of Johnson County Community College, provides teaching strategies specifically designed for paralegal educators. It concentrates on how to teach and is organized in three parts: the WHO of paralegal education—students and teachers; the WHAT of paralegal education—goals and objectives; and the HOW of paralegal education—methods of instruction, methods of evaluation, and other aspects of teaching. A copy of this pamphlet is available to each adopter. Quantities for distribution to adjunct instructors are available for purchase at a minimal price. A coupon in the pamphlet provides ordering information.

Survival Guide for Paralegal Students

A pamphlet by Kathleen Mercer Reed and Bradene Moore covers practical and basic information to help students make the most of their paralegal courses. Topics covered include choosing courses of study and note-taking skills.

Westlaw®

West's online computerized legal-research system offers students "hands-on" experience with a system commonly used in law offices. Qualified adopters can receive ten free hours of Westlaw®. Westlaw® can be accessed with Macintosh and IBM PCs and compatibles. A modem is required.

West's Paralegal Video Library

West Legal Studies is pleased to offer the following videos at no charge to qualified adopters:

- *The Drama of the Law II: Paralegal Issues Video*
  ISBN: 0-314-07088-5
- *The Making of a Case Video*
  ISBN: 0-314-07300-0
- *ABA Mock Trial Video—Product Liability*
  ISBN: 0-314-07342-6
- *Arguments to the United States Supreme Court Video*
  ISBN: 0-314-07070-2

Court TV Videos

West Legal Studies is pleased to offer the following videos from Court TV for a minimal fee:

- *New York v. Ferguson—Murder on the 5:33: The Trial of Colin Ferguson*
  ISBN: 0-7668-1098-4
- *Ohio v. Alfieri*
  ISBN: 0-7668-1099-2
- *Flynn v. Goldman Sachs—Fired on Wall Street: A Case of Sex Discrimination?*
  ISBN: 0-7668-1096-8
- *Dodd v. Dodd—Religion and Child Custody in Conflict*
  ISBN: 0-7668-1094-1
- *In Re Custody of Baby Girl Clausen—Child of Mine: The Fight for Baby Jessica*
  ISBN: 0-7668-1097-6
- *Fentress v. Eli Lilly & Co., et al—Prozac on Trial*
  ISBN: 0-7668-1095-x
- *Garcia v. Garcia—Fighting over Jerry's Money*
  ISBN: 0-7668-0264-7
- *Hall v. Hall—Irretrievably Broken—A Divorce Lawyer Goes to Court*
  ISBN: 0-7668-0196-9
- *Maglica v. Maglica—Broken Hearts, Broken Commitments*
  ISBN: 0-7668-0867-x
- *Northside Partners v. Page and New Kids on the Block—New Kids in Court: Is Their Hit Song a Copy?*
  ISBN: 0-7668-9426-7

Please note that Internet resources are of a time-sensitive nature and URL addresses may often change or be deleted.

Contact us at westlegalstudies@delmar.com

ACKNOWLEDGMENTS FOR PREVIOUS EDITIONS

Numerous careful and conscientious individuals have helped us in this undertaking from the beginning. We continue to be indebted to those whose contributions helped to make previous editions of *West's Paralegal Today* a valuable teaching/learning text. We particularly thank the following paralegal educators for their insightful criticisms and comments:

Laura Barnard
Lakeland Community College, OH

Linda S. Cioffredi
Woodbury College, VT

Jeptha Clemens
Northwest Mississippi Community College, MS

Arlene A. Cleveland
Pellissippi State Technical Community College, TN

Lynne D. Dahlborg
Suffolk University, MA

Kevin R. Derr
Pennsylvania College of Technology, PA

Donna Hamblin Donathan
Marshall University Community College, OH

Wendy B. Edson
Hilbert College, NY

Pamela Faller
College of the Sequoias, CA

Gary Glascom
Cedar Crest College, PA

Dolores Grissom
Samford University, AL

Paul D. Guymon
William Rainey Harper College, IL

Sharon Halford
Community College of Aurura, CO

Jean A. Hellman
Loyola University, Chicago, IL

Melinda Hess
College of Saint Mary, NE

Marlene L. Hoover
El Camino College, CA

Susan J. Howery
Yavapai College, AZ

Melissa M. Jones
Samford University, AL

Jennifer Allen Labosky
Davidson County Community College, NC

Dora J. Lew
California State University, Hayward, CA

Mary Hatfield Lowe
Westark Community College, AZ

Gerald A. Loy
Broome Community College, NY

Linda Mort
Kellogg Community College, MI

Constance Ford Mungle
Oklahoma City University, OK

H. Margaret Nickerson
William Woods College, MO

Martha G. Nielson
University of California, San Diego, CA

Elizabeth L. Nobis
Lansing Community College, MI

Joy D. O'Donnell
Pima Community College, AZ

Anthony Piazza
David N. Myers College, OH

Francis D. Polk
Ocean County College, NJ

Ruth-Ellen Post
Rivier College, NH

Elizabeth Raulerson
Indian River Community College, FL

Kathleen Mercer Reed
University of Toledo, OH

Lynn Retzak
Lakeshore Technical Institute, WI

Evelyn L. Riyhani
University of California, Irvine, CA

Melanie A. P. Rowand
California State University,
Hayward, CA

Vitonio F. San Juan
University of La Verne, CA

Susan F. Schulz
Southern Career Institute, FL

Loretta Thornhill
Hagerstown Community College, MD

Julia Tryk
Cuyahoga Community College, OH

ACKNOWLEDGEMENTS FOR THE THIRD EDITION

During the preparation of the Third Edition of *West's Paralegal Today*, a number of professionals offered us penetrating criticisms, comments, and suggestions for improving the text. While we haven't been able to comply with every request, each of the reviewers listed below will see that many of his or her suggestions have been taken to heart.

Lia Barone
Norwalk Community College, CT

Chelsea Campbell
Lehman College, NY

Bob Diotalevi
Florida Gulf Coast University, FL

Dora Dye
City College of San Francisco, CA

Wendy B. Edson
Hilbert College, NY

Leslie Sturdivant Ennis
Samford University, AL

Linda Wilke Heil
Central Community College, NE

Louise Hoover
Rockford Business College, IL

Jill Jasperson
Utah Valley State College, UT

Deborah Winfrey Keene
Lansing Community College, MI

John G. Thomas, III
North Hampton County Community College, PA

We also are grateful to the following paralegal educators, our featured guests in *West's Paralegal Today*, Third Edition, for enhancing the quality of our book with their tips and illuminating insights into paralegal practice:

Deborah E. Bouchoux
Georgetown University, Washington, DC

Daniel G. Cantone
Private Law Practice/Syracuse University, NY

John DeLeo
Central Pennsylvania Business School, PA

Ramona P. DeSalvo
Private Law Practice/Southeastern Career College, TN

Wendy B. Edson
Hilbert College, NY

Fernaundra Ferguson
University of West Florida, FL

Anne Geraghty-Rathert
Webster University, MO

Marci S. Johns
Faulkner University, AL

Judy A. Long
Rio Hondo College, CA

Lisa L. Newcity
Roger Williams University, RI

P. David Palmiere
Oakland University, MI

Lloyd G. Pearcy
Private Law Practice

Brent Roper
Private Law Practice/Author

Karen Sanders-West
Private Law Practice

Richard M. Terry
Baltimore City Community College,
MD

Pamela Poole Weber
Seminole Community College, FL

Joseph F. Whalen
Southeastern Career College, TN

E. J. Yera
Holmes Regional Medical Center, FL

Additionally, we extend our gratitude to those on-the-job paralegals who agreed to appear in the *Paralegal Profiles* of *West's Paralegal Today*, Third Edition.

In preparing *West's Paralegal Today,* Third Edition, we were also the beneficiaries of the expertise brought to the project by the editorial and production staff of the West Legal Studies program. Our editor, Pamela Fuller, successfully guided the project through each phase and put together a supplements package that is without parallel in the teaching and learning of paralegal skills. Melissa Riveglia, our developmental editor, was also incredibly helpful in putting together the teaching/learning package. We also wish to thank our production manager, Carolyn Miller, and production editor, Betty Dickson, for their assistance throughout the production process.

A number of other individuals contributed significantly to the quality of *West's Paralegal Today*, Third Edition. We wish to thank Katherine M. Silsbee for her assistance in creating what we believe is the best introductory paralegal text on the market today. We also thank Lavina Leed Miller and Roxie Lee for their help in coordinating the authors' work on the project and for their research and proofreading efforts. We were fortunate to have had the copyediting skills of Beverly Peavler. We are grateful to Pat Lewis and Suzie Franklin Defazio, whose proofreading skills will not go unnoticed, and to Suzanne Jasin for her assistance.

We know that we are not perfect. If you or your students have suggestions on how we can improve this book, write to us. That way, we can make *West's Paralegal Today*, Third Edition, an even better book in the future. We promise to answer every single letter that we receive.

Roger LeRoy Miller
Mary Meinzinger Urisko

INTRODUCTION TO THE STUDENT

The law sometimes is considered a difficult subject because it uses a specialized vocabulary and requires substantial time and effort to learn. Those who work with and teach law believe that the subject matter is exciting and definitely worth your efforts. Everything in *West's Paralegal Today: The Legal Team at Work,* Third Edition, has been written for the precise purpose of helping you learn the most important aspects of law and legal procedures.

Learning is a lifelong process. Your learning of legal concepts and procedures will not end when you finish your paralegal studies. On the contrary, the end of your paralegal studies marks the beginning of your learning process in regard to law and legal procedures. Just as valuable to you as the knowledge base you can acquire from mastering the legal concepts and terms in *West's Paralegal Today,* Third Edition, is a knowledge of *how to learn* those legal concepts and terms. The focus in this introduction, therefore, is on developing learning skills that you can apply to any subject matter and at any time throughout your career.

The suggestions and study tips offered in this introduction can help you "learn how to learn" law and procedures and maximize your chances of success as a paralegal student. They can also help you build lifelong learning habits that you can use in other classes and throughout your career as a paralegal.

MASTERING YOUR TEXT

A mistake commonly made by students is the assumption that the best way to understand the content of written material is to read and reread that material. True, if you have read through a chapter ten times, you have probably acquired a knowledge of its contents, but think of the time you have spent in the process. What you want to strive for is using your time *effectively*. We offer here some suggestions on how to study the chapters of *West's Paralegal Today* most effectively.

Read One Section at a Time

A piano student once said to her teacher, "This piece is so complicated. How can I possibly learn it?" The teacher responded, "It's simple: measure by measure." That advice can be applied to any challenging task. As a paralegal student, you are faced with the task of learning complicated legal concepts and procedures. By dividing up your work into manageable units, you will find that before long, you have achieved your goal. Each chapter in *West's Paralegal Today,* Third Edition, is divided into several major sections. By concentrating on sections, rather than chapters, you will find it easier to master the chapter's contents.

Assume, for example, that you have been assigned to read Chapter 9 of *West's Paralegal Today,* Third Edition. That chapter covers basic concepts and principles involving real property, estates, and family law. Mastering each of these topics requires you to learn a number of different legal concepts and terms. You will find it easier to master all of these topics if you concentrate on just one topic at a time. For example, you might begin with the section on real property and focus only on that section.

Once you have read through a section, do not stop there. Go back through the section again and organize the material in your mind. Outlining the section is one way to mentally organize what you have read.

Make an Outline

An outline is simply a method for organizing information. The reason an outline can be helpful is that it illustrates visually how concepts relate to each other. Outlining can be done as part of your reading of each section, but your outline will be more accurate (and more helpful later on) if you have already read through a section and have a general understanding of the topics covered in that section.

THE BENEFITS OF OUTLINING.   Although you may not believe that you need to outline, our experience has been that the act of *physically* writing an outline for a chapter helps most students to improve greatly their ability to retain and master the material being studied. Even if you make an outline that is no more than the headings in the text, you will be studying more efficiently than you otherwise would be.

Outlining is also a paralegal skill. As a paralegal, you will need to present legal concepts and fact patterns in an outline format. For example, paralegals frequently create legal memoranda to summarize their research results. The legal memorandum is usually presented in an outline format, which indicates how the topics covered in the memo relate to one another logically or sequentially. There is no better time to master the skill of outlining than the present, while you are a student. You can learn this skill by outlining sections and chapters of *West's Paralegal Today,* Third Edition.

IDENTIFY THE MAIN CONCEPTS IN EACH SECTION.   In outlining a chapter, you can use the outline at the beginning of the chapter as a starting point. The chapter-opening outlines include the headings of the major sections within the chapter. Use these headings as a guide when creating a more thorough and detailed outline. Be careful, though. To make an effective outline, you have to be selective. Outlines that contain all the information in the text are not very useful. Your objective in outlining is to identify main concepts and to arrange more detailed concepts under those main concepts. Therefore, in outlining, your first goal is to *identify the main concepts in each section.* Often the headings within your textbook and in the chapter-opening outlines are sufficient as identifiers of the major concepts. You may decide, however, that you want to phrase an identifier in a way that is more meaningful to you.

OUTLINE FORMAT.   Your outline should consist of several levels written in a standard outline format. The most important concepts are assigned upper-case roman numerals; the second most important, capital letters; the third most important, numbers; the fourth most important, lower-case letters; and the fifth most important, lower-case roman numerals. The number of levels you use in an outline varies, of course, with the complexity of the subject matter. In some outlines, or portions of outlines, you may need to use only two levels. In others, you may need five or more levels.

As an example of how to use numerals and letters in an outline, we present below a partial outline of the contracts section in Chapter 8 of *West's Paralegal Today*, Third Edition.

FUNDAMENTAL LEGAL CONCEPTS: CONTRACTS

I. Definition of a contract: A contract is any agreement (based on a promise or an exchange of promises) that can be enforced in court. A promise is an assurance that one will or will not do something in the future.

II. Requirements to form a valid contract

   A. Agreement—Agreement is divided into two events: an offer and an acceptance. One party must offer to enter into a legal agreement, and another party must accept the terms of the offer.

      1. The offer—Three elements are necessary:

         a. The offeror (the party making the offer) must have the intent to be bound by the offer.

         b. The terms of the offer must be reasonably certain or definite (note that some terms may be left open in sales contracts).

         c. The offer must be communicated to the offeree (the party to whom the offer is made).

      2. Termination of the offer—The offeror can normally revoke (take back) an offer at any time prior to acceptance.

         a. Both a rejection of the offer and the making of a counteroffer (by the offeree) terminate the original offer.

      3. Acceptance—Acceptance by the offeree results in a legally binding contract (provided that all of the other requirements of a valid contract are met).

         a. The terms of the offer must be accepted exactly as stated by the offeror (the mirror image rule).

         b. Acceptance must be timely—within the time period designated by the offeror or within a reasonable time.

         c. Under the mailbox rule, acceptance becomes valid the moment it is deposited in the mail (even if it is never received by the offeror).

   B. Consideration . . .

Consider Marking Your Text

From kindergarten through high school, you typically did not own your own textbooks. They were made available by the school system. You were told not to mark in them. Now that you own your own text for a course, you can greatly improve your learning by marking your text. There is a trade-off here. The more you mark up your textbook, the less you will receive from the bookstore when you sell it back at the end of the semester. The benefit is a better understanding of the subject matter, and the cost is the reduction in the price you receive for the resale of the text. Additionally, if you want a text that you can mark with your own notations, you necessarily have to buy a new one or a used one that has no markings. Both carry a higher price tag than a used textbook with markings.

THE BENEFITS OF MARKING.   Marking is helpful because it assists you to become an *active* participant in the mastery of the material. Researchers have shown that the physical act of marking, just like the physical act of outlining, helps you better retain the material. The better the material is organized in your mind, the more you will remember. There are two types of readers—passive and active. The active reader outlines and/or marks. Active readers typically do better on exams. Perhaps one of the reasons that active readers retain more is because the physical act of outlining and/or marking requires greater concentration. It is through greater concentration that more is remembered.

DIFFERENT WAYS OF MARKING.   The most commonly used form of marking is to underline important points. The second most commonly used method is to use a felt-tipped highlighter, or marker, in yellow or some other transparent color. Marking also includes circling, numbering, using arrows, making brief notes, and any other method that allows you to locate things when you go back to skim the pages in your textbook prior to an exam—or when creating your outline, if you mark your text first and then outline it.

POINTS TO REMEMBER WHEN MARKING.   Here are two important points to remember when marking your text:

1. *Read the entire section before you begin marking.* You cannot mark a section until you know what is important, and you cannot know what is important until you read the whole section.
2. *Do not mark too extensively.* You should mark your text selectively. If you fill up each page with arrows, asterisks, circles, and underlines, marking will be of little use. When you go back to review the material, you will not be able to find what was important. The key is *selective* activity. Mark each page in a way that allows you to see the most important points at a glance.

Memory Devices

During the course of your study of *West's Paralegal Today,* Third Edition, you will encounter numerous legal terms that will most likely be new to you. Your challenge will be to remember these terms and incorporate them into your own "working" vocabulary. You will also need to remember legal concepts and principles. We look here at some techniques for learning and retaining legal terms and concepts.

FLASH CARDS.   Using flash cards is a remarkably effective method of learning new terms or concepts. Through sheer repetition, or drilling, flash cards force you to recall certain ideas and repeat them. Although published flash cards are available in many bookstores, you should try to create your own by writing terms or concepts on index cards. Write the key term or concept on one side and the definition, process, or description on the other side.

There are several advantages to creating your own flash cards. First, the exercise of writing the information will help you insert the term into your permanent memory. Second, you do not need flash cards for terms that you already know or that you will not need to know for your particular course. Third, you can phrase the answer in a meaningful way, with unique cues that are designed just for your purposes. This personalizes the flash card, making the information easier to remember. Finally, you can modify the definition, if need be, so that it matches more closely the particular definition preferred by your instructor.

It is helpful to create your flash cards consistently and routinely at a given point in the learning process. One good moment is when you are reading or outlining your text. Make a flash card for each boldfaced term and write the margin definition on the flash card. Also include pronunciation instructions, if appropriate, on the card.

Take your flash cards with you everywhere. Review them at lunch, while you wait in line, or when you ride on the bus. When a flash card contains a term that is difficult to pronounce, say the term aloud, if possible, as often as you can. When you have a term memorized, set that card aside but save it as an exam-review device for later in the term. Prepare new cards as you cover new terms or concepts in class.

MNEMONICS.   One method that students commonly employ to remember legal concepts and principles is the use of mnemonic (pronounced "nee-*mahn*-ick") devices. Mnemonic devices are merely aids to memory. A mnemonic device can be a word, a formula, or a rhyme. As an aid to remembering the elements of a cause of action in negligence (see Chapter 7), for example, you might use the mnemonic ABCD, in which the letters represent the following concepts:

A represents "A duty of care."
B represents "Breach of the duty of care."
C represents "Causation (the breach must cause an injury)."
D represents "Damage (injury or harm)."

Similarly, to remember the basic activities that paralegals may not legally undertake (see Chapter 3), you might use the mnemonic FACt, in which the letters represent the following concepts:

F represents "fees"—paralegals may not set legal fees.
A represents "advice"—paralegals may not give legal advice.
Ct represents "court"—paralegals, with some exceptions, may not represent clients in court.

Whenever you want to memorize various components of a legal doctrine or concept, consider devising a mnemonic. Mnemonics need not make sense in themselves. The point is, if they help you remember something, then use them. Any association you can make with a difficult term to help you pronounce it, spell it, or define it more easily is a useful learning tool.

Identify What You Do Not Understand

One of the most important things you can do prior to class is clarify in your mind which terms, concepts, or procedures you *do not* understand. You can do this when marking your text by placing check marks or question marks by material that you find difficult to comprehend. Similarly, you can include queries in your outline. For example, in the sample partial outline of contracts presented earlier in this introduction, you might add a query following the subsection on acceptance that reads, "What is considered to be a 'reasonable time'"?

Once you have outlined and marked your text, go back to any problem areas that you have encountered and *think about them*. You will find that it is very exciting to figure out difficult material on your own. If you still do not understand a concept thoroughly, make a note to follow up on this topic later in the classroom. Perhaps the instructor's lecture will clarify the issue. If not, make a point of asking for clarification.

As a paralegal, you may be frequently asked to undertake preliminary investigations of legal claims. Identifying what facts are *not known* is the starting point for any investigation and focuses investigatory efforts. As a student, you might think about class time as an opportunity to "investigate" further the subject matter of your course. Identifying before class what you do not know about a topic allows you to focus your "investigative" efforts, particularly your listening efforts, during class and to maximize classroom opportunities for learning.

LEARNING IN THE CLASSROOM

The classroom is the heart of your learning experience as a paralegal student. Each instructor develops an overall plan for a course that includes many elements, which are integrated, or brought together, during class sessions. A major element in your instructor's course plan will be, of course, the material presented in your textbook, *West's Paralegal Today,* Third Edition. As discussed in the preceding section, reading your textbook assignments thoroughly, before class, is one way to enhance your chances of truly mastering the subject matter of the course. Equally important to this goal, though, are listening carefully to your instructor and taking good notes.

Be an Active Listener

The ability to listen actively is a learned skill and one that will benefit you throughout your career as a paralegal. When your supervising attorney gives instructions, for example, it is crucial that you understand those instructions clearly. If you do not, you will need to ask the attorney to further clarify the instructions until you know exactly what your assignment is. Similarly, when you are interviewing clients or witnesses, you will need to be constantly interacting, mentally, with the information the client or witness is giving you so that you can follow up, immediately if necessary, on that information with further questions or actions.

As a paralegal student, you can practice listening skills in the classroom that you will need to exercise later on the job. The more immediate benefit of listening actively is, of course, a better chance of obtaining an excellent course grade.

In a nutshell, active listening as a student requires you to do the following:

1. *Listen attentively.* For anything to be communicated verbally by one person to another, the listener has to pay attention. Otherwise, no communication will take place. If you find your attention wandering in the classroom, make a conscious effort to become alert and focus on what is being said.

2. *Mentally interact with what is being said.* Active listening involves mentally "acting" on the information being conveyed by the speaker (your instructor). For example, if your instructor is discussing the elements required for a cause of action in negligence, you do not want simply to write down, word for word, what the instructor is saying. Rather, you first make sure that you *understand* the meaning of what is being said. This requires you to think about what is being said in the context of what else you know about the topic. Does the information make sense within that context? Does what you are hearing raise further questions in your mind? If so, make a note of them.

3. *Ask for clarification.* If you do not understand what the instructor is saying or if something is confusing, ask for clarification. How you do this will depend to some extent on the size of your class and the degree of classroom formality. In some classes, you might feel comfortable raising your hand and questioning the instructor at that point during the lecture or discussion. In other classes, you might make a note to talk to the instructor about the topic after class or later, during the instructor's office hours.

Take Good Notes

The ability to take good notes is another skill that will help you excel both in your paralegal studies and on the job as a paralegal. Ideally, you will understand clearly everything that is being said in the classroom, and note taking will simply consist of jotting down, in your own words, brief phrases and sentences to remind you of what was stated. Often, however, you may not understand fully what the instructor is talking about, or the class period may be half over before it becomes clear to you where your instructor is going with a certain idea or topic. In the meantime, should you take notes?

The best answer to this question is, of course, "Ask for clarification." But in some situations, interrupting a lecturer may be awkward or perceived as discourteous. In these circumstances, the wiser choice might be to take notes. Write down, to the extent possible, what the instructor is saying, including brief summaries of any examples the instructor is presenting. Later, when you have more knowledge of the subject, what the instructor said during that period may fall into place. If not, find an opportunity to ask for clarification.

Two other suggestions for taking good notes and making effective use of them are the following: (1) develop and use a shorthand system and (2) review and summarize your notes as soon as possible after class.

DEVELOP AND USE A SHORTHAND SYSTEM.   There may be times during a lecture when you want to take extensive notes. For example, your instructor may be discussing a hypothetical scenario to illustrate a legal concept. Because you know that hypothetical examples are very useful in understanding (and later reviewing) legal concepts, you want to include a description of the hypothetical example in your notes. Using abbreviations and symbols can help you include more information in your notes in less time.

In taking notes of a hypothetical example, consider using a single letter to represent each person or entity involved in the example. This eliminates the need to write and rewrite the names as they are used. For example, if a hypothetical involves three business firms, you could designate each firm by a letter: *A* could stand for Abel Electronics, *B* for Brentwood Manufacturing, and *C* for Crandall Industries.

Certain symbols and abbreviations, including those listed below, are fairly widely used as a kind of "shorthand" by legal professionals and others to designate certain concepts, parties, or procedures:

Δ or D	defendant
π or P	plaintiff
≈	similar to
≠	not equal to, not the same as
[	therefore
a/k/a	also known as
atty	attorney
b/c or b/cz	because
b/p	burden of proof
cert	*certiorari*
dely	delivery
dep	deposition
disc	discovery
JML	judgment as a matter of law
JNOV	judgment *non obstante veredicto* (notwithstanding the verdict)
JOP	judgment on the pleadings

juris or **jx**	jurisdiction
K	contract
mtg	mortgage
n/a	not applicable
neg	negligence
PL	paralegal
Q	as a consequence, consequently
re	regarding
§ or **sec**	section
s/b	should be
S/F	Statute of Frauds
S/L	statute of limitations

You will want to expand on this short list by creating and using other symbols or abbreviations. Once you develop a workable shorthand system, routinely use it in the classroom and then carry it over to your job. Most firms or corporations you will work for will also commonly use symbols and abbreviations, which you can add to your shorthand system later. It may also be helpful to become familiar with proofing symbols, which are listed under "proofreading" in the dictionary.

REVIEW AND REVISE YOUR NOTES AFTER EACH CLASS.   An excellent habit to form is reviewing and revising your class notes as soon as possible after the class period ends. Often, at the moment you write certain notes, you are not sure of how they fit in the overall design of the lecture. After class, however, you usually have a better perspective and know how the "pieces of the puzzle" fit together. Reviewing and summarizing your notes while the topic is still fresh in your mind—at the end of each day, for example—gives you the opportunity to reorganize them in a logical manner.

If you have a computer available, consider also typing up your notes. That way, when you want to review them, you will be able to read them quickly. Using a basic outline format when typing your notes (or rewriting them, if you do not have a computer available) will be particularly helpful later. You can tell at a glance the logical relationships between the various statements made in class.

Although reviewing and summarizing your notes each day or at other frequent intervals may seem overly time consuming, in the long run it pays off. First, as with outlining and marking a text, reviewing your notes after class allows you to learn actively—you can think about what was covered during the class period, place various concepts in perspective, and decide what you do or do not understand after you complete your review. Second, you have probably already learned that memory is fickle. Even though we think we will not forget something we learned, in fact, we often do. When preparing for an exam, for example, you will want to remember what the instructor said in class about a particular topic. But, if you are like most people, your memory of that day and that class period may be rather fuzzy several weeks later. If you have taken good notes and summarized them legibly and logically, you will be able to review the topic quickly and effectively.

Networking in the Classroom

Several times in *West's Paralegal Today*, Third Edition, the authors, the featured guests, and the paralegals profiled mention the importance of networking. The best time to begin networking is in the classroom. Consciously make an effort to get to know your instructor. Let him or her come to know you and your interests. Later, when looking for a job, you may want to ask that instructor for a reference.

Similarly, make an effort to become acquainted with other students in your class. Compared with students who are taking other college courses, such as math and history courses, those of you in paralegal studies are more likely to be working in the same geographic area and may eventually belong to the same paralegal associations. Establishing connections with your classmates now may lead to networking possibilities later on the job, which offers many benefits for paralegals. One good way to establish long-term relationships with other students is by forming a study group.

Forming and Organizing a Study Group

Many paralegal students join together in study groups to exchange ideas, to share the task of outlining subjects, to prepare for examinations, and to lend support to each other generally. If you want to start a study group, a good way to find potential members is to observe your classmates and decide which students participate actively and frequently in class. Then approach those individuals with your idea of forming a study group. The number of participants in a study group can vary. Ordinarily, three to five members is sufficient for a good discussion. Including more than six members may defeat the goal of having each member actively participate, to the greatest extent possible, in group discussions.

Some paralegal students form study groups that meet on an "as needed" basis. For example, any member can call a meeting when there is an upcoming exam or difficult subject matter to be learned. Other students establish ongoing study groups that meet throughout the year (and sometimes for the entire paralegal program). The group works as a team and as such is an excellent preparatory device for working as part of a legal team in a law firm. Study groups can also continue on after course work is completed to prepare for certification exams. These groups are also a great way to build relationships with other future paralegals with whom you may want to network later, on the job.

MEETING TIMES AND PLACES.   It is helpful to set up a regular meeting time and hold that time sacred. The members must be committed to the meeting times and to completing their assignments, or the group will not serve its purpose. Study groups can meet anywhere. You might meet in a classroom, another school room, a member's home, a park, or a restaurant. Many paralegal schools and colleges have multipurpose rooms or study areas available to students who wish to meet in small groups. Some rooms are equipped with easels or drawing boards, which facilitate discussions. Audiovisual equipment may also be available for the group's use, such as a television with a VCR for viewing videotaped lectures. The group should select a meeting place that has limited distractions and sufficient space to accommodate each member's opened books, notes, and other materials.

WORK ALLOCATION.   Teamwork is very important in the paralegal profession. Study groups can help you learn to function as a member of a team by distributing the workload among the group. Work (such as outlining chapters) should be allocated among the group members. It is important to define clearly who will be doing what work. It may be a good idea at the close of each meeting to have each member state out loud what work he or she will be responsible for completing prior to the next meeting. Whatever work one member does, he or she should make copies to distribute to the other members at the meeting.

EVALUATING YOUR GROUP.   You should realize from the outset that your study group will be of little help if you are doing most of the work. You need to make sure that everyone who joins the group is as committed to learning the material as you are and that you make this concern known to the others. The teamwork approach is only effective if everybody does his or her share. Teamwork involves trust and reliance. If you cannot trust one of the members to form an accurate outline of a topic, you will not be able to rely on that outline. You will end up doing the work yourself, just as a precaution. Therefore, be very selective about whom you invite to join the group. If you joined an already existing group, leave it if it turns out to be a waste of your time.

ORGANIZING YOUR WORK PRODUCT

A part of the learning experience takes place through special homework assignments, research projects, and possibly study-group meetings. For example, if you are studying pretrial litigation procedures, you will read about these procedures in Chapter 12 of *West's Paralegal Today*, Third Edition. Your instructor will also likely devote class time to a discussion of these procedures. Additionally, you may be asked to create a sample complaint or to check your state's rules governing the filing of complaints in state courts. You also might have notes on a study-group discussion of these procedures.

How can you best organize all the materials generated during the coverage of a given topic? Here are a few suggestions that you might find useful. If you follow these suggestions, you will find that reviewing your work prior to exams is relatively easy—most of the work will already have been done.

Consider Using a Three-Ring Binder

An excellent way to integrate what you have learned is by using a three-ring binder and divider sheets with tabs for the different topics you cover. As you begin studying *West's Paralegal Today*, Third Edition, for example, consider having a different section in your binder for each chapter. Within that section, you can place your chapter outline (formed while reading the text), notes taken in the classroom or during other reading assignments, samples of projects you have done relating to topics in that chapter, and so on.

Integrate Your Notes into One Document, If Possible

If you have used a computer to key in your chapter outlines and class notes, consider incorporating everything you have learned about a topic into one document—a master, detailed outline of the topic. You can do this relatively easily by using the "cut and paste" feature of word-processing programs. The result will be a comprehensive outline of a particular topic that will make reviewing the topic prior to an exam (and perhaps later, on the job) a simple matter.

THE BENEFITS OF USING A COMPUTER

Many of the paralegals profiled in *West's Paralegal Today*, Third Edition, mentioned that if they were students again, they would spend more time developing computer skills. If you do not already have a personal computer, consider acquiring one, if possible. Alternatively, see if you can arrange with someone else to use his or her personal computer on a routine basis. If your school or college has computers available in the library or some other place for student use, you might use one of those computers. Find out when there is usually a computer available—such as early in the morning—and use the computer routinely at this time.

Using a computer provides many benefits. First, you can practice your keyboarding and word-processing skills (essential paralegal skills) simultaneously as you take notes or work on research or other class projects. Second, if you have a computer available, you can type up and better organize your notes. Such time is well spent because it not only increases your knowledge of the topics but also makes it easy to review what you have learned prior to exams.

Finally, a key benefit of using a computer is the quality of any work product or homework assignment that you submit to your instructor. The editing and formatting features of word-processing programs allow you to correct misspelled words, reorganize your presentation, and generally revise your document with little effort. The spell-checker and grammar-checker features help you avoid glaring errors. The formatting features allow you to present your document in an attractive format. You can change margins and use different fonts (such as italics or boldface) to emphasize certain words or phrases.

As a paralegal, you will be using a computer and a word-processing system to generate your work. You will also be expected to know how to use computers to create quality work products. The more you can learn about computers and word processing as a student, the easier it will be for you to perform your job as a paralegal.

GOING ONLINE

Another benefit of using a computer is, of course, the ability to go "online"—that is, connect to the Internet—and access the vast resources available on that worldwide computer network. In Chapter 17 of *West's Paralegal Today,* Third Edition, you will learn how the Internet can be used by legal professionals to obtain information on a variety of topics. A large number of colleges and universities offer free Internet access to their students. If you do not have a personal computer, check with your library to see if you can go online using one of the computers the library makes available to students.

You can obtain information online about most of the topics covered in this text. To help you learn how to find and evaluate specific online information, every chapter in this book ends with one or more Internet exercises in a section titled *Using Internet Resources.* Additionally, we have provided Internet addresses for numerous Web sites in the margins of the pages. If you go to these Web sites, you will find additional information about the topic being discussed in the text. In the *Technology and Today's Paralegal* features throughout this text, we have provided other Web sites when appropriate, and Chapter 17 (titled "Computer-Assisted Legal Research") contains numerous references to specific Web sites that offer useful information for paralegals and other legal professionals.

Realize that Internet sites tend to come and go, and there is no guarantee that a site referred to in this text will be there by the time this book is in print. We have tried, though, to include sites that so far have proved to be fairly stable. If you do have difficulty reaching a site (that is, if your destination is "Not Found" or has "No DNS Entry"), do not immediately assume that the site does not exist. First, recheck the Web site address (Uniform Resource Locator, or URL) shown in your browser. Remember you have to type the URL exactly as written: upper case and lower case are important. If it appears that the URL has been keyed in correctly, then try the following technique: delete all of the information to the right of the forward slash that is farthest to the right, and press "Enter."

For example, suppose that you have tried unsuccessfully to access the University of Washington's Internet Legal Resources at the following Web site: http://lib.law.washington.edu/research/research.html. First, check the URL as you keyed it in to make sure it is correct. Then delete the final "research.html" from the URL, and press "Enter." If you still have problems, delete "research," which is now the term farthest to the right. Eventually, you will get back to the home page and can attempt to locate the information you are looking for from there. If the home page is no longer functioning, you can try using the search function on your browser (enter "University of Washington Internet Legal Resources") to determine if the site still exists.

PREPARING FOR EXAMS

Being prepared for exams is crucial to doing well as a paralegal student. If you have followed the study tips and suggestions given in the preceding pages of this introduction, you will have little problem preparing for an exam. You will have at your fingertips detailed outlines of the topics covered, a marked textbook that allows you to review major concepts quickly and easily, and class notes. If you have integrated your outlines and class notes in one comprehensive, detailed outline, you will have an even easier task when it comes time to prepare for an examination.

In addition to mastering the material in *West's Paralegal Today*, Third Edition, and in the classroom, if you want to do well on an exam, you should develop an exam-taking strategy. For example, prior to any exam, you should find answers to the following questions:

- What type of exam are you going to take—essay, objective, or both?
- What reading materials and lectures will be covered on the exam?
- What materials should you bring to the exam? Will you need paper to write on, or will paper be provided?
- Will you be allowed to refer to your text or notes during the exam (as in an open-book exam)?
- Will the exam be computerized? If so, you will probably need to bring several number 2 pencils to the exam.
- How much time will be allowed for the exam?

The more you can find out in advance about an exam, the better you can prepare for it. For example, suppose you learn that there will be an essay question on the exam. One way to prepare for the question is to practice writing timed essays. In other words, find out in advance how much time you will have for each essay question—say, fifteen minutes—and then practice writing an answer to a sample essay question during a fifteen-minute time period. This is the only way you will develop the skills needed to pace yourself for an essay exam. Because most essay exams are "closed book," do your timed essay practice without using the book.

Usually, you can anticipate certain essay exam questions. You do this by going over the major concept headings in your lecture notes and in your text. Search for the themes that tie the materials together, and then think about questions that your instructor might ask you. You might even list possible essay questions as a review device. Then write a short outline for each of the questions that will most likely be asked. Some instructors give their students a list of questions from which the essay questions on the exam will be drawn. This gives you an opportunity to prepare answers for each of the questions in advance. Even though you cannot take your sample essays to class and copy them there, you will have organized the material in your mind.

TAKING EXAMS

There are several strategies you can employ while taking exams to improve your grade, including those discussed below.

Following Instructions

Students are often in such a hurry to start an exam that they take little time to read the instructions. The instructions can be critical, however. In a multiple-choice exam, for example, if there is no indication that there is a penalty for guessing, then you should never leave a question unanswered. Even if there are only a few minutes remaining at the end of the exam, you should guess at the answers for those questions about which you are uncertain.

You also need to make sure that you are following the specific procedures required for the exam. Some exams require that you use a number 2 lead pencil to fill in the dots on a machine-graded answer sheet. Other exams require underlining or circling. In short, read the instructions carefully.

Finally, check to make sure that you have all the pages of the examination. If you are uncertain, ask the instructor or the exam proctor. It is hard to justify not having done your exam correctly because you failed to answer all of the questions. Simply stating that you did not have them will pose a problem for both you and your instructor. Do not take a chance. Double-check to make sure.

Use Exam Time Effectively

Examinations are often timed. Timed examinations require that a question or cluster of questions be answered within a specified period of time. If you must complete thirty multiple-choice questions in one hour, then you have two minutes to work on each question. If you finish fifteen of those questions in one minute instead of two, then you will have banked fifteen minutes that can be spent elsewhere on the examination or used to double-check your answers.

Consider the following example. Assume that you have ninety minutes for the entire exam—thirty minutes to answer the multiple-choice questions, fifteen minutes to answer the true-false questions, and forty-five minutes to answer a long essay question. If you can shave ten minutes off the time it takes to answer the multiple-choice section and five minutes off the time it takes to answer the true-false questions, you will have fifteen additional minutes to complete the long essay question.

Taking Objective Examinations

The most important point to discover initially with any objective test is whether there is a penalty for guessing. If there is none, you have nothing to lose by guessing. In contrast, if a point or portion of a point will be subtracted for each incorrect answer, then you probably should not answer any question purely through guesswork.

Students usually commit one of two errors when they read objective-exam questions: (1) they read things into the questions that do not exist, or (2) they skip over certain words or phrases.

Most test questions include key words such as:

all
always
never
only

If you miss these key words, you will be missing the "trick" part of the question. Also, you must look for questions that are only *partly* correct, particularly if you are answering true-false questions.

Never answer a multiple-choice question without reading all of the alternatives. More than one of them may be correct. If several answers seem correct, make sure you select the one that seems the *most* correct.

Whenever the answer to an objective question is not obvious, start with the process of elimination. Throw out the answers that are clearly incorrect. Even when there is a penalty for guessing, if you can throw out several obviously incorrect answers, you may wish to guess by choosing among the remaining ones because your probability of choosing the correct answer is relatively high. Typically, the easiest way to eliminate incorrect answers is to look for those that are meaningless, illogical, or inconsistent. Often, test authors put in choices that make perfect sense and are indeed true but are not the answer to the question you are to answer.

Writing Essay Exams

As with objective exams, you need to read the directions to the essay questions carefully. It is best to write out a brief outline *before* you start answering the question. The outline should present your conclusion in one or two sentences, then your supporting argument. You should take care not to include in your essay information that is irrelevant, even if you think it is interesting. It is important to stay on the subject. We can tell you from firsthand experience that no instructor likes to read answers to unasked questions.

Finally, write as legibly as possible. Instructors will find it easier to be favorably inclined toward your essay if they do not have to reread it several times to decipher the handwriting.

PART I

THE PARALEGAL PROFESSION

C H A P T E R 1

TODAY'S PROFESSIONAL PARALEGAL

Chapter Outline

INTRODUCTION ✵ WHAT IS A PARALEGAL? ✵ WHAT DO PARALEGALS DO? ✵ PARALEGAL EDUCATION ✵ PARALEGAL SKILLS AND ATTRIBUTES ✵ THE FUTURE OF THE PROFESSION

After completing this chapter, you will know:

- What a paralegal is.
- What kinds of tasks paralegals perform.
- What are some of the professional associations of paralegals.
- The education and training available to paralegals.
- Whether paralegals must be certified or licensed.
- Some skills and attributes of the professional paralegal.

INTRODUCTION

If you are considering a career as a paralegal, be prepared to be part of an exciting and growing profession. In an effort to cut the cost of legal services to clients, law firms are giving more and more responsibilities to paralegals. The opportunities for paralegals who want to work outside of law firms (in corporations or government agencies, for example) are also expanding dramatically. Despite the economic slump in the early 2000s, the paralegal profession has continued to grow, and the average paralegal's salary has increased. In fact, according to one survey, paralegals in 2001 enjoyed one of the largest salary increases in more than six years (9.4 percent).[1]

How do you know if you want to become part of this dynamic profession? The first step in finding out if this is the right career for you is to become familiar with what a paralegal is, what kinds of work paralegals do, and what education and skills are needed. These are the topics we cover in this first chapter. In Chapter 2, you will learn about where paralegals work, how much they earn, and how they got their jobs. As you read through each of the chapters in this book, remember that this is only an introduction to the profession and the starting point of your education. You should supplement what you learn in the classroom by talking and networking with paralegals that work in various professional environments. After all, in today's competitive job market, whom you know can sometimes be as important as what you know in getting the job you desire.

On the Web
For more information on the definitions of *paralegal* and *legal assistant* given by the ABA, NALA, NFPA, and AAfPE, go to the following Web sites:
ABA: **http://www. abanet.org**
NALA: **http://www.nala.org**
NFPA: **http://www. paralegals.org**
AAfPE: **http://www. aafpe.org**

WHAT IS A PARALEGAL?

For years, there has been an ongoing debate among the various organizations of attorneys and paralegals on how to define exactly what a paralegal is. This debate probably stems from the fact that paralegals perform such a wide variety of duties that it is difficult to come up with a "one-size-fits-all" definition. Adding to the problem is the use of two different labels—*paralegal* and *legal assistant*—to describe essentially the same job or person. These different labels often confuse the public and have fueled debates within the profession as well.

In this book, we use the terms *paralegal* and *legal assistant* interchangeably, as is often done in the legal community. Although some individuals or groups may prefer one label to another, such disagreement does not mean that the labels describe different job duties. Indeed, some persons who are trained professional paralegals may be called something else entirely at their workplace, such as *legal technician* or *legal research specialist*.

After years of disagreement, two of the major organizations involved have finally reached a consensus on the definition of *paralegal*. The **American Bar Association (ABA)**, which is a national association for attorneys, and the **National Association of Legal Assistants (NALA)**, which is the largest national organization of paralegals, now jointly agree to the following definition:

> A **legal assistant** or **paralegal** is a person qualified by education, training, or work experience who is employed or retained by a lawyer, law office, corporation, governmental agency or other entity who performs specifically delegated substantive legal work, for which a lawyer is responsible.

The **National Federation of Paralegal Associations (NFPA)**, which is the second largest paralegal association, prefers the term *paralegal* to *legal assistant*.[2] Members of NFPA were concerned by the fact that many attorneys refer to their secretaries as legal assistants and wanted to distinguish the role of paralegals as professionals.

American Bar Association (ABA)
A voluntary national association of attorneys. The ABA plays an active role in developing educational and ethical standards for attorneys and in pursuing improvements in the administration of justice.

National Association of Legal Assistants (NALA)
One of the two largest national paralegal associations in the United States; formed in 1975. NALA is actively involved in paralegal professional development.

paralegal (or legal assistant)
A person qualified by education, training, or work experience who is employed or retained by a lawyer, law office, corporation, governmental agency, or other entity who performs specifically delegated substantive legal work, for which a lawyer is responsible.

National Federation of Paralegal Associations (NFPA)
One of the two largest national paralegal associations in the United States; formed in 1974. NFPA is actively involved in paralegal professional development.

Regardless of what they are called, paralegals or legal assistants today perform many functions that traditionally were performed by attorneys. The paralegal's work falls somewhere between that of an attorney and that of a legal secretary. As the definition above indicates, paralegals perform substantive legal work that they are trained to perform through education, experience, or (usually) both.

WHAT DO PARALEGALS DO?

Paralegals assist attorneys in many different ways. The following list is just a sampling of some of the tasks that legal assistants typically perform in a traditional setting—the law office. Keep in mind, though, that today's paralegals work in many nontraditional settings, including corporations, government agencies, courts, insurance companies, real estate firms, and virtually any other entity that uses legal services. Throughout this book, you will read about the specific things paralegals do in different settings.

A Sampling of Paralegal Tasks

Typically, legal assistants perform the following tasks:

- *Conduct client interviews and maintain general contact with clients*—provided that the client is aware of the status and function of the legal assistant and the legal assistant does not give legal advice.
- *Locate and interview witnesses*—to gather relevant facts and information about a lawsuit, for example.
- *Conduct legal investigations*—to obtain, organize, and evaluate information from a variety of sources, such as police reports, medical records, photographs, court documents, experts' reports, technical manuals, product specifications, and other statistical data.
- *Calendar and track important deadlines*—such as the date by which a certain document must be filed with the court or the date by which the attorney must respond to a settlement offer.
- *Organize and maintain client files*—to keep the multitudes of documents in each client's file readily accessible.
- *Conduct legal research*—to identify, analyze, and summarize the appropriate laws, court decisions, or regulations that apply to a client's case.
- *Draft legal documents*—such as legal correspondence, interoffice memoranda, documents to be filed with the court, contracts, wills, and mortgages.
- *Summarize witness testimony*—such as when depositions (sworn testimony) are taken of individuals out of court or when the parties have given written statements.
- *Attend legal proceedings*—such as real estate closings, depositions, executions of wills, court or administrative hearings, and trials with an attorney.
- *Use computers and technology*—to perform many of the above tasks.

Paralegals' Duties Vary

The specific tasks that paralegals perform vary dramatically depending on the size of the office, the kind of law that the firm practices, and the amount of experience or expertise the paralegal has. If you work in a one-attorney office, for example,

---

ETHICAL CONCERN

Paralegal Expertise and Legal Advice

Paralegals often become very knowledgeable in a specific area of the law. If you specialize in environmental law, for example, you will become very knowledgeable about environmental claims. In working with a client on a matter involving an environmental agency, you might therefore be tempted to advise the client on which type of action would be most favorable to him or her. Never do so. As will be discussed in detail in Chapter 3, only attorneys may give legal advice, and paralegals who give legal advice risk penalties for the unauthorized practice of law. Whatever legal advice is given to the client either must come directly from the attorney or, if from you, must reflect exactly (or nearly exactly) what the attorney said with no embellishment on your part. After consulting with your supervising attorney, for example, you can say to the client that Mr. X (the attorney) "advises that you do all that you can to settle the claim as soon as possible."

---

you may also perform certain secretarial functions. Your tasks might range from conducting legal research and investigating the facts, to photocopying documents, keying data into the computer, and answering the telephone while the secretary is out to lunch. If you work in a larger law firm, you usually have more support staff (secretaries, file clerks, and others) to whom you can delegate tasks. Your work might also be more specialized, and you may only work on certain types of cases. If you work in a law firm's real estate department, for example, you may deal only with legal matters relating to that area of law.

Although paralegal duties vary, document management, client relations, and research are the tasks that paralegals report spending the most time performing.[3] One way to better understand how a paralegal's functions might vary is to examine a typical scenario. The following hypothetical case illustrates the variety of tasks one paralegal might typically perform, as well as the roles that other paralegals may play in the same case.

The Paralegal at Work—A Hypothetical Case

Assume that you graduated from a paralegal program nine months ago and are currently working at Morris & Buckley. Morris & Buckley is a small firm in Florida with seven attorneys and two paralegals. For the most part, the firm handles personal-injury lawsuits and workers' compensation cases (benefits available under state law in order to compensate workers injured on the job; see Chapter 10). A client, Barbara Kaiser, comes in to the office to meet with attorney Ryan Buckley. The attorney asks you to sit in on the interview.

THE FACTS.   Kaiser was employed at a local plant nursery located directly across the street from her house until she was in an automobile accident on March 7, 2003. On the day of the accident, Kaiser was at her home when a huge thunderstorm sent a deluge of rain and hail down on the greenhouses at the rear of the plant nursery. The owner of the nursery was out of town. Although Kaiser was not scheduled to work that day, she received a telephone call from another employee at the nursery, who was in a panic. The plastic roofing on two of the greenhouses had ripped, and the ground was flooded. Kaiser, fearing the exotic plants inside would die, told the other employee that she would help.

Kaiser set out in her own car, planning to purchase some plastic roofing material for the greenhouse and some equipment to pump the water off the plants. While en route, Kaiser lost control of her vehicle at a stoplight and collided with a utility company truck that was rushing to repair a power outage. Paramedics extricated Kaiser from the wreckage and took her to the hospital, where she spent several weeks recovering after the accident. She had ruptured her spleen and broken several ribs and her jawbone. In addition, Kaiser's back was injured, although the doctors were unable to pinpoint what was causing her to suffer such severe back pain.

Kaiser had been off work for five months. She had applied for workers' compensation benefits, but the state had denied her claim on the ground that she was not at work at the time of the accident. The utility company's insurance had paid for her hospital expenses, but the insurance company had refused to pay for continuing therapy for her back injury. Because of the pain, Kaiser could not resume working after the accident and lost her job. Kaiser wants the attorney to advise her whether she can sue her employer, the utility company, and/or the state for denying her claim and to obtain compensation for her injuries.

YOUR ROLE AS A PARALEGAL IN A SMALL LAW FIRM.   In the above situation, a paralegal can do a number of things to assist attorney Buckley.

Case Management and Investigations.   First, you could draft a follow-up letter to Kaiser thanking her for choosing Morris & Buckley. In that letter, you might ask her to sign and return the enclosed forms authorizing the release of her medical records and other records to your office. You might next open a file for the case and enter Kaiser's information into the computerized case management system. Perhaps you will contact the hospital, doctors, police, insurance companies, the nursery, and the state to obtain whatever records and reports they have that will help the attorney evaluate Kaiser's claims. You will, of course, need to keep track of all evidence and information you discover as it comes in.

Legal Research, Drafting, and Client Relations.   Attorney Buckley might also ask you to research the issue of whether Kaiser was acting within the scope of her employment at the time of the accident and whether she had in any way contributed to the accident. He may want you to write a memorandum for him, summarizing your findings and telling him what you think would be the likely outcome of Kaiser's case. If it looks like Kaiser has a legitimate claim, Buckley may ask you to contact witnesses, request information and evidence from other parties, and set up depositions (meetings in which individuals give sworn testimony). You might also be asked to assist him in drafting the complaint—the initial document filed with the court that begins a lawsuit. You may also be instructed to arrange for an expert to evaluate Kaiser's injuries and provide testimony at trial. You could attend negotiations or hearings with the attorney. Often, it will be your responsibility to keep Kaiser apprised of what's happening on her case by e-mail, telephone, or letter.

Summarizing Witness Testimony and Trial Preparation.   If the case actually goes to trial, you will likely spend a lot of time getting prepared—contacting witnesses, organizing the evidence and documents, creating a trial notebook (which contains the trial briefs, legal research, documents, and strategy notes that the attorney will rely on at trial), summarizing witness testimony, obtaining background information on expert witnesses, preparing jury instructions, and researching issues that may come up at the trial. The attorney may even ask you to attend and assist in the trial.

THE ROLES OF OTHER LEGAL ASSISTANTS IN THE SAME CASE.   In the above scenario, other legal assistants are likely to be employed by the opposing parties—the utility company (whose driver was involved in the collision), the employer (if the employer retains the services of an attorney), and any insurance company that may be involved. Paralegals that work for the state's workers' compensation board or in the courts may also be involved in Kaiser's case. The individual functions that they perform depend on their level of experience and the specific policies of their employer. A legal assistant working for the utility company, for example, may research the company's potential liability under the law and the extent to which the company is covered by insurance. He or she may then prepare a memorandum for the attorney that will be defending the utility company. If the case does go to trial, that paralegal may have responsibilities similar to those that you would perform for the law firm representing Kaiser.

Paralegals and Technology

As technology advances, the role of many legal assistants is expanding, and they are increasingly becoming the technology experts at law firms. Because lawyers are busy with the practice of law and paralegals are often in the best position to know the firm's needs, many paralegals today take a leading role in reviewing and recommending new specialized legal software programs and online databases. In one survey conducted by *Legal Assistant Today,* 99.6 percent of paralegals polled reported using a computer on a daily basis, and 54.6 percent said that they were part of the technology decision-making process.[4]

Computer use and technical knowledge have thus become invaluable to today's paralegal. Paralegals use new computer software packages for internal case management and to track the number of hours billed to clients. Imaging software enables legal assistants to scan documents directly into a computer's database. The Internet and various CD-ROM packages allow paralegals to perform sophisticated legal research and investigation without leaving their desks. When preparing cases for trial that involve many documents, paralegals can now use litigation support software to retrieve, organize, and index the various materials for presentation. E-mail facilitates quick communication and improves efficiency. These technologies will be discussed in the appropriate chapters throughout this book. The point here is that technology is one of the foremost areas of expanding paralegal responsibility, and those entering the profession should realize that technological skills will greatly enhance their marketability.

PARALEGAL EDUCATION

The first paralegals were competent legal secretaries who learned from on-the-job training how to perform more complex legal tasks given to them by the attorneys for whom they worked. No formal paralegal education programs existed until the late 1960s, when the demand for lower-cost legal services increased. Once attorneys realized that using paralegals was extremely cost-effective and benefited both the client and the firm (as you will read in Chapter 4), the number of paralegal education programs increased dramatically. According to the ABA's Standing Committee on Legal Assistants, there are now more than a thousand programs operating in the United States. A great deal of variety exists, however, in the types of programs offered and the quality of the education provided.

On the Web
The Web site for the ABA's Standing Committee on Legal Assistants is: **http://www. abanet.org/legalassts/ approval.html**. (*Note:* No Web address ever ends in a comma, period, or semicolon. Consequently, you should ignore such punctuation when it appears at the ends of Web addresses cited in this book.)

On the Web
Information on paralegal education programs is available on both the NALA and NFPA Web sites (**http://www.nala. org** and **http://www. paralegals.org**).

Educational Options

The role of higher education and formal paralegal education has become increasingly important in the growth and development of the paralegal profession. Numerous colleges, universities, and business and private schools now offer programs. Generally, paralegal education programs fall into one of four categories:

- Two-year community college programs, culminating in the award of an associate of arts degree or a paralegal certificate. Such programs usually require the completion of approximately 60 semester hours and include some general education requirements.

- Four-year bachelor's degree programs with a major or minor in paralegal studies. A bachelor's degree in paralegal studies usually requires the completion of about 120 semester hours, with 50 to 60 of these hours spent on general education courses. A person may select a minor field that enhances her or his desirability in the job market. Conversely, an individual who majors in another field—for example, nursing—and obtains a minor in paralegal studies will also be very marketable to potential employers.

- Certificate programs offered by private institutions, usually 3 to 18 months in length. Typically, this type of program requires only a high school diploma or the equivalent for admission.

- Postgraduate certificate programs, usually 3 to 12 months in length, culminating in the award of a paralegal certificate. These programs require that the individual already have a degree in order to be admitted; some also require that the individual have achieved a certain grade point average.

Because those seeking to become paralegals have diverse educational backgrounds, capabilities, and work experience, no single type of program is best for everyone. Which program is most appropriate depends on the needs of the individual and the job market that he or she will enter.

Curriculum—A Blend of Substantive and Procedural Law

substantive law
Law that defines the rights and duties of individuals with respect to each other, as opposed to procedural law, which defines the manner in which these rights and duties may be enforced.

A legal assistant's education includes the study of both substantive law and procedural law. **Substantive law** includes all laws that define, describe, regulate, and create legal rights and obligations. For example, a law prohibiting employment discrimination on the basis of age falls into the category of substantive law. **Procedural law** establishes the methods of enforcing the rights established by substantive law. Questions about what documents need to be filed to begin a lawsuit, when the documents should be filed, which court will hear the case, which witnesses will be called, and so on are all questions of procedural law. In brief, substantive law defines our legal rights and obligations; procedural law specifies what methods, or procedures, must be employed to enforce those rights and obligations.

procedural law
Rules that define the manner in which the rights and duties of individuals may be enforced.

The Role of the AAfPE and ABA in Paralegal Education

American Association for Paralegal Education (AAfPE)
A national organization of paralegal educators; the AAfPE was established in 1981 to promote high standards for paralegal education.

The **American Association for Paralegal Education (AAfPE)** was formed in 1981 to promote high standards for paralegal education. The AAfPE and the ABA are the two major organizations responsible for developing the standards and curriculum for paralegal education programs across the nation. At present, the only state that requires a paralegal to meet certain minimum educational requirements is California.[5] Although education may not be mandated by the state, however, many employers today either require or prefer job candidates with a certain level of education. Some employers even select only graduates from well-established programs.

In 1974, the ABA first established a set of educational standards for paralegal training programs. Since then, the ABA guidelines have been revised several times to keep pace with changes in the paralegal profession. Paralegal schools are not required to be approved by the ABA. Rather, ABA approval is a voluntary process that gives extra credibility to the schools that successfully apply for it. Programs that meet the ABA's quality standards and that are approved by the ABA are usually referred to as **ABA–approved programs.** Of the paralegal education programs in existence today, the ABA has approved 254.

Certification

Certification refers to formal recognition by a professional group or state agency that an individual has met certain standards of proficiency specified by that group. Generally, this means passing an examination given by the organization and meeting certain requirements with respect to education and/or experience. Note that the term *certification,* as used here, does not refer to receiving a paralegal certificate. You may obtain a paralegal certificate after completing school, but you will not be considered a *certified paralegal* unless you complete the NALA, NFPA, or state certification process. Currently, no state *requires* paralegals to take a certification examination. Although most employers also do not require certification, earning a voluntary certificate from a professional society or the state can offer a competitive advantage in the labor market and lead to a higher salary (see Chapter 2).

NALA CERTIFICATION.   Paralegals who meet the standards set by NALA are eligible to take a two-day, comprehensive examination to become a **Certified Legal Assistant (CLA).** The exam is given three times a year at several regional testing centers and covers basic areas of substantive and procedural law. NALA also offers the **Certified Legal Assistant Specialist (CLAS)** exam to those who are already CLAs and who want to demonstrate special competence in a particular field of law. CLAS exams are offered in the following areas: bankruptcy, civil litigation, probate and estate planning, corporate and business law, criminal law and procedure, real estate, and intellectual property.[6] Appendix H provides more detailed information on NALA certification and requirements.

NFPA CERTIFICATION.   Paralegals with at least two years of work experience and a bachelor's degree can take the Paralegal Advanced Competency Exam (PACE) through NFPA. The PACE examination is broken down into two tests, one general and one specialized. Those who pass the examination use the designation **Registered Paralegal (RP).** Further information on the PACE program is provided in Appendix I of this book.

STATE CERTIFICATION.   Several states, including California, Florida, Louisiana, and Texas, have implemented voluntary statewide certification programs. Many more are considering implementing such programs. Generally, paralegal organizations (such as NALA and NFPA) are in favor of *voluntary* certification and oppose *mandatory* (legally required) certification or state licensing (as you will read in Chapter 3).

Continuing Legal Education

Paralegals, like attorneys, often supplement their formal education by attending **continuing legal education (CLE) programs.** CLE courses, which are offered by

---

ABA–approved program
A legal or paralegal educational program that satisfies the standards for paralegal training set forth by the American Bar Association.

certification
Formal recognition by a private group or a state agency that an individual has satisfied the group's standards of proficiency, knowledge, and competence; ordinarily accomplished through the taking of an examination.

 On the Web
You can learn about upcoming CLAS exams on the NALA Web site at **http://www.nala.org/ educ.htm.**
For more information on NFPA's PACE program, go to **http://www.paralegals.org/ PACE/home.html.**

Certified Legal Assistant (CLA)
A legal assistant whose legal competency has been certified by the National Association of Legal Assistants (NALA) following an examination that tests the legal assistant's knowledge and skills.

Certified Legal Assistant Specialist (CLAS)
A legal assistant whose competency in a legal specialty has been certified by the National Association of Legal Assistants (NALA) following an examination of the legal assistant's knowledge and skills in the specialty area.

Registered Paralegal (RP)
A paralegal whose competency has been certified by the National Federation of Paralegal Associations (NFPA) after the paralegal's successful completion of the Paralegal Advanced Competency Exam (PACE).

continuing legal education (CLE) programs
Courses through which attorneys and other legal professionals extend their education beyond school.

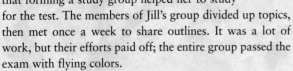

DEVELOPING PARALEGAL SKILLS

Preparing for the CLA Exam

Rita Barron received her paralegal certificate over a year ago and has been working in a law office since graduation. She plans to take the Certified Legal Assistant (CLA) exam in a few months. Rita consults with Jill Sanderson, a CLA, about taking the exam. Jill advises Rita that forming a study group helped her to study for the test. The members of Jill's group divided up topics, then met once a week to share outlines. It was a lot of work, but their efforts paid off; the entire group passed the exam with flying colors.

STUDY GROUP TIPS

- Select committed group members.
- Devise a plan for sharing the work.
- Clearly assign topics to be outlined.
- Share outlines and assignments regularly.
- Evaluate the group members' efforts.
- Consult online resources or a CLA review guide.

On the Web

NALA is implementing an online campus for continuing legal education (CLE) at **http://www.nalacampus.com**. For information on NFPA's online CLE offerings, go to **http://www.paralegals.org/CLE/home.html**.

state bar associations and paralegal associations, often take the form of special seminars and workshops that focus on specific topics or areas of law. Such programs are a good way to learn more about a specialized area of law or keep up to date on the latest developments in the law and in technology. Many employers today encourage their paralegals to take CLE courses and often pay some or all of the costs involved.[7]

Additionally, some paralegal organizations require their members to complete a certain number of CLE hours per year as a condition of membership. Both NALA and NFPA require paralegals that are certified to take CLE courses every year in order to maintain their status. California is the only state, as yet, to require a minimum number of CLE hours from *all* individuals who work as paralegals.

PARALEGAL SKILLS AND ATTRIBUTES

As noted earlier, paralegals today perform many tasks that lawyers used to perform. Thus, the demands on paralegals to be professional and efficient have increased. In order to be successful, a paralegal not only must possess specific legal knowledge but also should exhibit certain aptitudes and personality traits. For example, paralegals need to be able to think logically and to analyze complex issues of law and conflicting descriptions of fact. Some general characteristics that paralegals should have (or try to develop) are discussed below.

Analytical Skills

In any working environment, paralegals may be responsible for gathering and analyzing certain types of data. A corporate paralegal, for example, may be required to analyze new government regulations to see how they will affect the corporation. A paralegal working for the federal Environmental Protection Agency may be responsible for collecting and analyzing data on toxic waste disposal and drafting a memo setting forth his or her conclusions on the matter.

Legal professionals need to be able to take complex theories and fact patterns and break them down into smaller, more easily understandable components. That is how lawyers formulate arguments and judges decide cases. The process of legal analysis is critical to the paralegal's duties, especially when the paralegal is engaged in factual investigation, trial preparation, and legal research and writing. Analytical reasoning will be discussed in greater depth in Chapter 16 of this book. For now, it is important that you focus on developing a step-by-step approach to tackling each new subject or task that you encounter. Making analytical thinking a habit will improve your proficiency as a legal assistant.

Communication Skills

Good communication skills are critical when working in the legal area. In fact, it is sometimes said that the legal profession is a "communications profession" because effective legal representation depends to a great extent on how well a legal professional can communicate with clients, witnesses, court judges and juries, opposing attorneys, and others. Poor communication can damage a case, destroy a client relationship, and harm the legal professional's reputation. Good communication, in contrast, wins cases, clients, and sometimes promotions.

Communication skills include reading skills, speaking skills, listening skills, and writing skills. We look briefly at each of these skills here. Although we focus on communication skills in the law office setting, realize that good communication skills are essential to success in any work environment. For more information and tips on effective communication, see this chapter's *Featured Guest* article starting on the next page.

READING SKILLS.   Reading skills involve more than just being able to decipher the meaning of written letters and words. Reading skills also involve understanding the *meaning* of a sentence, paragraph, section, or page. As a legal professional, you will need to be able to read and understand many different types of written materials, including statutes and court decisions. You will therefore need to become familiar with legal terminology and concepts so that you grasp the meaning of these legal writings. You will also need to develop the ability to read documents *carefully* so that you do not miss important distinctions, such as the difference in meaning that can result from the use of *and* instead of *or*.

SPEAKING SKILLS.   Paralegals must also be able to speak well. In addition to using correct grammar, legal assistants need to be precise and clear in communicating ideas or facts to others. For example, when you discuss facts learned in an investigation with your supervising attorney, your oral report must communicate exactly what you found, or it could mislead the attorney. A miscommunication in this context could have serious consequences if it leads the attorney to take an action detrimental to the client's interests. Oral communication also has a non-verbal dimension—that is, we communicate our thoughts and feelings through gestures, facial expressions, and other "body language" as well as through words.

LISTENING SKILLS.   Good listening skills are extremely important in the context of paralegal work. Paralegals must follow instructions meticulously. To understand the instructions that you receive, you must listen carefully. Asking follow-up questions will help you to clarify anything that you do not understand. In addition, repeating the instructions will not only ensure that you understand them but also give the attorney a chance to add anything that he or she may have forgotten to tell you initially. Listening skills are particularly important in the interviewing context. In Chapter 13, you will read in greater detail about different types of listening skills and techniques that will help you conduct effective interviews with clients or witnesses.

Ten Tips for Effective Communication

BIOGRAPHICAL NOTE

Wendy B. Edson received her master's degree in library science (M.L.S.) from the University of Rhode Island and served as law librarian at the Buffalo, New York, firm of Phillips, Lytle, Hitchcock, Blain and Huber. In 1978, she joined the Paralegal Studies faculty at Hilbert College, in Hamburg, New York, and helped to develop an ABA-approved bachelor's degree program in 1992.

Edson teaches paralegalism and legal ethics, legal research and writing, law and literature, volunteerism, and alternative dispute resolution (ADR). She also developed and coordinates the internship program. Edson reviews and publishes on the topics of paralegal education, legal research and writing, and community service. She has lectured to legal professionals on legal research, teaching skills, internships, community service, environmental law, and ADR. Professor Edson is an AAfPE member and has presented papers at its national conferences and chaired model syllabi projects.

Words! They are the building blocks of human communication. Whether words are exchanged face to face—or by e-mail, phone, fax, or letter—communication is a two-way street. But how do we become skilled at maneuvering the *two-way* traffic of interpersonal communication? As in driving, we need to follow the "rules of the road." The rules of the road in regard to communication traffic are embodied in the following ten tips.

1. **Establish Communication Equality.** Communication equality does not require that individuals hold equal status in an office or organization but requires that each party believe in *equal rights* to speak and listen. Observe someone whom you consider to be a good communicator. You will note that he or she demonstrates equality by actively listening and responding appropriately to whoever is speaking. Workplace problems often reflect communication ailments rooted in inequality. A firm belief in communication equality, despite job titles, will help to create a cooperative, productive working environment.

2. **Plan for Time and Space.** Effective communication requires *time.* Imagine your reaction to a request to work overtime if your supervising attorney took thirty seconds to order you to do the work versus taking two minutes to explain the reason for the request and listening to your response. In the first situation, the attorney saved one and a half minutes but scored "zero" in terms of communication skills. In today's rushed world, it is easy to overlook the importance of communication skills in morale building and creating a cooperative, efficient work force.

Effective communicators are aware of how the physical environment in which a conversation takes place can affect the communication process. Communication is always enhanced when the parties have reasonable privacy and are not continually interrupted. Another important factor is physical comfort.

Choosing an inappropriate time and place for communication denies the importance of the matters being discussed and may send the wrong message to both the speaker and the listener.

3. **Set the Agenda.** Skilled communicators prepare an *agenda*—whether written or mental—of matters to be discussed in order of their priority. Frequently, both parties bring their respective agendas to a discussion, which means that priorities may need to be negotiated. A subordinate who brings up the topic of desired vacation time when the supervisor is preoccupied with a major project clearly demonstrates that his or her priorities are different from those of the supervisor.

Successful communication requires that the parties first negotiate a *common agenda*—that is, determine jointly the agenda for a particular discussion or meeting and what topics should take priority. Then, the topics can be dealt with one by one, in terms of their relative importance, to the satisfaction of both parties. *Agenda awareness* prevents parties from jumping from topic to topic without successfully resolving anything.

4. **Fine-Tune Your Speaking Skills.** Observe an individual whom you consider to be a good speaker, whether before a group of persons or on a one-on-one basis. What skills does that individual demonstrate? Effective

FEATURED GUEST, *Continued*

speakers work hard to express thoughts clearly; sometimes, they refer to notes or lists to refresh their memories. Skilled speakers also try to communicate accurately and to talk about matters that they know will interest their listeners. They cultivate *communication empathy*—the sincere effort to put themselves in their listeners' shoes. As you speak to others, pause occasionally and ask yourself: "Would I enjoy listening to what I am saying and how I am saying it?"

5. **Cultivate Listening Skills.**
Listening is not just refraining from speaking while another person is talking but an *active* process—the other half of the communication partnership. An active listener does not interrupt the speaker. If you sense that the speaker is engaging in a monologue, responsive behavior—including body language, attentiveness, and appropriate remarks—can steer the conversation back to a dialogue without cutting off the speaker.

An active listener realizes that listening is an investment in effective communication. By truly responding to what is being said, rather than regarding listening time as insignificant or time to plan his or her own remarks, the skilled listener establishes a bond of trust with the speaker. Active listeners avoid preconceived ideas about topics being discussed and assume that they do not know all the answers.

6. **Watch for Body Language.**
Body language is nonverbal communication that reflects our emotional state. Physical positions, such as leaning forward or away from the speaker while listening, can

reinforce or negate our spoken responses. Body attitudes, whether relaxed (comfortable posture, leaning forward, uncrossed arms and legs, relaxed neck and shoulders) or tense (stiff posture, backing away, crossed arms and legs, rigid neck and shoulders), vividly illustrate our responses before we utter a word. Eye contact is one of the most important tools in the body language tool kit for communication. Interviewers, social workers, and police officers have learned that steady and responsive eye contact means sincerity and credibility.

7. **Put Note Taking in Perspective.**
Overinvolvement in note taking detracts from the communication process because opportunities to listen actively, speak responsively, and be sensitive to body language are reduced. The speaker may ramble while the listener records the ramblings in extensive notes.

When it is necessary to take notes, it is helpful to establish some rapport with the speaker or listener before launching the note-taking process. Alternatively, follow-up notes can be a workable solution to the problem. The note taker can devote the interview time to communication and, after the interview, record his or her general impressions of the interview and identify specific issues that need to be discussed further.

8. **Recognize the Role of Criticism.**
Constructive criticism focuses on specific actions or behaviors rather than personalities. It is objective rather than subjective. Criticism that is stated calmly and objectively ("We need to rewrite the section on holographic wills") is much more palat-

"Eye contact is one of the most important tools in the body language tool kit for communication."

able for the person being criticized than is criticism in the form of a personal attack ("You did a terrible job"). By placing emphasis on actions instead of personalities, the parties can more easily work toward a satisfactory solution. If both the critic and the person being criticized can remain calm and can separate actions from personalities, then criticism will usually produce the desired result and *mutual* satisfaction.

9. **Aim for Satisfactory Closure.**
Closure means "wrapping up" the communication. Successful communicators know that handling closure properly can leave a participant with a good feeling even if the solution was not exactly what he or she initially desired. Summarizing the discussion and checking for agreement or a need for further discussion will encourage all participants to follow the tenth tip.

10. **Commit to Communicate.**
Excellent speakers and listeners have positive, self-confident attitudes that problems can be solved if the "rules of the road" are followed. Skilled communicators cultivate open minds, self-knowledge, and the ability to tolerate differences and empathize with others. They are committed to exercising their rights and responsibilities as speakers and listeners in the communication process.

WRITING SKILLS.   Finally, it is important for paralegals to have excellent writing skills. Legal assistants draft letters, memoranda, and a variety of legal documents. Letters to clients, witnesses, court clerks, and others must be clear and well organized and must follow the rules of grammar and punctuation. Legal documents must also be free of errors. Lawyers are generally scrupulously attentive to detail in their work, and they expect legal assistants to be equally so. Remember, you represent your supervising attorney when you write. You will learn more about writing skills in Chapter 18.

Computer Skills

In any workplace today, computer skills are essential. As mentioned earlier, advances in technology are transforming the way in which law firms and other organizations operate. At a minimum, you will be expected to have experience with word processing (generating and revising documents using a computer) and to have some data-entry skills. Realize, though, that paralegals who are well versed in computer technology will increasingly have an edge over those who are not in the paralegal job market. Already, some of the best-paying paralegal positions are held by paralegal specialists who know how to use sophisticated computer equipment and software, such as database management systems, and how to adapt new technology to their workplace needs to improve efficiency.

We cannot stress enough that to become a successful paralegal, the best thing you can do during your paralegal training is to become as knowledgeable as possible about computer technology, including online communications. Throughout this book, you will read about how technology is now being applied to all areas of legal practice. You will also learn how you can use technology, particularly the Internet, to perform various paralegal tasks and to keep up to date on the law.

As computer technology continues to advance, high-tech paralegals will increasingly be in demand. (See this chapter's *Technology and Today's Paralegal* feature for a glimpse at how technology is not only transforming the paralegal workplace but also creating new types of paralegal positions.)

Organizational Skills

Being a well-organized person is a plus for a legal assistant. Law offices are busy places. There are phone calls to be answered and returned, witnesses to get to court and on the witness stand on time, documents to be filed, and checklists and procedures to be followed. If you are able to organize files, create procedures and checklists, and keep things running smoothly, you will be doing a great service to the legal team and to clients.

If you work in a nontraditional setting, such as for a corporation or for the government, you will similarly find that good organizational skills are the key to success in your job. No matter where you work, you will need to organize files, certain types of data, and—most important—your time.

If organization comes naturally to you, you are ahead of the game. If not, now is the time to learn and practice organizational skills. You will find plenty of opportunities to do this as a paralegal student—by organizing your notebooks, devising an efficient tracking system for homework assignments, creating a study or work schedule and following it, and so on. Other suggestions for organizing your time and work, both as a student and as a paralegal on the job, are included at the beginning of this book. You will also find in any university or public library an abundance of books that offer guidelines on how to organize efficiently your work, your use of time, and your life generally.

The Changing Paralegal Workplace

In many ways, technology has simplified the work of legal assistants. Documents can be easily drafted and revised on the computer. Mistakes can be eliminated with the stroke of a key, and changes can be made in a matter of just seconds. Computerized forms make generating the paperwork for routine legal transactions, such as bankruptcy filings and divorce petitions, a relatively simple matter. Database management systems allow paralegals to track and analyze hundreds—if not thousands—of documents without having to search through boxes filled with papers. E-mail messages can be created and sent in a fraction of the time it takes to create, reproduce, and distribute hard-copy memos or letters. Online databases have made it possible to conduct legal research and find information relevant to a legal investigation without leaving the office.

MORE PARALEGAL OPPORTUNITIES

Indeed, it would seem that technology, by making legal work faster and easier to accomplish, might reduce the need for paralegals. That, however, is not true. Indeed, the opposite is occurring—technology is opening the door to new positions for paralegals. For example, some of today's paralegals are carving out a niche for themselves as Internet specialists. A paralegal who can conduct research efficiently using online resources is a valuable asset to any firm or agency. In a law office, efficient research saves time and money—for the firm and clients alike. Other paralegals are becoming experts in electronic evidence—encoding

documents relating to a particular legal matter so that those documents can be easily retrieved in the event of a lawsuit.

DOCUMENT RETENTION ISSUES

Another emerging field in which paralegals may play a significant role has to do with the types of documents that should be entered into, or retained on, electronic systems. Even documents that have been previously deleted from a hard drive may be retrieved and used as evidence in a lawsuit, and companies that want to prevent future problems with electronic evidence increasingly are turning to their lawyers for advice on this issue. A paralegal knowledgeable in this area is a valuable member of the legal team in such situations.

THE EMERGENCE OF A VIRTUAL WORKPLACE

Finally, technology has made it possible for some paralegals to perform at least some of their work at home. The virtual workplace, made feasible by telephones, faxes, and modems, is now becoming a reality.

TECHNOLOGY TIP

We cannot predict what the future may hold, but one thing seems certain: as technology advances, there will be an increasing need for creative adaptations of technology to the field of legal work. High-tech paralegals who can fill this need will very likely be the highest-paid—and the most valued—legal assistants in the future.

Interpersonal Skills

The ability to communicate and interact effectively with other people is an important asset for the paralegal. Paralegals work closely with their supervising attorneys, and the capacity to cultivate a positive working relationship helps get tasks done more efficiently. Paralegals also work with legal secretaries and other support staff in the law office, with attorneys and paralegals from other firms, with court personnel, and with numerous other people. Paralegals frequently interview clients and witnesses. As you will read in Chapter 13, if you can relate well to the person whom you are interviewing, your chances of obtaining useful information are increased.

There may be times when you will have to deal with clients who are experiencing difficulties in their lives, such as divorce or the death of a loved one. These people will need to be handled with sensitivity, tact, understanding, and courtesy. There will also be times when you will have to deal with people in your office who are under a great deal of stress or who for some other reason are demanding and

---

DEVELOPING PARALEGAL SKILLS

Interviewing a Client

Brenda Lundquist is a paralegal in a one-attorney firm. Brenda has multiple responsibilities, including interviewing prospective divorce clients. Using a standard set of forms, Brenda meets with the prospective client and obtains information about the reasons for the divorce, finances and assets, and desired custody arrangements. This information is needed to assist the supervising attorney in determining whether to take the case. The information also will help Brenda in preparing the documents to be filed with the court should the attorney decide to represent the client. Brenda enjoys the work because she likes helping people, and often people who are getting divorced need both emotional and legal support.

CHECKLIST FOR CLIENT INTERVIEWS

- Plan the interview in advance.
- Print out forms and checklists to use during the interview.
- Introduce yourself as a legal assistant.
- Explain the purpose of the interview to the client.
- Communicate your questions precisely.
- Listen carefully, and be supportive, as necessary.
- Summarize the client's major concerns.
- Give the client a "time line" for what will happen next in the legal proceedings.

---

less than courteous to you. You will need to know how to respond to these people in ways that promote positive working relationships.

The Ability to Keep Confidences

One of the requirements of being a paralegal is the ability to keep client information confidential. The word *requirement* is used here because being able to keep confidences is not just a desirable attribute in a paralegal, but a mandatory one. As you will read in Chapter 3, attorneys are ethically and legally obligated to keep all information relating to the representation of a client strictly confidential unless the client consents to the disclosure of the information.[8] The attorney may disclose this information only to people who are also working on behalf of the client and who therefore need to know it. Paralegals share in this duty imposed on all attorneys. If a paralegal reveals confidential client information to anyone outside the group working on the client's case, the lawyer (and the paralegal) may face legal consequences (including being sued by the client) if the client suffers harm as a result.

Keeping client information confidential means that you, as a paralegal, cannot divulge such information even to your spouse, family members, or closest friends. You should not talk about a client's case in hallways, elevators, or any areas in which others may overhear your conversation. Keeping work-related information confidential is an important part of being a responsible and reliable paralegal.

Professionalism

Paralegals should behave professionally at all times. That means you must be responsible and reliable in order to earn the respect and trust of the attorneys and clients with whom you work. It also means you must put aside any personal bias or emotion that interferes with your representation of a client or assessment of a case. Paralegals also need to be honest and assertive in letting others know what things they can and cannot do (for example, they cannot give legal advice). This

Trusts and Estates Paralegal

SUSAN J. MARTIN   *is a parale-gal in the Trusts and Estates department of Devine, Millimet & Branch, a large law firm, and has offices in the firm's Man-chester, New Hampshire, and Andover, Massachusetts, loca-tions. She has been in the legal profession for over twenty-two years. She worked for nine years as a legal secretary before becoming a paralegal and has worked in both large and small law firms in New Hampshire, Maine, Florida, Colorado, and Montana.*

Martin has a certificate from the National Association of Legal Secretaries, a certifi-cate in paralegal studies from the University of New Hampshire, and a bachelor's degree from Franklin Pierce College in New Hampshire. She has been a member of the PACE Development Committee of the National Federation of Paralegal Associations (NFPA) and was an item writer/content area expert for the PACE exam.

Martin served as president of the Paralegal Association of New Hampshire in 1998–1999 and chaired its Committee on Paralegal Education. She was editor of the association's bimonthly newsletter, The Annotator; *and also an adjunct member of the Delivery of Legal Services Committee of the New Hampshire Bar Association and a member of the bar association's Technology Section.*

What do you like best about your work?

"One of the benefits of working in the trusts and estates field is that you are not involved in contentious lawsuits in which, in many cases, there is no winner and everyone is unhappy. Although estate clients are fre-quently dealing with grief and loss, they are not openly hostile or defensive. For the most part, clients view the trusts and estates team in a very positive way, and this makes the job very enjoyable."

What is the greatest challenge that you face in your area of work?

"Probably the greatest challenge of my job is keeping informed about the changes in federal and state tax law. The Internal Revenue Code is complex and convoluted, and new rules and regulations are promulgated daily. Also, it is not unusual to have an estate that is subject not only to federal tax laws but also to the tax laws of several states. Sorting out tax obligations and coordi-nating the timely filing of several tax returns can some-times be a very difficult task."

> "To be successful in this field, you must be bright and articulate, and have a passion for detail."

What advice do you have for would-be paralegals in your area of work?

"To function well as a paralegal in the trusts and estates field, you must have a broad general knowledge of many other fields of law, including real estate, corpo-rations, family law, and even civil litigation. You must also have some knowledge of basic accounting principles. People who function well as paralegals in this field usually have excellent quantitative skills, are extremely organized, are able to man-age numerous files and deadlines simultaneously, can exercise sound independent judgment, and can work with a minimum of supervision. You must be computer literate and have proficient keyboarding skills."

What are some tips for success as a paralegal in your area of work?

"To be successful in this field, you must be bright and articulate and have a pas-sion for detail. You should love working with people. Working with the elderly requires compassion, humility, and resourcefulness. In this field in particular, you will meet clients from every social stratum, ethnic background, and cultural asso-ciation, and that requires patience, tolerance, and good humor."

TODAY'S PROFESSIONAL PARALEGAL

A Winning Combination

Susan Latham is a legal secretary for Melinda Oakwood, a real estate attorney who is a partner in the law firm of Morris, Crowther, Oakwood & Miller. The law firm is one of the largest in the state, employing over 300 attorneys, 75 paralegals, 130 secretaries, and many support staff members. Susan, who has become more of a  legal assistant than a secretary to Melinda, has decided, at the age of forty, to return to the local university to obtain a paralegal degree. This way, Susan can be rewarded (in the form of higher wages) for the work that she actually does already and can seek advancement in the firm.

Susan has worked for Melinda for eleven years. She has been given increased responsibility because she has shown Melinda that she is dependable and reliable in handling her work assignments. Her work is always turned in on time, and it is always accurate.

LEARNING ON THE JOB

Susan is very lucky to have Melinda as a supervising attorney. Melinda, who had been a teacher for ten years before she went to law school, likes to teach Susan how to undertake new work assignments. When Susan has a new type of document to prepare at work, Melinda gives her a sample document and very good instructions. Now that Susan is studying to be a paralegal, Melinda has started assisting Susan with her school assignments by giving her sample documents and copies of the laws that require those documents. Melinda also points out the differences between the class assignments and the sample documents and discusses with Susan why the differences matter from a legal perspective.

Additionally, Melinda encourages Susan to ask questions about school assignments and to take her time completing them so that when they are turned in, they are accurate. Susan has a strong sense of commitment, so she always sees a project through even if it seems to take forever.

USING PERSONAL ATTRIBUTES

Melinda is also lucky to have Susan as her secretary and, eventually, as her paralegal. Susan has many personal attributes that helped her on the job. She learns quickly and performs her work competently and efficiently. She also pays great attention to detail, which is one of the reasons Melinda encouraged Susan to get a paralegal degree. Unlike Melinda's former paralegal, who would send out letters and fail to include the documents that should have been enclosed, Susan is meticulous. And Melinda can always count on Susan to keep client information confidential.

Susan already had good computer and organizational skills when Melinda hired her. She did need to improve her analytical and listening skills, though. Susan's analytical skills are already improving as a result of a course she is taking in legal research, which requires case analysis. Over time, Susan has learned to listen to Melinda's instructions and to question Melinda when Susan is not exactly certain about what Melinda wants her to do.

THE RESULT: A WINNING TEAM

Melinda and Susan have developed a solid working relationship. It took time for Susan to develop some of the skills that she needed, but Melinda was a good and patient teacher. It also took time to develop a trusting relationship, but now Melinda can confidently delegate significant assignments to Susan, knowing that Susan will complete them accurately. Now that Susan is in a paralegal program, Melinda can also delegate more challenging work to Susan, and Susan will eventually be promoted to paralegal status. Melinda and Susan work productively and efficiently together. They like and rely on each other and enjoy their work. Theirs is a winning combination of talents and skills.

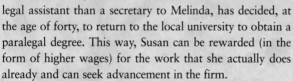

is particularly important because not everyone is sure what legal assistants are, and some people may have misconceptions about the role paralegals play.

As a paralegal, you will find that you are being judged not only by your actions and words but also by your appearance, demeanor, attitude, and a variety of other factors. When deadlines approach and the pace of office work becomes somewhat frantic, it can be difficult to meet the challenge of acting professionally. For example, you may have to complete a brief (a document to support an attorney's argument) and file it with the court by noon. It is 11 A.M., and you still have

a considerable portion of the brief to finish. When the pressure is on, it is important to remain calm and focus on completing your task quickly and accurately to
ensure quality work. If you are interrupted by a client's call or another attorney,
be aware that the way you react to that interruption (your attitude and demeanor)
is likely to affect whether others view you as professional. Strive to be courteous
and respectful during such interruptions. Remember that it is imperative that the
paralegal be detail oriented and accurate, even when working under pressure.

THE FUTURE OF THE PROFESSION

The paralegal profession is a dynamic, changing, and expanding field within the
legal arena. Legal assistants continue to assume a growing range of duties in the
nation's legal offices and perform many of the same tasks as lawyers. According
to the U.S. Department of Labor, the number of paralegal and legal assistant positions is projected to grow faster than the average for all occupations through
2010. In fact, the Bureau of Labor Statistics projects that the number of paralegal
positions will increase 62 percent by 2008, making it the sixth fastest growing
occupation in the United States. As suggested earlier, this growth stems from the
fact that law firms and other employers with legal staffs are hiring more paralegals to lower the cost—and increase the availability and efficiency—of legal services. Those entering the profession today will find a broader range of career
options than ever before. In addition, they will have the opportunity to help chart
the course the profession takes in the future.

✺ KEY TERMS AND CONCEPTS

ABA–approved program

American Association for Paralegal
  Education (AAfPE)

American Bar Association (ABA)

certification

Certified Legal Assistant (CLA)

Certified Legal Assistant Specialist
  (CLAS)

continuing legal education (CLE)
  program

legal assistant

National Association of Legal
  Assistants (NALA)

National Federation of Paralegal
  Associations (NFPA)

paralegal

procedural law

Registered Paralegal (RP)

substantive law

✺ CHAPTER SUMMARY

What Is a Paralegal?	1. *Paralegal or legal assistant*—Most people use the terms *paralegal* and *legal assistant* interchangeably. Some persons trained as paralegals may use a different label, such as *legal technician* or *legal research specialist*, at their workplace, however. Paralegals perform many of the tasks traditionally handled by attorneys.
	2. *Formal definition*—A legal assistant or paralegal is a person qualified by education, training, or work experience who is employed or retained by a lawyer, law office, corporation, governmental agency, or other entity who performs specifically delegated substantive legal work, for which a lawyer is responsible.

What Do Paralegals Do?	1. *Typical duties*—Legal assistants typically perform many of the following tasks: interviewing and maintaining general contact with clients, locating and interviewing witnesses, conducting legal investigations, calendaring and tracking important deadlines, organizing and maintaining client files, conducting legal research, drafting legal documents, summarizing witness testimony, attending legal proceedings, and using computers and technology.
	2. *Duties often vary*—Paralegals perform different functions depending on where they work and on their capabilities and experience. In law firms, paralegals' duties also vary according to the size of the firm and the kind of law practiced by the firm. Although their duties vary, paralegals commonly spend the bulk of their time performing document management, client relations, and research.
	3. *Paralegals and technology*—Technology is the number-one area of expanding paralegal responsibility. Paralegals who are skilled in using newly available technologies to assist them in performing their duties will excel in the profession.
Paralegal Education	Higher education and paralegal education programs have become increasingly important in the growth and development of the profession.
	1. *Educational options*—Colleges, universities, and private institutions now offer a wide variety of programs to train paralegals, ranging in length from eighteen months to four years.
	2. *ABA–approved programs*—Since 1974, the American Bar Association (ABA) has set educational standards for paralegal training programs. ABA–approved programs are those that meet with the ABA's approval. ABA approval is a voluntary process; paralegal programs are not required to be approved by the ABA.
	3. *Certification*—The term *certification* refers to formal recognition by a professional group or state agency that an individual has met certain standards of proficiency specified by that group. Generally, this means passing an examination and meeting certain requirements with respect to education and/or experience. Paralegals may be certified by NALA, NFPA, or a state organization. Currently, no state requires paralegal certification.
	4. *Continuing legal education (CLE)*—Continuing legal education courses are offered by state bar associations and paralegal associations. Such programs provide a way to learn more about a specialized area of law or keep up to date on the latest developments in law and technology.
Paralegal Skills and Attributes	Because paralegals today perform many of the tasks that lawyers used to perform, the demands on paralegals to be professional and efficient have increased. Paralegals also need to have a variety of skills. It is especially important for paralegals to have good analytical, communication, computer, organizational, and interpersonal skills, and be able to keep confidences.

❈ QUESTIONS FOR REVIEW

1. What is a paralegal? Is there any difference between a paralegal and a legal assistant?

2. What kinds of tasks do paralegals perform?

3. What needs within the legal profession do paralegals meet?

4. Name the two largest national paralegal associations in the United States. What are the benefits of belonging to a paralegal association?

5. What type of educational programs and training are available to paralegals? Must a person meet specific educational requirements to work as a paralegal?

6. What role does the American Bar Association play in paralegal education?

7. What does *certification* mean? What is a CLA? What is a CLAS? What does PACE stand for?

8. Name some states that have certification programs. Is state certification mandatory in those states?

9. List and describe the skills that are useful in paralegal practice. Do you have these skills?

10. List and describe some of the personal attributes of a professional paralegal. Do you feel that persons who do not have these attributes can cultivate them? If so, how?

❈ ETHICAL QUESTIONS

1. Richard attends a six-month paralegal course and earns a certificate. In the West Coast city where he lives, certified paralegals—those with a CLA designation—are in great demand in the job market. Richard responds to a newspaper advertisement for a certified paralegal, indicating that he is one. Has Richard done anything unethical? What is the difference between a certificate and certification?

2. Paula Abrams works as a paralegal for a small law firm that specializes in tax law. Recently, Paula purchased some new tax-return software and was trained in how to use it. Last week, Paula used the software to prepare tax returns for the Benedetto family. Paula saved the forms on a disk. She then retrieved the Benedetto forms and used them for the Marshalls' tax return. Paula entered much of the Marshalls' tax information into the computer. Mr. Marshall had not provided the children's Social Security numbers to Paula, though, so she only keyed in the information that she had available and decided to add the Social Security numbers later.

In the tax-season rush, Paula inadvertently neglected to enter the children's Social Security numbers on the Marshalls' tax return. Several months later, the Marshalls received a letter from the Internal Revenue Service stating that their exemptions had been denied because their children's Social Security numbers had been claimed on someone else's tax return. How might this situation be resolved? What other kinds of ethical problems might result from using computer-generated forms?

❈ PRACTICE QUESTIONS AND ASSIGNMENTS

1. Refer to Appendix F and Appendix G at the end of this book (or, if you have access to the Internet, you can go to http://www.findlaw.com), and find the answers to the following questions:

   a. What is the street address, e-mail address, and telephone number of the state bar association in your state?

   b. Is there an affiliate of the National Association of Legal Assistants or the National Federation of Paralegal Associations in your city? Where is the nearest affiliate of either of these organizations located?

   c. Are there any regional or local paralegal associations in your area? If so, what are their names, street and e-mail addresses, and phone numbers?

2. Using the material on paralegal skills presented in the chapter, identify which of the following are skills that a paralegal should have, and explain why.

   a. Reading skills.
   b. Interpersonal skills.
   c. Marketing skills.
   d. Oral communication skills.
   e. Math skills.
   f. Computer skills.
   g. Management skills.

3. Which of the following personal attributes, presented in the chapter, are helpful to a paralegal? Why?

   a. Insensitivity.   b. Commitment.   c. Integrity.   d. Unreliability.   e. Objectivity.   f. Inaccuracy.

✳ QUESTIONS FOR CRITICAL ANALYSIS

1. Tom and Sandy are having coffee after their first paralegal class. The instructor discussed the ongoing debate within the profession about whether to use the term *paralegal* or *legal assistant*. Tom says he agrees with NFPA that the term *paralegal* is preferable because no one will confuse paralegals with legal secretaries. Sandy, who has been working as a legal secretary for the last few years, is offended by Tom's remarks. What label do you prefer—*legal assistant* or *paralegal*—and why? Is it an important issue, in your opinion?

2. Joan McMahon is meeting with an adviser at her local college to discuss the possibility of enrolling in the school's legal-assistant program. Joan has completed two years of college-level courses in general education, which she could transfer, but she has had no legal-assistant classes. The adviser explains that there are three different degree options at the college: an associate's degree, a bachelor's degree, and a postgraduate certificate. Several for-profit business schools in the area offer certificate programs as well. How would you explain the differences in the degree and certificate options to Joan? Which options would Joan most likely favor? Why?

✳ PROJECTS

1. Write or telephone the National Association of Legal Assistants and the National Federation of Paralegal Associations (see Appendix F for the addresses and telephone numbers of these associations). See if they have affiliates in your area. Also, see if there are any state or local paralegal organizations in your area. Contact them for membership information. Do they accept student members?

2. Arrange an interview with an experienced paralegal, such as a graduate of your program or another paralegal that you may know. Ask the paralegal what he or she thinks are the most important skills and characteristics that paralegals should have.

✳ USING INTERNET RESOURCES

Browse through the materials on the Web sites of the National Association of Legal Assistants, or NALA (at http://www.nala.org), and the National Federation of Paralegal Associations, or NFPA (at http://www.paralegals.org). Then do the following:

1. Look closely at the benefits of membership listed by each of these organizations. How do they compare? Are there any significant differences?

2. Examine the information that is included on each site about the organization's certification program. For each program, summarize the requirements that a paralegal must meet to become certified.

3. Go to the Web site for West Legal Studies at http://westlegalstudies.com and click on "Online Resources," and then "State Resources." There, you will find a listing of state resources that provides links to relevant state-specific Web sites and to sites that furnish legal forms for the individual states. Click on your state's Web links and browse through the resources available. List the Web sites you find and briefly describe the kind of information available at each site. Can you access your state's bar association? Is there a way to view any of your state's codes (laws) or judicial opinions? Does the state attorney general or secretary of state have a Web site listed?

4. Go to "Paralegal Profession" at the NALA Web site (at http://www.nala.org) and click on "What is a Paralegal?". Which of the following tasks might legal

assistants perform, according to the information provided there?

a. Draft legal documents.

b. Try cases in court.

c. Locate witnesses.

d. Give legal advice.

e. Set legal fees.

f. Interview clients.

g. Perform legal investigations.

END NOTES

1. *Legal Assistant Today,* March/April 2002, p. 51.

2. The members of NFPA voted to remove the term *legal assistant* from their definition of *paralegal* at the annual conference in May 2002. The American Association for Paralegal Education (AAfPE) took a similar position at its annual meeting in 2002.

3. This is according to a survey conducted by *Legal Assistant Today* magazine in 2001, reported in March/April 2002, p. 54.

4. This is according to a survey conducted by *Legal Assistant Today* magazine in 2001, reported in *Legal Assistant Today,* June/July 2002, p. 54.

5. California Business and Professions Code, Sections 6450 through 6456. Enacted in 2000.

6. California Advanced Specialist (CAS) certification is also available as a specialty exam through NALA to paralegals that possess CLA certification. For more information on this state-specific NALA certification, see Appendix H.

7. According to a 2001 survey by *Legal Assistant Today,* 84.8 percent of employers paid at least part of the cost of continuing legal education. *Legal Assistant Today,* March/April 2002, p. 56.

8. Exceptions to the confidentiality rule are made in certain circumstances, as will be discussed in Chapter 3.

CHAPTER 2

CAREER OPPORTUNITIES

Chapter Outline

✴ INTRODUCTION   ✴ WHERE PARALEGALS WORK   ✴ PARALEGAL SPECIALTIES
✴ PARALEGAL COMPENSATION   ✴ PLANNING YOUR CAREER
✴ LOCATING POTENTIAL EMPLOYERS   ✴ JOB-PLACEMENT SERVICES
✴ MARKETING YOUR SKILLS   ✴ REEVALUATING YOUR CAREER

After completing this chapter, you will know:

- What types of firms and organizations hire paralegals.
- Some areas of law in which paralegals specialize.
- How much paralegals can expect to earn.
- How paralegals are compensated for overtime work.
- How to prepare a career plan and pursue it.
- What is involved in a job search and how to go about it.

INTRODUCTION

Paralegals today enjoy a wide range of employment opportunities in both the private and the public sector. Competent paralegals are in demand in law firms because attorneys realize that the use of legal assistants enables them to provide superior legal services at a lower cost to clients. Furthermore, although the majority of legal assistants continue to work in law offices, virtually any business that uses legal services can utilize the services of persons with paralegal training. Corporations, insurance companies, banks, and real estate agencies now regularly employ legal assistants. In addition, the government has created new positions for paralegals at many agencies. Paralegals now work in many court systems, in county offices, and in legal-services clinics across the nation.

This chapter provides you with a starting point for planning your career. In the pages that follow, you will read about where paralegals work and what compensation paralegals receive. You will also learn about the steps you will need to follow to plan your career, locate potential employers, and find a job.

On the Web

For helpful information on all aspects of paralegal careers, go to the National Association of Legal Assistants's Web site at **http://www.nala.org** and the National Federation of Paralegal Associations's Web site at **http://www.paralegals.org**.

WHERE PARALEGALS WORK

Paralegal employers fall into a number of categories. This section describes the general characteristics of each of the major types of working environments.

Law Firms

When paralegals first established themselves within the legal community in the 1960s, they assisted lawyers in a law firm setting. Today, law firms continue to hire more paralegals than do any other organizations, and over 70 percent of all paralegals work in law firms. Law firms vary in size from the small, one-attorney office to the huge "megafirm" with hundreds of attorneys. As you can see in Exhibit 2.1, the majority of paralegals work in settings that employ fewer than twenty attorneys.[1]

WORKING FOR A SMALL FIRM.   Many paralegals begin their careers working for small law practices, such as one-attorney firms or firms with just a few attorneys. To some extent, this is because of the greater number of small law firms, relative to large ones. It may also be due to geographic location. For example, a paralegal who lives in a relatively rural environment, such as a small community, may find that his or her only option is to work for a small legal practice.

On the Web

You can obtain a host of information on specific law firms by going to their Web pages. For example, go to Hale & Dorr's Web site at **http://www.haledorr.com**. (To find Web sites for law firms, check one of the legal directories discussed later in this chapter.)

EXHIBIT 2.1

Paralegal Employment and Compensation by Size of Firm or Legal Department

The authors compiled this chart using data from a variety of sources, including NALA, NFPA, *Legal Assistant Today* magazine, The Affiliates, and the Legal Assistant Manager Association (LAMA).

NUMBER OF ATTORNEYS	PERCENTAGE OF PARALEGALS	AVERAGE COMPENSATION (salary plus bonuses)
1	12%	$38,250
2–5	33%	$40,000
6–10	16%	$42,900
11–20	15%	$44,300
21–50	11%	$46,600
51–100	7%	$49,850
Over 100	6%	$54,000

Working for a small firm offers many advantages to the beginning paralegal, and you should be aware of them. If the firm is a general law practice, you will have the opportunity to gain experience in many different areas of the law. You will be able to learn whether you enjoy working in one area (such as family law) more than another area (such as personal-injury law) in the event that you later decide to specialize. Some paralegals also prefer the often more personal and less formal environment of the small law office, as well as the variety of tasks and greater flexibility that frequently characterize this setting.

A characteristic of small firms that may prove challenging has to do with compensation. Small firms pay, on average, lower salaries than larger firms do. As Exhibit 2.1 indicates, paralegal income is often related to firm size. Generally, the larger the firm, the higher the paralegal salaries. Small firms also may provide fewer employee benefits, such as pension plans or retirement plans.

Paralegals who work for small firms may also have less support staff to assist them. This means that if you work in a small law office, your job may involve a substantial amount of secretarial or clerical work.

WORKING FOR A LARGE FIRM.   In contrast to the (typically) more casual environment of the small law office, larger law firms usually are more formal. If you work for a larger firm, your responsibilities will probably be limited to specific, more well-defined types of tasks. For example, you may work for a department that handles (or for an attorney who handles) only certain types of cases, such as real estate transactions. Office procedures and employment policies will also be more clearly defined and may be set forth in a written employment manual.

The advantages of the large firm include greater opportunities for promotions and career advancement, higher salaries and (typically) better benefits packages, more support staff for paralegals, and (often) more sophisticated computer technology and greater access to research resources.

You may view certain characteristics of large law firms as either advantages or disadvantages, depending on your personality and preferences. For example, if you favor the more specialized duties and more formal working environment of the large law firm, then you will view these characteristics as advantages. If you prefer to handle a greater variety of tasks and enjoy the more personal, informal atmosphere of the small law office, then you might view the specialization and formality of the large law firm as disadvantages.

Corporations and Other Business Organizations

Over the past thirty-five years, paralegals have been given opportunities to work in business environments outside of law firms. Many of these businesses (such as insurance companies and banks) engage in activities that are highly regulated by government. Others (such as title insurance companies, law-book publishers, legal-software companies, and law schools) are in some way related to the practice of law. In addition, a vast number of businesses that need legal assistance hire paralegals.

An increasing number of paralegals work for corporate legal departments. Most major corporations hire in-house attorneys to handle corporate legal affairs. Some extremely large corporations have hundreds of attorneys on their payrolls. Legal assistants who are employed by corporations ordinarily work under the supervision of in-house attorneys.

Paralegals in a corporation perform a variety of functions, such as organizing corporate meetings and maintaining the necessary records, drafting employee contracts and benefit plans, and preparing financial and other reports for the corpo-

DEVELOPING PARALEGAL SKILLS

Contracts Administrator

Martha Parnell, a legal assistant, works as a contracts administrator for the Best Engines Corporation. Martha's job is to take calls from buyers who want to negotiate contracts with Best Engines. The corporation uses preprinted forms containing provisions that Best Engines prefers to have in its contracts, terms that are advantageous to Best Engines. Some customers buy large quantities of engines to use in factories or to pump oil out of oil wells or through pipelines. These companies usually want to negotiate contract terms that provide them with more rights.

Martha has just received a telephone call from a buyer who wants to negotiate an indemnity provision, which in the preprinted form contract requires the buyer to pay Best Engines for any losses arising under the contract.

She discusses alternative indemnity provisions, such as splitting the indemnity or leaving it out entirely, with the buyer. Martha then arranges to call the buyer back after discussing the various proposals with the general counsel (the attorney who heads the legal department).

TIPS FOR WORKING WITH CONTRACTS

- Know who—buyer or seller—holds the strongest bargaining position.
- Understand what the contract terms mean.
- Discuss all proposals with your client.
- Understand which terms your client will likely agree to and why.
- Determine which contract terms will be "deal busters."
- Set a timetable for finalizing the contract.

ration. Paralegals often are responsible for monitoring and reviewing government regulations to ensure that the corporation is operating within the law. When the corporation is involved in a lawsuit, paralegals may be assigned additional duties related to that lawsuit. (For more information on the duties of corporate paralegals, see Chapter 10.)

Nearly one-fifth of all paralegals now work in corporate environments. Paralegals who are employed by corporations frequently receive higher salaries than those working for law firms. In addition, paralegals who are employed by corporations normally work more regular hours and experience less stress than paralegals who work for law firms. For example, unlike the situation in law firms, in the corporate environment paralegals are not required to generate a specific number of "billable hours" per year (hours billed to clients for paralegal services performed, discussed in Chapter 4) because there are no clients to bill—the corporation is the client.

Government

A growing number of paralegals are employed by the government in various settings.

ADMINISTRATIVE AGENCIES.   Most paralegals who work for the government work for administrative agencies, such as the federal Environmental Protection Agency or a state environmental resources department. Paralegals who work for government agencies may be engaged in administrative appeals work (see Chapter 11), general or specialized legal research, welfare eligibility and claims, disability claims, the examination of documents (such as loan applications), and many other types of tasks. Your best source of information about employment positions in a particular administrative agency is the agency itself. You can find the names and telephone numbers of federal agencies, as well as a description of their functions, in the *United States Government Manual,* available in your public or college library.

On the Web
You can locate information on government agencies at numerous Web sites, including that of FindLaw at **http://www.findlaw.com.**

Paralegals who work for government agencies normally work regular hours, tend to work fewer total hours per year (have more vacation time) than paralegals in other environments, and, like paralegals who work for corporations, do not have to worry about billable hours. Additionally, paralegals who work for the government usually enjoy comprehensive employment benefits. Salaries, however, are sometimes lower than those offered by traditional law firms and other employers in the private sector.

LEGISLATIVE OFFICES.   Legislators in the U.S. Congress and in several state legislatures typically have staff members to help them with their various duties. These duties often include legal research and writing, and paralegals sometimes perform such services. For example, a senator who plans to propose an amendment to a law may ask a paralegal on her or his staff to research the legislative history of that law carefully (to discern the legislature's intention when passing the law—see Chapter 16) and write up a summary of that history.

LAW ENFORCEMENT OFFICES AND COURTS.   Many paralegals work for government law enforcement offices and institutions. As you will read in Chapter 15, which discusses criminal law and procedures in detail, a person accused of a crime is prosecuted by a *public prosecutor*. Public prosecutors (such as district attorneys, state attorneys general, and U.S. attorneys) are government officials who are paid by the government. Accused persons may be defended by private attorneys, or, if they cannot afford to hire a lawyer, by *public defenders*—attorneys paid for by the state to ensure that criminal defendants are not deprived of their constitutional right to counsel. Both public prosecutors and public defenders rely on paralegals to handle much of their legal work. (See Chapter 15 for a discussion of legal work relating to criminal law and procedures.)

Paralegals also find work in other government environments, such as federal or state court administrative offices. Court administrative work ranges from recording and filing court documents (such as the documents filed during a lawsuit—see Chapters 12 and 14) to handling collections for a regional tax authority for a local small claims court (a court that handles claims below a specified threshold amount—see Chapter 6). Paralegals may also work for bankruptcy courts (see page 32 for a discussion of bankruptcy law).

Legal Aid Offices

Legal aid offices provide legal services to those who find it difficult to pay for legal representation. During President Lyndon Johnson's "War on Poverty" in the 1960s, the government began to set aside funds for legal-services organizations around the country to help less advantaged groups obtain needed legal assistance at low or no cost. Most legal aid continues to be government funded, although some support comes from private legal foundations.

Many paralegals who work in this type of setting find their jobs rewarding, even though they often receive lower salaries than they would in other areas. In part, this is because of the nature of the work—helping needy individuals. Additionally, paralegals in legal aid offices generally assume a wider array of responsibilities than they would in a traditional law office or one of the other environments described earlier. For example, some federal and state administrative agencies, including the Social Security Administration at the federal level, allow paralegals to represent clients in agency hearings and judicial proceedings. As you will read in Chapter 3, paralegals normally are not allowed to represent clients—only attorneys can do so. Exceptions to this rule exist when a court or agency permits nonlawyers to represent others in court or in administrative agency hearings.

Freelance Paralegals

A number of experienced paralegals operate as freelancers. **Freelance paralegals** (also called *independent contractors* or *contract paralegals*) own their own businesses and perform specified types of legal work for attorneys on a contract basis. Attorneys who need temporary legal assistance sometimes contract with freelance paralegals to work on particular projects. In addition, attorneys who need legal assistance but cannot afford to hire full-time paralegals might hire freelancers to work on a part-time basis. (The suggestions offered later in this chapter on how you can find work as a paralegal apply to freelance jobs as well.)

Freelancing as a paralegal has both advantages and disadvantages. Because freelancers are their own bosses, they can set their own schedules. Thus, they enjoy a greater degree of flexibility in their working hours. In addition, depending on the nature of their projects, they may work at home or in attorneys' offices. With flexibility, however, comes responsibility. A freelance paralegal's income depends on the paralegal's ability to promote and maintain his or her business. If the paralegal has no clients for the month, there will be no paycheck. Also, freelancers do not enjoy job benefits such as medical insurance, sick time, or vacation time. A freelance paralegal needs to be self-motivated and driven to make the business work.

Realize that freelance paralegals work under attorney supervision. Freelancers are not to be confused with **legal technicians**—often called *independent paralegals*—who do *not* work under the supervision of an attorney and who provide (sell) legal services directly to the public. These services include helping members of the public obtain and fill out forms for certain types of legal transactions, such as bankruptcy filings and divorce petitions. As you will read in Chapter 3, legal technicians run the risk of violating state statutes prohibiting the unauthorized practice of law.

Paralegal Specialties

While many paralegals work for small firms that offer a wide range of legal services, other paralegals have found it useful and satisfying to specialize, in one area of law. The top three fields in which paralegals specialize, according to one survey, are litigation (47.3 percent), personal-injury law (22.1 percent), and corporate law (22.1 percent).[2] Numerous other specialty areas exist, however, some of which are listed in Exhibit 2.2 on the next page, along with the average compensation for paralegals in that area. Here, we discuss just a few of the areas in which paralegals may specialize.

Litigation Assistance

Working a lawsuit through the court system is called **litigation.** Paralegals who specialize in assisting attorneys in the litigation process are called **litigation paralegals.** Litigation paralegals work in general law practices, small litigation firms, litigation departments of larger law firms, and corporate legal departments. Litigation paralegals often specialize in a certain type of litigation, such as personal-injury litigation (which will be discussed shortly) or product liability cases (which involve injuries caused by defective products).

Work performed by litigation paralegals varies with the substantive law area being litigated. Some litigation paralegals investigate cases, review documents

freelance paralegal
A paralegal who operates his or her own business and provides services to attorneys on a contract basis. A freelance paralegal works under the supervision of an attorney, who assumes responsibility for the paralegal's work product.

legal technician (or independent paralegal)
A paralegal who offers services directly to the public, normally for a fee, without attorney supervision. Independent paralegals assist consumers by supplying them with forms and procedural knowledge relating to simple or routine legal procedures.

litigation
The process of working a lawsuit through the court system.

litigation paralegal
A paralegal who specializes in assisting attorneys in the litigation process.

EXHIBIT 2.2
Average Compensation by Specialty

The authors compiled this chart using data from a variety of sources, including NALA, NFPA, *Legal Assistant Today* magazine, The Affiliates, and the Legal Assistant Manager Association (LAMA).

AREA OF SPECIALTY	AVERAGE COMPENSATION
Bankruptcy	$40,500
Corporate	$45,410
Criminal	$38,090
Elder law	$39,970
Employment	$42,945
Environmental	$42,100
Family law	$38,150
Immigration	$40,500
Intellectual property	$53,050
Litigation	$42,500
Medical malpractice	$39,400
Mergers and acquisitions	$50,300
Personal injury	$39,270
Probate (wills and estates)	$39,180
Real estate law	$43,250

containing evidence, interview clients and witnesses, draft documents to file with the courts, and prepare for hearings and trials. The work that they do is somewhat similar to the work described in Chapter 1 in the hypothetical case of Barbara Kaiser. Note that the work performed by a litigation paralegal also varies depending on whether she or he works primarily on behalf of **plaintiffs** (those who bring lawsuits) or on behalf of **defendants** (those against whom lawsuits are brought). Lawyers in a personal-injury practice, for example, often represent plaintiffs. You will read in detail about litigation procedures and the important role played by paralegals in the litigation process in Chapters 12 through 15.

plaintiff
A party who initiates a lawsuit.

defendant
A party against whom a lawsuit is brought.

Personal-Injury Law

Much litigation involves claims brought by persons who have been injured in automobile accidents or other incidents as a result of the negligence of others. *Negligence* is a *tort,* or civil wrong, and someone who has been injured as a result of another's negligence is entitled under tort law to obtain compensation from the wrongdoer. (Tort law, including negligence, will be discussed in Chapter 7.)

Paralegals who specialize in personal-injury litigation often work for law firms that concentrate their efforts on this domain. Legal assistants in this area obtain and review medical and employment records to determine the client's injuries and lost wages. These items are needed to ascertain the plaintiff's damages in a personal-injury lawsuit. Personal-injury paralegals are also hired by insurance companies to investigate claims. Defendants in personal-injury cases are typically insured by automobile or other insurance, and a defendant's insurance company therefore has a duty to defend an insured customer who is being sued.

corporate law
Law that governs the formation, financing, merger and acquisition, and termination of corporations, as well as the rights and duties of those who own and run the corporation.

Corporate Law

Corporate law consists of the laws that govern the formation, financing, merger and acquisition, and termination of corporations, as well as the rights and duties of those who own and run the corporation. You will read in detail about the

---

DEVELOPING PARALEGAL SKILLS
Working for a Public Defender

Michele Sanchez works as a paralegal for the public defender's office in her county. Today, she has been assigned to go to the county jail to meet with a new client. The client has been jailed for child abuse and is very upset. She demands to be released from jail immediately. Michele notes her concerns and informs the client of the scheduling of the bail hearings.

TIPS FOR MEETING WITH A NEW CLIENT

- Review the case before meeting with the client.
- Listen carefully and supportively.
- Communicate with empathy.
- Minimize note taking.
- Do not appear to judge the client.

---

meaning of these terms and the tasks that corporate paralegals typically perform in Chapter 10.

Paralegals who specialize in corporate law may work for a corporation, in its legal department, or for a law firm that specializes in corporate law. Corporate paralegals often perform such tasks as preparing and filing documents with a state agency to set up corporations and to keep them in good standing, keeping corporate records, organizing and scheduling shareholders' meetings in accordance with state law, and preparing stock certificates. The demand for paralegals experienced in the area of corporate law is expanding. As you can see in Exhibit 2.2, which lists the average compensation by specialty, paralegals who work in corporate law generally receive higher salaries than paralegals in most other specialty areas. In addition, those corporate paralegals who further narrow their specialties to mergers and acquisitions are among the highest-paid paralegals today.

Criminal Law

Law is sometimes classified into the two categories of civil law and criminal law. **Civil law** is concerned with the duties that exist between persons or between citizens and their governments, excluding the duty not to commit crimes. Contract law, for example, is part of civil law. The whole body of tort law, which has to do with the infringement by one person of the legally recognized rights of another (see Chapter 7), is an area of civil law. **Criminal law,** in contrast, is concerned with wrongs committed against the public as a whole. Criminal acts are prohibited by federal, state, or local statutes (criminal law and procedures will be discussed in Chapter 15). In a criminal case, the government seeks to impose a penalty (a fine or jail time) on a person who has committed a crime. In a civil case, one party tries to make the other party comply with a duty or pay for the damage caused by the failure to so comply.

Paralegals who specialize in criminal law may work for public prosecutors, public defenders, or criminal defense attorneys. A legal assistant working for the prosecutor's office, for example, might draft search or arrest warrants. A paralegal working for the defense attorney (public or private) might obtain police reports, conduct research, and draft documents to be filed with the court—for example, a document arguing that the police violated the defendant's constitutional rights. Although criminal law and civil law are very different, the trial process is similar, and paralegals perform similar types of tasks (investigation, summarizing witness testimony, and so forth) in preparation for litigation.

civil law
The branch of law dealing with the definition and enforcement of private rights, as opposed to criminal matters.

criminal law
The branch of law that governs and defines those actions that are crimes and that subjects persons convicted of crimes to punishment imposed by the government (a fine or jail time).

On the Web
You can gain insight into criminal law and procedures by looking at some of the famous criminal law cases included on Court TV's Web site. Go to **http://www.courttv.com/index.html.**

Bankruptcy Law

Bankruptcy law is a body of law that allows debtors to obtain relief from their debts. Bankruptcy law is federal law, and bankruptcy proceedings take place in federal courts (see the discussion of the federal court system in Chapter 6). The twin goals of bankruptcy law are (1) to protect a debtor by giving him or her a fresh start, free from creditors' claims; and (2) to ensure that creditors who are competing for a debtor's assets are treated fairly. Bankruptcy law provides for several types of relief, and both individuals and business firms may petition for bankruptcy.

Both large and small firms practice bankruptcy law and hire paralegals who specialize in the area of bankruptcy law. Corporations undergoing bankruptcy proceedings may also hire paralegals experienced in bankruptcy to assist them on a temporary basis. If you specialize in bankruptcy, you might be responsible for interviewing the debtor to obtain information about the debtor's income, assets, and debts; reviewing creditors' claims to verify their validity; and preparing documents that will be submitted to the federal bankruptcy court.

On the Web
If you are interested in bankruptcy law, a good site for learning about current bankruptcy issues is that of the American Bankruptcy Institute at **http://www.abiworld.org**.

Employment and Labor Law

As will be discussed in Chapter 10, laws governing employment relationships are referred to collectively as *employment and labor law.* Employment and labor law includes laws governing health and safety in the workplace, labor unions and union-management relations, employment discrimination, sexual harassment, wrongful termination, pension plans, retirement and disability income (Social Security), employee privacy rights, the minimum wage that must be paid, and overtime wages.

Paralegals who are experienced in one or more of these areas may work for law firms, corporations and other business entities, or government agencies. Often, paralegals specialize in just one area of employment law. For example, many paralegals specialize in the area of workers' compensation. Under state **workers' compensation statutes,** employees who are injured on the job are compensated from state funds (obtained from taxes paid by employers). Paralegals working in this area assist persons injured on the job in obtaining compensation from the state workers' compensation board. As mentioned earlier, some government agencies allow paralegals to represent clients during agency hearings, which are conducted by agencies to settle disputes, or during negotiations with the agencies. Many state workers' compensation boards allow paralegals to represent clients in such hearings.

Frequently, working in the area of employment law involves interacting with numerous administrative agencies, such as the Occupational Safety and Health Administration and the Equal Opportunity Employment Commission. Each governmental agency has its own set of rules, requirements, and legal procedures. Paralegals who work in employment or labor law need to be familiar with the relevant federal and state agencies, as well as with their specific roles in resolving disputes. Many of the administrative agencies that regulate employment issues also hire paralegals. You will learn more about employment law in Chapter 10 and administrative agencies in Chapter 11.

On the Web
Several law firms that specialize in labor and employment issues have posted their newsletters on the Web. One such firm is Arent Fox, which you can access at **http://www.arentfox.com/home.html**.

Estate Planning and Probate Administration

Estate planning and probate administration both have to do with the transfer of an owner's property, or *estate,* on the owner's death. Through **estate planning,** the owner decides, *before* death, how his or her property will be transferred to others. The owner may make a **will,** for example, to designate the persons to whom his or her property is to be transferred. If someone contests the validity of the will, or if the property in the deceased person's estate is of a certain value, the will must be **probated** (proved) in a **probate court.** Depending on the size of the estate, it may take months—in some cases, over a year—for the probate court to approve the property distribution and for the property to be transferred to the rightful heirs. Furthermore, inheritance taxes and attorneys' fees (incurred in administering the estate) will reduce the value of the property that is given to heirs.

Because the probate process is time consuming and expensive, today many people engage in estate planning to avoid probate. For example, a person may opt to establish a **trust** agreement, which is a legal arrangement in which the ownership of property is transferred to a third person (the *trustee*) to be used for the benefit of another (the beneficiary). Paralegals often are responsible for interviewing clients to obtain information necessary to draft wills and trust agreements, for gathering information on debts and assets, and for locating heirs if necessary (see Chapter 9). A paralegal who is sensitive and caring toward the client, yet professional and conscientious in explaining and expediting procedures, is particularly well suited for this specialty.

Intellectual Property Law

Intellectual property consists of the products of individuals' minds—products that result from intellectual, creative processes. Those who create intellectual property acquire certain rights over the use of that property, and these rights are protected by law. Literary and artistic works are protected by *copyright law. Trademark law* protects business firms' distinctive marks or mottos. Inventions are protected by *patent law.* The primary benefit of intellectual property rights to the owner is that he or she controls the commercial use of the property. The owner, for example, may sell the intellectual property rights to another, may collect royalties on the use of the property (such as a popular song) by others, and may prevent unauthorized publishers from reproducing the property (such as a novel). In Chapter 8, you will read in greater detail about laws governing intellectual property.

will
A document directing how and to whom the maker's property and obligations are to be transferred on his or her death.

probate
The process of "proving" the validity of a will and ensuring that the instructions in a valid will are carried out.

probate court
A court that probates wills; usually a county court.

trust
An arrangement in which title to property is held by one person (a trustee) for the benefit of another (a beneficiary).

 On the Web
To find the wills of famous people (John Lennon, Jacqueline Kennedy Onassis, Elvis Presley, and dozens of others), go to **http://www. ca-probate.com/wills.htm.**

intellectual property
Property that results from intellectual, creative processes. Copyrights, patents, and trademarks are examples of intellectual property.

Many law firms (or special departments of large law firms) specialize in intellectual property law, such as patent law. Other firms provide a spectrum of legal services to their clients, of which intellectual property law is only a part. In addition, corporate legal departments may be responsible for registering copyrights, patents, or trademarks with the federal government.[3]

In the area of intellectual property, paralegals frequently research existing patents and trademarks. They also assist in compiling complex patent applications in accordance with detailed regulations, draft documents necessary to apply for trademark and copyright protection, and assist in litigating disputes. Because this area requires very specific knowledge that is currently in demand, paralegal intellectual property specialists are presently paid more than specialists in any other area (see Exhibit 2.2). This is an especially good practice area for paralegals with a science background. In fact, anyone, including a paralegal, with three years of undergraduate science courses can apply to the U.S. Patent and Trademark Office to become a registered patent agent, who prepares patent applications.

Environmental Law

environmental law
All state and federal laws or regulations enacted or issued to protect the environment and preserve environmental resources.

Environmental law consists of all laws that have been created to protect the environment. Environmental law involves the regulation of air and water pollution, natural resource management, endangered species protection, hazardous waste disposal and the cleanup of hazardous waste sites, pesticide control, and nuclear power regulation.

Employers of paralegal specialists in environmental law include administrative agencies (such as the federal Environmental Protection Agency, state natural resource departments, and local zoning boards), environmental law departments of large law firms, law firms that specialize in environmental law, and corporations. Corporations with legal departments often employ environmental specialists as well. For example, a corporation may employ a paralegal as an *environmental coordinator* to assist the corporation in maintaining compliance with government regulations, overseeing company environmental programs, and obtaining proper permits to use land in certain ways. Paralegals working in law firms that handle environmental matters often assist in litigation concerning alleged violations of environmental laws. They perform tasks similar to those described previously for litigation and personal-injury paralegals.

Real Estate Law

real estate
Land and things permanently attached to the land, such as houses, buildings, and trees and foliage.

Real estate, or *real property,* consists of land and all things permanently attached to the land, such as houses, buildings, and trees and foliage. Because of the value of real estate (for most people, a home is the most expensive purchase they will ever make), attorneys frequently assist persons or business firms that buy or sell real property to make sure that nothing important is overlooked. Paralegals who specialize in real estate may find employment in a number of environments, including small law firms that specialize in real estate transactions, real estate departments in large law firms, corporations or other business firms that frequently buy or sell real property, banking institutions (which finance real estate purchases), title companies, and real estate agencies. Paralegals working in the field of real estate law often draft contracts for the sale of real estate, draft mortgage agreements, draft and record deeds, and schedule closings on the sale of property. You will read in greater detail about real property law in Chapter 9.

PARALEGAL PROFILE

Real Estate Paralegal

TERRYE PRYBYLSKI *is a real estate paralegal at a full-service law firm that has represented businesses and individuals since 1890, when the industrial age created a boomtown for the city of Detroit. The firm handled Detroit's incredible growth and survived and prospered during the trials of the twentieth century, including the stock market crash, two World Wars, the introduction of unions, race riots, and the onset of the information age and the explosion of technology. Today, the firm has approximately a hundred attorneys and twenty paralegals in offices located throughout Michigan. Prybylski works in the real estate group's transactional practice in downtown Detroit.*

Prybylski has been a paralegal since 1992. She earned a postgraduate paralegal–legal assistant certificate from the American Institute for Paralegal Studies, Inc., and a master of business administration degree from the University of Detroit–Mercy.

Before specializing in real estate, Prybylski worked as a paralegal at a natural gas utility company and a national bank, where she was considered a "jack of all trades." At the bank, she worked in the areas of litigation and corporate, employment, banking, and regulatory law in addition to real estate law. She is a member of the State Bar of Michigan–Legal Assistants Section, Detroit Metropolitan Bar Association, and National Association of Legal Assistants (NALA) and is a notary public.

What do you like best about your work?

"What I like best about my work is the diversity of the client base and the variety of duties that I perform. I interact with developers, national banks, national and local tenants (particularly retail clients), corporate owners, individual buyers and sellers, surveyors, environmental consulting firms, title companies, and local governments. Each deal is unique, with its own specific set of circumstances, and each poses a challenge."

What is the greatest challenge that you face in your area of work?

"I am responsible for obtaining the title work, surveys, zoning letters, certificates of occupancy, corporate documents, and related due diligence. It is not uncommon for a transaction to involve multiple properties located in a variety of states. It is often a challenge to coordinate the acquisition of all of the required information from the various sources in a timely manner. Time frames and closing dates do not always allow for the time desired, and it takes persistence and a great deal of organizational skill to guarantee that all of the required elements have been obtained, reviewed, and approved prior to the closing date."

> **"In any area of specialization, a good paralegal is a team player who is willing to go the distance to do whatever it takes to get the job done."**

What advice do you have for would-be paralegals in your area of work?

"You must recognize the important role you play in the grand scheme of things. Not all of your assignments will be glamorous, but your efforts are vital to the success of the matter. A simple mistake—such as an incorrect legal description of property, an incorrect tax parcel identification number, or failure to conform to geographical recording requirements—will result in a document's not being recorded in a timely manner. This may have serious consequences for the client. It is important to perform all job duties with professionalism. Even a mundane task, such as compiling the closing binder, must be done to the best of your ability because your work product reflects on you and your firm's reputation."

What are some tips for success as a paralegal in your area of work?

"Knowing how to navigate on the Internet is crucial. I have discovered valuable resources and obtained all sorts of useful information in a fraction of the time that more traditional methods would take to obtain the same results. Information on business entities, whom to contact for zoning approval at the county level, statutes, local surveyors, and other data are now available online. Being detail oriented and accurate is a necessity for a real estate paralegal. This comes into play in many aspects of the job, such as when reviewing surveys, title work, and legal descriptions. In any area of specialization, a good paralegal is a team player who is willing to go the distance to do whatever it takes to get the job done. Excellent verbal and written communication skills, as well as a willingness to learn and experience new challenges, will guarantee success in your profession."

Family Law

family law
Law relating to family matters, such as marriage, divorce, child support, and child custody.

Family law, as the term implies, deals with family matters, such as marriage, divorce, alimony, child support, and child custody. We discuss family law in detail in Chapter 9. Family law is governed primarily by state statutes. If you specialize in this area, you will need to become familiar with your state's requirements concerning marriage and divorce procedures, child support, and related issues.

As a family law specialist, you might work for a small family law practice, for a family law department in a large law firm, or with a state or local agency, such as a community services agency, that assists persons who need help with family-related problems. As a paralegal working in family law, you might research and draft documents that are filed with the court in divorce and adoption proceedings. You might also perform investigations into assets and the grounds for divorce. Paralegals in this area often have extensive client contact and need to be skilled at extracting relevant information from sometimes emotionally distraught persons. Those with a background or interest in social work or counseling are particularly well suited to this specialty.

Emerging Specialty Areas

elder law
A relatively new legal specialty that involves servicing the needs of older clients, such as estate planning and making arrangements for long-term care.

immigration law
All laws that set forth the requirements that persons must meet if they wish to visit or immigrate to the United States.

The above listing of specialty areas is by no means exhaustive. In addition to these domains, several emerging areas offer opportunities for paralegals who wish to specialize. For example, as the U.S. population ages, more and more attorneys are focusing on servicing the needs of older clients. **Elder law** is the term used to describe this broad specialty. Paralegals who work in this practice area may be asked to assist in a variety of tasks, including those relating to estate planning (discussed earlier), age-discrimination claims, financial arrangements for long-term care, Medicare and Medicaid, abuse suffered by elderly persons, and the visitation rights of grandparents.

An increasing number of paralegals are also finding work in the area of **immigration law.** In the 1990s, immigration rates climbed significantly from those of previous decades. As the number of immigrants increased, so did the need for legal services among immigrant groups. Today, a number of law firms specialize in immigration law, particularly in California, New York, and other states with large immigrant populations. If you specialize in this area, you might assist clients who need help in filling out applications for work permits or visas or who need information on how to become U.S. citizens. You may help clients contact foreign government offices about their immigration status or assist clients who are involved in deportation proceedings.

Over the past decade, many nurses have found profitable and challenging work as paralegals. A paralegal who is also a trained nurse is particularly well equipped to evaluate legal claims involving injuries, such as those involved in personal-injury, medical malpractice, or product liability lawsuits. A relatively new specialty area among nurses—and within the legal profession—is that of the **legal nurse consultant (LNC)**. An LNC consults with legal professionals and others on medical aspects of legal claims or issues. LNCs usually work independently (offering their services on a contract basis) and are typically well paid for their services—up to $200 per hour, in some cases. Some LNCs work for law firms, insurance companies, government offices, and risk management departments of companies as salaried employees. The American Association of Legal Nurse Consultants offers a certification program in which nurses who meet the eligibility criteria (including appropriate educational credentials and sufficient experience as a legal nurse) and pass an examination may become certified as LNCs.

As discussed in the *Technology and Today's Paralegal* feature in Chapter 1, developments in technology are transforming the legal workplace. These developments are also opening doors to possible areas of specialization for paralegals. Paralegals who acquire expertise in high-tech equipment and software applications can perform valuable services for their employers and command high salaries.

legal nurse consultant (LNC)
A nurse who consults with legal professionals and others about medical aspects of legal claims or issues. Legal nurse consultants normally must have at least a bachelor's degree in nursing and a significant amount of nursing experience.

PARALEGAL COMPENSATION

What do paralegals earn? This is an important question for anyone contemplating a career as a paralegal. You can get some idea of what paralegals make, on average, from paralegal compensation surveys. Following a discussion of these surveys, we look at some other components of paralegal compensation, including job benefits and compensation for overtime work.

Compensation Surveys

Paralegal income is affected by a number of factors. We have already mentioned the effects of the size of the firm or legal department (see Exhibit 2.1) and the specialty area in which the paralegal practices (see Exhibit 2.2). Another income-determining factor is the paralegal's years of experience, which is shown in Exhibit 2.3 on the following page. Typically, more experienced paralegals enjoy higher rates of compensation. This is particularly noticeable when a paralegal has worked for the same employer for a long period of time.

Another major factor that affects paralegal compensation is geographical location. The previous exhibits illustrate *national* averages. Exhibit 2.4 on the next page, by contrast, shows *regional* averages of paralegal income. As you can see, paralegals who work in the Far West and in the Northeast generally enjoy higher levels of compensation than paralegals in other regions of the country. Remember, though, that these figures still represent averages and can therefore be deceptive. For example, a paralegal working in a rural area of Washington state may not earn as much as a paralegal who works in a city in the Plains states. Also,

On the Web
To learn more about the American Association of Legal Nurse Consultants and its certification programs, go to **http://www.aalnc.org**.

EXHIBIT 2.3

Paralegal Compensation by Years of Experience

The authors compiled this chart using data from a variety of sources, including NALA, NFPA, *Legal Assistant Today* magazine, The Affiliates, and the Legal Assistant Manager Association (LAMA).

YEARS OF EXPERIENCE	AVERAGE COMPENSATION
1–2	$33,200
3–5	$36,750
6–10	$41,100
11–15	$44,350
16–20	$46,600
More than 20	$49,850

a paralegal who works in a major city (such as Chicago or Detroit) may be compensated in an amount that greatly exceeds the average for that region.

Keep in mind, too, that salary statistics do not tell the whole story. Although paralegals earn more in California than in a midwestern state such as Nebraska, the cost of living is higher in California than in Nebraska. This means that your real income—the amount of goods and services that you can purchase with your income—may, in fact, be the same in both states despite the differences in salary. Salary statistics also do not reveal another important component of compensation—job benefits.

Job Benefits

Part of your total compensation package as an employee will consist of various job benefits. These benefits may include paid holidays, sick leave, group insurance coverage (life, disability, medical, dental), pension plans, and possibly others. Benefits packages vary from firm to firm. For example, one employer may pay the entire premium for your life and health insurance, while another employer may require you to contribute part of the cost of the insurance. Usually, the larger the firm, the greater the value of the benefits package.

> ❋ **When evaluating any job offer, you need to consider the benefits that you will receive and what these benefits are worth to you.**

You will read more about the importance of job benefits later in this chapter, in the context of evaluating a job offer.

EXHIBIT 2.4

Average Paralegal Compensation by Region

The authors compiled this chart using data from a variety of sources, including NALA, NFPA, *Legal Assistant Today* magazine, The Affiliates, and the Legal Assistant Manager Association (LAMA).

REGION	2002 AVERAGE COMPENSATION (SALARY PLUS BONUSES)
Northeast	$45,800
Great Lakes	$41,600
Plains states	$38,300
Southeast	$42,500
Southwest	$44,300
Rocky Mountains	$38,050
Far West	$54,900

Salaries versus Hourly Wages

Most paralegals are salaried employees. In other words, they receive a specified annual salary regardless of the number of hours they actually work. Other paralegals are paid an hourly wage rate for every hour worked. Paralegals are frequently asked to work overtime, and how they are compensated for overtime work usually depends on whether they are salaried employees or are paid hourly wages. Many firms compensate their salaried paralegals for overtime work through year-end **bonuses,** which are special payments made to employees in recognition of their devotion to the firm and the high quality of their work. Paralegals often receive annual bonuses ranging from $1,500 to nearly $4,000, depending on years of experience, firm size, and so forth. Some firms allow salaried employees to take compensatory time off work (for example, an hour off for every hour worked beyond usual working hours). Employees who are paid an hourly wage rate are normally paid overtime wages.

bonus
An end-of-the-year payment to a salaried employee in appreciation for that employee's overtime work, work quality, diligence, or dedication to the firm.

Federal Law and Overtime Pay

A major issue in the paralegal profession in regard to compensation has to do with overtime pay. Some paralegals who receive year-end bonuses question whether their bonuses sufficiently compensate them for the amount of overtime they have worked. The debate over overtime pay is complicated by the fact that the Fair Labor Standards Act (Wage-Hour Law) of 1938 requires employers to pay employees **overtime wages**—one and a half times their normal hourly rate—for all hours worked beyond forty hours per week. The act exempts certain types of employees from this overtime-pay requirement, however. *Exempt employees* include those who qualify under the terms of the act as holding "administrative," "executive," or "professional" positions.

overtime wages
Wages paid to workers who are paid an hourly wage rate to compensate them for overtime work (hours worked beyond forty hours per week). Under federal law, overtime wages are at least one and a half times the regular hourly wage rate.

The issue, then, is whether paralegals are exempt or nonexempt employees under the Fair Labor Standards Act. If they are exempt, they need not be paid an hourly overtime rate. If they are nonexempt, by law they must be paid overtime wages. Many firms argue that their paralegals are professionals and thus exempt from the act. Other firms, fearing possible liability for unfair labor practices, are beginning to pay overtime wages to their paralegals. Paralegals seem to be split fairly evenly on the issue, as are their employers. According to a compensation survey conducted by *Legal Assistant Today,* 47 percent of paralegals are classified by their employers as exempt employees, while 53 percent are classified as nonexempt.[4]

In early 1994, a federal court addressed this issue for the first time. The case arose when twenty-three paralegals who worked for Page & Addison, a law firm in Dallas, Texas, sought $40,000 in back wages for overtime hours that they had worked. The Department of Labor, which enforces the Fair Labor Standards Act, had concluded that the paralegals were nonexempt employees and thus subject to the act's overtime provisions. The federal court, however, disagreed, finding that paralegals could be classified as exempt (or professional) employees because they perform important work and exercise discretion and independent judgment.[5] Although the court decision in the *Page & Addison* case is significant, it does not mean that all paralegals are now classified as exempt employees. Rather, the issue is decided on the basis of the specific facts of a given case. The question of how paralegals should be classified for labor-law purposes continues to divide the profession.

PLANNING YOUR CAREER

Career planning involves essentially three steps. The first step is defining your long-term goals. The second step involves devising short-term goals and adjusting these goals to meet the realities of the job market. We look at these two steps of career planning in this section. This chapter's *Featured Guest* Article, which begins on page 42, also provides useful information on career planning and development. Later in this chapter, we discuss the third step: reevaluating your career after you have had some on-the-job experience as a paralegal.

Defining Your Long-Term Goals

From the outset, you will want to define, as clearly as possible, your career goals, and this requires some personal reflection and self-assessment. What are you looking for in a career? Why do you want to become a paralegal? Is income the most important factor? Is job satisfaction (doing the kind of work you like) the most important factor? Is the environment in which you work the most important factor? What profession could best utilize your special talents or skills? Asking yourself these and other broad questions about your personal preferences and values will help you define more clearly your overall professional goals.

Do not be surprised to find that your long-term goals change over time. As you gain more experience as a paralegal and your life circumstances change, you may decide that your former long-term goals are no longer appropriate. For example, you may desire a level of career involvement as a single person that may not be appropriate to your situation should you marry and have children. Similarly, later in life, when your children leave home, you may have different goals with respect to your work.

Also, at the outset of your career, you cannot know what opportunities might present themselves in the future. Career planning is an ongoing challenge for paralegals, just as it is for everyone. Throughout your career as a paralegal, you will probably meet other paralegals who have made career changes. A high percentage of paralegals in today's work force, for example, decided to become paralegals after several years of working in another profession, such as nursing, law enforcement, business administration, or accounting. Changes within the profession, your own experiences, and new opportunities constantly affect the career choices before you. The realities you face during your career may play a significant role in modifying your long-term goals.

Short-Term Goals and Job Realities

Long-term goals are just that—goals that we hope to achieve over the long run. It may take many years or even a lifetime to attain certain long-term goals that we set for ourselves. Short-term goals are the steps that we take to realize our long-term goals. As an entry-level paralegal, one of your short-term goals is simply to find a job.

Ideally, you will find a job that provides you with a salary commensurate with your training and abilities, a level of responsibility that is comfortable (or challenging) for you, and excellent job benefits. The realities of the job market are not always what we wish them to be, however. You should be prepared for the possibility that you might not find the "right" employer or the "perfect" job for you when you first start your job search. You may be lucky from the outset, but then again, it may take several attempts before you find the employer and the job that best suits your needs, skills, and talents. Remember, though, that even if you do not find the perfect job right away, you can gain valuable skills and experience in *any* job environment—skills and experience that can help you achieve long-term goals in the future. In fact, you might want to "try on" jobs at different-sized firms and in different specialty areas to see how they "fit" with your particular needs.

LOCATING POTENTIAL EMPLOYERS

Looking for a job is time consuming and requires attention to detail, persistence, and creativity. Your paralegal education is preparing you, among other things, to do investigative research. The investigative skills that you will use on the job as a paralegal are the ones that you should apply when looking for a job.

Where do you begin your investigation? How can you find out what paralegal jobs are available in your area or elsewhere? How do you know which law firms practice the type of law that interests you? The following suggestions will help you find answers to all of these questions.

Networking

Career opportunities often go unpublished. Many firms post notices within their own organizations before publishing online or in the "Help Wanted" section of a newspaper or periodical. This opens doors to their own employees before the general public. It also spares employers from having to wade through hundreds of employment applications for a vacant position. If you have connections within an organization, you may be told that a position is opening before other candidates are aware that an opportunity exists.

More paralegals report finding employment through networking than through any other means.[6] For paralegals, **networking** is the process of making personal connections with the other paralegals, paralegal instructors, attorneys, and others who are involved in (or who know someone who is involved in) the paralegal or legal profession. Professional organizations and internships offer two means of networkings.

networking
Making personal connections and cultivating relationships with people in a certain field, profession, or area of interest.

JOIN A PROFESSIONAL ASSOCIATION.   Students can begin forming a network of paralegal connections through affiliation with professional associations and student clubs. You have already learned about NALA and NFPA, the two largest national associations for legal assistants. Many other organizations of paralegals exist across the country. Some of these organizations are listed in Appendix F at the end of this book. See if your local paralegal association allows students to be members. If it does, attend meetings and become acquainted with other paralegals, who may know of job opportunities in your area. Persons involved with other groups, such as the Legal Assistant Management Association (an association of individuals who manage legal assistants) and the **state bar association** (a state-level association of attorneys), can also provide valuable inside knowledge of potential job openings.

state bar association
An association of attorneys within a state. In most states, an attorney must be a member of the state bar association to practice law in the state.

NETWORK DURING INTERNSHIPS.   Most paralegal education programs include an internship in which students are placed temporarily in a law firm or other work setting. Cultivate connections during your internship. The people you meet and deal with in these settings often turn out to be very beneficial to you in finding future employment. In many situations, an intern who has performed well is offered a full-time position after graduation. Even if you are not presently interested in working for the firm with which you do your internship, be careful not to "burn your bridges." You will find that the legal community, even in cities, is relatively small and that lawyers are more inclined to hire paralegals about whom their colleagues have made positive remarks.

FEATURED GUEST: ANNE GERAGHTY-RATHERT

Paralegal Career Planning and Development

BIOGRAPHICAL NOTE

*Anne Geraghty-Rathert gradu-
ated from St. Louis University
in 1985 with a bachelor of
arts degree in political science
and a certificate in political
journalism. In 1992, she graduated from the St. Louis
University School of Law. She
is currently an assistant professor in the Department of
History, Politics, and Law at
Webster University in St.
Louis, where she has been
teaching since 1993.*

*In her years at Webster,
Geraghty-Rathert has taught
in the ABA–approved para-
legal program at both the master's and bachelor's levels. She
has taught a wide variety of
courses, including introduction
to law, American legal history,
and constitutional law. She is
in her third year as the faculty
adviser of legal internships,
and she also oversees paralegal
job placement in the legal
studies program. In addition
to her teaching responsibilities,
she is a principal in the
Rathert law firm, a private law
practice.*

By the time students graduate
from a paralegal program, they
must have the essential skills
necessary to perform well in the profession. Paralegal career development
is an ongoing process that should be
considered at every point in a legal
studies education.

SKILL BUILDING

When a law office wants to hire a
paralegal, the prospective employer
will start with a quick assessment of
the person's background and skills.
The more skills candidates possess
and are able to positively identify, the
more likely it is that they will find
jobs. Students should select courses
that provide them with the best
employment skills and opportunities.
Then they should identify what they
have learned, incorporate that information into their résumés, and highlight it during their interviews.

Written Communication Skills.
Perhaps the most critical paralegal job
skill—but not necessarily the one that
receives the most emphasis—is
effective and grammatically correct
writing. Future paralegals should
choose course work that gives them
the chance to hone their writing skills.
In the paralegal profession, good legal
research and writing skills are crucial.
One of the best ways for a paralegal
to stand out is to include a solid
writing sample with his or her résumé.

Oral Communication Skills. Paralegal
students should also choose classes that
enhance their oral communication
skills. Some courses give students the
chance to emphasize interviewing and
listening skills through the use of role-
playing and group interactions. Other

courses may require students to give in-
class presentations. In these settings,
students are encouraged to use effective
communication skills and to state
clearly their questions and answers.
Students and faculty evaluate the
quality and clarity of oral
presentations, and students may offer
suggestions to each other on how to
improve their speaking abilities.

Office Protocol. Hiring organizations
must be able to rely on student
preparedness and the appropriateness
of their behavior once they are on the
job. Because many students have not
had an opportunity to work in an
office environment prior to starting
their work as paralegals, the legal
studies program is often their first
exposure to the nuances of office
protocol. It is critical that students
gain a real sense of the expectations of
law firms and employment settings
with respect to job skills and what
kind of behavior is appropriate.
Internship programs and in-house
clinical programs are helpful because
they offer students a chance to engage
in actual legal work while still in the
educational environment.

RÉSUMÉ DEVELOPMENT

Many students are intimidated by the
prospect of writing a résumé. They
generally know that education and
previous employment should be
included, but they do not know what
will make their résumé stand out in
the paralegal field. Components of
résumé development must include an
assessment of a student's job skills,
and, perhaps even more critically, an
assessment of the student's goals.
Students must be alert to opportuni-

FEATURED GUEST, *Continued*

ties to develop marketable skills and experience that are available to them while still in school. Course work, career services, and résumé writing workshops are just a few of the many on-campus resources that students may be able to access. By utilizing such resources, students can learn to make informed decisions about career options in the profession.

Students should write a first draft of their résumé as early as possible after they begin their paralegal studies. Utilizing the assistance of faculty and campus career offices for feedback, future paralegals will be able to perfect their résumés as their program continues. Résumés will then be ready to send out when the student approaches the job market. Students should be encouraged to begin collecting references and letters of recommendation as soon as they enter a paralegal program. These references and letters may be from professors, adjunct professors, or former employers. In addition, students should collect samples of the work they do in class and during internships. These samples can then be placed in a "portfolio" that the student can refer to in his or her résumé and bring to the interview.

INTERVIEWING

Students should also learn about the interviewing process while still in school. Again, workshops and course work can play an important part in preparing the student for job interviews. Through the use of role-playing and small-group interactions, students can develop interviewing skills. They can learn

how to prepare for the interview by doing advance research, how to approach the interview, and how to use various strategies to follow up on the interview once it has been concluded.

Internship opportunities can also be useful. As part of an internship course, students may submit a résumé to the host site and request an initial placement meeting, which is similar to an interview situation. Host sites are often willing to offer students feedback on both their résumés and the mock interviews. In addition, the site supervisors generally complete extensive written evaluations at the end of student internships. This is the perfect opportunity for a student to sit down with the supervisor and ask questions about the student's strengths and weaknesses. This information will help the student prepare for an actual interview in the paralegal field.

NETWORKING

Establishing relationships within the paralegal field prior to graduation will usually increase the student's employment options. Membership, either as a student or as a working paralegal, in local and national associations such as NALA can be especially helpful to networking. Legal studies programs and large law firms also hold paralegal job fairs periodically. Job fairs provide excellent opportunities to students. At these fairs, students can learn about various employers, engage in informal interviews with firms, and submit résumés to hiring personnel.

"Perhaps the most critical paralegal job skill—but not necessarily the one that receives the most emphasis—is effective and grammatically correct writing."

Students should also alert faculty and career placement personnel to their job searches. Many individual faculty members and career placement offices keep copies of student résumés and alert students to job advertisements for openings in the field or actively place students in job openings when possible.

CONCLUSION

By participating in a wide variety of course work and experiences, students can become acquainted with how an office works and develop the necessary knowledge and critical-thinking skills to operate well in that environment. Yet it is not enough to prepare only for the job itself. Students also need to learn how to find that dream job. Job placement must be considered at every point in a legal studies education—in every formal course, workshop, and clinical experience. Finding a job is rarely an accident, nor does it necessarily happen quickly or easily. Requesting guidance and utilizing support from available resources help to broaden the student's chances of succeeding in the job market.

Finding Available Jobs

Your next effort should be to locate sources that list paralegal job openings. A good place to start is with the classified ads in your local newspaper. **Trade journals** and similar publications, such as your local or state bar association's journal or news-letters, usually list openings for legal professionals, including paralegals. Increasingly, employers advertise job openings in online publications and turn to online databases to find prospective employees. In fact, today the best starting point when launching your job search is probably the Internet. (For more information on how you can use the Internet to search for jobs, see this chapter's *Technology and Today's Paralegal* feature.)

Identifying Possible Employers

You should also identify firms and organizations for which you might like to work and submit an employment application to them. In a well-organized job search, you will locate and contact those organizations that offer the benefits, salary, opportunities for advancement, work environment, and legal specialty of your choice. Even though these organizations may not have vacancies in your field at the moment, you want your job application to be immediately available when an opening does occur. Most firms, if they are interested in your qualifications, will keep your application on file for six months or so and may contact you if a posi-tion becomes available.

It is a good idea to begin compiling employer information for your job search while you are still completing your paralegal studies. Many of the resources you will need are available at the college or university that you attend or through your paralegal program (or, increasingly, online).

On the Web
You can search the Yellow Pages online at a number of Web sites, including Yahoo's Yellow Pages at **http://yp. yahoo.com.**

THE YELLOW PAGES.   An obvious source of information is the Yellow Pages of your local telephone directory. Look under "Attorneys" for the names of attor-neys and law firms in your locale. If you want to work in a specialty area, such as real estate, you might look under other listings, such as "Title Companies." Many libraries have the Yellow Pages for major cities across the country, which allows you to broaden the geographic scope of your search. You may be able to find sim-ilar information in online Yellow Pages listings.

LEGAL DIRECTORIES.   There are numerous legal directories that provide lists of attorneys, their locations, and their areas of practice. The *Martindale-Hubbell Law Directory,* which you can find at most law libraries (or online at **http:// www.martindale.com**), lists the names, addresses, telephone numbers, areas of legal practice, and other data for many lawyers and law firms throughout the United States. It is an excellent resource for paralegals interested in working for law firms or corporate legal departments. *West's Legal Directory* is another valu-able source of information. It is on the Internet at **http://lawyers.findlaw.com.** The directory contains a detailed listing of U.S. attorneys and law firms, state and federal attorneys and offices, and corporate legal departments and general counsel.

On the Web
If you are looking for a job in a corporate legal department, you can access over 300,000 companies online at **http://www.clickit.com.** Hoovers Online offers company and contact information for many public and private companies worldwide at **http://www.hoovers.com.**

JOB-PLACEMENT SERVICES

Throughout your job search, make full use of your school's placement service. Many paralegal programs provide job-placement services, and ABA–approved schools are required to provide ongoing placement services for students. Placement offices are

TECHNOLOGY AND TODAY'S PARALEGAL

Online Job Searching

Given how the Internet has affected all aspects of business and professional life, it is not surprising that it has become an invaluable device for both employers looking for job candidates and people seeking jobs. Today's paralegal can take advantage of this tool to make job searches much easier than in the past.

ONLINE EMPLOYMENT ADS

Paralegals looking for employment can access an increasing number of online sources to find out what positions are available in their field. A good starting point is the Hieros Gamos Employment Center's Web site (at **http://www.hg.org/employment.html**), which calls itself "the largest source of jobs on the Internet." At this site, in addition to finding job vacancies in your field, you can indicate the type of position you are interested in and ask to be notified by e-mail when a position in that area is posted. If you go to **http://careers.findlaw.com**, you will find a state-by-state list of job openings for paralegals.

A site sponsored by Cornell University and *Human Resource Executive* magazine (at **http://www.workindex.com**) allows you to search for listings in your area and also provides links to numerous other job-information sites and search engines. You can find links to state employment offices, federal jobs, and employment ads from publications in various areas of the country at Job Bank USA's site (go to **http://www.jobbankusa.com/jobs.html**).

Many states now publish job openings for state government positions on their Web pages, and some include application forms on their sites as well. For example, Vermont publishes its biweekly job notices on its Web site (at **http://www.vtstatejobs.info**).

POST YOUR RÉSUMÉ ONLINE

Increasingly, employers are recruiting new employees by using online résumé banks. These sites allow employers to search through databases of job seekers to find job candidates whose skills and qualifications most closely correlate with the employers' needs. In a sense, résumé banks are the online world's version of the traditional "Positions Wanted" ads in newspapers. A key difference for job seekers is that, whereas they must pay to place ads in newspapers and other publications, there is little or no cost involved in posting a résumé online—or keeping it there for some time.

One of the oldest résumé sites is that offered by LAWMATCH (at **http://www.lawmatch.com**).

LAWMATCH, like many other sites now offering such services, has both public and confidential sections. In a public listing, the identity of the candidate is revealed online. In a confidential listing, the identity of the candidate is not revealed; rather, interested employers are directed to call LAWMATCH, which then notifies the candidate of the employment opportunity. Confidential listings typically are sought by people who do not want their current employers to know that they are interested in other employment. The Legal Employment Search Site (at **http://www.legalemploy.com**) has links to numerous sites where you can post your résumé online; this site also gives helpful suggestions on how to use the Internet in your job search.

WEB HOME PAGES

Virtually all large firms (and increasingly, many small firms) have Web pages, as do federal and state government agencies. Once you have the name of a firm or agency that interests you, you can go online to see if that organization has a Web page. The Web page of a firm or agency may contain much useful information for job seekers, including, in some cases, available positions and the name of the person you should contact about employment.

To find home pages of law firms, a good starting point is FindLaw's site at **http://www.findlaw.com/14firms/index.html**. Just keying in the name of the firm on a search engine may lead you to the firm's home page. You can also browse through FindLaw's employer directory or search for employers who match specified criteria at **http://www.infirmation.com/shared/lss**. To locate the home pages for federal government agencies, access Federal World's site at **http://www.fedworld.gov**. To locate information on state governments, including state agencies, try **http://www.law.cornell.edu/states/index.html** and **http://www.findlaw.com/11stategov**.

TECHNOLOGY TIP

These sites and the links they offer will help get you started on your job search. To find other sites, check with your paralegal program director, your school's placement office, or your local paralegal association. All of these sources will have information on current Web sites that you can access for job information. You can also search job listings and post your résumé on NFPA's Legal Career Center page (at **http://paralegals.legalstaff.com**).

DEVELOPING PARALEGAL SKILLS

A Career Plan

Rob Johnson, a paralegal student who is working toward a bachelor's degree with a legal assistant major, needs to find a job for the internship class that is required for graduation. Rob, however, does not want to take just any job. Rob wants his internship to be the springboard for his career as a paralegal. Rob thus begins to implement some career-planning strategies.

CHECKLIST FOR CAREER PLANNING

- Establish long-term goals.
- Review the current job market and establish short-term goals.
- Locate available jobs and employers.
- Network.
- Reevaluate your job every few years.

---

staffed with personnel trained to assist you in finding a job, as well as in preparing job-search tools, such as your résumé and a list of potential employers.

A growing trend is to use legal staffing or placement companies (also known as recruiters) to locate employment. Usually, the employer pays the fees for the placement company's services, and the company recruits candidates for the paralegal position and arranges interviews. Placement services can be located through paralegal program directors, local paralegal associations, state bar associations, or on the Web.

Legal staffing companies place paralegal employees in both temporary (called "contract") and full-time (called "direct-hire") positions. Temporary contract employees are often used when a regular employee needs to take emergency or medical leave or when a special project requires additional paralegals, such as in large-scale litigation cases. Contract jobs can last from a few days to over a year. For example, in 2001, a Fortune 500 corporation hired from fifteen to twenty legal professionals for over a year to review documents in a major product liability case. Such relatively long-term opportunities can provide valuable work experience in a particular specialty. Direct-hire positions typically provide long-term employment with salary and benefits, which are not provided in most temporary employment contracts.

MARKETING YOUR SKILLS

Once you have located potential employers, the next step in your job search is to market your skills and yourself effectively to those employers. Marketing your skills involves three stages: the application process, interviewing for jobs, and following up on job interviews.

You should keep in mind throughout your job search that each personal contact you make, whether it results in employment or not, has potential for your future. A firm may not hire you today, for example, because you lack experience. But it may hire you a year from now if by then you have the experience that it is seeking. Therefore, always keep track of the contacts you make during your search, be patient, and be professional. You may be surprised how many doors will open for you, if not today, then tomorrow.

The Application Process

As a paralegal looking for professional employment, you will need to assemble and present professional application materials. The basic materials you should create are a résumé, a cover letter, a list of professional references, and a portfolio. The following discussion explains each of these documents and gives some practical tips on how to create them.

THE RÉSUMÉ.   For almost all job applications, you must submit a personal *résumé,* which summarizes your employment and educational background. Your résumé is an advertisement, and you should invest the time to make that advertisement effective. Because personnel officers in law firms, corporations, and government agencies may receive a hundred or more résumés for each position they advertise, your résumé should create the best possible impression if you want to gain a competitive edge over other job seekers.

Either generate your résumé yourself, using a computer and a laser printer, or have a professional résumé-preparation service do it for you. Format each page so that the reader is able to scan it quickly and catch the highlights. You might vary the type size, but never use a type size or style that is difficult to read.

What to Include in Your Résumé.   Your name, address, telephone number, e-mail address, and fax number belong in the heading of your résumé. The résumé should be simple, brief, and clear. As a general rule, it should contain only information that is relevant to the job that you are seeking. A one-page résumé is usually sufficient, unless two pages are required to list relevant educational background and work experience. Exhibits 2.5 and 2.6 on the following page show two sample résumés—one of a person with paralegal experience and one of a person without paralegal experience. Note that you should avoid placing your name and address in the upper left-hand corner, as this area is often stapled.

Divide your résumé into logical sections with headings, such as those shown in Exhibits 2.5 and 2.6. Whenever you list dates, such as educational and employment dates, list them chronologically, in reverse order. In other words, list your most recent educational or work history first. When discussing your education, list the names, cities, and states of the colleges or universities that you have attended and the degrees that you have received. You may want to indicate your major and minor concentrations and those courses that are most related to your professional goal, such as "Major: Paralegal Studies" or "Minor: Political Science." When listing your work experience, specify what your responsibilities have been in each position that you have held. Also, include any volunteer work that you have done.

Scholarships or honors should also be indicated. If you have a high grade point average (GPA), you should include it in your résumé. Under the heading "Selected Accomplishments," you might indicate your ability to speak more than one language or other special skill, such as online research skills.

What if you are an entry-level paralegal and have no work experience to list? What can you include on your résumé to fill out the page? If you are facing this situation, add more information on your educational background and experience. You can list specific courses that you took, particular skills—such as computer skills—that you acquired during your paralegal training, and student affiliations.

Do Not Include Personal Data.   Avoid including personal data (such as age, marital status, number of children, gender, or hobbies) in your résumé. Employers are prohibited by law from discriminating against employees or job candidates on the basis of race, color, gender, national origin, religion, age, or disability. You can help them fulfill this legal obligation by not including in your résumé any information that could serve as a basis for discrimination. For the same reason, you would be wise not to include a photograph of yourself with your résumé. Also,

EXHIBIT 2.5
A Sample Résumé of a Person with Paralegal Experience

ELENA LOPEZ

1131 North Shore Drive
Nita City, NI* 48804
Telephone: (616) 555-0102 • Fax: (616) 555-2103 • E-mail: elopez@nitanet.net

EMPLOYMENT OBJECTIVE
A position as a paralegal in a private law firm that specializes in personal-injury practice.

EDUCATION

2000   Postbaccalaureate certificate
Midwestern Professional School for Paralegals, Green Bay, WI
Focus: Litigation Procedures, Legal Investigation, Torts, Arbitration and Medication, Case Preparation, and Trial. GPA 3.8.

1997   Bachelor of Arts degree
University of Wisconsin, Madison, WI 53706.
Political Science major. GPA 3.5.

PARALEGAL EXPERIENCE

- Caldwell Legal Clinic, Nita City, NI
  Paralegal: June 2002 to the present.
  Responsibilities: Legal research and document review; drafting discovery documents, including interrogatories, deposition summaries, and requests for admissions; and trial preparation in personal-injury cases.

- Legal Aid Society, Green Bay, WI
  Paralegal: June 2000 to May 2002.
  Responsibilities: Part-time assistance to legal aid attorneys in their representation of indigent clients in matters such as divorce, abuse, child custody, paternity, and landlord/tenant disputes.

- University of Wisconsin, Madison, WI
  Research Assistant: Political Science Department, January 1997 to May 2000.
  Responsibilities: Research on the effectiveness of federal welfare programs in reducing poverty in the United States.

AFFILIATIONS
Paralegal Association of Wisconsin
National Association of Legal Assistants

*The abbreviation NI stands for Nita, a hypothetical state.

most prospective employers are not interested in such information as personal preferences, pastimes, or hobbies.

Proofread Your Results.   Carefully proofread your résumé. Use the spelling checker and grammar checker on your computer, but do not rely on them totally. Have a friend or teacher review your résumé for punctuation, syntax, grammar,

EXHIBIT 2.6

A Sample Résumé of a Person without Paralegal Experience

MARCUS BOHMAN

335 W. Alder Street
Gresham, CA 90650
Home Phone: (562) 555-6868 • Mobile Phone: (562) 555-2468 • E-mail: mboh44@gresham.net

---

OBJECTIVE

To obtain a paralegal position in a firm that specializes in real estate transactions.

QUALIFICATIONS

I am a self-motivated, certified paralegal (CLA 2003) with knowledge and background in real estate and a strong academic record (3.7 GPA). In addition to the education listed below, I have completed several courses on real estate financing and possess excellent accounting skills.

EDUCATION

2003   *Baccalaureate Degree—ABA–Approved Program*
        University of LaVerne, Legal Studies Program, LaVerne, CA
        Major: Paralegal Studies; Minor: Business Management
        Emphasis on Real Property and Land Use Planning, Legal Research and Writing.

EMPLOYMENT

2003   *Intern, Hansen, Henault, Richmond & Shaw*
        Researched and drafted numerous real estate documents, including land sale contracts, commercial leases, and deeds. Scheduled meetings with clients. Participated in client interviews and several real estate closings. Filed documents with county.

1998–2002   *Office Assistant, Eastside Commercial Property*
        Maintained files and handled telephone inquiries at commercial real estate company. Coordinated land surveys and obtained property descriptions.

1997–1998   *Clerk, LandPro Title Company*
        Coordinated title searches and acted as a liaison among banks, mortgage companies, and the title company.

1995–1997   *Clerk, San Jose County Recorder's office*
        Handled inquiries from the public and provided instruction to those seeking to look up records via microfiche.

---

spelling, and content. If you find an error, you need to fix it, even if it means having new résumés printed. A mistake on your résumé tells the potential employer that you are a careless worker, and this message may ruin your chances of landing a job.

THE COVER LETTER.   To encourage the recruiter to review your résumé, you need to capture his or her attention with a *cover letter* that accompanies the résumé. Because the cover letter often represents your first contact with an employer, it should be written carefully and precisely. It should be brief, perhaps only two or three paragraphs in length. Exhibit 2.7 shows a sample cover letter. Whenever possible, you should learn the name of the individual in charge of hiring (by phone or e-mail, if necessary) and direct your letter to that person. If you do not know the name of the individual responsible for reviewing résumés, use a generic title, such as "Human Resources Manager" or "Legal Assistant Manager."

Your cover letter should point out a few things about yourself and your qualifications for the position that might persuade a recruiter to examine your résumé. As a recently graduated paralegal, for example, you might draw attention to your high academic standing at school, your eagerness to specialize in the same area of law as the employer (perhaps listing some courses relating to that specialty), and your willingness to relocate to the employer's city. Your job is to convince the recruiter that you are a close match to the mental picture that he or she has of the perfect candidate for the job. Make sure that the reader knows when and where you can be reached. Often this is best indicated in the closing paragraph of the letter, as shown in Exhibit 2.7.

As with your résumé, you should read through your letter several times and have someone else read it also to make sure that it is free from mistakes and easily understood. You should use the same type of paper for your cover letter as you use for your résumé.

What about e-mailing your cover letter and résumé to prospective employers? This is a difficult question. On the one hand, e-mail is much faster than regular mail or express delivery services. On the other hand, an e-mail résumé does not look as nice. Furthermore, while some firms are accustomed to receiving applications by e-mail, others are not. Generally, you need to use your own judgment. If the job you are applying for was advertised online or if the employer provided an e-mail address for interested job candidates to use, then e-mail is probably appropriate. Generally, though, keep in mind the following:

> ※ **Job candidates who submit applications via e-mail should also send, via regular mail, printed copies of their letters and résumés.**

LIST OF PROFESSIONAL REFERENCES.   If a firm is interested in your application, you will probably be asked to provide a list of references—people whom the firm can contact to obtain information about you and your abilities. A paralegal instructor who has worked closely with you on an academic project, an internship supervisor who has firsthand knowledge of your work, or a past employer who has observed your problem-solving ability would all make excellent references. You should have at least three professionally relevant references, but no more than five references are necessary (if an interviewer needs additional references, he or she will ask for them). Never include the names of family members, friends, or others who will be clearly biased in your favor.

You should list your references on a separate sheet of paper, making sure to include your name, address, and telephone number at the top of the page, in the same format as on your résumé. For each person included on your list of references, include his or her current institutional affiliation or business firm, address, telephone number, fax number, and, if you know it, e-mail address. Generally, try to make it easy for prospective employers to contact and communicate with your references.

When creating your list of references, always remember the following rule:

> ※ **Never list a person's name as a reference unless you have first obtained that person's permission to do so.**

After all, it will not help you win the position if one of your references is surprised by the call or is unavailable, such as a paralegal instructor who is out of the coun-

EXHIBIT 2.7
A Sample Cover Letter

ELENA LOPEZ

1131 North Shore Drive
Nita City, NI 48804
Telephone: (616) 555-0102 • Fax: (616) 555-2103 • E-mail: elopez@nitanet.net

August 22, 2003

Allen P. Gilmore, Esq.
Jeffers, Gilmore & Dunn
553 Fifth Avenue, Suite 101
Nita City, NI 48801

Dear Mr. Gilmore:

I am responding to your advertisement in the *University of Nita Law Journal* for a paralegal to assist you in personal-injury litigation. I am confident that I possess the skills and qualifications that you seek.

As you can see from the enclosed résumé, I received my paralegal certificate from Midwestern Professional School after obtaining a Bachelor of Arts degree from University of Wisconsin. My paralegal courses included litigation procedures, legal research, legal investigation, and legal writing, and I graduated with a G.P.A. of 3.8.

After completing school, I obtained a position with the legal aid office where I worked for several years and honed my legal research and writing skills. My current position with Caldwell Legal Clinic has provided me with valuable experience in preparing personal-injury cases for trial. I very much enjoy this area of law and hope to specialize in personal-injury litigation.

I am excited about the possibility of meeting with you to learn more about the position that you have available. I have enclosed my résumé, as well as a list of professional references and a brief writing sample for your perusal.

Please contact me to schedule an interview. I look forward to hearing from you.

Sincerely yours,

Elena Lopez

Elena Lopez

Enclosures

try for the year. Such events raise a red flag to the interviewer and indicate that you are not concerned with details.

Obtaining permission from legal professionals to use their names as references also gives you an opportunity to discuss your plans and goals with them, and they may be able to advise you and assist you in your networking. Additionally, it gives you a chance to discuss with them the kinds of experience and skills in which a prospective employer may be interested.

professional portfolio
A job applicant's collection of selected personal documents (such as school transcripts, writing samples, and certificates) for presentation to a potential employer.

YOUR PROFESSIONAL PORTFOLIO.   When a potential employer asks you for an interview, have your **professional portfolio** of selected documents ready to give to the interviewer. The professional portfolio should contain another copy of your résumé, a list of references, letters of recommendation written by previous employers or instructors, samples of legal documents that you have composed, college or university transcripts, and any other relevant professional information, such as proof of professional certification or achievement. This collection of documents should be well organized and professionally presented. Depending on the size of your portfolio, a cover sheet, a table of contents, and a commercial binder may be appropriate.

The interviewer may be very interested in your research and writing skills. Therefore, your professional portfolio should contain several brief samples of legal writing. If you are looking for your first legal position, go through your paralegal drafting assignments and pull out those that reflect your best work and that relate to the job skills you wish to demonstrate. Then, working with an instructor or other mentor, revise and improve those samples for inclusion in the portfolio. Documents that you have drafted while an intern or when working as a part-time or full-time paralegal might also be used. These documents make excellent writing samples because they involve real-life circumstances. Be careful, however, and always remember to do the following:

> ✳   **On any sample document, completely blacken out (or "white out") any identifying reference to the client unless you have the client's permission to disclose his or her identity or the information is not confidential.**

Always include a résumé, as well as a list of references, in your professional portfolio, even though you already sent your résumé to the prospective employer with your cover letter. Interviewers may not have the résumé at hand at the time of the interview, and providing a second copy with your professional portfolio is a thoughtful gesture on your part.

Some interviewers may examine your professional portfolio carefully. Others may retain it to examine later, after the interview has concluded. Still others may not be interested in it at all. If there is a particular item in your portfolio that you would like the interviewer to see, make sure you point this out before leaving the interview.

The Interview

Interviews with potential employers may be the most challenging (and most stressful) aspect of your search for employment. The interview ordinarily takes place after the employer has reviewed your cover letter and résumé. Often, if the employer is interested in your application, a secretary or legal assistant will contact you to schedule an interview.

Every interview will be a unique experience. Some interviews will go very well, but you may still lose out to another candidate. Nonetheless, you have made a good contact, and you may be able to use this interviewer as a resource for information about other jobs. Remember what went right about the interview, and try to use that information at the next one. Other interviews may go poorly. Good lessons can be learned from poor interviews, however.

You will also find that some interviewers are more skilled at interviewing than others. Some have a talent for getting applicants to open up and discuss candidly their work and backgrounds. Others are confrontational and put the already nervous candidate on the defensive. Still others may be unprepared for the interview. They may not have had time to check the job requirements, for example, or when

> ## ETHICAL CONCERN
> ### "Gilding the Lily"
>
> When applying and interviewing for a job, be honest about your skills and job qualifications. Even though you are trying to impress a prospective employer, never succumb to the temptation to "gild the lily" by exaggerating your experience and qualifications.
>
> Suppose that you are interviewing for a job and the interviewer asks you about your GPA. Wanting to impress the interviewer, you say that your GPA was 3.8 when in fact it was 3.4. This "little white lie" may cost you the job. Prospective employers usually check your credentials, including your transcripts. Any misrepresentation, no matter how minor it may seem, will create a negative impression. Professional responsibility requires, among other things, that you be honest and pay scrupulous attention to detail—not only on the job but also during the job-application process.

the position is available. Unfortunately, as the person being interviewed, you have no control over who will interview you. The following discussion will help you prepare for a first paralegal job interview and will also serve as a refresher for you when seeking a career change.

BEFORE THE INTERVIEW.   You can do many things prior to the interview to enhance your chances of getting the job. First of all, you should do your "homework." Learn as much about the employer as possible. Check with your instructors or other legal professionals to find out if they are familiar with the firm or the interviewer. Check the employer's Web site, if there is one, and consult relevant directories, such as legal and company directories, as well as business publications, to see what you can learn about the firm and its members. When you are called for an interview, learn the full name of the interviewer, so that you will be able to address him or her by name during the interview and properly address a follow-up letter. During the interview, use Mr. or Ms. unless directed by the interviewer to be less formal.

Anticipate and review in your mind the possible questions that you might be asked during the interview. Then prepare (and possibly rehearse with a friend) your answers to these questions. For example, if you did not graduate from high school with your class but later fulfilled the requirements to graduate and received a general equivalency diploma (GED), you might well be asked why you dropped out of school. If you have already prepared an answer for this question, it may save you the embarrassment of having to decide, on the spot, how to reduce a complicated story to a brief sentence or two.

You should also prepare yourself to be interviewed by a "team" of legal professionals, such as an attorney and another paralegal or perhaps two or more attorneys and/or paralegals. Many prospective employers today invite others who will be working with a new paralegal to participate in the interviewing process.

Promptness is an extremely important factor. When preparing for an interview, you should therefore do the following:

- **Arrive for the interview at least ten minutes early and allow plenty of extra time to get there. If the firm is located in an area that is unfamiliar to you, make sure that you know how to get there, how long it will take, and, if you are driving, whether parking space is available nearby.**

EXHIBIT 2.8
Objectionable or
Illegal Questions

> **Q. Are you married?**
>
> **A.** If you are concerned about my social life interfering with work, I can assure you that I keep the two very distinct.
>
> **Q. Do you have any children yet?**
>
> **A.** That question leads me to believe that you would be concerned about my ability to prioritize my job and other responsibilities. Is that something that you are worried about?
>
> **Q. Are you or your husband a member of the Republican Party?**
>
> **A.** That is a private matter. Please realize that my family and political life will not interfere with my ability to do excellent work for your firm.
>
> **Q. You're quite a bit more mature than other applicants. Will you be thinking of retiring in the next ten years?**
>
> **A.** I don't understand how my age relates to my ability to perform this job.

Appearance is also important. Wear a relatively conservative suit or dress to the interview, and limit your use of jewelry or other flashy accents. You can find further tips on how to prepare for a job interview by checking online career sites or by looking at books dealing with careers and job hunting at a local bookstore or the library.

AT THE INTERVIEW.   During the interview, pay attention and listen closely to the interviewer's questions, observations, and comments. The interviewer asks questions to learn whether the candidate will fit comfortably into the firm, whether the candidate is organized and competent and will satisfactorily perform the job, and whether the candidate is reliable and will apply himself or herself to mastering the tasks presented. Your answers should be directly related to the questions, and you should not stray from the point. If you are unsure of what the interviewer means by a certain question, ask for clarification.

Interviewers use certain question formats to elicit certain types of responses. Four typical formats for questions are the following:

- *Closed-ended questions*—to elicit simple "Yes" or "No" answers.
- *Open-ended questions*—which invite you to discuss, in some detail, a specific topic or experience.
- *Hypothetical questions*—to learn how you might respond to situations that could arise during the course of your employment.
- *Pressure questions*—to see how you deal with uncomfortable situations or unpleasant discussions.

You will learn more about question formats in Chapter 13, when we discuss some techniques that paralegals use when interviewing clients.

Be aware that certain types of questions are illegal, or at least objectionable. These include questions directed at your marital status, family, religion, race, color, national origin, age, health or disability, or arrest record. You do not have to answer such questions unless you choose to do so. Exhibit 2.8 shows some examples of how you might respond to these types of questions.

As odd as it may seem, one of the most difficult moments is when the interviewer turns the inquiry around by asking, "Now then, do you have any questions?" Be prepared for this query. Before the interview, take time to list your

EXHIBIT 2.9
Questioning the Interviewer

Questions that you might want to ask the interviewer include the following:

- What is the method by which the firm assigns duties to paralegals?
- How do paralegals function within the organization?
- What clerical support staff is available for paralegals?
- Does the job involve travel? How will travel expenses be covered?
- What computer technology is used by the firm?
- Does the firm support paralegal continuing education and training programs?
- Will client contact be direct or indirect?
- Does the firm have an in-house library and access to computerized research services that paralegals can use?
- Will the paralegal be assigned work in a given specialty, such as real estate or family law?
- When does the job begin?
- What method is used to review and evaluate paralegal performance?
- How are paralegals supervised and by whom?
- Are paralegals classified as exempt employees by this firm?
- Is there a written job description or employee policy manual for the job that I may

concerns. Bring the list to the interview with you. Questioning the interviewer gives you an opportunity to learn more about the firm and how it uses paralegal services. Questioning the interviewer also may also give the interviewer an opportunity to see how you might interview a client on behalf of the firm. Exhibit 2.9 lists some sample questions that you might ask the interviewer. Note that you should not raise the issue of salary at the first interview unless you are offered the job.

AFTER THE INTERVIEW.   You should not expect to be hired as the result of a single interview, although occasionally this does happen. Often, two and even three interviews take place before you are offered a job. After leaving the interview, jot down a few notes to provide a refresher for your memory should you be called back for a second (or third) interview. You will impress the interviewer if you are able to "pick up where you left off" from a discussion initiated several weeks earlier. Also, list the names and positions of the people you met during the interview or just before or after it.

The Follow-Up/Thank-You Letter

A day or two after the interview, but not longer than a week later, you should send a *follow-up letter* to the interviewer. In this brief letter, you can reiterate your availability and interest in the position, thank the interviewer for his or her time in interviewing you, and perhaps refer to a discussion that took place during the interview.

You may have left the interview with the impression that the meeting went poorly. But the interviewer may have a different sense of what happened at the meeting. Interviewers have different styles, and what you interpreted to be a bad interview may just have been a reflection of that interviewer's particular approach or style. You simply have no way of being certain, so follow through and make yourself available for the job or at least for another meeting. For an example of a follow-up letter, see Exhibit 2.10 on the next page.

EXHIBIT 2.10
A Sample Follow-Up Letter

ELENA LOPEZ

1131 North Shore Drive
Nita City, NI 48804
Telephone: (616) 555-0102 • Fax: (616) 555-2103 • E-mail: elopez@nitanet.net

September 3, 2003

Allen P. Gilmore, Esq.
Jeffers, Gilmore & Dunn
553 Fifth Avenue, Suite 101
Nita City, NI 48801

Dear Mr. Gilmore:

Thank you for taking time out of your busy schedule to meet with me last Thursday about your firm's paralegal position. I very much enjoyed our discussion, as well as the opportunity to meet some of your firm's employees.

I am extremely interested in the possibility of becoming a member of your legal team and look forward to the prospect of meeting with you again in the near future.

Sincerely yours,

Elena Lopez

Elena Lopez

Job-Hunting Files

In addition to keeping your professional portfolio materials up to date, you need to create a filing system to stay abreast of your job-search activities. You should create a separate file for each potential employer and keep copies of your letters, including e-mail messages, to that employer in your file, along with any responses. You might also want to keep lists or notes on addresses, telephone numbers, e-mail addresses, dates of contacts, advantages and disadvantages of employment with the various firms that you have contacted or by which you have been interviewed, topics discussed at interviews, and so on. Then, when you are called for an interview, you will have information on the firm at your fingertips. Always keep in mind that when looking for paralegal employment, your "job" is finding work as a paralegal—and it pays to be efficient.

Your files will also provide you with an excellent resource for networking even after you have a permanent position. The files may also provide useful information for a career change in the future.

BENEFITS

What benefits are included? • Will the benefits package include medical insurance? • Life insurance? • Disability insurance? • Dental insurance? • What portion, if any, of the insurance premium will be deducted from your wages? • Is there an employee pension plan? • How many paid vacation days will you have? • Will the firm cover your paralegal association fees? • Will the firm assist you in tuition and other costs associated with continuing paralegal education? • Will the firm assist in day-care arrangements and/or costs? • Will you have access to a company automobile? • Does the firm help with parking expenses (important in major cities)?

CAREER OPPORTUNITIES

Does the position offer you opportunities for advancement? You may be willing to accept a lower salary now if you know that it will increase as you move up the career ladder.

COMPENSATION

Will you receive an annual salary or be paid by the hour? • If you will receive an annual salary, will you receive annual bonuses? • How are bonuses determined? • Is the salary negotiable? (In some large firms and in government agencies, it may not be.)

COMPETITION

How stiff is the competition for this job? If you really want the job and are competing with numerous other candidates for the position, you might want to accept a lower salary just to land the job.

JOB DESCRIPTION

What are the paralegal's duties within the organization? Do you have sufficient training and experience to handle these duties? • Are you under- or overqualified for the job? • Will your skills as a paralegal be utilized effectively? • How hard will you be expected to work? • How much overtime work will likely be required? • How stressful will the job be?

JOB FLEXIBILITY

How flexible are the working hours? • If you work eight hours overtime one week, can you take a (paid) day off the following week? • Can you take time off during periods when the workload is less?

LOCATION

Do you want to live in this community? • What is the cost of living in this area? Remember, a $40,000 salary in New York City, where housing and taxes are very expensive, may not give you as much real income as a $30,000 salary in a smaller, midsized community in the Midwest.

PERMANENCE

Is the job a permanent or temporary position? Usually, hourly rates for temporary assistance are higher than for permanent employees.

TRAVEL

Will you be required to travel? • If so, how often or extensively? • How will travel expenses be handled? Will you pay them up-front and then be reimbursed by the employer?

EXHIBIT 2.11
**Salary Negotiations:
What Is This Job Worth to You?**

Salary Negotiations

Sometimes a firm states a salary or a salary range in its advertisement for a paralegal. During a first interview, a prospective employer may offer that information as well. In other situations, an applicant does not know what the salary for a certain position will be until he or she is offered the job.

When you are offered a job, be prepared for the prospective employer to indicate a salary figure and ask you if that figure is acceptable to you. If it is acceptable, then you have no problem. If you think it is too low, then the situation becomes more delicate. If you have no other job offer and really need a job, you may not want to foreclose this job opportunity by saying that the salary is too low. You might instead tell the prospective employer that the job interests you and that you will consider the offer seriously. Also, remember that salary is just one factor in deciding what a job is worth to you. In addition to salary, you need to consider job benefits and other factors, including those listed in Exhibit 2.11.

Some prospective employers do not suggest a salary or a salary range but rather ask the job applicant what kind of salary he or she had in mind. You should be prepared for this question and should have researched paralegal salaries in the area.

✂   **Unless you are already familiar with the firm's salary structure, you should research the compensation given to paralegals in similar job situations in your community before you discuss salary with a prospective employer.**

You can find information on salaries by checking local, state, and national paralegal compensation surveys. Check first with your local paralegal association to see if it has collected data on local paralegal salaries. You might also find helpful information in your school's placement office.

Suppose that you have found in your research that paralegals in the community usually start at $32,000 but that many with your education and training start at $39,000. If you ask for an annual salary of $41,000, then you may be unrealistically expensive—and the job offer may be lost. If you ask for $39,000, then you are still "in the ballpark"—and you may win the job.

Negotiating salaries can be difficult. On the one hand, you want to obtain a good salary and do not want to underprice your services. On the other hand, overpricing your services may extinguish an employment opportunity or eliminate the possibility of working for an otherwise suitable employer. Your best option might be to state a salary range that is acceptable to you. That way, you are not pinned down to a specific figure. Note, though, that if you indicate an acceptable salary range, you invite an offer of the lowest salary—so the low end of the salary range should be the threshold amount that you will accept.

Reevaluating Your Career

Once you have gained experience working as a paralegal, you can undertake the third step in career planning: reevaluation. Assume that you have worked for a long enough period (two to four years, for example) to have acquired experience in certain types of paralegal work. At this point, you should reevaluate your career goals and reassess your abilities based on your accumulated experience.

Paralegals who want to advance in their careers normally have three options: (1) being promoted or transferring to another department or branch office of the firm, (2) moving to another firm—and perhaps another specialty, and (3) going back to school for additional education.

Career Paths

Larger firms often provide career paths for their paralegal employees. Moving from the entry-level position of *legal-assistant clerk* to the position of *legal-assistant manager*, for example, may be one career track within a large law firm. A career track with a state government agency might begin at a *legal-technician* level and advance to a *legal-specialist* level.

Creating Opportunities

Smaller firms, in contrast, usually have no predetermined career path or opportunities for promotion and career advancement. If you are the only paralegal in a small law firm, there will be no specified career path within the firm for you to follow. If you find yourself in this situation, you might consider staying with the firm and creating your own position or career ladder. Moving up the ladder is often a matter of bringing in someone new to assist you with your paralegal responsibilities. Are you prevented from taking on more complicated tasks (which you are capable of performing) because of your heavy workload, much of which could be handled by a paralegal with less experience? Suggest a plan to your

TODAY'S PROFESSIONAL PARALEGAL

Conducting a Title Exam

Kim Murphy is a paralegal working for the real estate law firm of Clark & Clark. Today, Kim is going to the Winston County Register of Deeds office to examine the title to the Spartan Shopping Center, located in Winston County. The owner of the shopping center, one of Clark & Clark's clients, has received an offer to sell the center, which has recently become very valuable. Kim's supervising attorney must prepare an abstract of title, which is a history of who owned the property, when past transfers were made, and other significant events. The abstract will be used to assure the buyer that he or she will receive clear and marketable title to the property.

Kim arrives at the county offices. She takes the elevator to the third floor, where the Register of Deeds office is located. As Kim approaches the counter, a clerk asks her, "What do you need today?" Kim recognizes the clerk, Sam McGrath, who has worked there for as long as Kim has worked for Clark & Clark. He often assists Kim and is very helpful.

"Sam, I need to run a title search and then I need copies of the deeds for the Spartan Shopping Center," responds Kim. "Okay, fill out this form, and I'll run the title search for you on the computer," says Sam. Kim writes down the name and address of the shopping center and hands the form to Sam.

EXAMINING OWNERSHIP RECORDS

Sam leaves the counter and goes to a room behind it, which contains computers. He runs the search through the computer that contains all of the records that were originally held in a book called the *Liber*. This is where all of the deeds, liens, and other documents affecting title to real estate are filed. Sam returns with a computerized list and copies of the deeds that show who has owned the property.

Kim thanks Sam and sits down at a nearby table to review the information that Sam has given her. Kim reads through each deed. She checks to see that each deed contains the same description of the property—to ensure that the entire parcel of land was conveyed (transferred) with each sale. Kim sees that it was. She also checks to make sure that the seller of the Spartan Shopping Center is the legal owner of the property.

CHECKING FOR LIENS

Next, Kim reviews the computer printout for any *liens* (rights of creditors against the property for payment of debts) that might have been filed against the property. Kim notes the mortgage lien, which is normal and expected. Typically, when the purchase of real property is financed by a mortgage loan, the lending institution places a lien on the property until the buyer has made all payments due under the terms of the loan contract. She also notes that the Internal Revenue Service (IRS) has placed a tax lien on the property. A tax lien means that the current owner is behind in the payment of taxes and that the IRS has the right to *foreclose on* (take temporary ownership of) the shopping center and sell it, using the proceeds to pay the overdue taxes. Any remaining proceeds would be returned to the shopping center's owner. If the IRS is not paid at the time of the new mortgage, the IRS will have priority over the new lender. Most lenders will not grant a loan under these circumstances.

THE CONSEQUENCES OF THE TAX LIEN FOR THE CLIENT

Kim realizes that the tax lien creates serious problems for Clark & Clark's client. Once the abstract is prepared, the buyer's attorney will learn about the lien and warn the buyer of the obvious risk. This tax lien must be resolved before Clark & Clark's client can sell the property.

Kim makes a copy of the computer printout and walks over to the cashier to pay for the title search and the copies of the deeds. The cost is $5 for the title search and $1 for each deed. She makes certain to get a receipt so that she can be reimbursed by the firm for the expense. Kim then returns to the office to inform her supervising attorney of the tax lien.

employer that shows how you can provide more complex legal services if you delegate many of your existing responsibilities to a new paralegal employee. One of the advantages of working for a small firm is the lack of any set, formal structure for promotions. If the firm is expanding, the paralegal may have significant input into how and to whom responsibilities will be assigned as new people are hired.

You can also create opportunities by acquiring additional education. If you are interested in a particular specialty area, course work in that area, in addition to your existing paralegal training and experience, may help land a job that can advance your career ambitions. Alternatively, you might decide to work toward an advanced degree, such as a master's in business administration (MBA), to create new career opportunities. Some paralegals opt to go to law school and become attorneys.

Other Options

There are many other alternatives. You may apply for a job with another firm that offers you a better position or more advancement opportunities. You might apply for a position that has become available in a branch office of your firm. You might volunteer to speak to paralegal classes and seminars and, in so doing, establish new contacts and contribute to paralegal professional development. Researching and writing law-related articles for your paralegal association's newsletter or trade magazine improves your professional stature in the legal community as well. Any of these activities will increase your visibility both inside and outside the firm. In a broad sense, these activities are part of networking. The people you meet when engaging in these activities may offer you employment opportunities that you did not even know existed but that are perfect for you.

 ## Key Terms and Concepts

bankruptcy law	**freelance paralegal**	**professional portfolio**
bonus	**immigration law**	**probate**
civil law	**intellectual property**	**probate court**
corporate law	**legal nurse consultant (LNC)**	**real estate**
criminal law	**legal technician**	**state bar association**
defendant	**litigation**	**trade journal**
elder law	**litigation paralegal**	**trust**
environmental law	**networking**	**will**
estate planning	**overtime wages**	**workers' compensation statutes**
family law	**plaintiff**	

 ## Chapter Summary

Where Paralegals Work	
	1. *Law firms*—Today, over 70 percent of paralegals work in law firms. The majority of these paralegals work in small law firms—those employing fewer than twenty attorneys. Working for a small firm enables a legal assistant to gain experience in a number of areas of law and is characterized by a more personal and less formal environment. The drawback is that paralegals in small firms often earn less than those in larger firms and often need to perform secretarial duties. Paralegals working for larger firms tend to specialize in one or more areas of law, receive higher salaries, enjoy better employee benefits, and have more support staff.

END NOTES

1. One of the difficulties in describing law firm environments is that the terms *small law firm* and *large law firm* mean different things to different people. In a large city, for example, a firm with twenty attorneys might qualify as a small law firm. In a smaller, more rural community, however, a firm with twenty attorneys would be considered a very large law firm. In this text, we refer to law firms with twenty or fewer attorneys as small law firms and firms with more than twenty attorneys as large firms.

2. "How Big Is Your Piece of the Pie? Paralegals Carved Out a Large Salary Increase in 2001," *Legal Assistant Today,* March/April 2002, p. 52.

3. Copyrights are registered with the U.S. Copyright Office, Library of Congress, Washington, DC 20559. Patents and trademarks are registered with the Patent and Trademark Office, U.S. Department of Commerce, Washington, DC 20231.

4. *Legal Assistant Today,* March/April 2002, p. 53.

5. *U.S. Department of Labor v. Page & Addison, P.C.,* U.S. District Court, Dallas, Texas, No. 91-2655, March 15, 1994.

6. "How Big Is Your Piece of the Pie? Paralegals Carved Out a Large Salary Increase in 2001," *Legal Assistant Today,* March/April 2002, p. 62.

CHAPTER 3

ETHICS AND PROFESSIONAL RESPONSIBILITY

Chapter Outline

❋ INTRODUCTION ❋ THE REGULATION OF ATTORNEYS ❋ ATTORNEY ETHICS AND PARALEGAL PRACTICE ❋ THE INDIRECT REGULATION OF PARALEGALS ❋ THE UNAUTHORIZED PRACTICE OF LAW ❋ SHOULD PARALEGALS BE LICENSED? ❋ A FINAL NOTE

After completing this chapter, you will know:

- Why and how legal professionals are regulated.

- Some important ethical rules governing the conduct of attorneys.

- How the rules governing attorneys affect paralegal practice.

- The kinds of activities that paralegals are and are not legally permitted to perform.

- Some of the pros and cons of regulation, including the debate over paralegal licensing.

INTRODUCTION

As discussed in the previous chapter, paralegals preparing for a career in today's legal arena have a variety of career options. Regardless of which career path you choose to follow, you should have a firm grasp of your state's ethical rules governing the legal profession. When you work under the supervision of an attorney, as most paralegals do, you and the attorney become team members. You will work together on behalf of clients and share in the ethical and legal responsibilities arising as a result of the attorney-client relationship.

In preparing for a career as a paralegal, you must know what these responsibilities are, why they exist, and how they affect you. The first part of this chapter is devoted to the regulation of attorneys because the ethical duties imposed on attorneys by state law affect paralegals as well. If a paralegal violates one of the rules governing attorneys, that violation may result in serious consequences for the client, for the attorney, and for the paralegal. As you read through the rules governing attorney conduct that are discussed in this chapter, keep in mind that these rules also govern paralegal practice, if indirectly.

Although attorneys are subject to direct regulation by the state, paralegals are not, except in California. Other states may directly regulate paralegals in the near future, however, in the form of licensing requirements. Paralegals are regulated indirectly both by attorney ethical codes and by state laws that prohibit nonlawyers from practicing law.[1] As the paralegal profession develops, professional paralegal organizations, the American Bar Association, and state bar associations of attorneys continue to issue guidelines that also serve to indirectly regulate paralegals.

THE REGULATION OF ATTORNEYS

The term *regulate* derives from the Latin term *regula*, meaning "rule." According to Webster's dictionary, to regulate means "to control or direct in agreement with a rule." To a significant extent, attorneys engage in **self-regulation** because they themselves establish the majority of the rules governing their profession. One of the hallmarks of a profession is the establishment of minimum standards and levels of competence for its members. The accounting profession, for example, has established such standards, as have physicians, engineers, and members of virtually every other profession.

Attorneys are also regulated externally by the state, because the rules of behavior established by the legal profession are adopted and enforced by state authorities. The purpose of regulating attorney behavior is to protect the public interest. First, by establishing educational and licensing requirements, state authorities ensure that anyone practicing law is competent to do so. Second, by defining specific ethical requirements for attorneys, the states protect the public against unethical attorney behavior that may affect clients' welfare. We will discuss these requirements and rules shortly. Before we do, however, you should know how these rules are created and enforced.

self-regulation
The regulation of the conduct of a professional group by members of the group. Self-regulation usually involves the establishment of ethical or professional standards of behavior with which members of the group must comply.

Who Are the Regulators?

Key participants in determining what rules should govern attorneys and the practice of law, as well as how these rules should be enforced, are bar associations, state supreme courts, state legislatures, and, in some cases, the United States Supreme Court. Procedures for regulating attorneys vary, of course, from state to state. What follows is a general discussion of some of the possible regulators.

On the Web
You can access information on state bar associations, legislatures, and courts, including the United States Supreme Court, at **http://www.findlaw.com**. The American Bar Association is online at **http://www.abanet.org**.

BAR ASSOCIATIONS.   Lawyers themselves determine the requirements for entering the legal profession and the rules of conduct they will follow. Traditionally, lawyers have joined together in professional groups, or bar associations, at the local, state, and national levels to discuss issues affecting the legal profession and to decide on standards of professional conduct.

Although membership in local and national bar associations is always voluntary, membership in the state bar association is mandatory in over two-thirds of the states. In these states, before an attorney can practice law, he or she must be admitted to the state's bar association. Approximately half of the lawyers in the United States are members of the American Bar Association (ABA), the voluntary national bar association discussed in Chapter 1. As you will read shortly, the ABA plays a key regulatory role by proposing model (uniform) codes, or rules of conduct, for adoption by the various states.

STATE SUPREME COURTS.   Typically, the state's highest court, often called the state supreme court, is the ultimate regulatory authority in that state.[2] The court's judges decide what conditions (such as licensing requirements, discussed below) must be met before an attorney can practice law within the state and under what conditions that privilege will be suspended or revoked. In many states, the state supreme court works closely with the state bar association. The state bar association may recommend rules and requirements to the court. If the court so orders, these rules and requirements become state law. Under the authority of the courts, state bar associations often perform routine regulatory functions, including the initiation of disciplinary proceedings against attorneys who fail to comply with professional requirements.

STATE LEGISLATURES.   State legislatures regulate the legal profession by enacting legislation affecting attorneys—statutes prohibiting the unauthorized practice of law, for example. In a few states, the states' highest courts delegate significant regulatory responsibilities to the state legislatures, which may include the power to bring disciplinary proceedings against attorneys.

THE UNITED STATES SUPREME COURT.   Occasionally, the United States Supreme Court decides issues relating to attorney conduct. For example, until a few decades ago, state ethical codes, or rules governing attorney conduct, prohibited lawyers from advertising their services to the public. These restrictions on advertising were later determined to be an unconstitutional limitation on attorneys' rights to free speech by the United States Supreme Court.[3]

Licensing Requirements

licensing
A government's official act of granting permission to an individual, such as an attorney, to do something that would be illegal in the absence of such permission.

The **licensing** of attorneys, which gives them the right to practice law, is accomplished at the state level. Each state has different requirements that individuals must meet before they are allowed to practice law and give legal advice. Generally, however, there are three basic requirements:

1. In most states, prospective attorneys must have obtained a bachelor's degree from a university or college[4] and must have graduated from an accredited law school (in many states, the school must be accredited by the ABA), which requires an additional three years of study.

2. In all states, a prospective attorney must pass a state bar examination—a very rigorous and thorough examination that tests the candidate's knowledge of the law and (in some states) the state's ethical rules governing attorneys. The

examination covers both state law (law applicable to the particular state in which the attorney is taking the exam and wishes to practice) and multistate law (law applicable in most states, including federal law).[5]

3. The candidate must pass an extensive personal background investigation to verify that he or she is a responsible individual and otherwise qualifies to engage in an ethical profession. An illegal act committed by the candidate in the past, for example, might disqualify the individual from being permitted to practice law.

Only when these requirements have been met can an individual be admitted to the state bar and legally practice law within the state.

Licensing requirements for attorneys are the result of a long history of attempts to restrict entry into the legal profession. The earliest of these restrictions date to the colonial era. During the 1700s, local bar associations began to form agreements to restrict membership to those who fulfilled certain educational and apprenticeship requirements. At the same time, to curb unnecessary litigation and the detrimental effects of incompetent legal practitioners, courts began to require that individuals representing clients in court proceedings had to be licensed by the court to do so.

Beginning in the mid-1850s, restrictions on who could (or could not) practice law were given statewide effect by state statutes prohibiting the **unauthorized practice of law (UPL)**. Court decisions relating to unauthorized legal practice also date to this period. By the 1930s, virtually all states had enacted legislation prohibiting anyone but licensed attorneys from practicing law. As you will see in subsequent sections, many of the regulatory issues facing the legal profession—and particularly paralegals—are directly related to these UPL statutes.

unauthorized practice of law (UPL)
The performance of actions defined by a legal authority, such as a state legislature, as constituting the "practice of law" without legal authorization to do so.

Ethical Codes and Rules

The legal profession is also regulated through ethical codes and rules adopted by each state—in most states, by order of the state supreme court. These codes of professional conduct—the names of the codes vary from state to state—evolved over a long period of time. A major step toward ethical regulation was taken in 1908, when the ABA approved the Canons of Ethics, which consisted of thirty-two ethical principles. In the following decades, various states adopted these canons as law.

Today's state ethical codes are based, for the most part, on two subsequent revisions of the ABA canons: the Model Code of Professional Responsibility (published in 1969) and the Model Rules of Professional Conduct (first published in 1983 to replace the Model Code and revised numerous times since then). Although most states have adopted laws based on the Model Rules, the Model Code is still in effect in some states. You should therefore be aware of both the Model Code and the Model Rules and become familiar with the set of rules that is in effect in your state.

THE MODEL CODE OF PROFESSIONAL RESPONSIBILITY.   The ABA Model Code of Professional Responsibility, often referred to simply as the Model Code, consists of nine canons. In the Model Code, each canon is followed by sections entitled "Ethical Considerations" (ECs) and "Disciplinary Rules" (DRs). The ethical considerations are "aspirational" in character—that is, they suggest ideal conduct, not necessarily behavior that is required by law. For example, Canon 6 ("A lawyer should represent a client competently") is followed by EC 6–1, which states (in part) that a lawyer "should strive to become and remain proficient in his

On the Web
To read the ethics code adopted by your state, go to **http://www.law.cornell.edu/ethics** and click on "Listing by jurisdiction" under the heading "Ways to access material." Then click on the appropriate state. You can also access ethics opinions—formal statements addressing specific problem areas issued by the state bar association—on this site.

For a comprehensive collection of ethics articles and laws, as well as links to other ethics sources, go to **http://www.legalethics.com**.

On the Web
You can access the entire text of the 2002 revisions to the Model Rules of Professional Conduct, along with an explanation of the changes to the rules, on the ABA's Web site at http://www.abanet.org/cpr/e2k-report_home.html.

practice." In contrast, disciplinary rules are mandatory in character—an attorney may be subject to disciplinary action for breaking one of the rules. For example, DR 6–101 (which follows Canon 6) states that a lawyer "shall not . . . [n]eglect a legal matter entrusted to him."

THE MODEL RULES OF PROFESSIONAL CONDUCT.   The 1983 revision of the Model Code—referred to as the Model Rules of Professional Conduct or, more simply, as the Model Rules—represented a thorough revamping of the code. The Model Rules replaced the canons, ethical considerations, and disciplinary rules of the Model Code with a set of rules organized under eight general headings, as outlined in Exhibit 3.1. Each rule is followed by comments shedding additional light on the rule's application and how it compares with the Model Code's treatment of the same issue.

2002 REVISIONS TO THE MODEL RULES.   Over the years, the Model Rules have been amended many times, and the states have adopted different versions. Because of the growing disparity in states' ethical rules, the ABA set up an ethics commission to reevaluate the Model Rules in light of the realities of modern law practice. The goal of the commission was to encourage greater uniformity throughout the states and to address new ethical concerns raised by technological developments (for example, e-mail and client confidentiality). After several years of meetings and public hearings, the ABA released its revised Model Rules of Professional Conduct in February 2002.

The revisions to the Model Rules are substantial in some areas but minor in others. Sometimes, the wording of a rule has been modified merely to clarify the intent of the rule. In this text, we use the 1983 Model Rules as the basis for discussion because the 2002 revisions had not yet been adopted by any state when the text was written. By the time you read this, however, the state you live in may have adopted the 2002 revisions. We therefore point out in the following discussion the areas in which the revisions significantly alter the existing rules.

Sanctions for Violations

Attorneys who violate the rules governing professional conduct are subject to disciplinary proceedings brought by the state bar association, state supreme court, or state legislature—depending on the state's regulatory scheme. In most states, unethical attorney actions are reported (by clients, legal professionals, or others) to the ethics committee of the state bar association, which is obligated to investigate each complaint thoroughly. For serious violations, the state bar association or the court initiates disciplinary proceedings against the attorney.

Sanctions range from a **reprimand** (a formal "scolding" of the attorney—the mildest sanction[6]) to **suspension** (a more serious sanction by which the attorney is prohibited from practicing law in the state for a given period of time, such as one month or one year, or for an indefinite period of time) to **disbarment** (revocation of the attorney's license to practice law in the state—the most serious sanction).

In addition to these sanctions, attorneys may be subject to civil liability for negligence. As will be discussed in Chapter 7, *negligence* (called **malpractice** when committed by a professional, such as an attorney) is a tort (a wrongful act) that is committed when an individual fails to perform a legally recognized duty. Tort law allows one who is injured by another's wrongful or careless act to bring a civil lawsuit against the wrongdoer for **damages** (compensation in the form of money). Of course, a client is permitted to bring a lawsuit against an attorney only if the client has suffered harm because of the attorney's failure to perform a legal duty.

reprimand
A disciplinary sanction in which an attorney is rebuked for his or her misbehavior. Although a reprimand is the mildest sanction for attorney misconduct, it is nonetheless a serious one and may significantly damage the attorney's reputation in the legal community.

suspension
A serious disciplinary sanction in which an attorney who has violated an ethical rule or a law is prohibited from practicing law in the state for a specified or an indefinite period of time.

disbarment
A severe disciplinary sanction in which an attorney's license to practice law in the state is revoked because of unethical or illegal conduct.

malpractice
Professional misconduct or negligence—the failure to exercise due care—on the part of a professional, such as an attorney or a physician.

damages
Money awarded as a remedy for a civil wrong, such as a breach of contract or a tortious act.

EXHIBIT 3.1
The ABA Model Rules of Professional Conduct (Headings Only)

CLIENT-LAWYER RELATIONSHIP

1.1	Competence
1.2	Scope of Representation
1.3	Diligence
1.4	Communication
1.5	Fees
1.6	Confidentiality of Information
1.7	Conflict of Interest: General Rule
1.8	Conflict of Interest: Prohibited Transactions
1.9	Conflict of Interest: Former Client
1.10	Imputed Disqualification: General Rule
1.11	Successive Government and Private Employment
1.12	Former Judge or Arbitrator
1.13	Organization as Client
1.14	Client under a Disability
1.15	Safekeeping Property
1.16	Declining or Terminating Representation

COUNSELOR

2.1	Advisor
2.2	Intermediary
2.3	Evaluation for Use by Third Persons

ADVOCATE

3.1	Meritorious Claims and Contentions
3.2	Expediting Litigation
3.3	Candor toward the Tribunal
3.4	Fairness to Opposing Party and Counsel
3.5	Impartiality and Decorum of the Tribunal
3.6	Trial Publicity
3.7	Lawyer as Witness
3.8	Special Responsibilities of a Prosecutor
3.9	Advocate in Nonadjudicative Proceedings

TRANSACTIONS WITH PERSONS OTHER THAN CLIENTS

4.1	Truthfulness in Statement to Others
4.2	Communication with Person Represented by Counsel
4.3	Dealing with Unrepresented Person
4.4	Respect for Rights of Third Persons

LAW FIRMS AND ASSOCIATIONS

5.1	Responsibilities of a Partner or Supervisory Lawyer
5.2	Responsibilities of a Subordinate Lawyer
5.3	Responsibilities Regarding Nonlawyer Assistants
5.4	Professional Independence of a Lawyer
5.5	Unauthorized Practice of Law
5.6	Restrictions on Right to Practice

PUBLIC SERVICE

6.1	*Pro Bono Publico* Service
6.2	Accepting Appointments
6.3	Membership in Legal Services Organization
6.4	Law Reform Activities Affecting Client Interests

INFORMATION ABOUT LEGAL SERVICES

7.1	Communications Concerning a Lawyer's Services
7.2	Advertising
7.3	Direct Contact with Prospective Clients
7.4	Communication of Fields of Practice
7.5	Firm Names and Letterheads

MAINTAINING THE INTEGRITY OF THE PROFESSION

8.1	Bar Admission and Disciplinary Matters
8.2	Judicial and Legal Officials
8.3	Reporting Professional Misconduct
8.4	Misconduct
8.5	Jurisdiction

If a paralegal's breach of a professional duty causes a client to suffer substantial harm, the client may sue not only the attorney but also the paralegal. Although law firms' liability insurance policies typically cover paralegals as well as attorneys, if the paralegal is working on a contract (freelance) basis, he or she will not be covered under a liability policy covering the firm's employees. Just one lawsuit could ruin a freelance paralegal financially—as well as destroy that paralegal's reputation in the legal community. (Note that liability insurance is especially important for independent paralegals, or legal technicians, as well.)

Attorneys and paralegals are also subject to potential criminal liability under criminal statutes prohibiting fraud, theft, and other crimes.

ATTORNEY ETHICS AND PARALEGAL PRACTICE

Because most state codes are guided by the Model Rules of Professional Conduct, the rules discussed in this section are drawn from the Model Rules. Keep in mind, though, the following important guideline:

> ※   **Your own state's code of conduct is the governing authority on attorney conduct in your state.**

As a paralegal, one of your foremost professional responsibilities is to meticulously follow the rules set forth in your state's ethical code. You will thus want to obtain a copy of your state's ethical code and become familiar with its contents. A good practice is to keep the code near at hand in your office (or on your desk).

Professional duties—and the possibility of violating them—are involved in virtually every task you will perform as a paralegal. Even if you memorize every one of the rules governing the legal profession, you can still quite easily violate a rule unintentionally (you should realize that paralegals rarely breach professional duties intentionally). To minimize the chances that you will unintentionally violate a rule, you need to know not only what the rules are but also how they apply to the day-to-day realities of your job.

The rules relating to competence, confidentiality, and conflict of interest deserve special attention here because they pose particularly difficult ethical problems for paralegals. Other important rules that affect paralegal performance—including the duty to charge reasonable fees, the duty to protect clients' property, and the duty to keep the client reasonably informed—will be discussed elsewhere in this text as they relate to special topics.

The Duty of Competence

Rule 1.1 of the Model Rules states one of the most fundamental duties of attorneys—the duty of competence. The rule reads as follows:

> A lawyer shall provide competent representation to a client. Competent representation requires the legal knowledge, skill, thoroughness and preparation reasonably necessary for representation.

breach
To violate a legal duty by an act or a failure to act.

Competent legal representation is a basic requirement of the profession, and **breaching** (failing to perform) this duty may subject attorneys to one or more of the sanctions discussed earlier. As a paralegal, you should realize that when you undertake work on an attorney's behalf, you share in this duty. If your supervising attorney asks you to research a particular legal issue for a client, for example, you must make sure that your research is careful and thorough—because the attorney's reputation (and the client's welfare) may depend on your performance.

You should also realize that careless conduct of the research, if it results in substantial injury to the client's interests, may subject you personally to liability for negligence, not to mention the loss of a job or career opportunities.

HOW THE DUTY OF COMPETENCE CAN BE BREACHED.   Most breaches of the duty of competence are inadvertent. Often, breaches of the duty of competence have to do with missed deadlines and errors in legal documents filed with the court.

Missed Deadlines.   Paralegals frequently work on several cases simultaneously, and keeping track of every deadline in every case can be challenging—especially for paralegals who are pressed for time. Organization is the key to making sure that all deadlines are met. All important dates relating to every case or client should be entered on a calendar. Larger firms typically use computerized calendaring and "tickler" (reminder) systems. Even the smallest firm normally has calendaring procedures and tickler systems in place. In addition to making sure that all deadlines are entered into the appropriate systems, you may want to have your own personal calendar for tracking dates that are relevant to the cases on which you are working—and then make sure that you consistently use it. You should develop a habit of checking your calendar every morning when you arrive at work or some other convenient time. Also, you should check frequently with your attorney about deadlines that he or she may not have mentioned to you.

Errors in Documents.   Breaches of the duty of competence can also involve errors in documents. For example, erroneous information might be included (or crucial information omitted) in a legal document to be filed with the court. If the attorney fails to notice the error before signing the document, and the document is delivered to the court containing the erroneous information, a breach of the duty of competence has occurred. Depending on its legal effect, this breach may expose the attorney and the paralegal to liability for negligence. To prevent these kinds of violations, you need to be especially careful in drafting and proofreading documents.

Generally, if you are ever unsure about what to include in a document, when it must be completed or filed with the court, how extensively you should research a legal issue, or any other aspect of an assignment, you should ask your supervising attorney for special instructions. You should also make sure that your work is adequately overseen by your attorney, to reduce the chances that it will contain costly mistakes or errors.

ATTORNEY'S DUTY TO SUPERVISE.   Rule 5.3 of the Model Rules defines the responsibilities of attorneys in regard to nonlawyer assistants. This rule states, in part, that "A lawyer should give . . . assistants appropriate instruction and supervision. . . . The measures employed in supervising nonlawyers should take account of the fact that they do not have legal training and are not subject to professional discipline." The rule also states that "a lawyer shall be responsible for the conduct of [a nonlawyer] that would be a violation of the rules of professional conduct if engaged in by a lawyer."

The 2002 revision specifies that this rule applies not only to lawyers who work in private law firms but also to lawyers in corporate legal departments, government agencies, and elsewhere. In addition, in the statements outlining attorneys' responsibilities toward nonlawyer employees in this area, the ABA commission changed the word *should* to *must*. Attorneys must both instruct and supervise nonlawyer employees on the appropriate ethical conduct and can be held personally responsible for the ethical violations of their subordinates.

On the Web
The Web sites of the two national paralegal associations, the National Association of Legal Assistants (NALA) and the National Federation of Paralegal Associations (NFPA), are good sources for information on the ethical responsibilities of paralegals, including new, technology-related ethical challenges. You can access NALA's site at **http://www. nala.org**. The URL for NFPA'S site is **http://www. paralegals.org**.

ETHICAL CONCERN
Missed Deadlines

As a paralegal, you will find that one of your most useful allies is a calendar. Consistently entering important deadlines on a calendaring system (computerized or otherwise) will help to ensure that you and your supervising attorney do not breach the duty of competence simply because a document was not filed with the court on time. For example, if a *complaint* (the document that initiates a lawsuit—see Chapter 12) is served on one of your firm's clients, you must file with the court the client's *answer* to the complaint within a specified number of days. If you fail to file the answer during that time period, the court could enter a judgment in favor of the party bringing the lawsuit. As you might imagine, the consequences of this judgment—called a *default judgment*—can be extremely detrimental to the client. As a paralegal, you need to be aware of the seriousness of the consequences of missed deadlines for your clients, especially the consequences of failing to file an answer on time.

INADEQUATE SUPERVISION.   Because attorneys are held legally responsible for their assistants' work, it may seem logical to assume that attorneys will take time to direct that work carefully. In fact, paralegals may find it difficult to ensure that their work is adequately supervised. For one thing, most paralegals are kept very busy, and making sure that all their tasks are properly overseen can be time consuming. Similarly, an attorney often does not want to take the time to read through every document drafted by his or her paralegal—particularly if the attorney knows that the paralegal is competent. Nonetheless, as a paralegal, you have a duty to assist your supervising attorney in fulfilling his or her ethical obligations, including the obligation to supervise your work.

If you ever feel that your attorney is not adequately supervising your work, there are several things you can do. You can try to improve communications with the attorney—generally, the more you communicate with your supervising attorney, the more likely it is that the attorney will take an active role in directing your activities. You can also ask the attorney for feedback on your work. Sometimes, it helps to place reminders on your personal calendar to discuss particular issues or questions with the attorney. Then, when an opportunity to talk to him or her arises, these issues or questions will be fresh in your mind. Another tactic is to attach a note to a document that you have prepared for the attorney, requesting him or her to review the document (or revised sections of the document) carefully before signing it.

Confidentiality of Information

Rule 1.6 of the Model Rules concerns attorney-client confidentiality. The rule of confidentiality is one of the oldest and most important rules of the legal profession, primarily because it would be difficult for a lawyer to properly represent a client without such a rule. A client must be able to confide in his or her attorney so that the attorney can best represent the client's interest. Because confidentiality is one of the easiest rules to violate, a thorough understanding of the rule is essential.

The general rule of confidentiality, as stated in the first paragraph of Rule 1.6, is that all information relating to the representation of a client must be kept confidential unless the client consents to disclosure. The 2002 revision of this rule

DEVELOPING PARALEGAL SKILLS
Inadequate Supervision

Michael Patton is a paralegal in a small, busy, general practice law firm. His supervising attorney, Muriel Chapman, answers his question about the amount of temporary alimony to be inserted into the judgment of divorce that he is preparing. She tells Michael that the $5,000 figure is the total amount, not the annual amount. Next, Michael requests that Muriel review the judgment before it is signed by the parties and filed with the court. Muriel tells Michael that she does not need to review his work—she is confident that he has prepared the document correctly because he always asks questions when he is uncertain. Michael remembers the adequate supervision rule and asks Muriel again to review his work. She finally agrees, stating, "You know, Michael, you are rather persistent in making me do 'the right thing.'"

TIPS FOR OBTAINING ADEQUATE SUPERVISION

- Request your supervising attorney to review your work.
- Use notes or ticklers as reminders to ask for a review.
- Make the review as convenient as possible for your supervising attorney.
- Discuss your ethical concerns with the attorney.
- Be persistent.

requires the client to give "informed consent" to the disclosure—that is, the lawyer must fully explain the risks and alternatives to the client.

Note that the rule does not make any qualifications about what kind of information is confidential. It simply states that a lawyer may not reveal "information relating to representation of a client." Does this mean that if a client tells you that he is the president of a local company, you have to keep that information confidential, even when the whole community knows that fact? For example, could you tell your spouse, "Mr. X is the president of XYZ Corporation"? It may seem permissible, because that fact is, after all, public knowledge. But in so doing, you must not indicate, by words or conduct, that Mr. X is a client of your firm. In such a situation, it is hard to know just what assumptions might be made based on what you have said. Consider another example. Suppose that one evening at dinner you told your spouse that you had met Mr. X that day. Your spouse might reasonably assume that your firm was handling some legal matter involving Mr. X. Because it may be difficult to decide what information is or is not confidential, a good rule of thumb is the following:

> ✳ **Paralegals should regard all information about a client or a client's case as confidential information.**

EXCEPTIONS TO THE CONFIDENTIALITY RULE.   Rule 1.6 provides for certain exceptions, each of which we look at here.

Client Consents to the Disclosure.   Paragraph (a) of the rule indicates that an attorney may reveal confidential information if the client consents to the disclosure. For example, suppose that an attorney is drawing up a will for a client, and the client is making his only son the sole beneficiary under the will and leaving nothing to his daughter. The daughter calls and wants to know how her father's will reads. The attorney cannot divulge this confidential information to the daughter because the client has not consented to such disclosure. Now suppose that the client has told the attorney that if his daughter calls the attorney to find out if she will inherit anything under the will, the attorney is to "go ahead and tell her that she gets nothing." In this situation, the attorney can disclose the information because the client has consented to the disclosure.

Impliedly Authorized Disclosures.   Paragraph (a) of Rule 1.6 also states that an attorney may make "disclosures that are impliedly authorized in order to carry out the representation." This exception is clearly necessary. Legal representation of clients necessarily involves the attorney's assistants, and they must have access to the confidential information to do their jobs. If a paralegal is working on the client's case, for example, he or she must know what the client told the attorney about the legal matter and must have access to information in the client's file concerning the case.

Client Intends a Harmful Act.   One of the most controversial exceptions to the confidentiality rule involves situations in which a client reveals to an attorney the client's intent to commit a harmful act. Paragraph (b) of Rule 1.6 states that the lawyer may reveal information to the extent that the lawyer deems it necessary "to prevent the client from committing a criminal act that the lawyer believes is likely to result in imminent death or substantial bodily harm."

One problem with this exception is that it is often difficult to ascertain whether the client really intends to do what he or she threatens. For example, a client might say during a prolonged custody battle, "I'm going to kill my ex-wife," but not really mean it. The lawyer must rely on her or his own judgment to determine if the threat is real and, if so, what to do about it. Another problem is that it is not always clear whether the client's intended behavior is in fact a criminal act that will result in bodily harm or death to another. As a paralegal, if a client communicates such a threat to you, you should immediately discuss the matter with your supervising attorney so that she or he can decide what should be done.

Defending against a Client's Legal Action.   The second exception in paragraph (b) of Rule 1.6 is particularly important for attorneys and paralegals. The classic example of this exception is a client's malpractice suit against an attorney. In this situation, it is essential for the lawyer to reveal confidential information to prove that he or she was not negligent. Note, though, that the attorney is permitted to disclose confidential information only to the extent that it is essential to defend against the lawsuit.

The Revised Model Rule Expands the Exceptions to Confidentiality.   The 2002 revision expands the grounds for disclosure under Model Rule 1.6 in several ways. First, it allows a lawyer to reveal client confidences to the extent the lawyer reasonably believes necessary "to prevent reasonably certain death or substantial bodily harm." In other words, the rule no longer requires that the act be criminal or that the client *intend* harm. The comments to the revised rule give an example in which a lawyer knows that a client has accidentally discharged toxic waste into a town's water supply and that a substantial risk exists that a person who drinks the water will contract a life-threatening or debilitating disease. Under these circumstances, the attorney would be authorized to disclose the information necessary to eliminate the threat or reduce the number of victims.

The revised Model Rule 1.6 also adds two new exceptions. The first allows a lawyer to reveal confidential information "to secure legal advice about the lawyer's compliance with these Rules." This exception is designed to prevent clients from utilizing a lawyer's services to commit fraud or cause substantial economic loss to another (which already is illegal under the ethical codes of thirteen states). The second change explicitly allows a lawyer to disclose confidential information to comply with the law or a court order. The comments to the revised rule

DEVELOPING PARALEGAL SKILLS
Client Intends to Commit a Crime

Samantha Serles, a legal assistant with a degree in psychology, is meeting with a client whom her firm is defending. The client, Jim Storming, has been charged with the murder of his mother-in-law. Samantha's job is to assess the client's mental state and consider whether he needs further evaluation. Samantha begins talking to Jim. She asks him how things are going and how he feels. He rolls his eyes at her questions and says, "How do you think I feel, being locked up in this place?" She decides to try to talk to him about the crime. "Jim," she says, "have you thought any more about how your mother-in-law died and about what happened that night?" "Yeah," he says. "I've thought about it plenty. I killed her, you know. But they aren't going to be able prove that I did it."

Samantha just listens as he continues. "I hated her. She talked my wife into divorcing me, and then she and my ex-

wife turned my kids against me. I'm going to get even with my ex-wife for that, too. I've been talking to some guys in here. They told me how I can have her taken care of while I'm in here. Then I won't have to take the rap for that one either." Samantha has seen enough to know that Jim needs psychiatric evaluation.

CHECKLIST FOR DETERMINING WHETHER A CLIENT INTENDS A HARMFUL ACT

- Is the threat one of a criminal act?
- If so, is it one that would cause bodily harm or death to another?
- Is the threat real?
- Always inform your supervising attorney of the threat.

explain that when disclosure appears to be required, the lawyer should discuss the matter with the client prior to making the necessary disclosures.

VIOLATIONS OF THE CONFIDENTIALITY RULE.   Paralegals, like other professionals, spend a good part of their lives engaged in their work. Naturally, they are tempted to discuss their work at home, with spouses and family members, or with others, such as co-workers and good friends. As a paralegal, perhaps one of the greatest temptations you will face is the desire to discuss a particularly interesting case, or some aspect of a case, with someone you know. You can deal with this temptation in two ways: you can decide, as a matter of policy, never to discuss anything concerning your work; or you can limit your discussion to issues and comments that will not reveal the identity of your client. The latter approach is, for many paralegals, a more realistic solution, but it requires great care. Something you say may reveal a client's identity, even though you are not aware of it.

Conversations Overheard by Others.   Violations of the confidentiality rule can happen simply by oversight. For example, suppose that you and the legal secretary in your office are both working on the same case and continue, as you walk down the hallway toward the elevator, a conversation that you have been having about the case. You pause in front of the elevator, not realizing that your conversation is being overheard by someone around the corner from you. You have no way of knowing the person is there, and you have no way of knowing whether the confidential information that you inadvertently revealed will have any adverse effect on your client's interests. One way to avoid the possibility of unwittingly revealing confidential information to **third parties** is to follow this rule of thumb:

> **Never discuss confidential information when you are in a common area, such as a hallway, an elevator, or a cafeteria, where a conversation might be overheard.**

third parties
A person or entity not directly involved in an agreement (such as a contract), legal proceeding (such as a lawsuit), or relationship (such as an attorney-client relationship).

> ## ETHICAL CONCERN
> ## Social Events and Confidentiality
>
> Assume that you are at a party with some other paralegals. You tell a paralegal whom you know quite well of some startling news—that a client of your firm, a prominent city official, is being investigated for drug dealing. Although your friend promises to keep this information strictly confidential, she nonetheless relays it to her husband, who in turn tells a co-worker, who in turn tells a friend, and so on. Within a few days, the news has reached the press, and the resulting media coverage results in irreparable harm to the official's reputation and standing in the community. If it can be proved that the harm is the direct result of your breach of the duty of confidentiality, the official could sue both you and the attorney for whom you work for damages.

Electronic Communications and Confidentiality.   Whenever you talk to or about a client on the telephone, make sure that your conversation will not be overheard by a third party. You may be sitting in your private office, but if your door is open, someone may overhear the conversation. Paralegals should take special care when using cellular phones. Cellular phones are not secure. Although conversations on digital cellular phones are more difficult to intercept than conversations on analog phones (which can be overheard by anyone in the vicinity with a scanner), there is still a security risk. As a precaution, you should thus never disclose confidential information when talking on a cellular phone. Because of the widespread use of mobile phones, paralegals today often, as a routine precaution, ask a client who is calling whether he or she is calling from a mobile unit. If the client is using a mobile phone, the paralegal can caution the client that confidential information should not be discussed.

Even such a simple operation as sending a fax can pose ethical pitfalls. Generally, you should exercise great care to make sure that you (1) send the fax to the right person (for example, when a letter is addressed to an opposing party in a lawsuit but is supposed to be sent to the client for his or her approval) and (2) dial the correct fax number.

You also need to be cautious when sending e-mail messages. For example, suppose that you are asked by your supervising attorney to send an e-mail message to a client and to attach a document containing the attorney's analysis of confidential information submitted by the client. The client's e-mail address is in your e-mail "address book," along with other numbers. You click on the client's name, type a brief message, attach the document, and click "send." Too late, you realize that you accidentally clicked on the opposing counsel's name instead of your client's. By a click of the mouse, you have disclosed important confidential information. To avoid this kind of problem, before you click "send," you should take a minute not only to review the message—grammar, sentence structure, and spelling—but also to verify the recipient's name and/or address. (For a further discussion of confidentiality problems posed by the use of e-mail, see this chapter's *Technology and Today's Paralegal* feature.)

Other Ways of Violating the Confidentiality Rule.   There are numerous other ways in which you can reveal confidential information without intending to do so. A file or document sitting on your desk, if observed by a third party, may reveal

Walling-Off Procedures.   Law offices usually have special procedures for "walling off" an attorney or other legal professional from a case when a conflict of interest exists. The firm may announce in a written memo to all employees that a certain attorney or paralegal should not have access to specific files, for example, and may set out procedures to be followed to ensure that access to those files is restricted. Computer documents relating to the case may be protected by warning messages or in some other way. Commonly, any hard-copy files relating to the case are flagged with a sticker to indicate that access to the files is restricted.

Firms normally take great care to establish and observe such procedures because if confidential information is used in a way harmful to a former client, the client may sue the firm seeking steep damages. In defending against such a suit, the firm will need to demonstrate that it took reasonable precautions to protect that client's interests.

On The Web
To read an article by NFPA's ethics coordinator entitled "The Ethical Wall: Its Application to Paralegals," go to **http://www.paralegals.org/ Development/Ethical Wall/toc.html.**

OTHER CONFLICT-OF-INTEREST SITUATIONS.   Several other types of situations may give rise to conflicts of interest. Gifts from clients may create conflicts of interest, because they tend to bias the judgment of the attorney or paralegal. Some types of gifts are specifically prohibited. For example, Rule 1.8(c) of the Model Rules of Professional Conduct prohibits an attorney from preparing documents (such as wills) for a client if the client gives the attorney or a member of the attorney's family a gift. (An exception to this rule exists, of course, when the attorney is a relative of the client.) Note that as a paralegal, you may be offered gifts from appreciative clients at Christmas or other times. Generally, such gifts pose no ethical problems. If a client offers you a gift that has substantial value, however, you should discuss the issue with your supervising attorney.

Attorneys also need to be careful about taking on a client whose case may create an "issue conflict" for the attorney. Generally, an attorney cannot represent a client with respect to a substantive legal issue if the client's position is directly contrary to that of another client being represented by the lawyer—or the lawyer's firm—in a case being brought within the same jurisdiction (the geographic area or subject matter over which a specific court has authority to decide legal disputes). The reason for this rule is that courts are obligated to follow precedents—earlier decisions on cases involving similar facts and issues (see Chapter 5). The court's ruling in one of the attorney's cases could therefore alter the outcome of the other case.

Occasionally, conflicts of interest may arise when two family members who are both attorneys or paralegals are involved in the representation of adverse parties in a legal proceeding. Model Rule 1.8(i) prohibits an attorney from representing a client if the adverse party to the dispute is being represented by a member of the attorney's family (such as a spouse, parent, child, or sibling). If you, as a paralegal, are married to or living with another paralegal or an attorney, you should inform your firm of this fact if you ever suspect that a conflict of interest might result from your relationship.

REVISION OF THE MODEL RULES PERTAINING TO CONFLICTS.   In 2002, the ABA amended the rules pertaining to conflicts of interest (Model Rules 1.7–1.10). Although the changes might appear significant (several of the titles have changed, for example), the primary purpose behind the revision was to clarify the meaning of the rules and to provide lawyers with more guidance regarding the complex rules on conflicts. Only a few substantive changes were made.

The main change in the 2002 revision is that in order to waive a conflict, each affected client must give his or her informed consent to the waiver. Also, the consent must be confirmed in writing. What this means is that if a conflict arises, the attorney must explain the risks and alternative courses of action to the client. Then

DEVELOPING PARALEGAL SKILLS
Building an Ethical Wall

Lana Smith, a paralegal, has been asked by her supervising attorney to set up an ethical wall because a new attorney, Sandra Piper, has been hired from the law firm of Nunn & Bush. While employed by Nunn & Bush, Piper represented the defendant, Seski Manufacturing, in the ongoing case of *Tymes v. Seski Manufacturing Co.* Lana's firm represents the plaintiff, Joseph Tymes, in that same case, so Piper's work for Nunn & Bush creates a conflict of interest. Lana makes a list of the walling-off procedures to use to ensure that the firm cannot be accused of violating the rules on conflict of interest.

CHECKLIST FOR BUILDING AN ETHICAL WALL

- Prepare a memo to the office manager regarding the conflict and the need for special arrangements.

- Prepare a memo to the team representing Tymes to inform them of the conflict of interest and the special procedures to be used.

- Prepare a memo to the firm giving the case name, the nature of the conflict, the parties involved, and instructions to maintain a blanket of silence with respect to Sandra Piper.

- Arrange for Piper's office to be on a different floor from the team to demonstrate, if necessary, that the firm took steps to prevent Piper and the team from having access to one another or each other's files.

- Arrange with the office manager for special computer passwords to be issued to the team members so that access to computer files on the *Tymes* case is restricted to team members only.

- Place "ACCESS RESTRICTED" stickers on the files for the *Tymes* case.

- Develop a security procedure for signing out and tracking the case files in the *Tymes* case—to prevent inadvertent disclosure of the files to Piper or her staff members.

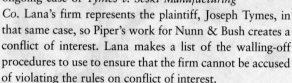

either the attorney must obtain the client's consent in writing or, if the client gives consent orally, the attorney must promptly draft a writing that confirms it. Additionally, the new rules make it clear that a client's consent will not be sufficient to overcome the conflict in certain situations. For example, a client cannot consent to a situation in which the lawyer would represent more than one defendant accused of committing a crime for which the defendants could receive the death penalty.

conflicts check
A procedure for determining whether an agreement to represent a potential client will result in a conflict of interest.

CONFLICTS CHECKS.   Whenever a potential client consults with an attorney, the attorney will want to make sure that no potential conflict of interest exists before deciding whether to represent the client. Running a **conflicts check** is a standard procedure in the law office and one that is frequently undertaken by paralegals. Before you can run a conflicts check, you need to know the name of the prospective client, the other party or parties that may be involved in the client's legal matter, and the legal issue involved. Normally, every law firm has some established procedure for conflicts checks, and in larger firms there is usually a computerized database containing the names of former clients and the other information you will need in checking for conflicts of interest.

THE INDIRECT REGULATION OF PARALEGALS

Paralegals are regulated *indirectly* in several ways. Clearly, the ethical codes for attorneys just discussed indirectly regulate the conduct of paralegals. Additionally, paralegal conduct is regulated indirectly by standards and guidelines created by paralegal professional groups as well as guidelines for the utilization of paralegals developed by the American Bar Association and various states.

EXHIBIT 3.2

Excerpts from Section 1 of NFPA's Code of Ethics and Professional Responsibility and Guidelines for Enforcement

Courtesy: National Federation of Paralegal Associations, Inc. Only the disciplinary rules are shown in this exhibit. The ethical considerations, which are important to a paralegal's understanding of these rules, can be read in Appendix C of this book.

Paralegal Ethical Codes

Paralegals are becoming increasingly self-regulated. Recall from Chapter 1 that the two major national paralegal associations in the United States—the National Federation of Paralegal Associations, or NFPA, and the National Association of Legal Assistants, or NALA—were formed to define and represent paralegal professional interests on a national level. Shortly after they were formed, both of these associations adopted codes of ethics defining the ethical responsibilities of paralegals.

NFPA's Code of Ethics.   In 1977, NFPA adopted its first code of ethics, called the Affirmation of Responsibility. The code has since been revised several times and, in 1993, was renamed the Model Code of Ethics and Professional Responsibility. In 1997, NFPA revised the code, particularly its format, and took the bold step of appending to its code a list of enforcement guidelines setting forth recommendations on how to discipline paralegals who violate ethical standards promulgated by the code. The full title of NFPA's current code is the Model Code of Ethics and Professional Responsibility and Guidelines for Enforcement.

Exhibit 3.2 presents excerpts from Section 1 of the code, entitled NFPA Model Disciplinary Rules and Ethical Considerations. For reasons of space, only the rules are included in the exhibit, not the ethical considerations that follow each rule. The ethical considerations are very important to paralegals, however, because they explain what conduct the rule prohibits. The full text of NFPA's code (including the rules, ethical considerations, and guidelines for enforcement) is presented in Appendix C of this book.

NALA's Code of Ethics.   In 1975, NALA issued its Code of Ethics and Professional Responsibility, which, like NFPA's code, has since undergone several revisions. Exhibit 3.3 on page 86 presents NALA's code in its entirety. Note that NALA's code, like the Model Code of Professional Responsibility discussed earlier in this chapter, presents ethical precepts as a series of "canons." (Prior to the 1997 revision of its code, NFPA also listed its ethical standards as "canons.")

Compliance with Paralegal Codes of Ethics.   Paralegal codes of ethics state the ethical responsibilities of paralegals generally, but they particularly apply to members of paralegal organizations that have adopted the codes. Any paralegal

On the Web

You can find NFPA's Model Code of Ethics and Professional Responsibility and Guidelines for Enforcement on the Web at **http://www. paralegals.org/ Development/ modelcode.html**.

On the Web

You can find NALA'S Code of Ethics and Professional Responsibility online at **http://www.nala. org/stand.htm**.

EXHIBIT 3.3
NALA's Code of Ethics and Professional Responsibility

© 1975, 1977, 1994 National Association of Legal Assistants, Inc. Reprinted with permission.

A legal assistant must adhere strictly to the accepted standards of legal ethics and to the general principles of proper conduct. The performance of the duties of the legal assistant shall be governed by specific canons as defined herein so justice will be served and goals of the profession attained. (See Model Standards and Guidelines for Utilization of Legal Assistants, Section II.)

The canons of ethics set forth hereafter are adopted by the National Association of Legal Assistants, Inc., as a general guide intended to aid legal assistants and attorneys. The enumeration of these rules does not mean there are not others of equal importance although not specifically mentioned. Court rules, agency rules and statutes must be taken into consideration when interpreting the canons.

Definition: Legal assistants, also known as paralegals, are a distinguishable group of persons who assist attorneys in the delivery of legal services. Through formal education, training and experience, legal assistants have knowledge and expertise regarding the legal system and substantive and procedural law which qualify them to do work of a legal nature under the supervision of an attorney.

Canon 1.
A legal assistant must not perform any of the duties that attorneys only may perform nor take any actions that attorneys may not take.

Canon 2.
A legal assistant may perform any task which is properly delegated and supervised by an attorney, as long as the attorney is ultimately responsible to the client, maintains a direct relationship with the client, and assumes professional responsibility for the work product.

Canon 3.
A legal assistant must not: (a) engage in, encourage, or contribute to any act which could constitute the unauthorized practice of law; and (b) establish attorney-client relationships, set fees, give legal opinions or advice or represent a client before a court or agency unless so authorized by that court or agency; and (c) engage in conduct or take any action which would assist or involve the attorney in a violation of professional ethics or give the appearance of professional impropriety.

Canon 4.
A legal assistant must use discretion and professional judgment commensurate with knowledge and experience but must not render independent legal judgment in place of an attorney. The services of an attorney are essential in the public interest whenever such legal judgment is required.

Canon 5.
A legal assistant must disclose his or her status as a legal assistant at the outset of any professional relationship with a client, attorney, a court or administrative agency or personnel thereof, or a member of the general public. A legal assistant must act prudently in determining the extent to which a client may be assisted without the presence of an attorney.

Canon 6.
A legal assistant must strive to maintain integrity and a high degree of competency through education and training with respect to professional responsibility, local rules and practice, and through continuing education in substantive areas of law to better assist the legal profession in fulfilling its duty to provide legal service.

Canon 7.
A legal assistant must protect the confidences of a client and must not violate any rule or statute now in effect or hereafter enacted controlling privileged communications.

Canon 8.
A legal assistant must do all other things incidental, necessary, or expedient for the attainment of the ethics and responsibilities as defined by statute or rule of court.

Canon 9.
A legal assistant's conduct is guided by bar associations' codes of professional responsibility and rules of professional conduct.

who is a member of an organization that has adopted one of these codes is expected to comply with the code's requirements. Note that compliance with these codes is not legally mandatory. In other words, if a paralegal does not abide by a particular ethical standard of a paralegal association's code of ethics, the association cannot initiate state-sanctioned disciplinary proceedings against the paralegal. The association can, however, expel the paralegal from the association, which may have significant implications for the paralegal's future career opportunities. See this chapter's *Featured Guest* article on the following page for a further discussion on how setting high ethical standards can enhance a paralegal's career opportunities.

Guidelines for the Utilization of Paralegals

As mentioned earlier in this chapter, the reason attorneys are regulated by the state is to protect the public from the harms that could result from incompetent legal advice and representation. Licensing requirements for attorneys thus serve the public interest. At the same time, they give lawyers something of a monopoly over the delivery of legal services—a monopoly that, in turn, may have detrimental effects on those who cannot afford to pay attorneys for their services. The increased use of paralegals stems, in part, from the legal profession's need to reduce the cost of legal services. The use of paralegals to do substantive legal work benefits clients because the hourly rate for paralegals is, of course, substantially lower than that for attorneys.

For this reason, bar associations (and courts, when approving fees) encourage attorneys to delegate work to paralegals whenever feasible to lower the costs of legal services for clients—and thus provide the public with greater access to legal services. In fact, some courts, when determining awards of attorneys' fees, have refused to approve fees at the attorney's hourly rate for work that could have been performed by a paralegal at a lower rate.

NALA, the ABA, and many of the states have adopted guidelines for the utilization of paralegal services. These guidelines were created in response to a variety of questions concerning the role and function of paralegals within the legal arena that had arisen during the 1970s and 1980s, including the following: What are paralegals? What kinds of tasks do they perform? What are their professional responsibilities? How can attorneys best utilize paralegal services? What responsibilities should attorneys assume with respect to their assistants' work?

NALA's Model Standards and Guidelines.   In 1984, NALA adopted its Model Standards and Guidelines for the Utilization of Legal Assistants. This document addresses and provides guidance on several issues of paramount importance to legal assistants today. It begins by listing the minimum qualifications that legal assistants should have and then, in a series of guidelines, indicates what legal assistants may and may not do. We will examine these guidelines in more detail shortly. (See Appendix B for the complete text of the annotated version of NALA's Model Standards and Guidelines, as revised in 1997.)

The ABA's Model Guidelines.   The ABA adopted its Model Guidelines for the Utilization of Legal Assistant Services in 1991. The ABA Standing Committee on Legal Assistants, which drafted the guidelines, based them on the NALA guidelines, various state codes and guidelines on the use of paralegals, and relevant state court decisions. The document consists of ten guidelines, each of which is followed by a lengthy comment on the derivation, scope, and application of the guideline. The ten guidelines are presented in Exhibit 3.4 on page 90. (For reasons

On the Web
NALA'S Model Standards and Guidelines are online at **http://www.nala. org/stand.htm.**

FEATURED GUEST: LISA L. NEWCITY

Ten Tips for Ethics and the Paralegal

BIOGRAPHICAL NOTE

Lisa L. Newcity has been a paralegal educator for approximately ten years. She is a full-time faculty member in the Legal Studies Department at Roger Williams University in Bristol, Rhode Island. She was formerly a practicing attorney specializing in the areas of personal injury, medical malpractice, product liability, and general liability.

Newcity currently chairs the NFPA Ethics Board and is a member of the Rhode Island Paralegal Association (RIPA). She and her students regularly participate in RIPA's community service and public education programs. She is also an active member of AAfPE.

Additionally, Newcity serves as the faculty adviser to the Roger Williams University Law Society and works with her students on such projects as Law Day and mock trials. Her areas of interest and research include legal ethics, tort reform, access to justice, and paralegal licensing and regulation.

A paralegal with a clear understanding of the rules of ethics is an invaluable asset to any law practice. Ethical behavior in the workplace increases client satisfaction, reduces the risk of liability for the employer, and, perhaps even more important, fosters a sense of respect and pride for the profession. The following tips offer some suggestions on how you can incorporate the rules of ethics and professional responsibility into your daily life as a practicing paralegal.

1. Set a High Standard for Competence.   The best paralegals know that in order to remain current and productive, they must keep abreast of changes in the law, in law office technology, and in legal ethics. Attend CLE (continuing legal education) seminars in your area of practice, as well as in ethics. Read your local, state, and national legal newspapers and journals for updates and changes in these areas. Take advantage of the educational opportunities offered by paralegal associations and bar associations. Understand that your paralegal education and experience provide a foundation on which you are expected to build throughout your career. The codes of professional responsibility for attorneys and paralegals require us to maintain a certain level of competence. Do this at a minimum, but always strive for the highest possible standard with respect to competence and skills.

2. Demonstrate Respect for Others and for the Profession.   In recent years, there has been much discussion regarding the "lack of civility" within the legal profession. Do your part to promote an atmosphere of mutual

respect and civility in your workplace by behaving professionally at all times. All legal professionals, attorneys and paralegals alike, should understand that clients and members of the public hold us to a higher standard of ethical conduct. We are expected to comport ourselves with dignity and to show respect for the law and for each other. Indeed, the codes of professional responsibility require us to avoid even the "appearance of impropriety." To that end, you must from time to time put your sense of professionalism and dignity before your own emotions when faced with uncivil conduct on the part of others. Do this for the good of your clients and for the good of the profession.

3. Become Active in Local and National Professional Associations. Collaborate with, and learn from, your colleagues as a member of a paralegal professional association, such as NFPA or NALA. Both organizations have made great strides in raising awareness about the paralegal profession, and both provide excellent sources of information for their members and for the public. In addition, these organizations (as well as state and local paralegal associations) have promulgated ethical guidelines for paralegals and publish ethics opinions and cases on ethics to guide their members.

4. Understand and Observe the Rules of Confidentiality.   The ethical rules on confidentiality create the underpinnings of the attorney-client relationship. Our ability to provide the best possible legal services for our clients hinges on the trust and confidence that our clients place in us. Do nothing that could jeopardize this. Recognize common "danger zones" for paralegals in preserving

FEATURED GUEST, *Continued*

confidentiality. Among other things, these danger zones include discussing clients and cases with family and friends, interviewing clients in your office when other clients' files and documents are in plain view, and discussing a client's case with a witness during an investigation.

5. **Demonstrate Loyalty to the Client by Recognizing Potential Conflicts of Interest.**   You know from studying the ethical rules concerning conflicts of interest that any conflict is a potential danger to the client and to your employer. Be diligent in following your firm's practices for conflict checking. Also, if you believe that a conflict may arise in a case that you are handling, speak to your supervising attorney immediately. It is always better to address conflict issues at the earliest possible opportunity. Waiting until later may result in unnecessary cost and embarrassment for you and for your employer.

6. **Demonstrate Loyalty to Your Employer through Your Professionalism.**   As a legal professional and an employee, you are a representative of your firm or agency. Paralegals interact with clients, witnesses, and court personnel on a regular basis. Refrain from gossip or negative remarks about your firm or employer. Attorneys and paralegals work together as integral members of a team on behalf of their clients. If difficulties or conflicts arise with your supervisor, speak to that person directly in an effort to resolve them. Your professionalism will be respected and appreciated.

7. **Practice Diligence in Completing Your Work Promptly and Efficiently.**

Prioritize your work to avoid neglecting important projects. Be scrupulous in maintaining your calendar and tickler system. Understand your own limits, and speak to your supervisor if the volume of work becomes so overwhelming that you run the risk of neglecting projects or missing deadlines. It is better to ask for assistance from your paralegal co-workers or from your supervisor than to ignore the problem until it is too late.

8. **Recognize Your Role as the Client's Contact, and Promote Responsiveness to the Client's Questions and Concerns.** Paralegals are often the persons within the firm to whom clients will look when questions arise. Unfortunately, one of the most common complaints about attorneys and their professional staff members is that they are unresponsive. Make it a point to return your clients' telephone calls in a prompt and courteous manner. When a client has a question calling for legal advice, bring it to the attorney's attention quickly, and encourage the attorney to respond to the client promptly. If the attorney is busy, offer to pass along the message (being careful to avoid giving legal advice yourself).

9. **Recognize UPL "Pitfalls for Paralegals."**   As you gain the confidence and trust of your firm's clients, you will, on occasion, be faced with questions calling for legal advice. Learn to develop strategies for handling these situations with tact and empathy. Remember that if a client has a pressing problem that calls for immediate attention, it is not sufficient to tell him or her that as a

> **"Ethical behavior in the workplace increases client satisfaction, reduces the risk of liability for the employer, and, perhaps even more important, fosters a sense of respect and pride for the profession."**

paralegal you are not permitted to give legal advice. Inform the client that you will find an attorney who can assist the client and that either you or the attorney will get right back to the client. Then be sure to do just that. Of course, paralegals may face other situations with serious UPL implications as well. When in doubt, consult the rules for guidance and speak with your supervising attorney.

10. **Know When to Ask for Help and Where to Get It.**   Every paralegal should have a copy of the ethical rules for attorneys and paralegals. Every paralegal should also regularly review ethics opinions, disciplinary proceedings, and cases interpreting the rules of professional conduct. Also, when questions or concerns about ethics arise, you should know where to turn for help. Many firms designate a particular individual within the firm as the "contact person" for ethical inquiries. Further, many state and local attorney licensing and regulatory agencies, bar associations, and paralegal associations provide services to legal professionals who have ethical questions. Inquire about your firm's policies regarding ethical questions, and take advantage of all available resources.

EXHIBIT 3.4

The ABA's Model Guidelines for the Utilization of Legal Assistant Services (Comments Not Included)

© 1999. Reprinted by permission of the American Bar Association. Annotations and commentary to the Guidelines are not included in this exhibit. A copy of the Guidelines with annotations and commentary is available through the ABA Legal Assistants Department staff office. Phone: 312-988-5616; Fax: 312-988-5677; E-mail: legalassts@abanet.org.

Guideline 1: A lawyer is responsible for all of the professional actions of a legal assistant performing legal assistant services at the lawyer's direction and should take reasonable measures to ensure that the legal assistant's conduct is consistent with the lawyer's obligations under the ABA Model Rules of Professional Conduct.

Guideline 2: Provided the lawyer maintains responsibility for the work product, a lawyer may delegate to a legal assistant any task normally performed by the lawyer except those tasks proscribed to one not licensed as a lawyer by statute, court rule, administrative rule or regulation, controlling authority, the ABA Model Rules of Professional Conduct, or these Guidelines.

Guideline 3: A lawyer may not delegate to a legal assistant:

(a) Responsibility for establishing an attorney-client relationship.
(b) Responsibility for establishing the amount of a fee to be charged for a legal service.
(c) Responsibility for a legal opinion rendered to a client.

Guideline 4: It is the lawyer's responsibility to take reasonable measures to ensure that clients, courts, and other lawyers are aware that a legal assistant, whose services are utilized by the lawyer in performing legal services, is not licensed to practice law.

Guideline 5: A lawyer may identify legal assistants by name and title on the lawyer's letterhead and on business cards identifying the lawyer's firm.

Guideline 6: It is the responsibility of a lawyer to take reasonable measures to ensure that all client confidences are preserved by a legal assistant.

Guideline 7: A lawyer should take reasonable measures to prevent conflicts of interest resulting from a legal assistant's other employment or interests insofar as such other employment or interests would present a conflict of interest if it were that of the lawyer.

Guideline 8: A lawyer may include a charge for the work performed by a legal assistant in setting a charge for legal services.

Guideline 9: A lawyer may not split legal fees with a legal assistant nor pay a legal assistant for the referral of legal business. A lawyer may compensate a legal assistant based on the quantity and quality of the legal assistant's work and the value of that work to a law practice, but the legal assistant's compensation may not be contingent, by advance agreement, upon the profitability of the lawyer's practice.

Guideline 10: A lawyer who employs a legal assistant should facilitate the legal assistant's participation in appropriate continuing education and *pro bono publico* activities.

of space, Exhibit 3.4 presents only the guidelines; for the current version of the comments, refer to the Model Guidelines in Appendix D of this text.)

STATE GUIDELINES.   Over two-thirds of the states have adopted some form of guidelines concerning the use of legal assistants by attorneys, the respective responsibilities of attorneys and legal assistants in performing legal work, the types of tasks paralegals may perform, and other ethically challenging areas of legal practice. Although the guidelines of some states reflect the influence of NALA's standards and guidelines, the state guidelines focus largely on state statutory definitions of the practice of law, state codes of ethics regulating the responsibilities of attorneys, and state court decisions. As a paralegal, you should make sure that you become familiar with your state's guidelines.

The Increasing Scope of Paralegal Responsibilities

The ethical standards and guidelines just discussed, as well as court decisions concerning paralegals, all support the goal of increasing the use of paralegals in the delivery of legal services. Today, paralegals can perform virtually any legal task as long as the work is supervised by an attorney (see Guideline 2 in Exhibit 3.4) and does not constitute the unauthorized practice of law (to be discussed shortly).

Paralegals working for attorneys may interview clients and witnesses, investigate legal claims, draft legal documents for attorneys' signatures, attend will executions (in some states), appear at real estate closings (in some states), and undertake numerous other types of legal work, as long as the work is supervised by attorneys. When state or federal law allows them to do so, paralegals can also represent clients before government agencies. Paralegals are allowed to perform freelance services for attorneys and, depending on state law and the type of service, perform limited independent services for the public.

Legal assistants are also permitted to give information to clients on many types of matters relating to a case or other legal concern. When arranging for client interviews, they let clients know what kind of information is needed and what documents to bring to the office. They inform clients about legal procedures and what clients should expect to experience during the progress of a legal proceeding. For example, in preparing for trial, legal assistants instruct clients on trial procedures, what they should wear to the trial, and so on. Clearly, as a legal assistant, you will be permitted to give clients all kinds of information. Nonetheless, you must make sure that you know where to draw the line between giving permissible types of advice and giving "legal advice"—advice that only attorneys are licensed to give under state laws.

The specific types of tasks that paralegals are legally permitted to undertake are described throughout this book; it would be impossible to list them all here. As you can see from the ABA's guidelines, paralegals may not perform tasks that only attorneys can legally perform. If they do so, they risk liability for the unauthorized practice of law—an important topic to which we now turn.

THE UNAUTHORIZED PRACTICE OF LAW

An awareness of what kinds of activities constitute the unauthorized practice of law (UPL) is vitally important for practicing paralegals. Paralegals judged to have engaged in UPL may be subject to fines and possibly imprisonment. UPL actions are complicated by the fact that state statutes stipulating that only licensed attorneys can engage in the practice of law rarely indicate with any specificity what constitutes the "practice of law." As you recall, most states' laws are based on either the ABA's Model Rules or the Model Code, neither of which clearly defines what constitutes the practice of law.

The lack of specificity with regard to the practice of law makes it difficult to predict with certainty what types of actions may constitute the unauthorized practice of law. Generally, however, state statutes regulating the practice of law, court decisions, and NALA identify certain activities that should *only* be performed by a licensed attorney. In other words, paralegals are prohibited from performing these activities. NALA's Model Standards and Guidelines summarize these prohibited activities in Guideline 2, which states that legal assistants should not perform any of the following actions:

- Establish attorney-client relationships.
- Set legal fees.

On the Web
A good starting point for locating your state's UPL statute and UPL court cases is FindLaw's Web site at **http://www. findlaw.com/casecode/ state.html.**

- Give legal opinions or advice.
- Represent a client before a court, unless authorized to do so by the court.
- Engage in, encourage, or contribute to any act that could constitute the unauthorized practice of law.

The first two activities in the list—establishing attorney-client relationships and setting legal fees—are fairly straightforward. The others, however, are less so and merit further discussion.

Giving Legal Opinions and Advice

Clearly, giving legal advice goes to the essence of legal practice. After all, a person would not seek out a legal expert if he or she did not want legal advice on some matter. Although a paralegal may communicate an attorney's legal advice to a client, the paralegal may not give legal advice.

THE NEED FOR CAUTION.   You need to be extremely careful to avoid giving legal advice even when discussing matters with friends and relatives. Although other nonlawyers often give advice affecting others' legal rights or obligations, paralegals may not do so. For example, when an individual receives a speeding ticket, a friend or relative who is a nonlawyer might suggest that the person should argue the case before a judge and explain his or her side of the story. When a paralegal gives such advice, however, he or she may be accused of engaging in the unauthorized practice of law. Legal assistants are prohibited from giving even simple, common-sense advice because of the understandably greater weight given to the advice of someone who has legal training.

Similarly, you need to be cautious in the workplace. Although you may have developed great expertise in a certain area of law, you must refrain from advising clients with respect to their legal obligations or rights. For example, suppose that you are a bankruptcy specialist and know that a client who wants to petition for bankruptcy has two realistic options to pursue under bankruptcy law. Should you tell the client about these options and their consequences? No, you should not. In effect, advising someone of his or her legal options is very close to advising a person of his or her legal rights and may therefore—in the view of many courts, at least—constitute the practice of law. Also, even though you may qualify what you say by telling the client that he or she needs to check with an attorney, this does not alter the fact that you are giving advice on which the client might rely.

BE ON THE SAFE SIDE.   What constitutes the giving of legal advice is difficult to pin down. As you read earlier, paralegals are permitted to advise clients on a number of matters, and drawing the line between permissible and impermissible advice may at times be difficult. To be on the safe side (and avoid potential liability for the unauthorized practice of law), a good rule of thumb is the following:

> **Never advise a client or other person on any matter if the advice may alter the legal position or legal rights of the one to whom the advice is given.**

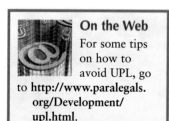

On the Web
For some tips on how to avoid UPL, go to **http://www.paralegals. org/Development/ upl.html.**

Whenever you are pressured to render legal advice—as you surely will be at one time or another, by your firm's clients or others—say that you cannot give legal advice because it is against the law to do so. Offer to find an attorney who can answer the client's questions. Paralegals usually find that a frank and honest approach provides the best solution to the problem.

DEVELOPING PARALEGAL SKILLS
Avoiding UPL Problems

Jenna Martin, a paralegal, is attending a client's holiday party. She is the first person from her firm to arrive at the party. As she enters the room, Mr. Holbrook, the president of the company, introduces himself to Jenna. She responds, saying, "It's nice to meet you. I'm Jenna Martin, with the firm of Atkins & White." Assuming that Jenna is an attorney, Holbrook begins to ask her for legal advice about a tax problem that the company is having. Jenna now needs to take action to avoid the unauthorized practice of law.

TIPS ON HOW TO AVOID UPL PROBLEMS

- Always introduce yourself as a paralegal or legal assistant.

- Always include your title when signing letters or other documents.

- If a letter contains information that may be construed as legal advice, make it clear that the attorney is the source of that advice.

- Make sure that your nonattorney status is clearly indicated on business cards and company letterhead.

- Always disclose your status to a court or other tribunal.

- If a client does not understand your role, explain it. Make it clear that paralegals may not give legal advice.

- Refer the client to an attorney for legal advice.

Representing Clients in Court

The rule that only attorneys—with limited exceptions—can represent others in court has a long history. Recall from the discussion of attorney regulation earlier in this chapter that attorney licensing was initially required only for court representation. In the last few decades, the ethical reasoning underlying this rule has been called into question by two developments.

First, in 1975 the United States Supreme Court held that people have a constitutional right to represent themselves in court.[7] Some people have questioned why a person can represent himself or herself in court but cannot hire a person more educated in the law to provide representation unless that person is a licensed attorney. Second, the fact that paralegals are allowed to represent clients before some federal and state government agencies, such as the federal Social Security Administration and state welfare departments (as will be discussed in Chapter 11), has called into question the ethical underpinnings of this rule. Nonetheless, as a paralegal you should know that you are not allowed to appear in court on behalf of your supervising attorney—although local courts in some states are carving out exceptions to this rule for limited purposes.

Disclosure of Paralegal Status

Because of the close working relationship between an attorney and a paralegal, a client may have difficulty perceiving that the paralegal is not also an attorney. For example, a client's call to an attorney may be transferred to the attorney's paralegal if the attorney is not in the office. The paralegal may assume that the client knows that he or she is not an attorney and may speak freely with the client about a legal matter, advising the client that the attorney will be in touch with the client shortly. The client, however, may assume that the paralegal is an attorney and may make inferences based on the paralegal's comments that result in actions with

Freelance Paralegal

DOROTHY SECOL has worked in the legal profession for over thirty years and has been a freelance paralegal since 1982. She maintains an office in Allenhurst, New Jersey. Secol is a graduate of Monmouth University, West Long Branch, New Jersey.

Secol is a member of the National Association of Legal Assistants (NALA) and received her CLA status in 1978. In addition, she is a former trustee of the Central Jersey Paralegal Association and a former vice president and trustee of the Legal Assistants Association of New Jersey. She is an associate member of the New Jersey State Bar Association and serves on its Paralegal Committee and Foreclosure Committee. She is also on the Paralegal Advisory Boards of Brookdale Community College and Ocean County College and is a mediator for three courts in her area.

Secol is the author of Starting and Managing Your Own Business: A Freelancing Guide for Paralegals, *published by Aspen Publishing Company, and has written articles for the* New Jersey Law Journal *and* New Jersey Lawyer. *In addition, Secol was a petitioner in the case of* In re Opinion 24 of the Committee on the Unauthorized Practice of Law, 128 N.J. 114 (1992). *In that case, the court held that "there is no distinguishable difference between an in-house and freelance paralegal working under the direct supervision of an attorney."*

What do you like best about your work?

"The aspect I like most about my work is the creativity. Whether it's defining an issue and then researching it, writing an argument to oppose or support your position, drafting a contract or a pleading, or working up a file, I am using my intellect and judgment. I love the fact that the law changes constantly—no day is ever the same. There is never any boredom to contend with, and you constantly have to be on your toes to keep up with the changes.

I love the excitement of running a business. The entrepreneurial aspect of being a freelance paralegal has allowed me the opportunity to grow and to learn how to be a businessperson as well as a paralegal. I have to deal with employees, vendors, clients, and suppliers, as well as provide for insurance, office equipment, advertising, marketing, technology, and much, much more. The flexibility of being in business has allowed me to spend time with my family when needed. I have had a chance to meet people from all over, to learn how different attorneys tackle problems, and to learn from different experiences. Working for many attorneys at one time gives you a different perspective than you would have if you worked for one attorney or for attorneys in one firm with a specific ideology."

What is the greatest challenge that you face in your area of work?

"The greatest challenge I have is consistently providing excellent services, maintaining professionalism at all times, and producing a product for the attorney that is as near perfect as it can get. Attorneys use the services of a freelance paralegal because they are short staffed, they do not have personnel with knowledge in a certain area of substantive law, or someone on their staff is on vacation or taking sick leave. It is up to me to ensure that the product they receive is perfect; otherwise, they don't need us. We must provide a better service than they are used to. Our services are our marketing tools."

What advice do you have for would-be paralegals in your area of work?

"Freelancing is not for the recent college graduate or someone with one or two years of experience; it is for the seasoned, experienced paralegal. To freelance, you must have a certain business acumen. Freelancing is more than just being a paralegal; it means running a business, whether it is out of your house or out of an office. You must have a certain temperament and personality. Some of the necessary characteristics are: (1) you must be a perfectionist—you are committed to be the very best you can be and you are not afraid of meeting change or of being different; (2) you must be a risk taker—you have to look for opportunities where your services are needed, and you also must learn to create a need where there was none before; (3) you must have a positive attitude and a good self-image, and you must know that you can do the job; and (4) you must have the necessary skills in order to be successful, which means being up to date on your market areas and

Freelance Paralegal *Continued*

"Freelancing is more than just being a paralegal; it means running a business . . . ."

your areas of substantive law, as well as having the very latest knowledge on which to base your business decisions (including knowledge of new technology, equipment, and so forth)."

What are some tips for success as a paralegal in your area of work?

"You must have a quality program for your services. Offer services above and beyond that which are required, and make your service indispensable. You should also know your market and your competition. If you are a real estate paralegal, be sure you are in an area where there is a need for those services. Choose your areas of substantive law based on your expertise, and then market them to those attorneys that will need your services. Additionally, you should establish goals. Be sure to have a business plan in place. Know where you want to be and how you expect to get there. You also need to plan your finances carefully. You will not have a weekly paycheck. Be sure you have enough capitalization to tide you over until your business picks up enough for you to meet all your financial obligations. Remember, you are now in business and will have certain responsibilities to meet, such as buying and maintaining equipment, supplies, rent, insurance, and subscriptions."

harmful consequences—in which event the paralegal might be charged with the unauthorized practice of law.

To avoid such problems, you should always do the following:

> ▓ **When dealing with clients or potential clients, disclose your paralegal status to ensure that they realize that you are a paralegal and not an attorney.**

Similarly, in correspondence with clients or others, you should indicate your nonattorney status by adding "Paralegal" or "Legal Assistant" after your name. If you have printed business cards or if your name is included in the firm's letterhead or other literature, also make sure that your nonlawyer status is clearly indicated there.

Guideline 1 of NALA's Model Standards and Guidelines emphasizes the importance of the disclosure of paralegal status by stating that all legal assistants have an ethical responsibility to "[d]isclose their status as legal assistants at the outset of any professional relationship with a client, other attorneys, a court or administrative agency or personnel thereof, or members of the general public." Disciplinary Rule 1.7 of NPFA's Model Code of Ethics and Professional Responsibility also stresses the importance of disclosing paralegal status. Guideline 4 of the ABA's Model Guidelines places on attorneys the responsibility for disclosing the nonattorney status of paralegals:

> It is the lawyer's responsibility to take reasonable measures to ensure that clients, courts, and other lawyers are aware that a legal assistant, whose services are utilized by the lawyer in performing legal services, is not licensed to practice law.

Paralegals Freelancing for Attorneys

Some paralegals have their own businesses and work as freelance paralegals for attorneys, as you learned in the previous chapter. In the early 1990s, there was some concern over whether freelance paralegals were, by definition, sufficiently supervised by attorneys to avoid liability for the unauthorized practice of law. In a landmark decision in 1992, the New Jersey Supreme Court stated that it could find no reason why freelance paralegals could not be just as adequately supervised by the attorneys for whom they worked as those paralegals working in attorneys' offices. Since that decision, courts in several other states and ethical opinions issued by various state bar associations have held that freelance paralegals who are adequately supervised by attorneys are not engaging in the unauthorized practice of law.

In its opinion, the New Jersey Supreme Court also called for the establishment of a Committee on Paralegal Education and Regulation to study the practice of paralegals and make recommendations to the court. The committee's report, submitted to the court in 1998, recommended that paralegals in New Jersey should be subject to state licensing requirements. This recommendation caused widespread debate among legal professionals in New Jersey and elsewhere—as you will read shortly.

Legal Technicians (Independent Paralegals) and UPL

As mentioned in Chapter 2, legal technicians (also called independent paralegals) provide "self-help" legal services directly to the public. Since the 1970s, when these types of services began to spring up around the country, the courts have had to wrestle with questions such as the following: If an independent paralegal advises a customer on what forms are necessary to obtain a simple, uncontested divorce, how those forms should be filed with the court, how the court hearing should be scheduled, and so on, do those activities constitute the practice of law?

Generally, the mere dissemination of legal information does not constitute the unauthorized practice of law. There is a fine line, however, between disseminating legal information (by providing legal forms to a customer, for example) and giving legal advice (which may consist of merely selecting the forms that best suit the customer's needs)—and the courts do not always agree on just where this line should be drawn.

EARLY CASES.   An early case on this issue was *The Florida Bar v. Brumbaugh*,[8] which was decided in 1978 by the Florida Supreme Court. The case was brought by the Florida Bar against Brumbaugh, who prepared legal documents for people who sought a simple, uncontested divorce. Brumbaugh prepared all the necessary court documents and told her customers how to file the documents with the court, how to schedule the court hearings, and—in a conference the day before the hearing—what would occur at the hearing.

The Florida Bar claimed that Brumbaugh was engaging in the practice of law in violation of the state's UPL statute. The Florida Supreme Court held that Brumbaugh could sell legal forms and other printed information regarding divorces and other legal procedures, that she could fill in the forms as long as the customer provided the information in writing, and that she could advertise her services. She could not, however, advise customers of their legal rights; tell them which forms should be used, how they should be filled out, and where to file them; or tell customers how to present their cases in court.

A year later, the same court decided *The Florida Bar v. Furman*,[9] which involved a woman who performed legal services very similar to those performed by Brumbaugh. The court held that the woman, Furman, had engaged in the unauthorized practice of law by failing to comply with the decision in *Brumbaugh*. The *Furman* case received substantial publicity when Furman disobeyed an *injunction* (a court order to cease engaging in the prohibited activities) and was sentenced to prison for **contempt of court** (failing to cooperate with a court order).

contempt of court
The intentional obstruction or frustration of the court's attempt to administer justice. A party to a lawsuit may be held in contempt of court (punishable by a fine or jail sentence) for refusing to comply with a court's order.

> ## ETHICAL CONCERN
> ### Saying "If I were you . . ." and UPL
>
> Any time that a paralegal, in responding to someone concerned about legal rights, says, "If I were you, I would . . . ," the paralegal is, in effect, giving legal advice—and engaging in the unauthorized practice of law. For example, assume that a client calls your law office, and you take the call. The client, Mrs. Rabe, is an older woman who is very upset about the fact that an insurance company has not paid on a $3,000 life insurance policy that she purchased covering the life of her grandson, who has just died. Mrs. Rabe tells you all of the details, and you feel that even though she might win a lawsuit against the insurance company, she would probably spend a lot more than $3,000 in the process. Mrs. Rabe wants to know if your supervising attorney will see her about the case, and when you tell her the attorney is out of town, she presses you for advice. Finally, you say, "Well, if I were you, I'd take the case to small claims court. You would not have to hire an attorney, it would be less costly, and you might recover some of the money." What you have not told Mrs. Rabe is that if she sues the insurance company, she might win not just the $3,000 payment but also substantial punitive damages for the insurance company's wrongful behavior—and might also benefit from other penalties imposed under the state's insurance statute.

AN ONGOING PROBLEM.   Legal technicians continue to face UPL allegations brought against them primarily by UPL committees and state bar associations. In 1997, an Oregon appellate court upheld the conviction of Robin Smith for engaging in UPL. In that case, the bar association complained that Smith provided consumers with various legal forms, advised them on which forms to use, and assisted them in completing the documents. The court reasoned that by drafting and selecting documents and giving advice with regard to their legal effect, Smith was practicing law.[10]

In 1998, a number of legal technicians were facing UPL charges in one case in California when the legislature enacted Senate Bill 1418. The new law authorized nonlawyers to provide certain types of legal services directly to the public. Under that law, a person who qualifies and registers with the county as a "legal document assistant" (LDA) may assist clients in filling out legal forms but cannot advise clients which forms to use.[11] After the LDA law passed, the case was settled.

THE CONTROVERSY OVER LEGAL SOFTWARE.   Notably, even publishers of self-help law books and computer software programs have come under attack for the unauthorized practice of law.[12] For example, in 1999 a Texas Court held that the legal software program *Quicken Family Lawyer* violated Texas's UPL statute. The program provided a hundred different legal forms (including contracts, real estate leases, and wills), along with instructions on how to fill out these forms. Because the program automatically adapted the content of a legal form to the responses of the user, the court held that it gave legal advice and thus constituted UPL.[13]

Shortly after the court's decision to prohibit the sale of the software, the Texas legislature amended the UPL statute to reverse the court's ruling. The new law in Texas explicitly authorizes the sale of legal self-help software, books, forms, and similar products to the public.[14] Note, however, that the Texas law authorizes these products to be used *only* for "self-help." The law does not permit persons who are not licensed to practice law (such as legal technicians) to utilize these programs to give legal advice or assistance to others.

DO PARALEGALS WHO OPERATE AS LEGAL TECHNICIANS VIOLATE UPL?
State courts and legislatures are still debating whether it is legal, at least in some situations, for legal technicians to operate without a lawyer's supervision. Generally, unless a state statute or rule specifically allows paralegals to assist the public directly without the supervision of an attorney, paralegals would be wise not to engage in such practices. Most state courts are much more likely to find that a paralegal is engaging in UPL than that a publisher of legal software is doing so. This is because of the special relationship of trust that develops between the paralegal and the client and the potential for abuse. In California, an LDA can assist a person by filling out forms, but the LDA must be careful not to suggest what forms to fill out. A legal technician in Texas who uses a software program designed to help people file for bankruptcy may be engaging in UPL. Because the consequences of violating state UPL statutes can be so serious, we cannot emphasize enough the following advice:

> ✖ **Any paralegal who contemplates working as a legal technician (independent paralegal) must thoroughly investigate the relevant state laws and court decisions on UPL before offering any services directly to the public and must rigorously abide by the letter of the law.**

SHOULD PARALEGALS BE LICENSED?

One of the major issues facing legal professionals and other interested groups today is whether paralegals should be subject to direct regulation by the state through licensing requirements. Unlike certification, which was discussed in Chapter 1, licensing involves direct and mandatory regulation, by the state, of an occupational or professional group. When licensing requirements are established for a professional group, such as for attorneys, a license is required in order for a member of the group to practice his or her profession.

Movements toward regulation of paralegals have been motivated in large part by the activities of legal technicians, or independent paralegals—those who provide legal services directly to the public without attorney supervision. Many legal technicians call themselves paralegals even though they have little, if any, legal training, background, or experience. Yet at the same time, those who cannot afford to hire an attorney can benefit from the self-help services provided by legal technicians who do have training and experience.

General Licensing

general licensing
A type of licensing in which all individuals within a specific profession or group (such as paralegals) must meet licensing requirements imposed by the state before they may legally practice their profession.

A number of states—including Arizona, Hawaii, Maine, Minnesota, New Jersey, New York, Oklahoma, Rhode Island, South Dakota, Texas, Utah, and Wisconsin— have considered implementing a **general licensing** program. A general licensing program would require all paralegals to meet certain educational requirements and other specified criteria before being allowed to practice their profession.

For example, after five years of study, the New Jersey Supreme Court Committee on Paralegal Education and Regulation recommended that paralegals be licensed to practice their profession. The committee's report proposed that paralegals be subject to state licensure based on demonstrated educational requirements and knowledge of the ethical rules governing the legal profession. Less than one week later, however, the New Jersey Supreme Court declined to follow the

9. What is the practice of law? What is the unauthorized practice of law (UPL)? How might paralegals violate state statutes prohibiting UPL?

10. What would the licensing of paralegals involve? What is limited licensing? What are some of the pros and cons in the debate over paralegal licensing?

❋ ETHICAL QUESTIONS

1. Anton Snow, a paralegal, has been asked to research the cases decided by courts in his state to see if he can find a case in which a landlord was held liable for crimes caused by a third party (someone other than the landlord or the tenant) on leased premises. Anton finds a case in which the trial court held that a landlord was liable for harms suffered by a plaintiff when she was mugged and robbed in an apartment complex's parking lot. Anton does not take the time to update the case. He therefore fails to find out that the state court of appeals later reversed the trial court's decision. Thus, the trial court's decision, which Anton gives to his supervising attorney, is no longer "good law." The supervising attorney, relying on Anton's research, advises the client accordingly. Discuss the potential problems that the client, the attorney, and Anton might face as a result of Anton's failure to update the trial court's decision.

2. Norma Sollers works as a paralegal for a small law firm. She is a trusted, experienced employee who has worked for the firm for twelve years. One morning, Linda Lowenstein, one of the attorneys, calls in from her home and asks Norma to sign Linda's name to a document that must be filed with the court that day. Norma has just prepared the final draft of the document and placed it on Linda's desk for her review and signature. Linda explains to Norma that because her child is sick, she does not want to leave home to come into the office. Norma knows that she should not sign Linda's name—only the client's attorney can sign the document. She mentions this to Linda, but Linda says, "Don't worry. No one will ever know that you signed it instead of me." How should Norma handle this situation?

3. Matthew Hinson is a legal technician. He provides divorce forms and typing and filing services to the public at very low rates. Samantha Eggleston uses his services. She returns with the forms filled out, but she has one question: How much in monthly child-support payments will she be entitled to receive? How may Matthew legally respond to this question?

❋ PRACTICE QUESTIONS AND ASSIGNMENTS

1. Kathryn Borstein works as a legal assistant for the legal department of a large manufacturing corporation. In the process of interviewing a middle-management accountant with the company relating to an employment discrimination lawsuit, Kathryn discovers that a few of the top executives cheat on their income tax returns by not declaring a portion of their bonuses. Kathryn becomes disenchanted with her job with the corporation for these and other reasons and finds a new job with a law firm. Her supervising attorney in the new law firm is involved in a case against her former employer. The attorney tells Kathryn that the only way to deal with these big corporations is to get whatever dirt you can on them and then threaten to go to the press. He wants to know if she can give him any such information. Can she tell him the "dirt" about the executives who cheat on their income taxes? Why or why not? What ethical rules are involved in her decision?

2. Peter Smith, a paralegal, is using the Internet to find property tax records for a client. The client has come to the firm because he wants to buy a parcel of property, but he also wants to make sure that the property taxes have been paid. Peter finds a Web site for the county register of deeds. He locates the property and notes that, according to the information given on the Web page, the taxes have been paid. He prints the page and writes a brief memo to the attorney. The attorney then advises the client that the taxes have been paid and that it is okay to go ahead and purchase the property. The client does so, but several weeks later he receives a notice that he owes $6,500 in back taxes. The client, who is understandably upset, complains to Peter's boss. Peter is sent to the county register of deeds to look up the records relating to the property. Peter finds that the correct information was in the county's records but was not on the Web site. He makes a copy of what he finds and

returns to the office. What ethical rule has been violated here? What do these "facts" reveal about the reliability of information posted on the Internet?

3. In which of the following instances may confidential client information be disclosed?

   a. A client's daughter calls to find out whether her mother has left her certain property in her will. The mother does not want the daughter to know that the daughter has been disinherited until the will is read after the mother's death.

   b. The client in a divorce case threatens to hire a hit man to kill her husband because she perceives that killing her husband is the only way that she can stop him from stalking her. It is clear that the client intends to do this.

   c. A former client sues her attorney for legal malpractice in the handling of a breach-of-contract case involving her cosmetics home-sale business. The attorney discloses that the client is having an affair with her next-door neighbor, a fact that is unrelated to the malpractice or breach-of-contract case.

4. According to this chapter's text, which of the following tasks may a paralegal legally perform?

   a. Draft a complaint at an attorney's request.

   b. Interview a witness to a car accident.

   c. Represent a client before an administrative agency.

   d. Investigate the facts of a car-accident case.

   e. Work as a freelance paralegal for attorneys.

   f. Work as a legal technician providing legal services directly to the public.

5. Review the facts in Ethical Question 3 above. What do the following ethical codes say about the unauthorized practice of law, and how would these statements apply to Hinson's situation? Could Hinson be disciplined if he gave Eggleston the information she requested?

   a. NFPA's Model Code of Ethics and Professional Responsibility (see Appendix C or visit NFPA's Web site at **http://www.paralegals.org**).

   b. NALA's Code of Ethics and Professional Responsibility (see Appendix A or visit NALA's Web site at **http://www.nala.org**).

Do your answers differ? If so, how?

✳ QUESTIONS FOR CRITICAL ANALYSIS

1. What could happen if the legal profession were not regulated? Why are ethical rules needed? What might happen if, for example, there were no rule governing competence in the profession?

2. The material in the chapter indicates that lawyers are largely responsible for regulating their own conduct. What do you think of a system in which members of a profession regulate themselves? Is this a good system? Can you think of a better alternative?

3. An experienced legal secretary opened a business, Northside Secretarial Services, for the purpose of delivering certain legal services directly to the public. Specifically, she prepared legal documents—and provided detailed instructions for filing the documents with the court and for service of process—in divorce and adoption cases. She held briefing sessions during which she gave detailed instructions about trials and hearings, including the types of questions that the court would ask and the responses that her "clients" should give to the court. The secretary advertised her services in a local newspaper, holding herself out to be an "expert in family law." She also advertised the sale of "do-it-yourself" divorce kits. She charged no more than $50 for her services, and many of her "clients" were indigent and illiterate.

The bar association in her state charged her with the unauthorized practice of law. A former client gave testimony that the secretary had advised her to lie about the date of her second marriage, because she could not remember it, in the complaint filed with the court to start divorce proceedings. Another former client testified that when he had found out that his wife was abusing the children, he had been advised he should not try to change the petition for divorce to seek custody of the minor children but should leave it to the state agency to handle abuse and custody issues.

What was the likely result of the state bar association's filing of unauthorized-practice-of-law charges against the legal secretary? How might the legal secretary have responded to these charges? What would result if the legal secretary was enjoined by court order from engaging in these activities and continued to do so anyway?

4. In your view, are personal and legal ethics totally distinct? How, generally, do (or should) personal and legal ethical standards interrelate?

5. If it were up to you to devise a set of ethical standards for the legal profession, would they be any different from those presented in the chapter? If so, in what ways?

6. Compare the activities that constitute the unauthorized practice of law with the activities in which paralegals may lawfully engage under the guidelines for the utilization of legal assistants. Why do you think that the activities that constitute the unauthorized practice of law are prohibited for nonlawyers? Could someone with training as a legal assistant compe-

tently handle some of these activities? If so, which ones?

7. What is the difference between a freelance paralegal and a legal technician? What are the advantages and disadvantages of each type of status? Would you prefer to work as a freelance paralegal or as a legal technician? Why?

8. Do you think that paralegals should be licensed? Why or why not? If you think that they should be licensed, what type of license should they be granted—general or limited? What impact would this have on paralegals? What impact would it have on the legal profession as a whole?

✳ PROJECTS

1. Go to the library and find out the requirements for becoming licensed to practice law in your state. These rules may be located in your state's court rules. Do your state's rules differ from the requirements mentioned in the text? If so, how?

2. Obtain a copy of your state's ethics rules for attorneys. These rules may be located in your state's court rules. How do the competence, confidentiality, and conflict-of-interest rules in your state compare with the ABA's Model Rules on these topics presented in this chapter? Using Microsoft's *PowerPoint* software or Corel's *Presentations* software, prepare a slide show comparing the two sets of rules.

3. Look in your local telephone book or in a directory of attorneys issued by your state bar association for an agency or commission that is responsible for dis-

ciplining attorneys. Contact the agency or commission to find out how attorneys are disciplined in your state. Learn about the various degrees of discipline that may be imposed. If disciplinary hearings are open to the public, try to attend one of the hearings. What is your impression?

4. Contact your state bar association to find out if paralegals may join. If they may, present the material, including the requirements for admission and fees, to the class.

5. Go to the library and find materials on the ethical standards of professions other than the legal profession. What ethical concerns do the rules of other professions cover? How are the rules of other professions similar to or different from the legal profession's ethical rules?

✳ USING INTERNET RESOURCES

1. Go to http://www.paralegals.org, the home page for the National Federation of Paralegal Associations (NFPA). Click on the box titled "Profession Development," and then click on "Ethics," which will take you to a page that lists, among other things, NFPA's ethics opinions. Then do the following:

   a. List five issues that NFPA has addressed in these opinions.

   b. Choose one opinion and write a paragraph explaining why the issue dealt with in the opinion is important for paralegals.

   c. Choose the same or a different opinion, read completely through it, and write a paragraph summa-

rizing NFPA's advice on the issue being addressed in the opinion.

2. Go online and find the case *In re Powell*, 266 Bankr. 450 (N.D.Cal. 2001). It can be accessed through the FindLaw Web site at http://www.findlaw.com. Under "Legal Professionals," click on "US State Resources" and scroll down to "California." When the California page appears, select "CA Judicial Decisions" under "Laws: Cases & Codes." Then, under "Federal," select "US Bankruptcy Court—Northern District of California Opinions." You will find that to access this case, you need to know the name of the judge who authored the opinion. Click on "Judge Alan

Jaroslovsky," and a list of the opinions written by this judge will appear. To retrieve the case, you can either browse through the list of opinions for 2001 and click on the opinion titled "Memorandum of Decision Re: Unauthorized Practice of Law" (on 5/7/01) or click on the search box and enter the word "Powell." Once you obtain the court's opinion for *In re Powell*, read through it and answer the following questions:

a. Why were Randy Wilson and Terry L. Clark (doing business as Professional Paralegal Services) charged with the unauthorized practice of law? What specific acts did they perform?

b. Why is the case being heard by a bankruptcy court?

c. From your reading of the case, are paralegals generally allowed to help members of the public fill out forms (bankruptcy petitions) to initiate bankruptcy proceedings? If so, what did these paralegals do wrong?

d. What does the court say that Section 110 of the Bankruptcy Code requires of paralegals who prepare bankruptcy forms?

e. What sanctions did the court impose on Wilson and Clark for engaging in the unauthorized practice of law?

3. Go online to **http://www.findlaw.com** to access information on state bar associations, membership rules, ethics rules, and attorney discipline. Then answer the following questions:

a. What are the requirements for an attorney to become licensed to practice law in your state? (Hint: The way that these requirements are listed varies from state to state. You may find these requirements under such listings as "Admissions," "Board of Law Examiners," "Supreme Court Rules," or "Court of Appeals Rules.") Do they differ from the requirements described in this chapter? If so, how?

b. Look up your state's ethical rules on competence, confidentiality, and conflict of interest. Are those rules the same as the rules discussed in this chapter? If not, what are the differences? Are the rules in your state stricter or more lenient?

c. Look for rules on the admission of paralegals to the state bar association in your state. Also look for your state's guidelines on the utilization of legal assistants. What did you find?

END NOTES

1. Some legal professionals maintain that statutes that prohibit nonlawyers from practicing law constitute a form of direct regulation, because paralegals who violate such statutes may be directly sanctioned (in the form of criminal penalties) under those laws. In this chapter, we use the term *direct regulation* to mean state regulation of a specified professional group, particularly through state licensing requirements.

2. There are exceptions, however. In some states, a lower state appellate court performs this function.

3. *Bates v. State Bar of Arizona,* 433 U.S. 350, 97 S.Ct. 2691, 53 L.Ed.2d 810 (1977). (See Chapter 16 for a discussion of how to read case citations.)

4. In some states, including Vermont, one need not have completed a bachelor's degree but must have completed a specified number of credits toward a degree.

5. Note that a few states allow individuals who have not attended law school but who have undertaken a form of independent study and practice (usually as paralegals) to take the bar exam and be admitted to the practice of law.

6. Even this mildest sanction can seriously damage an attorney's reputation within the legal community. In some states, state bar associations publish in their monthly journals the names of violators and details of the violations for all members of the bar to read (see the discus-

sion of attorney disciplinary proceedings in the feature *Today's Professional Paralegal* at the end of this chapter).

7. *Faretta v. California,* 422 U.S. 806, 95 S.Ct. 2525, 45 L.Ed.2d 562 (1975).

8. 355 So.2d 1186 (Fla. 1978).

9. 376 So.2d 378 (Fla. 1979).

10. *Oregon State Bar v. Smith,* 149 Or.App. 171, 942 P.2d 793 (1997).

11. This law is codified in California Business and Professions Code, Sections 6400–6416.

12. *In re Nolo Press/Folk Law, Inc.,* 42 Tex.Sup.Ct.J. 539, 991 S.W.2d 768 (1999).

13. *Unauthorized Practice of Law Committee v. Parsons Technology, Inc.,* 1999 WL 47235 (N.D.Tex. 1999). Note that this case has been overturned.

14. Texas Government Code Section 81.101(c) (Vernon Supp. 2000).

15. California Business and Professions Code, Sections 6450–6456. Enacted in 2000.

16. "Panacea or Pandora's Box—Has the Time Come for Regulation?" *Legal Assistant Today,* July/August 2001, pp. 93–95.

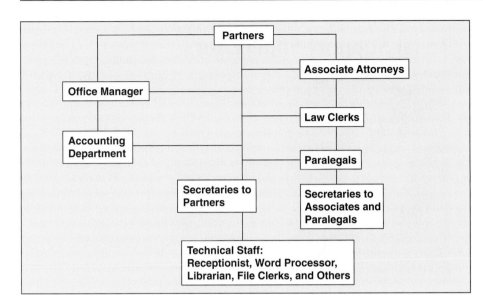

EXHIBIT 4.1
A Sample Organizational Chart for a Law Partnership

technology, such as new docketing software; ordering and monitoring supplies; and generally making sure that the office runs smoothly and that office procedures are established and followed. In a small firm, the office manager might also handle client billing procedures. The hypothetical firm represented in Exhibit 4.1 has an accounting department to perform this function.

The **support personnel** in a large law office may include secretaries, receptionists, bookkeepers, file clerks, messengers, and others. Depending on their functions and specific jobs, support personnel may fall under the supervision of any number of other personnel in the firm. In a very small firm, just one person—the legal secretary, for example—may perform all of the above-mentioned functions.

support personnel
Employees who provide clerical, secretarial, or other support to the legal, paralegal, and administrative staff of a law firm.

EMPLOYMENT POLICIES

Employees of a law firm, which include all personnel other than the partners or those who work for the firm on a contract basis, are subject to the firm's specific employment policies and procedures. A firm's basic rules or policies governing employment relationships may be set forth in an **employment manual** in larger firms. In smaller firms, these rules and policies are often unwritten. In either situation, when you take a job as a paralegal, or perhaps before you accept a position, you will want to become familiar with the firm's basic conditions of employment. There will be an established policy, for example, on how much vacation time you are entitled to during the first year, second year, and so on. There will also be a policy governing which holidays are observed by the firm, how much sick leave you can take, when you are expected to arrive at the workplace, and what will serve as grounds for the employer to terminate your employment.

employment manual
A firm's handbook or written statement that specifies the policies and procedures that govern the firm's employees and employer-employee relationships.

Employment policies and benefits packages vary from firm to firm. A foremost concern of paralegals (and employees generally) is how much they will be paid for their work, how they will be paid (that is, whether they will receive salaries or hourly wages), and what job benefits they will receive. These issues were discussed in detail in Chapter 2, so we will not examine them here. Rather, we look at some other areas of concern to paralegals in regard to employment policies, including performance evaluations and termination procedures.

PARALEGAL PROFILE

Legal Support Supervisor

ANITA HONG *graduated from the paralegal program of St. Mary's College in 1984. She has worked as a paralegal since 1985. Her first paralegal job was with the Oakland city attorney's office, where she started out as one of two paralegals in a pilot program. The program was a success. Since then, Hong has gone on to supervise a paralegal staff for that office and subsequently to become the legal support supervisor for the Oakland city attorney's office.*

Today, in addition to her supervisory duties, Hong also provides paralegal and administrative assistance to the city attorney's office's executive management team. Hong is currently serving as a primary representative in the National Federation of Paralegal Associations (NFPA) on behalf of the San Francisco Paralegal Association.

What do you like best about your work?
"Challenge! From day one, I've been challenged to succeed in various tasks given to me since I began my career as a paralegal in 1985. From there, I was promoted to a legal-assistant supervisor in 1989, and I went on to supervising a staff of paralegals and legal secretaries in 1994. This eventually evolved into a legal support supervisor position in 1997. What I enjoy most is the camaraderie among legal secretaries, paralegals, and attorneys."

What is the greatest challenge that you face in your area of work?
"Communication and customer service. When problems arise, I am one of the problem solvers and troubleshooters for my staff and the office as a whole. The types of problem solving range from customer service, to discovery issues, to staff issues. I have to be fast on my feet and resolve issues as quickly as possible. As a supervisor, I work very hard to stay on top of my work and deal with staff and office issues as they come up."

What advice do you have for would-be paralegals in your area of work?
"Be a mentor to paralegals new to the field. Give back what you've gained. As with any profession, it's okay to be the 'new kid on the block.' Look for mentors to guide you. I was very blessed to have a mentor to guide me as a paralegal and, eventually, as a supervisor. Also, I am fortunate to have a supervisor to help me to become a better supervisor."

"As paralegals, we must hold ourselves to the same level of professional and ethical standards as the attorneys in the legal profession."

What are some tips for success as a paralegal in your area of work?
"Besides having excellent analytical skills and common sense, you must have good people skills. It is important to have good relationships with your clients and your co-workers. Be a quick learner and be a team player. Show a 'can do' attitude, and be flexible about new tasks given to you. Show that you are 'in control.' Be ready to ask for guidance. If you make a mistake, be accountable for your actions without being defensive. Otherwise, people will lose confidence in your credibility and professional ability. As paralegals, we must hold ourselves to the same level of professional and ethical standards as the attorneys in the legal profession."

EXHIBIT 4.2

Factors That May Be Considered in a Performance Evaluation

1. RESPONSIBILITY
Making sure that all tasks are performed on time and following up on all pending matters.

2. EFFICIENCY
Obtaining good results in the least amount of time.

3. PRODUCTIVITY
Producing a sufficient quantity of work in a given time period.

4. COMPETENCE
Knowledge level and skills.

5. INITIATIVE
Applying intelligence and creativity to tasks and making appropriate recommendations.

6. COOPERATION
Getting along well with others on the legal team.

7. PERSONAL FACTORS
Appearance, grooming habits, friendliness, poise, and so forth.

8. DEPENDABILITY
Arriving at work consistently on time and being available when needed.

Performance Evaluations

Many law firms have a policy of conducting periodic performance evaluations, and these evaluations are used to determine if the employee receives a raise. Usually, performance is evaluated annually, but some firms conduct evaluations every six months.

Know What Is Expected of You.   Because paralegal responsibilities vary from firm to firm, no one evaluation checklist applies to every paralegal. Some of the factors that may be considered during a performance evaluation are indicated in Exhibit 4.2. Note, though, that performance evaluations are much longer and more detailed than the list shown in the exhibit. For example, each major item in that list may have several subheadings and perhaps further subheadings under those subheadings. Normally, under each item listed on a performance evaluation is a series of options—ranging from "very good" to "unsatisfactory" or something similar—for the supervisor or attorney to check.

When you begin work as a paralegal, you should learn at the outset exactly what your duties will be and what performance is expected of you. This way, you will be able to prepare for your first evaluation from the moment you begin working. You will not have to wait six months or a year before you learn that you were supposed to be doing something that you failed to do.

Be Prepared.   Make sure that you prepare for the evaluation and conduct yourself professionally at all times. Be your own advocate. Keep track of your accomplishments, such as the number of billable hours per week or month that you normally generate, so that you can point them out to your supervisor. If you were part of the team that worked many extra hours to win a big case for the firm, mention it during the evaluation. Make your supervisor aware of any way in which you have saved the firm money or contributed to the firm's success. If you have mastered a new software program or passed the CLA or PACE exam, tell this to your supervisor.

Get the Most from Your Performance Evaluation.   Both paralegals and their employers can benefit from the discussions that take place during a performance evaluation. In the busy workplace, you will probably not have much time available to talk with your supervisor about issues that do not relate to immediate work needs. Even if you do find a moment, you may feel awkward bringing up the topic of your performance or discussing a workplace problem. Performance evaluations are designed specifically to allow both sides to exchange their views on such matters.

During performance reviews, you will also learn how the firm rates your performance. You can gain valuable feedback from your supervisor, learn more about your strengths and weaknesses, and identify the areas in which you need to improve your skills. Be sure that you do not react negatively to any criticisms of your performance. Remember that even during an evaluation you are being evaluated. Adopting the right outlook and showing that you appreciate constructive criticism will impress your supervisor.

You can also utilize the evaluation to give your supervisor feedback on the workplace. This is especially useful if you feel you are capable of handling more complex tasks than you are currently being assigned. Attorneys sometimes underutilize paralegals simply because they do not know a paralegal's capabilities. If you gently suggest ways in which your knowledge and experience could be put to better use, sometimes that is all it takes to earn more challenging and rewarding job responsibilities. Also, if you and your supervising attorney never seem to have the time to meet face-to-face for the evaluation, consider writing up your own evaluation and presenting it to him or her for review.

Employment Termination

Virtually all policy manuals deal with the subject of employment termination. If you work for a firm that has prepared such a manual for its employees, the manual will likely specify what kind of conduct serves as a basis for firing employees. For example, the manual might specify that if an employee is absent more than twelve days a year for two consecutive years, the employer has grounds to terminate the employment relationship. The manual will also probably describe employment-termination procedures. For example, the firm might require that it be notified one month in advance if an employee decides to leave the firm; if the employee fails to give one month's notice, he or she may forfeit accumulated vacation time or other benefits on termination.

Employment Discrimination

Traditionally, employment relationships have been governed by the common law doctrine of employment at will. Under this doctrine, employers may hire and fire employees "at will"—that is, for any reason or no reason. Today, courts have created several exceptions to this doctrine, and state and federal statutes now regulate numerous aspects of the employment relationship. Under federal law (and many state statutes), employers may not refuse to hire job applicants, refuse to promote employees, or fire employees for discriminatory reasons—because of the employee's age, gender, or race, for example. These and other laws regulating employment relationships will be discussed in Chapter 10, but it should be mentioned here that virtually every large law firm today has special policies and procedures that must be followed with respect to claims of employment discrimination.

For example, an employee who experiences sexual harassment—a form of gender-based discrimination that is prohibited by federal law and most state laws—may be required by the firm's harassment policy to follow formal complaint channels to resolve the issue. If an employee fails to follow the required proce-

On the Web
For information on federal laws governing employment discrimination, access the Equal Employment Opportunity Commission's Web site at **http://www.eeoc.gov.**

dures, the firm may be able to avoid legal responsibility for the harassment. Similarly, if an employer does not have established procedures in place for dealing with harassment or other forms of discrimination, the employer may find it difficult to avoid liability for the harassment or discriminatory treatment initiated by supervisors or others against a particular employee.

FILING PROCEDURES

Every law firm, regardless of its size or organizational structure, has some kind of established filing procedures. Efficient filing procedures are important in any law firm, because the paperwork generated by even a small firm can be substantial. Efficient filing procedures are particularly necessary in law offices because important and confidential documents must be safeguarded yet be readily retrievable when they are needed. If a client file is misplaced or lost, the client may suffer irreparable harm.

Additionally, documents must be filed in such a way as to protect client confidentiality. The duty of confidentiality was discussed at length in Chapter 3, but it deserves special mention here because of the extent to which it frames all legal work and procedures. This is particularly true of filing procedures. All information received from or about clients, including client files and documents, is considered confidential.

> ※ **A breach of confidentiality by a paralegal or other employee can cause the firm to incur potentially extensive liability.**

If you work for a small firm, filing procedures may be rather informal, and you may even assume the responsibility for organizing and developing an efficient filing system. Larger firms normally have specific procedures concerning the creation, maintenance, use, and storage of office files. If you take a job with a large firm, a supervisor will probably spend some time training you in routine office procedures, including filing procedures. Although the trend today, particularly in larger firms, is toward computerized filing systems, firms routinely create "hard copies" to ensure that files are not lost if a computer system crashes.

Generally, law offices maintain several types of files. Typically, a law firm's filing system will include client files, work product files and reference materials, and forms files (as well as personnel files, which we do not discuss here).

Client Files

To illustrate client filing procedures, we present below the phases in the "life cycle" of a hypothetical client's file. The name of the client is Katherine Baranski; she has just retained one of your firm's attorneys to represent her in a lawsuit that she is bringing against Tony Peretto. Because Baranski is initiating the lawsuit, she is referred to as the *plaintiff*. Peretto, because he has to defend against Baranski's claims, is the *defendant*. The name of the case is *Baranski v. Peretto*. Assume that you will be working on the case and that your supervising attorney has just asked you to open a new case file. Assume also that you have already verified, through a "conflicts check" (discussed in Chapter 3), that no conflict of interest exists.

OPENING A NEW CLIENT FILE.   The first step that you (or a secretary, at your request) will take in opening a new file is to assign the case a file number. For reasons of both efficiency and confidentiality, many firms identify their client files by numbers or some kind of numerical and/or alphabetical sequence instead of the

DEVELOPING PARALEGAL SKILLS
Client File Confidentiality

Robert James, a paralegal with the law firm of Jenkins & Fitzgerald, takes a client's file with him to the law library to do some legal research. While he walks several aisles away to look for a particular legal reference book, Lori Sanger, an attorney from another firm, walks by and notices the file. She can see on the file the law firm's name, the client's name (Purdy Contracting, Inc.), the court's docket number, and the firm's file number. Because she recognizes the client's name, she writes down the docket number, goes to the court clerk's office, and requests the court's file, which is public information. She reads through the file and sees that Purdy Contracting, Inc., a construction company, is being sued for a substantial amount of damages.

Lori has a client who is about to award a big construction project to Purdy Contracting. She calls her client and warns the client that this lawsuit could bankrupt Purdy. As a result, Purdy Contracting does not get the job and complains to Jenkins & Fitzgerald. The firm changes its

policy so that client names no longer appear on the outside of client files.

CHECKLIST FOR CLIENT FILE CONFIDENTIALITY

- Create a confidential name for the client file, using alphabetical and/or numerical sequences.
- Do not leave files out in the open in public places, such as libraries or courts, where their contents can be observed by others.
- Do not leave files in areas within the law firm where other clients might observe a file and its contents.
- Follow the law firm's procedures for closing a file to ensure that extra copies of the documents and letters are destroyed.
- Destroy old files that no longer need to be retained by shredding them.

---

clients' names, as mentioned earlier. The *Baranski v. Peretto* case file might be identified by the letters BARAPE—the first four letters of the plaintiff's name followed by the first two letters of the defendant's name.

Increasingly, law firms are using computerized databases to record and track case titles and files. For example, some firms have file labels containing bar codes in which are embedded attorney codes, subject-matter codes, the client's name and file number, and so forth.

Typically, law firms maintain a master client list on which clients' names are entered alphabetically and cross-referenced to the clients' case numbers. If file numbers consist of numerical sequences, there is also a master list on which the file numbers are listed in numerical order and cross-referenced to the clients' names.

ADDING SUBFILES.   As the work on the *Baranski* case progresses and more documents are generated or received, the file will expand. To ensure that documents will be easy to locate, you will create subfiles. A special subfile might be created for client documents (such as a contract, will, stock certificate, or photograph) that the firm needs for reference or for evidence at trial. As correspondence relating to the *Baranski* case is generated, you will probably add a correspondence subfile. You will also want a subfile for your or the attorney's notes on the case, including research results.

As you will read in Chapters 12 through 14, litigation involves several stages. As the *Baranski* litigation progresses through these various stages, subfiles for documents relating to each stage will be added to the *Baranski* file. Many firms find it useful to color-code or add tabs to subfiles so that they can be readily identified. Often, in large files, an index of each subfile's contents is created and attached to the inside cover of the subfile.

DEVELOPING PARALEGAL SKILLS

A Client Complains about a Bill

Joni Winston takes a phone call for her supervising attorney, Mary Perkins. The caller, Joe Hendry, wants to leave a message regarding the bill for settling his father's estate. Joni tells Hendry that she worked with him on the estate matter and identifies herself as Mary's legal assistant. She asks Hendry for the details of the billing problem. He tells her that he was "double-billed" for the filing of the letters of authority with the probate court and threatens to file a grievance against Mary with the bar association if the matter is not resolved by 5:00 P.M. that day.

Joni sympathizes with Hendry and promises to look into the problem and call him back by the end of the day. Joni and Mary review the bill and determine that a temporary secretary mislabeled the second billing entry. The entry should have read "Preparing estate tax return" instead of "Filing letters of authority with the probate court." The amount billed remains the same. Joni returns Hendry's call, as promised, and explains to him what happened.

TIPS FOR AVOIDING BILLING ERRORS

- Select a billing system that is "user friendly."
- Carefully record your time.
- Establish procedures for regularly turning in time sheets and for recording your time.
- Assign billing tasks to one reliable staff member.
- Have attorneys review bills before they are sent to clients.

necessary in working on behalf of Client A. You spend two hours in the airplane summarizing a document relating to a case for Client B. Who should pay for those two hours, Client A, Client B, or both? In this situation, you could argue—as many attorneys do in similar circumstances—that you generated five billable hours, three on Client A's work and two on Client B's case. This is an example of how double billing can occur.

Double billing also occurs when a firm bills a new client for work that was done for a previous client. For example, suppose that an attorney is working on a case for Client B that is very similar to a case handled by the firm a year ago for Client A. The firm charged Client A $2,000 for the legal services. Because much of the research, writing, and other work done on Client A's case can transfer over to Client B's case, the firm is able to complete the work for Client B in half the time. In this situation, would it be fair to bill Client B $2,000 also? After all, $1,000 of that amount represents hours spent on Client A's case (and for which Client A has already been billed). At the same time, would it be fair to Client A to bill Client B less for essentially the same services? Would it be fair to the firm if it was not allowed to profit from cost-efficiencies generated by overlapping work?

Some firms today are tackling this ethical problem by splitting the benefits derived from cost-efficiencies between the client and the firm. For example, the attorney in the above example might split the savings created by the overlapping research ($1,000) with Client B by billing Client B $1,500 instead of $2,000. Other firms still bill their clients for the time spent on previous work that transfers over to new clients' cases.

THE AMERICAN BAR ASSOCIATION'S RESPONSE TO DOUBLE BILLING.   The American Bar Association (ABA) addressed double billing in a formal ethical opinion issued in 1993. In that opinion, the ABA stated that attorneys are prohibited (under the Model Rules discussed in Chapter 3) from charging more than one client for the same hours of work. Additionally, the ABA rejected the notion that the firm,

TECHNOLOGY AND TODAY'S PARALEGAL

Cyberspace Communications

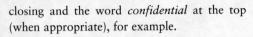

E-mail has become a standard communication tool used by business and professional firms, including law firms. The reason why e-mail is among the fastest-growing technologies is simple: it is a quick, easy-to-use, and inexpensive way to communicate. In large law firms or corporate enterprises, as well as in government agencies, e-mail messages are rapidly replacing the printed "interoffice memos" of the past. E-mail is also becoming a standard way for attorneys and paralegals to communicate with clients, opposing counsel, witnesses, and others.

APPLY PROFESSIONAL STANDARDS TO E-MAIL COMMUNICATIONS

Because e-mail is transmitted almost instantaneously through an electronic medium—computer networks—it may be difficult to remember that it is also a *written communication*. People using e-mail have a tendency to adopt a casual, conversational tone and to ignore the traditional rules of writing, such as sentence structure, spelling, and capitalization. E-mail is still mail, however, and it should reflect the same professional tone and quality that you use in the firm's paper correspondence. If you want to convey a message to someone (especially a client), you need to use clear and effective language.

There are several things you can do to ensure that your e-mail messages are professional and error free. First, choose an e-mail program that has a spell checker. Typos, misspellings, punctuation errors, and grammatical problems all detract from the message and can easily be avoided. Make sure that you also proofread your e-mail carefully. Many times, it is helpful to print out an important message, let it sit for a while, and then review it later when you can see it from a fresh perspective. Also, make sure that you use the same form as you would in an ordinary letter (see Chapter 18), with perhaps a few variations—adding your e-mail address below your name in the

closing and the word *confidential* at the top (when appropriate), for example.

TIPS FOR FORMATTING E-MAIL MESSAGES

Because e-mail often looks different on the recipient's computer screen than it does on your screen, keep the format as simple as possible. Use double spacing between paragraphs rather than indenting with tabs, and do not underline or boldface text (these features often do not transmit clearly from one e-mail system to another). If the message concerns a personal matter and is being sent to a client's workplace or a shared e-mail address, be careful what you identify in the subject line of the e-mail. For example, you could write "documents ready for signature" rather than "bankruptcy petition complete." Also, if your e-mail has an attachment, tell the recipient what word processing program you used to create the attachment, and offer to resend it as a text document if the recipient cannot open it on his or her computer.

TECHNOLOGY TIP

Always print out a copy of your e-mail and retain it in the client's file so that a record exists of important communications. Be sure that any e-mail you send discloses your status as a paralegal (to avoid liability for the unauthorized practice of law). Request the recipient to verify that any important messages have been received (such as when you are notifying the person of a court date). E-mail systems often have a function that allows senders to request a "return receipt," which will confirm that the message you sent was received. You should also respond to incoming e-mail promptly so that the sender knows that you have received the e-mail. Finally, make sure that you know the policies of your firm regarding confidential e-mail. If used carefully, e-mail can be a very efficient way to fulfill your duties and communicate with the firm's clients.

and not the client, should benefit from cost efficiencies created by the firm's work for previous clients. "The lawyer who has agreed to bill solely on the basis of time spent is obliged to pass the benefit of these economies on to the client."

Although ABA opinions are not legally binding on attorneys unless they are adopted by the states as law, they do carry significant weight in the legal community. Courts, for example, have tended to follow the ABA's position in resolving fee disputes. Typically, a court will not award attorneys' fees that it finds to be "excessive, redundant, or otherwise unnecessary."[1] In addition, some states will sanction or even disbar an attorney for double-billing a client.[2]

COMMUNICATING WITH CLIENTS

Sending monthly bills to clients is one way to keep attorney-client communication channels open. Such communication is important because attorneys have a duty to keep clients reasonably informed. Rule 1.4 of the Model Rules of Professional Conduct reads as follows:

> (a) A lawyer shall keep a client reasonably informed about the status of a matter and promptly comply with reasonable requests for information.
> (b) A lawyer shall explain a matter to the extent reasonably necessary to permit the client to make informed decisions regarding the representation.

As a paralegal, you need to be aware that keeping clients reasonably informed about the progress being made on their cases goes beyond courtesy and the cultivation of a client's goodwill—it is a legal duty of attorneys. The meaning of "reasonably informed" varies, of course, depending on the client and on the nature of the work being done by the attorney. In some cases, a phone call every week or two will suffice to keep the client informed. In other cases, the attorney may ask the paralegal to draft a letter to a client explaining the status of the client's legal matter. Some firms institute a regular monthly mailing to update clients on the status of their claims or cases. Generally, as a paralegal, you should discuss with your supervising attorney how each client should be kept informed of the status of his or her case.

Copies of all letters to a client should, of course, be placed in the client's file. Additionally, the client's file should contain a written record of each phone call made to or received from a client. That way, there is a "paper trail" in the event it is ever necessary to provide evidence of communication with the client. (Actually, this is a good practice for all phone calls relating to a client's matter.) You will learn about the various forms of letters that attorneys send to clients in Chapter 18. Increasingly, attorneys and paralegals communicate with clients via e-mail, which can pose special problems—as discussed in this chapter's *Technology and Today's Paralegal* feature on the facing page.

LAW OFFICE CULTURE AND POLITICS

As a paralegal, you will find that each law firm you work for is unique. Even though two firms may be the same size and have similar organizational structures, they will have different cultures, or "personalities." The culture of a given legal workplace is ultimately determined by the attitudes of the firm's owners (the partners, for example) in regard to the fundamental goals of the firm.

Additionally, you will find that each firm has a political infrastructure that may have little to do with the lines of authority and accountability that are spelled out in the firm's employment manual or other formal policy statement. An up-and-coming younger partner in the firm, for example, may in fact exercise more authority than one of the firm's older partners who is about to retire. There may be rivalry between associate attorneys for promotion to partnership status, and you may be caught in the middle of it. If you are aware (and you may not be) of the rivalry and your position relative to it, you may find yourself tempted to take sides—which could jeopardize your own future with the firm.

Unfortunately, paralegals have little way of knowing about the culture and politics of a given firm until they have worked for the firm awhile. Of course, if you know someone who works for or who has worked for a firm and value that

TODAY'S PROFESSIONAL PARALEGAL
Managing Conflict in the Legal Workplace

On Cheryl Hardy's first day at her new job as a legal assistant at Comp-Lease, Inc., a computer leasing corporation, Cheryl is introduced to the department staff by her boss, Dennis Hoyt. Dennis then takes her to meet the legal team. When she meets Jackie, the team secretary, Jackie gives her a frosty "Hello," without  a handshake or smile, and then looks down at the desk. Cheryl does not understand why Jackie seems hostile. She has just met Jackie and has not done or said anything to offend her.

After her lunch break, Cheryl is given her first lease package to prepare. The work consists of drafting a lease (rental) agreement and giving it to the secretary to input into the computer and print out the agreement form. Cheryl prepares the draft and gives it to Jackie. Cheryl is very polite and tells Jackie not to rush because the agreement does not have to be sent out for two days. When Cheryl asks Jackie for the lease two days later, it is not done. Jackie tells Cheryl to check with her after lunch to see how it is coming. "Great," thinks Cheryl to herself, as she walks back to her desk. "My first week on the job and I'll be in trouble because of Jackie."

ANALYZING THE PROBLEM

Cheryl decides to talk to a co-worker, Sandy, about the problem. At lunch, Cheryl explains the situation to Sandy. "She probably resents you," says Sandy. "You see, Jackie has always wanted to be a paralegal. The company has a policy that you have to have a degree or a certificate, even if you have experience, and so she cannot move into a paralegal position without some education. She has not been able to attend a paralegal training program because of family obligations and the expense involved. I'm sure that she knows that you were a legal secretary and that you worked your way through school. When Dennis told us that he had hired a new paralegal, he made your experience and education quite clear."

"Thanks, Sandy," says Cheryl. "That clears up the situation a lot. Now I can understand why she reacted the way she did to me."

SOLVING THE PROBLEM

Cheryl has an idea. She invites Jackie to lunch. Jackie talks about her interest in becoming a paralegal, her frustration with the company's policy, and her inability to get a certificate or degree because of her family obligations and the cost of going back to school. Cheryl tells Jackie that she was in a similar situation and that she got a scholarship from her school to pay for most of her education. She tells Jackie that she might be able to get one, too. She encourages Jackie by telling her, truthfully, that she is obviously bright enough to be a paralegal. Cheryl gives Jackie the name and phone number of Lois Allison, the director of the program that Cheryl attended. "Why don't you call her and tell her that I referred you? Explain that you are in the same situation that I was in when I started. She can tell you what might be available," suggested Cheryl.

When Cheryl returns to her office from lunch, she calls Lois Allison. She explains Jackie's situation and tells Lois that Jackie might be calling to get information on the program and scholarships. Lois replies that she will be happy to talk to Jackie and to help her if she can.

Later that afternoon, when Cheryl gives Jackie a lease package to prepare, Jackie prepares it right away. She even brings it into Cheryl's office, which she does not have to do. "I just want to thank you for going out of your way for me," says Jackie. "I called Lois Allison, and she wants me to come in and fill out some application forms. She thinks that I might qualify for a scholarship. So I might get to go to school after all." Cheryl smiles and replies, "I am glad that Lois could help you."

employee's opinion, you might gain some advance knowledge about the firm's environment from that source. Otherwise, when you start to work for a firm, you will need to learn for yourself about interoffice politics. One way to do this is to listen carefully whenever a co-worker discusses the firm's staff and ask discreet questions to elicit information from co-workers about office politics and unwritten policies. This way, you can both prepare yourself to deal with these issues and protect your own interests. Ultimately, after you've worked for the firm for a time, you will be in a position to judge whether the firm you have chosen is really the "right firm" for you.

KEY TERMS AND CONCEPTS

associate attorney	**legal administrator**	**retainer**
billable hours	**legal-assistant manager**	**retainer agreement**
contingency fee	**limited liability partnership (LLP)**	**shareholder**
double billing	**managing partner**	**sole proprietorship**
employment manual	**office manager**	**staff attorney**
expense slip	**partner**	**statute of limitations**
fixed fee	**partnership**	**support personnel**
forms file	**personal liability**	**time slip**
law clerk	**professional corporation (P.C.)**	**trust account**

 ## CHAPTER SUMMARY

The Organizational Structure of Law Firms	Law firms can be organized in the following ways:
	
	1. *Sole proprietorship*—In a sole proprietorship, one individual attorney owns the business and is entitled to all the firm's profits. That individual also bears the burden of any losses and is personally liable for the firm's debts or other obligations.
	
	2. *Partnership*—In a partnership, two or more individual lawyers jointly own the firm and share in the firm's profits and losses. Attorneys who are employed by the firm but who are not partners (such as associates and staff attorneys) do not share in the profits and losses of the firm.
	
	   a. Generally, partners are subject to personal liability for all of the firm's debts or other obligations.
	
	   b. In many states, firms can organize as *limited liability partnerships,* in which partners are not held personally liable for the malpractice of other partners in the firm.
	
	3. *Professional corporation*—In a professional corporation, two or more individuals jointly own the business as shareholders. The owner-shareholders of the corporation share the firm's profits and losses (as partners do) but are not held personally liable for the firm's debts or obligations beyond the amount they invested in the corporation.

Law Office Management and Personnel	Each law firm has a unique system of management and lines of authority. Generally, the owners of the firm (partners, for example) oversee and manage all other employees. Law firm personnel include associate attorneys; law clerks (sometimes called summer associates); paralegals; administrative personnel, who are supervised by the legal administrator or the office manager; and support personnel, including receptionists, secretaries, file clerks, and others.

Employment Policies	Employment policies relate to compensation and employee benefits, performance evaluations, employment termination, and other rules of the workplace, such as office hours. Frequently (particularly in larger firms), the policies of the firm are spelled out in an employment manual or other writing. Most large firms today have specific policies and procedures that apply to discrimination in the workplace.
Filing Procedures	Every law firm follows certain procedures in regard to its filing system. In larger firms, these procedures may be written down. In smaller firms, procedures may be more casual and based on habit or tradition.
	1. *Confidentiality*—Confidentiality is a major concern and a fundamental policy of every law firm. A breach of confidentiality by anyone in the law office can subject the firm to extensive legal liability. The requirement of confidentiality shapes, to a significant extent, filing procedures.
	2. *Types of files*—A typical law firm has client files, work product files and reference materials, forms files, and personnel files.
	3. *Objective*—Proper file maintenance is crucial to a smoothly functioning firm. An efficient filing system helps to ensure that important documents will not be lost or misplaced and will be available when needed. Filing procedures in a law office must also maximize client confidentiality and the safekeeping of documents.
Financial Procedures	A foremost concern of any law firm is to establish a clear policy on fee arrangements and efficient billing procedures so that each client is billed appropriately.
	1. *Fee arrangements*—Types of fee arrangements include fixed fees, hourly fees, and contingency fees. Clients who pay hourly fees are billed monthly for the time spent by attorneys and other legal personnel on the clients' cases or projects, as well as all costs incurred on behalf of the clients.
	2. *Client trust accounts*—Law firms are required to place all funds received from a client into a special account called a client trust account. This is to ensure that the client's money remains separate from the firm's money. It is extremely important that the funds held in the trust account be used only for expenses relating to the costs of serving that client's needs.
	3. *Billing and timekeeping*—Firms require attorneys and paralegals to document how they use their time. Because the firm's income depends on the number of billable hours produced by the firm's employees, firms usually require attorneys and paralegals to generate a certain number of billable hours per year. This requirement subjects legal personnel to significant pressure. Double billing presents a major ethical problem for law firms.
Communicating with Clients	Attorneys have a duty to keep their clients reasonably informed on matters they are handling for the clients. Paralegals should be aware that this is a legal duty and that they can play a significant role in keeping clients informed. Sending billing statements to clients is one way to communicate with them. Periodic phone calls, letters, and e-mail messages are other ways to keep clients informed.

Law Office Culture and Politics	Each office has its own culture, or personality, which is largely shaped by the attitudes of the firm's owners and the qualities they look for when hiring employees. Each firm also has a political infrastructure that is not apparent to outsiders. Office culture and politics make a great difference in terms of job satisfaction and comfort. Wise paralegals will learn as soon as possible after taking a job, from co-workers or others, about these aspects of the law office.

✳ QUESTIONS FOR REVIEW

1. What are the three basic organizational structures of law firms?

2. What is the difference between an associate and a partner?

3. Who handles the administrative tasks of a law firm? Who supervises the work performed by paralegals in a law firm?

4. Name some of the topics that might be included in an employment policy manual. How do firms evaluate paralegal performance?

5. Why is maintaining confidentiality so important in law offices? How does the confidentiality requirement affect law office procedures and practices?

6. What kinds of files do law firms maintain? What general procedures are typically followed in regard to client files?

7. How does a law firm arrange its fees with its clients? What ethical obligations do attorneys have with respect to legal fees?

8. How do lawyers and legal assistants keep track of their time? What is the difference between billable and nonbillable hours? What is a client trust account?

9. Describe some of the ways that attorneys communicate with clients. Why is communicating with clients important?

10. What is meant by the phrase "law office culture and politics"? How might law office culture and politics affect a paralegal?

✳ ETHICAL QUESTIONS

1. Catherine works as a paralegal for a sole practitioner. Catherine and the legal secretary both work in a large reception area. A client is waiting in the reception area to see the attorney. The legal secretary brings Catherine a fax of a real estate contract that she has just received from a client, Mrs. Henley, and then transfers Mrs. Henley's telephone call to her. Mrs. Henley tells Catherine that the attorney has promised to review the contract prior to the *closing* (the final step in the sale of real estate), which is scheduled for 4 P.M. today. Mrs. Henley is aware that Catherine, before she became a paralegal, worked as a real estate agent and is very experienced in real estate closings. Mrs. Henley insists that Catherine review and approve of the sales contract if the attorney is not available. What ethical problems is Catherine facing? What should she do?

2. Carla Seegen is an experienced legal assistant who is also a licensed realtor. She sold real estate for eight years before becoming a paralegal. Carla works in a small law firm and has recently been assigned to work for Mike McAllister, who is a new attorney and the son of one of the firm's founding partners, John McAllister. Mike is handling a real estate closing for the firm's biggest client. Mike is unfamiliar with the client's business and has no experience in real estate transactions. Carla soon learns of Mike's lack of knowledge and experience because he does not ask her to draft the appropriate documents and undertake the kinds of tasks that are necessary for the closing. Whenever she mentions these things to Mike, however, or offers to show him what must be done, Mike becomes annoyed. Carla likes her job and fears that if she continues to annoy Mike, she will be fired. At the same time, she is concerned about the client's welfare and legal protection. Should she talk to one

of the partners about the problem? Should she discuss the issue with John McAllister, Mike's father? How would you handle the situation?

3. Roberta Miller works as a paralegal, secretary, and receptionist for a sole practitioner. She is working on a bankruptcy file for a client, Gina Thomas. Because Roberta is running late for a meeting with a client, James Archer, she leaves the file—which is clearly marked, "Gina Thomas/Bankruptcy"—on her desk. Mr. Archer comes into her office for the meeting. During the meeting, Roberta turns to her computer to print a document for Mr. Archer to sign. While her back is turned, Mr. Archer notices the Gina Thomas file on Roberta's desk. Gina Thomas is his neighbor. When Roberta turns around, Mr. Archer begins to ask her questions about the file. Has an ethical violation occurred? If so, what rule has been violated, and how could Roberta have avoided the situation?

4. Attorney Smith represents Mrs. White in a divorce and custody action against Mr. White. At the outset of the representation, Mrs. White makes it clear that all that she is interested in is obtaining custody of her children. She even suggests that they propose trading the house for custody of the children in the settlement of the dispute. Attorney Smith tells Mrs. White, "Don't worry, I can get your kids. I don't suggest offering to trade the house for the children, though, because custody rights can always change, and once you give away the house, it's gone and you have nothing." The case drags on for over three years. Mrs. White pays attorney Smith $30,000. At the end of the trial, which lasts for three months, the outstanding bill is over $100,000, and while Mrs. White loses custody of the children, she is awarded the house. The house has enough equity to pay attorney Smith's bill, including significant fees for his legal assistant's time. The attorney demands that Mrs. White give him a lien against her house. She refuses to do so, and they are thrown into a fee dispute. Mrs. White discovers that attorney Smith's fees for his services are significantly higher than what other family law attorneys in her area normally charge. What ethical rule comes into play here? What arguments would Mrs. White make against attorney Smith? What would be his counterarguments?

5. Sam Martin, an attorney, receives a settlement check for a client's case. It is made out jointly to Sam and his client. Sam signs it and instructs his paralegal to deposit it into his law firm's bank account, instead of the client's trust account, because he wants to take out his fee before he gives the client his portion of the money. Can Sam do this? Why or why not? What should Sam's paralegal do?

6. Tom Baker, a paralegal, has been doing research for a client using Westlaw® (a computerized research service discussed in Chapter 17). Tom's supervising attorney tells him to bill the Westlaw® charges that he has just incurred on behalf of one client to both that client's and another client's account. The second client to be billed is a large and prosperous corporation, and the research applies to the second client as well. What ethical violation has occurred? What should Tom do?

❈ PRACTICE QUESTIONS AND ASSIGNMENTS

1. Using the material presented in the chapter, identify the following law practices by their organizational structure:

a. Bill James is an attorney who practices law on his own. He owns his legal practice, the building in which he works, and most of the office furniture. He leases his office equipment. Bill has one secretary and one paralegal who work for him.

b. Roberta Wagner owns a law firm with Joe Rosen. They own equal interests in the firm, participate equally in the firm's management, and share jointly in its profits and losses. Wagner & Rosen has three associates, six secretaries, and three paralegals who work for the firm.

c. Randall Smith and Susan Street own a law firm together as shareholders. They employ eight asso-

ciate attorneys, twelve secretaries, and five legal assistants.

2. Using the material presented in the chapter, identify the following law office personnel:

a. Martha Marsh worked as a paralegal in a large law firm. After thirteen years with the firm, Martha was promoted. She now oversees paralegal staffing, assignments, and professional development.

b. Mark James was hired by the partners of a large law firm, Smith & Smith, to manage the day-to-day operations of the firm.

c. Rhonda Allen is an attorney who works as an employee for Marsh & Martin, a law firm with 250 attorneys.

d. Tom is a file clerk for Jepp & Allen, P.C.

e. Michael O'Dowd is a lawyer. He owns O'Dowd & O'Dowd, P.C., with his sister, Jane.

3. Mary Anne is a paralegal student who has taken a job with a sole practitioner. The attorney has a general practice and handles legal matters relating to family law, real estate, estate planning and probate, and general civil litigation. He is very busy and, consequently, very disorganized. Mary Anne's first task is to help him organize his office, especially his client files. When Mary Anne arrives for her first day of work, she finds that he does not keep his files in the filing cabinets in the office. Rather, they are piled up on his desk, on the credenza, on the floor, and anywhere else that he happens to leave them. Using the material in this chapter, how would you create a filing system for the attorney's office? Be sure to include a discussion of how you would store, maintain, and destroy files.

4. Identify the type of billing that is being used in each of the following examples:

a. The client is billed $150 per hour for a partner's time, $100 per hour for an associate attorney's time, and $70 per hour for a legal assistant's time.

b. The attorney's fee is one-third of the amount that the attorney recovers for the client, either through a pretrial settlement or through a trial.

c. The client is charged $175 to change the name of the client's business firm.

5. Louise Lanham hires John J. Roberts, an attorney with the law firm of Sands, Roberts & Simpson, located at 1000 Plymouth Road, Phoenix, Arizona, to represent her in a divorce. She agrees to pay attorney Roberts a rate of $150 per hour and to pay a legal-assistant rate of $75 per hour. She also agrees to pay all costs and expenses, such as filing fees, expert-witness fees, court-reporter fees, and other fees incurred in the course of her representation. Using Exhibit 4.3, *A Sample Retainer Agreement,* draft a retainer agreement between Louise Lanham and John J. Roberts.

❋ QUESTIONS FOR CRITICAL ANALYSIS

1. Explain what *personal liability* means. What do you think of this concept? Is it fair to require that the personal assets of a partner, such as his or her house, be used to pay partnership debts?

2. Legal assistants, who started out as support personnel in most law firms (because they evolved from the secretarial staff), are increasingly treated as professional staff members. Make a list of the reasons why paralegals should be treated as professional staff members instead of support staff.

3. Do you think that performance evaluations are beneficial? What would happen if performance evaluations were not used? What types of information are included in them? What would you include to make them better?

4. Do you think that it is fair that employers are allowed to hire and fire employees for any reason or no reason under the employment-at-will doctrine? What might have led to the creation of the exceptions to the doctrine that now exist?

5. An employee who experiences sexual harassment may have to file a formal complaint and follow the firm's established procedures for resolving the issue. What impact might this requirement have on sexual-harassment complaints? What might happen if these procedures are not followed?

6. Why are efficient and confidential filing systems and procedures particularly necessary in law offices, more so than in other types of businesses? What might happen without them?

7. Why is it so important for members of a legal team to meticulously keep track of their hours? Why are some hours billable and others not? What happens if accurate billing records are not kept? Why are client trust funds required? Why are these accounts so important? What can happen if client funds are misused?

8. James Johnson is a sole practitioner. His office is about an hour's drive from the federal district court in which he files many of his lawsuits. He used to talk on the car phone to clients as he traveled the two hours to and from the courthouse. He would then bill the client on whose behalf he was going to the courthouse for two hours and the clients with whom he talked on the phone for increments of the same two hours. When the American Bar Association issued its rule prohibiting double billing, he was concerned that the rule would drive him out of business. Johnson feels that there should be different billing rules for lawyers in large firms and lawyers in small practices, such as his. What do you think?

9. Many law firms require their legal assistants to meet a quota of billable hours. Often, legal assistants can

only generate the number of billable hours required per week by working more than the number of hours that they are paid to work. This can lead to the temptation to "pad the bill." Can you think of ways to meet the quota without breaching ethical standards?

10. Other than courtesy and building good client relations, what are the reasons for communicating with clients? Make a list of the ways in which good client communication can be accomplished.

11. Every workplace, business, or law firm has its own personality or culture. How can you find out what a particular firm's culture is? Is this something you should try to determine before accepting employment with a particular firm? Why or why not?

✿ PROJECTS

1. Obtain a page from the "want ads" in your local newspaper or from another source that advertises for legal professionals. Try to determine from the ads whether the firms advertising openings are organized as sole proprietorships, partnerships, or professional corporations.

2. Research legal periodicals, such as *Legal Assistant Today* and the ABA's *Journal of Law Practice Management,* for articles on document/case management software. Write a one-page paper summarizing your findings. Be sure to describe how the software works and how its features and cost compare with other software on the market.

3. Research *Law Office Computing* magazine for articles on law office accounting software. Can you find any software specifically designed for trust accounts? Write a one-page paper summarizing your findings. Include a discussion of the pros and cons of each type of software, the cost, and which one was the most highly recommended.

4. Research various computer publications, such as *PC World, Computerworld,* and *Law Office Computing,* for articles discussing Zip disks and Zip drives. Write a one-page paper summarizing what they are, how they are used, and any pitfalls encountered in using this technology. Explain the uses for this technology in a law firm.

✿ USING INTERNET RESOURCES

1. Go online and access the following site: **http://www.bizfilings.com**. Under the heading "Learn about Incorporating," click on the link for "Incorporation." Summarize in writing the answers given to the following questions:

   a. What are the advantages of incorporation?

   b. What are the disadvantages of incorporation?

   c. How many directors must a corporation have?

   d. What factors should be considered when deciding on a corporate name?

2. Find legal forms on the Internet by going to the following Web site: **http://www.legaldocs.com**. Make a general list of the types of forms that are available.

Are they free? If not, how much do the forms cost? How can they be purchased? What methods of payment are accepted?

3. Research time-and-billing software on the Internet by going to the following Web site: **http://www.timeslips.com**. Under the pull-down menu for Products, select *"Timeslips,"* then click "More details" to read about the latest version of *Timeslips*. What are some of the features of this software? Is it limited to one type of billing arrangement, or is it flexible? Can it create reports? What else can it do? Select "Download Demo" from the Products menu, if you want to try out the program for yourself.

END NOTES

1. *EEOC v. Clear Lake Dodge,* 60 F.3d 1146 (5th Cir. 1995).

2. See, for example, *In re Entin,* 732 N.Y.S.2d 648, 287 A.D.2d 943 (N.Y.A.D. 2001) (attorney disbarred for double-billing New York state).

PART II

INTRODUCTION TO LAW

CHAPTER 5

SOURCES OF AMERICAN LAW

Chapter Outline

✤ INTRODUCTION   ✤ THE FRAMEWORK OF AMERICAN LAW   ✤ PRIMARY SOURCES
OF AMERICAN LAW   ✤ CONSTITUTIONAL LAW   ✤ STATUTORY LAW
✤ ADMINISTRATIVE LAW   ✤ CASE LAW AND THE COMMON LAW TRADITION
✤ NATIONAL AND INTERNATIONAL LAW

After completing this chapter, you will know:

- The meaning and relative importance in the American legal system
  of constitutional law, statutory law, administrative law, and case law.

- How English law influenced the development of the American legal
  system.

- What the common law tradition is and how it evolved.

- The difference between remedies at law and equitable remedies.

- Some of the terms that are commonly found in case law.

- How national law and international law differ and why these bodies
  of law sometimes guide judicial decision making in American courts.

INTRODUCTION

The American legal system is based largely on tradition. For the most part, the colonists who first came to America were governed by English law. As a result, the law of England continued to be the paramount model for American jurists and legislators after the colonists declared their independence from England in 1776. English common law from medieval times onward thus became part of the American legal tradition as well, modified as necessary to suit conditions unique to America.

This chapter opens with a discussion of the nature of law and then focuses on the sources of American law, including constitutional law, statutory law, administrative law, and case law. We then examine the common law tradition and its significance in the American legal system. You will also read how the law of other countries and international law affect judicial decision making in American courts. Another component of the American legal structure—the court system—will be examined in Chapter 6.

On the Web

The University of Michigan maintains a useful site with links to almost all U.S. government Web sites and many foreign government Web sites at **http://www.lib.umich.edu/ govdocs/govweb.html**.

THE FRAMEWORK OF AMERICAN LAW

As you probably realize, the law means different things to different people. Before beginning your study of American law, it is therefore useful to have a basic understanding of what the law is and some of the different approaches to the law that influence judges' decisions. These topics are covered in the following subsections.

What Is the Law?

Most paralegals and lawyers can spend their entire careers dealing with legal matters and still not be able to provide you with a useful definition of **law**. How law is defined frequently depends on the speaker's personal views on such matters as morality, ethics, and truth. The following is a general definition.

> ✖ **Law is a body of rules of conduct established and enforced by the controlling authority (the government) of a society.**

law
A body of rules of conduct established and enforced by the controlling authority (the government) of a society.

These "rules of conduct" may consist of unwritten principles of behavior, such as those established by a nomadic tribe. They may be set forth in a law code, such as the law code of one of today's European nations. They may consist of written laws and court decisions created by modern legislative and judicial bodies, as they do in the United States. Regardless of how such rules are created, they all have one thing in common: they establish rights, duties, and privileges that are consistent with the values and beliefs of their society or its ruling group.

One of the important functions of law in any society is to provide stability, predictability, and continuity so that people can be sure of how to order their affairs. If any society is to survive, its citizens must be able to determine what is legally right and legally wrong. They must know what sanctions will be imposed on them if they commit wrongful acts. If they suffer harm as a result of others' wrongful acts, they need to know whether and how they can receive compensation for their injuries. By setting forth the rights, obligations, and privileges of citizens, the law enables individuals to go about their business and personal lives with confidence and a certain degree of predictability. The stability and predictability created by the law provide an essential framework for all civilized societies.

Judicial Approaches to the Law

In the United States, judges have a hand in determining what the law is and how it should be applied in individual cases (this is because of the common law system that you will read about later in this chapter). Although a judge's function is not to *make* the laws—that is the function of the legislative branch of government—the courts play a significant role in defining what the law is.

In order to predict how a court will interpret and apply the law in a given case, legal scholars have identified a number of different philosophical theories of the law that affect judicial decision making. The study of theories of law, often referred to as **jurisprudence,** involves learning about the various schools of jurisprudential thought and discovering how the approaches of each school can affect how the law is understood and applied.

You may think that legal philosophy is far removed from the work of a paralegal. Actually, it is not. How judges interpret the written law and apply the law to a specific set of circumstances depends in part on their philosophical views. Paralegals, like the lawyers for whom they work, often are asked to analyze and predict how the court will apply the law to the facts of a case. Some background knowledge of the different approaches that exist is thus beneficial.

jurisprudence
The science or philosophy of law.

THE NATURAL LAW SCHOOL.   The **natural law school** is one of the oldest and most significant schools of jurisprudence. It dates back to the days of the Greek philosopher Aristotle (384–322 B.C.E.), who distinguished between *natural law* and law created by people (nations). Those who adhere to the natural law tradition believe that natural law consists of moral and ethical principles that are inherent in human nature and that a nation's written laws should reflect these universal principles.

The notion that people have "natural rights" stems from the natural law tradition. Those who claim that a specific foreign government is depriving certain citizens of their human rights implicitly are appealing to a higher law that has universal applicability. For example, suppose you work as a paralegal for a corporation that operates a manufacturing plant in South Africa. An employee in that plant claims that the corporation has engaged in employment discrimination that is illegal under U.S. law but not under South African law. A judge who believes that the law is designed to protect the natural rights of all individuals may be more inclined to rule in favor of the employee in that situation and against the corporation.

natural law school
A school of legal thought that holds that government and the legal system should reflect the universal moral and ethical principles that are inherent in human nature. The natural law school is the oldest and one of the most significant schools of legal thought.

THE POSITIVIST SCHOOL.   In contrast, those who adhere to the **positivist school** believe that there can be no higher law than a nation's positive law (the law that is enacted by the government). According to the positivist school, there is no such thing as "natural rights." Rather, human rights exist solely because of laws. If the laws are not enforced, anarchy (chaos) will result. Thus, whether a law is "bad" or "good" is irrelevant. The law is the law and must be obeyed until it is changed—in an orderly manner through a legitimate lawmaking process. A judge with positivist leanings probably would be more inclined to defer to an existing law than would a judge who adheres to the natural law tradition.

positivist school
A school of legal thought centered on the assumption that there is no law higher than the laws created by the government. Laws must be obeyed, even if they are unjust, to prevent anarchy.

THE HISTORICAL SCHOOL.   The **historical school** of legal thought emphasizes the evolutionary development of law by concentrating on the origin and history of the legal system. Thus, this school looks to the past to discover what the principles of contemporary law should be. The legal doctrines that have withstood the passage of time—those that have worked in the past—are deemed best suited for shaping present laws. Adherents of the historical school are more likely than those of other schools to strictly follow decisions made in past cases.

historical school
A school of legal thought that emphasizes the evolutionary development of law and that looks to the past to discover what the principles of contemporary law should be.

LEGAL REALISM.   Legal realism is based on the idea that law is just one of many institutions in society and that it is shaped by social forces and needs. The law is a human enterprise, and judges should take social and economic realities into account when deciding cases. Legal realists also believe that the law can never be applied with total uniformity. Given that judges are human beings with unique personalities, value systems, and intellects, different judges will obviously bring different reasoning processes to the same case.

Legal realism strongly influenced the growth of what is sometimes called the **sociological school** of jurisprudence. This school views law as a tool for promoting justice in society. In the 1960s, for example, the justices of the United States Supreme Court played a leading role in the civil rights movement by upholding long-neglected laws calling for equal treatment for all Americans, including African Americans and other minorities. Generally, judges who adhere to this philosophy of law are more likely to depart from past decisions than are those jurists who adhere to the other schools of legal thought.

sociological school
A school of legal thought that views the law as a tool for promoting justice in society.

As discussed, a judge's personal philosophy of law can affect how the judge interprets and applies the law in a particular case. The preceding discussion highlights only some of the many theories of law that affect judicial decision making. We next examine the various sources of law in the United States.

PRIMARY SOURCES OF AMERICAN LAW

American law has numerous sources. *Primary sources of law,* or sources that establish the law, include the following:

1. The U.S. Constitution and the constitutions of the various states.
2. Statutory law—including laws passed by Congress, state legislatures, and local governing bodies.
3. Regulations created by administrative agencies, such as the U.S. Food and Drug Administration.
4. Case law and common law doctrines.

We describe each of these important sources of law in the following pages.

Secondary sources of law are books and articles that summarize and clarify the primary sources of law. Examples include legal encyclopedias, treatises, articles in law reviews, and compilations of law, such as the *Restatements of the Law* (which will be discussed shortly). Courts often refer to secondary sources of law for guidance in interpreting and applying the primary sources of law discussed here.

On the Web
The national Constitution Center provides extensive information on the Constitution, including its history and current debates over constitutional provisions, at **http://www. constitutioncenter.org.**

CONSTITUTIONAL LAW

The federal government and the states have separate written constitutions that set forth the general organization, powers, and limits of their respective governments. **Constitutional law** is the law as expressed in these constitutions.

constitutional law
Law based on the U.S. Constitution and the constitutions of the various states.

The Federal Constitution

The U.S. Constitution, as amended, is the highest law of the land. This principle is set forth in Article VI of the Constitution, which provides that the Constitution, laws, and treaties of the United States are "the supreme Law of the Land." This provision is commonly referred to as the **supremacy clause.** A law in violation of

supremacy clause
The provision in Article VI of the U.S. Constitution that declares the Constitution, laws, and treaties of the United States are "the supreme Law of the Land."

the Constitution (including its amendments), no matter what its source, will be declared unconstitutional if it is challenged. For example, if a state legislature enacts a law that conflicts with the federal Constitution, a person or business firm that is subject to that law may challenge its validity in a court action. If the court agrees with the complaining party that the law is unconstitutional, it will declare the law invalid and refuse to enforce it.

The U.S. Constitution sets forth the powers of the three branches of government and the relationship between the three branches. Article I of the U.S. Constitution creates and empowers the legislature. It provides that Congress shall consist of a Senate and a House of Representatives and fixes the composition of each house and the election procedures, qualifications, and compensation for senators and representatives. Article I also establishes the procedures for enacting legislation and the areas of law in which Congress has the power to legislate. Article II establishes the executive branch, the process for electing and removing a president from office, the qualifications to be president, and the powers of the president. Article III creates the judicial branch and authorizes the appointment, compensation, and removal of judges. It also sets forth the jurisdiction of the courts and defines *treason*.

Bill of Rights
The first ten amendments to the U.S. Constitution.

CONSTITUTIONAL RIGHTS.   The need for a written declaration of rights of individuals eventually caused the first Congress of the United States to submit twelve amendments to the Constitution to the states for approval. Ten of these amendments, commonly known as the **Bill of Rights,** were adopted in 1791 and embody a series of protections for individuals—and in some cases, business entities—against various types of interference by the federal government. Summarized below are the protections guaranteed by the Bill of Rights. The full text of the Constitution, including its amendments (of which there are now twenty-seven), is presented in Appendix J at the end of the book.

1. The First Amendment guarantees the freedoms of religion, speech, and the press and the rights to assemble peaceably and to petition the government.

2. The Second Amendment guarantees the right to keep and bear arms.

3. The Third Amendment prohibits, in peacetime, the lodging of soldiers in any house without the owner's consent.

4. The Fourth Amendment prohibits unreasonable searches and seizures of persons or property.

5. The Fifth Amendment guarantees the rights to indictment by grand jury and to due process of law and prohibits compulsory self-incrimination and double jeopardy. (These terms and concepts will be defined in Chapter 15, which deals with criminal law and procedures.) The Fifth Amendment also prohibits the taking of private property for public use without just compensation.

6. The Sixth Amendment guarantees the accused in a criminal case the right to a speedy and public trial by an impartial jury and the right to counsel. The accused has the right to cross-examine witnesses against him or her and to solicit testimony from witnesses in his or her favor.

7. The Seventh Amendment guarantees the right to a trial by jury in a civil case involving at least twenty dollars.[1]

8. The Eighth Amendment prohibits excessive bail and fines, as well as cruel and unusual punishment.

9. The Ninth Amendment establishes that the people have rights in addition to those specified in the Constitution.

10. The Tenth Amendment establishes that those powers neither delegated to the federal government nor denied to the states are reserved for the states.

As originally intended, the Bill of Rights limited only the powers of the national government. Over time, however, the Supreme Court incorporated most of these rights into the protections against state actions afforded by the Fourteenth Amendment to the Constitution. That amendment, passed in 1868 after the Civil War, provides in part that "[n]o State shall . . . deprive any person of life, liberty, or property, without due process of law." Starting in 1925, the Supreme Court began to define various rights and liberties guaranteed in the national Constitution as comprising "due process of law," which was required of state governments under the Fourteenth Amendment. Today, most of the rights and liberties set forth in the Bill of Rights—such as the freedom of speech and religion guaranteed by the First Amendment—apply to state governments as well as the national government.

On the Web

Information on the role of the United States Supreme Court in interpreting the Constitution is available at **http://www. usscplus.com.**

THE COURTS AND CONSTITUTIONAL LAW.   You should realize that the rights secured by the Bill of Rights are not absolute. The broad principles enunciated in the Constitution are given form and substance by the courts. Courts often have to balance the rights and freedoms enunciated in the Bill of Rights against other rights, such as the right to be free from the harmful actions of others. Ultimately, it is the United States Supreme Court, as the final interpreter of the Constitution, that both gives meaning to our constitutional rights and determines their boundaries.

Courts Balance the Right to Free Speech.   An example of how the courts must balance the rights and freedoms granted by the Constitution can be found by looking at our right to free speech. Even though the First Amendment guarantees the right to free speech, we are not, in fact, free to say anything we want. In interpreting the meaning of the First Amendment, the Supreme Court has made it clear that certain types of speech will not be protected. Speech that harms the good reputation of another, for instance, is commonly considered to be a tort, or civil wrong. If the speaker is sued, he or she may be ordered by a court to pay damages to the harmed person (as you will read in Chapter 7).

Free Speech and the Internet.   The Internet has raised new problems for the courts in determining how to define and apply the protections conferred by the Constitution, particularly with regard to free speech. For example, the Supreme Court has ruled that obscene speech, though difficult to define, is not entitled to First Amendment protection. Congress first attempted to prohibit *online obscenity* in the Communications Decency Act (CDA) of 1996, which made it a crime to make available to minors online any "obscene or indecent" message.[2] Civil rights groups immediately claimed the act was an unconstitutional restraint on speech. The Supreme Court held that portions of the act were unconstitutional in *Reno v. American Civil Liberties Union.*[3] Subsequent attempts by Congress to curb pornography on the Internet have also encountered constitutional stumbling blocks.[4]

State Constitutions

Each state also has a constitution that sets forth the general organization, powers, and limits of the state government. The Tenth Amendment to the U.S. Constitution, which defines the powers and limitations of the federal government, reserves all powers not granted to the federal government to the states. Unless they conflict with the U.S. Constitution, state constitutions are supreme within the states' respective borders. State constitutions are thus important sources of law.

On the Web

If you are interested in looking at state constitutions, including the one for your state, go to **http://www.findlaw.com/ casecode/state.html.**

DEVELOPING PARALEGAL SKILLS

State versus Federal Regulation

Stephanie Wilson works as a paralegal in the legal department of National Pipeline, Inc., whose business is transporting natural gas to local utilities, factories, and other sites throughout the country. Last month, a pipeline running under a residential street in Minneapolis, Minnesota, exploded, resulting in several severe injuries and one death.

The federal government has regulated pipeline safety and maintenance since 1968, under the Natural Gas Pipeline Safety Act. As a result of the explosion, the state of Minnesota wants to regulate pipeline safety as well. Stephanie's boss, the general counsel, and several other executives believe that the federal act preempts, or occupies, this field of law, preventing the state from enacting another layer of safety legislation. Stephanie is assigned the task of researching the statute and relevant case law to determine if the federal law does in fact preempt the state's regulation.

TIPS FOR DETERMINING FEDERAL PREEMPTION

- Read through the statute to see if it expressly states that Congress intended to preempt the field.
- Look for an actual conflict between a federal and state law.
- Look for indications that Congress has impliedly occupied the field: Is the federal regulatory scheme pervasive? Is federal occupation of the field necessitated by the need for national uniformity? Is there a danger of conflict between state laws and the administration of the federal program?
- Locate and read cases discussing the issue of federal preemption in this area.

Constitutional Law and the Paralegal

Many paralegals assist attorneys in handling cases that involve constitutional provisions or rights. For example, a corporate client might claim that a regulation issued by a state administrative agency, such as the state department of natural resources, is invalid because it conflicts with a federal law or regulation. (Administrative agencies are discussed later in this chapter.) You may be assigned the task of finding out which regulation takes priority. Many cases arise in which the plaintiff claims that his or her First Amendment rights have been violated. Suppose that a plaintiff's religious beliefs forbid working on a certain day of the week. If he or she is required to work on that day, the plaintiff may claim that the employer's requirement violates the First Amendment, which guarantees the free exercise of religion.

No matter what kind of work you do as a paralegal, you will find that a knowledge of constitutional law will be beneficial. This is because the authority and underlying rationale for the substantive and procedural laws governing many areas of law are ultimately based on the Constitution. For example, knowledge of constitutional law is helpful to paralegals working in the area of criminal law, because criminal procedures are essentially designed to protect the constitutional rights of accused persons—as you will read in Chapter 15.

statute
A written law enacted by a legislature under its constitutional lawmaking authority.

statutory law
The body of written laws enacted by the legislature.

STATUTORY LAW

Statutes, which are laws enacted by legislative bodies at any level of government, make up another source of law. The body of written laws created by the legislature is generally referred to as **statutory law.**

Federal Statutes

Federal statutes are laws that are enacted by the U.S. Congress and that apply to every state. As mentioned, any law—including a federal statute—that violates the U.S. Constitution will be held unconstitutional. Examples of federal statutes include laws protecting intellectual property rights (see Chapter 8), laws regulating the purchase and sale of corporate stock (see Chapter 10), statutes prohibiting employment discrimination (see Chapter 10), and many environmental and consumer protection statutes (discussed in Chapter 11).

> **On the Web**
> A good starting point to access federal statutes, as well as state statutes online is **http://www.findlaw.com**.

State and Local Statutes and Ordinances

State statutes are laws enacted by state legislatures. Any state law that is found to conflict with the U.S. Constitution or with the state's constitution will be deemed unconstitutional. If a state statute is found to conflict with a federal statute, the federal statute will control. State statutes include state laws governing real property, estates, and family law issues (see Chapter 9); state statutes governing the formation of corporations and other business entities (see Chapter 10); state criminal statutes (see Chapter 15); and state versions of the Uniform Commercial Code (to be discussed shortly).

Statutory law also includes local ordinances. An **ordinance** is an order, rule, or law passed by a city or county government unit to govern matters not covered by federal or state law. Ordinances may not violate the U.S. Constitution, the relevant state constitution, or federal or state law. Local ordinances often have to do with land use (zoning ordinances), building or safety codes, construction or appearance of local housing, and other matters affecting the local unit. Persons who violate ordinances may be fined, jailed, or both.

ordinance
An order, rule, or law enacted by a municipal or county government to govern a local matter unaddressed by state or federal legislation.

Uniform Laws

A federal statute, of course, applies to all states. A state statute, in contrast, applies only within the state's borders. State laws thus vary from state to state. The differences among state laws were particularly notable in the 1800s, when conflicting state statutes frequently created problems for the rapidly developing trade and commerce among the states. To counter these problems, a group of legal scholars and lawyers formed the National Conference of Commissioners on Uniform State Laws (NCCUSL) in 1892 to draft uniform ("model") statutes for adoption by the states. The NCCUSL still exists today and continues to issue uniform statutes, often in conjunction with the American Law Institute.

Adoption of a uniform law is a state matter, and a state may reject all or part of the statute or rewrite it as the state legislature wishes. Hence, even when a uniform law is said to have been adopted in many states, those states' laws may not be entirely "uniform." Once adopted by a state legislature, a uniform act becomes a part of the statutory law of that state. A good example of a uniform law that has been adopted (at least in part) by all fifty states is the Uniform Commercial Code (UCC), which provides a uniform, yet flexible, set of rules governing commercial transactions and sales contracts. The UCC will be discussed in Chapter 8.

The Expanding Scope of Statutory Law

Today, legislative bodies and administrative agencies assume an ever-increasing share of lawmaking. Much of the work of modern courts consists of interpreting what the rulemakers intended to accomplish when a particular law was drafted and enacted and deciding how the law applies to a specific set of facts.

Statutory Law and the Paralegal

As a paralegal, you may often be dealing with cases that involve violations of statutory law. If you work for a small law firm, you may become familiar with the statutory law governing a wide spectrum of activities. If you specialize in one area, such as bankruptcy law, you will become very familiar with the federal statutory law governing bankruptcy and bankruptcy procedures. Here are just a few examples of areas in which you might work that are governed extensively by statutory law:

- *Corporate law*—governed by state statutes.
- *Patent, copyright, and trademark law*—governed by federal statutes.
- *Employment law*—governed to an increasing extent by federal statutes concerning discrimination in employment, workplace safety, labor unions, pension plans, Social Security, and other aspects of employment. Each state also has statutes governing certain areas of employment, such as safety standards in the workplace and employment discrimination.
- *Antitrust law*—governed by federal statutes prohibiting specific types of anti-competitive business practices.
- *Consumer law*—governed by state and federal statutes protecting consumers against deceptive trade practices (such as misleading advertising), unsafe products, and generally any activities that threaten consumer health and welfare.
- *Wills and probate administration* (relating to the transfer of property on the property owner's death)—governed by state statutes.

You will read about some of these areas of law in later chapters. A paralegal working in an area (or on a case) governed by statutory law needs to know how to both locate and interpret the relevant state or federal statutes. You will learn how to find and analyze statutory law in Chapters 16 through 18.

ADMINISTRATIVE LAW

There is virtually no way for the federal Congress or a state legislature to oversee the actual implementation of all the laws that it enacts. To assist them in their governing responsibilities, legislatures at all levels of government often delegate such tasks to **administrative agencies,** particularly when the issues relate to highly technical areas. By creating and delegating some of its authority to an administrative agency, a legislature may indirectly monitor a particular area in which it has passed legislation without becoming bogged down in the details relating to enforcement.

Agency Creation and Function

administrative agency
A federal or state government agency established to perform a specific function. Administrative agencies are authorized by legislative acts to make and enforce rules relating to the purpose for which they were established.

enabling legislation
A statute enacted by a legislature that authorizes the creation of an administrative agency and specifies the name, purpose, composition, and powers of the agency being created.

To create an administrative agency at the federal level, Congress passes **enabling legislation,** which specifies the name, purpose, composition, and powers of the agency being created. The Occupational Safety and Health Act of 1970, for example, provided for the creation of the Occupational Safety and Health Administration to administer and implement the provisions of the act, to issue rules as necessary to protect employees from dangerous conditions in the workplace, and to enforce the act's provisions and the agency's rules.

There are dozens of federal administrative agencies, each of which has been established to perform specific governing tasks. For example, the federal Environmental Protection Agency coordinates and enforces federal environmental laws. The Food and Drug Administration enforces federal laws relating to the safety of foods and drugs. The Federal Trade Commission issues and enforces

PARALEGAL PROFILE

General Law Practice Paralegal

DEBRA RUDOLPH *earned a bachelor of arts degree in English literature form the University of Tennessee, Knoxville, and graduated* summa cum laude *from the paralegal studies program at Pellissippi State Technical Community College.*

While a student in the paralegal studies program, Rudolph was the recipient of two paralegal scholarships and winner of West's Award for Outstanding Academic Achievement for 2000. She also was elected a member of Who's Who in American Junior Colleges *and* Lambda Chi *honor society. She presently serves on the advisory committee for the paralegal studies program at Pellissippi State.*

Rudolph is editor-in-chief of The Paralegal Advocate, *a statewide newsletter for members of the Tennessee Paralegal Association. She has also taught a seminar for the Institute for Paralegal Education on the topics of depositions, legal research, and investigative techniques.*

Rudolph works in a small general law practice in downtown Knoxville, where she specializes in the areas of civil litigation, business organizations, and estate and inheritance taxes.

What do you like best about your work?

"I love the variety of assignments, cases, and clients that I've been exposed to while working in a small general law practice. In a typical week, I might be researching the side effects of a prescription drug, interviewing witnesses about a fatal train accident, reviewing discovery in a felony murder file, ordering forms for a tax return, summarizing lengthy pleadings, performing legal research on fiduciary relationships, and photographing a client's wrecked vehicle. I am very grateful for the continual opportunities to learn and experience new things as a paralegal in a general law practice."

What is the greatest challenge that you face in your area of work?

"There is a great deal of pressure and worry associated with supervising and tracking deadlines, statutes of limitations, task schedules, case status reports, and calendars. All of these functions are constantly and quickly changing, and it is a challenge to juggle and maintain these crucial administrative tasks while also working on legal projects."

What advice do you have for would-be paralegals in your area of work?

"Read! Being well read is vital to performing investigations, interviews, and legal research. Having an understanding of the human condition is the key to successfully working the legal arena. Also, knowledge of local, national, and world events will aid a paralegal in working with the variety of clients and cases encountered in a general law practice. An understanding of the business world is also an asset to a paralegal working in a general law practice because some of your work may relate to investments, taxes, estates, and business organizations."

What are some tips for success as a paralegal in your area of work?

"Keeping up with technology is a must in a general law practice. In addition to strong keyboarding and Internet skills, knowledge of word processing, spreadsheets, and slide-show programs is a necessity. Strong organizational skills and the ability to think ahead are also important assets. A paralegal who really wants to

> **"Keeping up with technology is a must in a general law practice."**

shine will always maintain organized files and will anticipate anything his or her attorney may need. Things to anticipate may include a summary of a pleading, phone numbers and directions, or even having extralarge garbage bags available when traveling with oversized exhibits in times of inclement weather."

---

rules relating to unfair advertising or sales practices. Each state also has a number of administrative agencies, many of which parallel agencies at the federal level. For example, state environmental laws are implemented by state environmental agencies, such as a state's department of natural resources. The rules, orders, and decisions of administrative agencies at all levels of government constitute what is known as **administrative law.**

administrative law
A body of law created by administrative agencies in the form of rules, regulations, orders, and decisions in order to carry out their duties and responsibilities.

Administrative Law and the Paralegal

Paralegals frequently deal with administrative agencies. If you work for a law firm that has many corporate clients, you may be involved extensively in researching and analyzing agency regulations and their applicability to certain business activities. If you work for a corporate legal department, you will probably assist the attorneys in the department in a vital task—determining which agency regulations apply to the corporation and whether the corporation is complying with those regulations. If you work for an administrative agency, you may be involved in drafting new rules, in analyzing survey results to see if a new rule is necessary, in mediating disputes between a private party and an agency, in conducting investigations to gather facts about compliance with agency rules, and numerous other tasks. In any law practice, you may be asked to assist clients who are involved in disputes with administrative agencies.

Paralegals often become very familiar with administrative process when helping clients obtain needed benefits from state or federal administrative agencies. You may work with local agencies in helping homeless persons to obtain medical assistance, for example. As noted in Chapter 2, some administrative agencies, including the Social Security Administration, allow paralegals to represent clients at administrative agency hearings and other procedures.

We list below a few federal government agencies and describe how paralegals may be involved with administrative law and procedures relating to those agencies. (Administrative law and agency procedures will be covered in greater detail in Chapter 11.)

- *Equal Employment Opportunity Commission (EEOC).* If a client wants to pursue a claim against his or her employer for employment discrimination, the client must first contact the EEOC. The EEOC may investigate and try to settle the claim. If the problem cannot be resolved by the EEOC or if the EEOC decides not to take action on the matter, the client will be entitled to sue the employer directly. You may be involved in contacting the EEOC and assisting the client in complying with procedures required by the EEOC for handling complaints of employment discrimination.

- *Internal Revenue Service (IRS).* If you work for a corporate law department, you might be asked to assist corporate counsel in handling corporate taxes and related IRS requirements. If you work in a law firm, a corporate client may request legal assistance in settling a dispute with the IRS or in complying with tax laws.

- *Securities and Exchange Commission (SEC).* If you work for a corporation that sells shares of stock in its company to the public, you may be asked to assist in drafting the documents necessary to fulfill registration requirements under federal securities law. If you work for a law firm, you may perform similar tasks for corporate clients. You may also assist in the defense of a client who has been charged with "insider trading" in violation of securities law (which prohibits the purchase or sale of securities for personal gain based on knowledge available only to corporate officers or employees and not to the general public).

- *Food and Drug Administration (FDA).* Any firm that places foods or drugs on the market must make sure that those products are safe and properly labeled. If you work for a corporation or on behalf of a corporate client that markets food or drug products, you may be involved in procedures required by the FDA for product testing and labeling or for seeking FDA approval to market a product.

CASE LAW AND THE COMMON LAW TRADITION

Another important source of law consists of the decisions rendered by judges in cases that come before the courts. This body of law is called **case law.** To understand the importance of case law in the United States, you need to first understand what is meant by the common law tradition, which originated in medieval England.

As mentioned earlier, because of our colonial heritage much of American law is based on the English legal system. After the United States declared its independence from England, American jurists continued to be greatly influenced by English law and English legal writers. Indeed, much of American law in such areas as contracts, torts (types of civil wrongs), property law, and criminal law derives in large part from the English legal system.

case law
Rules of law announced in court decisions.

Early English Courts of Law

In 1066, the Normans conquered England, and William the Conqueror and his successors began the process of unifying the country under their rule. One of the means they used to this end was the establishment of the king's courts, or *curiae regis*. Before the Norman Conquest, disputes had been settled according to the local legal customs and traditions in various regions of the country. The king's courts sought to establish a uniform set of customs for the country as a whole. What evolved in these courts was the beginning of the **common law**—a body of general rules that prescribed social conduct and applied throughout the entire English realm.

Courts developed the common law rules from the principles underlying judges' decisions in actual legal controversies. Judges attempted to be consistent. When possible, they based their decisions on the principles suggested by earlier cases. They sought to decide similar cases in a similar way and considered new cases with care because they knew that their decisions would make new law. Each interpretation became part of the law on the subject and served as a legal **precedent.** Later cases that involved similar legal principles or facts could be decided with reference to that precedent. The courts were thus guided by traditions and legal doctrines that evolved over time.

In the early years of the common law, there was no single place or publication in which legal opinions could be found. In the late thirteenth and early fourteenth centuries, however, decisions of each year were gathered together and recorded in *Year Books*. These books were informal, containing only notes of cases made by lawyers and law students, and were not organized according to different legal topics. They were not official reports, did not include every case, and sometimes did not include cases until two or three years after the cases had been decided. Nevertheless, the *Year Books* were useful to lawyers and judges. In the sixteenth century, the *Year Books* were discontinued, and other compilations of cases became available.

common law
A body of law developed from custom or judicial decisions in English and U.S. courts and not by a legislature.

precedent
A court decision that furnishes an example or authority for deciding subsequent cases in which identical or similar facts are presented.

The Doctrine of *Stare Decisis*

The practice of deciding new cases with reference to former decisions, or precedents, eventually became a cornerstone of the English and American judicial systems. It forms a doctrine called *stare decisis*[5] ("to stand by things decided"). Under this doctrine, judges are obligated to follow the precedents established by their own courts or by higher courts within their jurisdictions (the areas over which they have authority—see Chapter 6).

stare decisis
The doctrine of precedent, under which a court is obligated to follow the earlier decisions of that court or a higher court within the jurisdiction if the same points arise again in litigation. This is a defining characteristic of the common law system.

The doctrine of *stare decisis* performs many useful functions. It helps the courts to be more efficient because if other courts have carefully reasoned through a similar case, their legal reasoning and opinions can serve as guides. *Stare decisis* also creates consistency. It makes the law more stable and predictable, because if the law on a given subject is well settled, someone bringing a case to court can usually rely on the court to make a decision based on what the law has been.

DEPARTURES FROM PRECEDENT.   Sometimes a court will depart from the rule of precedent if it decides that the precedent should no longer be followed. If a court decides that a ruling precedent is simply incorrect or that technological or social changes have rendered the precedent inapplicable, the court might rule contrary to the precedent. Cases that overturn precedent often receive a great deal of publicity.

In *Brown v. Board of Education of Topeka*[6] (decided in 1954), for example, the United States Supreme Court expressly overturned precedent when it concluded that separate educational facilities for whites and African Americans, which had been upheld as constitutional in numerous previous cases,[7] were inherently unequal. The Supreme Court's departure from precedent in *Brown* received a tremendous amount of publicity as people began to realize the ramifications of this change in the law. It also spearheaded the civil rights movement, which led to further lawsuits involving claims of racial discrimination.

CASES OF FIRST IMPRESSION.   Sometimes, there is no precedent on which to base a decision. For example, in 1986, a New Jersey court had to decide whether a surrogate-parenting contract should be enforced against the wishes of the surrogate parent (the natural mother).[8] This was the first such case to reach the courts, and there was no precedent in any jurisdiction to which the court could look for guidance. Developments in technology, which often outpace the law, sometimes result in cases for which there is no precedent. For example, suppose that an employee views sexually offensive images on a co-employee's computer monitor, and the employee claims that this constitutes "hostile-environment" sexual harassment. There may be no controlling state or federal law that deals with the employee's complaint.

When deciding cases such as these, called **cases of first impression,** or when there are conflicting precedents, courts may consider a number of factors, including legal principles and policies underlying previous court decisions or existing

On the Web
To learn how the Supreme Court justified its departure from precedent in the 1954 *Brown* decision, you can access the Court's opinion online at **http://www.findlaw.com.**

case of first impression
A case presenting a legal issue that has not yet been addressed by a court in a particular jurisdiction.

TECHNOLOGY AND TODAY'S PARALEGAL

Cases of First Impression and the Internet

Normally, if asked to research a legal problem, a paralegal can find a statute or some case law (or both) that clearly applies to the matter at hand. On occasion, however, you may be asked to perform research on an issue or question for which no legal precedent exists in your jurisdiction. In other words, the case is one of first impression. One area of law that has been significantly affected by the Internet—and that, as a result, often presents cases of first impression—is copyright law.

TECHNOLOGY AND COPYRIGHT LAW

As you will read in Chapter 8, federal copyright law grants the author or creator of certain literary or artistic productions the exclusive right to use and reproduce that work for a specific time period. Whenever the work is copied or used without the author's permission, an *infringement* of copyright occurs, and the author can sue for damages. When a work is published, the publisher receives from the author, in return for a payment of a negotiated sum of money, the exclusive right to publish the author's works for a specified period of time.

What happens, though, if a publisher, after publishing a work in print, later "republishes" it electronically over the Internet? Is this a "new" publication for which the publisher needs to renegotiate the right to publish the book? Clearly, traditional copyright law, which was created long before cyberspace was even imagined, does not provide the answer to this specific question. How, then, have the courts decided this issue? The answer is that they have looked to the principles underlying the traditional law and applied them to the situation at hand.

For example, in one case, *New York Times v. Tasini*,[a] several freelance writers sued the *New York Times* for publishing their articles online. Although the writers had given the newspaper permission to print the articles, the writers claimed that the *Times* did not have the right to electronically republish the articles. Ultimately, the United States

Supreme Court agreed with the writers in concluding that publishing an article in electronic form was essentially a new publication. The Court's decision was based entirely on the wording of the Copyright Act and its interpretation of the purpose behind the act. In another case involving a similar issue, the court decided that the relevant law was not copyright law but the common law governing contracts (also discussed in Chapter 8). The court thus looked to the language of the contract between the publishers and the authors to determine the nature of the rights that the authors granted to the publisher.[b]

RESEARCHING CASES OF FIRST IMPRESSION

Clearly, the Internet has posed many new difficulties for the courts in attempting to adapt traditional legal principles to cyberspace. Your approach to research thus needs to be flexible. First, look to see if there is any existing statutory law that the judge might determine *should* apply to your case (or that your supervising attorney can argue should apply). This is particularly important given that new technology, and especially the Internet, has forced the courts to adapt many existing statutes, such as federal copyright law, to meet the needs of modern society. Second, look to see if any other court (in a different state or district, for example) has considered a similar legal issue and, if so, what that court concluded. Although cases decided in other jurisdictions will not be binding precedents, courts often look at the way other courts have handled the issue when deciding matters of first impression.

TECHNOLOGY TIP

Generally, when researching cases of first impression involving Internet transactions, you will need to broaden the scope of your search of the sources of law. A wise paralegal will be creative and adopt a research strategy that is aimed at discovering both which laws *may* apply and which laws *should* apply given the specific facts of the case.

---

a. 533 U.S. 483, 121 S.Ct. 2381, 120 L.Ed.2d 500 (2001).

b. *Random House, Inc. v. Rosetta Books, LLC,* 283 F.3d 490 (2d Cir. 2002).

---

statutes, fairness, social values and customs, **public policy** (a governmental policy based on widely held societal values), and data and concepts drawn from the social sciences. (See this chapter's *Technology and Today's Paralegal* feature for an example of how two courts looked at different factors in deciding cases of first

public policy
A governmental policy based on widely held societal values.

impression involving copyright law and the Internet.) Which of these sources is chosen or receives the greatest emphasis will depend on the nature of the case being considered and the particular judge hearing the case.

Judges always strive to be free of subjectivity and personal bias in deciding cases. Each judge, however, has his or her own unique personality, set of values or philosophical leanings, and intellectual attributes—all of which necessarily frame the decision-making process.

Remedies at Law versus Remedies in Equity

remedy
The means by which a right is enforced or the violation of a right is prevented or compensated for.

In the early English king's courts, the kinds of **remedies** that the courts could grant were severely restricted. If one person wronged another in some way, the king's court could award as compensation only land, items of value, or money. The courts that awarded these things became known as **courts of law,** and the three remedies awarded by these courts—land, items of value, and money—became known as **remedies at law.**

court of law
A court in which the only remedies that could be granted were things of value, such as money damages. In early England, courts of law were distinct from courts of equity.

Even though this system helped to standardize the ways in which disputes were settled, those parties who wanted a remedy other than economic compensation could not be helped. Because the courts of law could not grant noneconomic remedies, many disappointed litigants became very frustrated with the court system. Some of the more persistent parties petitioned the king for relief. Most of these petitions were decided by an adviser to the king, called a **chancellor.** The chancellor, who was also the head of the Church of England, was said to be the "keeper of the king's conscience." When the chancellor thought that the claim was a fair one for which there was no adequate remedy at law, he would fashion new and unique remedies, called **remedies in equity,** to resolve the case. In this way, a new body of rules and remedies came into being and eventually led to the establishment of formal courts of chancery, or **courts of equity.**

remedy at law
A remedy available in a court of law. Money damages are awarded as a remedy at law.

chancellor
An adviser to the king in medieval England. Individuals petitioned the king for relief when they could not obtain an adequate remedy in a court of law, and these petitions were decided by the chancellor.

Equity is that branch of law, founded on what might be described as notions of justice and fair dealing, that seeks to supply a remedy when there is no adequate remedy available at law. Once the courts of equity were established, plaintiffs could pursue their claims in either courts of law (if they sought money damages) or courts of equity (if they sought equitable remedies). Plaintiffs had to specify whether they were bringing an "action at law" or an "action in equity," and they chose their courts accordingly. Only one remedy could be granted for a particular wrong.

remedy in equity
A remedy allowed by courts in situations where remedies at law are not appropriate. Remedies in equity are based on settled rules of fairness, justice, and honesty.

court of equity
A court that decides controversies and administers justice according to the rules, principles, and precedents of equity.

EQUITABLE PRINCIPLES AND MAXIMS.   Courts of equity often supplemented the common law by making decisions based on considerations of justice and fairness. Today, the same court can award both legal and equitable remedies, so plaintiffs may request both equitable and legal relief in the same case. Yet judges continue to be guided by so-called **equitable principles and maxims** when deciding whether to grant equitable remedies. Maxims are propositions or general statements of rules of law that courts often use in arriving at a decision. Some of the most influential maxims of equity are listed in Exhibit 5.1.

equitable principles and maxims
Propositions or general statements of rules of law that are frequently involved in equity jurisdiction.

laches
The equitable doctrine that bars a party's right to legal action if the party has neglected for an unreasonable length of time to act on his or her rights.

The last maxim listed in the exhibit ("Equity aids the vigilant, not those who slumber on their rights") has become known as the equitable doctrine of **laches.** The doctrine of laches encourages people to bring lawsuits while the evidence is still fresh. What constitutes a reasonable time, of course, varies depending on the circumstances of the case. The time period for pursuing a particular claim against another party is now usually fixed by a **statute of limitations.** After the time allowed under the statute of limitations has expired, further action on that claim is barred.

statute of limitations
A statute setting the maximum time period within which certain legal actions can be brought or rights enforced. After the period of time has run, normally no legal action can be brought.

> ### ETHICAL CONCERN
> ## What to Do When Someone
> ## Asks You about Remedies
>
> Suppose you learn that Lewis, one of your friends, recently broke his hip when he fell off a new ladder while painting his house. He fell because one of the steps wasn't securely attached and came loose as he was climbing the ladder. He had to pay $1,000 of the medical costs out-of-pocket. Also, his doctor told him that he probably wouldn't be able to work at his construction job for at least two months and maybe longer. Knowing that you are trained in law, Lewis asks you whether he can obtain compensation for the out-of-pocket medical expenses and for the lost wages. Should you advise him that he could sue the ladder's manufacturer and the owner of the hardware store that sold him the ladder for money damages, a remedy at law? No, you should not. Such a statement could subject you to liability for the unauthorized practice of law. The best thing to do in this situation is simply tell Lewis that because you are a paralegal, you cannot give legal advice, but that he should check with an attorney to see what remedies he might pursue to compensate him for his injuries.

JUDGES AND JUSTICES.   The terms *judge* and *justice* are usually synonymous and represent two designations given to judges in various courts. All members of the United States Supreme Court, for example, are referred to as justices. Justice is also the formal title usually given to judges of appeals courts, although this is not always the case. Justice is commonly abbreviated to J., and justices to JJ. A Supreme Court case might refer to Justice Kennedy as Kennedy, J., or to Chief Justice Rehnquist as Rehnquist, C.J.

In a trial court, a case is heard by one judge. In an appeals court, normally a panel of three or more judges (or justices) sit on the bench. Most decisions reached by appeals courts are explained in written court opinions.

DECISIONS AND OPINIONS.   The **opinion** contains the court's reasons for its decision, the rules of law that apply, and the judgment. There are four types of opinions. When all judges or justices unanimously agree on an opinion, the opinion is written for the entire court and can be deemed a *unanimous opinion*. When there is not a unanimous opinion, a *majority opinion* is written, outlining the views of the majority of the judges or justices deciding the case. The name of the judge or justice immediately preceding the unanimous or majority opinion indicates the author of the opinion—that is, the judge or justice who wrote the opinion on behalf of the others.

Often, a judge or justice who feels strongly about making or emphasizing a point that was not made or emphasized in the majority opinion writes a *concurring opinion,* which appears just following the majority opinion. In a concurring opinion, the judge or justice agrees (concurs) with the decision given in the majority opinion but for different reasons. In other than unanimous opinions, a *dissenting opinion* may also be written by a judge or justice who does not agree with the majority. The dissenting opinion, which follows the concurring opinion, if any, is important because it may form the basis of the arguments used years later in overruling the precedential majority opinion. The names of the judges or justices

opinion
A statement by the court setting forth the applicable law and the reasons for its decision in a case.

DEVELOPING PARALEGAL SKILLS

Following Up with a Client

Maggie Sufuentes is a paralegal with the law firm of Ramirez & Sanchez in Miami, Florida. Maggie's parents immigrated to the United States from Cuba and speak only Spanish at home. Maggie is bilingual, which makes her invaluable to her firm because she can talk with the firm's Spanish-speaking clients and act as an interpreter. She also handles all of the follow-up meetings and interviews with clients. Today, Maggie and Sanchez have interviewed Bianca Martinez, a college student who wants to immigrate to the United States from Cuba and work her way through college as a nanny. Sanchez has decided that it is best for Bianca to obtain an immigrant visa under the Cuban Adjustment Act of 1980. Bianca will return tomorrow with her visa, college applications, and other documents.

TIPS FOR COLLECTING DOCUMENTS FROM A CLIENT

- Prepare a written list of documents for the client to bring in.
- Make sure that the client knows what the documents are.
- Clearly explain the significance of the documents to the client.
- Make sure that the client understands the necessary time frame.
- Meet with the client briefly to collect and review the documents.

---

authoring any concurring or dissenting opinions are also indicated at the beginning of those opinions.

Common Law and the Paralegal

As a paralegal, you will find that a basic understanding of the common law tradition is necessary whenever you need to research and analyze case law. The doctrine of *stare decisis* and the distinction between legal and equitable remedies are critical concepts when applied to real-life situations faced by clients.

For example, suppose that a client wants to sue another party for breaching a contract to perform computer consulting services. In this situation, the common law of contracts would apply to the case. (In contrast, as you will read in Chapter 8, contracts for the sale of *goods* are governed by statutory law in virtually all of the states.) If you were asked to research the case, you would search for previous cases dealing with similar issues to see how those cases were decided. You would want to know of any precedents set by a higher court in your jurisdiction—and, of course, by the United States Supreme Court—on that issue. Even in an area governed by statutory law, such as sales contracts, you will want to find out how the courts have interpreted and applied the relevant state statute or statutory provision.

In addition to lawsuits involving contract law, the common law also applies to *tort law* (the law governing civil wrongs, such as negligence or assault and battery, as opposed to criminal wrongs). As a paralegal, you may be working on behalf of clients bringing or defending against the following types of actions, all of which involve tort law:

- *Personal-injury lawsuits*—actions brought by plaintiffs to obtain compensation for injuries allegedly caused by the wrongful acts of others, either intentionally or through negligence.

- *Malpractice lawsuits*—actions brought by plaintiffs against professionals, such as physicians and attorneys, to obtain compensation for injuries allegedly caused by professional negligence (breach of professional duties).
- *Product liability lawsuits*—actions brought by plaintiffs to obtain compensation for injuries allegedly caused by defective products.

Numerous other areas, such as property law and employment law, are also still governed to some extent by the common law. Depending on the nature of your job as a paralegal, you may be dealing with many issues that are governed by the common law. Because of the adversarial nature of our system, you may also be asked to work on cases that you do not believe in or for clients whom you do not like.

The Adversarial System of Justice

As discussed, the common law, or case law, is extremely important in defining what the law is in America. It is therefore important to keep in mind that American courts, like English courts, follow the **adversarial system of justice,** in which the parties act as adversaries, or opponents. Parties to a lawsuit come before the court as contestants, both sides presenting the facts of their cases in the light most favorable to themselves, in an attempt to "win" the "battle." The parties do not come together in the courtroom with the idea of working out a compromise solution to their problems or of looking at the dispute from each other's point of view. Rather, they take sides, present their best case to the judge or jury (if it is a jury trial), and hope that this impartial decision maker rules in their favor.

adversarial system of justice
A legal system in which the parties to a lawsuit are opponents, or adversaries, and present their cases in the light most favorable to themselves. The impartial decision maker (the judge or jury) determines who wins and who loses based on the evidence presented.

THE GOAL IS TO WIN.   Most people do not fully appreciate the impact that the adversarial nature of the legal system has on those who work within the system. For one thing, in an adversarial system, the goal of the attorneys (and paralegals) is not so much to determine the truth as to win the case. An attorney's job is not to seek out or reveal the truth to judges (although ethical rules clearly prohibit attorneys from presenting evidence that they know to be untrue). Rather, the role of the attorney is to discover and present the strongest legal argument on behalf of a client, regardless of the attorney's personal feelings about the client or the client's case.

CRITICISMS OF THE ADVERSARIAL SYSTEM.   The adversarial nature of proceedings frames the practice of law in many respects. Lawyers are under a great deal of pressure to win cases. Lawyers may also be pressured by the other attorneys in a law firm to win a particular client's case. Additionally, others who work in the lawyer's firm will likely be affected by the lawyer's success or failure in court.

Many people criticize our adversarial system of justice, believing that it contributes to a lack of integrity in the legal profession. After all, the idea is that a trial is supposed to lead to justice. Some attorneys in our system actually make higher incomes by prolonging disputes and obscuring the truth. The public may even view a lawyer who has successfully defended a criminal client as unethical because the client was found not guilty due to a "technicality."

Although our system is not perfect, most Americans agree that everyone should be allowed her or his "day in court" and should be given the opportunity to have legal advice and guidance in presenting her or his case. (For a discussion of how *pro bono* work, or uncompensated legal services, can help to ensure all Americans have equal access to justice, see this chapter's *Featured Guest* article on the next page.) These are the foundations of the concept of due process of law (which you will read about in Chapter 15). The adversarial system is therefore fundamental to what we consider to be justice in the United States.

FEATURED GUEST: MARCI S. JOHNS
Pro Bono Opportunities and the Paralegal

BIOGRAPHICAL NOTE

Marci S. Johns is an assistant professor of criminal justice and the director of legal studies for Faulkner University in Montgomery, Alabama. She has taught paralegal courses and continuing education programs for paralegals since 1999.

Johns is also an attorney with the law firm of Pettus, Smith, Brown & Associates, L.L.C. Her primary emphasis is elder law, which includes estate planning, probate, Medicaid, and Medicare. Other areas of practice include civil litigation and domestic relations.

Johns received her law degree from Faulkner University and is a member of the American Bar Association, the Alabama State Bar Association, the Montgomery County Bar Association, the National Academy of Elder Law Attorneys, AAfPE, NALA, and the Alabama Association of Legal Assistants.

The true spirit of the legal profession inherently includes servicing the needs of the less fortunate in society. One avenue to increasing equal access to justice and maintaining the affordability of legal services for all less fortunate clients is *pro bono* service (volunteer work). As legal professionals, paralegals should recognize *pro bono* efforts as being an integral part of their career. Like the traditional law office environment, the *pro bono* legal environment invites an opportunity for paralegals to use their legal skills to prepare legal documents and undertake legal research and investigation. *Pro bono* service also offers an excellent opportunity for the paralegal to network within the legal community and to develop skills in diverse areas of the law. Above all, helping those who desperately need legal representation can be an immensely gratifying experience for the paralegal.

Pro bono service is encouraged and endorsed by many bar associations and paralegal organizations. The American Bar Association's Standing Committee on Legal Assistants encourages *pro bono* service for paralegals in Guideline 10 of its *Model Guidelines on the Utilization of Legal Assistant Services*. Additionally, both NFPA and NALA recognize and promote the importance of *pro bono* work and regularly recognize paralegals engaging in *pro bono* work.

PRO BONO OPPORTUNITIES

Opportunities for the delivery of *pro bono* services vary greatly. For example, many in society suffer from problems associated with collection actions, bankruptcy, domestic relations, and obtaining public benefits. More specialized areas of *pro bono* legal work may involve the civil rights of prisoners, arbitration, tax claims, and elder law. Finally, paralegals fluent in various languages are certainly valuable in all areas of *pro bono* work.

Sources of *pro bono* opportunities are abundant. When searching for *pro bono* opportunities, paralegals should always start by consulting with their supervising attorneys for in-house *pro bono* opportunities. Many law firms maintain yearly *pro bono* service requirements for partners and associates. It is likely that the attorneys at these firms will welcome any assistance offered by paralegals. In the absence of in-house *pro bono* opportunities, paralegals should utilize their investigative skills to uncover opportunities within their communities. For instance, many paralegal organizations, local bar associations, and legal aid organizations maintain a directory of *pro bono* opportunities available on the national and state levels. These directories are a great starting point in finding suitable *pro bono* opportunities. Finally, paralegals should never hesitate to initiate organized *pro bono* services within their communities. Some of the most outstanding programs have been created by identifying needs within the community and using determination and initiative to meet those needs with *pro bono* legal services.

FEATURED GUEST, *Continued*

ETHICAL CHALLENGES OF *PRO BONO* WORK

As *pro bono* service becomes an important aspect of the paralegal career, special attention must be given to the ethical challenges that accompany this work. *Pro bono* service is typically delivered free of charge to the client. The absence of legal fees does not correlate to a lack of ethical responsibility, however. In fact, paralegals should participate in the delivery of *pro bono* services with a heightened sense of ethical awareness. In the *pro bono* setting, a lack of adequate lawyer supervision is often apparent. Therefore, it is the paralegal's responsibility to identify and appreciate ethical challenges presented by the *pro bono* client.

Observe the Duty of Competence. *Pro bono* clients are entitled to the same quality of legal services as paying clients. Paralegals must thus make sure that they are competent in the area in which they provide *pro bono* services. It is not uncommon for legal professionals to volunteer for a variety of *pro bono* services. Paralegals not familiar with a particular area of law should endeavor to utilize legal research and investigative skills to determine the proper forms or procedures required in the *pro bono* client's case. This initial research and investigation, followed by consultation with the supervising attorney, will most likely ensure that the ethical challenge of competency is met.

Avoid the Unauthorized Practice of Law. Perhaps the most pervasive ethical challenge presented to the paralegal in any context is the unauthorized practice of law (UPL). This is particularly true in the delivery of *pro bono* services. Many paralegals may feel compelled to offer legal advice to needy individuals simply out of compassion and sensitivity. Additionally, paralegals may have more direct client contact in *pro bono* matters. The more direct the contact, the more likely it is that a UPL situation could arise. Remember that the prohibition against UPL is not lifted simply because you are serving nonpaying clients. Indeed, paralegals must be ever watchful to avoid UPL regardless of the setting or the client's ability to pay for legal services.

Confidentiality Issues. Ethical challenges relating to confidentiality will undoubtedly arise in the *pro bono* setting. *Pro bono* clients may present interesting dilemmas and legal obstacles, yet the paralegal must adhere to the strict ethical obligation of confidentiality. When in doubt as to whether certain information is confidential, paralegals should remember to rely on the discretion of their supervising attorneys in making this determination and in assessing the potential ramifications of information disclosure.

Conflicts of Interest. Another challenge in *pro bono* work has to do with conflicts of interest. A

> **"[H]elping those who desperately need legal representation can be an immensely gratifying experience for the paralegal."**

paralegal working for a large law firm may be accustomed to computer-assisted conflicts-check procedures that can be performed easily and quickly. Many organizations that sponsor *pro bono* services, however, do not possess the capabilities to perform a conflicts check. Therefore, the responsibility to ensure that no conflict exists remains with the paralegal in many situations. This challenge is easily overcome by a heightened awareness of a potential conflict in any *pro bono* service.

CONCLUSION

Pro bono legal work is an important aspect of a responsible legal community. As a part of the legal community, paralegals should be dedicated to increasing equal access to justice and to maintaining the affordability of legal services for less fortunate clients through *pro bono* work. Through investigation and initiative, paralegals can uncover unlimited opportunities for personal and professional gratification through *pro bono* work.

NATIONAL AND INTERNATIONAL LAW

On the Web
The Library of Congress offers extensive information on national and international law at **http://www.loc.gov.**

Because business and other activities are becoming increasingly global in scope, numerous cases now brought before American courts relate to issues involving foreign parties or governments. The laws of other nations and international doctrines or agreements may affect the outcome of these cases, and thus those laws, doctrines, and agreements are also sources of law that guide judicial decisions in American courts. Many paralegals, particularly those who work for law firms that service clients operating in foreign countries, may need to become familiar with the legal systems of other nations during the course of their careers. For example, if you work in a firm in Arizona, California, New Mexico, or Texas, you may assist in the representation of Mexican clients. In this situation, you will want to have some familiarity with Mexican law and any international agreements that regulate U.S.–Mexican relations, such as the North American Free Trade Agreement.

National Law

national law
Law that pertains to a particular nation (as opposed to international law).

The law of a particular nation is referred to as **national law.** The laws of nations differ from country to country because each country's laws reflect that nation's own unique cultural, historical, economic, and political background. Broadly speaking, however, there are two types of legal systems used by the various countries of the world. We have already discussed one of these systems—the common law system of England and the United States. Generally, those countries that were once colonies of Great Britain retained their English common law heritage after they achieved their independence. Today, common law systems exist in several countries, including Australia, Canada, India, Ireland, and New Zealand.

On the Web
To find information on the laws governing other nations, including constitutions around the world, go to **http://www.oefre.unibe.ch/law/icl/home.html.**

In contrast to Great Britain and the common law countries, most of the other European nations base their legal systems on Roman *civil law,* or "code law." The term *civil law,* as used here, refers not to civil as opposed to criminal law but to *codified law*—an ordered grouping of legal principles enacted into law by a legislature or governing body. In a **civil law system,** the primary source of law is a statutory code, and case precedents are not judicially binding, as they normally are in a common law system. This is not to say that precedents are unimportant in a civil law system. On the contrary, judges in such systems commonly refer to previous decisions as sources of legal guidance. The difference is that judges in a civil law system are not obligated to follow precedent to the extent that judges in a common law system are; in other words, the doctrine of *stare decisis* does not apply.

civil law system
A system of law derived from that of the Roman Empire and based on a code rather than case law; the predominant system of law in the nations of continental Europe and the nations that were once their colonies.

Today, the civil law system is followed in most of the continental European countries, as well as in the Latin American, African, and Asian countries that were once colonies of the continental European nations. Japan and South Africa also have civil law systems. Ingredients of the civil law system are also found in the Islamic courts of predominantly Muslim countries. In the United States, the state of Louisiana, because of its historical ties to France, has in part a civil law system. The legal systems of Puerto Rico, Québec, and Scotland are similarly characterized as having elements of a civil law system.

International Law

international law
The law that governs relations among nations. International customs and treaties are generally considered to be two of the most important sources of international law.

Relationships between countries are regulated to an extent by international law. **International law** can be defined as a body of written and unwritten laws observed by independent nations and governing the acts of individuals as well as governments. The key difference between national law and international law is the fact that national law can be enforced by government authorities, whereas international law is enforced primarily for reasons of courtesy or expediency. In essence, international law is the result of centuries-old attempts to reconcile the traditional need of each nation to be the final authority over its own affairs with the desire of nations to benefit economically from trade and harmonious relations with one another. Although no independent nation can be compelled to obey a law external to itself, nations can and do voluntarily agree to be governed in certain respects by international law for the purpose of facilitating international trade and commerce and civilized discourse.

Traditional sources of international law include the customs that have been historically observed by nations in their dealings with each other. Other sources are treaties and international organizations and conferences. A **treaty** is an agreement between two or more nations that creates rights and duties binding on the parties to the treaty, just as a private contract creates rights and duties binding on the parties to the contract. To give effect to a treaty, the supreme power of each nation that is a party to the treaty must ratify it. For example, the U.S. Constitution requires approval by two-thirds of the Senate before a treaty executed by the president will be binding on the U.S. government. *Bilateral agreements,* as their name implies, occur when two nations form an agreement that will govern their commercial exchanges or other relations with one another. *Multilateral agreements* are formed by several nations. The European Union, for example, which regulates commercial activities among its European member nations, is the result of a multilateral trade agreement. Other multilateral agreements have led to the formation of regional trade associations, such as the North American Free Trade Agreement, which was formed by Canada, Mexico, and the United States.

International organizations and conferences also play an important role in the international legal arena. International organizations and conferences adopt resolutions, declarations, and other types of standards that often require a particular behavior of nations. The General Assembly of the United Nations, for example, has adopted numerous resolutions and declarations that embody principles of international law and has sponsored conferences that have led to the formation of international agreements. The United States is a member of more than one hundred multilateral and bilateral organizations, including at least twenty through the United Nations.

treaty
An agreement, or compact, formed between two independent nations.

International Law and the Paralegal

Communications technology, improved transportation facilities, and international organizations and treaties have all helped to form a global environment of business. What this means for attorneys and paralegals is that an increasing amount of legal work has an international dimension. As a paralegal, you may be asked to assist your supervising attorney in many tasks that involve an international aspect, including the following:

- Research the law of a foreign country on a particular issue, such as labor law, to determine whether a corporate client (or your corporate employer) with business operations overseas is complying with the laws of the host country.

- Assist a client who has a manufacturing plant overseas in forming employment policies that are consistent with the national law of the host country and (if U.S. employees work at the plant) with U.S. employment laws.

- Determine whether a client's patented product will be protected under the patent laws of a specific foreign country or whether an international treaty provides for such protection.

- Determine what special contractual provisions should be included in a client's contract for the international sale of goods to protect the client's interest.

TODAY'S PROFESSIONAL PARALEGAL

Legal and Paralegal Practice in England

Linda Lowden, a legal assistant with the large New York firm of Stone & Stone, has just received an exciting new assignment. She is going to work in the firm's London, England, office for several months to perform "due-diligence" work for a joint venture involving an American client, USA-Tech, Inc., and a British company, BritTech, Inc. Due-diligence work is the background research that is done on a company's financial records to make sure that these records accurately reflect the true financial situation of the company.

PARALEGALS IN ENGLAND

Linda arrives at Heathrow Airport and is greeted by RuthAnne Coddens, a legal executive with whom she will be working. In England, legal assistants are called legal executives. On the drive into London, RuthAnne explains that legal executives have been used for many years in England and are very well accepted. They are required to earn a degree and to obtain work experience prior to accepting employment as legal executives. Once they are employed, they assist attorneys by preparing legal documents, interviewing clients, and representing clients in the inferior (lower) courts. Legal executives work for solicitors' firms.

ATTORNEYS IN ENGLAND

"What is a solicitor's firm?" asks Linda. RuthAnne explains that in England, lawyers practice either as solicitors or as barristers. Solicitors advise clients on legal matters and prepare briefs, contracts, wills, and other legal documents for their clients. Barristers, in contrast, only represent clients in court. They are not allowed to form law partnerships, which is why most legal executives work for solicitors' firms. RuthAnne drops Linda off at the apartment where she will be living for the next several months.

LINDA'S WORK BEGINS

On Monday, RuthAnne picks Linda up for work, and they drive to the London offices of Stone & Stone. Linda begins her day with a tour of the offices. She meets the people with whom she will be working. She also talks to Stephen Markham, the attorney for BritTech, on the phone and arranges to meet with him at BritTech's offices the next day. Finally, by the end of the day, she settles into her temporary office and begins to organize a plan for tackling the due-diligence work that she has come to London to perform.

She begins her due-diligence research the next day by going to BritTech and talking to Stephen Markham. She requests that she be given access to BritTech's financial records so that she can review them and, if necessary, make copies to be examined by a certified public accountant. She also needs to verify the number of years that BritTech has been in business, which she can tell from its financial data.

TITLE SEARCHES AND INSURANCE POLICIES

As a result of her preliminary review of the financial records, Linda finds that the company owns all of the real estate on which its manufacturing operations are located. The next step is to perform title searches on the property to be certain that there are no liens on (legal claims to) the property. Linda returns to the office to find out how to go about a title search in London. She completes the title searches, finds nothing unusual, and forwards the results to her supervising attorney in New York.

The next step is to go to BritTech and look at the insurance policies for the business. It is important to verify that they exist and to look at the type of coverage they provide. Linda returns once more to the offices of BritTech and spends many days reviewing and copying the company's insurance policies.

LINDA COMPLETES HER TASK

Linda has now been in London for four months. Her research has gone well. She has one more major project. It is to review court dockets for litigation pending against BritTech. For this project, she needs the assistance of RuthAnne, who is familiar with the courts in London. She can tell Linda which courts would be handling cases in which BritTech would be a defendant and in which BritTech could lose large sums of money if the plaintiffs won. Linda and RuthAnne begin their tour of the courts in London. After two weeks, they find one case that may have significant financial consequences for BritTech, should the company lose the case. They obtain a copy of the documents relating to the case from the file, and Linda sends them to New York for further analysis of the potential liability. She is now ready to return home.

- Send communications via mail, express delivery services, telephone, e-mail, or fax to the foreign offices of an American firm or a foreign firm with which an American client has business dealings.

✺ KEY TERMS AND CONCEPTS

administrative agency	enabling legislation	precedent
administrative law	equitable principles and maxims	public policy
adversarial system of justice	historical school	remedy
Bill of Rights	injunction	remedy at law
case law	international law	remedy in equity
case of first impression	jurisprudence	rescission
chancellor	laches	sociological school
citation	law	specific performance
civil law system	national law	*stare decisis*
codify	natural law school	statute
common law	opinion	statute of limitations
constitutional law	ordinance	statutory law
court of equity	party	supremacy clause
court of law	positivist school	treaty

✺ CHAPTER SUMMARY

The Framework of American Law	1. *Definition of law*—The law has been defined variously over the ages, yet all definitions of law rest on the following assumption about the nature of law: law consists of a body of rules of conduct established and enforced by the controlling authority (the government) of a society.
	2. *Judicial approaches to the law*—The following are some of the leading schools of jurisprudential thought:
	a. The natural law school believes that some laws are universal and stem from moral and ethical principles that are inherent in human nature (as opposed to written laws). This is one of the oldest and most significant schools of jurisprudence.
	b. The positivist school believes that there is no higher law than a nation's positive (written) laws.
	c. The historical school believes that history has proved over time which legal doctrines work the best and should continue to be applied.
	d. Legal realists and the sociological school believe that judges should take into account the social and economic realities of the situation when deciding cases.

Primary Sources of American Law	There are four primary sources of American law: the U.S. Constitution and the constitutions of various states; statutory law, including laws passed by Congress, state legislatures, and local governing bodies; regulations created by administrative agencies; and the common law doctrines developed in cases.
Constitutional Law	Constitutional law is all law that is based on the provisions in the U.S. Constitution, as amended, and the various state constitutions. The U.S. Constitution creates and empowers the three branches of government, sets forth the relationship between the states and the federal government, and establishes procedures for amending the Constitution. 1. *Supremacy*—The U.S. Constitution is the supreme law of the land. A law in violation of the Constitution or one of its amendments, no matter what its source, will be declared unconstitutional and will not be enforced. A state constitution, so long as it does not conflict with the U.S. Constitution, is the supreme law within the state's borders. 2. *The Bill of Rights*—The first ten amendments to the federal constitution are known as the Bill of Rights. These amendments embody a series of protections for individuals—and in some cases, business entities—against various types of government actions. The Bill of Rights originally limited only the powers of the federal government. After the Fourteenth Amendment was passed, the Supreme Court began to apply the protections of the Bill of Rights against state government actions. 3. *The courts and constitutional law*—The rights secured by the constitution are not absolute. The courts, and ultimately the Supreme Court, interpret and define the boundaries of the rights guaranteed by the Constitution.
Statutory Law	Statutory law consists of all laws enacted by the federal Congress, a state legislature, a municipality, or some other governing body. Laws passed by Congress and state legislatures are called *statutes* and are published in federal and state codes. Laws passed by local governing units (cities and counties) are called *ordinances*. Statutory law takes precedence over the common law.
Administrative Law	Administrative law consists of the rules, regulations, orders, and decisions of administrative agencies at all levels of government. 1. *Agency creation*—Federal administrative agencies are created by enabling legislation enacted by the U.S. Congress, which specifies the name, purpose, composition, and powers of each agency created. State administrative agencies are created in a similar manner. 2. *Agency powers*—Agencies have the power to administer and enforce legislation and to issue rules that implement the goals of specific legislation.
Case Law and the Common Law Tradition	Case law (also referred to as judge-made law or the common law) consists of the decisions rendered by judges in cases that come before the court. Case law is a major source of law in the United States. 1. *The origins of common law*—The common law tradition originated in medieval England with the creation of the king's courts and was adopted in America during the colonial era.

Case Law and the Common Law Tradition—Continued

2. Stare decisis—*Stare decisis* means "to stand on things decided" and is the doctrine of precedent, which is a defining characteristic of the common law system. Under this doctrine, judges are obligated to follow the earlier decisions of that court or a higher court within their jurisdiction if the same points arise again in litigation.

   a. A court will depart from precedent if the court decides that the precedent should no longer be followed, such as if the ruling was incorrect or does not apply in view of changes in the social or technological environment.

   b. If no precedent exists, the court considers the matter as a case of first impression and looks to other areas of law and public policy for guidance.

3. *Remedies at law versus remedies in equity*—In medieval England, two types of courts emerged: courts of law and courts of equity. Courts of law granted remedies at law (such as money damages). Courts of equity arose in response to the need for other types of relief. In the United States today, the same court can typically grant either legal or equitable remedies.

4. *Remedies in equity*—Remedies in equity, which are normally available only when the remedy at law (money damages) is inadequate, include the following:

   a. Specific performance—A court decree ordering a party to perform a contractual promise.

   b. Injunction—A court order directing someone to do or refrain from doing a particular act.

   c. Rescission—An action to undo a contract and return the parties to their original positions; all duties under the contract are abolished.

5. *Statutory law and the common law* —The common law governs all areas of law not covered by statutory law. As the body of statutory law grows to meet different needs, the common law covers fewer areas. Even if an area is governed by a statutory law, however, the common law plays an important role because statutes are interpreted and applied by the courts, and court decisions may become precedents that must be followed by lower courts within the jurisdiction.

6. *Case law terminology*—

   a. Case title and citation—A case title consists of the surnames of the parties, such as *Baranski v. Peretto*. The *v.* stands for *versus*. The citation indicates the volume and page number of the reporter in which the case can be found.

   b. Party—The plaintiff or the defendant. Some cases involve multiple parties—that is, more than one plaintiff or defendant.

   c. Judge and justice—These terms are often used synonymously. Usage of the terms varies among courts. The term *justice* is traditionally used to designate judges who sit on the bench of the United States Supreme Court.

   d. Opinion—A document containing the court's reasons for its decision, the rules of law that apply, and the judgment. If the opinion is not unanimous, a majority opinion—reflecting the view of the majority of judges or justices—will be written. Concurring and dissenting opinions may also be written.

7. *The adversarial system of justice*—American courts, like English courts, follow a system of justice in which the parties to a lawsuit are opponents, or adversaries, and present their cases in the light most favorable to themselves. The impartial decision maker (the judge or jury) then determines who wins and who loses based on the evidence presented.

National Law	National law is the law of a particular nation. National law differs from nation to nation because each nation's laws have evolved from that nation's unique customs and traditions. Most countries have one of the following types of legal systems: 1. *The common law system*—Great Britain and the United States have a common law system. Generally, countries that were once colonies of Great Britain retained their English common law heritage after achieving independence. Under the common law, case precedents are judicially binding. 2. *The civil law system*—Many of the continental European countries and the nations that were formerly their colonies have civil law systems. Based on Roman codified law, civil law (or code law) is an ordered grouping of legal principles enacted into law by a governing body. The primary source of law is a statutory code. Although important, case precedents are not judicially binding.
International Law	International law is a body of laws that govern relationships among nations. International law allows nations to enjoy harmonious relations with each other and to benefit economically from international trade. Sources of international law include international customs and traditions developed over time, treaties among nations, and international organizations and conferences.

QUESTIONS FOR REVIEW

1. What is law? Does everyone agree on a single definition of law? What are some schools of jurisprudential thought, and how can these theories affect how the law is interpreted and applied in a specific case?
2. What is constitutional law? If a state constitution conflicts with the U.S. Constitution, which constitution takes priority?
3. What is a statute? How is statutory law created? What is an ordinance? What happens when a state statute conflicts with a federal statute?
4. What is an administrative agency? How are such agencies created?
5. Where, when, and how did the common law tradition begin?
6. What does *stare decisis* mean? Why is it said that the doctrine of *stare decisis* is the cornerstone of English and American law?
7. What is the difference between courts of law and courts of equity? Why did courts of equity evolve?
8. What kinds of remedies could be granted by courts of law? Name three remedies that could be granted by courts of equity.
9. How has statutory law affected the common law? What happens to a common law doctrine once it is codified in a statute?
10. What impact does the adversarial nature of our legal system have on court proceedings and attorneys in the United States? What are some pros and cons of the adversarial system?

ETHICAL QUESTIONS

1. Lon Thompson is a paralegal who works for a New York law firm. One of the firm's clients wants to open a chain of restaurants (including bars) in Michigan, and Lon has been asked to research the Michigan statutes to find out the legal drinking age in that state. Lon looks in the hardbound volume of the Michigan statutes and sees that the legal drinking age is eighteen. Lon forgets to check the "pocket part," which is inserted into a "pocket" in the inside back cover of the book. The pocket part contains amendments, indicates if a statute has been repealed, and generally updates the law as described in the volume. Because

of this oversight, Lon does not learn that the legal drinking age in Michigan was recently raised to twenty-one. He tells his supervising attorney that the legal drinking age in Michigan is eighteen, and the attorney passes that information on to the client. Has Lon violated any ethical rule? If so, which one? What consequences might the attorney face as a result of Lon's oversight? What consequences might Lon face?

2. John Scott, an attorney, has asked his legal assistant, Nanette Lynch, to do some research. Nanette is to research the state statutes to find out how many persons are required to witness a will. Nanette looks up the relevant state statute and finds it difficult to understand because it is so poorly written. After studying the statute for a while, Nanette decides that two witnesses are required and conveys this information to John. Actually, the statute requires that three persons witness a will or it will not be valid. John, relying on Nanette's conclusion, has two persons witness a client's will the next day. Have John and Nanette violated any ethical rules? Explain.

3. Marilyn Clark works as a paralegal in a small general law practice. After work one day, she receives a telephone call from her Aunt May, who is in distress. Her Aunt May and Uncle Bill went to open their summer cottage and found that beavers had made a dam in the lake, which caused severe flooding on their property and in their basement. Uncle Bill is threatening to take his rifle and put an end to the beavers and their mess. Aunt May, an environmentalist, does not want Uncle Bill to shoot the beavers, so she asks Marilyn if it is illegal to shoot beavers. Marilyn knows that beavers are protected as an endangered species under federal or state environmental statutes. How should Marilyn answer this question?

4. A legal assistant in your law firm is working on a case law research project for a class that she is taking. She spends two hours doing personal case law research for her project on a computerized legal-research service that charges the firm several dollars per minute of online time. The legal assistant bills the two hours to a major client's file, assuming that no one will ever learn what she has done. You happen to be sitting at the terminal next to her, and you notice that she bills the time to one of the firm's clients. What should you do? What would you do if you learned that your supervising attorney had billed personal research time to a client's file?

❋ PRACTICE QUESTIONS AND ASSIGNMENTS

1. Identify the constitutional amendment being violated in the following hypothetical situations:

   a. Jeremy's boss threatens to fire him if he does not work on Saturday nights, even though that is when he attends worship services.

   b. The city proposes an ordinance requiring that anyone caught stealing be punished by having his or her hand cut off for the first offense and the other hand cut off for the second offense.

   c. Because Robert's house is located in a poor neighborhood, the police decide that he must be a drug dealer. The police burst in and tear the place apart searching for drugs. They find nothing.

   d. The federal government bans all advertising of cigarettes.

2. In the following hypothetical situations, identify the type of case (criminal or civil), the remedy being sought, and whether it is a remedy at law or a remedy in equity:

   a. Beth files a petition with the court. She is seeking a decree that would undo a contract into which she entered.

   b. Jim sues Bob, seeking to be compensated for the cost of replacing several trees that Bob's dog has destroyed.

   c. Laurie seeks to have a contract for the sale of an antique Mercedes enforced.

   d. Sam files a petition seeking to prevent the electric company from cutting down a large tree on his property.

3. Identify the type of law (common law, constitutional law, statutory law, or administrative law) that applies in each of the following scenarios:

   a. Jean Gorman strongly disagrees with the U.S. government's decision to declare war on a foreign country. She places an antiwar sign in the window of her home. The city passes an ordinance that bans all such signs.

   b. An official of the state department of natural resources learns that the Ferris Widget Company has violated the state's Hazardous Waste Management Act. The official issues a complaint against the company for not properly handling and labeling its toxic waste.

c. Mrs. Sams was walking down a busy street when two teenagers on in-line skates crashed into her because they weren't watching where they were going. As a result of the teenagers' conduct, Mrs. Sams broke her hip, and according to her doctor, she will never walk normally again. She sues the teenagers for damages.

d. Joseph Barnes is arrested and charged with the crime of murder.

4. Identify the following statutory law concepts:

a. A state law enacted to require that teenagers receive expanded driving privileges at the ages of sixteen and seventeen.

b. A rule requring that trash be placed on the curb no sooner than 3:00 P.M. on the day before trash pickup.

c. The changing and organizing of criminal law into a statute.

5. Which of the following legal specialties are governed primarily by statutory law?

a. Tort law.

b. Family law.

c. Corporate law.

d. Property law.

6. Which of the following is an example of an administrative law case?

a. An employment-discrimination case that is filed with the EEOC.

b. A family law case pending in circuit court.

c. A dispute pending before the Internal Revenue Service.

d. An issue of securities law.

e. A tax matter pending before the Court of Federal Claims.

7. Identify whether each of the following is a national or international law concept:

a. The rule that in Germany there is no speed limit on the *autobahn*.

b. The French legal system, in which the doctrine of *stare decisis* does not apply.

c. The World Trade Organization, which governs trade among all member nations.

d. The documents governing and establishing the European Union.

✳ QUESTIONS FOR CRITICAL ANALYSIS

1. Rosa Jennings is an experienced paralegal. One day, while visiting with one of her neighbors, Lori Dolan, Lori asks Rosa some general questions about American law. Lori wants to know, for example, what the Bill of Rights is and what is meant by the common law tradition. Write one paragraph on each amendment in the Bill of Rights and a one-paragraph description of the common law tradition. Explain these concepts in your own words and include examples.

2. The rights guaranteed by the U.S. Constitution would be of little significance if they were not enforced by the government. In view of this fact, is a written constitution really necessary? Would the rights and privileges enjoyed by Americans be any different if we did not have a written constitution?

3. Locate *Clinton v. Jones*, 520 U.S. 681, 117 S.Ct. 1636, 137 L.Ed.2d 945 (1997). Answer the following questions about the case:

a. Read the first paragraph of the Supreme Court's syllabus, or summary. Who filed the lawsuit in the federal district court? For what reason(s)? What did the federal district court decide?

b. The Eighth Circuit Court of Appeals affirmed, or upheld, the district court's decision in part and reversed it in part. Using the syllabus, explain what the Eighth Circuit Court of Appeals did.

c. Find the heading, *"Held."* Paragraph 2 contains subparagraphs (a)–(d). This is a summary of the Supreme Court's reasons for affirming the decision of the Eighth Circuit Court of Appeals. For each subparagraph, summarize the Court's reasoning in one to two sentences.

4. Laws in the United States come primarily from four sources: the federal Constitution and state constitutions, statutes, administrative agencies, and the courts. Why are there so many different sources? What might happen if there were not?

How could the law be changed if only courts made the law?

5. Judges, particularly the justices of the United States Supreme Court, play a paramount role in the American legal system. Why is this?

6. Why does the body of statutory law continue to expand?

7. Why do legislatures delegate authority to administrative agencies? How is the delegation of authority to agencies accomplished? Give examples of two federal administrative agencies and the type of work that paralegals might perform with respect to the areas regulated by these agencies.

8. Of what does law consist? How does common law fit into the definition of law given in this chapter? How did the common law develop?

9. What does the phrase *stare decisis* mean? What obligation does *stare decisis* impose on judges? How did this doctrine develop? What do courts do when declining to follow precedent? What do they do when there is no precedent?

10. Why were the courts of law and the courts of equity separate? Are they still separate? How do legal and equitable remedies differ?

✳ PROJECTS

1. Look at the Constitution in Appendix J of this text. Identify the amendment and quote the relevant language in the Bill of Rights that gives U.S. citizens the following rights and protections:

   a. The right to freely exercise one's religion.

   b. Protection against unreasonable searches and seizures.

   c. Protection against self-incrimination.

   d. The right to counsel in criminal prosecutions.

   e. The right to free speech.

2. Look in the white pages of your local telephone directory for your federal representative and senator. Write down their names, addresses, and telephone numbers. Consider writing or calling their offices to request information on internships.

3. Look in your local telephone directory for listings under the name of your state. Write down the names of three administrative agencies listed there, and see if you can determine from their names what areas or activities they regulate. Write down your conclusions.

4. Find out if your state's courts use different procedures for cases that involve equity matters than for cases that do not. Are there any trial courts in your state that cannot grant equitable remedies?

5. Read through the sample court case presented as Exhibit 16.17 in Chapter 16. Identify the case name, the citation, the parties, the judge or justice who authored the opinion, the type of opinion (for example, majority, unanimous, and so on), and the first five words of the opinion.

6. Research the North American Free Trade Agreement (NAFTA) in periodicals, such as *Time* magazine or *Newsweek*. Write a one-page paper explaining what the treaty involves and who the signatories are.

✳ USING INTERNET RESOURCES

1. Go to FindLaw's home page at http://www.findlaw. com. This site offers links to many of the federal and state sources of law that you have read about in this chapter. In this exercise, you will be examining state laws, so click on "U.S. State Resources." The page you reach will list all of the states in alphabetical order. Open the site for your state, and then select "Primary Materials." Browse through the state sources of law that can be accessed online, and then answer the following questions:

   a. Were you able to access the text of your state's constitution?

   b. Did the site include your state's code (compilation of statutes) and administrative regulations?

   c. What other primary materials were included in the site?

   d. Now browse through the "Primary Materials" sites for three other states. How does your state's site compare to those of other states in terms of comprehensiveness and ease of use?

2. A database of the United States Supreme Court, located at http://www.usscplus.com, contains a description of the Court's role in interpreting the

Constitution. Go to this Web site, click on "Supreme Court FAQ," and then click on "The Court and Constitutional Interpretation." What is judicial review? What role did the case *Marbury v. Madison* have in shaping the Supreme Court's power of judicial review? Can the Supreme Court give "advisory opinions"? Why or why not?

3. Go to the Web site for World Constitutions and International Treaties at http://library.tamu.edu/ govdocs/workshop. Using the country index, pick a country in which you are interested. Does the country have a constitution? When was it adopted? Can you view it in any language other than English? Now go back to the home page. How many categories of international treaties are available through this site? Click on "Trade and Commercial Relations." How many treaties are listed under this heading?

END NOTES

1. Twenty dollars was forty days' pay for the average person when the Bill of Rights was written.

2. 47 U.S.C. Section 223(d)(1)(B). Specifically, the CDA prohibited any obscene or indecent message that "depicts or describes, in terms patently offensive as measured by contemporary community standards, sexual or excretory activities or organs." (You will read about the citation form for federal laws in Chapter 16.)

3. 521 U.S. 844, 117 S.Ct. 2329, 138 L.Ed.2d 874 (1997).

4. For example, a U.S. District Court held that the Children's Internet Protection Act of 2000, 17 U.S.C. Sections 1701–1741, was unconstitutional in *American Library Association, Inc. v. United States,* 201 F.Supp.2d 401 (E.D.Pa. 2002). The Children's Online Privacy Protection Act (COPA) of 1998, 15 U.S.C. Sections 6501–6506, was also challenged as unconstitutional. The Supreme Court, however, determined that its provisions did not violate the Constitution. See *Ashcroft v. American Civil Liberties Union,* 535 U.S 564, 122 S.Ct. 1700, 152 L.Ed.2d 771 (2002).

5. Pronounced *stahr-ee* dih-*si*-ses.

6. 347 U.S. 483, 74 S.Ct. 686, 98 L.Ed. 873 (1954).

7. See, for example, *Plessy v. Ferguson,* 163 U.S. 537, 16 S.Ct. 1138, 41 L.Ed. 256 (1896). In *Plessy,* the United States Supreme Court upheld a Louisiana statute providing for separate railway cars for whites and African Americans. The Court held that the statute did not violate the U.S. Constitution, which mandates equal protection under the laws, because the statute provided for equal facilities for African Americans. Lower courts interpreted this decision to apply to other types of facilities as well, and the "separate-but-equal doctrine" prevailed until the *Brown* decision in 1954.

8. *In re Baby M,* 217 N.J.Super. 313, 525 A.2d 1128 (1987).

9. Pronounced reh-*sih*-zhen.

CHAPTER 6

THE COURT SYSTEM AND ALTERNATIVE DISPUTE RESOLUTION

Chapter Outline

✳ INTRODUCTION ✳ BASIC JUDICIAL REQUIREMENTS
✳ STATE COURT SYSTEMS ✳ THE FEDERAL COURT SYSTEM
✳ ALTERNATIVE DISPUTE RESOLUTION

After completing this chapter, you will know:

- The requirements that must be met before a lawsuit can be brought in a particular court by a particular party.

- The difference between jurisdiction and venue.

- The types of courts that make up a typical state court system and the different functions of trial courts and appellate courts.

- The organization of the federal court system and the relationship between state and federal jurisdiction.

- How cases reach the United States Supreme Court.

- The various ways in which disputes can be resolved outside the court system.

INTRODUCTION

As explained in Chapter 5, American law is based on numerous elements—the federal Constitution and state constitutions, statutes passed by federal and state legislatures, administrative law, the case decisions and legal principles that form the common law, and, to an extent, the laws of other nations and international law. But the laws would be meaningless without the courts to interpret and apply them, and for this reason the court system is a vital component of the American legal system.

Paralegals working in all areas of the law, and particularly litigation paralegals, need to have a basic understanding of the different types of courts that make up the American court system. Even though there are fifty-two court systems—one for each of the fifty states, one for the District of Columbia, and a federal system—similarities abound. Keep in mind that the federal courts are not superior to the state courts. They are simply an independent court system, which derives its authority from Article III, Section 2, of the U.S. Constitution.[1]

In the first part of this chapter, we examine the structure of the American court system. Because of the costs, in both time and money, and the potential publicity attending court trials, many individuals and firms today are turning to alternative methods of dispute resolution that allow parties to resolve their disputes outside of court. In some cases, parties are required by the courts to try to resolve their disputes by one of these methods before they can take their cases to court. In the latter part of this chapter, we provide an overview of these alternative methods of dispute resolution and the role that attorneys and paralegals play in facilitating out-of-court dispute settlements.

BASIC JUDICIAL REQUIREMENTS

Before a lawsuit can be brought before a court, certain requirements must be met. We examine here these important requirements and some of the basic features of the American system of justice.

Types of Jurisdiction

jurisdiction
The authority of a court to hear and decide a specific action.

In Latin, *juris* means "law," and *diction* means "to speak." Thus, "the power to speak the law" is the literal meaning of the term **jurisdiction.** Before any court can hear a case, it must have jurisdiction over the person against whom the suit is brought or over the property involved in the suit. The court must also have jurisdiction over the subject matter.

JURISDICTION OVER PERSONS.   Generally, a court can exercise personal jurisdiction (*in personam* jurisdiction) over residents of a certain geographical area. A state trial court, for example, normally has jurisdictional authority over residents within the state or within a particular area of the state, such as a county or district. A state's highest court (often called the state supreme court[2]) has jurisdictional authority over all residents within the state.

long arm statute
A state statute that permits a state to obtain jurisdiction over nonresident individuals and corporations. Individuals or corporations, however, must have certain "minimum contacts" with that state for the statute to apply.

In some cases, under the authority of a long arm statute, a court can exercise personal jurisdiction over nonresidents as well. A **long arm statute** is a state law permitting courts to exercise jurisdiction over nonresident defendants. Before a court can exercise jurisdiction over a nonresident under a long arm statute, though, it must be demonstrated that the nonresident had sufficient contacts (*minimum contacts*) with the state to justify the jurisdiction. For example, if a

California citizen committed a wrong within the state of Arizona, such as causing an automobile injury or selling defective goods, an Arizona state court usually could exercise jurisdiction over the California citizen. Similarly, a state may exercise personal jurisdiction over a nonresident defendant who is sued for breaching a contract that was formed within the state.

In regard to corporations, the minimum-contacts requirement is usually met if the corporation does business within the state. A Maine corporation that has a branch office or manufacturing plant in Georgia, for example, has sufficient minimum contacts with the state of Georgia to allow a Georgia court to exercise jurisdiction over the Maine corporation. If the Maine corporation advertises and sells its products in Georgia, those activities may also suffice to meet the minimum-contacts requirements. A state court may also be able to exercise jurisdiction over a corporation in another country if it can be demonstrated that the foreign corporation has met the minimum-contacts test. For example, consider an Italian corporation that markets its products through an American distributor. If the corporation knew that its products would be distributed to local markets throughout the United States, it could be sued in any state by a plaintiff who was injured by one of the products.

JURISDICTION OVER PROPERTY.   A court can also exercise jurisdiction over property that is located within its boundaries. This kind of jurisdiction is known as *in rem* jurisdiction, or "jurisdiction over the thing." For example, suppose that a dispute arises over the ownership of a boat in dry dock in Fort Lauderdale, Florida. The boat is owned by an Ohio resident, over whom a Florida court cannot normally exercise personal jurisdiction. The other party to the dispute is a resident of Nebraska. In this situation, a lawsuit concerning the boat could be brought in a Florida state court on the basis of the court's *in rem* jurisdiction.

JURISDICTION OVER SUBJECT MATTER.   Jurisdiction over subject matter is a limitation on the types of cases a court can hear. In both the state and federal court systems, there are courts of *general jurisdiction* and courts of *limited jurisdiction*. The basis for the distinction lies in the subject matter of cases heard. For example, **probate courts**—state courts that handle only matters relating to the transfer of a person's assets and obligations on that person's death, including matters relating to the custody and guardianship of children—have limited subject-matter jurisdiction. A common example of a federal court of limited subject-matter jurisdiction is a bankruptcy court. **Bankruptcy courts** handle only bankruptcy proceedings, which are governed by federal bankruptcy law (bankruptcy law allows debtors to obtain relief from their debts when they cannot make ends meet). In contrast, a court of general jurisdiction can decide virtually any type of case.

The subject-matter jurisdiction of a court is usually defined in the statute or constitution creating the court. In both the state and federal court systems, a court's subject-matter jurisdiction can be limited not only by the subject of the lawsuit but also by the amount of money in controversy, by whether a case is a felony (a more serious type of crime) or a misdemeanor (a less serious type of crime), or by whether the proceeding is a trial or an appeal.

ORIGINAL AND APPELLATE JURISDICTION.   The distinction between courts of original jurisdiction and courts of appellate jurisdiction normally lies in whether the case is being heard for the first time. Courts having **original jurisdiction** are courts of the first instance, or **trial courts**—that is, courts in which lawsuits begin, trials take place, and evidence is presented. In the federal court system, the *district courts* are trial courts. In the various state court systems, the trial courts are

probate court
A court having jurisdiction over proceedings concerning the settlement of a person's estate.

bankruptcy court
A federal court of limited jurisdiction that hears only bankruptcy proceedings.

original jurisdiction
The power of a court to take a case, try it, and decide it.

trial court
A court in which cases begin and in which questions of fact are examined.

known by different names. The key point here is that normally, any court having original jurisdiction is known as a trial court. Courts having **appellate jurisdiction** act as reviewing courts, or **appellate courts.** In general, cases can be brought before them only on appeal from an order or a judgment of a trial court or other lower court. State and federal trial and appellate courts will be discussed more fully later in this chapter.

Jurisdiction of the Federal Courts

Because the federal government is a government of limited powers, the jurisdiction of the federal courts is limited. Article III of the U.S. Constitution establishes the boundaries of federal judicial power. Section 2 of Article III states that "[t]he judicial Power shall extend to all Cases, in Law and Equity, arising under this Constitution, the Laws of the United States, and Treaties made, or which shall be made, under their Authority."

FEDERAL QUESTIONS.   Whenever a plaintiff's cause of action is based, at least in part, on the U.S. Constitution, a treaty, or a federal law, then a **federal question** arises, and the case comes under the judicial power of federal courts. Any lawsuit involving a federal question can originate in a federal court. People who claim that their constitutional rights have been violated can begin their suits in a federal court.

DIVERSITY JURISDICTION.   Federal district courts can also exercise original jurisdiction over cases involving **diversity of citizenship.** Such cases may arise between (1) citizens of different states, (2) a foreign country and citizens of a state or of different states, or (3) citizens of a state and citizens or subjects of a foreign country. The amount in controversy must be more than $75,000 before a federal court can take jurisdiction in such cases. For purposes of diversity-of-citizenship jurisdiction, a corporation is a citizen of the state in which it is incorporated and of the state in which its principal place of business is located. A case involving diversity of citizenship can be filed in the appropriate federal district court.

As an example of diversity jurisdiction, assume that the following events have taken place. Maria Ramirez, a citizen of Florida, was walking near a busy street in Tallahassee, Florida, one day when a large crate flew off a passing truck and hit and seriously injured her. She incurred numerous medical expenses and could not work for six months. She now wants to sue the trucking firm for $500,000 in damages. The trucking firm's headquarters are in Georgia, although the company does business in Florida.

In this situation, Maria could bring suit in a Florida court because she is a resident of Florida, the trucking firm does business in Florida, and that is where the accident occurred. She could also bring suit in a Georgia court, because a Georgia court could exercise jurisdiction over the trucking firm, which is headquartered in that state. As a third alternative, Maria could bring suit in a federal court because the requirements of diversity jurisdiction have been met—the lawsuit involves parties from different states, Florida and Georgia, and the amount in controversy (the damages Maria is seeking) exceeds $75,000.

Note that in a case based on a federal question, a federal court will apply federal law. In a case based on diversity of citizenship, however, a federal court will normally apply the law of the state in which the court sits. This is because cases based on diversity of citizenship normally do not involve activities that are regulated by the federal government. Therefore, federal laws do not apply, and state law will govern the issue.

---

appellate jurisdiction
The power of a court to hear and decide an appeal; that is, the power and authority of a court to review cases that have already been tried in a lower court and to make decisions about them without actually holding a trial. This process is called appellate review.

appellate court
A court that reviews decisions made by lower courts, such as trial courts; a court of appeals.

federal question
A question that pertains to the U.S. Constitution, acts of Congress, or treaties. A federal question provides a basis for jurisdiction by the federal courts. This jurisdiction is authorized by Article III, Section 2, of the Constitution.

diversity of citizenship
Under Article III, Section 2, of the Constitution, a basis for federal district court jurisdiction over a lawsuit between (1) citizens of different states, (2) a foreign country and citizens of a state or states, or (3) citizens of a state and citizens or subjects of a foreign country. The amount in controversy must be more than $75,000 before a federal court can exercise jurisdiction in such cases.

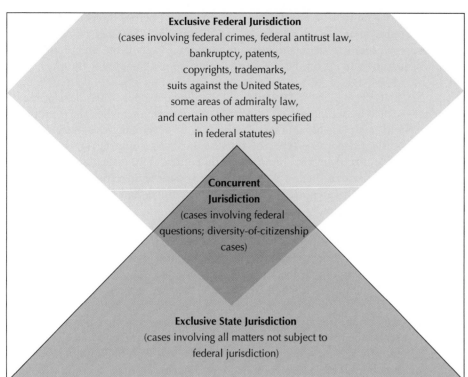

EXHIBIT 6.1
**Exclusive and
Concurrent Jurisdiction**

Exclusive Federal Jurisdiction
(cases involving federal crimes, federal antitrust law,
bankruptcy, patents,
copyrights, trademarks,
suits against the United States,
some areas of admiralty law,
and certain other matters specified
in federal statutes)

**Concurrent
Jurisdiction**
(cases involving federal
questions; diversity-of-citizenship
cases)

Exclusive State Jurisdiction
(cases involving all matters not subject to
federal jurisdiction)

EXCLUSIVE VERSUS CONCURRENT JURISDICTION.   When both federal and state courts have the power to hear a case, as is true in suits involving diversity of citizenship (such as Maria's case described above), **concurrent jurisdiction** exists. When cases can be tried only in federal courts or only in state courts, **exclusive jurisdiction** exists. Federal courts have exclusive jurisdiction in cases involving federal crimes, bankruptcy, patents, trademarks, and copyrights; in suits against the United States; and in some areas of admiralty law (law governing transportation on the seas and ocean waters). States also have exclusive jurisdiction in certain subject matters—for example, in divorce and adoptions. The concepts of concurrent and exclusive jurisdiction are illustrated in Exhibit 6.1.

When concurrent jurisdiction exists, a party has a choice of whether to bring a suit in, for example, a federal or a state court. The party's lawyer will consider several factors in counseling the party as to which choice is preferable. The lawyer may prefer to litigate the case in a state court because he or she is more familiar with the state court's procedures, or perhaps the attorney believes that the state's judge or jury would be more sympathetic to the client and the case.

Alternatively, the lawyer may advise the client to sue in federal court. Perhaps the state court's **docket** (the court's schedule listing the cases to be heard) is crowded, and the case could be brought to trial sooner in a federal court. Perhaps some feature of federal practice or procedure could offer an advantage in the client's case. Other important considerations include the law in an available jurisdiction, how that law has been applied in the jurisdiction's courts, and what the results in similar cases have been in that jurisdiction.

concurrent jurisdiction
Jurisdiction that exists when two different courts have the power to hear a case. For example, some cases can be heard in either a federal or a state court.

exclusive jurisdiction
Jurisdiction that exists when a case can be heard only in a particular court, such as a federal court.

docket
The list of cases entered on the court's calendar and thus scheduled to be heard by the court.

Jurisdiction in Cyberspace

The Internet's capacity to bypass political and geographic boundaries undercuts traditional basic limitations on a court's authority to exercise jurisdiction. These limits include a party's contacts with a court's geographic jurisdiction. As already discussed, for a court to compel a defendant to come before it, there must be at least minimum contacts—the presence of a company's salesperson within the state, for example. Are there sufficient minimum contacts if the only connection to a jurisdiction is an ad on the Web originating from a remote location?

THE "SLIDING-SCALE" STANDARD.   Gradually, the courts are developing a standard—called a "sliding-scale" standard—for determining when the exercise of jurisdiction over an out-of-state party is proper. In developing this standard, the courts have identified three types of Internet business contacts: (1) substantial business conducted over the Internet (with contracts or sales, for example); (2) some interactivity through a Web site; and (3) passive advertising. Jurisdiction is proper for the first category, is improper for the third, and may or may not be appropriate for the second.

INTERNATIONAL JURISDICTIONAL ISSUES.   Because the Internet is international in scope, international jurisdictional issues understandably have come to the fore. What seems to be emerging in the world's courts is a standard that echoes the requirement of minimum contacts applied by the U.S. courts. Most courts are indicating that minimum contacts—doing business within the jurisdiction, for example—are enough to compel a defendant to appear and that the defendant's physical presence is not required for the court to exercise jurisdiction.[3] The effect of this standard is that a company may have to comply with the laws of any jurisdiction in which it targets customers for its products.

Venue

venue
The geographical district in which an action is tried and from which the jury is selected.

Jurisdiction has to do with whether a court has authority to hear a case involving specific persons, property, or subject matter. **Venue**[4] is concerned with the most appropriate location for a trial. For example, two state courts may have the authority to exercise jurisdiction over a case, but it may be more appropriate or convenient to hear the case in one court than in the other.

Basically, the concept of venue reflects the policy that a court trying a suit should be in the geographic neighborhood (usually the county) in which the incident leading to the lawsuit occurred or in which the parties involved in the lawsuit reside. Pretrial publicity or other factors, though, may require a change of venue to another community, especially in criminal cases in which the defendant's right to a fair and impartial jury has been impaired. For example, suppose that a bomb has exploded in a federal building in Oklahoma City, killing more than 160 persons and injuring hundreds of others. Two defendants are indicted in connection with the bombing and scheduled for trial in an Oklahoma state court. Given these facts, the defense attorneys may argue—and the court will likely agree—that the defendants could not receive a fair trial in Oklahoma because an impartial jury could not be chosen. Although the Oklahoma court has jurisdiction, the court will order a change of venue to another location for trial.

Standing to Sue

standing to sue
A sufficient stake in a controversy to justify bringing a lawsuit. To have standing to sue, the plaintiff must demonstrate that he or she has been either injured or threatened with injury.

To bring a lawsuit before a court, a party must have **standing to sue,** or a sufficient "stake" in a matter to justify seeking relief through the court system. In other words, a party must have a legally protected and tangible interest at stake in the litigation in order to have standing. The party bringing the lawsuit must have suffered a harm as a result of the action about which he or she complained. For example, assume that a friend of one of your firm's clients was injured in a car

DEVELOPING PARALEGAL SKILLS

Choice of Courts: State or Federal?

Susan Radtke, a lawyer specializing in the area of employment discrimination, and her legal assistant, Joan Dunbar, are meeting with a new client. The client wants to sue her former employer for gender discrimination. The client complained to her employer when she was passed over for a promotion. She was fired, she claims, as a result of her complaint. The client appears to have a strong case, because several of her former co-workers have agreed to testify that they heard the employer say on many occasions that he would never promote a woman to a managerial position.

Since both state and federal laws prohibit gender discrimination, the case could be brought in either state or federal court. The client tells Susan that because of Susan's experience, she wants her to decide whether the case should be filed in a state or federal court. Joan will be drafting the complaint, so Susan and Joan discuss the pros and cons of filing the case in each court. Joan reviews a list of considerations with Susan.

TIPS FOR CHOOSING A COURT

- Review the jurisdiction of each court.
- Evaluate the strengths and weaknesses of the case.
- Evaluate the remedy sought.
- Evaluate the jury pool available for each court.
- Evaluate the likelihood of winning in each court.
- Evaluate the length of time it will take each court to decide the case.

---

accident caused by defective brakes. The client's friend would have standing to sue the automobile manufacturer for damages. The client, however, would not have standing because the client was not injured and therefore has no legally recognizable stake in the controversy.

Note that in some cases, a person will have standing to sue on behalf of another person. For example, suppose that a child suffered serious injuries as a result of a defectively manufactured toy. Because the child is a minor, a lawsuit could be brought on his or her behalf by another person, such as the child's parent or legal guardian.

Standing to sue also requires that the controversy at issue be justiciable. A **justiciable**[5] **controversy** is one that is real and substantial, as opposed to hypothetical or academic. For example, in the above situation, the child's parent could not sue the toy manufacturer merely on the ground that the toy was defective. The issue would become justiciable only if the child had actually been injured due to a defect in the toy as marketed. In other words, the parent normally could not ask the court to determine what damages might be obtained *if* the child had been injured, because this would be merely a hypothetical question.

justiciable controversy
A controversy that is real and substantial, as opposed to hypothetical or academic.

Judicial Procedures

Litigation in court, from the moment a lawsuit is initiated until the final resolution of the case, must follow specifically designated procedural rules. The procedural rules for federal court cases are set forth in the Federal Rules of Civil Procedure. State rules, which are often similar to the federal rules, vary from state to state—and even from court to court within a given state. Rules of procedure also differ in criminal and civil cases. Paralegals who work for trial lawyers need to be familiar with the procedural rules of the relevant courts. Because judicial procedures will be examined in detail in Chapters 12 through 15, we do not discuss them here.

On the Web
The Federal Rules of Civil Procedure are available online at **http:// www.law.cornell.edu/ rules/frcp/overview.htm.**

ETHICAL CONCERN
Meeting Procedural Deadlines

One of the paralegal's most important responsibilities is making sure that court deadlines are met. For example, suppose that your supervising attorney asks you to file with the court a motion to dismiss (a document requesting the court to dismiss a lawsuit for a specific reason). You know that the deadline for filing the motion is three days away. You plan to deliver the motion to the court the next day, so you don't place a reminder note on your calendar. In the meantime, you place the motion in the client's file. The next morning, you arrive at work and immediately are called to help your supervising attorney with last-minute trial preparations on another case. You are busy all afternoon interviewing witnesses in still another case. You have totally forgotten about the motion to dismiss and do not think of it again until a week later—when the deadline for filing the motion has passed. Because you forgot to file the motion, your supervising attorney has breached the duty of competence. How can you make sure that you remember important deadlines? The answer is simple: *always* enter deadlines on the office calendaring system and *always* check your calendar several times a day. Also, realize that missed deadlines provide the basis for many malpractice suits against attorneys.

Basic Judicial Requirements and the Paralegal

Paralegals should be familiar with the concepts of jurisdiction, venue, and standing to sue because these concepts affect pretrial litigation procedures. For example, a defendant in a lawsuit may claim that the court in which the plaintiff filed the lawsuit cannot exercise jurisdiction over the matter—or over the defendant or the defendant's property. If you are working on behalf of the defendant, you may be asked to draft a motion to dismiss the case on this ground. You may also be asked to draft a legal memorandum in support of the motion, outlining the legal reasons why the court cannot exercise jurisdiction over the case. (Motions to dismiss and supporting documents are discussed in Chapter 12.) Additionally, a party to a lawsuit may request that a case filed in a state court be "removed" to a federal court (if there is a basis for federal jurisdiction) or vice versa. You may be asked to draft a document requesting a change of venue (or objecting to an opponent's request for a change of venue) or requesting that the court dismiss the case because the plaintiff lacks standing to sue.

If you work for a plaintiff's attorney, you might be asked to draft a complaint to initiate a lawsuit. Once the attorney reviews the facts with you, he or she may expect you to know whether concurrent jurisdiction exists. If concurrent jurisdiction exists, the attorney may expect you to ask whether the suit should be filed in a state or a federal court. If concurrent jurisdiction does not exist, the attorney may assume that you know in which court the case will be filed and that you know how to prepare the complaint for the appropriate court.

Recall from Chapter 1 that paralegal education and training emphasize both substantive and procedural law. A paralegal can be a valuable member of a legal team if he or she has adequate knowledge of the procedural requirements relating to litigation and to different types of legal proceedings. You will read in detail about litigation procedures in Chapters 12 through 15.

EXHIBIT 6.2
State Court Systems

State court systems vary widely from state to state, and it is therefore impossible to show one "typical" state court system. This exhibit is typical of the court systems in several states, however, including Arizona, California, Nevada, and Texas.

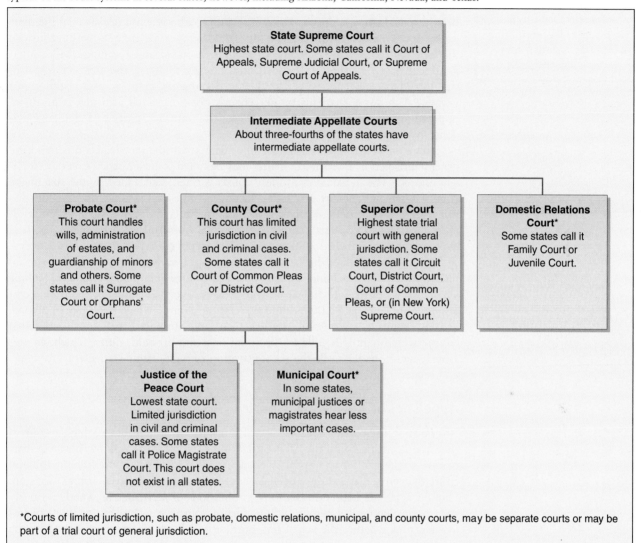

State Supreme Court
Highest state court. Some states call it Court of Appeals, Supreme Judicial Court, or Supreme Court of Appeals.

Intermediate Appellate Courts
About three-fourths of the states have intermediate appellate courts.

Probate Court*
This court handles wills, administration of estates, and guardianship of minors and others. Some states call it Surrogate Court or Orphans' Court.

County Court*
This court has limited jurisdiction in civil and criminal cases. Some states call it Court of Common Pleas or District Court.

Superior Court
Highest state trial court with general jurisdiction. Some states call it Circuit Court, District Court, Court of Common Pleas, or (in New York) Supreme Court.

Domestic Relations Court*
Some states call it Family Court or Juvenile Court.

Justice of the Peace Court
Lowest state court. Limited jurisdiction in civil and criminal cases. Some states call it Police Magistrate Court. This court does not exist in all states.

Municipal Court*
In some states, municipal justices or magistrates hear less important cases.

*Courts of limited jurisdiction, such as probate, domestic relations, municipal, and county courts, may be separate courts or may be part of a trial court of general jurisdiction.

STATE COURT SYSTEMS

Each state has its own system of courts, and no two state systems are the same. As Exhibit 6.2 indicates, there may be several levels, or tiers, of courts within a state court system: (1) state trial courts of limited jurisdiction, (2) state trial courts of general jurisdiction, (3) appellate courts, and (4) the state's highest court (often called the state supreme court). Judges in the state court system are usually elected by the voters for a specified term.

Generally, any person who is a party to a lawsuit has the opportunity to plead the case before a trial court and then, if he or she loses, before at least one level of appellate court. Finally, if a federal statute or federal constitutional issue is involved in the decision of a state supreme court, that decision may be further appealed to the United States Supreme Court.

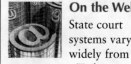

On the Web
State court systems vary widely from state to state. To learn about your state's court system, go to the Center for Information Law and Policy's Web site at **http://www.infoctr.edu/swl.**

On the Web
The Web site of the National Center for State Courts offers links to the Web pages of all state courts. Go to **http://www. ncsconline.org**.

Trial Courts

Trial courts are exactly what their name implies—courts in which trials are held and testimony taken. You will read in detail about trial procedures in Chapter 14. In that chapter, we follow a hypothetical case through the various stages of a trial. Briefly, a trial court is presided over by a judge, who issues a decision on the matter before the court. If the trial is a jury trial (many trials are held without juries), the jury will decide the outcome of factual disputes, and the judge will issue a judgment based on the jury's conclusion. During the trial, the attorney for each side introduces evidence (such as relevant documents, exhibits, and testimony of witnesses) in support of his or her client's position. Each attorney is given an opportunity to cross-examine witnesses for the opposing party and challenge evidence introduced by the opposing party.

State trial courts have either general or limited jurisdiction. Trial courts that have general jurisdiction as to subject matter may be called county, district, superior, or circuit courts.[6] The jurisdiction of these courts is often determined by the size of the county in which the court sits. State trial courts of general jurisdiction have jurisdiction over a wide variety of subjects, including both civil disputes (such as landlord-tenant matters or contract claims) and criminal prosecutions. In some states, trial courts of general jurisdiction may hear appeals from courts of limited jurisdiction.

Courts with limited jurisdiction as to subject matter are often called special inferior trial courts or minor judiciary courts. Courts of limited jurisdiction include small claims courts, which hear only civil cases involving claims of less than a certain amount, such as $5,000; domestic relations courts, which handle only divorce actions, paternity suits, and child-custody and support cases; local municipal courts, which mainly handle traffic violations; and probate courts, which, as previously mentioned, handle the administration of wills, estate-settlement problems, and related matters.

Appellate, or Reviewing, Courts

After a trial, the parties have the opportunity to file an appeal to a higher court if they are unsatisfied with the trial court's ruling. Practically speaking, however, parties are unlikely to file an appeal unless a reversible error was committed by the trial court that would cause the appellate court to overturn the trial court's decision. Usually, appellate courts do not look at questions of *fact* (such as whether a party did, in fact, commit a certain action, such as burning a flag) but at questions of *law* (such as whether the act of flag burning is a form of speech protected by the First Amendment to the Constitution). Only a judge, not a jury, can rule on questions of law.

Appellate courts normally defer to a trial court's findings on questions of fact because the trial court judge and jury were in a better position to evaluate testimony by directly observing witnesses' gestures, demeanor, and nonverbal behavior during the trial. When a case is appealed, an appellate panel of three or more judges reviews the record (including the written transcript of the trial) of the case on appeal, and the record does not include these nonverbal elements. Generally, then, appellate courts look for errors of law rather than evaluating the trial court judge's or jury's conclusions on questions of fact.

Every state has at least one appellate court, which may be either an intermediate appellate court or the state's highest court.

INTERMEDIATE APPELLATE COURTS.   About three-fourths of the states have intermediate appellate courts, or courts of appeals. The subject-matter jurisdiction of these courts is substantially limited to hearing appeals. Usually, appellate courts

PARALEGAL PROFILE

Litigation Paralegal

LEE A. PAIGE *graduated from the University of West Los Angeles School of Paralegal Studies with an ABA–approved paralegal certificate. He holds paralegal specialist certificates in litigation, real estate, environmental law, and intellectual property law. His experience includes state and federal litigation, copyrights, patent and trademark prosecution, assignments, and licensing. He is currently employed as a senior paralegal in the Los Angeles office of the Seattle-based law firm of Preston, Gates & Ellis, where he assists attorneys with railroad litigation and environmental law research.*

In 1998, Paige served as president of the Los Angeles Paralegal Association, the largest association of paralegals in the nation. He has been extremely active in the promotion and development of the paralegal profession both in California and nationally. He is frequently called on to serve as a motivational speaker and paralegal expert by high schools, colleges, paralegal schools, and paralegal and legal associations.

As a representative of the California Alliance of Paralegal Associations, Paige has lobbied the state bar association and the state legislature in an effort to codify a legal definition of the term paralegal *and specific educational standards for traditional paralegals. He has authored several articles on the paralegal profession and is a contributing writer to* Legal Assistant Today *magazine.*

What do you like best about your work?

"I very much enjoy research! To some paralegals, such a statement might sound a little crazy, but I really do enjoy researching more than any other part of my job. As a former news writer, my natural penchant for 'digging' for a story comes in quite handy. It is very gratifying to me for an attorney to give me a problem and rely on me to find the answer. I get quite an adrenaline rush from 'fact-finding' missions and a wealth of satisfaction from 'delivering the goods' that are the result of my computerized or manual research."

What is the greatest challenge that you face in your area of work?

"The greatest challenge I currently face is keeping ahead of our ever-mounting litigation schedule. I primarily assist a partner in my firm who represents a major railway company and juggles a huge caseload. My boss is an excellent attorney, but, as is the case with many litigators, he is frequently overloaded. His secretary and I must be constantly vigilant with his weekly calendar and daily schedule to prevent time conflicts and make sure that he does not miss any crucial dates or court appearances."

> **"One success tip that I always give to students and working paralegals is to never stop learning."**

What advice do you have for would-be paralegals in your area of work?

"I frequently lecture at local paralegal schools, and the advice I normally give paralegal students is to focus their studies on areas of law that are of interest to them. This will give them an idea of where their real strengths are. I work in litigation, but it is not for everyone. Litigation is very complex and demanding, and if students go into it blindly they may be disappointed. Many people enter into the paralegal profession as a second career, perhaps as a result of a layoff, forced relocation, or downsizing. Other people see becoming a paralegal as a way of getting a "foot in the door" of the legal profession, and still others use it as a proving ground in anticipation of going on to law school and becoming an attorney. Whatever their reasons for becoming paralegals, I always advise would-be paralegals to investigate the profession before they jump in, and to only attend an ABA–approved school."

What are some tips for success as a paralegal in your area of work?

"One success tip that I always give to students and working paralegals is to never stop learning. Paralegals should voluntarily take additional classes and seminars beyond their paralegal certificates. Such classes will keep them abreast of new developments in law and procedure that can affect their ability to assist their attorneys in the representation of their clients and increase their value to their employers."

DEVELOPING PARALEGAL SKILLS
Trial Emergency

David Garner, a legal assistant, arrives at work a few minutes before 9:00 A.M. Shirley, the secretary, is overjoyed to see him. It seems that Helen Schmidt, the attorney for whom they work, is in trial, and the judge has decided to instruct the jury this morning between 9:30 and 10:00 A.M. The judge started the trial an hour earlier today because her docket was so congested. Shirley has just finished typing the jury instructions and wants David to deliver them to Helen in the court.

TIPS FOR HANDLING TRIAL EMERGENCIES

- Stay calm and think clearly.
- Gather all necessary/requested materials.
- Try to anticipate any additional materials that might be needed.
- Find out the judge's name and courtroom number.
- Be familiar with the court by having visited it early on.
- Anticipate security problems caused by metal detectors and other devices.

will review the records, read appellate briefs filed by the parties, and listen to the oral arguments presented by the parties' attorneys. Then the panel of judges renders a decision. If a party is unsatisfied with the appellate court's ruling, that party can appeal to the highest state court.

HIGHEST STATE COURTS.   The highest appellate court in a state is usually called the supreme court but may be called by some other name. For example, in both New York and Maryland, the highest state court is called the Court of Appeals. The decisions of each state's highest court on all questions of state law are final. Only when issues of federal law are involved can a decision made by a state's highest court be overruled by the United States Supreme Court.

State Court Systems and the Paralegal

On the Web Superior Information Services, a Michigan Internet consulting company, provides a single site from which you can access Web pages for trial courts. Go to **http://www.courts.net**.

Because each state has its own unique system of courts, you will need to become familiar with the court system of your particular state. What is the official name of your state's highest court? How many intermediate state appellate courts are in your state, and to which of these courts should appeals from your local trial court or courts be appealed? What courts in your area have jurisdiction over what kinds of disputes?

In addition to knowing the names of your state's courts and their jurisdictional authority, you will also need to become familiar with the procedural requirements of specific courts. Paralegals frequently assist their attorneys in drafting legal documents to be filed in state courts, and the required procedures for filing these documents may vary from court to court. You will read more about court procedures in Chapters 12 and 14.

As indicated earlier and illustrated in Exhibit 6.1, state courts exercise exclusive jurisdiction over all matters that are not subject to federal jurisdiction. Family law and probate law (both discussed in Chapter 9), for example, are two areas in which state courts exercise exclusive jurisdiction. If you work in an area of the law over which state courts exercise exclusive jurisdiction, you will need to be familiar with procedural requirements established by state (or local) courts relating to those areas.

Realize also that many paralegals work within the court system, in both state courts and county courts (which are part of the state court system). Some paralegals work as assistants to court clerks. In addition, many paralegals work for bankruptcy courts, which are part of the federal court system—a topic to which we now turn.

THE FEDERAL COURT SYSTEM

On the Web
The Web site for the federal courts offers information on the federal court system and links to all federal courts at **http:// www.uscourts.gov**.

The federal court system is basically a three-tiered model consisting of (1) U.S. district courts (trial courts of general jurisdiction) and various courts of limited jurisdiction, (2) U.S. courts of appeals (intermediate courts of appeals), and (3) the United States Supreme Court, located in Washington, D.C. Exhibit 6.3 on the next page shows the organization of the federal court system.

According to the language of Article III of the U.S. Constitution, there is only one national Supreme Court. All other courts in the federal system are considered "inferior." Congress is empowered to create other inferior courts as it deems necessary. The inferior courts that Congress has created include those on the first and second tiers in our model—the district courts and various courts of limited jurisdiction, as well as the U.S. courts of appeals.

Unlike state court judges, who are usually elected, federal court judges—including the justices of the Supreme Court—are appointed by the president of the United States and confirmed by the U.S. Senate. Federal judges receive lifetime appointments (because under Article III they "hold their Offices during good Behavior").

U.S. District Courts

At the federal level, the equivalent of a state trial court of general jurisdiction is the district court. There is at least one federal district court in every state. The number of judicial districts can vary over time, primarily owing to population changes and corresponding case loads. Currently, there are ninety-four judicial districts.

U.S. district courts have original jurisdiction in federal matters. Federal cases typically originate in district courts. There are other trial courts with original but special (or limited) jurisdiction, such as the federal bankruptcy courts and others shown in Exhibit 6.3.

U.S. Courts of Appeals

In the federal court system, there are thirteen U.S. courts of appeals—also referred to as U.S. circuit courts of appeals. The federal courts of appeals for twelve of the circuits (including the District of Columbia Circuit) hear appeals from the federal district courts located within their respective judicial circuits. The court of appeals for the thirteenth circuit, called the Federal Circuit, has national appellate jurisdiction over certain types of cases, such as cases involving patent law and cases in which the U.S. government is a defendant.

On the Web
At the following Web site, you can search the opinions of U.S. circuit courts: **http:// www.law.cornell.edu/ opinions.html**.

A party who is dissatisfied with a federal district court's decision on an issue may appeal that decision to a federal circuit court of appeals. As in state courts of appeals, the decisions of the circuit courts are made by a panel of three or more judges. The judges review decisions made by trial courts to see if any errors of law were made, and the judges generally defer to a district court's findings of fact. The decisions of the circuit courts of appeals are final in most cases, but appeal to the United States Supreme Court is possible. Exhibit 6.4 on page 191 shows the

EXHIBIT 6.3

The Organization of the Federal Court System

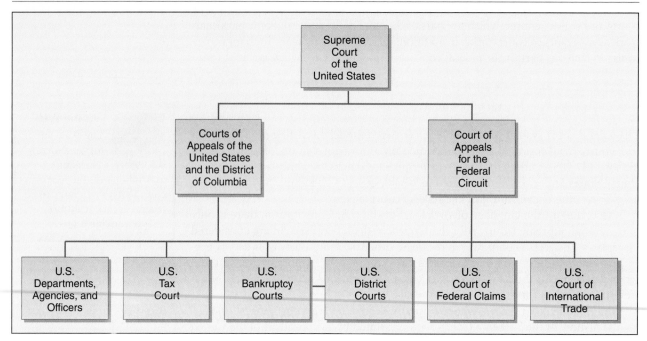

On the Web
An excellent site for information on the United States Supreme Court—including its basic functions and procedures, biographies and photographs of the justices, and even the history of the Supreme Court building—is the following: **http://www.usscplus.com/info/index.htm.**

geographical boundaries of U.S. circuit courts of appeals and the boundaries of the U.S. district courts within each circuit.

The United States Supreme Court

The highest level of the three-tiered model of the federal court system is the United States Supreme Court. The Supreme Court consists of nine justices. Although the Supreme Court has original, or trial, jurisdiction in rare instances (set forth in Article III, Section 2, of the Constitution—see Appendix J), most of its work is as an appeals court. The Supreme Court can review any case decided by any of the federal courts of appeals, and it also has appellate authority over some cases decided in the state courts.

HOW CASES REACH THE SUPREME COURT.   Many people are surprised to learn that there is no absolute right of appeal to the United States Supreme Court. Thousands of cases are filed with the Supreme Court each year, yet in recent years, it has heard fewer than one hundred cases each year.

To bring a case before the Supreme Court, a party requests the Court to issue a writ of *certiorari.* A **writ of *certiorari***[7] is an order issued by the Supreme Court to a lower court requiring the latter to send it the record of the case for review. Parties can petition the Supreme Court to issue a writ of *certiorari,* but whether the Court will issue one is entirely within its discretion. The Court will not issue a writ unless at least four of the nine justices approve of it. This is called the **rule of four.** The Court is not required to issue a writ of *certiorari,* and most petitions for writs are denied. A denial is not a decision on the merits of a case, nor does it indicate agreement with the lower court's opinion. It simply means that the Supreme Court declines to grant the request (petition) for appeal. Furthermore, denial of the writ has no value as a precedent.

writ of *certiorari*
A writ from a higher court asking the lower court to send it the record of a case for review. The United States Supreme Court uses *certiorari* to review most of the cases it decides to hear.

rule of four
A rule of the United States Supreme Court under which the Court will not issue a writ of *certiorari* unless at least four justices approve of the decision to issue the writ.

FEATURED GUEST, *Continued*

---

parties agree and propose solutions to the parties.

- Encourage the parties to settle their dispute.
- Formalize any agreement reached by the parties.
- Believe in the process.

ASSISTING ATTORNEYS IN THE MEDIATION PROCESS

Paralegals play a major role in assisting attorneys in the mediation of disputes, both before and during the mediation itself. Prior to the mediation, paralegals interview clients, assist in gathering any information (such as police reports, medical records, or child-care expenses) that will help the attorney when advising the client, draft documents that may be needed for the mediation, and prepare a list of mediators in the relevant geographic and specialty area. During the mediation, the paralegal may be asked to provide additional information and draft other documents (such as a settlement agreement). If the attorney serves as the mediator, the paralegal may be asked to schedule dates with the parties or their attorneys for the mediation, prepare any necessary forms, and draft a final settlement agreement.

PARALEGALS AS MEDIATORS

Paralegals with mediation training are employed in a variety of dispute-resolution settings outside the law office. For example, some paralegals with mediation training work for administrative agencies that offer dispute-resolution services. Other paralegals who are trained in mediation have supervised and trained volunteer mediators in community centers. Increasingly, mediation is being utilized to address community issues, including hostilities leading to violence in the schools. Peer mediation, for example, helps to diffuse such feelings as anger, distrust, and fear before those feelings escalate into violent acts. Paralegals may also serve as mediators in disputes between communities and the local police force or between city governments and representatives of the local citizenry.

Organizations promoting community mediation have sprung up

> **"Paralegals play a major role in assisting attorneys in the mediation of disputes, both before and during the mediation itself."**

around the country. There is now a national association of such groups—the National Association for Community Mediation (NAFCM). The NAFCM is an association of community mediation centers, their staff and volunteer mediators, and other individuals and organizations interested in the community mediation movement. Paralegals who are interested in participating in community mediation should check to see what community mediation organizations exist in their city or state.

Mediation training also provides the paralegal with opportunities in international settings. Some paralegals have exciting careers as members of a team mediating disputes between countries.

---

involved in the dispute, the place of arbitration, and the powers that the arbitrator will exercise. Frequently, the agreement includes a signed statement that the parties intend to be bound by the arbitrator's decision.

The next step in the process is the *hearing.* Normally, the parties agree prior to arbitration—in an arbitration clause or in a submission-to-arbitrate agreement, for example—on what procedural rules will govern the proceedings. In a typical hearing, the parties begin as they would at a trial by presenting opening arguments to the arbitrator and stating what remedies should or should not be granted. After the opening statements have been made, evidence is presented. Witnesses may be called and examined by both sides. After all evidence has been presented, the parties give their closing arguments. Although arbitration is in some ways similar to a trial, the rules (such as those regarding what kinds of evidence may be introduced) are usually much less restrictive than those involved in formal litigation.

After each side has had an opportunity to present evidence and to argue its case, the arbitrator reaches a decision. The final decision of the arbitrator is called an **award,** even if no money is conferred on a party as a result of the proceedings.

award
In the context of ADR, the decision rendered by an arbitrator.

ETHICAL CONCERN
Potential Arbitration Problems

Many individuals and business firms prefer to arbitrate disputes rather than take them to court. For that reason, they often include arbitration clauses in their contracts. These clauses normally specify who or what organization will arbitrate the dispute and where the arbitration will take place. To safeguard a client's interests, when drafting and reviewing arbitration clauses in contracts, the careful paralegal will be alert to the possibility that those who arbitrate the dispute might not be totally neutral or that the designated place of arbitration is so geographically distant from the client's location that it may pose a great inconvenience and expense for the client should an arbitrable dispute arise. The paralegal should call any such problems to his or her supervising attorney's attention. The attorney can then discuss the problem with the client and help the client negotiate an arbitration clause that is more favorable to the client's position.

Under most arbitration statutes, the arbitrator must render an award within thirty days of the close of the hearing.

A paralegal may become extensively involved in preparations for arbitration, just as he or she would in preparing for a trial. The paralegal will assist in obtaining and organizing all evidence relating to the dispute, may interview witnesses and prepare them for the hearing, and generally will assist in other tasks commonly undertaken prior to a trial (see Chapter 12).

THE ROLE OF THE COURTS IN PREARBITRATION.   The role of the courts in the arbitration process is limited. One important role is played at the prearbitration stage. When a dispute arises as to whether the parties have agreed in an arbitration clause to submit a particular matter to arbitration, one party may file suit to compel arbitration. The court before which the suit is brought will not decide the basic controversy but must decide whether the dispute is *arbitrable*—that is, whether the matter is one that can be resolved through arbitration. For example, if the dispute involves a claim of employment discrimination on the basis of age, the court will have to decide whether the Age Discrimination in Employment Act of 1967 (which protects persons forty years of age and older against employment discrimination on the basis of age) permits claims brought under this act to be arbitrated.

If the court finds that the subject matter in controversy is covered by the agreement to arbitrate, then a party may be compelled to arbitrate the dispute. Even when a claim involves a violation of a statute passed to protect a certain class of people, such as a statute prohibiting age discrimination against employees at the workplace, a court may determine that the parties must nonetheless abide by their agreement to arbitrate the dispute. Usually, a court will allow the claim to be arbitrated if the court, in interpreting the statute, can find no legislative intent to the contrary.

No party, however, will be ordered to submit a particular dispute to arbitration unless the court is convinced that the party has consented to do so.[9] Additionally, the courts will not compel arbitration if it is clear that the prescribed arbitration rules and procedures are inherently unfair to one of the parties. For example, if an employer's arbitration agreement with an employee states that it is the employee's responsibility to establish the procedure and the rules for the arbitration, the court may conclude that the rules are one-sided and unfair and thus refuse to enforce the arbitration agreement.[10]

THE POSTARBITRATION ROLE OF THE COURTS.   Courts also may play an important role at the postarbitration stage. If the arbitration has produced an award, one of the parties may appeal the award or may seek a court order compelling the other party to comply with the award. In determining whether an award should be enforced, a court conducts a review that is much more restricted in scope than an appellate court's review of a trial court decision. The general view is that because the parties were free to frame the issues and set the powers of the arbitrator at the outset, they cannot complain about the result. An arbitration award may be set aside, however, if the award resulted from the arbitrator's misconduct or "bad faith" or if the arbitrator exceeded his or her powers in arbitrating the dispute. An arbitrator is permitted to resolve only those issues that are covered by the agreement to submit to arbitration.

Other ADR Forms

The three forms of ADR just discussed are the oldest and traditionally the most commonly used forms. In recent years, a variety of new types of ADR have emerged. Some of them combine elements of mediation and arbitration. For example, in **binding mediation,** a neutral mediator tries to facilitate agreement between the parties, but if no agreement is reached the mediator issues a legally binding decision on the matter. In **mediation arbitration (med-arb),** an arbitrator first attempts to help the parties reach an agreement, just as a mediator would. If no agreement is reached, then formal arbitration is undertaken, and the arbitrator issues a legally binding decision.

Other ADR forms are sometimes referred to as "assisted negotiation" because they involve a third party in what is essentially a negotiation process. For example, in **early neutral case evaluation,** the parties select a neutral third party (generally an expert in the subject matter of the dispute) to evaluate their respective positions. The parties explain their positions to the case evaluator however they wish. The case evaluator then assesses the strengths and weaknesses of the parties' positions, and this evaluation forms the basis of negotiating a settlement.

The mini-trial is a form of assisted negotiation that is often used by business parties. In a **mini-trial,** each party's attorney briefly argues the party's case before representatives of each firm who have the authority to settle the dispute. Typically, a neutral third party (usually an expert in the area being disputed) acts as an adviser. If the parties fail to reach an agreement, the adviser renders an opinion as to how a court would likely decide the issue. The proceeding assists the parties in determining whether they should negotiate a settlement of the dispute or take it to court.

Court-Referred ADR

Today, the majority of states either require or encourage parties to undergo mediation or arbitration prior to trial. Generally, when a trial court refers a case for arbitration, the arbitrator's decision is not binding on the parties. If the parties do not agree with the arbitrator's decision, they can go forward with the lawsuit.

The types of court-related ADR programs in use vary widely. In some states, such as Missouri, ADR is voluntary. In other states, such as Minnesota, parties are required to undertake ADR before they can have their cases heard in court.

---

binding mediation
A form of ADR in which a mediator attempts to facilitate agreement between the parties but then issues a legally binding decision if no agreement is reached.

mediation arbitration (med-arb)
A form of ADR in which an arbitrator first attempts to help the parties reach an agreement, just as a mediator would. If no agreement is reached, then formal arbitration is undertaken, and the arbitrator issues a legally binding decision.

early neutral case evaluation
A form of ADR in which a neutral third party evaluates the strengths and weaknesses of the disputing parties' positions; the evaluator's opinion forms the basis for negotiating a settlement.

mini-trial
A private proceeding that assists disputing parties in determining whether to take their case to court. During the proceeding, each party's attorney briefly argues the party's case before the other party and (usually) a neutral third party, who acts as an adviser. If the parties fail to reach an agreement, the adviser renders an opinion as to how a court would decide the issue.

Some states, such as Minnesota, offer a menu of options. Other states, including Florida (which has a statewide, comprehensive mediation program), offer only one alternative.

Today's courts are also experimenting with a variety of ADR alternatives to speed up (and reduce the cost of) justice. Numerous federal courts now hold **summary jury trials (SJTs)**, in which the parties present their arguments and supporting evidence (other than witness testimony—witnesses are not called in an SJT). The jury renders a verdict, but unlike the verdict in an actual trial, the jury's verdict is not binding. The verdict does, however, act as a guide to both sides in reaching an agreement during the mandatory negotiations that immediately follow the SJT. If no settlement is reached, both sides have the right to a full trial later. Other alternatives being employed by the courts include summary procedures for commercial litigation and the appointment of special masters to assist judges in deciding complex issues.

Providers of ADR Services

ADR services are provided by both government agencies and private organizations. A major provider of ADR services is the **American Arbitration Association (AAA)**, which was founded in 1926. Most of the nation's largest law firms are members of this nonprofit association. Currently, about 200,000 disputes are submitted to the AAA for resolution each year in its numerous offices around the country. Cases brought before the AAA are heard by an expert or a panel of experts in the area relating to the dispute and are usually settled quickly. Generally, about half of the panel members are lawyers. To cover its costs, the AAA charges a fee, paid by the party filing the claim. In addition, each party to the dispute pays a specified amount for each hearing day, as well as a special additional fee for cases involving personal injuries or property loss.

Hundreds of for-profit firms around the country also provide ADR services. Typically, these firms hire retired judges to conduct arbitration hearings or otherwise assist parties in settling their disputes. Private ADR firms normally allow the parties to decide on the date of the hearing, the presiding judge, whether the judge's decision will be legally binding, and the site of the hearing—which may be a conference room, a law school office, or a leased courtroom. The judges follow procedures similar to those of the federal courts and use similar rules. Usually, each party to the dispute pays a filing fee and a designated fee for a hearing session or conference.

As mentioned, courts also have ADR programs in which disputes are resolved by court-appointed attorneys or paralegals who are qualified to act as arbitrators or mediators in certain types of disputes. Many paralegals have found that becoming a mediator or an arbitrator is an especially rewarding career option.

Online Dispute Resolution

Today, a number of companies and organizations offer dispute-resolution services via the Internet. The settlement of disputes in these online forums is known as **online dispute resolution (ODR)**. The disputes resolved in these forums usually involve disagreements over the right to use a certain Web site address or the quality of goods purchased over the Internet (including goods sold through Internet auction sites). Those who do business in cyberspace (and the attorneys who represent them) should therefore be aware of this ADR option.

Most online forums do not automatically apply the law of any specific jurisdiction. Instead, results are often based on general, universal legal principles. As with offline methods of dispute resolution, a party normally may appeal to a court

summary jury trial (SJT)
A method of settling disputes (used in some federal courts) in which a trial is held but the jury's verdict is not binding. The verdict acts only as a guide to both sides in reaching an agreement during the mandatory negotiations that immediately follow the trial. If a settlement is not reached, both sides have the right to a full trial later.

American Arbitration Association (AAA)
The major organization offering arbitration services in the United States.

On the Web
To obtain information on the services offered by the American Arbitration Association (AAA), as well as forms used to submit a case for arbitration, go to the AAA's Web site at **http://www. adr.org**.

online dispute resolution (ODR)
The resolution of disputes with the assistance of an organization that offers dispute-resolution services via the Internet.

TODAY'S PROFESSIONAL PARALEGAL

Arbitrating Commercial Contracts

Julia Lorenz has worked as a legal assistant for International Airlines (IA) for ten years. She works in the legal department on the staff of the general counsel. Her job has been to work with Jim Manning, senior attorney. This attorney is responsible for all of the corporation's contracts, including the following: major contracts with jet manufacturers for the purchase of aircraft, contracts with catering companies to supply food during flights, fuel contracts, employment and labor contracts, and many small contracts for the purchase and lease of equipment and supplies for the numerous airline offices and ticket counters.

REVIEWING PROPOSED CONTRACTS

Julia's job is to review the provisions of proposed major contracts, such as the contracts to purchase jet aircraft, and to provide Jim with an article-by-article summary of the contracts' provisions. Jim then negotiates these contracts to obtain the most favorable terms possible for the airline. Once he has negotiated a contract, Julia makes the final changes and forwards it to the appropriate IA corporate official to review and sign.

ATTENDING ARBITRATION PROCEEDINGS

All of the airline's major contracts contain arbitration clauses that require all contract disputes to be resolved through binding arbitration services provided by the American Arbitration Association (AAA). On numerous occasions, Julia has attended arbitration proceedings with Jim. In preparing for arbitration, Julia obtains affidavits, prepares subpoenas, and arranges for witnesses to be present to testify. During the arbitration proceedings, she assists in presenting material into evidence. She and Jim have developed a good rapport with several arbitrators at the local AAA office, and they usually request these arbitrators when they have a case that must be arbitrated.

BECOMING AN ARBITRATOR

Julia's knowledge of arbitration procedures and her outstanding work in preparing for arbitration, as well as during the proceedings, wins her significant recognition from this group of arbitrators. One of the arbitrators eventually approaches Julia and suggests that she apply for approval as an arbitrator. She says that she will consider it.

Julia later mentions the arbitrator's suggestion to Jim. He thinks that Julia had been paid quite a compliment and encourages her to contact the AAA to inquire about the possibility of being approved as an arbitrator. When Julia calls the AAA, she learns that arbitrators in the area of commercial arbitration are not required to be attorneys. She would need eight years of experience in her field and would have to meet certain educational requirements. When Julia realizes that she has the necessary qualifications, she submits an application. About two months later, she is approved as an arbitrator.

---

at any time. Negotiation, mediation, and arbitration services are all available to disputants over the Internet.

ONLINE NEGOTIATION.   Several Web-based firms offer online forums for negotiating monetary settlements. Typically, one party files a complaint, and the other party is notified by e-mail. Password-protected access to the online forum site is available twenty-four hours a day, seven days a week. Fees are generally low (often 2 to 4 percent, or less, of the disputed amount). The parties can drop the negotiations at any time.

ONLINE MEDIATION.   Mediation providers have also tried resolving disputes online. SquareTrade, for example, has provided mediation services for the online auction site eBay and also resolves disputes among other parties. SquareTrade uses Web-based software that walks participants through a five-step e-resolution process. Negotiation between the parties occurs on a secure page within SquareTrade's Web site. The parties may consult a mediator. The entire process takes as little as ten to fourteen days, and there is at present no fee unless the parties use a mediator.

ONLINE ARBITRATION.   A number of organizations, including the American Arbitration Association, offer online arbitration services. For example, Resolution Forum, Inc. (RFI), a nonprofit organization associated with the Center for Legal Responsibility at the South Texas College of Law, offers arbitration services through its CAN-WIN conferencing system. Using standard browser software and an RFI password, the parties to a dispute access an online conference room. When multiple parties are involved, private communications and break-out sessions are possible through private messaging facilities. RFI also offers mediation services.

ADR and the Paralegal

The time and money costs associated with litigating disputes in court continue to rise, and, as a result, disputing parties are increasingly turning to ADR as a means of settling their disagreements. As a way to reduce their caseloads, state and federal courts are also increasingly requiring litigants to undergo arbitration before bringing their suits in front of the courts. Although paralegals have always assisted attorneys in work relating to the negotiation of out-of-court settlements for clients, they may play an even greater role in the future. Some paralegals are qualified mediators and directly assist parties in reaching a mutually satisfactory agreement. Some paralegals serve as arbitrators. As more and more parties utilize ADR, paralegals will have increasing opportunities in this area of legal work.

If you are interested in becoming a mediator, you need to be thoroughly familiar with ADR law in the state in which you work. Some states do not require mediators to meet any special training requirements. For example, Florida law requires that a family mediator "shall be a person with the appropriate attributes who can demonstrate sensitivity toward the parties involved and facilitate solutions to the problem." Other states require mediators to have up to sixty hours of training in certain fields, such as family law, child development, or family dynamics.

❋ KEY TERMS AND CONCEPTS

alternative dispute
   resolution (ADR)

American Arbitration
   Association (AAA)

appellate court

appellate jurisdiction

arbitration

arbitration clause

award

bankruptcy court

binding mediation

concurrent jurisdiction

diversity of citizenship

docket

early neutral case evaluation

exclusive jurisdiction

federal question

jurisdiction

justiciable controversy

long arm statute

mediation

mediation arbitration (med-arb)

mini-trial

negotiation

online dispute resolution (ODR)

original jurisdiction

probate court

rule of four

settlement agreement

standing to sue

submission agreement

summary jury trial (SJT)

trial court

venue

writ of *certiorari*

CHAPTER SUMMARY

Basic Judicial Requirements	**1.** *Jurisdiction*—Before a court can hear a case, it must have jurisdiction over the person against whom the suit is brought (*in personam* jurisdiction) or the property involved in the suit (*in rem* jurisdiction), as well as jurisdiction over the subject matter.
	a. Limited versus general jurisdiction—Limited jurisdiction exists when a court is limited to a specific subject matter, such as probate or divorce. General jurisdiction exists when a court can hear any kind of case.
	b. Original versus appellate jurisdiction—Courts that have authority to hear a case for the first time (trial courts) have original jurisdiction. Courts of appeals, or reviewing courts, have appellate jurisdiction; generally, these courts do not have original jurisdiction.
	c. Federal jurisdiction—Arises (1) when a federal question is involved (when the plaintiff's cause of action is based, at least in part, on the U.S. Constitution, a treaty, or a federal law) or (2) when a case involves diversity of citizenship (as in disputes between citizens of different states, between a foreign country and citizens of a state or states, or between citizens of a state and citizens or subjects of a foreign country) and the amount in controversy exceeds $75,000.
	d. Concurrent versus exclusive jurisdiction—Concurrent jurisdiction exists when two different courts have authority to hear the same case. Exclusive jurisdiction exists when only state courts or only federal courts have authority to hear a case.
	2. *Jurisdiction in cyberspace*—Because the Internet does not have physical boundaries, traditional jurisdictional concepts have been difficult to apply in cases involving activities conducted via the Web. Gradually, the courts are developing standards to use in determining when jurisdiction over a Web owner or operator in another state is proper.
	3. *Venue*—Venue has to do with the most appropriate location for a trial, which is usually the geographic area where the event leading to the dispute took place or where the parties reside.
	4. *Standing to sue*—A legally protected and tangible interest in a matter sufficient to justify seeking relief through the court system. The controversy at issue must also be a justiciable controversy—one that is real and substantial, as opposed to hypothetical or academic.
	5. *Judicial procedures*—Rules of procedure prescribe the way in which disputes are handled in the courts. The Federal Rules of Civil Procedure govern all civil litigation in federal courts. Each state has its own procedural rules (often similar to the federal rules), and each court within a state has specific court rules that must be followed.
State Court Systems	**1.** *Trial courts*—Courts of original jurisdiction, in which legal actions are initiated. State trial courts have either general jurisdiction or limited jurisdiction.
	2. *Intermediate appellate courts*—Many states have intermediate appellate courts that review the proceedings of the trial courts; generally these courts do not have original jurisdiction. Appellate courts ordinarily examine questions of law and procedure while deferring to the trial court's findings of fact.

State Court Systems—Continued	3. *Supreme (highest) courts*—Each state has a supreme court, although it may be called by some other name. Decisions of the state's highest court are final on all questions of state law. If a federal question is at issue, the case may be appealed to the United States Supreme Court. 4. *Judges and justices*—State court judges and justices are normally elected by the voters for specified terms.

The Federal Court System	1. *U.S. district courts*—The federal district court is the equivalent of the state trial court. The district court exercises general jurisdiction over claims arising under federal law or based on diversity of citizenship. Federal courts of limited jurisdiction include the U.S. Tax Court, the U.S. Bankruptcy Court, and the U.S. Court of Federal Claims.
	
	2. *U.S. courts of appeals*—There are thirteen intermediate courts of appeals (or circuit courts of appeals) in the federal court system. Of those courts, twelve hear appeals from the district courts within their circuits. The thirteenth circuit court has national appellate jurisdiction over certain types of cases, such as cases involving patent law and cases in which the U.S. government is a defendant.
	
	3. *United States Supreme Court*—The United States Supreme Court is the highest court in the land and the final arbiter of the Constitution and federal law. There is no absolute right of appeal to the Supreme Court, and the Court hears only a fraction of the cases that are filed with it each year.
	
	   a. Although the Supreme Court has original jurisdiction in some cases, it functions primarily as an appellate court.
	
	   b. If the Supreme Court decides to review a case, it will issue a writ of *certiorari*, an order to a lower court requiring the latter to send it the record of the case for review. As a rule, only petitions that raise the possibility of important constitutional questions are granted.
	
	4. *Judges and justices*—Federal court judges and justices are appointed by the president of the United States and confirmed by the Senate. They receive lifetime appointments.

Alternative Dispute Resolution	The costs and time-consuming character of litigation, as well as the public nature of court proceedings, have caused many to turn to various forms of alternative dispute resolution (ADR) for settling their disagreements. The methods of ADR include the following: 1. *Negotiation*—The simplest form of ADR, in which the parties come together, with or without attorneys to represent them, and try to reach a settlement without the involvement of a third party. 2. *Mediation*—A form of ADR in which the parties themselves reach an agreement with the help of a neutral third party, called a mediator, who proposes solutions and emphasizes areas of agreement. 3. *Arbitration*—The most formal method of ADR, in which the parties submit their dispute to a neutral third party, the arbitrator (or panel of arbitrators), who renders a decision. The decision may or may not be legally binding, depending on the circumstances. a. Arbitration clauses that are voluntarily agreed on in contracts require the parties to resolve their disputes in arbitration (rather than in court).

Alternative Dispute Resolution—Continued	**b.** Arbitrators' decisions, even when binding, may be appealed to the courts for review. The court's review, however, is much more restricted than an appellate court's review of a trial court record. **4.** *Other types of ADR*—These include binding mediation, mediation arbitration (med-arb), early neutral case evaluation, mini-trials, and summary jury trials; generally, these are forms of "assisted negotiation." **5.** *Providers of ADR services*—The leading nonprofit provider of ADR services is the American Arbitration Association. Hundreds of for-profit firms also provide ADR services. **6.** *Online dispute resolution*—A number of organizations and firms offer negotiation, mediation, and arbitration services through online forums. To date, these forums have been a practical alternative for the resolution of disputes over the right to use a certain Web site address or the quality of goods purchased over the Internet.

❈ QUESTIONS FOR REVIEW

1. Define *jurisdiction,* and explain why jurisdiction is important.

2. What is the difference between personal jurisdiction and subject-matter jurisdiction? What is a long arm statute?

3. Define *original jurisdiction* and *appellate jurisdiction.* What is the difference between the two?

4. Over what types of cases can federal courts exercise jurisdiction?

5. What is the relationship between state and federal jurisdiction?

6. What is venue? What is the difference between venue and jurisdiction?

7. Describe the functions of a trial court. How do they differ from the functions of an appellate court?

8. What are the typical courts in a state court system? What are the three basic tiers, or levels, of courts in the federal court system?

9. How do cases reach the United States Supreme Court?

10. List and explain the various methods of alternative dispute resolution.

❈ ETHICAL QUESTIONS

1. Larry Simpson is working on a lawsuit that was recently filed in a federal district court on the basis of diversity-of-citizenship jurisdiction. Larry, a legal assistant, just received the plaintiff's answers to interrogatories (attorneys' written questions to the parties in a lawsuit), which he has been assigned by his supervising attorney to summarize. Larry discovers that the plaintiff's damages are nowhere near the $75,000 required for diversity jurisdiction. What should Larry do?

2. Diane Post, a paralegal, is working on the defense team in a civil lawsuit that has just been filed in the county court, which has limited jurisdiction over civil lawsuits. The plaintiff is seeking an injunction and

$3,000 in damages. (Recall from Chapter 5 that an injunction is an equitable remedy in which a court orders a person to do or refrain from doing a particular act.) The superior court is the only court with jurisdiction over equitable remedies. No one but Diane has noticed that the plaintiff is seeking a remedy that the county court does not have the jurisdictional authority to grant. What should Diane do?

3. Suzanne Andersen's supervising attorney, Amy Lynch, works occasionally as a mediator for family law cases in the local courts. Amy has mediated a divorce case today involving the property settlement of a wealthy businessperson, who happens also to be a defendant in another lawsuit in which Amy represents the plaintiff.

As a result of her mediation today, Amy has learned some confidential financial information about this man. She now has come to Suzanne, her paralegal, and asked her to use this information to his disadvantage in the lawsuit. How should Suzanne handle this situation?

4. Steve is a paralegal with an Ohio law firm that specializes in intellectual property law. He is working on a case in which the client claims that a competitor misappropriated trade secrets in violation of the Uniform Trade Secrets Act. The supervising attorney asks Steve to prepare and submit a complaint with the federal court on behalf of the client. After the attorney has reviewed the complaint, Steve files it electronically, via the Internet, as is permitted by the court. The complaint is not encrypted (encoded) and contains confidential information about the client's company that pertains to the lawsuit. Has Steve or the attorney violated any ethical obligation? If so, which ethical rule has been violated? Can the client sue Steve or the firm for negligence? What could Steve and the attorney have done differently to better protect the client's interests?

✻ PRACTICE QUESTIONS AND ASSIGNMENTS

1. A plaintiff and defendant are involved in an auto accident. Both are residents of the county and state in which the accident takes place. The plaintiff files an auto negligence lawsuit in the county circuit court where the trial will occur. What types of jurisdiction does the court have? (The types to be considered include *in personam* jurisdiction, *in rem* jurisdiction, subject-matter jurisdiction, limited jurisdiction, general jurisdiction, original jurisdiction, appellate jurisdiction, concurrent jurisdiction, and exclusive jurisdiction.)

2. The Brown family from Chicago, Illinois, owns a vacation home in Harbor Springs, Michigan. A dispute arises over the ownership of the property, and an action to partition, or divide, the ownership of the property is filed in the Michigan courts. What types of jurisdiction does the Michigan court have?

3. Renee Clark is a victim of gender discrimination in the workplace. She can file a lawsuit against her employer either under Title VII, a federal statute, in a federal district court or under her state's civil rights act in a state court. When both federal and state courts have authority to hear a case, as in this example, what kind of jurisdiction is involved?

4. Family courts hear cases involving divorce, custody, and other family matters. What types of jurisdiction do family courts have?

5. The court system in the state of Utopia has two levels of trial courts. The lower-level trial court has jurisdiction over civil cases involving damages under $25,000, misdemeanors, local ordinance violations, and small claims. The upper-level trial court has jurisdiction over civil cases involving damages exceeding $25,000, felonies and serious misdemeanors, divorce, and injunctions and can review the lower-level trial court's decisions. What are the various types of jurisdiction that each trial court in the state of Utopia has?

6. Marcia, who is from Toledo, Ohio, drives to Troy, Michigan, and shops at a popular mall. When leaving the parking lot, Marcia causes a car accident when she runs a stop sign. On what basis could a Michigan court obtain jurisdiction over Marcia?

7. Louise sues the manufacturer of her automobile, which is defective, under the Magnuson-Moss Warranty Act, a federal consumer protection statute. In which court can Louise bring her action, and on what jurisdictional basis?

8. Identify each of the following courts:

   a. This state court takes testimony from witnesses and receives evidence. It may have either general or limited subject-matter jurisdiction.

   b. This court has appellate jurisdiction and is part of a court system that is divided into geographical units called *circuits*.

   c. This state court usually has a panel of three or more judges who review the record of a case for errors of law and procedure. It does not have original jurisdiction.

   d. This court can exercise diversity-of-citizenship jurisdiction and receives testimony and other evidence.

   e. The decisions of this court are usually final. It is the highest appellate court in its geographical area.

   f. This federal court has nine justices. It has original jurisdiction over a few types of cases but functions primarily as an appellate court. There is no automatic right to appeal cases to this court.

9. Look at Exhibit 6.4. In which federal circuit is your state located? How many federal judicial districts are located in your state? In which federal district is your community located?

10. Based on the information provided in this chapter, including the exhibits, determine which federal court (or courts) could hear the following cases and on what jurisdictional grounds:

    a. A case in which the Internal Revenue Service sues a taxpayer for back taxes.

    b. A case involving an automobile accident between a citizen of Chicago, Illinois, and a citizen of St. Louis, Missouri, in which the plaintiff is seeking damages of $100,000.

    c. A bankruptcy case.

    d. A lawsuit claiming sexual harassment in violation of Title VII of the federal Civil Rights Act of 1964.

    e. A lawsuit claiming that the defendant violated the federal statute prohibiting racketeering crimes.

11. Suppose that you are a plaintiff in a case brought against the defendant for damages in the amount of $250,000. The case arose as a result of injuries and property damage that you incurred in a car accident caused by the defendant's reckless driving. You know that you have a good chance of winning that amount of damages if the case goes to trial. The defendant offers to settle the case for $175,000. Assume that it would take three years before the court could hear the case. What factors would you consider in deciding this question? What would your decision be?

12. Using Exhibit 6.5 as a model, draft a settlement agreement for a lawsuit involving the following facts:

    Harry Jones is suing Burt Gaston in the U.S. District Court for the Western District of Kentucky, docket number 99-123456. On June 12, 2003, Harry agrees to accept $100,000 in settlement of the lawsuit. Harry's attorney will prepare a settlement agreement for their signatures on June 30. Harry will be paid in one lump-sum cash payment on the execution of the settlement agreement, and he will give up his right to all claims against Burt and release Burt from all future liability for all claims arising out of this occurrence.

13. Using the materials presented in the chapter, identify the following methods of alternative dispute resolution:

    a. The parties to a divorce meet with a neutral third party who emphasizes points of agreement and proposes solutions to resolve their dispute. After several hours, the parties come to a solution.

    b. The parties to a contract dispute submit it to a neutral third party for a legally binding resolution. The neutral third party is not a court.

    c. The plaintiff and defense attorneys in a personal-injury case propose settlement figures to one another and their clients in an effort to voluntarily resolve the lawsuit.

    d. The attorneys from the personal-injury example above are able to reach an acceptable settlement figure of $100,000. They draft an agreement whereby the plaintiff gives up her right to sue in exchange for a payment of $100,000 by the defendant.

    e. A commercial dispute involving $95,000 in damages is filed in a federal court. The judge requires the parties' attorneys to present their arguments and supporting evidence, excluding witnesses, to the jury. The jury then renders a nonbinding verdict. Once the nonbinding verdict is rendered, the parties reach a settlement.

✳ QUESTIONS FOR CRITICAL ANALYSIS

1. Before a case can be heard by a court, the court must have jurisdiction to hear and decide the case. What types of jurisdiction exist? What would happen if a case were filed in a court that did not have jurisdiction over it?

2. The federal courts have jurisdiction primarily over diversity cases and over questions of federal law. State courts have jurisdiction over matters such as wills, divorces, and property concerns. Why? What would happen if federal courts decided divorce cases, for example? What would happen if state courts decided cases between a citizen of the state and a foreign citizen?

3. A change of venue from Oklahoma City to Denver, Colorado, was ordered for the trials of Timothy McVeigh and Terry Nichols after they had been

indicted in connection with the 1995 bombing of the Alfred P. Murrah Federal Building in Oklahoma City, which killed more than 160 persons and injured hundreds of others. The decision changing the venue of the trial is *United States v. McVeigh,* 918 F.Supp. 1467 (1996). Review this case. What constitutional issues were involved in the court's decision allowing a change of venue? Do death-penalty cases require a different standard? If so, what is the standard? What evidence did the court review in reaching its decision? Why did the court conclude that the federal district court in Denver, Colorado, met the requirements for an alternative venue? Given the outcome of the case, was the change of venue effective? Given the pretrial publicity, would the defendants have been convicted if venue had been changed to Maine?

4. What is the difference in the roles that the trial and appellate courts play in a lawsuit? Why is it that appellate courts only rarely decide questions of fact? When does an appellate court review facts?

5. Most state court judges are elected, while federal court judges are appointed. Which system, in your opinion, is fairer? Does either system affect the quality of the judiciary?

6. Do you think that it is fair that in most cases there is no right to appeal to the United States Supreme Court? Should citizens have to petition for *certiorari* to be heard by the Supreme Court? What does the requirement of a grant of *certiorari,* coupled with the limited number of cases that the Supreme Court hears, tell you about the role and purpose of the Supreme Court?

7. Why are Americans increasingly turning to ADR as a way of settling their disputes? What are the implications of ADR, including the increased use of "private justice," for the American system of justice generally?

8. Some individuals have claimed that mandatory ADR infringes on a person's constitutional right to a jury trial. Do you agree with this view? Why or why not?

❈ PROJECTS

1. Contact a local trial court and request a copy of a chart, pamphlet, or other publication that lists the courts in your state and describes the jurisdiction of each. Check with your instructor prior to undertaking this assignment for any special instructions.

2. Contact the local federal district court clerk's office and ask if electronic filings are accepted. If accepted, ask whether filings are accepted via e-mail or CD-ROM. Ask if any other form of filings, such as tax filings, are accepted. Find out if electronic filing is limited to certain types of documents or cases. Check with your instructor prior to undertaking this assignment for any special instructions.

3. Review a local legal newspaper or bar association journal. Locate advertisements for firms offering ADR services. Call one of these firms and find out what services are offered and what rates are charged.

4. Contact the American Arbitration Association and ask what kinds of disputes (contract disputes, employment disputes, and so on) it arbitrates. Request a copy of its procedural rules for the arbitration of disputes in one of the areas it handles. Review the rules and summarize the procedures involved.

5. Review the table of contents of the court rules of your state courts or the federal courts. What subjects are covered? How do these subjects relate to the topics discussed in this chapter? You should be able to locate these rules in your school's library or in a law school library.

❈ USING INTERNET RESOURCES

1. Paralegals frequently assist in ADR proceedings and even, in some cases, serve as mediators or arbitrators. To learn more about ADR procedures, go to http://www.adr.org, the home page for the American Arbitration Association (AAA). Browse through the site's offerings and find the answers to the following questions:
   a. When was the AAA founded? What types of services does it offer?

   b. Where is the AAA regional office nearest you? Does the AAA engage in arbitration outside the United States?

   c. According to the AAA glossary, who are case administrators, and what role do they play in arbitration proceedings?

   d. How many arbitration forms are available to download from this site? Is there any cost for downloading these forms? How many states provide state-specific forms on this site?

e. Click on "File a Case Online" and then on "FAQs." What is required in order to file a claim online? Is there any cost involved?

2. Go to the official site of the United States Supreme Court at **http://www.supremecourtus.gov**, and answer the following questions:

a. Click on "About the Supreme Court," and then click on "The Court and Its Procedures." When does the Supreme Court session begin and end each year? How long does each side normally have to argue a case before the Supreme Court justices? When the Court is in recess, approximately how many petitions do the justices have to review per week to determine if they will hear the case?

b. Click on "Orders and Journal" from the home page menu, and then click on "Orders of the Court" from the most recent time period. What is an order in the language of the Supreme Court? Do the justices sign orders? Are they used often?

c. Click on "Opinions," and then click on "Latest Slip Opinions." What is a slip opinion? Select a Supreme Court opinion that contains a syllabus, or summary of the court's opinion. Review it, and identify and briefly describe the parties, the general nature of the dispute, the dates the case was argued and decided, and the name of the justice who delivered the opinion of the court and any justice(s) who dissented.

d. Click on "Related Websites." Can you access the executive and legislative branches of government through the links provided in this Web site?

3. Go to the Web site, **http://www.courts.net**. This useful Web site provides a directory to courts throughout the country. This information is helpful for learning about the court system in a particular state, as well as locating the court. Click on your state. What information is available about the courts in your state? Make a list of the courts that are included, and note the types of information available. For example, are the addresses, telephone numbers, and judges' names provided? Do the trial courts and appellate courts have their own Web sites? Are the courts' rules and court calendars available online? Can you file any documents with the courts online? Can you access the opinions of the courts in your state via the Internet?

END NOTES

1. See Appendix J for the full text of the U.S. Constitution.

2. As will be discussed shortly, a state's highest court is often referred to as the state supreme court, but there are exceptions. For example, in New York the supreme court is a trial court.

3. Currently under negotiation is the Hague Convention on Jurisdiction, an international treaty intended to make civil judgments enforceable across national borders. One issue in the negotiations is whether to require that all disputes be settled in the country of the seller or the country of the buyer. It has also been suggested that mandatory jurisdiction provisions be left out of the treaty.

4. Pronounced *ven*-yoo.

5. Pronounced jus-*tish*-a-bul.

6. The name in Ohio is Court of Common Pleas; the name in New York is Supreme Court.

7. Pronounced sur-shee-uh-*rah*-ree.

8. The American Arbitration Association is a leading provider of arbitration services in the United States.

9. See, for example, *Wright v. Universal Maritime Service Corp.*, 525 U.S. 70, 119 S.Ct. 391, 142 L.Ed.2d 361 (1998).

10. *Hooters of America, Inc. v. Phillips*, 173 F.3d 933 (4th Cir. 1999). See also *Circuit City Stores, Inc. v. Adams*, 279 F.3d 889 (2002).

TORT LAW AND PRODUCT LIABILITY

Chapter Outline

✖ INTRODUCTION ✖ THE BASIS OF TORT LAW ✖ INTENTIONAL TORTS
✖ NEGLIGENCE ✖ CYBER TORTS: DEFAMATION ONLINE ✖ STRICT LIABILITY
✖ PRODUCT LIABILITY ✖ DEFENSES TO PRODUCT LIABILITY ✖ TORT LAW
AND THE PARALEGAL

After completing this chapter, you will know:

- What a tort is, the purpose of tort law, and the three basic categories of torts.

- The four elements of negligence.

- What is meant by strict liability and under what circumstances strict liability is applied.

- The meaning of strict product liability and the underlying policy for imposing strict product liability.

- What defenses can be raised in product liability actions.

Introduction

Torts are wrongful actions. In fact, the word *tort* is French for "wrong." Through tort law, society compensates those who have suffered injuries as a result of the wrongful conduct of others. Although some torts, such as trespass, originated in the English common law, the field of tort law continues to expand. As new ways to commit wrongs—such as the use of the Internet to commit wrongful acts—are discovered, the courts are extending tort law to cover these wrongs. Torts committed via the Internet are sometimes referred to as **cyber torts.**

In the pages that follow, you will read about some of the primary concepts of tort law and how they are being applied today in the context of the online environment, as well as other environments. You will also read about *product liability,* which is the area of tort law under which sellers can be held liable for defective products.

The common law of torts is an area of particular importance for paralegals. Tort lawsuits are frequent occurrences in the American legal arena, and many attorneys and paralegals devote a substantial amount of their time to serving clients who either want to bring or defend against tort lawsuits. Many attorneys who practice tort law also specialize in product liability actions. Because of the significance of these two areas of substantive law in litigation today, we begin our study of substantive law with an examination of tort law. The following four chapters are devoted to other fundamental areas of substantive law.

tort
A civil wrong not arising from a breach of contract; a breach of a legal duty that proximately causes harm or injury to another.

cyber tort
A tort committed in cyberspace.

The Basis of Tort Law

Two notions serve as the basis of all torts: wrongs and compensation. Tort law recognizes that some acts are wrong because they cause injuries to others. In a tort action, one person or group brings a personal-injury suit against another person or group to obtain compensation (money damages) or other relief for the harm suffered. Because tort suits involve "private" wrongs, they are distinguishable from criminal actions, which involve "public" wrongs. The state prosecutor brings criminal actions against individuals who commit acts that are considered to be wrongs against society as a whole (crimes are usually defined by statute, as you will read in Chapter 15). Sometimes an act may result in both a tort lawsuit and a criminal prosecution.

Generally, the purpose of tort law is to provide remedies for the invasion of various interests—such as people's interests in their physical safety and security, privacy, freedom of movement, and reputation—that society seeks to protect. In this chapter, we will discuss the two broad categories of torts: *intentional torts* and *negligence.* The classification of a particular tort depends largely on how the tort occurs (intentionally or unintentionally) and the surrounding circumstances. We will also examine the concept of *strict liability,* a tort doctrine under which a defendant may be held liable for harm or injury to another regardless of intention or fault.

On the Web
You can find cases and articles on torts in the tort law library at the Internet Law Library's Web site. Go to **http://www. lawguru.com/ilawlib.**

Intentional Torts

An **intentional tort,** as the term implies, requires *intent.* In tort law, intent does not necessarily mean that the actor (who is sometimes referred to as the **tortfeasor**) intended to harm someone; rather, it means only that the actor intended the consequences of his or her act or knew with substantial certainty that certain consequences would result from the act.

intentional tort
A wrongful act knowingly committed.

tortfeasor
One who commits a tort.

    ✖   **The law generally assumes that individuals intend the *normal* consequences of their actions.**

Thus, forcefully pushing another—even if done in jest and without any evil motive—is an intentional tort (if injury results), because the object of a strong push can ordinarily be expected to go flying.

Intentional Torts against Persons

There are two kinds of intentional torts: intentional torts against persons and intentional torts against property. In this section, we discuss intentional torts against persons, which include assault and battery, false imprisonment, intentional infliction of emotional distress, defamation, invasion of the right to privacy, appropriation, misrepresentation, and wrongful interference.

assault
Any word or action intended to make another person fearful of immediate physical harm; a reasonably believable threat.

ASSAULT AND BATTERY.   An **assault** is any intentional act that causes another to reasonably fear immediate harmful or offensive contact. Apprehension is not the same as fear. If a contact is such that a reasonable person would want to avoid it, and if there is a reasonable basis for believing that the contact will occur, then the plaintiff suffers apprehension regardless of whether he or she is afraid. The interest protected by tort law concerning assault is the freedom from having to expect harmful or offensive contact. The occurrence of apprehension is enough to justify compensation.

battery
The intentional and offensive touching of another without lawful justification.

The *completion* of the fear-inducing act, if it results in harm to the plaintiff, is a **battery,** which is defined as harmful or offensive physical contact *intentionally* performed. For example, suppose that Ivan threatens Jean with a gun, then shoots her. The pointing of the gun at Jean is an assault; the firing of the gun (if the bullet hits Jean) is a battery. The interest protected by tort law concerning battery is the right to personal security and safety. The contact can be harmful, or it can be merely offensive (such as an unwelcome kiss). Physical injury need not occur. The contact can involve any part of the body or anything attached to it—for example, a hat or other item of clothing, a purse, or a chair or an automobile in which one is sitting. Whether the contact is offensive or not is determined by the *reasonable person standard.*[1] The contact can be made by the defendant or by some force the defendant sets in motion—for example, a rock thrown, food poisoned, or a stick swung.

Compensation.   If the plaintiff shows that there was contact, and the jury agrees that the contact was offensive, the plaintiff has a right to compensation. There is no need to show that the defendant acted out of malice; the person could have just been joking or playing around. The underlying motive does not matter, only the intent to bring about the harmful or offensive contact to the plaintiff. In fact, proving a motive is never necessary (but is sometimes relevant). A plaintiff may be compensated for the emotional harm or loss of reputation resulting from a battery, as well as for physical harm.

defense
The reasons that a defendant offers and alleges why the plaintiff should not recover what she or he seeks in a lawsuit.

Defenses to Assault and Battery.   A number of legally recognized **defenses** (reasons why plaintiffs should not obtain what they are seeking) can be raised by a defendant who is sued for assault, battery, or both:

- *Consent.* When a person consents to the act that damages her or him, there is generally no liability (legal responsibility) for the damage done. For example, if Sue consents to being kissed, Bryan can raise this as a defense if she sues for battery.
- *Self-defense.* An individual who is defending his or her life or physical well-being can claim self-defense. In situations of both *real* and *apparent* danger, a person may use whatever force is *reasonably* necessary to prevent harmful con-

tact. Thus, if Simon is sexually assaulting Linda, she may claim this as a defense if Simon sues her for hitting him with a baseball bat.

- *Defense of others.* An individual can act in a reasonable manner to protect others who are in real or apparent danger. That is, if Fred offensively touches your wife and you hit Fred, you can raise this as a defense if Fred subsequently tries to sue you for battery.
- *Defense of property.* People can use reasonable force in attempting to remove intruders from their homes, although force that is likely to cause death or great bodily injury can never be used just to protect property. For example, if you catch someone in the act of breaking into your garage, you can use nondeadly force to stop that person without being liable for battery.

FALSE IMPRISONMENT.   *False imprisonment* is defined as the intentional confinement or restraint of another person's activities without justification. False imprisonment interferes with the freedom to move without restraint. The confinement can be accomplished through the use of physical barriers, physical restraint, or threats of physical force. Moral pressure or threats of future harm do not constitute false imprisonment. It is essential that the person being restrained not comply with the restraint willingly.

Stores are often sued for false imprisonment after they have attempted to confine a suspected shoplifter for questioning. Under the "privilege to detain" granted to merchants in some states, a merchant can use the defense of *probable cause* to justify delaying a suspected shoplifter. Probable cause exists when the evidence to support the belief that a person is guilty outweighs the evidence against that belief. Although laws governing false imprisonment vary from state to state, generally they require that any detention be conducted in a *reasonable* manner and for only a *reasonable* length of time.

INTENTIONAL INFLICTION OF EMOTIONAL DISTRESS.   The tort of *intentional infliction of emotional distress* can be defined as an intentional act that amounts to extreme and outrageous conduct resulting in severe emotional distress to another. For example, suppose a prankster telephones an individual and says that the individual's spouse has just been in a horrible accident. As a result, the individual suffers intense mental pain or anxiety. The caller's behavior is deemed to be extreme and outrageous conduct that exceeds the bounds of decency accepted by society and is therefore **actionable** (capable of serving as the basis for a lawsuit). Note that courts in some jurisdictions require that the emotional distress be evidenced by some physical symptom or illness or some emotional disturbance that can be documented by a psychiatric consultant or other medical professional.

actionable
Capable of serving as the basis of a lawsuit. An actionable claim can be pursued in a lawsuit or other court action.

DEFAMATION.   Wrongfully hurting a person's good reputation constitutes the tort of **defamation.** The law imposes a general duty on all persons to refrain from making false, defamatory statements about others. Breaching this duty orally involves the tort of **slander;** breaching it in writing involves the tort of **libel.** The tort of defamation also arises when a false statement is made about a person's product, business, or title to property.

defamation
Anything published or publicly spoken that causes injury to another's good name, reputation, or character.

The common law defines four types of false utterances that are considered slander *per se* (meaning that no proof of injury or harm is required for these false utterances to be actionable):

slander
Defamation in oral form.

- A statement that another has a loathsome communicable disease.
- A statement that another has committed improprieties while engaging in a profession or trade.

libel
Defamation in writing or some other form (such as videotape) having the quality of permanence.

DEVELOPING PARALEGAL SKILLS

Handling Emotional Distress Claims

Roxanne Stalker is a paralegal at the law firm of Meyers & Johnson. Bill Meyers represented Sheila Reisner in a divorce case two years ago. Since that time, Sheila has called the office on numerous occasions complaining about her former husband's conduct. This afternoon, Sheila has an appointment with Bill Meyers to discuss a tort claim that she wishes to bring against her former husband for emotional distress. Meyers, who thinks that Sheila is overly emotional and difficult, is too busy to talk with Sheila today. He asks Roxanne to interview Sheila, write down the pertinent information, and assess whether Sheila has a good claim for intentional infliction of emotional distress. After Meyers has reviewed Roxanne's notes, he will telephone Sheila to discuss the matter with her.

TIPS FOR INTERVIEWING THE EMOTIONALLY DISTRESSED CLIENT

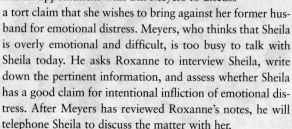

- Make some advance preparations when you know that a client is in a distressed state. Have some tissues at hand, a glass, and some drinking water. Tell others in the office not to disturb you.
- Stay calm and focused, and be professional. Adopt a demeanor that tells the client that you are listening and that you care.
- Keep in mind that you are not a counselor. Your role is to discover the facts underlying the client's legal claim.
- Steer the client's conversation to the facts that you need to know. For example, has Sheila's former husband engaged in extremely outrageous conduct with the intent to cause her distress?
- Concentrate on proof of damages. Remember that in many states an individual must exhibit objective physical symptoms or illness (through physicians' testimony, for example) in order to recover for emotional distress claims.

- A statement that another has committed or has been imprisoned for a serious crime.
- A false statement that an unmarried woman is unchaste.

The Publication Requirement.   The basis of the tort of defamation is the publication of a statement or statements that hold an individual up to contempt, ridicule, or hatred. *Publication* here means simply that the defamatory statements are communicated to persons other than the defamed party. For example, if Sally writes Andrew a private letter accusing him of embezzling funds, the action does not constitute libel. If John calls Rita dishonest, unattractive, and incompetent when no one else is around, the action does not constitute slander. In neither case was the message communicated to a third party.

The courts have generally held that even dictating a letter to a secretary constitutes publication, although the publication may be privileged (the meaning of privileged communications in defamation law will be discussed shortly). Moreover, if a third party overhears defamatory statements by chance, the courts usually hold that this also constitutes publication. Defamatory statements made via the Internet are actionable as well. Note further that any individual who republishes or repeats defamatory statements is liable even if that person reveals the source of the statements.

Defenses against Defamation.   Truth is normally an absolute defense against a defamation charge. In other words, if the defendant in a defamation suit can prove that his or her allegedly defamatory statements were true, the defendant will not be liable.

Another defense that is sometimes raised is that the statements were **privileged** communications and thus the defendant is immune from liability. Privileged communications are of two types: absolute and qualified. Only in judicial proceedings and certain legislative proceedings is an *absolute* privilege granted. For example, statements made in the courtroom by attorneys and judges during a trial are absolutely privileged, as are statements made by legislators during congressional floor debate.

In general, false and defamatory statements that are made about *public figures* (public officials who exercise substantial governmental power and any persons in the public limelight) and that are published in the press are privileged if they are made without **actual malice.**[2] To be made with actual malice, a statement must be made *with either knowledge of falsity or a reckless disregard of the truth*. Statements made about public figures, especially when they are made via a public medium, are usually related to matters of general public interest; they are made about people who substantially affect all of us. Furthermore, public figures generally have some access to a public medium for responding to disparaging (belittling, discrediting) falsehoods about themselves; private individuals do not. For these reasons, public figures have a greater burden of proof in defamation cases (they must prove actual malice) than do private individuals.

INVASION OF THE RIGHT TO PRIVACY.   A person has a right to solitude and freedom from prying public eyes—in other words, to privacy. The Supreme Court has held that a fundamental right to privacy is also implied by various amendments to the U.S. Constitution. Some state constitutions explicitly provide for privacy rights. In addition, a number of federal and state statutes have been enacted to protect individual rights in specific areas. Tort law also safeguards these rights through the tort of *invasion of privacy*. Four acts qualify as an invasion of privacy:

- *The use of a person's name, picture, or other likeness for commercial purposes without permission*. This tort, which is usually referred to as the tort of appropriation, will be examined shortly.
- *Intrusion in an individual's affairs or seclusion*. For example, invading someone's home or illegally searching someone's briefcase is an invasion of privacy. The tort has been held to extend to eavesdropping by wiretap, the unauthorized scanning of a bank account, compulsory blood testing, and window peeping.
- *Publication of information that places a person in a false light*. This could be a story attributing to the person ideas not held or actions not taken by the person. (Publishing such a story could involve the tort of defamation as well.)
- *Public disclosure of private facts about an individual that an ordinary person would find objectionable*. A newspaper account of a private citizen's sex life or financial affairs could be an actionable invasion of privacy.

APPROPRIATION.   The use by one person of another person's name, likeness, or other identifying characteristic, without permission and for the benefit of the user, constitutes the tort of **appropriation.** Under the law, an individual's right to privacy normally includes the right to the exclusive use of her or his identity.

A good example of appropriation can be found in the case brought by Vanna White, the hostess of the popular television game show *Wheel of Fortune*, against Samsung Electronics America, Inc. Without White's permission, Samsung included in an advertisement for its videocassette recorders a depiction of a robot dressed in a wig, gown, and jewelry, posed in a scene that resembled the *Wheel of Fortune* set, in a stance for which White is famous. The court held in White's favor, holding

privilege
In tort law, the ability to act contrary to another person's right without that person's having legal redress for such acts. Privilege may be raised as a defense to defamation.

actual malice
Real and demonstrable evil intent. In a defamation suit, a statement made about a public figure normally must be made with actual malice (with either knowledge of its falsity or a reckless disregard of the truth) for liability to be incurred.

On the Web
The Cyberspace Law Center of FindLaw, which is now a part of West Group, offers numerous links to privacy laws and cases at **http://cyber.lp. findlaw.com/privacy.**

appropriation
In tort law, the use by one person of another person's name, likeness, or other identifying characteristic without permission and for the benefit of the user.

ETHICAL CONCERN

Online Privacy

A pressing issue in today's online world has to do with the privacy rights of Internet users, especially in the employment context. For example, law firms today routinely provide their paralegals and other employees with e-mail access to facilitate the performance of job duties. What if, however, a paralegal uses e-mail to spread rumors or to make sexually explicit or unprofessional comments about other employees? Can a paralegal claim a right to privacy in the personal e-mail sent from his or her office computer? Most courts that have considered the question have concluded that employees have no reasonable expectation of privacy in e-mails sent from their office computers. This is true even when employees were not informed that their e-mails could be read by the employer. After all, the employer has both a legal and an ethical obligation to prevent harassment and discrimination in the workplace. Although employers who provide Internet access to employees can usually monitor or access their employees' e-mail messages without liability for invasion of privacy, they would not be allowed by most courts to publicly disclose the contents of an employee's personal e-mail.

---

that the tort of appropriation does not require the use of a celebrity's name or likeness. The court stated that Samsung's robot ad left "little doubt" as to the identity of the celebrity whom the ad was meant to depict.[3]

MISREPRESENTATION (FRAUD).   A misrepresentation leads another to believe in a condition that is different from the condition that actually exists. This is often accomplished through a false or an incorrect statement. The tort of **fraudulent misrepresentation,** or fraud, involves intentional deceit for personal gain—not misrepresentations innocently made by someone who is unaware of the existing facts.

fraudulent misrepresentation
Any misrepresentation, either by misstatement or omission of a material fact, knowingly made with the intention of deceiving another and on which a reasonable person would and does rely to his or her detriment.

Elements of Fraud.   The tort of fraudulent misrepresentation includes several elements:

- Misrepresentation of facts or conditions with knowledge that they are false or with reckless disregard for the truth.
- Intent to induce another to rely on the misrepresentation.
- Justifiable reliance by the deceived party.
- Damages suffered as a result of the reliance.
- Causal connection between the misrepresentation and the injury suffered.

Fraud exists only when a person represents as a fact something he or she knows is untrue. For example, it is fraud to claim that a building does not leak when one knows it does. Facts are objectively ascertainable, whereas *seller's talk* is not. If Harry says, "I am the best accountant in town," for example, that would be considered seller's talk, not fraud. The speaker is not trying to represent something as fact, because the term *best* is subjective (open to interpretation) and because a "reasonable person" would not rely on Harry's statement.

On the Web
The 'Lectric Law Library's Legal Lexicon includes an informative discussion of the elements of fraud as well as different types of fraud. To access this page, go to **http://www.lectlaw.com/def/f079.htm.**

Fact versus Opinion.   Normally, the tort of misrepresentation or fraud occurs only when there is reliance on a *statement of fact.* Sometimes, however, reliance on a *statement of opinion* may involve the tort of misrepresentation if the individual making the statement of opinion has a superior knowledge of the subject matter. For example, when a lawyer makes a statement of opinion about the law in a state in which the lawyer is licensed to practice, a court would construe reliance on such a statement to be equivalent to reliance on a statement of fact.

WRONGFUL INTERFERENCE.   Today, many lawsuits involve situations in which an individual or business is accused of wrongfully interfering with the business of another. These **business torts** are generally divided into two categories: wrongful interference with a contractual relationship (contract law will be discussed in Chapter 8) and wrongful interference with a business relationship.

business tort
Wrongful interference with another's business rights.

Wrongful Interference with a Contractual Relationship.   The body of tort law relating to *intentional interference with a contractual relationship* has expanded greatly in recent years. Three elements are necessary to establish the tort of wrongful interference with a contractual relationship:

- A valid, enforceable contract must exist between two parties.
- A third party must know that this contract exists.
- The third party must *intentionally* cause either of the two parties to breach the contract.

The contract may be between a firm and its employees or a firm and its customers. Sometimes, for example, a competitor of a firm draws away one of the firm's key employees. If the original employer can show (1) that the competitor induced the employee to leave (a breach of the contract) and (2) that the employee would not otherwise have broken the contract, then the employer may be entitled to compensation from the competitor.

Wrongful Interference with a Business Relationship.   Wrongful interference with a business relationship involves situations in which a party unreasonably interferes with another's business in an attempt to gain a share of the market. There is a difference between competitive methods that do not give rise to tort liability and **predatory behavior**—actions undertaken with the intention of unlawfully driving competitors completely out of the market. The distinction usually depends on whether a business is attempting to attract customers in general or to solicit only those customers who have shown an interest in a similar product or service of a specific competitor. If a shopping center contains two shoe stores, for example, an employee of Store A cannot be positioned at the entrance of Store B for the purpose of diverting customers to Store A. This type of activity constitutes the tort of wrongful interference with a business relationship, which is commonly considered to be an unfair trade practice. If this type of activity were permitted, Store A would reap the benefits of Store B's advertising.

predatory behavior
Business behavior that is undertaken with the intention of unlawfully driving competitors out of the market.

Defenses to Wrongful Interference.   A person will not be liable for the tort of wrongful interference with a contractual or business relationship if it can be shown that the interference was justified, or permissible. Good faith competitive behavior is a permissible interference even if it results in the breaking of a contract. For example, if Antonio's Meats advertises so effectively that it induces Beverly's Restaurant Chain to break its contract with Otis Meat Company, Otis Meat Company will be unable to recover against Antonio's Meats on a wrongful interference theory. After all, the public policy that favors free competition in advertising outweighs any possible instability that such competitive activity might cause in contractual relations.

Intentional Torts against Property

Intentional torts against property include trespass to land, trespass to personal property, and conversion. These torts are wrongful actions that interfere with individuals' legally recognized rights with regard to their land or personal property. The law distinguishes real property from personal property (see Chapter 9). *Real property* is land and things "permanently" attached to the land. *Personal property* consists of all other items, which are basically movable. Thus, a house and lot are real property, whereas the furniture inside a house is personal property. Money and stocks and bonds are also personal property.

trespass to land
The entry onto, above, or below the surface of land owned by another without the owner's permission or legal authorization.

TRESPASS TO LAND.   A **trespass to land** occurs whenever a person, without permission, enters onto land that is owned by another, causes anything to enter onto the land, remains on the land, or permits anything to remain on it. Actual harm to the land is not an essential element of this tort because the tort is designed to protect the right of an owner to exclusively possess his or her property. Common types of trespass to land include walking or driving on the land, shooting a gun over the land, throwing rocks at a building that belongs to someone else, causing water to back up on someone else's land, and placing part of one's building on an adjoining landowner's property.

Trespass Criteria, Rights, and Duties.   The owner of the real property must show that a person is a trespasser. For example, if a person ignores "posted" trespass signs and enters onto the property, he or she is established as a trespasser. A guest in your home is not a trespasser—unless she or he has been asked to leave but refuses. Any person who enters onto your property to commit an illegal act (such as a thief) is established impliedly as a trespasser, without posted signs. Normally, a trespasser must pay for any damage caused to the property and can be removed from the premises through the use of reasonable force without the owner's being liable for assault and battery.

Defenses against Trespass to Land.   The most common defense to trespass is that the trespass was warranted. For example, when a trespasser enters to assist someone in danger, a defense exists. Another defense exists when the trespasser can show that he or she had permission to come onto the land for a specified purpose, such as to read an electric meter. Note that the property owner can revoke such permission. If the property owner asks a meter reader to leave and the meter reader refuses, the meter reader at that point becomes a trespasser.

trespass to personal property
The unlawful taking or harming of another's personal property; interference with another's right to the exclusive possession of his or her personal property.

TRESPASS TO PERSONAL PROPERTY.   Whenever any individual unlawfully harms the personal property of another or otherwise interferes with the owner's right to exclusively possess that personal property, **trespass to personal property** occurs. For example, if a student takes another student's paralegal book as a practical joke and hides it so that the owner is unable to find it for several days prior to a final examination, the student has engaged in a trespass to personal property.

If it can be shown that trespass to personal property was warranted, then a complete defense exists. Most states, for example, allow automobile repair shops to hold a customer's car (under what is called a *mechanic's lien*) when the customer refuses to pay for repairs already completed.

conversion
The act of wrongfully taking or retaining a person's personal property and placing it in the service of another.

CONVERSION.   Whenever personal property is wrongfully taken from its rightful owner, the act of **conversion** occurs. Conversion is any act depriving an owner of personal property without that owner's permission and without just cause.

When conversion occurs, the lesser offense of trespass to personal property usually occurs as well. If the initial taking of the property was unlawful, there is trespass; retention of that property is conversion. Even if the owner permitted the initial taking of the property, failure to return it may still be conversion. Conversion is the civil side of crimes related to theft. A store clerk who steals merchandise from the store commits a crime and engages in the tort of conversion at the same time.

Even if a person mistakenly believed that she or he was entitled to the goods, a tort of conversion may occur. Someone who buys stolen goods, for example, is guilty of conversion even if he or she did not know that the goods were stolen. If the true owner brings a tort action against the buyer, the buyer must either return the property to the owner or pay the owner the full value of the property (despite having already paid money to the thief). If the person accused of conversion can show that the purported owner did not in fact own the property, however, a defense exists. Necessity is another possible defense against conversion.

NEGLIGENCE

The tort of **negligence** occurs when someone suffers injury because of another's failure to live up to a required *duty of care*. In contrast to intentional torts, in torts involving negligence, the one committing the tort neither wishes to bring about the consequences of the act nor believes that they will occur. The actor's conduct merely creates a *risk* of such consequences. If no risk is created, there is no negligence. The risk must also be foreseeable; that is, it must be such that a reasonable person engaging in the same activity would anticipate the risk and guard against it.

Many of the actions discussed in the section on intentional torts constitute negligence if the element of intent is missing. For example, if Juan intentionally shoves Naomi, who falls and breaks an arm as a result, Juan will have committed the intentional tort of assault and battery. If Juan carelessly bumps into Naomi, however, and she falls and breaks an arm as a result, Juan's action will constitute negligence. In either situation, Juan has committed a tort.

To succeed in a negligence action, the plaintiff must prove the following:

- That the defendant owed a duty of care to the plaintiff.
- That the defendant breached that duty.
- That the plaintiff suffered a legally recognizable injury.
- That the defendant's breach caused the plaintiff's injury.

We discuss here each of these four elements of negligence.

The Duty of Care and Its Breach

Central to the tort of negligence is the concept of a **duty of care.** The concept arises from the notion that if we are to live in society with other people, some actions can be tolerated and some cannot; some actions are right and some are wrong; and some actions are reasonable and some are not. The basic principle underlying the duty of care is that people are free to act as they please so long as their actions do not infringe on the interests of others.

The law of torts defines and measures the duty of care by the **reasonable person standard.** In determining whether a duty of care has been breached, for example, the courts ask how a reasonable person would have acted in the same circumstances. The reasonable person standard is said to be (though in an absolute sense it cannot be) objective. It is not necessarily how a particular person

negligence
The failure to exercise the standard of care that a reasonable person would exercise in similar circumstances.

duty of care
The duty of all persons, as established by tort law, to exercise a reasonable amount of care in their dealings with others. Failure to exercise due care, which is normally determined by the reasonable person standard, constitutes the tort of negligence.

reasonable person standard
The standard of behavior expected of a hypothetical "reasonable person"; the standard against which negligence is measured and that must be observed to avoid liability for negligence.

DEVELOPING PARALEGAL SKILLS
Medical Records

Derek Busset is a legal assistant for the small personal-injury firm of McNair and Iverson. Ralph McNair is handling a case in which Blanche Rosenthal's car was struck by an automobile driven by Daniel Gomez, who is insured by Reliable Insurance. The police report indicates that at the time of the accident, Gomez was speeding through a yellow light at the intersection when his car collided with Rosenthal's 1999 Cadillac, which had just entered the intersection on a green light. The insurance company has already compensated Rosenthal for the damages to her vehicle but disputes the amount of damages she is claiming for medical bills. The insurance company believes that Rosenthal's back injury was a preexisting condition, not caused by the accident. After speaking with a representative from the insurance company, attorney McNair asks Derek to contact Rosenthal and acquire the medical records to support her claims. McNair also wants Derek to write up a summary of what the records show.

TIPS FOR OBTAINING AND EVALUATING MEDICAL RECORDS

- Find out from the client the names of all of the physicians who treated the client and the names of hospitals or other facilities in which the client received medical care.

- Prepare—and have the client sign—medical release forms, which authorize the treating physicians to provide the patient's medical records directly to the law firm.

- Keep a log of the records as they come in.

- If a claim involves the possibility of a preexisting condition, make certain to request the client's complete medical history (from before the injury as well as after it). You will need these records to determine whether a preexisting condition might have caused or contributed to the plaintiff's injury.

- Obtain a medical dictionary or reference book so that you can decipher the terminology and abbreviations frequently used by medical personnel in charts and records.

---

would act. It is society's judgment of how an ordinarily prudent person should act. If the so-called reasonable person existed, he or she would be careful, conscientious, prudent, even tempered, and honest. That individuals are required to exercise a reasonable standard of care in their activities is a pervasive concept in the law, and many of the issues dealt with in subsequent chapters of this text have to do with this duty.

In negligence cases, the degree of care to be exercised varies depending on the defendant's occupation or profession, her or his relationship with the plaintiff, and other factors. Generally, whether an action constitutes a breach of the duty of care is determined on a case-by-case basis. The outcome depends on how the trial court judge (or jury, if it is a jury trial) decides a reasonable person in the position of the defendant would have acted in the particular circumstances of the case. In the following subsections, we examine the degree of care typically expected of landowners and professionals.

THE DUTY OF LANDOWNERS.   Landowners are expected to exercise reasonable care to protect persons coming onto their property from harm. As suggested earlier, in some jurisdictions, landowners are held to owe a duty to protect even trespassers against certain risks. Landowners who rent or lease premises to tenants are expected to exercise reasonable care to ensure that the tenants and their guests are not harmed in common areas, such as stairways, entryways, laundry rooms, and the like.

ETHICAL CONCERN
Malpractice Suits

Paralegals are not perfect and occasionally fail to perform a required duty. But the law will not "look the other way" if a client is harmed as a result of that negligence and then brings a malpractice suit against the attorney. It will not matter that the attorney specifically requested his or her paralegal to send a settlement letter to a defendant's attorney by a certain date. Nor will it matter that the attorney was under the impression that the letter had actually been sent by that date. The attorney, as the person responsible for the paralegal's work, will bear the legal consequences of the paralegal's negligent action if the client is harmed as a result and brings suit. The paralegal might also be held liable. As a paralegal, you should always make sure that you carry out instructions to the letter and perform your tasks accurately and in a timely manner, so that you do not expose your supervising attorney or yourself to liability for malpractice.

Duty to Business Invitees.   Retailers and other firms that explicitly or implicitly invite persons to come onto their premises are usually charged with a duty to exercise reasonable care to protect those persons, who are considered **business invitees**. For example, if you entered a supermarket, slipped on a wet floor, and sustained injuries as a result, the owner of the supermarket would be liable for damages if, when you slipped, there was no sign warning that the floor was wet. A court would hold that the business owner was negligent because the owner failed to exercise a reasonable degree of care in protecting the store's customers against foreseeable risks about which the owner knew or *should have known.* That a patron might slip on the wet floor and be injured as a result was a foreseeable risk, and the owner should have taken care to avoid this risk or to warn the customer of it. The owner also has a duty to discover and remove any hidden dangers that might injure a customer or other invitee.

business invitee
A person, such as a customer or a client, who is invited onto business premises by the owner of those premises for business purposes.

Open and Obvious Risks.   Some risks, of course, are so obvious that the owner need not warn of them. For instance, a business owner does not need to warn customers to open a door before attempting to walk through it. Other risks, however, even though they may seem obvious to a business owner, may not be so in the eyes of another, such as a child. For example, a hardware store owner may not think it is necessary to warn customers that a stepladder leaning against the back wall of the store could fall down and harm them. It is possible, though, that a child could tip the ladder over and be hurt as a result and that the store could be held liable.

THE DUTY OF PROFESSIONALS.   If an individual has knowledge, skill, or intelligence superior to that of an ordinary person, the individual's conduct must be consistent with that status. Professionals—including physicians, dentists, psychiatrists, architects, engineers, accountants, lawyers, and others—are required to have a standard minimum level of special knowledge and ability.

On the Web
You can locate the professional standards for various organizations at **http://www.lib.uwaterloo. ca/society/standards.html.**

   ▨   **Therefore, in determining what constitutes reasonable care in the case of professionals, their training and expertise are taken into account.**

In other words, an accountant cannot defend against a lawsuit for negligence by stating, "But I was not familiar with that principle of accounting."

FEATURED GUEST: JOSEPH F. WHALEN

The Facts and the Law: The Important Role of the Paralegal in Our Justice System

BIOGRAPHICAL NOTE

Joseph Whalen earned a J.D. in 1985 from Boston University School of Law and a B.A. in 1981 from Boston University. He is a former assistant district attorney and assistant attorney general in Massachusetts and presently serves as an assistant state attorney general in Tennessee.

Whalen has developed and presented regular law enforcement training programs in Massachusetts, where he also served as an instructor for police in-service and academy

training. In 1999, he traveled to the former Soviet republic of Ukraine, where he provided training to Ukrainian law enforcement and community groups. He has taught criminal justice ethics at the graduate level and currently teaches at a Nashville-area paralegal institute.

"Equal Justice under Law." These words are etched high above the magnificent steps and imposing front doors of the Supreme Court of the United States in Washington, D.C. They serve as a reminder to all those who enter that venerable institution or pass by it of the ultimate goal of our legal system. Indeed, the framework upon which our system of laws has been built— the U.S. Constitution—was created over two hundred years ago expressly to "establish justice."

For the paralegal who is spending yet another day at his or her desk, engrossed in the details of legal documents, such grandiose notions of "justice" and "the supremacy of the law" may appear quite distant and abstract. In actuality, though, the

paralegal's relationship to the law and our justice system is a far closer one than might be imagined by the paralegal who has just completed drafting a litigation document for the fifth time.

THE FACTS ARE IMPORTANT

The law provides a basis upon which to resolve the disputes and conflicts that give rise to the litigation in which many paralegals become involved. The law also operates in the absence of dispute—it governs an individual's or an organization's day-to-day conduct and thus provides a source of guidance so that disputes and conflicts can be avoided in the first place. Attorneys are thus called upon to provide legal advice for this latter purpose as well. In either instance—litigating a dispute or trying to avoid one—one of the first things that a paralegal student learns is that existing law must be applied to the particular facts and circumstances of the matter at hand. A litigant can ask little more from an impartial arbiter than that the case be decided based "on the facts and the law." And once that case is decided, the application of

---

If a professional violates her or his duty of care toward a client, the professional may be sued for malpractice. For example, a patient might sue a physician for *medical malpractice*. A client might sue an attorney for *legal malpractice* (discussed in Chapter 3).

The Injury Requirement and Damages

To recover damages (receive compensation), the plaintiff in a tort lawsuit must prove that she or he suffered a *legally recognizable* injury. That is, the plaintiff must have suffered some loss, harm, wrong, or invasion of a protected interest. This is true in lawsuits for intentional torts as well as lawsuits for negligence. The facts of the case must clearly establish a basis for recovery. (See this chapter's *Featured Guest* article, which emphasizes how paralegals play an important role in our legal system because they are often responsible for investigating and developing the relevant facts of a case.)

FEATURED GUEST, *Continued*

the law to those particular facts creates new law—that is, a precedent that may be used in the future when the law is to be applied to a similar factual situation.

The complete investigation, gathering, development, and presentation of relevant facts, therefore, is absolutely crucial in our legal system. Our adversarial system of justice relies on the effective presentation of the facts and the law by both parties. In the words of Judge William Koch of the Tennessee Court of Appeals, "Justice is fact-dependent." Indeed, a fact that has been overlooked in the investigation stage, or ignored in the presentation stage, has been effectively removed from the equation—it will not be included among the facts to which the law is applied. Such an oversight is not without consequence. The ultimate judgment in a case, or the assessment of whether a certain type of conduct is lawful, can oftentimes turn on a single, significant fact.

PARALEGALS PLAY A VITAL ROLE IN THIS PROCESS

Paralegals play a vital role in this process, for it is the paralegal,

under the guidance and supervision of an attorney, who is often called upon to investigate, develop, and present the relevant facts of a matter. When viewed in this light, tasks that involve utilization of a paralegal's investigative tools (such as reviewing or summarizing records or culling notes from client interviews) assume new significance. Ironically, the very tasks that may be regarded as routine, if not tedious, parts of a paralegal's day are the tasks that provide the paralegal's connection to the law and reflect the importance of the paralegal's role in our justice system.

A PARALEGAL CAREER IS MORE THAN JUST AN OCCUPATION

One could legitimately point out, of course, that our justice system is by no means perfect. Certainly, the legal profession itself has its fair share of critics, and that criticism is often not undeserved. Nevertheless, despite its flaws, one can really only marvel at how remarkably well the system of justice established by the framers of the Constitution has performed for more than two hundred years. While the daily realities of a frenetic law

> **"While the daily realities of a frenetic law practice may distract one's focus from time to time, a paralegal should never lose sight of the important position that he or she occupies in that legal system."**

practice may distract one's focus from time to time, a paralegal should never lose sight of the important position that he or she occupies in that legal system.

In the end, a paralegal career is so much more than just an occupation. The call for justice that emanates from the Supreme Court building in our nation's capital speaks directly to those who have made the law their career—paralegals and attorneys alike. Heeding that call will serve to ensure that our justice system will continue to operate effectively for at least another two hundred years.

Essentially, the purpose of tort law is to compensate for legally recognized injuries resulting from wrongful acts. If no harm or injury results from a given negligent action, there is nothing to compensate—and no tort exists. For example, if you carelessly bump into a passerby, who stumbles and falls as a result, you may be liable in tort if the passerby is injured in the fall. If the person is unharmed, however, there normally could be no suit for damages, because no injury was suffered. Although the passerby might be angry and suffer emotional distress, few courts recognize negligently inflicted emotional distress as a tort unless it results in some physical disturbance or dysfunction.

As already mentioned, the purpose of tort law is not to punish people for the torts that they commit but to compensate injured parties for damages suffered. **Compensatory damages** are intended to compensate, or reimburse, a plaintiff for actual losses—to make the plaintiff whole. Occasionally, however, punitive damages are also awarded in tort lawsuits. **Punitive damages** are intended to punish the wrongdoer and deter others from similar wrongdoing. Punitive damages are

compensatory damages
A money award equivalent to the actual value of injuries or damages sustained by the aggrieved party.

punitive damages
Money damages that may be awarded to a plaintiff to punish the defendant and deter future similar conduct.

rarely awarded in lawsuits for ordinary negligence and usually are given only in cases involving intentional torts. They may be awarded, however, if the defendant's negligent conduct was particularly reckless or willful.

Causation

Another element necessary to a tort is *causation*. If a person fails in a duty of care and someone suffers injury, the wrongful activity must have caused the harm for a tort to have been committed. In deciding whether there is causation, the court must address two questions:

causation in fact
Causation brought about by an act or omission without which an event would not have occurred.

- *Is there causation in fact?* Did the injury occur because of the defendant's act, or would it have occurred anyway? If an injury would not have occurred without the defendant's act, then there is causation in fact. **Causation in fact** can usually be determined by the use of the *but for* test: "but for" the wrongful act, the injury would not have occurred. Theoretically, causation in fact is limitless. One could claim, for example, that "but for" the creation of the world, a particular injury would not have occurred. Thus, as a practical matter, the law has to establish limits, and it does so through the concept of proximate cause.

proximate cause
Legal cause; exists when the connection between an act and an injury is strong enough to justify imposing liability.

- *Was the act the proximate cause of the injury?* **Proximate cause,** or legal cause, exists when the connection between an act and an injury is strong enough to justify imposing liability. For example, suppose Arnie carelessly leaves a campfire burning. The fire not only burns down the forest but also sets off an explosion in a nearby chemical plant that spills chemicals into a river, killing all the fish for a hundred miles downstream and ruining the economy of a tourist resort. Should Arnie be liable to the resort owners? To the tourists whose vacations were ruined? These are questions of proximate cause that a court must decide.

Both questions must be answered in the affirmative for liability in tort to arise. If a defendant's action constitutes causation in fact but a court decides that the action is not the proximate cause of the plaintiff's injury, the causation requirement has not been met—and the defendant normally will not be liable to the plaintiff.

Defenses to Negligence

Defendants often defend against negligence claims by asserting that the plaintiffs have failed to prove the existence of one or more of the required elements for negligence. Additionally, there are three basic *affirmative* defenses in negligence cases (defenses that defendants can use to avoid liability even if the facts are as the plaintiffs state): (1) assumption of risk, (2) superseding cause, and (3) contributory negligence.

assumption of risk
Voluntarily taking on oneself a known risk. Assumption of risk is a defense against negligence that can be used when the plaintiff has knowledge of and appreciates a danger and voluntarily exposes himself or herself to the danger.

ASSUMPTION OF RISK.   A plaintiff who voluntarily enters into a risky situation, knowing the risk involved, will not be allowed to recover. This is the defense of **assumption of risk.** The requirements of this defense are (1) knowledge of the risk and (2) voluntary assumption of the risk.

The risk can be assumed by express agreement, or the assumption of risk can be implied by the plaintiff's knowledge of the risk and subsequent conduct. For example, a driver entering a race knows that there is a risk of being killed or injured in a crash. Of course, the plaintiff does not assume a risk different from or greater than the risk normally carried by the activity. In our example, the race driver does not assume the risk that the banking in the curves of the racetrack will give way during the race because of a construction defect.

In emergency situations, risks are not considered assumed. Neither are they assumed when a statute protects a class of people from harm and a member of the class is injured by the harm. For example, employees are protected by statute from harmful working conditions and therefore do not assume the risks associated with the workplace. If an employee is injured, he or she will generally be compensated regardless of fault under state workers' compensation statutes (discussed in Chapter 10).

SUPERSEDING CAUSE.   An unforeseeable intervening event may break the connection between a wrongful act and an injury to another. If so, it acts as a *superseding cause*—that is, it relieves a defendant of liability for injuries caused by the intervening event. For example, suppose that Derrick keeps a can of gasoline in the trunk of his car. The presence of the gasoline creates a foreseeable risk and is thus a negligent act. If Derrick's car skids and crashes into a tree, causing the gasoline can to explode, Derrick will be liable for injuries sustained by passing pedestrians because of his negligence. If lightning striking the car had caused the explosion, however, the lightning would supersede Derrick's original negligence as a cause of the damage, because the lightning was not foreseeable.

CONTRIBUTORY NEGLIGENCE.   All individuals are expected to exercise a reasonable degree of care in looking out for themselves. In a few jurisdictions, recovery for injury resulting from negligence is prevented if the plaintiff was also negligent (failed to exercise a reasonable degree of care). This is the defense of **contributory negligence.** Under the common law doctrine of contributory negligence, no matter how insignificant the plaintiff's negligence is relative to the defendant's negligence, the plaintiff will be precluded from recovering any damages.

contributory negligence
A theory in tort law under which a complaining party's own negligence contributed to or caused his or her injuries. Contributory negligence is an absolute bar to recovery in a minority of jurisdictions.

The majority of states now allow recovery based on the doctrine of **comparative negligence.** This doctrine enables both the plaintiff's and the defendant's negligence to be computed and the liability for damages distributed accordingly. Some jurisdictions have adopted a "pure" form of comparative negligence that allows the plaintiff to recover, even if the extent of his or her fault is greater than that of the defendant. For example, if the plaintiff was 80 percent at fault and the defendant 20 percent at fault, the plaintiff may recover 20 percent of his or her damages. Many states' comparative negligence statutes, however, contain a "50 percent" rule by which the plaintiff recovers nothing if she or he was more than 50 percent at fault.

comparative negligence
A theory in tort law under which the liability for injuries resulting from negligent acts is shared by all persons who were guilty of negligence (including the injured party) on the basis of each person's proportionate carelessness.

Special Negligence Doctrines and Statutes

There are a number of special doctrines and statutes relating to negligence. We examine only a few of them here.

NEGLIGENCE *PER SE.*   Certain conduct, whether it consists of an action or a failure to act, may be treated as **negligence *per se*** (*per se* means "in or of itself"). Negligence *per se* may occur if an individual violates a statute or an ordinance providing for a criminal penalty and that violation causes another to be injured. The injured person must prove (1) that the statute clearly sets out what standard of conduct is expected, when and where it is expected, and of whom it is expected; (2) that he or she is in the class intended to be protected by the statute; and (3) that the statute was designed to prevent the type of injury that he or she suffered. The standard of conduct required by the statute is the duty that the defendant owes to the plaintiff, and a violation of the statute is the breach of that duty.

negligence *per se*
An action or failure to act in violation of a statutory requirement.

For example, a statute may require a landowner to keep a building in safe condition and may also subject the landowner to a criminal penalty, such as a fine, if the building is not kept safe. The statute is meant to protect those who are rightfully in the building. Thus, if the owner, without a sufficient excuse, violates the statute and a tenant is thereby injured, then a majority of courts will hold that the owner's unexcused violation of the statute conclusively establishes a breach of a duty of care—that is, that the owner's violation is negligence *per se.*

SPECIAL NEGLIGENCE STATUTES.   A number of states have enacted statutes prescribing duties and responsibilities in certain circumstances. For example, most states now have what are called **Good Samaritan statutes.** Under these statutes, persons who are aided voluntarily by others cannot turn around and sue the "Good Samaritans" for negligence. These laws were passed largely to protect physicians and medical personnel who voluntarily render their services in emergency situations to those in need, such as individuals hurt in car accidents.

Many states have also passed **dram shop acts,** under which a tavern owner or bartender may be held liable for injuries caused by a person who became intoxicated while drinking at the bar or who was already intoxicated when served by the bartender. In some states, statutes impose liability on *social hosts* (persons hosting parties) for injuries caused by guests who became intoxicated at the hosts' homes. Under these statutes, it is unnecessary to prove that the tavern owner, bartender, or social host was negligent.

> **Good Samaritan statute**
> A state statute stipulating that persons who provide emergency services to, or rescue, others in peril—unless they do so recklessly, thus causing further harm—cannot be sued for negligence.

> **dram shop act**
> A state statute that imposes liability on the owners of bars and taverns, as well as those who serve alcoholic drinks to the public, for injuries resulting from accidents caused by intoxicated persons when the sellers or servers of alcoholic drinks contributed to the intoxication.

CYBER TORTS: DEFAMATION ONLINE

A significant issue that has come before the courts in recent years relates to the question of who should be held liable for *cyber torts,* or torts committed in cyberspace. For example, who should be held liable when someone posts a defamatory message online? Should an Internet service provider (ISP)—a company, such as America Online (AOL), that provides access to the Internet through a local phone line, cable, or DSL connection—be liable for the remark if the ISP was unaware that it was being made?

Cyber torts (like cyber crimes, which will be discussed in Chapter 15) are not new torts as much as they are new ways of committing torts that present special issues of proof. How, for example, can it be proved that an online defamatory remark was "published" (which requires that a third party see or hear it)? How can the identity of the person who made the remark be discovered? We explore some of these questions in this section. Generally, determining what tort duties apply in cyberspace and at what point one of those duties is breached is not an easy task for the courts.

Online forums allow anyone—customers, employees, or crackpots—to complain about a business firm's personnel, policies, practices, or products. Regardless of whether the complaint is justified or whether it is true, it might have an impact on the business of the firm. One of the early questions in the online legal arena was whether the providers of such forums could be held liable for defamatory statements made in those forums.

Liability of Internet Service Providers

Newspapers, magazines, and television and radio stations may be held liable for defamatory remarks that they disseminate, even if those remarks are prepared or created by others. Under the Communications Decency Act of 1996, however,

Internet service providers, or "interactive computer service providers," are not liable for such material.[4]

Piercing the Veil of Anonymity

One initial problem for anyone who seeks to bring an action for online defamation is discovering the identity of the person who posted the defamatory message online. ISPs can disclose personal information about their customers only when ordered to do so by a court. Because of this, businesses and individuals are increasingly resorting to lawsuits against unidentified "John Does." Then, using the authority of the courts, they can obtain from the ISPs the identities of the persons responsible for the messages.

In one case, for example, Eric Hvide, a former chief executive of a company called Hvide Marine, sued a number of "John Does" who had posted allegedly defamatory statements about his company on various online message boards. Hvide, who eventually lost his job, sued the John Does for libel in a Florida court. The court ruled that Yahoo! and AOL had to reveal the identities of the defendant Does.[5]

In some other cases, though, the rights of plaintiffs in such situations have been balanced against the defendants' rights to free speech. For example, some courts have concluded that more than a bare allegation of defamation is required to outweigh an individual's right to anonymity in the exercise of free speech.

STRICT LIABILITY

Intentional torts and torts of negligence involve acts that depart from a reasonable standard of care and cause injuries. Under the doctrine of **strict liability,** liability for injury is imposed for reasons other than fault. Strict liability for damages proximately caused by an abnormally dangerous or exceptional activity is one application of this doctrine.

strict liability
Liability regardless of fault. In tort law, strict liability may be imposed on a merchant who introduces into commerce a good that is so defective as to be unreasonably dangerous.

Abnormally Dangerous Activities

Abnormally dangerous activities have three characteristics:

* The activity involves potential harm, of a serious nature, to persons or property.
* The activity involves a high degree of risk that cannot be completely guarded against by the exercise of reasonable care.
* The activity is not commonly performed in the community or area.

Clearly, the primary basis of liability is the creation of an extraordinary risk. For example, even if blasting with dynamite is performed with all reasonable care, there is still a risk of injury. Balancing that risk against the potential for harm, it seems reasonable to ask the person engaged in the activity to pay for any injury it causes. Although there is no fault, there is still responsibility because of the dangerous nature of the undertaking.

Other Applications of Strict Liability

Strict liability may also apply to harm caused by animals. Persons who keep wild animals are strictly liable for any harm inflicted by the animals. The basis for applying strict liability is that wild animals, should they escape from confinement, pose a serious risk of harm to persons in the vicinity. An owner of domestic animals (such as dogs, cats, cows, or sheep) may be strictly liable for harm caused by those animals if the owner knew, or should have known, that the animals were dangerous or had a propensity to harm others.

A significant application of strict liability is in the area of *product liability*—liability of manufacturers and sellers for harmful or defective products. Because of the importance of product liability in tort litigation, we discuss this type of liability at length in the following sections.

Product Liability

product liability
The legal liability of manufacturers, sellers, and lessors of goods to consumers, users, and bystanders for injuries or damages that are caused by the goods.

Those who manufacture, sell, or lease goods can be held liable for injuries and damages caused by defective goods under the law of **product liability**. Liability here is a matter of social policy. It is based on the notion that manufacturers are better able to bear the cost of injury than innocent victims and that requiring them to pay for damages caused by their products encourages them to make safer products. Injured parties can sue under theories of negligence and misrepresentation, as well as strict liability. (See this chapter's *Technology and Today's Paralegal* feature on page 232 for tips on how paralegals can utilize the Internet in product liability cases.)

Product Liability Based on Negligence

If a manufacturer fails to exercise due care to make a product safe, *any person* who is injured by the product can sue the manufacturer for negligence. The plaintiff does not have to be the person who purchased the product. Due care must be exercised in designing the product, selecting the materials, producing and assembling the product, and placing adequate warnings on the label to inform the user of dangers. The duty of care also requires the inspection and testing of any item purchased that is incorporated into the final product.

Product Liability Based on Misrepresentation

When a manufacturer or seller misrepresents the quality, nature, or appropriate use of the product, and the user is injured as a result, the basis of liability may be the tort of fraud. Generally, the misrepresentation must have been made knowingly or with reckless disregard for the facts, and the party must have intended the user to rely on the statement. An example is the intentional concealment of a product's defects. In contrast to actions based on negligence and strict liability, the plaintiff does not have to show that the product was defective or malfunctioned in fraud cases.

Strict Product Liability

 On the Web
For updates and information regarding Firestone Tires/Ford Explorer product liability cases, go to **http://www. safetyforum.com/tires/ tires-news.html.**

Under the doctrine of strict liability, a manufacturer that has exercised a reasonable degree of care can still be held liable if a product is defective and injures someone. Strict product liability reflects the general principle that the law should protect consumers from unsafe and dangerous products. The rule of strict liability is also applicable to the suppliers of component parts that are used in the final product.

Strict liability will only be imposed if the plaintiff can establish the following six requirements:

- The product must be in a defective condition when the defendant sells it.
- The defendant must normally be engaged in the business of selling (or otherwise distributing) that product.

ETHICAL CONCERN
Confidentiality and Product Liability

Recall from Chapter 3 that as a paralegal you are prohibited under ethical rules from revealing confidential client information. Although this sounds simple, paralegals in product liability firms may find themselves in a sticky situation. For example, suppose that your firm represents a particular toy manufacturer. The toy firm has produced and distributed a toy that is very popular for children two through four years of age. The toy, however, is apparently defective and has caused serious injuries to some children across the country. The product has not yet been recalled, and no information about the problems with the toy has appeared in the press. Everything you know about this toy you have learned from the work you have done on the case.

Now suppose that *you* are the parent of a child who is three years old, and many of your friends and family members have children around that age. Clearly, you would decide not to purchase that toy for your child, but what about telling others? Can you warn your friends and family about the defective toy? Can you tell your day-care provider? If you tell one person, even if it is a family member, you have technically violated the ethical rule of confidentiality. Yet what if you don't warn someone, and that person's child is injured as a result? This is just one example of ethical dilemmas that may arise for paralegals who work in the area of product liability.

- The product must be unreasonably dangerous to the user or consumer because of its defective condition (in most states).
- The plaintiff must incur physical harm to self or property by use or consumption of the product.
- The defective condition must be the proximate cause of the injury or damage.
- The goods must not have been substantially changed from the time the product was sold to the time the injury was sustained.[6]

Note that the plaintiff is not required to show why or in what manner the product became defective. The plaintiff must only prove that the product was so "defective" as to be "unreasonably dangerous"; that the product caused the injury; and that the condition of the product was essentially the same as when it was sold. A court will find the product to be an **unreasonably dangerous product** if either (1) the product is dangerous beyond the expectation of the ordinary consumer or (2) a less dangerous alternative was *economically* feasible for the manufacturer, but the manufacturer failed to produce it. A product may be unreasonably dangerous due to a flaw in the manufacturing process, a design defect, or an inadequate warning.

unreasonably dangerous product
In product liability, a product that is defective to the point of threatening a consumer's health and safety. A product will be considered unreasonably dangerous if it is dangerous beyond the expectation of the ordinary consumer or if a less dangerous alternative was economically feasible for the manufacturer, but the manufacturer failed to produce it.

MANUFACTURING DEFECTS.   A product that departs from its intended design, even though all possible care was exercised in the preparation and marketing of the product, has a manufacturing defect. Liability is imposed on the manufacturer (and on the wholesaler and retailer) regardless of whether the manufacturer acted "reasonably."

DESIGN DEFECTS.   A product has a design defect if the foreseeable risks of harm posed by the product could have been reduced or avoided by adopting a reasonable alternative design.

TECHNOLOGY AND TODAY'S PARALEGAL

Online Access to Information in Product Liability Suits

Evidence is critical in proving a product liability case. Attorneys typically hire experts to examine the product at issue and its safety. Experts also help formulate theories, opinions, and conclusions about the product and the injury, which will be presented as evidence at trial. As you can imagine, this service is expensive and time consuming. The Internet has dramatically improved the ability of attorneys and paralegals to quickly locate and access important information pertaining to product liability suits.

ONLINE DATABASES OF SIMILAR LITIGATION

Frequently, the product involved in a specific case—whether it be a cosmetic, cigarettes, a car, or something else—has been distributed nationwide and may have resulted in injuries and litigation elsewhere. Paralegals can now track down relevant product information via the Internet. For example, Minnesota's Blue Cross/Blue Shield (BC/BS), after it won its landmark case against tobacco firms, established an online database so that other potential plaintiffs could easily obtain the materials used in the trial. Over thirty-five million pages of information and evidentiary materials from that case are currently available online. Today, a paralegal wishing to view these documents can search through this database at no cost (although other online databases may charge a fee).

GATHERING INFORMATION FROM CYBERSPACE

Even if no other litigation has dealt with the product or company in question, paralegals can sometimes gain valuable information online from others who have complaints about a particular company's products or services. Many Web sites, sometimes called "sucks" sites, are specifically devoted to customers' complaints about a company. For example, suppose that you are working on a case involving a woman who was injured by a product made by MedRx (a fictional company). You could go online to the "MedRx sucks" site to find out if anyone else has complaints about this product or another MedRx product that contains the same chemicals. You may even find additional plaintiffs or witnesses for the case through these sites.

TECHNOLOGY TIP

The proliferation of online databases, such as those containing information about tobacco litigation, has been a boon for paralegals working on product liability cases. If a database exists that is dedicated to litigation of similar claims, you can save hours of research time and obtain valuable evidence quickly. In addition, searching the Internet for others who have complaints about a particular product or company can sometimes lead to useful information.

WARNING DEFECTS.   A product may also be deemed defective because of inadequate instructions or warnings in situations where the risk of harm was foreseeable and could have been avoided if a proper warning had been given. In evaluating the adequacy of warnings, courts consider the risks of the product and whether the content of the warning was understandable and clear to the expected user.[7] For example, children would likely respond readily to bright, bold, simple warning labels, whereas educated adults might need more detailed information.

Note that there is no duty to warn about risks that are obvious or commonly known. Warnings about *obvious risks* do not add to the safety of a product and could even detract from it by making other warnings seem less significant. Also, a seller must warn those who purchase its product of the harm that can result from the *foreseeable misuse* of the product. The key is the foreseeability of the misuse; sellers are not required to foresee and take precautions against every conceivable mode of use and abuse to which their products might be put.

DEFENSES TO PRODUCT LIABILITY

To avoid liability under any theory of product liability, the defendant can show that there is no basis for the plaintiff's claim or that the plaintiff has not met the requirements for liability. For example, if the suit alleges negligence and the defendant proves that the product did not cause the plaintiff's injury, the defendant will not be liable. If the defendant in a strict product liability suit can establish that the goods were subsequently altered, normally the defendant will not be held liable.[8] Defendants may also assert the affirmative defenses discussed next.

Assumption of Risk

The obviousness of a risk and a user's decision to proceed in the face of that risk may sometimes be a defense in a product liability suit. For example, if a buyer failed to heed a product recall by the seller, a court might conclude that the buyer had assumed the risk. To establish this defense, the defendant must show that (1) the plaintiff knew and appreciated the risk created by the product defect and (2) the plaintiff voluntarily assumed the risk, even though it was unreasonable to do so.

Product Misuse

Defendants can also claim that the plaintiff misused the product. This defense is similar to claiming that the plaintiff has assumed the risk. Here, however, the injured party *did not know that the product was dangerous for a particular use*, but the use was not the one for which the product was designed. The courts have severely limited this defense. Even if the injured party does not know about the inherent danger of using the product in a wrong way, if the misuse is reasonably foreseeable, the seller must take measures to guard against it.

Comparative Negligence

Developments in the area of comparative negligence (discussed previously in this chapter) have affected the doctrine of strict liability—the most extreme theory of product liability. Previously, the plaintiff's conduct was not a defense to strict liability. Today, many jurisdictions consider the negligent or intentional actions of both the plaintiff and the defendant when apportioning liability and damages. Even if the plaintiff misused the product, though, she or he may be able to recover at least some damages for injuries caused by a defective product.

Commonly Known Dangers

The dangers associated with certain products (such as sharp knives and guns) are so commonly known that manufacturers need not warn users of those dangers. If a defendant shows that a plaintiff's injury resulted from a *commonly known danger*, the defendant normally will not be liable. A related defense is the *knowledgeable user* defense. If a particular danger (such as electrical shock) is or should be commonly known by particular users of the product (such as electricians), the manufacturer need not warn these users of the danger.

TORT LAW AND THE PARALEGAL

Many paralegals become involved in tasks relating to tort lawsuits. If you work for a litigation firm, chances are that you will handle numerous assignments involving tort claims. Many law firms specialize in personal-injury litigation and

On the Web

For information on product liability litigation against tobacco companies, including defenses raised by tobacco manufacturers in trial-related documents, go to the State Tobacco Information Center's Web site at **http://stic.neu.edu/index.html.**

PARALEGAL PROFILE

Product Liability Paralegal

Lori A. Gray *has worked in the legal profession for more than twenty years. She has been a paralegal specializing in product liability litigation since 1986. Gray began her career working on the plaintiff side and then defected to the defense side in 1995.*

In October 2002, Gray left traditional law firm practice and moved into the corporate legal environment at Rockwell Automation, Inc. Gray attended Cuyahoga Community College and the American Institute for Paralegal Studies and is a member of the National Federation of Paralegal Associations. From 1998 to 2000, she served as the president of the Cleveland Association of Paralegals. She has taught many seminars and authored various articles for litigation paralegals.

What do you like best about your work?

"The most interesting aspect of my career has been learning about different products, including their design and application. It never ceases to amaze me how many hundreds of products we use in everyday life. Determining the cause of a product's failure is an exciting aspect of my work that allows me to continually build new skills. Every case is unique because of the product or combination of products involved. As modern technology continues to advance, this area of law will always offer fresh and exciting challenges."

What is the greatest challenge that you face in your area of work?

"One of the greatest challenges in my work lies in the investigation phase of every claim. Before I attend any site investigation, I learn all I can about the product, its history, and its application. Often, it is also helpful for me to research the design process and determine the original intended function of a product. This can sometimes be an arduous task, as a product may have originated long ago and its design may have changed dramatically since it entered the marketplace."

What advice do you have for would-be paralegals in your area of work?

"I have been fortunate throughout my career to have been surrounded by experts in the field. My paralegal education did not provide me with a background in engineering or product design. To excel in this area of the law, it is tremendously important to understand the product involved from the inception of its design through every possible application by the end user. It's always a great idea to see the product and even operate the product yourself, so you have firsthand knowledge. Also, it's important to know the applicable standards that govern the design and use of the product."

> **"To excel in this area of the law, it is tremendously important to understand the product involved from the inception of its design through every possible application by the end user."**

What are some tips for success as a paralegal in your area of work?

"Be open to learning everything you can about the product line, as well as similar and alternative designs. Also be aware of the human element involved in any product liability case. While a bad design can lead to a defective product, products are often altered and misused by the end user, resulting in serious injury or death. Never be afraid to ask questions of experts and engineers who are most familiar with the product."

represent plaintiffs who have been injured in car accidents or other incidents resulting from the defendant's alleged negligence.

If you work for a law firm that specializes in personal-injury litigation, you might be responsible for some of the following tasks:

- Interview a client (plaintiff) to obtain details about the accident and the injuries sustained in the accident.

DEVELOPING PARALEGAL SKILLS

Product Liability Paralegals

Sylvia is a paralegal working in the legal department of an automobile company. The company is frequently the defendant in product liability lawsuits. In these lawsuits, during the discovery phase of the litigation (see Chapter 12), attorneys for the plaintiffs normally request information about the design and manufacturing process used by the company in producing its vehicles.

Sylvia's job is to work with the corporate attorneys to gather this information and provide it to the plaintiffs' attorneys, as allowed or required by court rules. Frequently, Sylvia meets with the company's engineers to discuss these information requests and to obtain the necessary information. Sylvia then reviews with her supervising attorney the material to be sent out.

TIPS FOR OBTAINING INFORMATION

- Good communication skills help when making requests for information.
- Good interpersonal skills help you develop positive relationships with those from whom you need information.
- Analytical skills help determine what information is needed.
- Good writing skills assist you in preparing the responses to requests for information.
- Send out the responses in a timely fashion.

- Locate and interview witnesses to gather additional information about the accident.
- Obtain medical reports from physicians and hospitals describing the plaintiff's injuries.
- Attend depositions, and summarize the testimony of witnesses, parties, and experts in the case.
- Obtain employment data to verify the amount of lost wages that should be claimed as damages if the client's current or future employment is affected by the injury.
- Obtain a copy of the police report, and, if necessary, consult with police officers and investigators who worked on the case.
- Prepare documents to initiate a lawsuit, respond to the other party's documents, and file documents and responses with the court.
- Prepare exhibits for trial, create a trial notebook for the attorney to refer to during the trial, and prepare the client and witnesses for trial.
- Generally, provide litigation assistance (which will be discussed at length in Chapters 12 through 14).

Many law firms or departments of law firms specialize in areas of tort litigation other than personal-injury liability, such as medical malpractice and product liability. Paralegals who work for corporations may also become involved in tort and product liability litigation. A person who was injured in an accident caused by one of the company's truck drivers might sue the company for damages under negligence theory. A consumer who was injured by one of the corporation's products might initiate a product liability action against the corporation. No matter where you work, you will benefit from knowing the basic concepts of tort law discussed in this chapter.

TODAY'S PROFESSIONAL PARALEGAL

Developing a Life-Care Plan

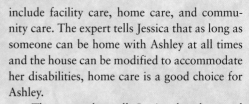

Attorney Long asks her paralegal, Jessica, to assist in developing a life-care plan for one of the firm's clients, Ashley. Ashley, a sixteen-year-old girl, passed out at school one day and was taken to Dr. Shafley, who diagnosed her as having the flu and sent her home. Less than a week later, Ashley's arms and legs had to be amputated because of Dr. Shafley's failure to diagnose the symptoms of bacterial spinal meningitis. Dr. Shafley wishes to settle out of court to avoid the publicity of a trial (his brother is running for mayor). Attorney Long therefore needs to establish the amount of damages to be requested.

THE LIFE-CARE PLAN

Following a serious injury, health-care costs can accumulate into millions of dollars. An attorney who represents an injured plaintiff often must develop a plan that identifies and establishes the cost of the health care that the client will need for the rest of his or her life. The life-care plan is basically a tool used to quantify the health-care needs of a client and establish the amount of damages that the client will seek in any settlement or trial of the case. Typically, developing a life-care plan involves hiring an expert qualified to assess the plaintiff's limitations and care needs and assigning a paralegal to coordinate and assist.

MEETING WITH THE CLIENT

Jessica talks with the attorney, and they go together to meet Ashley and her parents at the hospital in which Ashley has been a patient for several months. Ashley is more cheerful than Jessica anticipated, and Jessica admires the young woman's courage. Attorney Long tells Ashley that an expert will be coming to evaluate her condition and that Jessica will always be available to answer any questions she might have. After meeting Ashley, Jessica vows to do whatever she can to help Ashley receive the best possible care in the future. Jessica then contacts the expert whom the attorney has hired.

KEY COMPONENTS OF A LIFE-CARE PLAN

Jessica learns that there are several main components of any life-care plan. The first is what type of care is needed and where it will be provided. The options available include facility care, home care, and community care. The expert tells Jessica that as long as someone can be home with Ashley at all times and the house can be modified to accommodate her disabilities, home care is a good choice for Ashley.

The expert then tells Jessica that they need to assess the types of equipment, supplies, and medication that Ashley currently requires and what she will need in the future. For example, Ashley will be confined to a wheelchair until the proper prosthetics (artificial limbs) can be obtained. Her parents' house will need to have wheelchair ramps installed and other modifications made in order to accommodate Ashley's needs. The prosthetic devices, which are very expensive, will need to be replaced during Ashley's lifetime. Other supplies and medications will be required. The cost of all of these items must be determined and estimated for the future.

Jessica also learns that the life-care plan must take into account long-term therapy and additional medical services. Ashley will need physical therapy on a regular basis to enable her to function with her limitations and to learn how to use the prosthetics. She will also need some psychological counseling and recreational therapy, given the extent of her injuries. Additionally, persons who have had their limbs amputated have an increased risk of infections, bedsores, and other problems, and the cost of treating these foreseeable medical problems must be included.

HOW A PARALEGAL CAN ASSIST

Paralegals can play a significant role by serving as a liaison between the expert and the client, the family, physicians, and educators. Injured plaintiffs benefit from knowing that someone can always be reached if they need assistance. Paralegals also can keep track of health-care bills, set up necessary appointments, research costs, and order equipment and supplies. If the case goes to trial, the paralegal can assist in formulating the questions to ask the expert and can create useful exhibits for the jury. Moreover, helping clients who have been seriously injured to regain a degree of independence and plan their future can be very rewarding work.

KEY TERMS AND CONCEPTS

actionable	cyber tort	product liability
actual malice	defamation	proximate cause
appropriation	defense	punitive damages
assault	dram shop act	reasonable person standard
assumption of risk	duty of care	slander
battery	fraudulent misrepresentation	strict liability
business invitee	Good Samaritan statute	tort
business tort	intentional tort	tortfeasor
causation in fact	libel	trespass to land
comparative negligence	negligence	trespass to personal property
compensatory damages	negligence *per se*	unreasonably dangerous product
contributory negligence	predatory behavior	
conversion	privilege	

 CHAPTER SUMMARY

The Basis of Tort Law	Two notions serve as the basis of all torts: wrongs and compensation. Tort law recognizes that some acts are wrong because they cause injuries to others. 1. *Definition*—A *tort* is a civil wrong. In a tort action, one person or group brings a personal-injury suit against another person or group to obtain compensation (money damages) or other relief for the harm suffered. 2. *Objective of tort law*—Generally, the purpose of tort law is to provide remedies for the invasion of various interests such as physical security, privacy, freedom of movement, and reputation. 3. *Classification of torts*—There are two broad classifications of torts: *intentional torts* and *negligence*. In addition, in certain circumstances, defendants may be held liable for harm caused to others under the tort doctrine of *strict liability*.

Intentional Torts	1. *Intentional torts against persons*—
	
	  a. Assault and battery—An assault is an intentional act that causes another person to be apprehensive of immediate harm. A battery is an assault that results in physical contact.
	
	  b. False imprisonment—The intentional confinement or restraint of another person's movement without justification.
	
	  c. Intentional infliction of emotional distress—An intentional act that amounts to extreme and outrageous conduct resulting in severe emotional distress to another.
	
	  d. Defamation (libel or slander)—A false statement of fact, not made under privilege, that is communicated to a third person and that causes damage to a person's reputation. For public figures, the plaintiff must also prove actual malice.

Intentional Torts—Continued	e. Invasion of the right to privacy—The use of a person's name or likeness for commercial purposes without permission, wrongful intrusion into a person's private activities, publication of information that places a person in a false light, or disclosure of private facts that an ordinary person would find objectionable. f. Appropriation—The use of another person's name, likeness, or other identifying characteristic without permission and for the benefit of the user. g. Misrepresentation (fraud)—A false representation made by one party, through misstatement of facts or through conduct, with the intention of deceiving another and on which the other reasonably relies to his or her detriment. h. Wrongful interference—Knowing, intentional interference by a third party with an enforceable contractual relationship or an established business relationship between other parties for the purpose of advancing the economic interests of the third party. 2. *Intentional torts against property*— a. Trespass to land—The invasion of another's real property without consent or privilege. Specific rights and duties apply once a person is expressly or impliedly established as a trespasser. b. Trespass to personal property—Unlawfully damaging or interfering with the owner's right to use, possess, or enjoy his or her personal property. c. Conversion—A wrongful act in which personal property is taken from its rightful owner.
Negligence	1. *Negligence*—The careless performance of a legally required duty or the failure to perform a legally required act. Elements that must be proved are that a legal duty of care exists, that the defendant breached that duty, and that the breach caused damage or injury to another. 2. *Defenses to negligence*—The basic affirmative defenses in negligence cases are assumption of risk, superseding cause, and contributory negligence. 3. *Special negligence doctrines and statutes*— a. Negligence *per se*—A type of negligence that may occur if a person violates a statute or an ordinance providing for a criminal penalty and the violation causes another to be injured. b. Special negligence statutes—State statutes, such as dram shop acts and Good Samaritan laws, that prescribe duties and responsibilities in certain circumstances. The violation of such statutes will impose civil liability.
Cyber Torts: Defamation Online	General tort principles are being extended to cover cyber torts, or torts that occur in cyberspace, such as online defamation. Cyber torts often present special issues of proof. Federal and state statutes may also apply to certain forms of cyber torts.
Strict Liability	Under the doctrine of strict liability, a person or company may be held liable, regardless of the degree of care exercised, for damages or injuries caused by a product or activity. Strict liability includes liability for harms caused by abnormally dangerous activities, by dangerous animals, and by defective products (product liability).

Product Liability	Manufacturers and sellers can be held liable for injuries and damages caused by defective goods under the law of product liability. A person who is injured can sue under the theories of negligence, misrepresentation, or strict product liability.
	1. *Product liability based on negligence*—Due care must be used by the manufacturer in designing the product; selecting materials; producing, assembling, and testing the product; and placing adequate warnings on the label or product.
	2. *Product liability based on misrepresentation*—When the seller misrepresents the quality, nature, or appropriate use of the product, and the user is injured as a result, the basis of liability may be the tort of fraud. The plaintiff does not have to show that the product was defective in such cases.
	3. *Strict product liability*—A manufacturer that has exercised a reasonable degree of care can still be held liable if a product is defective and injures someone. This reflects the general principle that the law should protect consumers from unsafe and dangerous products. Liability extends to suppliers of component parts.
	a. The product must have been defective when purchased and unreasonably dangerous to the user.
	b. A product is unreasonably dangerous if (1) it is dangerous beyond the expectation of the ordinary consumer or (2) a less dangerous alternative was economically feasible but was not used by the manufacturer.
	c. The product's defective condition must have caused the injury.
	d. The product must not have been substantially changed since sold.
	e. The three types of product defects are manufacturing defects, design defects, and warning defects.
Defenses to Product Liability	A defendant can claim that there is no basis for the plaintiff's claim or that the plaintiff has not met the requirements for liability. The defendant can also raise the following defenses.
	1. *Assumption of risk*—The user or consumer knew of the risk of harm and voluntarily assumed it.
	2. *Product misuse*—The user or consumer misused the product in a way unforeseeable by the manufacturer.
	3. *Comparative negligence and liability*—Liability may be distributed between the plaintiff and the defendant under the doctrine of comparative negligence if the plaintiff's misuse of the product contributed to the risk of injury.
	4. *Commonly known dangers*—If a defendant succeeds in convincing the court that a plaintiff's injury resulted from a commonly known danger, such as the danger associated with using a sharp knife, the defendant will not be liable.

✳ QUESTIONS FOR REVIEW

1. What is a tort? What is the underlying purpose of tort law? What are the three main categories of torts, and how do they differ?

2. List and describe some of the defenses available to defendants in intentional tort actions, such as assault and battery.

3. What are the four elements of negligence? Why is the duty of care for professionals different from the duty of an ordinary person? If the defendant acted negligently but the plaintiff was not injured, can the plaintiff still recover damages?

4. What are the affirmative defenses to a negligence action? What is contributory negligence, and how is it different from comparative negligence?

5. How do cyber torts differ from traditional torts? What are some of the difficulties that a plaintiff faces in proving that online defamation occurred?

6. What is meant by strict liability? In what circumstances is strict liability applied?

7. What is product liability? What is the underlying policy reason for imposing liability on those who manufacture, sell, or lease goods?

8. Under which tort theories can product liability actions be brought? What elements must the plaintiff prove in a strict product liability action?

9. List and explain the three types of product defects that may lead a court to conclude a product is unreasonably dangerous.

10. What are some of the defenses that can be raised in product liability actions? Can the plaintiff's negligent conduct be a defense in product liability cases?

✳ Ethical Questions

1. Monica is a legal assistant in a law firm that specializes in representing business defendants in tort cases. Monica's supervising attorney has just been asked to defend a firm against a toxic-tort claim. The attorney asks Monica to do some legal research on toxic torts—an area with which she is not familiar. It takes Monica twelve hours to complete the research assignment, which is twice as long as the attorney told her to spend on the project. Monica is uncomfortable in billing the client for twelve hours of research time, and she is contemplating billing another client for six of the twelve hours. Should she? Why or why not?

2. Jeffrey Singleman is an experienced legal assistant in a tort law practice. He is given a great deal of responsibility and has minimal supervision. One day, Georgia Wellington, an associate with the firm, has two court appearances scheduled at the same time. One appearance is in federal court, which is on one side of town, and the other is in the county circuit court, which is on the other side of town. Georgia asks Jeffrey to handle the hearing in the county circuit court for her. What should Jeffrey do?

3. Dawn Mercer is a paralegal at Clarkson & Deichler, a firm that handles many tort law claims. Dawn is having dinner with Phil at a fish restaurant when a person sitting at a table near them begins to choke on a fish bone. When Phil stands up as if to go to the stranger's assistance, Dawn tells him not to—that he can be sued for negligence if something goes wrong. Dawn knows that the state they live in has not passed a Good Samaritan law. Because of Dawn's statements, Phil does not go to the individual's aid. Has Dawn violated any ethical duty? Does her statement constitute the unauthorized practice of law?

4. Claire is a new legal assistant interviewing a client who wants to sue the manufacturer of an allegedly defective treadmill. The client claims that while walking on the treadmill, he received an electrical shock that caused him to fall off and seriously injure his hip. Near the end of the interview, the client asks Claire whether she thinks he has a good case. Claire responds, "Well, as you know, I'm a paralegal, and I cannot give legal advice. Personally, though, I think that you do have a good case." Has Claire violated her ethical duties? How would you have handled the situation?

✳ Practice Questions and Assignments

1. Using the information on intentional torts and negligence presented in this chapter, identify the following torts:

   a. Mary receives a telephone call at 5:25 P.M. while she is making dinner for her husband, who will be home shortly. The caller says, "I've got your husband and his money, and I'm taking him to Brazil. You'll never see him again." In a panic, Mary, knowing that her husband has just received a large bonus from his employer, suffers a heart attack. The call was actually made by her husband's friend, Joe. Joe frequently plays practical jokes on Mary and her husband, and the call was another one of his pranks.

b. Susan Stetson has difficulty paying a large bill for a business dinner in a restaurant because of an error by her credit-card company. The restaurant owner takes Susan's purse, which contains her car keys, and prevents Susan from leaving for over two hours while the matter is being resolved.

c. The *Local Inquirer* publishes an article that claims that the sister of a famous movie star, whose name it mentions, is dying from AIDS. The article is false and is published without having been investigated by the reporter.

d. Jennifer is driving her children home from school. The two oldest children are fighting in the back seat. She turns to scold them, taking her eyes off the road temporarily. When she turns back, there is a child on a bike crossing the street in front of her. Jennifer tries but is unable to swerve to avoid hitting the boy.

2. Shirley, an elderly woman, was taking a walk down the street in Santa Monica. Two teenaged boys confronted her, and one of the boys demanded that she hand over her purse. Shirley refused and began scolding the boys, telling them that their mothers would be ashamed of them. One of the boys then grabbed at the straps of her purse but was unable to dislodge it from her shoulder. When the boys realized they were not going to get the purse, they ran away. Does Shirley have a tort claim against the boys? Which tort or torts have been committed?

3. Sarah and David are divorced. While they were married, David continually accused Sarah in private of being "unfaithful" to him and sexually promiscuous. Now that the divorce is final, Sarah learns that David is sending e-mails to all their mutual friends claiming that she is promiscuous. Can Sarah sue David for defamation? Could she have brought a defamation action prior to the divorce? What would happen to Sarah's claim if David could prove that Sarah was, in fact, promiscuous?

4. Gerald Guerrero grew up in Small Town, U.S.A., where his family owned a local diner. He then moved to New York City and worked in retail for twenty years. After his father's death, Gerald inherited the business and returned to Small Town to reopen the diner as "Gerry's Place." Tourists have begun visiting Small Town because it is mentioned in a popular song. Gerald decides to capitalize on the new tourist industry by posting a three-foot wooden sign in front of the door to the diner that states "Gerald Guerrero is the best cook in town" and presents testimonials of people who have supposedly eaten there and loved the food. The locals know that Gerald never cooked in the restaurant at all until last week, and no one has ever heard of any of the people named in the testimonials. One day, a group of tourists who have just eaten at Gerry's Place become seriously ill. While at the hospital, they speak to some locals and decide to file suit against Gerald Guerrero for fraudulent misrepresentation. Evaluate whether the facts presented meet the requirements of fraud.

5. Sam owns a bakery shop. He has been trying to obtain a long-term contract with the owner of Julie's Tea Salon for some time. Sam starts a local advertising campaign on radio and television and in the newspaper. The campaign is so persuasive that Julie decides to break the contract she has had for several years with Goody's Bakery so that she can buy her baked goods from Sam's bakery. Is Sam liable to Goody's Bakery for the tort of wrongful interference with a contractual relationship?

6. In which of the following situations will the acting party be liable for the tort of negligence? Explain fully.

a. Mary goes to the golf course on Sunday morning, eager to try out a new set of golf clubs she has just purchased. As she tees off on the first hole, the head of her club flies off and injures a nearby golfer.

b. Mary's doctor gives her some pain medication and tells her not to drive after she takes it, as the medication induces drowsiness. In spite of the doctor's warning, Mary decides to drive to the store while on the medication. Owing to her lack of alertness, she fails to stop at a traffic light and crashes into another vehicle, injuring a passenger.

7. Ruth carelessly parks her car on a steep hill, leaving the car in neutral and failing to engage the parking brake. The car rolls down the hill, knocking down an electric line. The sparks from the broken line ignite a grass fire. The fire spreads until it reaches a barn one mile away. The barn houses dynamite, and the burning barn explodes, causing part of the roof to fall on and injure a passing motorist, Jim. Can Jim recover from Ruth? Why or why not?

8. Kim went to Ling's Market to pick up a few items for dinner. It was a rainy, windy day, and the wind

had blown water through the door of Ling's Market each time the door opened. As Kim entered through the door, she slipped and fell in the approximately one-half inch of rainwater that had accumulated on the floor. The manager knew of the weather conditions but had not posted any sign to warn customers of the water hazard. Kim injured her back as a result of the fall and sued Ling's for damages. Can Ling's be held liable for negligence in this situation? Discuss.

9. Carmen buys a television set manufactured by AKI Electronics. She is going on vacation, so she takes the set to her mother's house for her mother to use. Because the set is defective, it explodes, causing considerable damage to her mother's house. Carmen's mother sues AKI for the damages to her house. Discuss the product liability theories under which Carmen's mother can recover from AKI.

10. When Patsy drove her new Chrysler, she sat very close to the steering wheel—less than a foot away from the steering-wheel enclosure of the driver's side air bag. At the time, Chrysler did not provide any warning that a driver should not sit close to the air bag. In an accident with another car, Patsy's air bag deployed. The bag caused her elbow to strike the windshield pillar and fracture in three places, resulting in repeated surgery and physical therapy. Patsy filed a suit against Chrysler, alleging that her injuries had been caused by Chrysler's failure to warn consumers about sitting near the air bag. At the trial, an expert testified that the air bag was not intended to prevent arm injuries, which were "a predictable, incidental consequence" of the bag's deploying. Should Chrysler be required to pay for Patsy's injuries? Why or why not?

11. Ingersoll-Rand Co. makes a machine that is used for stripping asphalt from roads that are being repaved. The maintenance manual that comes with the machine warns that users should stay ten feet away from the rear of the machine while it is operating, verify that the back-up alarm is working, and check the area for the presence of others. There is also a sign on the machine that tells users to stay ten feet away. Terrill Wilson, a road worker, was operating the machine in the street one day. The alarm did not sound, and Cosandra Rogers, who was standing with her back to the machine, was run over and severely injured. Rogers filed a suit against Ingersoll-Rand, alleging strict liability on the basis of a design defect. The jury awarded Rogers $10.2 million in compensatory damages and $6.5 million in punitive damages. Ingersoll-Rand appealed, emphasizing the adequacy of its warnings. Can an adequate warning shield a manufacturer from liability for a defectively designed product? Explain your answer.

✱ QUESTIONS FOR CRITICAL ANALYSIS

1. Tort law distinguishes between intentional acts that harm others and unintentional acts that harm others. How are they different? Are the consequences any different? Should they be?

2. The tort of intentional infliction of emotional distress imposes liability on a person who engages in extreme and outrageous conduct that causes another to suffer severe emotional distress. How can these types of "injuries" be measured? How can they be compensated for? Should this tort be allowed?

3. Negligence law imposes a duty on every member of society to act like a "reasonable person." How did the concept of a duty of care arise? What societal judgment does the reasonable person standard reflect?

4. A plaintiff in a negligence case must prove proximate cause, also known as legal cause, to succeed in the action. Foreseeability is one commonly used test of proximate cause. What impact does foreseeability have on the issue of causation? What might happen without such a test?

5. Mrs. Palsgraf was standing on a platform at a train station waiting for a train. Another train pulled up, and two men ran to catch it. The first man boarded the train without incident. The second man, however, ran into difficulty because the train had already begun to move. As he attempted to board the train, a guard on the train pulled him forward, and another guard on the platform pushed him from the platform onto the train. Unbeknownst to the guards, the package carried by the man, which was covered in newspaper, contained fireworks. When the package fell, it exploded. The explosion caused baggage scales some distance away to tip over and injure Palsgraf, who was standing near the scales. Palsgraf sued the Long Island Railroad. Do you think a court would find that the railroad owed a duty of care to Palsgraf? How would a court view

the issue of proximate cause in this case? Write two paragraphs, one analyzing the issue of duty of care and the other the issue of proximate cause.

6. Even if the elements of duty, breach of duty, and causation are met, there can be no recovery in a negligence action if the injury requirement is not met. Why not? Is this principle of tort law fair?

7. In a few states, if a plaintiff in a negligence case can be shown to have contributed at all to the injury, then the plaintiff is completely barred from recovering any damages by the defense of contributory negligence. Is this a fair outcome? With what doctrine have the majority of the states replaced the contributory negligence doctrine?

8. Strict liability imposes liability for injuries suffered by defendants without considering fault. Is this fair in any situation? If so, in which situations? What is the underlying rationale behind imposing strict product liability on defendants?

9. What general principle underlies the common law doctrine that business owners have a duty of care toward their customers? Does the duty of care unfairly burden business owners? Why or why not?

10. The United States has the strictest product liability laws in the world today. Why do you think many other countries, particularly developing countries, are more lax with respect to holding manufacturers liable for product defects?

✳ PROJECTS

1. Find out what defenses against negligence are used in your state. Do the courts in your state allow the defense of contributory negligence, or have they adopted the comparative negligence doctrine?

2. Contact your local police department to find out what is required in your area to obtain a police report. Is there a specific form that you need to fill out? Does the request have to be written and/or signed by an attorney, or can the request be made on the telephone or via e-mail? How much does it cost? How long does it take? Do you get a copy of any supplemental or investigative reports in addition to the original incident report?

3. Contact two local hospitals to find out what is required in order for them to release a person's medical records. Does one consent form authorize you to get all the medical records for an individual or only records within a specified time frame? What if the person had blood tests or other laboratory tests that were sent out of the hospital for processing—do you need a separate consent form for such tests? How much does the hospital charge to make copies of records? How long does it typically take to get medical records? Compare the information-release requirements of the two hospitals as well as the costs of obtaining the records and the time required.

4. Find a newspaper article on a serious injury accident. Read the article carefully, and write a two-page memo evaluating the potential negligence claim and indicating what you think is needed to "work up" the case. For example, you might make a list of any witnesses that need to be interviewed and any reports that should be obtained. Make sure to attach the article, or a copy of it, to the memo you prepare.

✳ USING INTERNET RESOURCES

1. Go to the Web site maintained by the Tobacco Control Resource Center at **http://www.library.ucsf.edu/ tobacco/litigation** for information on state tobacco litigation. Click on the link for "Key Litigation Documents by State and Other Jurisdictions." Select a state. If there is more than one case listed, select one case, and click on "Browse." You will find an electronic version of the complaint filed in the case. Use that document to answer the following questions.

   a. Who is the plaintiff in the action? How many tobacco companies are named as defendants in the complaint?

   b. How many "counts" or "causes of action" are listed in the complaint? (Hint: Usually the counts appear as headings.)

   c. What theory or theories of *tort* liability that were discussed in this chapter are alleged in the complaint?

2. Go to FindLaw's Injury and Tort Law Web Guide at **http://www.findlaw.com/01topics/22tort/index.html** to find answers to the following questions.

   a. Under the heading "Injury and Tort Law Web Guide," click on "Databases." What kind of information generally is available at this location? How might you use this information in a tort lawsuit? Can you access any data or reports from governmental agencies? Which agencies?

b. Now click on "Software." What kinds of software are listed?

c. Under the heading "Journals, Newsletters, and Articles," you can find many articles on tort law. Read an article that interests you, and write a one-page summary.

d. Now click on "Web Sites" and browse through the listings. Note how many of the listings are dedicated to providing information about defective products and product liability actions. Explore one of the Web sites provided, and write a short synopsis of what you found at that site.

e. Under "FindLaw Resources," click on "FindLaw Demonstrative Evidence Marketplace—Medical Illustrations & Anatomical Models." What kinds of products and services are available at this online marketplace? How might these products and services be useful to you as a paralegal in a tort case?

END NOTES

1. The reasonable person standard is an objective test of how a reasonable person would have acted under the same circumstances. See the discussion under "The Duty of Care and Its Breach" later in this chapter.

2. *New York Times Co. v. Sullivan,* 376 U.S. 254, 84 S.Ct. 710, 11 L.Ed.2d 686 (1964).

3. *White v. Samsung Electronics America, Inc.,* 971 F.2d 1395 (9th Cir. 1992).

4. 47 U.S.C. Section 230.

5. *Does v. Hvide,* 770 So.2d 1237 (Fla.App.3d 2000).

6. *Restatement (Second) of Torts,* Section 402A.

7. *Restatement (Third) of Torts: Products Liability,* Section 2, Comment h.

8. Under some state laws, the failure to properly maintain a product may constitute a subsequent alteration. See, for example, *LaPlante v. American Honda Motor Co.,* 27 F.3d 731 (1st Cir. 1994).

C H A P T E R 8

Contracts and Intellectual Property Law

Chapter Outline

- Introduction
- Requirements to Form a Valid Contract
- Defenses to Contract Enforceability
- Sales Contracts and Warranties
- Contract Performance and Remedies
- Electronic Contracting and Electronic Signatures
- Contract Law and the Paralegal
- Intellectual Property Law

After completing this chapter, you will know:

- The requirements for forming a valid contract and the kinds of circumstances under which contracts are not enforceable.
- The remedies available to the innocent party when a contract is breached, or broken.
- The nature of an electronic signature and the legal validity of such signatures.
- The nature of intellectual property and some forms of intellectual property.
- What conduct gives rise to a copyright infringement action.

INTRODUCTION

The law governs virtually every transaction or activity that individuals engage in across the nation. Simple, everyday transactions—such as purchasing a carton of milk from your corner grocer or installing a new software program on your home computer—are subject to specific laws that define the rights and duties of the parties involved in the transaction. In this chapter, you will learn about two of the most important areas of law—contracts and sales. Paralegals routinely help attorneys deal with contract and sales law disputes in which their clients are involved. Because the disputes often deal with complicated issues, paralegals need an understanding of the basic principles of these substantive law areas to follow the arguments involved in such disputes.

Another area of law that has become increasingly important involves the world's intellectual property, such as patents, trademarks, and copyrights. As you will learn later in the chapter, the value of intellectual property has become very important because of the freer flow of ideas throughout the world. Attorneys and their paralegals are frequently called on to help their clients register and protect some form of intellectual property.

REQUIREMENTS TO FORM A VALID CONTRACT

promise
An assurance that one will or will not do something in the future.

contract
An agreement or bargain struck between parties in which each party assumes a legal duty to the other party. The requirements for a valid contract are agreement, consideration, contractual capacity, and legality.

Contract law deals with, among other things, the keeping of promises. A **promise** is an assurance that one will or will not do something in the future. Simply put, a **contract** is any agreement (based on a promise or an exchange of promises) that can be enforced in court. (Today, forms for numerous types of contracts are available online—see this chapter's *Technology and Today's Paralegal* feature on page 250 for information on how to access Web sites offering contract forms.)

If a client alleges that a party has breached a contract, the first issue that you and your supervising attorney need to determine is whether a *valid contract* (a contract that will be enforced by a court) was ever formed. To form a valid contract, four basic requirements must be met. These requirements are listed below and explained more fully in the following subsections. It is important that you understand as you read this chapter that each requirement is separate and independent.

- *Agreement.* An agreement includes an offer and an acceptance. One party must offer to enter into a legal agreement, and another party must accept the terms of the offer.
- *Consideration.* Any promises made by parties must be supported by legally sufficient and bargained-for consideration (which is something of value that is received or promised to convince a person to make a deal, as you will read shortly).
- *Contractual capacity.* Both parties entering into the contract must have the contractual capacity to do so; the law must recognize them as possessing characteristics that qualify them as competent parties.
- *Legality.* The contract's purpose must be to accomplish some goal that is legal and not against public policy.

> ※ **If any of these four elements is lacking, no contract will have been formed.**

We look next at each of these requirements.

agreement
A meeting of the minds, and a requirement for a valid contract. Agreement involves two distinct events: an offer to form a contract and the acceptance of that offer by the offeree.

Agreement

A contract is, in essence, an **agreement** between two or more parties. Therefore, if the parties fail to reach an agreement on the terms of the contract, no contract exists.

Ordinarily, agreement is evidenced by two events: an *offer* and an *acceptance*. One party offers a certain bargain to another party, who then accepts that bargain.

OFFER.   An **offer** is a promise or commitment to do or refrain from doing some specified thing in the future. Three elements are necessary for an offer to be effective:

- The **offeror** (the party making the offer) must have the *intent to be bound* by the offer. Offers made in jest, in undue excitement, or in obvious anger do not meet this requirement.
- The terms of the offer must be *reasonably certain, or definite,* so that the parties and the court can ascertain the terms of the contract. (Note that in contracts for the sale of goods, discussed later in this chapter, the requirement of definiteness is relaxed somewhat so that a contract can still arise even if certain terms are left "open," or unspecified.[1])
- The offer must be communicated to the **offeree** (the party to whom the offer is made).

Intention.   For example, suppose that Al and Sue ride to work together each day in Sue's car, which she bought for $18,000 six months ago. One cold morning, Al and Sue get into the car, but Sue cannot get it started. She yells in anger, "I'll sell you my car for $600!" Al writes Sue a check for $600. Has a contract to sell the car been formed? If Al consulted with your supervising attorney, claiming that Sue had breached a contract because she had refused to give him the car, what would the attorney say? Most likely, the attorney would tell Al that a reasonable person would have recognized under the circumstances that Sue's offer was not serious—she did not intend to be bound but was simply frustrated. Therefore, no valid contract was formed.

Definiteness.   Similarly, the courts will not enforce an offer that is too ambiguous in terms. Suppose, for example, that Kim wants to sell her set of legal encyclopedias but has not mentioned a price. James then says to Kim, "I'll buy your encyclopedias and pay you some money for them next week." In this situation, no contract will result, because "some money" is not a definite term.

Termination of the Offer.   Once an offer has been communicated, the party to whom the offer was made can accept the offer, reject the offer, or make a counteroffer. If a party accepts the offer, a contract is formed (provided all the other requirements to form a contract are met). If the party rejects the offer, the offer is terminated. In other words, the offer no longer stands (and the offeree cannot take the offeror up on the offer). The offeree also has the option of rejecting the offer and simultaneously making another offer—called a counteroffer.

In a counteroffer, the offeree becomes the offeror—offering to form a contract with different terms. For example, suppose that Dillon offers to perform work for Wayne for $50,000. Wayne responds, "Your price is too high. I'll hire you for $40,000." Wayne's response is a counteroffer, because it terminates Dillon's offer and creates a new offer by Wayne.

Both a rejection of the offer and the making of a counteroffer terminate the original offer. The original offer can also be terminated if the party making the offer withdraws the offer before it has been accepted (which is called *revoking the offer*).[2] If the offer has already been accepted, however, then both parties are bound in contract. An offer will also terminate automatically in some circumstances, such as when the specific subject matter of the offer is destroyed, one of the parties dies or becomes incompetent, or a new law is passed that makes the

On the Web
The 'Lectric Law Library provides information on many legal topics, including contracts. Go to **http://www.lectlaw. com**. Click on "The Library's ROTUNDA," then click on "Laypeople's Law Lounge."

offer
A promise or commitment to do or refrain from doing some specified thing in the future.

offeror
The party making the offer.

offeree
The party to whom the offer is made.

acceptance
In contract law, the offeree's indication to the offeror that the offeree agrees to be bound by the terms of the offeror's offer, or proposal to form a contract.

mirror image rule
A common law rule that requires that the terms of the offeree's acceptance adhere exactly to the terms of the offeror's offer for a valid contract to be formed.

mailbox rule
A rule providing that an acceptance of an offer takes effect at the time it is communicated via the mode expressly or impliedly authorized by the offeror, rather than at the time it is actually received by the offeror. If acceptance is to be by mail, for example, it becomes effective the moment it is placed in the mailbox.

click-on agreement
An agreement that arises when a buyer, engaging in a transaction on a computer, indicates his or her assent to be bound by the terms of an offer by clicking on a button that says, for example, "I agree"; sometimes referred to as a *click-on license* or a *click-wrap agreement.*

consideration
Something of value, such as money or the performance of an action not otherwise required, that motivates the formation of a contract. Each party must give consideration for the contract to be binding.

On the Web
To learn more about how the courts decide such issues as whether consideration was lacking for a particular contract, look at relevant case law, which can be accessed through Cornell University's School of Law site at **http:// www.law.cornell.edu/ topics/contracts.html.**

contract illegal. Additionally, an offer will terminate if a period of time is specified in the offer and the offer is not accepted within that period. If no time for acceptance is specified in the offer, the offer expires when a *reasonable* period of time has passed. (What constitutes a reasonable period of time in the eyes of the court varies, depending on the circumstances.)

ACCEPTANCE.   As mentioned, a party's **acceptance** of the offer results in a legally binding contract (if all of the other elements of a valid contract are present). The acceptance must be *unequivocal*—that is, the terms of the offer must be accepted exactly as stated by the offeror. This principle of contract law is known as the **mirror image rule**—the terms of the acceptance must be the same as ("mirror") the terms of the offer. If the acceptance is subject to new conditions or if the terms of the acceptance materially change the original offer, the acceptance may be deemed a counteroffer that implicitly rejects the original offer.

Another requirement, for most types of contracts, is that the acceptance be communicated to the offeror. A significant problem with respect to contract formation has to do with the timeliness of acceptances. The general rule is that acceptance of an offer is timely if it is made before the offer is terminated. Problems arise, however, when the parties involved are not dealing face-to-face. In such cases, acceptance takes effect at the time the acceptance is communicated via the mode expressly or impliedly authorized by the offeror. This is the **mailbox rule.** Under this rule, if the offer states that it must be accepted by mail, the acceptance becomes valid the moment it is deposited in the mail (even if it is never received by the offeror).

Most of the time, the party making the offer does not indicate the preferred method of acceptance. In those cases, acceptance of an offer may be made by any medium that is *reasonable under the circumstances.* Several factors determine whether the acceptance was reasonable: the nature of the circumstances at the time the offer was made, the means used to transmit the offer, and the reliability of the offer's delivery. If, for example, an offer was sent by FedEx overnight delivery because an acceptance was urgently required, the offeree's attempt to accept by fax would be deemed reasonable. In contracts formed on the Internet, the issues of timeliness and method of acceptance usually do not arise. This is because persons often accept online offers simply by clicking on a box stating "I agree" or "I accept." Such **click-on agreements** are becoming widely used in the formation of contracts online (as discussed later in this chapter).

Consideration

Another requirement for a valid contract is consideration. **Consideration** is usually defined as something of value—such as money or the performance of an action not otherwise required—that is given in exchange for a promise. No promise is enforceable without consideration. For example, suppose that you give your friend $1,000 in exchange for her promise to take care of your house and garden for six months. This promise normally will be enforceable, because consideration has been given. Your consideration is $1,000; your friend's consideration is the assumption of an obligation (taking care of the house and garden) that she otherwise would not assume. Note that both parties to the contract must have consideration for the contract to be enforced.

Often, consideration is broken down into two parts: (1) something of *legal value* must be given in exchange for the promise, and (2) there must be a *bargained-for* exchange. The "something of legal value" may consist of a return promise that is bargained for. It may also consist of performance, which may be an act, a forbearance (refraining from action), or the creation, modification, or destruction of a legal relationship. For example, when you are twenty-one, your grandfather might promise to pay you $10,000 if you agree not to smoke any cigarettes before the age of twenty-five. Your consideration in this situation is refraining from the act of smoking cigarettes.

> ※   **Once a contract has been formed, the general common law rule is that the terms of the contract cannot be modified without further consideration.**

For instance, after making the deal in the example just mentioned, your grandfather cannot modify the terms by requiring you not to drink alcohol for the same $10,000—you would have to get additional consideration for this new agreement.

LEGAL SUFFICIENCY OF CONSIDERATION.   For a binding contract to be created, consideration must be *legally sufficient.* To be legally sufficient, consideration for a promise must be either *legally detrimental to the promisee* or *legally beneficial to the promisor.* A party can incur legal detriment either by promising to give legal value (such as the payment of money) or by a forbearance or a promise of forbearance—that is, by refraining from or promising to refrain from doing something that the party had a legal right to do.

The requirement of consideration distinguishes contracts from gifts. For example, if you promise to give your friend $1,000 as a gift and she promises to accept your gift, no contract results, because your friend has given no legally sufficient consideration for the contract.

ADEQUACY OF CONSIDERATION.   Adequacy of consideration refers to the fairness of the bargain. In general, a court will not question the adequacy of consideration if the consideration is legally sufficient. Parties are normally free to bargain as they wish. If people could sue merely because they had entered into a bad bargain, the courts would be overloaded with frivolous suits. In other words, Jack is free to sell his 1999 Mercedes Benz, which is in perfect condition, to Herb for $1,000, even if the car is worth more (the court will not invalidate the contract).

In extreme cases, a court may consider the adequacy of consideration in terms of its amount or worth because inadequate consideration may indicate fraud, duress, undue influence, or a lack of bargained-for exchange. It may also reflect a party's incompetence (for example, an individual might have been too intoxicated or simply too young to make a contract).

PROMISSORY ESTOPPEL.   In some circumstances, contracts will be enforced even though consideration is lacking. Under the doctrine of **promissory estoppel,** a person who has reasonably and substantially relied on the promise of another may be able to obtain some measure of recovery. The following elements are required:

promissory estoppel
A doctrine under which a promise is binding if the promise is clear and definite, the promisee justifiably relies on the promise, the reliance is reasonable and substantial, and justice will be better served by enforcement of the promise.

- There must be a clear and definite promise.
- The promisee must justifiably rely on the promise.
- The reliance normally must be of a substantial and definite character.
- Justice will be better served by enforcement of the promise.

If these requirements are met, a promise may be enforced even though it is not supported by consideration. In essence, the promisor will be *estopped* (prevented) from asserting the lack of consideration as a defense. For example, suppose that your uncle tells you, "I'll pay you $300 a week so you won't have to work anymore." In reliance on your uncle's promise, you quit your job, but your uncle

---

TECHNOLOGY AND TODAY'S PARALEGAL

Contract Forms

Before the printing press was invented, every contract form had to be handwritten. Since the advent of printing, most standard contract forms have been readily available at low cost. The introduction of computers into legal practice obviated the need to use preprinted forms and further allowed attorneys and paralegals to customize contract forms for each situation. This procedure has been both simplified and expanded by the inclusion of contract forms on simple-to-use CD-ROMs, such as *Quicken's Business Law Partner.*

ONLINE CONTRACT FORMS

Now the Internet has made available an even larger variety of contract forms, as well as other legal and business forms. For example, at http://biz.findlaw.com/states_new.html, you can find over 25,000 legal forms for lawyers, businesses, and the public. The contracts range from basic sales contracts to sample software licensing agreements. Many are available free of charge. The Internet Legal Resource Guide also offers a number of free contract forms and links to other online resources at http://www.ilrg.com/forms/index.html#other.

Yet another source for contract forms is 'Lectric Law Library's collection of forms at http://www.lectlaw.com/formb.htm. This site includes forms for the assignment of a contract, a contract for the sale of a business, and many others (some free, some for purchase). In addition, if you

become a member of the 'Lectric Law Library, you can access document assembly software that uses the forms to build a final contract for your case.

There are many other sources for contract forms on the Internet. For example, http://www.uslegalforms.com has numerous forms available in many areas of practice. Not only can you search for contracts by topic (such as corporate or construction contracts), but you can also look up state-specific forms (separation agreements, for example). Most of the forms are available for a nominal fee (ten to fifteen dollars) and can be obtained in printed form (mailed to you) or downloaded in the electronic format of your choice (*Microsoft Word, WordPerfect,* or rich text format). Similar types of services are available at many other sites, including http://www.legal-forms-now.com, http://myshoppingonline.com/my/600forms1.htm, and http://www.allaboutforms.com.

TECHNOLOGY TIP

Online contract forms are a tremendous resource for paralegals. Thousands of forms can be easily accessed and customized for use in a particular case. Keep in mind, though, that the contracts you find online will not necessarily be valid or upheld in your state or situation. You must always research the contract requirements in your state to verify that you are using the appropriate form.

---

refuses to pay you. Under the doctrine of promissory estoppel, you may be able to enforce such a promise.

Capacity

contractual capacity
The threshold mental capacity required by law for a party who enters into a contract to be bound by that contract.

For a contract to be deemed valid, the parties to the contract must have **contractual capacity**—the legal ability to enter into a contractual relationship. Courts generally presume the existence of contractual capacity, but there are some situations in which capacity is lacking or questionable. In many situations, a party may have the capacity to enter into a valid contract but also have the right to avoid liability under it.

Minors usually are not legally bound by contracts. Subject to certain exceptions, the contracts entered into by a minor are *voidable* (capable of being canceled, or avoided) at the option of that minor. The minor has the option of *disaffirming* (renouncing) the contract and setting aside the contract and all legal obligations arising from it. An adult who enters into a contract with a minor, how-

---

DEVELOPING PARALEGAL SKILLS

Assessing Capacity

Suppose you are a legal assistant for Jeffrey Barlow. Barlow asks you to draft a contract for Margaret Klaus, a seventy-six-year-old widow. In the contract, Margaret will convey all of her shares in NAPO Corporation to her nephew Jeremy. In return, Jeremy will take care of Margaret for the rest of her life. The attorney is leaving on vacation and asks you to have the document completed and arrange a meeting with the client and her nephew to sign the contract when he returns in two weeks.

   While drafting the agreement, you learn that the stock being conveyed is worth a great deal of money. Also, you begin to have doubts about Margaret's mental status. She has called you at least once a day for the past week. During the conversations, she often calls you by different names, repeats herself, and does not remember what you just told her. Although you know that Jeremy has been living with Margaret for the past six months (and is unemployed), whenever Margaret calls, she is alone and seems to be frightened. Now that you have finished the contract, you wonder if Margaret is capable of consenting to it and whether Jeremy has exerted too much influence over her. What should you do?

TIPS FOR DEALING WITH SUSPICIONS OF INCOMPETENCE

- Document everything. Keep a record of all the conversations you had with the client that led you to suspect a lack of contractual capacity, as well as any other facts that contributed to your suspicions (if you discovered the person was taking medication for mental illness, for example).

- Do not discuss your suspicions with anyone except the attorney in the case (particularly not with the client or the client's family). Making such statements about a person can be very damaging to his or her reputation, and you may even be held liable for defamation.

- Remember that it is the attorney's job to evaluate the client's contractual capacity, not yours. You just want to make the attorney aware of the situation in an effort to protect the client's best interests.

---

ever, cannot avoid his or her contractual duties on the ground that the minor can do so. Unless the minor exercises the option to set aside the contract, the adult party is bound by it.

   Intoxication is a condition in which a person's normal capacity to act or think is inhibited by alcohol or some other drug. If the person was sufficiently intoxicated to lack mental capacity, the transaction is voidable at the option of the intoxicated person even if the intoxication was purely voluntary. Although this is the common law rule, most courts today rarely permit contracts to be avoided because of a party's intoxication.

   If a person has been adjudged mentally incompetent by a court of law and a guardian has been appointed, any contract made by the mentally incompetent person is *void*—no contract exists. Only the guardian can enter into binding legal duties on the incompetent person's behalf. Even if the court has not previously ruled that the person is mentally incompetent, the contract may be avoided if incompetence is proved. For example, suppose Rita, who suffers from Alzheimer's disease, signs a contract to buy sixty new vacuums. If it can be proved that Rita did not understand what she was doing at the time she signed the contract, the contract will not be valid.

Legality

A contract to do something that is prohibited by federal or state statutory law is illegal and, as such, void from the outset and thus unenforceable. For example, a contract to buy a kidney from another person is void because it is illegal. No court would enforce the contract if a lawsuit were brought for breach of contract. Any contract to commit a crime is unenforceable.

In some cases, the subject matter of the contract is not illegal, but one of the parties is not legally authorized to perform the contract. For example, all states require that members of certain occupations—including physicians, lawyers, real estate brokers, architects, electricians, contractors, and stockbrokers—obtain licenses allowing them to practice. When a person enters into a contract with an unlicensed individual, the contract may still be enforceable, depending on the nature of the licensing statute. Some states expressly provide that the lack of a license in certain occupations (such as lawyers) bars the enforcement of work-related contracts. If the statute does not expressly declare this, one must look to the underlying purpose of the licensing requirements for a particular occupation. If the purpose is to protect the public from unauthorized practitioners, a contract involving an unlicensed individual normally is illegal and unenforceable. If the underlying purpose of the statute is to raise government revenues, however, a contract entered into with an unlicensed practitioner generally is enforceable—although the unlicensed person is usually fined.

Additionally, some contracts are not enforced because the court deems them to be contrary to public policy. For example, contracts that restrain trade (anti-competitive contracts) and contracts that are so oppressive to innocent parties that they "shock the conscience" of the court are not enforceable owing to the negative impact they would have on society.

DEFENSES TO CONTRACT ENFORCEABILITY

Two competent parties have entered into a contract for a legal purpose. The agreement is supported by consideration. The contract thus meets the four requirements for a valid contract. Nonetheless, the contract may be unenforceable if the parties have not genuinely assented (agreed) to its terms or if the contract is not in the proper form—such as in writing, if the law requires it to be in writing.

Genuineness of Assent

genuineness of assent
Knowing and voluntary assent to the contract terms. If a contract is formed as a result of mistake, misrepresentation, undue influence, or duress, genuineness of assent is lacking, and the contract will be voidable.

Lack of **genuineness of assent** can be used as a defense to the contract's enforceability. Genuineness of assent may be lacking because of a mistake, misrepresentation, undue influence, or duress.

unilateral mistake
Mistake as to a material fact on the part of only one party to a contract. In this situation, the contract is normally enforceable against the mistaken party, with some exceptions.

MISTAKE.   It is important to distinguish between *mistakes of fact* and *mistakes of value or quality*. If a mistake concerns the future market value or quality of the object of the contract, the mistake is one of *value,* and either party normally can enforce the contract. Each party is considered to have assumed the risk that the value would change or prove to be different from what he or she thought. Without this rule, almost any party who did not receive what he or she considered a fair bargain could argue mistake.

material fact
A fact that is important to the subject matter of the contract.

Only a mistake of fact allows a contract to be avoided. Mistakes of fact occur in two forms—*unilateral* and *mutual (bilateral)*. A **unilateral mistake** occurs when one party to the contract makes a mistake as to some **material fact**—that is, a fact important to the subject matter of the contract. The general rule is that a unilateral mistake does not afford the mistaken party any right to relief from the contract. There are some exceptions to this rule, however. For example, if a contractor's bid was significantly low because he or she made a mistake in addition when totaling the estimated costs, any contract resulting from the bid normally can be rescinded. (**Rescission** is the act of canceling, or nullifying, a contract.)

rescission
A remedy in which the contract is canceled and the parties are returned to the positions they occupied before the contract was made.

ETHICAL CONCERN
Potential Conflicts of Interest

Many times in a law office, two parties come in together and want the attorney (and paralegal) to write a contract that represents their agreement. This raises an obvious conflict-of-interest issue. Can the attorney represent both parties in a contract? Recall from Chapter 3 that conflict rules prevent an attorney from simultaneously representing adverse parties in a legal proceeding. On the one hand, drafting a contract is not really a legal proceeding, since the parties could write up a legally binding contract without an attorney. On the other hand, should a dispute arise over the contract, assisting one party will necessarily be adverse to the other. In this situation, the attorney and paralegal need to carefully research the rules on waiving conflicts in their state. If the state has adopted the 2002 Revision of the Model Rules, then the attorney must obtain the informed consent of each party, and the consent must be confirmed in writing. This means the attorney must explain the risks of having one attorney draw up a contract for two people and also must discuss the alternatives. Then the attorney must have the two parties sign a consent form or, if the parties give consent orally, must promptly draft a written document evidencing the consent.

When *both* of the parties are mistaken about the same material fact, a **mutual mistake** has occurred, and either party can cancel the contract. To illustrate, assume that at Perez's art gallery, Diana buys a painting of a landscape. Both Diana and Perez believe that the painting is by the artist Van Gogh. Later, Diana discovers that the painting is a very clever fake. Because neither Perez nor Diana was aware of this material fact when they made their deal, Diana can rescind (cancel) the contract and recover the purchase price of the painting.

mutual mistake
Mistake as to the same material fact on the part of both parties to a contract. In this situation, either party can cancel the contract.

FRAUDULENT MISREPRESENTATION.   When an innocent party is fraudulently induced to enter into a contract, the contract usually can be avoided because that party has not *voluntarily* consented to its terms. Normally, the innocent party can either rescind (cancel) the contract and be restored to his or her original position or enforce the contract and seek damages for any injuries resulting from the fraud.

You read about the tort of fraudulent misrepresentation in Chapter 7. In the context of contract law, fraudulent misrepresentation occurs when one party to a contract misrepresents a material fact to the other party, with the intention of deceiving the other party, and the other party justifiably relies on the misrepresentation. To collect damages, a party must also have been injured. A party may still be able to avoid the contract in some states without proving that he or she was injured by the fraud, however.

Note that the misrepresentation may be based on conduct as well as oral or written statements. For example, suppose Gene is contracting to buy Rachelle's horse for racing. While showing Gene the horse, Rachelle skillfully keeps the horse's head turned away so that Gene does not see that the horse is blind in one eye. Rachelle's conduct constitutes fraud.

UNDUE INFLUENCE.   Undue influence arises from special kinds of relationships in which one party can greatly influence another party, thus overcoming that party's free will. For example, elderly people may be unduly influenced by their caretakers, clients may be unduly influenced by their attorneys, and children may be unduly influenced by their parents. The essential feature of undue influence is that the party being taken advantage of does not, in reality, exercise free will in entering into a contract. A contract entered into under excessive or undue influence lacks genuine assent and is therefore voidable.

DURESS.   Assent to the terms of a contract is not genuine if one of the parties is *forced* into the agreement. Forcing a party to do something, including entering into a contract, through fear created by threats is legally defined as *duress*. In addition, blackmail or extortion to induce consent to a contract constitutes duress. Duress is both a defense to the enforcement of a contract and a ground for the rescission of a contract.

The Statute of Frauds

An otherwise valid contract may be unenforceable if it is not in the proper form. To ensure that there is reliable proof of the agreement, certain types of contracts are required to be in writing. If a contract is required by law to be in writing and there is no written evidence of the contract, it may not be enforceable.

Every state has a statute that specifies what types of contracts must be in writing (or be evidenced by a written document). This statute is commonly referred to as the **Statute of Frauds**.[3] Although the state statutes vary slightly, the following types of contracts are normally required to be in writing:

Statute of Frauds
A state statute that requires certain types of contracts to be in writing to be enforceable.

- Contracts involving interests in land (or anything attached to land, such as buildings, plants, minerals, or timber).
- Contracts that cannot by their terms be performed within one year from the date of formation.
- Collateral, or secondary, contracts, such as promises to answer for the debt or duty of another.
- Promises made in consideration of marriage, such as prenuptial agreements (which will be discussed in Chapter 9).
- Contracts for the sale of goods priced at $500 or more.

Note that the test for determining whether an oral contract is enforceable under the "one-year rule" stated in the second item above is not whether an agreement is *likely* to be performed within one year but whether performance is *possible* within one year. Also, the one-year period begins to run the day *after* the contract is formed. Exhibit 8.1 illustrates the one-year rule.

In some states, an oral contract that would otherwise be unenforceable under the Statute of Frauds may be enforced under the doctrine of promissory estoppel, based on detrimental reliance. Recall that if one party makes a promise on which the other party justifiably relies to his or her detriment, a court may prevent the party who made the promise from denying that a contract exists. In these circumstances, an oral promise can be enforceable if the reliance was foreseeable and if injustice can be avoided only by enforcing the promise.

sales contract
A contract for the sale of goods, as opposed to a contract for the sale of services, real property, or intangible property. Sales contracts are governed by Article 2 of the Uniform Commercial Code.

Uniform Commercial Code (UCC)
A uniform code of laws governing commercial transactions that has been adopted in part or in its entirety by all of the states. Article 2 of the UCC governs contracts for the sale of goods.

SALES CONTRACTS AND WARRANTIES

Sales contracts, or contracts for the sale of goods, are governed by state statutes that are based on Article 2 of the **Uniform Commercial Code** (UCC). The UCC is one of the many—and one of the most significant—uniform laws created by the

FEATURED GUEST, *Continued*

audit questionnaire. The audit questionnaire will typically ask the following:

- Does the client use any specific names, logos, or slogans in advertising its products and services?
- Are any written materials used in marketing (such as brochures, newspaper advertisements, and slides and written materials used for presentations)?
- Does the client develop any products or software?
- Does the client use any confidential methods or processes in developing and marketing its products and services, including financial forecasts, marketing plans, and customer lists?
- Has the company ever been sued for or accused of infringing another party's intellectual property rights?

The questionnaire should be tailored to the needs of the client. For example, companies engaged in telecommunications services or software development will need detailed sections designed to obtain information on software products and proprietary information. In contrast, companies engaged in consulting will likely have no "products" that need protection but will have a wealth of written materials that should be protected as trade secrets or registered as copyrights.

Conducting the Audit.   On receiving the questionnaire, the client should begin gathering the

materials that are responsive to the questionnaire. The legal team will then review the materials that the client has assembled to determine which materials can be protected under intellectual property law. If the client has a Web site, it should be carefully reviewed to ensure that the site is not only protected under copyright law but also that it does not infringe the rights of another party. Paralegals often coordinate the time and manner of the audit by scheduling the audit date, arranging for a conference room, and ensuring a photocopy machine is available to copy documents that are responsive to the questionnaire. Generally, the audit is conducted at the client's office because this is where the pertinent materials and documents are located.

The Audit Report.   After conducting the audit, the legal team prepares a written report for the client summarizing the results of the audit. The report identifies all of the intellectual property owned by the client and makes recommendations for its continued protection and maintenance. For example, the audit may disclose that the client uses a distinctive slogan in its advertising materials. The legal team will then recommend that the slogan be registered as a trademark.

POSTAUDIT ACTIVITY

After the audit is complete, the legal team, and particularly the paralegal, will begin preparing applications to

> ## "Paralegals play a significant role in drafting the audit questionnaire."

register trademarks, copyrights, and patents and will develop written policies to protect the client's trade secrets. Contracts will need to be drafted for the client to use when it hires independent contractors to develop certain products, such as software. Such contracts will clarify that the company will own all rights to any work products produced by those independent contractors. License agreements may need to be drafted so that the company can license its intellectual property to others to use. An Internet use policy may be needed so that all employees are aware of the confidential nature of the company's electronic communications.

The company will be advised to review materials used by its competitors to ensure that its competitors do not infringe on the company's valuable intellectual property rights—such as by using a trademark that is confusingly similar to one owned by the company, for example. Finally, the paralegal will create a docketing system to ensure that the client's intellectual property rights are maintained. For example, the paralegal should calendar the dates for maintenance and renewal of company trademarks. The paralegal should also schedule the date of the next intellectual property audit.

idea and an expression are inseparable, the expression cannot be copyrighted. Generally, anything that is not an original expression of an idea does not qualify for copyright protection. Facts widely known to the public are not copyrightable. Page numbers are normally not copyrightable because they follow a sequence known to everyone. Mathematical calculations are not copyrightable. The key requirement to obtain copyright protection is originality.

COPYRIGHT INFRINGEMENT.   Whenever the form or expression of an idea is copied, an infringement of copyright occurs. The reproduction does not have to be exactly the same as the original, nor does it have to reproduce the original in its entirety.

Penalties or remedies can be imposed on those who infringe copyrights. These range from actual damages (damages based on the actual harm caused to the copyright holder by the infringement) or statutory damages (damages provided for under the Copyright Act, not to exceed $100,000) to criminal proceedings for willful violations (which may result in fines and/or imprisonment).

An exception to liability for copyright infringement is made under the "fair use" doctrine. Under the Copyright Act, a person or organization can in certain situations reproduce copyrighted material without paying royalties (fees paid to the copyright holder for the privilege of reproducing the copyrighted material).[10] For example, an educator typically would be allowed under the fair use doctrine to make photocopies of new articles and distribute them to students for teaching purposes, but could not sell the copies commercially. Generally, the courts determine whether a particular use is fair on a case-by-case basis.

Trademarks and Related Property

trademark
A distinctive mark, motto, device, or emblem that a manufacturer stamps, prints, or otherwise affixes to the goods it produces so that they may be identified on the market and their origins made known. Once a trademark is established (under the common law or through registration), the owner is entitled to its exclusive use.

trade name
A term that is used to indicate part or all of a business's name and that is directly related to the business's reputation and goodwill. Trade names are protected under the common law (and under trademark law, if the business's name is the same as its trademark).

A **trademark** is a distinctive mark, motto, device, or emblem that a manufacturer stamps, prints, or otherwise affixes to the goods it produces so that those goods can be distinguished from the goods of other manufacturers and merchants. Examples of trademarks are brand-name labels on jeans, luggage, and other products. Generally, to be protected under trademark law, a mark must be distinctive. A distinctive mark might consist of an uncommon word (such as *Kodak* or *Xerox*) or words used in an uncommon or fanciful way (such as *English Leather* for an after-shave lotion instead of for leather processed in England).

Note that trademarks apply to *products*. The term **trade name** is used to indicate part or all of a business's name, such as McDonald's. Unless the trade name is also used as a trademark (as with Kodak, Xerox, and Coca-Cola, for example), the name is not protected under federal trademark law. Trade names are protected under the common law, however. Holiday Inns, Inc., for example, could sue a motel owner who used that name or a portion of it (such as "Holiday Motels") without permission. As with trademarks, words must be unusual or fanciful if they are to be protected as trade names. The word *Safeway*, for example, was considered by a court to be sufficiently fanciful to obtain protection as a trade name for a chain of food stores.

At common law, the person who used a symbol or mark to identify a business or product was protected in the use of that trademark. Today, trademarks may be registered with the state or with the federal government. Under current law, a mark can be registered federally (1) if it is currently in commerce or (2) if the applicant intends to put the mark into commerce within six months.

TRADEMARK INFRINGEMENT.   Registration of a trademark with the U.S. Patent and Trademark Office gives notice on a nationwide basis that the trademark

PARALEGAL PROFILE

ALLEN F. MIHECOBY *is an in-house paralegal for a publicly traded corporation involved in high-end retail and luxury goods. His experience has been primarily in large firms and multinational corporations. In 1997, he received a paralegal certificate from the ABA–approved program at Southeastern Paralegal Institute in Dallas, Texas.*

Mihecoby received both the PACE Registered Paralegal (RP) designation from NFPA and the Certified Legal Assistant (CLA) from NALA in 2002. He is an associate member of the American Bar Association and a member of the National Association of Legal Assistants; the National Federation of Paralegal Associations; the Legal Assistants Division of the State Bar of Texas; the College of the State Bar of Texas, Legal Assistants Division; the Metroplex Association of Corporate Paralegals; and the Dallas Area Paralegal Association and is a founding member of Legal Assistants of North Texas.

Intellectual Property Paralegal

What do you like best about your work?

"I like the variety of my work. As an in-house paralegal, I am exposed to the full gamut of intellectual property law on a daily basis. My day may begin by drafting a trademark application and then progress to negotiating a license agreement for a celebrity endorsement. I might then review documents that are to be given over to the other side in litigation to ensure that we comply with our company's privacy policy. In the same day, I may contact a foreign correspondent to discuss use of a patent in the European Union, review a vendor contract providing for the electronic transmission of orders, and work with U.S. Customs to halt the influx of counterfeit merchandise into the United States. Each day, I am presented with unique challenges and opportunities to learn and expand my skills."

What is the greatest challenge that you face in your area of work?

"Intellectual property changes from day to day and is constantly evolving. I spend a lot of time attending continuing legal education events and reviewing court cases, as well as decisions from administrative agencies, such as the Trademark Trials and Appeals Board. Each morning, I review online resources to see what events transpired the day before. Keeping abreast of changes is particularly important in the areas of e-commerce and privacy regulation. You might become accustomed to drafting an e-contract in a specific way, only to discover that a decision in another jurisdiction changes the standard."

What advice do you have for would-be paralegals in your area of work?

"Find a seasoned, veteran paralegal to serve as your mentor. It is a great asset both personally and professionally to have a group of skilled paralegal friends that have over sixty years of combined experience in the field. Each practice area is demanding, so make sure that you choose the field that is right for you. Should you choose intellectual property, be prepared to be married to the field."

What are some tips for success as a paralegal in your area of work?

"Networking is vital. This is a dynamic field, and chances are that you will be presented with some of the same challenges that your colleagues have faced. There are many national and international organizations you can use to stay connected with others who can provide valuable guidance. Also, creative thinking is a must. Learn to think 'outside of the box.' You will often find that a specific project does not fit neatly within a particular 'box,' or category. Your job is to organize the abstract. Finally, learn from everyone—from the senior partner in a law firm, to the courier who delivers your office's documents, to the professional who handles the electronic data for your client or company."

> **"Each day, I am presented with unique challenges and opportunities to learn and expand my skills."**

belongs exclusively to the registrant. The registrant is also allowed to use the symbol ® to indicate that the mark has been registered. Whenever that trademark is copied to a substantial degree or used in its entirety by another (intentionally or unintentionally), the trademark has been *infringed* (used without authorization), and the owner can sue. A person need not have registered a trademark in order to sue for trademark infringement, but registration does furnish proof of the date the owner began using the trademark. Only those trademarks that are deemed sufficiently distinctive from all competing trademarks will be protected, however.

TRADEMARK DILUTION.   Historically, federal trademark law only prohibited the unauthorized use of the same mark on competing or "related" goods or services when such use would be likely to confuse consumers. Trademark dilution laws, which have been passed by the federal government and about half of the states, extend that protection.

A famous mark may be diluted not only by the use of an *identical* mark but also by the use of a *similar* mark. For example, Ringling Bros.–Barnum & Bailey, Combined Shows, Inc., brought a suit against the state of Utah, claiming that Utah's use of the slogan "The Greatest Snow on Earth"—to attract visitors to the state's recreational and scenic resorts—diluted the distinctiveness of the circus's famous trademark, "The Greatest Show on Earth." Utah moved to dismiss the suit, arguing that the law protected owners of famous trademarks only against the unauthorized use of identical marks. A federal court disagreed and refused to grant Utah's motion to dismiss the case.[11]

Trademark *dilution* occurs when a trademark is used, without authorization, in a way that diminishes the distinctive quality of the mark. Unlike trademark infringement, a dilution cause of action does not require proof that consumers are likely to be confused by a connection between the unauthorized use and the mark. For this reason, the products (or services) involved do not have to be similar.

Trade Secrets

Some business processes and information that are not (or cannot be) patented, copyrighted, or trademarked are nevertheless protected against appropriation by a competitor as trade secrets. **Trade secrets** consist of customer lists, plans, research and development, pricing information, marketing techniques, production techniques, and generally anything that makes an individual company unique and that would have value to a competitor.

WHAT IS PROTECTED?   Unlike copyright and trademark protection, protection of trade secrets extends both to ideas and to their expression. (For this reason, and because a trade secret involves no registration or filing requirements, trade secret protection may be well suited for software.) Of course, the secret formula, method, or other information must be disclosed to some persons, particularly to key employees. Businesses generally attempt to protect their trade secrets by having all employees who use the process or information agree in their contracts, or in confidentiality agreements, never to divulge it.

MISAPPROPRIATION OF TRADE SECRETS.   One who discloses or uses another's trade secret, without a privilege to do so, is liable to the other if (1) he or she discovered the secret by improper means or (2) the disclosure or use constitutes a breach of confidence. The theft of confidential business data through industrial espionage, such as when a business taps into a competitor's computer, is a theft of trade secrets and is actionable.

trade secret
Information or processes that give a business an advantage over competitors who do not know the information or processes.

✳ QUESTIONS FOR REVIEW

1. Name and describe the four basic requirements to form a valid contract. Are there any circumstances in which the court will enforce the parties' agreement even though it lacks consideration?

2. Under what circumstances are contracts that meet the four basic requirements generally unenforceable?

3. What is the UCC, and to what types of contracts does it apply? How does the UCC affect the common law of contracts?

4. What is the doctrine of substantial performance? Why is it important in contract law? What happens if it becomes impossible to perform a contract? Are there any other situations in which one's performance will be excused?

5. What remedies are available to the innocent party when a contract is breached, or broken? What is specific performance, and in what kinds of circumstances is it available?

6. Explain what is meant by the terms *click-on agreement, shrink-wrap agreement,* and *browse-wrap terms.* How are they different? How are they similar? Which of the three do courts usually enforce?

7. What constitutes an electronic signature, and what is the legal validity of such signatures?

8. What is intellectual property, and why is it an important topic in the law today? Name four major forms of intellectual property.

9. What is a patent? How does one acquire a patent?

10. What types of property can be copyrighted? Must a copyright be registered with the U.S. Copyright Office in order to be protected under the law? What conduct gives rise to a copyright infringement action?

✳ ETHICAL QUESTIONS

1. Douglas Coleman works as a paralegal for an oil company. The attorney he works for is responsible for negotiating franchise contracts with people who want to purchase gas-station franchises. Most of those applying for franchises have lawyers who negotiate for them. Bob Little is applying for a franchise without a lawyer to represent him. It is apparent from talking to Little that he does not have much education, and he has indicated that he has never owned a gas station before. He has, however, recently inherited some money, and he wants to achieve his lifelong dream of owning his own gas station.

He has been sent a copy of the standard-form franchise agreement. The standard-form contract is very one-sided and unfair to the franchisee (the person purchasing the franchise). Little calls and says that he is ready to negotiate his franchise agreement with the oil company and asks Douglas to set up a telephone conference for that purpose. Douglas would like to tell Little that he really should have a lawyer represent his interests during the negotiations. Can he recommend to Little that he retain a lawyer? Should he give Little any tips about how to negotiate a franchising arrangement with the oil company? What might happen if Douglas does either of these things? What might happen if he does nothing?

2. Zachary Daniels is an experienced paralegal at a business law firm. He has drafted numerous contracts and is given a certain amount of independence in his work. Zachary frequently meets with clients without an attorney present. After each of these meetings, Zachary writes up a contract that reflects what the client is seeking and gives it to the attorney who is handling the case, along with a memorandum explaining why he has included certain provisions in the contract. Zachary is careful not to give legal advice to the clients during such meetings.

Today, Zachary is meeting with one of the firm's long-time clients, Jack Johnson, who owns a chain of well-known specialty stores worth several million dollars. With Jack is his fiancée, Oneida Kurtz, who is foreign born and speaks little English. Jack wants Zachary to draft a prenuptial agreement for him and his fiancée. In it, she will agree not to pursue any of Jack's business assets in the event that their marriage ends in divorce. Oneida does not have an attorney and says little during the meeting. How should Zachary handle this situation? Can he draft a contract that represents the interests of both parties? Why or why not?

3. Joanne has been your best friend since the seventh grade. You and she share a lot of common interests,

including music. She writes articles for the entertainment section of the local newspaper, and you recently landed a job as a paralegal with a firm that specializes in intellectual property. One day, you and Joanne are out to lunch discussing your favorite music group. She tells you that she heard from a reliable source that the lead guitarist, Jon, is leaving the group and going "solo" and will be playing the group's biggest hits on his first solo tour. You blurt out "I know, my firm is representing the band" without thinking. Joanne then continues to question you and presses you to tell her the "scoop" about the case. What should you do? Have you revealed confidential client information just by telling her the band is a client? What might be the consequences of your actions? What could happen if you told her what the case was about?

PRACTICE QUESTIONS AND ASSIGNMENTS

1. Using the material on contract law presented in this chapter, identify which defenses the defendants in the following hypothetical cases might use to defend against an action for breach of contract:

   a. Mrs. Martinez, a Spanish-speaking immigrant, buys a washing machine and signs a financing agreement that allows her to pay for it in monthly installments. The agreement contains a clause that allows the store to repossess the appliance if she misses a payment. Mrs. Martinez misses the next-to-the-last payment. The store notifies Mrs. Martinez that she has breached their contract and that it intends to repossess the washing machine. How might Mrs. Martinez defend against the store's action?

   b. Sally orally agrees to purchase a farm from her lifelong friend Fred. She promises to pay Fred $120,000 for the farm. She trusts Fred, so she does not put the deal in writing. A few days later, Fred sells the same property to Nell for $140,000. Fred and Nell put their agreement in writing. When Sally learns of Fred's contract with Nell, she sues Fred for breach of contract. What is Fred's defense?

   c. Rob enters into a contract with Tom to sell Tom fifty sweaters in Christmas colors and featuring Christmas designs. The first shipment of sweaters is due on October 1, 2003. When the sweaters are not delivered, Tom calls Rob and learns that the factory where the sweaters are produced has burned down. Tom, who is upset because he needed the sweaters for his Christmas catalogue sales, sues Rob for breach of contract. What is Rob's defense?

2. Using the material presented in this chapter on remedies for breach of contract, identify the remedies available to the innocent parties in the following situations:

   a. Mike sells two hundred computers to Heartland University for $100,000. Mike's secretary makes a typographical error when she types the contract, keying in $1,000,000 instead of $100,000. Heartland signs the contract without noticing the error but later refuses to pay more than $100,000. Mike, taking advantage of the error and Heartland's unwitting agreement to a price of $1,000,000 for the computers, sues Heartland for the full $1,000,000. What remedy will the court likely grant in this situation?

   b. Mrs. Wilcox sells her house to a young couple, the Warners. Among other things, Mrs. Wilcox guarantees that the basement does not leak. Two weeks after the Warners move into the house, the basement floods severely during a rainstorm. The Warners are upset and investigate the problem. They learn that the foundation is cracked and that the basement has always leaked. They contact their lawyer, demanding to get their money back in exchange for returning the house to Mrs. Wilcox. What remedy will the Warners' lawyer seek?

   c. Martha discovers an old painting in the attic of her grandmother's house. Martha has an antiques dealer come to the house and appraise the painting. The dealer offers her $1,000 for it. Martha accepts the dealer's offer and signs a contract of sale. The dealer is to pick up the painting, along with other items that Martha is selling to him, on the following Tuesday. Before the dealer returns, Martha's sister says that she would like to have the painting. Martha then calls the dealer and tells him that she will not be selling him the painting after all. The dealer sues Martha for breach of contract. What remedy might he seek?

3. On Saturday, Arthur mailed Tanya an offer to sell his car to her for $2,000. On Monday, having changed his mind and not having heard from Tanya, Arthur sent her a letter revoking his offer. On Wednesday, before she had received Arthur's letter of revocation,

Tanya mailed a letter of acceptance to Arthur. When Tanya demanded that Arthur sell his car to her as promised, Arthur claimed that no contract existed because he had revoked his offer prior to Tanya's acceptance. Is Arthur correct? Explain.

4. Bernie, the sole owner of a small business, has a large piece of used farm equipment for sale. He offers to sell the equipment to Hank for $10,000. Discuss what happens to the offer in the following situations:

  a. Bernie dies prior to Hank's acceptance; at the time he accepts, Hank is unaware of Bernie's death.

  b. The night before Hank accepts, a fire destroys the equipment.

5. Jerome is an elderly man who lives with his nephew, Philip. Jerome is totally dependent on Philip's support. Philip tells Jerome that unless Jerome transfers a tract of land he owns to Philip for a price 30 percent below market value, Philip will no longer support and take care of him. Jerome enters into the contract. What defense can Jerome raise to set aside this contract?

6. Based on the material on intellectual property law presented in the chapter, in which of the following situations would a court likely hold Maruta liable for copyright infringement?

  a. At the library, Maruta photocopies ten pages from a scholarly journal relating to a topic on which she is writing a term paper.

  b. Maruta makes leather handbags and sells them in her small leather shop. She advertises her handbags as "Vutton handbags," hoping that customers might mistakenly assume that they were made by Vuitton, the well-known maker of high-quality luggage and handbags.

  c. Maruta owns a video store. She purchases one copy of all the latest videos from various video manufacturers. Then, using blank videotapes, she makes copies to rent or sell to her customers.

  d. Maruta teaches Latin American history at a small university. She has a videocassette recorder and frequently tapes television programs relating to Latin America. She then takes the videos to her classroom so that her students can watch them.

7. Max plots a new Batman adventure and carefully and skillfully imitates the art of DC Comics to create an authentic-looking Batman comic. Max is not affiliated with the owners of the copyright to Batman. Can Max publish the comic without infringing on the owners' copyright?

8. Using the material on intellectual property presented in this chapter, identify the type of legal protection that applies to each form of intellectual property described below:

  a. Karen Wilson designs book bags for students. Her logo is a small schoolhouse stamped on the book bag. Karen's logo distinguishes her book bags from those of other manufacturers.

  b. Mike Pierson has developed a highly successful strategy for marketing his pizza and for locating his pizza shops. This strategy has made his company, Pizza Express, unique and prosperous.

  c. Carol Garcia writes a textbook, which is published. The publisher's payments to Carol are in the form of royalties.

  d. Dr. Alston invents a unique type of windshield wipers. He wants the right to sell his invention.

9. John and Andrew Doney invented a device for balancing rotors. Although they registered their invention with the U.S. Patent and Trademark Office, it was never put on the market as an automobile wheel balancer. Some time later, Exetron Corp. produced an automobile wheel balancer that used a device similar to that of the Doneys. Given the fact that the Doneys had not put the patented product in commerce, does Exetron's use of a similar device infringe on the Doneys' patent? Explain your answer.

✳ QUESTIONS FOR CRITICAL ANALYSIS

1. Consideration, a requirement for a valid contract, is defined as *something of value*. What items, other than money, meet this definition? How does consideration distinguish a contract from a gift?

2. Under what circumstances should courts examine the adequacy of consideration?

3. Why are minors allowed to avoid contractual obligations by canceling or disaffirming contracts? Are there any types of contracts that minors may *not* disaffirm? If so, what types of contracts, and why?

4. Legality, a requirement for a valid contract, makes contracts in violation of federal or state laws illegal

and void from the outset. Give examples of three different types of contracts that would violate federal or state laws.

5. Generally, courts hold that gambling contracts are illegal and thus void. Do you think that the advent of legalized forms of gambling, such as state-operated lotteries, is consistent with a continued public policy against the enforcement of gambling contracts? Why or why not?

6. Describe the types of individuals who might be capable of exerting undue influence on others.

7. The concept of substantial performance permits a party to be discharged from a contract even though the party has not fully performed his or her obligations according to the contract's terms. Is this fair? What policy interests are at issue here?

8. Many of our day-to-day transactions, such as buying a can of cola from a vending machine or purchasing groceries with a debit card, involve contracts. Explain how these contracts meet the requirements of a valid contract. Do they meet the requirements of the Statute of Frauds? Would a court enforce these contracts?

9. What does the Statute of Frauds require? How is it used in a contract dispute? Is the one-year rule fair? Why or why not?

10. Why are patents, trademarks, and copyrights known as intellectual property? What type of property is protected by a patent, a trademark, and a copyright, respectively? How is a trade secret protected?

✳ PROJECTS

1. Find out what the law is in your state regarding surrogate-parenting contracts. Are they regulated at all? If so, are they legal or illegal? Write a one-page paper summarizing your state's law on this topic.

2. Obtain a copy of the *Wall Street Journal*, and find in it an article on a lawsuit involving breach of contract. Write a one-page paper explaining the issues in the dispute. Remember to note the name and date of the article for your instructor.

3. Using the requirements for an offer that are stated in the chapter, draft a simple offer to purchase a laptop computer (used, including software) from a fellow paralegal student. Make sure that the offer is definite and certain. Then write an explanation (in one or two paragraphs) of how you would communicate the offer to the person, how long the offer would remain open, and what method of acceptance you would prefer.

4. Interview a paralegal who works in an intellectual property firm. Find out what his or her day-to-day work entails. Draft an outline covering the topics you discussed, and then give an oral presentation to the class.

✳ USING INTERNET RESOURCES

1. Go to FindLaw's site on contracts, which is located at http://www.findlaw.com/01topics/07contracts/index.html.

a. Under "FindLaw Resources," click on "FindLaw Summaries of Law—Contract Law." There, you will find a collection of articles on particular topics of interest. Scroll down to the listing titled "Contracts Law." Click on it, and browse around to see what information is available. Click on "Consideration," and read the summary provided. How many examples are given? Click on "Typical Contract Provisions," and read this section. How many different types of clauses are discussed? Note on a piece of paper the types of clauses identified.

b. Return to the FindLaw page indicated above. Now click on "FindLaw Corporate Deals—Sample Contracts," under "FindLaw Resources." There, you can access contracts listed by industry, by type, or by company name, or you can browse through the most recent contracts added to the site. Using any of the methods available, select a contract to view. Note the name of the contract and its general purpose. Does the contract use all of the clauses you noted in part a of this question (typical contract provisions)? Does it use any? Which of the typical clauses are used?

c. Return to the main FindLaw page again. Spend a few minutes browsing to see all that is available at (or through) this site. How do you think this site might be useful to a paralegal working in contract law? What links would be of particular interest to a paralegal working with sales contracts?

2. Go to the Web site of the U.S. Patent and Trademark Office (USPTO) at http://www.uspto.gov. This site offers a wealth of information concerning applying for patents and registering trademarks. You can also search existing patents and trademarks, get copies of records, and check the status of applications (among other things).

   a. You will find answers to the most frequently asked questions at http://www.uspto.gov/web/menu/helpfaq.htm#a29. Browse through the questions and answers for a few minutes, and then answer the following questions.

      1. What are the two categories of patents that are available? Briefly describe them.

      2. On average, how long does it take for a patent application to be processed?

      3. How long does it take to register a trademark?

      4. Where is the U.S. Patent and Trademark Office located?

5. Can you download the forms to apply for a patent or register a trademark?

6. Can you apply for a patent electronically?

7. Can you apply for trademark protection electronically?

   b. Although paralegals may fill out trademark registration documents, only paralegals who are authorized as "agents" by the USPTO can complete patent applications. You can find information about becoming a patent agent at http://www.uspto.gov/go/oed. Go to that page, and scroll down to the most recent general requirements bulletin. Click on it, and skim through the document. What is required generally to become an agent? Must the applicant meet certain minimum educational requirements? Take a test? Pay a fee? Write a one-page summary of your findings. Conclude by stating whether you might be interested in becoming a patent agent in the future.

END NOTES

1. See Section 204 of Article 2 of the Uniform Commercial Code (UCC)—or, as citations to the UCC are usually given, UCC 2–204. You can access the UCC and its provisions by going to the Web site given in this chapter in the *On the Web* feature on page 255.

2. Some offers are considered irrevocable—that is, they cannot be revoked by the offeror. For example, UCC 2–205 provides that a "merchant's firm offer," which arises when a merchant-offeror gives assurances in a signed writing that the offer will remain open, cannot be revoked during the time period stated in the offer or, if no time period is stated, for a reasonable period of time.

3. The name is misleading because the statute does not apply to fraud. Neither does it invalidate any type of contract. Rather, it denies *enforceability* to certain contracts that do not comply with its requirements in an effort to prevent fraud in the enforcement of contracts.

4. The Thirteenth Amendment to the U.S. Constitution prohibits involuntary servitude, and thus a court will not order a person to perform under a personal-service contract. A court may grant an order (injunction) prohibiting that person from engaging in similar contracts in the future for a period of time, however.

5. Similarly, courts often refuse to order specific performance of construction contracts because courts are not set up to operate as construction supervisors or engineers.

6. UETA 102(8).

7. 15 U.S.C. Sections 7001 *et seq.*

8. The E-SIGN Act applies only to agreements covered by Articles 2 and 2A and UCC 1–107 and 1–206.

9. 17 U.S.C. Sections 101 *et seq.*

10. 17 U.S.C. Section 107.

11. *Ringling Bros.–Barnum & Bailey, Combined Shows, Inc. v. Utah Division of Travel Development*, 935 F.Supp. 763 (E.D.Va. 1996); *cert.* denied, 528 U.S. 923, 120 S.Ct. 286, 145 L.Ed.2d 239 (1999).

REAL PROPERTY, ESTATES, AND FAMILY LAW

Chapter Outline

※ INTRODUCTION ※ REAL PROPERTY

※ WILLS, TRUSTS, AND ESTATES ※ FAMILY LAW

After completing this chapter, you will know:

- The difference between real property and personal property.

- How one acquires, holds, and transfers ownership rights in property and what procedures are involved in the sale of real estate.

- Devices used in estate planning and the laws and procedures that come into play when property is transferred on a person's death.

- The legal rights and obligations of parents and children.

- How marital property and debts are divided when a marriage is dissolved.

INTRODUCTION

As a paralegal, you will find that much of the legal work in this country involves activities in which every person, or nearly every person, engages at some point. For example, most people purchase a home within their lifetimes. Those who do not, rent. Nearly everyone gets married or has children, and everyone dies. In this chapter, you will learn about the sale and lease of real property, what happens to people's property when they die, and what legal rights and responsibilities are inherent in getting married and having children.

Although the three topics examined in this chapter are distinct bodies of law, in the real world they are often interrelated. For example, how real property is owned will affect who inherits the property if the owner dies. Similarly, if an illegitimate child's biological father dies, whether the child is entitled to inherit from the father's estate will depend on whether family law procedures have established the father's relationship to that child. Divorce also deals with division of property, and paralegals often are asked to draft deeds that transfer the title of property after a divorce judgment. Many paralegals today specialize in real estate, estate planning, and family law (as discussed in Chapter 2). Even paralegals working in other areas of practice will profit from a basic understanding of the legal concepts presented in this chapter.

REAL PROPERTY

From an early period, the law has divided property into two classifications: real property and personal property. **Real property,** or *real estate,* is land and all things attached to the land (such as trees and buildings), as well as the minerals below the surface of the land and the air above the land. **Personal property** is all other property. Personal property can be either tangible or intangible. *Tangible* personal property, such as a television set or a car, has physical substance. *Intangible* personal property represents a set of rights and interests but has no real physical existence. Stocks, bonds, and intellectual property rights (discussed in Chapter 8) are examples of intangible personal property.

real property
Immovable property consisting of land and the buildings and plant life thereon.

personal property
Any property that is not real property. Generally, any property that is movable or intangible is classified as personal property.

Ownership Rights in Property

Property ownership is often viewed as a "bundle of rights." One who owns the entire bundle of rights—ownership rights to the greatest degree possible—is said to own the property in **fee simple.**

※   **An owner in fee simple is entitled to use, possess, or dispose of the real or personal property (by sale, gift, or other means) however he or she chooses during his or her lifetime. On the owner's death, the interests in the property descend to the owner's heirs.**

Of course, those who own real property even in fee simple may be subject to certain restrictions on their right to use the property absolutely as they choose. For example, zoning laws may prohibit an owner of property in a given area from conducting certain types of activities (such as running a business) on the property. Also, under its power of **eminent domain,** the government has a right to take private property for public use (for a highway, for example), as long as the government compensates the owner for the value of the land taken.

Property owned in fee simple may also be subject to an **easement,** which is the right of another to use the owner's land for a limited purpose—a neighbor's right

fee simple
Ownership rights entitling the holder to use, possess, or dispose of the property however he or she chooses during his or her lifetime.

eminent domain
The power of a government to take land for public use from private citizens for just compensation.

easement
The right of a person to make limited use of another person's real property without taking anything from the property.

to use the land to reach a roadway, for example, or a utility company's right to erect and maintain power lines and poles or gas lines on the land.

In contrast to ownership in fee simple, other forms of ownership, including those discussed below, involve limited ownership rights.

CONCURRENT OWNERSHIP.   Persons who share the bundle of ownership rights to either real or personal property are said to be concurrent owners. There are two principal types of concurrent ownership: tenancy in common and joint tenancy.

tenancy in common
A form of co-ownership of property in which each party owns an undivided interest that passes to his or her heirs at death.

A **tenancy in common** is a form of co-ownership in which two or more persons own undivided interests in certain property. The interest is undivided because each tenant has rights in the whole property (not just one-half, for example). If a tenant in common dies, the tenant's ownership rights pass to his or her heirs.

joint tenancy
The joint ownership of property by two or more co-owners in which each co-owner owns an undivided portion of the property. On the death of one of the joint tenants, his or her interest automatically passes to the surviving joint tenant or tenants.

A **joint tenancy** is also a form of co-ownership in which two or more persons own undivided interests in property. The key feature of a joint tenancy is the "right of survivorship." When a joint tenant dies, that tenant's interest passes to the surviving joint tenant or tenants and not to the deceased tenant's heirs, as it would with a tenancy in common. If a joint tenant transfers his or her interest in the property while he or she is living, the joint tenancy terminates. The new co-owner (the one to whom the rights were transferred) and the other tenant or tenants become tenants in common.

Two other types of concurrent ownership take the form of a tenancy by the entirety and community property. A *tenancy by the entirety* is a form of co-ownership by husbands and wives that is similar to a joint tenancy, except that the spouses cannot separately transfer their interests in the property during their lifetimes. In a few states, husbands and wives can hold property as community property. In those states, *community property* is all property acquired during the marriage; each spouse technically owns an undivided one-half interest in the property.

LIFE ESTATES.   A *life estate* is an interest in real property that is transferred to another for the life of that individual. A conveyance "to Allison for her life" creates a life estate. In a life estate, the life tenant cannot injure the land in a manner that would adversely affect its value for the owner of the future interest in it.

FUTURE INTERESTS.   When someone who owns real property in fee simple conveys the property to another conditionally or for a limited period of time (such as with a life estate), the original owner still retains an interest in the land. This interest is called a *future interest* because it will only arise in the future. The holder of a future interest may transfer it to another during his or her lifetime. If the interest is not transferred, it will pass to the owner's heirs on his or her death.

The Transfer and Sale of Real Property

Property can be transferred in numerous ways. Property can be given to another as a gift or transferred to another by inheritance, leased to another, or sold. Most commonly, property is transferred by sale. The sale of tangible personal property (goods) is covered by the common law of contracts, as modified by Article 2 of the Uniform Commercial Code, which we discussed in Chapter 8. Rights in certain types of intangible property (such as checks, money orders, and other documents) are covered by other articles of the UCC. The sale of real property is governed by the common law of contracts as well as state (and, to a limited extent, federal) statutory law.

Here we look at some of the basic steps and procedures involved in the sale of real estate. These steps and procedures are summarized in Exhibit 9.1.

EXHIBIT 9.1
**Steps Involved in
the Sale of Real Estate**

BUYER'S PURCHASE OFFER

Buyer offers to purchase seller's property. The offer may be conditioned on buyer's ability to obtain financing, on satisfactory inspections of the premises, and so on. Included with the offer is earnest money.

SELLER'S RESPONSE

If seller accepts buyer's offer, then a contract is formed. Seller can also reject the offer or make a counteroffer that modifies buyer's terms. Buyer may accept or reject seller's counteroffer or make a counteroffer that modifies seller's terms.

PURCHASE AND SALE AGREEMENT

Once an offer or a counteroffer is accepted, a purchase and sale agreement is formed.

TITLE EXAMINATION AND INSURANCE

Title examiner investigates and verifies seller's rights in the property and discloses any claims or interests held by others. Buyer (and/or seller) may purchase title insurance to protect against a defect in title.

CLOSING

After financing is obtained and all inspections have been completed, the closing takes place. The escrow agent (such as a title company or a bank) transfers the deed to buyer and the proceeds of the sale to seller. The proceeds are the purchase price less any amount already paid by buyer and any closing costs to be paid by seller. Included in the closing costs are fees charged for services performed by the lender, escrow agent, and title examiner. The purchase and sale of the property is complete.

CONTRACT FORMATION—OFFER AND ACCEPTANCE.   The common law contractual requirements of agreement (offer and acceptance), consideration, contractual capacity, and legality all apply to real estate contracts. When a buyer wishes to purchase real estate, he or she submits an offer to the seller. The offer specifies all of the terms of the proposed contract—a description of the property, the price, and any other conditions that the buyer wishes to include. Often, a buyer conditions the offer on the buyer's ability to obtain financing. The offer might also specify which party will bear the cost of any repairs that need to be made. Typical provisions included in a real estate sales agreement are illustrated in Exhibit 9.2 on the following page. When signed by the buyer and the seller, the offer constitutes a contract for the sale of land that is binding on the parties.

The buyer normally tenders a sum of money, called *earnest money,* along with the offer. By paying earnest money, the buyer indicates that he or she is making a serious offer. Normally, the offer will provide that if the seller accepts the offer (and forms a contract with the buyer), the buyer will forfeit this money if he or she breaches the contract. Other damages for breach might also be specified in the agreement. If the deal goes through, the earnest money is usually applied to the purchase price of the real estate.

Once the offer is submitted to the seller, the seller has three options: he or she can accept the offer, reject it, or modify its terms—thus creating a counteroffer. The buyer, in turn, can then accept, reject, or modify the terms of the counteroffer—

EXHIBIT 9.2
**Typical Provisions in
Real Estate Sales Agreements**

- Names of parties and/or real estate agents
- Date of agreement and how long seller has to accept agreement
- Legal description of the property's location and size
- Amount of the purchase offer
- Amount of cash to be paid at the time of sale
- Amount of earnest money deposit
- Type of loan or financing the buyer plans to use
- Whether the sale is contingent on the buyer's obtaining financing
- Condition of the title and debt that buyer will assume
- Warranties of title (restrictions, rights, or limitations)
- Condition of property and zoning or use rights
- Prorations of taxes, insurance, or other obligations
- Description of any fixtures, appliances, and furnishings that will be included in sale and any warranty as to the condition of such items
- Inspection rights given to buyer (for example, water, well, mechanical, structural, electrical, termite), who will pay the costs of inspections, and whether the sale is contingent on inspector's approval
- Statement of who will bear the cost for such items as transfer fees, abstracts of title, and closing costs
- Conditions under which the offer may be canceled

thus creating yet another counteroffer for the seller to consider. In real estate transactions, bargaining over price and other conditions of the sale frequently involves the exchange of one or more counteroffers. Once one of the parties accepts an offer or counteroffer, a contract is formed by which both parties normally must abide.

THE ROLE OF THE ESCROW AGENT.   The sale of real property normally involves three parties: the seller, the buyer, and the escrow agent. Frequently, both the buyer and the seller are assisted by real estate agents, attorneys, and paralegals. The escrow agent, which may be a title company, bank, or special escrow company, acts as a neutral party in the transaction and facilitates the sale by allowing the buyer and the seller to complete the transaction without having to exchange documents and funds directly with each other.

To understand the vital role played by the escrow agent, consider the problems that might otherwise arise. Essentially, in the sale of property, the buyer gives the seller money, and the seller conveys (transfers) to the buyer a deed, representing ownership rights in the property (deeds will be discussed shortly). Neither the buyer nor the seller wishes to part with the money or the deed until all conditions of the sale and purchase have been met.

The solution is the use of an escrow agent. The escrow agent holds the deed until the buyer pays the seller for the property at the closing (the final step in the sale of real estate). The escrow agent also holds any money paid by the buyer, including the earnest money mentioned above, until the sale is completed. At the closing, the escrow agent receives money from the buyer, the buyer is given the deed, and the seller is given the money. The triangular relationship that exists among the buyer, the seller, and the escrow agent is depicted in Exhibit 9.3.

FINANCING.   Because few buyers want to—or can—pay cash for real property, buyers generally need to secure financing. Commonly, a buyer of real property

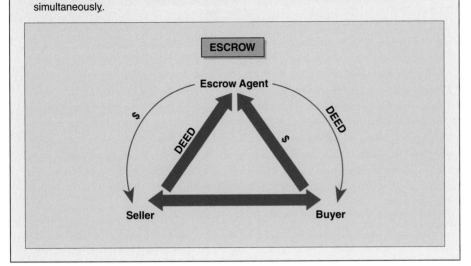

EXHIBIT 9.3
The Concept of Escrow

This exhibit illustrates the triangular relationship among the escrow agent, the seller, and the buyer in a transfer of real estate. As the exhibit indicates, the seller gives the escrow agent the deed, the buyer gives the escrow agent the money, and at the time of the closing, the escrow agent gives the seller the money and the buyer the deed—simultaneously.

ESCROW

Escrow Agent

$

DEED

DEED

$

Seller

Buyer

finances the purchase by obtaining a loan—called a **mortgage**—from a bank, a mortgage company, or some other party. When a buyer obtains a mortgage, the bank or mortgage company takes a security interest in the property. That is, the bank or mortgage company secures the right to claim ownership of the property if the buyer fails to make the scheduled payments.

mortgage
A written instrument giving a creditor an interest in the debtor's property as security for a debt.

INSPECTION OF THE PREMISES.   In addition to obtaining financing, buyers may have the premises inspected to see if there are any major electrical or plumbing problems, structural defects, termite or insect infestations, or other problems. Often, the contract of sale is conditioned on the outcome of these inspections. If problems surface during the inspections, the buyer and seller may negotiate (or may have included in the contract) arrangements specifying which party will pay what portion of the costs of any necessary repairs.

TITLE EXAMINATION AND INSURANCE.   Whenever title to property is transferred from one party to another, that transfer is recorded by the county recording office. A *title examination* involves checking these records carefully to make sure that the seller is actually the owner of the property described in the purchase offer and to determine whether claims (such as a tax lien for overdue taxes) on the property exist that were not disclosed by the seller. The title examination is an important task to be accomplished prior to the purchase of real estate. The title examination may be undertaken by the buyer or the buyer's attorney (paralegals frequently assume this responsibility) or by the lending institution, a title insurance company, or another party.

Normally, the history of past ownership and transfers of the property is already summarized in a document called an *abstract,* which may be in the possession of the seller (or the holder of the seller's mortgage or other company or institution). After examining the abstract, the title examiner gives an opinion as to the validity of the title. Title examinations are not foolproof, though, and buyers of real property generally purchase title insurance to protect their interests in the event that some defect in the title was not discovered during the examination.

ETHICAL CONCERN

Accurate Paperwork and the Sale of Real Estate

A rt Guthrie, a paralegal, was drafting a real estate offer for one of the firm's clients. Instead of keying in $90,000 as the amount being offered for the property, Art accidentally entered $900,000. No one detected the error. The seller accepted the offer, and only when Art was reviewing the closing package did he notice the mistake and tell his supervising attorney about it. The seller agreed to cancel the contract (because in the meantime she had received an offer of $110,000 for the property). Eventually the client paid $115,000—$25,000 more than he otherwise would have had to pay—for the desired property. The client sued the attorney for negligence, alleging that the attorney had breached the duty of competence and seeking the extra $25,000 in damages. The picture emerging from this hypothetical scenario is clear: when handling paperwork relating to real estate transactions, as with other legal documents, the paralegal must make absolutely sure that the documents are accurate.

THE CLOSING.   One of the terms specified in the contract is when the closing will take place. The closing—also called the settlement or the closing of escrow—is coordinated by the escrow agent. At the closing, several events happen nearly simultaneously: the buyer signs the mortgage note (if the purchase was financed by a mortgage), title insurance is obtained, the seller receives the proceeds of the sale (the purchase price less the amount previously paid by the buyer and less closing costs), and the deed to the property is delivered to the buyer.

deed
A document by which title to property is transferred from one party to another.

A **deed** is the instrument of conveyance (transfer) of real property. As indicated on the sample deed in Exhibit 9.4, a deed gives the names of the seller (grantor) and buyer (grantee), describes the property being transferred, evidences the seller's intent to convey (for example, "I hereby bargain, sell, grant, or give") the property, and contains the seller's signature.

Closing costs comprise fees for services, including those performed by the lender, escrow agent, and title company. These costs can range from several hundred to several thousand dollars, depending on the amount of the mortgage loan and other conditions of the sale, and must be paid, in cash, at the closing. Usually, the buyer and seller can learn in advance, by checking (or having their attorneys or real estate agents check) with the escrow agent handling the closing, what the closing costs will be. Also, under the federal Real Estate Settlement Procedures Act of 1976, lending institutions must notify—within a specified time period—each applicant for a mortgage loan of the precise costs that must be paid at the closing.

Leases

An owner of either personal or real property can lease, or rent, the property to another person or a business firm. A **lease** is a contractual agreement under which a property owner (the lessor) agrees to rent his or her property to another (the lessee) for a specified period of time. Leases of personal property (cars or equipment) are covered by the Uniform Commercial Code, which spells out the rights and duties of lessors and lessees.

lease
In real property law, a contract by which the owner of real property (the landlord) grants to a person (the tenant) an exclusive right to use and possess the property, usually for a specified period of time, in return for rent or some other form of payment.

Leases of real property are governed in part by the common law of contracts and in part (and to an increasing extent) by state statutory law. Although under the common law, an oral lease is valid, a party who seeks to enforce an oral lease

EXHIBIT 9.4
A Sample Deed

Date: May 31, 2003

Grantor: RAYMOND A. GRANT AND WIFE, JOANN H. GRANT

Grantor's Mailing Address (including county):
                   4106 North Loop Drive
                   Austin, Travis County, Texas
Grantee: DAVID F. FRIEND AND WIFE, JOAN E. FRIEND, AS
                   JOINT TENANTS WITH RIGHT OF SURVIVORSHIP
Grantee's Mailing Address (including county):
                   5929 Fuller Drive
                   Austin, Travis County, Texas

Consideration:
For and in consideration of the sum of Ten and No/100 Dollars ($10.00) and other
valuable consideration to the undersigned paid by the grantees herein named, the receipt
of which is hereby acknowledged, and for which no lien is retained, either express or
implied.

Property (including any improvements):
Lot 23, Block "A", Northwest Hills, Green Acres Addition, Phase 4, Travis County, Texas,
according to the map or plat of record in volume 22, pages 331-336, of the Plat Records
of Travis County, Texas.

Reservations from and Exceptions to Conveyance and Warranty:

This conveyance with its warranty is expressly made subject to the following:
Easements and restrictions of record in volume 7863, page 53, volume 8430, page 35,
volume 8133, page 152, of the Real Property Records of Travis County, Texas; and to
any other restrictions and easements affecting said property which are of record in
Travis County, Texas.

   Grantor, for the consideration and subject to the reservations from and exceptions to conveyance and
warranty, grants, sells, and conveys to Grantee the property, together with all and singular the rights and
appurtenances thereto in any wise belonging, to have and hold it to Grantee, Grantee's heirs, executors,
administrators, successors, or assigns forever. Grantor binds Grantor and Grantor's heirs, executors,
administrators, and successors to warrant and forever defend all and singular the property to Grantee and
Grantee's heirs, executors, administrators, successors, and assigns against every person whomsoever
lawfully claiming or to claim the same or any part thereof, except as to the reservations from and exceptions
to conveyance and warranty.

When the context requires, singular nouns and pronouns include the plural.

                                          BY: *Raymond A. Grant*
                                               Raymond A. Grant
                                          BY: *JoAnn H. Grant*
                                               JoAnn H. Grant

STATE OF TEXAS
COUNTY OF TRAVIS
   This instrument was acknowledged before me on the   31st   day of   May 2003
by   Raymond A. and JoAnn H. Grant

                                          Rosemary Potter
                                          Notary Public, State of Texas
                                          Notary's name (printed): ROSEMARY POTTER

Notary Seal

                                          Notary's commission expires: 1/31/2006

On the Web
If you are
interested in
learning why
the Real Estate Settlement
Procedures Act of 1976 was
passed and what it requires
of lending institutions, you
can find the act online at
**http://www.law.cornell.edu/
uscode/12/2601.shtml.**

may have difficulty proving its existence. In most states, statutes mandate that
leases exceeding one year's duration must be in writing. When real property is
leased, the lessor (landlord) retains ownership rights to the property, but the lessee
(tenant) obtains the right to the exclusive possession of the property. Most leases,
however, give the landlord the right to come onto the property for certain purposes—to make repairs, for example.

PARALEGAL PROFILE

Real Estate Paralegal

CAROL D. HOLLER, *a Certified Legal Assistant Specialist (CLAS), has worked in the largest law firm in Fort Lauderdale, Florida, for more than fifteen years and practices in the area of commercial real estate. She is also the supervisor in the real estate department in her firm and oversees fourteen real estate paralegals.*

Holler started her career in law with a small law firm in Towson, Maryland. The firm performed all of the closings for a Maryland savings and loan association. Holler's career took her to various law firms and corporations throughout the country, but her work always dealt primarily with real estate. This extensive experience, coupled with a real estate sales and appraisal background, has proved invaluable in her paralegal career.

Holler has been actively involved in Florida Legal Assistants, Inc., as its president for two years and in numerous other board positions. She has also served on the Continuing Education Council of the National Association of Legal Assistants, Inc., for many years.

What do you like best about your work?

"The everyday challenges of different real property issues keep my work varied and interesting. The variety of problems with each commercial real property transaction makes every closing exciting and new; I never get bored with the work. I feel this is one of the best parts about my work because I am constantly learning something new. Additionally, there is a great deal of client contact as well as contact with opposing counsel."

What is the greatest challenge that you face in your area of work?

"Millions of real property issues and people problems are associated with real property. Every day, we learn of another problem on a parcel of property, caused by either humans or the environment. Our job is to find a resolution to the problem and to create a smooth and pleasant closing for our client. Many of our clients feel that we are miracle workers, and keeping them thinking that way is the greatest challenge of my job."

What advice do you have for would-be paralegals in your area of work?

"When I have the opportunity to discuss becoming a paralegal with would-be paralegals (and it seems these opportunities are frequent), I tell them to take any job they can get in a law firm or title company and become a sponge—absorb everything they can from the people that work there and volunteer for everything they can to learn more. Prior knowledge is one of the best things you can have when you are finding a better job. Use your prior work experiences to build into the position you ultimately want."

What are some tips for success as a paralegal in your area of work?

"Knowledge, knowledge, knowledge are the best tips for success in my area of work. Much of this comes from years of experience and from handling a variety of transactions. Do not get stuck in a job where you are not continuously learning something new. Take the knowledge you have gained from one job and move on to something better and more challenging; keep the learning curve always moving upward."

> **"Do not get stuck in a job where you are not continuously learning something new."**

Paralegals frequently draft or review lease agreements for clients (or for corporate employers), and you should be familiar with the types of terms that are typically included in a lease agreement, or contract. Normally, a lease contract will specify the names of the lessor and lessee, the location of the premises being leased, the amount of rent to be paid by the lessee, the duration of the lease, and the respective rights and duties of the parties in regard to the use and maintenance of the leased premises. Exhibit 9.5 illustrates the kinds of provisions that are commonly included in lease agreements.

EXHIBIT 9.5
Typical Lease Terms

Term of lease: Indicates the duration of the lease, including the beginning and ending dates.

Rental: Indicates the amount of the rent payments and the intervals (monthly or yearly, for example) at which rent will be paid.

Maintenance and use of leased premises: Describes which areas will be repaired and maintained by the landlord and which by the tenant.

Utilities: Stipulates which utilities (electricity, water, and so forth.) will be paid by the landlord and by the tenant.

Alterations: Normally states that no structural alterations to the property will be made by the tenant without the landlord's consent.

Assignment: States whether the tenant's rights in the lease can be assigned (transferred) by the tenant to a third party.

Insurance: Indicates whether the landlord or the tenant will insure the premises against damage. (Normally, the landlord secures insurance coverage for the building, and the tenant obtains a "renter's policy" for his or her own personal property—furniture and other possessions—that will be housed in the building.)

Taxes: Designates which party will be liable for taxes or special assessments on the property. (Normally, the landlord assumes this responsibility, but in some commercial leases, the tenant agrees to take on this obligation.)

Destruction: States what will happen in the event that the premises are totally destroyed by fire or other casualty.

Quiet enjoyment: A covenant (promise) by the landlord that the tenant shall possess and enjoy the premises without interference by any third party.

Termination: Usually specifies that the tenant's right to possession of the premises ends when the lease expires.

Renewal: Indicates that the tenant has an option to renew the lease if the landlord is notified of the intent to renew within a certain period of time (such as one month or three months) before the lease expires.

Property Law and the Paralegal

Paralegals frequently undertake tasks that require an understanding of the law governing real property. If you work for a small legal practice, some of your work may involve assisting your supervising attorney in handling real estate transactions. If you work for a law firm (or a department within a law firm) that specializes in real estate transactions, you will have extensive contact with buyers and sellers of real property, as well as with real estate agents, title companies, banking institutions that finance real estate purchases, and the attorneys and paralegals who work on behalf of the other parties in real estate sales.

If a real estate agent is involved, the agent will assist the seller or the buyer in drawing up a purchase contract, in arranging for inspections, in having the title examined and title insurance procured, and in preparing the closing papers. In this situation, your job will be to assist the attorney in verifying, on behalf of your

DEVELOPING PARALEGAL SKILLS
Reviewing the Closing Package

Andy Casmis, a paralegal, is reviewing a closing package for his supervising attorney, a sole practitioner. Andy's job is to request the closing package from the lender and review it before the closing takes place. The closing package consists of the purchaser's requirements, closing statement, settlement statement, deed, bill of sale, mortgage documents, and title insurance policy. Andy needs to make sure that there are no mistakes in the closing documents.

CHECKLIST FOR REVIEWING A CLOSING PACKAGE

- Order the closing package as far in advance as possible.
- Set aside uninterrupted time for reviewing the closing package.

- Review the address and legal description of the property in the mortgage note and the deed for accuracy.
- Using a calculator, review the purchaser's requirements sheet, the closing statement, the bill of sale, and the mortgage documents to make sure that there are no numerical errors.
- Review each document to make sure that the parties' names are listed and spelled correctly.
- Review the deed to ensure that the ownership rights are accurately listed and that the names are correct.
- Contact the client and remind him or her of the items that need to be brought to the closing.

client, that all of the documents needed have been prepared and that the documents contain the correct purchase price, mortgage amount, property description, and other terms. Generally, you will be responsible for making sure that the documents are in order and that the client's interests are fully protected.

Here are just some of the types of tasks that you might perform as a real estate paralegal working for a law firm:

- Interview a client who wants to buy or sell property.
- Assist the client with the preliminary negotiations (offers and counteroffers) leading up to the purchase contract.
- Draft the offers and counteroffers, as well as other documents necessary to the sale.
- Conduct a title examination by going to the county courthouse and examining previous property transfers.
- Obtain or create a title abstract.
- Contact the title company to arrange for the closing.
- Handle the escrow account.
- Attend the closing. (In some states, paralegals are allowed to represent clients at closings.)

Corporations also purchase and sell property, and some larger corporations have real estate groups within their legal departments. If you work for a corporation that buys and sells a significant amount of property, your employer will be the "client," and you will perform similar tasks on the corporation's behalf.

The law governing real property also comes into play in contexts other than real estate purchases or sales. If you work in the area of probate administration, for example, you will need to have an understanding of how ownership rights in property are acquired and transferred.

ETHICAL CONCERN
Wills and Paralegal Supervision

It goes without saying that wills must accurately reflect the testator's wishes and that special care must be exercised in preparing a client's will. After all, unless the will is modified or revoked, it is indeed the "final word" on how the testator intends his or her property to be distributed. You will rest easier if you make sure that your supervising attorney reviews carefully any will that you draft, any subsequent modifications that are made, and particularly the document in its final form. Attorneys have a duty to supervise paralegal work. In regard to wills, as a paralegal you should hold your supervising attorney to this duty.

WILLS, TRUSTS, AND ESTATES

All of the real and personal property that a person owns will be transferred to others on that person's death. For that reason, the laws governing the succession of property are a necessary corollary to the concept of private ownership of property. As discussed in Chapter 2, people usually undertake *estate planning* to control how their property ("estate") will be transferred when they die. *Wills* and *trusts* are two basic devices used in the estate-planning process. We look at these devices, as well as others, in this section. We also discuss the process of *estate administration*, which involves collecting and transferring a decedent's (deceased person's) property.

Wills

As you learned in Chapter 2, a *will* is the final declaration of how a person desires to have his or her property disposed of after death. The maker of a will is also called a **testator** (from the Latin *testari,* "to make a will"). A will is referred to as a *testamentary disposition* of property, and one who dies after having made a valid will is said to have died **testate.** If no valid will has been executed, a decedent is said to have died **intestate.** When a person dies intestate, state **intestacy laws** govern the distribution of the property among heirs or next of kin.

A will can serve other purposes besides the distribution of property. It can appoint a guardian for minor children or incapacitated adults. It can also appoint a *personal representative* to settle the affairs of the deceased. An **executor** is a personal representative named in a will. An **administrator** is a personal representative appointed by the court for a decedent who dies without a will or who fails to name an executor in the will.

LAWS GOVERNING WILLS.   The laws governing wills come into play when a will is probated. To **probate** (prove) a will means to establish its validity and carry the administration of the estate through a process supervised by a *probate court.* When drafting wills for clients, attorneys and paralegals must make sure that the wills meet the specific requirements imposed by state statute. (See this chapter's *Featured Guest* article on the next page for a further discussion of this issue.)

Probate laws vary from state to state. In 1969, however, the American Bar Association and the National Conference of Commissioners on Uniform State Laws approved the Uniform Probate Code (UPC). The UPC, which has since been significantly revised, codifies general principles and procedures for the resolution

testator
One who makes a valid will.

testate
The condition of having died with a valid will.

intestate
The state of having died without a valid will.

intestacy laws
State statutes that specify how property will be distributed when a person dies intestate (without a valid will).

executor
A person appointed by a testator to serve as a personal representative on the testator's death.

administrator
A person appointed by a court to serve as a personal representative for a person who died intestate (without a valid will) or if the executor named in the will cannot serve.

probate
To prove and validate a will. The process of proving and validating a will and settling matters pertaining to the administration of a decedent's estate, guardianship of a decedent's children, and similar matters.

FEATURED GUEST: JOHN D. DELEO

The Paralegal's Relationship to the Law

BIOGRAPHICAL NOTE

John D. DeLeo received his bachelor of arts degree in political science from Pennsylvania State University. He received his paralegal certificate from Long Island University and was a practicing paralegal for two years before starting law school. He earned a J.D. degree from Loyola University School of Law, New Orleans, in 1984 and has been licensed to practice law in Louisiana and Pennsylvania.

After practicing law for a time, DeLeo joined the faculty of Central Pennsylvania College in Summerdale, Pennsylvania, in 1989. DeLeo teaches a variety of courses in the paralegal program at that school, including torts, constitutional law, evidence, and civil procedure. DeLeo was named faculty member of the year in 1990 and 1993.

Working in the legal field can be a daunting and sometimes mystifying experience. "The law" is so vast that no matter how long you study, you can never completely master it. Here are some suggestions on how you, as a paralegal, can start to get a handle on this potential quagmire.

WHAT IS THE PURPOSE OF YOUR TASK?

Whenever you receive an assignment, you should ask yourself why you are being asked to do it. What is the legal purpose of the task? The answer to this question will aid you in your work and bring things into focus.

DOES THE ISSUE RELATE TO PROCEDURAL OR SUBSTANTIVE LAW?

Also ask yourself whether the issue relates to procedural or substantive law. Procedural law concerns the method of enforcing legal rights. Substantive law defines what those rights are. Examples of substantive law are contract law, tort law, and property law. You will learn more about these areas of law in your paralegal program. Procedural law involves knowing the appropriate court in which to file a case, the

---

On the Web
To learn more about wills and probate procedures, you can access the UPC online at **http://www.law.cornell.edu/uniform/probate.html**.

On the Web
To find the wills of more than a hundred famous people from 1493 to the present, go to **http://www.ca-probate.com/wills.htm**.

of conflicts in settling estates and relaxes some of the requirements for a valid will contained in earlier state laws. Like other "uniform" laws, the UPC is a model act that does not become law in a state until adopted by that state's legislature. Many states have enacted some part of the UPC and incorporated it into their own probate codes. Nonetheless, inheritance laws vary widely among states, and paralegals should always check the particular laws of the state involved.

REQUIREMENTS FOR A VALID WILL.   A will must comply with state statutory requirements and formalities. If it does not, it will be declared void, and the decedent's property will be distributed according to state intestacy laws. Generally, most states uphold the following basic requirements for executing a will:

- *The testator must have testamentary capacity.* In other words, the testator must be of legal age (usually eighteen) and sound mind *at the time the will is made.*
- *Generally, a will must be in writing.* In some states, a will can be handwritten. In a few states, oral "deathbed" wills, made before witnesses, that dispose of personal property are permitted.
- *A will must be signed by the testator, generally at the end of the document.*
- *A will must be witnessed.* The number of witnesses (often two, sometimes three), their qualifications, and the manner in which the witnessing must be done are generally determined by state law.

---

appropriate time for filing various documents relating to litigation, and other rules. With the procedural and substantive distinction in mind, you can better separate and analyze the issues of the case. It is also important to know that when you do legal research, you will use different references for procedural issues than for substantive issues.

BE AWARE OF THE LARGER PICTURE

A key factor in paralegal work is the ability to be aware of the overarching situation in any case on which you are assigned to work. Different rules and procedures apply depending on the facts of the case before you. When working on a file, you should know, for example, that state law governs the areas of real property, estates, and family law. You must know what rules apply in your state and which

courts in your state have jurisdiction over the case on which you are working. The answers to these questions will direct your actions and your work on the case.

For example, many states have created special courts to deal with estates. These courts are often called surrogate court, probate court or orphan's court. These courts in turn will publish special rules of court to govern procedures in these courts. You must study the court system in your state and follow the rules of these special courts.

If you are working on a divorce case you may be confronted with such issues as the type of divorce, the distribution to the spouses of marital property, alimony, and child custody. Again, the law of the state in which you practice will govern the resolution of these issues and the court in your state system will have formulated rules of procedure on how to

> **"A key factor in paralegal work is the ability to be aware of the overarching situation in any case on which you are assigned to work."**

proceed in that court. Be sure you follow the rules of procedure. There is no worse feeling than to have done what you think is a great job on a case, and then have the document rejected by the court for not following one of its procedural rules.

Generally, a paralegal who can keep in mind the larger framework of an issue while still doing a particular assignment will be a valuable asset to a law firm. When you receive an assignment and you know why this task is important as well as the legal basis of the lawsuit, you will be able to do your job in a more effective way.

- *In some states, a will must be published.* A will is "published" by an oral declaration by the maker to the witnesses that the document they are about to sign is his or her "last will and testament."

THE PROBATE PROCESS.   Typically, probate procedures vary depending on the size of the decedent's estate. For smaller estates, most state statutes provide for the distribution of assets without formal probate proceedings. Faster and less expensive methods are then used. For example, property can be transferred by *affidavit* (a written statement taken in the presence of a person who has authority to affirm it), and problems or questions can be handled during an administrative hearing. In addition, some state statutes provide that title to cars, savings and checking accounts, and certain other property can be passed merely by filling out forms.

A majority of states also provide for *family settlement agreements,* which are private agreements among the beneficiaries. Once a will is admitted to probate, the family members can agree to settle among themselves the distribution of the decedent's assets. Although a family settlement agreement speeds the settlement process, a court order is still needed to protect the estate from future creditors and to clear title to the assets involved. The use of these and other types of summary procedures in estate administration can save time and money.

For larger estates, formal probate proceedings are normally undertaken, and the probate court supervises every aspect of the settlement of the decedent's estate.

DEVELOPING PARALEGAL SKILLS

Drafting a Client's Will

Mr. Perkins has come to the law firm of Smith & Hardy to have his will prepared. He has previously met with attorney Jennifer Hardy, who has been assisting him in estate planning. Today, Perkins meets with Jennifer Hardy's paralegal, James Reese, who will review with Perkins the information that is needed to prepare the will. After the meeting, James returns to his office, inserts a disk into his computer, and begins drafting Perkins's will. Later in the week, after going over the will with Jennifer Hardy, James will meet with Perkins so that Perkins can review and sign the will.

CHECKLIST FOR DRAFTING A WILL

- Start with a standard will form.
- Review each provision, or clause, in the standard form.
- Input the client's name, address, and other information.
- Modify the clauses as necessary to fit the client's needs.
- Specifically describe all of the client's assets in the will.
- Number each page and clause of the will.

Additionally, in some situations—such as when a guardian for minor children or for an incompetent person must be appointed and a trust has been created to protect the minor or the incompetent person—more formal probate procedures cannot be avoided. Formal probate proceedings may take several months to complete. As a result, a sizable portion of the decedent's assets (up to perhaps 10 percent) may have to go toward payment of fees charged by attorneys and personal representatives, as well as court costs.

Trusts

trust
An arrangement in which property is transferred by one person (the grantor, or settlor) to another (the trustee) for the benefit of a third party (the beneficiary).

Trusts are important estate-planning devices that are being increasingly utilized to avoid the costs associated with probating a will. A **trust** involves any arrangement by which legal title to property is transferred from one person to be administered by a trustee for another's benefit. If Mendel conveys his farm to Western Bank to be held for the benefit of his daughters, Mendel has created a trust. Mendel is the *settlor,* or *grantor* (the one creating the trust), Western Bank is the *trustee,* and Mendel's daughters are the *beneficiaries* (Exhibit 9.6 illustrates this trust arrangement.) A trust can be created for any purpose that is not illegal or against public policy.

There are numerous kinds of trusts, each with its own special characteristics. We look here at some of the most common types of trusts.

inter vivos trust
A trust created by the grantor (settlor) and effective during the grantor's lifetime—that is, a trust not established by a will.

LIVING TRUSTS.   A living trust—or ***inter vivos* trust** (*inter vivos* is Latin for "between or among the living")—is a trust executed by a grantor during his or her lifetime. A living trust may be an attractive estate-planning option because living trusts are not included in the property of a decedent's estate that is probated.

Living trusts can be irrevocable or revocable. The distinction between these two types of living trusts is an important one for estate planners. In an *irrevocable* living trust, the grantor permanently gives up control over the property. In a *revocable* living trust, in contrast, the grantor retains control over the trust property during his or her lifetime.

To establish an irrevocable living trust, the grantor executes a trust deed, and legal title to the trust property passes to the named trustee. The trustee has a duty

Marriage Requirements

Despite the fact that many couples today live together (cohabit) without first marrying, most Americans do marry at least once during their lifetimes. Marriage confers certain legal and practical advantages. The marriage establishes the rights and duties of the spouses, as well as of any children born during the marriage. Married couples may also have an easier time obtaining insurance and credit and adopting children. Additionally, many companies offer health insurance to spouses but not to unmarried partners.

States place some limitations on who can marry. The betrothed must be man and woman, currently unmarried, not closely related by blood, and over a certain age—usually eighteen years. State laws vary, and some states prohibit marriages among those who are closely related even if the relation is only by marriage. Persons who are under the required age can marry with parental consent or if they are emancipated from their parents. (**Emancipation** normally occurs when a child leaves home to support himself or herself.) Below a certain age, such as fourteen or sixteen, marriage may be absolutely prohibited by state law except with court approval.

emancipation
The legal relinquishment by a child's parents or guardian of the legal right to exercise control over the child. Usually, a child who moves out of the parents' home and supports himself or herself is considered emancipated.

PROCEDURAL REQUIREMENTS.   Certain procedures are generally required for a legally recognized marriage to take place. The parties must first obtain a *marriage license* from the state government, usually through the county clerk's office. Many states also require a *blood test* to check for certain diseases, such as venereal disease and rubella. Some states require couples to go through a *waiting period* before getting the license or between the time of acquiring the license and officially getting married.

In the majority of the states, some form of *marriage ceremony* is also required. The parties must present the license to someone authorized by the state to perform marriages, such as a justice of the peace, a judge, or a member of the clergy. The marriage ceremony must involve a public statement of the agreement to marry. After the ceremony, the *marriage license must be recorded.*

SAME-GENDER COUPLES.   One of the most controversial family law topics today involves the ability of gay or lesbian couples to marry. Many homosexual couples live in stable, long-term relationships. Sometimes, homosexual couples hold what are known as "commitment ceremonies," which are similar to marriage ceremonies, to formalize their relationships.

Although no state legally recognizes same-sex marriages—and about twenty-five states expressly prohibit such marriages—the legislature of Vermont passed a law in 2000 permitting homosexual couples to form "civil unions." Vermont's law puts same-sex unions on a par with marriages to a certain extent. The law entitles same-sex partners who form civil unions to receive some of the state benefits available to married couples, including the right to inherit a partner's property and to decide on medical treatment for an incapacitated partner. The future of civil unions in Vermont is uncertain, however, as efforts to repeal the law are in progress. Homosexual couples in all states may provide for similar protections through contract.

Common Law Marriages

A **common law marriage** is one in which the parties become married solely by mutual consent and without a license or ceremony. At one time, common law marriages were frequent in Europe. England abolished the common law marriage

common law marriage
A marriage that is formed solely by mutual consent and without a marriage license or ceremony. The couple must be eligible to marry, must have a present and continuing agreement to be husband and wife, must live together as husband and wife, and must hold themselves out to the public as husband and wife. Only fourteen states recognize common law marriages.

in 1753, although it remained lawful in Scotland and in the American colonies. Today in the United States, only fourteen states[2] and the District of Columbia recognize the common law marriage.

There are four general requirements for a common law marriage. The parties (1) must be eligible to marry, (2) must have a present and continuing intention and agreement to be husband and wife, (3) must live together as husband and wife, and (4) must hold themselves out to the public as husband and wife. Note that cohabitation alone cannot produce a common law marriage. The parties must additionally *hold themselves out to others as husband and wife.* Note that common law marriage does not require that a couple live together for a certain number of years.

A common law marriage is legal. Once a couple is regarded as married, they have all of the rights and obligations of a traditionally married couple—including the obligation to support each other and their children. Furthermore, those states that do not recognize common law marriages nonetheless acknowledge the validity of a common law marriage that was formed in one of the states that do permit common law marriages. Once a couple is regarded as married by common law, they must obtain a court decree to dissolve the marriage.

Marital Duties

In the old days, marriages were arranged between families through private contracts. Part of the contractual arrangement was that the husband would support and provide for his wife and children. The wife, in turn, had certain duties in the home. Although we still hear the term *marriage contract,* in fact, marriage represents a special type of contract that is governed not by contract law but by the state. In the United States, each state has laws that govern marriage and divorce and establish the spousal obligations of married partners.

FINANCIAL SUPPORT.   Generally, spouses are allowed to arrange their own affairs however they see fit. Nonetheless, the law still holds that one spouse has a duty to support the other spouse and children financially by providing such basics as food, shelter, and medical care—insofar as the spouse is able to do so. In many states, this duty lasts throughout the marriage, even if the spouses are living apart. Failure to provide support for a child may be a criminal violation. Additional duties may be created by a separate agreement between the spouses. Some courts will not enforce certain types of agreements, though, such as agreements to dole out sexual relations in return for money or some other consideration.

SPOUSAL ABUSE.   Each state creates its own definition of domestic violence through legislation and court decisions. In all states, however, it is illegal to batter a spouse. Unlawful abuse has been extended to include extreme cases of harassment and threats of physical beating or confinement. In some cases, an emergency restraining order may be necessary. A **restraining order** is a court order that requires one person (such as an abusing spouse) to stay away from another (such as the victim of spousal abuse). Many shelters are available to assist abused spouses.

restraining order
A court order that requires one person (such as an abusing spouse) to stay away from another (such as an abused spouse).

Parental Rights and Obligations

Legally, a child is defined as an unmarried minor (under the age of eighteen) who is not emancipated. Prior to a child's emancipation, parents have certain rights of control over the child. Parents can direct the upbringing of their children and con-

---

ETHICAL CONCERN
Dealing with Spousal Abuse

In family law, situations often arise in which paralegals face a conflict between personal and legal ethics. For example, suppose that Lena, a paralegal, is asked to assist in a divorce case. Her firm's client is the divorcing husband. During an interview, the client not only admits to Lena that he has abused his wife but also appears proud of it. In the husband's mind, he's simply exercising his right as head of the household. Lena finds the man personally offensive and does not want to have anything further to do with him. What can she do in this situation? One option would be to explain her feelings to her supervising attorney and see if another paralegal might handle the work instead. Often, though, either there is no other paralegal available or the attorney will not agree to the replacement. If this is the case in Lena's situation, she will either have to work with the client or place her job in jeopardy. If you ever find yourself in this kind of situation, it may help to remind yourself that paralegals have a duty of loyalty to their employers. Additionally, part of the paralegal's job is to be professionally objective.

---

trol where they live, what school they attend, and even what religion they practice. Parents also generally control the medical care to be given, although a parent's refusal to provide for such care in life-threatening situations (usually for religious reasons) can be a crime. Parents have broad legal authority to control the behavior of their children and even physically punish them—so long as the punishment does not constitute child abuse (to be discussed shortly).

Parents also have obligations toward their children. Parents are obligated to provide food, shelter, clothing, medical care, and other necessities. Parents must also ensure that their children attend school (normally until the age of sixteen). If a couple is married, the law presumes that any newborn child was fathered by the husband, and the husband must support the child unless he can prove that he is not the biological father. (Some states do not allow the husband an opportunity to prove his lack of paternity, however.) Although parental duties to a child generally end when the child reaches the age of eighteen, these duties may continue for a longer period if the child is seriously disabled.

LIABILITY FOR CHILDREN'S WRONGFUL ACTS.   Generally, parents are not liable for the wrongful actions of their children, *unless the actions result from the parents' negligence.* For example, suppose that a parent permits her fifteen-year-old son to drive the family car to the grocery store by himself, without supervision, although he has no driver's license. En route to the store, the boy causes an accident in which a passenger in the other car is seriously injured. The passenger would probably succeed in a negligence suit against the boy's parent in this situation.

Parents may also be liable for their children's intentional torts. About half of the states now provide for partial parental liability for their children's intentional torts, up to a limit of about $10,000 (depending on state law).

CHILD ABUSE AND NEGLECT.   All states allow parents to physically punish their children within reason. A parent, for example, may slap or spank a child without violating the laws prohibiting child abuse. Some states allow corporal (physical) punishment in the schools. In all states, however, laws prohibit sexual molestation and extreme punishment of children by anyone. For punishment to constitute physical child abuse, the punishment normally must result in injuries—such as broken skin or bones, excessive bruising, or swelling.

Child neglect is also a form of child abuse. Child neglect occurs when parents or legal guardians fail to provide for a child's basic needs, such as food, shelter, clothing, and medical treatment. Child abuse may even extend to emotional abuse, as when a person publicly humiliates a child in an extreme way.

CHILDREN BORN OUT OF WEDLOCK.　　Today, an increasing number of children are born to unmarried parents. In response, the law is evolving to provide added rights and protections for children born out of wedlock. One important right is the right of the child to be supported by the biological father. The biological father has a legal obligation to provide support for the child that is identical to that of a married father. The obligation usually lasts until the child is no longer a minor. The mother's subsequent marriage to another man does not necessarily extinguish the obligation of the biological father to support the child. In most states, the eventual marriage of the parents of a child born out of wedlock "legitimizes" the child.

paternity suit
A lawsuit brought by an unmarried mother to establish that a certain person is the biological father of her child. DNA testing or a comparable procedure is often used to determine paternity.

Paternity Suits.　　An unmarried mother may file a **paternity suit** to establish that a certain person is the biological father of her child. If the unwed mother is on public-welfare assistance, the government may file a paternity suit on the mother's behalf to obtain reimbursement for welfare payments given to the mother. Fathers may also file paternity actions in order to obtain visitation rights or custody of the child. The paternity of a child can be proved scientifically. DNA testing or comparable procedures that check for genetic factors can now determine, with almost 100 percent accuracy, whether an alleged person parented a particular child.

Inheritance Rights.　　Under the common law, an illegitimate child had no right to inherit. Today, inheritance laws governing illegitimate children vary from state to state. Generally, an illegitimate child is treated as the child of the mother and can inherit from her and her relatives. The child is usually not regarded as the legal child of the father unless paternity is established through some legal proceeding. Many state statutes permit the illegitimate child to inherit from the father if paternity has been established prior to the father's death. Even if paternity has been established, however, the illegitimate child will not necessarily have inheritance rights identical to those of legitimate children. Generally, the courts have upheld state probate statutes that discriminate between legitimate and illegitimate children for valid state purposes.

On the Web
The National Adoption Information Clearinghouse provides information on adoption laws and links to individual state statutes at **http://www. calib.com/naic/laws/ index.cfm.**

Adoption

adoption
A procedure in which persons become the legal parents of a child who is not their biological child.

foster care
A temporary arrangement in which a family is paid by the state to care for a child for a limited period of time, often pending adoption.

In contrast to children born out of wedlock, adopted children normally have the same legal rights as biological children, including the right to inherit property from their adoptive parents upon the parents' death. **Adoption** is a procedure in which persons become the legal parents of a child that is not their biological child. Once an adoption is formally completed, the adoptive parents have all the responsibilities of biological parents. Should they divorce, each adoptive parent has all the child-support obligations of a biological parent. Note that adoption is not the same as **foster care,** which is a temporary arrangement in which a family is paid by the state to care for a child for a limited period of time, often pending adoption.

REQUIREMENTS FOR ADOPTIONS.   Adoptions are governed by state laws, and these laws vary substantially from state to state. Generally, however, there are three minimum requirements for an adoption to be legal. First, the child's biological parents must give up their legal rights (either by consent, by death, or by order of the court). The adopting parents must then follow all procedures required by the state in which the adoption occurs. Finally, the adoption must be formally approved by a judge. There may be additional requirements in specific circumstances. For example, adopting a teenaged child generally requires the child's official consent.

All states permit single persons to adopt children, but married couples are generally preferred. Although some courts have approved adoptions by same-gender couples, generally such couples find it difficult to adopt children. Several states—including Florida, Mississippi, and Utah—have enacted laws that explicitly prohibit homosexual couples from adopting children.

AGENCY ADOPTIONS.   Adoption is often done through social-service agencies that are licensed by the state to place children for adoption. The biological parents terminate their parental rights, essentially giving up these rights to the agency and authorizing the agency to find legal parents for their child. Traditionally, in agency adoptions, the identities of the biological and the adoptive parents were kept confidential. Increasingly, though, state laws are allowing for the disclosure of this information in certain circumstances. In some states, for example, if an adopted child wants to meet with his or her birth parent or vice versa, the court will contact the child or parent to see if he or she will agree to such a meeting.

INDEPENDENT ADOPTIONS.   Prospective adoptive parents may also pursue independent adoption. An **independent adoption** is one that is arranged privately, as when a doctor, lawyer, or other individual puts a couple seeking to adopt a child in contact with a pregnant woman who has decided to give up her child for adoption. These parties make their own private arrangements. Usually, the adopting parents pay for the legal and medical expenses associated with the childbirth and adoption. The intermediary may also receive a fee. Because this method of adoption has the potential for abuse, it is prohibited by some states.

independent adoption
A privately arranged adoption, as when a doctor, lawyer, or other individual puts a couple seeking to adopt a child in contact with a pregnant woman who has decided to give up her child for adoption.

STEPPARENT ADOPTIONS.   Many adoptions today are so-called "stepparent adoptions," which occur when a married partner adopts his or her spouse's children from a former marriage. Usually, in such adoptions, the parental rights of the children's other biological parent are terminated either by consent or through a court proceeding.

COURT APPROVAL AND PROBATION.   All adoptions must be approved in court. The primary standard for approving an adoption is the "best interests of the child." Because this standard is so vague, the courts have a great deal of leeway in deciding whether to place children with prospective adoptive parents. The court considers the financial resources of the adopting parents, their family stability and home environment, their ages, their religious and racial compatibility, and other factors relevant to the child's future health and welfare.

After the adoption, many states place the new parents on probation for a time—usually from six months to one year. The agency or court appoints an individual to monitor developments in the home to ensure that the adoptive parents are caring appropriately for the child's well-being. If not, the child may be removed and returned to an agency for placement in another home.

Marriage Termination

A marriage can only be terminated by the state. In other words, even though partners want to end their marriage, and even though they separate, and live apart, they will continue to have the legal rights and obligations of spouses until their marriage is legally terminated. There are two ways in which a marriage can be terminated: by annulment or by divorce.

annulment
A court decree that invalidates (nullifies) a marriage. Although the marriage itself is deemed nonexistent, children of a marriage that is annulled are deemed legitimate.

ANNULMENT.   An **annulment** is a court decree that essentially invalidates (nullifies) a marriage. This means that the marriage was never effective in the first place. Today, annulments are rarely granted. Many of those seeking annulments do so because their religion does not condone divorce. In such situations, an annulment allows a subsequent marriage to be recognized as valid in the eyes of the church.

Grounds for invalidating a marriage through an annulment are similar to those for invalidating other contracts (even though marriage is not governed by contract law). If one of the parties did not genuinely assent to the marriage, if one of the parties lacked capacity, or if the marriage was based on fraud or duress, an annulment may be granted. An annulment may also be granted if the marriage was unconsummated. Other grounds for annulment include **bigamy**, which is the act of marrying one person while already legally married to another.

bigamy
The act of entering into marriage with one person while still legally married to another.

Even though the marriage is deemed invalid, children born during the marriage are considered legitimate in the eyes of the law. Also, as in a divorce, when a marriage is annulled, issues involving child support, spousal support, child custody, and property settlement must be decided by the couple or by the court.

divorce
A formal court proceeding that legally dissolves a marriage.

DIVORCE.   The most common way to end a marriage, of course, is divorce. A **divorce** is a formal court proceeding that legally dissolves a marriage. Divorce laws vary among the states, with some states having much simpler divorce procedures than others.

Fault-Based versus No-Fault Divorces.   Until the 1960s, to obtain a divorce a petitioning party had to allege reasons for the divorce—such as adultery, desertion, cruelty, or abuse—that were acceptable grounds for divorce under state law. This is called *fault-based divorce.* Unless the petitioning party could prove that his or her partner was "at fault" for the breakdown of the marriage in one of these ways, a divorce would not be granted. Eventually, changing economic and social conditions in America led to new attitudes toward divorce, which resulted in less stringent requirements for divorce. Thus arose the **no-fault divorce**—a divorce in which neither party is deemed to be at fault for the breakdown of the marriage.

no-fault divorce
A divorce in which neither party is deemed to be at fault for the breakdown of the marriage.

Today, all states allow no-fault divorces. Generally, a no-fault divorce may be based on one of three grounds:

* Irreconcilable differences (the most common ground).
* Living separately for a period of time specified by state statute (ranging from six months to three years).
* Incompatibility.

No-fault divorces make it practically impossible for one spouse to prevent a divorce desired by the other. Even in no-fault divorces, however, fault may be taken into consideration by the court in determining a couple's property settlement or spousal support arrangements.

The majority of the states permit *both* fault-based and no-fault divorces. Sometimes, a party may seek a fault-based divorce in an attempt to gain a more

On the Web
The Legal Information Institute offers an excellent tool for finding information regarding each state's laws pertaining to marriage, grounds for divorce, and child custody, as well as links to other sites related to family law issues. Go to **http://www. law.cornell.edu/topics/ child_custody.html.**

favorable property settlement (to be discussed shortly) than he or she could get in a no-fault divorce.

Divorce Procedures.   The first step in obtaining a divorce is to file a **petition for divorce** with the appropriate state court. Although the form and content of the petition vary, generally the petition includes:

- The names and addresses of both spouses.
- The date and place of their marriage.
- The names and addresses of any minor children and whether the wife is currently pregnant.
- The reasons for the divorce.
- A summary of any arrangements made by the divorcing couple as to support, custody, or visitation.
- The relief sought.

petition for divorce
The document filed with the court to initiate divorce proceedings. The requirements governing the form and content of a divorce petition vary from state to state.

The petition is served on the other spouse, who must file an answer to the petition within the number of days specified by state law. If the couple cannot agree on certain matters while the divorce is pending—such as who gets the children or who pays the mortgage—the court will hold a hearing to decide which partner should assume what responsibilities temporarily. Unless the case is settled through mediation or negotiation, a trial will be conducted, and the judge will decide the terms of the parties' final divorce decree.

Negotiation and Mediation.   Very few divorces actually go to trial. Usually, the parties settle their differences themselves prior to trial—though often only after lengthy negotiations, which are facilitated by their attorneys. If the parties agree to a settlement concerning contested issues, the agreement will be put in writing and presented to the court for its approval.

Divorcing spouses increasingly use mediation to settle disagreements, and in many states, mediation is mandatory in divorce cases. The mediator typically meets with the parties in the absence of lawyers and tries to guide the parties into agreeing on a mutually satisfactory settlement. Paralegals often assist clients during the mediation process. Some paralegals are trained mediators and conduct mediation proceedings.[3]

Child Custody

In many divorces, the issue of child custody—the right to live with and to care for the children on an everyday basis—is the most contentious issue to be resolved. In some cases, a court may appoint a guardian *ad litem* for the child. A **guardian *ad litem*** is a person appointed by the court (often an attorney) to represent the interests of a child or a mentally incompetent person before the court.

guardian *ad litem*
A person appointed by the court to represent the interests of a child or a mentally incompetent person before the court.

FACTORS CONSIDERED IN DETERMINING CHILD CUSTODY.   Traditionally, the mother almost always received custody. Mothers still usually receive custody, but courts now explicitly consider a number of factors when awarding custody. These factors include the following:

- The nature of the relationship and emotional ties with each parent.
- The ability of each parent to provide for the child's needs and education and each parent's interest in doing so.
- The ability of each parent to provide a stable environment for the child.

- The mental and physical health of each parent.
- The wishes of the child—especially older children.

In determining custody, courts may also consider other factors, such as whether one parent is a smoker (because secondary smoke can damage the child's lungs). Custodial arrangements are not permanent and may be changed by a court in view of the parents' changing circumstances.

legal custody

Custody of a child that confers on the parent the right to make major decisions about the child's life without consulting the other parent.

joint custody

Custody of a child that is shared by the parents following the termination of a marriage.

TYPES OF CUSTODIAL ARRANGEMENTS.   The parent who has **legal custody** of a child has the right to make major decisions about the child's life without consulting the other parent. Often, the parent who has legal custody also has physical custody.

Many states now provide for **joint custody**—shared custody—of the children of divorcing parents. Joint *legal* custody means that both parents together make major decisions about the child. Some procedure, such as mediation, is usually available in the event of disagreement. In some states, including California, mediation is mandatory in child-custody disputes. Joint legal custody may also involve joint *physical* custody, in which both parents maintain a home for the child and have physical custody of the child for roughly comparable time periods. Joint physical custody usually works best if both parents live in the same school district or if the child attends a private school to which both parents have access.

visitation rights

The right of a noncustodial parent to have contact with his or her child. Grandparents and stepparents may also be given visitation rights.

VISITATION RIGHTS.   Typically, the noncustodial parent receives **visitation rights**—the right to have contact with the child. The parent may get to spend weekends, alternate holidays, or other time periods with the child. The times and duration of the noncustodial parent's visits are often stated in the divorce settlement. In some situations, the court may order supervised visitation to ensure the child's safety. This means that the noncustodial parent's visits will take place in the presence of a third party. Only in extreme situations—such as when child abuse is involved—will a court completely deny visitation rights to the noncustodial parent.

Child Support

child support

The financial support necessary to provide for a child's needs. Commonly, when a marriage is terminated, the noncustodial spouse agrees or is required by the court to make child-support payments to the custodial spouse.

Regardless of the custody arrangements, a court must make some provision for **child support**—the financial support necessary to provide for the child's needs. States now have official, standardized guidelines determining child-support duties. These guidelines are often percentage formulas based on parental income. Judges must follow the guidelines, unless special circumstances justify a departure or the parents agree to a different arrangement. A child with a disability, for example, may require more support than provided for under the guidelines. Child-support orders may be revised and adjusted according to the changing needs of the child and incomes of the parents.

It is a common misconception that if one former spouse fails to meet his or her obligations under a divorce settlement or other court order (such as by withholding visitation rights), the other party can withhold payment of child support. Child support is a separate court order—it cannot be withheld because an ex-spouse does something that the other ex-spouse does not like. (Similarly, a parent cannot withhold visitation rights because the other parent did not pay support.)

Because so many noncustodial parents failed to make child-support payments in the past, state laws now provide for automatic withholding of support payments from the wages of the parent.

Spousal Support

In some situations, a divorce decree may also require that one spouse provide for the other spouse's support. **Alimony** is money paid to support a former spouse. Historically, the husband was the wage earner and was expected to pay alimony to his former wife so that she could maintain her standard of living. Today, the law governing alimony has changed significantly, largely because so many couples are both income earners. At least one state (Texas) has prohibited court-ordered alimony payments.

Alimony may be permanent or temporary. If a court orders one spouse to pay *permanent alimony* to the other, the alimony must be paid until the former spouse receiving the alimony remarries or dies (unless the court modifies the order for some reason). A more common form of alimony is temporary, or *rehabilitative, alimony,* which is designed to provide the ex-spouse with the education, training, or job experience necessary to support himself or herself. In deciding whether rehabilitative alimony is appropriate, a court usually considers the recipient's prospects of developing a new career. If the recipient is relatively advanced in age, for example, the court may grant permanent rather than rehabilitative alimony.

The amount of alimony awarded usually depends on the specific circumstances of the parties—their age, education, and incomes, for example. In about half the states, courts may also consider the reason for the divorce. If one party was more responsible than the other for the breakdown of the marriage, the alimony paid by that spouse might be higher than it would otherwise have been. Courts will also consider whether one spouse supported the other through college or graduate school in determining alimony awards.

alimony
Money paid to support a former spouse after a marriage has been terminated. The alimony may be permanent or temporary (rehabilitative).

Property Division

When a marriage is terminated, the property owned by the couple (including their debts) must be divided. **Property settlement**—the division of property on divorce—is often a main area of dispute. Although most divorcing couples eventually settle their financial disputes, the settlement reached is colored by the requirements of state law.

The way in which any court divides a couple's property depends largely on whether the property is considered marital property or separate property. **Marital property** is all property acquired during the course of a marriage (apart from inheritances and gifts received by one of the spouses). **Separate property** is property that a spouse owned before the marriage, plus inheritances and gifts acquired during the marriage. This property belongs to the spouse personally and not to the marital unit. On dissolution of the marriage, separate property is not divided but is retained by the owner.

The ownership right in separate property may be lost, however, if it is combined with marital property during marriage. For example, suppose that a wife owns a lot on which the couple builds a house after their marriage. The wife has lost her separate property rights in the land. Merely renovating separately held property (sprucing up a vacation home, for instance) may transform the separate property into joint property. Placing separate property (money) into a jointly held bank account may also transform the money into joint property.

COMMUNITY PROPERTY.   In ten states,[4] husbands and wives can hold property as community property. In those states, **community property** is all property acquired during the marriage (not including inheritances or gifts received by either

property settlement
The division of property between spouses on the termination of a marriage.

marital property
All property acquired during the course of a marriage, apart from inheritances and gifts made to one or the other of the spouses.

separate property
Property that a spouse owned before the marriage, plus inheritances and gifts acquired by the spouse during the marriage.

community property
Defined in ten states as all property acquired during the marriage, except for inheritances or gifts received during the marriage by either marital partner. Each spouse has a one-half ownership interest in community property.

party during the marriage). Even if only one party supplied all of the income and assets during the marriage, both spouses share equally (half and half) in the ownership of that property. Property owned by either partner before the marriage—and inheritances or gifts that partner received during the marriage—remain the property of that individual, or separate property, however.

EQUITABLE DISTRIBUTION.   All of the other states provide for the *equitable distribution* (fair distribution) of property to the divorcing spouses. That is, the marital property is divided according to the equities of the case (not necessarily split evenly). In some of these states, only the marital property is subject to distribution. In other states, all of the property owned by the couple, including separate property, may be factored into the property distribution. While in most cases, separate property remains with the owner, the courts exercise substantial discretion in deciding which person should receive what property. In deciding how to divide property between divorcing spouses, the courts consider a number of factors, including the following:

- The duration of the marriage.
- The health of the parties.
- The individuals' occupations and vocational skills.
- The individuals' relative wealth and income.
- The standard of living during the marriage.
- The relative contributions to the marriage (both financial and homemaker contributions).
- The needs and concerns of any children.
- Tax and inheritance considerations.

A typical property controversy in divorce cases concerns rights to the marital residence. If there are minor children, the house is usually given to the parent with custody of the children. It may be difficult to balance the grant of the house with other property (many families have few substantial assets other than their homes). Once the children are grown, the court may order the house to be sold and the proceeds divided to ensure that the property distribution is equitable.

Prenuptial Agreements

prenuptial agreement
A contract formed between two persons who are contemplating marriage to provide for the disposition of property in the event of a divorce or the death of one of the spouses after they have married.

Increasingly, couples are using prenuptial agreements to avoid problems over property division that may arise in the future. A **prenuptial agreement** (also known as an *antenuptial agreement*) is a contract between the parties that is entered into before marriage and that provides for the disposition of property in the event of a divorce or the death of one of the spouses. Prenuptial agreements must be in writing to be enforceable.

Most states now uphold prenuptial agreements, even if the agreements eliminate financial support in the event of divorce. Courts do look closely at such agreements for evidence of unfairness, though. Often courts find a prenuptial agreement is unfair if the parties did not retain independent counsel prior to signing the agreement. To enforce a prenuptial agreement, a party must also show that the agreement was made voluntarily and without threats or unfair pressure. Courts have refused to enforce prenuptial agreements in some circumstances, such as when a party was pressured into signing the agreement or when a party failed to disclose all of his or her assets.

Family Law and the Paralegal

The opportunities for paralegals in the area of family law are extensive and probably will continue to be so. The United States has the highest divorce rate in the world

TODAY'S PROFESSIONAL PARALEGAL

Family Law Specialists: Investigations

Janice Fong is a paralegal working for a small family law firm in Georgia, a state that allows both fault-based and no-fault divorce. She is working on a case for a client, Bridgett Hanson, who is seeking a divorce from her husband, a wealthy real estate developer. Janice's supervising attorney asks her to gather any facts that will establish grounds for a fault-based divorce—namely, Mr. Hanson's adultery.

MEETING WITH THE CLIENT

Janice calls Bridgett Hanson and sets up an appointment to get more details to substantiate her claims that Mr. Hanson has been unfaithful. Janice knows that this will be a difficult interview and arranges to have a private conference room, a box of tissues handy, and no interruptions.

In the interview, Janice chooses her words carefully and conveys her sympathy to the client. The client tells Janice that she knows that her husband has had an affair with his secretary. She relates to Janice that on two occasions she saw her husband's car at a local hotel in the middle of the day when he was supposed to be working. She also tells Janice that several of her close friends reported seeing Mr. Hanson and his secretary together outside the office—in restaurants, in bars, and once in the parking lot at the airport prior to one of his business trips.

Janice writes down the names and phone numbers of the friends and makes a note to speak with them. She also asks the client for the dates on which she saw her husband at the hotel and any dates on which he supposedly traveled out of town "on business" during the time he was having the affair. During the conversation, Janice learns that Mr. Hanson controlled all the couple's finances and that Bridgett Hanson never paid any of the bills, including credit-card bills (although she did use the credit cards).

LOOKING AT THE OPTIONS

After interviewing the other witnesses and reviewing her notes, Janice talks with her supervising attorney about how the investigation should proceed. The attorney tells her that there are several options for obtaining the information they need to prove adultery. The firm could hire a private investigator, could take Mr. Hanson's deposition (sworn out-of-court testimony—see Chapter 12) or the deposition of his secretary or others at the office, or could ask Mr. Hanson to admit the relationship during discovery (the formal process by which the parties to a lawsuit exchange information prior to trial—see Chapter 12). The firm could also ask the court for an order (called a *subpoena*) to request records from hotels, credit-card companies, and any other business that might show Mr. Hanson was having an extramarital affair.

DECIDING WHICH OPTION IS MOST APPROPRIATE

Janice's supervising attorney explains that while the firm often uses a private investigator's services, such services are rather expensive and may not be necessary in this case if the affair can be proved by other means. The attorney also indicates that she would like to have evidence of the affair before asking Mr. Hanson to admit it in a deposition or other discovery. The attorney says that in her experience, asking people to admit adultery is rarely productive. The attorney prefers evidence that is independent of a witness's or party's testimony in order to avoid the battle of "he said, she said" in court.

The attorney tells Janice to prepare a subpoena to obtain the hotel records. The attorney also tells Janice that the client, if she is an authorized user on any of the credit-card accounts, should be able to request records directly from the company. If the client is not an authorized user (for any business accounts, for example), then Janice and the attorney can either ask the husband's attorney to provide the records or subpoena them. Once they get those records, they will meet again to evaluate the best course of action.

REMAINING FLEXIBLE

Janice prepares a *subpoena duces tecum,* a court order commanding the hotel to produce or permit inspection and copying of the specified records. Once the subpoena has been prepared and signed by the court, Janice arranges for it to be delivered to (served on) the hotel. Janice also assists the client in filing a request with the credit-card companies to supply copies of account statements.

When the firm receives the requested information back from one of the credit-card companies, Janice discovers that Mr. Hanson charged a cruise and airline tickets for two six months ago—during a time when his wife (the client) thought he was on a business trip. Based on this discovery, Janice and her supervising attorney will need to reassess the investigation and will probably need to subpoena records from the airline and cruise companies.

(statistically, one out of every two couples who marry end up getting a divorce), and there is no indication that this high rate will decline in the future. Many paralegals work for law practices that specialize in handling divorces and legal work related to divorces, such as child-custody arrangements and property settlements.

Divorce is just one specialty within the broad area of family law, however, and paralegals often work in other types of family law, such as adoptions. Paralegals today may work for state welfare departments, publicly sponsored legal aid foundations, or groups that assist persons of low income with family-related legal problems. Paralegals working in the area of probate and estate administration also deal with questions relating to inheritance by children. Finally, paralegals who work for general law practices will likely be involved in family law matters, such as prenuptial agreements, adoptions, and divorce cases.

Because the area of family law involves many special legal areas, paralegals working in family law perform many different types of work. Here are some examples of the kinds of tasks you might perform if you work in this area of the law:

- Interview a client who is seeking a divorce to obtain information about the married couple, their property and debts, the reasons for the marriage breakdown, and their children, if any.
- Draft a petition for divorce and file divorce-related documents with the court.
- Assist in pretrial divorce proceedings, negotiations, and mediation.
- Assist in preparing a divorcing client for trial and in other trial-preparation matters.
- Draft a settlement agreement or prenuptial agreement.
- Assist in making arrangements for a private adoption.
- Research state laws governing marriage requirements, divorce procedures, child-custody arrangements, property settlements, and other matters.
- Help battered spouses obtain protection from their abusing spouses.

✳ KEY TERMS AND CONCEPTS

administrator	fee simple	personal property
adoption	foster care	petition for divorce
alimony	guardian *ad litem*	prenuptial agreement
annulment	independent adoption	probate
bigamy	*inter vivos* trust	property settlement
child support	intestacy laws	real property
common law marriage	intestate	restraining order
community property	joint custody	separate property
deed	joint tenancy	tenancy in common
divorce	lease	testamentary trust
easement	legal custody	testate
emancipation	marital property	testator
eminent domain	mortgage	trust
estate administration	no-fault divorce	visitation rights
executor	paternity suit	

✳ Chapter Summary

Real Property	Real property (also called real estate or realty) includes land and all things attached to the land (such as buildings and plants), as well as subsurface and air rights. All other types of property, both tangible and intangible, are personal property.
	1. *Ownership rights in property*—
	a. Fee simple—The most complete form of ownership, entitling the holder to use, possess, or dispose of the property however he or she chooses during his or her lifetime.
	b. Tenancy in common—Co-ownership in which each party owns an undivided interest in the property that passes to his or her heirs at death.
	c. Joint tenancy—Co-ownership in which each party owns an undivided interest in the property that automatically passes to the surviving joint tenant or tenants on his or her death.
	d. Life estate—An interest in property that entitles a specified individual to possess, use, and benefit from the property for the duration of the person's life.
	e. Future interest—An interest in property that will arise in the future.
	2. *The transfer and sale of real property*—Real property can be transferred as a gift, by inheritance, by lease, or by sale. Most of the time, real property is transferred by sale, which typically involves the following steps.
	a. The buyer makes a purchase offer, often conditioned on obtaining financing, and pays an earnest money deposit.
	b. If the seller accepts the offer, a contract is formed. Real estate agents may assist both the buyer and the seller in negotiating the terms.
	c. An escrow agent acts as a neutral party in the transaction, holding the deed and any money paid by the buyer until the sale is completed.
	d. Most buyers obtain a mortgage loan to finance the purchase. The holder of the mortgage then has a security interest in the property.
	e. Often, the sale is contingent on certain inspections of the property.
	f. A title examination is performed to ensure that the seller is actually the owner of the property and that no liens exist of which the buyer was not aware.
	g. At the closing, the buyer signs the mortgage note (if the sale is financed), title insurance is obtained, the seller is paid the purchase price (less any closing costs), and the buyer is given the deed to the property.
	3. *Leases*—The owner of real property (the lessor) may agree (contract) to rent the property out to another (the lessee) for a specified period of time. The lessee has the exclusive right to use the property. Leases are governed by contract law and by state statutes. Leases are usually in writing and must be written if the lease period exceeds one year.
Wills, Trusts, and Estates	1. *Wills*—A will is the final declaration of how a person desires to have his or her property disposed of after death.
	2. *Terminology*—A person who dies without leaving a will is said to have died intestate, and the decedent's property is distributed under state intestacy statutes. A person who makes a will is called a testator. The personal representative named in a will to settle the affairs of the decedent is called an executor. If the court appoints the personal representative, she or he is called an administrator.

Wills, Trusts, and Estates—Continued	**3.** *Requirements of a valid will*—A will must comply with state statutory requirements, which usually involve the following: 　**a.** The testator must have testamentary capacity (be of sound mind at the time the will is made). 　**b.** The will must be in writing (with some exceptions). 　**c.** The testator must sign the will. 　**d.** The will must be witnessed by a specified number of persons (usually two). 　**e.** In some states, the will must be published. **4.** *Probate procedures*—To probate a will means to establish its validity and administer the estate through a court process. Probate laws vary from state to state. Procedures may be formal or informal, depending on the size of the estate and other factors, such as whether a guardian for minor children must be appointed. **5.** *Trusts*—A trust is any arrangement by which property is transferred from one person (the grantor, or settlor) to be administered by another (the trustee) for the benefit of a third party (the beneficiary). 　**a.** A living (*inter vivos*) trust is executed by the grantor during his or her lifetime and can be revocable or irrevocable. 　**b.** A testamentary trust is created by will and comes into existence on the grantor's death. 　**c.** Special types of trusts include charitable trusts, spendthrift trusts, and Totten trusts. **6.** *Other estate-planning devices*—Several other strategies may be used to transfer property. These include owning property as joint tenants, giving gifts to children or others while one is still alive, and purchasing life insurance policies.
Family Law	**1.** *Marriage requirements*—Marriage is a status conferred by state law that establishes the rights and duties of spouses to one another and to any children born. Typically, the couple must be a man and a woman, currently unmarried, not closely related by blood, and over the age of eighteen (unless they have parental consent or are emancipated). **2.** *Marriage procedures*—Certain procedures may be required by the state in order for a marriage to be legally recognized. These procedures may involve a marriage license, a blood test, a waiting period, and a marriage ceremony, after which the license must be recorded. **3.** *Common law marriage*—A minority of states allow parties to be married solely by mutual consent and without a ceremony or license. Generally, the parties must be eligible to marry, must have an intention and agreement to be married, must live together as husband and wife, and must hold themselves out to others as husband and wife. If these requirements are met, the marriage is legal. **4.** *Marital duties*—Spouses have the duty to support the other spouse and children financially by providing basic necessities. Abusing one's spouse is illegal in all states. **5.** *Parental rights and obligations*—Parents have the legal right to control the upbringing of their minor children and to punish them within reason. They also must provide for the children's necessities and ensure that the children attend school (until the age of sixteen).

CHAPTER 10

AGENCY, BUSINESS ORGANIZATIONS, AND EMPLOYMENT

Chapter Outline

- INTRODUCTION
- AGENCY LAW
- FORMS OF BUSINESS ORGANIZATION
- EMPLOYMENT LAW

After completing this chapter, you will know:

- What agency relationships are and why they are established.
- The significance of agency law for business relationships.
- The most common forms of business organizations and how each type of business organizational form is created and operated.
- How profits, losses, risks, and liabilities are distributed in each business organizational form.
- How the government regulates employer-employee relationships.

INTRODUCTION

A basic knowledge of the substantive law discussed in the preceding chapters is fundamental for practicing paralegals. Even if you specialize in just one area of the law, you will find that legal concepts overlap considerably. This is certainly true with *agency law*, which we discuss in the beginning of this chapter. Tort law and contract law both overlap with the law of agency, as do many other areas of law, such as employment (discussed later in this chapter).

Agency is an important common law concept that permeates the business world. Because of this, a discussion of agency relationships provides an excellent background for an examination of business organizations, a topic with which much of this chapter is concerned. Following a description of the various types of business organizations available today, we look at employment law, an area in which many paralegals specialize.

AGENCY LAW

agency
A relationship between two persons in which one person (the agent) represents or acts in the place of the other (the principal).

agent
A person who is authorized to act for or in the place of another person (the principal).

principal
In agency law, a person who, by agreement or otherwise, authorizes another person (the agent) to act on the principal's behalf in such a way that the acts of the agent become binding on the principal.

The common law of agency involves concepts and principles with which all paralegals should be familiar. Agency is a pervasive concept in our society because little work could get done without agents. An **agency** relationship exists when one party, called the **agent,** agrees to represent or act for another party, called the **principal.** If you are working as a paralegal employee, in essence you are an agent of your employer. Attorneys, because they represent and act for their clients, are agents of those clients. All forms of business organizations involve agents. Indeed, a business world without agents is hard to imagine. Picture Henry Ford trying to sell all of the cars that Ford Motor Company manufactured. Obviously, other people must be appointed to fill in—act as agents—for the owner of a large company—the principal.

Employees and Independent Contractors

Normally, all employees who deal with third parties are deemed to be agents. A salesperson in a department store, for example, is an agent of the store's owner (the principal) and acts on the owner's behalf. Any sale of goods made by the salesperson to a customer is binding on the principal. Similarly, most representations of fact made by the salesperson with respect to the goods sold are binding on the principal.

independent contractor
A person who is hired to perform a specific undertaking but who is free to choose how and when to perform the work. An independent contractor may or may not be an agent.

Agency relationships can also arise between employers and independent contractors (such as real estate agents) who are hired to perform special tasks or services (such as the sale of property). An **independent contractor** is a person who is hired to perform a specific undertaking but who is free to choose how and when to perform the work. For example, building contractors and subcontractors are independent contractors because the property owner does not control the acts of either of these professionals. Truck drivers who own their equipment and hire themselves out on a per-job basis are independent contractors, but truck drivers who drive company trucks on a regular basis are usually classified as employees. Generally, courts look at the degree of control and supervision the employer exercised over the work performed to determine if the individual was an employee or an independent contractor. *An independent contractor may or may not be an agent.*

Agency Formation

Normally, agency relationships come about voluntarily by agreement of the parties. Although the parties often sign a contract (such as an agreement to list a house for sale with a real estate agent), the agreement need not be in writing. For example, if Deborah asks Ling, a gardener, to contract with others to landscape her yard, and Ling agrees, an agency relationship is created. If Ling then enters a contract with a landscape architect to design Deborah's yard, Deborah, as the principal, is legally bound by that contract.

An agency agreement can also be implied by conduct. Suppose that a hotel allows Dwight to park cars, even though Dwight does not have an employment contract there. The hotel's manager tells Dwight when to work, as well as where and how to park the cars. The hotel's conduct implies that Dwight has authority to act as a parking valet, and Dwight will be considered the hotel's agent for that purpose.

An agency relationship can also arise if the *principal* causes a third person to reasonably believe that another person is his or her agent, thus creating the *appearance* of an agency that does not in fact exist.[1] For example, Carmen, a sales representative, brings her friend with her to solicit orders from a customer and repeatedly refers to her friend as her assistant. The customer reasonably believes that the friend works with Carmen and proceeds to place orders with the friend. Carmen will not be allowed to deny that the friend is her agent. Similarly, if a principal approves or affirms a contract after the fact—by filling orders placed with a person who was not truly an agent, for example—an agency relationship is created.

Fiduciary Duties

An important concept in agency law is that an agency is a **fiduciary relationship—** one involving a high degree of trust and confidence. Because of this, certain legal (fiduciary) duties arise whenever an agency relationship comes into existence. Basically, this means that each party owes the other the duty to act honestly and to pursue faithfully the objective of the agency.

The principal is obligated to cooperate with the agent, provide safe working conditions for the agent, and reimburse the agent for work performed and for any expenses incurred while working on the principal's behalf. The agent, in turn, must perform his or her tasks competently, and must obey and be loyal to the principal. The duty of loyalty means that the agent's actions must be strictly for the benefit of the principal and must not result in any secret profit for the agent. In addition, the agent cannot represent two principals in the same transaction unless both know of the dual capacity and consent to it. The agent also has a duty to notify the principal of all matters that come to her or his attention concerning the subject matter of the agency and to render an accounting to the principal of all property and money received and paid out on behalf of the principal.

Duties also imply rights. In general, the principal has a right corresponding to every duty owed by the agent, and vice versa. If you read through your state's ethical rules governing attorneys, you will find that many of the rules governing attorney-client relationships are rooted in these agency concepts.

fiduciary relationship
A relationship involving a high degree of trust and confidence.

Agency Relationships and Third Parties

Agency law also comes into play when disputes arise over who should be liable—the principal, agent, or both—when an agent either forms a contract with a third party or causes injury to a third party. Generally, a principal is liable only for the authorized actions of his or her agent. Because the principal is frequently an employer or company that has greater resources with which to pay damages (has "deeper pockets") than the employee, the injured party usually seeks to hold the principal liable for the loss or damage caused by an agent.

> ### ETHICAL CONCERN
> # The Paralegal as Agent and Subagent
>
> Whenever an attorney agrees to represent a client, the attorney becomes an agent of the client. But what is the status of the paralegal who works for the attorney-agent on the client's behalf? In this situation, the paralegal becomes both an agent (of the attorney) and a subagent (of the client). Subagents also owe fiduciary duties to the principal. A paralegal who works for a law firm thus has fiduciary duties (as an agent) to the firm and (as a subagent) to the client. As a general rule, you should treat both your attorney and the client as principals and serve their interests with the utmost loyalty and care.

CONTRACT LIABILITY.   If an agent is not authorized to enter into a contract on behalf of the principal, then normally the principal will not be bound by the contract unless he or she voluntarily accepts (ratifies) it. An agent may be clearly authorized, either orally or in writing, to form certain contracts. The agent's authority may also be implied by custom—that is, an agent normally has the authority to do whatever is customary or necessary to fulfill the purpose of the agency. A paralegal office manager, for example, has the implied authority to enter into a contract to purchase office supplies on behalf of the firm because the authority to purchase supplies is necessary to the duties of office manager.

TORT LIABILITY.   Obviously, any person, including an agent, is liable for her or his own torts. Whether a principal can also be held liable for an agent's torts depends largely on whether the agent was an employee and whether the agent was acting within the scope of his or her employment at the time of committing the tort.

respondeat superior
A doctrine in agency law under which a principal-employer may be held liable for the wrongful acts committed by agents or employees acting within the scope of their agency or employment.

Under the doctrine of *respondeat superior,*[2] the principal-employer is liable for any harm caused to a third party by an agent-employee *acting within the scope of employment*. The doctrine imposes **vicarious liability** on the employer—that is, liability without regard to the personal fault of the employer—for torts committed by an employee in the course or scope of employment. The theory of *respondeat superior* is similar in this respect to the theory of strict liability covered in Chapter 7.

vicarious liability
Legal responsibility placed on one person for the acts of another.

Today's courts consider a number of factors in determining whether a particular act occurred within the course and scope of employment. For example, if the employer authorized the act or had reason to know that the employee would do the act in question, if the injury occurred during work hours, or if the employer furnished the means or tools (for example, a truck or a machine) that caused the injury, that fact would point toward employer liability. By contrast, if the injury occurred after work hours or while the employee was on a "frolic" of his or her own unrelated to performing the job, the employer might not be held responsible.

LIABILITY FOR INDEPENDENT CONTRACTORS' TORTS.   Generally, the principal is not liable for physical harm caused to a third person by the negligent act of an independent contractor in the performance of the contract. This is because the employer does not have the right to control the details of an independent contractor's performance. Exceptions to this rule are made in certain situations, however, as when exceptionally hazardous activities are involved or when the employer does in fact exercise a significant degree of control over the contractor's performance.

Agency Law and the Paralegal

A knowledge of agency law is important for the paralegal for several reasons. As a paralegal employee, you will be directly involved in an agency relationship, and it is to your advantage to know what kinds of rights and duties are involved in that relationship. A knowledge of agency law also helps you understand the ethical rules of the legal profession, many of which are derived from the common law of agency.

Furthermore, in your work as a paralegal, you will often be dealing with agents and issues of agency. As you will read shortly, for example, each partner in a partnership is considered an agent of every other partner in the firm and thus has fiduciary duties to the other partners. Corporate officers (such as corporate presidents and vice presidents) are agents of the corporation and, as such, assume the fiduciary duties that arise in agency relationships. Paralegals who work on behalf of corporate clients or who specialize in the area of corporate law will find that agency law permeates the corporate environment.

For paralegals working in the employment context, the doctrine of *respondeat superior* is particularly important because the outcome of many employment cases is influenced by this legal concept. For example, when an employee sues an employer for a supervisor's harassment, the employer may have to pay damages to the employee even though the employer was unaware of the supervisor's actions.

> **On the Web**
> To learn more about how agency doctrines apply to sexual harassment in today's workplace, access the Supreme Court opinions at **http://www.findlaw.com**, and browse through the following two cases decided by the Court in 1998: *Burlington Industries, Inc. v. Ellerth* and *Faragher v. City of Boca Raton.*

FORMS OF BUSINESS ORGANIZATION

Traditionally, there were three basic forms of business organization: the sole proprietorship, the partnership, and the corporation. These forms continue to be used. In addition, today's business owners and professionals are turning to newer, alternative business organizational forms known as limited liability companies and limited liability partnerships.

Each business form involves different relationships, rights, obligations, and regulatory schemes. In your work as a paralegal, you will want to have some idea of what these rights and duties are when you work on behalf of clients.

Sole Proprietorships

Remember from Chapter 4 that the simplest form of business is the *sole proprietorship,* in which one person—the sole proprietor—owns the business. The sole proprietor is entitled to all of the business's profits and bears personal responsibility for all of the business's debts and other obligations. Sole proprietors can own and manage any type of business, from an informal, home-office undertaking to a large restaurant or construction firm. Sole proprietorships are very common. In fact, they constitute over two-thirds of all American businesses. They are also usually small enterprises—only about 1 percent of the sole proprietorships in the United States earn over $1 million per year. Generally, anyone who does business without creating a separate business entity, such as a partnership or a corporation, has a sole proprietorship.

FORMATION OF A SOLE PROPRIETORSHIP.   The sole proprietorship is usually easier and less costly to start than any other kind of business, as few legal forms are involved. No partnership agreement need be devised, because there are no partners. No papers need be filed with the state (as when a corporation is formed) to establish the business. At most, there will be only minor paperwork involved, depending on the law of the city in which the business is located.

DEVELOPING PARALEGAL SKILLS

A Case of *Respondeat Superior*

Tom Mintin works as a paralegal in a plaintiff's personal-injury litigation firm. A new client, Ms. Bolls, has come into the office seeking representation and has met with Tom's supervising attorney, Jared Mills. Bolls, a single parent, and her son Steven were driving home from the grocery store one winter evening in their late-model Volkswagen. They were slowly making their way down an icy street. As they approached an intersection with a stop sign for oncoming traffic, their car was hit by an oncoming Jaguar, which failed to stop at the stop sign. The car was speeding, and the driver went through the stop sign at forty-five miles per hour. In the accident, Steven sustained a severe head injury that resulted in irreparable brain damage.

The wealthy occupants of the Jaguar, a married couple, had gone out for dinner, had several drinks, and then stopped to purchase Christmas cards for clients of the husband's employer, a multimillion-dollar business. Jared Mills asks Tom to research the issue of whether the multimillion-dollar business can be held liable for the car accident under a theory of *respondeat superior*. Tom researches the issue and learns that an employer is liable under *respondeat superior* for the negligent acts of an employee if the acts are committed in the scope of his or her employment. The employer may also be liable for an employee's acts if the acts occur while the employee is on a brief "detour" from the employer's work—such as when a paralegal employee stops by the dry cleaner's for personal reasons while on the way to the courthouse for his employer. The employer is not liable, however, if the employee is on a "frolic" of his or her own and is not pursuing work that he or she was hired to perform.

CHECKLIST FOR DETERMINING LIABILITY UNDER THE DOCTRINE OF *RESPONDEAT SUPERIOR*

- Did the employee's act constitute a tort?
- Did the employee commit the act within the course and scope of his or her employment?
- Was the act committed during work hours or after work hours?
- Did the employer authorize the act or have reason to know that the employee would do the act?
- Did the employer furnish the means by which the injury was inflicted (the car, for example)?
- Was the act committed during a brief detour from the employee's course of employment, or was the employee on a "frolic" of his or her own when the act occurred?

Because it is the simplest business form to create, persons first starting up a business often choose to operate as sole proprietors. An attorney or a freelance paralegal might begin doing business as a sole proprietor. (Recall from Chapter 4 that an attorney who practices law as a sole proprietor is often called a *sole practitioner.*)

ADVANTAGES OF SOLE PROPRIETORSHIPS.   A major advantage of the sole proprietorship is that the sole proprietor is entitled to all the profits made by the firm (because he or she takes all the risk). The sole proprietor is also free to make any decision he or she wishes concerning the business—whom to hire, when to take a vacation, what kind of business to pursue, and so on. Additionally, sole proprietors are allowed to establish tax-exempt retirement accounts, such as Keogh plans. (A Keogh plan is a retirement program designed for self-employed persons by which such persons can shelter a certain percentage of their income from taxation. The principal and interest earnings are not taxed until funds are withdrawn from the plan.)

DISADVANTAGES OF SOLE PROPRIETORSHIPS.   A major disadvantage of the sole proprietorship is that the proprietor alone, as the firm's sole owner, is personally liable for any losses, debts, and obligations incurred by the business enter-

Paralegal Entrepreneur

MELISSA L. HOWE *worked for many years as a paralegal for private attorneys before founding two paralegal-related businesses. The first, a paralegal freelance business, was opened in 1999. She sold this business in 2001 and opened a private paralegal college licensed by the Oklahoma Board of Private Vocational Schools. The college has a very successful job-placement program for students.*

Howe takes great pride in her students' accomplishments and is always willing to give them advice on how to open and operate their own businesses successfully. She is a former associate director of Women of Vision, a group that seeks to assist women in meeting their career challenges. In addition to running the paralegal college, Howe works as a consultant in the paralegal job field and consults and trains individuals on various legal software programs.

In 2003, Howe received her associate's degree in criminal justice from Cameron University, Lawton, Oklahoma. She is continuing her studies to complete her bachelor of science degree in criminal justice and plans to begin law school in the fall of 2004. Howe's latest endeavor is writing a book, The Paralegal Entrepreneur, *to be published by Delmar Learning.*

What do you like best about your work?

"I derive great pleasure from working in a business organization and assisting others with paralegal career training and employment. I am able to work with a variety of clients daily. I also enjoy the fact that I am able to use my own ideas and business plans and turn these ideas into profits. Each time my profits grow, or I find employment for a graduating paralegal student, I feel good inside."

What is the greatest challenge that you face in your area of work?

"The greatest challenge is meeting deadlines on a tight schedule. Another important challenge is staying current with certain permits, licenses, and business regulations. Sometimes it is difficult when you are very busy to take the time to complete these types of documents, but all successful organizations must update them on a regular basis."

What advice do you have for would-be paralegals in your area of work?

"You must possess excellent oral communication skills as well as writing skills. Stay on top of deadlines associated with regulations, licenses, and permits. Begin preparing these documents long before they are actually due. Preparing ahead will allow you to make last-minute changes and correct mistakes. Meeting these deadlines is very important to the organizations that need to approve or certify a license renewal."

What are some tips for success as a paralegal in your area of work?

"Tips for success are to not only dress professionally, but be professional. Stay current with ever-changing laws and administrative regulations. Make it a priority to know what type of organization you are working in. There are several types of business organization, and each has certain rules and regulations that must be followed. You should become very familiar with these rules and regulations, as well as with the expirations of certain permits and licenses. You should also have strong interpersonal skills and be able to work with all types of people. You should be a good troubleshooter for human resource and other computer software programs."

> **"The greatest challenge is meeting deadlines on a tight schedule. Another important challenge is staying current with certain permits, licenses, and business regulations."**

prise. As discussed in Chapter 4, *personal liability* means that the personal assets of the business owner (such as a home, car, savings account, or other tangible or intangible property) may be subject to creditors' claims if the business fails.

As a paralegal, if you are asked to do a preliminary investigation of a client's claim against a business entity, one of the first things you should check is the form of the business. For example, suppose that your firm's client wants to sue a business firm for damages. If you learn that the firm is a sole proprietorship, then you will know that if the firm itself has insufficient assets to pay damages to the client (should the client win in court), the firm's owner will personally be liable for the damages. Depending on what you learn about the firm's financial condition, you may want to investigate the owner's personal financial position as well.

Another disadvantage of the sole proprietorship is that if its owner wishes to expand the business, it is difficult to obtain capital. The sole proprietor is dependent on loans made by lending institutions and others. For this reason, sole proprietors sometimes decide to take on partners, who will contribute capital to the business, or to incorporate and sell shares in the business to raise funds.

TAXATION AND SOLE PROPRIETORSHIPS.   A sole proprietor must pay income taxes on business profits, but he or she does not have to file a separate tax return for the business. Rather, the profits are reported on the sole proprietor's personal tax return and taxed as personal income.

TERMINATION OF THE SOLE PROPRIETORSHIP.   In a sole proprietorship, the owner is the business. For that reason, when the owner dies, so does the business—it is automatically dissolved. If the business is to be transferred to family members or other heirs, a new proprietorship is created. Similarly, if the proprietor sells the business, whoever purchases it must establish either a new sole proprietorship or some other business form, such as a partnership or a corporation.

Partnerships

As discussed in Chapter 4, many law firms organize their business in the form of a *partnership*, which arises when two or more individuals undertake to do business together as *partners*. Each partner owns a portion of the business and shares jointly in the firm's profits or losses. Partners are personally liable for the debts and obligations of the business if the business fails, just as sole proprietors are.

The Uniform Partnership Act (UPA) governs the operation of partnerships. (The UPA is one of a number of "uniform" laws drafted by legal experts and submitted to the states for adoption. Uniform laws, like the American Bar Association's codes and rules, are model laws. They become actual law only when adopted by the states.) The UPA has been adopted in all of the states except Louisiana, as well as in the District of Columbia. A revised version of the UPA, known as the Revised Uniform Partnership Act (RUPA), has been adopted by several states, and other states are considering its adoption. Always keep in mind, however, the following rule:

> ※   **The provisions of the UPA (or the RUPA) govern a partnership** *only if the partners have not expressly agreed otherwise.*

PARTNERSHIP FORMATION.   Under the UPA, a partnership is defined as "an association of two or more persons to carry on as co-owners a business for profit." To create a partnership, two or more persons interested in establishing a profit-making business simply agree to do so, as partners. The partnership agreement can be expressed orally or in writing, or it can be implied by conduct. If the partnership is to continue for over a year, then the agreement must be in writing to satisfy the Statute of Frauds, a state statute that specifies what types of contracts must be in writing to be enforceable (discussed in Chapter 8).

RIGHTS AND DUTIES OF PARTNERS.   When two or more persons agree to do business as partners, they enter into a special relationship with one another. To an

On the Web
You can find a listing of which states have adopted the Uniform Partnership Act by going to the Web site for the NCCUSL at **http://www. nccusl.org**. Select the act title "Partnership Act," and then click on the search box. On the page that opens, click on the link titled "Legislative Facts Sheet."

EXHIBIT 10.1
Rights of Partners

PARTNERS HAVE THE RIGHT:

- To hold an ownership interest in the firm and to receive a share of the profits.
- To inspect partnership books and records.
- To an accounting of partnership assets and profits (for example, to determine the value of each partner's share in the partnership). An accounting can be performed voluntarily or can be compelled by a court order. Formal accounting occurs by right in connection with partnership dissolution proceedings.
- To participate in the management of the business operation unless the partnership agreement specifies otherwise.

extent, their relationship is similar to an agency relationship because each partner is deemed the agent of the other partners and of the partnership.

Partnership law is distinct from agency law in one significant way, however. A partnership is based on a voluntary contract between two or more competent persons who agree to place some or all of their money or other assets, labor, and skill in a business, with the understanding that profits and losses will be proportionately shared. In a nonpartnership agency relationship, the agent usually does not have an ownership interest in the business, nor is he or she obligated to bear a portion of the ordinary business losses.

The rights of partners are often written into the partnership agreement. If the agreement does not specify these rights, then the UPA comes into play (the state's version of the UPA or RUPA, as adopted). Some of the important rights of partners are listed in Exhibit 10.1.

LIABILITY OF PARTNERS.   Historically, a partnership could not be sued or initiate a lawsuit in its own name. This traditional rule treated all partnerships as aggregates of individuals. Under this rule, which is still followed in some states, only the individual partners—not the partnership—can be sued. Because this approach is so cumbersome, most states today recognize the partnership as an entity that may sue or be sued and collect judgments in the partnership's name.

A distinguishing feature of the partnership, and one that is often regarded as a disadvantage of this form of business, is the potentially extensive personal liability faced by partners for partnership obligations and for the actions of the other partners. Partners have **joint liability,** or shared liability. In other words, partners may be held personally liable not only for their own actions and those of the partnership as an entity but also for the actions of other partners.

Partners may also be subject to **joint and several liability**—*several* liability means *individual* liability.[3] Joint and several liability allows a plaintiff to sue and seek judgment against any one—or all—of the jointly liable defendants. Fault is not an issue. In a partnership, joint and several liability gives a third party the option of suing any one or more of the partners without suing all of them or the partnership itself. The third party may even sue a partner who had no knowledge of the circumstances that gave rise to the cause of action.

For example, suppose that a plaintiff wants to recover for damages allegedly caused by a physician's negligence (medical malpractice). The physician is one of four partners who own a partnership. Because partners are jointly and severally liable, the plaintiff could sue the physician who allegedly caused the harm, the partnership, one of the other physicians (even if that physician had nothing to do with the plaintiff's treatment), or all of the physicians to recover damages. The liability faced by partners is a major reason for the rapid growth of a new form of partnership, the limited liability partnership, which will be discussed later.

joint liability
Shared liability. In partnership law, partners incur joint liability for partnership obligations and debts.

joint and several liability
Shared and individual liability. In partnership law, joint and several liability means that a third party may sue one or more of the partners separately or all of them together. This is true even if one of the partners sued did not participate in or know about whatever gave rise to the cause of action.

ETHICAL CONCERN
The Paralegal as an Apparent Partner

If you work as a paralegal for a law partnership, you need to be especially careful to ensure that clients do not mistakenly conclude that you are an attorney-partner in the firm. For example, assume that you and your supervising attorney are waiting for a client to arrive for an intake interview. You are sitting in the attorney's office talking about another matter when the client arrives. During the course of the interview, the attorney asks you about an ordinance just passed by the city that might affect the client's planned renovations of an office building. Your answer indicates that you are knowledgeable in the law. The client leaves the office assuming that you are an attorney, even though you were introduced as the attorney's legal assistant. Should the client ever sue the firm and/or the partners, you may be subject to liability as an "apparent partner" if the client convinces the court that you "held yourself out as an attorney."

---

dissolution
The formal disbanding of a partnership or a corporation.

winding up
The process of winding up all business affairs (collecting and distributing the firm's assets) after a partnership or corporation has been dissolved.

limited partnership
A partnership consisting of one or more general partners and one or more limited partners.

general partner
A partner who participates in managing the business of a partnership and has all the rights and liabilities that arise under traditional partnership law.

limited partner
One who invests in a limited partnership but does not play an active role in managing the operation of the business. Unlike general partners, limited partners are only liable for partnership debts up to the amount that they have invested.

TAXATION OF PARTNERSHIPS.   The partnership itself, as an entity, does not pay federal income taxes. The partnership as an entity files an information return with the Internal Revenue Service on which the income received by the partnership is reported. The partners declare their shares of the partnership's profits on their personal income tax returns and pay taxes accordingly.

PARTNERSHIP TERMINATION.   The partnership agreement may specify the duration of the partnership by indicating that the partnership will end on a certain date or on the occurrence of a certain event. It would be a breach of the partnership agreement for one partner to withdraw from the partnership before the specified date arrived or the specified event occurred. The withdrawing partner would be liable to the remaining partners for any related losses.

When an agreement does not specify the duration of the partnership, the partners are free to withdraw at any time without incurring liability to the remaining partners. Under the UPA, withdrawal by a partner results in the **dissolution** (the formal disbanding) of the partnership (although a new partnership may arise among those who stay with the enterprise). Under the revised UPA (RUPA), however, the withdrawal of a partner causes a partnership to be dissolved only if the withdrawal results in the breakup of the partnership itself and the business cannot continue. The occurrence of certain events also results in partnership termination. The death or bankruptcy of a partner, for example, terminates the partnership.

Partnership termination is a two-step process. Dissolution is the first step in the process. The second step is the **winding up** of partnership affairs. Once the firm is dissolved, it continues to exist legally until the process of winding up all business affairs (collecting and distributing the firm's assets) is complete.

LIMITED PARTNERSHIPS.   Ordinary partnerships, such as those just discussed, are often referred to as *general partnerships*. The **limited partnership**, in contrast, is a special form of partnership involving two different types of partners—general partners and limited partners. The **general partners** manage the business and have the rights and liabilities of partners in a general partnership. The **limited partners** are, for the most part, simply investors in the business. A limited partnership may be formed, for example, to purchase and develop real estate. The limited partners play a passive role. Their funds help to finance the venture, and they receive a share of the profits in return.

The limited partner does not participate in the management of the partnership and, in return, enjoys limited liability status. Unlike general partners, who are personally liable for partnership obligations, limited partners are liable only up to the amount that they have invested. In other words, if the partnership goes bankrupt they will lose their investments but cannot be held liable for partnership debts beyond that amount.

In contrast to the informal, private, and voluntary agreement that usually suffices to create a general partnership, the formation of a limited partnership is a public and formal proceeding that must follow state statutory requirements. The partners must sign a *certificate of limited partnership*, which requires information similar to that found in a corporate charter. The certificate must be filed with the designated state official (usually, the secretary of state). In this respect, the limited partnership resembles the corporation—another creature of statute.

Corporations

Paralegals frequently work on behalf of corporate clients or on legal matters involving corporations. An increasing number of paralegals are also now working for corporate employers. As a paralegal, you should thus have a basic knowledge of how corporations are formed and operated. You should also be familiar with the basic rights and responsibilities of corporate personnel. Corporate personnel include the **shareholders** (the owners of the business, called shareholders because they purchase corporate **shares,** or stock), the **directors** (persons elected by the shareholders to direct corporate affairs), and the **officers** (persons hired by the directors to manage the day-to-day operations of the corporation).

Although it is owned by individuals, the corporation is a separate legal entity, which is created and recognized by state law. In the eyes of the law, a corporation is a legal "person" that enjoys many of the rights and privileges that U.S. citizens enjoy, such as the right of access to the courts as an entity that can sue or be sued. It also has, among other rights, the right to due process of law and the right to freedom from unreasonable searches and seizures.

The Model Business Corporation Act (MBCA) is a codification of modern corporation law that has been influential in the codification of corporation statutes. Today, the majority of state statutes are guided by a revision of the MBCA known as the Revised Model Business Corporation Act (RMBCA). There is, however, considerable variation among the statutes of the states that have based their statutes on the MBCA or the RMBCA, and several states do not follow either act.

> ⬛ **Because of this, as a paralegal you will need to rely on individual state corporation laws rather than the MBCA or RMBCA.**

We look now at corporate formation; various classifications of corporations; the rights and responsibilities of corporate personnel; and corporate mergers, consolidations, and termination.

CORPORATE FORMATION.   Generally, forming a corporation involves two steps. The first step consists of preliminary organizational and promotional undertakings—particularly, obtaining capital for the future corporation. Before a corporation becomes a reality, people invest in the proposed corporation as *subscribers*. The subscribers become the shareholder-owners of the corporation when the corporation becomes a legal entity.

shareholder
One who has an ownership interest in a corporation through the purchase of corporate shares, or stock.

share
A unit of stock; a measure of ownership interest in a corporation.

director
A person elected by the shareholders to direct corporate affairs.

officer
A person hired by corporate directors to assist in the management of the day-to-day operations of the corporation. Corporate officers include the corporate president, vice president, secretary, treasurer, and possibly others, such as a chief financial officer and chief executive officer. Corporate officers are employees of the corporation and subject to employment contracts.

On the Web
Corporate statutes for all but a few states are online at **http://www. law.cornell.edu/topics/ state_statutes.html.**

EXHIBIT 10.2
Articles of Incorporation

Filed with Secretary of State
_____, 20_____

SHORT FORM
ARTICLES OF INCORPORATION
OF
_____Hiram, Inc._____

ARTICLE I

The name of this corporation____Hiram, Inc._____

ARTICLE II

The purpose of this corporation is to engage in any lawful act or activity for
which a corporation may be organized under the General Corporation Law of
New Pacum other than the banking business, the trust company business, or
the practice of a profession permitted to be incorporated by the New Pacum
Corporation Code.

ARTICLE III

The name and address in the State of New Pacum of this corporation's initial
agent for service of process is:_____Hiram Galliard,_____
   8934 Rathburn Avenue, North Bend, New Pacum 98754_____

ARTICLE IV

The corporation is authorized to issue only one class of shares of stock; and
the total number of shares that this corporation is authorized to issue
is_____10,000._____

ARTICLE V

The corporation is a close corporation. All the corporation's issued shares
of stock shall be held of record by not more than ten (10) persons.

DATED: ____June 3, 2003_____

   Hiram Galliard   _Martha Bonnell_
   _____   _____
      [Signature(s) of Incorporator/Directors(s)]
I (we) hereby declare that I (we) am (are) the person(s) who executed the
foregoing Acticles of Incorporation, which execution is my (our) act and deed.

   Hiram Galliard   _Martha Bonnell_

prospectus
A document that discloses relevant
facts about a company and its
operations so that those who wish
to purchase stock (invest) in the
corporation have a basis for making
an informed decision.

articles of incorporation
The document filed with the
appropriate state official, usually the
secretary of state, when a business
is incorporated. State statutes
usually prescribe what kind of
information must be contained in
the articles of incorporation.

Contracts to purchase corporate shares (stock) are frequently made by
promoters on behalf of the future corporation. Promoters are those who, for themselves or others, take the preliminary steps in organizing a corporation. One of the
tasks of the promoter is to issue a prospectus. A **prospectus** is a document that
describes the corporation and its operations so that those who wish to purchase
stock (invest) in the corporation have a basis for making an informed decision.

The second step in forming a corporation is the process of incorporation.
Exact procedures for incorporation differ among states, but the basic requirements are similar. The primary document needed to begin the incorporation
process is called the **articles of incorporation** (see Exhibit 10.2 for sample articles
of incorporation for a small corporation). The articles include basic information

about the corporation and serve as a primary source of authority for its future organization and business functions. Once they have been filed in the appropriate state office, the articles of incorporation become a public record.

Paralegals frequently assist their supervising attorneys in preparing incorporation papers and filing them with the appropriate state office. (See this chapter's *Technology and Today's Paralegal* feature starting on page 338 for a discussion of the resources available on the Internet.) Also, as a paralegal, you may need to obtain information about a corporation—for example, when you are conducting an investigation. For both of these reasons, you should know what information is generally included in the articles of incorporation. Exhibit 10.3 on the next page lists and describes this information.

After the articles of incorporation have been prepared, signed, and authenticated by the incorporators, they are sent to the appropriate state official, usually the secretary of state, along with the appropriate filing fee. In many states, the secretary of state then issues a **certificate of incorporation** representing the state's authorization for the corporation to conduct business. (This may be called the **corporate charter.**) The certificate and a copy of the articles are returned to the incorporators, who then hold the initial organizational meeting that completes the details of incorporation. At this first organizational meeting, the corporation adopts a set of rules to govern the management of the corporation, called the **bylaws.** These bylaws grant or restrict the powers of the corporation.

CLASSIFICATIONS OF CORPORATIONS.   How a corporation is classified depends on its purpose, ownership characteristics, and location. A *private corporation* is, as the term indicates, a corporation that is privately owned. A *public corporation* is formed by the government for a political or governmental purpose, as when a town incorporates. Note that a public corporation is not the same as a publicly held corporation. A **publicly held corporation** is any corporation whose shares are publicly traded in securities markets, such as the New York Stock Exchange.

Corporations may also be classified as either *for-profit corporations* or *not-for-profit* (or *nonprofit*) *corporations.* Not-for-profit corporations may be formed by a group—such as a charitable association, a hospital, or a religious organization—to conduct its business without exposing the individual owners to personal liability.

Corporations owned by a small group of shareholders, such as family members, are called **close corporations,** or *closely held corporations.* Unlike large corporations, close corporations cannot sell their shares on public securities markets and usually place restrictions on the transfer of corporate shares—to keep the business in the family, for example, or for some other reason. State laws may provide more flexibility for close corporations, in terms of statutory formalities that must be observed, than for other corporations. Also, certain close corporations are permitted to elect a special corporate tax status under Subchapter S of the Internal Revenue Code. These corporations are called *S corporations.*

Lawyers, physicians, accountants, architects, engineers, and other professionals frequently incorporate as *professional corporations.* As discussed in Chapter 4, law firms often prefer to incorporate as professional corporations (P.C.s) rather than operate as partnerships.

DIRECTORS AND OFFICERS.   The articles of incorporation name the initial board of directors, which is appointed by the incorporators. Thereafter, the board of directors is elected by a majority vote of the shareholders. The board holds formal meetings and records the minutes (formal notes of what transpired at the meetings). Each director has one vote, and generally the majority rules. The

certificate of incorporation (corporate charter)
The document issued by a state official, usually the secretary of state, granting a corporation legal existence and the right to function.

bylaws
A set of governing rules adopted by a corporation or other association.

publicly held corporation
A corporation whose shares are publicly traded in securities markets, such as the New York Stock Exchange.

close corporation
A corporation owned by a small group of shareholders, often family members; also called a *closely held corporation.* Shares in close corporations cannot be publicly traded on the stock market, and often other restrictions on stock transfer apply. Some close corporations qualify for special tax status as *S corporations.*

 On the Web
For a site that offers online incorporation services, go to **http://www. bizfilings.com.**

EXHIBIT 10.3
Information Generally Included in the Articles of Incorporation

THE NAME OF THE CORPORATION

- The choice of a corporate name is subject to state approval to ensure against duplication or deception. State statutes usually require that the secretary of state run a check on the proposed name in the state of incorporation. Once cleared, a name can be reserved for a short time, for a fee, pending the completion of the articles of incorporation.

THE NATURE AND PURPOSE OF THE CORPORATION

- The intended business activities of the corporation must be specified in the articles, and, naturally, they must be lawful. Stating a general corporate purpose (for example, "to engage in the production and sale of agricultural products") is usually sufficient to give rise to all of the the powers necessary or convenient to the purpose of the organization.

THE DURATION OF THE CORPORATION

- A corporation can have perpetual existence under most state corporate statutes. A few states, however, prescribe a maximum duration, after which the corporation must formally renew its existence.

THE CAPITAL STRUCTURE OF THE CORPORATION

- The capital structure of the corporation is generally set forth in the articles. A few state statutes require a relatively small capital investment (for example, $1,000) for ordinary business corporations but a greater capital investment for those engaged in insurance or banking. The number of shares of stock authorized for issuance, their valuation, the various types or classes of stock authorized for issuance, and other relevant information concerning equity, capital, and credit must be outlined in the articles.

THE INTERNAL ORGANIZATION OF THE CORPORATION

- Whatever the internal management structure of the corporation, it should be described in the articles, although it can be included in bylaws adopted after the corporation is formed.

THE REGISTERED OFFICE AND AGENT OF THE CORPORATION

- The corporation must indicate the location and address of its registered office within the state. Usually, the registered office is also the principal office of the corporation. The corporation must give the name and address of a specific person who has been designated as an agent and who can receive legal documents (including service of process) on behalf of the corporation.

THE NAMES AND ADDRESSES OF THE INCORPORATORS

- Each incorporator must be listed by name and must indicate an address. An incorporator is a person—often the corporate promoter—who applies to the state on behalf of the corporation to obtain its corporate charter. The incorporator need not be a shareholder and need not have any interest at all in the corporation. Many states do not impose residency or age requirements for incorporators. States vary on the required number of incorporators; it can be as few as one or as many as three. Incorporators are required to sign the articles of incorporation when they are submitted to the state; often this is their only duty. In some states, they participate at the first organizational meeting of the corporation.

Jon Thomas is a paralegal in a law firm that specializes in corporate law. Jon and his supervising attorney have just concluded a meeting with new clients who want to incorporate their existing partnership. They want to use their current name, L&J Building Construction. Jon's assignment is to find out if the name is available and then, if it is, to reserve it. Jon knows that in his state he must contact the secretary of state's Department of Business Services to perform a preliminary inquiry regarding corporate name availability. He can do this in three ways: by telephone, by a search of the department's online database, or by e-mail using the department's corporate name availability inquiry form. Jon decides to search the online database at the department's Web site and discovers

that the name is available. He then downloads and prints the corporate name reservation form, prepares it, and immediately faxes it to the department.

TIPS FOR RESERVING A CORPORATE NAME

- Have the preferred name and several alternatives available.
- Make sure the client understands that the name selected may not be available.
- Determine whether the name is available before reserving it.
- Once you learn that the name is available, file the corporate name reservation form immediately.

directors' rights include the right to participate in board meetings and the right to inspect corporate books and records. The director's responsibilities to the corporation and its shareholders include declaring and paying **dividends** (payments to shareholders representing their share of corporate profits), appointing and removing officers, and making significant policy decisions.

The board of directors appoints the corporate officers, who manage the day-to-day operations of the firm. They may include a president, vice president, secretary, treasurer, chief financial officer, and chief executive officer. The officers are employees of the corporation and are subject to employment contracts. As employees, they are also agents of the corporation.

Directors and officers have fiduciary duties to the corporation and its shareholder-owners, including the duty of loyalty and the duty to exercise reasonable care when conducting corporate business. The duty of loyalty is breached when an officer or director uses corporate funds or confidences for personal gain, as when an officer discloses company secrets (such as a proposed merger) to an outsider. The duty of care is breached when a director's or officer's negligence—failure to exercise reasonable care in corporate operations or decision making—results in harmful consequences for the corporate entity.

dividend
A distribution of profits to corporate shareholders, disbursed in proportion to the number of shares held.

SHAREHOLDERS.   Any person who purchases a share in a corporation becomes an owner of the corporation. Through shareholders' meetings, the shareholders play an important role in the corporate entity—they elect the directors who control the corporation, and they have a right to vote (one vote per share) on decisions that significantly affect the corporation. They also have a right to share in corporate profits proportionate to the number of shares they hold. Shareholders do not manage the daily affairs of the corporation, nor are they liable for corporate debts or other obligations beyond the amount of their investments. Corporate owners, or shareholders, thus have *limited liability*—a key advantage of the corporate form of business.

EXHIBIT 10.4
Merger and Consolidation

A merger involves the legal combination of two or more corporations in such a way that only one of the corporations continues to exist. For example, Corporation A and Corporation B decide to merge. It is agreed that A will absorb B, so after the merger, B ceases to exist as a separate entity, and A continues as the surviving corporation. Consolidation occurs when two or more corporations combine in such a way that both corporations cease to exist and a new one emerges. For example, Corporation A and Corporation B consolidate to form an entirely new organization, Corporation C. In the process, both A and B are terminated as legal entities, and C comes into existence as an entirely new entity.

CORPORATE TAXATION.   The corporation as an entity pays income taxes on corporate profits. Then, when the profits are distributed to the shareholders in the form of dividends, the shareholders pay personal income taxes on the income they receive. This double-taxation feature of the corporate form of business is one of its major disadvantages.

Some small (close) corporations are permitted to avoid the double taxation of corporate profits by electing S corporation status under Subchapter S of the Internal Revenue Code. An S corporation, like a partnership, is a "pass-through" entity for tax purposes. This means that the corporation itself does not pay income taxes. Instead, it files an information return only, as a partnership does, indicating the corporation's net profits. The S corporation shareholders declare their proportionate shares of the corporation's net income on their personal tax returns and pay taxes on that income accordingly.

CORPORATE MERGER AND CONSOLIDATION.   As a paralegal, you may be asked to help corporate clients in procedures relating to major corporate changes, such as mergers and consolidations. A **merger** is a process through which one corporation (the surviving corporation) acquires all of the assets and liabilities of another corporation (the merged corporation). The shareholders of the merged corporation receive payment for their shares, either in cash or in shares in the surviving corporation. A **consolidation** is a similar process. The difference is that in a consolidation, both existing corporate entities disappear and a completely new corporation is formed. The differences between a merger and a consolidation are illustrated graphically in Exhibit 10.4.

State laws vary somewhat as to the procedures that must be undertaken to accomplish a merger or a consolidation. As a paralegal, you will need to find out

merger
A process in which one corporation (the surviving corporation) acquires all of the assets and liabilities of another corporation (the merged corporation).

consolidation
A process in which two or more corporations join to become a completely new corporation. The original corporations cease to exist.

what the specific requirements are in your state. Generally, the following requirements must be met:

- The boards of directors and the shareholders of each corporation involved must approve the merger or consolidation.
- Once the merger or consolidation is approved by these groups, articles of merger or articles of consolidation must be filed with the state, usually with the secretary of state's office.
- When state formalities have been satisfied, the state issues a certificate of merger to the surviving corporation or a certificate of consolidation to the newly consolidated corporation.

As a paralegal, you should realize the difference in legal effect between a merger or a consolidation and an *acquisition,* which occurs when one corporation acquires or purchases all or almost all of the assets of another company. In a merger or a consolidation, the surviving corporation or the newly consolidated corporation assumes not only the assets but also the liabilities of the previously existing entities. If a person has a valid claim against one of those entities, this claim is a liability that will be assumed by the surviving or newly consolidated corporation. A person injured by a defective product manufactured by one of the previously existing corporations, for example, could sue the surviving or new corporation and recover damages. In contrast, if an acquisition has occurred, the acquiring corporation has acquired the assets of the other corporation but normally has not assumed responsibility for the liabilities of that corporation.

On the Web
Hoover's Online has an extensive collection of data on U.S. corporations at **http://www.hoovers.com.**

CORPORATE TERMINATION.   As with partnership termination, corporate termination involves two steps. The first step, dissolution, extinguishes the legal existence of the corporation. The second step, **liquidation,** involves the winding up of the corporation's business affairs. After creditors have been paid, all remaining assets are distributed to the shareholders.

Corporations can be terminated at a time specified in the articles of incorporation or by the agreement of the shareholders and the board of directors. In certain circumstances, a court may dissolve a corporation. For example, if the directors are deadlocked and cannot agree on the management of the corporation, a court may grant a shareholder's petition to dissolve the corporation. A corporation may also be terminated by law if it fails to meet certain statutory requirements, such as the payment of taxes or annual fees.

liquidation
In regard to corporations, the process by which corporate assets are converted into cash and distributed among creditors and shareholders according to specific rules of preference.

Limited Liability Organizations

In recent years, two new forms of limited liability business organizations have emerged, the limited liability company and the limited liability partnership. The use of these new forms is spreading quickly because of the advantages they offer to businesspersons in regard to business taxation and liability—advantages not available through the partnership and corporate forms of business. (For a detailed discussion of the factors to consider when forming various types of business organizations, including limited liability organizations, see the chapter's *Featured Guest* article starting on page 340.)

For example, one of the major tax advantages of a partnership is that the partnership's income passes through to the partners as personal income. Consequently, partners avoid the double-taxation feature of the corporate form of business. But there is a price to pay for this tax advantage: partners face unlimited personal liability. The partners can avoid unlimited personal liability by incorporating their business, because corporate owners (shareholders) have limited liability. But again,

TECHNOLOGY AND TODAY'S PARALEGAL

Online Incorporation

Today, just about anybody can form a corporation for any lawful purpose in any state. The requirements differ from state to state. As a paralegal, your supervising attorney may ask you to assist a client who wishes to incorporate his or her business. The client may wish to incorporate in the state in which he or she currently does business, in another state (such as Delaware), or even in another country. As a paralegal, you may not advise clients on where to form a corporation. You can, however, assist in the process by finding out the formal requirements and cost of incorporation in various states using the Internet. You can also help to locate potential investors for the corporation online. In addition, you can find numerous online providers of company formation and registered agent services. (The registered agent acts as the original incorporator, files the articles of incorporation, and remains the registered agent for the life of the corporation.)

RESEARCHING STATE REQUIREMENTS

Nearly every state has a Web site at which you can find out the state's requirements for incorporation. Typically, incorporation is handled by the secretary of state's office. You can locate the state's site by performing a general search using the state's name, or you can go to a directory site such as that offered by the Library of Congress (http://lcweb.loc.gov/global/state/stategov.html) or Piper Resources

(http://www.statelocalgov.net). Most state sites post guidelines or instructions on forming corporations (and other business entities), fee schedules, and frequently asked questions (FAQs). Many also provide downloadable corporate forms. The majority of states also have searchable databases of corporate names and registered agents.

LOCATING POTENTIAL INVESTORS

The Internet allows promoters and others to access, easily and inexpensively, a large number of potential investors. Several online services specialize in matching potential investors with companies (or future companies) that are seeking investors. For example, the American Venture Capital Exchange, or AVCE (at http://www.avce.com), lists hundreds of companies that seek financing. Some of these companies are just starting up, while others are existing firms that wish to expand their businesses. AVCE provides a summary of each company's business plan for potential investors to review. Potential investors can then contact the companies in which they are interested. AVCE's listings include companies in Asia, Australia, Canada, Europe, Mexico, Russia, and South America as well as the United States.

Some companies specialize in matching entrepreneurs in specific industries with potential investors. For example, Garage.com (at http://www.garage.com) provides a list of start-up high-tech companies and summaries of their busi-

---

there is a price to pay for this limited liability: the double taxation of profits characteristic of the corporate form of business.

As mentioned, one way to achieve both goals—limited liability and single taxation of profits—is to elect S corporation status. Certain requirements must be met, however, before a corporation can qualify for S corporation status. One requirement is that the corporation have seventy-five or fewer shareholders, thus excluding large firms. Another requirement is that an S corporation may only have one class of stock (meaning that there is little flexibility in how corporate profits are distributed). Additionally, certain entities (such as partnerships and, with some exceptions, corporations) cannot be shareholders in an S corporation.

limited liability company (LLC)
A hybrid form of business organization authorized by a state in which the owners of the business have limited liability and taxes on profits are passed through the business entity to the owners.

LIMITED LIABILITY COMPANIES.   The **limited liability company (LLC)** is a hybrid form of business enterprise that combines the pass-through tax benefits of S corporations and partnerships with the limited liability of limited partners and corporate shareholders. Like the limited partnership and the corporation, an LLC must be formed and operated in compliance with state law. To form an LLC, *articles of organization* must be filed with a central state agency, such as the secretary

TECHNOLOGY AND TODAY'S PARALEGAL, CONTINUED

ness plans and a list of potential investors. Potential investors who are interested in one of the listed start-up companies can contact the company directly. The site also features articles of interest, research materials, and forums where users can ask questions of experts in certain areas. Other companies, such as BizWiz (http://www.clickit.com/capitalist), introduce capital seekers (companies) to capital sources (investors) worldwide.

ONLINE INCORPORATION SERVICES

Hundreds of companies provide incorporation services online that will assist you with incorporation. Although many sites are aimed at persons seeking to incorporate, some target law firms as clients and provide additional beneficial services. For example, if your client is interested in forming a Delaware corporation, Harvard Business Services (http://www.delawareinc.com) offers a fast and efficient way to incorporate. In addition, it provides free downloadable forms and will act as the corporation's registered agent for a fixed annual fee of fifty dollars.

Another Web site of use to corporate attorneys and paralegals is that of the Corporate Service Company (CSC) at http://www.incspot.com/public. CSC, a company with more than a hundred years' experience, offers an extensive range of services, including corporate forma-

tion and registered agent services. In addition, the company will scan and upload all the documents related to a transaction or litigation into an online database, providing centralized access to important documents for authorized users anywhere in the world and allowing multiple parties to track ongoing negotiations. Useful news and substantive law updates (federal and state) are provided at this site as well. CSC also sponsors the Paralegal Leadership Institute, which provides educational seminars (and CLE credits) to paralegals at locations across the country.

TECHNOLOGY TIP

The Web can assist paralegals with the incorporation process in many ways. It provides an efficient means of finding out state requirements, obtaining the proper forms, locating investors, and keeping abreast of current developments affecting corporations. The usefulness of a particular site will depend on the paralegal's level of experience and the individual needs of the client or firm. In some cases, it may be more cost-effective for a firm to hire a service provider than to conduct the research and prepare the paperwork for start-up companies.

---

of state's office. The business's name must include the word "Limited Liability Company" or the initials "L.L.C."

A major advantage of the LLC is that, as indicated, it does not pay taxes as an entity. Rather, profits are "passed through" the LLC and paid personally by the owners of the company, who are called *members* instead of shareholders. Another key advantage is that the liability of members is limited to the amount of their investments. In an LLC, members are also allowed to participate fully in management activities, and under some state statutes, the firm's managers need not even be members of the LLC. Yet another advantage is that corporations and partnerships, as well as foreign investors, can be LLC members. Additionally, in contrast to S corporations, there is no limit on the number of members of the LLC. Finally, part of the LLC's attractiveness to businesspersons is the flexibility it offers. The members can themselves decide how to operate the various aspects of the business through a simple operating agreement.

The disadvantages of the LLC are relatively few. Generally, the major disadvantage has been the lack of uniformity among state statutes with respect to LLCs. The differences among the states are rapidly disappearing, however.

FEATURED GUEST: LLOYD G. PEARCY

The Paralegal and Projects Involving Business Organizations

BIOGRAPHICAL NOTE

Lloyd G. Pearcy, an attorney for over thirty years, has taught business organizations at Denver Paralegal Institute for two decades and business law classes in both undergraduate and MBA programs at the University of Phoenix. He has presented Continuing Legal Education seminars on business organizations to trade associations throughout the United States. He has contributed to a book on employment law and has written numerous columns on business law in various trade journals.

The paralegal who is assigned projects involving business organizations will experience many opportunities to excel and achieve personal satisfaction. An understanding of the practical and frequently overlooked issues discussed here may help you attain recognition and professional fulfillment.

PRACTICAL CONSIDERATIONS IN ANALYZING JURISDICTIONAL CHOICES

Today, states compete to attract new businesses by making their statutes regulating business organizations more user friendly. Yet the statutes tend to level out. As soon as one state modifies its statute or regulations, other states quickly copy the modifications. The tendency of state legislatures to enact model acts more or less intact adds to this process.

In most cases, I advise clients to charter their businesses in their home states. The business owners and their legal counsel will be more familiar with all of the home state's statutes, not just those directly pertaining to business entities. They will also be more likely to keep abreast of periodic legislative revisions.

There are some situations, however, in which it is strategically, if not legally, advantageous to incorporate in another state. If the company's business plan is to make a public stock offering several years down the line, some underwriters will counsel the business owners to incorporate in the state of Delaware, because prospective investors often regard Delaware corporations as more sophisticated. If the company that is going public is in the medical field, the preferred state of incorporation may be Tennessee. If it is a credit-card–issuing company, the jurisdiction of choice may be South Dakota, not because that state's corporation statute is preferred but because its law governing lenders is considered desirable.

AN UNEXPECTED ADVANTAGE OF PAR-VALUE STOCK

Par-value stock has always been misunderstood. The term is a misnomer.

It has nothing to do with the book value or market value of stock. It is a minimum issuance price in that the corporation cannot sell par stock for less than the designated par value. Another rule is that the funds the corporation receives from the issuance of par stock cannot be used for the payment of dividends.

Many legal scholars believe that the usefulness of the distinction between par-value and no-par-value stock has ended. With the development of sophisticated accounting procedures, the information that the designation conveys has become outdated. Some states have abolished the distinction or made it optional.

Designating stock as par value may nonetheless be advantageous to your firm's client. This is because some states base their franchise taxes or registration fees on a formula computed by multiplying the number of authorized shares by their par value. If the stock is no-par stock, these states impute a value to those shares, often $1 per share. A corporation operating in numerous states and thus needing to qualify as a foreign corporation in multiple jurisdictions can incur significant qualification fees. This is especially true if its articles of incorporation authorize a large number of shares. By designating a par value below one dollar—for example, one cent per share—the corporation is assured that it will qualify for the lowest tax or fee available.

> **"Limited liability companies (LLCs) are the 'new kid on the block' in the world of business entities."**

FEATURED GUEST, *Continued*

DO NOT OVERLOOK SHARES IN SERIES

An underutilized feature of corporation law is the opportunity to designate a corporation's stock as "shares in series." When a class of stock is so designated in the articles of incorporation, it enables the company to vary the attributes of different blocks of *the same class of stock* at different issuance dates. Such shares are known informally as "blank stock."

Suppose that your law firm has a business client who is incorporating. The client wants maximum flexibility in conforming the sale of its shares of stock to market conditions, which change from time to time. The client does not want to bother with several classes of stock, nor with having to amend the articles of incorporation in the future. The "shares in series" alternative is designed for this scenario. There is a single class of stock, but certain characteristics can be varied each time the corporation sells a different block of shares. Attributes that can be varied in this way include such matters as voting rights, dividend rates, liquidation priorities, conversion rights, and redemption terms. The allowable variations are defined in each state's statute. To reserve this flexibility, the class must be designated as "series shares" in the articles of incorporation. Thereafter, each time the corporation issues a block of shares the board of directors defines the specific attributes of the stock.

CONSIDER THE ADVANTAGES OF A LIMITED LIABILITY COMPANY

Limited liability companies (LLCs) are the "new kid on the block" in the world of business entities. Most states have adopted enabling legislation that not only authorizes the formation of domestic LLCs but also allows foreign LLCs to qualify to do business within the state.

LLCs are a blend of other business forms. Like limited and general partnerships and S corporations, the LLC is a "pass-through" entity. The LLC does not pay income taxes as an entity and files only an "informational tax return" with the Internal Revenue Service. Available tax credits or deductions pass through the entity to the owners personally. None of the owners of an LLC (called "members") is personally liable for business debts. Furthermore, none of the limitations placed on S corporations applies to LLCs. There is no limit on the number of owners, there can be more than one class of securities, nonresident aliens are allowed to be owners, affiliated ownership with other entities is not disqualifying, and so on.

MAKE THE LIMITED LIABILITY ELECTION FOR GENERAL OR LIMITED PARTNERSHIPS

In recent years, virtually all states have enacted laws allowing general partnerships to register as limited liability partnerships (LLPs). Generally, limited partnerships are allowed to register as limited liability limited partnerships (LLLPs). Registration as an LLP or LLLP affords significant protection against personal liability for all partners in a general partnership and for the general partners of limited partnerships. Without the election to operate as an LLP, general partners are personally liable for all of the business debts. If the assets of the business are insufficient to pay its creditors, the personal assets of the partners can be reached. If a partner cannot pay his or her proportionate share, the entire obligation falls on the partner or partners who can.

If the LLP election is made, partners remain liable for their own misconduct but not for that of their partners. This protection is acquired by filing the appropriate document with the secretary of state. The name of the general partnership is required to include the words "Limited Liability Partnership," or the abbreviation "L.L.P." Similarly, the name of a limited partnership that makes the election must include the words "Limited Liability Limited Partnership," or the abbreviation "L.L.L.P." Thereafter, businesses that extend credit to, or enter into other business relationships with, the partnership are deemed to have notice that the partners will not be personally liable for payment of business debts. Consistent with the law governing other entity forms that limit personal liability, such as corporations and limited liability companies, it is not sufficient for the partnership to merely *acquire* the limited liability designation through registration. It must consistently display the designation in its business documents so there is a continuing notice as to the limitation on personal liability of the partners.

limited liability partnership (LLP)
A hybrid form of business organization authorized by a state that allows professionals to enjoy the tax benefits of a partnership while limiting in some way the normal joint and several liability of partners.

LIMITED LIABILITY PARTNERSHIPS.   The **limited liability partnership (LLP)** is similar to the LLC. The difference is that the LLP is designed more for professionals, such as attorneys, who normally do business as partners in a partnership. Like LLCs, LLPs must be formed and operated in compliance with state statutes. The appropriate form must be filed with a central state agency, usually the secretary of state's office, and the business's name must include either "Limited Liability Partnership" or the initials "L.L.P."

The major advantage of the LLP is that it allows a partnership to function as a pass-through entity for tax purposes but limits the personal liability of the partners for partnership tort liability. Although LLP statutes vary from state to state, generally each state statute limits in some way the liability of partners. In most states, it is relatively easy to convert a traditional partnership into an LLP because the firm's basic organizational structure remains the same. Additionally, all of the laws governing partnerships still apply (apart from those modified by the LLP statute). Normally, an LLP statute is simply an amendment to a state's already existing partnership law.

Business Organizations and the Paralegal

We have already mentioned many of the ways in which paralegals benefit from a knowledge of business organizations. Because so much legal work has to do with business clients, it is impossible to summarize the many tasks involving business organizations that paralegals carry out. The following list, however, will give you an idea of some of the types of work that paralegals frequently perform in this area:

- Reserve a corporate name for an incorporator.
- Draft a partnership agreement and the documents necessary to form a limited partnership or limited liability company. File the required papers with the appropriate state office.
- Prepare articles of incorporation or articles of consolidation or merger and file them with the appropriate state office.
- Prepare minutes of corporate meetings and maintain a minutes binder.
- Draft a corporate prospectus, corporate bylaws, or a stock-option agreement for corporate clients. (A stock-option agreement is an option to purchase the corporation's stock at a specified price.)
- Review or prepare documents relating to the sale of corporate securities (stocks and bonds); assist a supervising attorney in making sure that federal and state requirements relating to the sale of corporate securities are met.
- Assist in the dissolution of a partnership or corporation.
- Assist in litigation relating to a corporation or other form of business.
- Research state laws governing partnerships, corporations, and limited liability organizations.

EMPLOYMENT LAW

Whenever a business organization hires an employee, an employment relationship is established. In the United States, employment relationships traditionally have been governed primarily by the common law. Today, though, federal and state statutes regulate the workplace extensively and provide employees with many rights and protections. Common law doctrines apply to areas *not* covered by statutory law.

Because attorneys and paralegals are frequently involved in legal work relating to employment relationships, you should have a basic understanding of employment law. In this section, we look at the common law doctrine governing employment relationships and at some of the ways in which the government regulates today's workplace.

Employment at Will

Traditionally, employment relationships have been governed by the common law doctrine of employment at will, as well as by the common law rules governing contracts, torts, and agency (discussed previously). Under the doctrine of **employment at will,** either party may terminate an employment contract at any time and for any reason, unless a contract or statute specifically provides otherwise. Today, the majority of American workers continue to have the legal status of "employees at will." In other words, this common law doctrine is still in widespread use, and only one state (Montana) does not apply the doctrine.

Nonetheless, as mentioned, federal and state statutes governing employment relationships prevent the doctrine from being applied in a number of circumstances. Today's employer is not permitted to fire an employee if to do so would violate a federal or state employment statute, such as one prohibiting employment termination for discriminatory reasons (to be discussed shortly).

employment at will
A common law doctrine under which employment is considered to be "at will"—that is, either party may terminate the employment relationship at any time and for any reason, unless a contract or statute specifies otherwise.

Wrongful Discharge

Whenever an employer discharges an employee in violation of an employment contract or a statutory law protecting employees, the employee may bring an action for **wrongful discharge.** For example, most states have a statute prohibiting employers from discharging or taking other actions against an employee because the employee has filed a workers' compensation claim. If an employee who was injured on the job files a claim for workers' compensation, and the employer then fires the employee, the employee can sue for wrongful discharge.

Even in situations where an employer's actions do not violate any express employment contract or statute, an employee may be able to bring a wrongful discharge action in certain circumstances. This is particularly true if the employer has violated some common law principle of contract, tort, or agency law. For example, suppose that a retail store employee is fired for no reason, despite the manager's earlier statements that the employee could only be fired for "good cause." Some courts have held that in such situations, even though no written contract exists, an *implied* employment contract exists that prohibits the employer from firing without a good reason. Similarly, if the employer engages in abusive discharge procedures or makes defamatory statements about the employee who is being terminated, the employee may sue for wrongful discharge under tort theories.

wrongful discharge
An employer's termination of an employee's employment in violation of the law.

Labor Laws

In the early decades of the twentieth century, employees began to organize to protect their interests. They formed associations called *labor unions* and elected union representatives to bargain with employers for improved wages and working conditions. The ultimate weapon of the labor union was, of course, the *strike*. By their organized refusal to work, employees could bring their employer's operations to a halt—to the financial detriment of the employer.

In 1932, Congress established the legal right of employees to organize labor unions with the passage of the Norris-LaGuardia Act. The act protected peaceful strikes, picketing, and boycotts and restricted the power of the federal courts to enjoin (stop or prohibit) labor unions from engaging in peaceful strikes.

The Norris-LaGuardia Act was strengthened by the enactment of the National Labor Relations Act (NLRA) of 1935. The twin goals of the NLRA were to protect workers' efforts to organize into unions and to promote **collective bargaining** (bargaining between union representatives and employers) as a peaceful method of dispute resolution. The NLRA sought to curb activities that would discourage or prevent collective bargaining efforts conducted on behalf of the workers. The NLRA also created the National Labor Relations Board (NLRB) to oversee the enforcement of the statute. Congress gave the NLRB the power to investigate alleged NLRA violations and to prevent continued violations by particular employers.

Another law to protect workers was the Fair Labor Standards Act (FLSA) of 1938. Among other things, the act prohibited the oppression or exploitation of children by regulating the employment of minors. For example, under the act, children below the age of sixteen cannot be employed on a full-time basis except in very limited circumstances. The FLSA also established guidelines regulating overtime pay and minimum hourly wages. The act provided that if in any week an employee works more than forty hours, the hours in excess of the first forty must be compensated at one and a half times the employee's regular hourly rate. As for the minimum hourly wage, it represents the absolute minimum amount that an employer can pay an employee per hour. The minimum wage rate, which is set by Congress, is changed periodically to reflect inflation.

Family and Medical Leave

In 1993, Congress passed the Family and Medical Leave Act (FMLA) to protect employees who need time off work for family or medical reasons. A majority of the states also have legislation allowing for employment leave for family or medical reasons, and many employers maintain private family-leave plans for their workers.

The FMLA requires employers who have fifty or more employees to provide employees with up to twelve weeks of family or medical leave during any twelve-month period. During the employee's leave, the employer must continue the worker's health-care coverage and guarantee employment in the same position or a comparable position when the employee returns to work. An important exception to the FMLA, however, allows the employer to avoid reinstatement of a *key employee*—defined as an employee whose pay falls within the top 10 percent of the firm's work force. Additionally, the act does not apply to employees who have worked less than one year or less than twenty-five hours a week during the previous twelve months.

Generally, an employee may take family leave when he or she wishes to care for a newborn baby, a newly adopted child, or a foster child just placed in the employee's care. An employee may take medical leave when the employee or the employee's spouse, child, or parent has a "serious health condition" requiring care. For most absences, the employee must demonstrate that the health condition requires continued treatment by a health-care provider and includes a period of incapacity of more than three days.

Remedies for violations of the FMLA include (1) damages for unpaid wages (or salary), lost benefits, denied compensation, and actual monetary losses (such as the cost of providing for care) up to an amount equivalent to the employee's wages for twelve weeks; (2) job reinstatement; and (3) promotion. The successful plaintiff is entitled to court costs, attorneys' fees, and—in cases involving bad faith on the part of the employer—double damages.

---

collective bargaining
The process by which labor and management negotiate the terms and conditions of employment, including wages, benefits, working conditions, and other matters.

On the Web
Several law firms that specialize in labor law publish online newsletters that discuss current issues relating to labor and employment law. For examples of the kind of information that you can find in such newsletters, go to the following Web sites: **http://www.arentfox.com/ quickGuide/business Lines/employ/employ. htm** and **http://www. haledorr.com.**

ETHICAL CONCERN
The Unauthorized Practice of Law

To illustrate how easy it is to give legal advice without intending to, consider this example. Lara, a paralegal, was interviewing a client who was considering petitioning for bankruptcy. The client's right arm was in a sling. After Lara asked him about the injury, he described how it had happened. He also said that he had been unable to work at his job as a mechanic for two weeks and that he was worried because his employer was threatening to fire him if he couldn't return to work within another week or two. When Lara looked puzzled at this news, the client asked her what was wrong. She said, "Well, I'm wondering how you could be fired, because employers are required by law to give their employees medical leave for up to twelve weeks during any one-year period." Lara said that she would check with her supervising attorney about that matter, and then she continued the interview. In the meantime, what if the client, relying on Lara's statement, later confronted his employer and demanded a twelve-week leave? What if the employer fired him on the spot? What if the employer had only a few employees and was not subject to the leave requirements of the Family and Medical Leave Act of 1993? As you can see, Lara's "legal advice" might have caused the client to suffer harm.

State Workers' Compensation Laws

State **workers' compensation laws** establish an administrative procedure for compensating workers injured on the job. Instead of suing, an injured worker files a claim with the administrative agency or board that administers the local workers' compensation claims. State workers' compensation statutes normally allow employers to purchase insurance from a private insurer or a state fund to pay workers' compensation benefits in the event of a claim. Most states also allow employers to be *self-insured*—that is, employers who show an ability to pay claims do not need to buy insurance.

In general, the right to recover benefits is based wholly on the existence of an employment relationship and the fact that the injury was *accidental* and *occurred on the job or in the course of employment,* regardless of fault. Intentionally inflicted self-injury, in contrast, would not be considered accidental and hence would not be covered. If an injury occurred while an employee was commuting to or from work, it would not usually be considered to have occurred on the job or in the course of employment and hence would not be covered.

An employee must notify his or her employer of an injury promptly (usually within thirty days of the injury's occurrence). Generally, an employee also must file a workers' compensation claim with the appropriate state agency or board within a certain period (sixty days to two years) from the time the injury is first noticed, rather than from the time of the accident.

An employee's acceptance of workers' compensation benefits bars the employee from suing for injuries caused by the employer's negligence. By barring lawsuits for negligence, workers' compensation laws also bar employers from raising common law defenses to negligence, such as contributory negligence. For example, an employer can no longer raise such defenses as contributory negligence or assumption of risk (see Chapter 7) to avoid liability for negligence. A worker may sue an employer who *intentionally* injures the worker, however.

workers' compensation laws
State statutes that establish an administrative procedure for compensating workers for injuries that arise out of or in the course of their employment, regardless of fault.

Employment Discrimination

Federal laws prohibiting employment discrimination have done much to further employees' rights to fair treatment in the workplace. State laws also protect employees from discriminatory treatment, sometimes to a greater extent than federal laws do. The major federal laws prohibiting employment discrimination are the following:

- Title VII of the Civil Rights Act of 1964 (prohibits discrimination based on race, color, national origin, religion, and gender).
- The Age Discrimination in Employment Act of 1967 (prohibits discrimination based on age).
- The Americans with Disabilities Act of 1990 (prohibits discrimination based on disability).

TITLE VII OF THE CIVIL RIGHTS ACT OF 1964.   The most significant federal law prohibiting discrimination is the Civil Rights Act of 1964. The law was enacted to protect certain groups from the discriminatory practices of business owners, educational institutions, employers, and other groups. One section of the act, known as Title VII, pertains to employment practices. Title VII prohibits employers from discriminating against employees or potential employees on the basis of race, color, national origin, religion, or gender. The Pregnancy Discrimination Act of 1978 amended Title VII to expand the definition of gender-based discrimination to include discrimination based on pregnancy.

Title VII has been interpreted by the courts to prohibit both intentional and unintentional discrimination. The latter occurs when certain employer practices or procedures have a discriminatory effect, even though they were not intended to be discriminatory. For example, suppose that a city requires all of its firefighters to be at least six feet tall. In effect, that job requirement discriminates against women, because few women are that tall. The effect of the rule is discriminatory, even though the intent in adopting the rule might have been merely to ensure an able-bodied firefighting crew.

sexual harassment

In the employment context, (1) the hiring or granting of job promotions or other benefits in return for sexual favors (*quid pro quo* harassment) or (2) language or conduct that is so sexually offensive that it creates a hostile working environment (hostile-environment harassment).

Sexual Harrassment.   The courts have also extended Title VII protection to those who are subject to **sexual harassment** in the workplace. There are two types of sexual harassment. *Quid pro quo harassment* occurs when a superior doles out awards (promotions, raises, benefits, or other advantages) to a subordinate in exchange for sexual favors. (*Quid pro quo*, a Latin term, means "this for that" or "something for something.") In contrast, *hostile-environment harassment* occurs when an employee is subjected to offensive sexual comments, jokes, or physical contact in the workplace that make it difficult or impossible for the employee to perform a job satisfactorily.

Generally, an employer is held responsible (liable) for the conduct of certain employees, such as managers and supervisors, even if the employer was unaware of the conduct, under the doctrine of *respondeat superior* (discussed earlier in this chapter). In a sexual-harassment case, if an employee in a supervisory position did the harassing, the employer will usually be held liable *automatically* for the behavior. If the person who did the harassing was not a supervisor but a co-worker, the employer will be held liable only if the employer knew, or should have known, about the harassment and failed to take immediate corrective action. An employer may even be held liable at times for the actions of nonemployees (customers or clients, for example) if the employer knew about the harassment and let it continue.

Note that Title VII prohibits not only sexual harassment but also the harassment of any employee on the basis of race, color, national origin, religion, age, or disability. In other words, racial or ethnic slurs against an employee may give rise to a hostile work environment claim under Title VII, just as sexually offensive comments would.

The Equal Employment Opportunity Commission.   The Equal Employment Opportunity Commission (EEOC) is a federal agency that administers and enforces Title VII and the laws prohibiting employment discrimination based on disability or age (to be discussed shortly), as well as some other federal antidiscrimination laws. Claims of Title VII violations must first be filed with the EEOC. The EEOC will either investigate and take action on the claim on behalf of the employee or allow the employee to file a civil suit against the employer. The EEOC also has established guidelines that are often used by the courts to determine if the actions complained of constitute harassment under the law.

Employers' Liability under Title VII.   An employer's liability under Title VII can be extensive. In general, the court can order injunctive relief against the employer (a judicial order to prevent future discrimination), retroactive promotions that were wrongfully withheld from the employee, and past wages to compensate the employee for the time he or she was wrongfully unemployed. Damages are also available in cases involving *intentional* discrimination.

On the Web
You can find the complete text of Title VII, the ADEA, and the ADA (and other federal antidiscrimination laws), as well as information about the activities of the EEOC, at the EEOC's Web site. Go to **http://www.eeoc.gov**.

DISCRIMINATION BASED ON AGE.   The Age Discrimination in Employment Act (ADEA) of 1967 prevents employers from discriminating against workers between the ages of forty and seventy on the basis of their age. The act was passed, in part, in response to an increasing tendency on the part of employers to reduce costs by excluding older workers from their work forces and hiring younger workers (at lower salaries) instead. For the ADEA to apply, however, an employer must have twenty or more employees, and the employer's business activities must affect interstate commerce.

DISCRIMINATION BASED ON DISABILITY.   Congress enacted the Americans with Disabilities Act (ADA) in 1990 to strengthen existing laws prohibiting discrimination in the workplace against individuals with disabilities. Employers with fifteen or more employees are obligated to satisfy the requirements of the ADA.

As defined by the 1990 statute, disabilities include heart disease, cancer, blindness, paralysis, acquired immune deficiency syndrome, emotional illnesses, and learning disabilities. Under the ADA, an employer is not permitted to discriminate against a person with a disability if *reasonable accommodations* can be provided to assist the worker in satisfactorily performing the job. An employer is not required to accommodate a worker with a disability if the accommodation would constitute an undue hardship for the employer, however. For example, if the cost of accommodating the employee is extremely high, that high cost might constitute an undue hardship for the employer. Although enforcement of the ADA falls within the jurisdiction of the EEOC, the paralegal should note that the worker alleging discrimination in violation of the ADA may also file a civil lawsuit against the employer for violation of the act.

Employment Law and the Paralegal

Employment law necessarily affects the paralegal. As an employee, you will be subject to the laws governing employment relationships. As a legal professional, you may be extensively involved in tasks relating to labor and employment laws. You may work in the corporate counsel's office of a large corporate enterprise, for example. If the corporation's employees belong to a labor union, the corporate counsel's office will handle matters governed by labor laws, such as collective

TODAY'S PROFESSIONAL PARALEGAL

Developing a Policy on Sexual Harassment

Erika Delong, a legal assistant, works in the office of the general counsel at ABC Manufacturing Corporation. She works closely with the personnel department. Today, she is attending a meeting with her supervisor, Gene Tompkins, who is the general counsel, to discuss the company's policy on sexual harassment with the vice president of human resources, the president of the corporation, and the vice presidents of several of the corporation's divisions. Erika has been asked to attend the meeting because her supervisor will ultimately be responsible for preparing the policy and he wants her to draft it. Erika has already obtained copies of other companies' policies to use as samples in the meeting.

The meeting is held in a large conference room. The president opens the meeting by explaining its purpose—to develop a policy on sexual harassment. "We want to discourage it and to have a written policy that includes reporting and investigation procedures. Erika and Gene have several samples that we can review," says the president.

SETTING POLICY GOALS AND DEFINING SEXUAL HARASSMENT

Erika passes out the sample policies. The group then reviews the various policies, with Gene explaining the legal ramifications of each one. The president remarks that he thinks the policy should begin with a statement that the corporation wants to promote an atmosphere in which authority and power are not abused and in which sexual harassment is not condoned. He points out some language that he likes in one of the samples. Erika high-

lights it so she will have an idea of how to draft the introduction.

Gene then states, "After an introduction and general statement of the corporation's policy, we should give the legal definition of what constitutes sexual harassment. The definition in sample three is very good from both a legal and a practical point of view because it also gives examples." Erika highlights the definition paragraph in sample three and puts a number 2 next to it, so she knows that it should come second. She flips back to the sample the president referred to and puts a number 1 next to it.

DEVELOPING PROCEDURES

As the discussion continues, the vice president of human resources comments on the procedure for filing a complaint, the investigation that will take place, and the disciplinary measures that will be imposed for sexual harassment. The vice president does not like any of the samples, and the group spends quite a bit of time working through specific language to pin down what he wants. When the meeting is over, the group goes to lunch in the executive dining room. After lunch, Gene informs the others that Erika will prepare a draft of the policy and will circulate it among them for review and comment. Once all of their comments have been collected, the group will meet again to decide on the final provisions. Erika will then prepare and circulate a final draft of the policy. Erika returns to her office to begin working on the initial draft.

---

bargaining agreements and labor-management disputes. As a paralegal in a law firm or a government agency, you might assist in work relating to claims of employment discrimination, which might require you to interact with the EEOC or a relevant state agency. Here are just a few tasks that paralegals commonly undertake in the area of labor and employment law:

- Draft employment contracts for an employer.
- Assist with contract negotiations between labor and management.
- Prepare for arbitration proceedings before the NLRB.
- Respond to inquiries from the NLRB regarding a client's alleged unfair labor practices.
- Prepare for and attend administrative hearings before the EEOC.
- Gather factual information to counter or support a claim of employment discrimination.

- Prepare reports and furnish documentation in response to an EEOC investigation into an employee's claim of employment discrimination.
- Draft a policy manual for a business client concerning what actions constitute discriminatory employment practices.
- Research the EEOC's guidelines on sexual harassment and relevant case law to determine what types of policies and procedures will help a client avoid liability for sexual harassment.
- Prepare notices regarding a firm's employment policies, important changes in employment laws, and so on.
- Assist in litigation involving multiple plaintiffs.

Key Terms and Concepts

agency
agent
articles of incorporation
bylaws
certificate of incorporation (corporate charter)
close corporation
collective bargaining
consolidation
director
dissolution
dividend
employment at will
fiduciary relationship
general partner
independent contractor
joint and several liability
joint liability
limited liability company (LLC)
limited liability partnership (LLP)
limited partner
limited partnership
liquidation
merger
officer
principal
prospectus
publicly held corporation
respondeat superior
sexual harassment
share
shareholder
vicarious liability
winding up
workers' compensation law
wrongful discharge

Chapter Summary

Agency Law	An agency relationship arises when one person (called the *agent*) agrees to act for or in the place of another person (called the *principal*). 1. *Employees versus independent contractors*—Employees who deal with third parties are normally considered to be agents of their employers. An independent contractor differs from an employee in that the employer does not control the details of the independent contractor's job performance. The independent contractor may or may not be an agent. 2. *Agency formation*—An agency relationship may be formed by express agreement (oral or written) or implied by conduct. It can also arise if the principal causes a third party to believe the agency existed. 3. *Duties of the principal*—The principal must cooperate with the agent, provide safe working conditions for the agent, and reimburse the agent for work performed and for any expenses incurred on the principal's behalf.

Agency Law—Continued	4. *Duties of the agent*—The agent must perform his or her tasks competently, obey and be loyal to the principal, notify the principal of matters concerning the agency, and render an accounting to the principal of how and for what purpose the principal's funds were used.
	5. *Liability for an agent's contracts*—The principal normally is bound by any contract formed by the agent on behalf of the principal, as long as the action was authorized. If the action was not authorized, the principal will not be liable unless he or she voluntarily agrees to be bound by (ratifies) the contract.
	6. *Liability for an agent's torts*—Agents are personally liable for the torts that they commit. If an agent commits a tort within the scope of his or her employment as an agent, the principal may also be held liable under the doctrine of *respondeat superior.*
	7. *Liability for independent contractor's torts*—A principal is not liable for harm caused by an independent contractor's negligence, unless hazardous activities are involved (in which situation the principal is strictly liable for any resulting harm) or other exceptions apply.
Forms of Business Organization	1. *Sole proprietorships*—The simplest form of business organization; used by anyone who does business without creating a separate business entity. The owner is the business, even though he or she may hire employees to run the business.
	a. The owner is personally liable for all business debts and obligations.
	b. The owner pays personal income taxes on all profits.
	c. The proprietorship terminates on the death of the sole proprietor or the sale or transfer of the business.
	2. *Partnerships*—Created by the written or oral agreement of the parties to do business jointly as partners. All partners share equally in management, unless otherwise provided for in the partnership agreement. The partners may hire employees to assist them in running the business.
	a. Partners are personally liable for partnership debts and obligations.
	b. The partnership as an entity does not pay income taxes but files an informational tax return with the Internal Revenue Service each year. Each partner pays personal income tax on his or her share of the profits of the partnership.
	c. A partnership may be terminated by the agreement of the partners or by the occurrence of certain events, such as the death or bankruptcy of a partner.
	d. The creation of a limited partnership is a formal proceeding that must comply with state statutory requirements. Only the general partners may participate in management in a limited partnership, and only the general partners have unlimited personal liability; the liability of limited partners is limited to the amount of their investments.
	3. *Corporations*—
	a. A corporation is created by a state-issued charter. The shareholders elect directors, who set policy and appoint officers to manage day-to-day corporate affairs.
	b. Shareholders have limited liability and are not personally liable for the debts of the corporation (beyond the amount of their investments).
	c. The corporation pays income tax on net profits; shareholders again pay income tax on profits distributed as dividends.

EXHIBIT 11.1
Executive Departments and Important Subagencies

DEPARTMENT	DATE FORMED	IMPORTANT SUBAGENCIES
State	1789	Passport Office; Bureau of Diplomatic Security; Foreign Service; Bureau of Human Rights and Humanitarian Affairs; Bureau of Consular Affairs
Treasury	1789	Internal Revenue Service; U.S. Mint
Interior	1849	U.S. Fish and Wildlife Service; National Park Service; Bureau of Indian Affairs; Bureau of Land Management
Justice	1870[a]	Federal Bureau of Investigation; Drug Enforcement Administration; Bureau of Prisons
Agriculture	1889	Soil Conservation Service; Agricultural Research Service; Food Safety and Inspection Service; Federal Crop Insurance Corporation; Farmers Home Administration
Commerce	1913[b]	Bureau of the Census; Bureau of Economic Analysis; Minority Business Development Agency; U.S. Patent and Trademark Office; National Oceanic and Atmospheric Administration
Labor	1913[b]	Occupational Safety and Health Administration; Bureau of Labor Statistics; Employment Standards Administration; Office of Labor-Management Standards
Defense	1949[c]	National Security Agency; Joint Chiefs of Staff; Departments of the Air Force, Navy, Army
Housing and Urban Development	1965	Office of Block Grant Assistance; Emergency Shelter Grant Program; Office of Urban Development Action Grants; Office of Fair Housing and Equal Opportunity
Transportation	1967	Federal Aviation Administration; Federal Highway Administration; National Highway Traffic Safety Administration; Federal Transit Administration
Energy	1977	Office of Civilian Radioactive Waste Management; Office of Nuclear Energy; Energy Information Administration
Health and Human Services	1980[d]	Food and Drug Administration; Health Care Financing Administration; Public Health Service; Administration for Children and Families
Education	1980[e]	Office of Special Education and Rehabilitation Services; Office of Elementary and Secondary Education; Office of Postsecondary Education; Office of Vocational and Adult Education
Veterans Affairs	1989	Veterans Health Administration; Veterans Benefits Administration; National Cemetery System
Homeland Security	2002	U.S. Customs Service; Immigration and Naturalization Service; U.S. Coast Guard; Secret Service; Federal Emergency Management Agency

a. Formed from the Office of the Attorney General (created in 1789).
b. Formed from the Department of Commerce and Labor (created in 1903).
c. Formed from the Department of War (created in 1789) and the Department of the Navy (created in 1798).
d. Formed from the Department of Health, Education, and Welfare (created in 1953).
e. Formed from the Department of Health, Education, and Welfare (created in 1953).

ments. The Occupational Safety and Health Administration, for example, is a subagency within the Department of Labor. Exhibit 11.1 lists the executive departments and important subagencies of the U.S. government.

Although all administrative agencies are part of the executive branch of government, **independent regulatory agencies,** some of which are listed and described in Exhibit 11.2 on the next page, are outside the major executive departments. The Federal Trade Commission and the Securities and Exchange Commission are examples of independent regulatory agencies.

The significant difference between the two types of agencies lies in the accountability of the regulators. Agencies that are considered part of the executive

independent regulatory agency
A type of administrative agency that is more independent of presidential control than an executive agency. Officials of independent regulatory agencies cannot be removed without cause.

EXHIBIT 11.2
Selected Independent Regulatory Agencies

NAME	DATE FORMED	PRINCIPAL DUTIES
Federal Reserve System Board of Governors (Fed)	1913	Determines policy with respect to interest rates, credit availability, and the money supply.
Federal Trade Commission (FTC)	1914	Prevents businesses from engaging in unfair trade practices; stops the formation of monopolies in the business sector; protects consumer rights.
Securities and Exchange Commission (SEC)	1934	Regulates the nation's stock exchanges, in which shares of stock are bought and sold; enforces the securities laws, which require full disclosure of the financial profiles of companies that wish to sell stock and bonds to the public.
Federal Communications Commission (FCC)	1934	Regulates all communications by telegraph, cable, telephone, radio, satellite, and television.
National Labor Relations Board (NLRB)	1935	Protects employees' rights to join unions and bargain collectively with employers; attempts to prevent unfair labor practices by both employers and unions.
Equal Employment Opportunity Commission (EEOC)	1964	Works to eliminate discrimination in employment based on religion, gender, race, color, disability, national origin, or age; investigates claims of discrimination.
Environmental Protection Agency (EPA)	1970	Undertakes programs aimed at reducing air and water pollution; works with state and local agencies to help fight environmental hazards. (It has been suggested recently that its status be elevated to that of a department.)
Nuclear Regulatory Commission (NRC)	1975	Ensures that electricity-generating nuclear reactors in the United States are built and operated safely; regularly inspects operations of such reactors.

branch are subject to the authority of the president, who has the power to appoint and remove federal officers. In contrast, those who run independent agencies serve for fixed terms and cannot be removed without just cause.

Agency Powers

Federal administrative agencies are created by Congress. Because Congress cannot possibly oversee the actual implementation of all the laws it enacts, it must delegate such tasks to others, particularly when the issues relate to highly technical areas, such as air and water pollution. By delegating some of its authority to make and implement laws, Congress is able to monitor indirectly a particular area in which it has passed legislation without becoming bogged down in the many details relating to enforcement—details that are often best left to specialists.

On the Web
The home pages for all of the federal administrative agencies discussed in this chapter, as well as many other federal agencies, can be located easily using the Federal Web Locator. Go to **http://www.infoctr.edu/fwl.**

ENABLING LEGISLATION.   As you learned in Chapter 5, when Congress wants to create an administrative agency, it passes enabling legislation, which specifies the name, purpose, function, and powers of the agency being created. The agency may exercise only those powers delegated to it by Congress in the enabling act. State agencies are created by state legislatures through similar enabling acts.

Enabling acts are important sources of information for paralegals who are researching legal matters involving administrative agencies. Suppose, for example, that you are employed by a law firm and that a client is being investigated by the Federal Trade Commission (FTC) for deceptive advertising practices. In your research, you would learn that the FTC was created by the Federal Trade Commission Act of 1914, which prohibits unfair and deceptive trade practices. You would learn what procedures the agency must follow to charge persons or organizations with a violation and whether the act provides for judicial review of agency orders. You would also discover that the act grants to the FTC the power to do the following:

- Create "rules and regulations for the purpose of carrying out the Act."
- Conduct investigations of business practices.
- Obtain reports from interstate corporations concerning their business practices.
- Investigate possible violations of federal antitrust statutes (laws prohibiting certain kinds of anticompetitive business behavior).
- Publish the findings of its investigations.
- Recommend new legislation.
- Hold trial-like hearings to resolve certain kinds of trade disputes that involve FTC regulations or federal antitrust laws.

AGENCY POWERS AND THE CONSTITUTION.   Administrative agencies occupy an unusual niche in the American legal system because they exercise powers that are normally divided among the three branches of government. Notice that the FTC's enabling legislation, discussed above, grants to the FTC powers associated with the legislature (rulemaking), the executive branch (enforcement of the laws), and the courts (**adjudication,** or the formal resolution of disputes). The constitutional principle of *checks and balances* allows each branch of government to act as a check on the actions of the other two branches. Furthermore, under the Constitution, only the legislative branch is authorized to create laws. Yet administrative agencies, which are not specifically referred to in the Constitution, make **legislative rules** that are as legally binding as laws passed by Congress.

adjudication
The act of resolving a controversy and rendering an order or decision based on a review of the evidence presented.

legislative rule
A rule created by an administrative agency that is as legally binding as a law enacted by a legislature.

The Delegation Doctrine.   Courts generally hold that Article I of the U.S. Constitution authorizes delegation of power to administrative agencies. In fact, courts typically conclude that Article I is the basis for *all* administrative law. Section 1 of that article grants all legislative powers to Congress and requires Congress to oversee the implementation of all laws. Article I, Section 8, gives Congress the power to make all laws necessary for executing its specified powers. The courts interpret these passages, under what is referred to as the **delegation doctrine,** as granting Congress the power to establish administrative agencies that can create rules for implementing those laws.

delegation doctrine
A doctrine that authorizes Congress to delegate some of its lawmaking authority to administrative agencies. The doctrine is implied by Article I of the U.S. Constitution, which grants specific powers to Congress to enact and oversee the implementation of laws.

Limitations on Agency Power.   The three branches of government exercise certain controls over agency powers and functions. For example, the courts (the judicial branch) have the authority to invalidate legislative acts that violate the Constitution (see Chapter 6). Thus, if a court concludes that Congress has enabled an agency to exercise lawmaking powers that rightfully should be exercised only by Congress, the court can invalidate the law. Courts also sometimes review agencies' decisions, as will be discussed later in this chapter. Additionally, Congress (the legislative branch) exerts some control over administrative agencies. Just as Congress can delegate powers to an agency, so can it take away those powers, or even abolish the agency. Congress can also revise funding limits to restrict an agency's scope of operations.

Although the other branches of government control agencies to some extent, in many ways administrative agencies function independently. For this reason,

FEATURED GUEST: JUDY A. LONG

Paralegal Positions in Government

BIOGRAPHICAL NOTE

Judy A. Long received her bachelor's degree and master's degree in business administration from California State University at Long Beach. She received her J.D. with honors from Western State University College of Law and is a member of the California State Bar Association. She developed the ABA–approved paralegal program at Rio Hondo College in Whittier, California, and is presently the paralegal coordinator at Rio Hondo College, where she also teaches classes.

Long has been involved in the legal profession for many years as a paralegal, an attorney, and a professor. She has authored a text on law office procedures, published by West Legal Studies, and co-authored a textbook on basic business law.

The federal government and state, county, and local governments all offer positions for paralegals.

Duties and responsibilities are as varied as the different government departments and agencies.

Unlike paralegals in private law firms, who often work long hours, paralegals employed by the government usually work a standard thirty-five or forty hours a week. There are many other advantages to working for the government. These advantages include good salaries, excellent benefits (such as medical and dental insurance), and time off for vacations, government holidays, and sick leave. Paralegals receive regularly scheduled performance reviews and are usually given annual salary increases. In some cases, however, they must pass tests to receive promotions.

The working environment is generally more structured in government offices than in private law firms, corporations, or other organizations. Depending on your preferences, this may also be perceived as an advantage.

THE FEDERAL GOVERNMENT

Paralegals are employed by the federal government in several different departments. To obtain a position with the federal government, you must contact the Office of Personnel Management (OPM), which has thirty-nine branch offices in various areas of the country. You can learn the location of these offices by writing the OPM at 1900 E Street N.W., Washington, DC 20415-0001, or contacting the OPM by phone at 1-202-606-1800. You can also check the OPM's Web site at http://www.opm.gov for information. The OPM administers examinations to all entry-level paralegal applicants. After the results have been obtained, the applicants' names are placed on a register from which federal agencies select job candidates.

When applying for a federal position, you need to complete Form 171. This form, which can be obtained from the OPM, is similar to an employment application. You must complete a separate form for each position for which you apply. It is therefore a good idea to fill out the form, leaving the specific position blank, and make several copies. Then, as you apply for different jobs, all you have to do is type in the position. You should also keep a copy of each form that you submit. Before completing the form, read through the booklet titled *Hiring Standards for Paralegals*, which can also be obtained from the OPM, so that your application will be geared to the qualifications required for the open position.

The largest employer of paralegals in the federal government is the Department of Justice (DOJ), which has branches in many cities throughout the country. Paralegals who work for the DOJ may be involved in investigating criminal cases, conducting legal research, interviewing witnesses, and gathering and documenting exhibits and other evidence needed for prosecuting criminal violations. Subagencies within the DOJ include the Drug Enforcement Administration (DEA), and the Office of the Solicitor General. Other government departments and agencies that employ paralegals include the military, the Civil Rights Commission, the Equal Employment Opportunity

Commission (EEOC), the Department of Transportation, the United States Postal Service, and the Federal Deposit Insurance Corporation. The kinds of cases paralegals might work on vary depending on the agency and range from prosecuting drug dealers (DEA) to employment discrimination (EEOC) to securities fraud (the Securities and Exchange Commission, or SEC), along with numerous other possibilities.

STATE AND COUNTY GOVERNMENTS

Many state and county departments employ paralegals in the criminal justice field. Paralegals in these areas assist in preparing cases for trial, undertaking legal research, finding and preparing witnesses for trial, and investigating cases. If they work for the public defender's office, they may spend time interviewing accused persons and investigating their backgrounds. The state attorney general's office employs paralegals for investigation, legal research, document preparation, and assistance with litigation.

County governments also employ paralegals in various capacities. For instance, some of my former paralegal students are employed as consumer counselors and investigators for the Los Angeles County Department of Consumer Affairs. Their duties and responsibilities include handling and investigating consumer complaints against businesses.

"GETTING YOUR FOOT IN THE DOOR"

Spending time as a student intern in a government office prepares you for a government position after graduation. Volunteer assistance from student interns is often welcomed. When these interns graduate, they have an inside track to a permanent position with a government office.

Our paralegal program also includes an internship class in which students work for unit credits but are not paid. Some of the students work in government offices.

If there is a particular government office in which you are interested, invite a guest speaker from that office to speak to your class (with your instructor's permission, of course). Not only will this enable you to learn more about what paralegals do in that office, but you will have made a contact that may prove valuable when you graduate and are looking for a job.

Visiting government offices is an excellent way to learn about different areas of government. If you would like to know more about the state attorney general's office, for instance, call that office and set up an appointment to interview an attorney or paralegal there to see what this person does. Again, you will establish a contact that you may be able to use after graduation.

In our paralegal program, a fieldwork class has been established in conjunction with the Los Angeles County Department of Consumer

> **"Spending time as a student intern in a government office prepares you for a government position after graduation."**

Affairs. Students learn consumer law in the classroom and then work as volunteers doing consumer counseling in the Department of Consumer Affairs. They also assist litigants in Small Claims Court. Several of the students have obtained positions as a direct result of this experience.

If you are interested in a position that has regular hours, good benefits, and a competitive salary, you should consider working for the government. Start your investigation today by contacting the departments in which you are interested, or call the nearest branch of the federal Office of Personnel Management to obtain more information about positions in the federal government. You may find that the steady, secure government position suits you better than the stress and long hours associated with working for a private law firm. It is never too early to start your job search! Every contact you make while you are a student is a potential employer when you graduate.

bureaucracy
In relation to government, the organizational structure, consisting of bureaus and agencies, through which the government implements and enforces the laws.

administrative process
The procedure used by administrative agencies in the administration of law.

On the Web
You can access the text of the APA online at
http://www.oalj.dol.gov.

rulemaking
The actions undertaken by administrative agencies when formally adopting new regulations or amending old ones.

administrative agencies, which constitute the **bureaucracy,** are sometimes referred to as the "fourth branch" of the U.S. government.

Administrative Process

Rulemaking, enforcement, and adjudication constitute the three main functions of an administrative agency. How these functions are carried out make up what has been termed **administrative process.** Administrative process involves the administration of law by administrative agencies, in contrast to judicial process, which involves the administration of law by the courts.

All federal agencies must follow specific procedural requirements in their rulemaking, adjudication, and other functions. Sometimes, Congress specifies certain procedural requirements in an agency's enabling legislation. If Congress does not spell out the procedures to be followed by a particular agency, the Administrative Procedure Act (APA) of 1946 applies. The APA establishes detailed procedures that all federal agencies must follow in making formal rules and adjudicating disputes. The APA is therefore an important part of the administrative process and administrative law. It does not apply to informal rulemaking and hearings by agencies, however.

RULEMAKING.   A major function of an administrative agency is **rulemaking**—the formulation of new regulations. As mentioned, Congress confers the agency's power to make legislative rules in the agency's enabling legislation. For example, the Occupational Safety and Health Administration (OSHA) was authorized by the Occupational Safety and Health Act of 1970 to develop and issue rules governing safety in the workplace. In formulating its rules, OSHA has to follow specific rulemaking procedures required under the APA. The most common rulemaking procedure involves three basic steps: notice of the proposed rulemaking, a comment period, and the final rule.

When a federal agency decides to create a new rule, it publishes a notice of the proposed rulemaking proceedings in the *Federal Register,* a daily publication of the executive branch that prints government orders, rules, and regulations. The

PARALEGAL PROFILE

Immigration Paralegal

DIANE S. GALLO *has been a practicing paralegal for more than twelve years, concentrating in the regulatory law areas of immigration and naturalization, telecommunications, and environment. She coordinates the firm's immigration practice, which meets the ongoing needs of corporations that employ foreign nationals as professionals and managers. She is generally well versed in the requirements of immigration law.*

Gallo graduated from Georgia State University with a bachelor of arts degree in sociology. In 1985, she earned a paralegal certificate with honors from the National Center for Paralegal Training. She is actively involved with the National Federation of Paralegal Associations and has held several offices, including the presidency.

What do you like best about your work?

"What I like most about my job is the client contact. I work primarily with immigration and naturalization. A typical day for me involves planning strategies and assisting clients. I enjoy working with people and building relationships to achieve goals. The failure or success of our efforts in areas such as immigration can dramatically affect clients' lives."

What is the greatest challenge that you face in your area of work?

"The greatest challenge for me is the cross-cultural dimension of my job. I deal with many international clients, and cultural differences can be challenging. I have to be sensitive to other perspectives, viewpoints, and customs."

What advice do you have for would-be paralegals in your area of work?

"I recommend a focus on both communication and writing skills. Organizational skills are also critical for all paralegal work and especially in the area of immigration law."

What are some tips for success as a paralegal in your area of work?

"Tips for success as an immigration paralegal include having excellent writing, communication, and computer skills. People skills are also an important asset. Don't be afraid to carve out a niche for yourself and aggressively seek what you want to do."

> "The greatest challenge for me is the cross-cultural dimension of my job."

notice states where and when the proceedings will be held, the agency's legal authority for making the rule (usually, its enabling legislation), and the terms or subject matter of the proposed rule.

A "comment period" follows during which interested parties can express their views on the proposed rule in an effort to influence agency policy. Finally, after the comments have been received and reviewed, the agency drafts the final rule and publishes it in the *Federal Register.* The agency must respond to any significant comments that it has received concerning the proposed rule by either modifying its final rule or explaining, in a statement accompanying the final rule, why it has not made any changes. Later, the rule is compiled in the *Code of Federal Regulations,* an important source for paralegals researching administrative law, as you will learn in Chapter 16.

INVESTIGATION.   Administrative agencies conduct investigations of the entities that they regulate. One type of agency investigation occurs during the rule-making process. The purpose of this type of investigation is to obtain information about a certain individual, firm, or industry in order to ensure that the rule issued is based on a consideration of relevant factors (rather than being arbitrary and

On the Web
The *Code of Federal Regulations* and the *Federal Register* can be found online at the following government Web site: **http://www.access.gpo. gov/nara/cfr/index.html.**

DEVELOPING PARALEGAL SKILLS

Preparing for an Administrative Hearing

Brent Moore is a nurse and a paralegal. He represents clients before the Social Security Administration (SSA). His nursing background helps him to evaluate medical claims and to argue on behalf of his client when a dispute arises between a client and the SSA. One of his clients, Margarete Sufuentes, has just been denied disability benefits by the SSA. Brent is preparing to argue Margarete's case at an agency hearing.

TIPS FOR PREPARING FOR AN ADMINISTRATIVE HEARING

- Be certain to file the hearing request form within the required time limits.

- Obtain copies of all reports and other documents well in advance of the hearing.
- Explain the hearing procedure to the client.
- Prepare exhibits to display critical evidence, such as reports, medical records, and so on.
- Compile all documents and other evidence in the order in which it will be presented at the hearing.
- Include documents and other evidence that you will attempt to discredit at the hearing.
- Prepare and submit a written argument, or brief, if necessary.
- Rehearse your oral argument.

capricious). After final rules are issued, agencies conduct investigations to monitor compliance with those rules. A typical agency investigation of this kind might begin when a paralegal working for the agency takes a statement from a citizen who reports a possible violation of an agency rule. Agencies may then request additional documents or conduct inspections to determine whether a violation has occurred.

Normally, business firms comply with agency requests to inspect facilities or business records because it is in any firm's interest to maintain good relationships with regulatory bodies. In some instances, though, such as when a firm thinks an agency request is unreasonable and may be detrimental to the firm's interest, the firm may refuse to comply with the request. In such situations, an agency may need to resort to the use of a subpoena (see Chapter 13) or a search warrant (see Chapter 15).

ENFORCEMENT—ADJUDICATION.   After conducting an investigation of a suspected rule violation, an agency may begin to take administrative action against an individual or organization. Most administrative actions are resolved through negotiated settlements at their initial stages, without the need for formal adjudication.

Negotiated Settlements.   Depending on the agency, negotiations may take the form of a simple conversation or a series of informal conferences. Whatever form the negotiations take, their purpose is to rectify the problem to the agency's satisfaction and eliminate the need for additional proceedings. Both sides are usually motivated to settle in order to avoid the expense and time (and sometimes negative publicity) associated with formal proceedings.

Formal Complaints.   If a settlement cannot be reached, the agency may issue a formal complaint against the suspected violator. For example, suppose that the Environmental Protection Agency (EPA) finds that a factory is polluting groundwater in violation of federal pollution laws. The EPA will issue a complaint

---

ETHICAL CONCERN
Decorum before Agency Hearings

What do you do when an administrative law judge (ALJ) is obviously biased against you or your client? Suppose that you are authorized to represent a client before a certain state agency, and your client, who is suffering from alcoholism and related medical problems, is trying to obtain disability benefits from the agency. The ALJ makes it clear that he does not believe that those who voluntarily abuse alcohol should be entitled to state disability or medical assistance for alcohol-related problems. Throughout the hearing, your patience and poise are put to the test by the judge's perceptibly hostile attitude and intimidating words. In situations such as these, you need to remember that you are at the hearing not to serve your own interests but to serve the interests of the client. Angry responses to the ALJ will only worsen your client's chances for a favorable decision, and if the decision is appealed, your heated responses will be on the record for review. As Rule 3.5 of the Model Rules of Professional Conduct points out, no matter what judges may do, the advocate must "protect the record for subsequent review and preserve professional integrity by patient firmness."

---

against the violator in an effort to bring the plant into compliance with federal regulations. This complaint is a public document, and a press release may accompany it. The factory charged in the complaint will respond by filing an answer to the EPA's allegations. If the factory and the EPA cannot agree on a settlement, the case will be adjudicated.

When a case is adjudicated, it is heard by an **administrative law judge (ALJ)**. The ALJ presides over the hearing and has the power to administer oaths, take testimony, rule on questions of evidence, and make determinations of fact. Although the ALJ works for the agency prosecuting the case, he or she is required by law to be an unbiased adjudicator (judge). Hearing procedures vary widely from agency to agency. They may be informal meetings conducted at a table in a conference room, or they may be formal adjudicatory hearings resembling trials. In some agencies, paralegals are allowed to represent clients at these hearings (paralegal practice before administrative agencies will be discussed shortly).

administrative law judge (ALJ)
One who presides over an administrative agency hearing and who has the power to administer oaths, take testimony, rule on questions of evidence, and make determinations of fact.

Agency Orders.   Following the hearing, the ALJ renders a decision on the case. Either party can appeal the ALJ's decision to the board or commission that governs the agency. If, in the example just mentioned, the factory is dissatisfied with the ALJ's decision, it can appeal the decision to the commission that governs the EPA. Then, if the factory is dissatisfied with the commission's decision, it can appeal the decision to a federal court of appeals. If no party appeals the case, the ALJ's decision becomes final. The ALJ's decision also becomes final if a party appeals but the commission and the court decline to review the case.

If an appellate court does review the ALJ's decision, the court normally defers to agency decisions on questions of fact—just as appellate courts do when reviewing trial court decisions. Usually, the court will look only at certain factors, such as whether the agency exceeded its authority and whether it followed the proper procedures. The court will also determine whether the ALJ interpreted applicable laws properly and whether the decision was based on substantial evidence or was "arbitrary and capricious," thus constituting an abuse of discretion.

On the Web
To find information on state administrative agencies, use the State Web Locator at **http://www.infoctr.edu/swl.**

State Administrative Agencies

So far, you have been reading about federal administrative agencies. State agencies, however, also play a significant regulatory role. As a paralegal, you may find yourself working with a state agency, a federal agency, or perhaps both simultaneously. Not all states publish agency regulations in a compiled form, as the federal government does. In states that do not provide compilations, it may be difficult to research state regulations, at least until you become familiar with the workings of a particular agency. Many states, however, do have administrative codes, which make it easier to locate the rules and regulations of specific agencies.

Commonly, a state creates an agency as a parallel to a federal agency to provide similar services on a more localized basis. Such parallel agencies include the federal Social Security Administration and the state welfare agency, the Internal Revenue Service and the state revenue agency, and the Environmental Protection Agency and the state pollution-control agency. Not all federal agencies have parallel state agencies, however. The U.S. Postal Service, the Federal Bureau of Investigation, and the Nuclear Regulatory Commission have no parallel state agencies.

In the event that the actions of parallel state and federal agencies come into conflict, the actions of the federal agency will prevail. For example, if the Federal Aviation Administration specifies the hours during which airplanes may land at and depart from airports, a state or local government is prohibited from issuing inconsistent laws or regulations governing the same activity. The priority of federal law over conflicting state laws is based on the supremacy clause of the U.S. Constitution. This clause, which is found in Article VI, states that the U.S. Constitution and "the Laws of the United States which shall be made in Pursuance thereof . . . shall be the supreme Law of the Land."

Paralegal Practice before Administrative Agencies

Paralegals, as well as other qualified nonlawyers, are permitted to practice administrative law in some situations under Section 555 of the APA, which reads, in part, as follows:

> A person compelled to appear in person before an agency or representative thereof is entitled to be accompanied, represented, and advised by counsel or, if permitted by the agency, by other qualified representative[s].

By allowing "other qualified representative[s]" to practice administrative law, an agency increases efficiency while reducing the costs involved—the client is not required to hire an attorney to pursue an administrative claim (unless, of course, court action is required). Federal agencies that allow representation by nonlawyers include the Social Security Administration and the Wage and Appeals Board within the Department of Labor.

One agency, the Federal Maritime Commission, requires nonlawyer representatives to register, pay a small fee, and satisfy certain educational requirements. To represent someone before the Social Security Administration, in contrast, one need only obtain from the agency an "Appointment of Representative" form and have the client sign it. Other agencies that allow nonlawyers to represent clients may require the nonlawyer to pass an examination or to meet specific educational requirements.

Although only federal agencies must follow the APA, state agency procedures are usually similar to those required by the APA, and both federal and state agen-

PENALTIES FOR VIOLATING THE CLEAN AIR ACT.   The EPA can assess civil penalties of up to $25,000 per day for violations of emission limits under the Clean Air Act. Additional fines of up to $5,000 per day can be assessed for other violations, such as failing to maintain required records. To penalize those for whom it is more cost-effective to violate the act than to comply with it, the EPA is authorized to obtain a penalty equal to the violator's economic benefits from noncompliance. Persons who provide information about violators may be paid up to $10,000. Private citizens can also sue violators. Those who knowingly violate the act may be subject to criminal penalties, including fines of up to $1 million and imprisonment for up to two years (for false statements or failures to report violations). Corporate officers are among those who may be subject to these penalties.

Water Pollution

Federal regulations governing water pollution can be traced back to the Rivers and Harbors Appropriations Act of 1899. These regulations prohibited ships and manufacturers from discharging or depositing refuse in navigable waterways.

NAVIGABLE WATERS.   Navigable waters include coastal waters, freshwater wetlands, and lakes and streams used by interstate travelers and industry. In 1948, Congress passed the Federal Water Pollution Control Act (FWPCA), but its regulatory system and enforcement proved inadequate. In 1972, amendments to the FWPCA—known as the Clean Water Act—were enacted to (1) make waters safe for swimming, (2) protect fish and wildlife, and (3) eliminate the discharge of pollutants into the water. The amendments required that municipal and industrial polluters apply for permits before discharging wastes into navigable waters.

They also set forth specific time schedules, which were extended by amendment in 1977 and by the Water Quality Act of 1987. Under these schedules, the EPA establishes limits for discharges of different types of pollutants based on the technology available for controlling them. Regulations, for the most part, specify that the "best available control technology" be installed. The EPA issues guidelines as to what equipment meets this standard, which essentially requires the most effective pollution-control equipment available.

Under the Clean Water Act, violators are subject to a variety of civil and criminal penalties. Civil penalties for each violation range from a maximum of $10,000 per day, and not more than $25,000 per violation, to as much as $25,000 per day. Criminal penalties range from a fine of $2,500 per day and imprisonment for up to one year to a fine of $1 million and fifteen years' imprisonment. Injunctive relief and damages can also be imposed. The polluting party can be required to clean up the pollution or pay for the cost of doing so. Criminal penalties apply only if a violation was intentional.

DRINKING WATER.   Another statute governing water pollution is the Safe Drinking Water Act of 1974, which requires the EPA to set maximum levels for pollutants in public water systems. Operators of public water supply systems must come as close as possible to meeting the EPA's standards by using the best available technology that is economically feasible. The EPA is particularly concerned about contamination from underground sources. Pesticides and wastes leaked from landfills or disposed of in underground injection wells are among the more than two hundred pollutants known to exist in groundwater used for drinking in at least thirty-four states. The act was amended in 1996 to give the EPA more flexibility in setting regulatory standards governing drinking water.

OCEAN DUMPING.   The Marine Protection, Research, and Sanctuaries Act of 1972 (known popularly as the Ocean Dumping Act), as amended in 1983, prohibits entirely the ocean dumping of certain materials, including chemical and high-level radioactive waste. The act establishes a permit program for transporting and dumping other materials. There are specific exemptions, including pollutants subject to the permit provisions of other environmental legislation.

Each violation of any provision or permit may result in a civil penalty of not more than $50,000 or revocation or suspension of the permit. A knowing violation is a criminal offense that may result in a $50,000 fine, imprisonment for not more than a year, or both. An injunction may also be imposed.

OIL POLLUTION.   In 1989, the supertanker *Exxon Valdez* caused the worst oil spill in North American history in the waters of Alaska's Prince William Sound. A quarter of a million barrels of crude oil—more than ten million gallons—leaked out of the ship's broken hull. In response to the *Exxon Valdez* oil-spill disaster, Congress passed the Oil Pollution Act of 1990. Any onshore or offshore oil facility, oil shipper, vessel owner, or vessel operator that discharges oil into navigable waters or onto an adjoining shore may be liable for cleanup costs, as well as damages. The act created a $1 billion oil cleanup and economic compensation fund and decreed that by the year 2011, oil tankers using U.S. ports must be double hulled to limit the severity of accidental spills.

Under the act, damage to natural resources, private property, and the local economy, including the increased cost of providing public services, is compensable. The act provides for civil penalties of $1,000 per barrel spilled or $25,000 for each day of the violation. The party held responsible for the cleanup costs can bring a civil suit for contribution from other potentially liable parties.

Toxic Chemicals

Originally, most environmental cleanup efforts were directed toward reducing smog and making water safe for fishing and swimming. Over time, however, control of toxic chemicals became an important part of environmental law.

PESTICIDES AND HERBICIDES.   The first toxic chemical problem to receive widespread public attention was that posed by pesticides and herbicides. Using these chemicals to kill insects and weeds has increased agricultural productivity, but their residue remains in the environment. In some instances, accumulations of this residue have killed animals, and scientists have identified potential long-term effects that are detrimental to humans. Under the Federal Insecticide, Fungicide, and Rodenticide Act of 1947, pesticides and herbicides must be registered before they can be sold, used only for approved applications, and used in limited quantities when applied to food crops. If a substance is identified as harmful, the EPA can cancel its registration.

Under 1996 amendments to the act, for a pesticide to remain on the market, there must be a "reasonable certainty of no harm" to people from exposure to the pesticide. This means that there must be no more than a one-in-a-million risk to people of developing cancer from exposure in any way, including eating food that contains residues from the pesticide.

Penalties for registrants and producers for violating the act include imprisonment for up to one year and a fine of no more than $50,000. Penalties for commercial dealers include imprisonment for up to one year and a fine of no more than $25,000. Farmers and other private users of pesticides or herbicides who violate the act are subject to a $1,000 fine and imprisonment for up to thirty days.

TOXIC SUBSTANCES.   The Toxic Substances Control Act of 1976 regulates chemicals and chemical compounds that are known to be toxic (such as asbestos and polychlorinated biphenyls, popularly known as PCBs) and authorizes investigation of any possible harmful effects from new chemical compounds. The regulations permit the EPA to require that manufacturers, processors, and other organizations planning to use chemicals first determine their effects on human health and the environment. The EPA may require special labeling, limit the use of a substance, set production quotas, or prohibit the use of a substance altogether.

HAZARDOUS WASTES.   Some industrial, agricultural, and household wastes pose more serious threats than others. If not properly disposed of, these toxic chemicals may present a substantial danger to human health and the environment. If released into the environment, they may contaminate public drinking water resources.

Resource Conservation and Recovery Act.   In 1976, Congress passed the Resource Conservation and Recovery Act (RCRA) in reaction to an ever-increasing concern about the effects of hazardous waste materials on the environment. The RCRA required the EPA to establish regulations to monitor and control hazardous waste disposal and to determine which forms of solid waste should be considered hazardous and thus subject to regulation. The act authorized the EPA to promulgate various technical requirements for some types of facilities for storage and treatment of hazardous waste. The act also requires all producers of hazardous waste materials to label and package properly any hazardous waste that is to be transported.

The RCRA was amended in 1984 and 1986 to decrease the use of land containment in the disposal of hazardous waste and to require compliance with the act by some generators of hazardous waste—such as those generating less than 1,000 kilograms (2,200 pounds) a month—that had previously been excluded from regulation under the RCRA.

Under the RCRA, a company may be assessed a civil penalty based on the seriousness of the violation, the probability of harm, and the extent to which the violation deviates from RCRA requirements. The assessment may be up to $25,000 for each violation. Criminal penalties include fines up to $50,000 for each day of violation, imprisonment for up to two years (in most instances), or both. Criminal fines and the time of imprisonment can be doubled for certain repeat offenders.

Superfund.   In 1980, Congress passed the Comprehensive Environmental Response, Compensation, and Liability Act (CERCLA), commonly known as Superfund. The basic purpose of Superfund, which was amended in 1986, is to regulate the cleanup of disposal sites in which hazardous waste is leaking into the environment. A special federal fund was created for this purpose.

Superfund provides that when a release or a threatened release of hazardous chemicals from a site occurs, the following persons are responsible for cleaning up the site: (1) the person who generated the wastes disposed of at the site, (2) the person who transported the wastes to the site, (3) the person who owned or operated the site at the time of the disposal, and (4) the current owner or operator. A person falling within one of these categories is referred to as a **potentially responsible party (PRP).** If the PRPs do not cleanup the site, Superfund authorizes the EPA to clean up the site and recover cleanup costs from the PRPs.

Superfund imposes strict liability on PRPs. Also, liability under Superfund is usually joint and several—that is, a PRP who generated only a fraction of the hazardous waste disposed of at the site may nevertheless be liable for all of the cleanup costs. CERCLA authorizes a party who has incurred cleanup costs to

potentially responsible party (PRP) A party who may be liable under the Comprehensive Environmental Response, Compensation, and Liability Act, or Superfund. Any person who generated hazardous waste, transported hazardous waste, owned or operated a waste site at the time of disposal, or currently owns or operates a site may be responsible for some or all of the cleanup costs involved in removing the hazardous chemicals.

DEVELOPING PARALEGAL SKILLS

Monitoring the *Federal Register*

Robin Hayes is a legal assistant for CARCO, Inc., a large company that manufactures automobile parts. She works in the environmental law practice group, within the corporation's legal department. One of her responsibilities is to monitor the *Federal Register* on a daily basis for newly proposed environmental regulations and for changes to existing rules. Today, Robin notices a change to the hazardous waste manifest, a form that CARCO is required to use when shipping hazardous waste to a disposal facility. The change requires the company to certify its efforts in reducing the amount of hazardous waste that it generates. Robin prepares a memo to the attorneys in the group, because they will need to inform management of the change.

CHECKLIST FOR MONITORING THE *FEDERAL REGISTER*

• Have your name put at the top of the routing slip that circulates the *Federal Register* to personnel in your firm or department.

• Review the *Federal Register* every day without fail.

• Begin by perusing the table of contents to locate topics affecting your client.

• Next, review the subtopics to determine if notices, rules, or proposed rules have been issued on topics affecting your client.

• Skim through any notices, rules, and proposed rules that may apply to your client.

• Read in detail the relevant notices, rules, and proposed rules that may apply to your client.

• Photocopy relevant notices, rules, and proposed rules for circulation to the attorneys and others who should be advised of this information.

• Notify the attorneys and others of upcoming deadlines for comments on proposed rules and changes.

---

bring a "contribution action" against any other person who is liable or potentially liable for a percentage of the costs.

State and Local Regulation

Many states regulate the degree to which the environment may be polluted. Thus, for example, even when state zoning laws permit a business's proposed development, the proposal may have to be altered to change the development's impact on the environment. State laws may restrict a business's discharge of chemicals into the air or water or regulate its disposal of toxic wastes. States may also regulate the disposal or recycling of other wastes, including glass, metal, and plastic containers and paper. Additionally, states may restrict emissions from motor vehicles.

City, county, and other local governments control some aspects of the environment. For instance, local zoning laws control some land use. These laws may be designed to inhibit or direct the growth of cities and suburbs or to protect the natural environment. Numerous other environmental concerns, including methods of waste and garbage removal, are typically subject to local regulation.

Environmental Law and the Paralegal

Paralegals who specialize in environmental law find employment in a number of settings. A paralegal specialist in this area may work for a federal or state environmental agency, a local government agency concerned with natural resources, a law firm's environmental department, or a corporate legal department.

TODAY'S PROFESSIONAL PARALEGAL

Working for an Administrative Agency

The Environmental Protection Agency (EPA) employs several paralegals. One of them is Mary Ulrich, who works for the Freedom of Information Act (FOIA) officer. The Freedom of Information Act of 1966 requires federal government agencies to disclose certain records to any person on request. Some types of records, however, such as those containing information relating to trade secrets, are exempt from this requirement. Anyone who wishes to obtain information from a government agency must submit a written request to the agency. Mary Ulrich's job involves responding to FOIA requests on behalf of the EPA. FOIA requests must be made in writing, but often legal assistants or attorneys from law firms or corporations call before they submit written requests.

RECEIVING AN INFORMATION REQUEST

Mary's telephone rings. It is Scott Webb, a paralegal with Sims and Howard in Chicago. He wants to talk to Mary about the EPA's file on the Black Hole landfill, a toxic waste site to which one of Sims and Howard's clients has allegedly contributed hazardous waste. Scott wants to know the size of the file on the landfill and the type of information that it contains. If the EPA's file is small enough, Scott will request copies of most of its relevant contents. He will request the copies over the phone and will also follow up on the conversation with a letter. Mary will be able to tell Scott if there are documents in the file that might have to be reviewed by an agency attorney before they can be reproduced.

Mary pulls the file and finds that it contains at least ten thousand pages of documents. She informs Scott of this. Because the agency charges for copying costs, including the time that Mary spends copying the records, Scott asks for specific types of documents. One kind of record that he wants is a list of the types and quantities of hazardous waste that other parties have allegedly contributed to the site.

DEALING WITH FOIA EXEMPTIONS

Mary looks for this information in the file. She finds it but also sees that information on several of the alleged contributors is exempt from FOIA disclosure requirements under trade secrets exemptions. Mary informs Scott of this fact. Scott also wants information on why the agency decided to include his firm's client in the list of contributors to the toxic waste site. Mary reminds Scott that interagency memos are usually privileged and that his request will have to be reviewed by agency counsel to determine if the agency could disclose this information.

Mary and Scott finish their conversation. Mary decides to wait for Scott's formal FOIA letter before starting to work on the request because so many of the documents will have to be reviewed by counsel before they can be sent out. Maybe Scott and the attorney for whom he works will rethink their strategy or make a different request now that they know they will have to wait for a decision from the agency's counsel office, especially when a good part of their request might be denied.

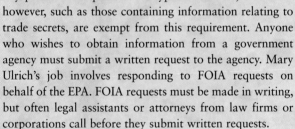

If you work for a government environmental agency, you may be involved in the research and writing necessary to create new rules or revise existing ones. You may be asked to assist in monitoring compliance with a particular regulation. You might draft documents relating to legal actions brought against violators. In a corporate environment, you may be asked to help draft the firm's environmental policies and procedures or to obtain and fill out forms the firm is required to submit to an environmental agency.

Some paralegals working in the area of environmental law may be involved in extensive litigation concerning environmental claims. For example, a government agency may bring an action against a business that has failed to comply with a particular law or regulation. A company may sue another company that refuses to contribute to the cost of cleaning up a hazardous site to which it furnished materials. An individual or group of individuals may sue a company for health injuries suffered because of the company's polluting activities. Often, such litigation involves massive amounts of paperwork and exhibits, and case management becomes a challenge. A paralegal who can meet this challenge will be a valuable asset to his or her employer.

Here are some of the many types of tasks that you might perform as a paralegal working in the area of environmental law:

- Obtain permits from federal, state, or local environmental agencies to use property in certain ways (such as clearing trees or filling wetlands).
- Draft and file the documents necessary to include another polluting company as a defendant in an action brought by a government agency.
- Monitor the *Federal Register* on a routine basis to determine if new environmental regulations have been proposed by the EPA.
- Research the scope and applicability of a particular regulation to find out whether a client's planned action may violate that rule, whether a permit is required, and so on.
- Prepare for and perhaps attend hearings before environmental agencies.
- Assist in negotiations between an environmental agency and a business firm or group of firms to settle a dispute over a claimed violation of an environmental law or regulation.
- Coordinate a corporate employer's environmental programs and policies and monitor corporate activities to ensure proper compliance with environmental laws.

 ## KEY TERMS AND CONCEPTS

adjudication	**counteradvertising**	**independent regulatory agency**
administrative law judge (ALJ)	**deceptive advertising**	**legislative rule**
administrative process	**delegation doctrine**	**potentially responsible party (PRP)**
bureaucracy	**environmental impact statement (EIS)**	**rulemaking**
cease-and-desist order		**toxic tort**
consumer	**executive agency**	
consumer law	**garnishment**	

 ## CHAPTER SUMMARY

| Administrative Law | Administrative agencies combine functions normally associated with the three branches of government (executive, legislative, and judicial). Administrative agencies issue and enforce specific rules and regulations.

1. *Types of administrative agencies*—There are two basic types of federal administrative agencies:

   a. Executive agencies are cabinet departments or subagencies within cabinet departments and are accountable to the president. The president has the power to appoint and remove officers of executive agencies.

   b. Independent regulatory agencies are also part of the executive branch but are outside the major executive departments and subject to less presidential control. Officers serve for fixed terms and cannot be removed without just cause. |

Administrative Law—Continued	2. *Agency creation and powers*—Congress (and state legislatures) create administrative agencies by passing enabling legislation, which specifies the name, purpose, function, and powers of the agency being created.
	
	3. *Agency powers and the Constitution*—Courts generally hold that Article I of the U.S. Constitution authorizes Congress to delegate power to agencies so that the agencies can make the rules necessary for implementing the laws enacted by Congress. This is known as the delegation doctrine and is the basis for all administrative law.
	
	4. *Limitations on agency power*—In many ways, agencies function independently, although the other branches of government may exercise some control over them. A court will invalidate an agency rule if it is unconstitutional and may sometimes review an agency's decision on appeal. Congress can take certain powers away from an agency or can limit an agency's operations by reducing its funding. The president can remove officers of executive agencies.
	
	5. *Administrative process*—Administrative agencies exercise three basic functions:
	
	   a. Rulemaking—Agencies make rules governing activities within the areas of their authority. Typically, rulemaking procedure involves publishing notice of the proposed rulemaking, allowing a comment period, and then drafting the final rule.
	
	   b. Investigation—Agencies conduct investigations of regulated entities both to gather information and to monitor compliance with agency rules.
	
	   c. Adjudication—When a regulated entity fails to comply with agency rules, the agency can take administrative action. Most violations are resolved through negotiated settlements. If a settlement cannot be reached, the agency may issue a formal complaint, and an administrative law judge (ALJ) will conduct a hearing and decide the issue. Either party can appeal the ALJ's order to the board or commission that governs the agency if dissatisfied. Most agency decisions can also then be appealed to a court.
	
	6. *State administrative agencies*—State administrative agencies regulate state affairs. Often, a state agency is created as a parallel to a federal agency. If the actions of parallel state and federal agencies come into conflict, the federal agency will prevail, based on the supremacy clause of the U.S. Constitution.
	
	7. *Paralegals in agency hearings*—Paralegals and other nonlawyers are permitted to represent clients before certain federal and state agencies.

Consumer Law	All statutes, agency rules, and common law judicial decisions that serve to protect the interests of consumers are classified as consumer law. Today, there are many federal consumer protection statutes, in addition to a wide variety of state consumer protection statutes. Some state statutes provide more protection than that afforded by the federal laws discussed below.
	
	1. *Deceptive advertising*—Advertising that misleads consumers or that is based on false claims is prohibited by the Federal Trade Commission (FTC). Generally, the test for whether an ad is deceptive is whether a reasonable consumer would be deceived by the ad.
	
	   a. Cease-and-desist orders—The FTC can require the advertiser to stop the challenged advertising.
	
	   b. Counteradvertising—The FTC may also require the advertiser to advertise to correct the earlier misinformation.

Consumer Law—Continued	2. *Labeling and packaging*—Manufacturers must comply with labeling or packaging requirements for their specific products. In general, labels must be accurate and not misleading. Food products must bear labels detailing their nutritional content, and standards must be met before a product can use terms like *fresh* and *organic* on the label.
	3. *Sales transactions*—Many federal and state laws regulate the disclosure of terms to consumers in sales transactions, particularly in door-to-door and mail-order sales. The FTC conducts most of the federal regulation of sales. Numerous provisions of the Uniform Commercial Code also protect consumers from unfair trade practices at the state level.
	4. *Consumer health and safety*—Laws protecting the health and safety of consumers regulate the content of a food, drug, or other item, as opposed to regulating what appears on the label.
	a. The Federal Food, Drug and Cosmetic Act protects consumers against adulterated and misbranded foods and drugs. The act establishes food standards, specifies safe levels of potentially hazardous food additives, and sets classifications of foods and food advertising.
	b. The Consumer Product Safety Act seeks to protect consumers from risk of injury from hazardous products. The Consumer Product Safety Commission has the power to remove products that are deemed imminently hazardous from the market and to ban the manufacture and sale of hazardous products.
	5. *Consumer credit protection*—Credit protection has become an important area regulated by consumer protection legislation.
	a. Truth-in-Lending Act (TILA)—A disclosure law requiring sellers and lenders to disclose credit terms or loan terms so that individuals can shop around to compare terms. Also provides for the following:
	1. Equal credit opportunity—Prohibits creditors from discriminating on the basis of race, religion, national origin, color, gender, marital status, or age.
	2. Credit-card protection—Limits the liability of cardholders for unauthorized charges made on unsolicited credit cards.
	3. Credit-card rules—Allows credit-card users to withhold payment for faulty products purchased by credit card and to withhold payment for charges billed in error until disputes are resolved.
	b. Fair Credit Reporting Act—Protects consumers against inaccurate credit reporting and provides that credit reports can only be issued for certain purposes. Consumers are entitled to receive a copy of their credit report on request and to be notified any time they are denied credit or insurance based on the report. The reporting agency must conduct an investigation if the consumer contests any information on the credit report.
Environmental Law	1. *Common law actions*—Parties may recover damages for injuries sustained as a result of a firm's pollution-causing activities under the theories of negligence and strict liability. Businesses engaging in ultrahazardous activities are liable for whatever injuries the activities cause, regardless of whether they exercise reasonable care.

Environmental Law—Continued	**2.** *Federal regulation of the environment—* **a.** The federal Environmental Protection Agency (EPA) was created in 1970 to coordinate federal environmental programs. The EPA administers most federal environmental policies and statutes. **b.** The National Environmental Policy Act of 1969 imposes environmental responsibilities on all federal agencies and requires the preparation of an environmental impact statement (EIS) for every major federal action. An EIS must analyze the action's impact on the environment, its adverse effects and possible alternatives, and its irreversible effects on environmental quality. **3.** *Important areas regulated by federal law—*Important areas regulated by the federal government include the following: **a.** Air pollution—Regulated under the authority of the Clean Air Act of 1963 and its amendments, particularly those of 1970 and 1990. **b.** Water pollution—Regulated under the authority of the Rivers and Harbors Appropriation Act of 1899, as amended, and the Federal Water Pollution Control Act of 1948, as amended by the Clean Water Act of 1972. **c.** Toxic chemicals and hazardous waste—Pesticides and herbicides, toxic substances, and hazardous waste are regulated under the authority of the Federal Insecticide, Fungicide, and Rodenticide Act of 1947, the Toxic Substances Control Act of 1976, and the Resource Conservation and Recovery Act of 1976, respectively. The Comprehensive Environmental Response, Compensation, and Liability Act (CERCLA) of 1980, as amended, regulates the cleanup of hazardous waste–disposal sites. **4.** *State and local regulation—*Activities affecting the environment are controlled at the local and state levels through regulations relating to land use, the disposal and recycling of garbage and waste, and pollution-causing activities in general.

✻ QUESTIONS FOR REVIEW

1. How are administrative agencies created? What are two types of federal agencies?

2. What powers can an administrative agency exercise? Why is it said that administrative agencies exercise powers—executive, legislative, and judicial—that are usually divided among the three branches of government?

3. How are agency powers constitutionally justified? How are agency powers held in check?

4. Describe the most commonly used procedure for agency rulemaking. Where can a paralegal find an agency rule?

5. How do agencies enforce laws and regulations? What is the role of the administrative law judge?

6. What are some areas of consumer law regulated by statute? Name and describe some of the most important consumer protection statutes.

7. How does the Federal Food, Drug and Cosmetic Act protect consumers? What are the major federal statutes providing for consumer protection in credit transactions?

8. What are the major federal statutes that protect the environment? What federal agency is charged with administering federal environmental laws? Do states also pass laws and issue regulations protecting the environment?

9. What is an environmental impact statement (EIS), and when is one required? What factors does an EIS evaluate?

10. What is Superfund? What parties are responsible for the cleanup of hazardous waste sites?

✳ ETHICAL QUESTIONS

1. Ting Li is a paralegal on the staff at Fountain Square, an exclusive retirement community and assisted living facility. Ting has been asked by one of the attorneys she works with to assist a resident, Charles Koehn, in a dispute with the Veterans Benefits Administration. Charles, who is eighty-nine, suffers from periods of dementia, in addition to having several other medical problems. Charles's only living relative is Linda Moore, a daughter with whom he has not spoken in several years. One day, a woman calls Fountain Square and asks to speak with Ting. She states that she is from the Veterans Administration and asks a number of questions about Charles, his medical condition, his current income, and the veteran's benefits he is receiving. Assuming the woman is from the Veterans Administration, Ting answers her questions. Has Ting violated any ethical obligation? How should she have handled the situation? How would you go about verifying the identity of an agency representative over the phone?

2. Lucinda Dunlop is a paralegal for a busy employment law firm. She is working on a case in which a client, Jamar Howell, claims he was fired from his job because of his race. Lucinda's supervising attorney asks her to contact the Equal Employment Opportunity Commission (EEOC) to find out what procedural requirements must be followed before Jamar's case can be filed in court. Lucinda has never contacted the EEOC before. Now, she makes a number of calls to the agency. Each time, she speaks to a different person and gets a different response to her questions. She is frustrated and has many other cases on which she needs to work. Finally, Lucinda writes down the response that she knows the attorney wants to hear, even though it is not exactly what she was told. Has Lucinda breached an ethical duty? Which one? If it turns out that the information she has given the attorney is inaccurate, could the attorney be sued for negligence?

3. The state Department of Environmental Quality is holding a hearing. FastCar, an automobile manufacturing company, has been accused of violating the air-emissions standards in the state. An administrative law judge (ALJ) is presiding over the hearing. The ALJ makes several comments about lawless corporate polluters and refers to the state's environmental laws as "polluter pay acts." Julie Marks, a paralegal, is attending the hearing with Jeffrey Nelson, a FastCar attorney. How should they respond to the ALJ's remarks?

✳ PRACTICE QUESTIONS AND ASSIGNMENTS

1. Using the material on administrative agencies presented in Exhibits 11.1 and 11.2, identify the agencies described below by name and type (independent or executive):

   a. This department oversees education and reports to the secretary of education.

   b. This department oversees the Food and Drug Administration.

   c. The Immigration and Naturalization Service is an important subagency of this department.

   d. This department oversees the Internal Revenue Service.

   e. This agency oversees issues related to consumer products and protects consumer rights.

   f. This agency investigates claims of employment discrimination.

2. Using the material in the chapter discussing the functions of administrative agencies, identify which function is being carried out in each of the following scenarios:

   a. The Environmental Protection Agency publishes a notice of proposed rulemaking in the *Federal Register*. The proposed rule creates three categories of generators of hazardous waste and imposes various regulations on the different types of generators.

   b. Robert is denied disability benefits by the Social Security Administration (SSA). Robert's attorney challenges the denial, and a hearing on the matter is held by the SSA's administrative law judge.

   c. Louise calls the state department of health to report unsanitary conditions that she has observed at a local restaurant. The health department visits the restaurant to determine whether the conditions there are unsanitary.

3. Using the material on the agency rulemaking process discussed in this chapter, discuss the steps that an agency would follow if it wanted to create the following rule:

   Every paralegal shall be entitled to have the day off on his or her birthday. If the birthday falls on a weekend or a holiday, the paralegal shall be given a day off during the week to celebrate his or her birthday.

4. Rhonda Raines works as a paralegal for a busy attorney. While the attorney is taking a deposition in the firm's conference room, a client calls. The client owns a restaurant and has just returned from out of town to find an inspector from the state's health department at the restaurant's door. The client has not inspected the kitchen yet, and he wants to look it over himself before the inspector sees it. If the restaurant receives another citation for violating the health code, the agency could put the restaurant out of business permanently.

   The client wants to know if there is any way he can prevent the inspector from coming in and inspecting the restaurant. Rhonda tells him the attorney is tied up but she can slip into the conference room and hand him a note asking him what the client can do to put off the inspection. On the basis of what you have learned in this chapter, write a note from the attorney to Rhonda instructing the client on how to keep the inspector out of his kitchen.

5. Using the material on consumer law presented in this chapter, identify the law that would apply to each of the following situations and explain how it would resolve the problem:

   a. Mary purchases a new computer system for $2,500 and pays for it with a credit card. The first week that Mary has her new computer, she has serious difficulty operating many of the programs, the computer constantly freezes up, and she loses work that she has prepared on the word processor. Mary complains to the company from which she purchased the computer. When the problem is not resolved, she withholds payment to her credit-card company and notifies it of the reason.

   b. Dick has a credit card with an $8,000 balance. He loses his job and stops paying the credit-card company. A collection agency begins to harass him at all hours of the day and even calls his former employer to verify that Dick had been fired.

6. Using the materials on environmental law presented in the chapter, identify the law that applies to each of the following situations and explain how it would resolve the problem:

   a. The foreman at a manufacturing plant disposes of a fifty-five-gallon drum of spent solvents, a toxic waste, every week by pouring it on the ground "out back."

   b. An investigation reveals that the local gas utility company has PCBs in its pipeline in excess of those allowed.

   c. An oil company releases hundreds of gallons of oil into a local river, contaminating the river, which is a major source of drinking water for the area.

   d. A manufacturing plant that produces metallic paint for use on motor vehicles releases more pollutants into the air than the allowable emissions limits for its vicinity.

   e. In the 1950s, five large manufacturing companies disposed of hazardous waste by burying the waste on the property of a farmer forty miles away from the city and its inhabitants. The rural farm is now part of a suburb. The suburb's groundwater and drinking water are found to be contaminated by the waste buried on the site of the former farm. The citizens demand that the site be cleaned up.

❋ QUESTIONS FOR CRITICAL ANALYSIS

1. Why are so many administrative agencies needed? What do they regulate? Do government agencies assist those groups that they were created to help, or are agencies unnecessarily burdensome?

2. The heads of independent regulatory agencies serve fixed terms and cannot be removed without cause. What are the benefits of this arrangement? What problems might it cause? Is this a good system?

3. The U.S. Constitution provides for a separation of powers among the executive, legislative, and judicial branches of government. Why, then, are administrative agencies allowed to exercise executive, legisla-

tive, and judicial powers? What would be the result if agencies could not exercise this combination of powers?

4. Federal administrative agencies typically have parallel agencies at the state level. Why? What happens if there is a conflict between a state and a federal regulation? If a citizen wants to challenge an agency rule or decision, must he or she go through two layers of government bureaucracy to do so? If so, is this a good system?

5. Some administrative agencies allow nonlawyers, including paralegals, to represent clients before the

agencies, yet paralegals are not allowed to represent clients in courts. What is the difference between paralegals' representing clients before agencies and representing clients in courts?

6. What debt-collection practices does the Fair Debt Collection Practices Act prohibit? How would these practices assist a debt-collection agency in collecting debts? What can debt-collection agencies legally do to collect debts?

7. Why do employers dislike garnishment proceedings? What action might an employer take to avoid a garnishment situation with a specific employee? How can the employee be protected? Is garnishment fair to the employer? Is it fair to the employee? Why or why not?

8. Make a list of the consumer laws presented in this chapter. What rights do these laws protect? Why are they needed? What does the necessity for consumer protection laws say about our society?

9. What tort actions exist for environmental pollution? How do tort actions fit into the environmental regulatory scheme? What would happen if tort actions were the only remedy for environmental pollution?

10. The Clean Air Act, the Clean Water Act, and the Toxic Substances and Control Act, among others, regulate the amount of pollution allowed into the air, water, and other aspects of the environment. Should any pollution be allowed into the environment? Who should determine how "clean" air or water should be? What might happen if no pollution at all were allowed?

11. In addition to imposing joint liability, Superfund also imposes strict liability—that is, liability without regard to fault—on generators and transporters of hazardous waste and on those who own and operate the site at the time of the disposal and at the time of the cleanup. Is it fair to hold companies liable if they did not know that the waste they were disposing of was harmful? Is it fair to hold a subsequent purchaser of contaminated property liable who did not know that the property was polluted when he or she purchased it? Who ultimately pays for the cleanup costs?

✳ PROJECTS

1. Visit a local law library to determine if your state has an administrative code similar to the federal government's *Code of Federal Regulations*. If your state has such a code, what is it called? Does your state also have a publication similar to the *Federal Register*? If so, what is it called? How often is it published?

2. Using a telephone book or a state directory (or an online directory of state agencies), make a list of five state administrative agencies for which you would be interested in working, along with the phone number of each agency. Call each agency and ask if nonlawyers are allowed to practice before it. Record your results, and report them to the class. Discuss with others in the class what agency each would prefer to work for and why.

3. Contact one of the agencies identified in your answer to Project 2. Arrange to visit the agency to observe what kind of work paralegals perform at that agency. Discuss this project with your instructor before you undertake it to learn if any limitations apply.

4. Contact the Federal Trade Commission by telephone at 1-202-382-4357 or in writing at the following address: Federal Trade Commission, CRC-240, Washington, DC 20580. Find out how to file a complaint for deceptive advertising. Does the agency resolve complaints submitted by individuals?

5. Contact a credit reporting agency and obtain a credit report on yourself, if one exists. Does the report contain accurate information about your credit transactions? If not, and if a denial of credit, employment, or insurance might have been based on the report, you can and should have it corrected, as permitted under the Fair Credit Reporting Act.

✳ USING INTERNET RESOURCES

1. You can read the *Federal Register* online by going to **http://www.access.gpo.gov/nara/cfr/index.html** and clicking on *Federal Register* in the left-hand column. Browse through this site for few minutes. Note that you can search the database by using key words and can narrow your search by picking sections of the *Register* that you wish to search, such as proposed regulations. You can also browse the *Register* table of contents by date.

a. Browse through the table of contents for the current *Federal Register* and become familiar with the layout. What versions of the document are available on the Web site?

b. Assume you work for a corporation that manufactures pesticides. Determine how many rules, proposed rules, and notices might affect your employer in just one issue.

2. The Federal Trade Commission (FTC) provides information on consumer law issues through its Web site, located at **http://www.ftc.gov**. Go to this Web site, and follow the directions given below.

a. Select "Who We Are and How We Serve You." What are the vision, mission, and goals of the FTC?

b. Click on "How the FTC Brings an Action." Summarize in two paragraphs how the FTC brings an action.

c. Click on "Privacy" at the bottom of the screen. What is the FTC's privacy policy regarding those who visit its Web site?

d. Click on "Where to Go for More Information." Make a list of the offices, including their names and addresses, to contact for additional information, along with any other sources included.

e. Go back to the home page and select "Consumer Protection." What areas of consumer protection does the FTC regulate?

f. From the home page, access "Current News Releases." Do any of these news releases deal with false advertising? Prepare a one-paragraph summary of one of the news releases.

END NOTES

1. Administrative law is variously defined. Some scholars define administrative law as the law that governs the authority, powers, and functions of administrative agencies.

PART III

LEGAL PROCEDURES AND PARALEGAL SKILLS

CHAPTER 12

CIVIL LITIGATION—BEFORE THE TRIAL

Chapter Outline

INTRODUCTION ※ CIVIL LITIGATION—A BIRD'S EYE VIEW ※ THE PRELIMINARIES ※ THE PLEADINGS ※ PRETRIAL MOTIONS ※ TRADITIONAL DISCOVERY TOOLS ※ THE DUTY TO DISCLOSE UNDER FRCP 26 ※ DISCOVERY OF ELECTRONIC EVIDENCE

After completing this chapter, you will know:

- The basic steps involved in the civil litigation process and the types of tasks that may be required of paralegals during each step of the pretrial phase.
- What a litigation file is, what it contains, and how it is organized, maintained, and reviewed.
- How a lawsuit is initiated and what documents are filed during the pleadings stage of the civil litigation process.
- What a motion is and how certain pretrial motions, if granted by the court, will end the litigation before the trial begins.
- What discovery is and what kind of information attorneys and their paralegals obtain from parties to the lawsuit and from witnesses when preparing for trial.

DEVELOPING PARALEGAL SKILLS

File Workup

Once a litigation file has been created, the paralegal typically "works up" the file. In the Baranski case, after paralegal Lopez has completed her initial investigation into Baranski's claim, she will review and summarize the information that she has amassed so far, including the information that she has gathered through the initial client interview, subsequent client interviews, and any investigation that she has conducted.

Lopez will also identify areas that might require the testimony of an expert witness. For example, if Baranski claimed that as a result of the accident she had broken her hip and would always walk with a limp, Gilmore would want a medical specialist to give expert testimony to support Baranski's claim. (How to locate expert witnesses will be discussed in later chapters.) Lopez would prepare a list of potential experts for Gilmore to review.

Once Lopez has worked up the file, she will prepare a memo to Gilmore summarizing the file. This memo will provide Gilmore with factual information for deciding which legal remedy or strategy to pursue, what legal issues need to be researched, and generally how to proceed with the case.

TIPS FOR PREPARING A FILE WORKUP MEMO

- Summarize the information that has been obtained about the case.
- Suggest a plan for further investigation in the case (you will read about investigation plans in Chapter 13).
- Suggest additional information that might be obtained during discovery (discussed later in this chapter).
- Include a list of expert witnesses to contact, explaining which witnesses might be preferable and why.

lawsuit progresses, Lopez will make sure that special subfiles are created for documents relating to the pleadings and discovery stages (to be discussed shortly). Depending on the office filing system, the file folders for these subfiles may be color coded or numbered so that each subfile can be readily recognized and retrieved. Lopez will also prepare an index for each subfile to indicate what documents are included in it. The index will be placed at the front of the folder for easy reference.

A properly created and maintained litigation file will provide a comprehensive record of the case so that others in the firm who become involved with it can quickly acquaint themselves with the progress of the proceedings. Because well-organized files are critical to the success of any case, Lopez should take special care to properly maintain the file.

THE PLEADINGS

The next step will be for plaintiff Baranski's attorney (Gilmore) to file a complaint in the appropriate court. The **complaint**[4] is a document that states the claims the plaintiff is making against the defendant. The complaint also contains a statement regarding the court's jurisdiction over the dispute and a demand for a remedy (such as money damages).

The filing of the complaint is the initial step that begins the legal action against the defendant, Peretto. The plaintiff's complaint and the defendant's answer—both of which are discussed below—are **pleadings.** The pleadings inform each party of the claims of the other and specify the issues (disputed questions) involved in the case. We examine here the complaint and answer, two basic pleadings.

The complaint must be filed within the period of time allowed by law for bringing legal actions. The allowable period is fixed by state statutes of limitations

complaint
The pleading made by a plaintiff or a charge made by the state alleging wrongdoing on the part of the defendant.

pleadings
Statements by the plaintiff and the defendant that detail the facts, charges, and defenses involved in the litigation.

(discussed in Chapter 5), and this period varies for different types of lawsuits. For example, actions concerning breaches of sales contracts must usually be brought within four years. For negligence lawsuits, statutes of limitations vary from state to state. After the time allowed under a statute of limitations has expired, normally no action can be brought, no matter how strong the case was originally. For example, if the statute of limitations covering the auto-negligence lawsuit that plaintiff Baranski is bringing against defendant Peretto allows two years for bringing an action, Baranski normally has to initiate the lawsuit within that two-year period or forgo (give up) forever the possibility of suing Peretto for damages caused by the car accident.

Drafting the Complaint

The complaint itself may be no more than a few paragraphs long, or it may be many pages in length, depending on the complexity of the case. In the Baranski case, the complaint will probably be only a few pages long unless special circumstances justify additional details. The complaint will include the following sections, each of which we discuss below:

- Caption.
- Jurisdictional allegations.
- General allegations (the body of the complaint).
- Prayer for relief.
- Signature.
- Demand for a jury trial.

Exhibit 12.2 starting on page 402 shows a sample complaint. The sections of the complaint are indicated in the marginal annotations.

Baranski's case is being filed in a federal court, so the Federal Rules of Civil Procedure (FRCP) apply. If the case were being filed in a state court, paralegal Lopez might need to review the appropriate state rules of civil procedure. The rules for drafting pleadings in state courts differ from the FRCP. The rules also differ from state to state and even from court to court within the same state. Lopez could obtain pleading forms, either from "form books" available in the law firm's files or library (or on computer disk or online) or from pleadings drafted previously in similar cases litigated by the firm in the court in which the Baranski case will be filed.

docket
The list of cases entered on a court's calendar and thus scheduled to be heard by the court.

THE CAPTION.   All documents submitted to the court or other parties during the litigation process begin with a caption. The caption is the heading, which identifies the name of the court, the title of the action, the name of the parties, the type of document, and the court's file number. Note that the court's file number may also be referred to as the case number or *docket number,* depending on the jurisdiction. (A **docket** is the list of cases entered on a court's calendar that are scheduled to be heard.) The caption for a complaint leaves a space for the court to insert the number that it assigns to the case. Courts typically assign the case a number when the complaint is filed. Any document subsequently filed with the court in the case will list the file, case, or docket number on the front page of the document. Exhibit 12.2 shows how the caption will read in the case of *Baranski v. Peretto.*

allegation
A party's statement, claim, or assertion made in a pleading to the court. The allegation sets forth the issue that the party expects to prove.

JURISDICTIONAL ALLEGATIONS.   Because attorney Gilmore is filing the lawsuit in a federal district court, he will have to include in the complaint an allegation that the federal court has jurisdiction to hear the dispute. (An **allegation** is an assertion, claim, or statement made by one party in a pleading that sets out what the party expects to prove to the court.) Recall from Chapter 6 that federal courts can exercise jurisdiction over disputes involving either a *federal question* or *diversity of citizenship*. A federal question arises whenever a claim in a civil lawsuit relates to a federal law, the U.S. Constitution, or a treaty executed by the U.S. government. Diversity of citizenship exists when the parties involved in the lawsuit are citizens of different states and the amount in controversy exceeds $75,000. Because Baranski and Peretto are citizens of different states (Nita and Zero, respectively) and because the amount in controversy exceeds $75,000, the case meets the requirements for diversity-of-citizenship jurisdiction. Gilmore thus asserts that the federal court has jurisdiction on this basis, as illustrated in Exhibit 12.2.

As explained in Chapter 6, certain matters—such as those involving patent or copyright disputes, the Internal Revenue Service, or bankruptcy—can *only* be brought in federal courts. Certain other cases, however, including those involving diversity of citizenship, may be brought in either a state court or a federal court. Thus, an attorney in Gilmore's position can advise the client that he or she has a choice. Gilmore probably considered several factors when advising Baranski on which court would be preferable for her lawsuit. An important consideration is how long it would take to get the case to trial. Many courts are overburdened by their case loads, and sometimes it can take years before a court will be able to hear a case. If Gilmore knows that the case could be heard two years earlier in the federal court than in the state court, that will be an important factor to consider.

GENERAL ALLEGATIONS (THE BODY OF THE COMPLAINT).   The body of the complaint contains a series of allegations, stated in numbered paragraphs, which set forth a claim for relief. In plaintiff Baranski's complaint, the allegations outline the factual events that gave rise to Baranski's claims.[5] The events are described in a series of chronologically arranged, numbered allegations so that the reader can understand them easily. As Exhibit 12.2 shows, the numbers of the paragraphs in the body of the complaint continue the sequence begun in the section on jurisdictional allegations.

Advocate Plaintiff's Position.   When drafting the complaint, paralegal Lopez will play the role of advocate. She must present the facts forcefully and in a way that supports and strengthens the client's claim. The recitation of the facts should demonstrate that defendant Peretto engaged in conduct that entitles plaintiff Baranski to relief. Even though she will want to present the facts in a light most favorable to Baranski, Lopez must be careful not to exaggerate the facts or make false statements. Rather, she must present the facts in such a way that the reader could reasonably infer that defendant Peretto was negligent and that Peretto's negligence caused Baranski's injuries and losses.

What if her research into the case had given Lopez reason to believe that a fact was probably true even though she could not be certain as to its validity? She could still include the statement in the complaint by prefacing it with the phrase, "On information and belief . . . ." This language would indicate to the court that the plaintiff, Baranski, had good reason to believe the truth of the statement but that the evidence for it either had not yet been obtained or might not hold up under close scrutiny.

Be Clear and Concise.   The most effective complaints are those that are clear and concise. Moreover, brevity and simplicity are required under FRCP 8(a). As in all legal writing, Lopez should strive for clarity. When drafting the complaint,

EXHIBIT 12.2
The Complaint

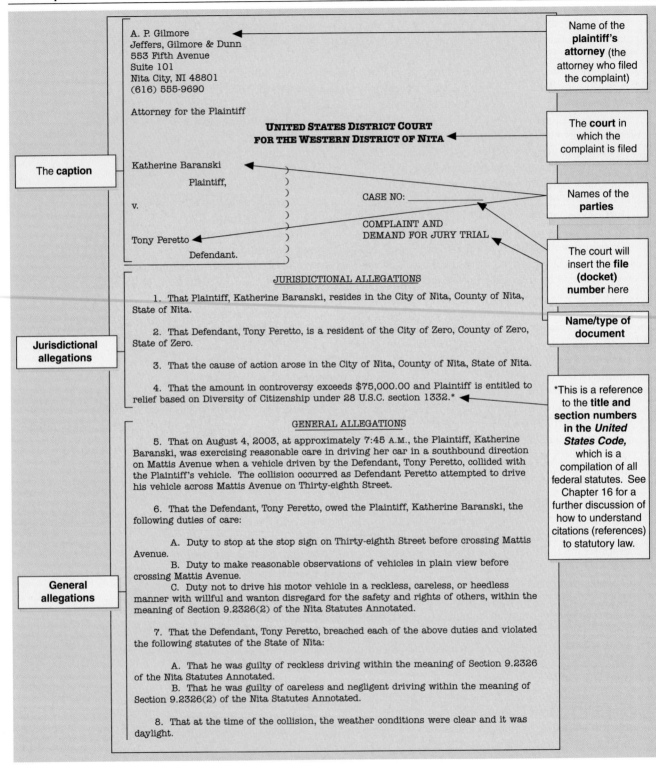

A. P. Gilmore
Jeffers, Gilmore & Dunn
553 Fifth Avenue
Suite 101
Nita City, NI 48801
(616) 555-9690

Attorney for the Plaintiff

**UNITED STATES DISTRICT COURT
FOR THE WESTERN DISTRICT OF NITA**

Katherine Baranski
    Plaintiff,

v.

Tony Peretto
    Defendant.

CASE NO: _____

COMPLAINT AND
DEMAND FOR JURY TRIAL

Name of the **plaintiff's attorney** (the attorney who filed the complaint)

The **court** in which the complaint is filed

Names of the **parties**

The court will insert the **file (docket) number** here

Name/type of document

The caption

Jurisdictional allegations

General allegations

JURISDICTIONAL ALLEGATIONS

1. That Plaintiff, Katherine Baranski, resides in the City of Nita, County of Nita, State of Nita.

2. That Defendant, Tony Peretto, is a resident of the City of Zero, County of Zero, State of Zero.

3. That the cause of action arose in the City of Nita, County of Nita, State of Nita.

4. That the amount in controversy exceeds $75,000.00 and Plaintiff is entitled to relief based on Diversity of Citizenship under 28 U.S.C. section 1332.*

*This is a reference to the **title and section numbers** in the *United States Code,* which is a compilation of all federal statutes. See Chapter 16 for a further discussion of how to understand citations (references) to statutory law.

GENERAL ALLEGATIONS

5. That on August 4, 2003, at approximately 7:45 A.M., the Plaintiff, Katherine Baranski, was exercising reasonable care in driving her car in a southbound direction on Mattis Avenue when a vehicle driven by the Defendant, Tony Peretto, collided with the Plaintiff's vehicle. The collision occurred as Defendant Peretto attempted to drive his vehicle across Mattis Avenue on Thirty-eighth Street.

6. That the Defendant, Tony Peretto, owed the Plaintiff, Katherine Baranski, the following duties of care:

    A. Duty to stop at the stop sign on Thirty-eighth Street before crossing Mattis Avenue.
    B. Duty to make reasonable observations of vehicles in plain view before crossing Mattis Avenue.
    C. Duty not to drive his motor vehicle in a reckless, careless, or heedless manner with willful and wanton disregard for the safety and rights of others, within the meaning of Section 9.2326(2) of the Nita Statutes Annotated.

7. That the Defendant, Tony Peretto, breached each of the above duties and violated the following statutes of the State of Nita:

    A. That he was guilty of reckless driving within the meaning of Section 9.2326 of the Nita Statutes Annotated.
    B. That he was guilty of careless and negligent driving within the meaning of Section 9.2326(2) of the Nita Statutes Annotated.

8. That at the time of the collision, the weather conditions were clear and it was daylight.

DEVELOPING PARALEGAL SKILLS

Federal Court Rules—Creating a Complaint Checklist

Ann Marston is a paralegal who works in a firm with a federal court practice. A new paralegal, Brian Blake, is joining the firm, and Ann has been asked to train Brian. Her supervising attorney has suggested that she create a checklist for drafting federal court complaints. The checklist could be used to train not only Brian but also new associates in the firm.

Before she begins drafting a complaint, Ann meets with Brian and explains what she does. Ann tells Brian that she starts by getting the file and reviewing her notes, memos from the client interview, and any reports, such as police reports, that are in the file. She explains that these sources will assist her in describing how, for example, a personal injury occurred in an accident case. She also checks to see if she made any notes, during her meeting with the attorney who will handle the case, regarding the court in which the case will be filed, because in some cases the state and federal courts have concurrent jurisdiction. Next, she finds out the plaintiff's and the defendant's correct legal names. If necessary, she contacts the secretary of state to obtain the legal name of a corporation. Last, she takes out her copy of the Federal Rules of Civil Procedure and reviews Rules 8, 10, and 11, which specify the kind of information that should be included in complaints filed in a federal court.

CHECKLIST FOR DRAFTING A COMPLAINT

- Determine when the statute of limitations expires by checking the file for the relevant dates.
- Locate a previously drafted complaint form for the type of cases involved.
- Determine the court's basis for jurisdiction in the case, and draft an allegation explaining it.
- Determine the facts that create the cause of action, or the legal basis for the lawsuit.
- Draft the "general allegations," or the body of the complaint. If the plaintiff has more than one legal basis for the relief sought, draft as many "counts" as the plaintiff has.
- Determine the specific type of relief, such as money damages, that the plaintiff is seeking, and draft a prayer for relief.
- Insert a signature block for an attorney to sign after conducting a reasonable inquiry into the facts that support the claim.
- Determine if a jury trial is desired, and draft a demand for a jury trial if needed.

Filing the Complaint

Once the complaint has been prepared, carefully checked for accuracy, and signed by attorney Gilmore, paralegal Lopez will file the complaint with the court in which the action is being brought. To file the complaint, Lopez will either deliver the paper document to the court—the traditional method—or file the complaint with the court electronically via e-mail, fax, or CD-ROM.

TRADITIONAL METHOD OF FILING.   Traditionally, a person filing a complaint personally delivers the complaint to the clerk of the court, together with a specified number of copies of the complaint and a check payable to the court in the amount of the required filing fee. Usually, a summons (which will be discussed shortly) is also attached. If Lopez uses this method of filing, she can either deliver the complaint to the court clerk or have someone deliver it for her. If she is not aware of the court's specific procedures for filing the complaint, she will need to contact the court to verify the amount of the filing fee and how many copies of the complaint need to be filed. Typically, the original (signed) complaint is filed with at least two copies (the court keeps the original, and the plaintiff and defendant receive a copy),

On the Web
To find out whether a particular court permits documents to be filed electronically and, for some courts, to obtain the appropriate forms, visit that court's Web page (or the home page for the state court system). You can find links to federal and state courts at **http://www. findlaw.com.**

although additional copies may be required, particularly if there are multiple plaintiffs or defendants in the case.

The court clerk files the complaint by stamping the date on the first page of all the documents (original and copies); assigning the case a file number, or docket number; and assigning the case to a particular judge. (In some state courts, the file number or judge may not be assigned until later.) The clerk then returns the date-stamped copies to the person who delivered the documents for service on the defendant (to be discussed shortly).

ELECTRONIC FILING METHODS.   The FRCP provides that federal courts *may* permit filing by fax or "other electronic means." Today, as you read in the *Technology and Today's Paralegal* feature in Chapter 6, many courts at both the federal and state levels are experimenting with various methods of electronic filing. Some courts allow faxed pleadings, others allow e-mail transmission, and others allow filing of documents on CD-ROM. The requirements to file documents electronically (in the jurisdictions that permit such filing) vary dramatically. If Lopez wants to file plaintiff Baranski's complaint via electronic means, she will need to contact the individual court to find out the specific requirements.

Paralegals should keep in mind that in the future, filing court documents electronically is likely to become increasingly common. Even today, a few courts prefer certain types of complaints to be filed electronically. For example, the U.S. District Court for the Northern District of California has ordered that all complaints and pleadings in certain types of securities actions be filed electronically through a clearinghouse maintained by the Stanford University Law School. In that court, if a party chooses to file paper documents, the documents must also be posted electronically within three days after filing. The electronic filings are then indexed and made available to the public online. Paralegals thus need to keep up to date on local court rules that may affect the method by which certain complaints are filed.

Service of Process

Before the court can exercise jurisdiction over the defendant—in effect, before the lawsuit can begin—the court must have proof that the defendant was notified of the lawsuit. Serving the summons and complaint—that is, delivering these documents to the defendant in a lawsuit—is referred to as **service of process.**

service of process
The delivery of the summons and the complaint to a defendant.

summons
A document served on a defendant in a lawsuit informing the defendant that a legal action has been commenced against him or her and that the defendant must appear in court or respond to the plaintiff's complaint within a specified period of time.

THE SUMMONS.   The **summons** identifies the parties to the lawsuit, as well as the court in which the case will be heard, and directs the defendant to respond to the complaint within a specified period of time. In the Baranski case, paralegal Lopez will prepare a summons by filling out a form similar to that shown in Exhibit 12.3. Lopez will also prepare a cover sheet for the case (a preprinted form), which is required in the federal courts and in most state courts.

If the case were being brought in a state court, paralegal Lopez would deliver the summons to the court clerk at the same time she delivered the complaint. (In federal court cases, as will be discussed, the complaint may already have been filed under the FRCP provisions relating to waiver of notice.)

After the clerk files the complaint and signs, seals, and issues the summons, attorney Gilmore will be responsible for making sure that the summons and complaint are served on defendant Peretto. The service of the complaint and summons must be effected within a specified time—120 days under FRCP 4(m)—after the complaint has been filed.

EXHIBIT 12.3
A Summons in a Civil Action

UNITED STATES DISTRICT COURT
FOR THE WESTERN DISTRICT OF NITA

Katherine Baranski   )
                  Plaintiff,)
v.   )
)
Tony Peretto   )
             Defendant.)

Civil Action, File Number 99-14335-NI

Summons

To the above-named Defendant:

You are hereby summoned and required to serve upon A. P. Gilmore, Jeffers, Gilmore & Dunn, plaintiff's attorney, whose address is 553 Fifth Avenue, Suite 101, Nita City, NI 48801, an answer to the complaint which is herewith served upon you, within 20 days after service of this summons upon you, exclusive of the day of service. If you fail to do so, judgment by default will be taken against you for the relief demanded in the complaint.

C. H. Hynek   February 10, 2004

CLERK   DATE

John Dolan

BY DEPUTY CLERK

SERVING THE COMPLAINT AND SUMMONS.   How service of process occurs depends on the rules of the court or jurisdiction in which the lawsuit is brought. Under FRCP 4(c)(2), service of process in federal court cases may be effected "by any person who is not a party and who is at least 18 years of age." Paralegal Lopez, for example, could serve the summons by personally delivering it to defendant Peretto. Alternatively, she could make arrangements for someone else to do so, subject to the approval of attorney Gilmore. Many law firms contract with independent companies that provide process service in the local area. In some types of cases, the attorney might request that the court have a U.S. marshal or other federal official serve the summons.

Under FRCP 4(e)(1), service of process in federal court cases may also be effected "pursuant to the law of the state in which the district court is located." Some state courts require that the complaint and summons be served by a public officer, such as a sheriff.

Alternative Service Methods.   Although the most common way to serve process on a defendant is through personal service, or actual delivery, as described above, other methods of service are permissible at times, depending on the jurisdiction. *Substituted service* is any method of service allowed by law in place of personal service, such as service by mail or fax. Most states allow a process server to effect service by leaving a copy of the documents at the defendant's place of work, at his or her home address, or with someone else who resides in the home (such as a wife or an older child). In some circumstances, if the defendant cannot be physically located, the law may allow the process server to effect service by mailing a copy of the summons and complaint to the defendant's last known address and/or publishing a notice in the local newspaper. In other situations, delivering the documents

EXHIBIT 12.4
A Return-of-Service Form

RETURN OF SERVICE

Service of the Summons and Complaint was made by me	DATE 2/11/04
NAME OF SERVER Elena Lopez	TITLE Paralegal

Check one box below to indicate appropriate method of service

☒ Served personally upon the defendant. Place where served: Defendant Peretto's Home: 1708 Johnston Drive, Zero City, Zero 59806

☐ Left copies thereof at the defendant's dwelling house or usual place of abode with a person of suitable age and discretion then residing therein.
Name of person with whom the summons and complaint were left: _____

☐ Returned unexecuted: _____

☐ Other (specify): _____

DECLARATION OF SERVER

I declare under penalty of perjury under the laws of the United States of America that the foregoing information contained in the Return of Service and Statement of Service Fees is true and correct.

Executed on ___2/11/04___   *Elena Lopez*
                    Date   *Signature of Server*

308 University Avenue, Nita City, Nita 48804
Address of Server

---

to an authorized agent is sufficient. The paralegal and attorney thus need to know the types of service authorized by the laws of civil procedure in their own state.

Proof of Service.   Regardless of how the summons is served, attorney Gilmore will need some kind of proof that defendant Peretto actually received the summons. In federal court cases, unless service is made by a U.S. marshal or other official, proof of service is established by having the process server fill out and sign a form similar to the **return-of-service form** shown in Exhibit 12.4. This form is then submitted to the court as evidence that service has been effected.

Jurisdictions May Vary.   Paralegal Lopez must be very careful to comply with the service requirements of the court in which plaintiff Baranski's suit has been filed. If service is not properly made, defendant Peretto will have a legal ground (basis) for asking the court to dismiss the case against him, thus delaying the litigation. As mentioned earlier, the court will not be able to exercise jurisdiction over Peretto until he has been properly notified of the lawsuit being brought against him.

return-of-service form
A document signed by a process server and submitted to the court to prove that a defendant received a summons.

SERVING CORPORATE DEFENDANTS.   In cases involving corporate defendants, the summons and complaint may be served on an officer or a *registered agent* (representative) of the corporation. The name of a corporation's registered agent is usually obtainable from the secretary of state's office in the state in which the company incorporated its business (and, usually, the secretary of state's office in any state in which the corporation does business).

FINDING THE DEFENDANT.   Because some defendants may be difficult to locate, paralegals sometimes have to investigate and attempt to locate a defendant so that process can be served. Helpful information sources include telephone directories, banks, former business partners or fellow workers, credit bureaus, Social Security offices, insurance companies, landlords, state and county tax rolls, utility companies, automobile-registration bureaus, bureaus of vital statistics, and the post office. (Chapter 13 discusses these and other possible sources, including various online sources, that the paralegal might consult when trying to locate parties or witnesses involved in lawsuits.)

THE DEFENDANT CAN WAIVE SERVICE.   In many instances, the defendant is already aware that a lawsuit is being filed (often the plaintiff's attorney has been in contact with the defendant and has indicated that a complaint would be filed). In such cases, a plaintiff can request the defendant to *waive* (give up) her or his right to be formally served with a summons. FRCP 4(d) sets forth the procedure by which a plaintiff's attorney can request the defendant to accept service of the documents through the mail or "other reliable means." Many states have similar laws, which allow the defendant to waive formal service requirements.

   The aim of FRCP 4(d) is to eliminate the costs associated with service of process and to foster cooperation among adversaries. As an incentive, defendants who agree to waive formal service of process under the federal rules receive additional time to respond to the complaint (sixty days, compared with the twenty days that a defendant normally has to respond to the complaint under FRCP 12). Some state rules of civil procedure provide other types of incentives, such as making a party who will not agree to waive service pay for reasonable expenses thereafter incurred in serving or attempting to serve the party.

The Defendant's Response

Once a defendant receives the plaintiff's complaint, the defendant must respond to the complaint within a specified time period (typically twenty to thirty days). If the defendant fails to respond within that time period, the court, on the plaintiff's motion, will enter a **default judgment** against the defendant. The defendant will then be liable for the entire amount of damages that the plaintiff is claiming and will lose the opportunity to either defend against the claim in court or settle the issue with the plaintiff out of court.

   In the Baranski case, assume that defendant Peretto consults with an attorney, Elizabeth A. Cameron, to decide on a course of action. Before Cameron advises Peretto on the matter, she will want to investigate plaintiff Baranski's claim and obtain evidence of what happened at the time of the accident. She may ask her paralegal, Gordon McVay, to call anyone who may have witnessed the accident and any police officers who were at the scene. Attorney Cameron will also ask McVay to gather relevant documents, including the traffic ticket that Peretto received at the time of the accident and any reports that might have been filed by the police. If all goes well, attorney Cameron and paralegal McVay will complete their investigation in a few days and then meet to assess the results.

default judgment
A judgment entered by a clerk or court against a party who has failed to appear in court to answer or defend against a claim that has been brought against him or her by another party.

As mentioned earlier, most cases are settled out of court before they go to trial. But even if Peretto's attorney suspects that an out-of-court settlement might be financially preferable to a trial, she will still draft a response to plaintiff Baranski's claim. She knows that if defendant Peretto does not respond to the plaintiff's complaint within the proper time period, the court will enter a default judgment against Peretto. In deciding how best to respond to the complaint, Peretto's attorney, Cameron, must consider whether to file an answer or a motion to dismiss the case.

answer
A defendant's response to a plaintiff's complaint.

THE ANSWER.   A defendant's **answer** must respond to each allegation in the plaintiff's complaint. FRCP 8(b) permits the defendant to admit or deny the truth of each allegation. Defendant Peretto's attorney may advise Peretto to admit to some of the allegations in plaintiff Baranski's complaint, because doing so narrows the number of issues in dispute.

> ✖ **Any allegations that are not denied by the defendant will be deemed to have been admitted.**

If defendant Peretto has no knowledge as to whether a particular allegation is true or false, then his attorney, Cameron, may indicate that in the answer. This puts the burden of proving the allegation on plaintiff Baranski, just as if it were an outright denial. It is not necessary for Peretto's attorney to include in the answer any of the reasons for the denial of particular allegations in Baranski's complaint. These reasons may be revealed during the discovery phase of the litigation process (discussed later in this chapter).

Exhibit 12.5 illustrates the types of responses that defendant Peretto might make in his answer. Like the complaint, the answer begins with a caption and ends with the attorney's signature. It may also include, following the attorney's signature, an affidavit signed by the defendant, as well as a demand for a jury trial, as in Exhibit 12.5.

> ### Case at a Glance
>
> **The Plaintiff—**
> Plaintiff: Katherine Baranski
> Attorney: Allen P. Gilmore
> Paralegal: Elena Lopez
>
> **The Defendant—**
> Defendant: Tony Peretto
> Attorney: Elizabeth A. Cameron
> Paralegal: Gordon McVay

Answer and Affirmative Defenses.   A defendant may assert, in the answer, a reason why he or she should not be held liable for the plaintiff's injuries even if the facts, as alleged by the plaintiff, are true. This is called raising an **affirmative defense.**

affirmative defense
A response to a plaintiff's claim that does not deny the plaintiff's facts but attacks the plaintiff's legal right to bring an action.

For example, Peretto might claim that someone else was driving his Dodge van when it crashed into Baranski's car. Peretto's attorney might also raise the defense of *contributory negligence.* That is, she could argue that even though defendant Peretto's car collided with Baranski's, plaintiff Baranski was also negligent because she was exceeding the speed limit when the accident occurred and was thus unable to avoid being hit by Peretto's car. As discussed in Chapter 7, in a few states, if it can be shown that the plaintiff was contributorily negligent, the plaintiff will be completely barred from recovery. Most states, however, have abandoned the doctrine of contributory negligence in favor of a *comparative negligence* standard. In these states, a plaintiff whose own negligence contributed to an injury can still recover damages, but the damages are reduced by a percentage that represents the degree of the plaintiff's negligence. Although affirmative defenses are directed toward the plaintiff, the plaintiff is not required to file additional pleadings in response to these defenses.

counterclaim
A claim made by a defendant in a civil lawsuit against the plaintiff; in effect, a counterclaiming defendant is suing the plaintiff.

Answer and Counterclaim.   Peretto's attorney may follow the answers to the plaintiff's allegations with one or more counterclaims. A **counterclaim** is like a reverse lawsuit in which the defendant asserts a claim against the plaintiff for injuries that the defendant suffered from the same incident. For example, defendant Peretto might contend that plaintiff Baranski lost control of her car and

EXHIBIT 12.5
The Answer

Elizabeth A. Cameron
Cameron & Strauss, P.C.
310 Lake Drive
Zero City, ZE 59802
(616) 955-6234

Attorney for Defendant

UNITED STATES DISTRICT COURT
FOR THE WESTERN DISTRICT OF NITA

Katherine Baranski	)	
Plaintiff,	)	CASE NO. 99-14335-NI
	)	Honorable Harley M. Larue
v.	)	
	)	ANSWER AND
Tony Peretto	)	DEMAND FOR JURY TRIAL
Defendant.	)	

JURISDICTIONAL ALLEGATIONS

1. Defendant lacks sufficient information to form a belief as to the truth of the allegations contained in paragraph 1 of Plaintiff's Complaint.

2. Defendant admits the allegations contained in paragraph 2 of Plaintiff's Complaint.

3. Defendant admits the allegations contained in paragraph 3 of Plaintiff's Complaint.

4. Defendant lacks sufficient information to form a belief as to the truth of the allegations contained in paragraph 4 of Plaintiff's Complaint.

GENERAL ALLEGATIONS

5. Defendant admits the allegations contained in paragraph 5 of Plaintiff's Complaint.

6. Defendant admits the allegations contained in paragraph 6 of Plaintiff's Complaint.

7. Defendant contends that he was operating his vehicle properly and denies the allegations contained in paragraph 7 of Plaintiff's Complaint for the reason that the allegations are untrue.

8. Defendant admits the allegation contained in paragraph 8 of Plaintiff's Complaint.

9. Defendant lacks sufficient information to form a belief as to the truth of the allegation contained in paragraph 9 of Plaintiff's Complaint.

10. Defendant lacks sufficient information on the proximate cause of Plaintiff's injuries to form a belief as to the truth of the averments contained in paragraph 10 of Plaintiff's Complaint.

11. Defendant denies the allegation of negligence contained in paragraph 11 of Plaintiff's Complaint.

EXHIBIT 12.5
The Answer—Continued

<u>NEW MATTER AND AFFIRMATIVE DEFENSES</u>

Although denying that the Plaintiff is entitled to the relief prayed for in the Plaintiff's Complaint, Defendant further states that the Plaintiff is barred from recovery hereunder by reason of the following:

1. That the Plaintiff's injuries were proximately caused by her own contributory negligence and want of due care under the circumstances prevailing at the time of the accident.

2. That the Plaintiff was exceeding the posted speed limit at the time and place of the accident and therefore was guilty of careless and negligent driving within the meaning of Section 9.2325(1) of the Nita Statutes Annotated.

3. That the Plaintiff failed to exercise that standard of care that a reasonably prudent person would have exercised under the same or similar conditions for her own safety and that her own negligence, contributory negligence, and/or comparative negligence caused or was a contributing factor to the incident out of which the Plaintiff's cause of action arises.

4. The Defendant reserves the right, by an appropriate Motion, to move the Court to amend the Defendant's Answer to the Plaintiff's Complaint, to allege other New Matters and Affirmative Defenses as may be revealed by discovery yet to be had and completed in this case.

WHEREFORE, the Defendant prays for a judgment of no cause of action with costs and attorneys' fees to be paid by the Plaintiff.

Cameron & Strauss, P.C.

Elizabeth A. Cameron

Date: ___2/25/04___

Elizabeth A. Cameron
Attorney for the Defendant

310 Lake Drive
Zero City, ZE 59802

Tony Peretto, being first duly sworn, states that he has read the foregoing Answer by him subscribed and that he knows the contents thereof, and the same is true, except those matters therein stated to be upon information and belief, and as to those matters, he believes to be true.

Tony Peretto

Defendant

Laura Curtis

Sworn and subscribed before me this __25th__ day of February, 2004.

Notary Public, Zero County,
State of Zero

My Commission Expires:
December 8, 2005

<u>DEMAND FOR A JURY TRIAL</u>

The Defendant demands a trial by jury.

Cameron & Strauss, P.C.

Elizabeth A. Cameron

Date: _2/25/04_____

Elizabeth A. Cameron
Attorney for the Defendant
310 Lake Drive
Zero City, Zero 59802

skidded into Peretto's car, causing Peretto to be injured. This allegation would be a counterclaim. The plaintiff is required to reply to any counterclaims made by the defendant.

Answer and Cross-Claim.   In cases in which a complaint names multiple defendants, the answer filed by one defendant might be followed by a **cross-claim,** in which the defendant asserts a claim against another defendant. (Note that cross-claims may also be filed by one plaintiff against another plaintiff in the same case.) For example, suppose that plaintiff Baranski had been struck by two vehicles, one belonging to defendant Peretto and one belonging to Leon Balfour. If Peretto and Balfour had been named as co-defendants in Baranski's complaint, Peretto's attorney might have filed an answer to Baranski's complaint that included a cross-claim against Balfour. The party against whom the cross-claim is brought is required to reply to (answer) the claim.

MOTION TO DISMISS.   A **motion** is a procedural request submitted to the court by an attorney on behalf of his or her client. When one party files a motion with the court, that party must also send to, or serve on, the opposing party a *notice of motion.* The notice of motion informs the opposing party that the motion has been filed and indicates when the court will hear the motion. The notice of motion gives the opposing party an opportunity to prepare for the hearing and argue before the court why the motion should not be granted.

The **motion to dismiss,** as the phrase implies, requests the court to dismiss the case for reasons provided in the motion. Defendant Peretto's attorney, for example, could file a motion to dismiss if she believed that Peretto had not been properly served, that the complaint had been filed in the wrong court, that the statute of limitations for that type of lawsuit had expired, or that the complaint did not state a claim for which relief (a remedy) could be granted. See Exhibit 12.6 on the next page for an example of a motion to dismiss.

If defendant Peretto's attorney decides to file a motion to dismiss plaintiff Baranski's claim, she may want to attach one or more **supporting affidavits**—sworn statements as to certain facts that may contradict the allegations made in the complaint. Peretto's attorney may also have her paralegal draft a **memorandum of law** (which is called a *brief* in some states) to be submitted along with the motion to dismiss and the accompanying affidavits. The memorandum of law will present the legal basis for the motion, citing any statutes and cases that support it. A supporting affidavit gives factual support to the motion to dismiss, while the memorandum of law provides the court with the legal grounds for the dismissal of the claim.[6]

The Scheduling Conference

After the complaint and answer have been filed, the court will typically schedule a conference to consult with the attorneys for both sides. (A party who is not represented by an attorney will attend the conference himself or herself.) Following this meeting, the judge will enter a *scheduling order* that sets out the time limits within which pretrial events (such as the pleadings, the discovery, and the final pretrial conference) must be completed, as well as the date of the trial. Under FRCP 16(b), the scheduling order should be entered "as soon as practicable but in any event within 90 days after the appearance of a defendant and within 120 days after the complaint has been served on a defendant." The purpose of this meeting is to enable the court to manage the case efficiently and establish time restrictions that are appropriate given the specific facts and circumstances involved in the case.

▦ Case at a Glance

The Plaintiff—
Plaintiff: Katherine Baranski
Attorney: Allen P. Gilmore
Paralegal: Elena Lopez

The Defendant—
Defendant: Tony Peretto
Attorney: Elizabeth A. Cameron
Paralegal: Gordon McVay

---

cross-claim
A claim asserted by a defendant in a civil lawsuit against another defendant or by a plaintiff against another plaintiff.

motion
A procedural request or application presented by an attorney to the court on behalf of a client.

motion to dismiss
A motion filed by the defendant in which the defendant asks the court to dismiss the case for a specified reason, such as improper service, lack of personal jurisdiction, or the plaintiff's failure to state a claim for which relief can be granted.

supporting affidavit
An affidavit accompanying a motion that is filed by an attorney on behalf of his or her client. The sworn statements in the affidavit provide a factual basis for the motion.

memorandum of law
A document (known as a brief in some states) that delineates the legal theories, statutes, and cases on which a motion is based.

EXHIBIT 12.6
A Motion to Dismiss

Elizabeth A. Cameron
Attorney for the Defendant
Cameron & Strauss, P.C.
310 Lake Drive
Zero City, ZE 59802
(616) 955-6234

UNITED STATES DISTRICT COURT
FOR THE WESTERN DISTRICT OF NITA

Katherine Baranski) 　　　　　　Plaintiff,) 　　　　　　　　　　　) vs.) 　　　　　　　　　　　) Tony Peretto) 　　　　　Defendant.)	CASE NO. 99-14355-NI Honorable Harley M. Larue MOTION TO DISMISS

　　The Defendant, Tony Peretto, by his attorney, moves the court to dismiss the above-named action because the statute of limitations governing the Plaintiff's claim has expired, as demonstrated in the memorandum of law that is being submitted with this motion. The Plaintiff therefore has no cause of action against the Defendant.

Cameron & Strauss, P.C.

Elizabeth A Cameron

Date: 2/20/04

Elizabeth A. Cameron
Attorney for the Defendant
310 Lake Drive
Zero City, ZE 59802

Amending the Pleadings

An attorney may be called on by a client to file a complaint or an answer without having much time to become familiar with the facts of the case. Because no attorney can anticipate how a case will evolve, the complaint or answer may have to be amended to account for newly discovered facts or evidence. Amendments may also be desirable when circumstances dictate that a different legal theory or defense be put forward.

PRETRIAL MOTIONS

Many motions may be made during the pretrial litigation process, including those listed and described in Exhibit 12.7. Some pretrial motions, if granted by the court, will end a case before trial. These motions include the motion to dismiss (which has already been discussed), the motion for judgment on the pleadings, and the motion for summary judgment. Here we examine the latter two motions.

Motion for Judgment on the Pleadings

Once the two attorneys in the Baranski case, Gilmore and Cameron, have finished filing their respective pleadings and amendments, either one of them may file a **motion for judgment on the pleadings**. Motions for judgment on the pleadings are

motion for judgment on the pleadings
A motion that may be filed by either party in which the party asks the court to enter a judgment in his or her favor based on information contained in the pleadings. A judgment on the pleadings will only be made if there are no facts in dispute and the only question is how the law applies to a set of undisputed facts.

EXHIBIT 12.7
Pretrial Motions

MOTION TO DISMISS

A motion filed by the defendant in which the defendant asks the court to dismiss the case for a specified reason, such as improper service, lack of personal jurisdiction, or the plaintiff's failure to state a claim for which relief can be granted.

MOTION TO STRIKE

A motion filed by the defendant in which the defendant asks the court to strike (delete) from the complaint certain of the paragraphs contained in the complaint. Motions to strike help to clarify the underlying issues that form the basis for the complaint by removing paragraphs that are redundant or irrelevant to the action.

MOTION TO MAKE MORE DEFINITE AND CERTAIN

A motion filed by the defendant to compel the plaintiff to clarify the basis of the plaintiff's cause of action. The motion is filed when the defendant believes that the complaint is too vague or ambiguous for the defendant to respond to it in a meaningful way.

MOTION FOR JUDGMENT ON THE PLEADINGS

A motion that may be filed by either party in which the party asks the court to enter a judgment in his or her favor based on information contained in the pleadings. A judgment on the pleadings will only be made if there are no facts in dispute and the only question is how the law applies to a set of undisputed facts.

MOTION TO COMPEL DISCOVERY

A motion that may be filed by either party in which the party asks the court to compel the other party to comply with a discovery request. If a party refuses to allow the opponent to inspect and copy certain documents, for example, the party requesting the documents may make a motion to compel production of documents.

MOTION FOR SUMMARY JUDGMENT

A motion that may be filed by either party in which the party asks the court to enter judgment in his or her favor without a trial. Unlike a motion for judgment on the pleadings, a motion for summary judgment can be supported by evidence outside the pleadings, such as witnesses' affidavits, answers to interrogatories, and other evidence obtained prior to or during discovery.

often filed when the pleadings indicate that no facts are in dispute and the only question is how the law applies to a set of undisputed facts. For example, assume for a moment that in the Baranski case, defendant Peretto admitted to all of plaintiff Baranski's allegations in his answer and raised no affirmative defenses. In this situation, Baranski's attorney, Gilmore, would file a motion for judgment on the pleadings in Baranski's favor.

Motion for Summary Judgment

A **motion for summary judgment** is similar to a motion for judgment on the pleadings in that the party filing the motion is asking the court to grant a judgment in its favor without a trial. As with a motion for judgment on the pleadings, a court will only grant a motion for summary judgment if it determines that no facts are in dispute and the only question is how the law applies to a set of facts agreed on by both parties.

motion for summary judgment
A motion that may be filed by either party in which the party asks the court to enter judgment in his or her favor without a trial. Unlike a motion for judgment on the pleadings, a motion for summary judgment can be supported by evidence outside the pleadings, such as witnesses' affidavits, answers to interrogatories, and other evidence obtained prior to or during discovery.

<table>
<tr><td>

ETHICAL CONCERN

Deadlines and the Duty of Competence

Experienced paralegals often emphasize how easy it is to miss deadlines. A very important deadline that the paralegal should always check is when the statute of limitations expires for the type of claim being made. For example, suppose that the state of Nita's statute of limitations requires Baranski to file her complaint against Peretto within two years or forever forgo the right to sue him. Also suppose that Baranski did not realize that she would always have a limp until a year or so after the accident. Baranski consults with attorney Gilmore about the matter a month before the two-year statute of limitations expires. Gilmore and his paralegal, Lopez, should immediately check the statute of limitations to make sure that they do not miss any deadlines. Otherwise, by the time Lopez completes her initial investigation into the matter, has further consultations with Baranski, and completes other preliminaries—including the drafting of the complaint—the statute might expire before the complaint is filed. All attorneys (and their paralegals) are charged with a duty of competence, and a breach of this duty (such as failing to notice and advise a client of the date on which a statute of limitations expires) may subject the attorney to a lawsuit for professional negligence (malpractice).

</td></tr>
</table>

Case at a Glance

The Plaintiff—
   Plaintiff: Katherine
      Baranski
   Attorney: Allen P.
      Gilmore
   Paralegal: Elena Lopez

The Defendant—
   Defendant: Tony Peretto
   Attorney: Elizabeth A.
      Cameron
   Paralegal: Gordon
      McVay

When the court considers a motion for summary judgment, it can take into account *evidence outside the pleadings*. This distinguishes the motion for summary judgment from the motion to dismiss and the motion for judgment on the pleadings. To support a motion for summary judgment, one party can submit evidence obtained at any point prior to trial (including during the discovery stage of litigation—to be discussed shortly) that refutes the other party's factual claim. In the Baranski case, for example, suppose that Peretto was in another state at the time of the accident. Defendant Peretto's attorney could make a motion for summary judgment in Peretto's favor and attach to the motion a witness's sworn statement that Peretto was in the other state at the time of the accident. Unless plaintiff Baranski's attorney could bring in sworn statements by other witnesses to show that Peretto was at the scene of the accident, Peretto would normally be granted his motion for summary judgment.

A motion for summary judgment would be particularly appropriate if plaintiff Baranski had previously signed a release waiving her right to sue defendant Peretto on the claim. In that situation, Peretto's attorney, Cameron, would attach a copy of the release to the motion before filing the motion with the court. Cameron would also prepare and attach a memorandum of law in support of the motion. When the motion was heard by the court, Cameron would argue that the execution of the waiver barred plaintiff Baranski from pursuing her claim against defendant Peretto.

The burden would then shift to plaintiff Baranski's attorney, Gilmore, to demonstrate that the release was invalid or otherwise not binding on Baranski. If the judge believed that the release had been voluntarily signed by plaintiff Baranski, then the judge might grant the motion for summary judgment in Peretto's favor. If attorney Gilmore convinced the judge that the release signed by Baranski had been procured by coercive or fraudulent practices, however, then the judge would deny the motion for summary judgment and permit the case to go to trial.

PARALEGAL PROFILE

Litigation Paralegal

CHARISSE A. CHARLES-HAMPTON *received her bachelor of arts degree,* cum laude, *in legal administration in December 1993 from the University of West Florida. Her first paralegal job was as an intern for a judge. After graduation, she was hired by a small law firm as a workers' compensation litigation paralegal and is currently working as a litigation paralegal, primarily in the area of personal injury.*

She is an active member of the Pensacola Legal Assistants Association and serves as chairperson for the Scholarship Awards Committee.

What do you like best about your work?

"What I like best about my work is being able to communicate with people in various offices to assist our clients in defending their claims. I have met a lot of people via the telephone and in so doing, have established great working relationships with many doctors' offices, judges' offices, clerks at the courthouse, and adjusters at various insurance companies, to just list a few. My working relationships with these people make my job much easier when I need to call on their assistance for our clients."

What is the greatest challenge that you face in your area of work?

"The greatest challenge for me is playing the role of both a plaintiff's paralegal and a defense paralegal. Some days it is very hard to empathize with clients who I know in my heart are not seriously injured and are only looking for a handout. On the flip side, it is sometimes very difficult to not allow my emotions to come into play when defending a matter for an insurance company regarding an individual who has been seriously injured."

"Communication can help you or destroy you."

What advice do you have for would-be paralegals in your area of work?

"I suggest that they focus heavily on their communication skills. Communication can help you or destroy you. I encourage them to attend workshops that focus on communicating with clients who are both difficult and not so difficult. I also encourage would-be paralegals to be detail oriented. Lastly, I suggest that they welcome challenges, big or small."

What are some tips for success as a paralegal in your area of work?

"Tips for success as a personal-injury paralegal include good communication skills, organizational skills, computer skills, timeliness, a willingness to accept changes, and a willingness to make changes that will benefit all parties involved."

TRADITIONAL DISCOVERY TOOLS

Before a trial begins, the parties can use a number of procedural devices to obtain information and gather evidence about the case. Plaintiff Baranski's attorney, for example, will want to know how fast defendant Peretto was driving, whether he had been drinking, and whether he saw the stop sign. The process of obtaining information from the opposing party or from other witnesses is known as **discovery.**

Discovery serves several purposes. It preserves evidence from witnesses who might not be available at the time of the trial or whose memories will fade as time passes. It can pave the way for summary judgment if both parties agree on all of the facts. It can lead to an out-of-court settlement if one party decides that the

discovery
Formal investigation prior to trial. During discovery, opposing parties use various methods, such as interrogatories and depositions, to obtain information from each other and from witnesses to prepare for trial.

ETHICAL CONCERN
Keeping Client Information Confidential

As it happens, attorney Gilmore's legal assistant, Lopez, is a good friend of plaintiff Baranski's daughter. Lopez learns from the results of Baranski's medical examination that Baranski has a terminal illness. Lopez is sure that the daughter, who quarreled with her mother two months ago and hasn't spoken to her since, is unaware of the illness and would probably be very hurt if she learned that Lopez knew of it and didn't tell her. Should Lopez tell her friend about the illness? No. This is confidential information at this point, which Lopez only became aware of by virtue of her job. Should the information be revealed publicly during the course of the trial, then Lopez would be free to disclose it to her friend if the friend still remained unaware of it. In the meantime, Lopez is ethically (and legally) obligated not to disclose the information to anyone who is not working on the case, including her friend.

opponent's case is too strong to challenge. Even if the case does go to trial, discovery prevents surprises by giving parties access to evidence that might otherwise be hidden. This allows both parties to learn as much as they can about what to expect at a trial before they reach the courtroom. It also serves to narrow the issues so that trial time is spent on the main questions in the case.

The FRCP and similar rules in the states set forth the guidelines for discovery activity. Discovery includes gaining access to witnesses, documents, records, and other types of evidence. The rules governing discovery are designed to make sure that a witness or a party is not unduly harassed, that **privileged information** (communications that ordinarily may not be disclosed in court) is safeguarded, and that only matters relevant to the case at hand are discoverable. Currently, the trend is toward allowing more discovery and thus fewer surprises.

Traditional discovery devices include interrogatories, depositions, requests for production and physical examination, and requests for admission. Each of these discovery tools is examined below.

privileged information
Confidential communications between certain individuals, such as an attorney and his or her client, that are protected from disclosure except under court order.

Interrogatories

Interrogatories are written questions that must be answered, in writing, by the parties to the lawsuit and then signed by the parties under oath. Typically, the paralegal drafts the interrogatories for the attorney's review and approval. In the Baranski case, for example, attorney Gilmore will probably ask paralegal Lopez to draft interrogatories to be sent to defendant Peretto.

interrogatories
A series of written questions for which written answers are prepared and then signed under oath by a party to a lawsuit (the plaintiff or the defendant).

DRAFTING INTERROGATORIES.   All discovery documents, including interrogatories, normally begin with a caption similar to the complaint caption illustrated earlier in this chapter. Following the caption, Lopez will add the name of the party who must answer the interrogatories, instructions to be followed by the party, and definitions of certain terms that are used in the interrogatories. The body of the document consists of the interrogatories themselves—that is, the questions that the opposing party must answer. The interrogatories should end with a signature line for the attorney below which appears the attorney's name and address.

Before drafting the questions, Lopez will want to review carefully the contents of the case file (including the pleadings and the evidence and other information that she obtained during her preliminary investigation into plaintiff Baranski's claim) and consult with attorney Gilmore on what litigation strategy should be pursued. For further guidance, she might consult form books containing sample interrogatories as well as interrogatories used in similar cases previously handled by the firm. (For tips on how to draft effective interrogatories, see this chapter's *Featured Guest* article starting on the following page.)

Depending on the complexity of the case, interrogatories may be few in number, or they may run into the hundreds. Exhibit 12.8 starting on page 422 illustrates the types of interrogatories that have traditionally been used in cases similar to the Baranski-Peretto case. Depending on the rules of the court in which the Baranski case is being filed, paralegal Lopez might draft similar interrogatories for defendant Peretto to answer. Realize that many state courts now limit the number of interrogatories that can be used, and FRCP 33 limits the number of interrogatories in federal court cases to twenty-five (unless a greater number is allowed by stipulation of the parties or by court order). Therefore:

Before drafting interrogatories, the paralegal should always check the rules of the court in which an action is being filed to find out if that court limits the number of interrogatories that can be used.

ANSWERING INTERROGATORIES. After receiving the interrogatories, defendant Peretto must answer them within a specified time period (thirty days under FRCP 33) in writing and under oath, as mentioned above. Very likely, he will have substantial guidance from his attorney and his attorney's paralegal in forming his answers. Peretto must answer each question truthfully, of course, because he is under oath. His attorney and her paralegal would counsel him, though, on how to phrase his answers so that they are both truthful and strategically sound. For example, they would advise Peretto on how to limit his answers to prevent disclosing more information than necessary.

Depositions

Like interrogatories, **depositions** are given under oath. Unlike interrogatories, however, depositions are usually conducted orally (except in certain circumstances, such as when the party being deposed is at a great distance and cannot be deposed via telephone). Furthermore, they may be taken from witnesses. As indicated earlier, interrogatories can only be taken from the parties to the lawsuit.

deposition
A pretrial question-and-answer proceeding, usually conducted orally, in which an a party or witness answers an attorney's questions. The answers are given under oath, and the session is recorded.

When an attorney takes the deposition, the attorney is able to question the person being deposed (the **deponent**) *in person* and then follow up with any other questions that come to mind. The attorney is not limited in the number of questions that she or he may ask in a deposition, whereas many courts limit the number of interrogatory questions. Moreover, because the questioning is usually done in person, the deponent must answer the questions without asking an attorney or paralegal how he or she should respond. Thus, the answers to deposition questions are not filtered through counsel in the same way answers to interrogatories are.

deponent
A party or witness who testifies under oath during a deposition.

Normally, the defendant's attorney deposes the plaintiff first, and then the plaintiff's attorney deposes the defendant. Following these depositions, the attorneys may depose witnesses and other parties to obtain information about the event leading to the lawsuit. When both the defendant and the plaintiff are located in the same jurisdiction, the site of the deposition will usually be the offices of the attorney requesting the deposition. When the parties are located in different

FEATURED GUEST: P. DAVID PALMIERE

Ten Tips for the Effective Use of Interrogatories

BIOGRAPHICAL NOTE

P. David Palmiere received his bachelor's degree magna cum laude *in economics from the University of Michigan in 1972 and his law degree from the University of Michigan Law School in 1975. Palmiere, currently a member of the firm of Secrest, Wardle, Lynch, Hampton, Truex & Morley in Farmington Hills, Michigan, has practiced litigation for more than twenty-five years in courts from California to New York.*

For the past twenty-four years, Palmiere has also been an adjunct professor in an ABA–accredited legal-assistant program at Oakland University in Rochester, Michigan, where he teaches litigation and also assisted in designing the litigation specialty curriculum. Palmiere has been a guest lecturer at Wayne State University School of Law and a featured speaker at the state convention of the Legal Assistants Association of Michigan.

Interrogatories are written questions to an opposing party requiring written answers. Interrogatories are a mainstay of discovery, but often interrogatory effort is wasted because of poor topic selection or ineffective drafting. Here are some guidelines for the effective use of interrogatories.

1. Interrogatories and Answers Are a Struggle between Adversaries. Good answers start with good questions. An interrogatory (question) is wasted if the answer is not meaningful. There are sanctions for bad faith answers to good questions. Ambiguous questions, however, allow the opponent to dodge the question without incurring sanctions. The more direct, crisp, and clear your phrasing, the more a fear of sanctions will compel informative answers. Always assume that your opponent will seize any excuse to decline to answer, and minimize such opportunities. If your questions pass the clarity test, they will probably be effective.

2. Limit Interrogatories to Appropriate Subjects. There are five basic discovery tools: interrogatories, requests for production of documents and things, requests for admission, depositions, and physical or mental examinations of persons. Each tool has its own role in discovery. Interrogatories are best used to elicit concrete items of factual information, such as names, addresses, dates, times, and places. Interrogatories are usually ineffective in asking for narrative accounts of complex facts

or for the basis for opinions—tasks that are more appropriate to a deposition. Similarly, instead of wasting interrogatories asking for specifics about documents (other than who has them), it is better practice to join the interrogatories to a request for production of the documents themselves. Limit interrogatories to their most appropriate purpose—learning hard, factual data.

3. Use Contention Interrogatories. One exception to the foregoing is a "contention interrogatory," which asks the opponent for all facts supporting some assertion from the opponent's pleading. If the defendant asserts that the plaintiff's claim is barred by the statute of limitations, the plaintiff's contention interrogatory says, "Please state each fact that supports your contention that the plaintiff's claim is barred by the statute of limitations." Contention interrogatories can effectively smoke out and dispose of sham issues. Note, however, that contention interrogatories have a major blind spot: they do not elicit, except indirectly, information to *refute* the opponent's contentions. Other questions are needed for that.

4. Use Several Sets of Interrogatories at Strategic Points during the Discovery Process. Interrogatories are primarily used early in the case to gather leads for further investigation. But interrogatories are not "just for breakfast." They are also useful to follow up on leads developed in other discovery, such as document productions or depositions. As you

FEATURED GUEST, *Continued*

read every new document and deposition, list new or unanswered questions, and consider interrogatories as the tool of choice for following up on the matter.

5. Be Aware of Court Rules Concerning Interrogatories.   The court hearing the case will have rules about interrogatories. Know those rules. For example, the Federal Rules of Civil Procedure allow interrogatories only *after* the lawyers have conferred about a discovery schedule. The federal rules also require court permission to ask more than twenty-five questions, including subparts. State courts have their own rules limiting or affecting the use of interrogatories. These limitations must be observed.

6. Each Interrogatory Must Stand on Its Own—The "Stranger in the Street" Test.   Interrogatory questions are often flawed because they lack context. Give every question this test: If a stranger approached you in the street, and asked the question just as you have written it, without more, could you answer it? For example, a stranger approaches you and says, "What time was it?" Your natural response would be, "What time was *what*?" or "What are you talking about?" This question does not pass the "stranger in the street" test. Any question that fails the test will probably not bring a meaningful answer from the opponent.

7. Use Definitions to Supply Context for Questions.   Open your interrogatories with definitions of terms to be used, such as "the incident." Be sure that your definitions are nonargumentative— for example, if a plaintiff defines "the incident" as "the collision caused by defendant's negligence," the defendant will object to every question using the term. Then, in the interrogatories, you may ask what time "the incident" took place or who saw any part of "the incident" without having to repeat the entire description to supply the necessary context. Once you define a term, however, use it consistently. Remember that this word now has a special meaning and cannot be used as if it were ordinary English.

8. Some Questions You *Always* Ask.   Questions that you should always ask include questions about eyewitnesses, about the opponent's trial witnesses, and about the opponent's expert witnesses. Ask these even if you ask nothing else.

9. Master Standard Phrasing.   Like other legal drafting, interrogatories tend to fall into standard patterns and phrases. Master these. Many lawyers begin each interrogatory, "Please state . . . ." If you do so, each item that follows must be an item of information. (Students often submit questions reading, "Please state each car that you own." One cannot "state" a car, but only

> ## "Limit interrogatories to their most appropriate purpose—learning hard, factual data."

information about the car, which is not what the question asks.) When an interrogatory contains a condition, description, or qualification, place it at the beginning of the question: "For each lawsuit to which you have ever been a party, please state . . . ." This phrasing is an effective substitute for questions that would otherwise have an "if-then" structure ("If you have ever been a party to a lawsuit, then please state . . ."). Drafting will be simpler if you use singular word forms rather than plural. When using subparts, make sure each one follows grammatically from the body of the main question.

10. Make Effective Use of the Duty to Supplement Responses. Federal Rule 26(e) and many state rules establish a duty to supplement interrogatory responses. This duty is often overlooked. Send periodic letters to the opposition, requesting supplements of prior interrogatory answers under the applicable rule. This places your side in a strong position to object if surprises are sprung at the trial.

EXHIBIT 12.8
Sample Interrogatories

A. P. Gilmore
Attorney for Plaintiff
Jeffers, Gilmore & Dunn
553 Fifth Avenue
Suite 101
Nita City, NI 48801
(616) 555-9690

**UNITED STATES DISTRICT COURT
FOR THE WESTERN DISTRICT OF NITA**

Katherine Baranski)
       Plaintiff,)
)
v.)
)
)
Tony Peretto)
       Defendant.)

CASE NO. 99-14335-NI
Honorable Harley M. Larue

PLAINTIFF'S FIRST
INTERROGATORIES
TO DEFENDANT

PLEASE TAKE NOTICE that the following Interrogatories are directed to you under the provisions of Rule 26(a)(5) and Rule 33 of the Federal Rules of Civil Procedure. You are requested to answer these Interrogatories and to furnish such information in answer to the Interrogatories as is available to you.

You are required to serve integrated Interrogatories and Answers to these Interrogatories under oath, within thirty (30) days after service of them upon you. The original answers are to be retained in your attorney's possession and a copy of the answers are to be served upon Plaintiff's counsel.

The answers should be signed and sworn to by the person making answer to the Interrogatories.

When used in these Interrogatories the term "Defendant," or any synonym thereof, is intended to and shall embrace and include, in addition to said Defendant, all agents, servants and employees, representatives, attorneys, private investigators, or others who are in possession or who may have obtained information for or on behalf of the Defendant.

These Interrogatories shall be deemed continuing and supplemental answers shall be required immediately upon receipt thereof if Defendant, directly or indirectly, obtains further or different information from the time answers are served until the time of trial.

1. Were you the driver of an automobile involved in an accident with plaintiff on August 4, 2003, at about 7:45 A.M. at the intersection of Mattis Avenue and Thirty-eighth Street, in Nita City, Nita? If so, please state:

    (a) Your name;
    (b) Every name you have used in the past;
    (c) The dates you used each name;
    (d) The date and place of your birth.

2. Please list your current residence and all residences you occupied in the five years preceding your move to your currrent residence, including complete addresses, dates of residence, and names of owners or managers.

3. Please indicate where you are presently employed and where you were employed during the five years preceding the beginning of your current employment. In so doing, please indicate the following:

    (a) The names, addresses, and telephone numbers of each employer or place of business, including the dates during which you worked there;
    (b) How many hours you worked, on average, per week;
    (c) The names, addresses, and telephone numbers of your supervisors (or owners of the business);
    (d) The nature of the work that you performed.

EXHIBIT 12.8
Sample Interrogatories—Continued

4. At the time of the incident, were you acting as an agent or employee for any person? If so, state:

    (a) The name, address, and telephone number of that person;
    (b) A description of your duties.

5. At the time of the incident, did you have a driver's license? If so, state:

    (a) The state or other issuing entity;
    (b) The license number and type;
    (c) The date of issuance and expiration;
    (d) Any violations, offenses, or restrictions against your license.

6. Indicate whether you have ever had your driver's license suspended, revoked, or canceled, and whether you have ever been denied the issuance of a driver's license for mental or physical reasons. If you have, please indicate the date and state of such occurrence as well as the reasons for it.

7. At the time of the incident, did you or any other person have any physical, emotional, or mental disability or condition that may have contributed to the occurrence of the incident? If so, for each person state:

    (a) The name, address, and telephone number;
    (b) The nature of the disability or condition;
    (c) The name, address, and telephone number or any qualified person who treated or diagnosed the condition, and the dates of such treatment.
    (d) The manner in which the disability or condition contributed to the occurrence of the incident.

8. Within twenty-four hours before the incident, did you or any person involved in the incident use or take any of the following substances: alcoholic beverage, marijuana, or other drug or medication of any kind (prescription or not)? If so, for each person state:

    (a) The name, address, and telephone number;
    (b) The nature or description of each substance;
    (c) The quantity of each substance used or taken;
    (d) The date and time of day when each subtance was used or taken;
    (e) The address where each substance was used or taken;
    (f) The name, address, and telephone number of each person who was present when each substance was used or taken;
    (g) The name, address, or telephone number of any health-care provider that prescribed or furnished the subtance and the condition for which it was prescribed or furnished.

9. For each time you have had your vision checked within the last five years, please indicate the following:

    (a) The date and reason for the vision examination;
    (b) The name, address, and telephone number of the examiner;
    (c) The results and/or actions taken.

10. For each time you have had your hearing checked within the last five years, please indicate the following:

    (a) The date and reason for the hearing examination;
    (b) The name, address, and telephone number of the examiner;
    (c) The results and/or actions taken.

[Additional questions would be asked relating to the scene of the accident, including road conditions and surface, posted speed limits, shoulders and curbs on the side of the road, the general character of the neighborhood, when the defendant noticed the plaintiff's vehicle, where it was located and the speed at which the plaintiff was traveling, whether there were other vehicles between the plaintiff's and the defendant's vehicles, and so forth.]

Dated:

                                    Allen P. Gilmore
                                    Attorney for Plaintiff

EXHIBIT 12.9
Notice of Taking Deposition

UNITED STATES DISTRICT COURT
FOR THE WESTERN DISTRICT OF NITA

Katherine Baranski)
      Plaintiff,)
)
v.)
)
)
Tony Peretto)
      Defendant.)

CASE NO. 99-14335-NI
Honorable Harley M. Larue

NOTICE OF TAKING
DEPOSITION

TO: Elizabeth A. Cameron
      Cameron & Strauss, P.C.
      310 Lake Drive
      Zero City, ZE 59802

     PLEASE TAKE NOTICE that Katherine Baranski, by and through her attorneys, Jeffers, Gilmore & Dunn, will take the deposition of Tony Peretto on Wednesday, April 15, 2004, at 1:30 P.M., at the law offices of Cameron & Strauss, P.C., 310 Lake Drive, Zero City, ZE 59802, pursuant to the Federal Rules of Civil Procedure, before a duly authorized and qualified notary and stenographer.

Dated: March 20, 2004

Jeffers, Gilmore & Dunn

Allen P. Gilmore

Allen P. Gilmore
Attorney for Katherine Baranski
553 Fifth Avenue, Suite 101
Nita City, NI 48801

jurisdictions, other arrangements may be made. In the Baranski case, attorney Gilmore will travel to defendant Peretto's city, which is located in another state, and depose Peretto in the office of Peretto's attorney, Cameron.

PROCEDURE FOR TAKING DEPOSITIONS.   The attorney wishing to depose a party or witness must give reasonable notice in writing to all other parties in the case. This is done by serving the opposing attorney (or attorneys) with a notice of taking deposition, which states the time and place of the deposition and the name of the person being examined (see Exhibit 12.9).

    If the person scheduled to be deposed would not attend voluntarily, a paralegal may also need to prepare a subpoena for deposition and submit it to the court for signature. Generally, a **subpoena** is an order issued by the court clerk directing a party to appear and to testify at trial, as will be discussed in Chapter 14. A *subpoena for deposition* orders the person to appear at a deposition rather than in a court proceeding. A subpoena should also be prepared if the attorney wants the deponent to bring certain documents or tangible things to the deposition (this is called a *subpoena duces tecum*).

    Under FRCP 30, depositions may not be taken (without court permission) before the parties have made the initial disclosures required by Rule 26 and discussed later in this chapter. Also, Rule 30 requires court approval if either party wants to take more than one deposition from the same person or more than a total of ten depositions in the case.

subpoena
A document commanding a person to appear at a certain time and place to give testimony concerning a certain matter.

EXHIBIT 12.10
Deposition Questions

<u>DEPOSITION QUESTIONS</u>

1. Please state your full name and address for the record.
2. What is your age, birth date, and Social Security number?
3. What is your educational level, and what employment position do you hold?
4. Do you have a criminal record, and if so, for what?
5. Have you ever been involved in previous automobile accidents? What driving violations have you had? Has your driver's license ever been suspended?
6. What is your medical history? Have you ever had health problems? Are you in perfect health? Were you in perfect health at the time of the accident?
7. Do you wear glasses or contact lenses? If so, for what condition? Were you wearing your glasses or contacts at the time the accident occurred?
8. Do you take medication of any kind?
9. Do you have any similar lawsuits or any claims pending against you?
10. Who is your automobile insurer? What are your policy limits?
11. Were there any passengers in your vehicle at the time of the accident?
12. Describe your vehicle. What was the mechanical condition of your vehicle at the time of the accident? Do you do your own mechanical work? What training do you have in maintaining and repairing automobiles? Had you taken your vehicle to a professional mechanic's shop prior to the accident?
13. State the date the accident occurred.
14. Where were you prior to the accident, at least for the six hours preceding the accident?
15. Where were you going when the accident occurred, and for what purpose?
16. What were you doing during the last few moments before the accident? Were you smoking, eating, drinking, or chewing gum?
17. What were you thinking about just before the accident occurred?
18. What route did you take to reach your destination, and why did you take this particular route?
19. Describe the weather conditions at the time of the accident.
20. Please recite the facts of how the accident occurred.
21. Please describe the area in which the accident occurred. Were there many cars and pedestrians on the streets? Were there traffic controls, obstructions, or the like?
22. What was your location, and in what direction were you going?
23. When did you see the Plaintiff's automobile approaching?
24. How far away were you when you first saw the auto? What was your rate of speed?
25. Did your vehicle move forward, or was it pushed backward by the impact?
26. When did you first apply your brakes? Were your brakes functioning properly?
27. Did you attempt to avoid the accident? If so, how?
28. Did you receive a traffic ticket as a result of the accident?
29. Do you own the vehicle that you were driving at the time of the accident?
30. Were you acting within the scope of your employment when the accident occurred?
31. What were the conditions of the parties affected by the accident just after the accident occurred?
32. Did you attempt to provide first aid to any party?
33. How did the Plaintiff leave the scene, and what was her physical condition?
34. What was the damage to your vehicle, and has it been repaired?

DRAFTING DEPOSITION QUESTIONS.   Depositions are conducted by attorneys. Although paralegals may attend depositions, they do not ask questions during the deposition. Deposition questions are often drafted by paralegals, however. In the Baranski case, for example, attorney Gilmore might ask paralegal Lopez to draft questions for a deposition of defendant Peretto or someone else, such as an eyewitness to the accident. For Peretto's deposition, Lopez might draft questions similar to those presented in Exhibit 12.10. Attorney Gilmore can then use Lopez's questions as a kind of checklist during the deposition. Note, though, that Gilmore's questions will not be limited to the questions included in the list. Other,

DEVELOPING PARALEGAL SKILLS
Deposition Summaries

After a deposition is taken, each attorney orders a copy of the deposition transcript. Copies may be obtained in printed form or on a computer disk. When the transcript is received, the legal assistant's job is to prepare a summary of the testimony that was given. The summary is typically only a few pages in length.

The legal assistant must be very familiar with the lawsuit and the legal theories that are being pursued so that he or she can point out inconsistencies in the testimony and how the testimony varies from the pleadings. The paralegal might also give special emphasis to any testimony given by deponents that will help to prove the client's case in court.

After the deposition summary has been created, the paralegal places the summary in the litigation file, usually in a special discovery folder or binder within the larger file. The deposition summary will be used to prepare for future depositions, to prepare pretrial motions, and to impeach witnesses at the trial, should they give contradictory testimony.

TIPS FOR SUMMARIZING A DEPOSITION

- Find out how the deposition is to be summarized—by chronology, by legal issue, by factual issues, or otherwise.
- Read through the deposition transcript and mark important pages.
- Using a dictaphone or dictation software, dictate a summary of the information on the marked pages.
- Be sure to include a reference to the page and line that is being summarized.
- Take advantage of software that will assist in summarizing the deposition transcript.

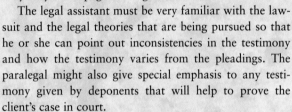

Case at a Glance

The Plaintiff—
 Plaintiff: Katherine Baranski
 Attorney: Allen P. Gilmore
 Paralegal: Elena Lopez

The Defendant—
 Defendant: Tony Peretto
 Attorney: Elizabeth A. Cameron
 Paralegal: Gordon McVay

unforeseen questions may arise as Gilmore learns new information during the deposition. Also, the deponent's answer to one question may reveal the answer to another, so that not all questions will need to be asked.

PREPARING THE CLIENT FOR A DEPOSITION.   No attorney can predict a deponent's answers beforehand. Spontaneous and perhaps even contradictory statements can seriously damage the deponent's case. For this reason, the deposed party and his or her lawyer will want to prepare for the deposition by formulating mock answers to anticipated questions. For example, if defendant Peretto's attorney plans to depose plaintiff Baranski, attorney Gilmore and paralegal Lopez might have Baranski come into their office for a run-through of possible questions that Peretto's attorney might ask her during the deposition. This kind of preparation does not mean that the lawyer tells the deponent what to say. Instead, the lawyer offers suggestions as to how the answers to certain questions should be phrased. The answers must be truthful, but the truth can be presented in many ways.

Gilmore would also caution Baranski to limit her responses to the questions and not to engage in speculative answers that might prejudice her claim. If plaintiff Baranski was asked whether she had ever been involved in an automobile accident before, for example, Gilmore would probably caution her to use a simple (but truthful) "yes" or "no" answer. Attorney Gilmore normally would permit Baranski to volunteer additional information only in response to precisely phrased questions.

THE ROLE OF THE DEPONENT'S ATTORNEY.   The deponent's attorney will attend the deposition, but the attorney's role will be limited. Under FRCP 30, the attorney may instruct a deponent not to answer a question only when necessary to preserve a privilege, to enforce a limitation directed by the court, or to present a motion to terminate the deposition. In other words, if plaintiff Baranski was being deposed by defendant Peretto's attorney, Cameron, she would have to answer Cameron's questions even if the questions were not clearly relevant to the issues of the case—unless the court had previously limited this line of questioning. The deponent's attorney, Gilmore, could object only to questions that called for privileged information to be disclosed. Under Rule 30, that attorney is also required to state objections concisely, in a nonargumentative and nonsuggestive manner.

As will be discussed shortly, deposition proceedings are recorded. If both attorneys agree to do so, however, they can go "off the record" to clarify a point or discuss a disputed issue. Depositions are stressful events, and tempers often flare. In the event that the deposition can no longer be conducted in an orderly fashion, the attorney conducting the deposition may have to terminate it.

THE DEPOSITION TRANSCRIPT.   Every utterance made during a deposition is recorded. A court reporter will usually record the deposition proceedings and create an official **deposition transcript.** Methods of recording a deposition include stenographic recording (a traditional method that involves the use of a shorthand machine), tape recording, videotape recording, or some combination of these methods. Rule 30(b)(2) of the FRCP states that unless the court orders otherwise, a deposition "may be recorded by sound, sound-and-visual, or stenographic means."

deposition transcript
The official transcription of the recording taken during a deposition.

The deposition transcript may be used by either party during the trial to prove a particular point or to **impeach** (call into question) the credibility of a witness who says something during the trial that is different from what he or she stated during the deposition. For example, a witness in the Baranski case might state during the deposition that defendant Peretto *did not* stop at the stop sign before proceeding to cross Mattis Avenue. If, at trial, the witness states that Peretto *did* stop at the stop sign before crossing Mattis Avenue, plaintiff Baranski's attorney (Gilmore) could challenge the witness's credibility on the basis of the deposition transcript. Exhibit 12.11 on the next page shows a page from a transcript of a deposition conducted by attorney Gilmore in the Baranski case. The deponent was Julia Williams, an eyewitness to the accident. On the transcript, the letter "Q" precedes each question asked by Gilmore, and the letter "A" precedes each of Williams's answers.

impeach
To call into question the credibility of a witness by challenging the truth or accuracy of his or her trial statement.

SUMMARIZING AND INDEXING THE DEPOSITION TRANSCRIPT.   Typically, the paralegal will summarize the deposition transcript. The summary, which along with the transcript will become part of the litigation file, allows the members of the litigation team to review quickly the information obtained from the deponent during the deposition.

In the Baranski case, assume that paralegal Lopez is asked to summarize the deposition transcript of Julia Williams. A commonly used format for deposition summaries is to summarize the information sequentially—that is, in the order in which it was given during the deposition—as shown in Exhibit 12.12 on page 429. Notice that the summary includes the page and line numbers in the deposition transcript where the full text of the information can be found.

Often, in addition to summarizing the transcript, the paralegal provides an index to the document. The index consists of a list of topics (such as education, employment status, injuries, medical costs, and so on) followed by the relevant page and line numbers of the deposition transcript. Together, the summary and the index allow anyone involved in the case to locate information quickly. Today, keyword indexes allow attorneys and paralegals to locate within seconds deposition testimony on a particular topic. Often, court reporters will provide key-word indexes on request.

On the Web
If you are interested in the history of court reporting, visit the Web site of the National Court Reporters Association at **http://www.ncraonline.org/ about/history/Court Reporter.shtml.**

EXHIBIT 12.11
A Deposition Transcript (Excerpt)

67	Q: Where were you at the time of the accident?
68	A: I was on the southwest corner of the intersection.
69	Q: Are you referring to the intersection where Thirty-eighth Street crosses Mattis Avenue?
70	A: Yes.
71	Q: Why were you there at the time of the accident?
72	A: Well, I was on my way to work. I usually walk down Mattis Avenue to the hospital.
73	Q: So you were walking to work down Mattis Avenue and you saw the accident?
74	A: Yes.
75	Q: What did you see?
76	A: Well, as I was about to cross the street, a dark green van passed within three feet of me and ran the
77	stop sign and crashed into another car.
78	Q: Can you remember if the driver of the van was a male or a female?
79	A: Yes. It was a man.
80	Q: I am showing you a picture. Can you identify the man in the picture?
81	A: Yes. That is the man who was driving the van.
82	Q: Do you wear glasses?
83	A: I need glasses only for reading. I have excellent distance vision.
84	Q: How long has it been since your last eye exam with a doctor?
85	A: Oh, just a month ago, with Dr. Sullivan.

page 4

Requests for Production and Physical Examination

> **⊞ Case at a Glance**
>
> **The Plaintiff—**
>   Plaintiff: Katherine
>   Baranski
>   Attorney: Allen P.
>   Gilmore
>   Paralegal: Elena Lopez
>
> **The Defendant—**
>   Defendant: Tony Peretto
>   Attorney: Elizabeth A.
>   Cameron
>   Paralegal: Gordon
>   McVay

Another traditional method of discovery is the request for the production of documents or tangible things or for permission to enter on land or other property for inspection and other purposes. FRCP 34 authorizes each party to request documents and other forms of evidence from any other party. If the item requested is very large or cannot be "produced" for some reason (Baranski's car, for example), then the party can request permission to enter on the other party's land to inspect, test, sample, and photograph the item. In federal courts, the duty of disclosure under FRCP 26 (discussed shortly) has greatly decreased the need to file such production requests.

When the mental or physical condition of a party is in controversy, the opposing party may also request the court to order the party to submit to a physical or mental examination by a licensed examiner. For example, if defendant Peretto claims that plaintiff Baranski's injuries were the result of a preexisting medical condition, rather than the collision, defense attorney Cameron may file a request to have Baranski examined by a licensed physician. Because the existence, nature,

EXHIBIT 12.12
**A Deposition
Summary (Excerpt)**

Case:	Baranski v. Peretto Plaintiff 15773	Attorney: Allen P. Gilmore Legal Assistant: Elena Lopez
Deponent:	Julia Williams 3801 Mattis Avenue Nita City, Nita 48800	Date: March 16, 2004

Page	Line(s)	
		* * * *
4	72–77	Williams stated that she was on the way to work at the time of the accident. She was about to cross the street when Peretto's car ("a dark green van") passed within three feet of her, ran the stop sign, and crashed into Baranski's car.
4	80–81	When shown a picture of Peretto, she identified him as the driver of the green van.
4	82–83	Williams has excellent distance vision and does not require corrective lenses. She does need reading glasses for close work.
		* * * *

and extent of Baranski's injuries are important in calculating the damages that she might be able to recover from Peretto, the court may order Baranski to undergo a physical examination if requested.

Requests for Admission

During discovery, a party can also request that the opposing party admit the truth of matters relating to the case. For example, plaintiff Baranski's attorney can request that defendant Peretto admit that he did not stop at the stop sign before crossing Mattis Avenue at Thirty-eighth Street. Such admissions save time at trial because the parties will not have to spend time proving facts on which they already agree. Any matter admitted under such a request is conclusively established as true for the trial. FRCP 36 permits requests for admission but stipulates that a request for admission cannot be made, without the court's permission, prior to the prediscovery meeting of the attorneys. In view of the limitations on the number of interrogatories under the FRCP (and under some state procedural rules), requests for admission are a particularly useful discovery tool.

THE DUTY TO DISCLOSE UNDER FRCP 26

In federal courts prior to 1993, if an attorney wanted to obtain information or evidence that was in the possession of another party, she or he had to ask for it using one of the traditional discovery methods already discussed. In 1993, amendments to the FRCP significantly changed the discovery rules in federal courts, and these changes have influenced state rules on civil procedure. Today, each party to a lawsuit has a duty to disclose to the other party specified types of information prior to the discovery stage of litigation. Under Rule 26(f), once a lawsuit is brought, the parties (the plaintiff and defendant and/or their attorneys, if the parties are represented by counsel) must schedule a prediscovery meeting to discuss the nature of the lawsuit, any defenses that may be raised against the claims being brought, and possibilities for promptly settling or otherwise resolving the dispute. The meeting should take place as soon as practicable but at least fourteen days before a scheduling conference is held or a scheduling order issued. Either at this meeting or within ten days after it, the parties must also make the initial disclosures described below and submit to the court a plan for discovery. As the trial date approaches, the attorneys must make subsequent disclosures relating to witnesses, documents, and other information that is relevant to the case.

These rules do not replace the traditional methods of discovery discussed in the preceding section. Rather, the rules impose a duty on attorneys to disclose specified information automatically to opposing counsel early in the litigation process so that the time and costs of traditional discovery methods can be reduced. Attorneys may still use the traditional discovery tools (depositions and interrogatories, for instance) to obtain information, but they cannot use these methods until the prediscovery meeting has been held and initial disclosures have been made. Also, to save the court's time, the rules give attorneys a freer hand in crafting a discovery plan that is appropriate to the nature of the claim and the parties' needs.[7]

Initial Disclosures

FRCP 26(a)(1) requires each party to disclose the following information to the other party either at an initial meeting of the parties or within ten days following the meeting:

- The name, address, and telephone number of any person who is likely to have "discoverable information" and the nature of that information.
- A copy or "description by category and location" of all documents, data, and other "things in the possession, custody, or control of the party" that are relevant to the dispute.
- A computation of the damages being claimed by the disclosing party. The party must make available to the other party, for inspection and copying, documents or other materials on which the computation of damages is based, "including materials bearing on the nature and extent of injuries suffered."
- Copies of any insurance policies that cover the injuries or harms alleged in the lawsuit and that may pay part or all of a judgment (damages, for example) resulting from the dispute.

In the Baranski case, attorney Gilmore and paralegal Lopez must work quickly to assemble all relevant information, documents, and other evidence that Lopez has gathered during client interviews and during her preliminary investigation into the case. Lopez will prepare copies of the documents or other information—or a description of them—for attorney Gilmore's review and signature. The copies or descriptions will then be filed with the court and delivered to defendant Peretto's attorney.

Note that in the information disclosed to defendant Peretto's attorney, paralegal Lopez must include even information that might be damaging to Baranski's position. Lopez need not disclose *privileged information*, however. If defendant Peretto's attorney seeks information that attorney Gilmore claims is privileged, Peretto's attorney will be able to obtain that information only through a court order.

- A list of exhibits that indicates which exhibits will be offered and which exhibits may be offered if the need arises.

These disclosures must be made at least thirty days before trial, unless the court orders otherwise. Once the disclosures have been made, the opposing party has fourteen days within which to file with the court any objections to the use of any deposition or exhibit. If objections are not made, they are deemed to be waived (unless a party can show good cause why he or she failed to object to the disclosures within the fourteen-day time period).

An attorney's duty to disclose relevant information is ongoing throughout the pretrial stage. Any time an attorney learns about relevant supplemental information concerning statements or responses made earlier, that information must be disclosed to the other party.

DISCOVERY OF ELECTRONIC EVIDENCE

Over the last few years, electronic evidence has significantly changed litigation and has become a major consideration in pretrial discovery. Electronic evidence, or e-evidence, consists of all computer-generated or electronically recorded information, such as e-mail, voice mail, spreadsheets, word processing documents, and other data. E-evidence has become increasingly important because it can reveal significant facts that are not discoverable by other means. The Federal Rules of Civil Procedure and most state rules (as well as court decisions) specifically allow discovery of electronic "data compilations" (or e-evidence).

The discovery of e-evidence is fundamentally different from the discovery of paper documents and physical evidence, although traditional discovery methods, such as interrogatories and depositions, are still used in obtaining it. The following subsections describe the features of e-evidence that make it uniquely important. They are intended only as an introduction to the rapidly advancing area of electronic evidence. For additional suggestions about electronic discovery, see this chapter's *Technology and Today's Paralegal* feature starting on the next page.

The Advantages of Electronic Evidence

E-evidence has several distinct advantages over paper discovery. People and businesses use computers to store and communicate enormous amounts of data. A great deal of the information stored on computers (20 to 30 percent) is never printed on paper. In addition, whenever a person is working on a computer, information is being recorded on the hard disk without being saved by the user. This information, called **metadata,** is the hidden data kept by the computer about a document, including the file's location, path, creator, date created, date last accessed, hidden notes, earlier versions, passwords, and formatting. It reveals information about how, when, and by whom a document was created, accessed, modified, and transmitted. This information can only be obtained from the file in its electronic format—not from printed versions.

metadata
Embedded electronic data recorded by a computer in association with a particular file, including the file's location, path, creator, date created, date last accessed, hidden notes, earlier versions, passwords, and formatting. Metadata reveals information about how, when, and by whom a document was created, accessed, modified, and transmitted.

E-MAIL COMMUNICATIONS.   Today, millions of e-mail messages are sent each year, and it has become commonplace to use e-mail at work and at home. Because e-mail is so widespread, it has become a fertile ground for gathering evidence in litigation. In fact, some believe that e-mail is the "smoking gun" of the future. This is largely due to the fact that most people converse freely and informally in their e-mail communications, as if talking to a close friend or business

TECHNOLOGY AND TODAY'S PARALEGAL

Electronic Discovery

Paralegals today, particularly litigation paralegals, need to be prepared to deal with electronic discovery. This means not only formulating electronic discovery plans but also making sure to preserve the integrity of any electronic evidence acquired. It is important, too, to remember that e-evidence is fragile. Although—as discussed in the chapter text—it may be difficult to truly delete files from a computer system, it is certainly not impossible. Every time a user enters new data, loads new software, or performs routine maintenance procedures, the data on the computer is permanently altered. Just booting up a computer can change dates and times on numerous files. The following are some general guidelines to follow in conducting e-discovery.

PRESERVATION-OF-EVIDENCE LETTER

To preserve the maximum amount of information, you must put all parties—including your own client—on notice that you are seeking the electronic evidence in their control. You do this by writing a preservation-of-evidence letter at the outset of discovery. This letter informs the parties that they have a duty to take immediate action to preserve the evidence. It is your best protection against the other side's arguing that someone has inadvertently modified or destroyed the e-evidence you seek.

Be specific in the letter about what you want preserved (e-mail, word processing documents, databases, spreadsheets, telephone logs, backup and removable media). Also explain in detail what the party should not do (load new software, perform certain maintenance procedures, save new files on existing drives or media, or destroy old back-up media). If you suspect the other side will ignore your request, you can ask the court for a protective order.

USE INTERROGATORIES TO GATHER INFORMATION

In order to find out where to look for the evidence that you seek, you need to find out as much as you can about the system with which you are dealing. If the target system is your opponent's system, you can use interrogatories to get answers to the following types of questions:

- System layout: How many computers are there? What are the operating systems and software applications? Are the computers networked? Are there any files with restricted access?

- E-mail system: What e-mail system is being used and by how many users?

- Back-up system and office procedures: How and when are files backed up? What routines does the company use to archive and purge data? Are back-up media rotated? Does the company use any monitoring software?

- System administrator: Who is responsible for overseeing and maintaining the system?

- Other electronic evidence: Does anyone use laptops, personal digital assistants, cell phones, or other electronic devices? Does anyone use a home computer for work or to access e-mail?

associate. This makes e-mail very believable and compelling evidence—evidence that can be very damaging if discovered by outsiders.

In addition, in its electronic form, e-mail contains information that provides links to other e-mails, e-mail attachments, erased files, and metadata. These metadata reveal any person who received copies of the e-mail message (even "blind" copies). Thus, e-evidence can be used to trace a message to its true originator, reconstruct an e-mail conversation, and establish a timeline of the events in dispute (who knew what, when). Attorneys also use it to verify the client's claims or discredit the claims of the opposition. Whether it is evidence of adultery, sexual harassment, employment discrimination, fraud, or the theft of trade secrets, e-mail often contains the most compelling evidence in a case.

DELETED FILES CAN BE RETRIEVED.   Another major advantage of e-evidence is that even deleted files can often be retrieved from the "residual data" within

TECHNOLOGY AND TODAY'S PARALEGAL, CONTINUED

FOLLOW UP WITH DEPOSITIONS

Once you know the names of the parties who oversee the system or have special knowledge of it, take depositions. Make sure that you receive full information about the back-up system and any other data sources. Obtain user names and e-mail addresses. Find out whether any security measures (passwords or encryption) are in place. Ask about audit trails. Don't forget to ask *every* witness who is deposed about his or her computing habits. For example, ask the witness whether he or she makes individual back-ups, saves to a different computer or to portable media, works from home, uses a laptop, and so forth.

REQUEST FOR PRODUCTION

Once you find out the details of where electronic evidence is located, draft a request for production of the evidence. As mentioned in the text, after you have gained access to the evidence, it is imperative that you make an exact image copy and preserve it so that it will be admissible as evidence at trial. It is usually best to hire an outside computer forensic expert to accomplish this task and avoid chain-of-custody disputes. Have the expert make a working copy of the data that is write-protected so that you can review the data without inadvertently making changes. Several reputable computer forensic companies are accessible online, including Kroll Ontrack (http://www.krollontrack.com),

New Technologies, Inc. (http://www.forensics-intl.com), and Electronic Evidence Discovery, Inc. (http://www.eedinc.com). These sites also provide articles, research notes, and related information. In addition, you can download sample practice forms at the Kroll Ontrack site (including preservation letters, interrogatories, and a motion to compel electronic discovery).

TECHNOLOGY TIP

Electronic discovery is likely to become commonplace in the near future. Paralegals should learn, at minimum, the right questions to ask in depositions and interrogatories. Remember that your client will be expected to provide e-discovery to the other side as well. Once the e-evidence is acquired, the legal team must figure out how to manage, review, and interpret what is likely to be a tremendous amount of data. A single CD can hold up to 20,000 pages, and a DVD can hold nearly 100,000 pages. Most firms do not yet have the staff, facilities, or technical expertise necessary to convert such massive amounts of data into a format that can be loaded onto existing legal software. Outside digital-discovery processing companies, however, can provide such services. (See, for example, Applied Discovery, Inc., at http://applieddiscovery.com, and DocuLex (formerly Advocate Solutions, Inc.), at http://www.doculex.com/index.htm.

the computer. This is because deleting a file does not actually destroy the data but simply makes the space occupied by that data available to be overwritten by new information. Until that space is actually used for new data (which may be in weeks, in months, or never), the deleted record can be retrieved with special software.

Most people believe that when they delete a record or e-mail and empty the recycle bin, the message is gone from their computer. This increases the probability of candid e-mail communications. As just described, however, deleted data remains on the computer until overwritten by new data (or wiped out by certain utility software). In fact, experts have even been able to retrieve data, in whole or in part, from computers that have been damaged by water, fire, or severe impact. Therefore, don't assume that e-evidence is not available just because a file was deleted, a computer was damaged, or a utility program was run.

The Sources of Electronic Evidence

Key to conducting electronic discovery is developing an understanding of the kinds of information that computers can provide so that you will know where to look for particular kinds of information. Generally, computer data can be located in active files, in back-up files, or as residual data. Active files are those currently accessible on the computer (word processing documents, e-mail, and spread-sheets, for example). Back-up files are those that have been copied to removable media such as Zip disks, CDs, or DVDs. As mentioned, residual data is data that appears to be gone but is still recoverable from somewhere on the computer system. Residual data no longer has pointers to indicate its location and can only be retrieved by special software.

BACK-UP DATA.   Back-up files can be a source of hidden treasure for the legal team. Reviewing back-up copies of documents and e-mail provides useful information about how a particular matter progressed over several weeks or months.

Many companies back up data at routine intervals (weekly or monthly), while others have no formal back-up schedule. Some companies have back-up routines for word processing documents but not for e-mail. Back-up copies may also be made automatically by word processing software or individually by a user. Sometimes, a person makes back-up copies of work files for use on his or her home computer. Because the current location of the data depends on which back-up process is used, you need to find out the individual's or business's back-up policy (or practice) as soon as you can during discovery.

Note that back-up files contain not only the e-mail messages and word processing documents but also other embedded information that can be useful. For example, when computers are networked, computer logs and audit trails that keep track of network usage may be available. An audit trail will tell you who accessed the system, when it was accessed, and whether those that accessed the system copied, downloaded, modified, or deleted any files. In addition, back-up data files include certain nonprinting information, such as the date and time the files were created. Some word processing software allows users to insert hidden comments or track changes while drafting and revising documents. These comments and revisions can also be accessed from the electronic version of the back-up file.

OTHER SOURCES OF E-EVIDENCE.   It is important to remember that electronic evidence is not limited to the data found on computer systems. As stated, e-evidence includes *all* electronically recorded information, such as voice mail, back-up voice mail, video, electronic calendars, phone logs, Palm Pilots and other personal digital assistants, laptops, cell phones, and any other devices that digitally store data. You should not overlook any possible sources of e-evidence during discovery. Use traditional discovery tactics (such as interrogatories and depositions) to find out about other sources of potential e-evidence. Consider and ask about all possible sources that might prove fruitful.

The Special Requirements of Electronic Evidence

The law has been developing to accommodate electronic evidence. It is clear that while most courts allow discovery of electronic evidence, judges also recognize that electronic evidence can be easily manipulated. To ensure that the evidence you obtain during discovery will be admissible as evidence in court, you must do two things. First, make sure that you obtain an exact image copy of the electronic evidence, as described shortly. Second, make sure that you can prove that nothing has been altered or changed from the time the image copy was made.

TODAY'S PROFESSIONAL PARALEGAL

Witness Coordination

Barbara Lyons works as a paralegal for a busy litigation firm. Today she is assisting with a medical-malpractice trial. Susan Weiss, the attorney for whom Barbara works, has asked Barbara to coordinate Susan's witnesses. It is 8:30 A.M., and Barbara and Susan are waiting in the courtroom for Dr. Max Brennan, the first witness that Susan will call today.

PLANNING A WITNESS'S ARRIVAL TIME

While they are waiting, Susan fills Barbara in on how the trial went yesterday and what she expects to happen today. Susan tells Barbara that she expects Dr. Brennan to be on the stand testifying from 9 A.M. until at least the lunch break. Then she expects that he will be cross-examined for an hour or two after lunch. Susan wants Barbara to have the next witness, Laura Lang, at the court-house and ready to testify by 11 A.M., though, in the event that Dr. Brennan is excused earlier than expected.

Barbara has already arranged with the witness to arrive at the courthouse by 11 A.M. but is concerned that Lang will not be on time. Barbara has met with Lang two times to review her testimony and prepare her for the trial experience, and Lang has always been late. Barbara tells Susan about her concerns. Susan tells Barbara to go out into the hallway at 9 A.M. and call Lang. "Tell her that things are moving along more quickly than planned and to be here at ten o'clock. That should help to make sure that she will be here by eleven."

A WITNESS IS DELAYED

It is 8:35 A.M., and Dr. Brennan has not yet arrived. Susan asks Barbara to go out to the hallway and call him, first in his car and then in his office, to find out where he is. Barbara opens her trial notebook to the witness section. Dr. Brennan's page is first because he is the first witness scheduled to appear. She locates the number for his cell phone, jots it down on a scrap of paper, and leaves the courtroom. As she starts dialing Dr. Brennan's number, she sees him walk out of the elevator. Barbara puts the phone back and greets Dr. Brennan. "Sorry I'm running late, but I had an emergency this morning and I had to stop by the hospital before I came here," explains Dr. Brennan.

"I'm just glad to see you!" exclaims Barbara. "Let's go into the courtroom. You are the first witness, and Susan wants to see you." Barbara and Dr. Brennan enter the courtroom, and Susan and Dr. Brennan talk briefly before the judge enters. The court is called to order, and the trial resumes. Barbara sits at the counsel table while Susan questions Dr. Brennan on the stand. At 9 A.M., Barbara leaves the courtroom and calls Laura Lang.

TAKING PRECAUTIONS—ARRANGING FOR A WITNESS TO ARRIVE EARLY

Lang answers the phone. "Hello Ms. Lang. It's Barbara Lyons from Smith, White & White. Susan Weiss asked me to call you and tell you that the trial is moving faster than we anticipated. Susan would like you to be here at ten o'clock instead of eleven, if that's possible," advises Barbara. "Oh. Well, I suppose I can be there by then," responds Lang. "Do you remember how to get here?" asks Barbara. "Yes, I have the directions," answers Lang. "Good. I'll see you soon then, at ten o'clock," says Barbara. She returns to the courtroom.

At 9:55 A.M., Barbara leaves the courtroom again to wait in the hallway for Laura Lang. By 10:15 A.M., Lang has still not arrived. Barbara opens the courtroom door to listen. The testimony is going faster than Susan had anticipated, and Barbara can tell that Susan will probably be ready to put Lang on the stand in another thirty minutes or so. Barbara closes the courtroom door. She gets out her cell phone and dials Lang's telephone number. There is no answer. "I hope that she is on her way," thinks Barbara.

A TIMELY ARRIVAL

Now it is 10:45 A.M., and Lang has still not arrived. Barbara opens the courtroom door again and can tell that there is only about five minutes left in Dr. Brennan's testimony. She dials Lang's number again. No answer. Barbara continues to wait in the hallway, and a few minutes later Lang appears. Barbara breathes a sigh of relief. She opens the courtroom door, catches Susan's eye, and nods her head.

ACQUIRING AN IMAGE COPY. In order to use any evidence in court, you must convince the court that the evidence is authentic. In the case of electronic evidence, you must show that the electronic version of the evidence that you have acquired is exactly the same as the version that was present on the target system. The only way to do this is to have an image copy made.

Suppose the target system is a computer drive. Making an image copy would involve creating a sector-by-sector mirror image of the drive being copied. The image copy would capture all data, including residual data. This is much different from the usual file-by-file back-up copying method.

Making an image copy of a computer drive is complicated and is best left to an expert in computer forensics. Computer forensics experts collect, preserve, and analyze electronic evidence and testify in court if needed. Unskilled attempts to acquire an image of a computer's drive can easily lead to disaster, wrecking the evidence and rendering it inadmissible at trial.

chain of custody
A series describing the movement and location of evidence from the time it is obtained to the time it is presented in court. The court requires that evidence be preserved in the condition in which it was obtained if it is to be admitted into evidence at trial.

PRESERVING THE CHAIN OF CUSTODY. Once you have acquired an exact copy of the electronic evidence, you must establish and maintain a chain of custody to avoid any claims that the evidence has been tampered with. The phrase **chain of custody** refers to the movement and location of evidence from the time it is obtained to the time it is presented in court. It is particularly crucial when dealing with electronic evidence to make sure that you can track the evidence from its original source to its admission in court. This will provide the court with the necessary assurance that nothing has been added, changed, or deleted. The original image copy should be write-protected so that it is tamperproof, labeled as the original, and kept in a secure location. Typically, a forensic specialist will make working copies of the original data that are write-protected and scanned for viruses. You should always use the working copies rather than the original when reviewing e-evidence.

KEY TERMS AND CONCEPTS

affidavit
affirmative defense
allegation
answer
chain of custody
complaint
counterclaim
cross-claim
default judgment
deponent
deposition
deposition transcript
discovery
discovery plan
docket
Federal Rules of Civil Procedure (FRCP)
impeach
interrogatories
judgment
memorandum of law
metadata
motion
motion for judgment on the pleadings
motion for summary judgment
motion to dismiss
pleadings
prayer for relief
privileged information
return-of-service form
service of process
subpoena
summons
supporting affidavit
witness

✳ CHAPTER SUMMARY

Civil Litigation—A Bird's Eye View	1. *Pretrial settlements*—Throughout the pretrial stage of litigation, the attorney and paralegal will attempt to help the parties reach a settlement at the same time as they are preparing the case for trial.
	
	2. *Procedural requirements*—Although civil lawsuits vary from case to case in terms of complexity, cost, and detail, all civil litigation involves similar procedural steps, as described in Exhibit 12.1.
	
	    a. The Federal Rules of Civil Procedure (FRCP) govern all civil cases heard in federal courts and specify what must be done during the various stages of litigation.
	
	    b. Each state has adopted its own rules of civil procedure, which in many states are similar to the FRCP.
	
	    c. Many courts also have (local) rules of procedure that supplement the federal or state rules.

The Preliminaries	1. *The initial client interview*—The first step in the civil litigation process occurs when the attorney initially meets with a client who wishes to bring a lawsuit against another party or parties. The attorney normally conducts this initial client interview, although the paralegal often attends the interview and may make arrangements with the client for subsequent interviews. 2. *Preliminary investigation*—Once the attorney agrees to represent the client in the lawsuit and the client has signed the retainer agreement, the attorney and the paralegal undertake a preliminary investigation to ascertain the facts alleged by the client and gain other factual information relating to the case. 3. *The litigation file*—A litigation file is created to hold all documents and records pertaining to the lawsuit. Each law firm or legal department has its own specific procedures for organizing and maintaining litigation files. Generally, the file will expand, as the case progresses, to include subfiles for the pleadings, discovery, and other documents and information relating to the litigation.

The Pleadings	The pleadings inform each party of the claims of the other and detail the facts, charges, and defenses involved in the litigation. Pleadings typically consist of the plaintiff's complaint, the defendant's answer, and any counterclaim or cross-claim.
	
	1. *The complaint*—A complaint states the claim or claims that the plaintiff is making against the defendant. A lawsuit in a federal or state court normally is initiated by the filing of a complaint with the clerk of the appropriate court.
	
	    a. The complaint includes a caption, jurisdictional allegations, general allegations (body of the complaint) detailing the cause of action, a prayer for relief, a signature, and, if appropriate, a demand for a jury trial.
	
	    b. A complaint can be filed either by personal delivery of the papers to the court clerk or, if the court permits, by electronic filing via e-mail, fax, or CD-ROM. The procedural requirements of courts that allow electronic filing vary dramatically and should be researched prior to any electronic filing.

The Pleadings—Continued	**2.** *Service of process*—Typically, the defendant is notified of a lawsuit by delivery of the complaint and a summons (which is called service of process). The summons identifies the parties to the lawsuit, identifies the court in which the case will be heard, and directs the defendant to respond to the complaint within a specified time period.
	
	    a. Although often the complaint and summons are personally delivered to the defendant, other methods of service are allowed in some cases, depending on the jurisdiction.
	
	    b. In federal cases and in many states, the defendant can waive or give up the right to be personally served with the summons and complaint (and accept service by mail, for example).
	
	    c. Under FRCP 4, if the defendant waives service of process, the defendant receives additional time to respond to the complaint.
	
	3. *The defendant's response*—On receiving the complaint, the defendant has several options.
	
	    a. The defendant may submit an answer. The answer may deny any wrongdoing or may assert an affirmative defense against the plaintiff's claim, such as the plaintiff's contributory negligence. The answer may be followed by a counterclaim, in which the defendant asserts a claim against the plaintiff arising out of the same incident; or it may be followed by a cross-claim, in which the defendant makes claims against another defendant named in the complaint.
	
	    b. Alternatively or simultaneously, the defendant might make a motion to dismiss the case. A motion to dismiss asserts that, even assuming the facts of the complaint are true, the plaintiff has failed to state a cause of action or there are other grounds for dismissal of the suit.

Pretrial Motions	**1.** *Motion for judgment on the pleadings*—A pretrial motion that may be filed by either party after all pleadings and amendments have been filed. The motion asks the court to enter a judgment in favor of one party based on information contained in the pleadings alone. A judgment on the pleadings will only be made if there are no facts in dispute and the only question is how the law applies to the facts. **2.** *Motion for summary judgment*—A motion that may be filed by either party during or after the discovery stage of litigation. This motion, like the motion for judgment on the pleadings, asks the court to enter judgment without a trial. Unlike a motion for judgment on the pleadings, however, a motion for summary judgment can be supported by evidence outside the pleadings (including affidavits, depositions, and interrogatories). The motion for summary judgment will not be granted if any facts are in dispute.
Traditional Discovery Tools	In preparing for trial, the attorney for each party undertakes a formal investigative process called discovery to obtain evidence helpful to his or her client's case. **1.** *Interrogatories*—Interrogatories are written questions that the parties to the lawsuit must answer, in writing and under oath. The FRCP and some states' rules limit the number of questions that may be asked. **2.** *Depositions*—Like interrogatories, depositions are given under oath, but unlike interrogatories, depositions may be taken from witnesses as well as

Traditional Discovery Tools—Continued	from the parties to the lawsuit. Also, the attorney is able to question the deponent (the person being deposed) in person. There is no limit on the number of questions that may be asked. Usually, a court reporter records the official transcript of the deposition. 3. *Requests for production*—During discovery, the attorney for either side may request another party to produce documents or tangible things or to allow him or her access to documents or tangible things for inspection and other purposes. 4. *Physical or mental examinations*—When the mental or physical condition of a party is in controversy, the opposing party may request the court to order the party to submit to an examination by a licensed examiner. 5. *Requests for admission*—A party can request the opposing party to admit the truth of matters relating to the case. Such admissions save time at trial because the parties do not have to spend time proving facts on which they agree.
The Duty to Disclose under FRCP 26	In federal court cases, FRCP 26 requires that the attorneys cooperate in forming a discovery plan early in the litigation process. The rule also requires attorneys to disclose relevant information *automatically*. Under FRCP 26, only after initial disclosures have been made can attorneys resort to the use of traditional discovery tools. An attorney's duty to disclose relevant information under FRCP is ongoing throughout the pretrial stage.
Discovery of Electronic Evidence	Electronic evidence consists of all computer-generated or electronically recorded information, such as e-mail, voice mail, spreadsheets, and word processing documents. The federal rules and most state rules allow discovery of evidence in electronic form. E-evidence has significantly changed discovery in civil litigation because it can reveal facts not discoverable by other means. 1. *Advantages of e-evidence*—Electronic evidence often provides more information than paper discovery, since much data that is on the computer is never printed out. In addition, the computer records hidden data (called metadata) about documents and e-mail, which can be very useful to the legal team. Even files that were deleted by the user can be retrieved from the residual data within the computer. 2. *Sources of e-evidence*—E-evidence may be located in the active data of the computer, the back-up data that has been copied to removable media, or the residual data that appears to be gone from the computer. Back-up data is particularly useful to the legal team. Not all e-evidence is located on computers, and you should investigate other potential sources, such as voice mail, phone logs, personal digital assistants, and so forth. 3. *Requirements of e-evidence*—In order to ensure that e-evidence will be admissible as evidence in the trial, you must obtain an exact image copy of the original data and then preserve the chain of custody until the time of trial, making sure to do nothing that will alter the evidence.

QUESTIONS FOR REVIEW

1. What happens during the initial client interview? Who normally conducts this interview, the attorney or the paralegal? Why?
2. What are the basic steps in the litigation process prior to the trial? How does the paralegal assist the attorney in each of these steps?
3. What kinds of documents are contained in a litigation file? How might these documents be classified, or organized, within the file?
4. What documents constitute the pleadings in a civil lawsuit? What is the effect of each type of document on the litigation?
5. How are defendants notified of lawsuits that have been brought against them? What procedures are required under FRCP 4 for notifying the defendant in a lawsuit?
6. What is service of process? Why is it important?
7. Name three pretrial motions, and state the purpose of each.
8. What is a counterclaim? What is an affirmative defense? What is the effect of each of these on the litigation?
9. What is discovery? When does it take place? List three discovery devices that can be used to obtain information prior to trial.
10. How has the duty to disclose under FRCP 26 changed the discovery process in federal court cases?

ETHICAL QUESTIONS

1. Pamela Hodges has just started working as a paralegal for Lawyers, Inc., a high-volume, low-overhead law firm that handles mostly simple and routine litigation. Her supervising attorney, Carol Levine, has two initial client meetings scheduled at the same time. Carol tells Pam to handle one, and she (Carol) will come in to sign the retainer agreement. After one and a half hours, Carol is still tied up, and the client is demanding that Pam sign the retainer agreement or he will find another attorney. Should Pam let the client leave and risk losing his business, or should Pam sign the retainer agreement? Does she have other options?
2. Your next-door neighbor's son was beaten up while at school. The boy's mother is facing over $1,000 in medical and dental expenses as a result of his injuries, which she cannot afford to pay. She knows that you work as a paralegal in a law firm that specializes in personal-injury litigation, so she asks you if you will help her. She wants you to write a letter threatening legal action, which she will then sign, and she also wants to know whether she can sue the parents of the boys who beat up her son. Should you write the letter? Should you advise her on what action she might take against the other boys' parents? What are your ethical obligations in this situation? How could you help her without violating professional ethical standards?
3. Bruce Miller, a paralegal, is meeting with a client, Callie Nelson, to prepare answers to interrogatories. In the course of preparing the answers, Callie asks Bruce if he thinks that she has a good case, if there are better legal theories that she could pursue to win her case, and what her options are if she loses. How should Bruce answer these questions?
4. Scott Emerson takes a job as a paralegal with a large law firm that specializes in defending clients against product liability claims. The firm's clients are some of the largest manufacturing companies in the country. Mark Jones, an associate attorney, assigns Scott the job of drafting and sending out interrogatories to the plaintiff in a case brought against one of the firm's clients. Specifically, Scott is told to send out a standard set of one hundred interrogatories, each with five parts. Scott eventually learns that one of the favorite discovery tactics of the firm is to inundate plaintiffs with discovery requests, interrogatories, and depositions to cause continuous delays and to outspend the plaintiffs. Scott knows that the relevant state court rules do not limit the number of interrogatories that can be used, but he suspects that the firm's tactics are ethically questionable. Are they? What should Scott do?

✳ PRACTICE QUESTIONS AND ASSIGNMENTS

1. Assume that you work for attorney Tara Jolans of Adams & Tate, 1000 Town Center, Suite 500, White Tower, Michigan. Jolans has decided to represent Sandra Nelson in her lawsuit against David Namisch. Based on the following information, draft a complaint to be filed in the U.S. District Court for the Eastern District of Michigan.

   Sandra Nelson is a plaintiff in a lawsuit resulting from an automobile accident. Sandra was turning left at a traffic light at the intersection of Jefferson and Mack Streets, while the left-turn arrow was green, when she was hit from the side by a car driven by David Namisch, who failed to stop at the light. The accident occurred on June 3, 2003, at 11:30 P.M. David lives in New York, was visiting his family in Michigan, and just prior to the accident had been out drinking with his brothers. Several witnesses saw the accident. One of the witnesses called the police.

   Sandra was not wearing her seat belt at the time of the accident, and she was thrown against the windshield, sustaining massive head injuries. When the police and ambulance arrived, they did not think that she would make it to the hospital alive, but she survived. She wants to claim damages of $500,000 for medical expenses, $65,000 for lost wages, and $55,000 for property damage to her Rolls Royce. The accident was reported in the local newspaper, complete with photographs.

2. Using Exhibit 12.3, *A Summons in a Civil Action,* draft a summons to accompany the complaint against David Namisch. David's address is 1000 Main Street, Apartment 63, New York, NY 10009. The court clerk's name is David T. Brown.

3. Using Exhibit 12.4, *A Return-of-Service Form,* draft a form to show that you, a paralegal for Whitman, Schultz & Horowitz, 325 Cleveland Avenue, Suite 407, New York, NY 10009, personally delivered a complaint and summons to Jarred Ramul at his residence. Jarred's address is 10833 Main Street, Apartment 63, on the sixth floor of the Baker Building in New York City, 10009. Include all required information.

4. Draft the first ten questions for a set of interrogatories to be directed to the plaintiff, Sandra Nelson, based on the facts given in Question 1 above.

5. Using Exhibit 12.9, *Notice of Taking Deposition,* draft a notice that Sandra Nelson's attorneys will be taking the deposition of David Namisch on September 10, 2004, at 9:00 A.M., at the law offices of Adams & Tate. Mr. Namisch's attorney is Mark Simmons of Simmons & Smith, 444 Park Avenue, New York, NY 10007.

6. Using the material presented in the chapter on pre-trial motions, identify each of the following motions:

   a. Tom Smith is a defendant in an auto-negligence case. His attorney files a motion requesting that a judgment be granted in Tom's favor without a trial. He attaches to the motion an affidavit of an eyewitness, who saw the plaintiff run a stop sign.

   b. Dr. Higgins is sued for medical malpractice. The plaintiff recovered completely and has no damages. Dr. Higgins's attorney files a motion asking that the case against his client be dismissed for failure to state a claim on which relief can be granted.

   c. After the answer is filed in a case brought by a plaintiff who slipped on a broken egg and fell on a grocery store floor, her attorney files a motion requesting that the court enter a judgment in the plaintiff's favor based on the undisputed facts contained in both the answer and the complaint.

   d. Dr. Higgins's attorney loses the motion discussed above. When the plaintiff's attorney requests medical records, Dr. Higgins instructs his attorney to refuse to provide the records. The plaintiff's attorney files a motion to obtain the records.

✳ QUESTIONS FOR CRITICAL ANALYSIS

1. Most cases are settled before trial. Why is this? What does it say about our system of justice? Does it place certain parties at a disadvantage? Why or why not?

2. What is the difference between preliminary investigation and discovery? What impact does this difference have on a case? Which would you prefer to undertake to determine the facts of a case?

3. A complaint must be served on the defendant in a lawsuit. What happens if the defendant is not properly served? Is this a fair result? Why or why not?

4. Why are defendants in federal courts and some state courts allowed to waive service of process? What is it that these defendants actually waive?

5. Why does a complaint contain jurisdictional allegations and general allegations? What is the difference between these types of allegations? Why is each type necessary? What might happen if jurisdictional allegations were not included in a complaint?

6. How can a legal professional include a fact in a complaint if he or she has reason to believe that the fact is true but is uncertain as to its truth? Does including such a fact have any impact on the attorney's signing of the complaint or an affidavit?

7. If a defendant fails to respond to the plaintiff's complaint within a specified time period, what can happen? Is this a fair rule? Why?

8. What happens if a defendant fails to deny an allegation in answering a complaint? Is this fair to the defendant? What happens if a defendant is uncertain as to the truth of a matter being alleged by a plaintiff in a complaint?

9. What is the difference between a motion for summary judgment and a motion for judgment on the pleadings? Is one motion preferable to the other? Give an example of how each motion is used.

10. What is the difference between interrogatories and depositions? Which is more efficient? Which is more cost-effective? Which would you prefer to use?

11. Some state court rules require the use of traditional discovery tools. The FRCP, in contrast, imposes a duty on parties and their attorneys to disclose certain information automatically, without waiting for traditional discovery requests. Which system of discovery is better, and why? Which is faster? Which is more realistic?

✶ PROJECTS

1. Litigation is paper and document intensive, and computers can help tame the "paper dragon." Software has been developed and is constantly being updated that can organize and coordinate various pieces of evidence and testimony by using a combination of imaging software, database software, and full-text searching. This allows evidence, including documents and deposition transcripts, to be scanned into the computer, indexed, and easily located or retrieved. Two of the companies that sell the software are Summation Legal Technologies, Inc., and INMAGIC. Contact one of these companies for a free demonstration CD or free online demonstration. Summation can be reached at 1-800-735-7866 or via the Internet at http://www.summation.com. From its Web site, you can view an online demonstration, order a free CD demonstration, or register for a live demonstration. INMAGIC can be reached at 1-800-229-8398 or online at http://www.inmagic.com. At the Web site, you can download a demonstration (several modules are available). After trying a demonstration of one of these companies' products, write a one-page paper describing how the software works.

2. Visit the county court clerk's office (or the clerk's office of a local court) and obtain the following: local court rules, summons and return-of-service forms, and a filing-fee schedule.

3. Review your state's court rules to determine which, if any, of the pretrial motions covered in this chapter are used in the courts in your state. Are the rules the same for all courts in your state? If not, what are some differences among courts?

4. Find out when a local court's "motion day" is, and attend court for two to three hours on that day. Observe as many motions as possible. Write a one-page summary of what you observed. Be sure to include the name of the court you visited, the date, and the judge's name.

✶ USING INTERNET RESOURCES

1. Access the Web site of the National Court Reporters Association at http://www.verbatimreporters.com.

   a. Click on "Site Map." Under the heading "About NCRA," click on "History of Court Reporters."

Read the article, and then answer the following questions:

• When was the stenotype first invented? How does this machine work?

- What is computer-aided transcription? What is "realtime" translation?

b. Now click on "Find a Reporter or Caption," and search for your city (if you live in a smaller community, enter the name of a large city in your area or state).

- How many court reporters or court-reporting firms offer services in that area?

- List five types of services that one (or more) of these court reporters or firms offer.

2. The legal documents in the case brought by Paula Corbin Jones against Bill Clinton for sexual harassment can be found at a site maintained by the *Washington Post*. Go to this site at **http://www. washingtonpost.com/wp-srv/politics/special/pjones/ legal.htm**, and answer the following questions:

a. Under the heading "Complaint and Responses," go to the complaint filed by Paula Corbin Jones.

- In what court was the complaint filed?

- Who were the defendants?

- How many causes of action did plaintiff Jones allege?

- What was the amount of the damages (compensatory and punitive) that the plaintiff requested?

- Did the plaintiff ask for a jury trial?

b. Under the heading "Complaint and Responses," go to President Clinton's response (answer).

- What case number was assigned to the case?

- Does the president admit to or deny the allegations of the complaint?

- How many affirmative defenses does the president's answer raise?

c. Scroll down to "President Clinton's Deposition," and click on it to view excerpts from the deposition. Find the part of the deposition titled "Events at the Excelsior Hotel." Answer the following questions:

- When was the president's deposition taken?

- Where was the president's deposition taken?

- How many objections were made by the president's attorney during this section of the deposition?

- What did the president say about his relationship with Paula Jones?

END NOTES

1. Some practitioners use the abbreviation FRCivP to distinguish the Federal Rules of Civil Procedure from the Federal Rules of Criminal Procedure.

2. Nita and Zero are fictitious states invented for the purpose of this hypothetical.

3. See Chapter 4 for a discussion of legal fees and the form and function of the retainer agreement.

4. In some courts and in certain types of cases, this document may be called a *petition*.

5. The body of the complaint described in this section is a *fact pleading*, in which sufficient factual circumstances must be alleged to convince the court that the plaintiff has a cause of action. State courts often require fact pleadings, whereas federal courts only require *notice pleading*. FRCP 8(a)

requires only that the complaint have "a short and plain statement of the claim showing that the pleader is entitled to relief." Fact pleading and notice pleading are not totally different—that is, the same allegation of facts could be in the body of a complaint submitted to either a federal or a state court. Federal courts simply have fewer requirements in this respect, and therefore they are often more attractive to litigants.

6. The memorandum of law described here should not be confused with the legal memorandum discussed in Chapter 18. The latter is an internal memorandum (that is, a memo submitted—usually by the paralegal—to an attorney).

7. Under the provisions of the FRCP, federal district courts can modify, or opt not to follow, the rules requiring early disclosures.

CHAPTER 13

CONDUCTING
INTERVIEWS
AND INVESTIGATIONS

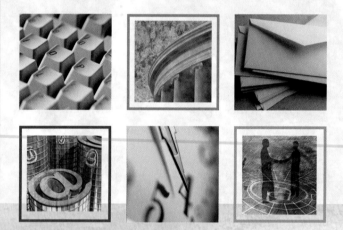

Chapter Outline

✳ INTRODUCTION ✳ PLANNING THE INTERVIEW ✳ INTERVIEWING SKILLS
✳ INTERVIEWING CLIENTS ✳ INTERVIEWING WITNESSES
✳ PLANNING AND CONDUCTING INVESTIGATIONS

After completing this chapter, you will know:

- How to prepare for an interview and the kinds of skills employed during the interviewing process.

- The common types of client interviews paralegals may conduct and the different types of witnesses paralegals may need to interview during a preliminary investigation.

- How to create an investigation plan.

- The variety of sources that you can use to locate information or witnesses.

- Rules governing the types of evidence that are admissible in court.

- How to summarize your investigation results.

INTRODUCTION

Paralegals frequently interview clients. After the initial client interview (which is usually conducted by the supervising attorney), the paralegal may conduct one or more subsequent interviews to obtain detailed information from the client. How the paralegal relates to the client has an important effect on the client's attitude toward the firm and the attorney or legal team handling the case.

Additionally, paralegals often conduct pretrial investigations. As part of a preliminary investigation into a client's claim, the paralegal may interview one or more witnesses to gain as much information as possible. The more factual evidence that can be gathered in support of a client's claim, the better the client's chances in court—or in any other dispute-settlement proceeding.

Learning how to conduct interviews and investigations is thus an important part of preparing for your career as a paralegal. In this chapter, you will read about the basic skills and concepts that you can apply when interviewing clients or witnesses and when conducting investigations.

PLANNING THE INTERVIEW

Planning an interview involves organizing many details. As a paralegal, you may be responsible for locating a witness, scheduling the interview, determining where the interview should take place, arranging for the use of one of the firm's conference rooms or other office space for the interview, and managing additional related details. Crucial to the success of any interview is how well you prepare for it.

Know What Information You Want to Obtain

Prior to any interview, you should have clearly in mind the kind of information you want to obtain from the client or witness being interviewed—the **interviewee.** If possible, discuss with your supervising attorney the goal of the interview and the type of information that the attorney hopes to obtain. This will ensure that you and the attorney share an understanding of what topics need to be covered in the interview. Once you know the questions that you want to ask, prepare a checklist or outline in advance so that you can refer to it during the interview.

interviewee
The person who is being interviewed.

PREPRINTED INTERVIEW FORMS.   Many law firms have created preprinted or computerized forms indicating the kinds of information that should be gathered during client interviews relating to particular types of claims. Firms that frequently handle personal-injury claims, for example, often use a personal-injury intake sheet such as that shown in Exhibit 13.1 starting on the next page. Standardized client intake forms are also available as part of many legal software programs and from a variety of online sources. Using preprinted forms helps to ensure that all essential information will be obtained, especially for the beginning interviewer.

In some cases, the information needed will be clear from the legal forms or documents that will ultimately be filed with the court. For example, a paralegal interviewing a client who is petitioning for bankruptcy or divorce can look at the bankruptcy or divorce court forms during the interview to make sure all required information is obtained.

REMAIN FLEXIBLE.   Keep in mind, however, that prepared questions and preprinted forms should only be used as guidelines during the interview. Do not simply read the questions word for word from a prepared list or stick rigidly to a

EXHIBIT 13.1
Personal-Injury Intake Sheet

PERSONAL-INJURY INTAKE SHEET

Prepared for Clients of
Jeffers, Gilmore & Dunn

1. Client Information:

Name: Katherine Baranski

Address: 335 Natural Blvd.

Nita City, NI   48802

Social Security No.: 206-15-9858

Marital Status: Married   Years Married: 3

Spouse's Name: Peter Baranski

Children: None

Phone Numbers: Home (616) 555-2211   Work (616) 555-4849

Employer: Nita State University

Mathematics Department

Position: Associate Professor of Mathematics

Responsibilities: Teaching

Salary: $ 48,000

2. Related Information:

Client at Scene: Yes

Lost Work Time: 5 months

Client's Habits: Normally drives south on Mattis Avenue on way to university each morning at about the same time.

planned outline of topics. If you do, you throw away an opportunity to interact with the interviewee and gain the interviewee's trust, and he or she will probably not disclose any information other than what is specifically asked for.

During any interview, the interviewer should remain flexible, listen carefully to the interviewee's responses, and let those responses guide the questioning. (Remember that you can always ask the interviewee to return to a certain topic later on in the interview.) By focusing too much on your own role and on what your next question will or should be, you can easily overlook the importance of what the client or witness is saying right now.

⬚ **Make sure that you listen to the interviewee's responses and modify your questions accordingly.**

EXHIBIT 13.1
**Personal-Injury Intake Sheet—
Continued**

3. Incident/Accident:

Date: August 4, 2003   Time: 7:45 A.M.

Place: Mattis Avenue and 38th Street, Nita City, Nita

Description: Mrs. Baranski was driving south on Mattis Avenue when a car driven by Tony Peretto, who was attempting to cross Mattis at 38th Street, collided with Mrs. Baranski's vehicle.

Witnesses: None known by Mrs. Baranski

Defendant: Tony Peretto

Police: Nita City

Action Taken: Mrs. Baranski was taken to City Hospital by ambulance (Nita City Ambulance Co.).

4. Injuries Sustained:

Nature: Multiple fractures to left hip and leg; lacerations to left eye and left side of face; multiple contusions and abrasions

Medical History: No significant medical problems prior to the accident

Treating Hospital: Nita City Hospital

Treating Physician: Dr. Swanson

Hospital Stay: August 4, 2003   to November 20, 2003

Insurance: Southwestern Insurance Co. of America

Policy No: 00631150962 -B

Interview Conducted by:

Allen P. Gilmore
Attorney   January 30, 2004
                                            Date

Elena Lopez
Paralegal/Witness   January 30, 2004
                                            Date

Effective listening techniques are discussed later in this chapter.

PLAN TO ASK FOLLOW-UP QUESTIONS.   Another important point to remember is to ask for details and clarification after the interviewee has made a statement. Find out who, what, when, where, and how. If an interviewee says, for example, that he saw someone hit Jane in the face, you will need to ask for more specifics, such as:

• How far away was he at the time?
• What exactly did he see?
• How many times was she hit and with what (open hand, fist, weapon)?

- Who else was present?
- Was it light or dark? Inside or outside?
- From what angle did he view the incident?
- Does he know Jane or her assailant? How?
- What were Jane and the assailant doing before and after the incident?
- What was the witness doing before the incident?

Also, although you should read the case file thoroughly before the interview, try to set aside what you have read or heard about the case. Let the interviewee tell you the story from his or her own perspective and avoid preconceived notions about what the person will say. One approach is to pretend that you know nothing about the case and let the interviewee tell you her or his version of the facts. Then, as the interview unfolds, think about what the person is saying from the perspective of your opponent—why should anyone believe that story? Ask follow-up questions aimed at establishing what makes the person's story more or less believable. If a witness says a car was going fifty-five miles per hour, for example, ask how he or she could tell the speed. If it turns out the witness has been racing cars recreationally for the past fifteen years, this fact can be used to help make the witness's testimony more believable.

Recording the Interview

Some interviewers tape-record their interviews. Before you tape-record an interview, you should always do the following:

> ※   **Obtain permission to tape-record the interview from both your supervising attorney and the person being interviewed.**

When you are using a tape recorder, you should state or include at the beginning of the tape the following identifying information:

- The name of the person being interviewed and any other relevant information about the interviewee.
- The name of the person conducting the interview.
- The names of other persons present at the interview, if any.
- The date, time, and place of the interview.
- On the record, the interviewee's consent to having the interview tape-recorded.

If more than one tape is used, you should indicate at the end of each tape that the interview will be continued on the next tape in the series, and each subsequent tape should contain identifying information.

There are several advantages to tape-recording an interview. For one thing, having a record of the interview on tape reduces the need to take extensive notes during the interview. You can either have the tape transcribed for future reference or listen to the tape later (when creating an interview summary, for example, as discussed later) to refresh your memory of how the interviewee responded to certain questions. You may also want to have other members of the legal team read the transcript or listen to the tape. Sometimes, what seemed insignificant to you may seem significant to someone else working on the case. Also, as a case progresses, a remark made by an interviewee that did not seem important at the time of the interview may take on added importance in view of evidence gathered later.

There are also some disadvantages to tape-recording interviews. A major disadvantage is that clients and witnesses may feel uncomfortable and be less willing to disclose information freely if they know everything they are saying is being

DEVELOPING PARALEGAL SKILLS

The Tape-Recorded Interview

Justin Hooper is preparing for an interview that will be tape-recorded. He takes the tape recorder to the conference room where the interview will take place and sets up the tape recorder. The witness arrives and is shown into the conference room by the receptionist. Justin takes a prepared statement from a file folder containing the introductory remarks used in a tape-recorded interview. He reads it into the tape recorder:

"My name is Justin Hooper. I am a paralegal at the law firm of Smith & Howard. The firm is representing Mr. Barry Buckner, the defendant in *Jones v. Buckner*. This tape-recorded interview is taking place in the law offices of Smith & Howard on January 6, 2004. The time is two o'clock in the afternoon."

Justin then turns to the witness and asks her to state and spell her name into the tape recorder. Justin also asks the witness for her consent to have the interview tape-recorded, so that the witness's consent will be on record. Then the interview begins.

TIPS FOR CONDUCTING A TAPE-RECORDED INTERVIEW

- Test the tape recorder before the interview to ensure that it is working properly.
- Create a prepared introductory statement that gives the name of the interviewer; the date, time, and location of the interview; the case name; and other relevant information.
- Ask the witness to state and spell his or her name into the tape recorder.
- Ask the witness for permission to tape-record the interview—be certain the witness's answer is tape-recorded.
- Ask all others present during the interview to state and spell their names.
- Have additional tapes available, and immediately label additional tapes as they are used.
- If more than one tape is used, be certain to state on each tape which number the tape is and how many tapes were used.

recorded. Such reluctance is understandable in view of the fact that the interviewee does not know what exactly will transpire during the course of the interview or how the tape may later be used. When asking an interviewee for his or her permission to tape-record an interview, you should therefore evaluate carefully how the interviewee responds to this question. Depending on the interviewee's response, you might consider taking notes instead of tape-recording the session. Another option is to go through the questions you will ask with the interviewee once before asking permission to turn on the tape recorder.

INTERVIEWING SKILLS

Interviewing skills are essentially any skills—particularly interpersonal and communication skills—that help you to conduct a successful interview. In this section, you will learn how the use of interpersonal and communication skills can help you establish a comfortable relationship with the interviewee. Then, you will read about specific questioning and listening techniques that can help you control the interview and elicit various types of information.

Interpersonal Skills

At the outset of any interview, remember that your primary goal is to obtain information from the client or witness being interviewed. Although some people communicate information and ideas readily and effectively, others may need considerable prompting and encouragement. If they feel comfortable in your presence and in the interviewing environment, they will generally be more willing to disclose information.

As you begin an interview, you should remember that the interviewee may be very nervous or at least uncomfortable. Because the time you have to talk with a client or witness will be limited, you should put that individual at ease as quickly as possible. A minute or two spent chatting casually with the client or witness is time well spent. Also, saying or doing something that shows your concern for the interviewee's physical comfort helps to make the interviewee feel more relaxed. For example, you might offer the individual a cup of coffee or other beverage.

Using language that the interviewee will understand is essential in establishing a good working relationship with that person. If you are interviewing a client with only a grade-school education, for example, do not use the phrase "facial lacerations" when talking about "cuts on the face." If you are interviewing a witness who does not speak English very well, arrange to have an interpreter present unless you are fluent in the witness's native language. Because most clients and witnesses are not familiar with legal terminology, you should always abide by the following rule of thumb when conducting interviews:

> ※ **Avoid using legal terms that will not be clearly understood by the interviewee.**

If you must use a specific legal term to express an idea, be sure that you define the term and that it is clearly understood.

Questioning Skills

When questioning witnesses or clients, you should remember to remain objective at all times and gather as much relevant factual information as possible. Sometimes, you may have difficulty remaining objective when questioning witnesses because you sympathize with the client and may not want to hear about facts that are contrary to the client's position. But relevant factual information includes those details that adversely affect the client's case as well as those that support his or her position. Indeed, your supervising attorney must know *all* of the facts, especially any that might damage the client's case in court.

In some situations, it may be difficult to remain objective not because of your sympathy *for* the client but because of your own personal biases *against* the client, the witness, or the case. Interviewers must be especially careful to evaluate their own feelings prior to conducting an interview. If you feel a person's conduct or situation is morally reprehensible, you may convey those feelings during the interview either verbally or nonverbally. Once the interviewee senses your disapproval, he or she is likely to limit the information disclosed. For example, suppose that you are interviewing Sandra, a client who is trying to regain custody of her children. The state took Sandra's children away because she abused "crack" cocaine and failed to properly care for them. You have read through the file and strongly disapprove of Sandra's past conduct. You also have doubts about whether she has sufficiently recovered from her drug problem. If you do not set aside your personal feelings prior to meeting with Sandra, it may unconsciously affect your interaction and thwart the success of the interview.

The experienced legal interviewer uses certain questioning techniques to prompt interviewees to communicate the information needed. There are several types of questions, including open-ended, closed-ended, hypothetical, and leading questions. Exhibit 13.2 provides some examples of the types of questions discussed in the following subsections.

EXHIBIT 13.2
Types of Interview Questions

Type of Question	Open-Ended Questions	Closed-Ended Questions	Leading Questions	Hypothetical Questions
Definition	A broad, exploratory question that elicits a lengthy response.	A question phrased in such a way that it elicits a "yes" or "no" response.	A question phrased in such away that it suggests the desired answer.	A question that asks the interviewee to assume a certain set of facts in forming an answer.
Typical Uses	Used mostly with friendly witnesses and clients.	Used to clarify a witness's statement or to keep her or him on track. Used with adverse or reluctant witnesses.	Used at times with adverse witnesses in interviews. Used often by attorneys to cross-examine witnesses in trial (see Chapter 14).	Used primarily with expert witnesses in interviews and during trial.
Examples	• Describe the morning of the accident. What did you do that morning? • What did you observe prior to entering the intersection? • When did you first observe the defendant's car and where was it? • How fast was the defendant going at the time of the accident?	• Were you late for work that morning? • Was there anyone in the car with you at the time? • Were you already in the intersection at the time you first saw the plaintiff's car? • Were you exceeding the speed limit at the time the accident occurred?	• You were running late for work that morning, correct? • You saw that the light had turned red before you entered the intersection, didn't you? • Isn't it true that you were driving in excess of the speed limit at the time of the accident? • Isn't it true that you had been out drinking at a bar until late on the night before the accident?	• If a full-sized van is traveling at fifty-five miles per hour, how far before an intersection must the driver apply the brakes in order to stop the vehicle? • If a 200-pound man consumed fourteen beers in six hours, how long would it take before the alcohol was out of his system so that it would not affect his ability to drive? • What type of treatment does a person who has suffered the kinds of injuries just described ordinarily receive?

OPEN-ENDED QUESTIONS.   The **open-ended question** is a broad, exploratory question that invites any number of possible responses. The open-ended question can be used when you want to give the interviewee an opportunity to talk at some length about a given subject. "What happened on the night of October 28—the night of the murder?" is an open-ended question. Other examples of open-ended questions are "And what happened next?" and "What did you see as you approached the intersection?" When you ask a question of this kind, be prepared for a lengthy response. If a witness has difficulty narrating the events he or she observed or if a lull develops during the explanation, you will need to encourage the witness to continue through the use of various prompting responses (which will be discussed shortly in the context of listening skills).

Open-ended questions are useful in interviewing clients or friendly witnesses (witnesses who favor the client's position). This is because these kinds of interviewees are usually forthcoming, and you will be able to gain information from them by indicating in broad terms what you want them to describe. Open-ended questions are also a good way for the interviewer to evaluate whether the interviewee's demeanor and overall effectiveness would make him or her a good witness at trial.

open-ended question
A question phrased in such a way that it elicits a relatively unguided and lengthy narrative response.

closed-ended question
A question phrased in such a way that it elicits a simple "yes" or "no" answer.

CLOSED-ENDED QUESTIONS.   The **closed-ended question**, in contrast, is intended to elicit a "yes" or "no" response from the interviewee. "Did you see the murder weapon?" is an example of a closed-ended question. Although closed-ended questions tend to curb communication, they are useful in some situations. For example, if an interviewee tends to digress frequently from the topic being discussed, using closed-ended questions can help keep him or her on track. Closed-ended questions, because they invite specific answers, also may be useful to clarify the interviewee's previous response and to relax the interviewee in preparation for more difficult questions that follow. In addition, closed-ended questions may help to elicit information from adverse witnesses (those who are not favorable to the client's position), who may be reluctant to volunteer information.

leading question
A question that suggests, or "leads to," a desired answer. Interviewers may use leading questions to elicit responses from witnesses who otherwise would not be forthcoming.

LEADING QUESTIONS.   The **leading question** is one that suggests to the listener the answer to the question. "Isn't it true that you were only ten feet away from where the murder took place?" is a leading question. This question, of course, invites a "yes" answer. Leading questions can be very effective for drawing information out of eyewitnesses or clients, particularly when they are reluctant to disclose information. They can also be useful for interviewing adverse witnesses who are hesitant to communicate information that may be helpful to the client's position. (In fact, they are the primary method of questioning used by attorneys when cross-examining witnesses at trial, as you will read in Chapter 14.) When used with clients and friendly witnesses, however, leading questions have a major drawback:

> ※   **Leading questions may lead to distorted answers because the client or witness may tailor the answer to fit his or her perception of what the interviewer wants to know.**

For this reason, in the interviewing context, leading questions should be used cautiously and only when the interviewer is fully aware of the possible distortions that might result.

hypothetical question
A question based on hypothesis, conjecture, or fiction.

HYPOTHETICAL QUESTIONS.   As a paralegal, you may be asked to interview an expert witness either to gather information about a case or to evaluate whether that person would be an effective expert witness at trial (expert witnesses will be discussed later in this chapter). The **hypothetical question** is frequently used with expert witnesses. Hypothetical questions allow you to obtain an answer to an important question without giving away the facts (and confidences) of a client's case. For example, you might invent a hypothetical situation involving a certain type of knee injury (the same kind of injury as that sustained by a client) and then ask an orthopedic surgeon what kind of follow-up care would ordinarily be undertaken for that type of injury.

Listening Skills

The interviewer's ability to listen is perhaps the most important communication skill used during the interviewing process. Whenever you conduct an interview, you will want to absorb fully the interviewee's verbal answers, as well as his or her nonverbal messages. Prior to the interview, you should make sure that the room in which it is to be held will be free of noises, phone calls, visitors, and other interruptions or distractions. During the interview itself, you can use several listening techniques to maximize communication and guide the interviewee toward the fullest disclosure of needed information.

Locating Witnesses

Perhaps one of the most challenging tasks for the legal investigator is locating a witness whose address is unknown or who has moved from a previous, known address. Suppose, for example, that in the Baranski case the police investigation report lists the name, address, and telephone number of Edna Ball, a witness to the accident. When you call her number, a recording informs you that the phone has been disconnected. You go to her address, and the house appears to be vacant. What is your next step?

At this point, many paralegals suggest to their supervising attorneys that a professional investigator take over the search. But if you alone must locate the witness, there are several sources to which you can turn. A good starting point is to visit other homes in the neighborhood. Perhaps someone living nearby knows Edna Ball and can give you some leads as to where she is or what happened to her. Other sources are discussed below.

TELEPHONE AND CITY DIRECTORIES.   The telephone directory can sometimes be a valuable source of information for the investigator. In trying to locate Edna Ball, for example, you might check to see if her name is listed in the current directory and, if so, whether it is listed jointly with someone, such as her husband. Your local telephone information service might have a new number listed for her. If the information-service operator indicates that the number is unlisted, you can explain the nature of your concern and request that the operator phone Edna Ball at that number to see if she is willing to call you.

City directories are also good potential sources of information. Such directories may be available in the local library or the law firm's library. A city directory generally contains more information than a phone book. For example, some city directories list places of employment and spouses' names in addition to addresses and telephone numbers. Typically, city directories provide a listing of names and phone numbers by street address. In the Baranski case, if you wanted to obtain the telephone numbers of persons who live in the area of the Baranski-Peretto accident, you could consult a city directory for addresses near the intersection where the accident occurred.

ONLINE PEOPLE FINDERS.   Today, paralegals can use one of the numerous Internet people-finding services to locate witnesses (and witness's assets, if needed). Some of these online services charge a nominal fee (ranging from three dollars to seventy dollars) for each search, depending on the type of report requested (simple address record, background check, e-mail address, assets). The services will check public records, telephone directories, court and criminal records, and a variety of other sources and provide results quickly and efficiently. (For an example, go to **http://www.people-finder.com**, **http://bigfoot.com**, **http://www.searchbug.com/ peoplefinder**, or **http://www.infousa.com/fs/consumer.htm** and enter the name, city, and state of the person you wish to locate.) Both of the largest online legal research services (Westlaw® and Lexis®, which will be discussed in Chapter 17) offer people-finding services as well. In addition, several software programs that conduct Internet searches, such as *NetDetective* and *OnlineDetective,* are available for a one-time charge.

On the Web
To find telephone book Web sites, you can do a broad search using a search engine, such as that of Infoseek at **http://www. infoseek.com**.

OTHER INFORMATION SOURCES.   Other sources of information include media reports (newspaper and magazine articles and television videos covering the event being investigated); court records (probate proceedings, lawsuits, and so on); deeds to property (usually located in the county courthouse); birth, marriage, and death certificates; voter-registration lists; the post office (at which the witness may

TECHNOLOGY AND TODAY'S PARALEGAL

Online Medical Research

Attorneys and paralegals frequently deal with cases involving personal injuries, medical malpractice, product liability, and other health-related problems. In such cases, paralegals may be asked to do some research on a particular medical topic, procedure, or device. (A paralegal may also be asked to locate an expert witness in the medical field; you will read about online databases of expert witnesses in Chapter 17.)

KNOW THE TERMINOLOGY

You might want to begin your research by familiarizing yourself with the relevant medical terminology. To do this, you can access medical dictionaries and glossaries online. For example, you can find the online medical dictionary maintained by CancerWEB at http://cancerweb.ncl.ac.uk/omd. To find online medical glossaries, you can go to http://www.interfold.com/translator/medsites.htm, which provides links to a number of glossaries in eighteen different languages, or to http://www.glossarist.com, which provides links to hundreds of medical glossaries on both general topics and specific conditions and disorders. Another useful site for legal professionals can be found at http://www.legal-med-ware.com/files/Medical_Glossaries.htm, which includes links to sites providing such things as manuals on diagnosis and treatment, terms used in managed health care, and information on health-care standards.

ONLINE MEDICAL JOURNALS AND TEXTBOOKS

Many medical journals are available online. For example, the American Medical Association publishes a number of journals, including the well-known *Journal of the American Medical Association* (JAMA), which can be accessed from http://pubs.ama-assn.org. Cambridge University provides online access to the full text of articles for over a hundred medical journals at http://www.uk.cambridge.org/journals/medicine, as does Stanford University at http://www.med.stanford.edu/medworld/research_journals.html. At sites such as http://www.emedicine.com and http://www.medbioworld.com, you will find searchable databases of some of the leading medical journals. You simply type in a key word, such as HIV, and the articles that mention that topic are instantly available to you.

Numerous medical textbooks are also available online. Two of the best resources for accessing medical textbooks are Martindale's Health Science Guide, located at http://www.sci.lib.uci.edu/HSG/HSGuide.html, and the Multimedia Medical Reference Library at http://www.medlibrary.com/medlibrary. Both sites give the paralegal access to hundreds of medical textbooks (as well as journal articles), results from clinical trials, case studies, teaching files, and audio and video tutorials. Information about medical devices, drugs, and medical procedures can be found at Yahoo's medical site (at http://d4.dir.scd.yahoo.com/health/medicine) and at http://www.healthgate.com.

GOVERNMENT MEDICAL RESOURCES

Other sites useful to paralegals engaged in medical research are maintained by the U.S. government. For example, the Food and Drug Administration's site (at http://www.fda.gov) provides information about recent topics of concern involving prescription drugs, new medical devices, food safety, dietary supplements, cosmetics, animal feed and drugs, and radiation-emitting products. The National Institutes of Health—which is part of the U.S. Department of Health and Human Services—maintains a site (at http://www.nih.gov) that provides a wealth of health-related information. Through this site, you can read about general medical topics and research studies or use MEDLINEplus, a searchable database of health information provided through the National Library of Medicine.

TECHNOLOGY TIP

Paralegals involved in litigation that requires medical research can access numerous resources over the Internet. This can save hours of time that would have been spent researching medical topics in the books and journal articles found in libraries. There are so many online resources, however, that dealing with them can be overwhelming to a paralegal who is just becoming familiar with medical literature. A wise paralegal may want to spend a few hours browsing through the sites mentioned above before being assigned a particular research project. Once you find a site that you personally find useful and easy to navigate, bookmark the site on your computer or add it to your favorites for future reference.

Insurance Paralegal

KIRTRENA S. DEEN *received her bachelor of arts degree in legal administration from the University of West Florida in Pensacola, Florida, in 1996. On graduation, she worked at a large law firm as a legal assistant for approximately a year and a half in the area of personal-injury and employment law. She then accepted a position as a claims representative for a national automobile insurance company.*

In September 1998, Deen received her Florida Department of Insurance Adjusters license. Additionally, she serves on the University of West Florida Legal Administration Program Advisory Board as a paralegal representative in the corporate/public sector.

What do you like best about your work?

"I enjoy the responsibility and exposure of investigating, evaluating, and negotiating a variety of automobile claims as opposed to adjusting only specific types of automobile claims. Some examples of the claims I am assigned to adjust include property, bodily-injury, arson, theft, vandalism, and weather-related claims. I also enjoy the investigative process of meeting the parties involved, securing recorded statements, conducting scene investigations, and canvassing for witnesses."

What is the greatest challenge that you face in your area of work?

"Once a claim has been reported, the claims representative must investigate to establish coverage, finalize legal liability, and inspect the reported damage. Once the claim has been thoroughly investigated, it must be evaluated to determine a fair settlement and negotiated accordingly. Therefore, the greatest challenge of adjusting claims is completing the investigation, evaluation, and negotiation process promptly and fairly while complying with the terms of the insurance policy and governing statutory laws."

What advice do you have for would-be paralegals in your area of work?

"My advice is to possess strong interpersonal skills, as well as superior writing and oral communication skills. Due to the variety of claims assigned, claims representatives in my area daily communicate and negotiate with insureds, claimants, and other claims representatives, as well as attorneys, regarding the settlement of claims. Additionally, regular meetings and communication with paint and body shop managers is needed regarding the assessment of automobile damage. Thus, the ability to communicate effectively with all kinds of people is a great asset to possess in my area of work."

What are some tips for success as a paralegal in your area of work?

"Know the terms and conditions of the insurance policy and regularly refer to the policy to substantiate them. The insurance policy is the contract between the insurance company and the insured to which they must adhere. Know the statutory laws governing claims handling in your area and keep abreast of changes. Be detail oriented and analytical in the investigation process. Feel passionate about your work. Passion for your work will enable you to go that extra mile to handle claims promptly and fairly."

> "[T]he ability to communicate effectively with all kinds of people is a great asset to possess in my area of work."

have left a forwarding address); credit bureaus; the tax assessor's office; and city utilities, such as the local electric or water company.

Professional organizations may be useful sources as well. For example, if you have learned from one of Edna Ball's neighbors that she is a paralegal, you can check with state and local paralegal associations to see if they have current information on her. You might also check with federal, state, or local governmental agencies or bureaus (discussed in the following section) to see if the information contained in public records will be helpful in locating Edna Ball.

Accessing Government Information

On the Web
You can access the home pages of federal agencies by going to **http://www.findlaw.com**.

Records and files acquired and stored by government offices and agencies can be a tremendous resource for the legal investigator. Public records available at local government buildings or offices (such as the county courthouse or post office) were mentioned above. Additionally, it is possible to obtain information from federal agencies, such as the Social Security Administration, and from state departments or agencies, such as the state revenue department or the secretary of state's office. If you wish to obtain information from any government files or records, you should check with the specific agency or department to see what rules apply.

The Freedom of Information Act (FOIA), which was enacted by Congress in 1966, requires the federal government to disclose certain records to any person on request. A request that complies with the FOIA procedures need only contain a reasonable description of the information sought. Exhibit 13.8 illustrates the proper format for a letter requesting information under the FOIA. Note that the FOIA exempts some types of information from the disclosure requirement, including classified information (information concerning national security), confidential material dealing with trade secrets, government personnel rules, and personal medical files.

Investigation and the Rules of Evidence

Because an investigation is conducted to obtain information and verify facts that may eventually be introduced as evidence at trial, you should know what kind of evidence will be admissible in court before undertaking your investigation.

evidence
Anything that is used to prove the existence or nonexistence of a fact.

rules of evidence
Rules governing the admissibility of evidence in trial courts.

Evidence is anything that is used to prove the existence or nonexistence of a fact. Whether evidence will be admitted in court is determined by the **rules of evidence**—rules that have been created by the courts to ensure that any evidence presented in court is fair and reliable. The Federal Rules of Evidence govern the admissibility of evidence in federal courts. For cases brought in state courts, state rules of evidence apply. (Many states have adopted evidence rules patterned on the federal rules.) Of course, you will not need to become an expert in evidentiary rules, but a basic knowledge of how evidence is classified and what types of evidence are admissible in court will greatly assist your investigative efforts.

direct evidence
Evidence establishing the existence of a fact that is in question without relying on inferences.

circumstantial evidence
Indirect evidence that is offered to establish, by inference, the likelihood of a fact that is in question.

DIRECT VERSUS CIRCUMSTANTIAL EVIDENCE.   Two types of evidence may be brought into court—direct evidence and circumstantial evidence. **Direct evidence** is any evidence that, if believed, establishes the truth of the fact in question. For example, bullets found in the body of a shooting victim provide direct evidence of the type of gun that fired them. **Circumstantial evidence** is indirect evidence that, even if believed, does not establish the fact in question but only the degree of likelihood of the fact. In other words, circumstantial evidence can create an inference that a fact exists.

For example, suppose that your firm's client owns the type of gun that shot the bullets found in the victim's body. This circumstantial evidence does not estab-

EXHIBIT 13.8
**Freedom of Information
Act Request Form**

Agency Head or FOIA Officer
Title
Name of Agency
Address of Agency
City, State, Zip

Re: Freedom of Information Act Request.

Dear_____:

    Under the provisions of the Freedom of Information Act,
5 U.S.C. 552, I am requesting access to [identify the records as clearly
and specifically as possible].

    If there are any fees for searching for, or copying, the records I have requested, please
inform me before you fill the request. [Or: . . . please supply the records without informing
me if the fees do not exceed $_____.]

    [Optional] I am requesting this information [state the reason for your request if you think
it will assist you in obtaining the information].

    [Optional] As you know, the act permits you to reduce or waive fees
when the release of the information is considered as "primarily benefiting
the public." I believe that this request fits that category and I therefore
ask that you waive any fees.

    If all or any part of this request is denied, please cite the specific
exemption(s) that you think justifies your refusal to release the information,
and inform me of the appeal procedures available to me under the law.

    I would appreciate your handling this request as quickly as possible,
and I look foward to hearing from you within ten days, as the law stipulates.

Sincerely,

Signature
Name
Address
City, State, Zip

On the Web
For further
information on
how to make
an FOIA request, go to
**http://www.nist.gov/
admin/foia/foia.htm.**

lish that the client shot the victim. Combined with other circumstantial evidence, however, it could help to convince a jury that the client committed the crime. For instance, if other circumstantial evidence indicates that your firm's client had a motive for harming the victim and that the client was at the scene of the crime at the time the crime was committed, a jury might conclude that the client committed the crime.

RELEVANCE.   Evidence will not be admitted in court unless it is relevant. **Relevant evidence** is evidence that tends to prove or disprove the fact in question. For example, evidence that the gun belonging to your firm's client was in the home of another person when the victim was shot would be relevant, because it would tend to prove that the client did not shoot the victim.

    Even relevant evidence may not be admitted in court if its probative (proving) value is substantially outweighed by other important considerations. For example, even though evidence is relevant, it may not be necessary—the fact at issue may have been sufficiently proved or disproved by previous evidence. In that situation, the introduction of further evidence would be a waste of time and would cause undue delay in the trial proceedings. Relevant evidence may also be excluded if it would tend to distract the jury from the main issues of the case, mislead the jury, or cause the jury to decide the issue on an emotional basis.

relevant evidence
Evidence tending to prove or disprove the fact in question. Only relevant evidence is admissible in court.

DEVELOPING PARALEGAL SKILLS

Accessing Government Information

Ellen Simmons has started a new job as a paralegal for Smith & Case, a law firm that handles Superfund cases (see Chapter 11). Ellen is about to request copies of documents from the EPA. Ellen calls and speaks to Christopher Peter, a paralegal with the EPA. She identifies herself as a paralegal from Smith & Chase, which is representing a client involved at the Suburban Landfill Superfund site. Ellen is greeted with an icy silence and wonders what she might have said to offend Christopher. She asks if the EPA has the waste-in/waste-out report that gives the total volume of hazardous waste at the site and lists the potentially responsible parties.

Christopher responds, in a surprised voice, that the EPA does have the documents. "Are you new?" asks Christopher. "Is it that obvious?" jokes Ellen. Christopher responds that it's not really that obvious and explains that her predecessor always just sent in FOIA requests for everything that the EPA had in its files and that it took weeks to respond to these requests. "Believe me, your firm has quite a reputation around here," says Christopher.

Ellen knows that she is off to a good start in her new job and with an important legal assistant at the EPA. She

smiles to herself as she promises to submit the FOIA request for only the waste-in/waste-out report.

TIPS FOR WORKING WITH GOVERNMENT AGENCIES

- Review the file to familiarize yourself with the case before calling the agency.
- Review the agency's regulations to ascertain which documents the agency prepares in specific types of cases, such as Superfund cases.
- Make a list of the various documents.
- Determine in advance (from the list) which documents you will be requesting.
- Develop a list of alternatives to use in the event that the documents that you request have not been prepared or are not available.
- Make reasonable requests from the agency.
- Cultivate good working relationships with agency staff members.

---

authentication
The process of establishing the genuineness of an item that is to be introduced as evidence in a trial.

AUTHENTICATION OF EVIDENCE.   At trial, an attorney must lay the proper foundation for the introduction of certain evidence, such as documents, exhibits, and other objects, and must demonstrate to the court that the evidence is what the attorney claims.[1] The process by which this is accomplished is referred to as **authentication.** The authentication requirement relates to relevance, because something offered in evidence becomes relevant to the case only if it is authentic, or genuine.

> ※   **As a legal investigator, you therefore need to make sure that the evidence you obtain is not only relevant but also capable of being authenticated if introduced at trial.**

Commonly, evidence is authenticated by the testimony of witnesses. For example, if an attorney wants to introduce an autopsy report as evidence in a case, he or she can have the report authenticated by the testimony of the medical examiner who signed it. Generally, an attorney must offer enough proof of authenticity to convince the court that the evidence is, in fact, what it is purported to be.

The rules of evidence require authentication because certain types of evidence, such as exhibits and objects, cannot be cross-examined by opposing counsel, as witnesses can, yet such evidence may have a significant effect on the jury. The authentication requirement provides a safeguard against the introduction of non-verified evidence that may strongly influence the outcome of the case.

The Federal Rules of Evidence provide for the self-authentication of specific types of evidence. In other words, certain documents or records need not be authenticated by testimony. Certified copies of public records, for example, are automatically deemed authentic. Other self-authenticating evidentiary documents include official publications (such as a report issued by the federal Environmental Protection Agency), documents containing a notary public's seal or the seal of a public official, newspaper or magazine articles, and manufacturers' trademarks or labels.

HEARSAY.   When interviewing witnesses, keep in mind that the witness's testimony *in court* must be based on the witness's own knowledge and not hearsay. **Hearsay** is defined as testimony that is given in court by a witness who relates not what he or she knows personally but what another person said. Literally, it is what someone heard someone else say. Hearsay is generally not admissible in court when offered to prove the truth of the matter asserted.

For example, a witness in the Baranski case cannot testify in court that she heard another observer say, "that van is going ninety miles per hour"—even if the other observer was a police officer. Such testimony would be inadmissible under the hearsay rule. The witness can only testify about what she personally observed regarding the accident. Of course, during the investigation, witnesses often tell you what other people said (and you should not discourage them from doing so). If you wish to use information obtained this way as evidence in court, however, you need to find an alternative method of proving it (such as by the testimony of the people who made the original statements, for example).

Policy Underlying the Hearsay Rule.   There are several reasons why hearsay is generally not allowed. First, the person who made the out-of-court statements (referred to as the declarant) was not under oath at the time of making the statements. Second, the witness who is testifying may have misunderstood what the other person said. Third, because there is no opportunity to cross-examine the person who actually made the statements, there is no way to verify that the statements were actually made, much less that the witness heard them correctly. In other words, hearsay evidence is inadmissible because it is unreliable, not because it is irrelevant.

Exceptions to the Hearsay Rule.   Exceptions to the hearsay rule are made in specific circumstances, often because the statements are made in situations that indicate a high degree of reliability. For example, a witness is usually allowed to testify about what a dying person said concerning the cause or circumstances of his or her impending death. This is because the courts have concluded that a person facing imminent death will usually not lie about who or what caused that death. Similarly, if a person makes an excited statement at the time of a stressful or startling event (such as "Oh no! That woman has just dropped her baby out the window"), a witness can usually testify as to that statement in court. If one of the parties to a lawsuit makes an out-of-court admission (for example, if defendant Peretto in the Baranski case admits to his friends that he was driving too fast at the time of the accident), a witness's testimony about what the party said will be admissible.[2] Exhibit 13.9 on the following page lists and describes some of the traditional exceptions to the hearsay rule.

Summarizing Your Results

The final step in any investigation is summarizing the results. Generally, your investigation report should provide an overall summary of your findings, a

hearsay
Testimony that is given in court by a witness who relates not what he or she knows personally but what another person said. Hearsay is generally not admissible as evidence.

EXHIBIT 13.9
Some Exceptions to the Hearsay Rule

Present Sense Impression—A statement describing an event or condition made at the time the declarer perceived the event or condition or immediately thereafter [FRE 803(1)].* Example: "I smell smoke."

Excited Utterance—A statement relating to a startling event or condition made while the declarer was under the stress or excitement caused by the startling event or condition [FRE 803(2)]. Example: "Oh no! The brakes aren't working!"

State of Mind—A statement of the declarer's then existing state of mind, emotion, sensation, or physical condition (such as intent, plan, motive, design, mental feeling, pain, or bodily health). Such statements are considered trustworthy because of their spontaneity [FRE 803(3)]. Example: "My leg is bleeding and hurts terribly."

Recorded Recollection—A memorandum or record indicating a witness's previous statements concerning a matter that the witness cannot now remember with sufficient accuracy to testify fully about the matter. If admitted in court, the memorandum or record may be read into evidence but may not itself be received as an exhibit unless offered by an adverse party [FRE 803(5)]. Example: An employer's memo to one of his or her employees in which the employer responds to the employee's complaint about safety violations in the workplace.

Former Testimony—Testimony that was given at another hearing or deposition by a witness who is now unavailable, if the party against whom the testimony is now offered was a predecessor in interest and had an opportunity to examine the witness in court during the previous hearing or deposition [FRE 804(b)(1)]. Example: An employee's testimony about his or her employer that was introduced at a trial brought by the employee's co-worker against that employer for sexual harassment. The employer is now being sued by another employee for sexual harassment, and the employee who testified in the previous trial is out of the country. The employee's testimony in the previous trial may be admissible.

Business Records—A document or compilation of data made in the course of a regularly conducted business activity, unless the source of the information or the method or circumstances of the document's preparation indicate that it is not trustworthy as evidence. The source of information must be from a person with firsthand knowledge, although this person need not be the person who actually made the entry or created the document [FRE 803(6)]. Example: Financial statement of a business firm.

Dying Declarations—In a prosecution for homicide or in a civil action or proceeding, a statement made by a person who believes that his or her death is impending about the cause or circumstances of his or her impending death [FRE 804(b)(2)]. Example: Derek said just before he died, "Jethro stabbed me."

Statement against Interest—A statement that was made by someone who is now unavailable and that was, at the time of its making, so far contrary to the declarer's financial, legal, or other interests that a reasonable person in the declarer's position would not have made the statement unless he or she believed it to true [FRE 804(b)(3)]. Example: Sanchez says that Jackson, who is now missing, made the following statement to Sanchez just before leaving town: "I committed the perfect crime!"

Miscellaneous Exceptions—Miscellaneous exceptions include records of vital statistics [FRE 803(9)]; records of religious organizations [FRE 803(11)]; marriage, baptismal, or similar certificates [FRE 803(12)]; family records (including charts, engravings on rings, inscriptions on family portraits, and engravings on tombstones) [FRE 803(13)]; and statements offered as evidence of a material fact that are trustworthy because of the circumstances in which they were uttered [FRE 804(b)(5) and FRE 803(24)].

*Federal Rules of Evidence.

summary of the facts and information gathered from each source that you investigated, and your general conclusions and recommendations based on the information obtained during the investigation.

OVERALL SUMMARY.   The overall summary of the investigation should thoroughly describe for the reader all of the facts you have gathered about the case. This section should be written in such a way that someone not familiar with the case could read it and become adequately informed of the case's factual background.

TODAY'S PROFESSIONAL PARALEGAL

Interviewing a Client

Amanda Blake, a paralegal, works for John Kerrigan, a sole practitioner. A new client, Joel Sontag, calls for an appointment to make his will. The attorney has to go out of town for a court hearing. Because Sontag seems to be anxious to get the will done, the attorney asks Amanda to meet with Sontag and interview him to obtain some basic information. The attorney will review the information when he returns from his trip and then call Sontag to advise him on the will and other estate-planning possibilities.

PREPARING FOR THE INTERVIEW

Amanda reserves the conference room. On the day of Sontag's visit, she has it set up for the interview. She has already made a copy of the will and estate-planning checklist that she will use to ensure that she gets all of the essential information from Sontag. The secretary shows Sontag into the conference room when he arrives.

MEETING THE CLIENT

Amanda introduces herself, saying, "Hello, Mr. Sontag, I'm Amanda Blake, John Kerrigan's legal assistant. I'll be meeting with you today to obtain the estate-planning information that Mr. Kerrigan needs if he is to advise you." Sontag responds, "Mr. Kerrigan told me that we would be meeting today. He also told me how capable you are." Amanda smiles and says, "Thanks. And did Mr. Kerrigan explain to you that I'm not an attorney?" Sontag responds, "Yes, he did." Amanda then removes her checklist and note pad from her file.

OBTAINING INFORMATION ABOUT THE CLIENT

"I'll be reviewing this checklist to make sure that we obtain all of the information that we need for your will," Amanda informs Joel. "First, I need you to fill out the client information form," instructs Amanda. "As you can see, it requires you to give us personal information, such as your name, legal residence, date of birth, and other data." Joel takes the form and fills it out. When he is finished, he hands it to Amanda.

"Now I need some other information. First, I need to know if you're married," states Amanda. "Yes, I am," responds Joel. "Your wife's name is?" asks Amanda. "Nicole Lynn Sontag," answers Joel. "And your wife resides with you at the address that you've given on the client information form?" asks Amanda. "Yes, she does,"

Joel states. "When was she born, and what's her Social Security number?" asks Amanda. "She was born on January 17, 1968, and her Social Security number is 363-46-2350," says Joel.

"Now, Joel, do you have any children?" asks Amanda. "Yes, we have one son, Joel, Jr., aged four," answers Joel. "Do you want to provide for both of them in your will?" asks Amanda. "Yes," responds Joel. "Do you have any other relatives for whom you want to provide?" asks Amanda. "Yes, I have a brother, Alfred Sontag, who lives in a home for autistic people," answers Joel. "I'll need the address for the home," responds Amanda. Joel takes an address book out of his briefcase and gives her the address. "Is there anyone else whom you want to provide for in your will?" asks Amanda. "No," responds Joel.

OBTAINING INFORMATION ABOUT THE CLIENT'S PROPERTY

"Now we need to discuss property," Amanda informs Joel. "Do you own a home?" she asks. "Yes," he answers. Amanda says, "I need to know if the home is located at the address you gave on the form, when you bought it, what it cost, what its present approximate market value is, whether you own it jointly with your wife, and the balance on your mortgage." Joel gives her all of the requested information. Amanda continues questioning Joel about his property holdings until she has covered all the items on her checklist.

CONCLUDING THE INTERVIEW

"Well," says Amanda, "we've covered everything on the checklist. Now we need to set up a time for you to meet with Mr. Kerrigan to discuss estate-planning procedures and your will. Because you jointly own property with your wife, Mr. Kerrigan may want both of you to meet with him. Would two o'clock next Tuesday afternoon be a good time for you both to come in to meet with Mr. Kerrigan?" Joel tells Amanda that he thinks that both he and his wife could arrange to meet with the attorney at that time. They tentatively schedule an appointment for that date. Joel will call Amanda if the appointment must be changed. Joel gets up to leave the office, saying that he'll probably see her again next Tuesday. "I'll look forward to that," says Amanda. Amanda then begins to prepare a detailed summary of the interview to give to her supervising attorney on his return.

SOURCE-BY-SOURCE SUMMARIES.   You should also create a list of your information sources, including witnesses, and summarize the facts gleaned from each of these sources. Each "source section" should contain all of the information gathered from that source, including direct quotes from witnesses. Each source section should also contain a subsection giving your personal comments on that particular source. You might comment on a witness's demeanor, for example, or on whether the witness's version of the facts was consistent or inconsistent with that of other witnesses. Your impressions of the witness's competence or reliability could be noted. If the witness provided you with further leads to be explored, this information could also be included.

GENERAL CONCLUSIONS AND RECOMMENDATIONS.   In the final section, you will present your overall conclusions about the investigation, as well as any suggestions that you have on the development of the case. Attorneys rely heavily on their investigators' impressions of witnesses and evaluations of investigative results because the investigators have firsthand knowledge of the sources. Your impression of a potentially important witness, for example, may help the attorney decide whether to arrange for a follow-up interview with the witness. Usually, the attorney will want to interview only the most promising witnesses, and your impressions and comments will serve as a screening device. Based on your findings during the investigation, you might also suggest to the attorney what further information can be obtained during discovery, if necessary, and what additional research needs to be done.

 KEY TERMS AND CONCEPTS

active listening	eyewitness	lay witness
authentication	friendly witness	leading question
circumstantial evidence	hearsay	open-ended question
closed-ended question	hostile witness	passive listening
direct evidence	hypothetical question	relevant evidence
evidence	interviewee	rules of evidence
expert witness	investigation plan	witness statement

 CHAPTER SUMMARY

Planning the Interview	Paralegals often interview clients and witnesses. Prior to the interview, the paralegal should prepare the interview environment to ensure that interruptions, noises, and delays will be minimized, that the client will be comfortable, and that any necessary supplies, forms, and equipment are at hand.

Planning the Interview—Continued	1. *Planning the questions*—In preparing for an interview, the interviewer should have in mind the kind of information being sought from the interviewee. Preprinted interview forms provide helpful guidelines, but the interviewer should remain flexible during the interview, tailor questions to the interviewee's responses, and ask follow-up questions.
	2. *Recording the interview*—Some paralegals tape-record their interviews for future reference. If you do, make sure to obtain permission from your supervising attorney and the person being interviewed before taping. Also, keep in mind that some clients and witnesses will be less willing to disclose information freely when being taped. If the interviewee appears hesitant, consider taking notes instead.
Interviewing Skills	Interviewing skills include interpersonal skills, questioning skills, and communication skills, particularly listening skills.
	1. *Interpersonal skills*—The interviewer should put the interviewee at ease, use language that the person will understand, and avoid using legal terms.
	2. *Questioning skills*—Types of questions used during the interviewing process include open-ended, closed-ended, leading, and hypothetical questions. The questioning technique will depend on the person being interviewed and the type of information sought (see Exhibit 13.2).
	3. *Communication skills*—The ability to listen is perhaps the most important skill for an interviewer to develop.
	a. Passive listening involves listening attentively to the speaker and using either verbal or nonverbal cues (such as nodding) to encourage him or her to continue.
	b. Active listening involves not just listening attentively but also giving feedback that indicates to the speaker that you understand what he or she is saying.
	c. One effective active listening technique is for the interviewer to "reflect back," or restate, what the interviewee has said. This gives the speaker an opportunity to clarify or correct previous statements.
	d. Active listening enables the interviewer to control the flow of the interview. It allows the interviewer to put the interviewee's statements into the larger context and facilitates smooth transitions between topics.
Interviewing Clients	There are three types of client interviews: initial interviews (usually conducted by the attorney but often attended by the paralegal), subsequent interviews (often conducted by the paralegal), and informational interviews (or meetings, also typically handled by the paralegal).
	1. *Scheduling interviews*—In setting up an interview, the paralegal should tell the client what documents to bring to the interview and follow up with a confirmation letter giving the date and time of the interview and listing the items the client is to bring.
	2. *Summarizing the interview*—As soon as possible after an interview is concluded, the paralegal should summarize in a written memorandum the information gathered in the interview. The memorandum should include the paralegal's general impressions of the client's statements and nonverbal behaviors.

Interviewing Witnesses	1. *Types of witnesses*—Types of witnesses include expert witnesses (who have specialized training that qualifies them to testify as to their opinion in a given area), lay witnesses (ordinary witnesses who have factual information about the matter being investigated), eyewitnesses (who have firsthand knowledge of an event—because they saw it happen, for example), friendly witnesses (who are favorable to the client's position), and hostile witnesses (who are biased against the client, friendly to the opponent, or resent being interviewed for other reasons).
	2. *Questioning witnesses*—Investigative questions should be open ended so that they elicit the most complete answers possible. Additional questions should ascertain whether the witness is competent, credible, and reliable and whether the witness has any bias relevant to the case.
	3. *Winding up the interview*—The paralegal should ask the witness at the end of the interview if the witness would like to add anything to her or his statement. This gives the witness an opportunity to explain an answer or expand on the areas discussed.
	4. *Witness statements*—Following an interview of a witness, the paralegal should prepare a memo to the supervising attorney relating what the witness said during the interview and asking if the attorney wants a formal witness statement prepared. The formal witness statement identifies the witness, discloses what was discovered during the interview, and is signed by the witness.
Planning and Conducting Investigations	Factual evidence is crucial to the outcome of a legal problem, and paralegals are often asked to conduct investigations to discover any factual evidence that supports (or contradicts) a client's claims. Before starting an investigation, the paralegal should create an investigation plan—a step-by-step list of what sources will be investigated to obtain specific types of information (police reports, medical and employment records, and so forth). The paralegal should discuss the plan with his or her supervising attorney before embarking on the investigation.
	1. *Locating witnesses*—Sources of factual information regarding witnesses or other persons include telephone and city directories; online people finders; media reports; court records; utility companies; professional organizations; and information recorded, compiled, or prepared by federal, state, and local government entities. The Freedom of Information Act of 1966 requires that federal agencies disclose certain records to any person on request, provided that the form of the request complies with the procedures mandated by the act.
	2. *Rules of evidence*—Evidence is anything that is used to prove the existence or nonexistence of a fact. Rules of evidence established by the federal and state courts spell out what types of evidence may or may not be admitted in court.
	a. Direct evidence is any evidence that, if believed, establishes the truth of the fact in question.
	b. Circumstantial evidence is evidence that does not directly establish the fact in question but that establishes, by inference, the likelihood of the fact.
	c. Only relevant evidence, which tends to prove or disprove a fact in question, is admissible as evidence in court.
	d. For evidence to be admitted at trial, the attorney must prove to the court that the evidence is what it purports to be. This is called authentication.

Planning and Conducting Investigations—Continued	e. Hearsay is testimony given in court by a witness who relates not what he or she knows personally, but what someone else said. Generally, hearsay evidence is not admissible in court. Exceptions are made in circumstances that indicate a high degree of reliability—for example, when the hearsay involves a party's out-of-court admissions or a dying person's statement about who caused his or her death.
	3. *Summarize results*—When the investigation is complete, the paralegal should summarize the results. The summary should include an overall summary, a source-by-source summary, and a final section giving the paralegal's conclusions and recommendations.

✳ QUESTIONS FOR REVIEW

1. What kinds of skills do interviewers employ during interviews?

2. What are the types of questions that can be used in an interview? When would you use each type?

3. What takes place during the initial client interview? What is the paralegal's role at this interview? What other types of client interviews are commonly conducted by paralegals? What is the purpose of each type?

4. List and describe the various types of witnesses. In what kinds of situations might each of these types of witnesses be used?

5. What is a witness statement? How is it used?

6. Why and how do you create an investigation plan? What types of actions might be included in an investigation plan?

7. List five sources that you would consult in attempting to locate a witness. Which would be the most useful? Which would be the least useful? Why?

8. What is evidence? How are the rules of evidence used?

9. Define and give examples of the following types of evidence: direct evidence, circumstantial evidence, relevant evidence, authenticated evidence, and hearsay.

10. What is included in an investigation summary? Why should one be prepared?

✳ ETHICAL QUESTIONS

1. Leah Fox, a legal assistant, has been asked by the attorney for whom she works to contact several potential witnesses to see what they know about an event. The first witness that Leah calls says, "I don't know if I should get involved. I don't want to get in trouble. You see, I was supposed to be at work, but I called in sick. If I get involved and my employer finds out where I really was, I might get fired. You're a lawyer, what do you think?" How should Leah respond?

2. Kirsten Piels, a legal assistant, is conducting a follow-up interview with a new client, who is seeking a divorce. Kirsten is asking the client about the couple's marital property. According to the client, both spouses want to divide the property evenly on their divorce. When Kirsten asks the client about checking

or savings accounts, the client says to Kirsten, "You know, Kirsten, I have this 'secret' savings account, but I don't want anybody to know about it. Please don't tell Mr. Harcourt [Kirsten's supervising attorney] what I've just told you." What should Kirsten do in this situation?

3. Jeffrey Jones starts a new job as a paralegal. He reviews a file and notices that the client has not been contacted and updated on the status of the case in three months. He also notices that there is a settlement conference scheduled for tomorrow and that the client needs to be in court. What should Jeffrey do?

4. Peter Romano is asked to review the *Clemmons v. Auto Manufacturer of America* file and to investigate in the case. His boss represents the auto manufacturer

in this product liability case and believes, based on the evidence uncovered so far, that he has an open-and-shut case against the plaintiff, who claims that her husband was killed when the car exploded on impact during an auto accident. Peter begins interviewing witnesses, including an engineer who works for the company. The engineer states that he knew the car was defective and would explode on impact. Peter is worried that his boss will be upset about this fact, because it damages his "open-and-shut" case. What should Peter do?

5. Thomas Lent is a new legal assistant with a law firm that specializes in personal-injury cases. He is reviewing a request to produce documents that was recently received in a case that his supervising attorney is handling for the plaintiff. The document requests the plaintiff's medical records, but it does not state specifically which records or for what injuries. Thomas's supervising attorney instructs Thomas to obtain copies of all of the plaintiff's medical records. The plaintiff's medical-records file is several inches thick because the plaintiff is an elderly person and has various medical problems. Thomas is instructed to bury the relevant medical records in the stack and not to make them obvious to the defendant's attorney. If she wants these records, she will have to sort through the file, says the attorney. What should Thomas do? Can the attorney be disciplined for this kind of behavior?

6. In response to a discovery request, Lynnette Banks, a paralegal in a corporate law firm, receives a package of documents in the mail. She opens the package and begins to read through the documents. As she does so, she discovers some that have the words "Privileged and Confidential" stamped on them. She scans a document and realizes that it is a letter from the opposing counsel to his client. The letter reveals the opposing attorney's legal strategy for the case on which Lynnette is now working. What should Lynnette do?

✳ PRACTICE QUESTIONS AND ASSIGNMENTS

1. Review the Baranski-Peretto hypothetical case discussed earlier in this text (see Chapter 12). Then write sample questions that you would ask when interviewing eyewitnesses to the accident. Phrase at least one question in each of the question formats discussed in this chapter.

2. Using the information in this chapter on questioning skills, identify the following types of questions:

   a. "Did you go on a cruise in the Bahamas with another woman, Mr. Johnson?"

   b. "Isn't it true, Mr. Johnson, that someone other than your wife accompanied you on a cruise in the Bahamas?"

   c. "Mr. Johnson, will you please describe your whereabouts between January 10 and January 17, 2004?"

3. Lena Phillips, a fifty-two-year-old, self-employed seamstress, fell down the three steps in front of her house and fractured her right wrist. She was treated in the emergency room at the Neighborhood Hospital by Dr. Ralph Dean on the day that she fell, January 10, 2003, and released. On January 17, January 25, and February 11, 2003, she visited Dr. Dean's office for follow-up care to make sure that the wrist was healing properly. It appeared that the wrist was healing properly during the month in which she was treated by Dr. Dean. She noticed, however, that even though she had a full range of motion in her wrist, the wrist angled inward somewhat. When she queried Dr. Dean about this, he told her that some angling of the wrist was inevitable.

Over the course of the following year, her wrist became increasingly crooked and bent inward. She went to an orthopedist, Dr. Alicia Byerly, on March 30, 2004. Dr. Byerly tried a splint, but without success. Dr. Byerly eventually performed surgery on the wrist at the Neighborhood Hospital on May 3, 2004, but was unable to correct the problem. Dr. Byerly told Ms. Phillips that she should have had surgery on the wrist during the first three weeks after it was broken to correct the angling problem.

Lena Phillips has come to the firm for which you work, the law firm of Samson & Gore, 5000 West Avenue, Northville, NH 12345, because she wants to sue Dr. Dean for medical malpractice. On May 15, 2004, you are asked to investigate her case. Draft an investigation plan.

4. Using Exhibit 13.3, *A Sample Follow-Up Letter to a Client,* as an example, draft a follow-up letter to Lena Phillips based on the facts from question 3 above. The attorney who gave you the assignment is Alan Samson. You will need to include a retainer agreement and instruct the client not to talk to Dr. Dean.

※   **Unless the paralegal knows from prior experience what his or her supervising attorney wants to include in the trial notebook and how it should be organized, the paralegal should discuss these matters with the attorney.**

Typically, the trial notebook is a three-ring binder (or several binders, depending on the complexity of the case). The contents of the notebook are separated by divider sheets with tabs on them. Paralegal Lopez will create a general index to the notebook's contents and place this index at the front of the notebook. She may also create an index for each section of the binder and place those indexes at the beginnings of the sections. Some paralegals use a computer notebook and a software retrieval system to help them quickly locate documents, especially in complicated cases involving thousands of documents.

When preparing the trial notebook, always remember the following:

※   **The documents in the trial notebook should not be the original documents but rather copies of them.**

The original documents (unless they are needed as evidence at trial) should always remain in the firm's files, both for reasons of security (should the trial notebook be misplaced) and to ensure that Lopez or others in the office will have access to the documents while the notebook is in court with the attorney.

Paralegal Lopez will not wait until the last minute to prepare the trial notebook. Rather, at the outset of the lawsuit, she will make copies of the pleadings and other documents as they are generated to include in the notebook. That way, she will not have to spend valuable time just before the trial, when there are other pressing needs, to do work that could have been done earlier. For further suggestions on how to prepare a trial notebook, see this chapter's *Featured Guest* article starting on the next page.

> ■ **Case at a Glance**
>
> **The Plaintiff—**
>   Plaintiff: Katherine
>   Baranski
>   Attorney: Allen P.
>   Gilmore
>   Paralegal: Elena Lopez
>
> **The Defendant—**
>   Defendant: Tony Peretto
>   Attorney: Elizabeth A.
>   Cameron
>   Paralegal: Gordon
>   McVay

PRETRIAL CONFERENCE

Before the trial begins, the attorneys usually meet with the trial judge in a **pretrial conference** to explore the possibility of resolving the case and, if a settlement is not possible, at least agree on the manner in which the trial will be conducted. In particular, the parties may attempt to clarify the issues in dispute and establish ground rules to restrict such matters as the admissibility of certain types of evidence. For example, attorney Gilmore might have paralegal Lopez draft a **motion in limine**[1] (a motion to limit evidence) to submit to the judge at this time. The motion will request the judge to order that certain types of evidence not be brought out at trial.

To illustrate: Suppose that plaintiff Baranski had been arrested in the past for illegal drug possession. Gilmore knows that evidence of the arrest, if introduced by the defense at trial, might prejudice the jury against Baranski. In this situation, Gilmore might submit a motion *in limine* to keep the defense from presenting the evidence. Exhibit 14.3 on page 498 presents a sample motion *in limine*. Note that with the motion Gilmore would include affidavits and/or a memorandum of law (a brief)—these documents were discussed in Chapter 12—to convince the judge that the motion should be granted.

Once the pretrial conference has concluded, both parties turn their attention to the trial itself. Assuming that the trial will be heard by a jury, however, one more step is necessary before the trial begins: selecting the jurors who will hear the trial and render a verdict on the dispute.

pretrial conference
A conference prior to trial in which the judge and the attorneys litigating the suit discuss settlement possibilities, clarify the issues in dispute, and schedule forthcoming trial-related events.

motion *in limine*
A motion requesting that certain evidence not be brought out at the trial, such as prejudicial, irrelevant, or legally inadmissible evidence.

FEATURED GUEST: KAREN SANDERS-WEST

The Trial Notebook

BIOGRAPHICAL NOTE

Karen Sanders-West is a certified legal-assistant specialist with the Wichita, Kansas, firm of Foulston Siefkin, LLP, specializing in business and commercial litigation. Sanders-West received her bachelor's degree in political science and history and her associate's degree in legal-assistant studies from Wichita State University. She received her juris doctorate in June 2002, graduating magna cum laude *from the Presidents College School of Law.*

Sanders-West has taught in the legal-assistant program at Wichita State University and has extensive experience as a lecturer and speaker. She has also authored a number of articles on legal topics and legal-assistant issues. She is a former president of NALA, a former chair of the NALA Certifying Board, and a former member of the ABA School Approval Commission. She is an instructor in NALA's CLA review course and recently received NALA's President's Award in recognition of her outstanding service to the legal-assistant profession.

A trial notebook serves as a road map for presenting a case to a judge or a jury. The term *trial notebook* has become a generic label because we have moved far beyond thinking of the trial notebook as simply a three-ring black binder that holds all of the information needed to successfully maneuver through the course of a trial. That is not to say that the three-ring notebook no longer ever serves this purpose. In relatively simple matters (if there is such a thing when it comes to trying any lawsuit), the notebook may still be perfectly adequate. In more complex matters, the trial notebook has "morphed" into something much different. In most cases, there will be multiple notebooks. In fact, one notebook may be nothing more than a comprehensive index to the contents of all of the materials contained in the multivolume set of notebooks. In some cases, the trial notebook is not even physical, but virtual—in a laptop computer.

HOW THE TRIAL NOTEBOOK MAY BE USED

In the ideal world, it would be apparent from the time a petition or a complaint is filed whether a case will actually end up being tried (only about 3 percent of the cases filed in the federal courts actually go to trial). There is, of course, no way to make such a prediction. Therefore, it is important to start planning what form and substance your trial notebook will take from day one, or shortly thereafter. That way, in the statistically unlikely event that the case you are working on goes to trial, you will be prepared. The savvy and time-conscious legal assistant will begin to assemble the trial notebook

as soon as he or she becomes a part of the trial team. Tossing documents in a file folder may be all it takes to get the trial notebook off to a good start.

Despite the name and ultimate purpose of a trial notebook, it will also be a valuable tool and resource for tracking the progress of the case, as well as for use in any settlement negotiations, mediations, and/or arbitration proceedings that may occur. Note, though, that several of these purposes will only be served if the trial notebook is developed early in the case.

CONTENTS OF THE TRIAL NOTEBOOK

Before going any further, it is necessary to indicate the basic documents that will be part of any trial notebook, regardless of its form. The following list is not necessarily inclusive, but it is representative of the types of documents that typically are included in the notebook:

- Primary pleadings, including the petition/complaint, the answer, pretrial orders, any motions and rulings, trial briefs, and discovery pleadings that may be significant for trial purposes (not all discovery pleadings will fall into this category). One discovery pleading that would be potentially significant is a response to a request for admissions. Regardless of whether they are included in the trial notebook, all pleadings should be readily available for reference during the trial.

- Witness information, including phone numbers (so that witnesses can be reached on a moment's notice, if necessary, to get the witness on the stand at the appropriate time).

- Service providers—for example, copy services, reprographic services, office supply sources, stenographic services, pharmacies, dentists, physicians, hospitals, emergency medical services, and technology resources.

- An outline of the issues, both factual and legal, to be addressed during the trial.

- A chronology/time line of the case.

- A cast of characters.

- An outline or script of questions that will be addressed to each witness, including references to exhibits that will be used with each witness.

- Deposition outlines and summaries.

- An exhibit list. An exhibit list will also be in the actual exhibit notebook or notebooks. The copy in the trial notebook will be used to track the exhibits; to indicate which witness each exhibit is used with and whether the exhibit was offered, admitted, or objected to; and to indicate how each exhibit is to be used during the trial.

- Copies of relevant case law.

- Opening and closing statements.

- Any information or aid unique to the particular lawsuit being tried.

Note that the above points are not listed in any particular order. In fact, the order in which documents and information are physically arranged should be based on two factors: first, the ease of finding what the legal assistant or attorney

is looking for; and, second, the preference of the attorney in how the information should be arranged.

THE PARALEGAL'S TRIAL NOTEBOOK

The legal assistant may find that it is a good idea to create a mirror notebook for his or her specific use during the trial. As an experienced courtroom legal assistant, I would never be without a mirror notebook that contains, at the very least, those things for which I know I will be responsible. Examples include witness information, the exhibit list, and service provider information.

THE VIRTUAL TRIAL NOTEBOOK

Any discussion of trial notebooks would be sorely dated if it did not mention the virtual trial notebook—a trial notebook that is maintained entirely on a laptop computer. The advantages of using a virtual trial notebook are obvious to anyone familiar with computers. Here are just a few of them:

- The virtual trial notebook is easier to transport than multiple notebooks.

- Incredible amounts of information and data can be stored on the computer.

- Full-volume depositions can be available on the laptop for full-text searches. Deposition summaries can be hyperlinked to relevant portions in the actual deposition transcript.

- Laptops can allow the attorney or the legal assistant to access the Internet for factual or legal research during the trial.

"A trial notebook serves as a road map for presenting a case to a judge or a jury."

- Exhibits, pleadings, and correspondence can be scanned to be accessible on the laptop. Outlines of witness examinations can be hyperlinked to pleadings and exhibits.

- Outlines, drafts, notes, and so on can be easily prepared or edited on the laptop.

Of course, an in-depth discussion of virtual trial notebooks would have to include the software and technology that make the virtual trial notebook work. That discussion is beyond the scope of this article.

IS A TRIAL NOTEBOOK ALWAYS NECESSARY?

Does every case that goes to trial need a trial notebook? The answer is yes. There must always be some form of trial notebook, whether it be a file folder, a three-ring notebook, or a laptop. Remember the road-map analogy. Why would anyone—lawyer or legal assistant—risk overlooking the means for successfully navigating a client's case in the courtroom? A myriad of justifications exist for using legal assistants to assist in the delivery of legal services to the client. Certainly, one of the most persuasive justifications is organization, which equates to efficiency. The creation and use of trial notebooks is an example of organization/efficiency at its highest level for litigation legal assistants and attorneys.

EXHIBIT 14.3
Motion *in Limine*

A. P. Gilmore
Jeffers, Gilmore & Dunn
553 Fifth Avenue
Suite 101
Nita City, NI 48801
(616) 555-9690

Attorney for Plaintiff

UNITED STATES DISTRICT COURT
FOR THE WESTERN DISTRICT OF NITA

Katherine Baranski) Plaintiff,)) v.))) Tony Peretto) Defendant.)	CASE NO. 99-14335-NI Honorable Harley M. Larue MOTION IN LIMINE

The Plaintiff respectfully moves the Court to prohibit counsel for the Defendant from directly or indirectly introducing or making any reference during the trial to the Plaintiff's arrest in 1994 for the possession of illegal drugs.

The grounds on which this motion is based are stated in the accompanying affidavits and memorandum.

Date: 6/18/04

Allen P. Gilmore
Allen P. Gilmore
Attorney for the Plaintiff

On the Web

Numerous firms offer trial consulting services, including assistance in jury selection. You can access the Web site of one such firm, Jury Research Institute, at **http://www. jri-inc.com.**

voir dire
A proceeding in which attorneys for the plaintiff and the defendant ask prospective jurors questions to determine whether any potential juror is biased or has any connection with a party to the action or with a prospective witness.

JURY SELECTION

Before the trial gets under way, a panel of jurors must be assembled. The clerk of the court usually notifies local residents by mail that they have been selected for jury duty. The process of selecting prospective jurors varies, depending on the court, but often they are randomly selected by the court clerk from lists of registered voters or those to whom driver's licenses have been issued. The persons selected then report to the courthouse on the date specified in the notice. At the courthouse, they are gathered into a single pool of jurors, and the process of selecting those jurors who will actually hear the case begins. Although some types of trials require twelve-person juries, civil matters can be heard by a jury of as few as six persons in many states.

Voir Dire

Both the plaintiff's attorney and the defendant's attorney have some input into the ultimate make-up of the jury. Each attorney will question prospective jurors in a proceeding known as *voir dire.*[2] Experienced litigators know how important the

DEVELOPING PARALEGAL SKILLS

Trial Support

Scott Greer, a paralegal with the firm of Dewey & Stone, is helping an attorney prepare for a trial in a personal-injury lawsuit. The client was injured in an automobile accident and is now a paraplegic. Scott has received a memo from his supervising attorney requesting that he prepare a diagram of the accident and arrange to have a "day in the life" videotape created for presentation to the jury. The video will show what a typical day in the life of the plaintiff is like as a result of the injuries sustained in the accident. Scott contacts Trial Support Services, Inc., a firm that specializes in litigation support, to make the video. Scott also obtains permission

to have Trial Support Services, Inc., create the diagram as well.

TIPS FOR CREATING TRIAL VIDEOS

- Use a reliable trial-support services provider or vendor.
- Arrange to meet the vendor at the location where the videotape will be made.
- Make sure that the videotape is realistic, so that the court will allow its use.
- Preview the video before giving it to the attorney.
- Make sure that the vendor is paid on time.

---

voir dire process is—not only to picking the right jury but also as a time for attorneys to introduce themselves and their clients and make a favorable impression on the jury before the trial begins.

Legal assistants often work with their attorneys to write up the questions that will be asked of jurors during *voir dire*. Because all of the jurors will have previously filled out forms giving basic information about themselves, the attorneys and their paralegals can tailor their questions accordingly. They fashion the questions in such a way as to uncover any biases on the part of prospective jurors and to find persons who might identify with the plights of their respective clients.

Typically, the legal team for each side has already developed an idea of what kind of person would be most sympathetic toward or most likely to vote in favor of its client. Indeed, sometimes experts are hired to help create a juror profile (see the *Today's Professional Paralegal* feature later in this chapter). The paralegals and attorneys then formulate questions based on this notion of the ideal juror in the case.

Jury selection may last a few hours or many days, depending on the complexity of the case and the rules and preferences of the particular court or judge. In some courts, the judge queries prospective jurors using questions prepared and submitted by the attorneys. In other courts, the judge has each juror answer a list of standard questions and then gives each attorney a small amount of time to ask follow-up questions. When large numbers of prospective jurors are involved, the attorneys (or judge) may direct their questions to groups of jurors as opposed to individual jurors in order to minimize the time spent choosing a jury.

On the Web
You can read the *Handbook for Trial Jurors Serving in the United States District Courts* at **http://www.txed.uscourts.gov/jhandbook.htm.**

Challenges during *Voir Dire*

During *voir dire*, the attorney for each side will decide if there are any individuals he or she would like to prevent from serving as jurors in the case. The attorney may then exercise a **challenge** to exclude a particular person from the jury. There are two types of challenges available to both sides in a lawsuit: challenges for cause and peremptory challenges.

challenge
An attorney's objection, during *voir dire,* to the inclusion of a particular person on the jury.

ETHICAL CONCERN

Should You Tell Your Supervising Attorney What You Know about a Prospective Juror?

During *voir dire,* paralegal Lopez notices one of her neighbors among the prospective jurors. Lopez knows that her neighbor is strongly biased against foreigners and will probably not be an impartial juror in the case against Tony Peretto, who has a slight foreign accent. Lopez also knows that she and attorney Gilmore want their client, plaintiff Baranski, to win the case, and a juror biased against Peretto would definitely help them achieve this goal. Should Lopez tell Gilmore what she knows about this prospective juror? Yes. It is to Gilmore's—and his client's—advantage to know all he can about the prospective jurors, and it is up to Gilmore to decide how to use whatever information he obtains. Furthermore, Lopez has no duty to keep confidential any information that she has learned about her neighbor.

---

challenge for cause
A *voir dire* challenge for which an attorney states the reason why a prospective juror should not be included in the jury.

peremptory challenge
A *voir dire* challenge to exclude a potential juror from serving on the jury without any supporting reason or cause. Peremptory challenges based on racial or gender criteria are illegal.

CHALLENGES FOR CAUSE.   The attorney can exercise a **challenge for cause** if the prospective juror is biased against the client or case for some reason. For example, if a juror states during *voir dire* that he or she hates all immigrants and the client is foreign born, the attorney can exercise a challenge for cause. Each side's attorney can exercise an *unlimited* number of challenges for cause. Because most people are not forthcoming about their biases, the attorney must be able to prove sufficiently to the court that the person cannot be an objective juror in the case. Often, the judge will ask the challenged juror follow-up questions and then determine that the juror can be objective after all.

PEREMPTORY CHALLENGES.   Both attorneys may exercise a *limited* number of **peremptory challenges** without giving any reason to the court as to why they object to a particular juror. In most cases, peremptory challenges are the only challenges exercised (because there is no proof that an individual juror is biased). A juror may thus be excused from serving on the jury for any reason, including his or her facial expressions or nonverbal behavior during the questioning. Peremptory challenges based on racial criteria or gender, however, are illegal.[3]

Because the number of peremptory challenges is limited (a court may allow only three, for example), attorneys must exercise peremptory challenges carefully. Experienced litigators try to conserve their peremptory challenges so that they can eliminate the prospective jurors who appear the most hostile.

PROCEDURE FOR CHALLENGES.   Typically, *voir dire* takes place in the courtroom, and the attorneys question the six to twelve prospective jurors who are seated in the jury box. Other prospective jurors may be seated in the audience area of the courtroom, so that as one person is excused, another person can walk up to take his or her place in the jury box. The procedure varies, of course, depending on the jurisdiction. Often, rather than making challenges orally in front of the jury, the attorneys simply write down on a piece of paper which juror they wish to challenge and the paper is given to the judge. The judge thanks and dismisses the prospective juror, and the process starts over again with the next individual. When this method is used, the remaining prospective jurors do not know which side dismissed the individual and so are less likely to make guesses about the underlying reasons.

The Paralegal's Role during *Voir Dire*

As mentioned, paralegals help develop a jury profile and draft questions that will be asked during *voir dire*. In addition, a paralegal can assist an attorney by providing another pair of eyes and ears during the jury selection process. Attorneys frequently rely on the observations of other members of the legal team (including paralegals) who are present during the questioning.

If paralegal Lopez attends *voir dire* with attorney Gilmore in the Baranski case, for example, she will carefully watch all of the jurors as the attorneys question them. Lopez, because she is not participating in the questioning, is free to observe the prospective jurors more closely than Gilmore. She will then report to Gilmore any verbal or nonverbal response she observed that Gilmore might not have noticed. For example, suppose that as Gilmore is questioning one juror, another juror is staring at plaintiff Baranski and frowning with disapproval. Gilmore might not notice this behavior, and Lopez can bring it to his attention.

Alternate Jurors

Because unforeseeable circumstances or illness may necessitate that one or more of the sitting jurors be dismissed, the court seats several *alternate jurors* who will also hear the entire trial. Depending on the rules of the particular jurisdiction, a court might have two or three alternate jurors present throughout the trial. If a juror has to be excused in the middle of the trial, then an alternate can take his or her place without disrupting the proceedings. Unless they replace jurors, alternate jurors do not participate in jury deliberations at the end of the trial.

The Trial

Once the jury members are seated, the judge swears in the jury, and the trial itself can begin. During the trial, the attorneys, Allen Gilmore and Elizabeth Cameron, will present their cases to the jury. Because the attorneys will be concentrating on the trial, it will fall to their paralegals to coordinate the logistical aspects of the trial and observe as closely as possible the trial proceedings. Because paralegal Lopez is thoroughly familiar with the case and Gilmore's legal strategy, she will be a valuable ally during the trial. She will be able to anticipate Gilmore's needs and provide appropriate reminders or documents as Gilmore needs them.

Prior to each trial day, for example, Lopez will assemble the documents and materials that will be needed in court. During the court proceedings, Lopez will make sure that attorney Gilmore has within reach any documents or exhibits that he needs for questioning parties or witnesses. When attorney Gilmore no longer needs the documents or exhibits, Lopez will put them aside in an appropriate place. At the end of the day, she will again organize the documents and materials, decide what will be needed for the next day, and file the documents that can remain in the office.

Paralegal Lopez must also monitor each witness's testimony to ensure that it is consistent with previous statements made by the witness. Lopez will have the relevant deposition transcript (and summary) at hand when a witness takes the stand. She will follow the deposition transcript (or summary) of each witness as that witness testifies. This way, she can pass a note to Gilmore if he misses any inconsistencies in the witness's testimony.

Case at a Glance

The Plaintiff—
Plaintiff: Katherine Baranski
Attorney: Allen P. Gilmore
Paralegal: Elena Lopez

The Defendant—
Defendant: Tony Peretto
Attorney: Elizabeth A. Cameron
Paralegal: Gordon McVay

Litigation Paralegal

What do you like best about your work?

"As a member of both litigation and maritime/admiralty sections at my firm, I work on an assortment of cases, including construction, product liability, and toxic torts on the litigation side and maritime personal injury, wrongful death, vessel stranding, collision, sinking, and shipping-related cases on the maritime/admiralty side. Although I enjoy the variety of work, I especially enjoy working on the maritime cases. Living and working in Hawaii, the 'Gateway to the Pacific Rim,' I am afforded the opportunity to work with many shipping agents, ship owners, marine underwriters, and marine consultants/experts throughout the world."

What is the greatest challenge that you face in your area of work?

"The greatest challenge I face in my area of work is the ability to balance my typically smaller maritime cases with my larger and more complex litigation cases. Approximately 90 percent of my maritime cases are in federal court, and therefore they follow a pretty set time line as directed by scheduling and pretrial orders, while my nonmaritime cases (such as an action filed by the Hawaii state attorney general against the tobacco industry) are filed in state court with no set pretrial dates provided until a week before trial. Just recently, I was faced with preparing a maritime case for a jury trial in a federal court while simultaneously preparing a product liability case in a state court—that was a challenge! But I faced it head-on. What helped me get through preparing the two cases for trial was knowing the rules and procedures of both courts and properly managing both of my cases."

Lopez will also observe how the jury is responding to various witnesses and their testimony or to the attorneys' demeanor and questions. She will take notes during the trial on these observations as well as on the points being stressed and the types of evidence introduced by the opposing counsel, Cameron. At the end of the day, Lopez and Gilmore may review the day's events, and Lopez's "trial journal" will provide a ready reference to the major events that transpired in the courtroom.

Opening Statements

opening statement
An attorney's statement to the jury at the beginning of the trial. The attorney briefly outlines the evidence that will be offered during the trial and the legal theory that will be pursued.

The trial both opens and closes with attorneys' statements to the jury. In their **opening statements,** the attorneys will give a brief version of the facts and the supporting evidence that they will use during the trial. Because some trials can drag on for weeks or even months, it is extremely helpful for jurors to hear a summary of the story that will unfold during the trial. Otherwise, they may be left wondering how a particular piece of evidence fits into the dispute.

In short, the opening statement is a kind of "road map" that describes the destination that each attorney hopes to reach and outlines how he or she plans to reach it. Plaintiff Baranski's attorney, Gilmore, will focus on such things as his client's lack of fault and the injuries that she sustained when she was hit by defendant Peretto's

Litigation Paralegal, *Continued*

What advice do you have for would-be paralegals in your area of work?

"Learn all you can about the area of the law with which you are dealing, whether it is maritime law, construction law, or personal-injury law; attend continuing legal education seminars and read legal reference materials, hornbooks, and treaties; know your court rules (this includes state, federal, and local rules); always be one step ahead of your attorney—if you know a discovery response is due, take the initiative to draft it without being asked; continually offer your assistance with anything that needs to be done. Attorneys appreciate the interest you show in a case, as well as the initiative you take."

What are some tips for success as a paralegal in your area of work?

"Here are my 'Top Ten Tips' for success as a paralegal: (1) take the initiative; (2) be confident in your role as the paralegal (you can do this by knowing and/or learning court procedures, applicable court rules, and elements of the law with which you are dealing); (3) be organized; (4) develop document-management skills (document management and organization are crucial to your success as a paralegal); (5) take an interest in the issues of a case and focus on how you can efficiently and effectively assist the attorney in proving or disproving those issues; (6) learn to use a database program and apply it to a case (using a database will help you with document management, especially with larger, more complex litigation cases); (7) develop your online factual research skills (Internet; public-information computer databases such as InfoTech, DBT Autotrek, and LexisNexis; and so forth); (8) expand your communication skills to include familiarity with and/or knowledge of other languages and cultures; (9) develop and follow a tickler and calendaring system that will assist in your efforts to ensure that your attorney meets pretrial deadlines; and last but surely not least, (10) be a team player—do not exhibit an attitude because you are the paralegal. Remember, you are a member of a team with a common goal: to achieve the best results for your client. You should never be above photocopying, date stamping, or filing documents with a court."

car. Peretto's attorney, Cameron, will highlight the points that weaken plaintiff Baranski's claim (for example, Cameron might point out that Baranski was speeding) or otherwise suggest that defendant Peretto did not commit any wrongful act.

The Plaintiff's Case

Once the opening statements have been made, Gilmore will present the plaintiff's case first. Because he is the plaintiff's attorney, he has the burden of proving that defendant Peretto was negligent.

DIRECT EXAMINATION.   Attorney Gilmore will call several eyewitnesses to the stand and ask them to tell the court about the sequence of events that led to the accident. This form of questioning is known as **direct examination.** For example, Gilmore will call Julia Williams, an eyewitness who saw the accident occur, and ask her questions such as those presented in Exhibit 14.4 on the following page. He will also call other witnesses, including the police officer who was summoned to the accident scene and the ambulance driver. Gilmore will try to elicit responses from these witnesses that strengthen plaintiff Baranski's case—or at least that do not visibly weaken the claim.

direct examination
The examination of a witness by the attorney who calls the witness to the stand to testify on behalf of the attorney's client.

EXHIBIT 14.4
**Direct Examination—
Sample Questions**

ATTORNEY:	Mrs. Williams, please explain how you came to be at the scene of the accident.
WITNESS:	Well, I was walking north on Mattis Avenue toward Nita City Hospital, where I work as a nurse.
ATTORNEY:	Please describe for the court, in your own words, exactly what you observed when you reached the intersection of Mattis Avenue and Thirty-eighth Street.
WITNESS:	I was approaching the intersection when I saw the defendant run the stop sign on Thirty-eighth Street and crash into the plaintiff's car.
ATTORNEY:	Did you notice any change in the speed at which the defendant was driving as he approached the stop sign?
WITNESS:	No. He didn't slow down at all.
ATTORNEY:	Mrs. Williams, are you generally in good health?
WITNESS:	Yes.
ATTORNEY:	Have you ever had any problems with your vision?
WITNESS:	No. I wear reading glasses for close work, but I see well in the distance.
ATTORNEY:	And how long has it been since your last eye examination?
WITNESS:	About a month or so ago, I went to Dr. Sullivan for an examination. He told me that I needed reading glasses but that my distance vision was excellent.

During direct examination, attorney Gilmore will not usually be permitted to ask *leading questions*, which are questions that lead the witness to a particular desired response (see Chapter 13). A leading question might be something like the following: "So, Mrs. Williams, you noticed that the defendant ran the stop sign, right?" If Mrs. Williams answers "yes," she has, in effect, been "led" to this answer by Gilmore's leading question. The fundamental purpose behind a trial is to establish what actually happened, not to tell witnesses what to say.

> ▓ **Leading questions may distort the testimony by discouraging witnesses from telling their stories in their own words.**

When Gilmore is dealing with *hostile witnesses* (uncooperative witnesses or those who are testifying on behalf of the other party), however, he is normally permitted to ask leading questions. This is because hostile witnesses may be uncommunicative and unwilling to describe the events they witnessed. If Gilmore asked a hostile witness what he or she observed on the morning of August 4 at 7:45 A.M., for example, the witness might respond, "I saw two trucks driving down Mattis Avenue." That answer might be true, but it has nothing to do with the Baranski-Peretto accident. Therefore, to elicit information from this witness, Gilmore would be permitted to use leading questions, which would force the witness to respond to the question at issue.

cross-examination
The questioning of an opposing witness during the trial.

CROSS-EXAMINATION.   After attorney Gilmore has finished questioning a witness on direct examination, defendant Peretto's attorney, Cameron, will begin her **cross-examination** of that witness. During her cross-examination, Cameron will be

EXHIBIT 14.8
**Motion for Judgment
as a Matter of Law
or for a New Trial**

Elizabeth A. Cameron
Cameron & Strauss, P.C.
310 Lake Drive
Zero City, ZE 59802
(616) 955-6234

Attorney for Defendant

UNITED STATES DISTRICT COURT
FOR THE WESTERN DISTRICT OF NITA

Katherine Baranski) 　　　　Plaintiff,)) v.)) Tony Peretto) 　　　　Defendant.)	CASE NO. 99-14335-NI Honorable Harley M. Larue MOTION FOR JUDGMENT AS A MATTER OF LAW OR, IN THE ALTERNATIVE, MOTION FOR A NEW TRIAL

The Defendant, Tony Peretto, moves this Court, pursuant to Rule 50(b) of the Federal Rules of Civil Procedure, to set aside the verdict and judgment entered on August 15, 2004, and to enter instead a judgment for the Defendant as a matter of law. In the alternative, and in the event the Defendant's motion for judgment as a matter of law is denied, the Defendant moves the Court to order a new trial.

The grounds for this motion are set forth in the attached memorandum.

Date:　8/16/04 _____

Elizabeth A Cameron
Elizabeth A. Cameron
Attorney for the Defendant

---

instructions, excessive or inadequate damages, or the existence of newly discovered evidence (but not if the evidence could have been discovered earlier through the use of reasonable care). As with other posttrial motions in federal courts, the motion for a new trial must be filed within ten days following the entry of the judgment. Exhibit 14.8 illustrates a motion for judgment as a matter of law or, in the alternative, for a new trial.

Appealing the Verdict

If attorney Cameron's posttrial motions are unsuccessful or if she decides not to file them, she may still file an **appeal**. The purpose of an appeal is to have the trial court's decision either reversed or modified by an appellate court. As discussed in Chapter 6, appellate courts, or courts of appeals, are *reviewing* courts, not trial courts. In other words, no new evidence will be presented to the appellate court, and there is no jury. The appellate court will review the trial court's proceedings to decide whether the trial court erred in applying the law to the facts of the case, in instructing the jury, or in administering the trial generally. Appellate courts

On the Web
The Federal Rules of Appellate Procedure are online at **http://www.law.cornell. edu/topics/appellate_ procedure.html**.

appeal
The process of seeking a higher court's review of a lower court's decision for the purpose of correcting or changing the lower court's judgment or decision.

rarely tamper with a trial court's findings of fact because the judge and jury were in a better position than the appellate court to evaluate the credibility of witnesses, the nature of the evidence, and so on.

As grounds for the appeal, defendant Peretto's attorney, Cameron, might argue that the trial court erred in one of the ways mentioned in the preceding paragraph. Unless she believes that a reversal of the judgment is likely, however, she will probably advise Peretto not to appeal the case, as an appeal will simply add to the costs and expenses already incurred by Peretto in defending against plaintiff Baranski's claim.

NOTICE OF APPEAL.   When the appeal involves a federal district court decision, as in the Baranski case, the **appellant** (the party appealing the decision) must file a notice of appeal with the district court that rendered the judgment. The clerk of the court then notifies the **appellee** (the party against whom the appeal is taken) as well as the court of appeals. The clerk also forwards to the appellate court a transcript of the trial court proceedings, along with any related pleadings and exhibits; these materials together constitute the **record on appeal.**

THE APPELLATE BRIEF AND ORAL ARGUMENTS.   When a case is appealed, the attorneys for both parties submit written *briefs* that present their positions regarding the issues to be reviewed by the appellate court. The briefs outline each party's view of the proper application of the law to the facts. (Appellate briefs will be discussed further in Chapter 18.)

After the appellate court has had an opportunity to review the briefs, the court sets aside a time for both attorneys to argue their positions before the panel of judges. The attorneys will then present their arguments and answer any questions that the judges might have. Generally, the attorneys' arguments before an appellate court are limited in terms of both the time allowed for argument and the scope of the argument. Following the oral arguments, the judges will decide the matter and then issue a formal written opinion, which normally will be published in the relevant reporter (see Chapter 16 for a detailed discussion of how court opinions are published).

THE APPELLATE COURT'S OPTIONS.   Once they have reviewed the record and heard oral arguments, the judges have several options. For example, in the Baranski case, if the appellate court decided to uphold the trial court's decision, then the judgment for plaintiff Baranski would be **affirmed.** If the judges decided to **reverse** the trial court's decision, however, then Peretto would no longer be obligated to pay the damages awarded to Baranski by the trial court. The court might also affirm or reverse a decision *in part.* For example, the judges might affirm the jury's finding that Peretto was negligent but **remand** the case—that is, send it back to the trial court— for further proceedings on another issue (such as the extent of Baranski's damages). An appellate court can also *modify* a lower court's decision. If, for example, the appellate court decided that the jury awarded an excessive amount in damages, the appellate court might reduce the award to a more appropriate, or fairer, amount.

The decision of the appellate court may sometimes be appealed further. A state appellate court's decision, for example, may be appealed to the state supreme court. A federal appellate court's decision may be appealed to the United States Supreme Court. It will be up to these higher courts to decide whether they will review the case. In other words, these courts are not normally *required* to review cases. Recall from Chapter 6 that although thousands of cases are submitted to the United States Supreme Court each year, it hears less than one hundred. (An action decided in a state court, however, has a somewhat greater chance of being reviewed by the state supreme court.)

appellant
The party who takes an appeal from one court to another; sometimes referred to as the petitioner.

appellee
The party against whom an appeal is taken—that is, the party who opposes setting aside or reversing the judgment; sometimes referred to as the respondent.

record on appeal
The items submitted during the trial (pleadings, motions, briefs, and exhibits) and the transcript of the trial proceedings that are forwarded to the appellate court for review when a case is appealed.

affirm
To uphold the judgment of a lower court.

reverse
To overturn the judgment of a lower court.

remand
To send a case back to a lower court for further proceedings.

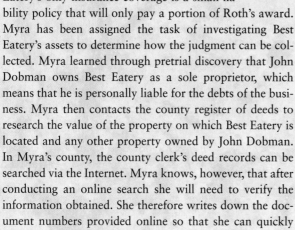

DEVELOPING PARALEGAL SKILLS

Locating Assets

Paralegal Myra Cullen works for a law firm that represented Jennifer Roth in a lawsuit brought against Best Eatery, a local restaurant. Roth won $100,000 in a lawsuit for damages resulting from falling and breaking her leg in the restaurant's lobby on a rainy morning. Best Eatery's only insurance coverage is a small liability policy that will only pay a portion of Roth's award. Myra has been assigned the task of investigating Best Eatery's assets to determine how the judgment can be collected. Myra learned through pretrial discovery that John Dobman owns Best Eatery as a sole proprietor, which means that he is personally liable for the debts of the business. Myra then contacts the county register of deeds to research the value of the property on which Best Eatery is located and any other property owned by John Dobman. In Myra's county, the county clerk's deed records can be searched via the Internet. Myra knows, however, that after conducting an online search she will need to verify the information obtained. She therefore writes down the document numbers provided online so that she can quickly

access the information at the clerk's office. Myra determines that Dobman's equity in the property on which Best Eatery is located is $110,000, which will cover any shortfall in the damages. Because the equity is sufficient to cover the award, Myra simply notes the record number of Dobman's other real property (his house) in the client's file.

TIPS FOR LOCATING ASSETS

* Ask what property the defendant owns during discovery, such as in interrogatories.
* Ask for the address of the property.
* Go to the register of deeds to learn about any liens filed against the property and the amount of any mortgage loan.
* Check with a real estate agent or an appraiser as to the market value of the property.
* Deduct the liens and the mortgage debt from the market value to determine the defendant's equity.

ENFORCING THE JUDGMENT

The uncertainties of the litigation process are compounded by the lack of guarantees that any judgment will be enforceable. It is one thing to have a court enter a judgment in your favor; it is quite another to collect the money to which you are entitled from the opposing party. Even if the jury awarded Baranski the full amount of damages requested ($130,000), for example, she might not, in fact, "win" anything at all. Peretto's auto insurance coverage might have lapsed, in which event the company would not cover any of the damages. Alternatively, Peretto's insurance coverage might be limited to $30,000, meaning that Peretto would have to pay personally the remaining $100,000. If Peretto did not have that amount of money available, then Baranski would need to go back to court and request that the court issue a **writ of execution**—an order, usually issued by the clerk of the court, directing the sheriff to seize (take temporary ownership of) and sell Peretto's assets. The proceeds of the sale would then be used to pay the damages owed to Baranski. Any excess proceeds of the sale would be returned to Peretto.

Even as a **judgment creditor** (one who has obtained a court judgment against his or her debtor), Baranski may not be able to obtain the full amount of the judgment from Peretto. Laws protecting debtors provide that certain property (such as a debtor's home up to a specific value, tools used by the debtor in his or her trade, and so on) is *exempt*. Exempt property cannot be seized and sold to pay debts owed to judgment creditors. Similar exemptions would apply if Peretto declared bankruptcy. Thus, even though Baranski won at trial, she, like many others who

writ of execution
A writ that puts in force a court's decree or judgment.

judgment creditor
A creditor who is legally entitled, by a court's judgment, to collect the amount of the judgment from a debtor.

TODAY'S PROFESSIONAL PARALEGAL

Drafting *Voir Dire* Questions Like a Pro

Andrea Leed, a legal assistant, is preparing for trial. Her boss is a famous trial attorney, Mary Marshall. Mary rarely loses a case. One of her many secrets to success is that she always draws up a jury profile and prepares carefully for *voir dire*.

Mary is defending a corporation in an environmental liability case. The case involves many complex engineering and scientific issues that the jury will need to understand in order to reach its verdict. It is a common practice in these types of cases to select a "blue ribbon" jury—a jury consisting of persons who are very well educated. Mary has suggested that Andrea locate and hire a psychologist to prepare a jury profile.

CONSULTING WITH AN EXPERT WITNESS

Andrea contacts TrialPsych, Inc., a consulting firm headed by Dr. Linda Robertson, who specializes in jury selection. Dr. Robertson would be delighted to work on the case, but her services are very expensive, and Andrea must find out whether the client is willing to pay Dr. Robertson's fee. The client agrees to pay the fee, so Andrea meets with Dr. Robertson to discuss the case. Andrea explains that the client is a corporation and that the case involves complex scientific and engineering issues. Dr. Robertson consults her files for statistical information on these types of cases. She finds that the ideal jury would be made up of white-collar professionals holding advanced degrees in engineering or another applied science. Also, the prospective jurors would ideally be against extensive government regulation of the corporate world.

DRAFTING *VOIR DIRE* QUESTIONS

Andrea returns to the office and discusses with Mary the results of her consultation with Dr. Robertson. Mary and Andrea decide to draft questions for *voir dire* that are designed to elicit the type of information recommended by Dr. Robertson. Andrea then drafts a list of about twenty questions, including such questions as the following:

1. Please state your name and address.
2. Where are you employed, and how long have you been employed there?
3. What is the highest level of education that you have attained: high school diploma, some college but no degree, college degree, advanced degree (please specify)?
4. If you have attended college or received a college degree, what was your field of study?
5. Have you ever been fired by a corporate employer in a way that you believed was unfair?
6. Have you ever worked for a government regulatory agency, and, if so, what were your responsibilities in that position?
7. Have you, or persons or business firms with whom you are or have been associated, ever been sued for violating environmental statutes or regulations? If so, what were the violations?
8. In your opinion, what should be the government's role in regulating a company's operations?

REVIEWING THE *VOIR DIRE* QUESTIONS

Andrea faxes the list of questions to Dr. Robertson, who reviews them and faxes back some suggested changes, which Andrea incorporates. When the final list of questions is drawn up, she presents it to Mary and places a copy of the list in the trial notebook. Mary asks Andrea to call Dr. Robertson and ask her if she is available to sit in on the actual *voir dire* process to ensure that jury selection goes smoothly.

---

are awarded damages, might not be able to collect them. Realize, though, that judgments constitute liens (legal claims) for significant time periods. If the financial circumstances of the debtor—such as Peretto—change in the future, recovery may be possible.

The difficulty of enforcing court judgments, coupled with the high costs accompanying any litigation (including attorneys' fees, court costs, and the litigants' time costs), is a major reason why most disputes are settled out of court, either before or during the trial.

✳ KEY TERMS AND CONCEPTS

affirm

appeal

appellant

appellee

challenge

challenge for cause

charge

closing argument

cross-examination

direct examination

judgment creditor

motion for a directed verdict

motion for a new trial

motion for judgment
   notwithstanding the verdict

motion *in limine*

opening statement

peremptory challenge

pretrial conference

record on appeal

recross-examination

redirect examination

remand

reverse

trial notebook

verdict

voir dire

writ of execution

✳ CHAPTER SUMMARY

Preparing for Trial	1. *Trial-preparation checklist*—Before the trial begins, attorneys for both sides and their paralegals gather and organize all evidence, documents, and other materials relating to the case. It is helpful to create a checklist to ensure that nothing is overlooked during this stage.
	2. *Witnesses and subpoenas*—Paralegals often assist in contacting and issuing subpoenas to witnesses, as well as in preparing witnesses for trial.
	3. *Prepare exhibits and trial notebook*—Paralegals also assume responsibility for making sure that all exhibits and displays are ready by the trial date and that the trial notebook is complete.
Pretrial Conference	Prior to the trial, the attorneys for both sides meet with the trial judge in a pretrial conference to decide whether a settlement is possible or, if not, to decide how the trial will be conducted and what types of evidence will be admissible.
	1. *Motions* in limine—One or both of the attorneys may make a motion *in limine,* which asks the court to keep certain evidence from being offered at the trial.
Jury Selection	1. Voir dire—During the *voir dire* process, attorneys for both sides question potential jurors to determine whether certain potential jurors should be excluded from the jury.
	2. *Challenges for cause*—Attorneys for both sides can exercise an unlimited number of challenges for cause on the basis of prospective jurors' bias against the client or case.
	3. *Peremptory challenges*—Both attorneys can exercise a limited number of peremptory challenges without giving any reason to the court for excluding a particular juror.

The Trial	Once the jury has been selected and seated, the trial begins. The paralegal, if he or she attends the trial, coordinates witnesses' appearances, tracks the testimony of witnesses and compares it with sworn statements that the witnesses made prior to the trial, and provides the attorney with appropriate reminders or documents when necessary.
	1. *Opening statements*—The trial begins with opening statements in which the attorneys briefly outline their versions of the facts of the case and the evidence they will offer to support their views.
	2. *Plaintiff's case*—Following the attorneys' opening statements, the plaintiff's attorney presents evidence supporting the plaintiff's claims, including the testimony of witnesses.
	a. The attorney's questioning of a witness whom he or she calls is referred to as direct examination.
	b. Following direct examination by the plaintiff's attorney, the defendant's attorney may cross-examine the witness.
	c. If the witness was cross-examined, the plaintiff's attorney may question the witness on redirect examination, after which the defendant's attorney may question the witness on recross-examination.
	3. *Motion for a directed verdict*—After the plaintiff's attorney has presented his or her client's case, the defendant's attorney may make a motion for a directed verdict, also called *a motion for judgment as a matter of law*. This motion asserts that the plaintiff has not offered enough evidence to support the validity of the plaintiff's claim against the defendant. If the judge grants the motion, the case will be dismissed.
	4. *Defendant's case*—The attorneys then reverse their roles, and the defendant's attorney presents evidence and testimony to refute the plaintiff's claims. Any witnesses called to the stand by the defendant's attorney will be subject to direct examination by that attorney, cross-examination by the plaintiff's attorney, and possible redirect examination and recross-examination.
	5. *Closing arguments*—After the defendant's attorney has finished his or her presentation, both attorneys give their closing arguments. A closing argument includes all the major points that support the client's case and emphasizes shortcomings in the opposing party's case.
	6. *Jury instructions*—Following the attorneys' closing arguments, the judge instructs the jury in a charge—a document that includes statements of the applicable law and a review of the facts as they were presented during the trial. The jury must not disregard the judge's instructions as to what the applicable law is and how it should be applied to the facts of the case as interpreted by the jury.
	7. *Verdict*—Once the jury reaches a decision, it issues a verdict in favor of one of the parties and is discharged. The court then enters a judgment consistent with the jury's verdict.
Posttrial Motions and Procedures	After the verdict has been pronounced and the trial concluded, the losing party's attorney may file a posttrial motion or an appeal.

Posttrial Motions and Procedures—Continued	1. *Motion for judgment notwithstanding the verdict*—A motion for judgment notwithstanding the verdict (also called a *motion for judgment as a matter of law*) asks the judge to enter a judgment in favor of the losing party in spite of the verdict because the verdict was not supported by the evidence or was otherwise erroneous.
	2. *Motion for a new trial*—A motion for a new trial asserts that the trial was so flawed—by judge or juror misconduct or other pervasive errors—that a new trial should be held.
	3. *Appealing the verdict*—The attorney may, depending on the client's wishes, appeal the decision to an appellate court for review. Appeals are usually filed only when the attorney believes that a reversal of the judgment is likely.
	a. If an appeal is pursued, the appellant must file a notice of appeal with the court that rendered the judgment. Then the clerk will forward the record on appeal to the appropriate reviewing court.
	b. The parties then file appellate briefs arguing their positions. Later, they will be given the opportunity to present oral arguments before the appellate panel.
	c. The appellate court decides whether to affirm, reverse, remand, or modify the trial court's judgment.
	d. The appellate court's decision may sometimes be appealed further (to the state supreme court, for example).
Enforcing the Judgment	Even though a plaintiff wins a lawsuit for damages, it may be difficult to enforce the judgment against the defendant, particularly if the defendant has few assets. The paralegal is often involved in locating assets so that the attorney can request a writ of execution (court order to seize property) in an attempt to collect the amount the client is owed.

✳ QUESTIONS FOR REVIEW

1. What role does the paralegal play in preparing witnesses, exhibits, and displays for trial? How can the paralegal assist the attorney in preparing the trial notebook?

2. What is a pretrial conference? What issues are likely to be raised and decided at a pretrial conference?

3. How are jurors selected? What role does the attorney play in the selection process? Does the paralegal play a role in the process?

4. What is the difference between a peremptory challenge and a challenge for cause?

5. What role might the paralegal play during the trial? What types of trial-related tasks may the paralegal perform?

6. How are witnesses examined during trial? What is the difference between direct examination and cross-examination?

7. What is a jury charge? Can the jury decide matters of law?

8. Name the posttrial motions that are available. In what situation is each of them used?

9. Describe the procedure for filing an appeal. What factors does an attorney consider when deciding whether a case should be appealed?

10. Why do appellate courts defer to trial courts' findings of fact? What options might an appellate court pursue after it has completed its review of a case?

✺ ETHICAL QUESTIONS

1. Anthony Paletti, a paralegal, is attending a trial with his supervising attorney. Anthony leaves the courtroom to meet a witness. On his way down the hall, he runs into the defendant in the case. The defendant says to Anthony, "You work for the plaintiff's attorney, don't you? I have a question for you about that contract that your attorney offered into evidence." Should Anthony answer the defendant's question? Why or why not?

2. A client claiming to have severely injured his back at work comes into the office of a law firm. The client, in a wheelchair, seeks legal advice about filing a lawsuit, and the attorney decides to take the case. Two days later, Alvin Kerrigan, the attorney's paralegal, sees the new client on the roof of a building installing shingles. What should Alvin do?

3. During a lunch break in the course of a trial, Louise Lanham, a paralegal, was washing her hands in the rest room. One of the members of the trial jury came up to her and said, "I don't understand what negligence is. Can you explain it to me?" How should Louise answer this question?

✺ PRACTICE QUESTIONS AND ASSIGNMENTS

1. Paralegal Patricia Smith is assisting her supervising attorney, who has received a trial date for an auto-accident case. The trial is set to begin in ten weeks. Discovery has been completed in the case. The depositions of the plaintiff and defendant have been taken, along with those of two eyewitnesses, a police officer, and Dr. Black, the plaintiff's physician. Additionally, the plaintiff and the defendant have answered interrogatories. Patricia's firm represents the plaintiff, and her supervising attorney plans to call not only the client, but also the defendant, Mr. Sams (an eyewitness), and the police officer to testify. All of the witnesses are local. The case file contains police reports, newspaper articles about the accident, and medical records in addition to the deposition and interrogatory materials. Using the material presented in Exhibit 14.1, *Trial-Preparation Checklist*, prepare a checklist for Patricia to complete.

2. A product liability trial is about to begin. It involves the death of Tom Bert, which resulted from a defective industrial press. The plaintiff's wife is suing as Tom's personal representative. One of her claims is for *loss of consortium*, which is a claim for the loss of her relationship with her husband. Tom's wife remarried three weeks after his funeral, however, and there exists evidence that she was having an affair with her second husband prior to Tom's death. The defense attorney wants to be able to address the plaintiff as Mrs. Ross, her new name resulting from her recent marriage, throughout the trial. Calling the wife by her new name in front of the jury will emphasize to the jury that she did not have much of a relationship with Tom Bert. The defense attorney hopes that this will significantly decrease any damages that might be awarded to Mrs. Ross on the loss-of-consortium claim. The plaintiff's attorney assigns you the task of drafting a motion *in limine* to keep the defense attorney from addressing the plaintiff as Mrs. Ross during the trial. Prepare an outline of the argument that would be included in the motion.

3. Using Exhibit 14.2, *A Subpoena*, draft a subpoena for a friendly witness using the following facts:

Simon Kolstad, whose address is 100 Schoolcraft Road, Del Mar, California, is a witness to be subpoenaed in *Sumner v. Hayes*, a civil lawsuit filed in the U.S. District Court for the Eastern District of Michigan, docket number 99–123492. He is being subpoenaed by the plaintiff's attorney, Marvin W. Green, whose office is located at 300 Penobscot Building, Detroit, Michigan. Kolstad is to appear in room number 6 of the courthouse, which is located at 231 Lafayette Boulevard, Detroit, Michigan, at 2:30 P.M. on January 10, 2004. Kolstad is to bring with him a letter from the defendant to Kolstad dated February 9, 2001.

4. Draft a series of questions for the plaintiff's attorney and for the two defendants' attorneys (the attorneys representing the doctor and the pharmaceutical company) to use during *voir dire* in a case involving the following facts:

The plaintiff's daughter died five days after starting a regimen of taking weight-loss pills. The daughter died because the pills were incompatible with her blood type. Prior to taking the pills, she was a perfectly healthy twenty-five-year-old law student. The mother is bringing a medical-malpractice suit against the doctor for prescribing the wrong type of pill. The mother is also suing the pharmaceutical company that manufactured the pill on the ground that it failed to warn of the dangers of its pill for those persons, including her daughter, whose blood types were incompatible with the pill.

5. Using the scenario from question 4 above, involving the law student who died after taking weight-loss pills that were incompatible with her blood type, conduct the *voir dire*. Plaintiff and defense teams, each consisting of at least one attorney and one paralegal, will need to be selected. The rest of the class will serve as the jury pool to be questioned during *voir dire*. Each legal team, using the questions drafted for question 4 above, is to select the jurors most favorable to its client's position. Additional factual information relating to the two defendants includes the following:
   a. The physician has prescribed this pill on numerous occasions and has never had a patient die as a result of taking it. The doctor did not take a thorough medical history of the plaintiff, nor did he note her blood type.
   b. The pharmaceutical company does include a package insert warning physicians of the dangers involved in taking the drug and instructing them as to the types of tests that should be undertaken before the pill is prescribed.
6. Your client, a surgeon, is suing a lawyer for slander (a tort arising when someone makes a verbal statement that harms another's good name or reputation—see Chapter 7). The lawyer was representing the surgeon in a malpractice case. In the presence of several other physicians, the lawyer told the surgeon that he "ought to have his head examined" and that he was "so incompetent at his job" that the lawyer had decided not to defend him against the malpractice claim. The surgeon is suing the lawyer for slander because, as a result of the lawyer's comments, the physician's staff privileges at a major hospital have been suspended and he can no longer perform surgery there.

   Using the material presented in the chapter, draft questions for your supervising attorney to ask your client, the surgeon, during trial.
7. Using the material presented in the chapter, identify the motion that would be filed in each of the following situations:
   a. A plaintiff's attorney loses a case, and she believes that her loss is due to prejudicial jury instructions given by the judge.
   b. The defendant's key witness was hospitalized during a trial and was unable to testify. As a result, key evidence was not presented, and the defendant was unable to prove his case.
   c. In the example above, the plaintiff's attorney made the appropriate motion, which was not granted, and ultimately lost the lawsuit. Thus, according to the plaintiff's attorney, the judgment was not supported by the evidence.
   d. The defense attorney has seen grisly photographs of an accident that the plaintiff's attorney has in her file. The defense attorney is concerned that these photographs would unfairly prejudice a jury against the defendant during the trial.
8. Using the material presented in the chapter, indicate whether the appellate court will affirm, modify, or reverse the trial court's decision or remand the case for further proceedings:
   a. A trial court finds for the plaintiff in the amount of $150,000 in a case in which the plaintiff slipped and fell in a grocery store. The court of appeals finds that while the plaintiff is entitled to damages, the damages awarded by the jury are excessive. The appellate court sends the case back to the trial court for reevaluation of the amount of damages awarded.
   b. A trial court finds that the plaintiff was slandered by the defendant. On appeal, the court of appeals finds that the trial court admitted evidence that it should not have allowed and holds that without this evidence, there was no slander.
   c. A trial court finds that the defendant breached a contract and owes the plaintiff $1,000,000 in damages. The defendant appeals, claiming that the damages are not supported by the evidence. The court of appeals agrees with the trial court's decision.

Questions for Critical Analysis

1. Typically, all witnesses called to appear at a trial are served with subpoenas, even friendly witnesses. Why is this? What might happen if they were not subpoenaed? How can the service of subpoenas be handled with friendly witnesses so that they are not offended?

2. Most prudent attorneys do not put a witness on the stand without discussing the witness's testimony beforehand or at least learning what the witness will say. What might happen if a witness whose testimony has not been discussed ahead of time, or whose testimony is unknown, takes the stand? What effect might this have on the outcome of the case?

3. Much preparation and organization goes into trial work, from preparing witnesses and trial notebooks, to drafting questions, to creating exhibits and displays. Why is this done? What impact do these preparations have on the jury? What impact would (or does) disorganization and lack of preparation have on the jury?

4. Certain types of cases, such as product liability cases, require complex evidence. Should certain types of jurors be required in these complex cases? Why or why not?

5. What is the difference between redirect examination and recross-examination? When is each type of examination used? What is allowed during each type of examination?

6. Why are leading questions not allowed during direct examination? Why are leading questions allowed during cross-examination? Is the use of leading questions fair to the witness being cross-examined?

7. What is the basis for a motion for a directed verdict? Why would a trial start if the grounds for a motion for a directed verdict existed? Are these motions frequently granted?

8. Why do you think that attorneys and paralegals, instead of judges, draft jury instructions? Does this surprise you? Why or why not?

9. Is there a difference between a verdict and a judgment? If so, what is the difference? Who do you think drafts the judgment? Why?

10. After a trial, the losing party may file a motion for a judgment notwithstanding the verdict and/or a motion for a new trial. What is the likelihood that a judge will grant such motions? Why would a losing party file these types of motions as opposed to appealing the case?

11. How is a judgment paid when there is no insurance or other cash assets available to pay the judgment? Is all of a defendant's property subject to the judgment? If not, what property is exempt? Why might these exemptions have been created?

❋ PROJECTS

1. Call a local court clerk or administrator (not a judge) to obtain a list of the cases on the court's trial docket. Arrange to attend a trial that is not expected to last longer than a few days. Attend the trial for as many days as you can, and observe carefully the following proceedings: *voir dire,* opening statements, the presentation of evidence, and closing arguments. Also note how paralegals are used. Prepare a three-page summary of your observations, making sure to include the name and docket number of the case, the name of the court, and the name of the judge.

2. Look up your state's court rules and find out how many challenges for cause are allowed during *voir dire.* How many peremptory challenges are permitted during *voir dire?*

3. Call your local sheriff's office and find out what happens when a writ of execution is carried out. Ask if any printed information on this procedure is available. If so, request a copy. Share the results of your research with the class. (Discuss this assignment with your instructor prior to undertaking it.)

4. Look through some computer magazines, such as *Law Office Computing* and *Law Technology Product News,* for articles on the use of technology, such as digital cameras or scanners, to prepare or present evidence during a trial. If possible, obtain demo disks or videos of the technology. Present your findings to the class.

❋ USING INTERNET RESOURCES

1. If you are assisting an attorney in litigating a case, you may be asked to do some research on jury verdicts in similar cases. To date, not many fully searchable databases that contain this information are available on the Web, although the number is expanding. One site is that offered by MoreLaw at **http://www.**

morelaw.com. Access this site, and spend some time browsing through its offerings. Then click on "Recent Decisions," and select a large state, such as California or New York.

a. How many cases/verdicts were listed for the state you selected?

b. Choose five cases. For each case, describe briefly what it was about, who "won" the case (the plaintiff or the defendant), and, if the plaintiff won, what amount of damages was awarded.

c. Choose one of these cases, and describe it in further detail. Who initiated the lawsuit? Why? Who was the defendant? What general area of law was involved (torts, product liability, contracts, and so on)? How did the jury decide the issue? Did the jury award damages? If so, in what amount? Were punitive damages also awarded?

d. Generally, what are the advantages of this site for paralegals doing research on jury verdicts? What are the disadvantages?

2. Do a general search on the Internet for vendors of trial-support services, such as imaging and coding. Pick two of the vendors, and browse through their Web sites.

a. Write a one-page summary of the services that each company provides.

b. Write an additional two paragraphs comparing the vendors' services and stating which of the two companies you would recommend and why.

END NOTES

1. Pronounced in *lim*-uh-nay.

2. Pronounced vwahr *deehr.* Literally, these French verbs mean "to see, to speak." During the *voir dire* phase of litigation, attorneys do in fact see the jurors speak. In legal language, however, the phrase refers to the process of interrogating jurors to learn about their backgrounds, attitudes, and so on.

3. Discriminating against prospective jurors on the basis of race was prohibited by the United States Supreme Court in *Batson v. Kentucky*, 476 U.S. 79, 106 S.Ct. 1712, 90 L.Ed.2d 69 (1986). Discriminating against prospective jurors on the basis of gender was prohibited by the Supreme Court in *J.E.B. v. Alabama ex rel. T.B.*, 511 U.S

127, 114 S.Ct. 1419, 128 L.Ed.2d 89 (1994). See Chapter 16 for an explanation of how to read court citations.

4. Amendments to the Federal Rules of Civil Procedure designated both the motion for a directed verdict and the motion for judgment notwithstanding the verdict as motions for judgment as a matter of law. One of the reasons for the change was to make evident the common identity of these motions (both motions claim, at different times during the proceedings, that there is insufficient evidence against the defendant to justify a claim—or a verdict—against the defendant). Many judges and attorneys continue to use the former names of these motions, however, so we include them in our discussion.

CHAPTER 15

CRIMINAL LAW AND PROCEDURES

Chapter Outline

INTRODUCTION ✻ WHAT IS A CRIME? ✻ ELEMENTS OF CRIMINAL LIABILITY ✻ TYPES OF CRIMES ✻ CYBER CRIME ✻ CONSTITUTIONAL SAFEGUARDS ✻ CRIMINAL PROCEDURES PRIOR TO PROSECUTION ✻ THE PROSECUTION BEGINS ✻ THE TRIAL

After completing this chapter, you will know:

- The difference between crimes and other wrongful acts.
- The two elements that are required for criminal liability and some of the most common defenses that are raised in defending against criminal charges.
- Five broad categories of crimes and some common types of crimes.
- The constitutional rights of persons accused of crimes.
- The basic steps involved in criminal procedure from the time a crime is reported to the resolution of the case.
- How and why criminal litigation procedures differ from civil litigation procedures.

INTRODUCTION

More than one million people are arrested for crimes and enter the criminal justice system each year. As the crime rate continues to increase, so does the work of attorneys and legal assistants involved in criminal law cases. Criminal cases are prosecuted by **public prosecutors,** who are employed by the government. The public prosecutor in federal criminal cases is called a U.S. attorney. In cases tried in state or local courts, the public prosecutor may be referred to as a *prosecuting attorney, state prosecutor, district attorney, county attorney, or city attorney.*

Defendants in criminal cases may hire private attorneys to defend them. If a defendant cannot afford to hire an attorney, the court will appoint one for him or her. Everyone accused of a crime that may result in a jail sentence has a right to counsel, and this right is ensured by court-appointed attorneys, called **public defenders,** who are paid by the state.

Many employment opportunities exist for paralegals interested in working for public prosecutors or public defenders across the country. Private criminal defense attorneys also utilize paralegals. In addition, victims' rights organizations and police departments may employ legal assistants. Paralegals may also come into contact with criminal defendants in the course of their work in a general law practice or in a corporate legal department. A client of the firm may be arrested for driving while intoxicated or for possessing illegal drugs, for example, or a corporation might have to defend against alleged criminal violations of federal environmental laws.

In this chapter, we provide an overview of criminal law and procedure. We begin by explaining the nature of crime and the key differences between criminal law and civil law. We then discuss the elements of criminal liability and some of the many types of crime. Throughout the chapter, we emphasize the constitutional protections that come into play when a person is accused of a crime and focus on how and why criminal procedures differ from civil procedures.

public prosecutor
An individual, acting as a trial lawyer, who initiates and conducts criminal cases in the government's name and on behalf of the people.

public defender
A court-appointed attorney who is paid by the state to represent a criminal defendant who is unable to hire private counsel.

WHAT IS A CRIME?

What is a crime? To answer that question, we begin by distinguishing crimes from other wrongs, such as torts—and, hence, criminal law from tort, or civil, law. Major differences between civil and criminal law are summarized in Exhibit 15.1 on the next page. After discussing these differences, we explain how one act can qualify as both a crime and a tort. We then describe classifications of crimes and jurisdiction over criminal acts.

Key Differences between Civil and Criminal Law

A **crime** can be distinguished from other wrongful acts, such as torts, in that a crime is an *offense against society as a whole.* Criminal defendants are prosecuted by public officials on behalf of the state, as mentioned above, not by their victims or other private parties. In addition, those who have committed crimes are subject to penalties, including fines, imprisonment, and, in some cases, death. As discussed in Chapter 7, tort remedies—remedies for civil wrongs—are generally intended to compensate the injured party (by awarding money damages, for example). Criminal law, however, is concerned with punishing the wrongdoer in an attempt to deter others from similar actions.

Another factor distinguishing criminal law from tort law is that criminal law is primarily statutory law. Essentially, a crime is whatever a legislature has

crime
A broad term for violations of law that are punishable by the state and are codified by legislatures. The objective of criminal law is to protect the public.

EXHIBIT 15.1
Civil and Criminal Law Compared

ISSUE	CIVIL LAW	CRIMINAL LAW
Area of concern	Rights and duties between individuals and between persons and their government	Offenses against society as a whole
Wrongful act	Harm to a person or to a person's property	Violation of a statute that prohibits some type of activity
Party who brings suit	Person who suffered harm	The state
Standard of proof	Preponderance of the evidence	Beyond a reasonable doubt
Remedy	Damages to compensate for the harm, or a decree to achieve an equitable result	Punishment (fine, removal from public office, imprisonment, or death)

On the Web
Many state criminal codes are now online. To find your state's code, go to **http://www.findlaw.com** and select "State Codes."

beyond a reasonable doubt
The standard used to determine the guilt or innocence of a person charged with a crime. To be guilty of a crime, a suspect must be proved guilty "beyond and to the exclusion of every reasonable doubt."

declared to be a crime. Although federal crimes are defined by the U.S. Congress, most crimes are defined by state legislatures.

As mentioned in Chapter 5, at one time criminal law was governed primarily by the common law. Over time, common law doctrines and principles were codified, expanded on, and enacted in statutory form. Although many crimes were originally defined by the common law, the statutory definitions of those crimes may differ significantly from these common law definitions.

For example, under the common law, in order to be guilty of *burglary,* a person had to break into and enter another person's dwelling at night with intent to commit a felony. Today, under most state statutes, a burglary need not take place at night, and the building entered need not be a person's home. Statutes have thus modified the common law definition of burglary.

The standards of proof required in criminal and civil cases represent another area of difference. Because the state has extensive resources at its disposal when prosecuting criminal cases, there are numerous procedural safeguards to protect the rights of defendants. One of these safeguards is the higher standard of proof that applies in a criminal case. In a civil case, the plaintiff usually must prove his or her case by a *preponderance of the evidence.* Under this standard, the plaintiff must convince the court that, based on the evidence presented by both parties, it is more likely than not that the plaintiff's allegation is true.

In a criminal case, in contrast, the state must prove its case **beyond a reasonable doubt.** That is, every juror in a criminal case must be convinced, beyond a reasonable doubt, of the defendant's guilt. The higher standard of proof in criminal cases reflects a fundamental social value—a belief that it is worse to convict an innocent individual than to let a guilty person go free. We will look at other safeguards later in the chapter, in the context of criminal procedure.

Yet another factor that distinguishes criminal law from tort law is the fact that a criminal act does not necessarily involve a victim, in the sense that the act directly and physically harms another. If Marissa grows marijuana in her backyard for her personal use, she may not be physically or directly harming another's interests, but she is nonetheless committing a crime (in most states and under federal law). Why? Because she is violating a rule of society that has been enacted into law by duly elected representatives of the people. She has committed an offense against society's values.

THE RACKETEER INFLUENCED AND CORRUPT ORGANIZATIONS ACT (RICO).
In 1970, in an effort to curb the apparently increasing entry of organized crime into the legitimate business world, Congress passed the Racketeer Influenced and Corrupt Organizations Act (RICO).[7] The act makes it a federal crime to (1) use income obtained from racketeering activity to purchase any interest in an enterprise, (2) acquire or maintain an interest in an enterprise through racketeering activity, (3) conduct or participate in the affairs of an enterprise through racketeering activity, or (4) conspire to do any of the preceding activities. Today, RICO is used more often to attack white-collar crime than organized crime.

Racketeering activity is not a new type of crime created by RICO; rather, RICO incorporates by reference twenty-six separate types of federal crimes and nine types of state felonies[8] and declares that if a person commits *two* of these offenses, he or she is guilty of "racketeering activity." Any individual found guilty of a violation is subject to a fine of up to $25,000 per violation, imprisonment for up to twenty years, or both. Additionally, the statute provides that those who violate RICO may be required to forfeit any assets, in the form of property or cash, that were acquired as a result of the illegal activity or that were "involved in" or an "instrumentality of" the activity.

CYBER CRIME

Today, many crimes are committed with computers and occur in cyberspace. These crimes fall under the broad label of **cyber crime**. As we mentioned earlier, most cyber crimes are not "new" crimes. Rather, they are existing crimes in which the Internet is the instrument of wrongdoing. The challenge for law enforcement is to apply traditional laws—which were designed to protect persons from physical harm or to safeguard their physical property—to crimes committed in cyberspace. Here, we look at several types of cyber crimes against persons and property.

cyber crime
A crime that occurs online, in the virtual community of the Internet, as opposed to the physical world.

Cyber Theft

In cyberspace, thieves are not subject to the physical limitations of the "real" world. A thief with dial-in access can steal data stored in a networked computer from anywhere on the globe. Only the speed of the connection and the thief's computer equipment limit the quantity of data that can be stolen.

On the Web
The Bureau of Justice Statistics of the U.S. Department of Justice offers an impressive collection of statistics on crime, including cyber crime, at the following Web site: **http://www.ojp.usdoj.gov/bjs.**

FINANCIAL CRIMES.   Computer networks provide opportunities for employees to commit crimes that can involve serious economic losses. For example, employees of a company's accounting department can transfer funds among accounts with little effort and often with less risk than would be involved in paper transactions. Generally, the dependence of businesses on computer operations has left many companies vulnerable to sabotage, fraud, embezzlement, and the theft of proprietary data, such as trade secrets or other intellectual property (discussed in Chapter 8).

IDENTITY THEFT.   A form of cyber theft that has become particularly troublesome in recent years is **identity theft.** Identity theft occurs when the wrongdoer steals a form of identification—such as a name, date of birth, or Social Security number—and uses the information to access the victim's financial resources. This crime existed to a certain extent before the widespread use of the Internet. Thieves would "steal" calling-card numbers by watching people using public telephones,

identity theft
The theft of a form of identification, such as a name, date of birth, or Social Security number, which is then used to access the victim's financial resources.

or they would rifle through garbage to find bank account or credit-card numbers. The Internet, however, has turned identity theft into perhaps the fastest-growing financial crime in the United States. The Internet provides those who steal information offline with an easy medium for using items such as stolen credit-card numbers and e-mail addresses while protected by anonymity. An estimated 500,000 Americans are victims of identity theft each year.

Cyber Stalking

cyber stalker
A person who commits the crime of stalking in cyberspace. The cyber stalker usually finds the victim through Internet chat rooms, newsgroups, bulletin boards, or e-mail and proceeds to harass that person or put the person in reasonable fear for his or her safety or the safety of his or her immediate family.

Most states have laws against stalking. These laws make it a crime to harass or follow a person while making a "credible threat" that puts that person in reasonable fear for his or her safety or the safety of his or her immediate family. Traditionally, these laws required a physical act (following the victim). **Cyber stalkers** are stalkers who commit their crimes in cyberspace—usually finding their victims through Internet chat rooms, newsgroups, bulletin boards, or e-mail. To close this "loophole" in existing stalking laws, more than three-fourths of the states now have laws specifically designed to combat cyber stalking and other forms of online harassment.

Note that cyber stalking can be even more threatening than physical stalking in some respects. While it takes a great deal of effort to stalk physically, it is relatively easy to harass a victim with electronic messages. Furthermore, the possibility of personal confrontation may discourage a stalker from actually following a victim. This disincentive is removed in cyberspace. Finally, there is always the possibility that a cyber stalker will eventually pose a physical threat to her or his target.

Hacking

hacker
A person who uses one computer to break into another.

Persons who use one computer to break into another are sometimes referred to as **hackers.** Hackers who break into computers without authorization often commit cyber theft. Sometimes, however, their principal aim is to prove how smart they are by gaining access to others' password-protected computers and causing random data errors or making unpaid-for telephone calls.[9]

It is difficult to know how frequently hackers succeed in breaking into databases across the United States. The Federal Bureau of Investigation estimates that only 25 percent of all corporations that suffer such security breaches report the incident to a law enforcement agency. For one thing, corporations do not want it to become publicly known that the security of their data has been breached. For another, admitting to a breach would be admitting to a certain degree of incompetence, which could damage their reputations.

Prosecuting Cyber Crimes

The Internet has raised new issues in the investigation of crimes and the prosecution of offenders. As discussed in Chapter 6, the issue of jurisdiction presents difficulties in cyberspace. Identifying the wrongdoers can also be difficult. Cyber criminals do not leave physical traces, such as fingerprints or DNA samples, as evidence of their crimes. Even electronic "footprints" can be hard to find and follow. For example, e-mail can be sent through a remailer, an online service that guarantees that a message cannot be traced to its source.

For these reasons, laws written to protect physical property are difficult to apply in cyberspace. Nonetheless, governments at both the state and federal levels have taken significant steps toward controlling cyber crime, both by applying existing criminal statutes and by enacting new laws that specifically address wrongs committed in cyberspace.

THE COMPUTER FRAUD AND ABUSE ACT.   Perhaps the most significant federal statute specifically addressing cyber crime is the Counterfeit Access Device and Computer Fraud and Abuse Act of 1984. This act, as amended,[10] provides, among other things, that a person who accesses or attempts to access a computer online, without authority, to obtain classified, restricted, or protected data is subject to criminal prosecution. Such data could include financial and credit records, medical records, legal files, military and national security files, and other confidential information in government or private computers. The crime has two elements: accessing a computer without authority and taking the data. This theft is a felony if it is committed for a commercial purpose or for private financial gain or if the value of the stolen data (or computer time) exceeds $5,000. Penalties include fines and imprisonment for up to twenty years. A victim of computer theft can also bring a civil suit against the violator to obtain damages, an injunction, and other relief.

OTHER FEDERAL STATUTES.   The federal wire fraud statute, the Economic Espionage Act of 1996, and RICO, all of which were discussed earlier, extend to crimes committed in cyberspace as well. Two other federal statutes that may apply are the Electronic Fund Transfer Act of 1978, which makes unauthorized access to an electronic fund transfer system a crime, and the Anticounterfeiting Consumer Protection Act of 1996, which increased penalties for stealing copyrighted or trademarked property.

CONSTITUTIONAL SAFEGUARDS

From the very moment a crime is reported until the trial concludes, law enforcement officers and prosecutors must be careful to abide by the specific criminal procedures that have been established to protect an accused person's constitutional rights. Before allowing a case to go to trial, the prosecutor and paralegals assigned to the case review all pretrial events very closely to make sure that all requirements have been properly observed. Defense attorneys and their legal assistants also investigate and review closely the actions of arresting and investigating police officers in an attempt to obtain grounds for a dismissal of the charges against their clients.

The U.S. Constitution provides specific procedural safeguards to protect persons accused of crimes against the potentially arbitrary or unjust use of government power. These safeguards are stated in the first ten amendments to the Constitution, which constitute the Bill of Rights. As you will see in the following pages, criminal procedure is rooted in the constitutional rights and protections spelled out in the Fourth, Fifth, Sixth, and Eighth Amendments. These rights and protections are summarized below. The full text of the U.S. Constitution, including the Bill of Rights, is presented in Appendix J.

1. The Fourth Amendment prohibits unreasonable searches and seizures and requires a showing of probable cause (which will be discussed shortly) before a search or an arrest warrant may be issued.

2. The Fifth Amendment requires that no one shall be deprived of "life, liberty, or property without due process of law." **Due process of law** means that the government must follow a set of reasonable, fair, and standard procedures (that is, criminal procedural law) in any action against a citizen.

3. The Fifth Amendment prohibits **double jeopardy** (trying someone twice for the same criminal offense).

On the Web

The American Civil Liberties Union (ACLU) has long acted as a guardian of Americans' civil liberties. You can learn about some of the constitutional questions raised by various criminal laws and procedures by going to the ACLU's Web site at **http://www.aclu.org**.

due process of law
Fair, reasonable, and standard procedures that must be used by the government in any legal action against a citizen. The Fifth Amendment to the U.S. Constitution prohibits the deprivation of "life, liberty, or property without due process of law."

double jeopardy
To place at risk (jeopardize) a person's life or liberty twice. The Fifth Amendment to the Constitution prohibits a second prosecution for the same criminal offense in all but a few circumstances.

4. The Fifth Amendment guarantees that no person shall be "compelled in any criminal case to be a witness against himself." This is known as the privilege against compulsory **self-incrimination.**

5. The Sixth Amendment guarantees a speedy and public trial, a trial by jury, the right to confront witnesses, and the right to a lawyer at various stages in some proceedings.

6. The Eighth Amendment prohibits excessive bail and fines and cruel and unusual punishment.

self-incrimination
The act of giving testimony that implicates oneself in criminal wrongdoing. The Fifth Amendment to the Constitution states that no person "shall be compelled in any criminal case to be a witness against himself."

The Exclusionary Rule

exclusionary rule
In criminal procedure, a rule under which any evidence obtained in violation of the accused's constitutional rights, as well as any evidence derived from illegally obtained evidence, will not be admissible in court.

Under what is known as the **exclusionary rule,** all evidence obtained in violation of the constitutional rights spelled out in the Fourth, Fifth, and Sixth Amendments normally must be excluded from the trial, along with all evidence derived from the illegally obtained evidence. Evidence derived from illegally obtained evidence is known as the "fruit of the poisonous tree." For example, if during an illegal search drugs are obtained, the search is "the poisonous tree," and the drugs are the "fruit," which normally will be excluded from evidence if the case is brought to trial.

The purpose of the exclusionary rule is to deter police from conducting warrantless searches and from engaging in other misconduct. The rule is sometimes criticized because it can lead to injustice. Many a defendant has "gotten off on a technicality" because law enforcement personnel failed to observe procedural requirements. Even though a defendant may be obviously guilty, if the evidence of that guilt was obtained improperly (without a valid search warrant, for example), it normally cannot be used against the defendant in court.

The *Miranda* Rule

Miranda rights
Certain constitutional rights of accused persons taken into custody by law enforcement officials, such as the right to remain silent and the right to counsel, as established by the United States Supreme Court's decision in *Miranda v. Arizona.*

In *Miranda v. Arizona,*[11] a case decided in 1966, the United States Supreme Court established the rule that individuals who are arrested must be informed of certain constitutional rights, including their Fifth Amendment right to remain silent and their Sixth Amendment right to counsel. These rights, which have come to be called the *Miranda* **rights,** are listed in Exhibit 15.3. If the arresting officers fail to inform a criminal suspect of these constitutional rights, any statements the suspect makes normally will not be admissible in court. It is important to note that the police are not required to give *Miranda* warnings until the individual is placed in custody. Thus, if a person who is not in custody makes voluntary admissions to an officer, these statements are admissible.

 On the Web
If you are interested in reading the Supreme Court's opinion in *Miranda v. Arizona,* go to **http://supct.law.cornell. edu:8080/supct/cases/ name.htm.** Select "M" from the menu at the top of the page, scroll down to find the case name, and click on it.

CHALLENGES TO THE *MIRANDA* RULE.   The Supreme Court's *Miranda* decision was controversial, and in 1968 Congress attempted to overrule the decision when it enacted Section 3501 of the Omnibus Crime Control Act. Essentially, this act reinstated the rule that had been in effect for 180 years before *Miranda*—namely, that statements by defendants can be used against them as long as the statements are made voluntarily. The U.S. Justice Department immediately disavowed the act as unconstitutional, however, and the section has never been enforced. Although the U.S. Court of Appeals for the Fourth Circuit attempted to enforce the provision in 1999, the court's decision was reversed by the United States Supreme Court in 2000. The Supreme Court held that the *Miranda* rights enunciated by the Court in the 1966 case were constitutionally based and thus could not be overruled by a legislative act.[12] Today, both on television and in the real world, police officers routinely advise suspects of their "*Miranda* rights" on arrest.

EXHIBIT 15.3
The *Miranda* Rights

On taking a criminal suspect into custody and before any interrogation takes place, law enforcement officers are required to communicate the following rights and facts to the suspect:

1. **The right to remain silent.**
2. **That any statements made may be used against the person in a court of law.**
3. **The right to talk to a lawyer and have a lawyer present while being questioned.**
4. **If the person cannot afford to hire a lawyer, the right to have a lawyer provided at no cost.**

In addition to being advised of these rights, the suspect must be asked if he or she understands the rights and whether he or she wishes to exercise the rights or waive (not exercise) the rights.

EXCEPTIONS TO THE *MIRANDA* RULE.   Over time, as part of a continuing attempt to balance the rights of accused persons against the rights of society, the United States Supreme Court has carved out numerous exceptions to the *Miranda* rule. In 1984, for example, the Court recognized a "public safety" exception. The need to protect the public warranted the admissibility of statements made by the defendant (in this case, indicating where he placed a gun) as evidence at trial, even though the defendant had not been informed of his *Miranda* rights.[13]

In 1985, the Supreme Court further held that a confession need not be excluded even though the police failed to inform a suspect in custody that his attorney had tried to reach him by telephone.[14] In an important 1991 decision, the Court stated that a suspect's conviction will not be overturned solely on the ground that the suspect was coerced into making a confession by law enforcement personnel. If other, legally obtained evidence admitted at trial is strong enough to justify the conviction without the confession, then the fact that the confession was obtained illegally can, in effect, be ignored.[15]

In yet another case, in 1994, the Supreme Court ruled that a suspect must unequivocally and assertively request to exercise his or her right to counsel in order to stop police questioning. Saying, "Maybe I should talk to a lawyer" during an interrogation after being taken into custody is not enough. The Court held that police officers are not required to decipher the suspect's intentions in such situations.[16]

CRIMINAL PROCEDURES PRIOR TO PROSECUTION

Although the Constitution guarantees due process of law to individuals accused of committing crimes, the actual steps involved in bringing a criminal action vary significantly depending on the jurisdiction and type of crime. In this section, we provide an overview of the basic procedures that take place before an individual is prosecuted for a crime. Exhibit 15.4 on the following page illustrates a general outline of criminal procedure in both federal and state cases. Because of the many procedural variations, however, a paralegal involved in a criminal case will need to research the specific procedural requirements that apply to the case. (The many roles paralegals can play in criminal cases are described in this chapter's *Featured Guest* article starting on page 542.)

EXHIBIT 15.4

**Major Procedural
Steps in a Criminal Case**

ARREST

Police officer takes suspect into custody. Most arrests are made without a warrant. After the arrest, the officer searches the suspect, who is then taken to the police station.

BOOKING

At the police station, the suspect is searched again, photographed, fingerprinted, and allowed at least one telephone call. After the booking, charges are reviewed, and if they are not dropped, a complaint is filed and a magistrate reviews the case for probable cause.

INITIAL APPEARANCE

The suspect appears before the magistrate, who informs the suspect of the charges and of his or her rights. If the suspect requires a lawyer, one is appointed. The magistrate sets bail (conditions under which a suspect can obtain release pending disposition of the case).

GRAND JURY

A grand jury determines if there is probable cause to believe that the defendant committed the crime. The federal government and about half of the states require grand jury indictments for at least some felonies.

PRELIMINARY HEARING

In a court proceeding, a prosecutor presents evidence, and the judge determines if there is probable cause to hold the defendant over for trial.

INDICTMENT

An indictment is the charging instrument issued by the grand jury.

INFORMATION

An information is the charging instrument issued by the prosecutor.

ARRAIGNMENT

The suspect is brought before the trial court, informed of the charges, and asked to enter a plea.

PLEA BARGAIN

A plea bargain is a prosecutor's promise to make concessions (or promise to seek concessions) in return for a suspect's guilty plea. Concessions may include a reduced charge or a lesser sentence.

GUILTY PLEA

In most jurisdictions, most cases that reach the arraignment stage do not go to trial but are resolved by a guilty plea, often as a result of a plea bargain. The judge sets the case for sentencing.

TRIAL

Generally, most felony trials are jury trials, and most misdemeanor trials are bench trials (trials before judges). If the verdict is "guilty," the judge sets the case for sentencing. Everyone convicted of a crime has the right to an appeal.

Arrest and Booking

An **arrest** occurs when police officers take a person into custody and charge him or her with a crime. After the arrest, the police typically search the suspect and take the suspect to a *holding facility* (usually at the police station or a jail), where booking occurs. **Booking** refers to the process of entering a suspect's name, the offense for which the suspect is being held, and the time of arrival into the police log (computer). The suspect is then fingerprinted and photographed, told the reason for the arrest, and allowed to make a phone call. If the crime is not serious, the officer may then release the suspect on personal recognizance, if the suspect promises to appear before a court at some later date. Otherwise, the suspect may be held in custody pending his or her initial appearance (which generally occurs within a few days).

Obviously, law enforcement personnel are in control of the arrest and booking of suspects. Paralegals and attorneys are not usually involved until after an arrest has been made. The defense will, however, look closely to see that the proper procedure was followed in the arrest of the client. An officer can legally arrest a person with or without a warrant, as long as the officer had probable cause to believe that the person committed a crime (discussed shortly). Before an officer questions a suspect who has been arrested, the officer must give the *Miranda* warnings discussed earlier.

DETENTION IS NOT AN ARREST.   Before we discuss probable cause, it is important to note that an arrest differs from a *stop* or *detention,* such as a traffic stop. Police officers have a right to stop and detain a person if they have a *reasonable suspicion* that the person committed, or is about to commit, a crime. Reasonable suspicion is a much lower standard than probable cause—because stopping a person is much less invasive than arresting the person. That means, for example, that an officer can stop a person who matches the description of an assailant in the neighborhood based on reasonable suspicion. The officer can even "frisk" the person being detained (pat down the person's clothes) to make sure the person is not carrying a weapon. The officer cannot legally arrest any person, however, without probable cause.

PROBABLE CAUSE.   The requirement of **probable cause** is a key factor that is assessed repeatedly throughout the various stages of criminal proceedings. The first stage, arrest, requires probable cause. In the context of arrest, probable cause exists if there is a substantial likelihood that:

1. A crime was committed.
2. The individual committed the crime.

Note that probable cause involves a *likelihood*—not just a possibility—that the suspect committed the crime. It is not enough that the police officer suspects that the individual has committed a crime. It must be likely. The probable cause requirement stems from the Fourth Amendment, which prohibits unreasonable searches and seizures.

If a police officer observes a crime being committed, the officer can arrest the wrongdoer on the spot without a warrant, because the probable cause requirement is met. If a victim or some other person reports a crime to the police, the police must decide whether there is enough information about the alleged wrongdoer's guilt to establish probable cause to arrest. What is and is not considered probable cause can vary depending on the case law in the particular jurisdiction. Usually, if the suspect is at his or her home at the time of the arrest, the police will

arrest
To take into custody a person suspected of criminal activity.

booking
The process of entering a suspect's name, offense, and arrival time into the police log (blotter) following his or her arrest.

probable cause
Reasonable grounds to believe the existence of facts warranting certain actions, such as the search or arrest of a person.

FEATURED GUEST: PAMELA POOLE WEBER

Paralegals and Criminal Litigation

BIOGRAPHICAL NOTE

Pamela Poole Weber graduated from Stetson University College of Law and is licensed to practice law in Florida. In 1989, after working in both the corporate and public sectors as a litigator, she joined Seminole Community College in Central Florida. There, she developed and was the director of a two-year legal-assistant program as well as serving as the executive director of the Seminole Community College Foundation.

Weber has been active in various legal areas, teaching police recruits in the area of juvenile law and lecturing to seniors on issues relating to the rights of elderly persons.

The gavel strikes, the trial is over, and the jury is escorted to the jury room to deliberate. Your pulse begins to pound, and the gravity of the situation overwhelms you. This is the first time that you, as a paralegal, have assisted your supervising attorney in a criminal case. Now comes the most difficult time—waiting for the decision. But you take satisfaction in knowing that you have done the best job you can.

* * * *

Criminal litigation is a very fast-paced area of law that is continually changing. Many people do not understand what is involved in defending or prosecuting someone accused of a crime. First and foremost, both sides must be familiar with current laws and especially with changes or new interpretations of those laws. Attorneys do not always have the time required to keep up with these changes. A paralegal can be a valuable asset to a law office by keeping informed on current developments—by reading current court decisions, by reviewing summaries of new laws or modifications to existing laws, by being alert for emerging trends reported in the media, and by generally keeping their eyes and ears open. This behind-the-scenes work is in many ways just as interesting as the spectacular trial scenes on television, and a paralegal's input with respect to current law may well determine the outcome of a case.

Both the defense and the prosecution must review every aspect of the case. This requires combining legal research with critical analysis. Attorneys and paralegals work together in planning a course of action for each case, regardless of whether the case is simple or highly complex. This team approach is becoming more widely accepted because of the results it generates. As the old saying goes, "Two minds are better than one."

OPPORTUNITIES FOR PARALEGALS

Criminal litigation may present paralegals with a variety of opportunities, although paralegals are not utilized as extensively in criminal litigation as they are in civil litigation. Some attorneys do not use paralegals to their fullest capabilities because they do not know how to maximize paralegal services. Often, paralegals must suggest tasks that they can perform or, if appropriate, must simply go ahead and perform the tasks on their own. Remember, though, that paralegals cannot engage in any actions that only attorneys are licensed to perform.

What are some of the services that paralegals can provide? Obviously, legal research is critical to successful criminal litigation, and paralegals can perform this research for attorneys. Such research may involve a review and analysis of the law or laws that allegedly have been violated by the defendant, various defense strategies, procedural problems, and evidentiary problems—just to name a few. Sometimes, research is very detailed, requiring days and even weeks to complete. At other times, research may have to be done at the last minute within only an hour or two.

Paralegals who want more contact with people can involve themselves in the evidentiary side of the case. Both the defense attorney and the prosecuting attorney in a criminal case have some sort of evidence—physical evidence, witnesses' testimony, or confessions, for example—with which to

FEATURED GUEST, *Continued*

work. The paralegal may interview witnesses, prepare deposition questions, review police and laboratory reports, or identify photographs that may be useful at trial.

Many paralegals enjoy the challenge of critical analysis and strategic thinking. The criminal litigation paralegal is continually provided with challenges in this respect. In this area, the paralegal can assist in actually preparing the case for trial. The paralegal may be asked to draft pretrial motions, review the available research and documents, draft responses to the opposing side's motions, prepare questions for jury selection, and prepare jury instructions for the conclusion of the case.

HOW CAN I ASSIST IN THE DEFENSE OF A CRIMINAL?

This question, long asked by attorneys, is now being asked by paralegals. Many people look at this area of law and say that they could never represent such defendants as Ted Bundy and Jeffrey Dahmer (convicted serial killers). Perhaps these people believe that by representing such defendants, the attorneys are somehow condoning their criminal actions. Or perhaps they detest those defendants so much that they want them convicted and punished without the benefit of due process. But attorneys and their legal assistants must remind themselves that until the verdict is in, the defendants are only *accused* of committing the criminal acts. They are guilty of no crime until the jury decides they are guilty *beyond a reasonable doubt*. Our country's criminal justice system is founded

on the principle that a person is "innocent until proven guilty." The paralegal must remember that his or her job is not to decide the guilt or innocence of an accused person. Rather, it is to ensure that *justice* is being served.

A paralegal working for the prosecutor will strive to ensure that the people of a particular city, county, or state, or even the United States, are having their interests protected. The prosecution does not represent the victim of a criminal act but rather the citizens of a community.

The defense paralegal will work to ensure the protection of the rights of the accused. The U.S. Constitution guarantees that all persons have certain rights, including the right to a trial in which they may confront their accusers and the right to be represented by legal counsel during that trial. These rights apply to everyone—including those who actually commit the crimes with which they are charged. It is up to the defense team to make sure that the defendant has not been deprived of any of his or her constitutional rights.

The defense attorney and his or her legal assistants will examine closely all the circumstances, procedures, and evidence involving the defendant to make sure that the defendant has been allowed to exercise these rights. It may be the task of the paralegal to determine if evidence, including a confession, was properly obtained. If it was not, the paralegal may assist in drafting motions to bring this to the attention of the court. The defense team will also explore various defenses

> ## "The defense paralegal will work to ensure the protection of the rights of the accused."

that may be available to the accused.

Paralegals who wish to work in the area of criminal justice must be prepared to be highly objective about criminal proceedings. They must be able to separate their personal and emotional responses to a particular defendant's alleged criminal acts from their professional goal of serving that defendant's best interests by doing all they can to ensure that his or her rights have been observed.

CONCLUSION

Criminal litigation offers numerous opportunities for legal assistants, but it is important to remember that in some cases it may be difficult to achieve the necessary personal and emotional distance from a case to deal with it objectively and professionally.

* * * *

The bailiff returns and announces that the jury has reached a verdict. Your heart leaps into your throat. You take a deep breath and wait. The jury returns a verdict for your side, and you realize that you have just experienced a first victory as a paralegal. After all, you say to yourself, your efforts were crucial to the success of your attorney's case. You know that not all future cases will be "won," but you experience the rewarding feeling of being an integral part of the system seeking justice for all Americans.

DEVELOPING PARALEGAL SKILLS

The Prosecutor's Office—Warrant Division

Kathy Perello works as a legal assistant in the warrant division of the county prosecutor's office. Officer Ryan McCarthy is at her door with a burglary report. The police have a suspect they want to arrest. Officer McCarthy presents the paperwork from the prosecutor that authorizes the arrest and requests that Kathy prepare an arrest warrant. Officer McCarthy will then take the warrant to the court, swear to the truth of its contents, and ask the judge to sign the warrant so that McCarthy can make the arrest.

- Obtain a copy of the suspect's criminal history.
- Use the above to prepare the warrant.
- Verify that the criminal history matches the suspect.
- Make sure that the crime and the suspect are both specifically described.
- Review the typed warrant to ensure that it includes any other required terms.
- Call the officer to pick up the warrant and take it to a judge for a determination of probable cause.

CHECKLIST FOR PREPARING A WARRANT

- Obtain written authorization from a prosecutor before initiating the warrant procedure.

---

need to obtain an arrest warrant (unless the police pursued the suspect to the home or some other emergency circumstance exists).

arrest warrant
A written order, based on probable cause and issued by a judge or public official (magistrate), commanding that the person named on the warrant be arrested by the police.

search warrant
A written order, based on probable cause and issued by a judge or public official (magistrate), commanding that police officers or criminal investigators search a specific person, place, or property to obtain evidence.

WARRANTS.   Often, the police try to gather more information to help them determine whether a suspect should be arrested. If, after investigating the matter, the police decide to arrest the suspect, they must obtain an **arrest warrant** from a judge or other public official. To obtain this warrant, the police will have to convince the official, usually through supporting affidavits, that probable cause exists.

Probable cause is also required to obtain a **search warrant,** which authorizes police officers or other criminal investigators to search specifically named persons or property for evidence and to seize the evidence if they find it (see Exhibit 15.5). Probable cause requires law enforcement officials to have trustworthy evidence that would convince a reasonable person that the proposed search or seizure is more likely justified than not. Furthermore, the Fourth Amendment prohibits general warrants. It requires a particular description of that which is to be searched or seized (see Exhibit 15.5). Once a warrant is obtained, the search cannot extend beyond what is described in the warrant. General searches through a person's belongings are impermissible.

There are exceptions to the requirement for a search warrant. For example, if an officer is arresting a person (either with an arrest warrant or sufficient probable cause) and sees drug paraphernalia "in plain view," no search warrant is required to seize that evidence. Another exception exists when it is likely that the items sought will be removed or destroyed before a warrant can be obtained.

Investigation after the Arrest

As already mentioned, when a suspect is "caught red-handed," the police may arrest the suspect without an arrest warrant and may not have to undertake much of an investigation of the alleged offense after the arrest. In other cases, however, the police must find and interview witnesses and conduct searches (of the suspect's

EXHIBIT 15.5
A Search Warrant

Ch. 89   **SEARCH AND SEIZURE**   **§ 7942**
                                                                    Rule 41

§ **7942. Search Warrant**

AO 93 (Rev. 5/85) Search Warrant @

United States District Court

_____ DISTRICT OF_____

In the Matter of the Search of
(Name, address or brief description of person or property to be searched)

                                        SEARCH WARRANT

                          CASE NUMBER:

TO: _____ and any Authorized Officer of the United States

Affidavit(s) having been made before me by_____who has reason to
                                              Affiant
believe that ☐ on the person of or ☐ on the **premises known as** (name, description and/or location)

in the _____ District of_____ there is now
concealed a certain person or property, namely (describe the person or property)

I am satisfied that the affidavit(s) and any recorded testimony establish probable cause to believe that the person
or property so described is now concealed on the person or premises above-described and establish grounds for
the issuance of this warrant.

YOU ARE HEREBY COMMANDED to search on or before _____
                                                                  Date
(not to exceed 10 days) the person or place named above for the person or property specified, serving this warrant
and making the search (in the daytime—6:00 A.M. to 10:00 P.M.) (at any time in the day or night as I find
reasonable cause has been established) and if the person or property be found there to seize same, leaving a copy
of this warrant and receipt for the person or property taken, and prepare a written inventory of the person or property seized and promptly return this warrant to _____
                                                        U.S Judge or Magistrate
as required by law.

_____   at   _____
Date and Time Issued   City and State

_____   _____
Name and Title of Judicial Officer   Signature of Judicial Officer   [G13950]

home or car, for example) to collect evidence. Witnesses may view the suspect
individually in a *lineup,* in which the suspect appears with a group of several others. In more serious cases, detectives may take charge of the investigation.

    As the police review the evidence at hand, they may conclude there is insuf-
ficient evidence to justify recommending the case for prosecution. If so, the suspect is released, and no charges are filed. This does not preclude the police from
recommending prosecution later if more evidence is obtained. Alternatively, the
police may decide to change the offense with which the suspect is being charged.
The police may also decide to release the suspect with a warning or a referral to

On the Web
You can find
summaries of
famous criminal
cases, and sometimes related
pleadings and other
documents, at the Web site
of Court TV. Go to **http://
www.courttv.com/trials.**

EXHIBIT 15.5
A Search Warrant—Continued

§ **7942**
Rule 41   **SPECIAL PROCEEDINGS**   **Ch. 89**

AO 93 (Rev. 5/85)   Search Warrant

RETURN		
DATE WARRANT RECEIVED	DATE AND TIME WARRANT EXECUTED	COPY OF WARRANT AND RECEIPT FOR ITEMS LEFT WITH

INVENTORY MADE IN THE PRESENCE OF

INVENTORY OF PERSON OR PROPERTY TAKEN PURSUANT TO THE WARRANT

CERTIFICATION

I swear that this inventory is a true and detailed account of the person or property taken by me on the warrant.

_____

Subscribed, sworn to, and returned before me this date.

_____   _____

U.S. Judge or Magistrate   Date

[G13951]

a social service agency. Unless the suspect is released, at this point in the criminal process, control over the case moves from the police to the public prosecutor.

THE PROSECUTION BEGINS

The prosecution of a criminal case begins when the police inform the public prosecutor of the alleged crime, provide the reports written by the arresting and investigating officers, and turn over evidence relating to the matter. The prosecutor may choose to investigate the case further by personally interviewing the suspect, the arresting and investigating officers, and witnesses and gathering other evidence. The prosecutor's legal assistants often participate in these tasks. Based on a review of the police file or an investigation, the prosecutor decides whether to take the case to trial or drop the case and allow the suspect to be released. Major reasons for releasing the suspect include insufficient evidence and unreliable witnesses.

The prosecutor has broad discretion. If the prosecutor decides to pursue the case, he or she also decides what charges to file against the defendant. Because prosecutions are expensive and resources are limited, most prosecutors do not go forward with a case unless they think they can prove the case in court. Typically, if the prosecutor decides to file the case, he or she will allege as many criminal offenses as could possibly be proved based on the facts. If the defendant is facing numerous charges, the likelihood is greater that the prosecutor will get a conviction on at least one of them (the chances are also greater that the defendant will plead guilty to one or more of the offenses in exchange for having the others dropped).

If the decision is made to prosecute the case, then the prosecutor must undertake the necessary procedures to formally charge the person before the court. These procedures vary depending on the court and the type of case. Often, misdemeanor charges are handled somewhat differently than felony charges. In some states, prosecutors may file complaints involving misdemeanor charges, but a grand jury indictment (which will be discussed shortly) is required for felony charges. The way a criminal case is initiated is one area of criminal procedure that varies substantially among the states. Keep this in mind as you read the following subsections.

Complaint and Initial Appearance

The criminal litigation process may begin with the filing of a *complaint* (see Exhibit 15.6 on the next page). The complaint includes a statement of the charges that are being brought against the suspect. The suspect now becomes a criminal defendant. Because the defendant is in the court system, prosecutors must show that they have legal grounds to proceed. They must show probable cause that a crime was committed and that the defendant committed the crime.

In most jurisdictions, defendants are taken before a judge or magistrate (public official) very soon after arrest. During this *initial appearance,* the judge makes sure that the person appearing is the person named in the complaint, informs the defendant of the charge or charges made in the complaint, and advises the defendant of the right to counsel and the right to remain silent. If a defendant cannot afford to hire an attorney, a public defender or member of the private bar may be appointed to represent the defendant at this time (or the defendant may be asked to fill out an application for appointed counsel).

The judge must also make a decision whether to set bail in the case or release the defendant until the next court date. **Bail** is an amount of money paid by the defendant to the court as insurance that the defendant will show up for future court appearances. If the defendant shows up as promised, the court returns the money. Courts often use standard bail schedules, which set the bail for specific kinds of cases, and may deny bail for very serious crimes. The Eighth Amendment prohibits "excessive bail," and the defendant has a right to a bail hearing to reduce the amount set by the court. If the court sets bail in an amount that the defendant is unable to pay, the defendant (or his or her attorney or paralegal) can arrange with a *bail bondsperson* to post a bail bond on the defendant's behalf. The bail bondsperson promises to pay the bail amount to the court if the defendant fails to return for further proceedings. In return, the bail bondsperson receives a payment from the defendant, usually 10 percent of the bail amount.

On the Web
A good site for information on the criminal justice system is **http://library.thinkquest.org/2760.** Here, you can follow a fictional murder case through the courts, find a glossary of terms used in criminal law, view actual forms that are filled out during the course of an arrest, and learn about some controversial issues in criminal law.

bail
The amount of money or conditions set by the court to assure that an individual accused of a crime will appear for further criminal proceedings. If the accused person provides bail, whether in cash or by means of a bail bond, then the person is released from jail.

EXHIBIT 15.6
A Complaint

United States District Court

DISTRICT OF _____

UNITED STATES OF AMERICA
V.

CRIMINAL COMPLAINT

CASE NUMBER:

(Name and Address of Defendant)

I, the undersigned complainant being duly sworn state the following is true and correct to the best of my knowledge and belief. On or about _____ in _____ county, in the _____ District of _____ defendant(s) did, (Track Statutory Language of Offense)

in violation of Title _____ United States Code, Section(s) _____.

I further state that I am a(n) _____ and that this complaint is based on the following
Official Title

facts:

Continued on the attached sheet and made a part hereof: ☐ Yes   ☐ No

_____
Signature of Complainant

Sworn to before me and subscribed in my presence,

_____   at   _____
Date   City and State

Preliminary Hearing

preliminary hearing
An initial hearing in which a judge or magistrate decides if there is probable cause to believe that the defendant committed the crime with which he or she is charged.

The defendant again appears before a magistrate or judge at a **preliminary hearing.** During this hearing, the magistrate or judge determines whether the evidence presented is sufficient to establish probable cause to believe the defendant committed the crime with which he or she is charged. This may be the first adversarial proceeding in which both sides are represented by counsel. Paralegals may become extensively involved in the process at this point by assisting in preparation for the hearing. The prosecutor may present witnesses, who may be cross-examined by defense counsel (the defense rarely presents its witnesses prior to trial). If the defendant intends to plead guilty, he or she usually waives the right to a preliminary hearing to help move things along more quickly. In many jurisdictions, however, the preliminary hearing is required in certain felony cases.

If the magistrate finds the evidence insufficient to establish probable cause, either the charge is reduced to a lesser one or charges are dropped altogether and the defendant is released. If the magistrate believes there is sufficient evidence to establish probable cause, the prosecutor issues an information. The **information** is the formal charge against the defendant and binds over the defendant for further proceedings, which usually means that the defendant is arraigned and the case proceeds to trial.

information
A formal criminal charge made by a prosecutor without a grand jury indictment.

Grand Jury Review

The federal government and about half of the states require a grand jury, and not the prosecutor, to make the decision as to whether a case should go to trial. In other words, a grand jury's indictment is an alternative to a prosecutor's information to initiate the criminal litigation process.

A **grand jury** is a group of citizens called to decide whether there is probable cause to believe that the defendant committed the crime with which he or she is charged and therefore should go to trial. Even in cases in which grand jury review is not required, the prosecutor may call a grand jury to evaluate the evidence against a suspect, which will indicate to the prosecutor the relative strength or weakness of the case.

grand jury
A group of citizens called to decide whether probable cause exists to believe that a suspect committed the crime with which he or she has been charged and should stand trial.

The grand jury sits in closed session and hears only evidence presented by the prosecutor—the defendant cannot present evidence at this hearing. Normally, the defendant and his or her attorney are not even allowed to attend grand jury proceedings—although in some cases the defendant may be required to testify. The prosecutor presents to the grand jury whatever evidence the state has against the defendant, including photographs, documents, tangible objects, test results, the testimony of witnesses, and other items. If the grand jury finds that probable cause exists, it issues an **indictment** against the defendant called a *true bill.* Over 97 percent of the cases that prosecutors bring to grand juries result in indictment. The indictment is filed with the trial court and becomes the formal charge against the defendant. An example of an indictment is shown in Exhibit 15.7 on the following page.

indictment
A charge or written accusation, issued by a grand jury, that probable cause exists to believe that a person has committed a crime for which he or she should stand trial.

Arraignment

At the **arraignment,** the defendant is informed of the charges against him or her and must respond to the charges by entering a plea. Three possible pleas can be entered: guilty, not guilty, and *nolo contendere,* which is Latin for "I will not contest it" and is often called a no-contest plea. A plea of no contest is neither an admission of guilt nor a denial of guilt—but it operates like a guilty plea in that the defendant is convicted. The primary reason for pleading no contest is so that the plea cannot later be used against the defendant in a civil trial. For example, if a defendant pleads guilty to assault, the admission of guilt can be used to impose civil liability, whereas with a no-contest plea, the plaintiff in the civil suit must prove the defendant's guilt. No-contest pleas are thus useful for the defendant who could be sued in a civil action for damages caused to a person or property.

arraignment
A court proceeding in which the suspect is formally charged with the criminal offense stated in the indictment. The suspect then enters a plea (guilty, not guilty, or *nolo contendere*) in response.

nolo contendere
Latin for "I will not contest it." A criminal defendant's plea in which he or she chooses not to challenge, or contest, the charges brought by the government. Although the defendant will still be convicted and sentenced, the plea neither admits nor denies guilt.

At the arraignment, the defendant can move to have the charges dismissed, which happens in a fair number of cases for a variety of reasons. The defendant may claim, for example, that the case should be dismissed because the statute of limitations for the crime in question has lapsed. Most frequently, however, the defendant pleads guilty to the charge or to a lesser charge that has been agreed on through **plea bargaining** between the prosecutor and the defendant. If the defendant pleads guilty, no trial is necessary, and the defendant is sentenced based on the plea. If the defendant pleads not guilty, the case is set for trial.

plea bargaining
The process by which the accused and the prosecutor in a criminal case work out a mutually satisfactory disposition of the case, subject to court approval. Usually, plea bargaining involves the defendant's pleading guilty to a lesser offense in return for a lighter sentence.

EXHIBIT 15.7
An Indictment

[*Title of Court and Cause*]

The Grand Jury charges that:

On or about _____, 20__, at _____, _____, in the _____ District of _____, _____ having been convicted of knowingly acquiring and possessing food stamp coupons in a manner not authorized by the provisions of Chapter 51, Title 7, United States Code, and the regulations issued pursuant to said chapter, a felony conviction, in the federal district court for the _____ District of _____, and sentenced on _____, 20__, did knowingly possess a firearm that had been transported in and affecting commerce, to wit: an OMC Pistol, Back Up 380 Caliber, serial number _____; all in violation of Section 1202(a)(1) of Title 18, United States Code, Appendix.

A True Bill

_____,
Foreperson.

_____,
United States Attorney.

Pretrial Motions

Defense attorneys and their paralegals will search for and be alert to any violation of the defendant's constitutional rights. Many pretrial motions are based on possible violations of the defendant's rights as provided by the Constitution and criminal procedural law. We discuss here a few of the most common motions filed in a criminal case. Note, however, that the specific requirements for pretrial motions vary depending on the jurisdiction. Not every jurisdiction allows every type of pretrial motion, and the standards used by judges to evaluate such motions may differ as well. Also keep in mind that a motion is generally accompanied by a separate pleading that sets forth the legal argument in support of the motion; this pleading may be called a memorandum of law, a brief, or supporting points and authorities.[17] Affidavits may also be attached.

motion to suppress evidence
A motion requesting that certain evidence be excluded from consideration during the trial.

MOTIONS TO SUPPRESS.   One of the most common and effective motions made by defense attorneys (and often drafted by paralegals) is the **motion to suppress evidence.** A motion to suppress asserts that the evidence against the defendant was illegally obtained and should be excluded (inadmissible). Typically, this motion is filed when the officer performs a search without probable cause, seizes evidence, and then arrests the defendant based on that evidence. For example, suppose an officer stops the defendant's vehicle because his taillight is out and then proceeds to search through the contents of the defendant's trunk, finding illegal narcotics. The defendant is subsequently charged with possession. A motion to suppress would be appropriate here (and probably successful) because the officer did not have probable cause to search the trunk in carrying out a traffic stop.

The defense attorney normally prepares the motion and submits a memorandum of law (legal argument) with the motion. Exhibit 15.8 starting on page 552 shows a sample memorandum. Often, the attorney will request the court to allow

ETHICAL CONCERN
The Ethics of Plea Bargaining

Paralegals who work on criminal cases may be ethically troubled by plea bargaining. In such situations, it may be helpful to view the issues in the larger context of the American justice system and American society. American courts are overburdened with cases, and it is in the public interest to reduce their case loads. American jails and prisons are overcrowded, and reducing prison sentences is one way to deal with this issue. In the larger context, then, the ethical issue is whether you believe that it is fair to balance society's interest in obtaining strict justice against society's interest in lowering the social costs (more prisons, more courts, more judges, and so on) of that justice. Also, and more directly to the point, your job as a paralegal is to serve the client's best interests—and it may be in the client's best interests to plea bargain. In such a situation, you will need to set your personal feelings aside.

oral argument on the motion, although in some jurisdictions it is automatic. The court will then conduct a hearing on the motion. The attorneys for both sides may call witnesses (police officers and others who were present) to testify, and the judge will make a ruling. If the judge agrees that the evidence should be excluded and grants the motion, the defendant may be able to avoid trial. This is because frequently, without the evidence, the prosecution will not be able to prove its case against the defendant and will thus drop the charges.

MOTIONS TO DISMISS.   A motion can be filed to dismiss all of the charges or only some of the charges pending against the defendant (if multiple offenses are alleged). There are many grounds for filing a motion to dismiss. Motions to dismiss in criminal cases often assert that the defendant's constitutional rights—or criminal procedures stemming from the Constitution—have been violated. For example, the defense might argue that the prosecution has waited too long to prosecute the case in violation of the defendant's Sixth Amendment right to a speedy and public trial (sometimes called a *speedy trial motion*). The defense will file the motion along with a supporting memorandum, which may argue that the defendant has been prejudiced by the delay, that witnesses are no longer available, and that a fair trial cannot be had. If the judge grants the motion, the case is dismissed.

Because it may eliminate charges against a client without subjecting the client to the risks of a jury trial, the motion to dismiss is one of the most useful motions for the defense to file. A paralegal who becomes skilled at writing persuasive motions to dismiss will thus be a valuable asset to the defense team.

OTHER COMMON MOTIONS.   Just as in civil cases, attorneys in criminal cases often file motions *in limine* (discussed in Chapter 14) to keep certain evidence out of the trial. For example, a defense attorney whose client has prior criminal convictions may file a motion *in limine* requesting the court to prevent any evidence of these convictions from being offered by the prosecution. The prosecutor may also file such motions to keep possibly prejudicial evidence from being admitted (concerning a victim's reputation, for example).

EXHIBIT 15.8
Memorandum in Support of Motion to Suppress

[Attorney for Defendant]

SUPERIOR COURT OF THE STATE OF NITA
FOR THE COUNTY OF NITA

THE PEOPLE OF THE STATE OF NITA,	)	Case No.: C45778
Plaintiff,	)	D.A. No.: A39996
	)	
	)	**MEMORANDUM OF LAW IN SUPPORT**
v.	)	**OF MOTION TO SUPPRESS**
	)	
	)	DATE: 10-27-03
Eduardo Jose Mendez,	)	TIME: 1:15
Defendant.	)	Estimated Time: 45 min.
	)	No. of Witnesses: 1

Defendant, Eduardo Jose Mendez, by and through his attorney the Public Defender of the County of Nita, respectfully submits the following memorandum of law in support of his motion to Suppress.

STATEMENT OF FACTS

On or about September 23, 2003, at approximately 02:15, Officer Ramirez observed Mr. Mendez riding his bicycle in the area of 1300 Elm St. and 500 C St. It was drizzling, and few people walked the streets. Officer Ramirez indicated that the area is known for narcotic activity and that he believed Mr. Mendez had or was about to participate in narcotic activity.

Mr. Mendez was on his bicycle at the corner of Elm and C St. when Officer Ramirez approached him. He indicated that Mr. Mendez appeared to be nervous and was sweating profusely. He asked Mr. Mendez what he was doing, and Mr. Mendez responded that he was waiting for his girlfriend. Officer Ramirez conducted a pat-down search for weapons. He felt several hard objects inside Mr. Mendez's pants pockets and asked Mr. Mendez if he had a knife in his pocket. Mr. Mendez consented to a search of his pockets, and Officer Ramirez found only a wooden pencil.

Without asking for permission, and without notice, Officer Ramirez reached for and grabbed Mr. Mendez's baseball cap. The officer took the cap off of Mr. Mendez's head. He felt the outside of the cap and with his fingers manipulated a small soft lump in Mr. Mendez's cap. He went through the cap and moved the side material of the cap. He found a small plastic package burnt on one end. He opened the package. Officer Ramirez found a small amount of an off-white powder substance inside the package.

ARGUMENT

I. MR. MENDEZ'S FOURTH AMENDMENT RIGHT TO PRIVACY WAS VIOLATED BECAUSE THE OFFICER'S DETENTION OF MR. MENDEZ WAS NOT JUSTIFIED BY REASONABLE SUSPICION

A person has been seized within the meaning of the Fourth Amendment if, in view of all the circumstances surrounding the incident, a reasonable person would have believed that he was not free to leave. *United States v. Mendenhall*, 446 U.S. 544, 554 (1980). Here, Officer Ramirez seized Mr. Mendez when he stopped to question him. Mr. Mendez submitted to Officer Ramirez's show of authority when he responded to the questioning. Mr. Mendez's belief that he was not free to leave is evidenced by his actions during the seizure. He appeared nervous and kept looking around in all directions as if looking for someone to help him. A reasonable person such as Mr. Mendez, in view of all of the circumstances, would have believed and in fact did believe he was not free to leave. Therefore, the officer's initial stop was a seizure.

* * * *

EXHIBIT 15.8
Memorandum in Support of Motion to Suppress—Continued

Officer Ramirez did not have reasonable suspicion to stop Mr. Mendez. He fails to point to specific facts causing him to suspect criminal activity was afoot. Officer Ramirez notes in his police report that he "felt" that defendant "had been participating or was about to participate in narcotic activity." The officer also indicated that he believed the area was known for narcotic activity. However, "Persons may not be subjected to invasions of privacy merely because they are in or are passing through a high crime area." *McCally-Bey v. Kirner*, 24 F.Supp.3d 389 (N.D. Nita 2002).

These observations taken as a whole and Officer Ramirez's explanation do not rise to the requisite level of reasonable suspicion necessary to invade the privacy of a citizen.

II. OFFICER RAMIREZ'S PAT-DOWN SEARCH EXCEEDED ITS SCOPE WHEN HE SEARCHED THE BASEBALL CAP AND MANIPULATED ITS CONTENTS

Under the *Terry* doctrine, a search is referred to as a "frisk." *Terry v. Ohio* 392 U.S. 1 (1968). A frisk is justified only if the officer reasonably believes that the person is armed and dangerous. A frisk is a pat-down of a person's outer clothing. It is limited in scope to its purpose, which is to search for weapons. Even slightly lingering over a package because it feels like it contains drugs exceeds the scope of the search. *Minnesota v. Dickerson* 508 U.S. 366 (1993). An officer cannot manipulate a package or a substance that is clearly not a weapon through an individual's clothing during a *Terry* pat-down search.
* * * *

III. OFFICER RAMIREZ DID NOT HAVE PROBABLE CAUSE TO CONDUCT A WARRANTLESS SEARCH OF MR. MENDEZ
* * * *

IV. ALL EVIDENCE OBTAINED AS A RESULT OF AN UNLAWFUL DETENTION MUST BE SUPPRESSED AS TAINTED EVIDENCE; FRUIT OF THE POISONOUS TREE
* * * *
* * * *

As discussed above, the detention of Mr. Mendez did not meet constitutionally established standards of reasonableness. Hence, all evidence obtained as a result of such unlawful detention is inadmissible. In addition, all evidence seized as a result of the arrest that followed from his unlawful detention is inadmissible as fruit of the poisonous tree.
* * * *

For the above-mentioned reasons, all evidence obtained as a result of Mr. Mendez's detention, illegal search, and subsequent arrest in this case must be suppressed.

Dated:

Respectfully submitted,

_____
Attorney for Defendant

DEVELOPING PARALEGAL SKILLS
Discovery in the Criminal Case

The law firm of McCoy & Warner is defending Taylor Rogers in a case of attempted murder. Rogers allegedly shot a person in a drive-by shooting on the expressway. Lee Soloman, a paralegal, is working on the case. Today, as the result of a discovery motion that his supervising attorney won in court, Lee has received copies of all of the evidence that the prosecuting attorney has in his file. Lee's job is to create the discovery file and then to work with the material in the file to prepare the case.

- Review the evidence and prepare a memo summarizing it.
- Review the memo and/or evidence with your supervising attorney.
- If the supervising attorney agrees, contact witnesses and obtain statements.
- Interview the police officers who were involved in the arrest or who were at the crime scene.

TIPS FOR CRIMINAL DISCOVERY

- Create a discovery file containing sections for the defendant's statements, witnesses' statements, police reports, tests, and other evidence.

motion for a change of venue
A motion requesting that a trial be moved to a different location to ensure a fair and impartial proceeding, for the convenience of the parties, or for some other acceptable reason.

motion to recuse
A motion to remove a particular judge from a case.

motion to sever
A motion to try multiple defendants separately.

Sometimes—when there is a good deal of pretrial publicity, for instance—the defense may make a **motion for a change of venue** asking the court to relocate the trial. Other times, the defense may file a **motion to recuse** asking the trial judge to remove himself or herself from the case. Such a motion usually is filed only when the judge has publicly displayed some bias or personally knows the parties or witnesses in the case. If the motion is granted, a different judge will hear the defendant's case. When a case involves more than one defendant, the defense counsel may file a **motion to sever** (separate) the cases for purposes of trial.

Various other motions—including motions to reduce the charges against the defendant, to obtain evidence during discovery, or to extend the trial date—may also be made prior to the trial. As with motions made during the civil litigation process, each motion must be accompanied by supporting affidavits and/or legal memoranda.

Discovery

In preparing for trial, public prosecutors, defense attorneys, and paralegals engage in discovery proceedings (including depositions and interrogatories), interview and subpoena witnesses, prepare exhibits and a trial notebook, examine relevant documents and evidence, and do other tasks necessary to most effectively prosecute or defend the defendant. Although similar to civil litigation in these respects, criminal discovery is generally more limited, and the time constraints relating to discovery are different in criminal cases.

During discovery, defendants are generally entitled to obtain *any* evidence in the possession of the prosecutor relating to the case, including statements previously made by the defendant, objects, documents, and reports of tests and examinations. The prosecutor must hand over evidence that tends to show the defendant's innocence as well as evidence of the defendant's guilt. Defendants are given this right to

---

ETHICAL CONCERN
Preparing Exhibits for Trial

I n preparing exhibits for trial, especially when creating an exhibit from raw data, it is important that the paralegal ensure that the exhibit is accurate and not misleading. An attorney has a duty not to falsify evidence, and if erroneous evidence is introduced in court and challenged by opposing counsel, your supervising attorney may face serious consequences. By preparing an inaccurate exhibit (for example, by miscalculating a column of figures), the paralegal may jeopardize the attorney's professional reputation by causing the attorney to breach a professional duty.

---

offset the fact that the prosecution (the state) has more resources at its disposal than the defendant (an individual citizen).

THE TRIAL

Only a small fraction of the criminal cases brought by the state actually go to trial. Some defendants are released, or the charges against them are dropped. Most defendants plead guilty to the offense or to a lesser offense prior to trial. Plea bargaining occurs at every stage of criminal proceedings, from the arraignment to the date of trial (even during a trial, defendants can accept a plea bargain). Because a trial is expensive and the outcome uncertain, both sides in criminal cases have an incentive to negotiate a plea and thus avoid the trial—just as both sides in a civil dispute are motivated to reach a settlement.

Although some criminal trials go on for weeks and are highly publicized, most criminal trials last less than one week (often only a few days). The trial itself is conducted in much the same way as a civil trial. The prosecutor and the defense attorney make their opening statements, examine and cross-examine witnesses, and summarize their positions in closing arguments. The jury is instructed and sent to deliberate. When the jury renders a verdict, the trial comes to an end. There are, however, a few major procedural differences between criminal trials and civil trials, including those discussed below.

The Presumption of Innocence

In criminal trials, the defendant is innocent until proven guilty. The prosecutor bears the burden of proving the defendant is guilty of the offenses with which he or she is charged. The defendant does not have to prove that he or she did not commit the offenses. In fact, the defendant is not required to present any evidence whatsoever to counter the state's accusations (although clearly it might be in the defendant's best interests to put on a defense). Even if a defendant actually committed the crime, he or she will be innocent in the eyes of the law unless the prosecutor can substantiate the charges with sufficient evidence to convince the jury or judge of the defendant's guilt.

Not only does the state bear the burden of proving the defendant guilty, but it also is held to a very high standard of proof. Remember that in criminal cases the prosecution must prove its case *beyond a reasonable doubt*. It is not enough for the jury (or judge) to think that the defendant is probably guilty; the members of the jury must be firmly convinced of the defendant's guilt. The jurors receive instructions such as, "If you think there is a real possibility that he [or she] is not guilty, you *must* give him [or her] the benefit of the doubt and find him [or her] not guilty." The presumption of innocence and the high burden of proof are designed to protect the individual from the state.

The Privilege against Self-Incrimination

As already mentioned, the Fifth Amendment to the U.S. Constitution states that no person can be forced to give testimony that might be self-incriminating. Therefore, a defendant does not have to testify at trial. Witnesses may also refuse to testify on this ground. For example, if a witness, while testifying, is asked a question and answering the question would reveal his or her own criminal wrongdoing, the witness may "take the Fifth" and refuse to testify on the ground that the testimony may incriminate him or her.

The Right to a Speedy Trial

The Sixth Amendment requires a speedy and public trial for criminal prosecutions but does not specify what is meant by "speedy." Courts interpret whether a defendant's right to a speedy trial has been violated on a case-by-case basis. (Usually, the issue is raised in pretrial motions, as discussed earlier.) Generally, however, criminal cases are brought to trial much quicker than civil cases. A defendant who remains in custody prior to trial, for example, will often be tried within thirty to forty-five days from the date of arraignment. If the defendant (or the defendant's attorney) needs more time to prepare a defense, the defendant may give up the right to be tried within a certain number of days but will still go to trial within a relatively short period of time (a few months, typically).

The Requirement for a Unanimous Verdict

Of the criminal cases that go to trial, the majority are tried by a jury. In most jurisdictions, jury verdicts in criminal cases must be *unanimous* for **acquittal** or conviction. In other words, all twelve jurors (or all six jurors, if the state allows six-person juries) must agree that the defendant is either guilty or not guilty. If the jury cannot reach unanimous agreement on whether to acquit or convict the defendant, the result is a **hung jury.** When the jury is hung, the defendant may be tried again (although often the case is not retried). The requirement for unanimity is important because if even one juror is not convinced of the defendant's guilt, the defendant will not be convicted. Thus, the prosecuting attorney must make as strong a case as possible, while the defense attorney can aim at persuading one or more jurors to have doubts. (Trial graphics can be effective in persuading a jury, as this chapter's *Technology and Today's Paralegal* feature explains.)

Sentencing

When a defendant is found guilty by a trial court (or pleads guilty to an offense without a trial), the judge will pronounce a **sentence**, which is the penalty imposed on anyone convicted of a crime. Often, the sentence is pronounced in a separate proceeding at a later date.

Unless the prosecutor is seeking the death penalty, the jury is not normally involved in the sentencing of the defendant. Jurors are dismissed after they return a verdict, and the judge either sentences the defendant on the spot or schedules a future court appearance for sentencing. At the sentencing hearing,

acquittal
A certification or declaration following a trial that the individual accused of a crime is innocent, or free from guilt, in the eyes of the law and is thus absolved of the charges.

hung jury
A jury whose members are so irreconcilably divided in their opinions that they cannot reach a verdict. The judge in this situation may order a new trial.

sentence
The punishment, or penalty, ordered by the court to be inflicted on a person convicted of a crime.

Trial Graphics

Effective trial graphics can mean the difference between winning and losing a case in criminal as well as in civil litigation (see the feature on courtroom technology in Chapter 14). This is particularly true in cases that involve complex fact patterns, scientific evidence, or testimony from numerous or conflicting experts. Using presentation graphics simplifies complex evidence and makes it more understandable to the jury.

TYPES OF GRAPHIC PRESENTATIONS

Trial graphics are classified into three main types: fact graphics, concept graphics, and case graphics. Fact graphics show only the facts on which both parties agree. For example, time lines that indicate the order in which events occurred, if uncontested, are fact graphics.

Concept graphics are used to educate the judge and jury about ideas with which they are not familiar. Usually, concept graphics are supported by expert testimony about the particular topic. For example, charts outlining the general procedures involved in DNA fingerprinting would be concept graphics (provided there is no reference to the facts of the particular case).

Case, or analytical, graphics illustrate the basis of the defense or allegation. They include facts that are in dispute, as well as inferences that can be drawn from the facts. A flow chart showing how certain facts are related and how they lead to a specific conclusion is an example. Case graphics, while very effective, tend to be argumentative and are often challenged by the other side as being unfair or misleading. In some courtrooms, the use of case graphics may be restricted to closing arguments.

NO NEED TO BE HIGH TECH

Graphics do not have to be technologically sophisticated or expensive to be effective. The important factor is that the graphics chosen be appropriate and well used. As mentioned in Chapter 14, there are many different ways to create graphic presentations, including digital records and video, special presentation software, and outside vendors. The method used will depend on the size of the courtroom, the resources available, and the effectiveness of one method over another in highlighting the desired evidence. Cost is always a factor, particularly in criminal trials, in which the client (a defendant) may not have the same monetary resources as a company involved in civil litigation. That does not mean that graphic presentations are to be avoided in criminal trials, however. Most people, if facing criminal conviction and a possible jail sentence, will consider the expense of the presentations money well spent if the graphics may help convince the jury to acquit.

LESS IS OFTEN MORE

If you are preparing a presentation, remember that a good graphic presentation should be simple and straightforward. Trim excess words and punctuation from charts, lists, and diagrams. Using incomplete sentences and simple phrases is acceptable when you are presenting the information in graphic form. Use boldface text and easy-to-read fonts. Keep plenty of "white space" in your graphic displays. Know what you want the reader to focus on, and eliminate all distractions. Remember that it is your job to make it easy for the jury to see, read, and understand your points. Don't overburden the graphic displays with too much information or detail, and don't use so many graphics that the jury stops paying attention. Pick and choose wisely. The main purpose of trial graphics is to focus attention on the points you want to emphasize or highlight, not to focus attention on the actual presentation or display.

TECHNOLOGY TIP

Because graphic presentations are powerful tools, paralegals involved in criminal trial work should always consider whether graphics might be helpful to the judge's or jury's understanding of a case. Plan ahead—do not wait until the last minutes before trial to think about your graphic presentations. You can create graphics overnight (or have them created), but the most effective graphics take time to create. Make a file folder of possibilities early on in trial preparation so that you can develop and refine your graphic displays over time.

ETHICAL CONCERN

The Benefits of Good Record Keeping

One of your jobs as a paralegal is to make sure that witnesses are in court at the proper time. This job relates to the attorney's duty of competence, which, if breached, could expose the attorney to potential liability for malpractice. For all your efforts, however, a key witness fails to appear in court. Your supervising attorney is understandably upset about this and asks you how it could have happened. You show the attorney the memorandum of your interview with the client, in which you noted that the witness was willing to testify; the receipt from the certified letter that you sent to the witness, which contained the subpoena, indicating that the witness had received it; and a telephone memo of a call that you made to the witness a week prior to the trial in which the witness agreed to be in court on the date of the trial. Although your documentation is not a cure for the problem presented by the missing witness, it does provide evidence—should it be necessary—that neither you nor the attorney was negligent.

the judge usually listens to arguments from both attorneys concerning the factors in "aggravation and mitigation" (which involve why the defendant's punishment should be harsh or lenient).

Most criminal statutes set forth a maximum and minimum penalty that should be imposed for a violation. Thus, judges often have a range of options and a great deal of discretion in sentencing individual defendants. The judge typically sentences the offender to one or more of the following:

- Incarceration in a jail or a prison.
- Probation (formal or informal).
- Fines or other financial penalties.
- Public work service (for less serious offenders).
- Classes (for certain types of offenses, such as domestic violence and alcohol- or drug-related crimes).
- Death (in some states).

INCARCERATION.   Defendants sentenced to incarceration will go to a county jail for less serious offenses (involving sentences of less than one year) or a state prison for serious crimes (involving sentences of more than one year). In some cases, the judge may consider alternatives to jail time. A defendant may be placed on house arrest (and in many jurisdictions wear an electronic device around her or his ankle that will notify the authorities if she or he leaves a designated area). A defendant who has an alcohol or drug problem may sometimes be allowed to satisfy the incarceration portion of a sentence in an inpatient rehabilitation program. In some states, a defendant may be allowed to satisfy short periods of custody time (ten to thirty days) by checking in to the jail on weekends only or by participating in a supervised release program, which enables the defendant to stay employed.

PROBATION.   A standard part of almost every sentence (in both felony and misdemeanor cases) is probation. Typically, a person will be sentenced to substantially less than the maximum penalty and placed on probation with certain conditions for at least two or three years (depending on the maximum allowed by statute). If

On the Web
The U.S. Sentencing Guidelines can be found online at **http://www.ussc.gov**.

the person fails to meet the conditions of her or his probation, probation may be revoked, and the person may be sentenced to custody time up to the maximum for the offense.

For example, if convicted of driving while under the influence, a defendant might be sentenced to two days in custody, three years of informal probation, a fine of $3,000, ten days of public work service (picking up roadside trash), and a first-offenders program (meeting twice a week for six to eight weeks and costing several thousand dollars). If the defendant does not do all of the things he or she has been sentenced to do, the court can revoke probation and sentence the person to spend up to a year in jail.

Probation can be either formal or informal. In formal probation, which is typical in felony cases, the defendant is required to meet regularly with a probation officer, who monitors his or her progress. The defendant may be required to submit to drug and alcohol testing, to possess no firearms, and to avoid socializing with those who might be engaging in criminal activity, for example. Defendants on informal probation do not have a probation officer, but they also may be required to comply with certain conditions, such as paying the fine, performing public work service, participating in specified programs (such as attending Alcoholics Anonymous meetings or anger management classes), and not violating the law.

Diversion

In many states, **diversion programs** are available to defendants charged with certain types of offenses specified by statute. Diversion is an alternative to prosecution. Diversion programs vary. Basically, however, these programs suspend criminal prosecution for a certain period of time and require that the defendant complete specified conditions—such as attending special classes and not having contact with the police—during that time. If the person fulfills *all* of the requirements of diversion, the case will be dismissed. If the defendant fails to complete the diversion satisfactorily, the criminal prosecution springs back to life, and the defendant is prosecuted for the crime. The objective is to deter the defendant from further wrongdoing by offering an incentive—namely, a way to avoid any record of conviction. In essence, diversion is similar to a sentencing without a conviction.

A defendant who is charged with a first offense of driving under the influence, for example, may qualify for diversion on the charge (eligibility requirements vary among states). The defendant might be required to (1) attend an eight-month-long course educating him or her on the dangers of drunk driving, (2) pay for that course, (3) pay a certain sum of money to a victims' restitution fund, and (4) not have any contact with the police for a period of two years. If the defendant complies with all of the conditions, then after two years, the case will be dismissed. If the person completes only seven of the eight months required by the course, or is charged with another crime six months later, he or she will fail to complete the diversion successfully, and the charges against him or her will be reinstated immediately (or as soon as the court or prosecutor discovers the failure).

Diversion is a good option for the defendant who is guilty of the crime alleged and wants to avoid having a criminal conviction on her or his record. Most of the time, defendants who are eligible for diversion choose that option at the arraignment or soon after and thus do not proceed to trial. On occasion, however, judges may allow a person to divert even after a trial.

Appeal

Persons convicted of crimes have a right of appeal. (The prosecution may appeal certain types of decisions, but it may not appeal a verdict of not-guilty.) Most

diversion program
In some jurisdictions, an alternative to prosecution that is offered to certain felony suspects to deter them from future unlawful acts.

 On the Web
For an example of an appeal petition in an actual criminal case, go to **http://www.courttv.com/ trials/woodward/ appeal.html**.

TODAY'S PROFESSIONAL PARALEGAL

Working for the District Court

Amanda Bowin is a legal assistant who is assigned to work for six of the twelve judges who serve on the district court. Today is "criminal call," and she is in the courtroom observing an arraignment. She has in front of her a docket sheet for the defendant. She listens while the judge explains the criminal charges. The defendant pleads not guilty, and the date for the pretrial hearing is set. (If the defendant had pled guilty, then a sentencing date and probation interview would have been scheduled.) Amanda notes the plea and the pretrial hearing date on the docket sheet. She then observes five more arraignments and notes the defendants' pleas on their respective docket sheets.

"SHOW CAUSE" MOTIONS

Several attorneys enter the courtroom. They are present for "show cause" motions. A "show cause" motion is made when a defendant has violated the terms of his or her probation or sentence. The first motion is made by an assistant prosecutor against a defendant who was stopped on the highway for speeding and was found to be carrying a handgun. The judge evaluates the evidence and gives the defendant the option of either pleading guilty to the violation of probation or going to trial on the issue. The defendant chooses to plead guilty and is sentenced by the judge. Amanda notes all of the information on her docket sheet for this case. She listens to the remaining "show cause" motions and makes notes on the pleas and sentences.

SENTENCING HEARINGS

Next, the sentencing hearings begin. Amanda listens and notes the sentences on the relevant docket sheets. The last item up this morning is the sentencing of a woman who has been convicted for criminal neglect—she abandoned her two-year-old child at a gas station. The child has been placed in a foster home. The defense attorney is allowed to call a witness to testify as to the defendant's character and how well she cared for her daughter. This is an attempt to convince the judge to impose the lightest possible sentence allowable for this crime.

The attorney calls a social worker to the stand. The social worker testifies that the defendant-mother had pre-viously had a drug problem for which she had sought treatment. There had been no place for her to go for treatment where she could take her baby, and she had no one with whom she could leave her baby. For those reasons, she had opted for an outpatient program, a less effective form of treatment. She had tried hard to fight her addiction to "crack" cocaine and had been doing well, but sometimes it takes more than one attempt at treatment to succeed. The social worker continues by telling the court that unfortunately, the defendant-mother had strayed from her treatment and was under the influence of cocaine at the time that her friend talked her into abandoning her child.

The mother is very remorseful and regrets her actions. She truly loves her daughter and does not want to lose custody of her permanently. If the judge gives her a long jail sentence, she is afraid that she will ultimately lose custody of her child. After this testimony, the social worker steps down from the stand.

The judge considers the testimony. He knows that if he puts the defendant-mother in jail, she will not receive the treatment that she needs. This will not help either the defendant or her daughter. He sentences her to one year of drug rehabilitation in a live-in facility. This means that her child will remain in foster care for that time. The decision regarding her daughter's custody after that time will be left up to the agency that placed the daughter in the foster home. If the mother's treatment is successful, the agency might consider returning the child to the mother's custody. The defendant is to appear before the court every three months and give a progress report.

CRIMINAL CALL ENDS

Amanda notes this sentence on her docket sheet. She leaves the courtroom now that the criminal call is over. She takes the files containing the docket sheets and her notes for the cases to the Records Department. There the information will be entered into the county's computer system to update the status of these cases.

2. Janice Henley is a legal assistant to a criminal defense attorney. They are defending a notorious drug dealer who was arrested in a huge drug bust. The drug bust was videotaped by the agents of the Drug Enforcement Administration who carried it out. The videotape is their best evidence against the client.

   In the hall outside the courtroom, Janice observes the girlfriend of the defendant approach the federal prosecutor and talk to him. He happens to be holding the videotape, along with some papers, in his hand. The girlfriend pulls what appears to be a large magnet from her oversized purse and leans toward the videotape. If the magnet makes contact with the tape, it will erase it. What should Janice do?

3. Larry Dow works as a paralegal for the criminal defense firm of Rice & Rowen. He and his boss have just met with Joe Dollan, an attorney from another well-known law firm. Joe has been arrested for embezzling funds from an estate he was managing for a client and needs a criminal defense attorney to handle the case. Embezzlement is a felony, and if convicted, Joe will lose his license to practice law. Larry knows that a good friend of his recently retained Joe to handle the estate of her uncle. Should Larry tell his friend that Joe has been charged with embezzlement? Is there anything that Larry can do to help his friend?

4. Melinda Johns works as a legal assistant for the county prosecutor. She is working with Ms. Roberts, the victim of a robbery. They are preparing for trial. The prosecutor gives Ms. Roberts several options for proving the case and tells her to think about it overnight. The next morning, Ms. Roberts, still undecided, asks Melinda which strategy she should pursue. How should Melinda answer Ms. Roberts's question?

Practice Questions and Assignments

1. Using the material presented in the chapter, identify each of the following crimes by its classification:
   a. Jerry refuses to mow his lawn, and it grows to a height of seven inches. The local police department receives complaints from his neighbors and gives Jerry a citation for violating the local lawn-height ordinance.
   b. Nancy is arrested for being drunk in public. She faces a possible jail sentence of six months in prison.
   c. Susan is arrested for arson. The penalty includes confinement for over one year in prison on conviction.
2. The following situations are similar (all involve the theft of Makoto's television set), yet they represent three different crimes. Using the material presented in the chapter, identify which crime has been committed, noting the differences among them.
   a. While passing Makoto's house one night, Sarah sees a portable television set left unattended on Makoto's lawn. Sarah takes the television set, carries it home, and tells everyone she owns it.
   b. While passing Makoto's house one night, Sarah sees Makoto outside with a portable television set. Holding Makoto at gunpoint, Sarah forces him to give up the set. Then Sarah runs away with it.
   c. While passing Makoto's house one night, Sarah sees a portable television set in a window. Sarah breaks the front-door lock, enters, and leaves with the set.
3. Review the material presented in the chapter on types of crimes. Which, if any, of the following crimes necessarily involve illegal activity on the part of more than one person?
   a. Bribery.
   b. Forgery.
   c. Embezzlement.
   d. Larceny.
   e. Receiving stolen property.
4. Rafael stops Laura on a busy street and offers to sell her an expensive wristwatch for a fraction of its value. After some questioning by Laura, Rafael admits that the watch is stolen property, although he says he was not the thief. Laura pays for and receives the wristwatch. Has Laura committed any crime? Has Rafael? Explain.
5. Review the material presented in this chapter on the *Miranda* rights. Summarize these rights. Now review Appendix J, which includes the Bill of Rights. From which amendment(s) are the *Miranda* rights derived?
6. Review the material presented in the chapter on the major procedural steps in a criminal case. Prepare a one-page summary of these steps. Identify the steps that involve constitutional rights and the amendments on which these rights are based.
7. A suspect is arrested, taken into custody, and

interrogated at the police station. The police are determined to get him to confess to a murder. They confront him with an accomplice who accuses him of having committed the murder. The accused denies the allegation and says, "I didn't do it, you did." The police then take him, handcuffed, into an interrogation room and question him for hours until he confesses. He is never told that he has the right to remain silent or to consult an attorney. Additionally, they refuse him the right to talk to his attorney when he requests to do so during the interrogation, and they refuse to allow his retained attorney to speak with him when his attorney arrives at the police station.

Using the material presented in the chapter, analyze the facts of this situation, and explain what rights the accused should have been accorded and why.

8. Using the material presented in the chapter on state of mind, identify the type of homicide committed in each of the following situations:

   a. David, while driving in an intoxicated state, crashes into another car and kills its occupants.

   b. David, after pulling up next to his wife at a stoplight and observing her passionately kissing another man, smashes into her car and kills her.

   c. David, who is angry with his boss for firing him, plans to kill his boss by smashing his car into his boss's car, killing his boss and making it look like a car accident. David carries out his plan, kills his boss, and survives the accident.

9. Using the material presented in the chapter, discuss the following defenses:

   a. Mary is waiting for a bus at a dimly lit bus stop at 6:30 A.M. A man approaches her from behind and pulls out a gun. He puts the gun to her head and starts laughing, telling her that there is one bullet in the barrel and that he is going to pull the trigger until it goes off. Mary pulls a gun out of her pocket, puts her hand behind her back, and shoots her assailant in the stomach, killing him.

   b. Jennifer and Kathy are walking on a crowded downtown street. Suddenly, from behind, someone grabs Jennifer's purse. Kathy pulls a gun out of

her pocket and shoots and kills the purse-snatcher.

   c. Joan is lying in bed at night, drifting off to sleep, when her bedroom window breaks. A man dressed in black with a stocking over his head jumps through it and attacks her. Joan, aware that a serial rapist has attacked several of her neighbors, pulls out a gun from under her mattress and shoots and kills her assailant.

   d. Jan arrives home from grocery shopping on a Tuesday morning at 10:00 A.M. and enters her house through the kitchen door. She hears a noise upstairs and goes to investigate. She finds a burglar loading her jewelry into a small felt bag. Jan pulls out a handgun and shoots and kills the burglar.

10. Using the material presented in the chapter, identify the following criminal procedures:

   a. Tom is charged with the crime of arson. He pleads not guilty and is bound over for trial in the district court.

   b. Ned is taken to the police station, searched, photographed, fingerprinted, and allowed to make one telephone call.

   c. A jury of Barbara's peers reviews the evidence against her and determines whether probable cause exists and whether the prosecutor should proceed to trial for manslaughter.

   d. Police officers stop Larry on the street because his description matches that of a reported gas-station robber. He is three blocks from the gas station when they stop him. They question him, search him, and find that he has a pocketful of $20 and $50 dollar bills—the same denominations that were reported by the gas-station attendant as having been stolen. The police read Larry his rights and take him into the station.

   e. Larry is taken before a magistrate, where the charges against him are read and counsel is appointed. His request to be set free on bail is denied.

   f. In exchange for a guilty plea to manslaughter, the prosecutor agrees to drop the more serious murder charges against Mary.

✳ QUESTIONS FOR CRITICAL ANALYSIS

1. Crimes are classified into two major categories: felonies and misdemeanors (including petty offenses). What is the difference between these classifications? What does the difference indicate about the reasons for such classifications?

2. When is a crime a federal crime? Why is there a difference between state and federal crimes? Should there be?
3. A guilty act is typically required in order for a crime to be committed. Is it ever possible for a crime to be committed without a guilty act? If so, how? Give an example of such a crime.
4. What role does the mental state of an accused play in the definition of a crime? How does the degree of wrongfulness affect the crime? What would be the result if intent were not considered? Would this be a fair outcome for the accused? For society?
5. Should cyber crimes include the elements of traditional crimes (*actus reas* and *mens rea*)? Why or why not? Do you think the punishment for crimes committed in cyberspace should be more severe than the punishment for traditional crimes? Why or why not?
6. Should people who are insane be convicted of crimes? If so, should they be convicted of all crimes or only certain types of crimes? What should the test be for determining if someone is insane? Should insane persons who are convicted of crimes be placed in a mental institution instead of a prison?
7. The statute of limitations is a defense to some crimes. Should it be allowed as a defense to all crimes? What about the crime of murder?
8. Why do you think so many procedural safeguards were included in the Constitution for the protection of criminal defendants?
9. Look at the U.S. Constitution in Appendix J. Is there anything in the Bill of Rights that requires the police to give criminal suspects the *Miranda* warnings upon arrest?
10. The United States Supreme Court has made numerous exceptions to the *Miranda* rule. Additionally, juries are permitted to accept confessions without being convinced that they were voluntarily made. What does this say about the way in which the rule has been applied? What does it say about the way in which criminals' rights are enforced by the courts in general?
11. How is *probable cause* defined? What might be the historical reasons for this requirement?
12. Make a list of the differences between the requirements for a civil trial and for a criminal trial. What is the reason for these differences?
13. On conviction in federal court, the defendant is sentenced by a judge who applies the federal sentencing guidelines. These guidelines provide a range of penalties from which the judge may choose. Should the judge be able to choose a sentence, or should sentences be mandatory? Should the defendant be given the opportunity to present evidence to minimize his or her sentence?
14. Timothy McVeigh was sentenced to death for the bombing of a federal building in Oklahoma City, Oklahoma. Do you think that this was a fair penalty for the crime committed? Why or why not? He appealed his conviction and sentence to the United States Supreme Court, which ruled against him. What arguments might he have made in an attempt to persuade the Supreme Court to rule against the death penalty?

PROJECTS

1. Call the state court in your city that handles pretrial criminal procedures, such as initial hearings and arraignments. Arrange to be in court when these matters are being heard.
2. Call the state court in your city that handles the most serious crimes (felonies and/or serious misdemeanors), and obtain a list of the criminal trials that are on the docket. Arrange to attend one of the trials for as long as possible. Observe how legal assistants are used by the trial attorneys.
3. Call the county prosecutor's office in your area and ask if it gives tours to students. If so, arrange to go on a tour of the prosecutor's office, and try to learn how warrants are issued and how the prosecutor prepares for trial. Also observe how paralegals are utilized in the office.
4. Contact your local police department, and ask if it gives tours to students. If so, arrange to take a tour of the department and learn, to the extent possible, what procedures are followed in regard to booking and investigation.
5. Call your local criminal court. Ask if it has a copy of the state court's standard criminal search warrant. Request a copy. Compare the state court forms with the standard federal court search warrant contained in the chapter as Exhibit 15.5. Write a one-page paper summarizing the differences and similarities.
6. Review your state's court rules to see how the rules for criminal cases differ from those for civil cases. List and describe the major differences.

✳ USING INTERNET RESOURCES

1. Go to **http://library.thinkquest.org/2760**. This site, which has become well known primarily for its "Anatomy of a Murder," also provides a list of "Landmark Supreme Court Cases" in criminal law. Select "Rockin' Supreme Court Cases" to view a list of these cases. Select one of the cases, scan through it, and then answer the following questions:

    a. Who was the defendant, and with what crime or crimes was he or she charged?

    b. What defenses were raised by the defendant?

    c. What constitutional issue was involved?

    d. What was the Supreme Court's decision?

2. Go to the Web site of the Federal Bureau of Investigation (FBI) at **http://www.fbi.gov**.

    a. Click on "Library and Reference." Next, click on "History of the FBI."

    • When was the FBI founded, and by whom?

    • What was the agency's original name? When and how was it changed?

    • Prior to 1920, what types of crimes did the FBI investigate? Were there many crimes to be investigated? Why or why not?

    • When did the FBI become a large agency? Why?

    b. Return to the FBI home page. Click on "Freedom of Information Act."

    • When did the Freedom of Information Act (FOIA) first apply to FBI records? Why?

    • What is the FBI's procedure on receiving an FOIA request?

    • How many FOIA requests has the FBI handled since 1975? How many employees work in the FOIA section?

    c. Click on "Electronic Reading Room."

    • What is required to view the cases contained in the Electronic Reading Room? Do you have this software available on your computer? How can you obtain it? If you are not using your own computer, check with a supervisor to make sure that you can load this software.

    • Under "Categories," click on "Alphabetical Listing." List the names of four celebrities for whom the FBI has files. Why might the FBI have investigated these people?

END NOTES

1. The American Law Institute (mentioned in Chapter 5) issued the Official Draft of the Model Penal Code in 1962. The Model Penal Code was designed to assist state legislatures in reexamining and recodifying state criminal laws. Uniformity among the states is not as important in criminal law as in other areas of the law. Crime varies with local circumstances, and it is appropriate that punishments vary accordingly.

2. Pronounced *ak*-tuhs *ray*-uhs.

3. Pronounced mehns *ray*-uh.

4. *United States v. Park,* 421 U.S. 658, 95 S.Ct. 1903, 44 L.Ed.2d 489 (1975).

5. 18 U.S.C. Sections 1341–1342.

6. 18 U.S.C. Sections 1831–1839.

7. 18 U.S.C. Sections 1961–1968.

8. See 18 U.S.C. Section 1961(1)(A).

9. The total cost of crime on the Internet is estimated to be several billion dollars annually, but two-thirds of that total is said to consist of unpaid-for toll calls.

10. The National Information Infrastructure Protection Act of 1996, 18 U.S.C. Section 1030, amended the Computer Fraud and Abuse Act of 1984.

11. 384 U.S. 436, 86 S.Ct. 1602, 16 L.Ed.2d 694 (1966).

12. *Dickerson v. United States,* 530 U.S. 428, 120 S.Ct. 2326, 147 L.Ed.2d 405 (2000). The United States Supreme Court heard another case involving challenges to the *Miranda* rule in 2002 but has not yet issued a ruling. See *Chavez v. Martinez,* 122 S.Ct. 2326 (2002).

13. *New York v. Quarles,* 467 U.S. 649, 104 S.Ct. 2626, 81 L.Ed.2d 550 (1984).

14. *Moran v. Burbine,* 475 U.S. 412, 106 S.Ct. 1135, 89 L.Ed.2d 410 (1985).

15. *Arizona v. Fulminante,* 499 U.S. 279, 111 S.Ct. 1246, 113 L.Ed.2d 302 (1991).

16. *Davis v. United States,* 512 U.S. 452, 114 S.Ct. 2350, 129 L.Ed.2d 362 (1994).

17. At a minimum, the following states, as well as the District of Columbia, refer to the pleading that accompanies a motion as a memorandum of law: Alaska, Connecticut, Illinois, Maryland, Massachusetts, Michigan, Missouri, Montana, New York, North Carolina, Oregon, and Texas.

CHAPTER 16

LEGAL RESEARCH AND ANALYSIS

Chapter Outline

✳ INTRODUCTION ✳ PRIMARY AND SECONDARY SOURCES ✳ RESEARCHING CASE LAW—THE PRELIMINARY STEPS ✳ SECONDARY SOURCES OF CASE LAW ✳ THE CASE REPORTING SYSTEM ✳ ANALYZING CASE LAW ✳ RESEARCHING STATUTORY LAW ✳ ANALYZING STATUTORY LAW ✳ RESEARCHING ADMINISTRATIVE LAW ✳ FINDING CONSTITUTIONAL LAW ✳ UPDATING THE LAW—LEARNING TO USE CITATORS

After completing this chapter, you will know:

- How primary and secondary sources of law differ and how to use each of these types of sources in the research process.

- How court decisions are published and how to read case citations.

- How to analyze case law and summarize, or brief, cases.

- How federal statutes and regulations are published and the major sources of statutory and administrative law.

- How to read and interpret statutory law and what kinds of resources are available for researching the legislative history of a statute.

- Why finding current law is important and how to verify that your research results are up to date.

569

INTRODUCTION

For many paralegals, legal research is a fascinating part of their jobs. They find it intrinsically interesting to read the actual words of a court's opinion on a legal question or the text of a statute. Additionally, they acquire a firsthand knowledge of the law and how it applies to actual people and events. Research is also a crucial part of the paralegal's job, and the ability to conduct research thoroughly yet efficiently enhances a paralegal's value to the legal team.

As a paralegal, you may be asked to perform a variety of research tasks. Some research tasks will be simple. You may be asked to locate and copy a court case, for example. Other research tasks may take days or even weeks to complete. In almost all but the simplest of research tasks, legal research overlaps extensively with legal analysis. To find relevant case law, for example, you need to be able to analyze the cases you find to ensure that they are indeed relevant.

Many paralegals now conduct research without even entering a law library. Computerized legal services such as Westlaw® and Lexis® allow legal professionals to find the text of cases, statutes, and other legal documents without leaving their desks. As you will read in Chapter 17, these and an abundance of other sources are now available online. An increasing number of law firms today are also purchasing reference materials on CD-ROMs. To a great extent, how you do your research—that is, whether you conduct research online or in a law library—will depend on your employer and the computer facilities available to you.

Regardless of whether legal research is conducted online or in a law library, it is essential to know what sources to consult for different types of information. You will learn about these sources in this chapter. You will also learn how to make sure that the law you find is up to date and still "good law."

PRIMARY AND SECONDARY SOURCES

Generally, research sources fall into two broad categories—primary sources and secondary sources. Printed decisions of the various courts in the United States, statutes enacted by legislative bodies, rules and regulations created by administrative agencies, presidential orders, and generally any documents that *establish* the law are **primary sources** of law. **Secondary sources** of law consist of books and articles that summarize, systematize, compile, or otherwise interpret the law. Legal encyclopedias, which summarize the law, are secondary sources of law.

Normally, researchers in any field or profession begin their research with secondary sources. Secondary sources are often referred to as *finding tools*, because they help the researcher to find primary sources on the topics they are researching and to learn how those sources have been interpreted by others. If you are asked to research case law on a certain issue, you should do likewise. You should first refer to secondary sources to learn about the issue and find relevant primary sources concerning it. Then you can go to the primary sources themselves (such as statutes or court cases) to research the established law on the issue.

In the following sections, you will read about the primary and secondary sources that are most frequently used in researching case law, statutory law and legislative history, administrative law, and constitutional law.

RESEARCHING CASE LAW—THE PRELIMINARY STEPS

Any research project normally involves the following five steps:

- Defining the issue(s) to be researched.
- Determining the goal of the research project.

primary source
In legal research, a document that establishes the law on a particular issue, such as a case decision, legislative act, administrative rule, or presidential order.

secondary source
In legal research, any publication that indexes, summarizes, or interprets the law, such as a legal encyclopedia, a treatise, or an article in a law review.

ETHICAL CONCERN
Efficiency in Research

Attorneys have a duty to charge their clients reasonable fees. As a paralegal, you help your attorney fulfill this duty by working efficiently so as to minimize the number of hours you spend on work relating to the client's matter. Legal research can be extremely time consuming, as every paralegal knows. To reduce the time spent in researching a particular legal issue, start out on your quest with a clear idea of your research task. After all, your time is expensive not only for the client (who pays for it) but also for your supervising attorney (who may need your assistance on other cases as well). By knowing as precisely as possible what the goal of your research is, you can reach that goal more quickly and thus better serve the interests of both the client and your supervising attorney.

- Consulting relevant secondary sources.
- Researching relevant primary sources.
- Synthesizing and summarizing research results.[1]

To illustrate how you would follow the first two steps when researching case law, we present a hypothetical case. The case involves one of your firm's clients, Trent Hoffman, who is suing Better Homes Store for negligence. During the initial client interview, Hoffman explained to you and your supervising attorney that he had gone to the store to purchase a large mirror. As he was leaving the store through the store's side entrance, carrying the bulky mirror, he ran into a large pole just outside the door. He did not see the pole because the mirror blocked his view. On hitting the pole, the mirror broke, and a piece of glass entered Hoffman's left eye, causing permanent loss of eyesight in that eye. Hoffman claims that the store was negligent in placing a pole so close to the exit and is suing the store for $3 million in damages.

You have already undertaken a preliminary investigation into the matter and obtained evidence supporting Hoffman's account of the facts. Your supervising attorney now asks you to do some research. Your job is to research case law to find other cases with similar fact patterns and see how the courts decided the issue in those cases.

Defining the Issue

Before you consult any source, primary or secondary, you must know the legal issue that needs to be researched. Your first task will be to examine closely the facts of Hoffman's case to determine the nature of the legal issue involved. Based on Hoffman's description of the factual circumstances (verified through your preliminary investigation) and on his allegation that Better Homes Store should not have placed a pole just outside one of the store's entrances, you know that the legal issue relates to the tort of negligence. As a starting point, you should therefore review what you know about negligence theory.

Recall from Chapter 7 that the tort of negligence is defined as the failure to exercise reasonable care. To succeed in a negligence action, a plaintiff must establish that (1) the defendant had a duty of care to the plaintiff, (2) the defendant breached that duty, (3) the plaintiff suffered a legally recognizable injury, and

(4) the injury was caused by the defendant's breach of the duty of care. A knowledge of these elements will help you determine the issue that needs to be researched in Hoffman's case. There is little doubt that the third requirement has been met—Hoffman's loss of sight in his left eye is a legally recognizable injury for which he can be compensated—*if* he succeeds in proving the other three elements of negligence. Proving the fourth element, causation, is largely dependent on proving the first two elements. In your research, you will therefore want to focus on the first two elements. Specifically, you need to find answers to the following questions:

- Did Better Homes Store owe a duty of care to its customer, Hoffman? You might phrase this question in more general terms: Do business owners owe a duty of care to **business invitees**—customers and others whom they invite onto their premises?
- If so, what is the extent of that duty, and how is it measured? In other words, are business owners always liable, in all circumstances, when customers are injured on their premises? Or must some condition be met before store owners will be liable? For example, must a customer's injury be a *foreseeable* consequence of a condition on the premises, such as the pole outside the store's door, for the store owner to be liable for the injury?
- If the injury must be a foreseeable consequence of a condition, would a court find that Hoffman's injury in this case was a foreseeable consequence of the pole's placement just outside the store's door?

These, then, are the issues you need to research. Notice how the term *issue* has become plural. You will find that this is a common occurrence in legal research—only rarely will you be researching a single legal issue.

Determining Your Research Goals

Once you have defined the issue or issues to be researched, you will be in a better position to determine your research goals. Remember that you are working on behalf of a client, who is paying for your services. Your overall goal is thus to find legal support for Hoffman's claim. To achieve this goal, you will want to find two things: cases on point and cases that are mandatory authorities. Depending on what you find, you may also need to look for persuasive authorities.

CASES ON POINT.   One of your research goals is to find a case (or cases) on point in which the court held for the plaintiff. A **case on point** is a previous case involving fact patterns and legal issues that are similar to those in the case you are researching. In regard to Hoffman's negligence claim, a case on point would be one in which the plaintiff alleged that he or she was injured while on a store's premises because of a dangerous condition on those premises.

The ideal case on point, of course, would be a case in which all four elements of a case (the parties, the circumstances, the legal issues involved, and the remedies sought by the plaintiff) are very similar to those in your case. Such a case is called a **case on "all fours."**[2] In regard to Hoffman's claim, a case on "all fours" would be a case on point, such as just described, in which the plaintiff-customer did not expect a condition (such as an obstacle in his or her path) to exist and was prevented from seeing the condition by some action that a customer would reasonably undertake (such as carrying a large box out of a store). The parties and the circumstances of the case would thus be very similar to those in Hoffman's case. In addition, the plaintiff would have sustained a permanent injury, as Hoffman did, and sought damages for negligence.

---

business invitee
A person, such as a customer or client, who is invited onto business premises by the owner of those premises for business purposes.

case on point
A case involving factual circumstances and issues that are similar to those in the case being researched.

case on "all fours"
A case in which all four elements (the parties, the circumstances, the legal issues involved, and the remedies sought by the plaintiff) are very similar to those in the case being researched.

DEVELOPING PARALEGAL SKILLS
Defining the Issues to Be Researched

Federal government agents observed Bernie Berriman in his parked car talking on his cellular phone. Later, other cars were seen driving up to Bernie's car and stopping. The drivers received brown paper bags in exchange for money. Bernie was questioned, and his car was searched. Cocaine was found in the car. He was arrested for transporting and distributing cocaine, and the police took his car and cellular phone. Bernie's lawyer is arguing that the government agents did not have the authority to require Bernie to forfeit his car and cellular phone. Natalie Martin, a legal assistant with the U.S. attorney's office, has been assigned the task of researching the federal statutes and cases on this issue.

Before Natalie can begin her research project, she must thoroughly review the case to determine what specific issues need to be researched. Using a checklist method that she learned in school, she breaks the facts of the case

down into five categories and inserts the relevant facts from her assignment:

- **Parties:** Who are the people involved in the action or lawsuit?
- **Places and things:** Where did the events take place, and what items are involved in the action or lawsuit?
- **Basis of action or issue:** What is the legal claim or issue involved in the action or lawsuit?
- **Defenses:** What is the legal reason why the accused should not be held responsible?
- **Relief sought:** What is the legal remedy or penalty sought in the case?

Now Natalie is ready to go the library and begin her research.

MANDATORY AUTHORITIES.   In researching Hoffman's case, another goal is to find cases (on point or on "all fours") that are also mandatory authorities. A **mandatory authority** is any authority that the court must rely on in its determination of the issue. A mandatory authority may be a statute, regulation, or constitution that governs the issue, or it may be a previously decided court case that is controlling in your jurisdiction.

For a case to serve as a mandatory authority, it must be on point and decided by a superior court. A superior court, in the sense used here, is any court that is on a higher tier in the court system. Recall from Chapter 6 that both the federal and state court systems consist of several levels, or tiers, of courts. *Trial courts,* in which evidence is presented and testimony given, are on the bottom tier (which also includes lower courts handling specialized issues). Decisions from a trial court can be appealed to a higher court, which commonly is an intermediate *court of appeals,* or *appellate court.* Decisions from these intermediate courts of appeals may be appealed to an even higher court, such as a state supreme court or, if a federal question is involved, the United States Supreme Court.

A lower court is bound to follow the decisions set forth by a higher court in the same jurisdiction. An appellate court's decision in a case involving facts and issues similar to a case brought in a trial court in the same jurisdiction would thus be a mandatory authority—the trial court would be bound to follow the appellate court's decision on the issue. A higher court is never required to follow an opinion written by a lower court in the same jurisdiction, however.

State courts have the final say on state law, and federal courts have the final say on federal law. Thus, except in deciding an issue that involves federal law, state courts do not have to follow the decisions of federal courts. In deciding issues that involve federal law, however, state courts must abide by the decisions of the United States Supreme Court.

mandatory authority
Any source of law that a court must follow when deciding a case. Mandatory authorities include constitutions, statutes, and regulations that govern the issue before the court and court decisions made by a superior court in the jurisdiction.

⁂ **When you are performing research, look for cases on point decided by the highest court in your jurisdiction, because those cases carry the most weight.**

persuasive authority
Any legal authority, or source of law, that a court may look to for guidance but on which it need not rely in making its decision. Persuasive authorities include cases from other jurisdictions and secondary sources of law, such as scholarly treatises.

PERSUASIVE AUTHORITIES.   A **persuasive authority** is not binding on a court. In other words, the court is not required to follow that authority in making its decision. Examples of persuasive authorities are (1) prior court opinions of other jurisdictions, which, although they are not binding, may suggest how a particular case should be decided; (2) legal periodicals, such as law reviews, in which the issue at hand is discussed by legal scholars; (3) encyclopedias summarizing legal principles or concepts relating to a particular issue; and (4) legal dictionaries that describe how the law has been applied in the past.

Often, a court refers to persuasive authorities when deciding a *case of first impression,* which is a case involving an issue that has never been addressed by that court before. For example, if in your research of Hoffman's claim you find that no similar cases have ever reached a higher court in your jurisdiction, you would look for similar cases decided by courts in other jurisdictions. If courts in other jurisdictions have faced a similar issue, the court may be guided by those other courts' decisions when deciding Hoffman's case. Your supervising attorney will want to know about these persuasive authorities so that she can present them to the court for consideration.

SECONDARY SOURCES OF CASE LAW

Finding cases that are both on point and mandatory legal authorities is not always easy. The body of American case law consists of about five million decisions. Each year, more than forty thousand new cases are added to this collection. Because the decisions of the courts are published in chronological order, finding relevant precedents would be a Herculean task if it were not for secondary sources of law that classify decisions according to subject. A logical place to begin your research is thus with secondary sources of case law. In researching Hoffman's claim, you might look first at a legal encyclopedia to learn more about the topic of negligence and the duty of care of business owners to business invitees. Generally, to help you find topics that shed light on your subject, you should make a list of key terms and phrases before beginning the research process.

Legal Encyclopedias

Legal encyclopedias provide detailed summaries of legal rules and concepts. Legal encyclopedias also arrange topics alphabetically and refer readers to leading cases in that area of law.

Encyclopedias are helpful resources for the student who is new to legal research or for an experienced legal professional who is researching an unfamiliar area of law. By referring to an encyclopedia, you can obtain background information that will help you direct your research more effectively. Two popular legal encyclopedias are *American Jurisprudence,* Second Edition, and *Corpus Juris Secundum.* Another popular legal resource is *Words and Phrases.* We discuss each of these works here. (Note that there are also state-specific encyclopedias—that is, encyclopedias that refer readers to state cases or statutes relating to a specific topic. You can check with the reference librarian in your local law library to find a state-specific encyclopedia, if your state has one.)

AMERICAN JURISPRUDENCE, SECOND EDITION.   *American Jurisprudence,* Second Edition, is commonly referred to as *American Jurisprudence 2d* or, more briefly, as *Am. Jur. 2d.* (A photograph of one of the volumes of this encyclopedia is shown in Exhibit 16.1.) This encyclopedia is published by the Lawyers Cooperative Publishing Company. (Because this company is now part of West Group, in the remainder of this chapter we refer to its publications as West Group publications.) *American Jurisprudence 2d* offers a detailed discussion of virtually every area of American law. The encyclopedia covers more than 440 topics in 58 volumes. Each topic is further divided into various subtopics containing narrative descriptions of the general rules of law that have emerged from generations of court decisions. If there are conflicting decisions on an issue or topic, the encyclopedia indicates this and offers explanations for the differing opinions. The encyclopedia also provides various cross-references to specific court cases, annotations in *American Law Reports* (to be discussed shortly), law reviews, and other relevant sections of *American Jurisprudence.* The volumes are kept current through supplements called **pocket parts** (because they slip into a pocket in the front or back of the volume), which contain additions to the various topics and subtopics.

As in any encyclopedia, topics in *American Jurisprudence 2d* are presented alphabetically. Each general topic is organized to allow a researcher to find quickly the specific area of interest. Each volume of the encyclopedia also contains an index, located at the back of the volume. A separate index is provided for the entire encyclopedia once a series, or edition, is completed. The indexes can be very helpful to the researcher. For example, in researching the issue in Hoffman's lawsuit against Better Homes Store for negligence, you could look in the index for such terms as *premises liability, business invitees, duty of care, landowners,* or some other term or phrase. Exhibit 16.2 on the next page shows the first page of the discussion of premises liability. Although not shown in the exhibit, an outline of the major topics of the section follows, complete with descriptive subsections. The outline allows the researcher to locate easily any relevant areas within the general subject matter.

CORPUS JURIS SECUNDUM.   Another encyclopedia helpful to the legal researcher is *Corpus Juris Secundum,* or *C.J.S.,* which is published by West Group. This encyclopedia, like *American Jurisprudence 2d,* provides detailed information on almost every area of the law. *C.J.S.* consists of 101 volumes and covers 433 topics, each of which is further divided into subtopics. One of the volumes of this set is depicted in Exhibit 16.3 on page 577.

The approaches of *C.J.S.* and *American Jurisprudence 2d* are very similar. *C.J.S.* offers an explanation of contradictory court decisions on an issue, if there are any, and provides the names of these cases and of the published sources in which they can be found. *C.J.S.* also contains alphabetical entries as well as indexes for locating relevant legal information. The indexes are located at the ends of individual volumes and in a multivolume index at the end of a set. To keep its information up to date, *C.J.S.* also provides supplements (pocket parts) containing current materials. In regard to Hoffman's claim, if you looked up the word *business* in the *C.J.S.,* you would find a discussion of that topic, including a reference to business invitees (as shown on the page from the *C.J.S.* presented in Exhibit 16.4 on page 578).

WORDS AND PHRASES.   *Words and Phrases* is a forty-six-volume encyclopedia of definitions and interpretations of legal terms and phrases published by West Group. It is a useful tool for learning how the courts have interpreted a particular term or phrase. The words and phrases covered are arranged in alphabetical

EXHIBIT 16.1
American Jurisprudence 2d

Reproduced with permission of West Group.

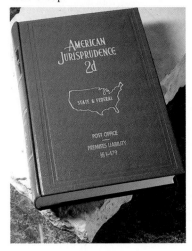

pocket part
A separate pamphlet containing recent cases or changes in the law that is used to update hornbooks, legal encyclopedias, and other legal authorities. It is called a "pocket part" because it slips into a sleeve, or pocket, in the front or back binder of the volume.

EXHIBIT 16.2
Excerpt from *American Jurisprudence 2d*

Reproduced with permission of West Group.

PREMISES LIABILITY

by

Irwin J. Schiffres, J.D. and Sheila A. Skojec, J.D.

Scope of topic: This article discusses the principles and rules of law applicable to and governing the liability of owners or occupants of real property for negligence causing injury to persons or property by reason of defects therein or hazards created by the activities of such owners or occupants or their agents and employees. Treated in detail are the classification of persons injured as invitees, licensees, or trespassers, and the duty owed them, as well as the rules applicable in those jurisdictions where such status distinctions are no longer determinative of the duty owed the entrant; the effect of "recreational use" statutes on the duty owed persons using the property for such purposes; the greater measure of duty owed by the owner to children as compared to adult licensees and trespassers, including the attractive nuisance doctrine; and the specific duties and liabilities of owners and occupants of premises used for business or residential purposes. Also considered is the effect of the injured person's negligence on the plaintiff's right to recover under principles of contributory or comparative negligence.

Federal aspects: One injured on premises owned or operated by the United States may seek to recover under general principles of premises liability discussed in this article. Insofar as recovery is sought under the Federal Torts Claims Act, see 35 Am Jur 2d, FEDERAL TORTS CLAIMS ACT § 73.

Treated elsewhere:
Mutual obligations and liabilities of adjoining landowners with respect to injuries arising from their acts or omissions, see 1 Am Jur 2d, ADJOINING LANDOWNERS AND PROPERTIES §§ 10, 11, 28 et seq., 37 et seq.

Liability for the acts or omissions of the owners or occupants of premises abutting on a street or highway which cause injury to those using the way, see 39 Am Jur 2d, HIGHWAYS, STREETS, AND BRIDGES §§ 517 et seq.

Liability for violation of building regulations, see 13 Am Jur 2d, BUILDINGS §§ 32 et seq.

Liability of employer for injuries caused employees on the employer's premises, see 53 Am Jur 2d, MASTER AND SERVANT §§ 139 et seq.

Liability for injuries caused by defective products on the premises, see 63 Am Jur 2d, PRODUCTS LIABILITY

Respective rights and liabilities of a landlord and tenant where one is responsible for an injury suffered by the other, or by a third person, on leased premises or on premises provided for the common use of tenants, see 49 Am Jur 2d, LANDLORD AND TENANT §§ 761 et seq.

Liability of a receiver placed in charge of property for an injury sustained thereby or thereon by someone other than the persons directly interested in the estate, see 66 Am Jur 2d, RECEIVERS § 364

Duties and liabilities of occupiers of premises used for various particular types of businesses or activities, see 4 Am Jur 2d, AMUSEMENTS AND EXHIBITIONS §§ 51 et seq.; 14 Am Jur 2d, CARRIERS §§ 964 et seq.; 38 Am Jur 2d, GARAGES, AND FILLING AND PARKING STATIONS §§ 81 et seq.; 40 Am Jur 2d, HOSPITALS AND ASYLUMS § 31; 40 Am Jur 2d, HOTELS, MOTELS, AND RESTAURANTS §§ 81 et seq.; 50 Am Jur 2d, LAUNDRIES, DYERS, AND DRY CLEANERS §§ 21, 22; 54 Am Jur 2d, MOBILE HOMES, TRAILER PARKS, AND TOURIST CAMPS § 17; 57 Am Jur 2d, MUNICIPAL, COUNTY, SCHOOL, AND STATE TORT LIABILITY; AND 59 AM JUR 2d, PARKS, SQUARES, AND PLAYGROUNDS §§ 43 et seq.

Duties and liabilities with respect to injuries caused by particular agencies, such as

317

---

order. Each is followed by abstracts (brief summary statements) from federal or state court decisions in which the word or phrase has been interpreted or defined. The abstract also indicates the names of the cases and the reporters in which they can be located. **Reporters** are publications containing the actual texts of court cases, as will be discussed later in this section. When researching Hoffman's claim, you could find out how various courts have defined *negligence* by looking up that term in *Words and Phrases*. Part of the entry for this term is shown in Exhibit 16.5 on page 579. *Words and Phrases* is updated by annual supplementary pocket parts.

reporter
A book in which court cases are published, or reported.

Case Digests

In researching the issue in Hoffman's case against Better Homes Store, you might want to check a case digest as well as a legal encyclopedia for references to relevant case law. **Digests,** which are produced by various publishers, are helpful research tools because they provide indexes to case law—from the earliest recorded cases through the most current opinions. Case digests arrange topics alphabetically and provide information to help you locate referenced cases, but they do not offer the detail found in legal encyclopedias. Collected under each topic heading in a case digest are annotations. **Annotations** are comments, explanatory notes, or case summaries. In case digests, annotations consist of very short statements of relevant points of law in reported cases.

The digests published by West Group offer the most comprehensive system for locating cases by subject matter. West publishes digests of both federal court opinions and state court opinions, as well as regional digests and digests that correspond with its reporters covering specialized areas, such as bankruptcy.

THE WEST KEY-NUMBER SYSTEM.   West's key-number system has simplified the task of researching case law. The system divides all areas of American law into specific categories, or topics, arranged in alphabetical order. The topics are further divided into many specific subtopics, each designated by a **key number,** which is accompanied by the West key symbol: ☞. Exhibit 16.6 on page 580 shows some of the key numbers used for subtopics under the topic of negligence.

West editors provide abstracts, or **headnotes,** for all areas of the law discussed within each decision appearing in the West reporters. Every headnote is described by its topic name, which is followed by a key number indicating the specific subject discussed. This system of arranging legal and factual issues by subject matter allows West to gather all headnotes under the same topic and key number into one published work—the digest. If you consulted a West digest when researching Hoffman's case, the digest would indicate the names of cases relating to the topic as well as the reporters in which the texts of those cases could be found.

WEST'S FEDERAL DIGESTS.   West's federal digests cover cases from the United States Supreme Court, the U.S. courts of appeals, the U.S. district courts, and various specialized federal courts, such as bankruptcy courts. Cases from all of these courts are organized according to the West key-number system. Headnotes from the United States Supreme Court are listed first, followed by appellate court and district court cases.

There are several separate sets of federal digests corresponding to different years and providing coverage from 1754 to the present. The *Federal Practice Digest 4th,* the current edition, begins with 1991. Exhibit 16.7 on page 581 shows excerpts from West's *Federal Practice Digest 4th* on the topic of negligence. As shown in the exhibit, the section begins with a general topical outline (shown in the lower right-hand portion of the exhibit). You can scan through the outline to find the specific subtopic covering the issue you are researching. Then, you can turn to the pages covering that subtopic (the beginning page of one of the subtopics is shown at the upper left-hand side of the exhibit) to find references to relevant case law.

Each of these federal digests provides headnotes for cases appearing in the *Supreme Court Reporter* (which reports cases decided by the United States Supreme Court), the *Federal Reporter* (which reports cases from the federal courts of appeals), the *Federal Supplement* (which reports cases from the federal district courts), and the *Federal Rules Decisions* (which covers federal rules of

digest
A compilation in which brief summaries of court cases are arranged by subject and subdivided by jurisdiction and court.

annotation
A brief comment, an explanation of a legal point, or a case summary found in a case digest or other legal source.

key number
A number (accompanied by the symbol of a key) corresponding to a specific topic within West's key-number system to facilitate legal research of case law.

headnote
A note near the beginning of a reported case summarizing the court's ruling on an issue.

EXHIBIT 16.3
Corpus Juris Secundum

Reproduced with permission of West Group.

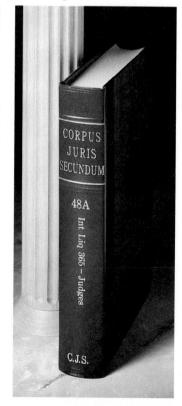

EXHIBIT 16.4
Excerpt from *Corpus Juris Secundum*

Reproduced with permission of West Group.

BUSINESS   12A C. J. S.

Business time. The term "business time" has been held to mean the ability to engage in a sustained effort of a character sufficiently substantial to negative the idea that there was not a total loss of power reasonably to continue a business or profession.[18]

Business use. The phrase "business use" may have different meanings in different statutes, ordinances, and other writings.[19] The generally accepted meaning of the term necessarily implies employment of one or more persons for the purpose of earning a livelihood, activities of persons to improve their economic conditions and desires, and generally relates to commercial and industrial engagements.[20]

Business visitor. "Business visitors" are deemed to fall into two classes, first, those who enter upon the premises of another for a purpose connected with the business which the possessor conducts thereon, and, second, those who come upon the premises for a purpose connected with their own business which is connected with any purpose, business or otherwise, for which the possessor uses the premises.[21]

The phrase "business visitor" has been held equivalent to "invitee,"[22] and has been compared or contrasted with "licensee"[23] and "gratuitous licensee."[24]

Other phrases employing the word "business," as an adjective, are set out in the note.[25]

Iowa.—Crane Co. v. City Council of Des Moines, 225 N.W. 344, 345, 208 Iowa 164.

N.J.—Duke Power Co. v. Hillsborough Tp., Somerset County, 26 A.2d 713, 729, 20 N.J.Misc. 240.

N.C.—Mecklenburg County v. Sterchi Bros. Stores, 185 S.E. 454, 457, 459, 210 N.C. 79.

Okl.—State v. Atlantic Oil Producing Co., 49 P.2d 534, 538, 174 Okl. 61—Grieves v. State ex rel. County Attorney, 35 P.2d 454, 456, 168 Okl. 642.

Or.—Endicott, Johnson & Co. v. Multnomah County, 190 P. 1109, 1111, 96 Or. 679.

18. Ark.—Pacific Mut. Life Ins. Co. v. Riffel, 149 S.W.2d 57, 59, 202 Ark. 94.

19. Ga.—Snow v. Johnston, 28 S.E.2d 270, 277, 197 Ga. 146.

Test

Definite test of business use would usually be whether or not profit was being made, directly or indirectly, by owner, on particular occasion.

N.Y.—Juskiewicz v. New Jersey Fidelity & Plate Glass Ins. Co., 206 N.Y.S. 566, 568, 210 App.Div. 675.

20. Ga.—Snow v. Johnston, 28 S.E.2d 270, 277, 197 Ga. 146.

21. Kan.—Bessette v. Ernsting, 127 P.2d 438, 440, 155 Kan. 540—Kurre v. Graham Ship by Truck Co., 15 P.2d 463, 465, 136 Kan. 356.

See generally C.J.S. Negligence §§ 63(41)–63(56).

What constitutes

Cal.—Crane v. Smith, 144 P.2d 356, 361, 362, 23 Cal.2d 288.

Held "business visitors"

Cal.—Turnipseed v. Hoffman, 144 P.2d 797, 798, 23 Cal.2d 532 —Hill v. Eaton & Smith, 149 P.2d 762, 763, 65 Cal.App.2d 11.

Mass.—Fortier v. Hibernian Bldg. Ass'n of Boston Highlands, 53 N.E.2d 110, 113, 315 Mass. 446.

N.Y.—Haefeli v. Woodrich Engineering Co., 175 N.E. 123, 125, 255 N.Y. 442.

Vt.—Rheaume v. Goodro, 34 A.2d 315, 316, 113 Vt. 370.

22. U.S.—Robey v. Keller, C.C.A.Va., 114 F.2d 790, 794—McCann v. Anchor Line, C.C.A.N.Y., 79 F.2d 338, 339.

Conn.—Knapp v. Connecticut Theatrical Corporation, 190 A. 291, 292, 122 Conn. 413.

Kan.—Kurre v. Graham Ship by Truck Co., 15 P.2d 463, 465, 136 Kan. 356.

Mo.—Stevenson v. Kansas City Southern Ry. Co., 159 S.W.2d 260, 263, 348 Mo. 1216.

Pa.—Hartman v. Miller, Super., 17 A.2d 652, 653, 143 Pa.Super. 143.

R.I.—Royer v. Najarian, 198 A. 562, 564, 60 R.I. 368.

23. U.S.—McCann v. Anchor Line, C.C.A.N.Y., 79 F.2d 338, 339.

Cal.—Oettinger v. Stewart, 148 P.2d 19, 20, 21, 24 Cal.2d 133, 156 A.L.R. 1221.

24. Cal.—Oettinger v. Stewart, 148 P.2d 19, 20, 21, 24 Cal.2d 133, 156 A.L.R. 1221.

N.H.—Sandwell v. Elliott Hospital, 24 A.2d 273, 274, 92 N.H. 41.

N.Y.—Haefeli v. Woodrich Engineering Co., 175 N.E. 123, 125, 255 N.Y. 442.

Petluck v. McGolrick Realty Co., 268 N.Y.S. 782, 786, 240 App.Div. 61.

25. **Particular terms**

(1) "Business compulsion" as analogous to "duress."

Cal.—Sistrom v. Anderson, 124 P.2d 372, 376, 51 C.A.2d 213.

(2) "Business assets" distinguished from "personal asset."

Cal.—In re Friedrichs' Estate, 290 P. 54, 55, 107 Cal.App. 142.

(3) "Business compulsion" contrasted with "duress."

Wash.—Ramp Buildings Corporation v. Northwest Bldg. Co., 4 P.2d 507, 509, 164 Wash. 603, 79 A.L.R. 651.

(4) "Business district" defined in statute and contrasted with "residential district."

N.C.—Mitchell v. Melts, 18 S.E.2d 406, 410, 220 N.C. 793.

(5) "Business enterprise" requires investment of capital, labor, and management.

U.S.—Helvering v. Jewel Mining Co., C.C.A.8, 126 F.2d 1011, 1015.

(6) One's home is not a "business enterprise."

Minn.—State v. Cooper, 285 N.W. 903, 905, 205 Minn. 333, 122 A.L.R. 727.

(7) Renting rooms in dwelling house is not engaging in a "business enterprise."

Tex.—Austin v. Richardson, Com.App., 288 S.W. 180, 181.

(8) "Business establishment" held to be a statutory phrase restricted to one resembling a mill, workshop, or other manufacturing establishment.

N.Y.—O'Connor v. Webber, 147 N.Y.S. 1053, 163 App.Div. 175, 178.

(9) "Business loss (or losses)" contrasted with "damage to property."

490

---

procedure). As mentioned, West also publishes specialized digests corresponding to its special federal reporters. Examples of these digests are *West's Bankruptcy Digest, Military Justice Digest, Education Law Digest, Reporting Services Digest,* and *United States Claims Digest.* West also provides exclusive digest coverage of the decisions of the United States Supreme Court in the *United States Supreme Court Digest.*

WEST'S STATE AND REGIONAL DIGESTS.   West's digest system also provides state digests for the cases of all states except Utah, Nevada, and Delaware. State digests include references to decisions issued by federal courts located within the state. Some state court decisions are also represented in West's regional digests.

EXHIBIT 16.5
Excerpt from
Words and Phrases

Reproduced with permission of
West Group.

NEGLIGENCE

Estoppel by Negligence
Fault
General Negligence
Gross Negligence
Hazardous Negligence
Heedlessness
High Degree of Negligence
Homicide by Negligence
Imputed Contributory Negligence
Imputed Negligence
Incurred Without Fault or Negligence
Independent Act of Negligence
Independent Negligence
Injury Resulting from Negligence
Insulated Negligence
Intentional Negligence
Joint Negligence
Legal Negligence
Liability Created by Law
Marine Cause
Mistake, Error or Negligence
Mutual Contributory Negligence
Negligent
Notice of Negligence
Nuisance
Nuisance Dependent Upon Negligence
Ordinary Care
Ordinary Negligence
Otherwise
Persistent Negligence
Preponderance
Presumption of Negligence
Prima Facie Case of Negligence
Prima Facie Negligence
Prior Negligence
Proof of Negligence
Proximate Contributory Negligence
Reckless; Recklessly; Recklessness
Separate Negligence
Simple Negligence
Situation Created by Actor's Negligence
Slight Negligence
Specific Negligence
Subsequent Negligence
Supervening Negligence
Trespass
Wanton Negligence
Wantonness
Willful and Intentional Negligence
Willful Negligence
Willfulness
Without Negligence

In general

"Negligence", in absence of statute, is defined as the doing of that thing which a reasonably prudent person would not have

In general—Cont'd

done, or the failure to do that thing which a reasonably prudent person would have done, in like or similar circumstances. Biddle v. Mazzocco, Or., 284 P.2d 364, 368.

"Negligence" is a departure from the normal or what should be the normal, and is a failure to conform to standard of what a reasonably prudent man would ordinarily have done under the circumstances, or is doing what such man would not have done under the circumstances. Moran v. Pittsburgh-Des Moines Steel Co., D.C.Pa., 86 F. Supp. 255, 266.

"Negligence" being failure to do that which ordinarily prudent man would do or doing of that which such a man would not do under same circumstances, an ordinary custom, while relevant and admissible in evidence of negligence, is not conclusive thereof, especially where it is clearly a careless or dangerous custom. Tite v. Omaha Coliseum Corp., 12 N.W.2d 90, 94, 144 Neb. 22, 149 A.L.R. 1164.

Whether or not an act or omission is "negligence" seems to be determined by what under like circumstances would men of ordinary prudence have done. Cleveland, C., C. & St. L. R. Co. v. Ivins, Ohio, 12 O.C.D. 570.

"Negligence" means simply the want of ordinary care under the circumstances surrounding that particular case and the transaction in question, and "negligently" simply means doing an act in such a manner that it lacks the care which men of ordinary prudence and foresight use in their everyday affairs of life under the same or similar circumstances. Smillie v. Cleveland Ry., Ohio, 31 O.C.D. 323, 325, 20 Cir.Ct.R.,N.S., 302.

"Negligence" is the failure to do what a reasonable and prudent man would ordinarily have done under circumstances of situation or doing what such a person, under existing circumstances, would not have done. Judt v. Reinhardt Transfer Co., 17 Ohio Supp. 105, 107, 32 O.O. 161.

By "negligence" is meant negligence of such character that in the discretion of the court, the defendant should have inflicted upon him the punative penalties of having his license suspended and that the public required such protection. Com. v. Galley, 17 Som. 54.

"Negligence" is a failure to use ordinary care, that is, such care as persons of ordinary prudence are accustomed to exercise

524

West currently publishes four regional digests, corresponding to four of its seven regional reporters (the names and coverage of West's regional reporters will be discussed later in this chapter).

EXHIBIT 16.6
**Subtopics and Key
Numbers in a West Digest**

Reproduced with permission of
West Group.

NEGLIGENCE

SUBJECTS INCLUDED

General civil negligence law and premises liability, including duty, standards of care, breach of duty, proximate cause, injury, defenses, and comparative fault, whether based on the common law or statute, as well as procedural aspects of such actions

General civil liabilities for gross negligence, recklessness, willful or wanton conduct, strict liability and ultrahazardous instrumentalities and activities

Negligence liabilities relating to the construction, demolition and repair of buildings and other structures, whether based on the common law or statute

General criminal negligence offenses and prosecutions

SUBJECTS EXCLUDED AND COVERED BY OTHER TOPICS

Accountants or auditors, negligence of, see ACCOUNTANTS ⌾8,9

Aircraft, accidents involving, see AVIATION ⌾141–153

Attorney's malpractice liability, see ATTORNEY AND CLIENT ⌾105–129.5

Banks, liabilities of, see BANKS AND BANKING ⌾100

Brokers, securities and real estate, liabilities of, see BROKERS

Car and highway accidents, see AUTOMOBILES

Common carriers, liabilities to passengers, see CARRIERS

Domestic animals, injuries by or to, see ANIMALS

Dram Shop liability and other liabilities for serving alcohol, see INTOXICATING LIQUORS ⌾282–324

*   *   *   *

For detailed references to other topics, see Descriptive-Word Index

_____

Analysis

   I. IN GENERAL, ⌾200–205.

  II. NECESSITY AND EXISTENCE OF DUTY, ⌾210–222.

 III. STANDARD OF CARE, ⌾230–239.

 IV. BREACH OF DUTY, ⌾250–259.

  V. HEIGHTENED DEGREES OF NEGLIGENCE, ⌾272–276.

 VI. VULNERABLE AND ENDANGERED PERSONS; RESCUES, ⌾281–285.

VII. SUDDEN EMERGENCY DOCTRINE, ⌾291–295.

VIII. DANGEROUS SITUATIONS AND STRICT LIABILITY, ⌾301–307.

WEST'S COMPREHENSIVE *AMERICAN DIGEST SYSTEM.*   West's *American Digest System* is a comprehensive set of volumes incorporating case abstracts from West's state, federal, and regional digests. Most of the cases catalogued are from appellate courts, although some trial court decisions are included. The *American Digest System* is particularly helpful when there is no case on point in your jurisdiction.

EXHIBIT 16.7
West's *Federal Practice Digest 4th* on Negligence

Reproduced with permission of West Group.

77A F P D 4th—173

NEGLIGENCE ⬅1037(4)

For references to other topics, see Descriptive-Word Index

E.D.Mich. 1998. Under Michigan law, a property owner is not an absolute insurer of the safety of invitees.
Meyers v. Wal-Mart Stores, East, Inc., 29 F.Supp.2d 780.

E.D.Mich. 1995. under Michigan law, property owner is not insurer of safety of invitees.
Bunch v. Long John Silvers, Inc., 878 F.Supp. 1044.

E.D.Mich. 1994. Under Michigan law, property owner is not insurer of safety of invitees.
Dose v. Equitable Life Assur. Soc., 864 F.Supp. 682.

E.D.N.C. 1993. Premises owner does not automatically insure safety of invitees and is not liable in absence of negligence.
Faircloth v. U.S., 837 F.Supp. 123.

E.D.Va. 1999. Under Virginia law, owner of premises is not insurer of his invitees safety; rather, owner must use ordinary care to render premises reasonably safe for invitee's visit.
Sandow-Pajewski v. Busch Entertainment Corp., 55 F.Supp.2d 422.

⬅**1037(4). Care required in general.**

C.A.7 (Ill.) 1986. Under Illinois law, landowner is liable for physical harm to his invitees caused by condition on his land: where landowner could by exercise of reasonable care have discovered condition; where landowner should realize that condition involves unreasonable risk of harm to invitees; where landowner should expect that invitees will not discover danger or will fail to protect against it; and where landowner fails to exercise reasonable care to protect invitees.
Higgins v. White Sox Baseball Club, Inc., 787 F.2d 1125.

C.A.7 (Ind.) 1994. Under Indiana law, landowner's duty to invitee while that invitee is on premises is that of reasonable care.
Salima v. Scherwood South, Inc., 38 F.3d 929.

Under indiana law, landowner is liable for harm caused to invitee by condition on land only if landowner knows of or through exercise of reasonable care would discover condition and realize that it involves unreasonable risk of harm to such invitees, should expect the invitee will fail to discover or realize danger or fail to protect against it, and fails to exercise reasonable care in protecting invitee against danger.
Salima v. Scherwood South, Inc., 38 F. 3d 929.

Under Indiana law, landowner is not liable for harm caused to invitees by conditions whose

For cited U.S.C.A. sections and legislative histo

danger is known or obvious unless landowner could anticipate harm despite obviousness.
Salima v. Scherwood South, Inc., 38 F.3d 929.

C.A.6 (Mich.) 1998. Under Michigan law, where invitor has reason to expect that, despite open and obvious nature of hazard, invitee will

---

NEGLIGENCE   77A F P D 4th—542

XVI. DEFENSES AND MITIGATING CIRCUMSTANCES.—Continued.

    570. _____ Professional rescuers; "firefighter's rule."
    575. Imputed contributory negligence.

XVII. PREMISES LIABILITY.
  (A) IN GENERAL.
    ⬅ 1000. Nature.
      1001. Elements in general.
      1002. Constitutional, statutory and regulatory provisions.
      1003. What law governs.
      1004. Preemption.

  (B) NECESSITY AND EXISTENCE OF DUTY.
    ⬅ 1010. In general.
      1011. Ownership, custody and control.
      1012. Conditions known or obvious in general.
      1013. Conditions created or known by defendant.
      1014. Foreseeability.
      1015. Duty as to children.
      1016. _____ In general.
      1017. _____ Trespassing children.
      1018. Duty to inspect or discover.
      1019. Protection against acts of third persons in general.
      1020. Duty to warn.
      1021. Duty of store and business proprietors.
      1022. _____ In general.
      1023. _____ Duty to inspect.
      1024. _____ Protection against acts of third persons.
      1025. Duty based on statute or other regulation.

  (C) STANDARD OF CARE.
    ⬅ 1030. In general.
      1031. Not insurer or guarantor.
      1032. Reasonable or ordinary care in general.
      1033. Reasonably safe or unreasonably dangerous conditions.
      1034. Status of entrant.
      1035. _____ In general.
      1036. _____ Care dependent on status.
        (1). In general.
        (2). Who are invitees.
        (3). Not insurer as to invitees.
        (4). Care required in general.
        (5). Public invitees in general.
        (6). Implied invitation.
        (7). Persons working on property.
        (8). Delivery persons and haulers.
      1040. _____ Licensees.
        (1). In general.
        (2). Who are licensees.

PARALEGAL PROFILE

Litigation Paralegal

PAMELA JO RAYBOURN *serves as a legal assistant in the areas of product liability, business and employment litigation, and antitrust. Her work includes undertaking factual investigations, drafting and responding to discovery requests (including motion practice), and organizing large documents. She has extensive experience in preparing for and assisting at trial, arbitration, and mediation. She is also involved in supervising and training support staff.*

Raybourn has served as chair of NFPA's Ethics Committee, has written numerous articles for newsletters published by the Oregon State Bar Association and the Oregon Legal Assistants Association, and has been a PACE exam preparer for NFPA.

What do you like best about your work?

"I like the responsibility of searching for the factual information that makes or breaks the case. I like digging and asking questions to gather all the information necessary to prepare the case. I also enjoy working with the employees of our corporate clients. It is easy to zealously represent a client when you know the client has integrity and strong business ethics."

What is the greatest challenge that you face in your area of work?

"It doesn't help the client if you complete the assignment and it sits on the attorney's desk for weeks. I find myself in the role of a prodder, checking to see that the work gets off the attorney's desk and out the door."

What advice do you have for would-be paralegals in your area of work?

"Get a well-rounded education in all areas of law. Because litigation can involve any legal theory, I have found it necessary to understand the legal principles involved in probate and estates, real estate, contracts, patents, bankruptcy, business organizations, and product liability in addition to understanding tort and negligence theory. The better you understand a legal theory, the more able you are to review documents and locate facts to support that theory."

"There is no such thing as a dumb question."

What are some tips for success as a paralegal in your area of work?

"Ask questions. There is no such thing as a dumb question. You will exert less wasted energy and effort if you ask a question to be sure you understand the assignment. Sometimes I go back to the attorney more than once to ensure that I am on the right track. Sometimes a review of documents will lead to other questions. If you ask questions, you can direct your efforts to efficiently completing the assignment. This will benefit you as well as the client."

To find persuasive authorities, you will want to consider cases from all jurisdictions. The *American Digest System* will help you locate them efficiently.

Sequential Sets.   The *American Digest System* is divided into three different sets, each covering a specific period of time. The *American Digest Century Edition* provides coverage of all cases from 1658 through 1896. The *Decennial Digest* includes all cases issued from 1896 to the present. Each volume in the set covers a ten-year period; for example, the *Eighth Decennial Digest* covers cases reported between 1966 and 1976. West has slightly changed the decennial digest publication schedule because of the increased number of reported cases. Today, "decennial" digests are issued every five years, rather than every ten years. The most recently published cases can be found in West's *General Digest*, which is an annual publication. Three volumes of these digests are shown in Exhibit 16.8.

Advantages of the **American Digest System.**   The advantage of the *American Digest System* is its vast coverage of cases from different courts. The digests cover almost every topic, and most key numbers are represented, even though they may relate to only a few cases. Some of the most common areas of the law contain hundreds of different case abstracts, offering the researcher a wide variety of resources to consider. Under each key number, cases are listed by type of court. Federal court cases appear first, starting with a listing of decisions issued by the United States Supreme Court. This listing is followed by listings of appellate court decisions and, finally, district court cases. State court cases follow the federal court listings and are arranged in alphabetical order by state.

Each of West's decennial digests also offers the researcher many helpful finding tools. The **table of cases** lists all of the cases included in the digest, in alphabetical order. This listing usually appears in the last volume of the set. The decennial digests also have topical outlines that list various subtopics. If you know the specific topic on which you want to focus, all you need to do is locate the digest containing that topic and review the outline for specific subtopics. Exhibit 16.9 on the following page shows outlines for the topic and subtopics relating to negligence, as well as key-numbered annotations. Each volume of the digest system lists the various topics that it contains.

OTHER DIGESTS.   There are other digests for specific jurisdictions and specialized interest areas. For example, the *Lawyers' Edition of the Digest of the Supreme Court Reports* corresponds to decisions listed in the *Lawyers' Edition of the Supreme Court Reports*. Both are published by West Group and are similar in organizational style to the West digests. Other publishers also publish state-specific digests, such as Callahan's *Michigan Digest*.

Annotations: *American Law Reports*

The *American Law Reports (A.L.R.)* and *American Law Reports Federal (A.L.R. Federal)*, published by West Group, are also useful resources for the legal researcher. An *A.L.R.* volume is shown in Exhibit 16.10 on page 585. These reports are multivolume sets that present the full text of selected cases in numerous areas of the law. They are helpful in finding cases from jurisdictions throughout the country with similar factual and legal issues.

There are five different series of *American Law Reports,* covering case law since 1919. The first and second series contain separate digests that provide references to cases and also have word indexes to assist the researcher in locating specific areas. The remaining sets of *A.L.R.* volumes use the *Quick Index* approach to access cases and information on a particular topic (see Exhibit 16.11 on page 586). The cases presented in these reporters are followed by annotations—that is, references to articles that explain or comment on the specific issues involved in the cases. These reporters can therefore be a good source to turn to for an overview of a specific area of law or current trend in the law.

When using any of the volumes of *A.L.R.,* the researcher must be sure to update her or his results. *A.L.R.* annotations are periodically updated by the addition of relevant cases. For the first series, the annotations are updated in a set of books called the *A.L.R. Blue Book of Supplemental Decisions.* The second series is updated in the *A.L.R. Later Case Service,* and the remaining series are made current by pocket-part supplements located in the front of each volume. In addition, the researcher can

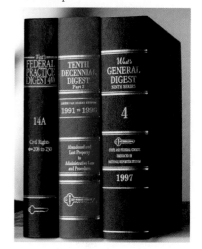

table of cases
An alphabetical list of the cases that have been cited or reproduced in a legal text, case digest, or other legal source.

EXHIBIT 16.9

Outlines for Topics and Subtopics in a West *Decennial Digest*

Reproduced with permission of West Group.

---

42 11th D Pt 1—175

NEGLIGENCE

XVII. PREMISES LIABIITY.—Cont'd

(C) STANDARD OF CARE.—Cont'd

1075. Care required of store and business proprietors.
1076. ____ In general.
1077. ____ Inspection and discovery.
1078. ____ Protection against act of third persons.
1079. Standard established by statute or other regulations.

(D) BREACH OF DUTY.

1085. In general.
1086. Defect or dangerous conditions generally.
1087. Knowledge or notice in general.
1088. ____ In general.
1089. ____ Constructive notice.
1090. Miscellaneous particular cases.
1095. Slips and falls in general.
1100. Buildings and structures.
1101. ____ In general.
1102. ____ Doors, entryways and exits.
1103. ____ Windows.
1104. ____ Floors.
    (1). In general.
    (2). Knowledge of condition or danger.
    (3). Falls in general.
    (4). Inequalities in surface.
    (5). Rugs, carpets and mats.
    (6). Water and other substances.
    (7). Objects and debris.
    (8). Cleaning and waxing.
1110. ____ Steps, stairs and ramps.
    (1). In general.
    (2). Substances and objects.
    (3). Handrails.
1115. ____ Walls and paint.
1116. ____ Roofs and ceilings.
1117. ____ Elevators and escalators.
1118. ____ Decks, balconies, and patios.
1119. ____ Furniture, shelves, displays, carts and other accessories
1125. ____ Exterior grounds in general.
1126. Private walkways and paths.
1127. Parking lots and driveways.
1128. Trees.
    * * * *
    * * * *

(F) RECREATIONAL USE DOCTRINE AND STATUTES

1191. In general.
1192. Purpose of doctrine.
1193. Construction of statutes in general.
1194. Property, conditions, activities and persons covered.
1195. Charges and fees for use.
1196. Duties and care required.
1197. Willful or malicious acts.

(G) LIABILITIES RELATING TO CONSTRUCTION, DEMOLITION AND REPAIR.

1201. In general.
1202. Defects in buildings and structures in general.
    (1). In general.
    (2). Design defects.
    (3). Construction defects.
1204. Accidents and injuries in general.
    (1). In general.
    (2). Covering or guarding dangerous places.

    * * * *

    * * * *

(I) PROXIMATE CAUSE.

1220. In general.
1221. Necessity of causation.
1222. Necessity of legal or proximate cause.
1223. Requisites, definitions and distinctions.
1224. Failure to act or warn; omissions in general.
1225. Miscellaneous particular cases.
1226. Slips and falls in general.
1227. Buildings and structures.
1228. ____ In general.
1229. ____ Floors; slips and falls.
1230. ____ Steps, stairs and ramps.
1231. ____ Elevators and escalators.
1232. Private walkways and paths.
1233. Parking lots and driveways.
1234. Pools, bodies of water and beaches.
1235. Snow and ice.

---

consult the annotation history table located at the end of the quick index to see whether any new annotations supplement or change an earlier annotation.

Treatises

treatise

In legal research, a work that provides a systematic, detailed, and scholarly review of a particular legal subject.

A **treatise** is a formal scholarly work that treats a given subject systematically and in detail. Treatises are written by individuals such as law professors, legal scholars, and practicing attorneys. Law treatises are commentaries that summarize, interpret, or evaluate different areas of substantive and procedural law. Some treatises are published in multivolume sets, and others are contained in a single book. Each text contains a table of contents and an index or indexes for efficient reference, and most contain a table of cases referred to within the text. Although treatises are secondary materials and have no binding effect on courts, they may merit particular judicial respect and recognition when written by leading scholars in the field. Many of these scholarly works are classics and serve as valuable sources of information many years after publication.

Hornbooks are single-volume treatises that synthesize the basic principles of an area of the law. Paralegals who seek to familiarize themselves with a particular area of the law, such as torts or contracts, should review one of the many available hornbooks. For example, in researching the issue in Trent Hoffman's negligence case, you might want to locate the learned treatise *Prosser and Keeton on the Law of Torts,* Fifth Edition, which is included in West's Hornbook Series, and read the sections on negligence in that volume. (Exhibit 16.12 on page 587 shows the page of this book that opens the chapter on defenses to negligence.) This text was written by distinguished lawyers from leading law schools. In addition to providing a clear and organized discussion of the subject matter, hornbooks present many examples of case law and references to cases that may be helpful to the researcher seeking cases with similar facts and issues.

Treatises are usually organized by section numbers rather than by page numbers. As is characteristic of other legal sources, they are divided into topics and subtopics. Most treatises are updated by supplementary loose-leaf pages or pocket-part additions.

Restatements of the Law

The American Law Institute (ALI) has drafted and published compilations of the common law called *Restatements of the Law,* which generally summarize the common law rules followed by most states. There are *Restatements* in the areas of contracts, torts, agency, trusts, property, restitution, security, judgments, and conflict of laws. Many of the *Restatements* are now in their second or third editions. Exhibit 16.13 on page 587 shows a volume of the *Restatement (Third) of Torts.*

The *Restatements,* like other secondary sources of law, do not in themselves have the force of law but are an important source of legal analysis and opinion on which judges often rely in making their decisions. Each section in the *Restatements* contains a statement of the principles of law that are generally accepted by the courts and/or embodied in statutes, followed by a discussion of these principles. The discussions present particular cases as examples and also discuss variations.

Legal Periodicals

Legal periodicals, such as law reviews, are another secondary source of authority. Legal periodicals contain thoroughly researched information on specific areas of the law. The authors are usually law professors, attorneys prominent in their fields, judges, legal scholars, or law students. The periodicals discuss and evaluate specific laws and their implications. Additionally, they may advocate changes in the law.

Articles in legal periodicals can be extremely helpful to paralegals. Many law-review articles present well-written and informative overviews of areas of the law with which paralegals may be unfamiliar. Legal periodicals may be helpful case-finding aids as well. For example, suppose you have a case on point and find that a recent law-review article cites that case. The article contains numerous footnotes citing relevant cases and statutes and describing the rules in various jurisdictions. By reading the article, you can get an idea of the most important cases on your topic, form an understanding of the arguments involved, and discover the various rules applied by different courts. If the article is current, it may be a good source on recent developments and trends in the law as well. Most important, you can save the hours of research time you would have spent finding the cases or authorities cited by the author. As with all legal sources, however, you must verify and update any case information found in law-review articles.

hornbook
A single-volume scholarly discussion, or treatise, on a particular legal subject (such as property law).

EXHIBIT 16.10
American Law Reports

Reproduced with permission of West Group.

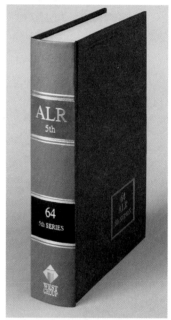

On the Web
You can learn more about the American Law Institute (ALI) and its publications, including information on which *Restatements of the Law* are in the process of being revised, by accessing the ALI's Web site at **http://www.ali.org.**

EXHIBIT 16.11

Excerpt from the *A.L.R. Federal's* Quick Index

Reproduced with permission of West Group.

ALR 3d

QUICK INDEX

ABANDONMENT

Contracts (this index)

Criminal enterprise: withdrawal from or abandonment of criminal enterprise, 8 Am Jur POF 2d, pp 231–266

Disclosure of trade secret in court proceedings as abandonment of secrecy, 58 ALR3d 1318

Easement: abandonment of easement, 3 Am Jur POF 2d, pp 647–674

Eminent domain: what constitutes abandonment of eminent domain proceeding so as to charge condemnor with liability for condemnee's expenses or the like, 68 ALR3d 610

Felony-murder: what constitutes termination of felony for purpose of felony-murder rule, 58 ALR3d 851

Fire insurance: obtaining new property insurance as cancellation of existing insurance, 3 ALR3d 1072

Harassment or other mistreatment by employer or supervisor as "good cause" justifying abandonment of employment, 76 ALR3d 1089, 9 Am Jur POF2d, pp 697–728

Home, abandonment of: what voluntary acts of child, other than marriage or entry into military service, terminate parent's obligation to support, 32 ALR3d 1055

Infestation of leased dwelling or apartment with vermin as entitling tenant to abandon premises or as constructive eviction by landlord in absence of express covenant of habitability, 27 ALR3d 924

Mechanics' lien: abandonment of construction or of contract as affecting time for filing mechanics' liens or time for giving notice to owner, 52 ALR3d 797

Mines and Minerals (this index)

Mitigation: landlord's duty, on tenant's failure to occupy, or abandonment of, premises,

to mitigate damages by accepting or procuring another tenant, 21 ALR3d 534

Nonconforming use: zoning-abandonment of lawful nonconforming use, 18 Am Jur POF 2d, pp 731–777

Oil or gas: duty and liability as to plugging oil or gas well abandoned or taken out of production, 50 ALR3d 240

Physician's abandonment of patient, 3 Am Jur POF 2d, pp 117–165

Principal and agent: insurance agent's statement or conduct indicating that insurer's cancellation of policy shall not take effect as binding on insurer, 3 ALR3d 1135

Proofs: abandonment, 1 Am Jur POF, pp 1–10

Real estate contract: purchaser's abandonment of land sales contract, 5 Am Jur POF 2d, pp 165–188

Trade Secrets (this index)

Unemployment Compensation (this index)

Withdrawal, after provocation of conflict, as reviving right of self-defense, 55 ALR3d 1000

Zoning (this index)

ABANDONMENT OF CASE

Condemnation of rural property for highway purposes, abandonment of action involving, 8 Am Jur Trials, pp 57–102

ABANDONMENT-OF-SHIP DRILL

Liability for injury to or death of passenger in connection with a fire drill or abandonment-of-ship drill aboard a vessel, 8 ALR3d 650

ABANDONMENT OF SPOUSE OR CHILD

Desertion (this index)

ABATEMENT

Action.

Consult POCKET PART for later annotations   **1**

Paralegals can locate articles relevant to a particular issue in a number of ways. As mentioned, many law books are annotated, and the annotation accompanying a particular case or statute may refer you to relevant law-review articles. The periodical guides that are available in the law library are also helpful. The two most popular are *Index to Legal Periodicals* (see Exhibit 16.14 on page 590), which indexes articles appearing in approximately five hundred periodicals, and the *Current Legal Index*, which covers over seven hundred legal periodicals. Both publications include subject indexes and indexes of authors and titles.

Chapter 11

NEGLIGENCE: DEFENSES

§ 65. Contributory Negligence

The two most common defenses in a negligence action are contributory negligence and assumption of risk. Since both developed at a comparatively late date in the development of the common law,[1] and since both clearly operate to the advantage of the defendant, they are commonly regarded as defenses to a tort which would otherwise be established. All courts now hold that the burden of plead-

ing and proof of the contributory negligence of the plaintiff is on the defendant.[2]

Contributory negligence is conduct on the part of the plaintiff, contributing as a legal cause to the harm he has suffered, which falls below the standard to which he is required to conform for his own protection.[3] Unlike assumption of risk, the defense does not rest upon the idea that the defendant is relieved of any duty toward the plaintiff. Rather, although the defendant has violated his duty, has been negligent, and would oth-

---

§ 65

1. The earliest contributory negligence case is Butterfield v. Forrester, 1809, 11 East 60, 103 Eng.Rep. 926. The first American case appears to have been Smith v. Smith, 1824, 19 Mass. (2 Pick.) 621. Assumption of risk first appears in a negligence case in 1799. See infra, § 68 n. 1.

2. E.g., Wilkinson v. Hartford Accident & Indemnity Co., La.1982, 411 So.2d 22; Moodie v. Santoni, 1982, 292 Md. 582, 441 A.2d 323; Addair v. Bryant, 1981, ___ W.Va. ___, 284 S.E.2d 374; Pickett v. Parks, 1981, 208 Neb. 310, 303 N.W.2d 296; Hatton v. Chem-Haulers, Inc., Ala.1980, 393 So.2d 950; Sampson v. W. F. Enterprises, Inc., Mo.App.1980, 611 S.W.2d 333; Howard v. Howard, Ky.App.1980, 607 S.W.2d 119; cf. Reuter v. United States, W.D.Pa.1982, 534 F.Supp. 731 (presumption that person killed or suffering loss of memory was acting with due care).

Illinois and certain other jurisdictions held to the contrary for some time. See West Chicago Street Railroad Co. v. Liderman, 1900, 187 Ill. 463, 58 N.E. 367; Kotler v. Lalley, 1930, 112 Conn. 86, 151 A. 433; Dreier v. McDermott, 1913, 157 Iowa 726, 141 N.W. 315. See Green, Illinois Negligence Law II, 1944, 39 Ill.L.Rev. 116, 125–130.

3. Second Restatement of Torts, § 463. See generally, Malone, The Formative Era of Contributory Negligence, 1946, 41 Ill.L.Rev. 151; James, Contributory Negligence, 1953, 62 Yale L.J. 691; Bohlen, Contributory Negligence, 1908, 21 Harv.L.Rev. 233; Lowndes, Contributory Negligence, 1934, 22 Geo.L.J. 674; Malone, Some Ruminations on Contributory Negligence, 1981, 65 Utah L.Rev. 91; Schwartz, Contributory and Comparative Negligence: A Reappraisal, 1978, 87 Yale L.J. 697; Note, 1979, 39 La.L.Rev. 637.

451

EXHIBIT 16.12
A Page from the *Hornbook on the Law of Torts*

Reproduced with permission of West Group.

EXHIBIT 16.13
Restatement (Third) of Torts: Products Liability

Reproduced with permission of West Group.

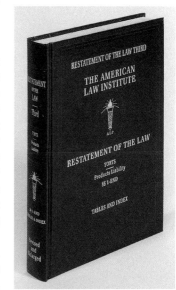

THE CASE REPORTING SYSTEM

The primary sources of case law are, of course, the cases themselves. Once you have learned what cases are relevant to the issue you are researching, you need to find the cases and examine the exact words of the court opinions. (See this chapter's *Featured Guest* article on the next page for tips on conducting legal research.) Assume, for example, that in researching the issue in Hoffman's case, you learn that your state's supreme court, a few years ago, issued a decision on a case with a very similar fact pattern. In that case, the state supreme court upheld a lower court's judgment that a retail business owner had to pay extensive damages to a customer who was injured on the store's premises. You know that the state supreme court's decision is a mandatory authority, and to your knowledge, the decision has not been overruled or modified. Therefore, the case will likely provide weighty support to your attorney's arguments in support of Hoffman's claim.

At this point, however, you have only read *about* the case in secondary sources. To locate the case itself and make sure it is applicable, you need to understand the case reporting system and the legal "shorthand" employed in referencing court cases.

FEATURED GUEST: E. J. YERA

Ten Tips for Effective Legal Research

BIOGRAPHICAL NOTE

In 1987, E. J. Yera graduated from the University of Miami School of Law, where he subsequently served as a research instructor until 1989.

After clerking for the U.S. District Court for the Southern District of Florida, Yera served as corporate counsel for Holmes Regional Medical Center in Melbourne, Florida, and its affiliates until 1995. He then became a member of the Health Care Task Force in the Antitrust Division of the U.S. Department of Justice in Washington, D.C.

In 1997, Yera became a member of the U.S. Attorney's Office in the Southern District of Florida. He has taught and lectured in various paralegal programs and has published several articles.

If you perform legal research frequently, you will develop a routine. The purpose of this article is not to give you ironclad rules but to set out ten guidelines that will help you find the routine that is most comfortable for you. You may come back to this article and reread it over time. Now, however, as you read it for the first time, think about how you can use the tips in your future research tasks.

1. Before You Start, Make Sure You Know the Exact Legal Issue You Will Be Researching. You would be surprised at how many students, paralegals, and lawyers research a question for hours only to discover they were not researching the correct legal question. Before you start your research, you should determine the legal question or issue that needs to be researched. You might learn this from reviewing information you already have available, such as a summary of a client interview. If you have an opportunity to ask questions of the attorney giving you a research assignment, do so. What counts, in the end, is coming back with the correct answers, not impressing the attorney by appearing to understand the research task completely when you first hear about it. It will take you twice as long to finish the assignment if you research the wrong issue or if you are unsure what the issue is.

2. Understand the Language of the Issue. Often, the researcher finds that he or she cannot find the answer because the legal terms used in defining the problem are unfamiliar to him or her. Legal terms, or "terms of art," as they are often called, are as unfamiliar to many people as a foreign language. If you are uncertain about the meaning of any term or phrase,

look it up in a law dictionary or encyclopedia to get a general idea of its meaning. Depending on how broad the term is, you may want to read a hornbook on the topic to give you a basic understanding of it. For example, assume you are researching an issue relating to securities law. If you do not have a clear understanding of what securities are, there is no way in the world that you can conduct effective research on the issue. You will need to acquire some background knowledge before you focus on the particular research topic.

3. Be Aware of the Circular Nature of Legal Research and Use It to Your Advantage. Students often ask whether primary or secondary sources should be researched first. The answer is that it does not matter, as long as you always research both types of sources. By researching both primary and secondary sources on a topic, you can be assured that you are almost always double-checking your own work. For example, in a case (primary source of law) on a particular issue, the judge writing the opinion will discuss any pertinent statutes on the issue. Similarly, most annotated versions of a statute (annotations are secondary sources of law) give a listing, following the text of the statute, of cases applying the statute and the context in which the statute was applied. The reason you check both sources is to make sure you have found all of the relevant materials.

4. Until You Submit the Assignment, Always Assume There Are Additional Relevant Materials to Find. You need to keep on your toes until you complete your research task. Always assuming that further relevant materials must be located will help

FEATURED GUEST, *Continued*

you do this. Of course, there comes a point when you have to assume that you *have* covered the research territory, and knowing when to stop doing research is perhaps one of the hardest things to learn. Certain legal issues can be researched for months and even years. The intent of this tip, though, is to encourage you not to cut corners when conducting research.

5. Keep a List of What Sources You Have Found and Where They Have Led You. You do not want to spend valuable time wondering if you have already checked certain sources. Therefore, it is important to construct a "road map" of where you have been and where you are going.

6. Take the Time to Become Familiar with the Sources You Are Using. It probably seems obvious that you need to become familiar with your sources, yet this requirement is sometimes overlooked. For example, a case digest (a volume summarizing cases) may indicate on its spine that the digest covers the years "1961 to Date." "To Date," however, does not mean that it is the most current digest; it only means that the digest covers cases up to the date of publication. You should take the time to read the first few pages of the digest to verify its contents. This is true generally for any source you are using—look it over carefully before assuming it contains the sources you need.

7. Always Be Aware of the Jurisdiction and the Time Frame You Are Researching. If you are researching an issue that will be resolved by a Florida state court, then your emphasis should be on

Florida cases. Of course, there are times when no case law is available, and you must then find cases on point from other states to use as persuasive authorities. You must also be aware of the time frame covered by the source you are using (as mentioned in Tip 6). Be aware when researching any area of the law that very often there is either a loose-leaf service or a pamphlet or pocket part (a small booklet that slips into a pocket of the bound volume) containing newer information. Always ask yourself the following question: Where can the most up-to-date material be found? If you don't know, ask a law librarian who does.

8. Always Use *Shepard's* to Make Sure the Cases You Are Using Are Up to Date. *Shepard's Citations* is a set of volumes that helps the researcher of case law in two ways. First, it lists other cases that have cited the cases you have found. This information is helpful because if another case has cited a case you have found, that other case may also be relevant to your issue, and thus you may be able to use it. Also, cases that cite your case are more recent, and using one or more of those cases may thus be advantageous. Second, *Shepard's* tells you, among other things, whether the cases that you have found are still "good law"—that is, whether the cases have been overruled, reversed, or the like. Knowing this information is crucial—because presenting a case to your attorney that no longer represents good law could well be a short cut to the unemployment line.

9. Use Computerized Legal-Research Services to Update Your Research Results. Computerized legal databases such as Westlaw®

"What counts, in the end, is coming back with the correct answers . . . ."

and Lexis® allow you to update your research results by using online citators. Also, these services allow you to search the available case law for words or phrases. By doing so, you can actually create your own indexing system. Additionally, the Internet is a great source for legal materials. Several state and federal courts, government agencies, law schools, and bar associations have developed Web sites containing different types of primary and secondary legal materials.

10. Twice a Year, Take Three or Four Hours and Browse through Your Local Law Library. You cannot use sources effectively if you do not know that they exist. You should periodically—say, twice a year—spend an afternoon in the law library browsing through the shelves. Read the first few pages of each new source; then make a note of what the source contains. Ask the librarian for new sources in your area. The time you save later will more than compensate for an afternoon's time spent in the library. You will be surprised at how quickly the new sources you discovered or were told about at the law library come to mind when you receive a research assignment, and they may figure significantly in your research.

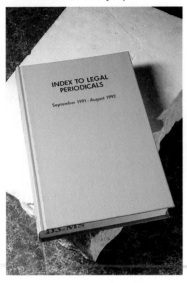

ETHICAL CONCERN
Avoiding Plagiarism

Plagiarism—copying the exact, or nearly exact, words of another without acknowledging the author of those words—may constitute a violation of federal copyright law (discussed in Chapter 8). You should realize that it is possible to plagiarize another's words *unintentionally*. Suppose, for example, that you are taking notes from a legal treatise, such as a hornbook on the law of torts, and you copy several paragraphs word for word for your future reference. You don't enclose the paragraphs in quotation marks because you know you will remember that those are not your words but the words of the hornbook's authors. A week or so later, you are preparing a brief and, referring to your notes, you include those paragraphs, assuming that they are your own version of what the authors said in the hornbook. In short, you have plagiarized a substantial portion of another's copyrighted work without even being aware of it. To ensure that your employer will not face a lawsuit for copyright infringement, always remember to include quotation marks (and the exact source of the quoted material) when copying another's words.

State Court Decisions

Most state trial court decisions are not published. Except in New York and a few other states that publish selected opinions of their trial courts, decisions from state trial courts are merely filed in the office of the clerk of the court, where the decisions are available for public inspection.

STATE REPORTERS.   Written decisions of the appellate, or reviewing, courts, however, are published and distributed. The reported appellate decisions are published chronologically in volumes called *reports* or *reporters,* which are numbered consecutively. State appellate court decisions are found in the state reporters of that particular state. The reporters may be either the "official" reporters, designated as such by the state legislature, or "unofficial" reporters, published by West Group. Although some states still have official reporters (and a few states, such as New York and California, have more than one official reporter), many states have eliminated their own official reporters in favor of West's National Reporter System, discussed next.

REGIONAL REPORTERS.   State court opinions also appear in regional units of the National Reporter System, published by West Group. Most lawyers and libraries have the West reporters because they report cases more quickly and are distributed more widely than the state-published reports. Also, the lawyer can look up cases in other neighboring states in the same book (thus saving the cost of buying multiple state-published reports).

The National Reporter System divides the states into the following geographic areas: *Atlantic* (A. or A.2d), *South Eastern* (S.E. or S.E.2d), *South Western* (S.W., S.W.2d, or S.W.3d), *North Western* (N.W. or N.W.2d), *North Eastern* (N.E. or N.E.2d), *Southern* (So. or So.2d), and *Pacific* (P., P.2d, or P.3d). The *2d* and *3d* in the abbreviations refer to *Second Series* and *Third Series,* respectively. The states included in each of these regional divisions are indicated in Exhibit 16.15, which illustrates West's National Reporter System. Note that the names of the areas may not be the same as what we commonly think of as a geographical region. For

EXHIBIT 16.15
National Reporter System—Regional and Federal

Regional Reporters	Coverage Beginning	Coverage
Atlantic Reporter (A. or A.2d)	1885	Connecticut, Delaware, Maine, Maryland, New Hampshire, New Jersey, Pennsylvania, Rhode Island, Vermont, and District of Columbia.
North Eastern Reporter (N.E. or N.E.2d)	1885	Illinois, Indiana, Massachusetts, New York, and Ohio.
North Western Reporter (N.W. or N.W.2d)	1879	Iowa, Michigan, Minnesota, Nebraska, North Dakota, South Dakota, and Wisconsin.
Pacific Reporter (P. or P.2d)	1883	Alaska, Arizona, California, Colorado, Hawaii, Idaho, Kansas, Montana, Nevada, New Mexico, Oklahoma, Oregon, Utah, Washington, and Wyoming.
South Eastern Reporter (S.E. or S.E.2d)	1887	Georgia, North Carolina, South Carolina, Virginia, and West Virginia.
South Western Reporter (S.W. or S.W.2d)	1886	Arkansas, Kentucky, Missouri, Tennessee, and Texas.
Southern Reporter (So. or So.2d)	1887	Alabama, Florida, Louisiana, and Mississippi.

Federal Reporters		
Federal Reporter (F., F.2d, or F. 3d)	1880	U.S. Circuit Court from 1880 to 1912; U.S. Commerce Court from 1911 to 1913; U.S. District Courts from 1880 to 1932; U.S. Court of Claims (now called U.S. Court of Federal Claims) from 1929 to 1932 and since 1960; U.S. Court of Appeals since 1891; U.S. Court of Customs and Patent Appeals since 1929; and U.S. Emergency Court of Appeals since 1943.
Federal Supplement (F.Supp. 2d)	1932	U.S. Court of Claims from 1932 to 1960; U.S. District Courts since 1932; and U.S. Customs Court since 1956.
Federal Rules Decisions (F.R.D.)	1939	U.S. District Courts involving the Federal Rules of Civil Procedure since 1939 and Federal Rules of Criminal Procedure since 1946.
Supreme Court Reporter (S.Ct.)	1882	U.S. Supreme Court since the October term of 1882.
Bankruptcy Reporter (Bankr.)	1980	Bankruptcy decisions of U.S. Bankruptcy Courts, U.S. District Courts, U.S. Courts of Appeals, and U.S. Supreme Court.
Military Justice Reporter (M.J.)	1978	U.S. Court of Military Appeals and Courts of Military Review for the Army, Navy, Air Force, and Coast Guard.

NATIONAL REPORTER SYSTEM MAP

example, the *North Western* reporter does not include the Pacific Northwest but does include states, such as Iowa, that most people do not think of as being in the Northwest.

CITATION FORMAT.   In order to locate a case, you must know where to look. After an appellate decision has been published, it is normally referred to (cited) by the name of the case, the volume number and the abbreviated name of the book in which the case is located, the page number on which the case begins, and the year. In other words, there are five parts to a standard **citation:**

citation
In case law, a reference to a case by the volume number, name, page number of the reporter in which a case can be found, and the year. In statutory and administrative law, a reference to the title number, name, and section of the code in which a statute or regulation can be found.

Case Name	Volume number	Name of book	Page number	(Year)

This basic format is used for every citation regardless of whether the case is published in an official state reporter or a regional reporter (or both). When more than one reporter is cited for the same case, each reference is called a **parallel citation** and is separated from the next citation by a comma. The first citation is to the state's official reporter (if there is one), although the text of the court's opinion will be the same (parallel) at any of the listed locations.

parallel citation
A second (or third) citation for a given case. When a case is published in more than one reporter, each citation is a parallel citation to the other(s).

To illustrate how to find case law from citations, suppose you want to find the following case: *Davidson v. Microsoft Corp.,* 143 Md.App. 43, 792 A.2d 336 (2002). You can see that the opinion in this case can be found in Volume 143 of the official *Maryland Appellate Reports,* on page 43. The parallel citation is to Volume 792 of the *Atlantic Reporter, Second Series,* page 336. In some cases, additional information may appear in parentheses at the end of a citation, usually indicating the court that heard the case (if that information is not clear from the citation alone). Exhibit 16.16 on pages 593 to 595 further illustrates how to read case citations.

When conducting legal research, you should write down the citations to the cases or other legal sources that you have consulted, quoted, or want to refer to in a written summary of your research results. Several guides have been published on how to cite legal sources. The most widely used guide is a book entitled *The Bluebook: A Uniform System of Citation,* which is published by the Harvard Law Review Association. This book explains the proper format for citing cases, statutes, constitutions, regulations, and other legal sources. It is a good idea to memorize the basic format for citations to cases and statutory law because these legal sources are frequently cited in legal writing. Another popular guide is a booklet entitled *ALWD Citation Manual: A Professional System of Citation,* which is published by the Association of Legal Writing Directors and Darby Dickerson.

Federal Court Decisions

As mentioned earlier, court decisions from the U.S. district courts (federal trial courts) are published in West's *Federal Supplement* (F.Supp. or F.Supp.2d), and opinions from the circuit courts of appeals are reported in West's *Federal Reporter* (F., F.2d, or F.3d). These are both unofficial reporters (there are no official reporters for these courts). Both the *Federal Reporter* and the *Federal Supplement* incorporate decisions from specialized federal courts. West also publishes separate reporters, such as its *Bankruptcy Reporter,* that contain decisions in certain specialized fields under federal law.

On the Web
To find Supreme Court opinions and opinions issued by the federal appellate courts, a good starting point is FindLaw's site at **http://www.findlaw.com.**

United States Supreme Court Decisions

Opinions from the United States Supreme Court are published in several reporters, including the *United States Reports,* West's *Supreme Court Reporter,* and the

EXHIBIT 16.16
How to Read Case Citations

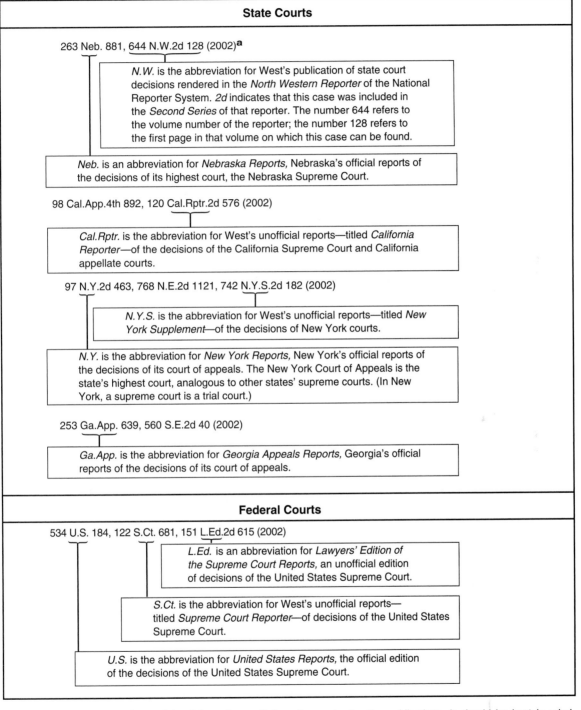

State Courts

263 Neb. 881, 644 N.W.2d 128 (2002)[a]

> *N.W.* is the abbreviation for West's publication of state court decisions rendered in the *North Western Reporter* of the National Reporter System. *2d* indicates that this case was included in the *Second Series* of that reporter. The number 644 refers to the volume number of the reporter; the number 128 refers to the first page in that volume on which this case can be found.

> *Neb.* is an abbreviation for *Nebraska Reports,* Nebraska's official reports of the decisions of its highest court, the Nebraska Supreme Court.

98 Cal.App.4th 892, 120 Cal.Rptr.2d 576 (2002)

> *Cal.Rptr.* is the abbreviation for West's unofficial reports—titled *California Reporter*—of the decisions of the California Supreme Court and California appellate courts.

97 N.Y.2d 463, 768 N.E.2d 1121, 742 N.Y.S.2d 182 (2002)

> *N.Y.S.* is the abbreviation for West's unofficial reports—titled *New York Supplement*—of the decisions of New York courts.

> *N.Y.* is the abbreviation for *New York Reports,* New York's official reports of the decisions of its court of appeals. The New York Court of Appeals is the state's highest court, analogous to other states' supreme courts. (In New York, a supreme court is a trial court.)

253 Ga.App. 639, 560 S.E.2d 40 (2002)

> *Ga.App.* is the abbreviation for *Georgia Appeals Reports,* Georgia's official reports of the decisions of its court of appeals.

Federal Courts

534 U.S. 184, 122 S.Ct. 681, 151 L.Ed.2d 615 (2002)

> *L.Ed.* is an abbreviation for *Lawyers' Edition of the Supreme Court Reports,* an unofficial edition of decisions of the United States Supreme Court.

> *S.Ct.* is the abbreviation for West's unofficial reports—titled *Supreme Court Reporter*—of decisions of the United States Supreme Court.

> *U.S.* is the abbreviation for *United States Reports,* the official edition of the decisions of the United States Supreme Court.

a. The case names have been deleted from these citations to emphasize the publications. It should be kept in mind, however, that the name of a case is as important as the specific numbers of the volumes in which it is found. If a citation is incorrect, the correct citation may be found in a publication's index of case names. The date of a case is also important because, in addition to providing a check on error in citations, the value of a recent case as an authority is likely to be greater than that of an earlier case.

EXHIBIT 16.16
How to Read Case Citations—Continued

Federal Courts (continued)

287 F.3d 122 (2d Cir. 2002)

> *2d Cir.* is an abbreviation denoting that this case was decided in the United States Court of Appeals for the Second Circuit.

187 F.Supp.2d 1288 (D.Colo. 2002)

> *D.Colo.* is an abbreviation indicating that the United States District Court for the District of Colorado decided this case.

Statutory and Other Citations

18 U.S.C. Section 1961(1)(A)

> *U.S.C.* denotes *United States Code,* the codification of *United States Statutes at Large.* The number 18 refers to the statute's U.S.C. title number and 1961 to its section number within that title. The number 1 refers to a subsection within the section and the letter A to a subdivision within the subsection.

UCC 2–206(1)(b)

> *UCC* is an abbreviation for *Uniform Commercial Code.* The first number 2 is a reference to an article of the UCC and 206 to a section within that article. The number 1 refers to a subsection within the section and the letter b to a subdivision within the subsection.

Restatement (Second) of Contracts, Section 162

> *Restatement (Second) of Contracts* refers to the second edition of the American Law Institute's *Restatement of the Law of Contracts.* The number 162 refers to a specific section.

17 C.F.R. Section 230.505

> *C.F.R.* is an abbreviation for *Code of Federal Regulations,* a compilation of federal administrative regulations. The number 17 designates the regulation's title number, and 230.505 designates a specific section within that title.

Westlaw® Citations[b]

2002 WL 10238

> *WL* is an abbreviation for Westlaw®. The number 2002 is the year of the document that can be found with this citation in the Westlaw® database. The number 10238 is a number assigned to a specific document. A higher number indicates that a document was added to the Westlaw® database later in the year.

---

b. Many court decisions that are not yet published or that are not intended for publication can be accessed through Westlaw®, an online legal database.

EXHIBIT 16.16
How to Read Case Citations—Continued

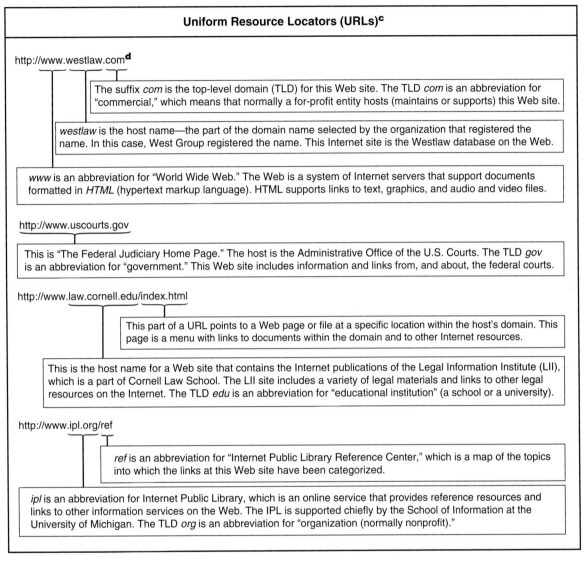

Uniform Resource Locators (URLs)^c

http://www.westlaw.com^d

The suffix *com* is the top-level domain (TLD) for this Web site. The TLD *com* is an abbreviation for "commercial," which means that normally a for-profit entity hosts (maintains or supports) this Web site.

westlaw is the host name—the part of the domain name selected by the organization that registered the name. In this case, West Group registered the name. This Internet site is the Westlaw database on the Web.

www is an abbreviation for "World Wide Web." The Web is a system of Internet servers that support documents formatted in *HTML* (hypertext markup language). HTML supports links to text, graphics, and audio and video files.

http://www.uscourts.gov

This is "The Federal Judiciary Home Page." The host is the Administrative Office of the U.S. Courts. The TLD *gov* is an abbreviation for "government." This Web site includes information and links from, and about, the federal courts.

http://www.law.cornell.edu/index.html

This part of a URL points to a Web page or file at a specific location within the host's domain. This page is a menu with links to documents within the domain and to other Internet resources.

This is the host name for a Web site that contains the Internet publications of the Legal Information Institute (LII), which is a part of Cornell Law School. The LII site includes a variety of legal materials and links to other legal resources on the Internet. The TLD *edu* is an abbreviation for "educational institution" (a school or a university).

http://www.ipl.org/ref

ref is an abbreviation for "Internet Public Library Reference Center," which is a map of the topics into which the links at this Web site have been categorized.

ipl is an abbreviation for Internet Public Library, which is an online service that provides reference resources and links to other information services on the Web. The IPL is supported chiefly by the School of Information at the University of Michigan. The TLD *org* is an abbreviation for "organization (normally nonprofit)."

c. URLs are frequently changed as sites are redesigned and may not be working for other reasons, such as when a Web site has been deleted. If you are unable to find sites in this text with the specified URLs, go to the text's Web site at **http://westlegalstudies.com**, where you may find an updated URL for the site or a URL for a similar site.
d. The basic form for a URL is "service://hostname/path." The Internet service for all of the URLs in this text is *http* (hypertext transfer protocol). Most Web browsers will add this prefix automatically when a user enters a host name or a hostname/path.

Lawyers' Edition of the Supreme Court Reports, each of which we discuss below. A sample citation to a Supreme Court case is also included in Exhibit 16.16.

THE *UNITED STATES REPORTS.*   The *United States Reports* (U.S.) is the official edition of all decisions of the United States Supreme Court for which there are written opinions. Published by the federal government, the series includes reports of Supreme Court cases dating from the August term of 1791. Approximately two to four weeks after the Supreme Court issues a decision, the official slip opinion is published by the U.S. Government Printing Office. The **slip opinion** is the first authoritative text of the opinion and is printed as an individual pamphlet. After a

slip opinion
A judicial opinion published shortly after the decision is made and not yet included in a case reporter or advance sheets.

TECHNOLOGY AND TODAY'S PARALEGAL

Looking Ahead

Every day, it seems, legislatures propose or pass new laws; administrative agencies propose or issue new regulations; and new cases begin to work their way through the court system. A few of these may reach the nation's highest court. As a paralegal, you can perform a valuable service for your supervising attorney by keeping up with new developments in the legal arena or in your specialty area. Online sources can help you in this task.

IS A NEW *RESTATEMENT* OF THE *LAW* IN PROGRESS?

Suppose you want to discover whether a new edition of one of the *Restatements* is being planned or developed. To find out, you can go to the Web site of the American Law Institute at http://www.ali.org. There, you can find information on all of the *Restatements,* including new editions. You can find out whether the American Law Institute is working on a new edition or has any new publications pertaining to your area of practice. You can also check to see whether an annual pocket part or supplementary pamphlet has been issued that updates the material in one of the bound *Restatement* volumes. If you find a publication you are interested in, you can order it online. In addition, you can request the American Law Institute to send you e-mail notification of any developments pertaining to a particular area or areas of law. As you know, the *Restatements* are secondary sources of law, but the courts are often guided by the principles set forth in these compilations.

ARE ANY NEW UNIFORM LAWS BEING DEVELOPED?

To find out about new uniform laws being developed by the National Conference of Commissioners on Uniform State Laws (NCCUSL), you can visit its Web site at http://www. nccusl.org. There, you will find the full text of all uniform acts, including every draft of the final uniform act. You can also find out which states have already adopted an act and which states currently have adoption legislation pending. In addition, the site provides comprehensive legislative reports by act or by state so that you can see the status of bills that are being considered by legislatures across the country. The site also includes the text of all in-process drafts and proposed revisions to existing uniform laws. While these drafts are just that—they are not yet law—they may become law in the future once approved by the NCCUSL and submitted to the states for adoption. In the meantime, provisions in these drafts may serve as persuasive authorities.

WHAT CASES WILL BE DECIDED BY THE SUPREME COURT THAT COULD AFFECT MY AREA OF PRACTICE?

You can find out what cases are pending before the Supreme Court from a number of online sources. For example, at http://washingtonpost.findlaw.com/supreme_court/docket, you will find a subject index that tells you if the Supreme Court has heard or is scheduled to hear in the current term any cases that involve a specific area of law. Once you click on the area you are interested in, you will find the case name(s) and docket number(s) of interest. You can then access the Court's decision (if a decision has been reached), the briefs submitted by the parties (and others), the transcripts of oral arguments, and the case history (what the lower courts held and why).

The Legal Information Institute of Cornell University provides useful information about the Supreme Court at http://supct.law.cornell.edu/supct/index.php. You can scan through the most recent Supreme Court decisions, view the decisions by month or by term, and search for decisions involving a specific topic. You can also see what cases are pending and what cases have been argued before the Court. You can even subscribe to a service (called the *LII Bulletin*) that will notify you, via e-mail, of Supreme Court rulings within *hours* after they have been handed down.

At http://supremecourt.newstrove.com, you can find a listing of recent articles published in newspapers and magazines relating to cases that were argued before the Supreme Court. This is also a good source of information on issues that the Supreme Court will be addressing. Finally, you can search the Supreme Court's database by docket number or case name and view case information and decisions at http://www.supremecourtus.gov/docket/docket.html.

TECHNOLOGY TIP

Paralegals today can readily access information online to stay current on new developments in the law. More difficult is sorting through the wealth of information available. Search for Web sites that will quickly and efficiently provide information that is pertinent to the area of law in which you are interested. After identifying a site as useful, bookmark it and check it regularly.

number of slip opinions have been issued, the advance sheets of the official *United States Reports* appear. These are issued in pamphlet form to provide a temporary resource until the official bound volume is finally published.

THE *SUPREME COURT REPORTER.*   Supreme Court cases are also published in West's *Supreme Court Reporter* (S.Ct.), which is an unofficial edition of Supreme Court opinions dating from the Court's term in October 1882. In this reporter, the case report—the formal court opinion—is preceded by a brief **syllabus** (summary of the case) and headnotes with key numbers (used throughout the West reporters and digests) prepared by West editors.

syllabus
A brief summary of the holding and legal principles involved in a reported case, which is followed by the court's official opinion.

THE *LAWYERS' EDITION OF THE SUPREME COURT REPORTS.*   The *Lawyers' Edition of the Supreme Court Reports* (L.Ed. or L.Ed.2d), also published by West Group, is an unofficial edition of the entire series of the Supreme Court reports containing many decisions not reported in early official volumes. The advantage offered to the legal researcher by the *Lawyers' Edition* is its research tools. In its second series, it precedes each case report with a full summary of the case and discusses in detail selected cases of special interest to the legal profession. Also, the *Lawyers' Edition* is the only reporter of Supreme Court opinions that provides summaries of the briefs presented by counsel.

UNOFFICIAL LOOSE-LEAF SERVICES.   Unofficial loose-leaf services publish Supreme Court decisions the day after a decision is announced. Two loose-leaf services cover Supreme Court opinions: *United States Law Week,* which is published by the Bureau of National Affairs, and the *Supreme Court Bulletin,* which is published by CCH, Inc.

ANALYZING CASE LAW

Attorneys often rely heavily on case law to support a given position or argument. One of the difficulties all legal professionals face in analyzing case law is the sheer length and complexity of some court opinions. While certain court opinions may be only two or three pages long, others can occupy hundreds of pages. Understanding the components of a case—that is, the basic format in which cases are presented—can simplify your task of reading and analyzing case law. You will find that over time, as you acquire experience, case analysis becomes easier. This section focuses on how to read and analyze cases, as well as how to summarize, or *brief,* a case.

The Components of a Case

Reported cases contain much more than just the court's decision. Cases have many different parts, and you should understand why each part is there and what information it communicates. The annotations on the sample court case shown in Exhibit 16.17 on pages 598 to 600 indicate the various components of a case.

The case presented in Exhibit 16.17 is an actual case that was decided by the United States Supreme Court in 2002. Ella Williams, a former employee of Toyota Motor Manufacturing, Kentucky, Inc., filed a suit against Toyota in a federal district court alleging in part that she had a disability (carpal tunnel syndrome), which Toyota failed to reasonably accommodate in violation of the Americans with Disabilities Act of 1990 (ADA).[3] The court issued a judgment in favor of Toyota. Williams appealed to the U.S. Court of Appeals for the Sixth Circuit, which reversed this judgment, concluding that Williams was disabled because she

EXHIBIT 16.17
A Sample Court Case

Supreme Court of the United States

TOYOTA MOTOR MANUFACTURING, KENTUCKY, INC., Petitioner,

v.

Ella WILLIAMS.

No. 00-1089.

Argued Nov. 7, 2001.

Decided Jan. 8, 2002.

Former employee sued former employer under Americans with Disabilities Act (ADA). The United States District Court for the Eastern District of Kentucky, Henry R. Wilhoit, Jr., Chief Judge, entered summary judgment for former employer. Former employee appealed. The United States Court of Appeals for the Sixth Circuit, 224 F.3d 840, reversed. Certiorari was granted. The Supreme Court, Justice O'Connor, held that: (1) to be substantially limited in performing manual tasks, an individual must have an impairment that prevents or severely restricts the individual from doing activities that are of central importance to most people's daily lives * * * (4) Court of Appeals applied wrong standard * * * and (6) medical conditions that caused employee to restrict certain activities did not constitute manual-task disability under ADA.

Reversed and remanded.

Justice O'CONNOR delivered the opinion of the Court.

* * * *

I

Respondent [Ella Williams] began working at petitioner's [Toyota Motor Manufacturing, Kentucky, Inc.,] automobile manufacturing plant in Georgetown, Kentucky, in August 1990. She was soon placed on an engine fabrication assembly line, where her duties included work with pneumatic tools. Use of these tools eventually caused pain in respondent's hands, wrists, and arms. She sought treatment at petitioner's in-house medical service * * * . [Respondent's] physician * * * placed her on permanent work restrictions that precluded her from [performing tasks required on the assembly line].

In light of these restrictions, for the next two years petitioner assigned respondent to various modified duty jobs. * * *

* * * *

* * * [S]he began to experience pain in her neck and shoulders. Respondent again sought care at petitioner's in-house medical service * * * .

* * * [O]n December 6, 1996, * * * she was placed under a no-work-of-any-kind restriction by her treating physicians. On January 27, 1997, respondent received a letter from petitioner that terminated her employment * * * .

* * * [R]espondent filed suit against petitioner in the United States District Court for the Eastern District of Kentucky. Her complaint alleged that petitioner had violated the [Americans with Disabilities Act of 1990 (ADA)] * * * by failing to reasonably accommodate her disability * * * .

Annotations (right column):

The *case title*.

The *docket number* assigned by the United States Supreme Court.

The *dates* on which the case was *argued* and *decided*.

The *syllabus*—a brief summary of the issues and decisions in the case. Prepared by West Group editors.

A Latin term meaning that the United States Supreme Court ordered the appellate court to send it the record of the case for review.

The Supreme Court concluded that the lower court erred in its interpretation of the law.

Sent back to the trial court for further proceedings consistent with this opinion.

This line gives the name of the justice who authored the opinion of the Court.

The Court divides the opinion into four parts, headed by roman numerals. The first part of the opinion summarizes the factual background of the case.

The party against whom the appeal is brought.

The party appealing the decision.

To make impossible or impracticable by prior action.

A federal trial court in which a lawsuit is initiated.

A document that, when filed with a court, initiates a lawsuit.

EXHIBIT 16.17
A Sample Court Case—Continued

A judgment that a court enters without beginning or continuing a trial. This judgment can be entered only if no facts are in dispute and the only question is how the law applies to the facts.	* * * * * * * [T]he District Court granted (summary judgment) to petitioner. * * * * * * *
A federal court that hears appeals from the federal district courts located within its geographic boundaries.	Respondent appealed * * *. The ([United States] Court of Appeals) for the Sixth Circuit reversed the District Court's ruling * * *. The Court of Appeals (held) that [respondent was disabled] because her ailments "prevented her from doing the tasks associated with certain types of manual assembly line jobs * * *."
The *holding* of a court is the legal principle drawn from the court's decision. In this case, it was this holding that was appealed.	* * * * (II)
The second major section of the opinion sets out parts of the ADA that are considered in this case.	The ADA requires (covered entities) including private employers, to provide "reasonable accommodations to the known physical or mental limitations of an otherwise qualified individual with a disability who is an applicant or employee, unless * * * the accommodation would impose an undue hardship." * * * [A] "disability" is: * * * "a physical or mental impairment that substantially limits one or more * * * major life activities * * *."
Individuals and organizations subject to the law, which in this case is the ADA.	* * * * (III)
The third major section of the opinion analyzes the terms of the statute quoted in the previous section.	* * * * Our consideration of this [case] is guided first and foremost by the words of the [ADA's] disability definition itself. "[S]ubstantially" in the phrase "substantially limits" suggests "considerable" or "to a large degree." The word "substantial" thus clearly precludes impairments that interfere in only a minor way with the performance of manual tasks from qualifying as disabilities. * * * "Major life activities" * * * refers to those activities that are of central importance to daily life. In order for performing manual tasks to fit into this category—a category that includes such basic abilities as walking, seeing, and hearing—the manual tasks in question must be central to daily life. * * * * * * * We therefore hold that to be substantially limited in performing manual tasks, an individual must have an impairment that prevents or severely restricts the individual from doing activities that are of central importance to most people's daily lives. * * *
The fourth major section of the opinion applies the law to the issue before the Court.	* * * * (IV) * * * *
In this case, the regulations include rules issued by the federal Equal Employment Opportunity Commission.	There is * * * no support in the [ADA], our previous opinions, or the (applicable [administrative] regulations) for the Court of Appeals' idea that the question of whether an impairment constitutes a disability is to be answered only by analyzing the effect of the impairment in the workplace. * * *
Proof is the establishment of a fact by evidence. Without evidence, there is no proof, although there may be evidence that does not amount to proof.	Even more critically, the manual tasks unique to any particular job are not necessarily important parts of most people's lives. * * * The [lower] court, therefore, should not have considered respondent's inability to do * * * manual work in her specialized assembly line job as sufficient (proof) that she was substantially limited in performing manual tasks. * * * *

EXHIBIT 16.17
A Sample Court Case—Continued

---

*   *   * [E]ven after her condition worsened, she could still brush her teeth, wash her face, bathe, tend her flower garden, fix breakfast, do laundry, and pick up around the house. *   *   * [H]er medical conditions caused her to avoid sweeping, to quit dancing, to occasionally seek help dressing, and to reduce how often she plays with her children, gardens, and drives long distances. But these changes in her life did not amount to such severe restrictions in the activities that are of central importance to most people's daily lives that they establish a manual-task disability as a matter of law. *   *   *

*   *   *   *

> A *matter of law* is a question decided by the application of legal rules or principles, as opposed to a *matter of fact,* which is determined by witnesses' testimony or other evidence.

   Accordingly, we reverse the Court of Appeals' judgment granting *   *   * summary judgment to respondent and remand the case for further proceedings consistent with this opinion.

> In this paragraph of the opinion, the Court states its decision and gives its order.

---

could not perform the manual work required by her specific job. Toyota appealed to the United States Supreme Court. The issue before the Court was whether Williams's condition qualified as a disability.

   Important sections, terms, and phrases in the case are defined or discussed in the margins. You will note also that triple asterisks (*   *   *) and quadruple asterisks (*   *   *   *) frequently appear in the exhibit. The triple asterisks indicate that we have deleted a few words or sentences from the opinion for the sake of readability or brevity. Quadruple asterisks mean that an entire paragraph (or more) has been omitted. Also, when the opinion cites another case or legal source, the citation to the referenced case or source has been omitted to save space and to improve readability.

   We discuss below the various components of a case. As you read through the descriptions of these components, refer to Exhibit 16.17, which illustrates most of them. Remember, though, that the excerpt presented in Exhibit 16.17, because it has been pared down for illustration, may be much easier to read than some court opinions you will encounter.

CASE TITLE.   The title of a case indicates the names of the parties to the lawsuit, and the *v.* in the case title stands for *versus,* or "against." In the trial court, the plaintiff's last name appears first, and the second name is the defendant's. If the case is appealed, however, the appellate court will *sometimes* place the name of the party appealing the decision first, so the parties' names may be reversed. Because some appellate courts retain the trial court order of names, it is often impossible to distinguish the plaintiff from the defendant in the title of a reported appellate court decision. You must therefore carefully read the facts of each case to identify the parties.

CASE CITATION.   Typically, the citation to the case is found just above or just below the case title (and often at the tops of consecutive printed pages). If the citation appears on Westlaw® and one of the parallel citations is not yet available, the citation may include an underlined space for the volume and page number to be filled in once it becomes available (such as "____ U.S. ____").

DOCKET NUMBER.   The docket number immediately follows the case title. Recall from Chapter 12 that a docket number is assigned by the court clerk when

On the Web
If you are interested in reading the entire opinion rendered by the United States Supreme Court in the sample case presented in Exhibit 16.17, you can access the case online at **http://supreme.lp. findlaw.com.**
Find the link to Supreme Court opinions, and then, when the link opens, click on "2002 decisions." When that link opens, scroll down to *Toyota Motor Mfg., KY., Inc. v. Williams* to access the case.

a case is initially filed. The number serves as an identifier for all papers submitted in connection with the case. A case published in a reporter should not be cited by its docket number, but the docket number may serve as a valuable tool in obtaining background information on the case. Cases appearing in slip-opinion form (cases that have been decided but that are not yet published in a reporter) are usually identified, filed, and cited by docket number. After publication of the decision, the docket number may continue to serve as an identifier for appellate records and briefs (appellate briefs will be discussed in Chapter 18).

DATES ARGUED AND DECIDED. An important component of a case is the date on which it was decided by the court. Usually, the date of the decision immediately follows the docket number. In addition to the date of the court's decision on the matter, the date on which the case was argued before the court (in appellate court cases) may also be included here, as in Exhibit 16.17.

SYLLABUS. Following the docket number is the *syllabus*—a brief synopsis of the facts of the case, the issues analyzed by the court, and the court's conclusion. In official reporters, the courts usually prepare the syllabi; in unofficial reporters, the publishers of the reporters usually prepare them. The syllabus is often a helpful research tool. It provides a clear overview of the case and points out various legal issues discussed by the court. But always keep in mind the following caution:

Reading the syllabus is not a substitute for reading the case.

HEADNOTES. Often, unofficial reporters, such as those published by West Group, make extensive use of case *headnotes*. As discussed earlier, headnotes are short paragraphs that serve to highlight and summarize specific rules of law mentioned in the case. In reporters published by West Group, they are correlated to the comprehensive West key-number system. In Exhibit 16.17, the headnotes were deleted for reasons of space, as were the names of counsel.

NAMES OF COUNSEL. The published report of the case usually contains the names of the lawyers (counsel) representing the parties. The attorneys' names are typically found just following the syllabus (and headnotes, if any).

NAME OF JUDGE OR JUSTICE AUTHORING THE OPINION. The name of the judge or justice who authored the opinion in the case will also be included in the published report of the case, just before the court's opinion. In the case presented in Exhibit 16.17, Justice O'Connor of the United States Supreme Court authored the opinion.

In some cases, instead of the name of a judge or justice, the decision will be authored *per curiam* (Latin for "by the court"), which means that the opinion is that of the whole court and not the opinion of any one judge or justice. Sometimes the phrase is used to indicate that the chief justice or presiding judge wrote the opinion. The phrase also may be used for an announcement of a court's disposition of a case that is not accompanied by a written opinion.

OPINION. As you may have noted in previous chapters, the term *opinion* is often used loosely to refer to a court case or decision. In fact, the term has a precise meaning. The formal opinion of the court contains the analysis and decision of the judge or judges that heard and decided the case. Most opinions contain a brief statement of the facts of the case, a summary of the legal issues raised by the facts, and the remedies sought by the parties. In appellate court cases, the court summarizes the errors of the lower court, if any, and the impact of these errors on the case's outcome. The main body of the court's opinion is the application of the law to the particular facts. The court often mentions case precedents, relevant statutes, and administrative rules and regulations to support its reasoning. Additionally, court opinions often contain discussions of policy and other factors that clarify the underlying reason for the court's decision.

When all of the judges unanimously agree in their legal reasoning and their decision, the opinion is deemed a *unanimous* opinion. When the opinion is not unanimous, a *majority* opinion is written, outlining the views of the majority of the judges deciding the case. If a judge agrees, or concurs, with the majority's decision, but for different reasons, that judge may write a *concurring opinion*. A *dissenting opinion* presents the views of one or more judges who disagree with the majority's decision. The dissenting opinion is important because it may form the basis of the arguments used years later in overruling the precedential majority opinion.

THE COURT'S CONCLUSION.   In the opinion, the judges indicate their conclusion, or decision, on the issue or issues before the court. If several issues are involved, as often happens, there may be a conclusion at the end of the discussion of each issue. Often, at the end of the opinion, the conclusions presented within the opinion are briefly reiterated and summarized. If no conclusions have yet been presented, they are presented in the concluding section of the opinion.

An appellate court also specifies what the *disposition* of a case should be. If the appellate court agrees with a lower court's decision, it will *affirm* that decision, which means that the decision of the lower court remains unchanged. If the appellate court concludes that the lower court erred in its interpretation of the law, the court may *reverse* the lower court's ruling. Sometimes, if an appellate court concludes that further factual findings are necessary or that a case should be retried and a decision made that is consistent with the appellate court's conclusions of law, the appellate court will *remand* the case to the lower court for further proceedings consistent with its opinion. In the sample case presented in Exhibit 16.17, the United States Supreme Court reversed the lower court's decision and remanded the case.

Analyzing Cases

When you are researching case law, your main focus should be on the opinion— the words of the court itself. You will inevitably find that some opinions are easier to understand than others. Some judges write more clearly and logically than others do. You may need to reread a case (or a portion of a case) to understand what is being said, why it is being said at that point in the case, and what the judge's underlying legal reasoning is. Some cases contain several pages describing facts and issues of previous cases and how those cases relate to the one being decided by the court. You might want to reread these discussions several times to distinguish between comments made in the previous case and comments that are being made about the case at bar (before the court).

LOOK FOR GUIDEPOSTS IN THE OPINION.   Often, the judge writing the opinion provides some guideposts, perhaps by indicating sections and subsections within the opinion by numbers, letters, or subtitles. Note that in Exhibit 16.17, Roman numerals are used to divide the opinion into basic sections. Scanning through the opinion for these types of indicators can help orient you to the opinion's format.

In cases that involve dissenting or concurring opinions, you need to make sure that you identify these opinions so that you do not mistake one of them for the majority opinion. Generally, you should scan through the case a time or two to

---

ETHICAL CONCERN

Citing Sources

Before returning a legal source to the library shelf (or signing off a computerized legal-research service), you should make sure that you have included in your research notes the proper reference or citation for that authority. If you forget to cite your source, you will have to spend additional time relocating the source once again to obtain the citation. As has been stressed elsewhere, your time is a valuable resource for your attorney and a costly one for your client. If you have to spend another hour's time going to and from a library to obtain a citation that you should have included in your notes in the first place, the client may not consider charges for that hour to be "reasonable"—and attorneys have a duty to charge their clients reasonable fees.

---

sent to the president or governor, who has the authority to sign it into law. Once legislation is signed into law, it is published.

To find the relevant statutory law governing a particular legal issue or area, you will need to know, first of all, the names of the various publications in which statutory law can be found. In this section, we look first at how federal statutes are published and how you can find, within these publications, statutes governing the issue you are researching. A more difficult task in researching statutory law is deciding whether a statute you have found is really applicable to the issue being researched. This determination requires a careful reading of the statute and may require further inquiry. You may need to analyze what the legislature intended when it passed the bill and how the courts have interpreted the statute.

The Publication of Federal Statutes

Federal statutes in the United States are published in three forms. The first official publication of a statute's text is the slip law. **Slip laws** present the text of statutes in the form of pamphlets or single sheets. These pamphlets or sheets are not indexed, but they can be identified by their **public law number,** or P.L. number—a number assigned to each statute on completion of the legislative process. Slip laws are available through the *United States Code Service (U.S.C.S.)* advance service and the *United States Code Congressional and Administrative News (U.S.C.C.A.N.)* advance service. They are published in pamphlet form by the U.S. Government Depository Library. (The *U.S.C.S.* and the *U.S.C.C.A.N.* will be discussed in greater detail shortly.)

The second form in which statutes are officially published is the session law. **Session laws** are collections of statutes contained in volumes and arranged by the year or legislative session during which they were enacted. Each volume contains an index. The session laws of the U.S. Congress appear in the *United States Statutes at Large,* which is published by the U.S. government. *Statutes at Large* volumes contain the language of the legislation as it appeared at the time of passage. They also include references to the House or Senate bill number, which can be helpful in directing the researcher to legislative sources, such as committee hearings and reports. These sources are valuable when you are trying to determine the intended meaning of a particular statute. Each state issues its own official

slip law
The first official publication of a statute, which comes out shortly after the legislation is passed (presented as a single sheet or pamphlet).

public law number
An identification number that has been assigned to a specific statute, or public law, following the legislative process.

session law
Law as officially published in volumes in which statutes are organized chronologically by year or legislative session.

EXHIBIT 16.19
Titles in the *United States Code*

TITLES OF UNITED STATES CODE

*1. General Provisions.	27. Intoxicating Liquors.
2. The Congress.	*28. Judiciary and Judicial Procedure; and Appendix.
*3. The President.	
*4. Flag and Seal, Seat of Government, and the States.	29. Labor.
	30. Mineral Lands and Mining.
*5. Government Organization and Employees; and Appendix.	*31. Money and Finance.
†6. [Surety Bonds.]	*32. National Guard.
7. Agriculture.	33. Navigation and Navigable Waters.
8. Aliens and Nationality.	‡34. [Navy.]
*9. Arbitration.	*35. Patents.
*10. Armed Forces; and Appendix.	36. Patriotic Societies and Observances.
*11. Bankruptcy; and Appendix.	*37. Pay and Allowances of the Uniformed Services.
12. Banks and Banking.	
*13. Census.	*38. Veterans' Benefits.
*14. Coast Guard.	*39. Postal Service.
15. Commerce and Trade.	40. Public Buildings, Property, and Works.
16. Conservation.	41. Public Contracts.
*17. Copyrights.	42. The Public Health and Welfare.
*18. Crimes and Criminal Procedure; and Appendix.	43. Public Lands.
	*44. Public Printing and Documents.
19. Customs Duties.	45. Railroads.
20. Education.	*46. Shipping; and Appendix.
21. Food and Drugs.	47. Telegraphs, Telephones, and Radiotelegraphs.
22. Foreign Relations and Intercourse.	
*23. Highways.	48. Territories and Insular Possessions.
24. Hospitals and Asylums.	*49. Transportation; and Appendix.
25. Indians.	50. War and National Defense; and Appendix.
26. Internal Revenue Code.	

*This title has been enacted as law. However, any Appendix to this title has not been enacted as law.
†This title was enacted as law and has been repealed by the enactment of Title 31.
‡This title has been eliminated by the enactment of Title 10.

Page III

session laws. Some states have both an official and an unofficial version. The titles of the volumes vary by state.

Finally, statutory material is published in compilations referred to as **codes.** Unlike the sources just discussed, codes arrange statutory provisions by topic, thus facilitating legal research. Most statutory codes are updated through the issuance of supplemental pocket parts or by loose-leaf services. Paralegals conducting research on statutory law should begin by reviewing the index provided for the relevant statutory code.

The *United States Code*

The *United States Code,* or *U.S.C.,* is published by the U.S. government every six years and is updated annually. The *U.S.C.* is divided into fifty topic classifications. As shown in Exhibit 16.19, each of these topics, called *titles* of the code, carries a descriptive title and a number. For example, laws relating to commerce and trade

code
A systematic and topically organized presentation of laws, rules, or regulations.

On the Web
You can access and search (by title and section number) the U.S. Code online at **http://www4.law. cornell.edu/uscode.**

are collected in Title 15. Laws concerning the courts and judicial procedures are collected in Title 28. Titles are subdivided into chapters (sections) and subchapters. A citation to the *U.S.C.* includes title and section numbers. Thus, a reference to "28 U.S.C. Section 1346" means that the statute can be found in Section 1346 of Title 28. "Section" may also be designated by the symbol §, and "Sections" by §§.

One approach to finding statutory law in the *U.S.C.* is simply to refer to the title descriptions listed in the front of each volume. This approach is most beneficial for researchers who can quickly find the applicable title for the statute they are researching. Alternatively, the researcher can consult the index to the *U.S.C.* The index provides an alphabetical listing of all federal statutes by subject matter and by the name of the act. The researcher should consider the various ways the statute could be listed and then review the index for the appropriate description. The more descriptive words the researcher can think of, the more likely it is that he or she will be able to locate a particular statute. The index provides the exact location of the statute, by title and section.

Sometimes a researcher may know the popular name of a legislative act but not its official name. In this situation, the researcher can consult the *U.S.C.* volume entitled *Popular Name Table,* which lists statutes by their popular names. Many legislative bills enacted into law are commonly known by a popular name. Some have descriptive titles reflecting their purpose; others are named after their sponsors. The Labor-Management Reporting and Disclosure Act of 1959, for example, is also known as the Landrum-Griffin Act. Searching by popular name will allow the researcher to find the title and section of the statute and therefore locate the statute in the *U.S.C.*

The *U.S.C.* also lists, after the text of the statute, citations to the *United States Statutes at Large.* These citations are helpful for paralegals who wish to examine previous versions of the statute in the *Statutes at Large.*

Unofficial Versions of the Federal Code

There are two unofficial versions of the federal code. Both are similar to the *U.S.C.,* but they contain some important differences. They provide annotations describing cases and other sources that have applied or interpreted a given statute. Additionally, they contain more cross-references to related sections of the code than does the *U.S.C.* These two unofficial federal codes are discussed next.

THE *UNITED STATES CODE ANNOTATED.*   One of the unofficial versions of the *U.S.C.* is West's *United States Code Annotated (U.S.C.A.).* The *U.S.C.A.* contains the full text of the *U.S.C.,* the U.S. Constitution, the Federal Rules of Evidence, and various other rules, including the Rules of Civil Procedure and the Rules of Criminal Procedure. This useful set of approximately two hundred volumes offers historical notes relating to the text of each statute and any amendments to the act. As shown in Exhibit 16.20 on the following page, cross-references to other titles and sections within the *U.S.C.A.* are also given. Annotations, referred to as "Notes of Decisions," offer additional research assistance by listing cases that have analyzed, discussed, or interpreted the particular statute.

The *U.S.C.A.* is more current than the *U.S.C.* The supplements updating the *U.S.C.* often lag behind current statutory law by more than a year, whereas the *U.S.C.A.* provides updated statutory information through supplemental pocket parts and pamphlets many times a year.

Locating statutory law in the *U.S.C.A.* is similar to locating statutes in the *U.S.C.* Researchers can use the topical or index approach and, if necessary, look through the *Popular Name Table.*

EXHIBIT 16.20

Excerpt from the *United States Code Annotated*

Reproduced with permission of West Group.

Ch. 11   PEACETIME DISABILITY   38 § 1131

CROSS REFERENCES

Rates of peacetime death compensation same as specified under this section, see 38 USCA § 1142.

LIBRARY REFERENCES

American Digest System

Veterans' benefits; rights and disabilities in general, see Armed Services ⬌101.

Encyclopedias

Veterans' benefits; compensation for dependents and survivors, see C.J.S. Armed Services § 254.

Veterans' benefits; general considerations, see C.J.S. Armed Services § 251.

Veterans' benefits; payment of benefits, see C.J.S. Armed Services § 265.

Law Reviews

Making intramilitary tort law more civil: A proposed reform of the Feres Doctrine. David Schwartz, 95 Yale L.J. 992 (1986).

WESTLAW ELECTRONIC RESEARCH

Armed services cases: 34k[add key number].

See, also, WESTLAW guide following the Explanation pages of this volume.

NOTES OF DECISIONS

Death of claimant   1
Withdrawal of claim   2

1. Death of claimant

Where the widow filed a claim but died before decision was made in her favor, awards were made as if there had been no surviving widow. 1943, A.D. V.A. 524.

2. Withdrawal of claim

Where the stepfather's claim for death compensation had not yet been favor-ably considered, a withdrawal of his claim had the effect of entitling the mother to be considered as the only person who had established a right to the benefit under former § 472b of this title, and she was accordingly entitled to the $45 rate therein provided for one parent. 1940, A.D.V.A. 458.

SUBCHAPTER IV—PEACETIME DISABILITY COMPENSATION

CROSS REFERENCES

Amounts payable under this subchapter exempt from tax levy, see 26 USCA § 6334.

§ 1131. Basic entitlement

For disability resulting from personal injury suffered or disease contracted in line of duty, or for aggravation of a preexisting injury suffered or disease contracted in line of duty, in the active military, naval, or air service, during other than a period of war, the United States will pay to any veteran thus disabled and who was discharged or released under conditions other than dishonorable from the period of service in which said injury or disease was incurred, or preexisting injury or disease was aggravated, compensation as provided in this subchapter, but no compensation shall be paid if

237

---

38 § 1131   DISABILITY, ETC., COMPENSATION   Ch. 11

the disability is a result of the veteran's own willful misconduct or abuse of alcohol or drugs.

(Pub.L. 85–857, Sept. 2, 1958, 72 Stat. 1122, § 331; Pub.L. 101–508, Title VIII, § 8052(a)(3), Nov. 5, 1990, 104 Stat. 1388–351; renumbered Pub.L. 102–83, § 5(a), Aug. 6, 1991, 105 Stat. 406.)

HISTORICAL AND STATUTORY NOTES

Revision Notes and Legislative Reports

1958 Act. Senate Report No. 2259 and House Report No. 1298, see 1958 U.S. Code Cong. and Adm.News, p. 4352.

1990 Act. House Report No. 101–881 and House Conference Report No. 101–964, see 1990 U.S.Code Cong. and Adm.News, p. 2017.

Amendments

1990 Amendment. Pub.L. 101–508 substituted "a result of the veteran's own willful misconduct or abuse of alcohol or drugs" for "the result of the veteran's own willful misconduct".

Effective Dates

1990 Act. Amendment by Pub.L. 101–508 effective with respect to claims filed after Oct. 31, 1990, see section 8052(b) of Pub.L. 101–508, set out as a note under section 105 of this title.

LIBRARY REFERENCES

American Digest System

Veterans' benefits; compensation for disability, see Armed Services ⬌104.

Veterans' benefits; rights and benefits in general, see Armed Services ⬌101.

Encyclopedias

Veterans' benefits; disability compensation, see C.J.S. Armed Services § 255.

Veterans' benefits; general considerations, see C.J.S. Armed Services § 251.

Law Reviews

Federal Tort Claims Act—Feres Doctrine. (1985) 24 Duquesne L.Rev. 309.

WESTLAW ELECTRONIC RESEARCH

Armed services cases: 34k[add key number].

See, also, WESTLAW guide following the Explanation pages of this volume.

NOTES OF DECISIONS

Action against government contractor   4
Civilian   2
Indemnity   3
Law governing   1

1. Law governing

The Veterans' Benefits Act did not preempt Navy enlisted man's action under state law against private corporation which operated government-owned nuclear reactor facility, to recover for injuries sustained while enlisted man was on duty and a deck on which he was standing collapsed, despite provision in contract between corporation and the Government that Government would reimburse corporation for all judgments incurred in connection with the contract; such clause apparently was added by the parties without specific statutory or regulatory direction and, even if indemnification would frustrate the Act, preemption would operate against corporation's indemnity claim and not against the enlisted man's claim against the corporation. Chapman v. Westinghouse Elec. Corp., C.A.9 (Idaho) 1990, 911 F.2d 267.

2. Civilian

A civilian is ineligible under this section for any injuries resulting from improper activation into military service. Vain v. U.S., C.A.Del.1983, 708 F.2d 116.

3. Indemnity

Where this chapter is present, it is sole or exclusive remedy for claims which involve service-related injuries, irrespective of who sues United States; thus, in a case growing out of service-connected injury, there cannot be a recovery of indemnity for payments to serviceman

238

THE *UNITED STATES CODE SERVICE.*   The second unofficial version of the federal code is the *United States Code Service (U.S.C.S.)*, published by West Group. The *U.S.C.S.* offers some of the same features offered by the *U.S.C.A.*, such as annotations. The *U.S.C.S.* and the *U.S.C.A.* are distinguishable by the research tools they provide. The research section of the *U.S.C.S.* provides references and citations to some sources that are not contained in the *U.S.C.A.*, including such publications as *American Law Reports*, legal periodicals, and *American Jurisprudence*.

Like the *U.S.C.A.*, the *U.S.C.S.* offers an effective updating service in the form of replacement volumes and pocket parts. The *U.S.C.S.* issues softbound updated volumes called *Cumulative Later Case and Statutory Service*, which compile cases—including annotations—that have been published since the last printed pocket-part supplement. Another *U.S.C.S.* updating service is the advance service, a monthly compilation of slip laws and other legislative decrees.

Paralegals can begin statutory research in the *U.S.C.S.* by reviewing the *Subject Index* or the *Popular Name Table*. Both annotated codes also have conversion charts listing all public acts by public law number, *Statutes at Large* references, and *U.S.C.* title and section numbers.

State Codes

State codes follow the *U.S.C.* pattern of arranging statutes by subject. They may be called codes, revisions, compilations, consolidations, general statutes, or statutes, depending on the preference of the states. In some codes, subjects are designated by number. In others, they are designated by name. For example, "13 Pennsylvania Consolidated Statutes Section 1101" means that the statute can be found in Section 1101 of Title 13 of the Pennsylvania code. "California Commercial Code Section 1101" means that the statute can be found in Section 1101 under the heading "Commercial" in the California Code. Abbreviations may be used. For example, "13 Pennsylvania Consolidated Statutes Section 1101" may be abbreviated to "13 Pa.C.S. § 1101," and "California Commercial Code Section 1101" may be abbreviated to "Cal. Com. Code § 1101."

In many states, official codes are supplemented by annotated codes published by private publishers. Annotated codes follow the numbering scheme set forth in the official state code but provide outlines and indexes to assist in locating information. These codes also provide references to case law, legislative history sources, and other documents in which the statute has been considered or discussed. Like their federal counterparts, the annotated codes at the state level are kept current with pocket parts and other supplementary materials.

ANALYZING STATUTORY LAW

Because of the tremendous growth in statutory and regulatory law in the last century, the legal issues dealt with by attorneys are frequently governed by statutes and administrative agency regulations. Paralegals must understand how to interpret and analyze this body of law. Although we use the terms *statute* and *statutory law* in this section, the following discussion applies equally well to the regulations issued by administrative agencies.

If a statute applies to the legal issues in your case, you must understand the statute thoroughly before evaluating how it does or does not apply to the issue that you are researching. The first step in statutory analysis is therefore to read the language of the statute very carefully. The next step is to interpret the meaning of the statute.

Reading Statutory Law

As with court cases, some statutes are more difficult to read than others. Some are extremely wordy or lengthy or difficult to understand for some other reason. By carefully reading and rereading a statute, however, you can usually determine the reasons for the statute's enactment, the class of people to which the statute applies, the kind of conduct being regulated by the statute, and the circumstances in which that conduct is prohibited, required, or permitted. You can also learn whether the statute allows for any exceptions and, if so, in what circumstances. When reading a statute, you can do several things to simplify your task, including those discussed below.

COVERAGE AND EFFECTIVE DATE.   When researching statutory law on behalf of a client, one of the first things you should find out is whether the statute is applicable to the client's case. Suppose your firm's client is a small corporation with ten employees. Your firm is defending the client against a lawsuit for employment discrimination based on disability in violation of the Americans with Disabilities Act (ADA) of 1990. In researching this statute, the first thing you will want to check is what firms are subject to the statute. (You will find that the ADA applies only to employers who have fifteen or more employees, and thus the client is not subject to the act's provisions.)

Each statute also indicates the date on which it will become legally effective. This is something you will want to verify at the outset of your inquiry. Note that the effective date may be a year or two later than the date on which the statute was enacted into law. For example, the provisions relating to employment in the Americans with Disabilities Act of 1990 did not become legally effective until July 26, 1992. Questions also arise in regard to whether the provisions of the act will apply *retroactively*—that is, to lawsuits filed before the effective date of the statute. If the statute is unclear on its applicability in this respect, you will want to research relevant case law to find out how the courts have decided this issue.

DEFINITIONS.   Usually, near the beginning of a statute or the beginning of each major section within the statute, you can find a list of terms followed by their definitions. In the example just mentioned, which involves a lawsuit based on discrimination against a person with a disability, you will want to read carefully the statutory definition of *disability.* You will also want to learn how the ADA defines other terms or phrases that may be important in determining the defendant firm's liability. For example, the ADA requires employers to reasonably accommodate persons with disabilities. You will want to find out how the act defines *reasonable accommodation.*

SUBDIVISIONS.   Another helpful tactic in reading statutory law is to identify the various sections and subsections in the statute. Often, statutes indicate subsections by letters or numbers, but it is easy to lose sight of the relationship between one subsection and another. Consider the excerpt from the ADA shown in Exhibit 16.21. You will find that this section of the statute contains several levels of subsections and that each subsection is preceded by a number or letter. You may find that you have to scan through the section more than once to determine how the subsections are related. Statutes frequently contain even more levels of subsections, and at times, you may want to diagram the structure of the text to discern the interrelationship of various subsections.

AND VERSUS OR.   When reading a statute, you should also pay careful attention to the words *and* and *or* in the text. For example, suppose that a section of a statute begins with the words "A contract which does not satisfy the requirements of subsection (1) but which is valid in other respects is enforceable if . . . ." Following these words, two conditions are listed. A crucial factor in interpreting the section is whether the conditions are connected by *and* or *or.* If *and* is used, then both conditions must be met before the contract is enforceable. If *or* is used, then only one of the conditions must be met. Consciously looking for these *connectors* in positions such as the one just described can help to clarify the meaning of a statutory provision.

§ 12112. Discrimination

(a) General rule
No covered entity shall discriminate against a qualified individual with a disability because of the disability of such individual in regard to job application procedures, the hiring, advancement, or discharge of employees, employee compensation, job training, and other terms, conditions, and privileges of employment.

(b) Construction
As used in subsection (a) of this section, the term "discriminate" includes—

(1) limiting, segregating, or classifying a job applicant or employee in a way that adversely affects the opportunities or status of such applicant or employee because of the disability of such applicant or employee;

(2) participating in a contractual or other arrangement or relationship that has the effect of subjecting a covered entity's qualified applicant or employee with a disability to the discrimination prohibited by this subchapter (such relationship includes a relationship with an employment or referral agency, labor union, an organization providing fringe benefits to an employee of the covered entity, or an organization providing training and apprenticeship programs);

(3) utilizing standards, criteria, or methods of administration—
  (A) that have the effect of discrimination on the basis of disability; or
  (B) that perpetuate the discrimination of others who are subject to common administrative control;

(4) excluding or otherwise denying equal jobs or benefits to a qualified individual because of the known disability of an individual with whom the qualified individual is known to have a relationship or association;

(5)(A) not making reasonable accommodations to the known physical or mental limitations of an otherwise qualified individual with a disability who is an applicant or employee, unless such covered entity can demonstrate that the accommodation would impose an undue hardship on the operation of the business of such covered entity; or
  (B) denying employment opportunities to a job applicant or employee who is an otherwise qualified individual with a disability, if such denial is based on the need of such covered entity to make reasonable accommodation to the physical or mental impairments of the employee or applicant;

(6) using qualification standards, employment tests, or other selection criteria that screen out or tend to screen out an individual with a disability or a class of individuals with disabilities unless the standard, test, or other selection criteria, as used by the covered entity, is shown to be job-related for the position in question and is consistent with business necessity; and

(7) failing to select and administer tests concerning employment in the most effective manner * * * .

EXHIBIT 16.21
Excerpt from the Americans with Disabilities Act of 1990

Interpreting Statutory Law

Generally, when trying to understand the meaning of statutes, you should do as the courts do. We therefore now look at some of the typical techniques used by courts when they are faced with the task of interpreting the meaning of a given statute or statutory provision.

RULES OF CONSTRUCTION.   Certain statutory rules of interpretation, called **rules of construction,** may prove helpful in your analysis of the statute's language

rules of construction
The rules that control the judicial interpretation of statutes.

DEVELOPING PARALEGAL SKILLS
Interpreting Statutes

Ralph Winter, a paralegal, works for an attorney who is representing the plaintiff in a negligence case. The plaintiff stepped on a broken stair step in her apartment building, fell, and broke her hip. She is suing the owner of the building for negligence. The attorney has successfully opposed the owner-defendant's motion for summary judgment in the case, but the defense is now trying a new tactic. The defense wants to get the venue of the case changed to a county in which the landlord owns and operates a restaurant and owns a significant amount of other commercial property on the assumption that a jury in that area might be more inclined to favor the defendant. The defense has filed a motion for change of venue, and Ralph is once again researching the law.

He has located a statute entitled "Venue in County Designated." It reads:

> Notwithstanding any provision of this article, the place of trial of an action shall be in the county designated by the plaintiff, unless the place of trial is changed to another county by order, upon motion, or by consent as provided in subdivision (b) of Rule 511. N.Y. Civil Practice Sec. 509 (McKinney 1976).

"This statute is pretty clear," thinks Ralph. Ralph turns to the annotations following section 509 to make sure the courts have applied it as he interprets it. Under note 5, he finds the title, "Motion for Change of Venue." Ralph finds a case involving an injured tenant. It holds that venue was proper in the county in which the plaintiff resided, the accident occurred, the plaintiff was treated for the resulting injuries, and the building's superintendent resided, rather than the county in which the building owner's residence and principal place of business were located. Ralph decides to pull this helpful case and read it to be certain it says what the annotation indicates.

TIPS FOR APPLYING STATUTES

• Read the language of the statute and summarize each provision in your mind or, if it is lengthy, on paper.

• Make sure that the statute has taken effect and has not been repealed, amended, or held unconstitutional—check the pocket part or a citator.

• Apply each requirement of the statute to the facts of the problem being researched.

• Review the case annotations following each section to determine how the courts have applied the law.

and intent. Examples of statutory rules of interpretation used in many jurisdictions are the following:

• Specific provisions are given greater weight than general provisions when there is a conflict between the two.

• Recent provisions are given greater weight than earlier provisions when there is a conflict between the two.

• Masculine pronouns refer to both males and females.

• Singular nouns also include the plural forms of the nouns.

plain-meaning rule
A rule of statutory interpretation. If the meaning of a statute is clear on its face, then that is the interpretation the court will give to it; inquiry into the legislative history of the statute will not be undertaken.

THE PLAIN-MEANING RULE.   In interpreting statutory language, courts also apply the **plain-meaning rule.** Under this rule, the words chosen by the legislature must be understood according to their common meanings. If the statute is clear and unambiguous *on its face* (in its apparent and obvious meaning), and therefore capable of only one interpretation, that interpretation must be given to it. No additional inquiries, such as inquiries into legislative intent or history, are permitted when the meaning of the statute is clear on its face.

The plain-meaning rule, although seemingly simple, is usually not so simple to apply. For one thing, the plain meaning of a statute is rarely totally clear, because legal language, especially in statutes, is difficult to understand and often inherently ambiguous. Also, each word or phrase in a statute takes on meaning only in con-

DEVELOPING PARALEGAL SKILLS
Researching the *U.S.C.A.*

Natalie Martin has completed her factual analysis of the case involving Bernie Berriman (see the *Developing Paralegal Skills* feature entitled "Defining the Issues to Be Researched") and begins her research. The issue she is researching is whether the government, which arrested Bernie for the transportation and distribution of cocaine, had the authority to confiscate Bernie's car and cell phone. Natalie's supervising attorney has told her to start her research by going to the *United States Code Annotated* (U.S.C.A.) to find the relevant federal statutes.

CHECKLIST FOR RESEARCHING THE *U.S.C.A.*

- Start with general index volumes unless you know the *U.S.C.A.* title (topic) number or a popular name.

- If you know the specific title number, begin in the title index. If you know the popular name of a statute, begin in the *Popular Name Table*.

- Look up topics, either by factual categories or legal categories, in the index. Here, the topic could be "drugs."

- Look up subtopics within topics. Here, "forfeiture" or "property" could be subtopics under "drugs."

- Write down the citations to the *U.S.C.A.* volumes containing the topics.

- Look up the citations in the volumes containing the titles or topics.

- Read the relevant sections of the statute to determine if they apply to the research.

- Update the relevant sections of the statute to determine if they apply to the research.

- Check the annotations following the statute sections for case law in which the statute has been applied and interpreted.

- Review any cases that appear relevant.

- "Shepardize" both statutes and cases to make sure they are still "good law." (*Shepard's* citators are discussed later in this chapter.)

---

text—as it relates to the surrounding text. Thus, the interpretation of the meaning of a statutory word, phrase, or provision remains ultimately subjective.

Furthermore, laws, by their very nature, cannot be too specific. When enacting a statute, the legislators often state a broad principle of law and then leave it up to the courts to apply this principle to specific circumstances—which vary from case to case. For example, consider the final two lines of the excerpt from the ADA presented in Exhibit 16.21 on page 611. What exactly does the clause "failing to select and administer tests concerning employment in the most effective manner" mean? In interpreting this provision, you would need to research case law to see how the courts have interpreted the provision or study the legislative history of the act to understand the legislators' intent in wording the clause in that particular way.

PREVIOUS JUDICIAL INTERPRETATION.   Paralegals often find that researching statutory law also involves researching case law—to see how the courts have interpreted and applied statutory provisions. As discussed, courts are obligated to follow the precedents set by higher courts in their jurisdictions. A statutory interpretation made by a higher court therefore must be accepted as binding by lower courts in the same jurisdiction. You can find citations to court cases relating to specific statutes by referring to annotated versions of state or federal statutory codes.

LEGISLATIVE INTENT.   Another common technique employed in statutory interpretation is learning the intent of the legislature. A court relying on this method determines the meaning of the statute by attempting to find out why the legislators chose to phrase the statute in the particular language they used or, more generally, what the

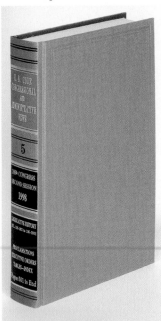

legislators sought to accomplish by enacting the statute. To discern the intent of the legislators who drafted a particular law, it is often necessary to investigate the legislative history of the statute. This can be done by researching such sources as committee reports and records of congressional hearings and other proceedings.

Before you can study these sources, of course, you need to know how to find them. The easiest way to locate them is to refer to the unofficial, annotated versions of the federal code, such as the *U.S.C.A.* and the *U.S.C.S.* These codes often contain information regarding the legislative history of a statute. For example, the statute's public law number and date of passage are included in these annotated codes, as are cross-references to sources that will provide you with more detailed information on a statute's legislative history. Each source that you discover will likely lead you to other useful sources.

Committee Reports.   Committee reports provide the most important source of legislative history. Congressional committees produce reports for each bill, and these reports often contain the full text of the bill, a description of its purpose, and the committee's recommendations. Several tables are also included to set out dates for certain actions. The dates can help the researcher locate floor debates and committee testimony in the *Congressional Record* (described below) and various other publications. Committee reports are published according to a numerical series and are available through the U.S. Government Printing Office.

The **Congressional Record.**   The *Congressional Record,* which is published daily while Congress is in session, contains *verbatim* (word-for-word) transcripts of congressional debates and proceedings. The transcripts include remarks made by various members of Congress, proposed amendments, votes, and occasionally the text of the bill under discussion.

Legislative hearings, another important source of legislative research, can be found in the transcripts of testimony before the House and Senate committees considering the proposed legislation. The purpose of conducting hearings is to determine if such legislation is needed. As a result, many types of testimony are presented. The researcher may find some helpful testimony in these sources, yet it is important to remember that much of it may be biased, because of the interested positions of the parties presenting the information. Hearings may be informative but are not as authoritative as committee reports in determining legislative intent.

Other Sources of Legislative History.   The two tools most frequently used in conducting research on legislative history are the *United States Code Congressional and Administrative News (U.S.C.C.A.N.)* and the *Congressional Information Service (C.I.S.).* The *U.S.C.C.A.N.,* a West publication shown in Exhibit 16.22, contains reprints of statutes as published in the *Statutes at Large* and sections describing the statutes' legislative history, including committee reports. Statutes in the *U.S.C.A.* are followed by notations directing the researcher to the corresponding legislative history in the *U.S.C.C.A.N.* The *C.I.S.,* a U.S. government publication, contains information from committee reports, hearing reports, documents from both houses, and special publications. Both the *C.I.S.* and the *U.S.C.C.A.N.* provide a system of indexing and abstracting that allows quick access to information.

RESEARCHING ADMINISTRATIVE LAW

Administrative rules and regulations constitute a growing source of American law. As discussed in Chapter 11, Congress frequently delegates authority to administrative agencies through enabling legislation. For example, in 1914 Congress passed the Federal Trade Commission Act, which established the Federal Trade Commission, or FTC. The act gave the FTC the authority to issue and enforce rules and regulations relating to unfair trade practices in the United States. Other federal administrative agencies include the Occupational Safety and Health Administration, the Consumer Product Safety Commission, and the Securities and Exchange Commission. The orders, regulations, and decisions of such agencies are legally binding and, as such, are primary sources of law.

The *Code of Federal Regulations*

The *Code of Federal Regulations (C.F.R.)* is a government publication containing all federal administrative agency regulations (see Exhibit 16.23). The regulations are compiled from the *Federal Register,* a daily government publication consisting of executive orders and administrative regulations, in which administrative regulations are first published. (See Chapter 11 for a discussion of administrative rulemaking procedure.)

The *C.F.R.* uses the same titles as the *United States Code* (shown previously in Exhibit 16.19). This subject-matter organization allows the researcher to determine the section in the *C.F.R.* in which a regulation will appear. Each title of the *C.F.R.* is divided into chapters, subchapters, parts, and sections.

Publication of the *C.F.R.*

The *C.F.R.* is revised and republished four times a year. Recent regulations appear in the *Federal Register* until they are later incorporated into the *C.F.R.* If, as a paralegal, you are searching for administrative regulations in the *C.F.R.,* you should begin with the index section of the *Index and Finding Aids* volume. This index will allow you to locate the relevant title and the section of the *C.F.R.* that pertains to the problem. The next step is locating the regulation in the most recent volume of that title in the *C.F.R.* You should also review the *List of C.F.R. Sections Affected,* issued in monthly pamphlets, to determine if any changes have been made to the section since the last revision.

Finding Tools for Administrative Law

The *Congressional Information Service (C.I.S.)* also provides an index to the *C.F.R.* The *C.I.S.* index is helpful in locating *C.F.R.* regulations by subject matter and also in determining the geographical areas affected by the regulation. The *American Digest System* can be of additional help to the paralegal, because it provides coverage of court cases dealing with administrative questions. The digests, however, do not contain any agency rulings. Additionally, certain loose-leaf services provide administrative decisions for particular specialty fields, such as taxation. If available, they are a useful research tool.

Whenever you need to research administrative law, remember that the most efficient way to find what you are looking for may be simply to call the agency and ask agency personnel how to access information relevant to your research topic.

FINDING CONSTITUTIONAL LAW

The federal government and all fifty states have their own constitutions describing the powers, responsibilities, and limitations of the various branches of government. Constitutions can be replaced or amended, and it is important that researchers have access to both current versions and older ones.

EXHIBIT 16.23
Code of Federal Regulations

Reproduced with permission of West Group.

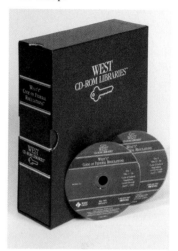

The text of the U.S. Constitution can be found in a number of publications. A useful source of federal constitutional law is *The Constitution of the United States of America,* published under the authority of the U.S. Senate and available through the Library of Congress. It includes the full text of the U.S. Constitution, corresponding United States Supreme Court annotations, and a discussion of each provision, including background information on its history and interpretation. Additional constitutional sources are found in the *U.S.C.A.* and the *U.S.C.S.,* both of which contain the entire text of the Constitution and its amendments as well as citations to cases discussing particular constitutional provisions. Annotated state codes provide a similar service for their state constitutions. Constitutional annotations are updated through supplementary pocket parts. State constitutions are usually included in the publications containing state statutes.

UPDATING THE LAW—LEARNING TO USE CITATORS

Almost every day, new court decisions are made, new regulations are issued, and new statutes are enacted or existing statutes amended. Because the law is ever changing, a critical factor to consider when researching a topic or point of law is whether a given court opinion, statute, or regulation is still valid. A case decided six months ago, for example, may prove to be "bad law" today if it has been reversed or significantly modified on appeal. The careful researcher will avoid assuming that the case law or statutory law on a specific issue is the same today as it was last month or last year. This section will show you how to make sure that a law or court interpretation of the law is up to date and still "good law"—that is, currently valid law.

Case Law

Shepard's Citations, which is published by Shepard's, is a research tool with which all paralegals should become familiar. *Shepard's* contains the most comprehensive system of case citators in the United States. A **citator** provides a list of legal references that have cited or interpreted a case or law. A *case citator* provides, in addition, a history of the particular case. *Shepard's* lists every case published in an official or unofficial reporter by its citation.

    Shepard's citators are available for nearly every jurisdiction. *Shepard's United States Citations* covers the decisions of the United States Supreme Court as reported in *United States Reports, Supreme Court Reporter,* and *Lawyers' Edition of the Supreme Court Reports. Shepard's Federal Reporter Citations* provides coverage of the various federal courts of appeal and district courts. Shepard's citators also exist for the reports of every state, the District of Columbia, and Puerto Rico. Every region of the National Reporter System is covered by *Shepard's.* Exhibit 16.24 shows a *Shepard's* case citator.

    One of the most valuable functions of *Shepard's* is that it provides the researcher with a means to verify the history of a case. For example, if a paralegal wants to know whether a certain court decision has been reversed by a higher court, *Shepard's* provides that information. Note, though, that it takes some time before the hardcover printed versions of *Shepard's* citators are updated. In conducting research in *Shepard's,* you will therefore need to check the softcover supplements that accompany and update the most recent hardbound volumes. The supplements are color coded (red, blue, or yellow) and placed next to the *Shepard's* volumes on the library shelf. In addition, to make absolutely sure that your research is truly up to date, you will want to use one of the online citators provided by computerized legal-research services and discussed later in this section.

citator
A book or online service that provides the history and interpretation of a statute, regulation, or court decision and a list of the cases, statutes, and regulations that have interpreted, applied, or modified a statute or regulation.

EXHIBIT 16.24
Shepard's Citations

Reproduced by permission of Shepard's. Further reproduction of any kind is strictly prohibited.

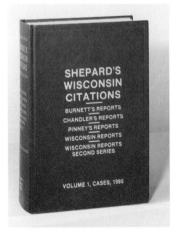

THE ORGANIZATION OF *SHEPARD'S CITATIONS.*   At first glance, the unique organizational structure and language of *Shepard's* can appear confusing. The researcher begins by finding the appropriate citator, the one that corresponds with the researched case's citation. For example, if the citation for the main case indicates that it is from the *Atlantic Reporter,* the citator to locate is *Shepard's Atlantic Citations.* Then, to locate the case in this publication, the researcher finds the pages covering the relevant volume of the *Atlantic Reporter.* The volume numbers are printed in the upper left-hand corner of each page for easy reference. Once the correct pages are found, the researcher reviews the listings to locate the page on which the case begins. Parallel citations to other reporters are listed in parentheses with the case. Following this is a listing of citations identifying any higher courts that have reviewed the case. Then comes a listing of cases that have cited the main case.

TYPES OF INFORMATION PROVIDED BY *SHEPARD'S CITATIONS.*   Paralegals can use *Shepard's* citators to accomplish several research objectives:

- Parallel citations—*Shepard's* provides parallel citations for the cited cases, allowing the paralegal to locate the case in other official or unofficial reporters.

- Other cases—*Shepard's* lists other cases ("citing cases") that have cited the main case ("the cited case"). For example, suppose that in researching a matter you have found a case on point. You can check *Shepard's Citations* to find out what other cases have dealt with one or more issues in your case (the cited case). Also, *Shepard's* listing of citing cases may include other cases on point that you will want to check.

- References to periodicals—If you are researching a case on point, *Shepard's* provides further research tips by referring to helpful periodical articles and annotations in the *American Law Reports.*

- Case history—As mentioned, *Shepard's* provides a history of the cited case. If the decision in your case on point has been overturned on appeal (or if any further action has been taken), *Shepard's* will indicate this.

Note that *Shepard's* has an elaborate abbreviation system to provide information on how the cited case has been used in the citing case. For example, if the ruling in the cited case has been followed by a citing case, the symbol *f* (for "followed") will appear after the name of the citing case. Exhibit 16.25 on the next page explains other symbols used in *Shepard's.*

Statutory and Constitutional Law

Shepard's citators for constitutions and statutes are similar to the case citators. The cited constitutional or statutory sources are listed by section number on each page and appear in boldfaced print for quick reference. *Shepard's* can serve as a valuable tool in constitutional and statutory research by identifying other sources that have discussed the researched provision and by providing information on the status of the provision.

On the federal level, the *Statutes Edition of Shepard's United States Citations* contains listings of the following publications:

- The U.S. Constitution.
- The *U.S.C., U.S.C.A.,* and *U.S.C.S.*
- The *United States Statutes at Large* provisions that have not yet been incorporated into the *U.S.C.*
- *Federal Reporter* citations.

ABBREVIATIONS—ANALYSIS

History of Case

a	(affirmed)	Same case affirmed on rehearing.
cc	(connected case)	Different case from case cited but arising out of same subject matter or intimately connected therewith.
m	(modified)	Same case modified on rehearing.
r	(reversed)	Same case reversed on rehearing.
s	(same case)	Same case as case cited.
S	(superseded)	Substitution for former opinion.
v	(vacated)	Same case vacated.
US	cert den	*Certiorari* denied by U.S. Supreme Court.
US	cert dis	*Certiorari* dismissed by U.S. Supreme Court.
US	reh den	Rehearing denied by U.S. Supreme Court.
US	reh dis	Rehearing dismissed by U.S. Supreme Court.

Treatment of Case

c	(criticized)	Soundness of decision or reasoning in cited case criticized for reasons given.
d	(distinguished)	Case at bar different either in law or fact from case cited for reasons given.
e	(explained)	Statement of import of decision in cited case. Not merely a restatement of the facts.
f	(followed)	Cited as controlling.
h	(harmonized)	Apparent inconsistency explained and shown not to exist.
j	(dissenting opinion)	Citation in dissenting option.
L	(limited)	Refusal to extend decision of cited case beyond precise issues involved.
o	(overruled)	Ruling in cited case expressly overruled.
p	(parallel)	Citing case substantially alike or on all fours with cited case in its law or facts.
q	(questioned)	Soundness of decision or reasoning in cited case questioned.

ABBREVIATIONS—COURTS

Cir. Fed.—U.S. Court of appeals, Federal Circuit
Cir (number)—U.S. Court of Appeals Circuit (number)
CIT—United States Court of International Trade
CCPA—Court of Customs and Patent Appeals
Cl Ct—Claims Court (U.S.)
Ct Cl—Court of Claims Reports (U.S.)
Cu Ct—Customs Court Decisions
DC—District of Columbia
EC or ECA—Temporary Emergency Court of Appeals
ML—Judicial Panel on Multidistrict Litigation
RRR—Special Court Regional Rail Reorganization Act of 1973

- Annotations from the *American Law Reports* and the *Lawyers' Edition of the Supreme Court Reports*.

Shepard's also cites publications for all state constitutions and statutes, including a listing of federal statutory and constitutional provisions that have been cited in state sources.

Analyzing Case Law	1. *Case format*—Reported cases contain more information than just the court's decision. Typically, case formats include the following components:
	a. The title (case name, usually plaintiff versus defendant).
	b. The name of the court that decided the case.
	c. The case citation.
	d. The docket number assigned by the court.
	e. The date on which the case was decided.
	f. The syllabus (a brief synopsis of the facts, issues, and ruling).
	g. The headnotes (short paragraphs that summarize the rules of law discussed in the case; in West's reporters, headnotes correlate with the key-number system).
	h. The names of counsel.
	i. The name of the judge who authored the opinion.
	j. The opinion (the court's own words on the matter).
	k. The conclusion (holding, ruling).
	2. *Briefing cases*—Legal professionals often brief, or summarize, the cases they research. Knowing how to read, analyze, and summarize cases makes it easier to compare and synthesize research results accurately and efficiently. Although the format of briefs varies, the following headings are typical: citation, facts, procedure, issue, decision, holding, and reasoning.
Researching Statutory Law	Bills and ordinances that are passed by legislative bodies (federal, state, and local) become statutory law, a primary source of American law. Statutes that are enacted are eventually published in codes, which are updated by supplemental pocket parts and loose-leaf services.
	1. *Federal statutes*—Federal laws are published officially in the *United States Code (U.S.C.)*. The *U.S.C.* organizes statutes into fifty subjects, or titles, and further subdivides each title into chapters (sections) and subchapters. The researcher can find a statute in the *U.S.C.* by searching through the topical outlines, by looking in the index, or by looking under the act's popular name in the volume entitled *Popular Name Table*. The *United States Code Annotated* and the *United States Code Service* are unofficial publications of federal statutes. Both of these sources are useful to researchers because they provide annotations and citations to other resources.
	2. *State statutes*—State codes follow the *U.S.C.* pattern of arranging statutes by subject. They may be called codes, revisions, compilations, general statutes, or statutes, depending on the state. In many states, official codes are supplemented by annotated codes published by private publishers.
Analyzing Statutory Law	1. *Reading statutory law*—Reading and analyzing statutory law is often difficult. You should first note the statute's provisions concerning its coverage and effective date to ensure that it applies to the case or claim being researched. You should also note the definitions given in the statute and determine the relationships among subsections within the statute.
	2. *Interpreting statutes*—In interpreting statutory law, the paralegal can turn to several helpful guidelines: the statutory rules of construction; the plain-meaning rule; previous judicial interpretations of the statute, if any exist; and the legislative history of the statute.

Analyzing Statutory Law—Continued	3. *Legislative intent*—The legislative history of a statute can reveal the intent of the legislature and thus help to establish the relevance of the statute to the issue being researched. Important sources for researching legislative history include transcripts of committee reports and hearings, transcripts of congressional proceedings, and the wording of statutes as first published in the *United States Statutes at Large*. Helpful resources in this area include the *Congressional Record*, the *United States Code Congressional and Administrative News,* and the *Congressional Information Service*.
Researching Administrative Law	Regulations issued by federal administrative agencies are primary sources of law. Agency regulations are published in the *Code of Federal Regulations (C.F.R.)*. The C.F.R. follows a format similar to that of the *United States Code (U.S.C.),* and the subject classifications (titles) of the C.F.R. correspond to the titles in the U.S.C. To locate recently published regulations, the researcher should refer to the *Federal Register*'s cumulative *List of C.F.R. Sections Affected,* which reflects changes made during the current month.
Finding Constitutional Law	Constitutions are also primary sources of law. The U.S. Constitution can be found in a number of publications, including *The Constitution of the United States of America* (available through the Library of Congress), the *U.S.C.A.,* and the *U.S.C.S.* Annotated versions of state constitutions are also available.
Updating the Law— Learning to Use Citators	Crucial in legal research is using citators to make sure that the research results are still valid. 1. Shepard's Citations—The various volumes of *Shepard's Citations* allow the researcher to verify whether a case has been overruled or reversed, a statute repealed or amended, an agency regulation voided or superseded, and the like. 2. *Online citators*—Online citators, including those provided by Lexis® and Westlaw®, enable the researcher to access cases, statutes, or regulations (or amendments or modifications to existing statutes or regulations) that have not yet been included in printed citators and thus ensure that research results are as up to date as possible.

✳ QUESTIONS FOR REVIEW

1. What are the differences between primary and secondary sources of law? How are each of these types of sources used in legal research?

2. What is a case on point? What is a case on "all fours"? Why is finding such a case important when researching case law? What is the difference between a mandatory authority and a persuasive authority?

3. How are legal encyclopedias, case digests, and other secondary sources used to find case law relevant to a research topic? What is the West key-number system, and how does it simplify the legal-research process?

4. Describe the forms in which court decisions are published, from their initial publication to their final published form.

5. Identify the various parts of a case citation. How do case citations help you locate a case? List and briefly describe the components of a reported case. Which part should you focus on when analyzing a case?

6. How do you brief a case? What is the purpose of briefing a case? What should be included in a case brief?

7. Describe the forms in which statutes are published, from their original issuance to their final published

form. Do the same for regulations. What are the major sources for statutes and regulations?

8. What are some points to consider when reading and interpreting statutory law? What guidelines do the courts traditionally use to interpret a statute?

9. What are some guidelines for reading and interpreting statutory law? What is meant by the term *leg-islative history?* What resources are available for researching the legislative history of a statute?

10. Why is it important to find the most current law? How can you verify that your research results are up to date?

✳ ETHICAL QUESTIONS

1. Kristine Connolly, a paralegal in a litigation firm, has finished reading a brief that the opposing side submitted to the court in support of a motion for summary judgment. In the brief, she notices a citation to a state supreme court case of which she is unaware. She is experienced in the field and keeps current with new cases as they are decided. She wants to look at the case because it gives the other side a winning edge. She checks in the advance sheets, digests, and state encyclopedias, as well as on Westlaw®. She finally calls the state supreme court clerk's office and asks about the case. The office has no record of such a case. She asks the legal assistant for the opposing counsel to give her a copy of the case. When she does not receive it, she decides that the case is probably fictional. What should Kristine do?

2. Barbara Coltiers is a legal assistant in a very busy litigation practice. She gets a call from a nervous attorney in her firm thirty minutes before the attorney is to appear in court. He wants her to do some research before he goes to court. He has just heard about a case that might help him win and gives her the citation. Because he is in a hurry, he gives her the wrong volume number. She has a hard time finding the case, but after about fifteen minutes of searching, she locates the citation. She quickly copies the case and runs to his office with it so that he can hurry across the street to the court for his appearance. She is in such a hurry that she forgets to check the subsequent history of the case.

It turns out that the case has been overruled by the state supreme court and is therefore no longer controlling in the jurisdiction. The attorney is chastised by the judge for citing it. In fact, the judge is so annoyed with the attorney for making an argument that is not based on existing law that he denies the attorney's motion and makes the attorney pay the other side's court costs. When the client finds out why the motion was denied, she is irate. Does the client have any remedy against the attorney? Against Barbara?

3. John Hernandez is studying at a local college to be a paralegal. The college has Westlaw® for its students to use. The software license specifically prohibits the faculty or students of the college from using the program for personal work. John knows that Kathy, a classmate, has a part-time job with a law firm, and he becomes aware that Kathy is using Westlaw® regularly to do research for her supervising attorney in that firm. What should John do?

✳ PRACTICE QUESTIONS AND ASSIGNMENTS

1. Using the material presented in the chapter, identify the case name, volume number, reporter abbreviation, page number, and year of decision for each of the following case citations, including the parallel citations:

   a. *Smith v. James,* 400 Mich. 19, 630 N.W.2d 98 (1999).

   b. *Johnson v. Fassler Wrecking, Inc.,* 10 Cal.4th 539, 27 Cal.Rptr.2d 201 (1999).

   c. *Barnes v. Barnes,* 95 N.Y.2d 101, 637 N.E.2d 23, 654 N.Y.S. 13 (1999).

   d. *Miranda v. Arizona,* 384 U.S. 436, 86 S.Ct. 1602, 16 L.Ed.2d 694 (1966).

2. Using the material presented in the chapter, identify the title number, code abbreviation, and section number for the following statutory citations:

   a. 42 U.S.C. Section 1161(a).

   b. 20 C.F.R. 404.101(a).

3. Using the material presented in the chapter, indicate whether the following sources are primary or secondary sources:

a. Digest.

b. Case reporter.

c. Legal encyclopedia.

d. Statute.

e. The *Code of Federal Regulations.*

4. Sleeping Beauty is awakened by a kiss from Prince Charming. She can think of nothing more repulsive than to be kissed by him. Sleeping Beauty suffers from nightmares and depression as a result of this incident and contacts a law firm regarding filing a lawsuit against the prince for the damages, which include medical expenses, that she has suffered as a result of the kiss. The paralegal is assigned the task of researching Sleeping Beauty's case to determine whether or not she can sue. What are the issue(s) to be researched? What would the paralegal's research goals be?

5. Mr. John D. Consumer bought a new car eight months ago. The car frequently stalls. The problem began the first week after he purchased the vehicle. It stalled late at night on an expressway while he was returning home from a business trip. It has stalled at least monthly since then, often in potentially dangerous areas. Not only has he taken the car to the dealer, who has repeatedly attempted to repair the problem without success, but he has also notified the manufacturer in writing of the problem.

   Most states have a lemon law that requires manufacturers to replace vehicles that cannot be repaired, even if the warranty has expired. Does your state have a lemon law? If so, would the lemon law help Mr. Consumer?

   Research this question and try to find the answer to Mr. Consumer's problem. Begin by analyzing the facts. Then make a list of relevant legal terms to look up in an index.

   Select a legal encyclopedia—either *American Jurisprudence* or *Corpus Juris Secundum*—to use in your research. Write down the name of the encyclopedia. Consult the general index volumes.

   a. Write down the index topics under which you found relevant information. (If you have difficulty locating relevant information, try checking the topic indexes in the individual volumes.)

   b. Write down the citations to encyclopedia sections containing relevant information.

   c. Look up these citations in the appropriate volumes of the encyclopedia to find an answer to Mr. Consumer's problem. Be sure to check the pocket part for more current citations. According

to the encyclopedia, what is the answer to John D. Consumer's problem?

6. After analyzing the facts of Mr. Consumer's problem and making a list of legally and factually relevant terms, as described in Practice Question 5, do the following:

   a. Locate the index to the annotated version of your state statutes. Using your list of terms, look in the index for citations to relevant statute sections. Write down the citations.

   b. If you did Practice Question 5 above, compare how you found the citations in the index to your state statutes with how you found them in the legal encyclopedia. Under what topics did you look in each situation?

   c. Now that you have found relevant citations, go to the volume of the statute containing the cited sections and read those sections. (Be sure to check the pocket part of the volume.) What answer does the statute in your state give to Mr. Consumer's problem? If you answered Practice Question 5 above, is the answer given in the encyclopedia? If not, how do the answers differ?

7. Using the annotated version of your state statutes, look for relevant case law on Mr. Consumer's problem. If no annotated version of your state statute exists or if no cases appear in the annotated version—or if you want to learn to use another source—locate a state digest. Find the relevant section(s) and locate case law that interprets the statute and that is as similar to Mr. Consumer's problem as possible.

   a. Write down the citations to no more than three relevant cases. Now look up those cases in the case reporters.

   b. Read through the summary and headnotes of each case. Do the cases still appear to be relevant? If not, go back to the annotated statute or digest and look for more relevant cases.

   c. What did you find? Did the courts' application of the statute change in any way your answer to the problem facing Mr. Consumer?

8. The hypothetical case discussed in the chapter involving a lawsuit brought by Trent Hoffman against Better Homes Store for negligence is based on an actual case: *Ward v. K-Mart Corp.,* 136 Ill.2d 132, 554 N.E.2d 223 (1990). Obtain a copy of the case. Using the materials presented in the chapter, answer the following questions about the case.

   a. What is the docket number?

b. What court rendered the decision in the case?

c. What are the names of the attorneys who were involved in the case?

d. What does headnote number 4 say?

e. What does the synopsis of the case say?

9. Read through the court's opinion in the case *Ward v. K-Mart Corp.*, 136 Ill.2d 132, 554 N.E.2d 223 (1990) and then do the following:

a. Find at least one statement made by the court that constitutes *dicta*.

b. Brief the case.

10. Obtain a copy of the case *Bragdon v. Abbott,* 524 U.S. 624, 118 S.Ct. 2196, 141 L.Ed.2d 540 (1998), which involves a claim arising under the Americans with Disabilities Act (ADA), and then answer the following questions:

a. How does the Americans with Disabilities Act (ADA) define the term *disability?*

b. What disease was the United States Supreme Court reviewing to determine whether it was a disability under the ADA?

c. What did the Court decide regarding whether the disease was a disability under the ADA?

d. How did the Court apply the statutory definition of disability to the disease?

e. Did the Court determine whether the disease constituted a "physical impairment"? If so, how did the Court reach this conclusion?

11. Using the material presented in Exhibit 16.25, *Abbreviations Used in* Shepard's, answer the following questions:

a. Under the section entitled "History of Case," what does the abbreviation, "a" stand for? The abbreviation "r"? Why are these abbreviations significant?

b. Under the section entitled "Treatment of Case," what does the abbreviation "d" stand for? The abbreviation "o"? Why are these significant?

✳ QUESTIONS FOR CRITICAL ANALYSIS

1. Sources of law are divided into two broad categories, primary and secondary sources. What is the difference between these two types? Why are only primary sources allowed to be cited in most briefs and other documents filed with the courts?

2. What is the difference between a mandatory and a persuasive authority? Why is this distinction important for the courts? Which source is preferable to find when doing legal research? Why?

3. What is the difference between a case on point and a case on "all fours"? Which is it preferable to locate? How do these cases fit into the research goals? How likely is it that you might find a case on point or on "all fours"?

4. Legal encyclopedias, legal digests, and *American Law Reports* are secondary sources. For what is each source used? How are these sources different? How are they similar? Which source is preferable to use, and why?

5. What is an annotation? How is it used in a digest? In the *American Law Reports?*

6. Explain the West key-number system. What is its purpose? Is its use limited to digests? How can the key-number system be of assistance to a researcher?

7. What is a parallel citation? Why are parallel citations used?

8. The written opinions of judges sitting on state and federal appellate courts are usually published in reporters. Why is it that trial court decisions are not routinely published in reporters?

9. What is West's National Reporter System? What geographical units does it include? Is it widely used? Why or why not? How might the West key-number system tie into it?

10. *The Bluebook* provides rules for citation. Why are these rules needed? What would happen without these rules? Can you think of a better system?

11. What is the difference between case law and statutory law? Why is the difference significant? In what forms are statutes published? What are the parallel codes for the statutes of the U.S. government?

12. Why is statutory language often difficult to read and understand? What factors must legislators consider when drafting statutes?

13. How is statutory law interpreted? What role do case law and legislative history play in its interpretation? How reliable are the sources?

14. What is the purpose of *Shepard's Citations?* What might result if *Shepard's* citators were not used? Are there other methods of accomplishing the same objective?

✳ PROJECTS

1. Using a state bar directory or other type of legal directory, find out which law libraries in your area are open to the public. Make arrangements to visit a law library. If tours of the library are offered, try to be present for a tour.

2. Make arrangements through your professor, a local bar association, or your personal contacts to visit the law library of a law firm or the legal department of a corporation or government office. If you also participated in Project 1 above, compare the materials available in the libraries of firms or government agencies with those available in law libraries. Why is it necessary for legal professionals to use law libraries other than those located in their offices?

3. Find out if your state has an official reporter for its appellate courts. If it does, find out where the reporter is printed and how often the advance sheets are compiled into a hardbound volume and distributed.

4. Obtain a copy of *The Bluebook: A Uniform System of Citation* and look up the citation formats for your state court reporters and statutes.

5. Using information from Chapter 6, make a diagram of the federal court system. List the reporters for each court in the system, using the information given in this chapter.

✳ USING INTERNET RESOURCES

1. Go to the home page of the American Law Institute (ALI) at http://www.ali.org. Browse through this site and its offerings, and then answer the following questions:

   a. Select "Press Releases" and look over the list of new press releases. Have any new *Restatements* been published by the ALI? If so, on what topics?

   b. Now click on "Publications Catalog" and access the ALI's "Catalog of Publications." How many *Restatements of the Law* have been published by the ALI? Make a list of the topics covered in the *Restatements*.

2. The *United States Code,* which contains the statutes passed by Congress, can be accessed through Cornell Law School's Legal Information Institute at http://www4.cornell.edu/uscode. Access this Web site.

   a. How many ways are there to access the *United States Code* within the Web site? What are they?

   b. Scroll down to the title listing. How many titles are there? Click on Title 42. What does it cover? How many chapters are in Title 42? In the "Search Title 42" box, enter "Superfund Act." Describe the results you obtain.

   c. Go back to the *United States Code* home page. Using the section entitled "Find U.S. Code Materials by Title and Section," enter "42" in the title box and "9601" in the section box; then click on "Go to title and section." Describe what you find. In what chapter is this act located? In addition to the statutory section, what else is available?

END NOTES

1. This final step—because it involves legal writing—is covered in part in Chapter 18.

2. Some scholars maintain that this phrase originated from the Latin adage that "nothing similar is identical unless it runs on all four feet."

3. In the context of employment, the ADA is designed to eliminate discriminatory practices that prevent otherwise qualified individuals with disabilities from working. See Chapter 10.

CHAPTER 17

COMPUTER-ASSISTED LEGAL RESEARCH

Chapter Outline

✴ INTRODUCTION ✴ CD-ROMs AND LEGAL RESEARCH
✴ WESTLAW® AND LEXIS® ✴ GOING ONLINE—INTERNET BASICS
✴ CONDUCTING ONLINE RESEARCH ✴ LOCATING PEOPLE AND INVESTIGATING
COMPANIES ✴ SOME OF THE BEST LEGAL-RESOURCE SITES ON THE INTERNET

After completing this chapter, you will know:

- How CD-ROMs and legal-research services provided by Westlaw®
  and Lexis® help legal professionals in computer-assisted legal
  research (CALR).

- What the Internet is, and how it can be accessed and navigated.

- Some strategies for planning and conducting research on the Internet.

- How you can find people and investigate companies using Internet
  search tools and databases.

- How to find some of the best legal resources available on the Internet.

INTRODUCTION

Computers and online databases have greatly simplified the tasks of paralegals in all areas of legal work. This is particularly true in the area of legal research. One of the great benefits of computer technology for legal practitioners is **computer-assisted legal research (CALR)**. As you learned in Chapter 16, thorough and up-to-date legal research requires access to voluminous source materials, including state and federal court decisions and statutory law. Today, attorneys and paralegals can access many of these materials online—either through the use of proprietary software and a modem connection or via the Internet. Additionally, a number of primary and secondary legal sources are available on CD-ROMs.

An obvious advantage of CALR is that you can locate and print out court cases, statutory provisions, and other legal documents within a matter of minutes without leaving your work station. Another key advantage of CALR is that new case decisions and changes in statutory law are entered almost immediately into certain online legal databases, including those of Westlaw® and Lexis®. This means that you can find out easily and quickly whether a case decided three months ago is still "good law" today.

In this chapter, after a discussion of CD-ROMs and legal research, we look at the legal-research services available through Westlaw® and Lexis®. We then look at the Internet—what it is and how it can be used to conduct online research efficiently. You will learn about service providers, browsers, and search engines. You will discover how to evaluate whether the Internet is the best tool for particular research projects. You will also read about some of the best resources currently available on the Internet.

By the time you read this chapter, some of what we say will have changed, particularly with respect to Internet resources. Some of these resources may have improved, others may have been removed, and still others may have been added. (See this chapter's *Featured Guest* article starting on page 632 for information on how to keep abreast of computer technology.) The general approach to conducting research online will not have altered, however. If you master the basic principles of online research discussed in this chapter, you will be able to conduct research on the Internet no matter how much it changes.

CD-ROMs AND LEGAL RESEARCH

Increasingly, today's law firms are using research materials available in CD-ROM ("compact disk, read-only memory") format. CD-ROMs are accessed through a CD-ROM reader, which reads and displays the contents of a CD-ROM when it is inserted into the reader. Depending on the computer system, the reader may be contained within the computer or attached to the computer with a cable. The software program accompanying a CD-ROM allows the computer operating system to communicate with the CD-ROM. A paralegal using CD-ROMs for legal research would find the CD-ROM containing the relevant reference materials—a legal encyclopedia, for example—and use the CD-ROM's index or search tool to quickly locate a given topic or subtopic.

Advantages of Using CD-ROMs

Most law firms have law libraries containing legal encyclopedias, case digests, statutory compilations, and other research materials frequently used by the firms' attorneys and paralegals. Law libraries and the physical space required to house them are expensive, particularly for small law firms. An obvious advantage of using legal reference materials on CD-ROMs is that they are far less costly to purchase and require much less space than their printed counterparts.

A CD-ROM holds the equivalent of over 600 megabytes of data. This means that one CD-ROM can store approximately 300,000 pages, or over a hundred volumes of legal reference materials. For example, the entire 215-volume *United States Code Annotated* (discussed in Chapter 16) is contained on only two CD-ROMs. Many federal government publications, legal encyclopedias, West reporters, and other research sources are also available in CD-ROM format. Exhibit 17.1 shows a photograph of CD-ROM legal libraries. CD-ROMs can also be easily transported. They can be used (on laptop or notebook computers) while traveling or even in the courtroom. A further advantage of using CD-ROMs is that searching their contents is easier and quicker than searching printed reference sources. For example, if you are researching a state statute, you can search through the statute for certain words or section numbers using the search command, which saves valuable research time. West's CD-ROM libraries offer the advantage of the key-number system. As discussed in Chapter 16, this system simplifies legal research by allowing you to search key numbers to find relevant case law or other legal sources. You can also copy segments of the statute directly to your computer, which reduces the amount of time you spend in document preparation as well as lessening the risk of error.

EXHIBIT 17.1
West CD-ROM Libraries

Reproduced with permission of West Group.

Disadvantages of Using CD-ROMs

The major disadvantage of using CD-ROMs in legal research is that, like their printed equivalents, they can become outdated. Suppose that you want to locate recent court cases interpreting a particular provision of the *United States Code*. If your CD-ROM containing the *United States Code Annotated* was purchased five years ago, clearly you will be unable to find the latest annotations on that CD-ROM. In other words, just as when conducting research using printed legal reference materials, you need to keep in mind the date of the materials included on the CD-ROM.

Note that even the most recently issued CD-ROM version of a legal encyclopedia or other reference work may be somewhat outdated, just as a printed text is, because of the time it takes to create and distribute the CD-ROM. The best way to ensure that your research is really up to date is to check an online legal database.

WESTLAW® AND LEXIS®

CALR has made it possible to access legal databases containing many of the most important legal resources. By accessing databases provided through commercial legal-research services, legal professionals can obtain case law or statutory law relating to a particular issue within seconds. Two premier legal-research services often used by attorneys and paralegals are Westlaw® and Lexis®. To use these legal-research services, a law firm or other user signs a contract with the provider of the services. Westlaw® users may be charged either by the hour or by the transaction. Lexis® users are typically charged based on the number of database searches performed.

The Westlaw® and Lexis® databases contain extensive legal and business information. Westlaw®, for example, is organized into more than 17,000 databases covering all areas of the law. It is possible to access such primary sources as federal and state statutes, court cases, and administrative regulations. Some of the materials are

FEATURED GUEST: BRENT ROPER

Keeping Current on Computer Technology

BIOGRAPHICAL NOTE

Brent Roper received his degree in law and his master's degree in business administration from Washburn University in Topeka, Kansas. Over the past fifteen years, he has published a number of textbooks and articles on law office computing and law office management.

Aside from ethics, competency, and meeting client needs, keeping up to date on changing computer technology in the law office is one of the most important tasks of any legal professional.

The widespread use of computers during the last thirty to forty years has had a profound impact on how law is practiced in the twenty-first century. In the 1960s and 1970s, only the largest of law firms used computers, and they were mainly used for "back-office" functions, such as accounting and billing. Today, computers are used daily by almost all law office staff members—senior partners, legal assistants, and mail clerks alike. The computer

is an indispensable tool that permeates nearly every function of any law practice, regardless of whether the practice consists of a global law firm with a thousand attorneys or a small-town solo practitioner. The accompanying table shows the many ways in which computers may be used in a law firm.

WHY IT IS CRITICAL TO BE SAVVY IN COMPUTER TECHNOLOGY

The list of computer uses in the law office grows longer every day. And while it is difficult to stay abreast of the changes in computer technology, it

FUNCTION/APPLICATION	DESCRIPTION
Accounting/budgeting	Tracking and managing the firm's finances
Asset management	Tracking and accounting relating to the firm's property
Calendar/docket control/case management	Tracking, controlling, and managing appointments, deadlines, and work to be done on client cases
Connectivity/network software/groupware/security	Linking and sharing information on a global basis in a secured environment
Database management	Tracking, sorting, and retrieving information
Electronic mail	Client, interoffice, court, and law practice communication, including the ability to electronically transfer documents
Factual/substantive research	Finding and discovering information via the Internet and other resources relating to client cases
Legal research	Computer-assisted legal research (Westlaw®, Lexis®, Internet legal resources, CD-ROM libraries, and other electronic law-related information resources)
Legal specific software	Managing, organizing, and producing client-related work information regarding specific legal functions or fields (for example, software designed to meet the needs of a law office in specific practice areas such as real estate, criminal law, estate planning, wills, and taxes)
Litigation support	Organizing, storing, retrieving, and summarizing case-related information for litigation
Marketing	Newsletters, Web sites, and other marketing materials
Payroll	Paying employees and accounting for taxes and withholdings
Presentation generation	Preparing electronic presentations
Project management	Organizing, tracking, and sequencing a large number of items for a complex project/assignment
Record keeping	Tracking and storing client case files
Spreadsheets	Electronic number processing
Timekeeping and billing	Invoicing and collecting monies from clients for services that have been rendered
Word processing	Electronic document preparation

FEATURED GUEST, *Continued*

is critical for every legal professional to do so. Keeping current on computer trends and how they affect law practices is not about "keeping up with the Joneses" or bragging about having the latest computer. Rather, it allows you to do the following:

- Provide the best-quality services to clients.
- Provide the most convenient services to clients.
- Increase productivity and efficiency.
- Meet ethical obligations to clients and courts and keep information secure.
- Keep costs down.
- Maintain a competitive advantage for clients.
- Have the tools to compete and survive in a very competitive legal environment.

Computer technology and innovation directly affect these matters in almost every law office function, so it is critical to continue to learn and to increase your computer skills. In this day and age, it is almost impossible to provide legal services to clients and stay competitive in the legal marketplace without using a computer, investing regularly in technology, and constantly learning about new computer techniques and software. It is *not* enough to know just the basics; most legal professionals *need* to know advanced features of many software products to really get the most out of them. It takes time, but the payoff can be substantial.

WAYS TO STAY ABREAST OF COMPUTER TECHNOLOGY

Most legal professionals are extremely busy, juggling a variety of client cases and responsibilities and constantly meeting deadlines. Listed next are some ideas on how you can keep current on legal technology issues:

- **Read and study computer articles in legal publications**—Most legal professionals subscribe to legal journals and periodicals. Most of these publications have articles that cover computer and technology topics. Instead of skimming the articles quickly to get them off your desk or skipping them entirely, take the time to read, study, and apply them in your everyday activities.
- **Subscribe to a general computer magazine**—Many general computer magazines are available. Even these general magazines have a wealth of information related to word processing programs, spreadsheets, databases, e-mail, and other software that is used every day in most law offices.
- **Subscribe to a law-specific computer magazine**—Several law-specific magazines, such as *Law Office Computing* and *Law Practice Management,* cover law office computing topics. These publications can help you keep current on law office computing trends and the most recent software created specifically for law offices.
- **Subscribe to electronic legal computing newsletters and discussion lists**—A number of resources exist on the Internet for information about legal computing, including legal computing newsletters via e-mail, discussion groups that focus on

> ## "The list of computer uses in the law office grows longer every day."

legal computing needs, and general Internet resources for legal professionals.

- **Take the time to learn from other users and take time to experiment**—Watch and learn from other legal professionals, ask questions about how others use their computers and software, and compare notes. Also, one of the best ways to learn techniques is to try new things and experiment when you have a new problem to be solved.
- **Obtain training in computing**—There are a wide variety of options for learning how to use computers and computer programs. These options may include on-site classes at your law office. Additional options are training workshops offered by vendors, computer courses or continuing education workshops on computing topics, and Web tutorials on software programs. Take advantage of these whenever possible.
- **Upgrade to new products**—Support product upgrades (some practices fail to upgrade to the latest versions of products because of the cost), and use new product features when you can.

also accessible through specialized databases, such as bankruptcy, insurance, and taxation. Secondary sources include legal texts and periodicals, public records, and other sources of business and financial information.

Accessing Westlaw® or Lexis®

To access Westlaw® or Lexis®, a subscriber can use the service's proprietary software, which allows the subscriber's computer to access the database through a modem connection. Traditionally, this was the only way to access these services. Today, both Westlaw® and Lexis® can be accessed online via the Internet as well—at http://www.westlaw.com and http://www.lexis.com, respectively. No special software is needed to access either service via the Internet.

An advantage of accessing these databases on the Web is that research can be done easily with a standard browser (browsers are discussed later in this chapter) and without the extensive training needed to use the proprietary software. A disadvantage is that users who do not have the software also do not have the accompanying manuals that instruct them on how to use the services. "Help" links at both Web sites, however, give users instructions on how to perform various tasks. Another disadvantage for Lexis® users is that not all of the Lexis® databases are included on the Web site. In contrast, Westlaw® offers the full panoply of its services on the Web.

When you access Westlaw® or Lexis® (using proprietary software or via the Internet), you will be asked to sign onto the service with your password. After you sign on, a welcome page is displayed. (The welcome page of Westlaw® is shown in Exhibit 17.2.) From this page, you can begin your research. You can retrieve documents by citation, check citations, or search databases for cases, statutes, or other documents on a given topic or issue.

Retrieving a Document by Citation

If you have the citation for a document, such as a court case or statute, you can enter the citation and call up the document. For example, on Westlaw® you would click on the "Find this document by citation" box on the left side of the screen.

Then you would key in the citation for a case, statute, regulation, or other document. Within seconds, the cited document would appear on the screen.

Checking a Citation

Westlaw® and Lexis® both provide online citators. Recall from Chapter 16 that a citator, such as one of *Shepard's* citators, shows the history of a case and provides a list of legal references that have cited or interpreted the case. Online citators are extremely useful to legal researchers because they are more up to date than printed citators.

For example, suppose that you want to find out whether the holding in a particular case decided by a California appellate court is still "good law." If you are using Lexis®, you can use the **Auto-Cite** citator to find out if the decision was appealed to the California Supreme Court (or to the United States Supreme Court) and, if so, whether the holding was affirmed, overturned, or modified on appeal. You can also "Shepardize" the case to find out how courts in other jurisdictions have dealt with the same issue.

If you are using Westlaw®, you can use the **KeyCite** citator service. An important editorial enhancement to documents accessible through Westlaw® is the KeyCite case status flag, which indicates when there is case history that should be investigated. A case status flag, depending on its color, will warn you that a case is not good law for at least one of its points, that the case has some negative history but its holding has not been reversed, or that the case has been overruled. KeyCite provides other features to make research more efficient as well. Suppose that you have found a case in the KeyCite database that cites the case you are researching. Stars added to the citation of the citing case show the extent to which your case is discussed in the citing case. For example, four stars indicate that the citing case contains an extended discussion of your case, usually more than a printed page of text. One star indicates the reference is brief, usually no more than as part of a list of case citations.

If your search results include a statute or an agency rule, Westlaw® enables you to check for any recent changes. The service displays any documents on Westlaw® that amend or repeal the statute or rule you are viewing. Westlaw® automatically retrieves references, notes, or annotations that apply to the title, chapter, or subchapter of a statute or rule you are viewing. It also displays tables that track statute numbers through amendments and other changes. The annotations are hyperlinked so that when you click on a reference, Westlaw® instantly brings up the document onto the screen.

These and other tools allow you to access updated law within seconds. As emphasized in Chapter 16, a crucial part of legal research is making sure your findings are accurate and up to date. If your supervising attorney is preparing for trial, for example, the attorney will want to base his or her legal argument on current authorities. A precedential case that may have been good law yesterday may not remain so today.

> ※ **Making sure that your research results reflect current law is a crucial step in legal research.**

Auto-Cite
An aid to legal research developed by the editors of Lexis®. On Lexis®, Auto-Cite can be used to find the history of a case, to verify whether the case is still good law, and to perform other functions.

KeyCite
An aid to legal research developed by the editors of Westlaw®. On Westlaw®, KeyCite can trace case history, retrieve secondary sources, categorize legal citations by legal issue, and perform other functions.

Selecting a Database

Much of the legal research that paralegals perform involves searching legal databases for cases or statutes relating to certain topics or legal issues. To do this, you first select a database that you want to search. If you are using Westlaw®, for

DEVELOPING PARALEGAL SKILLS

Cite Checking on Westlaw®

Katie, a paralegal, needs to quickly check a citation for a case from the court of appeals to see if it is still good law. Her supervising attorney wants to use the case in a brief that must be filed within a few hours. Katie accesses Westlaw®. She enters her password and client-identifying information. Once she has gained access, she clicks on the "KeyCite this citation" box and enters the case citation. The search turns up a red flag, which means that the case has been reversed or overruled and is no longer good law. Katie clicks on the red flag, which takes her to the decision in which the case was reversed or overruled. It turns out that the case was reversed on grounds that were not related to the rule of law for which her supervising attorney wants to cite the case. Katie and her supervisor can use the case in their brief after all. For their purpose, it is still good law.

TIPS FOR USING KEYCITE

* A red flag means that a case has been reversed or overruled and must be reviewed.
* A yellow flag means that the case has been questioned and should be checked.
* Never cite a case without verifying that it is still good law.
* Always read a citing case to find out why your case has a red or yellow flag and to determine what issue in your case has been questioned, reversed, or overruled.

---

example, you would click on the box labeled "Search These Databases" and enter a database identifier (for example, you could enter "ca-cs" to search all California cases). If you do not know the abbreviation for the database you wish to search, you can choose "View Westlaw Directory" or "Find a Database Wizard." The directory provides a list of databases and their identifiers. The database wizard service prompts you with on-screen questions, then directs you to the appropriate database. Either way, you will find the database you want.

For example, suppose that your supervising attorney has asked you to research case law on the liability of tobacco product manufacturers for cancer caused by the use of those products. To do a thorough investigation, you will need to search the databases containing decisions from all state courts as well as from all federal courts. By working your way through Westlaw® directories, you will be able to find the databases containing decisions from all state courts ("allstates") and all federal courts ("allfeds").

After you become familiar with the database identifiers on whatever service you are using, you can access that database more directly. For example, on the opening page of Westlaw® you can enter "allfeds" or "allstates" into the database box at the bottom left-hand corner of the screen.

Searching a Database

Once you have chosen a specific database, such as "allfeds," a search box will open on the screen into which you can enter your *search query*. Traditionally, searches of Westlaw® and Lexis® databases had to use the "terms and connectors" (Boolean) method of searching. Today, both services also allow users to draft search queries using natural language (or "plain English"). Before beginning your search, you should indicate in the search box which method you will use.

THE TERMS AND CONNECTORS METHOD.   In a search employing terms and connectors, you use numerical and grammatical connectors to specify the rela-

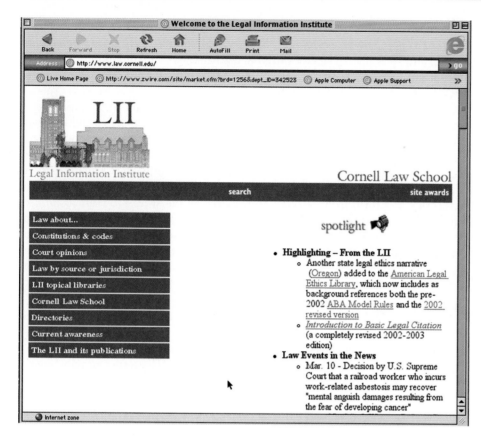

EXHIBIT 17.4
**The Home Page of the
Legal Information Institute**

Reproduced with permission.

zation might use this method. Setting up a gateway requires registering a domain name with a registrar accredited by the Internet Corporation for Assigned Names and Numbers, or ICANN (see http://www.icann.org), paying a registration fee, and operating a computer work station with software connected to a special high-speed phone line.

INTERNET SERVICE PROVIDERS (ISPs).   Most users gain access to the Internet through Internet service providers. An **Internet service provider (ISP)** is a service that provides dedicated access to the Internet. ISPs are usually the least expensive options for gaining access. Most ISPs serve local regions, but there are national ISPs, including America Online, Inc. (http://www.aol.com), Microsoft's MSN (http://www.msn.com), and Earthlink (http://www.earthlink.com). A list of thousands of ISPs, organized by area code and country, is available at http://thelist. internet.com. High-speed service is available in many regions, ranging from fast ISDN access to even faster DSL and cable systems.

Internet service provider (ISP)
A company that provides dedicated access to the Internet, generally through a local phone number.

Navigating the Internet

Once you have access to the Internet, the next important step is to navigate through the vast number of Internet resources until you find the information you are seeking. As stated earlier, the Internet is similar to an enormous library, but there is a key difference—the Internet has no centralized, comprehensive card catalogue. In place of a card catalogue, a researcher uses browsers, guides, directories, and search engines.

BROWSERS.   A browser is software that allows a computer to roam the Web. The most popular browsers are Microsoft Explorer (**http://www.microsoft. com/ie**) and Netscape Navigator (**http://www.netscape.com/computing/download/ index.html**). A free browser can be found at **http://www.opera.com**. These browsers can be used with any Internet service.

Improvements and other changes in browser interfaces and capabilities are so rapid and ongoing that almost any discussion of specific features would be outdated before it was published. Although each browser (and each version of each browser) has its own features, all browsers perform the same basic functions. These functions include the ability to set up automatic links (referred to as "Favorites" in Explorer and "Bookmarks" in Netscape) to Internet sites and to travel back and forth from resource to resource on the Web. Browsers also make it possible to copy text from Web sites and paste it into a word processing document. With a browser, you can download images, software, and documents to your computer. Finally, with a browser you can search only the document that appears in your window. This last feature is most helpful when the document is long and your time is short.

GUIDES AND DIRECTORIES.   The lack of a single, comprehensive catalogue of what's available on the Internet has led to hundreds of attempts to survey and map the Web. Lists of Web sites categorized by subject are organized into guides and directories, which can be accessed at Web sites online. These sites provide menus of topics that are usually subdivided into narrower subtopics, which themselves may be subdivided, until a list of URLs is reached. If you're uncertain of which menu to use, directories allow you to run a search of the directory site. Popular examples of online directories include Yahoo (**http://www.yahoo.com**) and, for legal professionals, FindLaw (**http://www.findlaw.com**). Exhibit 17.5 presents FindLaw's home page. FindLaw, now part of West Group, offers an increasingly complete array of resources. Topic areas include cases and codes, U.S. federal resources, forms, legal subjects, software and technology, reference resources, law student resources, and many others. You should familiarize yourself with FindLaw before you undertake any legal research.

SEARCH ENGINES.   Next to browsers, the most important tools for conducting research on the Web are search engines. A search engine scans the Web and indexes the contents of pages into a database. Whereas people compile directories, a computer generates most of the results delivered by a search engine. This means that the results are limited by the researcher's ability to phrase a query within the constraints of the search engine's capabilities. Search engines include the following:

- Google (**http://www.google.com**).
- Microsoft (**http://search.msm.com**).
- AltaVista (**http://altavista.com**).
- Profusion (**http://www.profusion.com**).
- Excite (**http://www.excite.com**).
- Lycos (**http://www.hotbot.lycos.com**).
- Infoseek (**http://infoseek.go.com**).
- AskJeeves (**http://www.ask.com**).

Search Engine Variations.   A so-called research engine is available at **http://www.iLOR.com**. This relatively new site offers more options than a regular search site. It allows you to pick only the results that are important to your

EXHIBIT 17.5
The Home Page for FindLaw

Reproduced with permission.

search needs. Moreover, you can put the best results in your personal "My List" for later use.

Some search engines will search only specific categories of resources, particularly for law research. For example, FindLaw provides a tool at http://lawcrawler.findlaw.com that searches only legal resources on the Web. This FindLaw tool can be further limited to search specified databases, such as federal government sites only.

Meta search engines run searches on more than one search engine simultaneously. They are the best tools for searching the most Web space possible. It should be noted that nothing searches the entire Web, however. Meta search engines include Copernic (http://www.copernic.com/en/index.html, which requires a free downloadable program), Mamma (http://www.Mamma.com), Metacrawler (http://wwwmetacrawler.com), Dogpile (http://www.dogpile.com), and Vivisimo (http://vivisimo.com).

Kinds of Searches.   There are two basic kinds of searches: by keyword and by concept. A keyword search generates Web sources that use the exact terms that the researcher types in. A concept search adds sources that use related words. In general, the best results are obtained in a search for Web pages that contain very specific terms. Exhibit 17.6 on the following page provides a look at the results of running a search.

EXHIBIT 17.6
Results of a Search Using a Search Engine

Excite is a trademark of Excite, Inc., and may be registered in various jurisdictions. Excite screen display © 1995–1999 Excite, Inc.

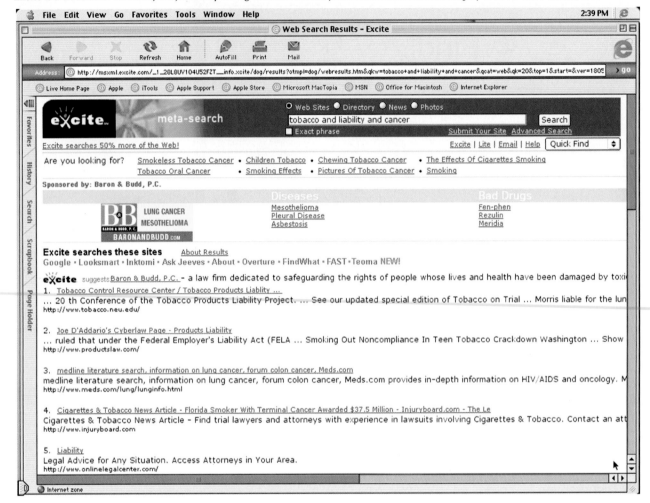

Using Search Engines Effectively.   Search engines vary in the size and scope of searches, in the flexibility of possible queries, and in the presentation of results. When contemplating whether the Internet is the best tool for a research project, however, you should always keep the following in mind:

> ✼ **For legal research, even the best search engine cannot match the results of a search conducted with the internal search engine of a commercial fee-based database such as Lexis® or Westlaw®.**

For example, all search engines have the capability to use connectors, such as "and," "or," and "not." For most search engines, this is the limit of their sophistication. More precise queries can be formulated with Westlaw® or Lexis®, especially for a researcher proficient in using the service. As discussed earlier in this chapter, search tools on Lexis® or Westlaw® allow a researcher to pinpoint any-

TECHNOLOGY AND TODAY'S PARALEGAL
Creative Online Searching

Information can be collected easily via the Internet. The only limit to what is collected and how it is analyzed is the ability of the researcher. What distinguishes a good researcher from an average researcher is the ability to obtain hard-to-find or obscure data from hard-to-reach sources that are especially reliable. Backing up a secondary source with hard-to-find primary data is qualitative, comprehensive research.

For example, the Web can be a good source for obtaining background information on people. Imagine that a lawyer for whom you work is scheduled to question a certain witness. Background information could be useful during the questioning. The witness's past can be investigated on the Web in several ways. A general search can be made to uncover any data concerning the witness. Newsgroups (discussed elsewhere in this chapter) can be searched to discover whether the person has said anything in these groups that relates to his or her testimony. Other ways to find people and information about them are discussed later in this chapter.

Interpreting the data in clever ways is another attribute that distinguishes good researchers. For example, one of your client's competitors advertises employment opportunities for engineers with certain skills. To an intelligent researcher, this may indicate a new direction for the competitor's research and development or a new product line.

TECHNOLOGY TIP

A competitor's Web links could give your client insight into the competitor's operations or indicate a new market for your client's products. To discover sites that link to your competitor's home page, you could use a feature such as the advanced search tool at the Alta Vista search engine site (http://www.altavista.com). In that tool, as a search term, use **link: <your competitor's home page address>**.

---

source material in a distant library delivered to a closer library, where you can more conveniently review it.

Another way to find out what resources are available is to begin with a listserv list or a newsgroup. These can also be used to update your research.

Listservers. A **listserv list** (or mailing list) is basically a list of e-mail addresses of persons interested in a particular topic. By placing their names on the list, they agree to receive e-mail from others about the topic. A message sent to the list's address is automatically sent to everyone on the list. Anyone on the list can respond to whoever sent the message. As a researcher, you might post a message that asks for suggestions about online resources for your research. You can also add your name to the list to receive mass e-mailings. In some cases, you may be able to browse an archive of messages to see if another researcher has previously called attention to a resource that matches your search.

Listserv lists (see **http://www.tile.net/lists**) provide more anonymity than newsgroups. Paralegals who are interested in subscribing to a list can go to the Web site maintained by the National Federation of Paralegal Associations to find links to a number of lists that might be appealing (see **http://www.paralegals. org/LegalResources/listservices.html**).

Newsgroups. A **newsgroup** (also known as a **Usenet group**) is a forum that resembles a community bulletin board. A newsgroup can be selected by topic. A researcher can post a question or problem (for example, "Does anyone know a good source for what I want to know?") and check back hours or days later for others' responses. A researcher might also browse the newsgroup's archive, although messages are typically stored only for limited periods of time. There are

listserv list
A list of e-mail addresses of persons who have agreed to receive e-mail about a particular topic.

newsgroup (Usenet group)
An online bulletin board service. A newsgroup is a forum, or discussion group, that usually focuses on a particular topic.

> ## ETHICAL CONCERN
> ## Surfing the Web
>
> A problem faced by paralegals who are novices in conducting online research is how to avoid spending hours surfing the Web for a site that contains the information being sought. You know the information is "out there" somewhere on the Web, but how can you locate it? What key terms can you use in your search that will find the information but that will also narrow the search sufficiently—so that you do not end up retrieving hundreds of thousands of documents? Over time, of course, you will become familiar with the best sites for information in your area of practice. In the meantime, how can you avoid giving the impression to your employer that you are "wasting" time surfing the Web? One thing you can do is explain to your employer at the outset that surfing the Web is part of the learning process and that this "learning time" is essential if you are to become efficient in online research.

thousands of newsgroups (a few hundred focus on law-related topics). Newsgroup directories can be skimmed at such sites as Liszt (http://www.liszt.com). Newsgroups can be searched with specialized search engines, such as Newsville at http://www.newsville.com/news/groups.

BROWSING THE LINKS.   Traveling around on the Internet to see what data are available is known as "surfing the Web." Clicking on links within a site to open other Web pages is called "browsing the links." As you browse through the links that could be potentially useful for your research, two problems will become apparent. First, you will need to keep track of the Web sites you visit. Second, the speed at which your computer browses may be slow.

Marking a site as a "Favorite" (Explorer) or adding a "Bookmark" (Netscape) for the site is an electronic substitute for keeping a book on your desk. As mentioned earlier, with one of these tools you can create an automatic link to any point on the Web and return to it at any time. For example, you might want an automatic link to the site at which you begin your research: a directory, a search engine, or one of the sites that have many links that relate to what you need.

Slow speed can be more of a problem. It may be the result of something that you can correct, such as an outmoded browser. It is not always so easily overcome, however. It can result from bad phone lines, your service provider's problems, the limits of equipment (yours or someone else's), quirks in the weather, and so on.

Before going online, you may want to take steps to avoid some of the causes of slow speed. For example, to avoid the difficulty of accessing a popular site during its busiest times, you might go online early in the morning or late in the day. You should be aware that if traffic is heavy at a particular site, there could be a **mirror site** with the same data. A site will note on its home page if a mirror site is available. You might also avoid downloading or uploading large files at a site's busy times. It may be possible to increase your speed by selecting the text-only option when you browse. This may be particularly helpful when you use a low-performance computer or modem to access a site that has rich graphics. With some sites, this may not be an option, however, because the graphics may be necessary to navigate the sites.

mirror site
A Web site that duplicates another site. A mirror site is used to improve the availability of access to the original site.

at online sites. See the international version at http://www.bartleby.com/110. Try also http://www.thesaurus.com.

ZIP CODES.   For zip codes, see the U.S. Postal Service site at http://www.usps.com/zip4.

University Sites

Many universities, colleges, law schools, and other academic institutions are dedicated to making the Internet and its related technology an essential part of professional research. Their Web sites are often good points from which to start because in general they provide updated material and links to other resources. Some of these sites are discussed in the following subsections.

LAW-RELATED STARTING POINTS.   The Legal Information Institute at Cornell Law School is a good starting place for online legal research. The URL is http://www.law.cornell.edu. This site includes many United States Supreme Court decisions (within hours of their release) and links to many other law-related sites and services.

Another good site is the World Wide Web Virtual Law Library maintained by the Indiana University School of Law at http://www.law.indiana.edu/law/v-lib/index.html. This is a comprehensive, up-to-date subject index of law-related topics.

LawLists, a site produced at the University of Chicago, is online at http://www.lib.uchicago.edu/~llou/lawlists/info.html. This site contains an extensive listing of law-related discussion groups, including legal listservs.

Meta-Index for Legal Research at Georgia State University College of Law (http://gsulaw.gsu.edu/metaindex) enables a researcher to use several Web sites' internal search tools simultaneously.

WashLaw WEB at http://www.washlaw.edu is produced by Washburn University. This site includes a comprehensive collection of links to legal resources on the Web.

Northwestern University, at Oyez Oyez Oyez: A Supreme Court Database (http://oyez.nwu.edu), provides digital audio (RealAudio) of the oral arguments in many important United States Supreme Court cases, as well as recordings of some of the announcements of the Court's opinions.

GOVERNMENT RESOURCES LISTINGS.   The site of the Documents Center of the University of Michigan Library is a reference point for local, state, federal, foreign, and international law resources on the Web. The URL is http://www.lib.umich.edu/govdocs/index.html. This site has one of the most comprehensive lists of links to government documents on the Web, with descriptions of what is included at each link.

LAW-RELATED DISCUSSION GROUPS.   To receive information about new and updated resources related to the law, subscribe to LAWSRC-L by sending an e-mail note to mailto:listserve@listserve.law.cornell.edu. In the note, state, "subscribe LAWSRC-L <your name>."

NET-LAWYERS is a discussion group that involves primarily practicing attorneys in how to use the Internet. To subscribe, send an e-mail message to mailto:net-lawyers-request@Webcom.com. In the message, state, "subscribe NET-LAWYERS <your name>."

WEB SITE EVALUATIONS.   Questions to use when considering the reliability and accuracy of a particular Web site are listed at a site titled "Ten Cs for Evaluating Internet Resources." The URL is http://www.uwec.edu/Library/Guides/tencs.html.

Questions are also listed at "Thinking Critically about World Wide Web Resources." The URL for this site is http://www.library.ucla.edu/libraries/college/help/critical/index.htm.

Government Sites

The government—the federal government, in particular—provides many excellent resources online. Nearly every federal agency has its own Web site. The following are some of the most useful sites for a paralegal.

LAW-RELATED STARTING POINTS.   The House of Representatives Library at http://www.house.gov is one of the best government-supported resources on the Web. This site contains the full text of pending legislation and congressional testimony. The "Law Library" section contains a wealth of legal resources. The Library of Congress's THOMAS site (http://thomas.loc.gov) duplicates some of the House site's materials, but it does not include the "Law Library."

BUSINESS AND ECONOMIC INFORMATION.   The Web site of the U.S. Department of Commerce, at http://www.commerce.gov, provides a wealth of business and economic statistical data and other information. Some of it is available only for a fee. There are links to other government agencies' sites, including the home page of the U.S. Patent and Trademark Office.

INFORMATION ABOUT PUBLIC COMPANIES.   As mentioned earlier, the EDGAR database of the Securities and Exchange Commission (at http://www.sec.gov/edgar.shtml) contains public companies' electronic filings of documents and forms that the commission requires. This is one of the best resources on the Web for information about public companies.

GOVERNMENT PUBLICATIONS.   GPO Access, the Government Printing Office's database, contains the full text of the *Code of Federal Regulations,* the *Congressional Record,* the *Federal Register,* all versions of all bills introduced in Congress, the current edition of the *United States Government Manual,* the *United States Code,* and other government publications. The URL for this site is http://www.gpoaccess.gov/databases.html.

DISCUSSION GROUP.   To learn about new government sources that appear on the Web, subscribe to GOVDOC-L. Send a message to mailto:listserv@psuvm.psu.edu or mailto:listserv@psuvm.bitnet. The message should read "subscribe GOVDOC-L <your name>."

Sites for Associations and Organizations

Some online databases that catalogue associations, professional organizations, and nonprofit organizations include the following.

ASSOCIATIONS.   Associations Online includes Web links to more than five hundred associations divided into categories. The address is http://www.ipl.org/div/aon. Yahoo's directory includes a list of professional associations at http://www.yahoo.com/Business_and_Economy/Organizations/Professional.

PROFESSIONAL ORGANIZATIONS.   Professional organizations indexed according to business category (accounting, banking, law, and so on) can be found at http://www.nvst.com/rsrc/proforg.htm. (For Web sites for bar associations and paralegal organizations, see Chapters 1 and 3.)

NONPROFIT ORGANIZATIONS.   More than a million nonprofit organizations are included in a database maintained by the Internet Nonprofit Center at http://www.nonprofits.org. This site includes links to the Web pages of many nonprofit organizations.

Free Commercial Sites

Commercial sites are Web pages that are maintained or supported by for-profit organizations (as opposed to academic institutions, the government, and nonprofit organizations). Some commercial sites, such as Westlaw® and Lexis®, are fee based. Other sites pay for themselves with on-site advertising. These are free commercial sites. Free commercial sites that may be of value to a legal professional include those discussed next.

ALL-PURPOSE STARTING POINTS.   Yahoo organizes, categorizes, and subdivides the most comprehensive list of URLs on the Web. New Web addresses are added at the rate of hundreds per day. Yahoo's address is http://www.yahoo.com. Another good starting point is the Google site located at http://www.google.com.

Internet orientation, Internet tools, and Internet guides are the subjects of the Internet Web Text Index at http://www.december.com/Web/text/index.html.

A collection of references to various subject guides can be found at the Internet Public Library at http://ipl.org.

LAW-RELATED STARTING POINTS.   The West Legal Studies site (http://www.westlegalstudies.com) is a paralegal resource center. The site provides access to resources for professionals, students, and instructors, including links to nearly a thousand legal and paralegal information Web sites.

Another West site with a similar name—West Legal Studies Resource Center—is at http://www.westbuslaw.com. This site includes daily law highlights, an overview of the U.S. court system, study aids for students, links to a law dictionary and a lawyers' directory, and more.

The "Internet Legal Resource Guide," at http://www.ilrg.com, is an index of approximately four thousand law-related Web sites, categorized by topic. The site also includes the "LawRunner: A Legal Research Tool," which is preprogrammed to run your search terms in templates across as many as thirty million Web pages.

"The Legal List" at http://www.heels.com/TLL/1995/TheLegalList_7.0_1095/Intro/SOC.html is both a guide to research on the Web and a good starting point with links to other online resources.

The producers of the periodical *legal.online* offer links at their site at http://www.legalonline.com to legal resources on the Web that the producers find to be particularly useful. These resources include government sites as well as sites maintained by libraries, law schools, law firms, private companies, and others.

Law-related search engines are linked at "Virtual Legal Search Engines," a site produced by Virtual Search Engines, at http://www.virtualfreesites.com/search.legal.html. This site also includes a number of basic references (dictionaries, for example) and links to search engines for other topics.

Thousands of law-related materials and products are available through the 'Lectric Law Library at http://lectlaw.com. Most of the information files are not

EXHIBIT 17.9

The Home Page of the 'Lectric Law Library

Reprinted with permission. Contact http://LectLaw.com or staff@LectLaw.com.

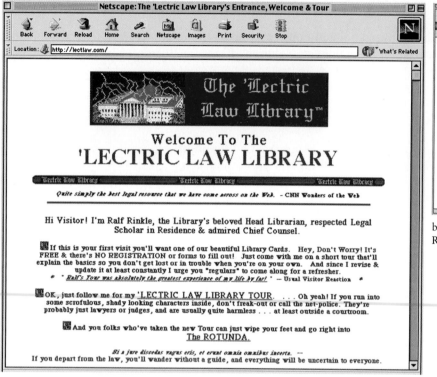

a. Home page

b. "Legal Professional's Lounge" in "The Rotunda"

links to other sites but are actually at this site, with plain text and simple graphics. Most of the larger items are compressed for downloading. Also included are legal forms and a law dictionary. An illustration of the home page of the 'Lectric Law Library is in Exhibit 17.9.

"Law Library Resource Xchange" (LLRX), at http://www.llrx.com, provides links to a number of resource sites on the Web, ranging from legal research to library products and services. This site, which is maintained by Law Library Resource Xchange, L.L.C., includes timely and updated articles relating to research and library topics.

MEDIA DIRECTORY.   The American Journalism Review site contains more than eight thousand links to the online pages of newspapers, magazines, and other media, at http://newslink.org/menu.html.

TODAY'S PROFESSIONAL PARALEGAL

Locating Guardians and Wards

Patrick Mitchell works as a legal assistant for a sole practitioner, Anne Urso. Anne takes probate court assignments in which the court appoints her guardian *ad litem*. (A guardian *ad litem* is a special guardian appointed by a court to protect the interests of minors or incapacitated persons in legal proceedings.) This requires Anne to determine whether someone who has previously been appointed as a legal guardian for an incapacitated person needs to continue as guardian. In order to make this determination, Anne must visit the ward and meet with the guardian.

Today, Anne has received an envelope in the mail appointing her guardian *ad litem* in five cases. The paperwork that comes from the court contains the names and addresses of both the guardian and the ward. Anne knows from experience that the court's records are often out of date and that this information needs to be updated.

Anne assigns the task of locating the guardians and wards to Patrick. He will call them first to see if the information from the court is accurate and to set up a meeting between them and either Anne or himself. The forms have to be submitted to the court within two weeks of their receipt by Anne, which is a quick turnaround time, especially in light of Anne's case load. Patrick calls the ward and the guardian on the first sheet and finds that their telephone numbers have been disconnected. He sets this sheet aside and calls the people listed on the next sheet. He succeeds in contacting the guardian and learns that the ward, an eighty-five-year-old man, Mr. Ahern, died almost a year ago. Patrick continues calling the guardians and wards listed on the sheets. He is able to contact the next three and sets up appointments with them.

Now Patrick must locate the guardian and the ward from the first sheet. He decides that the fastest way to do this is to use a people locator on the Internet. From past experience, Patrick is familiar with a number of reliable Web sites. These sites include KnowX, Bigfoot, and MapQuest. He accesses http://www.bigfoot.com. He enters the name of the ward, Thomas Ford, and the address, 1111 Three Mile Drive, Detroit, Michigan, and clicks on "Search." Within a few seconds, the computer retrieves a telephone number and an address for Mr. Ford. The telephone number is different from the one that was on the court's forms. Patrick runs another search for the guardian and turns up a new telephone number and address for him as well. Patrick then calls the guardian and the ward and schedules an appointment to meet with them.

Patrick then goes online to the Web site http://www.knowx.com to verify the death records of the second ward, Mr. Ahern. Using Mr. Ahern's Social Security number, he is able to access these records and print out a copy to include with his report. Patrick places a copy in the file.

Next, Patrick needs to use a mapping Web site to create maps for, and driving directions to, the five different locations to which he and Anne will need to go. Patrick accesses http://www.mapquest.com. He enters the address of the office and then the address of the first ward. He clicks on "Search," and a map with driving directions soon appears on the screen. Patrick prints out five maps with driving directions and places them in the file. Having finished this project, he then turns to his next task.

✳ KEY TERMS AND CONCEPTS

Auto-Cite	**home page**	**listserv list**
computer-assisted legal research (CALR)	**hypertext transfer protocol (http)**	**mirror site**
file transfer protocol (ftp)	**Internet service provider (ISP)**	**newsgroup (Usenet group)**
	KeyCite	**World Wide Web**

✳ CHAPTER SUMMARY

CD-ROMS and Legal Research	Computer-assisted legal research often involves using CD-ROMs. An advantage of using legal resources in CD-ROM format is that they are less costly to purchase and require less physical space than printed resources. CD-ROMs can also be easily transported, which means they can be used while traveling, in the courtroom, or anywhere outside the office. The major disadvantage of using CD-ROMs in legal research is that they, like their printed equivalents, eventually become outdated.
Westlaw® and Lexis®	For serious legal research, legal professionals often use online commercial legal-research services, particularly Lexis® and Westlaw®. Subscribers to these fee-based services can access the services' databases through the use of proprietary software and a modem connection or via the Internet. Both Lexis® and Westlaw® provide their users with access to an extensive collection of legal, business, and other resources. Using these fee-based legal services, paralegals can access specific documents, check citations, update the law, and search hundreds of databases. Both Lexis® and Westlaw® allow users to search databases with queries using terms and connectors or natural language.
Going Online—Internet Basics	Today's legal professionals can access a vast amount of information using the Internet, which is a global communication network of interconnected computers. Many online resources are available free, while others charge a fee for accessing their databases. 1. *Internet tools*—Internet tools include uniform resource locators (URLs), which are Internet "addresses"; e-mail, which transmits messages via the Internet to specific e-mail addresses; file transfer protocol (ftp), a basic interface that connects computers and allows files to be transferred from one computer to another; and the World Wide Web, a data service on the Internet that is accessed through a browser. 2. *Accessing and navigating the Internet*—The Internet is accessed through gateways, usually Internet service providers. To navigate the Internet, which has no card catalogue as a library does, one uses browsers (software such as Microsoft Explorer and Netscape Navigator that allows a computer to roam the Web); guides and directories (menus of topics at various Web sites); and search engines (such as Alta Vista and Google) that scan the Web for certain keywords or concepts. Meta search engines run searches on more than one search engine simultaneously and thus are the best tools for searching the most Web space possible.
Conducting Online Research	1. *Before going online*—Before beginning an online research session, you should first decide whether the Internet is the right tool for your research project. Ask yourself what sources you will need and whether they are available on the Internet. At this time, there are insufficient primary and secondary legal sources on the Web to conduct in-depth legal research. There are, however, an increasing number of primary sources online. For fact-based research, such as locating people and public records, the Internet offers an abundance of useful information. 2. *Plan ahead*—To avoid wasting time, define what you are seeking and determine which sources are most likely to lead you to the desired results.

Conducting Online Research—Continued	3. *Research strategies*—Once online, you can use various search tools and other resources (such as listservs and newsgroups) to locate information relevant to your topic. Often, researchers need to "browse the links" for a time before finding a site that is particularly relevant. Once you find a useful site, you can use your browser or the site's internal search tool to look for specific information within the site. 4. *Evaluating what you find*—In evaluating your research results, it is especially important to consider the reliability of any information obtained online. 5. *Updating your results*—To update results, you can access news sites online to look for articles or press releases concerning recent developments in the area you are researching.
Locating People and Investigating Companies	Paralegals often engage in online research to locate information about persons and to investigate companies. Sometimes, a person can be located through a broad search of the Web using a search engine such as Yahoo. Narrow searches can be conducted by accessing—for free or for a fee—specialized databases, such as compilations of physicians, lawyers, or expert witnesses. Searches for persons may also be conducted based on specific characteristics, such as veteran status or vehicle registration. Numerous online sites contain information about both private and public companies.
Some of the Best Legal-Resource Sites on the Internet	Basic resources that you can find on the Web range from almanacs to zip code directories. Various university and government sites offer links to a number of primary and secondary legal sources. There are also online databases that catalogue associations, professional organizations, and nonprofit organizations, as well as several free commercial sites that serve as all-purpose starting points for online research.

❋ QUESTIONS FOR REVIEW

1. What are some of the advantages and disadvantages of using legal resources in CD-ROM format when conducting legal research?

2. What is Westlaw®? What is Lexis®? How do legal professionals access these services? What kinds of legal sources do these services make available to users?

3. How can these services be used to update the law? Describe two ways in which you can search databases on Lexis® and Westlaw®.

4. What is the difference between the Internet and the World Wide Web? Name and define four useful Internet tools.

5. Define and give two examples of an Internet gateway. What is a browser? What are Internet guides and directories?

6. What should you do before going online to conduct a research session? Is the Internet a good research tool for serious legal research? Why or why not?

7. What are some starting points in doing online research? How can you discover what resources are available on the Web? Why is it important to evaluate the reliability of information found online and to update the results of an Internet research session?

8. What online search techniques could you use when trying to find information on a specific person? How would you go about finding company names and addresses in an Internet search?

9. List five basic, nonlegal resources that can be accessed via the Internet. Name five universities whose law schools or legal institutes provide extensive Internet legal libraries or links to Internet legal resources.

10. What kinds of legal resources can be accessed at various government sites? What resources or search tools can be found at sites for associations and organizations and at free commercial sites?

✳ ETHICAL QUESTIONS

1. Janice, a paralegal in a firm specializing in labor law, joins a listserv. It is called AWD@counterpoint.com. It is a discussion group about the Americans with Disabilities Act (ADA) of 1990 and related laws. Another member of the group posts a question about what companies the ADA applies to and whether his company is subject to the law. Janice knows the answer and could answer it. Should Janice answer the question? Why or why not?

2. The partners in the law firm of Dewey & Howe learn about a plane crash in the morning newspaper. They instruct their legal assistant to contact all of the families of the victims via e-mail to see if they are interested in filing a class-action lawsuit against the airline. Is this type of activity allowed under the ethical rules?

3. The law firm of Smith & Varney decides that it needs a Web page to advertise the law firm's services over the Internet. They assign the task to paralegal Mark Hampton. Mark develops a Web site for the firm. The site contains a biography of each attorney, e-mail addresses for all attorneys, and Web links to helpful and related practice areas. Is this type of Web site allowable advertising under the ethical rules?

4. Samantha, a paralegal, runs a credit check on a client over the Internet without using an encryption program. The client's Visa number is intercepted, and unauthorized purchases amounting to $4,320 are charged on the client's account. What kind of ethical problems result?

✳ PRACTICE QUESTIONS AND ASSIGNMENTS

1. Using the material presented in the chapter on Westlaw®, answer the following questions:

   a. How would you gain access to Westlaw®?

   b. How would you find the case *Tasini v. New York Times Co., Inc.*, 184 F.Supp.2d 350 (2002)? How would you find out whether the holding in that case is still good law?

   c. What specific steps would you take to find the database of decisions made by courts in your state?

2. Suppose that one of your clients is suing a restaurant that served her tainted oysters. The oysters contained bacteria that caused the client to suffer serious health injuries, including permanent nerve damage. What databases would you search on Westlaw® to find out whether there are any other cases involving this issue or a similar issue? How would you draft a query in natural language to retrieve these cases from the selected database(s)? To draft a query using terms and connectors, what key terms would you use?

3. Explain the parts of the following URL:

   http://www.urisko.edu

4. Create your own URL, using your name to create a Web site for commercial purposes.

5. Using the material presented in the chapter, make a list of the Web sites that you would search to find the name, address, and telephone number of a particular company. Would you search the same sites for more detailed information? If not, where would you search? Does it make a difference whether the company is public or private? If so, where would you search for information on public companies? Where would you search for information on private companies?

6. Assume that the legal researchers in the situations described below all have access to an excellent law library, to Westlaw® or Lexis®, and to the Internet. Which of these three research sources or tools would you advise the legal professional to use for his or her particular research need? Why?

   a. Matthew, a paralegal, needs to find out if a case cited in a legal motion he is drafting is still good law.

   b. Cindy, an attorney, needs to locate a psychiatric expert witness.

   c. Robert, a paralegal, has been asked to locate a statutory provision; he needs to make sure that the result is up to date.

   d. Tom, a paralegal, needs to locate a witness to a car accident.

   e. Megan, a paralegal, needs to find an heir who is to inherit $500,000 under her uncle's will.

✳ QUESTIONS FOR CRITICAL ANALYSIS

1. Why would an attorney invest in a legal encyclopedia contained on a CD-ROM instead of a printed set of encyclopedias? In conducting legal research, would you prefer to use legal sources in CD-ROM format rather than printed legal sources? Why or why not?

2. Legal professionals must pay a significant fee to access legal databases provided by commercial services such as Westlaw® and Lexis®. Why would it ever be preferable to use these fee-based services for research instead of the Internet, which offers free access to numerous online legal and other resources?

3. What are some advantages of using Westlaw® or Lexis® when doing legal research rather than using the printed resources in a law library? Are there any disadvantages?

4. What is the Internet? What is the World Wide Web? Are they different entities, or are these terms synonyms for the same entity?

5. The Internet offers vast resources and provides these resources instantly. What are the advantages of the Internet? Are there any disadvantages? If so, what are they?

6. What impact does the Internet have on how legal professionals perform their work? What impact does it have on society as a whole? Is the impact positive or negative, or both?

7. Chat rooms provide Internet users with the ability to communicate in "real time." How does "real-time" communication compare with talking on the telephone? How does it compare with writing letters or sending e-mail messages? Which method of communication do you prefer? Why?

8. What are the types of gateways to the Internet? Which one is the most useful? Which one is the most cost-effective? Which one is best suited for a law firm? Why?

9. What is the difference between a gateway to the Internet and a browser? How do directories and search engines differ?

10. Do you believe that the Internet will be the sole tool used by legal researchers in the future? Why or why not?

✳ PROJECTS

1. Most colleges and universities provide Internet access to students. Find out if the school you attend provides such access. If it does, find out which gateway to the Internet is used and which Web browser. Also, find out if it is possible for students to have an e-mail account at the school.

2. Do a research project on how and why the Internet was created. Write a two-page paper summarizing the results of your research.

3. Using Corel WordPerfect, create a Web page for yourself, your employer, or your paralegal program. What information needs to be included?

4. Contact the West Group sales representative for your area. Request information on West's CD-ROM research products. Write a one-page paper describing what is available, how much the CD-ROM products cost, and how they are updated.

✳ USING INTERNET RESOURCES

1. This chapter has presented many tips about how to use the Internet to do legal research and to find useful information relating to legal work. For additional information and links to sites that may be useful, go to the National Federal of Paralegals site (http://www. paralegals.org) and click on "Legal Resources." From that page, click on any of the headings, such as "Internet Directories and Search Engines" or "Legal-Related Sites," to find a list of hyperlinks to other Web sites. Follow the links to three different Web sites. Explore each for a few minutes, and then write a brief paper that answers the following questions about each site:

a. What is the URL of the site?

b. What kind of information is available, and how might it be used?

c. Does the site have an internal search engine?

d. In your opinion, is the site useful, reliable, and up to date? Why or why not?

2. The American Bar Association's Web site contains helpful information on legal-research sources on the Internet. Access the Web site at

http://www.abanet.org/lpm/var/research.shtml

Answer the following questions about the research sources available online:

a. What categories of research materials are available?

b. Go to the "Legal Resources" category. Click on the "Johns Hopkins University Law Collection." How is the collection organized?

c. Click on the "Back" button. Select the "Legal Information Institute at Cornell Law School." How does it compare with the Johns Hopkins University collection? How is it organized? Which legal-research Web site would you prefer to use, and why?

END NOTES

1. Note that Westlaw® and Lexis® have been "online" for years, in the sense that their databases can be accessed elec- tronically. In the remaining pages of this chapter, we use the term *online* to refer specifically to the Internet.

LEGAL WRITING: FORM AND SUBSTANCE

Chapter Outline

After completing this chapter, you will know:

- What factors you should consider before undertaking a legal-writing assignment.

- What factors you should consider when drafting a legal document.

- Some techniques for improving your writing skills.

- Some basic guidelines for structuring sentences and paragraphs.

- The purpose and format of the most common types of legal letters.

- How to prepare a legal memorandum.

- How to prepare an appellate brief.

INTRODUCTION

To a certain extent, legal research, analysis, and writing are all part of the same process. Once you locate the law that applies to a particular issue in dispute, you need to interpret that law and analyze how it applies to the facts of the client's case. After that, you must be able to summarize the results of your research and analysis in writing to communicate those results clearly to your supervising attorney.

Much legal writing, of course, is not directly related to the research process. As a paralegal, your day will frequently involve other types of writing responsibilities as well. You will be expected to know how to draft letters to clients and opposing counsel, internal memos, pleadings to be submitted to the court, and a variety of other documents.

Although a paralegal may be involved in drafting many kinds of legal documents, the same basic principles of writing apply to all. In this chapter, we provide some guidelines and suggestions for how to write effectively and describe some of the types and formats of legal documents commonly prepared by paralegals. We conclude the chapter with a special section on how to draft the appellate brief—the document submitted by each side's attorney on appeal to present the legal reasons why the court should rule in favor of the attorney's client.

LEGAL WRITING—THE PRELIMINARIES

Much of your work as a paralegal will involve writing assignments. We will look at writing skills and the kinds of legal materials that paralegals create in subsequent sections. Here, you will read about some general requirements involved in legal writing.

Whenever you receive a writing assignment, you need to understand at the outset (1) the nature of your writing assignment, (2) when it must be completed, and (3) what type of writing approach is appropriate to the assignment. We examine each of these basic requirements here.

Understanding the Assignment

The practice of law is often hectic, and frequently paralegals are asked to research, analyze, and report their results on particular issues within a short time period. When you receive a writing assignment, you should always make sure that you understand the exact nature of the request so that you can execute your task as efficiently as possible. The writing style, format, and methodological approach used in legal writing vary, depending on the specific objectives of the document you are supposed to create. If you need to ask questions, do so. You should never equate asking questions with incompetence. As the adage states, the only "dumb question" is the one that is not asked.

Time Constraints and Flexibility

The time factor is an important consideration in legal writing. When you receive a writing assignment, you need to understand clearly when the assignment must be completed. In some situations, you will be required to submit writings to a court by a certain date, which is inflexible. Additionally, clients usually demand quick responses to questions. And frequently, during the course of litigation or other legal activities, crucial new issues arise that must be addressed immediately, often overnight or within two or three days. As a paralegal, you will need to assess such situations realistically. If little time is given for the completion of a project, you will have to use your informed judgment, deciding what information is crucial to the writing and what can be omitted.

In addition to time constraints, other circumstances may influence the way a paralegal handles an assignment. For example, external circumstances, such as newly enacted laws, may affect the legal treatment of an issue. Additionally, a client may unexpectedly demand a change in the course of action. These situations require flexibility. Whenever you undertake a writing task, you should be prepared for the possibility that you may have to make quick changes and go in new directions before your assignment is completed.

Writing Approaches

Another thing you should determine when you receive a writing assignment is what type of writing is required. Some documents require an *objective* (unbiased) analysis, which either focuses on the facts or presents a balanced discussion of both sides of an issue. Other documents are *persuasive* and require you to advocate by presenting the facts and issues in the light most favorable to your client.

For example, assume that your supervising attorney hands you two lease agreements and asks you to compare them and note whether the differences in the wording of the agreements lead to different obligations. Your concern will not be to point out which agreement is better but to analyze and compare the documents objectively and point out which clauses lead to what kinds of obligations. Objective analysis may also be required when an attorney seeks assistance in providing clients with information regarding a particular legal matter. Clients often seek the advice of an attorney to determine whether they have a claim that merits the filing of a lawsuit. In this situation, an attorney may request the paralegal to investigate the issues thoroughly and provide a memorandum containing an accurate and unbiased analysis of the issue.

If the writing assignment is intended to advocate a position, the style of writing will be somewhat different. For example, if your supervising attorney asks you to draft a pretrial motion asking the court to exclude certain evidence from a trial, you will need to adopt a persuasive style of writing. Your goal will be to convince the judge that the argument proposed is stronger than the opposing party's position. You will therefore need to develop supportive legal arguments and present the matter in the light most favorable to the client. (Realize, though, that attorneys have a duty of candor toward the court. This duty requires an attorney to disclose mandatory authorities to the court even if those authorities are adverse to the client's position. The attorney can, of course, still argue that the client's case should be distinguished from the controlling authority.)

THE IMPORTANCE OF GOOD WRITING SKILLS

The legal profession is primarily a communications profession. Effective written communications are particularly crucial in the legal arena. For paralegals, good writing skills therefore go hand in hand with successful job performance. The more competent a writer you are, the more likely it is that your finished products will be satisfactory to the attorney with whom you are working. You should also keep in mind that some of your written projects, such as correspondence, represent the firm for which you work. A well-written document is a positive reflection on the firm and upholds the firm's reputation for good performance. For additional tips on effective legal writing, see this chapter's *Featured Guest* article on the next page.

FEATURED GUEST: RICHARD M. TERRY

Ten Tips for Effective Legal Writing

BIOGRAPHICAL NOTE

Richard M. Terry received his bachelor's degree and master's degree from the University of Baltimore. He worked as a legal assistant for ten years. During that time, he was a supervisor in the Office of the Public Defender for Baltimore City. He has also served as an assistant professor and the coordinator of the legal-assistant program at Baltimore City Community College.

Writing is a major form of communication. As a paralegal, you will be asked to write constantly throughout your career. Writing in this profession can take many forms, depending on your specialty and employer. You may be asked to prepare letters to clients and reports on client interviews and investigations, as well as responses to legal questions you have researched. Make no mistake—every document you prepare will be important. The tips for effective legal writing given below are not cast in stone. They are general guidelines that will make you a better legal writer, not only while you are in school but also when you enter the profession.

1. Plan before You Write. In this age of computerized word processing, there is a tremendous temptation just to sit down at the keyboard and begin to type, creating as you go along. Avoid this temptation at all costs. Instead, prepare a plan of action before you put the first word on paper. Your plan of action will consist of a few simple steps. First, if your supervising attorney has asked you to write the document, make sure that he or she has spelled out clearly what is needed. Second, if you are drafting a particular type of document (such as a pleading or memorandum) for the first time, ask for or find a sample to use, perhaps in your firm's files. Third, outline the document before you begin writing. Making an outline is the key to producing a well-organized document. Fourth, just

before printing out the final copy of the document, check with the attorney again, to make sure you have not missed any key points.

2. Write with a Purpose. Writing with a purpose means writing with an identifiable goal in mind. The document you produce must reflect that purpose. Generally, the purpose for any legal document is either objective or adversarial. A document with an objective purpose simply passes on information, without any appearance of bias. A document with an adversarial purpose emphasizes the strong points of one position versus the weak points of another. Adversarial writing will reflect a definite bias.

3. Write Clearly. Remember that simple is usually better. Try to say exactly what you mean, and use standard vocabulary and clear and concrete terms. It is not necessary to show that you have a mastery of legal language. Identify your audience, and write to the people who will ultimately read your document. The style and tone of your writing should change with the document's intended audience, as well as with the purpose of the document. When you write to a client, for example, try to avoid the use of technical or legal terms. Your tone should be explanatory, and you should define legal terms and describe the consequences of legal actions. In contrast, when you are writing to the court or to attorneys, you will not need to explain legal concepts or terms. Remember, too, that readers

FEATURED GUEST, *Continued*

normally do not have time to figure out what you are trying to say. Structure what you write, get to the point, and stick to it.

4. Use Proper Grammar and Sentence Structure. Legal documents once were routinely written in highly formal, complex language, but over the past few years, writing in plain English has become the rule. As a result, legal documents are no longer as long and complicated as they once were. No matter which style you use, however, you must observe the rules of basic grammar and punctuation you learned in junior and senior high school. Make sure, for example, that you write in complete sentences and punctuate long sentences correctly.

5. Use an Appropriate Writing Style. *Style* is a broad term. In a general sense, it refers to how you express what you have to say, as opposed to the content of your writing. For example, a piece of writing can have a formal or an informal style. More narrowly, style can refer to specific forms, such as the form of a legal citation or of the names of particular courts. A good style manual can assist in determining what is an appropriate style. Style manuals give many basic rules and explain how the rules apply in different contexts. Well-known style manuals include *The Elements of Style* by William Strunk, Jr., and E. B. White and the *Chicago Manual*

of Style, currently in its fourteenth edition. For the proper format for legal citations, the source to consult is *The Bluebook: A Uniform System of Citation.*

6. Edit Your Work. The first draft of a document is not necessarily correct in every detail. Always go back and review objectively what you have written. If possible, have someone else read it for you. If that is not possible, try reading the document backwards—that is, from the last line to the first line. More often than not, you will catch at least some spelling and punctuation errors this way.

7. Use Computers Effectively. The computer has come of age in the law office of today. Using computers saves time and reduces the potential for errors in legal writing. There is no excuse for sending out any document containing spelling and grammatical mistakes if the document was produced on a computer. Use the spell-checker and grammar-checker functions to ensure that the document has no spelling or grammatical errors before you print it. Because today's law office relies heavily on computers for both research and writing, legal assistants who wish to succeed on the job should become knowledgeable in the use of computers and legal software.

8. Keep Copies. Whenever you create a document, keep a copy for

"Identify your audience, and write to the people who will ultimately read your document."

your files. For one thing, this will help you to create a "forms file." Legal writing is somewhat repetitive. The form stays the same, and only the names and facts are changed. Creating a forms file will, in the long run, save you time and effort.

9. Consider New Writing Methods and Styles. Keeping abreast of what others in the field are doing and how they write may affect the format and style of your writing. Read as many trade publications as possible. Papers such as the *National Law Journal* are great sources of information, and magazines such as *Legal Assistant Today* often give interesting writing tips. Another way of keeping up with current information is to network with others in the profession. Maybe another legal assistant has a method or style of writing that is suited to your situation. Don't close your mind to it.

10. Practice, Practice, Practice. Good, effective writing is an art that requires a great deal of practice. The more you write, the better you become.

Each writing assignment you receive will give you an opportunity to improve and perfect your writing skills. In the following sections, we offer some guidelines you can follow as you strive to improve your writing. Paralegals seriously interested in improving their writing skills also will have close at hand a good dictionary, a thesaurus, a style manual (such as Strunk and White's *The Elements of Style* or the *Chicago Manual of Style),* and perhaps a book or two on basic English grammar.

Organize and Outline Your Presentation

Once you know what it is you want to demonstrate, discuss, or prove to your reader, you need to decide how best to organize your ideas to achieve this end. Because organization is essential to effective legal writing, you should have your organizational framework in mind before you begin writing. Most people find that an outline—whether it is a simple sketch in pencil on a scrap of paper or a detailed outline created by a specialized computer program—makes writing easier. It not only saves time but also produces a more organized result.

When creating an outline, you decide the sequence in which topics should be discussed. Often, lawyers put their strongest argument first in legal writing. Aside from that, some issues will need to be addressed before others, either for logical reasons or for purposes of clarity and readability. Similar issues should be grouped together, either in the same section or under the same topic heading. Other factors you will want to consider when organizing your presentation are format and structural devices.

CHOICE OF FORMAT.   An important requirement in legal writing is selecting the appropriate format. The format of a document concerns such things as the width of margins, the indentation of paragraphs, and the number of line spaces between paragraphs or other sections, for example. Documents to be filed with a court must conform to the procedural rules of the particular jurisdiction. Most law firms also adopt special formats for other types of documents, such as correspondence sent to clients and opposing counsel and internal legal memoranda. When writing these types of documents, you need to know what format your firm prefers to use.

STRUCTURAL DEVICES.   If you are writing about a complex legal research project involving numerous issues, you may want to divide your presentation into several sections, with each section dealing with one issue. You can make it easier for the reader to follow the discussion by including a "road map" to the document. For example, you might preface the writing with an introduction that highlights the points that will be discussed and the conclusion that will be reached, thus orienting the reader to the document's contents. You might also use numbered or bulleted lists as a device to let the reader know the structure of your argument or discussion. In addition, try to "walk" your reader through the analysis and discussion by including descriptive headings and subheadings in the body of the document so that the reader never gets lost.

chronologically
In a time sequence; naming or listing events in the time order in which they occurred.

Arranging events **chronologically**—that is, in a time sequence—can also serve as a structural device. A chronologically structured discussion is sometimes easier for the reader to follow. This is particularly true when you are describing the factual background leading to a lawsuit. Presenting the facts and events in chronological order helps to orient the reader. Even if you are discussing legal issues instead of facts, you might want to use a chronological structure for at least part of your discussion. For example, if you are writing about the historical development of a particular rule of law, you will want to structure that part of the discussion chronologically.

Write to Your Audience

Paralegals prepare legal documents and correspondence for a wide range of people. Whenever you draft legal correspondence or legal documents of any kind, you should keep in mind that legal documents are not ends in themselves. They are created for someone (a judge, an attorney, a client, a witness, or some other person) to read. The ultimate goal of legal writing is to *communicate* information or ideas to your reader. It is therefore important to tailor the writing to the intended audience. For example, a letter directed to an attorney may include legal terms and concepts that would be inappropriate in a letter to a layperson, who probably would not understand them. You must therefore consider to whom the legal writing is directed and what legal understanding the reader possesses.

In addition to the reader's legal knowledge, paralegals should consider how well the reader understands the subject matter. You cannot presume, especially in cases dealing with technical and scientific matters, that your reader knows as much as the attorney or yourself. Indeed, you should normally assume the contrary—that the reader has had neither the time nor the background to gain a comprehensive understanding of every legal or factual matter presented. Both in consideration of your reader's needs and in the interests of effective communication, you should present your information or analysis clearly, carefully leading the reader from point A to point B, from point B to point C, and so on.

Avoid Legalese: Use Everyday English

As a paralegal, writing to your audience often requires you to minimize or eliminate legal jargon, or legalese. Legalese consists of terms that are used by legal professionals but that are unknown to most people outside the legal profession. Therefore, if you are writing a letter to a client, either avoid using legal terms the client may not understand or define such terms for your reader. For example, if you are advising a client of the date on which *voir dire* will take place, consider saying "jury selection"—or perhaps "*voir dire* (jury selection)"—instead. Although a certain amount of legal terminology in legal writing is unavoidable, you should minimize the use of language that may confuse the reader. (See this chapter's *Technology and Today's Paralegal* feature on the next page for a discussion of online sources offering instructions on and some examples of "plain-English" writing.)

Lawyers have traditionally used certain terms in legal documents—words such as *hereof, therein,* and *thereto,* for example—that you should avoid whenever possible in your writing. These and similar words sound strange and excessively formal to the ordinary person. Legal documents are also often filled with redundancies. Consider, for example, the following sentence from an agreement to finance a business:

> ✳ **If Borrower shall have made any representation or warranty herein . . .
> which shall be in any material respect false and/or erroneous and/or
> incorrect . . .**

What is the difference between *false, erroneous,* and *incorrect?* Often, these terms are used synonymously, and it is hard to imagine that something could be erroneous and still be correct—so why should it be necessary to add *incorrect* to the clause?

Other commonly used legal phrases containing obvious redundancies include *all the rest, residue, and remainder; null and void; full and complete;* and *cease and desist.* In the first phrase, the words *rest, residue,* and *remainder* mean essentially the same thing. In the second phrase, the words *null* and *void* are synonymous, as

TECHNOLOGY AND TODAY'S PARALEGAL

Online "Plain-English" Guidelines

The ability to write clearly and effectively is a valuable asset to any paralegal, because virtually every paralegal is required to do a certain amount of writing as a part of his or her job. As mentioned elsewhere, clear and effective writing means keeping legalese— legal terminology typically understood only by legal professionals—to a minimum or even eliminating it entirely. The problem is how to convert traditional legal language into clear and understandable prose. Today's paralegals can find helpful instruction in the art of writing in plain English at many online locations.

GOVERNMENT PUBLICATIONS

The U.S. government publishes some of the best online plain-English guides. The "Plain English Handbook," put out by the Securities and Exchange Commission (SEC), is available at http://www.sec.gov/pdf/handbook.pdf. Although the handbook was intended to help individuals create clearer and more informative SEC disclosure documents, the guidelines given in the booklet can apply to any written communication. The Small Business Administration also publishes an online guide explaining how to write in plain language at http://www.sba.gov/plain/whatis.html. In addition, the Office of the Federal Register's booklet "Drafting Legal Documents" can be found at http://www.archives.gov/federal_register/drafting_legal_documents/drafting_legal_documents.html.

The U.S. government also has an official Web site dedicated to the use of plain language (http://www.plainlanguage.gov) and publishes a guide called "Writing User-Friendly Documents." Foreign governments also may provide useful information. For example, the Australian government publishes a booklet called "Plain English at Work" that can be accessed at http://www.dest.gov.au/archive/publications/plain_en.

WORLDWIDE ORGANIZATIONS

Since the 1970s, the plain-English movement, which is fighting for public information (such as laws) to be written in plain English, has received worldwide attention. A British organization, called the Plain English Campaign, is one of the most prominent groups in this movement. The Plain English Campaign has worked to promote the use of plain English in many nations, including the United States. You can find (and download) several helpful guides at its Web site (http://www.plainenglishcampaign.com), including "How to Write in Plain English" and "The A–Z of Alternative Words." Another campaign, called Fight the Fog, is directed at institutions in the European Union (EU). At its Web site, http://europa.eu.int/comm/translation/en/ftfog/index.htm, you can read a booklet called "How to Write Clearly," as well as other news and publications in several languages.

Clarity is a worldwide group of lawyers and interested laypersons who seek to promote the use of good, clear language by the legal profession. The group publishes a journal and a newsletter, holds seminars on legal drafting, provides an online discussion group, and even gives informal drafting help to members and others. You can find out about the group at http://www.clarity.international.net. Finally, anyone interested in keeping abreast of plain language legal information and education initiatives (such as books, videos, and Web sites) can subscribe free of charge to the online Plain Language Law Newsletter, which is published by the Law and Justice Foundation of New South Wales (http://www.lawfoundation.net.au/information/pll/index.html).

TECHNOLOGY TIP

Paralegals interested in improving their plain-English writing skills have many Internet resources to which they can turn. The guides mentioned above provide practical information and suggest alternative wording. In addition, paralegals can access a plain-English glossary of legalese at http://www.uchelp.com/database/law/glossary.htm and take online writing courses offered at Purdue University (http://owl.english.purdue.edu) and at http://www.web.ca/~plain/PlainTrain/Digest.html.

EXHIBIT 18.1
Using Words Efficiently

Do not write:
Ms. Carpenter never drives at night due to the fact that she has poor night vision.

Write instead:
Ms. Carpenter does not drive at night because she has poor night vision.

Do not write:
The new client who brought his business to our attention yesterday has a number of issues pertaining to his legal problems that he needs to discuss with us as soon as possible.

Write instead:
The client who hired us yesterday needs to discuss his legal problems immediately.

Do not write:
The defendant worked for one of the members of an organized crime ring for a period of seven years. During that seven-year period of time, the defendant witnessed crimes numbering in the hundreds.

Write instead:
During the seven years that the defendant worked for a member of an organized crime ring, he witnessed hundreds of crimes.

are the coupled terms in the other phrases. Yet these types of phrases are commonplace in legal documents, largely because they have traditionally been used in the legal profession and because of the natural inclination of lawyers to want to make sure that all aspects of a given subject are covered.

As a paralegal, you should strive to minimize the use of legalese, including redundancies, in your own writing—but be cautious:

> ✖ **When translating legalese into plain English, you need to make sure that you correctly understand the intent of the legal phrase. If you have any doubts, always ask your supervising attorney.**

Be Brief and to the Point

Just as the use of legalese can hinder communication, so, too, can the use of too many words. Writing effectively requires efficiency in word usage. Omit surplus words. Unnecessary words can become stumbling blocks for your reader and prevent a clear understanding of the point you wish to make. Moreover, concise statements are much more powerful and persuasive. When proofreading your document, take time to make sure that your statements are brief and to the point. Exhibit 18.1 offers some examples of how efficient word usage can enhance clarity.

Generally, you should only use words essential to the point you are making; unnecessary words may distract and confuse the reader. Similarly, you should include in your writing only concepts or factual information directly relevant to your topic.

Writing Basics: Sentences

A good writer uses a high proportion of short, concrete sentences because they are easier to understand. Additionally, forceful sentences include active, dynamic verbs rather than nominalizations (verbs transformed into nouns). For example, it is simpler and more effective to say "the plaintiff decided to settle the case" than "the plaintiff made a decision to settle the case." In the first example, the verb *decide* is direct and forceful. In the second example, the conversion of *decided* into *made a decision* detracts from the forcefulness of the verb.

Writing in the active voice also makes sentences easier to understand. The active voice sets up a subject-verb-object sentence structure, whereas the passive voice uses an object-verb-subject format. For example, "The defendant stole the diamond" uses the active voice. Contrast the simplicity and strength of this statement with its passive equivalent: "The diamond was stolen by the defendant." The use of the active voice puts people, actors, movers, and doers into your writing and thus makes your writing more reflective of reality. Sometimes, however, you may want to maintain the facelessness of the actor or doer. For example, if your firm is defending a plaintiff who has been accused of stealing a diamond, consider writing "the diamond that was stolen" instead of "the diamond that the plaintiff allegedly stole." In this situation, the passive voice effectively removes the plaintiff from the action.

You should also make sure you use correct grammar when writing legal documents. Grammatical and punctuation errors, such as those in the following sentences, distract your reader and may reflect poorly on your (and your firm's) professional reputation and status.

- *Incorrect:* The plaintiff should *of* consulted with the defendant.
- *Correct:* The plaintiff should *have* consulted with the defendant.
- *Incorrect:* The defendant could not possibly have *did* what the plaintiff alleged.
- *Correct:* The defendant could not possibly have *done* what the plaintiff alleged.
- *Incorrect:* The *plaintiffs* allegations were vague and ambiguous.
- *Correct:* The *plaintiff's* allegations were vague and ambiguous.

When proofreading your documents, make sure they are free of any errors involving subject-verb agreement, punctuation, spelling, the use of apostrophes, and other elements.

Writing Basics: Paragraphs and Transitions

A paragraph is a group of sentences that develops a particular idea. A paragraph should have unity and coherence. Each paragraph should begin with a *topic sentence* that indicates what the paragraph is about. Each subsequent sentence in the paragraph should contribute to the development of the topic; if it does not, consider placing the sentence elsewhere or simply deleting it. When you write, be conscious of why you begin a new paragraph—or why you do not. Keep paragraphs short, if possible. When you proofread, watch carefully for how you are using paragraphs and break up paragraphs that are too long. You should create a new paragraph whenever you start discussing another idea. Paragraphs that are not logically constructed are often confusing and pointless for the reader.

Take your reader with you as you move from one paragraph to another. Although the connection between paragraphs may be clear to you, the writer, it may not be clear to your reader. You need to show, by including transitional sentences or phrases, how a topic discussed in one paragraph relates to the subsequent paragraph. Exhibit 18.2 lists some terms and phrases writers commonly use to effect smooth transitions.

Be Alert for Sexist Language

The language of the law has traditionally used masculine pronouns inclusively—that is, to refer to both males and females. Jurists, legal scholars, and others in the legal profession are consciously moving away from this tradition. As a paralegal,

EXHIBIT 18.3
Components of a Legal Letter

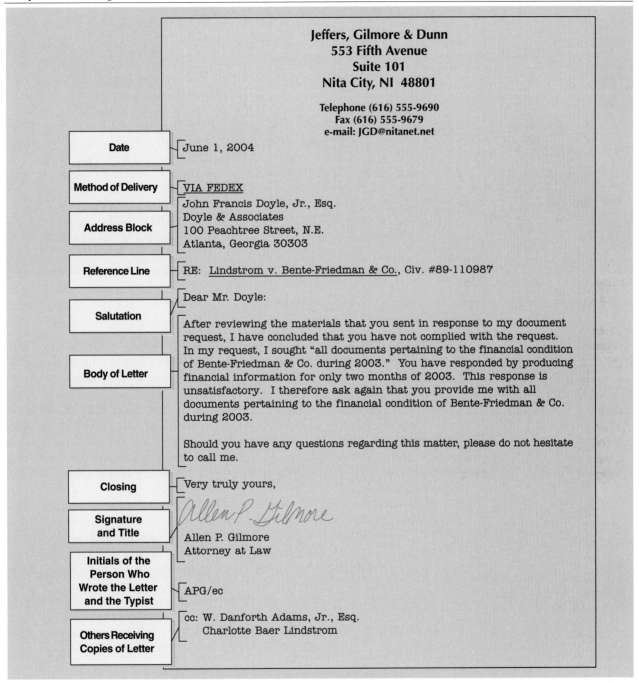

Jeffers, Gilmore & Dunn
553 Fifth Avenue
Suite 101
Nita City, NI 48801

Telephone (616) 555-9690
Fax (616) 555-9679
e-mail: JGD@nitanet.net

Date	June 1, 2004
Method of Delivery	VIA FEDEX
Address Block	John Francis Doyle, Jr., Esq. Doyle & Associates 100 Peachtree Street, N.E. Atlanta, Georgia 30303
Reference Line	RE: Lindstrom v. Bente-Friedman & Co., Civ. #89-110987
Salutation	Dear Mr. Doyle:
Body of Letter	After reviewing the materials that you sent in response to my document request, I have concluded that you have not complied with the request. In my request, I sought "all documents pertaining to the financial condition of Bente-Friedman & Co. during 2003." You have responded by producing financial information for only two months of 2003. This response is unsatisfactory. I therefore ask again that you provide me with all documents pertaining to the financial condition of Bente-Friedman & Co. during 2003. Should you have any questions regarding this matter, please do not hesitate to call me.
Closing	Very truly yours,
Signature and Title	*Allen P. Gilmore* Allen P. Gilmore Attorney at Law
Initials of the Person Who Wrote the Letter and the Typist	APG/ec
Others Receiving Copies of Letter	cc: W. Danforth Adams, Jr., Esq. Charlotte Baer Lindstrom

for a financing transaction may read "RE: Closing Procedures for ABC Company's $4,000,000 Financing Package."

The **salutation,** which appears just below the reference line, is a greeting to the addressee. Because legal correspondence is a professional means of communication, the salutation, as well as the body of the letter, should be formal in tone. There are, of course, circumstances in which a formal greeting may not be necessary. For example, if the addressee is someone you know quite well, it may be

salutation
The formal greeting to the addressee of the letter. The salutation is placed just below the reference line.

> ## ETHICAL CONCERN
> ## "Confidential" Correspondence
>
> As a paralegal, you may be faced with the question of whether you should open letters to the attorney for whom you work when the letters are marked "Confidential." For example, suppose that you work for an attorney who is out of the country for two weeks. Because she will be hard to reach during this time, she has instructed you to open all of her mail and respond appropriately to certain matters. She has explicitly told you to call her only if an emergency arises. While she is gone, you receive a letter to the attorney that is marked "Confidential." You recognize the sender's name (an attorney who is defending against a lawsuit brought by one of your supervising attorney's clients) and suspect that the letter pertains to the lawsuit. Should you open the letter? Should you hold it until your attorney returns? Or should you try to contact your attorney for advice? To avoid this kind of situation, ask your employer in advance how you should handle confidential mail. Some attorneys routinely have their paralegals open this type of mail; others do not.

appropriate to address the person by his or her first name, rather than by "Mr." or "Ms." In these situations, you must use your discretion to determine the appropriate level of formality. Generally, when in doubt, use a formal salutation.

BODY AND CLOSING.   The main part of the letter is the body of the letter. The body of the letter should be formal and should effectively communicate information to the reader. As a representative of the firm, the paralegal must be careful to proofread all outgoing correspondence to ensure that the letter contains accurate information, is clearly written, and is free of any grammatical or spelling errors.

Following the body of the letter are standard concluding sentences. These final sentences are usually courteous statements such as "Thank you for your time and attention to this matter," or "Should you have any questions or comments, please call me at the above-listed number." These brief concluding statements are followed by the **closing**. The closing in legal correspondence is formal—for example, "Sincerely" or "Very truly yours."

Finally, you should always include your title in any correspondence written by you on behalf of the firm. Your title ("Paralegal" or "Legal Assistant" or other title) should immediately follow your name. This, of course, is not a concern when you prepare correspondence for an attorney who will provide a signature.

closing
A final comment to a letter that is placed above the signature, such as "Sincerely" or "Very truly yours."

Types of Legal Letters

There are several types of legal correspondence, and each type serves a different purpose. Types of legal letters with which you should become familiar include the following:

- Informative letters.
- Confirmation letters.
- Opinion (advisory) letters.
- Demand letters.

EXHIBIT 18.4
A Sample Informative Letter

Jeffers, Gilmore & Dunn
553 Fifth Avenue
Suite 101
Nita City, NI 48801

Telephone (616) 555-9690
Fax (616) 555-9679
e-mail: JGD@nitanet.net

June 24, 2004

Bernadette P. Williams
149 Snowflake Drive
Irving, TX 75062

RE: Kempf/Joseph Arbitration Proceedings

Dear Ms. Williams:

The arbitration will resume on Monday, August 1, 2004. Please arrive at the offices of the American Arbitration Association (the AAA) before 8:30 A.M. The offices of the AAA are located at 400 West Ferry Boulevard in Dallas. You will be called as a witness sometime before 12:00 noon.

Should you have any questions or concerns regarding your responsibilities as a witness, please do not hesitate to contact me.

Sincerely,

Elena Lopez
Elena Lopez
Legal Assistant

INFORMATIVE LETTERS. A letter that conveys information to another party is an **informative letter.** As a paralegal, you will write many such letters—to clients, for example. Informative letters might be written to advise a client about current developments in a case, an upcoming meeting or procedure, the general background on a legal issue, or simply a breakdown of the firm's bill. The letters you write should be tailored to the client's level of legal understanding.

Informative letters are also sent to opposing counsel and other individuals. For example, law firms often send litigation-scheduling information to opposing counsel, witnesses, and other persons who may be involved in a trial. Informative letters may also be used as transmittal (cover) letters when documents or other materials are sent to a client, a court, opposing counsel, or some other person. Exhibit 18.4 shows a sample letter written to an individual who will testify during an arbitration procedure.

CONFIRMATION LETTERS. Another type of letter frequently written by paralegals is the confirmation letter. **Confirmation letters** are similar to informative letters in that they communicate certain information to the reader. Confirmation letters put into written form the contents of an oral discussion. In addition to providing attorneys with a permanent record of earlier conversations, confirmation letters also safeguard against any misinterpretation or misunderstanding of what was communicated orally. See Exhibit 18.5 on the next page for an example of a confirmation letter.

informative letter
A letter that conveys certain information to a client, a witness, an adversary's counsel, or some other person regarding some legal matter (such as the date, time, place, and purpose of a meeting) or a cover letter that accompanies other documents being sent to a person or court.

confirmation letter
A letter that states the substance of a previously conducted verbal discussion to provide a permanent record of the oral conversation.

EXHIBIT 18.5
A Sample Confirmation Letter

Jeffers, Gilmore & Dunn
553 Fifth Avenue
Suite 101
Nita City, NI 48801

Telephone (616) 555-9690
Fax (616) 555-9679
e-mail: JGD@nitanet.net

August 3, 2004

Pauline C. Dunbar
President
Minute-Magic Corporation
7689 Industrial Boulevard
San Francisco, CA 80021

RE: Purchase of real estate from C. C. Barnes, Inc.

Dear Ms. Dunbar:

The following information describes the current status of the negotiations between C. C. Barnes, Inc., and Minute-Magic Corporation:

    Selling Price: $800,000
    Financing Agreement: Citywide Bank
    Interest Rate: 7.5%

This information confirms what I told you on the phone today, August 3, 2004. I look forward to seeing you next week. Should you have any questions or comments in the meantime, please give me a call.

Very truly yours,

Allen P. Gilmore

Allen P. Gilmore
Attorney at Law

APG/ec

---

opinion (advisory) letter
A letter from an attorney to a client containing a legal opinion on an issue raised by the client's question or legal claim. The opinion is based on a detailed analysis of the law.

OPINION LETTERS.   The function of an **opinion letter,** or **advisory letter,** is to provide not only information but also advice. In contrast to informative letters, opinion letters actually give a legal opinion about the matter discussed. Attorneys providing opinion letters are required to provide a detailed analysis of the law and to bring the analysis to a definite conclusion, setting forth the firm's opinion on the matter.

In addition to rendering the law firm's legal opinion, opinion letters may also be used to inform a client of the legal validity of a specific action. For example, a company seeking to establish operations in a foreign country may seek a lawyer's opinion on whether a certain action it plans to undertake is legally permissible. The attorney (or a paralegal) will research the issue and then draft an advisory letter to the client. Opinion letters are commonly quite long and include detailed explanations of how the law applies to the client's factual situation. Sometimes, the attorney just summarizes his or her conclusion in the opinion letter (as in the opinion letter shown in Exhibit 18.6) and attaches a legal memorandum to the letter explaining the legal sources and reasoning used in forming that conclusion.

The Appellate Brief	When a case is appealed to a higher court, attorneys for both sides file appellate briefs with the court of appeals. The purpose of an appellate brief is to convince the appellate court of the merits of a client's position on appeal. A persuasive and forceful writing approach is therefore used.

1. *Types of appellate briefs—*

   a. The appellant's brief is filed on behalf of the party appealing the lower court's decision.

   b. The appellee's brief is filed on behalf of the party against whom the appeal is sought.

   c. A reply brief is filed by the appellant in response to the appellee's brief.

   d. The *amicus curiae* brief is filed by a "friend of the court" on behalf of one of the parties to the case in the interest of a broadly held public concern.

2. *Format*—Most courts require that appellate briefs be presented in a format that includes the following sections:

   a. Title page.

   b. Table of contents.

   c. Table of authorities.

   d. Statement of jurisdiction.

   e. Questions presented.

   f. Statement of the claim.

   g. Summary of the argument.

   h. Argument. Each section of the argument consists of a point heading and the body of the argument.

   i. Conclusion.

✳ QUESTIONS FOR REVIEW

1. What factors should you consider before undertaking a legal-writing assignment?

2. List and describe each of the guidelines for effective writing. What is meant by the statement "You should write to your audience"?

3. What is plain English? Why should you write in plain English?

4. What is the active voice? What is the passive voice? Why is it better to use the active voice in your legal writing?

5. What are some basic guidelines for the structure of a paragraph? List three transitional phrases that can be used to connect ideas between paragraphs.

6. List the component parts of a typical legal letter.

7. What are the four types of letters discussed in this chapter? What is the function of each type?

8. How is an internal memorandum organized? List and describe its components.

9. What must you know and understand before you begin to prepare a legal memorandum?

10. What is the purpose of an appellate brief?

❋ ETHICAL QUESTIONS

1. Lynette Bennett, a paralegal, works as a clerk for a judge in the county circuit court. She has just finished reviewing the plaintiff's and defendant's briefs in an auto-accident case. The plaintiff's brief described the injury as follows:

   > The plaintiff was struck by the defendant's car as she crossed Lincoln Avenue at the crosswalk. She sustained serious injuries to her left knee, for which she had surgery. She also experiences pain and discomfort in her back and neck.

   The defendant's brief described the injury as follows:

   > The plaintiff was struck when she suddenly stepped in front of the defendant's vehicle. The defendant's vehicle was traveling at a speed of five miles per hour. In her lawsuit against the defendant, the plaintiff claims that she sustained significant injuries from this minor accident.

   Lynette is disturbed by the disparity in the two descriptions of the plaintiff's injuries. It sounds to Lynette as if someone is lying. What do you think? What impact would falsifying the facts have on the writer's credibility?

2. Bill Richardson, a legal assistant, has been asked by his supervising attorney to prepare an internal memorandum analyzing a client's claim. When Bill reviews the facts, he realizes that the client has a very weak case and will probably lose. But Bill thinks that the client was taken advantage of and that she should be given a chance to try to recover at least something. He knows that his supervisor will not take a losing case to court, so he writes the memo in such a way as to favor the client's position as much as possible. He is not objective in analyzing the potential pitfalls of the case. Is what Bill has done ethical? Is it professional? How should he have handled the situation?

3. David Thomas, a paralegal, is sending out a letter to a client. It is an informative letter advising the client of the status of her case and explaining what the next step in the litigation process will be. David signs the letter without including his title. He mails the letter to the client. The client has questions, and she calls David, thinking that he is the attorney. How should David handle this situation? What should he have done to prevent it?

4. Ken Hall, a legal assistant, is handling all of his supervising attorney's mail while she is out of town on business for the week. The supervising attorney only wants to be contacted if absolutely necessary. She receives a letter marked "personal and confidential." Ken does not recognize the return address on the letter. How should Ken handle the situation?

❋ PRACTICE QUESTIONS AND ASSIGNMENTS

1. Clip an article out of the newspaper or a news journal. Then follow the instructions and answer the questions given below:

   a. Underline all of the active verbs and circle all of the passive verbs. Did the writer use more active verbs than passive verbs in writing the article?

   b. Count the number of words in each sentence. What is the average sentence length? Do short sentences predominate?

   c. Locate the topic sentence in each paragraph. Is the writer's paragraph construction effective?

   d. Notice how the author uses transitional sentences when moving from one paragraph to the next. Underline the key transitional words or phrases.

2. Analyze the construction of the following paragraphs. How could they be improved?

   The first is knowing of the danger. The second is voluntarily subjecting oneself to the danger. The defense of assumption of risk has two elements.

   She did not voluntarily subject herself to the danger when the stadium assigned seats to season-ticket holders. She knew that balls were often hit into the stands. The plaintiff knew of the danger involved in attending a baseball game.

3. Proofread the following paragraph, circling all of the mistakes. Then rewrite the paragraph.

   The defendant was arrested and charged with drunk driving. Blood alcohol level of .15. He refused to take a breathalyzer test at first. After the police explained to him that he would loose his license if he did not take it, he consented. He also has a blood test to verify the results of the breathalyzer.

4. Review the *Practice Questions and Assignments* at the end of Chapter 16. If you did the research required by those questions, use the lemon law and the cases that you found to prepare an internal memorandum analyzing Mr. Consumer's problem and whether the lemon law in your state will help him. Be sure to include your opinion of the strength of his case.

5. Using the research results from question 5 in the *Practice Questions and Assignments* at the end of Chapter 16, draft an opinion letter from your supervising attorney to Mr. Consumer, advising him as to how the state's lemon law applies to his case and what type of relief he can expect.

6. Using the material presented in this chapter, prepare an informative letter to a client using the following facts:

> The client, Dr. Brown, is being sued for medical malpractice and is going to be deposed on January 15, 2004, at 1:00 P.M. The deposition will take place at the law offices of Callaghan & Young. The offices are located at 151 East Jefferson Avenue, Cincinnati, Ohio. The client needs to call your supervising attorney's office to set up an appointment, so that the attorney can prepare Dr. Brown for the deposition.

7. Review Exhibit 16.21 in Chapter 16, *Excerpt from the Americans with Disabilities Act of 1990*. Summarize sections (a) and (b) in two to three paragraphs. Write one paragraph in plain English explaining what sections (a) and (b) mean.

❋ QUESTIONS FOR CRITICAL ANALYSIS

1. The Americans with Disabilities Act (ADA) of 1990 does not require employers to accommodate persons with disabilities if those persons pose a direct threat to the health and safety of others. Read the following case annotations and synthesize the annotations into the rule of law regarding the type of threat that is required to prevent employment under the "direct threat" provision of the ADA:

   a. Orthopedic surgeon posed a direct threat to the health of his patients as a result of his HIV-positive status, and thus, hospitals did not violate ADA by prohibiting the surgeon from performing surgery without patient consent given patients' knowledge of surgeon's HIV status; although current knowledge about HIV transmission from surgeon to patient is uncertain, because there is no known cure, the duration of risk posed by a surgeon in a surgical setting was permanent and the severity of the harm was that the disease was, at present, fatal in most cases. *Scoles v. Mercy Health Corp.,* 887 F.Supp. 765 (E.D.Pa.1994).

   b. Employers' executive director's inability to drive did not pose significant risk of substantial harm to health and safety of director or others that could not be eliminated or reduced by reasonable accommodation, as required to support employer's direct threat defense; driving was not an essential function of executive director's position, and providing the executive director with an alternative mode of transportation was a reasonable accommodation. *Equal Employment Opportunity Commission v. AIC Security Investigation, Ltd.,* 820 F.Supp. 1060 (N.D.Ill. 1993).

   c. Even if Georgia Ports Authority police officer had timely complained of his "benign essential tremor" disability which caused him to fail a firearms proficiency test and had requested an accommodation, the officer failed to show how this could be done so as to prevail on his ADA claim; GPA police officer who could not shoot straight posed an unacceptable risk to others and the officer did not show how his deficiency, and the direct threat to the health of others that it represented, could be reasonably accommodated. *Fussell v. Georgia Ports Authority,* 906 F.Supp. 1561 (S.D.Ga. 1995).

   d. Neurologist with attention deficit disorder (ADD) which affected his short-term memory and led to mistakes on patients' charts and in dispensing of medicine to patients posed a direct threat to the health and safety of others, and thus, the employer was not required under the ADA to accommodate his disability. *Robertson v. Neuromedical Center,* 983 F.Supp. 669 (M.D.La. 1997).

2. Why is it important to write to your audience? To what audience should legislators write when drafting legislation?

3. Using the material presented in the chapter, analyze the following hypothetical by applying the IRAC method and write a one-page paper reporting your results:

> Mr. Damien is a teacher at the Wabash Academy, a private boarding school. He has a twenty-one-year-old son who has bipolar affective disorder, formerly called manic-depressive psychosis, a mood disorder. While visiting Mr. Damien, his son has repeatedly threatened members of the school community. On one occasion, Mr. Damien's son abducted the headmaster's sixteen-year-old daughter and attempted to have the teenager admitted to a psychiatric hospital. Mr. Damien's son also made threatening phone calls to the headmaster. In one such call, he claimed to have drained several quarts of his own blood from his body because he was not permitted to communicate with the headmaster's sixteen-year-old daughter. Mr. and Mrs. Damien refuse to prevent their son from visiting their home on the school's campus. As a result, the school fired Mr. Damien. Mr. Damien claims that the termination of his employment violates the Americans with Disabilities Act (ADA) of 1990.

The case law interpreting the ADA does not require employment of an individual with disabilities if that individual, or that individual's disabled relative or associate, poses a direct threat to the health and safety of others.

✳ PROJECTS

1. Compare Microsoft's *Word* and Corel's *WordPerfect* word processing software. Write a one-page paper summarizing which you prefer and why. Be sure to note the legal applications each software package has available.

2. If possible, find a copy of a business letter. Identify its component parts. How does it differ from the sample legal letter presented in Exhibit 18.3? How is it similar?

3. Contact the court of appeals in your state. Ask if the court gives tours, has any programs available for college students, or allows observation of oral arguments. If so, arrange to take a tour and observe an oral argument. If available, it would be helpful if you could obtain a copy of each side's brief and read it prior to the oral argument. Check with your instructor for any special directions before contacting the court. Write a one-page paper summarizing your visit to the court of appeals.

4. Review your state's court rules that apply to the preparation of documents—such as pleadings, motions, and appellate briefs—to be filed with the courts. Are there any specific instructions for the format of these documents, such as page limits or requirements for double spacing or separately numbered paragraphs or allegations? Make a list of the rules, and summarize the requirements. Your list and accompanying summary should not exceed two typewritten pages.

✳ USING INTERNET RESOURCES

1. Access the Securities and Exchange Commission's "Handbook of Plain English" at the following site:

> http://www.sec.gov/pdf/handbook.pdf

Scroll through the handbook to find answers to the following questions:

a. Describe the "unoriginal but useful" writing tip given in the handbook's preface. Why did the writer of the preface find the tip useful?

b. How does Chapter 1 of the handbook describe a "plain-English" document?

c. Browse through Chapter 6, titled "Writing in Plain English." Write down two "before and after" examples showing how the use of plain English improved the writing.

d. What is a nominalization? Write a sentence including a nominalization (not one of those listed in Chapter 6), and then rewrite the sentence to make the nominalization the main verb of the sentence.

2. The American Bar Association's Web site contains helpful articles on legal writing, particularly in the section on law practice management.

a. Access the search home page of the Web site, at http://www.abanet.org/scripts/search/search_results.jsp, and perform a search. Using the arrows next to the box labeled "Search in," select "Law Practice Management Section" from the drop-down list. Then enter "legal writing" in the box next to "Keyword or Phrase." How many articles did your search retrieve? Scan the articles.

Do the titles of any of the articles listed refer to plain English or the plain-English movement? Now search on the words "plain English." How many articles does that search retrieve? What do you conclude based on your comparison of the numbers of articles retrieved by the searches?

b. Click on the article titled "Strategies for Revising Documents" (which can be found at **http://www.abanet.org/lpm/bestpractices/articles/bparticle 11100_front.shtml**). How many "Checklists for Revising" does the article present? What does the author mean by the expression "incubation time"? What does the author say about reading your work aloud?

c. Read one article that appeals to you, and write a one-page summary of the author's main points.

Include the name of the article for your instructor's reference. Your instructor may ask you to present your summary to the class. Did anyone else in the class read that same article? If so, compare the summaries to see if you and the other student or students interpreted the author's points differently.

d. Now click on "Online Writing Labs" under the heading "Best Practices" at the left side of the screen (or search for the topic using the search engine). How many resources are listed under this topic? Scan the services offered, and write a one-paragraph synopsis of what is available. Do you think these services could be useful to you as a paralegal? How?

END NOTES

1. Pronounced ah-*mee*-cuhs *kur*-ee-ay.

2. The record of the case, or record on appeal, consists of the following: (1) the pleadings, (2) a transcript of the trial testimony and copies of the exhibits, (3) the judge's rulings on motions made by the parties, (4) the arguments of counsel, (5) the instructions to the jury, (6) the verdict, (7) the post-trial motions, and (8) the judgment order from which the appeal is taken.

NALA's
Code of Ethics and
Professional
Responsibility

A legal assistant must adhere strictly to the accepted standards of legal ethics and to the general principles of proper conduct. The performance of the duties of the legal assistant shall be governed by specific canons as defined herein so that justice will be served and goals of the profession attained. (See Model Standards and Guidelines for Utilization of Legal Assistants, Section II.)

The canons of ethics set forth hereafter are adopted by the National Association of Legal Assistants, Inc., as a general guide intended to aid legal assistants and attorneys. The enumeration of these rules does not mean there are not others of equal importance although not specifically mentioned. Court rules, agency rules, and statutes must be taken into consideration when interpreting the canons.

Definition: Legal assistants, also known as paralegals, are a distinguishable group of persons who assist attorneys in the delivery of legal services. Through formal education, training, and experience, legal assistants have knowledge and expertise regarding the legal system and substantive and procedural law which qualify them to do work of a legal nature under the supervision of an attorney.

Canon 1

A legal assistant must not perform any of the duties that attorneys only may perform nor take any actions that attorneys may not take.

Canon 2

A legal assistant may perform any task which is properly delegated and supervised by an attorney, as long as the attorney is ultimately responsible to the client, maintains a direct relationship with the client, and assumes professional responsibility for the work product.

Canon 3

A legal assistant must not: (a) engage in, encourage, or contribute to any act which could constitute the unauthorized practice of law; and (b) establish attorney-client relationships, set fees, give legal opinions or advice, or represent a client before a court or agency unless so authorized by that court or agency; and (c) engage in conduct or take any action which would assist or involve the attorney in a violation of professional ethics or give the appearance of professional impropriety.

Canon 4

A legal assistant must use discretion and professional judgment commensurate with knowledge and experience but must not render independent legal judgment in place of an attorney. The services of an attorney are essential in the public interest whenever such legal judgment is required.

Canon 5

A legal assistant must disclose his or her status as a legal assistant at the outset of any professional relationship with a client, attorney, a court or administrative agency, or personnel thereof, or a member of the general public. A legal assistant must act prudently in determining the extent to which a client may be assisted without the presence of an attorney.

Canon 6

A legal assistant must strive to maintain integrity and a high degree of competency through education and training with respect to professional responsibility, local rules and practice, and through continuing education in substantive areas of law to better assist the legal profession in fulfilling its duty to provide legal service.

Canon 7

A legal assistant must protect the confidences of a client and must not violate any rule or statute now in effect or hereafter enacted controlling privileged communications.

Canon 8

A legal assistant must do all other things incidental, necessary, or expedient for the attainment of the ethics and responsibilities as defined by statute or rule of court.

Canon 9

A legal assistant's conduct is guided by bar associations' codes of professional responsibility and rules of professional conduct.

© Copyright 1998 NALA.

NALA's
MODEL STANDARDS
AND GUIDELINES
FOR THE UTILIZATION
OF LEGAL ASSISTANTS

NALA's study of the professional responsibility and ethical considerations of legal assistants is ongoing. This research led to the development of the NALA Model Standards and Guidelines for Utilization of Legal Assistants. This guide summarizes case law, guidelines, and ethical opinions of the various states affecting legal assistants. It provides an outline of minimum qualifications and standards necessary for legal assistant professionals to assure the public and the legal profession that they are, indeed, qualified. The following is a listing of the standards and guidelines.

The annotated version of the Model was revised extensively in 1997. It is online (NALA Model Standards and Guidelines) and may be ordered through NALA headquarters.

INTRODUCTION

Proper utilization of the services of legal assistants affects the efficient delivery of legal services. Legal assistants and the legal profession should be assured that some measures exist for identifying legal assistants and their role in assisting attorneys in the delivery of legal services. Therefore, the National Association of Legal Assistants, Inc., hereby adopts these Model Standards and Guidelines as an educational document for the benefit of legal assistants and the legal profession.

STANDARDS

A legal assistant should meet certain minimum qualifications. The following standards may be used to determine an individual's qualifications as a legal assistant:

1. Successful completion of the Certified Legal Assistant (CLA) certifying examination of the National Association of Legal Assistants, Inc.;

2. Graduation from an ABA–approved program of study for legal assistants;

3. Graduation from a course of study for legal assistants which is institutionally accredited but not ABA approved, and which requires not less than the equivalent of sixty semester hours of classroom study;

4. Graduation from a course of study for legal assistants, other than those set forth in (2) and (3) above, plus not less than six months of in-house training as a legal assistant;

5. A baccalaureate degree in any field, plus not less than six months in-house training as a legal assistant;

6. A minimum of three years of law-related experience under the supervision of an attorney, including at least six months of in-house training as a legal assistant; or

7. Two years of in-house training as a legal assistant.

For purposes of these Standards, "in-house training as a legal-assistant" means attorney education of the employee concerning legal assistant duties and these Guidelines. In addition to review and analysis of assignments, the legal assistant should receive a reasonable amount of instruction directly related to the duties and obligations of the legal assistant.

GUIDELINES

These Guidelines relating to standards of performance and professional responsibility are intended to aid legal assistants and attorneys. The responsibility rests with an attorney who employs legal assistants to educate them with respect to the duties they are assigned and to supervise the manner in which such duties are accomplished.

Guideline 1

Legal assistants should:

1. Disclose their status as legal assistants at the outset of any professional relationship with a client, other attorneys, a court or administrative agency or personnel thereof, or members of the general public;

2. Preserve the confidences and secrets of all clients; and

3. Understand the attorney's Code of Professional Responsibility and these guidelines in order to avoid any action which would involve the attorney in a violation of that Code, or give the appearance of professional impropriety.

Guideline 2

Legal assistants should not:

1. Establish attorney-client relationships; set legal fees, give legal opinions or advice; or represent a client before a court; nor

2. Engage in, encourage, or contribute to any act which could constitute the unauthorized practice of law.

Guideline 3

Legal assistants may perform services for an attorney in the representation of a client, provided:

1. The services performed by the legal assistant do not require the exercise of independent professional legal judgment;
2. The attorney maintains a direct relationship with the client and maintains control of all client matters;
3. The attorney supervises the legal assistant;
4. The attorney remains professionally responsible for all work on behalf of the client, including any actions taken or not taken by the legal assistant in connection therewith; and
5. The services performed supplement, merge with, and become the attorney's work product.

Guideline 4

In the supervision of a legal assistant, consideration should be given to:

1. Designating work assignments that correspond to the legal assistant's abilities, knowledge, training, and experience.
2. Educating and training the legal assistant with respect to professional responsibility, local rules and practices, and firm policies;
3. Monitoring the work and professional conduct of the legal assistant to ensure that the work is substantially correct and timely performed;
4. Providing continuing education for the legal assistant in substantive matters through courses, institutes, workshops, seminars, and in-house training; and
5. Encouraging and supporting membership and active participation in professional organizations.

Guideline 5

Except as otherwise provided by statute, court rule or decision, administrative rule or regulation, or the attorney's Code of Professional Responsibility and within the preceding parameters and proscriptions, a legal assistant may perform any function delegated by an attorney, including but not limited to the following:

1. Conduct client interviews and maintain general contact with the client after the establishment of the attorney-client relationship, so long as the client is aware of the status and function of the legal assistant, and the client contact is under the supervision of the attorney.
2. Locate and interview witnesses, so long as the witnesses are aware of the status and function of the legal assistant.
3. Conduct investigations and statistical and documentary research for review by the attorney.
4. Conduct legal research for review by the attorney.
5. Draft legal documents for review by the attorney.

6. Draft correspondence and pleadings for review by and signature of the attorney.

7. Summarize depositions, interrogatories, and testimony for review by the attorney.

8. Attend executions of wills, real estate closings, depositions, court or administrative hearings, and trials with the attorney.

9. Author and sign letters provided the legal assistant's status is clearly indicated and the correspondence does not contain independent legal opinions or legal advice.

The notes to accompany the NALA Model Standards and Guidelines for Utilization of Legal Assistants are updated regularly by the NALA Professional Development Committee. The standards and guidelines are adopted by the NALA membership, and changes to these provisions must be brought before NALA members during their annual meeting in July.

NFPA's
MODEL CODE OF ETHICS AND PROFESSIONAL RESPONSIBILITY AND GUIDELINES FOR ENFORCEMENT

Preamble

The National Federation of Paralegal Associations, Inc. ("NFPA") is a professional organization comprised of paralegal associations and individual paralegals throughout the United States and Canada. Members of NFPA have varying backgrounds, experiences, education, and job responsibilities that reflect the diversity of the paralegal profession. NFPA promotes the growth, development and recognition of the paralegal profession as an integral partner in the delivery of legal services.

In May 1993 NFPA adopted its Model Code of Ethics and Professional Responsibility ("Model Code") to delineate the principles for ethics and conduct to which every paralegal should aspire.

Many paralegal associations throughout the United States have endorsed the concept and content of NFPA's Model Code through the adoption of their own ethical codes. In doing so, paralegals have confirmed the profession's commitment to increase the quality and efficiency of legal services, as well as recognized its responsibilities to the public, the legal community, and colleagues.

Paralegals have recognized, and will continue to recognize, that the profession must continue to evolve to enhance their roles in the delivery of legal services. With increased levels of responsibility comes the need to define and enforce mandatory rules of professional conduct. Enforcement of codes of paralegal conduct is a logical and necessary step to enhance and ensure the confidence of the legal community and the public in the integrity and professional responsibility of paralegals.

In April 1997 NFPA adopted the Model Disciplinary Rules ("Model Rules") to make possible the enforcement of the Canons and Ethical Considerations contained in the NFPA Model Code. A concurrent determination was made that the Model Code of Ethics and Professional Responsibility, formerly aspirational in nature, should be recognized as setting forth the enforceable obligations of all paralegals.

The Model Code and Model Rules offer a framework for professional discipline, either voluntarily or through formal regulatory programs.

§1. NFPA Model Disciplinary Rules and Ethical Considerations

1.1 A Paralegal Shall Achieve and Maintain a High Level of Competence.

ETHICAL CONSIDERATIONS

EC–1.1(a) A paralegal shall achieve competency through education, training, and work experience.

EC–1.1(b) A paralegal shall aspire to participate in a minimum of twelve (12) hours of continuing legal education, to include at least one (1) hour of ethics education, every two (2) years in order to remain current on developments in the law.

EC–1.1(c) A paralegal shall perform all assignments promptly and efficiently.

1.2 A Paralegal Shall Maintain a High Level of Personal and Professional Integrity.

ETHICAL CONSIDERATIONS

EC–1.2(a) A paralegal shall not engage in any *ex parte* communications involving the courts or any other adjudicatory body in an attempt to exert undue influence or to obtain advantage or the benefit of only one party.

EC–1.2(b) A paralegal shall not communicate, or cause another to communicate, with a party the paralegal knows to be represented by a lawyer in a pending matter without the prior consent of the lawyer representing such other party.

EC–1.2(c) A paralegal shall ensure that all timekeeping and billing records prepared by the paralegal are thorough, accurate, honest, and complete.

EC–1.2(d) A paralegal shall not knowingly engage in fraudulent billing practices. Such practices may include, but are not limited to: inflation of hours billed to a client or employer; misrepresentation of the nature of tasks performed; and/or submission of fraudulent expense and disbursement documentation.

EC–1.2(e) A paralegal shall be scrupulous, thorough, and honest in the identification and maintenance of all funds, securities, and other assets of a client and shall provide accurate accounting as appropriate.

EC–1.2(f) A paralegal shall advise the proper authority of non-confidential knowledge of any dishonest or fraudulent acts by any person pertaining to the handling of the funds, securities, or other assets of a client. The authority to whom the report is made shall depend on the nature and circumstances of the possible misconduct, (e.g., ethics committees of law firms, corporations and/or paralegal associations, local or state bar associations, local prosecutors, administrative agencies, etc.). Failure to report such knowledge is in itself misconduct and shall be treated as such under these rules.

1.3 A Paralegal Shall Maintain a High Standard of Professional Conduct.

ETHICAL CONSIDERATIONS

EC–1.3(a) A paralegal shall refrain from engaging in any conduct that offends the dignity and decorum of proceedings before a court or other adjudicatory body and shall be respectful of all rules and procedures.

EC–1.3(b) A paralegal shall avoid impropriety and the appearance of impropriety and shall not engage in any conduct that would adversely affect his/her fitness to practice. Such conduct may include, but is not limited to: violence, dishonesty, interference with the administration of justice, and/or abuse of a professional position or public office.

EC–1.3(c) Should a paralegal's fitness to practice be compromised by physical or mental illness, causing that paralegal to commit an act that is in direct violation of the Model Code/Model Rules and/or the rules and/or laws governing the jurisdiction in which the paralegal practices, that paralegal may be protected from sanction upon review of the nature and circumstances of that illness.

EC–1.3(d) A paralegal shall advise the proper authority of non-confidential knowledge of any action of another legal professional that clearly demonstrates fraud, deceit, dishonesty, or misrepresentation. The authority to whom the report is made shall depend on the nature and circumstances of the possible misconduct, (e.g., ethics committees of law firms, corporations and/or paralegal associations, local or state bar associations, local prosecutors, administrative agencies, etc.). Failure to report such knowledge is in itself misconduct and shall be treated as such under these rules.

EC–1.3(e) A paralegal shall not knowingly assist any individual with the commission of an act that is in direct violation of the Model Code/Model Rules and/or the rules and/or laws governing the jurisdiction in which the paralegal practices.

EC–1.3(f) If a paralegal possesses knowledge of future criminal activity, that knowledge must be reported to the appropriate authority immediately.

1.4 A Paralegal Shall Serve the Public Interest by Contributing to the Improvement of the Legal System and Delivery of Quality Legal Services, Including *Pro Bono Publico* Services.

ETHICAL CONSIDERATIONS

EC–1.4(a) A paralegal shall be sensitive to the legal needs of the public and shall promote the development and implementation of programs that address those needs.

EC–1.4(b) A paralegal shall support efforts to improve the legal system and access thereto and shall assist in making changes.

EC–1.4(c) A paralegal shall support and participate in the delivery of *Pro Bono Publico* services directed toward implementing and improving access to justice, the law, the legal system, or the paralegal and legal professions.

EC–1.4(d) A paralegal should aspire annually to contribute twenty-four (24) hours of *Pro Bono Publico* services under the supervision of an attorney or as authorized by administrative, statutory, or court authority to:

1. persons of limited means; or
2. charitable, religious, civic, community, governmental, and educational organizations in matters that are designed primarily to address the legal needs of persons with limited means; or
3. individuals, groups, or organizations seeking to secure or protect civil rights, civil liberties, or public rights.

The twenty-four (24) hours of *Pro Bono Publico* services contributed annually by a paralegal may consist of such services as detailed in this EC-1.4(d), and/or administrative matters designed to develop and implement the attainment of this aspiration as detailed above in EC-1.4(a) B (c), or any combination of the two.

1.5 A Paralegal Shall Preserve All Confidential Information Provided by the Client or Acquired from Other Sources before, during, and after the Course of the Professional Relationship.

ETHICAL CONSIDERATIONS

EC–1.5(a) A paralegal shall be aware of and abide by all legal authority governing confidential information in the jurisdiction in which the paralegal practices.

EC–1.5(b) A paralegal shall not use confidential information to the disadvantage of the client.

EC–1.5(c) A paralegal shall not use confidential information to the advantage of the paralegal or of a third person.

EC–1.5(d) A paralegal may reveal confidential information only after full disclosure and with the client's written consent; or, when required by law or court order; or, when necessary to prevent the client from committing an act that could result in death or serious bodily harm.

EC–1.5(e) A paralegal shall keep those individuals responsible for the legal representation of a client fully informed of any confidential information the paralegal may have pertaining to that client.

EC–1.5(f) A paralegal shall not engage in any indiscreet communications concerning clients.

1.6 A Paralegal Shall Avoid Conflicts of Interest and Shall Disclose Any Possible Conflict to the Employer or Client, as Well as to the Prospective Employers or Clients.

ETHICAL CONSIDERATIONS

EC–1.6(a) A paralegal shall act within the bounds of the law, solely for the benefit of the client, and shall be free of compromising influences and loyalties. Neither the paralegal's personal or business interest, nor those of other clients or third persons, should compromise the paralegal's professional judgment and loyalty to the client.

EC–1.6(b) A paralegal shall avoid conflicts of interest that may arise from previous assignments, whether for a present or past employer or client.

EC–1.6(c) A paralegal shall avoid conflicts of interest that may arise from family relationships and from personal and business interests.

EC–1.6(d) In order to be able to determine whether an actual or potential conflict of interest exists a paralegal shall create and maintain an effective record-keeping system that identifies clients, matters, and parties with which the paralegal has worked.

EC–1.6(e) A paralegal shall reveal sufficient non-confidential information about a client or former client to reasonably ascertain if an actual or potential conflict of interest exists.

EC–1.6(f) A paralegal shall not participate in or conduct work on any matter where a conflict of interest has been identified.

EC–1.6(g) In matters where a conflict of interest has been identified and the client consents to continued representation, a paralegal shall comply fully with the implementation and maintenance of an Ethical Wall.

1.7 A Paralegal's Title Shall Be Fully Disclosed.

ETHICAL CONSIDERATIONS

EC–1.7(a) A paralegal's title shall clearly indicate the individual's status and shall be disclosed in all business and professional communications to avoid misunderstandings and misconceptions about the paralegal's role and responsibilities.

EC–1.7(b) A paralegal's title shall be included if the paralegal's name appears on business cards, letterhead, brochures, directories, and advertisements.

EC–1.7(c) A paralegal shall not use letterhead, business cards, or other promotional materials to create a fraudulent impression of his/her status or ability to practice in the jurisdiction in which the paralegal practices.

EC–1.7(d) A paralegal shall not practice under color of any record, diploma, or certificate that has been illegally or fraudulently obtained or issued or which is misrepresentative in any way.

EC–1.7(e) A paralegal shall not participate in the creation, issuance, or dissemination of fraudulent records, diplomas, or certificates.

1.8 A Paralegal Shall Not Engage in the Unauthorized Practice of Law.

ETHICAL CONSIDERATIONS

EC–1.8(a) A paralegal shall comply with the applicable legal authority governing the unauthorized practice of law in the jurisdiction in which the paralegal practices.

§2. NFPA GUIDELINES FOR THE ENFORCEMENT OF THE MODEL CODE OF ETHICS AND PROFESSIONAL RESPONSIBILITY

2.1 Basis For Discipline

2.1(a) Disciplinary investigations and proceedings brought under authority of the Rules shall be conducted in accord with obligations imposed on the paralegal professional by the Model Code of Ethics and Professional Responsibility.

2.2 Structure of Disciplinary Committee

2.2(a) The Disciplinary Committee ("Committee") shall be made up of nine (9) members including the Chair.

2.2(b) Each member of the Committee, including any temporary replacement members, shall have demonstrated working knowledge of ethics/professional responsibility–related issues and activities.

2.2(c) The Committee shall represent a cross-section of practice areas and work experience. The following recommendations are made regarding the members of the Committee.

1. At least one paralegal with one to three years of law-related work experience.
2. At least one paralegal with five to seven years of law-related work experience.
3. At least one paralegal with over ten years of law-related work experience.
4. One paralegal educator with five to seven years of work experience; preferably in the area of ethics/professional responsibility.
5. One paralegal manager.
6. One lawyer with five to seven years of law-related work experience.
7. One lay member.

2.2(d) The Chair of the Committee shall be appointed within thirty (30) days of its members' induction. The Chair shall have no fewer than ten (10) years of law-related work experience.

2.2(e) The terms of all members of the Committee shall be staggered. Of those members initially appointed, a simple majority plus one shall be appointed to a term of one year, and the remaining members shall be appointed to a term of two years. Thereafter, all members of the Committee shall be appointed to terms of two years.

2.2(f) If for any reason the terms of a majority of the Committee will expire at the same time, members may be appointed to terms of one year to maintain continuity of the Committee.

2.2(g) The Committee shall organize from its members a three-tiered structure to investigate, prosecute, and/or adjudicate charges of misconduct. The members shall be rotated among the tiers.

2.3 Operation of Committee

2.3(a) The Committee shall meet on an as-needed basis to discuss, investigate, and/or adjudicate alleged violations of the Model Code/Model Rules.

2.3(b) A majority of the members of the Committee present at a meeting shall constitute a quorum.

2.3(c) A Recording Secretary shall be designated to maintain complete and accurate minutes of all Committee meetings. All such minutes shall be kept confidential until a decision has been made that the matter will be set for hearing as set forth in Section 6.1 below.

2.3(d) If any member of the Committee has a conflict of interest with the Charging Party, the Responding Party, or the allegations of misconduct, that member shall not take part in any hearing or deliberations concerning those allegations. If the absence of that member creates a lack of a quorum for the Committee, then a temporary replacement for the member shall be appointed.

2.3(e) Either the Charging Party or the Responding Party may request that, for good cause shown, any member of the Committee not participate in a hearing or deliberation. All such requests shall be honored. If the absence of a Committee member under those circumstances creates a lack of a quorum for the Committee, then a temporary replacement for that member shall be appointed.

2.3(f) All discussions and correspondence of the Committee shall be kept confidential until a decision has been made that the matter will be set for hearing as set forth in Section 6.1 below.

2.3(g) All correspondence from the Committee to the Responding Party regarding any charge of misconduct and any decisions made regarding the charge shall be mailed certified mail, return receipt requested, to the Responding Party's last known address and shall be clearly marked with a "Confidential" designation.

2.4 Procedure for the Reporting of Alleged Violations of the Model Code/Disciplinary Rules

2.4(a) An individual or entity in possession of non-confidential knowledge or information concerning possible instances of misconduct shall make a confidential written report to the Committee within thirty (30) days of obtaining same. This report shall include all details of the alleged misconduct.

2.4(b) The Committee so notified shall inform the Responding Party of the allegation(s) of misconduct no later than ten (10) business days after receiving the confidential written report from the Charging Party.

2.4(c) Notification to the Responding Party shall include the identity of the Charging Party, unless, for good cause shown, the Charging Party requests anonymity.

2.4(d) The Responding Party shall reply to the allegations within ten (10) business days of notification.

2.5 Procedure for the Investigation of a Charge of Misconduct

2.5(a) Upon receipt of a Charge of Misconduct ("Charge"), or on its own initiative, the Committee shall initiate an investigation.

2.5(b) If, upon initial or preliminary review, the Committee makes a determination that the charges are either without basis in fact or, if proven, would not constitute professional misconduct, the Committee shall dismiss the allegations of misconduct. If such determination of dismissal cannot be made, a formal investigation shall be initiated.

2.5(c) Upon the decision to conduct a formal investigation, the Committee shall:

1. mail to the Charging and Responding Parties within three (3) business days of that decision notice of the commencement of a formal investigation. That notification shall be in writing and shall contain a complete explanation of all Charge(s), as well as the reasons for a formal investigation and shall cite the applicable codes and rules;

2. allow the Responding Party thirty (30) days to prepare and submit a confidential response to the Committee, which response shall address each charge specifically and shall be in writing; and

3. upon receipt of the response to the notification, have thirty (30) days to investigate the Charge(s). If an extension of time is deemed necessary, that extension shall not exceed ninety (90) days.

2.5(d) Upon conclusion of the investigation, the Committee may:

1. dismiss the Charge upon the finding that it has no basis in fact;

2. dismiss the Charge upon the finding that, if proven, the Charge would not constitute Misconduct;

3.   refer the matter for hearing by the Tribunal; or
4.   in the case of criminal activity, refer the Charge(s) and all investigation results to the appropriate authority.

2.6 Procedure for a Misconduct Hearing before a Tribunal

2.6(a) Upon the decision by the Committee that a matter should be heard, all parties shall be notified and a hearing date shall be set. The hearing shall take place no more than thirty (30) days from the conclusion of the formal investigation.

2.6(b) The Responding Party shall have the right to counsel. The parties and the Tribunal shall have the right to call any witnesses and introduce any documentation that they believe will lead to the fair and reasonable resolution of the matter.

2.6(c) Upon completion of the hearing, the Tribunal shall deliberate and present a written decision to the parties in accordance with procedures as set forth by the Tribunal.

2.6(d) Notice of the decision of the Tribunal shall be appropriately published.

2.7 Sanctions

2.7(a) Upon a finding of the Tribunal that misconduct has occurred, any of the following sanctions, or others as may be deemed appropriate, may be imposed upon the Responding Party, either singularly or in combination:

1.   letter of reprimand to the Responding Party; counseling;
2.   attendance at an ethics course approved by the Tribunal; probation;
3.   suspension of license/authority to practice; revocation of license/authority to practice;
4.   imposition of a fine; assessment of costs; or
5.   in the instance of criminal activity, referral to the appropriate authority.

2.7(b) Upon the expiration of any period of probation, suspension, or revocation, the Responding Party may make application for reinstatement. With the application for reinstatement, the Responding Party must show proof of having complied with all aspects of the sanctions imposed by the Tribunal.

2.8 Appellate Procedures

2.8(a) The parties shall have the right to appeal the decision of the Tribunal in accordance with the procedure as set forth by the Tribunal.

DEFINITIONS

APPELLATE BODY   means a body established to adjudicate an appeal to any decision made by a Tribunal or other decision-making body with respect to formally heard Charges of Misconduct.

CHARGE OF MISCONDUCT   means a written submission by any individual or entity to an ethics committee, paralegal association, bar association, law enforcement agency, judicial body, government agency, or other appropriate body or entity, that sets forth non-confidential information regarding any instance of alleged misconduct by an individual paralegal or paralegal entity.

CHARGING PARTY means any individual or entity who submits a Charge of Misconduct against an individual paralegal or paralegal entity.

COMPETENCY means the demonstration of: diligence, education, skill, and mental, emotional, and physical fitness reasonably necessary for the performance of paralegal services.

CONFIDENTIAL INFORMATION means information relating to a client, whatever its source, that is not public knowledge nor available to the public. ("Non-Confidential Information" would generally include the name of the client and the identity of the matter for which the paralegal provided services.)

DISCIPLINARY HEARING means the confidential proceeding conducted by a committee or other designated body or entity concerning any instance of alleged misconduct by an individual paralegal or paralegal entity.

DISCIPLINARY COMMITTEE means any committee that has been established by an entity such as a paralegal association, bar association, judicial body, or government agency to: (a) identify, define, and investigate general ethical considerations and concerns with respect to paralegal practice; (b) administer and enforce the Model Code and Model Rules and; (c) discipline any individual paralegal or paralegal entity found to be in violation of same.

DISCLOSE means communication of information reasonably sufficient to permit identification of the significance of the matter in question.

ETHICAL WALL means the screening method implemented in order to protect a client from a conflict of interest. An Ethical Wall generally includes, but is not limited to, the following elements: (1) prohibit the paralegal from having any connection with the matter; (2) ban discussions with or the transfer of documents to or from the paralegal; (3) restrict access to files; and (4) educate all members of the firm, corporation, or entity as to the separation of the paralegal (both organizationally and physically) from the pending matter. For more information regarding the Ethical Wall, see the NFPA publication entitled "The Ethical Wall—Its Application to Paralegals."

EX PARTE means actions or communications conducted at the instance and for the benefit of one party only, and without notice to, or contestation by, any person adversely interested.

INVESTIGATION means the investigation of any charge(s) of misconduct filed against an individual paralegal or paralegal entity by a Committee.

LETTER OF REPRIMAND means a written notice of formal censure or severe reproof administered to an individual paralegal or paralegal entity for unethical or improper conduct.

MISCONDUCT means the knowing or unknowing commission of an act that is in direct violation of those Canons and Ethical Considerations of any and all applicable codes and/or rules of conduct.

PARALEGAL is synonymous with "Legal Assistant" and is defined as a person qualified through education, training, or work experience to perform substantive legal work that requires knowledge of legal concepts and is customarily, but not exclusively performed by a lawyer. This person may be retained or employed by a lawyer, law office, governmental agency, or other entity or may be authorized by administrative, statutory, or court authority to perform this work.

PRO BONO PUBLICO means providing or assisting to provide quality legal services in order to enhance access to justice for persons of limited means; charitable, religious, civic, community, governmental, and educational organizations in matters that are designed primarily to address the legal needs of persons with limited means; or individuals, groups, or organizations seeking to secure or protect civil rights, civil liberties, or public rights.

PROPER AUTHORITY means the local paralegal association, the local or state bar association, Committee(s) of the local paralegal or bar association(s), local prosecutor, administrative agency, or other tribunal empowered to investigate or act upon an instance of alleged misconduct.

RESPONDING PARTY means an individual paralegal or paralegal entity against whom a Charge of Misconduct has been submitted.

REVOCATION means the rescission of the license, certificate, or other authority to practice of an individual paralegal or paralegal entity found in violation of those Canons and Ethical Considerations of any and all applicable codes and/or rules of conduct.

SUSPENSION means the suspension of the license, certificate, or other authority to practice of an individual paralegal or paralegal entity found in violation of those Canons and Ethical Considerations of any and all applicable codes and/or rules of conduct.

TRIBUNAL means the body designated to adjudicate allegations of misconduct.

APPENDIX D

THE ABA'S MODEL GUIDELINES FOR THE UTILIZATION OF LEGAL ASSISTANT SERVICES

The following Guidelines were adopted by the ABA's policy-making body, the House of Delegates, in 1991. Lawyers are the intended audience of these Guidelines. The Guidelines, therefore, are addressed to lawyer conduct and not directly to the conduct of legal assistants and paralegals. Both the National Association of Legal Assistants (NALA) and the National Federation of Paralegal Associations (NFPA) have adopted guidelines of conduct that are directed to legal assistants and paralegals.

The Guidelines were developed to conform with the ABA's Model Rules of Professional Conduct, decided authority, and contemporary practice. Lawyers are to be directed to Model Rule 5.3 of the Model Rules of Professional Conduct and nothing in these Guidelines is intended to be inconsistent with Rule 5.3. For more information see, the ABA Center for Professional Responsibility.

Note: The terms "legal assistant" and "paralegal" are used interchangeably. Annotations and commentary to the Guidelines (which were not adopted as official policy in 1991 by the House of Delegates) are included below. They are currently being reviewed by the Standing Committee on Legal Assistants to see if they should be revised in light of current case law. A copy of the Guidelines with annotations and commentary is available through the ABA Legal Assistants Department staff office. (Phone: 312/988-5616; Fax: 312/988-5677; E-Mail: legalassts@abanet.org.)

Guideline 1

A lawyer is responsible for all of the professional actions of a legal assistant performing legal assistant services at the lawyer's direction and should take reasonable measures to ensure that the legal assistant's conduct is consistent with the lawyer's obligations under the ABA Model Rules of Professional Conduct.

COMMENT TO GUIDELINE 1.   An attorney who utilizes a legal assistant's services is responsible for determining that the legal assistant is competent to perform the tasks assigned, based on the legal assistant's education, training, and experience, and for ensuring that the legal assistant is familiar with the responsibilities of attorneys and legal assistants under the applicable rules governing professional conduct.[1]

Under principles of agency law and rules governing the conduct of attorneys, lawyers are responsible for the actions and the work product of the non-lawyers they employ. Rule 5.3 of the Model Rules[2] requires that partners and supervising attorneys ensure that the conduct of non-lawyer assistants is compatible with the lawyer's professional obligations. Several state guidelines have adopted this language. E.g., Commentary to Illinois Recommendation (A), Kansas Guideline III(a), New Hampshire Rule 35, Sub-Rule 9, and North Carolina Guideline 4. Ethical Consideration 3–6 of the Model Code encouraged lawyers to delegate tasks to legal assistants provided the lawyer maintained a direct relationship with the client, supervised appropriately, and had complete responsibility for the work product. The adoption of Rule 5.3, which incorporates these principles, implicitly reaffirms this encouragement.

Several states have addressed the issue of the lawyer's ultimate responsibility for work performed by subordinates. For example, Colorado Guideline 1.c, Kentucky Supreme Court Rule 3.700, Sub-Rule 2.C, and Michigan Guideline I provide: "The lawyer remains responsible for the actions of the legal assistant to the same extent as if such representation had been furnished entirely by the lawyer and such actions were those of the lawyer." New Mexico Guideline X states "[the] lawyer maintains ultimate responsibility for and has an ongoing duty to actively supervise the legal assistant's work performance, conduct, and product." Connecticut Recommendation 2 and Rhode Island Guideline III state specifically that lawyers are liable for malpractice for the mistakes and omissions of their legal assistants.

Finally, the lawyer should ensure that legal assistants supervised by the lawyer are familiar with the rules governing attorney conduct and that they follow those rules. See Comment to Model Rule 5.3; Illinois Recommendation (A)(5), New Hampshire Supreme Court Rule 35, Sub-Rule 9, and New Mexico, Statement of Purpose; see also NALA's Model Standards and Guidelines for the Utilization of Legal Assistants, guidelines IV, V, and VIII (1985, revised 1990) (hereafter "NALA Guidelines").

The Standing Committee and several of those who have commented upon these Guidelines regard Guideline 1 as a comprehensive statement of general principle governing lawyers who utilize legal assistant services in the practice of law. As such it, in effect, is a part of each of the remaining Guidelines.

---

1. Attorneys, of course, are not liable for violation of the ABA Model Rules of Professional Conduct ("Model Rules") unless the Model Rules have been adopted as the code of professional conduct in a jurisdiction in which the lawyer practices. They are referenced in this model guideline for illustrative purposes; if the guideline is to be adopted, the reference should be modified to the jurisdiction's rules of professional conduct.
2. The Model Rules were first adopted by the ABA House of Delegates in August of 1983. Since that time many states have adopted the Model Rules to govern the professional conduct of lawyers licensed in those states. Since a number of states still utilize a version of the Model Code of Professional Responsibility ("Model Code"), which was adopted by the House of Delegates in August of 1969, however, these comments will refer to both the Model Rules and the predecessor Model Code (and to the Ethical Considerations and Disciplinary Rules found under the canons in the Model Code).

Paralegal Associations

NFPA Associations

REGION I

Alaska Association of Paralegals
P.O. Box 101956
Anchorage, AK 99510-1956

Hawaii Paralegal Association
P.O. Box 674
Honolulu, HI 96809

Oregon Paralegal Association
P.O. Box 8523
Portland, OR 97207

Paralegal Association of Southern
    Nevada
P.O. Box 1752
Las Vegas, NV 89125-1752

Sacramento Valley Paralegal
    Association
P.O. Box 453
Sacramento, CA 95812-0453

San Diego Paralegal Association
P.O. Box 87449
San Diego, CA 92138-7449

San Francisco Paralegal Association
P.O. Box 2110
San Francisco, CA 94126-2110

Washington State Paralegal Association
P.O. Box 58530
Seattle WA 98138

REGION II

Dallas Area Paralegal Association
P.O. Box 12533
Dallas, TX 75225

Illinois Paralegal Association
P.O. Box 452
New Lenox, IL 60451-0452

Kansas City Paralegal Association
1912 Clay Street
North Kansas City, MO 64116

Kansas Paralegal Association
P.O. Box 1675
Topeka, KS 66601

Minnesota Paralegal Association
1711 W. County Road B #300N
Roseville, MN 55113

New Orleans Paralegal Association
P.O. Box 30604
New Orleans, LA 70190

Paralegal Association of Wisconsin
P.O. Box 510892
Milwaukee, WI 53203-0151

Rocky Mountain Paralegal Association
P.O. Box 481864
Denver, CO 80248-1864

REGION III

Cincinnati Paralegal Association
P.O. Box 1515
Cincinnati, OH 45201

The Greater Dayton Paralegal
    Association, Inc.
P.O. Box 515, Mid-City Station
Dayton, OH 45402

Greater Lexington Paralegal
    Association, Inc.
P.O. Box 574
Lexington, KY 40586

Gulf Coast Paralegal Association
P.O. Box 66705
Mobile, AL 36660

Indiana Paralegal Association, Inc.
P.O. Box 44518
Indianapolis, IN 46204

Memphis Paralegal Association
P.O. Box 3646
Memphis, TN 38173

The Michiana Paralegal
Association, Inc.
P.O. Box 11458
South Bend, IN 46634

Memphis Paralegal Association
P.O. Box 3646
Memphis, TN 38173-0646

Middle Tennessee Paralegal
Association
P.O. Box 198006
Nashville, TN 37219

Northeast Indiana Paralegal
Association, Inc.
P.O. Box 13646
Fort Wayne, IN 46865

Northeastern Ohio Paralegal
Association
P.O. Box 80068
Akron, OH 44308-0068

Palmetto Paralegal Association
P.O. Box 11634
Columbia, SC 29211-1634

Paralegal Association of Central Ohio
P.O. Box 15182
Columbus, OH 43215-0182

Tampa Bay Paralegal Organization
P.O. Box 2840
Tampa, FL 33601

REGION IV

Central Pennsylvania Paralegal
Association
P.O. Box 11814
Harrisburg, PA 17108

Chester County Paralegal
Association
P.O. Box 295
West Chester, PA 19381-0295

Fredericksburg Paralegal Association
P.O. Box 7351
Fredericksburg, VA 22404

Lycoming County Paralegal
Association
P.O. Box 991
Williamsport, PA 17701

Maryland Association of
Paralegals, Inc.
550 M Ritchie Highway PMB, #203
Severna Park, MD 21146

Montgomery County Paralegal
Association
P.O. Box 1765
Blue Bell, PA 19422

National Capital Area Paralegal
Association
P.O. Box 27607
Washington, DC 20038-7607

The Philadelphia Association of
Paralegals
P.O. Box 59179
Philadelphia, PA 19102-9179

South Jersey Paralegal Association
P.O. Box 355
Haddonfield, NJ 08033

REGION V

Capital District Paralegal Association
P.O. Box 12562
Albany, NY 12212-2562

Central Connecticut Paralegal
Association
P.O. Box 230594
Hartford, CT 06123-0594

Central Massachusetts Paralegal
Association
P.O. Box 444
Worcester, MA 01614

Connecticut Association of Paralegals
P.O. Box 134
Bridgeport, CT 06601-0134

Long Island Paralegal Association
1877 Bly Road
East Meadow, NY 11554-1158

Manhattan Paralegal Association, Inc.
P.O. Box 4006
Grand Central Station
New York, NY 10163

Massachusetts Paralegal
Association, Inc.
P.O. Box 1381
Marblehead, MA 01945

The New Haven County Association
of Paralegals
P.O. Box 862
New Haven, CT 06504-0862

Paralegal Association of Rochester, Inc.
P.O. Box 40567
Rochester, NY 14604

Rhode Island Paralegals Association
P.O. Box 1003
Providence, RI 02901

Vermont Paralegal Organization
P.O. Box 5755
Burlington, VT 05402

West/Rock Paralegal Association
P.O. Box 668
New City, NY 10956

Western Massachusetts Paralegal
Association, Inc.
P.O. Box 30005
Springfield, MA 01103

Western New York Paralegal
Association, Inc.
P.O. Box 207
Niagara Square Station
Buffalo, NY 14201

NALA STATE AND LOCAL AFFILIATES

Alabama

Alabama Association of Legal
Assistants
P.O. Box 55921
Birmingham, AL, 35255-5921

Legal Assistant Society of Virginia
College
Dept of Paralegal Studies
800 28th Avenue
Birmingham, AL 35209

Samford Paralegal Association
Birmingham, AL

Arizona

Arizona Paralegal Association
P.O. Box 392
Phoenix, AZ 85001

Legal Assistants of Metropolitan
Phoenix
P.O. Box 13005
Phoenix, AZ 85002

Tuscon Association of Legal Assistants
Tucson, AL

Arkansas

Arkansas Association of Legal
Assistants
120 E. 4th Street
Little Rock, AR 72201

California

Los Angeles Paralegal Association
P.O. Box 71708
Los Angeles, CA 90071

Orange County Paralegal Association
P.O. Box 8512
Newport Beach, CA 92658

Palomar College
1140 West Mission Road
San Marcos, CA 92069-1487

Paralegal Association of Santa Clara
  County
P.O. Box 26736
San Jose, CA 95159-6736
(408) 235-0301

San Joaquin Association of Legal
  Assistants
P.O. Box 28515
Fresno, CA 93729-8515
(559) 433-2328

Santa Barbara Paralegal Association
1224 Coast Village Circle, Suite 32
Santa Barbara, CA 93108.

Ventura County Association of Legal
  Assistants
P.O. Box 24229
Ventura, CA 93002

Colorado

Association of Legal Assistants of
  Colorado
Colorado Springs, CO

Legal Assistants of the Western Slope

Florida

Central Florida Paralegal Association
P.O. Box 1107
Orlando, FL 32802

Gainesville Association of
  Paralegals, Inc.
P.O. Box 2519
Gainesville, FL 32602
(904) 462-2249

Northeast Florida Paralegal
  Association, Inc.
P.O. Box 52264
Jacksonville, FL 32201

Northwest Florida Paralegal
  Association
P.O. Box 1333
Pensacola, FL 32502

Paralegal Association of Florida
P.O. Box 7073
West Palm Beach, FL 33405
(800) 433-4352

South Florida Paralegal Association
P.O. Box 110603
Miami, FL 33111
(305) 944-0204

Southwest Florida Paralegal
  Association, Inc.
P.O. Box 2094
Sarasota, FL 34230-2094

Volusia Association of Paralegals
P.O. Box 15075
Daytona Beach, FL 32115-5075

Georgia

Southeastern Association of Legal
  Assistants

Illinois

Central Illinois Paralegal Association
P.O. Box 1948
Bloomington, IL 61702

Indiana

Indiana Legal Assistants, Inc.
230 East Ohio Street, 4th Floor
Indianapolis, IN 47204

Iowa

Iowa Association of Legal Assistants
P.O. Box 93153
Des Moines, IA 50393

Kansas

Heartland Association of Legal
  Assistants
P.O. Box 12413
Overland Park, KS 66282-2413
(913) 477-7625

Kansas Association of Legal
  Assistants
P.O. Box 47031
Witchita, KS 67201
(316) 291-9711

Louisiana

Louisiana State Paralegal Association
P.O. Box 1705
Lake Charles, LA 70602-1705
(337) 436-0522

Northwest Louisiana Paralegal
  Association
333 Texas Street, Suite 717
Shreveport, LA 71101-3673
(318) 227-1990

Michigan

Legal Assistants Association of
  Michigan
P.O. Box 80125
Lansing, MI 48908-0125

Mississippi

Mississippi Association of Legal
  Assistants
P.O. Box 996
Jackson, MS 39205

University of Southern Mississippi
  Society for Paralegal Studies
The University of Southern Mississippi
2701 Hardy Street
Hattiesburg, MS 39406

Missouri

PSI SIGMA CHI Paralegal Society of
  Springfield College
Springfield College
1010 West Sunshine Street
Springfield, MO 65807

Montana

Montana Association of Legal
  Assistants
P.O. Box 9016
Missoula, MT 59807-9016

Nebraska

Nebraska Association of Legal
  Assistants
P.O. Box 24943
Omaha, NE 68124

Nevada

Sierra Nevada Association of
  Paralegals
Reno, NV

New Jersey

The Legal Assistants Association of
  New Jersey, Inc.
P.O. Box 142
Caldwell, NJ 07006

North Carolina

Coastal Carolina Paralegal Club
Coastal Carolina Community
  College
444 Western Blvd.
Jacksonville, NC 28546

Metrolina Paralegal Association
P.O. Box 36260
Charlotte, NC 28236

North Carolina Paralegal Association
P.O. Box 36264
Charlotte, NC 28236-6264
(800) 479-1905

North Dakota

Red River Valley Legal Assistants

Western Dakota Association of Legal
Assistants
Bismarck, ND

Ohio

Toledo Association of Legal Assistants
Toledo, OH

Oklahoma

City College Legal Association
City College
2620 S Service Road
Moore, OK 73160
(405) 329-5627

Northeastern State University Legal
Assistant Association
Northeastern State University
600 N. Grand Ave.
Tahlequah, OK 74464

Oklahoma Paralegal Association
P.O. Box 5784
Enid, OK 73702-5784

TCC Student Association of Legal
Assistants
Tulsa Community College
Tulsa, OK

Tulsa Association of Legal Assistants
P.O. Box 1484
Tulsa, OK 74101-1484

Oregon

Pacific Northwest Legal Assistants
Association
P.O. Box 1835
Eugene, OR 97440

Pennsylvania

Keystone Legal Assistant Association
P.O. Box 25
Enola, PA 19381

South Carolina

Charleston Association of Legal
Assistants, Inc. (CALA)
P.O. Box 1511
Charleston, SC 29402

Greenville Association of Legal
Assistants, Inc. (GALA)

P.O. Box 10491, F.S.
Greenville, SC 29603

Tri-County Paralegal Association, Inc.
(TCPA)
P.O. Box 62691
North Charleston, SC 29419-2691

South Dakota

National American University Student
Association of Legal Assistants
321 Kansas City St.
Rapid City, SD 57701

South Dakota Paralegal Association
P.O. Box 8381
Rapid City, SD 57709

Tennessee

Greater Memphis Paralegal
Alliance, Inc.
P.O. Box 3846
Memphis, TN 38173
(901) 527-6254

Tennessee Paralegal Association
3295 Highway 45 South
Jackson, TN 38301
(800) 727-0622

Texas

Capital Area Paralegal Association
P.O. Box 773
Austin, TX 78767

El Paso Association of Legal Assistants
P.O. Box 6
El Paso, TX 79940

Legal Assistants of North Texas
Association
P.O. Box 131207
Dallas, TX 75313

Legal Assistants Association—Permian
Basin
Midland, TX

Northeast Texas Association of Legal
Assistants "NTALA"
P.O. Box 2284
Longview, TX 75606

Southeast Texas Association of Legal
Assistants
P.O. Box 813
Beaumont, TX 77704

Texas Panhandle Association of Legal
Assistants "TPALA"

P.O. Box 112775
Amarillo, TX

Tyler Area Association of Legal
Assistants
Tyler, TX

West Texas Association of Legal
Assistants
Laredo, TX

Utah

Legal Assistants Association of Utah
Salt Lake City, UT

Virgin Islands

Virgin Islands Association of Legal
Assistants, Inc.
P.O. Box 297
St. Thomas, VI 00804
(340) 775-8011

Virginia

Peninsula Legal Assistants, Inc.
115 Freemoor Dr.
Poquoson, VA 23662

Richmond Area Association of Legal
Assistants
P.O. Box 384
Richmond, VA 23218

Roanoke Valley Paralegal Association
P.O. Box 1505
Roanoke, VA 24007-1505

Tidewater Association of Legal
Assistants
P.O. Box 3566
Norfolk, VA 23514-3566

West Virginia

Legal Assistants of West Virginia, Inc.
P.O. Box 1744
Clarksburg, WV 26302-1744

Wisconsin

Madison Area Paralegal Association
P.O. Box 2242
Madison, WI 53701-2242

Wyoming

Legal Assistants of Wyoming
P.O. Box 155
Casper, WY 82602-0155

State and Major Local Bar Associations

Alabama

Alabama State Bar
Founded 1879
415 Dexter Avenue
Montgomery, AL 36104
(334) 269-1515
fax: (334) 261-6310

Birmingham Bar Assn.
Founded 1885
2021 2d Avenue N
Birmingham, AL 35203
(205) 251-8006
fax: (205) 251-7193

Alaska

Alaska Bar Assn.
Founded 1955
P.O. Box 100279
Anchorage, AK 99510
(907) 272-7469
fax: (907) 272-2932

Arizona

Maricopa County Bar Assn.
Founded 1914
303 E. Palm Lane
Phoenix, AZ 85004-1532
(602) 257-4200
fax: (602) 257-0522

State Bar of Arizona
Founded 1933
111 W. Monroe Street, Ste. 1800
Phoenix, AZ 85003-1742
(602) 252-4804
fax: (602) 271-4930

Arkansas

Arkansas Bar Assn.
Founded 1899
400 W. Markham
Little Rock, AZ 72201
(501) 375-4605
fax: (501) 375-4901

California

Bar Assn. of San Francisco
Founded 1872
465 California Street, Ste. 1100
San Francisco, CA 94104
(415) 982-1600

Beverly Hills Bar Assn.
Founded 1931
300 S. Beverly Drive, #201
Beverly Hills, CA 90212
(310) 553-6644
fax: (310) 284-8290

Eastern Alameda County Bar Assn.
Founded 1877
7901 Stoneridge Drive, Ste. 501
Pleasanton, CA 94588
(510) 893-7160
fax: (510) 893-3119

Lawyers' Club of Los Angeles
Founded 1930
P.O. Box 862170
Los Angeles, CA 90086
(213) 624-2525

Lawyers' Club of San Francisco
Founded 1946
685 Market Street, Ste. 750
San Francisco, CA 94105
(415) 882-9150
fax: (415) 882-7170

Los Angeles County Bar Assn.
Founded 1878
P.O. Box 55020
Los Angeles, CA 90055
(213) 896-6424
fax: (213) 896-6500

Orange County Bar Assn.
P.O. Box 17777
Irvine, CA 92623
(949) 440-6700
fax: (949) 440-6710

Sacramento County Bar Assn.
Founded 1925
901 H. Street, Ste. 101
Sacramento, CA 95814
(916) 448-1087
fax: (916) 448-6930

San Diego County Bar Assn.
Founded 1920
1333 Seventh Avenue
San Diego, CA 92101
(619) 231-0781
fax: (619) 338-0042

Santa Clara County Bar Assn.
Founded 1917
4 N. Second Street, Ste. 400
San Jose, CA 95113
(408) 287-2557
fax: (408) 287-6083

State Bar of California
Founded 1927
180 Howard Street
San Francisco, CA 94105
(415) 538-2000

Colorado

The Colorado Bar Assn.
Founded 1897
1900 Grant Street, Ste. 900
Denver, CO 80203
(303) 860-1115
fax: (303) 894-0821

Denver Bar Assn.
Founded 1891
1900 Grant Street, Ste. 900
Denver, CO 80203-4309
(303) 860-1115
fax: (303) 894-0821

Connecticut

Connecticut Bar Assn.
Founded 1875
30 Bank Street
New Britain, CT 06050
(860) 223-4400
fax: (860) 223-4488

Hartford County Bar Assn.
Founded 1783
179 Allen Street, Ste. 210
Hartford, CT 06103
(860) 525-8106
fax: (860) 293-1345

Delaware

Delaware State Bar Assn.
Founded 1923
301 N. Market Street

Wilmington, DE 19801
(302) 658-5279
fax: (302) 658-5212

District of Columbia

The Bar Assn. of the Dist. of Columbia
Founded 1871
1819 H Street, NW, 12th Floor
Washington, DC 20006-3690
(202) 223-6600
fax: (202) 293-3388

The District of Columbia Bar
Founded 1972
1250 H Street NW, 6th Floor
Washington, DC 20005-3908
(202) 737-4700
fax: (202) 626-3473

Florida

The Dade County Bar Assn.
Founded 1920
123 NW First Avenue, #214
Miami, FL 33128
(305) 371-2220
fax: (305) 539-9749

The Florida Bar
Founded 1950
650 Apalachee Parkway
Tallahassee, FL 32399-2300
(904) 561-5600
fax: (904) 561-5827

Hillsborough County Bar Assn.
Founded 1937
101 E. Kennedy Blvd., Ste. 2110
Tampa, FL 33647
(813) 221-7777
fax: (813) 221-7778

Orange County Bar Assn.
880 N. Orange Avenue, #100
Orlando, FL 32801
(407) 422-4551
fax: (407) 843-3470

Georgia

Atlanta Bar Assn.
Founded 1888
400 International Tower
229 Peachtree Street NE
Atlanta, GA 30303
(404) 521-0781
fax: (404) 522-0269

State Bar of Georgia
Founded 1964
104 Marietta Street NW, Ste. 100
50 Hurt Plaza

Atlanta, GA 30303
(404) 527-8700
fax: (404) 527-8717

Hawaii

Hawaii State Bar Assn.
Founded 1899
1132 Bishop Street,
Ste. 906
Honolulu, HI 96813
(808) 537-1868
fax: (808) 521-7936

Idaho

Idaho State Bar
Founded 1923
P.O. Box 895
Boise, ID 83701
(208) 334-4500
fax: (208) 334-4515

Illinois

The Chicago Bar Assn.
Founded 1874
321 South Plymouth Court
Chicago, IL 60604-3997
(313) 554-2000
fax: (312) 554-2054

Chicago Council of Lawyers
Founded 1969
220 S. State Street, Ste. 800
One Quincy Court
Chicago, IL 60604
(312) 427-0710
fax: (312) 427-0181

Illinois State Bar Assn.
Founded 1877
424 S. Second Street
Springfield, IL 62701
(217) 525-1760
fax: (217) 525-0712

Indiana

Indiana State Bar Assn.
Founded 1896
230 E. Ohio, 4th Floor
Indianapolis, IN 46204
317/639-5465
fax: 317/266-2588

Indianapolis Bar Assn.
Founded 1878
107 N. Pennsylvania Street,
Ste. 200
Indianapolis, IN 46204
317/269-2000
fax: 317/464-8118

Iowa

The Iowa State Bar Assn.
Founded 1874
521 E. Locust, 3rd Floor
Des Moines, IA 50309
(515) 243-3179
fax: (515) 243-2511

Kansas

Kansas Bar Assn.
Founded 1882
1200 SW Harrison
Topeka, KS 66612-1806
(785) 234-5696
fax: (785) 234-3813

Kentucky

Kentucky Bar Assn.
Founded 1871
514 West Main Street
Frankfort, KY 40601-1883
(501) 564-3795
fax: (502) 564-3225

Louisville Bar Assn.
Founded 1900
600 W. Main Street
Louisville, KY 40202-2633
(502) 583-5314
fax: (502) 583-4113

Louisiana

Louisiana State Bar Assn.
Founded 1941
601 St. Charles Avenue
New Orleans, LA 70130
(504) 566-1600
fax: (504) 566-0930

New Orleans Bar Assn.
Founded 1924
228 Saint Charles Avenue, Ste. 1223
New Orleans, LA 70130
(504) 525-7453
fax: (504) 525-6549

Maine

Maine State Bar Assn.
Founded 1891
P.O. Box 788
Augusta, ME 04332-0788
(207) 622-7523
fax: (207) 623-0083

Maryland

Bar Assn. of Baltimore City
Founded 1880
111 N. Calvert Street, Ste. 627

Baltimore, MD 21202
(410) 539-5936
fax: (410) 685-3420

Bar Association of Montgomery
County
Founded 1894
27 W. Jefferson Street
Rockville, MD 20850
(301) 424-3454
fax: (301) 217-9327

Maryland State Bar Assn., Inc.
Founded 1896
520 W. Fayette Street
Baltimore, MD 20201
(410) 685-7878
fax: (410) 685-1016

Massachusetts

Boston Bar Assn.
Founded 1761
16 Beacon Street
Boston, MA 02018
(617) 742-0615
fax: (617) 523-0127

Massachusetts Bar Assn.
Founded 1911
20 West Street
Boston, MA 02111-1218
(617) 542-3602

Michigan

Detroit Bar Assn.
Founded 1836
2100 Buhl Building
535 Griswold
Detroit, MI 48226
(313) 961-6120
fax: (313) 965-0842

Oakland County Bar Assn.
Founded 1934
1760 S. Telegraph, Ste. 100
Bloomfield Hills, MI 48302-0181
(248) 334-3400
fax: (248) 334-7757

State Bar of Michigan
Founded 1936
306 Townsend Street
Lansing, MI 48933-2083
(800) 968-1442
fax: (517) 482-6248

Minnesota

Hennepin County Bar Assn.
Founded 1919
600 Nicollet Mall, Ste. 390
Minneapolis, MN 55402

(612) 752-6600
fax: (612) 752-6601

Minnesota State Bar Assn.
Founded 1883
600 Nicollet Mall, #380
Minneapolis, MN 55402
(612) 333-1183
fax: (612) 333-4927

Ramsey County Bar Assn.
Founded 1883
E-1401 First National Bank Bldg.
332 Minnesota Street
St. Paul, MN 55101
(612) 222-0846
fax: (612) 223-8344

Mississippi

Mississippi Bar
Founded 1905
P.O. Box 2168
Jackson, MS 39225-2168
(601) 948-4471
fax: (601) 355-8635

Missouri

Bar Assn. of Metropolitan St. Louis
Founded 1874
720 Olive, Ste. 2900
St. Louis, MO 63101
(314) 421-4134
fax: (314) 421-0013

Kansas City Metropolitan Bar
Association
Founded 1884
1125 Grand, Ste. 400
Kansas City, MO 64106
(816) 474-4322
fax: (816) 474-0103

The Missouri Bar
Founded 1944
P.O. Box 119
Jefferson City, MO 65102
(314) 635-4128
fax: (314) 635-2811

Montana

State Bar of Montana
Founded 1975
P.O. Box 577
Helena, MT 59624
(406) 442-7660
fax: (406) 442-7763

Nebraska

Nebraska State Bar Assn.
Founded 1877
635 South 14th Street

Lincoln, NE 68501
(402) 475-7091
fax: (402) 475-7098

Nevada

State Bar of Nevada
Founded 1928
600 E. Charleston Blvd.
Las Vegas, NV 89104
(702) 382-2200
fax: (702) 385-2878

New Hampshire

New Hampshire Bar Assn.
Founded 1873
112 Pleasant Street
Concord, NH 03301
(603) 224-6942
fax: (603) 224-2910

New Jersey

Bergen County Bar
Founded 1898
15 Bergen Street
Hackensack, NJ 07601
(201) 488-0044
fax: (201) 488-0073

Essex County Bar Assn.
Founded 1898
One Riverfront Plaza
7th Floor
Newark, NJ 07102-5497
(201) 622-7753
fax: (201) 622-4341

New Jersey State Bar Assn.
Founded 1899
New Jersey Law Center
One Constitution Square
New Brunswick, NJ 08901-1500
(908) 249-5000
fax: (908) 249-2815

New Mexico

State Bar of New Mexico
Founded 1886
P.O. Box 25883
Albuquerque, NM 87125
(505) 842-6132
fax: (505) 843-8765

New York

The Assn. of the Bar of the City of
    New York
Founded 1871
42 W. 44th Street

New York, NY 10036
(212) 382-6620
fax: (212) 302-8219

Bar Assn. of Erie County
Founded 1887
438 Main St., Sixth Floor
Buffalo, NY 14202
(716) 852-8687
fax: (716) 856-7641

Bar Assn. of Nassau County, Inc.
Founded 1899
15th & West Streets
Mineola, NY 11501
(516) 747-4070
fax: (516) 747-4147

Brooklyn Bar Assn.
Founded 1872
123 Remsen Street
Brooklyn, NY 11201-4212
(718) 624-0675
fax: (718) 797-1713

Monroe County Bar Assn.
Founded 1892
One Exchange Street, 5th Floor
Rochester, NY 14614
(716) 546-1817
fax: (716) 546-1807

New York County Lawyers Assn.
Founded 1908
14 Vesey Street
New York, NY 10007
(212) 267-6646
fax: (212) 406-9252

New York State Bar Assn.
Founded 1876
One Elk Street
Albany, NY 12207
(518) 463-3200
fax: (518) 463-4276

Queens County Bar Assn.
Founded 1876
90-35 148th Street
Jamaica, NY 11435
(718) 291-4500
fax: (718) 657-1789

Suffolk County Bar Assn.
Founded 1908
560 Wheeler Road
Hauppauge, NY 11788-4357
(516) 234-5511
fax: (516) 234-5899

Westchester County Bar Assn.
Founded 1896
300 Hamilton Avenue, Ste. 400

White Plains, NY 10601
(914) 761-3707
fax: (914) 761-9402

North Carolina

North Carolina Bar Assn.
Founded 1899
P.O. Box 3688
Cary, NC 27513
(919) 677-0561
fax: (919) 677-0761

North Carolina State Bar
Founded 1933
208 Fayetteville Street Mall
P.O. Box 25908
Raleigh, NC 27605
(919) 828-4620
fax: (919) 821-9168

10th Judicial District Bar Assn.
800 Weston Pkwy.
Cary, NC 27513
(919) 677-9903
fax: (919) 677-0761

North Dakota

State Bar Assn. of North Dakota
Founded 1921
515½ E. Broadway, Ste. 101
Bismark, ND 58501
(701) 255-1404
fax: (701) 224-1621

Ohio

Cincinnati Bar Assn.
Founded 1873
The Cincinnati Bar Center
225 E. Sixth Street, 2nd Floor
Cincinnati, OH 45202-3209
(513) 381-8213
fax: (513) 381-0528

Cleveland Bar Assn.
Founded 1873
113 St. Clair Avenue, Ste. 100 NE
Cleveland, OH 44114-5193
(216) 696-3525
fax: (216) 696-2413

Columbus Bar Assn.
Founded 1869
175 South 3rd Street, Ste. 1100
Columbus, OH 43215-5193
(614) 221-4112
fax: (614) 221-4850

Cuyahoga County Bar Assn.
Founded 1928
526 Superior Avenue, Ste. 1240

Cleveland, OH 44114
(216) 621-5112
fax: (216) 523-2259

Ohio State Bar Assn.
Founded 1880
1700 Lake Shore Drive
Columbus, OH 43216-6562
(614) 487-2050
fax: (614) 487-1008

Oklahoma

Oklahoma Bar Assn.
Founded 1939
1901 N. Lincoln Blvd.
P.O. Box 53036
Oklahoma City, OK 73152
(405) 524-2365
fax: (405) 524-1115

Oklahoma County Bar Assn.
Founded 1902
119 N. Robinson, Ste. 240
Oklahoma, OK 73102
(405) 236-8421
fax: (405) 232-2210

Tulsa County Bar Assn.
Founded 1903
1446 South Boston
Tulsa, OK 74119
(916) 584-5243
fax: (918) 592-0208

Oregon

Multnomah Bar Assn.
Founded 1906
630 SW Fifth Avenue, Ste. 200
Portland, OR 97204
(503) 222-3275
fax: (503) 243-1881

Oregon State Bar
Founded 1890
5200 SW Meadows Road
Lake Oswego, OR 97035
(503) 620-0222
fax: (503) 684-1366

Pennsylvania

Allegheny County Bar Assn.
Founded 1870
436 Seventh Avenue
400 Kopper's Building
Pittsburgh, PA 15219
(412) 261-6161
fax: (412) 261-3622

Pennsylvania Bar Assn.
Founded 1895
P.O. Box 186, 100 South Street

Harrisburg, PA 17108
(717) 238-6715
fax: (717) 238-1204

Philadelphia Bar Assn.
Founded 1802
1101 Market Street, 11th Floor
Philadelphia, PA 19107-2911
(215) 238-6338
fax: (215) 238-1267

Puerto Rico

Puerto Rico Bar Assn.
Founded 1840
Appartado 9021900
San Juan, PR 00902-1900
(787) 721-3358
fax: (787) 721-0330

Rhode Island

Rhode Island Bar Assn.
Founded 1898
115 Cedar Street
Providence, RI 02903
(401) 421-5740
fax: (401) 421-2703

South Carolina

South Carolina Bar
Founded 1975
950 Taylor Street
Columbia, SC 29202
(803) 799-6653
fax: (803) 799-4118

South Dakota

State Bar of South Dakota
Founded 1931
222 E. Capitol Avenue
Pierre, SD 57501
(605) 224-7554
fax: (605) 224-0282

Tennessee

Tennessee Bar Assn.
Founded 1831
221 Fourth Avenue N, Ste. 400
Nashville, TN 37129-2198
(615) 383-7421
fax: (615) 297-8058

Tennessee Bar Assn.
Founded 1881
3622 West End Avenue
Nashville, TN 37205-2403

Texas

Dallas Bar Assn.
Founded 1873

2101 Ross Avenue
Dallas, TX 75201
(214) 969-7066
fax: (214) 880-0807

Houston Bar Assn.
Founded 1870
1001 Fannin, Ste. 1300
Houston, TX 77002-6708
(713) 759-1133
fax: (713) 759-1710

San Antonio Bar Assn.
Founded 1916
Bexar County Courthouse,
100 Dolorasa, 5th Floor
San Antonio, TX 78205
(210) 227-8822
fax: (210) 271-9614

State Bar of Texas
Founded 1939
P.O. Box 12487
Austin, TX 78711
(512) 463-1463 or
(800) 204-2222
fax: (512) 463-7388

Utah

Utah State Bar
Founded 1931
645 S. 200 East, #310
Salt Lake City, UT 84111
(801) 531-9077
fax: (801) 531-0660

Vermont

Vermont Bar Assn.
Founded 1878
35-37 Court Street, P.O. Box 100
Montpelier, VT 05601
(802) 223-2020
fax: (802) 223-1573

Virginia

Fairfax Bar Assn.
Founded 1935
4110 Chain Bridge Road, #303
Fairfax, VA 22030
(703) 246-2740
fax: (703) 273-1274

The Virginia Bar Assn.
Founded 1888
7th & Franklin Bldg.
701 E. Franklin Street, Ste. 1120
Richmond, VA 23219
(804) 644-0052

Virginia State Bar
Founded 1938

VA State Bar
707 E. Main Street, Ste. 1500
Richmond, VA 23219-2803
(804) 775-0500
fax: (804) 775-0501

Washington

King County Bar Assn.
Founded 1906
The Bank of CA Bldg., Suite 600
900 4th Avenue
Seattle, WA 98164
(206) 624-9365
fax: (206) 382-1270

Washington State Bar Assn.
Founded 1890
2101 Fourth Avenue, Ste. 400
Seattle, WA 98121-2330
(206) 443-9722
fax: (206) 727-8319

West Virginia

The West Virginia Bar Assn.
Founded 1886

904 Security Bldg.
P.O. Box 2162
Huntington, WV 25722
(304)522-2652
fax: (304) 522-2795

West Virginia State Bar
Founded 1947
2006 Kanawha Blvd. E
Charleston, WV 25311
(304) 558-2456
fax: (304) 558-2567

Wisconsin

Milwaukee Bar Assn.
Founded 1858
424 East Wells Street
Milwaukee, WI 53202
(414) 274-6760
fax: (414) 274-6765

State Bar of WI
P.O. Box 7158
Madison, WI 53707-7158
(608) 257-3838
fax: (608) 257-5502

Wyoming

Wyoming State Bar
Founded 1915
500 Randall Avenue
Cheyenne, WY 82001
(307) 632-9061
fax: (307) 632-3737

Guam

Guam Bar Assn.
259 Martyr Street, Ste. 101
Hagatna, Guam 96910
(011) 671/477-7010
fax: (011) 671/477-9734

Northern Mariana Islands Bar Assn.
Founded 1985

Virgin Islands

Virgin Islands Bar Assn.
Founded 1921
P.O. Box 4108
Christiansted, VI 00822
(809) 778-7497
fax: (809) 773-5060

APPENDIX H

INFORMATION ON NALA'S CLA AND CLAS EXAMINATIONS

BACKGROUND AND NUMBERS

Established in 1976, the Certified Legal Assistant program has enabled the profession to develop a strong and responsive self-regulatory program offering a nationwide credential for legal assistants. The Certified Legal Assistant program establishes and serves as a:

- National professional standard for legal assistants.
- Means of identifying those who have reached this standard.
- Credentialing program responsive to the needs of legal assistants and responsive to the fact that this form of self-regulation is necessary to strengthen and expand development of this career field.
- Positive, ongoing, voluntary program to encourage the growth of the legal-assistant profession, attesting to and encouraging a high level of achievement.

As of January 2003, there are 11,678 Certified Legal Assistants and over 1,010 Certified Legal Assistant Specialists in the United States. Over 24,000 legal assistants have participated in this program. The distribution of CLAs is as follows:

CLA Examination Data
States Represented at Time of
Certification as of January 31, 2003

Alabama	143	Maryland	15	Puerto Rico	2
Alaska	81	Massachusetts	14	Rhode Island	4
Arizona	842	Michigan	139	South Carolina	111
Arkansas	71	Minnesota	23	South Dakota	120
California	599	Mississippi	126	Tennessee	201
Colorado	214	Missouri	93	Texas	2,404
Connecticut	4	Montana	59	Utah	113
Delaware	2	Nebraska	115	Vermont	2
Florida	3,039	Nevada	222	Virginia	249
Georgia	153	New Hampshire	70	Virgin Islands	34
Hawaii	3	New Jersey	55	Washington	49
Idaho	41	New Mexico	176	Washington, D.C.	5
Illinois	56	New York	71	West Virginia	67
Indiana	46	North Carolina	318	Wisconsin	34
Iowa	113	North Dakota	94	Wyoming	110
Kansas	183	Ohio	103	Canada	2
Kentucky	19	Oklahoma	476	France	1
Louisiana	147	Oregon	108		
Maine	64	Pennsylvania	74		

On December 31, 1990, 3,974 legal assistants had achieved the CLA designation. As of the December 2002 testing session, there were 11,678 Certified Legal Assistants. Since the examination was first administered in 1976, over 24,000 legal assistants have participated in this program.

In order to pass, a legal assistant must successfully complete all five sections of the CLA examination. Approximately 40 percent of the examinees pass all sections on the first sitting; over 60 percent of the examinees pass four or more sections of the examination on the first sitting.

Use of the CLA credential signifies that a legal assistant is capable of providing superior services to firms and corporations. National surveys consistently show Certified Legal Assistants are better paid and better utilized in a field where attorneys are looking for a credible, dependable way to measure ability. The credential has been recognized by the American Bar Association as a designation which marks a high level of professional achievement. The CLA credential has also been recognized by over forty-seven legal-assistant organizations and numerous bar associations.

For information concerning standards of professional credentialing programs, see the article "The Certified Legal Assistant Program and the United States Supreme Court Decision in *Peel v. Attorney Registration and Disciplinary Committee of Illinois.*" In this case, the United States Supreme Court addressed the issue concerning the utilization of professional credentials awarded by private organizations. In *Peel v. Attorney Registration and Disciplinary Committee of Illinois,* 110 S.Ct. 2281 (1990), the Court suggested that a claim of certification is truthful and not misleading if it meets certain standards. This article details those standards in terms of the standards of the NALA Certified Legal Assistant Program.

CLA and CLA Specialist are certification marks duly registered with the U.S. Patent and Trademark Office (No. 113199 and No. 1751731 respectively). Any unauthorized use of these credentials is strictly forbidden.

ADMINISTRATION

The Certifying Board for Legal Assistants is responsible for content, standards, and administration of the Certified Legal Assistant Program. It is composed of legal assistants who have received a CLA Specialist designation, attorneys, and legal-assistant educators. In the technical areas of statistical analyses, examination construction, reliability, and validity tests, the Board contracts with a professional consulting firm offering expertise in these areas as well as in occupational research. Technical analyses of the CLA examination are conducted on an ongoing basis to ensure the integrity of the examination. Content analyses of the test design, accuracy of questions, and topic/subject mix for each exam section are ongoing processes of the Certifying Board. The Board also utilizes the occupational data available through surveys of legal assistants and other means, including review of textbooks and research within the field of legal-assistant education. Through these analyses and procedures, the Board is assured that the examination reflects and responds to workplace realities and demands.

THE EXAMINATION—ELIGIBILITY REQUIREMENTS

To be eligible for the CLA examination, a legal assistant must meet one of the following alternate requirements:

1. Graduation from a legal-assistant program that is:

- Approved by the American Bar Association; or
- An associate degree program; or
- A postbaccalaureate certificate program in legal-assistant studies; or
- A bachelor's degree program in legal-assistant studies; or
- A legal-assistant program which consists of a minimum of 60 semester hours (900 clock hours or 225 quarter hours) of which at least 15 semester hours (90 clock hours or 22.5 quarter hours) are substantive legal courses.

2. A bachelor's degree in any field plus one year's experience as a legal assistant. Successful completion of at least 15 semester hours (or 22.5 quarter hours or 225 clock hours) of substantive legal courses will be considered equivalent to one year's experience as a legal assistant.

3. A high school diploma or equivalent plus seven (7) years' experience as a legal assistant under the supervision of a member of the Bar, plus evidence of a minimum of twenty (20) hours of continuing legal education credit to have been completed within a two (2) year period prior to the examination date.

EXAMINATION SUBJECTS

The Certified Legal Assistant examination is a two-day comprehensive examination based on federal law and procedure. The major subject areas of the examination are:

- Communications
- Ethics
- Legal Research
- Human Relations and Interviewing Techniques*
- Judgment and Analytical Ability
- Legal Terminology*

---

*Note: Effective with the July 2001 testing session, the Human Relations and Interviewing Techniques questions are combined with the Communications section; questions from the Legal Terminology section are included in the Substantive Law Section.

Substantive Law—This section consists of five mini-examinations covering (1) the American Legal System and four (4) of the areas listed below as selected by examinees:

- Administrative Law
- Bankruptcy
- Business Organizations/Corporations
- Contracts
- Family Law
- Criminal Law and Procedure
- Litigation
- Probate and Estate Planning
- Real Estate

CLA Specialty Examinations

Those who have achieved the CLA credential may seek advanced certification in specialty practice areas. Specialty certification examinations are available in the areas of Bankruptcy, Civil Litigation, Corporations/Business Law, Criminal Law and Procedure, Intellectual Property, Estate Planning and Probate, and Real Estate. Each of these is a four-hour examination written to test specialized knowledge of the practice area.

The CLA Specialty program began in 1982 with the examinations for those working in the areas of Civil Litigation and Probate and Estate Planning. In 1984, the Corporations/Business and Criminal Law and Procedure examinations were offered. A Real Estate specialty examination was offered for the first time in 1987; Bankruptcy in 1992; and Intellectual Property in 1995. As of the December 2001 CLA Specialty examinations, 996 CLAs have received a CLA Specialist designation, as follows:

Bankruptcy	43
Civil Litigation	470
Corporate/Business	56
Criminal Law and Procedure	48
Intellectual Property	44
Probate and Estates	107
Real Estate	195
California Advanced Specialists	47

NALA is also working with individual states to established advanced specialty certification programs designed to test knowledge of state law and procedures. State certification programs are available to legal assistants in California, Florida, and Louisiana.

Maintaining Professional Certification

The Certified Legal Assistant credential is awarded for a period of five years. To maintain Certified Legal Assistant status, legal assistants must submit proof of participation in a minimum of fifty hours of continuing legal-education programs or individual study programs. Credit is also awarded for significant achievement in the area of continuing legal-assistant education such as successful completion of a state certification test, completion of a CLA Specialty examination, or teaching in a legal-assistant program.

REVOCATION OF THE CLA CREDENTIAL

The Certified Legal Assistant designation may be revoked for any one of the following reasons:

1. Falsification of information on the application form.
2. Subsequent conviction of the unauthorized practice of law.
3. Failure to meet educational and other recertification requirements.
4. Divulging the contents of any examination question or questions.
5. Subsequent conviction of a felony.
6. Violation of the NALA Code of Ethics and Professional Responsibility.

DATES AND DEADLINES AND TESTING CENTERS AND FEES

The CLA examination is offered three times a year: March/April (depending on the holiday schedule), July, and December. Application forms and the requisite fees must be received by the published filing dates. Filing deadline dates are January 15 for the March/April examination, May 15 for the July examination, and October 1 for the December examination session.

Many schools, universities, and junior colleges serve as testing centers through an arrangement with NALA. In cities in which a school testing center is not already established, NALA will establish a testing center where ten or more legal assistants apply. All testing center locations are subject to minimum registration.

The fee for the CLA examination is $225 for NALA members and $250 for nonmembers of NALA. Retake fees are $50 per section. CLA Specialty examination fees are $100 for NALA members and $125 for nonmembers. Effective August 2001, the CLA examination program has been approved by the Veterans Administration under the new licensing and certification benefit. The VA will pay the examination fee for qualified veterans. For further information, see http://www.gibill.va.gov/education/benefits.htm.

STUDY MATERIALS

A number of CLA study references are available, including the following:

- NALA Manual for Legal Assistants, Third Edition
- CLA Study Guide and Mock Examination
- Real Estate Law Specialty Review Manual
- Business Organizations Specialty Review
- Manual
- CLA Review Manual, Second Edition

For further information and online ordering, go to the NALA Campus Web site (http://www.nala.org).

Examination preparation seminars for selected topics are also available online at http://www.NALACampus.com.

CALIFORNIA ADVANCED SPECIALIZATION CERTIFICATION FOR PARALEGALS

Established in 1995, the California Advanced Specialist (CAS) Certification was created for California paralegals who have achieved the national CLA (Certified

Legal Assistant) credential and want to demonstrate advanced knowledge of California law and procedure. To qualify for the California Advanced Examination, these legal assistants have successfully completed a two-day examination covering general skills and knowledge required of legal assistants, and have demonstrated proficiency in the specialty practice area. Specialty certification in California is available in the areas of Civil Litigation, Business Organizations/Business Law, Real Estate, Estates and Trusts, and Family Law. As of December 1999, there are 30 legal assistants in California who have achieved the CAS credential. For further details about the program, contact NALA Headquarters or the Commission for Advanced California Paralegal Specialization, Inc., 3306 Ladrillo Aisle, Irvine, CA 92606.

Examination Date	Application Deadline Date
March 21 and 22, 2003	January 15, 2003
July 18 and 19, 2003	May 15, 2003
December 5 and 6, 2003	October 1, 2003
Spring 2004	January 15, 2004

FLORIDA CERTIFICATION PROGRAMS

Established in 1980, the Paralegal Association of Florida, Inc.'s, Certification program (the CFLA) complements NALA's CLA program. Its purpose is to provide a standard for measurement of advanced skills and knowledge in Florida law of those persons who have already achieved the national CLA certification.

The Paralegal Association of Florida, Inc., began administering the CFLA exam in 1983. As NALA's largest affiliate association in the State of Florida, FLA, Inc., was the first in the nation to administer such an exam for the state level. There are presently 124 CFLAs in the state of Florida.

The CFLA examination is administered through the Certifying Board of PAF, Inc., in conjunction with the PAF, Inc., mid-year meeting in the Spring and the annual meeting in September. The exam takes three hours and is limited to Florida law. A two-day CFLA review course has also been established. PAF, Inc., has developed a CFLA study guide which is available from PAF, Inc., headquarters at a cost of $85 plus shipping.

Upon successful completion of the CFLA examination, a legal assistant becomes authorized to use the designation "CFLA" with the "CLA" or "CLAS" designation. CFLAs are required to have 30 hours of continuing legal education credit over a five-year period to maintain their CFLA certification which must be directly applicable to Florida law. Proof of continuing legal education must be submitted to and is maintained by the Certifying Board.

For Further Information, contact:
Paralegal Association of Florida, Inc., Headquarters,
http://www.pafinc.org
800-433-4352
Certifying Board Chair—Patricia Tassinari, CLA, CFLA
e-mail address: **ptassinari@batemanharden.com**

LOUISIANA CERTIFIED PARALEGAL PROGRAM

At its 1992 annual meeting, the members of the Louisiana State Paralegal Association (LSPA) passed a resolution which endorsed voluntary certification as a means of establishing professional standards and promoting recognition of the paralegal profession. Subsequently, the LSPA determined a state voluntary certification credential should be developed and made available to all Louisiana paralegals who desire to demonstrate comprehensive knowledge, a high degree of proficiency in Louisiana law, and adherence to a Code of Ethics to enhance the quality of paralegal services available to the Louisiana legal community and to the public it serves.

The resulting certification program requires the candidate to sit for both the LCP (Louisiana Certified Paralegal) and CLA (Certified Legal Assistant) examinations. The LCP examination is designed to test the examinee's knowledge and understanding of the Louisiana legal and judicial system, Louisiana general law, ethics, civil procedure, and four areas of Louisiana substantive law. The CLA examination offered by the National Association of Legal Assistants tests the core paralegal skills, knowledge of the American legal and judicial system, and four areas of substantive law based on federal law and common law principles.

To qualify for the examination, one must either have a valid CLA credential or meet one of the alternate eligibility requirements of the CLA examination.

Testing Sessions

The examination is offered twice a year, in October and in the spring (March or April). Applications are due six weeks prior to the examination date.

Subjects

As a state-specific examination, the LCP examination is designed to test a paralegal's knowledge and comprehension of the law in the state of Louisiana. Each examinee will be required to take the general law, ethics, and civil procedures sections and must select four law topics, from a list of eight, that will comprise the substantive law section of that examinee's test. The substantive law areas are:

- Business Organizations
- Contracts/Obligations
- Criminal Law and Procedure
- Wills/Probate/Successions/Trusts
- Family Law
- Property
- Torts
- Evidence

Preparation

Those individuals who have not had formal substantive law paralegal courses in Louisiana would benefit from study of a current textbook covering the topics selected for the substantive law section. Much of the material covered in this section of the examination is acquired through experience in the legal field.

The LSPA will offer a review course once a year to assist interested parties in preparing for the examination. Written materials and a videotape of the seminar sessions are available from the Louisiana State Paralegal Association in care of NALA Headquarters, 1516 S. Boston, #200, Tulsa, OK 74119, (918) 587-6828.

INFORMATION ON NFPA's PACE EXAMINATION

INTRODUCTION

The legal service industry is facing great change. While containing costs, it is trying to respond to an increased number of pending cases, rapid changes in technology, and increased demands from consumers for a higher level of client service.

As an active and vital part of the legal service industry, the paralegal profession is facing possible regulation through certification, licensing, or other means. The National Federation of Paralegal Associations, Inc., gathered this information to describe the bold step it is undertaking—a step that may dramatically change the entire profession.

A BOLD STEP FORWARD

A grass-roots organization, NFPA is directed by its membership—each member association has one vote in the future of the national organization and the profession. During NFPA's 1994 Mid-Year Meeting, the membership voted overwhelmingly to develop an exam to test the competency level of experienced paralegals.

> ## PACE = Paralegal Advanced Competency Exam
>
> Offering experienced paralegals an option to
>
> - validate your experience and job skills;
> - establish credentials; and
> - increase your value to your organizations and clients.
>
> The only exam of its kind, PACE
>
> - developed by a professional testing firm;
> - administered by an independent test administration company;
> - tests concepts across practice areas;
> - offers the profession a national standard of evaluation; and
> - offered at multiple locations on numerous dates and at various times.
>
> ## PACE = Personal Advancement for the Experienced Paralegal

The overwhelmingly positive vote to develop this exam is a conscientious effort by these paralegals to direct the future of the paralegal profession and acknowledges the vital role of paralegals within the legal service industry. It is also a direct response to states that are considering regulation of the paralegal profession and are seeking a method to measure job competency. While NFPA believes in the criteria the members established to take this exam, it recognizes any state may adopt the exam and modify the criteria.

The Paralegal Advanced Competency Exam (PACE) will be developed in two stages, identified as tiers. Tier I, comprising general and ethics questions, is available; state-specific modules will be developed within particular jurisdictions as the need arises. Tier II will comprise specialty sections.

Paralegals receive two major benefits by taking PACE. The exam

- provides a fair evaluation of the competencies of paralegals across practice areas; and
- creates a professional level of expertise by which all paralegals can be evaluated.

EXPERIENCE AND EDUCATION

Requirements for a paralegal to take either tier of PACE include work experience and education. The paralegal cannot have been convicted of a felony nor be under suspension, termination, or revocation of a certificate, registration, or license by any entity. PACE has generated a great deal of interest since the resolution to develop it was passed. Based on this interest, and the number of paralegals who may apply to take the exam (a number reported by the U.S. Department of Labor to exceed 113,000), a need exists for global grandparenting.

Requirements for Tier I are

- a minimum of four (4) years' experience as a paralegal obtained by December 31, 2000 **OR**
- a bachelor's degree, and completion of a paralegal program within an institutionally accredited school (which may be embodied in the bachelor's degree), **and** a minimum of two (2) years' experience as a paralegal.

Requirements for Tier II are

- successful completion of Tier I, **AND**

    one of the following

- a minimum of six (6) years' experience as a paralegal **OR**
- a bachelor's degree, and completion of a paralegal program within an institutionally accredited school; (which may be embodied in the bachelor's degree), and a minimum of four (4) years' experience as a paralegal.

NFPA'S ROLE

First organized in 1974, NFPA was created to provide a communications network and develop channels to expand the role of the paralegal profession. In addition, NFPA has assisted the profession in evaluating educational standards and responding to organizations and entities that appear interested in regulating the profession.

NFPA membership has significantly increased since its inception. In 2000, it included 55 associations, located throughout the United States, with more than 17,000 members.

Independent and Fair

NFPA strongly believes PACE must produce legitimate and verifiable results and consistently pass only paralegals who demonstrate an established level of knowledge, skills, and competency. PACE was developed in cooperation with the independent test development firm, Professional Examination Service (PES).

PES was selected through an extensive proposal process and a personal interview with the NFPA Board of Directors. PES has developed professional exams for more than 50 years for groups such as the Federal Reserve System, the National Association of Securities Dealers, Inc., the Environmental Protection Agency, and the Emergency Medical Technicians and Paramedics. PES currently works with more than 75 professional associations and more than 300 licensing boards in 62 jurisdictions in the United States and Canada.

But PES does not work alone. An independent task force of paralegals, paralegal educators, attorneys, and other public members who are legal advocates in every step, from the preparation of the job analysis for paralegals through creation of the initial exam and ongoing revisions.

To ensure test results are valid, the test is administered by PES, an independent firm.

All profits received from the exam program will be passed to the "Foundation for the Advancement of the Paralegal Profession," an independent foundation, and will be used to further the entire paralegal profession.

Preparing for the Future

PACE presents a bold opportunity to all paralegals to advance the profession. This exam provides hard facts about the competency of experienced paralegals. While PACE does not address all the issues of regulation, including certification and licensing, it does provide the legal service industry with an option to evaluate the competency level of experienced paralegals.

As members of a self-directed profession, all paralegals should consider the vital role the profession performs within the legal service industry. PACE is independently monitored and well-structured. PACE provides test results across practice areas and, possibly, state-specific laws. While the test is offered on a voluntary basis, all experienced paralegals are encouraged to sit for the exam.

NFPA is committed to ensuring the paralegal profession responds to the changing needs of the public and legal service industry. In voting to develop PACE, NFPA's membership took a bold step toward addressing the future issues facing the profession.

Lexis-Nexis has sponsored a twenty minute presentation on paralegals which highlights PACE. This presentation is available on video or CD-ROM.

Credential

Those who pass PACE and maintain the continuing education requirement may use the designation "PACE—Registered Paralegal" or "RP."

To maintain the RP credential, 12 hours of continuing legal or specialty education is required every two years, with at least one hour in legal ethics.

Registered Paralegals should review the *"Facts Every RP Should Know"* found at http://www.paralegals.org to be aware of the ways the PACE credential can be used and information on registraton of CLE credits. Also included in the fact sheet is information on non-renewal status, inactive status, suspension and revocaton of the use of the RP credential, and the appeals process.

Inactive status may be granted by the PACE Standards Committee upon completion of an application. One-half of the CLE requirement is required while in inactive status.

How To Prepare and Register

To prepare for the exam, paralegals may use any of the following options:

* *a study manual*
* *sample exam disk* which contains 100 sample questions, grading of the answers and listing of further resources for incorrect answers
* *seminars* sponsored by local paralegal associations and NFPA which can be found on the NFPA's calendar
* *PACE Review Course,* a seven-week course provided through the Internet
* *Online seminars* can be found on NFPA's CLE page

To register to take the exam, send $15 to NFPA, P.O. Box 33108, Kansas City, MO 64114-0108, for a Candidate Handbook, which includes an application, information on exam content, sample exam questions, and logistical information on taking the exam. The $15 fee will be applied to the overall examination fee of $225. Once the application has been approved, the exam must be taken within 90 days.

PACE is a four-hour, computer-generated test and is offered at more than 200 Sylvan Technology Centers, also known as Prometric, throughout the country. Once approved, each applicant can schedule the date and time to take the test at his or her convenience on any day except Sundays and holidays. Please note: not all Sylvan Learning Centers are Technology Centers.

THE CONSTITUTION OF THE UNITED STATES

Preamble

We the People of the United States, in Order to form a more perfect Union, establish Justice, insure domestic Tranquility, provide for the common defence, promote the general Welfare, and secure the Blessings of Liberty to ourselves and our Posterity, do ordain and establish this Constitution for the United States of America.

Article I

SECTION 1.   All legislative Powers herein granted shall be vested in a Congress of the United States, which shall consist of a Senate and House of Representatives.

SECTION 2.   The House of Representatives shall be composed of Members chosen every second Year by the People of the several States, and the Electors in each State shall have the Qualifications requisite for Electors of the most numerous Branch of the State Legislature.

No Person shall be a Representative who shall not have attained to the Age of twenty five Years, and been seven Years a Citizen of the United States, and who shall not, when elected, be an Inhabitant of that State in which he shall be chosen.

Representatives and direct Taxes shall be apportioned among the several States which may be included within this Union, according to their respective Numbers, which shall be determined by adding to the whole Number of free Persons, including those bound to Service for a Term of Years, and excluding Indians not taxed, three fifths of all other Persons. The actual Enumeration shall be made within three Years after the first Meeting of the Congress of the United States, and within every subsequent Term of ten Years, in such Manner as they shall by Law direct. The Number of Representatives shall not exceed one for every thirty Thousand, but each State shall have at Least one Representative; and until such enumeration shall be made, the State of New Hampshire shall be entitled to chuse three, Massachusetts eight, Rhode Island and Providence Plantations one, Connecticut five, New York six, New Jersey four, Pennsylvania eight, Delaware one, Maryland six, Virginia ten, North Carolina five, South Carolina five, and Georgia three.

When vacancies happen in the Representation from any State, the Executive Authority thereof shall issue Writs of Election to fill such Vacancies.

The House of Representatives shall chuse their Speaker and other Officers; and shall have the sole Power of Impeachment.

SECTION 3.   The Senate of the United States shall be composed of two Senators from each State, chosen by the Legislature thereof, for six Years; and each Senator shall have one Vote.

Immediately after they shall be assembled in Consequence of the first Election, they shall be divided as equally as may be into three Classes. The Seats of the Senators of the first Class shall be vacated at the Expiration of the second Year, of the second Class at the Expiration of the fourth Year, and of the third Class at the Expiration of the sixth Year, so that one third may be chosen every second Year; and if Vacancies happen by Resignation, or otherwise, during the Recess of the Legislature of any State, the Executive thereof may make temporary Appointments until the next Meeting of the Legislature, which shall then fill such Vacancies.

No Person shall be a Senator who shall not have attained to the Age of thirty Years, and been nine Years a Citizen of the United States, and who shall not, when elected, be an Inhabitant of that State for which he shall be chosen.

The Vice President of the United States shall be President of the Senate, but shall have no Vote, unless they be equally divided.

The Senate shall chuse their other Officers, and also a President pro tempore, in the Absence of the Vice President, or when he shall exercise the Office of President of the United States.

The Senate shall have the sole Power to try all Impeachments. When sitting for that Purpose, they shall be on Oath or Affirmation. When the President of the United States is tried, the Chief Justice shall preside: And no Person shall be convicted without the Concurrence of two thirds of the Members present.

Judgment in Cases of Impeachment shall not extend further than to removal from Office, and disqualification to hold and enjoy any Office of honor, Trust, or Profit under the United States: but the Party convicted shall nevertheless be liable and subject to Indictment, Trial, Judgment, and Punishment, according to Law.

SECTION 4.   The Times, Places and Manner of holding Elections for Senators and Representatives, shall be prescribed in each State by the Legislature thereof; but the Congress may at any time by Law make or alter such Regulations, except as to the Places of chusing Senators.

The Congress shall assemble at least once in every Year, and such Meeting shall be on the first Monday in December, unless they shall by Law appoint a different Day.

SECTION 5.   Each House shall be the Judge of the Elections, Returns, and Qualifications of its own Members, and a Majority of each shall constitute a Quorum to do Business; but a smaller Number may adjourn from day to day, and may be authorized to compel the Attendance of absent Members, in such Manner, and under such Penalties as each House may provide.

Each House may determine the Rules of its Proceedings, punish its Members for disorderly Behavior, and, with the Concurrence of two thirds, expel a Member.

Each House shall keep a Journal of its Proceedings, and from time to time publish the same, excepting such Parts as may in their Judgment require Secrecy; and the Yeas and Nays of the Members of either House on any question shall, at the Desire of one fifth of those Present, be entered on the Journal.

Neither House, during the Session of Congress, shall, without the Consent of the other, adjourn for more than three days, nor to any other Place than that in which the two Houses shall be sitting.

SECTION 6.   The Senators and Representatives shall receive a Compensation for their Services, to be ascertained by Law, and paid out of the Treasury of the United States. They shall in all Cases, except Treason, Felony and Breach of the Peace, be privileged from Arrest during their Attendance at the Session of their respective Houses, and in going to and returning from the same; and for any Speech or Debate in either House, they shall not be questioned in any other Place.

No Senator or Representative shall, during the Time for which he was elected, be appointed to any civil Office under the Authority of the United States, which shall have been created, or the Emoluments whereof shall have been increased during such time; and no Person holding any Office under the United States, shall be a Member of either House during his Continuance in Office.

SECTION 7.   All Bills for raising Revenue shall originate in the House of Representatives; but the Senate may propose or concur with Amendments as on other Bills.

Every Bill which shall have passed the House of Representatives and the Senate, shall, before it become a Law, be presented to the President of the United States; If he approve he shall sign it, but if not he shall return it, with his Objections to the House in which it shall have originated, who shall enter the Objections at large on their Journal, and proceed to reconsider it. If after such Reconsideration two thirds of that House shall agree to pass the Bill, it shall be sent together with the Objections, to the other House, by which it shall likewise be reconsidered, and if approved by two thirds of that House, it shall become a Law. But in all such Cases the Votes of both Houses shall be determined by Yeas and Nays, and the Names of the Persons voting for and against the Bill shall be entered on the Journal of each House respectively. If any Bill shall not be returned by the President within ten Days (Sundays excepted) after it shall have been presented to him, the Same shall be a Law, in like Manner as if he had signed it, unless the Congress by their Adjournment prevent its Return in which Case it shall not be a Law.

Every Order, Resolution, or Vote, to which the Concurrence of the Senate and House of Representatives may be necessary (except on a question of Adjournment) shall be presented to the President of the United States; and before the Same shall take Effect, shall be approved by him, or being disapproved by him, shall be repassed by two thirds of the Senate and House of Representatives, according to the Rules and Limitations prescribed in the Case of a Bill.

SECTION 8.   The Congress shall have Power To lay and collect Taxes, Duties, Imposts and Excises, to pay the Debts and provide for the common Defence and general Welfare of the United States; but all Duties, Imposts and Excises shall be uniform throughout the United States;

To borrow Money on the credit of the United States;

To regulate Commerce with foreign Nations, and among the several States, and with the Indian Tribes;

To establish an uniform Rule of Naturalization, and uniform Laws on the subject of Bankruptcies throughout the United States;

To coin Money, regulate the Value thereof, and of foreign Coin, and fix the Standard of Weights and Measures;

To provide for the Punishment of counterfeiting the Securities and current Coin of the United States;

To establish Post Offices and post Roads;

To promote the Progress of Science and useful Arts, by securing for limited Times to Authors and Inventors the exclusive Right to their respective Writings and Discoveries;

To constitute Tribunals inferior to the supreme Court;

To define and punish Piracies and Felonies committed on the high Seas, and Offenses against the Law of Nations;

To declare War, grant Letters of Marque and Reprisal, and make Rules concerning Captures on Land and Water;

To raise and support Armies, but no Appropriation of Money to that Use shall be for a longer Term than two Years;

To provide and maintain a Navy;

To make Rules for the Government and Regulation of the land and naval Forces;

To provide for calling forth the Militia to execute the Laws of the Union, suppress Insurrections and repel Invasions;

To provide for organizing, arming, and disciplining, the Militia, and for governing such Part of them as may be employed in the Service of the United States, reserving to the States respectively, the Appointment of the Officers, and the Authority of training the Militia according to the discipline prescribed by Congress;

To exercise exclusive Legislation in all Cases whatsoever, over such District (not exceeding ten Miles square) as may, by Cession of particular States, and the Acceptance of Congress, become the Seat of the Government of the United States, and to exercise like Authority over all Places purchased by the Consent of the Legislature of the State in which the Same shall be, for the Erection of Forts, Magazines, Arsenals, dock-Yards, and other needful Buildings;—And

To make all Laws which shall be necessary and proper for carrying into Execution the foregoing Powers, and all other Powers vested by this Constitution in the Government of the United States, or in any Department or Officer thereof.

SECTION 9. The Migration or Importation of such Persons as any of the States now existing shall think proper to admit, shall not be prohibited by the Congress prior to the Year one thousand eight hundred and eight, but a Tax or duty may be imposed on such Importation, not exceeding ten dollars for each Person.

The privilege of the Writ of Habeas Corpus shall not be suspended, unless when in Cases of Rebellion or Invasion the public Safety may require it.

No Bill of Attainder or ex post facto Law shall be passed.

No Capitation, or other direct, Tax shall be laid, unless in Proportion to the Census or Enumeration herein before directed to be taken.

No Tax or Duty shall be laid on Articles exported from any State.

No Preference shall be given by any Regulation of Commerce or Revenue to the Ports of one State over those of another: nor shall Vessels bound to, or from, one State be obliged to enter, clear, or pay Duties in another.

No Money shall be drawn from the Treasury, but in Consequence of Appropriations made by Law; and a regular Statement and Account of the Receipts and Expenditures of all public Money shall be published from time to time.

No Title of Nobility shall be granted by the United States: And no Person holding any Office of Profit or Trust under them, shall, without the Consent of the Congress, accept of any present, Emolument, Office, or Title, of any kind whatever, from any King, Prince, or foreign State.

SECTION 10.   No State shall enter into any Treaty, Alliance, or Confederation; grant Letters of Marque and Reprisal; coin Money; emit Bills of Credit; make any Thing but gold and silver Coin a Tender in Payment of Debts; pass any Bill of Attainder, ex post facto Law, or Law impairing the Obligation of Contracts, or grant any Title of Nobility.

No State shall, without the Consent of the Congress, lay any Imposts or Duties on Imports or Exports, except what may be absolutely necessary for executing its inspection Laws: and the net Produce of all Duties and Imposts, laid by any State on Imports or Exports, shall be for the Use of the Treasury of the United States; and all such Laws shall be subject to the Revision and Controul of the Congress.

No State shall, without the Consent of Congress, lay any Duty of Tonnage, keep Troops, or Ships of War in time of Peace, enter into any Agreement or Compact with another State, or with a foreign Power, or engage in War, unless actually invaded, or in such imminent Danger as will not admit of delay.

Article II

SECTION 1.   The executive Power shall be vested in a President of the United States of America. He shall hold his Office during the Term of four Years, and, together with the Vice President, chosen for the same Term, be elected, as follows:

Each State shall appoint, in such Manner as the Legislature thereof may direct, a Number of Electors, equal to the whole Number of Senators and Representatives to which the State may be entitled in the Congress; but no Senator or Representative, or Person holding an Office of Trust or Profit under the United States, shall be appointed an Elector.

The Electors shall meet in their respective States, and vote by Ballot for two Persons, of whom one at least shall not be an Inhabitant of the same State with themselves. And they shall make a List of all the Persons voted for, and of the Number of Votes for each; which List they shall sign and certify, and transmit sealed to the Seat of the Government of the United States, directed to the President of the Senate. The President of the Senate shall, in the Presence of the Senate and House of Representatives, open all the Certificates, and the Votes shall then be counted. The Person having the greatest Number of Votes shall be the President, if such Number be a Majority of the whole Number of Electors appointed; and if there be more than one who have such Majority, and have an equal Number of Votes, then the House of Representatives shall immediately chuse by Ballot one of them for President; and if no Person have a Majority, then from the five highest on the List the said House shall in like Manner chuse the President. But in chusing the President, the Votes shall be taken by States, the Representation from each State having one Vote; A quorum for this Purpose shall consist of a Member or Members from two thirds of the States, and a Majority of all the States shall be necessary to a Choice. In every Case, after the Choice of the President, the Person having the greater Number of Votes of the Electors shall be the Vice President. But if there should remain two or more who have equal Votes, the Senate shall chuse from them by Ballot the Vice President.

The Congress may determine the Time of chusing the Electors, and the Day on which they shall give their Votes; which Day shall be the same throughout the United States.

No person except a natural born Citizen, or a Citizen of the United States, at the time of the Adoption of this Constitution, shall be eligible to the Office of President; neither shall any Person be eligible to that Office who shall not have attained to the Age of thirty five Years, and been fourteen Years a Resident within the United States.

In Case of the Removal of the President from Office, or of his Death, Resignation or Inability to discharge the Powers and Duties of the said Office, the same shall devolve on the Vice President, and the Congress may by Law provide for the Case of Removal, Death, Resignation or Inability, both of the President and Vice President, declaring what Officer shall then act as President, and such Officer shall act accordingly, until the Disability be removed, or a President shall be elected.

The President shall, at stated Times, receive for his Services, a Compensation, which shall neither be increased nor diminished during the Period for which he shall have been elected, and he shall not receive within that Period any other Emolument from the United States, or any of them.

Before he enter on the Execution of his Office, he shall take the following Oath or Affirmation: "I do solemnly swear (or affirm) that I will faithfully execute the Office of President of the United States, and will to the best of my Ability, preserve, protect and defend the Constitution of the United States."

SECTION 2.   The President shall be Commander in Chief of the Army and Navy of the United States, and of the Militia of the several States, when called into the actual Service of the United States; he may require the Opinion, in writing, of the principal Officer in each of the executive Departments, upon any Subject relating to the Duties of their respective Offices, and he shall have Power to grant Reprieves and Pardons for Offenses against the United States, except in Cases of Impeachment.

He shall have Power, by and with the Advice and Consent of the Senate to make Treaties, provided two thirds of the Senators present concur; and he shall nominate, and by and with the Advice and Consent of the Senate, shall appoint Ambassadors, other public Ministers and Consuls, Judges of the supreme Court, and all other Officers of the United States, whose Appointments are not herein otherwise provided for, and which shall be established by Law; but the Congress may by Law vest the Appointment of such inferior Officers, as they think proper, in the President alone, in the Courts of Law, or in the Heads of Departments.

The President shall have Power to fill up all Vacancies that may happen during the Recess of the Senate, by granting Commissions which shall expire at the End of their next Session.

SECTION 3.   He shall from time to time give to the Congress Information of the State of the Union, and recommend to their Consideration such Measures as he shall judge necessary and expedient; he may, on extraordinary Occasions, convene both Houses, or either of them, and in Case of Disagreement between them, with Respect to the Time of Adjournment, he may adjourn them to such Time as he shall think proper; he shall receive Ambassadors and other public Ministers; he shall take Care that the Laws be faithfully executed, and shall Commission all the Officers of the United States.

SECTION 4.   The President, Vice President and all civil Officers of the United States, shall be removed from Office on Impeachment for, and Conviction of, Treason, Bribery, or other high Crimes and Misdemeanors.

Article III

SECTION 1.   The judicial Power of the United States, shall be vested in one supreme Court, and in such inferior Courts as the Congress may from time to time ordain and establish. The Judges, both of the supreme and inferior Courts, shall hold their Offices during good Behaviour, and shall, at stated Times, receive for their Services a Compensation, which shall not be diminished during their Continuance in Office.

SECTION 2.   The judicial Power shall extend to all Cases, in Law and Equity, arising under this Constitution, the Laws of the United States, and Treaties made, or which shall be made, under their Authority;—to all Cases affecting Ambassadors, other public Ministers and Consuls;—to all Cases of admiralty and maritime Jurisdiction;—to Controversies to which the United States shall be a Party;—to Controversies between two or more States;—between a State and Citizens of another State;—between Citizens of different States;—between Citizens of the same State claiming Lands under Grants of different States, and between a State, or the Citizens thereof, and foreign States, Citizens or Subjects.

In all Cases affecting Ambassadors, other public Ministers and Consuls, and those in which a State shall be a Party, the supreme Court shall have original Jurisdiction. In all the other Cases before mentioned, the supreme Court shall have appellate Jurisdiction, both as to Law and Fact, with such Exceptions, and under such Regulations as the Congress shall make.

The Trial of all Crimes, except in Cases of Impeachment, shall be by Jury; and such Trial shall be held in the State where the said Crimes shall have been committed; but when not committed within any State, the Trial shall be at such Place or Places as the Congress may by Law have directed.

SECTION 3.   Treason against the United States, shall consist only in levying War against them, or, in adhering to their Enemies, giving them Aid and Comfort. No Person shall be convicted of Treason unless on the Testimony of two Witnesses to the same overt Act, or on Confession in open Court.

The Congress shall have Power to declare the Punishment of Treason, but no Attainder of Treason shall work Corruption of Blood, or Forfeiture except during the Life of the Person attainted.

Article IV

SECTION 1.   Full Faith and Credit shall be given in each State to the public Acts, Records, and judicial Proceedings of every other State. And the Congress may by general Laws prescribe the Manner in which such Acts, Records and Proceedings shall be proved, and the Effect thereof.

SECTION 2.   The Citizens of each State shall be entitled to all Privileges and Immunities of Citizens in the several States.

A Person charged in any State with Treason, Felony, or other Crime, who shall flee from Justice, and be found in another State, shall on Demand of the executive Authority of the State from which he fled, be delivered up, to be removed to the State having Jurisdiction of the Crime.

No Person held to Service or Labour in one State, under the Laws thereof, escaping into another, shall, in Consequence of any Law or Regulation therein, be discharged from such Service or Labour, but shall be delivered up on Claim of the Party to whom such Service or Labour may be due.

SECTION 3.   New States may be admitted by the Congress into this Union; but no new State shall be formed or erected within the Jurisdiction of any other State; nor any State be formed by the Junction of two or more States, or Parts of States, without the Consent of the Legislatures of the States concerned as well as of the Congress.

The Congress shall have Power to dispose of and make all needful Rules and Regulations respecting the Territory or other Property belonging to the United States; and nothing in this Constitution shall be so construed as to Prejudice any Claims of the United States, or of any particular State.

SECTION 4. United States shall guarantee to every State in this Union a Republican Form of Government, and shall protect each of them against Invasion; and on Application of the Legislature, or of the Executive (when the Legislature cannot be convened) against domestic Violence.

Article V

The Congress, whenever two thirds of both Houses shall deem it necessary, shall propose Amendments to this Constitution, or, on the Application of the Legislatures of two thirds of the several States, shall call a Convention for proposing Amendments, which, in either Case, shall be valid to all Intents and Purposes, as part of this Constitution, when ratified by the Legislatures of three fourths of the several States, or by Conventions in three fourths thereof, as the one or the other Mode of Ratification may be proposed by the Congress; Provided that no Amendment which may be made prior to the Year One thousand eight hundred and eight shall in any Manner affect the first and fourth Clauses in the Ninth Section of the first Article; and that no State, without its Consent, shall be deprived of its equal Suffrage in the Senate.

Article VI

All Debts contracted and Engagements entered into, before the Adoption of this Constitution shall be as valid against the United States under this Constitution, as under the Confederation.

This Constitution, and the Laws of the United States which shall be made in Pursuance thereof; and all Treaties made, or which shall be made, under the Authority of the United States, shall be the supreme Law of the Land; and the Judges in every State shall be bound thereby, any Thing in the Constitution or Laws of any State to the Contrary notwithstanding.

The Senators and Representatives before mentioned, and the Members of the several State Legislatures, and all executive and judicial Officers, both of the United States and of the several States, shall be bound by Oath or Affirmation, to support this Constitution; but no religious Test shall ever be required as a Qualification to any Office or public Trust under the United States.

Article VII

The Ratification of the Conventions of nine States shall be sufficient for the Establishment of this Constitution between the States so ratifying the Same.

Amendment I [1791]

Congress shall make no law respecting an establishment of religion, or prohibiting the free exercise thereof; or abridging the freedom of speech, or of the press; or the right of the people peaceably to assembly, and to petition the Government for a redress of grievances.

Amendment II [1791]

A well regulated Militia, being necessary to the security of a free State, the right of the people to keep and bear Arms, shall not be infringed.

Amendment III [1791]

No Soldier shall, in time of peace be quartered in any house, without the consent of the Owner, nor in time of war, but in a manner to be prescribed by law.

Amendment IV [1791]

The right of the people to be secure in their persons, houses, papers, and effects, against unreasonable searches and seizures, shall not be violated, and no Warrants shall issue, but upon probable cause, supported by Oath or affirmation, and particularly describing the place to be searched, and the persons or things to be seized.

Amendment V [1791]

No person shall be held to answer for a capital, or otherwise infamous crime, unless on a presentment or indictment of a Grand Jury, except in cases arising in the land or naval forces, or in the Militia, when in actual service in time of War or public danger; nor shall any person be subject for the same offence to be twice put in jeopardy of life or limb; nor shall be compelled in any criminal case to be a witness against himself, nor be deprived of life, liberty, or property, without due process of law; nor shall private property be taken for public use, without just compensation.

Amendment VI [1791]

In all criminal prosecutions, the accused shall enjoy the right to a speedy and public trial, by an impartial jury of the State and district wherein the crime shall have been committed, which district shall have been previously ascertained by law, and to be informed of the nature and cause of the accusation; to be confronted with the witnesses against him; to have compulsory process for obtaining witnesses in his favor, and to have the Assistance of Counsel for his defence.

Amendment VII [1791]

In Suits at common law, where the value in controversy shall exceed twenty dollars, the right of trial by jury shall be preserved, and no fact tried by jury, shall be otherwise re-examined in any Court of the United States, than according to the rules of the common law.

Amendment VIII [1791]

Excessive bail shall not be required, nor excessive fines imposed, nor cruel and unusual punishments inflicted.

Amendment IX [1791]

The enumeration in the Constitution, of certain rights, shall not be construed to deny or disparage others retained by the people.

Amendment X [1791]

The powers not delegated to the United States by the Constitution, nor prohibited by it to the States, are reserved to the States respectively, or to the people.

Amendment XI [1798]

The Judicial power of the United States shall not be construed to extend to any suit in law or equity, commenced or prosecuted against one of the United States by Citizens of another State, or by Citizens or Subjects of any Foreign State.

Amendment XII [1804]

The Electors shall meet in their respective states, and vote by ballot for President and Vice-President, one of whom, at least, shall not be an inhabitant of the same state with themselves; they shall name in their ballots the person voted for as President, and in distinct ballots the person voted for as Vice-President, and they shall make distinct lists of all persons voted for as President, and of all persons voted for as Vice-President, and of the number of votes for each, which lists they shall sign and certify, and transmit sealed to the seat of the government of the United States, directed to the President of the Senate;—The President of the Senate shall, in the presence of the Senate and House of Representatives, open all the certificates and the votes shall then be counted;—The person having the greatest number of votes for President, shall be the President, if such number be a majority of the whole number of Electors appointed; and if no person have such majority, then from the persons having the highest numbers not exceeding three on the list of those voted for as President, the House of Representatives shall choose immediately, by ballot, the President. But in choosing the President, the votes shall be taken by states, the representation from each state having one vote; a quorum for this purpose shall consist of a member or members from two-thirds of the states, and a majority of all states shall be necessary to a choice. And if the House of Representatives shall not choose a President whenever the right of choice shall devolve upon them, before the fourth day of March next following, then the Vice-President shall act as President, as in the case of the death or other constitutional disability of the President.—The person having the greatest number of votes as Vice-President, shall be the Vice-President, if such number be a majority of the whole number of Electors appointed, and if no person have a majority, then from the two highest numbers on the list, the Senate shall choose the Vice-President; a quorum for the purpose shall consist of two-thirds of the whole number of Senators, and a majority of the whole number shall be necessary to a choice. But no person constitutionally ineligible to the office of President shall be eligible to that of Vice-President of the United States.

Amendment XIII [1865]

SECTION 1.   Neither slavery nor involuntary servitude, except as a punishment for crime whereof the party shall have been duly convicted, shall exist within the United States, or any place subject to their jurisdiction.

SECTION 2.   Congress shall have power to enforce this article by appropriate legislation.

Amendment XIV [1868]

SECTION 1.   All persons born or naturalized in the United States, and subject to the jurisdiction thereof, are citizens of the United States and of the State wherein they reside. No State shall make or enforce any law which shall abridge the privileges or immunities of citizens of the United States; nor shall any State deprive any person of life, liberty, or property, without due process of law; nor deny to any person within its jurisdiction the equal protection of the laws.

SECTION 2.   Representatives shall be apportioned among the several States according to their respective numbers, counting the whole number of persons in each State, excluding Indians not taxed. But when the right to vote at any election for the choice of electors for President and Vice President of the United States, Representatives in Congress, the Executive and Judicial officers of a State, or the members of the Legislature thereof, is denied to any of the male inhabitants of such State, being twenty-one years of age, and citizens of the United States, or in any way abridged, except for participation in rebellion, or other crime, the basis of representation therein shall be reduced in the proportion which the number of such male citizens shall bear to the whole number of male citizens twenty-one years of age in such State.

SECTION 3.   No person shall be a Senator or Representative in Congress, or elector of President and Vice President, or hold any office, civil or military, under the United States, or under any State, who having previously taken an oath, as a member of Congress, or as an officer of the United States, or as a member of any State legislature, or as an executive or judicial officer of any State, to support the Constitution of the United States, shall have engaged in insurrection or rebellion against the same, or given aid or comfort to the enemies thereof. But Congress may by a vote of two-thirds of each House, remove such disability.

SECTION 4.   The validity of the public debt of the United States, authorized by law, including debts incurred for payment of pensions and bounties for services in suppressing insurrection or rebellion, shall not be questioned. But neither the United States nor any State shall assume or pay any debt or obligation incurred in aid of insurrection or rebellion against the United States, or any claim for the loss or emancipation of any slave; but all such debts, obligations and claims shall be held illegal and void.

SECTION 5.   The Congress shall have power to enforce, by appropriate legislation, the provisions of this article.

Amendment XV [1870]

SECTION 1.   The right of citizens of the United States to vote shall not be denied or abridged by the United States or by any State on account of race, color, or previous condition of servitude.

SECTION 2.   The Congress shall have power to enforce this article by appropriate legislation.

Amendment XVI [1913]

The Congress shall have power to lay and collect taxes on incomes, from whatever source derived, without apportionment among the several States, and without regard to any census or enumeration.

Amendment XVII [1913]

SECTION 1.   The Senate of the United States shall be composed of two Senators from each State, elected by the people thereof, for six years; and each Senator shall have one vote. The electors in each State shall have the qualifications requisite for electors of the most numerous branch of the State legislatures.

SECTION 2.   When vacancies happen in the representation of any State in the Senate, the executive authority of such State shall issue writs of election to fill such vacancies: *Provided*, That the legislature of any State may empower the executive thereof to make temporary appointments until the people fill the vacancies by election as the legislature may direct.

SECTION 3.   This amendment shall not be so construed as to affect the election or term of any Senator chosen before it becomes valid as part of the Constitution.

Amendment XVIII [1919]

SECTION 1.   After one year from the ratification of this article the manufacture, sale, or transportation of intoxicating liquors within, the importation thereof into, or the exportation thereof from the United States and all territory subject to the jurisdiction thereof for beverage purposes is hereby prohibited.

SECTION 2.   The Congress and the several States shall have concurrent power to enforce this article by appropriate legislation.

SECTION 3.   This article shall be inoperative unless it shall have been ratified as an amendment to the Constitution by the legislatures of the several States, as provided in the Constitution, within seven years from the date of the submission hereof to the States by the Congress.

Amendment XIX [1920]

SECTION 1.   The right of citizens of the United States to vote shall not be denied or abridged by the United States or by any State on account of sex.

SECTION 2.   Congress shall have power to enforce this article by appropriate legislation.

Amendment XX [1933]

SECTION 1.   The terms of the President and Vice President shall end at noon on the 20th day of January, and the terms of Senators and Representatives at noon on the 3d day of January, of the years in which such terms would have ended if this article had not been ratified; and the terms of their successors shall then begin.

SECTION 2.   The Congress shall assemble at least once in every year, and such meeting shall begin at noon on the 3d day of January, unless they shall by law appoint a different day.

SECTION 3.   If, at the time fixed for the beginning of the term of the President, the President elect shall have died, the Vice President elect shall become President.

If the President shall not have been chosen before the time fixed for the beginning of his term, or if the President elect shall have failed to qualify, then the Vice President elect shall act as President until a President shall have qualified; and the Congress may by law provide for the case wherein neither a President elect nor a Vice President elect shall have qualified, declaring who shall then act as President, or the manner in which one who is to act shall be selected, and such person shall act accordingly until a President or Vice President shall have qualified.

Section 4.   The Congress may by law provide for the case of the death of any of the persons from whom the House of Representatives may choose a President whenever the right of choice shall have devolved upon them, and for the case of the death of any of the persons from whom the Senate may choose a Vice President whenever the right of choice shall have devolved upon them.

Section 5.   Sections 1 and 2 shall take effect on the 15th day of October following the ratification of this article.

Section 6.   This article shall be inoperative unless it shall have been ratified as an amendment to the Constitution by the legislatures of three-fourths of the several States within seven years from the date of its submission.

Amendment XXI [1933]

Section 1.   The eighteenth article of amendment to the Constitution of the United States is hereby repealed.

Section 2.   The transportation or importation into any State, Territory, or possession of the United States for delivery or use therein of intoxicating liquors, in violation of the laws thereof, is hereby prohibited.

Section 3.   This article shall be inoperative unless it shall have been ratified as an amendment to the Constitution by conventions in the several States, as provided in the Constitution, within seven years from the date of the submission hereof to the States by the Congress.

Amendment XXII [1951]

Section 1.   No person shall be elected to the office of the President more than twice, and no person who has held the office of President, or acted as President, for more than two years of a term to which some other person was elected President shall be elected to the office of President more than once. But this Article shall not apply to any person holding the office of President when this Article was proposed by the Congress, and shall not prevent any person who may be holding the office of President, or acting as President, during the term within which this Article becomes operative from holding the office of President or acting as President during the remainder of such term.

Section 2.   This article shall be inoperative unless it shall have been ratified as an amendment to the Constitution by the legislatures of three-fourths of the several States within seven years from the date of its submission to the States by the Congress.

Amendment XXIII [1961]

SECTION 1.   The District constituting the seat of Government of the United States shall appoint in such manner as the Congress may direct:

A number of electors of President and Vice President equal to the whole number of Senators and Representatives in Congress to which the District would be entitled if it were a State, but in no event more than the least populous state; they shall be in addition to those appointed by the states, but they shall be considered, for the purposes of the election of President and Vice President, to be electors appointed by a state; and they shall meet in the District and perform such duties as provided by the twelfth article of amendment.

SECTION 2.   The Congress shall have power to enforce this article by appropriate legislation.

Amendment XXIV [1964]

SECTION 1.   The right of citizens of the United States to vote in any primary or other election for President or Vice President, for electors for President or Vice President, or for Senator or Representative in Congress, shall not be denied or abridged by the United States, or any State by reason of failure to pay any poll tax or other tax.

SECTION 2.   The Congress shall have power to enforce this article by appropriate legislation.

Amendment XXV [1967]

SECTION 1.   In case of the removal of the President from office or of his death or resignation, the Vice President shall become President.

SECTION 2.   Whenever there is a vacancy in the office of the Vice President, the President shall nominate a Vice President who shall take office upon confirmation by a majority vote of both Houses of Congress.

SECTION 3.   Whenever the President transmits to the President pro tempore of the Senate and the Speaker of the House of Representatives his written declaration that he is unable to discharge the powers and duties of his office, and until he transmits to them a written declaration to the contrary, such powers and duties shall be discharged by the Vice President as Acting President.

SECTION 4.   Whenever the Vice President and a majority of either the principal officers of the executive departments or of such other body as Congress may by law provide, transmit to the President pro tempore of the Senate and the Speaker of the House of Representatives their written declaration that the President is unable to discharge the powers and duties of his office, the Vice President shall immediately assume the powers and duties of the office as Acting President.

Thereafter, when the President transmits to the President pro tempore of the Senate and the Speaker of the House of Representatives his written declaration that no inability exists, he shall resume the powers and duties of his office unless the Vice President and a majority of either the principal officers of the executive department or of such other body as Congress may by law provide, transmit within four days to the President pro tempore of the Senate and the Speaker of the House of Representatives their written declaration that the President is unable to discharge the powers and duties of his office. Thereupon Congress shall decide the issue, assembling within forty-eight hours for that purpose if not in session. If the Congress, within twenty-one days after receipt of the latter written declaration, or, if Congress is not in session, within twenty-one days after Congress is required to assemble, determines by two-thirds vote of both Houses that the President is unable to discharge the powers and duties of his office, the Vice President shall continue to discharge the same as Acting President; otherwise, the President shall resume the powers and duties of his office.

Amendment XXVI [1971]

SECTION 1.   The right of citizens of the United States, who are eighteen years of age or older, to vote shall not be denied or abridged by the United States or by any State on account of age.

SECTION 2.   The Congress shall have power to enforce this article by appropriate legislation.

Amendment XXVII [1992]

No law, varying the compensation for the services of the Senators and Representatives, shall take effect, until an election of Representatives shall have intervened.

SPANISH EQUIVALENTS FOR IMPORTANT LEGAL TERMS IN ENGLISH

Abandoned property: bienes abandonados

Acceptance: aceptación; consentimiento; acuerdo

Acceptor: aceptante

Accession: toma de posesión; aumento; accesión

Accommodation indorser: avalista de favor

Accommodation party: firmante de favor

Accord: acuerdo; convenio; arregio

Accord and satisfaction: transacción ejecutada

Act of state doctrine: doctrina de acto de gobierno

Administrative law: derecho administrativo

Administrative process: procedimiento o metódo administrativo

Administrator: administrador (-a)

Adverse possession: posesión de hecho susceptible de proscripción adquisitiva

Affirmative action: acción afirmativa

Affirmative defense: defensa afirmativa

After-acquired property: bienes adquiridos con posterioridad a un hecho dado

Agency: mandato; agencia

Agent: mandatorio; agente; representante

Agreement: convenio; acuerdo; contrato

Alien corporation: empresa extranjera

Allonge: hojas adicionales de endosos

Answer: contestación de la demande; alegato

Anticipatory repudiation: anuncio previo de las partes de su imposibilidad de cumplir con el contrato

Appeal: apelación; recurso de apelación

Appellate jurisdiction: jurisdicción de apelaciones

Appraisal right: derecho de valuación

Arbitration: arbitraje

Arson: incendio intencional

Articles of partnership: contrato social

Artisan's lien: derecho de retención que ejerce al artesano

Assault: asalto; ataque; agresión

Assignment of rights: transmisión; transferencia; cesión

Assumption of risk: no resarcimiento por exposición voluntaria al peligro

Attachment: auto judicial que autoriza el embargo; embargo

Bailee: depositario

Bailment: depósito; constitución en depósito

Bailor: depositante

Bankruptcy trustee: síndico de la quiebra

Battery: agresión; física

Bearer: portador; tenedor

Bearer instrument: documento al portador

Bequest or legacy: legado (de bienes muebles)

Bilateral contract: contrato bilateral

Bill of lading: conocimiento de embarque; carta de porte

Bill of Rights: declaración de derechos

Binder: póliza de seguro provisoria; recibo de pago a cuenta del precio

Blank indorsement: endoso en blanco

Blue sky laws: leyes reguladoras del comercio bursátil

Bond: título de crédito; garantía; caución

Bond indenture: contrato de emisión de bonos; contrato del ampréstito

Breach of contract: incumplimiento de contrato

Brief: escrito; resumen; informe

Burglary: violación de domicilio

Business judgment rule: regla de juicio comercial

Business tort: agravio comercial

Case law: ley de casos; derecho casuístico

Cashier's check: cheque de caja

Causation in fact: causalidad en realidad

Cease-and-desist order: orden para cesar y desistir

Certificate of deposit: certificado de depósito

Certified check: cheque certificado

Charitable trust: fideicomiso para fines benéficos

Chattel: bien mueble

Check: cheque

Chose in action: derecho inmaterial; derecho de acción

Civil law: derecho civil

Close corporation: sociedad de un solo accionista o de un grupo restringido de accionistas

Closed shop: taller agremiado (emplea solamente a miembros de un gremio)

Closing argument: argumento al final

Codicil: codicilo

Collateral: garantía; bien objeto de la garantía real

Comity: cortesía; cortesía entre naciones

Commercial paper: instrumentos negociables; documentos a valores commerciales

Common law: derecho consuetudinario; derecho común; ley común

Common stock: acción ordinaria

Comparative negligence: negligencia comparada

Compensatory damages: daños y perjuicios reales o compensatorios

Concurrent conditions: condiciones concurrentes

Concurrent jurisdiction: competencia concurrente de varios tribunales para entender en una misma causa

Concurring opinion: opinión concurrente

Condition: condición

Condition precedent: condición suspensiva

Condition subsequent: condición resolutoria

Confiscation: confiscación

Confusion: confusión; fusión

Conglomerate merger: fusión de firmas que operan en distintos mercados

Consent decree: acuerdo entre las partes aprobado por un tribunal

Consequential damages: daños y perjuicios indirectos

Consideration: consideración; motivo; contraprestación

Consolidation: consolidación

Constructive delivery: entrega simbólica

Constructive trust: fideicomiso creado por aplicación de la ley

Consumer protection law: ley para proteger el consumidor

Contract: contrato

Contract under seal: contrato formal o sellado

Contributory negligence: negligencia de la parte actora

Conversion: usurpación; conversión de valores

Copyright: derecho de autor

Corporation: sociedad anómina; corporación; persona juridica

Co-sureties: cogarantes

Counterclaim: reconvención; contrademanda

Counteroffer: contraoferta

Course of dealing: curso de transacciones

Course of performance: curso de cumplimiento

Covenant: pacto; garantía; contrato

Covenant not to sue: pacto or contrato a no demandar

Covenant of quiet enjoyment: garantía del uso y goce pacífico del inmueble

Creditors' composition agreement: concordato preventivo

Crime: crimen; delito; contravención

Criminal law: derecho penal

Cross-examination: contrainterrogatorio

Cure: cura; cuidado; derecho de remediar un vicio contractual

Customs receipts: recibos de derechos aduaneros

Damages: daños; indemnización por daños y perjuicios

Debit card: tarjeta de dé bito

Debtor: deudor

Debt securities: seguridades de deuda

Deceptive advertising: publicidad engañosa

Deed: escritura; título; acta translativa de domino

Defamation: difamación

Delegation of duties: delegación de obligaciones

Demand deposit: depósito a la vista

Depositions: declaración de un testigo fuera del tribunal

Devise: legado; deposición testamentaria (bienes inmuebles)

Directed verdict: veredicto según orden del juez y sin participación activa del jurado

Direct examination: interrogatorio directo; primer interrogatorio

Disaffirmance: repudiación; renuncia; anulación

Discharge: descargo; liberación; cumplimiento

Disclosed principal: mandante revelado

Discovery: descubrimiento; producción de la prueba

Dissenting opinion: opinión disidente

Dissolution: disolución; terminación

Diversity of citizenship: competencia de los tribunales federales para entender en causas cuyas partes intervinientes son cuidadanos de distintos estados

Divestiture: extinción premature de derechos reales

Dividend: dividendo

Docket: orden del día; lista de causas pendientes

Domestic corporation: sociedad local

Draft: orden de pago; letrade cambio

Drawee: girado; beneficiario

Drawer: librador

Duress: coacción; violencia

Easement: servidumbre

Embezzlement: desfalco; malversación

Eminent domain: poder de expropiación

Employment discrimination: discriminación en el empleo

Entrepreneur: empresario

Environmental law: ley ambiental

Equal dignity rule: regla de dignidad egual

Equity security: tipo de participación en una sociedad

Estate: propiedad; patrimonio; derecho

Estop: impedir; prevenir

Ethical issue: cuestión ética

Exclusive jurisdiction: competencia exclusiva

Exculpatory clause: cláusula eximente

Executed contract: contrato ejecutado

Execution: ejecución; cumplimiento

Executor: albacea

Executory contract: contrato aún no completamente consumado

Executory interest: derecho futuro

Express contract: contrato expreso

Expropriation: expropriación

Federal question: caso federal

Fee simple: pleno dominio; dominio absoluto

Fee simple absolute: dominio absoluto

Fee simple defeasible: dominio sujeta a una condición resolutoria

Felony: crimen; delito grave

Fictitious payee: beneficiario ficticio

Fiduciary: fiduciaro

Firm offer: oferta en firme

Fixture: inmueble por destino, incorporación a anexación

Floating lien: gravamen continuado

Foreign corporation: sociedad extranjera; U.S. sociedad constituída en otro estado

Forgery: falso; falsificación

Formal contract: contrato formal

Franchise: privilegio; franquicia; concesión

Franchisee: persona que recibe una concesión

Franchisor: persona que vende una concesión

Fraud: fraude; dolo; engaño

Future interest: bien futuro

Garnishment: embargo de derechos

General partner: socio comanditario

General warranty deed: escritura translativa de domino con garantía de título

Gift: donación

Gift *causa mortis*: donación por causa de muerte

Gift *inter vivos*: donación entre vivos

Good faith: buena fe

Good faith purchaser: comprador de buena fe

Holder: tenedor por contraprestación

Holder in due course: tenedor legítimo

Holographic will: testamento ológrafico

Homestead exemption laws: leyes que exceptúan las casas de familia de ejecución por duedas generales

Horizontal merger: fusión horizontal

Identification: identificación

Implied-in-fact contract: contrato implícito en realidad

Implied warranty: garantía implícita

Implied warranty of merchantability: garantía implícita de vendibilidad

Impossibility of performance: imposibilidad de cumplir un contrato

Imposter: imposter

Incidental beneficiary: beneficiario incidental; beneficiario secundario

Incidental damages: daños incidentales

Indictment: auto de acusación; acusación

Indorsee: endorsatario
Indorsement: endoso
Indorser: endosante
Informal contract: contrato no formal; contrato verbal
Information: acusación hecha por el ministerio público
Injunction: mandamiento; orden de no innovar
Innkeeper's lien: derecho de retención que ejerce el posadero
Installment contract: contrato de pago en cuotas
Insurable interest: interés asegurable
Intended beneficiary: beneficiario destinado
Intentional tort: agravio; cuasi-delito intenciónal
International law: derecho internaciónal
Interrogatories: preguntas escritas sometidas por una parte a la otra o a un testigo
Inter vivos **trust:** fideicomiso entre vivos
Intestacy laws: leyes de la condición de morir intestado
Intestate: intestado
Investment company: compañia de inversiones
Issue: emisión

Joint tenancy: derechos conjuntos en un bien inmueble en favor del beneficiario sobreviviente
Judgment *n.o.v.***:** juicio no obstante veredicto
Judgment rate of interest: interés de juicio
Judicial process: acto de procedimiento; proceso jurídico
Judicial review: revisión judicial
Jurisdiction: jurisdicción

Larceny: robo; hurto
Law: derecho; ley; jurisprudencia
Lease: contrato de locación; contrato de alquiler
Leasehold estate: bienes forales

Legal rate of interest: interés legal
Legatee: legatario
Letter of credit: carta de crédito
Levy: embargo; comiso
Libel: libelo; difamación escrita
Life estate: usufructo
Limited partner: comanditario
Limited partnership: sociedad en comandita
Liquidation: liquidación; realización
Lost property: objetos perdidos

Majority opinion: opinión de la mayoría
Maker: persona que realiza u ordena; librador
Mechanic's lien: gravamen de constructor
Mediation: mediación; intervención
Merger: fusión
Mirror image rule: fallo de reflejo
Misdemeanor: infracción; contravención
Mislaid property: bienes extraviados
Mitigation of damages: reducción de daños
Mortgage: hypoteca
Motion to dismiss: excepción parentoria
Mutual fund: fondo mutual

Negotiable instrument: instrumento negociable
Negotiation: negociación
Nominal damages: daños y perjuicios nominales
Novation: novación
Nuncupative will: testamento nuncupativo

Objective theory of contracts: teoria objetiva de contratos
Offer: oferta
Offeree: persona que recibe una oferta

Offeror: oferente
Order instrument: instrumento o documento a la orden
Original jurisdiction: jurisdicción de primera instancia
Output contract: contrato de producción

Parol evidence rule: regla relativa a la prueba oral
Partially disclosed principal: mandante revelado en parte
Partnership: sociedad colectiva; asociación; asociación de participación
Past consideration: causa o contraprestación anterior
Patent: patente; privilegio
Pattern or practice: muestra o práctica
Payee: beneficiario de un pago
Penalty: pena; penalidad
Per capita: por cabeza
Perfection: perfeción
Performance: cumplimiento; ejecución
Personal defenses: excepciones personales
Personal property: bienes muebles
Per stirpes: por estirpe
Plea bargaining: regateo por un alegato
Pleadings: alegatos
Pledge: prenda
Police powers: poders de policia y de prevención del crimen
Policy: póliza
Positive law: derecho positivo; ley positiva
Possibility of reverter: posibilidad de reversión
Precedent: precedente
Preemptive right: derecho de prelación
Preferred stock: acciones preferidas
Premium: recompensa; prima
Presentment warranty: garantía de presentación
Price discrimination: discriminación en los precios

Principal: mandante; principal
Privity: nexo jurídico
Privity of contract: relación contractual
Probable cause: causa probable
Probate: verificación; verificación del testamento
Probate court: tribunal de sucesiones y tutelas
Proceeds: resultados; ingresos
Profit: beneficio; utilidad; lucro
Promise: promesa
Promisee: beneficiario de una promesa
Promisor: promtente
Promissory estoppel: impedimento promisorio
Promissory note: pagaré; nota de pago
Promoter: promotor; fundador
Proximate cause: causa inmediata o próxima
Proxy: apoderado; poder
Punitive, or exemplary, damages: daños y perjuicios punitivos o ejemplares

Qualified indorsement: endoso con reservas
Quasi contract: contrato tácito o implícito
Quitclaim deed: acto de transferencia de una propiedad por finiquito, pero sin ninguna garantía sobre la validez del título transferido

Ratification: ratificación
Real property: bienes inmuebles
Reasonable doubt: duda razonable
Rebuttal: refutación
Recognizance: promesa; compromiso; reconocimiento
Recording statutes: leyes estatales sobre registros oficiales
Redress: reporacíon
Reformation: rectificación; reforma; corrección
Rejoinder: dúplica; contrarréplica

Release: liberación; renuncia a un derecho
Remainder: substitución; reversión
Remedy: recurso; remedio; reparación
Replevin: acción reivindicatoria; reivindicación
Reply: réplica
Requirements contract: contrato de suministro
Rescission: rescisión
Res judicata: cosa juzgada; res judicata
Respondeat superior: responsabilidad del mandante o del maestro
Restitution: restitución
Restrictive indorsement: endoso restrictivo
Resulting trust: fideicomiso implícito
Reversion: reversión; sustitución
Revocation: revocación; derogación
Right of contribution: derecho de contribución
Right of reimbursement: derecho de reembolso
Right of subrogation: derecho de subrogación
Right-to-work law: ley de libertad de trabajo
Robbery: robo
Rule 10b-5: Regla 10b-5

Sale: venta; contrato de compreventa
Sale on approval: venta a ensayo; venta sujeta a la aprobación del comprador
Sale or return: venta con derecho de devolución
Sales contract: contrato de compraventa; boleto de compraventa
Satisfaction: satisfacción; pago
Scienter: a sabiendas
S corporation: S corporación
Secured party: acreedor garantizado

Secured transaction: transacción garantizada
Securities: volares; titulos; seguridades
Security agreement: convenio de seguridad
Security interest: interés en un bien dado en garantía que permite a quien lo detenta venderlo en caso de incumplimiento
Service mark: marca de identificación de servicios
Shareholder's derivative suit: acción judicial entablada por un accionista en nombre de la sociedad
Signature: firma; rúbrica
Slander: difamación oral; calumnia
Sovereign immunity: immunidad soberana
Special indorsement: endoso especial; endoso a la orden de una person en particular
Specific performance: ejecución precisa, según los términos del contrato
Spendthrift trust: fideicomiso para pródigos
Stale check: cheque vencido
Stare decisis: acatar las decisiones, observar los precedentes
Statutory law: derecho estatutario; derecho legislado; derecho escrito
Stock: acciones
Stock warrant: certificado para la compra de acciones
Stop-payment order: orden de suspensión del pago de un cheque dada por el librador del mismo
Strict liability: responsabilidad unconditional
Summary judgment: fallo sumario

Tangible property: bienes corpóreos
Tenancy at will: inguilino por tiempo indeterminado (según la voluntad del propietario)
Tenancy by sufferance: posesión por tolerancia

Tenancy by the entirety: locación conyugal conjunta

Tenancy for years: inguilino por un término fijo

Tenancy in common: specie de copropiedad indivisa

Tender: oferta de pago; oferta de ejecución

Testamentary trust: fideicomiso testamentario

Testator: testador (-a)

Third party beneficiary contract: contrato para el beneficio del tercero-beneficiario

Tort: agravio; cuasi-delito

Totten trust: fideicomiso creado por un depósito bancario

Trade acceptance: letra de cambio aceptada

Trademark: marca registrada

Trade name: nombre comercial; razón social

Traveler's check: cheque del viajero

Trespass to land: ingreso no authorizado a las tierras de otro

Trespass to personal property: violación de los derechos posesorios de un tercero con respecto a bienes muebles

Trust: fideicomiso; trust

Ultra vires: ultra vires; fuera de la facultad (de una sociedad anónima)

Unanimous opinion: opinión unámine

Unconscionable contract or clause: contrato leonino; cláusula leonino

Underwriter: subscriptor; asegurador

Unenforceable contract: contrato que no se puede hacer cumplir

Unilateral contract: contrato unilateral

Union shop: taller agremiado; empresa en la que todos los empleados son miembros del gremio o sindicato

Universal defenses: defensas legitimas o legales

Usage of trade: uso comercial

Usury: usura

Valid contract: contrato válido

Venue: lugar; sede del proceso

Vertical merger: fusión vertical de empresas

Voidable contract: contrato anulable

Void contract: contrato nulo; contrato inválido, sin fuerza legal

Voir dire: examen preliminar de un testigo a jurado por el tribunal para determinar su competencia

Voting trust: fideicomiso para ejercer el derecho de voto

Waiver: renuncia; abandono

Warranty of habitability: garantía de habitabilidad

Watered stock: acciones diluídos; capital inflado

White-collar crime: crimen administrativo

Writ of attachment: mandamiento de ejecución; mandamiento de embargo

Writ of *certiorari*: auto de avocación; auto de certiorari

Writ of execution: auto ejecutivo; mandamiento de ejecutión

Writ of mandamus: auto de mandamus; mandamiento; orden judicial

GLOSSARY

ABA–approved program A legal or paralegal educational program that satisfies the standards for paralegal training set forth by the American Bar Association.

acceptance In contract law, the offeree's indication to the offeror that the offeree agrees to be bound by the terms of the offeror's offer, or proposal to form a contract.

acquittal A certification or declaration following a trial that the individual accused of a crime is innocent, or free from guilt, in the eyes of the law and is thus absolved of the charges.

actionable Capable of serving as the basis of a lawsuit. An actionable claim can be pursued in a lawsuit or other court action.

active listening The act of listening attentively to the speaker's message and responding by giving appropriate feedback to show that you understand what the speaker is saying; restating the speaker's message in your own words to confirm that you accurately interpreted what was said.

actual malice Real and demonstrable evil intent. In a defamation suit, a statement made about a public figure normally must be made with actual malice (with either knowledge of its falsity or a reckless disregard of the truth) for liability to be incurred.

actus reus A guilty (prohibited) act. The commission of a prohibited act is one of the two essential elements required for criminal liability; the other element is the intent to commit a crime.

address block That part of a letter that indicates to whom the letter is addressed. The address block is placed in the upper left-hand portion of the letter, above the salutation (or reference line, if one is included).

adjudication The act of resolving a controversy and rendering an order or decision based on a review of the evidence presented.

administrative agency A federal or state government agency established to perform a specific function. Administrative agencies are authorized by legislative acts to make and enforce rules relating to the purpose for which they were established.

administrative law A body of law created by administrative agencies in the form of rules, regulations, orders, and decisions in order to carry out their duties and responsibilities.

administrative law judge (ALJ) One who presides over an administrative agency hearing and who has the power to administer oaths, take testimony, rule on questions of evidence, and make determinations otherwise authorized by law.

administrative process The procedure used by administrative agencies in the administration of law.

administrator A person appointed by a court to serve as a personal representative for a person who died intestate (without a valid will) or if the executor named in the will cannot serve.

adoption A procedure in which persons become the legal parents of a child who is not their biological child.

adversarial system of justice A legal system in which the parties to a lawsuit are opponents, or adversaries, and present their cases in the light most favorable to themselves. The impartial decision maker (the judge or jury) determines who wins and who loses based on the evidence presented.

affidavit A written statement of facts, confirmed by the oath or affirmation of the party making it and made before a person having the authority to administer the oath or affirmation.

affirm To uphold the judgment of a lower court.

affirmative defense A response to a plaintiff's claim that does not deny the plaintiff's facts but attacks the plaintiff's legal right to bring an action.

agency A relationship between two persons in which one person (the agent) represents or acts in the place of another (the principal).

agent A person who is authorized to act for or in the place of another person (the principal).

agreement A meeting of the minds, and a requirement for a valid contract. Agreement involves two distinct events: an offer to form a contract and the acceptance of that offer by the offeree.

alimony Money paid to support a former spouse after a marriage has been terminated. The alimony may be permanent or temporary (rehabilitative).

allegation A party's statement, claim, or assertion made in a pleading to the court. The allegation sets forth the issue that the party expects to prove.

alternative dispute resolution (ADR) The resolution of disputes in ways other than those involved in the traditional judicial process. Negotiation, mediation, and arbitration are forms of ADR.

American Arbitration Association (AAA) The major organization offering arbitration services in the United States.

American Association for Paralegal Education (AAfPE) A national organization of paralegal educators; the AAfPE was established in 1981 to promote high standards for paralegal education.

American Bar Association (ABA) A voluntary national association of attorneys. The ABA plays an active role in developing educational and ethical standards for attorneys and in pursuing improvements in the administration of justice.

amicus curiae brief A brief filed with the court by a third party (that is, a party not directly involved in the lawsuit) that is concerned about the outcome of the litigation. The purpose of such a brief is to convince the court to rule in favor of one of the parties because not to do so would affect a broad interest of society. (*Amicus curiae* is Latin for "friend of the court.")

annotation A brief comment, an explanation of a legal point, or a case summary found in a case digest or other legal source.

annulment A court decree that invalidates (nullifies) a marriage. Although the marriage itself is deemed nonexistent, children of a marriage that is annulled are deemed legitimate.

answer A defendant's response to a plaintiff's complaint.

appeal The process of seeking a higher court's review of a lower court's decision for the purpose of correcting or changing the lower court's judgment or decision.

appellant The party who takes an appeal from one court to another; sometimes referred to as the petitioner.

appellant's brief An appellate brief that argues in favor of the appellant's position. This brief will try to convince the court that the lower court's decision was erroneous.

appellate brief A document submitted to an appellate court setting forth legal arguments and supporting law in favor of the appellant or the appellee.

appellate court A court that reviews decisions made by lower courts, such as trial courts; a court of appeals.

appellate jurisdiction The power of a court to hear and decide an appeal; that is, the power and authority of a court to review cases that already have been tried in a lower court and the power to make decisions about them without actually holding a trial. This process is called appellate review.

appellee The party against whom an appeal is taken—that is, the party who opposes setting aside or reversing the judgment; sometimes referred to as the respondent.

appellee's brief An appellate brief that argues in favor of the appellee's position. This brief will attempt to rebut (counter) any arguments in the appellant's brief and will emphasize the accuracy of the earlier judgment rendered in its favor.

appropriation In tort law, the use by one person of another person's name, likeness, or other identifying characteristic without permission and for the benefit of the user.

arbitration A method of settling disputes in which a dispute is submitted to a disinterested third party (other than a court), who renders a decision that may or may not be legally binding.

arbitration clause A clause in a contract that provides that, in case of a dispute, the parties will determine their rights by arbitration rather than through the judicial system.

arraignment A court proceeding in which the suspect is formally charged with the criminal offense stated in the indictment. The suspect then enters a plea (guilty, not guilty, or *nolo contendere*) in response.

arrest To take into custody a person suspected of criminal activity.

arrest warrant A written order, based on probable cause and issued by a judge or public official (magistrate), commanding that the person named on the warrant be arrested by the police.

arson The willful and malicious burning of a building (and, in some states, personal property) owned by another; arson statutes have been extended to cover the destruction of any building, regardless of ownership, by fire or explosion.

articles of incorporation The document filed with the appropriate state official, usually the secretary of state, when a business is incorporated. State statutes usually prescribe what kind of information must be contained in the articles of incorporation.

assault Any word or action intended to make another person fearful of immediate physical harm; a reasonably believable threat.

associate attorney An attorney working for a law firm who is not a partner and does not have an ownership interest in the firm. Associates are usually less experienced attorneys and may be invited to become partners after working for the firm for several years.

assumption of risk Voluntarily taking upon oneself a known risk. Assumption of risk is a defense against negligence that can be used when the plaintiff has knowledge of and appreciates a danger and voluntarily exposes himself or herself to the danger.

attorney-client privilege A rule of evidence requiring that confidential communications between a client and his or her attorney (relating to their professional relationship) be kept confidential, unless the client consents to disclosure.

authentication The process of establishing the genuineness of an item that is to be introduced as evidence in a trial.

Auto-Cite An aid to legal research developed by the editors of Lexis®. On Lexis®, Auto-Cite can be used to find the history of a case, to verify whether the case is still good law, and to perform other functions.

award In the context of ADR, the decision rendered by an arbitrator.

bail The amount of money or conditions set by the court to assure that an individual accused of a crime will appear for further criminal proceedings. If the accused person provides bail, whether in cash or by means of a bail bond, then the person is released from jail.

bankruptcy court A federal court of limited jurisdiction that hears only bankruptcy proceedings.

bankruptcy law The body of federal law that governs bankruptcy proceedings. The twin goals of bankruptcy law are (1) to protect a debtor by giving him or her a fresh start, free from creditors' claims; and (2) to ensure that creditors who are competing for a debtor's assets are treated fairly.

battery The intentional and offensive touching of another without lawful justification.

beyond a reasonable doubt The standard used to determine the guilt or innocence of a person charged with a crime. To be guilty of a crime, a suspect must be proved guilty "beyond and to the exclusion of every reasonable doubt."

bigamy The act of entering into marriage with one person while still legally married to another.

Bill of Rights The first ten amendments to the Constitution.

billable hours Hours or fractions of hours that attorneys and paralegals spend in work that requires legal expertise and that can be billed directly to clients.

binding mediation A form of ADR in which a mediator attempts to facilitate agreement between the parties, but then issues a legally binding decision if no agreement is reached.

bonus An end-of-the-year payment to a salaried employee in appreciation for that employee's overtime work, work quality, diligence, or dedication to the firm.

booking The process of entering a suspect's name, offense, and arrival time into the police log (blotter) following his or her arrest.

breach To violate a legal duty by an act or a failure to act.

breach of contract The failure, without legal excuse, of a contractual party to perform the obligations assumed in a contract.

briefing a case Summarizing a case. A typical case brief will indicate the full citation for the case, the factual background and procedural history of the case, the issue or issues raised in the case, the court's decision, the court's holding, and the legal reasoning on which the court based its decision. The brief may also include conclusions or notes concerning the case made by the one briefing it.

browse-wrap terms Terms and conditions of use that are presented to an Internet user at the time the user downloads certain products, such as software, but that the user need not agree to (by clicking "I agree," for example) before being able to install or use the products.

bureaucracy In relation to government, the organizational structure, consisting of bureaus and agencies, through which the government implements and enforces the laws.

burglary Breaking and entering onto the property of another with the intent to commit a felony.

business invitee A person, such as a customer or client, who is invited onto business premises by the owner of those premises for business purposes.

business tort Wrongful interference with another's business rights.

bylaws A set of governing rules adopted by a corporation or other association.

case law Rules of law announced in court decisions.

case of first impression A case presenting a legal issue that has not yet been addressed by a court in a particular jurisdiction.

case on "all fours" A case in which all four elements of a case (the parties, the circumstances, the legal issues involved, and the remedies sought by the plaintiff) are very similar to those in the case being researched.

case on point A case involving factual circumstances and issues that are similar to those in the case being researched.

causation in fact Causation brought about by an act or omission without which an event would not have occurred.

cease-and-desist order An administrative or judicial order prohibiting a person or business firm from conducting activities that an agency or court has deemed illegal.

certificate of incorporation (corporate charter) The document issued by a state official (usually the secretary of state) granting a corporation legal existence and the right to function.

certification Formal recognition by a private group or a state agency that an individual has satisfied the group's standards of proficiency, knowledge, and competence; ordinarily accomplished through the taking of an examination.

Certified Legal Assistant (CLA) A legal assistant whose legal competency has been certified by the National Association of Legal Assistants (NALA) following an examination that tests the legal assistant's knowledge and skills.

Certified Legal Assistant Specialist (CLAS) A legal assistant whose competency in a legal specialty has been certified by the National Association of Legal Assistants (NALA) following an examination of the legal assistant's knowledge and skills in the specialty area.

chain of custody A series describing the movement and location of evidence from the time it is obtained to the time it is presented in court. The court requires that evidence be preserved in the condition in which it was obtained if it is to be admitted into evidence at trial.

challenge An attorney's objection, during *voir dire,* to the inclusion of a particular person on the jury.

challenge for cause A *voir dire* challenge for which an attorney states the reason why a prospective juror should not be included in the jury.

chancellor An adviser to the king in medieval England. Individuals petitioned the king for relief when they could not obtain an adequate remedy in a court of law, and these petitions were decided by the chancellor.

charge The judge's instruction to the jury, following the attorneys' closing arguments, setting forth the rules of law that the jury must apply in reaching its decision, or verdict.

child support The financial support necessary to provide for a child's needs. Commonly, when a marriage is terminated, the noncustodial spouse agrees or is required by the court to make child-support payments to the custodial spouse.

chronologically In a time sequence; naming or listing events in the time order in which they occurred.

circumstantial evidence Indirect evidence that is offered to establish, by inference, the likelihood of a fact that is in question.

citation In case law, a reference to the volume number, name, and page number of the reporter in which a case can be found. In statutory and administrative law, a reference to the title number, name, and section of the code in which a statute or regulation can be found. In criminal procedure, an order for a defendant to appear in court or indicating that a person has violated a legal rule.

citator A book or online service that provides the history and interpretation of a statute, regulation, or court decision and a list of the cases, statutes, and regulations that have interpreted, applied, or modified a statute or regulation.

civil law The branch of law dealing with the definition and enforcement of private or public rights, as opposed to criminal matters.

civil law system A system of law derived from that of the Roman Empire and based on a code rather than case law; the predominant system of law in the nations of continental Europe and the nations that were once their colonies.

click-on agreement An agreement that arises when a buyer, engaging in a transaction on a computer, indicates his or her assent to be bound by the terms of an offer by clicking on a button that says, for example, "I agree"; sometimes referred to as a *click-on license* or a *click-wrap agreement.*

close corporation A corporation owned by a small group of shareholders, often family members; also called a *closely held corporation.* Shares in close corporations cannot be publicly traded on the stock market, and often other restrictions on stock transfer apply. Some close corporations qualify for special tax status as *S corporations.*

closed-ended question A question phrased in such a way that it elicits a simple "yes" or "no" answer.

closing A final comment to a letter that is placed above the signature, such as "Sincerely" or "Very truly yours."

closing argument An argument made by each side's attorney after the cases for the plaintiff and defendant have been presented. Closing arguments are made prior to the jury charge.

code A systematic and topically organized presentation of laws, rules, or regulations.

codify To collect and organize systematically and logically a body of concepts, principles, decisions, or doctrines.

collective bargaining The process by which labor and management negotiate the terms and conditions of employment, including wages, benefits, working conditions, and other matters.

common law A body of law developed from custom or judicial decisions in English and U.S. courts and not by a legislature.

common law marriage A marriage that is formed solely by mutual consent and without a marriage license or ceremony. The couple must be eligible to marry, must have a present and continuing agreement to be husband and wife, must live together as husband and wife, and must hold themselves out to the public as husband and wife. Only fourteen states recognize common law marriages.

community property Defined in ten states as all property acquired during the marriage, except for inheritances or gifts received during the marriage by either marital partner. Each spouse has a one-half ownership interest in community property.

comparative negligence A theory in tort law under which the liability for injuries resulting from negligent acts is shared by all persons who were guilty of negligence (including the injured party) on the basis of each person's proportionate carelessness.

compensatory damages A money award equivalent to the actual value of injuries or damages sustained by the aggrieved party.

complaint The pleading made by a plaintiff or a charge made by the state alleging wrongdoing on the part of the defendant.

computer information Under the Uniform Computer Information Transactions Act, information in electronic form obtained from or through use of a computer, or that is in digital or an equivalent form capable of being processed by a computer.

computer-assisted legal research (CALR) Any legal research conducted with the assistance of computers. CALR includes the use of CD-ROMs, fee-based providers such as Westlaw® and Lexis®, and the Internet.

concurrent jurisdiction Jurisdiction that exists when two different courts have the power to hear a case. For example, some cases can be heard in either a federal or a state court.

confirmation letter A letter that states the substance of a previously conducted verbal discussion to provide a permanent record of the oral conversation.

conflict of interest A situation in which two or more duties or interests come into conflict, as when an attorney attempts to represent opposing parties in a legal dispute.

conflicts check A procedure for determining whether an agreement to represent a potential client will result in a conflict of interest.

consideration Something of value, such as money or the performance of an action not otherwise required, that motivates the formation of a contract. Each party must give consideration for the contract to be binding.

consolidation A process in which two or more corporations join to become a completely new corporation. The original corporations cease to exist.

constitutional law Law based on the U.S. Constitution and the constitutions of the various states.

consumer An individual who purchases products and services for personal or household use.

consumer law Statutes, agency rules, and judicial decisions protecting consumers of goods and services.

contempt of court The intentional obstruction or frustration of the court's attempt to administer justice. A party to a lawsuit may be held in contempt of court (punishable by a fine or jail sentence) for refusing to comply with a court's order.

contingency fee A legal fee that consists of a specified percentage (such as 30 percent) of the amount the plaintiff recovers in a civil lawsuit. The fee must be paid only if the plaintiff prevails in the lawsuit (recovers damages).

contract An agreement or bargain struck between parties in which each party assumes a legal duty to the other party. The requirements for a valid contract are agreement, consideration, contractual capacity, and legality.

contractual capacity The threshold mental capacity required by law for a party who enters into a contract to be bound by that contract.

continuing legal education (CLE) program Courses through which attorneys and other legal professionals extend their education beyond school.

contributory negligence A theory in tort law under which a complaining party's own negligence contributed to or caused his or her injuries. Contributory negligence is an absolute bar to recovery in a minority of jurisdictions.

conversion The act of wrongfully taking or retaining of a person's personal property and placing it in the service of another.

copyright The exclusive right of an author (or other creator) to publish, print, or sell an intellectual production for a statutory period of time.

corporate law Law that governs the formation, financing, merger and acquisition, and termination of corporations, as well as the rights and duties of those who own and run the corporation.

counteradvertising New advertising undertaken pursuant to a Federal Trade Commission order for the purpose of correcting earlier false claims that were made about a product.

counterclaim A claim made by a defendant in a civil lawsuit against the plaintiff; in effect, a counterclaiming defendant is suing the plaintiff.

court of equity A court that decides controversies and administers justice according to the rules, principles, and precedents of equity.

court of law A court in which the only remedies that could be granted were things of value, such as money damages. In early England, courts of law were distinct from courts of equity.

crime A broad term for violations of law that are punishable by the state and are codified by legislatures. The objective of criminal law is to protect the public.

criminal law The branch of law that governs and defines those actions that are crimes and that subjects persons convicted of crimes to punishment imposed by the government (a fine or jail time).

cross-claim A claim asserted by a defendant in a civil lawsuit against another defendant or by a plaintiff against another plaintiff.

cross-examination The questioning of an opposing witness during the trial.

cyber crime A crime that occurs online, in the virtual community of the Internet, as opposed to the physical world.

cybernotary A legally recognized authority that can certify the validity of digital signatures.

cyber stalker A person who commits the crime of stalking in cyberspace. The cyber stalker usually finds victims through Internet chat rooms, newsgroups, bulletin boards, or e-mail and proceeds to harass that person or put the person in reasonable fear for his or her safety or the safety of his or her immediate family.

cyber tort A tort committed in cyberspace.

damages Money awarded as a remedy for a civil wrong, such as a breach of contract or a tortious act.

deceptive advertising Advertising that misleads consumers, either by unjustified claims concerning a product's performance or by the failure to disclose relevant information concerning the product's composition or performance.

deed A document by which title to property is transferred from one party to another.

defamation Anything published or publicly spoken that causes injury to another's good name, reputation, or character.

default judgment A judgment entered by a clerk or court against a party who has failed to appear in court to answer or defend against a claim that has been brought against him or her by another party.

defendant A party against whom a lawsuit is brought.

defense The reasons that a defendant offers and alleges why the plaintiff should not recover or establish what she or he seeks in a lawsuit.

defense of others The use of reasonable force to protect others from harm.

defense of property The use of reasonable force to protect one's property from the harm threatened by another. The use of deadly force in defending one's property is seldom justified.

delegation doctrine A doctrine that authorizes Congress to delegate some of its lawmaking authority to administrative agencies. The doctrine is implied by Article I of the U.S. Constitution, which grants specific powers to Congress to enact and oversee the implementation of laws.

demand letter A letter in which one party explains its legal position in a dispute and requests that the recipient take some action (such as paying money owed).

deponent A party or witness who testifies under oath during a deposition.

deposition A pretrial question-and-answer proceeding, usually conducted orally, in which a party or witness answers an attorney's questions. The answers are given under oath, and the session is recorded.

deposition transcript The official transcription of the recording taken during a deposition.

dicta A Latin term referring to nonbinding (nonprecedential) judicial statements that are not directly related to the facts or issues presented in the case and thus not essential to the holding.

digest A compilation in which brief summaries of court cases are arranged by subject and subdivided by jurisdiction and court.

direct evidence Evidence establishing the existence of a fact that is in question without relying on inferences.

direct examination The examination of a witness by the attorney who calls the witness to the stand to testify on behalf of the attorney's client.

director A person elected by the shareholders to direct corporate affairs.

disbarment A severe disciplinary sanction in which an attorney's license to practice law in the state is revoked because of unethical or illegal conduct.

discovery Formal investigation prior to trial. During discovery, opposing parties use various methods, such as interrogatories and depositions, to obtain information from each other and from witnesses to prepare for trial.

discovery plan A plan formed by the attorneys litigating a lawsuit, on behalf of their clients, that indicates the types of information that will be disclosed by each party to the other prior to trial, the testimony and evidence that each party will or may introduce at trial, and the general schedule for pretrial disclosures and events.

dissolution The formal disbanding of a partnership or a corporation.

diversion program In some jurisdictions, an alternative to prosecution that is offered to certain felony suspects to deter them from future unlawful acts.

diversity of citizenship Under Article III, Section 2 of the Constitution, a bases for federal district court jurisdiction over a lawsuit between (1) citizens of different states, (2) a foreign country and citizens of a state or different states, or (3) citizens of a state and citizens or subjects of a foreign country. The amount in controversy must be more than $75,000 before a federal court can take juris-diction in such cases.

dividend A distribution of profits to corporate sharehold-ers, disbursed in proportion to the number of shares held.

divorce A formal court proceeding that legally dissolves a marriage.

docket The list of cases entered on a court's calendar and thus scheduled to be heard by the court.

double billing Billing more than one client for the same billable time period.

double jeopardy To place at risk (jeopardize) a person's life or liberty twice. The Fifth Amendment to the Constitution prohibits a second prosecution for the same criminal offense in all but a few circumstances.

dram shop act A state statute that imposes liability on the owners of bars and taverns, as well as those who serve alcoholic drinks to the public, for injuries resulting from accidents caused by intoxicated persons when the sellers or servers of alcoholic drinks contributed to the intoxication.

due process of law Fair, reasonable, and standard proce-dures that must be used by the government in any legal action against a citizen. The Fifth Amendment to the U.S. Constitution prohibits the deprivation of "life, liberty, or property without due process of law."

duty of care The duty of all persons, as established by tort law, to exercise a reasonable amount of care in their dealings with others. Failure to exercise due care, which is normally determined by the reasonable person stan-dard, constitutes the tort of negligence.

e-signature An electronic sound, symbol, or process attached to or logically associated with a record and executed or adopted by a person with the intent to sign the record, according to the Uniform Electronic Transactions Act.

early neutral case evaluation A form of ADR in which a neutral third party evaluates the strengths and weak-nesses of the disputing parties' positions; the evaluator's opinion forms the basis for negotiating a settlement.

easement The right of a person to make limited use of another person's real property without taking anything from the property.

elder law A relatively new legal specialty that involves servicing the needs of older clients, such as estate plan-ning and making arrangements for long-term care.

emancipation The legal relinquishment by a child's par-ents or guardian of the legal right to exercise control over the child. Usually, a child who moves out of the parents' home and supports himself or herself is considered emancipated.

embezzlement The fraudulent appropriation of the prop-erty or money of another by a person entrusted with that property or money.

eminent domain The power of a government to take land for public use from private citizens for just compensation.

employment at will A common law doctrine under which employment is considered to be "at will"—that is, either party may terminate the employment relationship at any time and for any reason, unless a contract speci-fies otherwise.

employment manual A firm's handbook or written state-ment that specifies the policies and procedures that govern the firm's employees and employer-employee relationships.

enabling legislation A statute enacted by a legislature that authorizes the creation of an administrative agency and specifies the name, purpose, composition, and powers of the agency being created.

environmental impact statement (EIS) A statement required by the National Environmental Policy Act for any major federal action that will significantly affect the quality of the environment. The statement must analyze the action's impact on the environment and explore alter-native actions that might be taken.

environmental law All state and federal laws or regula-tions enacted or issued to protect the environment and preserve environmental resources.

equitable principles and maxims Propositions or general statements of rules of law that are frequently involved in equity jurisdiction.

estate administration The process in which a decedent's personal representative settles the affairs of the dece-dent's estate (collects assets, pays debts and taxes, and distributes the remaining assets to heirs); the process is usually overseen by a probate court.

estate planning Making arrangements, during a person's lifetime, for the transfer of that person's property or oblig-ations to others on the person's death. Estate planning often involves executing a will, establishing a trust fund, or taking out a life insurance policy to provide for others, such as a spouse or children, on one's death.

ethical wall A term that refers to the procedures used to create a screen around a legal employee to shield him or her from information about a case in which there is a conflict of interest.

evidence Anything that is used to prove the existence or nonexistence of a fact.

exclusionary rule In criminal procedure, a rule under which any evidence that is obtained in violation of the accused's constitutional rights, as well as any evidence derived from illegally obtained evidence, will not be admissible in court.

exclusive jurisdiction Jurisdiction that exists when a case can be heard only in a particular court, such as a federal court.

executive agency A type of administrative agency that is either a cabinet department or a subagency within a cabinet department. Executive agencies fall under the authority of the president, who has the power to appoint and remove federal officers.

executor A person appointed by a testator to serve as a personal representative on the testator's death.

expense slip A slip of paper on which any expense, or cost, that is incurred on behalf of a client (such as the payment of court fees or long-distance telephone charges) is recorded.

expert witness A witness with professional training or substantial experience qualifying him or her to testify as to his or her opinion on a particular subject.

eyewitness A witness who testifies about an event that he or she observed or has experienced firsthand.

family law Law relating to family matters, such as marriage, divorce, child support, and child custody.

federal question A question that pertains to the U.S. Constitution, acts of Congress, or treaties. A federal question provides a basis for jurisdiction by the federal courts. This jurisdiction is authorized by Article III, Section 2, of the Constitution.

Federal Rules of Civil Procedure (FRCP) The rules controlling all procedural matters in civil trials brought before the federal district courts.

fee simple Ownership rights entitling the holder to use, possess, or dispose of the property however he or she chooses during his or her lifetime.

felony A crime—such as arson, murder, rape, or robbery—that carries the most severe sanctions. Sanctions range from one year in a state or federal prison to life imprisonment or (in some states) the death penalty.

fiduciary relationship A relationship involving a high degree of trust and confidence.

file transfer protocol (ftp) An interface program that connects one computer to another over the Internet to copy files.

fixed fee A fee paid to the attorney by his or her client for having rendered a specified legal service, such as the creation of a simple will.

forgery The fraudulent making or altering of any writing in a way that changes the legal rights and liabilities of another.

forms file A reference file containing copies of the firm's commonly used legal documents and informational forms. The documents in the forms file serve as a model for drafting new documents.

foster care A temporary arrangement in which a family is paid by the state to care for a child for a limited period of time, often pending adoption.

fraudulent misrepresentation Any misrepresentation, either by misstatement or by omission of a material fact, knowingly made with the intention of deceiving another and on which a reasonable person would and does rely to his or her detriment.

freelance paralegal A paralegal who operates his or her own business and provides services to attorneys on a contractual basis. A freelance paralegal works under the supervision of an attorney, who assumes responsibility for the paralegal's work product.

friendly witness A witness who is biased against your client's adversary or sympathetic toward your client in a lawsuit or other legal proceeding.

garnishment A proceeding in which a creditor legally seizes a portion of a debtor's property (such as wages) that is in the possession of a third party (such as an employer).

general licensing A type of licensing in which all individuals within a specific profession or group (such as paralegals) must meet licensing requirements imposed by the state before they may legally practice their profession.

general partner A partner who participates in managing the business of a partnership and has all the rights and liabilities that arise under traditional partnership law.

genuineness of assent Knowing and voluntary assent to the contract terms. If a contract is formed as a result of mistake, misrepresentation, undue influence, or duress, genuineness of assent is lacking, and the contract will be voidable.

Good Samaritan statute A state statute stipulating that persons who provide emergency services to, or rescue, others in peril—unless they do so recklessly, thus causing further harm—cannot be sued for negligence.

grand jury The group of citizens called to decide whether probable cause exists to believe that a suspect committed the crime with which he or she has been charged and should stand trial.

guardian *ad litem* A person appointed by the court to represent the interests of a child or a mentally incompetent person before the court.

hacker A person who uses one computer to break into another.

headnote A note near the beginning of a reported case summarizing the court's ruling on an issue.

hearsay Testimony that is given in court by a witness who relates not what he or she knows personally but what another person said. Hearsay is generally not admissible as evidence.

historical school A school of legal thought that emphasizes the evolutionary development of law and that looks to the past to discover what the principles of contemporary law should be.

holding The binding legal principle, or precedent, that is drawn from the court's decision in a case.

home page The main page of a Web site. Often, the home page serves as a table of contents to other pages at the site.

hornbook A single-volume scholarly discussion, or treatise, on a particular legal subject (such as property law).

hostile witness A witness who is biased against your client or friendly toward your client's adversary in a lawsuit or other legal proceeding; an adverse witness.

hung jury A jury whose members are so irreconcilably divided in their opinions that they cannot reach a verdict. The judge in this situation may order a new trial.

hypertext transfer protocol (http) An interface program that enables computers to communicate. Hypertext is a database system by which distinct objects, such as text and graphics, can be linked. A protocol is a system of formats and rules.

hypothetical question A question based on hypothesis, conjecture, or fiction.

identity theft The theft of a form of identification, such as a name, date of birth, or Social Security number, which is then used to access the victim's financial resources.

immigration law All laws that set forth the requirements that persons must meet if they wish to visit or immigrate to the United States.

impeach To call into question the credibility of a witness by challenging the truth or accuracy of his or her trial statement.

independent adoption A privately arranged adoption, as when a doctor, lawyer, or other individual puts a couple seeking to adopt a child in contact with a pregnant woman who has decided to give up her child for adoption.

independent contractor A person who is hired to perform a specific undertaking but who is free to choose how and when to perform the work. An independent contractor may or may not be an agent.

independent regulatory agency A type of administrative agency that is more independent of presidential control than an executive agency. Officials of independent regulatory agencies cannot be removed without cause.

indictment A charge or written accusation, issued by a grand jury, that probable cause exists to believe that a named person has committed a crime for which he or she should stand trial.

information A formal criminal charge made by a prosecutor without a grand jury indictment.

informative letter A letter that conveys certain information to a client, a witness, an adversary's counsel, or other person regarding some legal matter (such as the date, time, place, and purpose of a meeting) or a cover letter that accompanies other documents being sent to a person or court.

injunction A court decree ordering a person to do or refrain from doing a certain act or activity.

insider trading Trading in the stock of a publicly listed corporation based on inside information about the corporation that is not available to the public. One who possesses inside information and has a duty not to disclose it to outsiders may not profit from the purchase or sale of securities based on that information until that information is available to the public.

intellectual property Property that results from intellectual, creative processes. Copyrights, patents, and trademarks are examples of intellectual property.

intentional tort A wrongful act knowingly committed.

international law The law that governs relations among nations. International customs and treaties are generally considered to be two of the most important sources of international law.

Internet service provider (ISP) A company that provides dedicated access to the Internet, generally through a local phone number.

interrogatories A series of written questions for which written answers are prepared and then signed under oath by a party to a lawsuit (the plaintiff or the defendant).

interviewee The person who is being interviewed.

***inter vivos* trust** A trust created by the grantor (settlor) and effective during the grantor's lifetime—that is, a trust not established by a will.

intestacy laws State statutes that specify how property will be distributed when a person dies intestate (without a valid will).

intestate The state of having died without a valid will.

investigation plan A plan that lists each step involved in obtaining and verifying the facts and information that are relevant to the legal problem being investigated.

joint and several liability Shared and individual liability. In partnership law, joint and several liability means that a third party may sue one or more of the partners separately or all of them together. This is true even if one of the partners sued did not participate in or know about whatever gave rise to the cause of action.

joint custody Custody of a child following the termination of a marriage that is shared by the parents.

joint liability Shared liability. In partnership law, partners incur joint liability for partnership obligations and debts.

joint tenancy The joint ownership of property by two or more co-owners in which each co-owner owns an undivided portion of the property. On the death of one of the joint tenants, his or her interest automatically passes to the surviving joint tenant or tenants.

judgment The court's final decision regarding the rights and claims of the parties to a lawsuit.

judgment creditor A creditor who is legally entitled, by a court's judgment, to collect the amount of the judgment from a debtor.

jurisdiction The authority of a court to hear and decide a specific action.

jurisprudence The science or philosophy of law.

justiciable controversy A controversy that is real and substantial, as opposed to hypothetical or academic.

KeyCite An aid to legal research developed by the editors of Westlaw®. On Westlaw®, KeyCite can trace case history, retrieve secondary sources, categorize legal citations by legal issue, and perform other functions.

key number A number (accompanied by the symbol of a key) corresponding to a specific topic within West's key-number system to facilitate legal research of case law.

laches The equitable doctrine that bars a party's right to legal action if the party has neglected for an unreasonable length of time to act on his or her rights.

larceny The wrongful or fraudulent taking and carrying away of another person's personal property with the intent to deprive the person permanently of the property.

law A body of rules of conduct established and enforced by the controlling authority (the government) of a society.

law clerk A law student working as an apprentice with a law firm, during the summer or part-time during the school year, to gain practical experience. Some law firms refer to law clerks as *summer associates.*

lay witness A witness who can truthfully and accurately testify on a fact in question without having specialized training or knowledge; an ordinary witness.

leading question A question that suggests, or "leads to," a desired answer. Interviewers may use leading questions to elicit responses from witnesses who otherwise would not be forthcoming. Generally, in court leading questions may be asked only of hostile witnesses.

lease In real property law, a contract by which the owner of real property (the landlord) grants to a person (the tenant) an exclusive right to use and possess the property, usually for a specified period of time, in return for rent or some other form of payment.

legal administrator An administrative employee of a law firm who manages the day-to-day operations of the firm. In smaller law firms, legal administrators are usually called office managers.

legal assistant (or paralegal) A person qualified by education, training, or work experience who is employed or retained by a lawyer, law office, corporation, governmental agency or other entity who performs specifically delegated substantive legal work, for which a lawyer is responsible.

legal-assistant manager An employee in a law firm who is responsible for overseeing the paralegal staff and paralegal professional development.

legal custody Custody of a child that confers on the parent the right to make major decisions about the child's life without consulting the other parent.

legal nurse consultant (LNC) A nurse who consults with legal professionals and others about medical aspects of legal claims or issues. Legal nurse consultants normally must have at least a bachelor's degree in nursing and a significant amount of nursing experience.

legal technician (or independent paralegal) A paralegal who offers services directly to the public, normally for a fee, without attorney supervision. Independent paralegals assist consumers by supplying them with forms and procedural knowledge relating to simple or routine legal procedures.

legislative rule A rule created by an administrative agency that is as legally binding as a law enacted by a legislature.

libel Defamation in writing or some other form (such as videotape) having the quality of permanence.

licensing A government's official act of granting permission to an individual, such as an attorney, to do something that would be illegal in the absence of such permission.

limited liability company (LLC) A hybrid form of business organization authorized by a state in which the owners of the business have limited liability and taxes on profits are passed through the business entity to the owners.

limited liability partnership (LLP) A business organizational form designed for professionals who normally do business as partners in a partnership. The LLP is a pass-through entity for tax purposes, like the general partnership, but limits the personal liability of partners.

limited licensing A type of licensing in which a limited number of individuals within a specific profession or group (such as legal technicians within the paralegal profession) must meet licensing requirements imposed by the state before those individuals may legally practice their profession.

limited partner One who invests in a limited partnership but does not play an active role in managing the operation of the business. Unlike general partners, limited partners are only liable for partnership debts up to the amount that they have invested.

limited partnership A partnership consisting of one or more general partners and of one or more limited partners.

liquidation In regard to corporations, the process by which corporate assets are converted into cash and distributed among creditors and shareholders according to specific rules of preference.

listserv list A list of e-mail addresses of persons who have agreed to receive e-mail about a particular topic.

litigation The process of working a lawsuit through the court system.

litigation paralegal A paralegal who specializes in assisting attorneys in the litigation process.

long arm statute A state statute that permits a state to obtain jurisdiction over nonresident individuals and corporations. Individuals or corporations, however, must have certain "minimum contacts" with that state for the statute to apply.

magistrate A public civil officer or official with limited judicial authority, such as the authority to issue an arrest warrant.

mailbox rule A rule providing that an acceptance of an offer takes effect at the time it is communicated via the mode expressly or impliedly authorized by the offeror, rather than at the time it is actually received by the offeror. If acceptance is to be by mail, for example, it becomes effective the moment it is placed in the mailbox.

malpractice Professional misconduct or negligence—the failure to exercise due care—on the part of a professional, such as an attorney or a physician.

managing partner The partner in a law firm who makes decisions relating to the firm's policies and procedures and who generally oversees the business operations of the firm.

mandatory authority Any source of law that a court must follow when deciding a case. Mandatory authorities include constitutions, statutes, and regulations that govern the issue before the court, and court decisions made by a superior court in the jurisdiction.

marital property All property acquired during the course of a marriage, apart from inheritances and gifts made to one or the other of the spouses.

material fact A fact that is important to the subject matter of the contract.

mediation A method of settling disputes outside of court by using the services of a neutral third party, who acts as a communicating agent between the parties; a method of dispute settlement that is less formal than arbitration.

mediation arbitration (Med-Arb) A form of ADR in which an arbitrator first attempts to help the parties reach an agreement, just as a mediator would. If no agreement is reached, then formal arbitration is undertaken, and the arbitrator issues a legally binding decision.

memorandum of law A document (known as a brief in some states) that delineates the legal theories, statutes, and cases on which a motion is based.

mens rea A wrongful mental state, or intent. A wrongful mental state is a requirement for criminal liability. What constitutes a wrongful mental state varies according to the nature of the crime.

merger A process in which one corporation (the surviving corporation) acquires all of the assets and liabilities of another corporation (the merged corporation).

metadata Embedded electronic data recorded by a computer in association with a particular file, including the file's location, path, creator, date created, date last accessed, hidden notes, earlier versions, passwords, and formatting. Metadata reveals information about how, when, and by whom a document was created, accessed, modified, and transmitted.

mini-trial A private proceeding that assists disputing parties in determining whether to take their case to court. During the proceeding, each party's attorney briefly argues the party's case before the other party and (usually) a neutral third party, who acts as an adviser. If the parties fail to reach an agreement, the adviser renders an opinion as to how a court would likely decide the issue.

***Miranda* rights** Certain constitutional rights of accused persons taken into custody by law enforcement officials, such as the right to remain silent and the right to counsel, as established by the United States Supreme Court's decision in *Miranda v. Arizona*.

mirror image rule A common law rule that requires that the terms of the offeree's acceptance adhere exactly to the terms of the offeror's offer for a valid contract to be formed.

mirror site A Web site that duplicates another site. A mirror site is used to improve the availability of access to the original site.

misdemeanor A less serious crime than a felony, punishable by a fine or incarceration for up to one year in jail (not a state or federal penitentiary).

money laundering Falsely reporting income that has been obtained through criminal activity, such as illegal drug transactions, as income obtained through a legitimate business enterprise to make the "dirty" money "clean."

mortgage A written instrument giving a creditor an interest in the debtor's property as security for a debt.

motion A procedural request or application presented by an attorney to the court on behalf of a client.

motion for a change of venue A motion requesting that a trial be moved to a different location to ensure a fair and impartial proceeding, for the convenience of the parties, or for some other acceptable reason.

motion for a directed verdict (motion for judgment as a matter of law) A motion requesting that the court grant a judgment in favor of the party making the motion on the ground that the other party has not produced sufficient evidence to support his or her claim.

motion for a new trial A motion asserting that the trial was so fundamentally flawed (because of error, newly discovered evidence, prejudice, or other reason) that a new trial is needed to prevent a miscarriage of justice.

motion for judgment notwithstanding the verdict A motion (also referred to as a motion for judgment as a matter of law in federal courts) requesting that the court grant judgment in favor of the party making the motion on the ground that the jury verdict against him or her was unreasonable or erroneous.

motion for judgment on the pleadings A motion that may be filed by either party in which the party asks the court to enter a judgment in his or her favor based on information contained in the pleadings. A judgment on the pleadings will only be made if there are no facts in dispute and the only question is how the law applies to a set of undisputed facts.

motion for summary judgment A motion that may be filed by either party in which the party asks the court to enter a judgment in his or her favor without a trial. Unlike a motion for judgment on the pleadings, a motion for summary judgment can be supported by evidence outside the pleadings, such as witnesses' affidavits, answers to interrogatories, and other evidence obtained prior to or during discovery.

motion *in limine* A motion requesting that certain evidence not be brought out at the trial, such as prejudicial, irrelevant, or legally inadmissible evidence.

motion to dismiss A motion filed by the defendant in which the defendant asks the court to dismiss the case for a specified reason, such as improper service, lack of personal jurisdiction, or the plaintiff's failure to state a claim for which relief can be granted.

motion to recuse A motion to remove a particular judge from a case.

motion to sever A motion to try multiple defendants separately.

motion to suppress evidence A motion requesting that certain evidence be excluded from consideration during the trial.

mutual mistake Mistake as to the same material fact on the part of both parties to a contract. In this situation, either party can cancel the contract.

National Association of Legal Assistants (NALA) One of the two largest national paralegal associations in the United States; formed in 1975. NALA is actively involved in paralegal professional development.

National Federation of Paralegal Associations (NFPA) One of the two largest national paralegal associations in the United States; formed in 1974. NFPA is actively involved in paralegal professional development.

national law Law that pertains to a particular nation (as opposed to international law).

natural law school A school of legal thought that holds that government and the legal system should reflect the universal moral and ethical principles that are inherent in human nature. The natural law school is the oldest and one of the most significant schools of legal thought.

negligence The failure to exercise the standard of care that a reasonable person would exercise in similar circumstances.

negligence *per se* An action or failure to act in violation of a statutory requirement.

negotiation A process in which parties attempt to settle their dispute informally, with or without attorneys to represent them.

networking Making personal connections and cultivating relationships with people in a certain field, profession, or area of interest.

newsgroup (Usenet group) An online bulletin board service. A newsgroup is a forum, or discussion group, that usually focuses on a particular topic.

no-fault divorce A divorce in which neither party is deemed to be at fault for the breakdown of the marriage.

nolo contendere Latin for "I will not contest it." A criminal defendant's plea in which he or she chooses not to challenge, or contest, the charges brought by the government. Although the defendant will still be convicted and sentenced, the plea neither admits nor denies guilt.

offer A promise or commitment to do or refrain from doing some specified thing in the future.

offeree The party to whom the offer is made.

offeror The party making the offer.

office manager An administrative employee who manages the day-to-day operations of a business firm. In larger law firms, office managers are usually called legal administrators.

officer A person hired by corporate directors to assist in the management of the day-to-day operations of the corporation. Corporate officers include the corporate president, vice president, secretary, treasurer, and possibly others, such as a chief financial officer and chief executive officer. Corporate officers are employees of the corporation and subject to employment contracts.

online dispute resolution (ODR) The resolution of disputes with the assistance of an organization that offers dispute-resolution services via the Internet.

open-ended question A question phrased in such a way that it elicits a relatively unguided and lengthy narrative response.

opening statement An attorney's statement to the jury at the beginning of the trial. The attorney briefly outlines the evidence that will be offered during the trial and the legal theory that will be pursued.

opinion A statement by the court setting forth the applicable law and the reasons for its decision in a case.

opinion (advisory) letter A letter from an attorney to a client containing a legal opinion on an issue raised by the client's question or legal claim. The opinion is based on a detailed analysis of the law.

ordinance An order, rule, or law enacted by a municipal or county government to govern a local matter unaddressed by state or federal legislation.

original jurisdiction The power of a court to take a case, try it, and decide it.

overtime wages Wages paid to workers who are paid an hourly wage rate to compensate them for overtime work (hours worked beyond forty hours per week). Under federal law, overtime wages are at least one and a half times the regular hourly wage rate.

paralegal (or legal assistant) A person qualified by education, training, or work experience who is employed or retained by a lawyer, law office, corporation, governmental agency or other entity who performs specifically delegated substantive legal work, for which a lawyer is responsible.

parallel citation A second (or third) citation for a given case. When a case is published in more than one reporter, each citation is a parallel citation to the other(s).

partner A person who has undertaken to operate a business jointly with one or more other persons. Each partner is a co-owner of the business firm.

partnership An association of two or more persons to carry on, as co-owners, a business for profit.

party With respect to lawsuits, the plaintiff or the defendant. Some cases involve multiple parties (more than one plaintiff or defendant).

passive listening The act of listening attentively to the speaker's message and responding to the speaker by providing verbal or nonverbal cues that encourage the speaker to continue; in effect, saying "I'm listening, please go on."

patent A government grant that gives an inventor the exclusive right or privilege to make, use, or sell his or her invention for a limited time period.

paternity suit A lawsuit brought by an unmarried mother to establish that a certain person is the biological father of her child. DNA testing or a comparable procedure is often use to determine paternity.

peremptory challenge A *voir dire* challenge to exclude a potential juror from serving on the jury without any supporting reason or cause. Peremptory challenges based on racial or gender criteria are illegal.

performance In contract law, the fulfillment of one's duties arising under a contract with another; the normal way of discharging one's contractual obligations.

personal liability An individual's personal responsibility for debts or obligations. The owners of sole proprietorships and partnerships are personally liable for the debts and obligations incurred by their business firms. If their firms go bankrupt or cannot meet debts as they become due, the owners will be personally responsible for paying the debts.

personal property Any property that is not real property. Generally, any property that is movable or intangible is classified as personal property.

persuasive authority Any legal authority, or source of law, that a court may look to for guidance but on which it need not rely in making its decision. Persuasive authorities include cases from other jurisdictions and secondary sources of law, such as scholarly treatises.

petition for divorce The document filed with the court to initiate divorce proceedings. The requirements governing the form and content of a divorce petition vary from state to state.

petty offense In criminal law, the least serious kind of wrong, such as a traffic or building-code violation.

plain-meaning rule A rule of statutory interpretation. If the meaning of a statute is clear on its face, then that is the interpretation the court will give to it; inquiry into the legislative history of the statute will not be undertaken.

plaintiff A party who initiates a lawsuit.

plea bargaining The process by which the accused and the prosecutor in a criminal case work out a mutually satisfactory disposition of the case, subject to court approval. Usually, plea bargaining involves the defendant's pleading guilty to a lesser offense in return for a lighter sentence.

pleadings Statements by the plaintiff and the defendant that detail the facts, charges, and defenses involved in the litigation.

pocket part A separate pamphlet containing recent cases or changes in the law that is used to update hornbooks, legal encyclopedias, and other legal authorities. It is called a "pocket part" because it slips into a sleeve, or pocket, in the front or back binder of the volume.

point heading A brief recapitulation of the point being made in a section of an appellate brief. Point headings separate the text into logical sections and make the argument easier to follow.

positivist school A school of legal thought centered on the assumption that there is no law higher than the laws created by the government. Laws must be obeyed, even if they are unjust, to prevent anarchy.

potentially responsible party (PRP) A party who may be liable under the Comprehensive Environmental Response, Compensation, and Liability Act, or Superfund. Any person who generated hazardous waste, transported hazardous waste, owned or operated a waste site at the time of disposal, or currently owns or operates a site may be responsible for some or all of the clean-up costs involved in removing the hazardous chemicals.

prayer for relief A statement at the end of the complaint requesting that the court grant relief to the plaintiff.

precedent A court decision that furnishes an example or authority for deciding subsequent cases in which identical or similar facts are presented.

predatory behavior Business behavior that is undertaken with the intention of unlawfully driving competitors out of the market.

preliminary hearing An initial hearing in which a magistrate decides if there is probable cause to believe that the defendant committed the crime for which he or she is charged.

prenuptial agreement A contract formed between two persons who are contemplating marriage to provide for the disposition of property in the event of a divorce or the death of one of the spouses after they have married.

pretrial conference A conference prior to trial in which the judge and the attorneys litigating the suit discuss settlement possibilities, clarify the issues in dispute, and schedule forthcoming trial-related events.

primary source In legal research, a document that establishes the law on a particular issue, such as a case decision, legislative act, administrative rule, or presidential order.

principal In agency law, a person who, by agreement or otherwise, authorizes another person (the agent) to act on the principal's behalf in such a way that the acts of the agent become binding on the principal.

privilege In tort law, the ability to act contrary to another person's right without that person's having legal redress for such acts. Privilege may be raised as a defense to defamation.

privileged information Confidential communications between certain individuals, such as an attorney and his or her client, that are protected from disclosure except under court order.

probable cause Reasonable grounds to believe the existence of facts warranting certain actions, such as the search or arrest of a person.

probate The process of "proving" the validity of a will and ensuring that the instructions in a valid will are carried out, including settling matters pertaining to the administration of a decedent's estate and guardianship of a decedent's minor children.

probate court A court that handles proceedings relating to wills and the settlement of deceased persons' estates; usually a county court.

procedural law Rules that define the manner in which the rights and duties of individuals may be enforced.

product liability The legal liability of manufacturers, sellers, and lessors of goods to consumers, users, and bystanders for injuries or damages that are caused by the goods.

professional corporation (P.C.) A firm that is owned by shareholders, who purchase the corporation's stock, or shares. The liability of shareholders is often limited to the amount of their investments.

professional portfolio A job applicant's collection of selected personal documents (such as school transcripts, writing samples, and certificates) for presentation to a potential employer.

promise An assurance that one will or will not do something in the future.

promissory estoppel A doctrine under which a promise is binding if the promise is clear and definite, the promisee justifiably relies on the promise, the reliance is reasonable and substantial, and justice will be better served by enforcement of the promise.

property settlement The division of property between spouses on the termination of a marriage.

prospectus A document that discloses relevant facts about a company and its operations so that those who wish to purchase stock (invest) in the corporation have the basis for making an informed decision.

proximate cause Legal cause; exists when the connection between an act and an injury is strong enough to justify imposing liability.

public defender A court-appointed attorney who is paid by the state to represent a criminal defendant who is unable to hire private counsel.

public law number An identification number that has been assigned to a specific statute, or public law, following the legislative process.

publicly held corporation A corporation whose shares are publicly traded in securities markets, such as the New York Stock Exchange.

public policy A governmental policy based on widely held societal values.

public prosecutor An individual, acting as a trial lawyer, who initiates and conducts criminal cases in the government's name and on behalf of the people.

punitive damages Money damages that may be awarded to a plaintiff to punish the defendant and deter future similar conduct.

real estate Land and things permanently attached to the land, such as houses, buildings, and trees and foliage.

real property Immovable property consisting of land and the buildings and plant life thereon.

reasonable person standard The standard of behavior expected of a hypothetical "reasonable person"; the standard against which negligence is measured and that must be observed to avoid liability for negligence.

record on appeal The items submitted during the trial (pleadings, motions, briefs, and exhibits) and the transcript of the trial proceedings that are forwarded to the appellate court for review when a case is appealed.

recross-examination The questioning of an opposing witness following the adverse party's redirect examination.

redirect examination The questioning of a witness following the adverse party's cross-examination.

reference line The portion of the letter that indicates the matter to be discussed in the letter, such as "RE: Summary of Cases Applying the Family and Medical Leave Act of 1993." The reference line is placed just below the address block and above the salutation.

reformation An equitable remedy granted by a court to correct, or "reform," a written contract so that it reflects the true intentions of the parties.

Registered Paralegal (RP) A paralegal whose competency has been certified by the National Federation of Paralegal Associations (NFPA) after the paralegal's successful completion of the Paralegal Advanced Competency Exam (PACE).

relevant evidence Evidence tending to prove or disprove the fact in question. Only relevant evidence is admissible in court.

remand To send a case back to a lower court for further proceedings.

remedy The means by which a right is enforced or the violation of a right is prevented or compensated for.

remedy at law A remedy available in a court of law. Money damages are awarded as a remedy at law.

remedy in equity A remedy allowed by courts in situations where remedies at law are not appropriate. Remedies in equity are based on settled rules of fairness, justice, and honesty.

reply brief An appellate brief filed by the appellant to rebut (counter) arguments made by the appellee in the appellee's brief.

reporter A book in which court cases are published, or reported.

reprimand A disciplinary sanction in which an attorney is rebuked for his or her misbehavior. Although a reprimand is the mildest sanction for attorney misconduct, it is nonetheless a serious one and may significantly damage the attorney's reputation in the legal community.

rescission A remedy whereby a contract is terminated and the parties are returned to the positions they occupied before the contract was made.

respondeat superior A doctrine in agency law under which a principal-employer may be held liable for the wrongful acts committed by agents or employees while acting within the scope of their agency or employment.

responsible corporate officer doctrine A common law doctrine under which the court may impose criminal liability on a corporate officer for actions of employees under her or his supervision regardless of whether she or he participated in, directed, or even knew about those actions.

restitution An equitable remedy under which a person is restored to his or her original position prior to loss or injury, or placed in the position that he or she would have been in had the breach not occurred.

restraining order A court order that requires one person (such as an abusing spouse) to stay away from another (such as an abused spouse).

retainer An advance payment made by a client to a law firm to cover part of the legal fees and/or costs that will need to be incurred on that client's behalf.

retainer agreement A signed document stating that the attorney or the law firm has been hired by the client to provide certain legal services and that the client agrees to pay for those services in accordance with the terms set forth in the retainer agreement.

return-of-service form A document signed by a process server and submitted to the court to prove that a defendant received a summons.

reverse To overturn the judgment of a lower court.

robbery The taking of money, personal property, or any other article of value from a person by means of force or fear.

rule of four A rule of the United States Supreme Court under which the Court will not issue a writ of *certiorari* unless at least four justices approve of the decision to issue the writ.

rulemaking The actions undertaken by administrative agencies when formally adopting new regulations or amending old ones.

rules of construction The rules that control the judicial interpretation of statutes.

rules of evidence Rules governing the admissibility of evidence in trial courts.

sales contract A contract for the sale of goods, as opposed to a contract for the sale of services, real property, or intangible property. Sales contracts are governed by Article 2 of the Uniform Commercial Code.

salutation The formal greeting to the addressee of the letter. The salutation is placed just below the reference line.

search warrant A written order, based on probable cause and issued by a judge or public official (magistrate), commanding that police officers or criminal investigators search a specific person, place, or property to obtain evidence.

secondary source In legal research, any publication that indexes, summarizes, or interprets the law, such as a legal encyclopedia, a treatise, or an article in a law review.

self-defense The legally recognized privilege to protect oneself or one's property against injury by another. The privilege of self-defense only protects acts that are reasonably necessary to protect oneself or one's property.

self-incrimination The act of giving testimony that implicates one's own guilt or participation in criminal wrongdoing. The Fifth Amendment to the Constitution states that no person "shall be compelled in any criminal case to be a witness against himself."

self-regulation The regulation of the conduct of a professional group by members of the group. Self-regulation usually involves the establishment of ethical or professional standards of behavior with which members of the group must comply.

sentence The punishment, or penalty, ordered by the court to be inflicted on a person convicted of a crime.

separate property Property that a spouse owned before the marriage, plus inheritances and gifts acquired by the spouse during the marriage.

service of process The delivery of the summons and the complaint to a defendant.

session law Law as officially published in volumes in which statutes are organized chronologically by year or legislative session.

settlement agreement An out-of-court resolution to a legal dispute, which is agreed to by the parties in writing. A settlement agreement may be reached at any time prior to or during a trial.

sexual harassment In the employment context, (1) the hiring or granting of job promotions or other benefits in return for sexual favors (*quid pro quo* harassment) or (2) language or conduct that is so sexually offensive that it creates a hostile working environment (hostile-environment harassment).

share A unit of stock; a measure of ownership interest in a corporation.

shareholder One who purchases corporate stock, or shares, and who thus becomes an owner of the corporation.

shrink-wrap agreement An agreement whose terms are expressed in a document located inside the box in which the goods (usually software) are packaged.

slander Defamation in oral form.

slip law The first official publication of a statute, which comes out shortly after the legislation is passed (presented as a single sheet or pamphlet).

slip opinion A judicial opinion published shortly after the decision is made and not yet included in a case reporter or advance sheets.

sociological school A school of legal thought that views the law as a tool for promoting justice in society.

sole proprietorship The simplest form of business organization, in which the owner is the business. Anyone who does business without creating a formal business entity has a sole proprietorship.

specific performance An equitable remedy requiring exactly the performance that was specified in a contract; usually granted only when money damages would be an inadequate remedy and the subject matter of the contract is unique (for example, real property).

staff attorney An attorney hired by a law firm as an employee. A staff attorney has no ownership rights in the firm and will not be invited to become a partner in the firm.

standing to sue A sufficient stake in a controversy to justify bringing a lawsuit. To have standing to sue, the plaintiff must demonstrate that he or she has been either injured or threatened with injury.

stare decisis The doctrine of precedent, under which a court is obligated to follow the earlier decisions of that court or a higher court within the jurisdiction if the same points arise again in litigation. This is a defining characteristic of the common law system.

state bar association An association of attorneys within a state. In most states, an attorney must be a member of the state bar association to practice law in the state.

statute A written law enacted by a legislature under its constitutional lawmaking authority.

Statute of Frauds A state statute that requires certain types of contracts to be in writing to be enforceable.

statute of limitations A statute setting the maximum time period within which certain actions can be brought or rights enforced. After the period of time has run, no legal action can be brought.

statutory law The body of written laws enacted by the legislature.

strict liability Liability regardless of fault. In tort law, strict liability may be imposed on a merchant who introduces into commerce a good that is so defective as to be unreasonably dangerous.

submission agreement A written agreement to submit a legal dispute to an arbitrator or arbitrating panel for resolution.

subpoena A document commanding a person to appear at a certain time and place to give testimony concerning a certain matter.

substantive law Law that defines the rights and duties of individuals with respect to each other, as opposed to procedural law, which defines the manner in which these rights and duties may be enforced.

summary jury trial (SJT) A method of settling disputes (used in some federal courts) in which a trial is held but the jury's verdict is not binding. The verdict only acts as a guide to both sides in reaching an agreement during the mandatory negotiations that immediately follow the trial. If a settlement is not reached, both sides have the right to a full trial later.

summons A document served on a defendant in a lawsuit informing the defendant that a legal action has been commenced against him or her and that the defendant must appear in court or respond to the plaintiff's complaint within a specified period of time.

support personnel Employees who provide clerical, secretarial, or other support to the legal, paralegal, and administrative staff of a law firm.

supporting affidavit An affidavit accompanying a motion that is filed by an attorney on behalf of his or her client. The sworn statements in the affidavit provide a factual basis for the motion.

supremacy clause The provision in Article VI of the U.S. Constitution that declares the Constitution, laws, and treaties of the United States are "the supreme Law of the Land."

suspension A serious disciplinary sanction in which an attorney who has violated an ethical rule or a law is prohibited from practicing law in the state for a specified or an indefinite period of time.

syllabus A brief summary of the holding and legal principles involved in a reported case, which is followed by the court's official opinion.

table of cases An alphabetical list of the cases that have been cited or reproduced in a legal text, case digest, or other legal source.

tenancy in common A form of co-ownership of property in which each party owns an undivided interest that passes to his or her heirs at death.

testamentary trust A trust that is created by will and that does not take effect until the death of the testator.

testate The condition of having died with a valid will.

testator One who makes a valid will.

third party A person or entity not directly involved in an agreement (such as a contract), legal proceeding (such as a lawsuit), or relationship (such as an attorney-client relationship).

time slip A record documenting, for billing purposes, the hours (or fractions of hours) that an attorney or a paralegal worked for each client, the date on which the work was done, and the type of work that was undertaken.

tort A civil wrong not arising from a breach of contract; a breach of a legal duty that proximately causes harm or injury to another.

tortfeasor One who commits a tort.

toxic tort A wrongful act (tort) that occurs when a person or business fails to properly use or clean up toxic chemicals that cause harm to a person or to society; also used to refer to an action brought against a toxic polluter.

trade journal A newsletter, magazine, or other periodical that provides a certain trade or profession with information (products, trends, or developments) relating to that trade or profession.

trademark A distinctive mark, motto, device, or emblem that a manufacturer stamps, prints, or otherwise affixes to the goods it produces so that they may be identified on the market and their origins made known. Once a trademark is established (under the common law or through registration), the owner is entitled to its exclusive use.

trade name A term that is used to indicate part or all of a business's name and that is directly related to the business's reputation and goodwill. Trade names are protected under the common law (and under trademark law, if the business's name is the same as its trademark).

trade secret Information or processes that give a business an advantage over competitors who do not know the information or processes.

treatise In legal research, a work that provides a systematic, detailed, and scholarly review of a particular legal subject.

treaty An agreement, or compact, formed between two independent nations.

trespass to land The entry onto, above, or below the surface of land owned by another without the owner's permission or legal authorization.

trespass to personal property The unlawful taking or harming of another's personal property; interference with another's right to the exclusive possession of his or her personal property.

trial court A court in which cases begin and in which questions of fact are examined.

trial notebook A binder that contains copies of all of the documents and information that an attorney will need to have at hand during the trial.

trust An arrangement in which title to property is held by one person (a trustee) for the benefit of another (a beneficiary).

trust account A bank or escrow account in which one party (the trustee, such as an attorney) holds funds belonging to another person (such as a client); a bank account into which funds advanced to a law firm by a client are deposited.

unathorized practice of law (UPL) The act of engaging in actions defined by a legal authority, such as a state legislature, as constituting the "practice of law" without legal authorization to do so.

Uniform Commercial Code (UCC) A uniform code of laws governing commercial transactions that has been adopted in part or in its entirety by all of the states. Article 2 of the UCC governs contracts for the sale of goods.

unilateral mistake Mistake as to a material fact on the part of only one party to a contract. In this situation, the contract is normally enforceable against the mistaken party, with some exceptions.

unreasonably dangerous product In product liability, a product that is defective to the point of threatening a consumer's health and safety. A product will be considered unreasonably dangerous if it is dangerous beyond the expectation of the ordinary consumer or if a less dangerous alternative was economically feasible for the manufacturer, but the manufacturer failed to produce it.

venue The geographical district in which an action is tried and from which the jury is selected.

verdict A formal decision made by a jury.

vicarious liability Legal responsibility placed on one person for the acts of another.

visitation rights The right of a noncustodial parent to have contact with his or her child. Grandparents and stepparents may also be given visitation rights.

voir dire A proceeding in which attorneys for the plaintiff and the defendant ask prospective jurors questions to determine whether any potential juror is biased or has any connection with a party to the action or with a prospective witness.

warranty An express or implied promise by a seller that specific goods to be sold meet certain criteria, or standards of performance, on which the buyer may rely.

white-collar crime A crime that typically occurs only in a business context; popularly used to refer to an illegal act or series of acts committed by an individual or business entity using nonviolent means.

will A document directing how and to whom the maker's property and obligations are to be transferred on his or her death.

winding up The process of winding up all business affairs (collecting and distributing the firm's assets) after a partnership or corporation has been dissolved.

witness A person who is asked to testify under oath at a trial.

witness statement The written record of the statements made by a witness during an interview, signed by the witness.

work product An attorney's mental impressions, conclusions, and legal theories regarding a case being prepared on behalf of a client. Work product normally is regarded as privileged information.

workers' compensation laws State laws establishing an administrative procedure for compensating workers for injuries that arise in the course of their employment, regardless of fault.

World Wide Web A hypertext-based system through which specially formatted documents are accessible on the Internet.

writ of *certiorari* A writ from a higher court asking the lower court to send it the record of a case for review. The United States Supreme Court uses *certiorari* to review most of the cases it decides to hear.

writ of execution A writ that puts in force a court's decree or judgment.

wrongful discharge An employer's termination of an employee's employment in violation of the law.

INDEX